Fodor's 2011

FRANCE

Fodor's Travel Publications New York, Toronto, London, Sydney, Auckland

www.fodors.com

TIGRE D'OR
LONDON
L'IMPRESSIONNISTE
L'IMPRESSIONNISTE

Be a Fodor's Correspondent

Our latest guidebook to France—now in full color—owes its success to travelers like you. Throughout, you'll find photographs submitted by members of Fodors.com to our "Show Us Your France" photo contest.

Facing this page is a photograph of a beautiful river scene in central France as captured by dthomasdupont. On pages 1 and 310 you'll find the grand prize-winning photograph of Mont-St-Michel taken by Lane Clark.

We are especially proud of this color edition. No other guide to France is as up to date or has as much practical planning information, along with hundreds of color photographs and illustrated maps.

We've also included "Word of Mouth" quotes from travelers who shared their experiences with others on our forums. If you're inspired and can plan a better trip because of this guide, we've done our job.

We invite you to join the travel conversation: Your opinion matters to us and to your fellow travelers. Come to Fodors.com to plan your trip, share an experience, ask a question, submit a photograph, post a review, or write a trip report.

Tell our editors about your trip. They want to know what went well and how we can make this guide even better. Share your opinions at our feedback center at fodors.com/feedback, or email us at editors@fodors.com with the subject line "France Editor." You might find your comments published in a future Fodor's guide. We look forward to hearing from you.

Bon Voyage!

Evelyn Lanzillotti

Tim Jarrell

Tim Jarrell, Publisher

FODOR'S FRANCE 2011

Editor: Robert I. C. Fisher

Editorial Contributors: Andrew Collins, Linda Dannenberg, Jennifer Ditsler-Ladonne, John Fanning, Sarah Fraser, Linda Hervieux, Rosa Jackson, Christopher Mooney, George Semler, Heather Stimmler-Hall

Production Editor: Carrie Parker
Maps & Illustrations: Mark Stroud, Moon Street Cartography; David Lindroth; Ed Jacobus; Mapping Specialists, *cartographers;* Bob Blake, Rebecca Baer, *map editors;* William Wu, *information graphics*
Design: Fabrizio La Rocca, *creative director*; Guido Caroti, Siobhan O'Hare, *art directors*; Tina Malaney, Chie Ushio, Nora Rosansky, Ann McBride, Jessica Walsh, *designers*; Melanie Marin, *senior picture editor*
Cover Photo: (Chateau de Villandry, Loire Valley): SIME/eStock Photo
Production Manager: Amanda Bullock

COPYRIGHT

ISBN 978–1–4000–0473–7

ISSN 0532–5692

SPECIAL SALES

This book is available at special discounts for bulk purchases for sales promotions or premiums. Special editions, including personalized covers, excerpts of existing books, and corporate imprints, can be created in large quantities for special needs. For more information, write to Special Markets/Premium Sales, 1745 Broadway, MD 6-2, New York, New York 10019, or e-mail specialmarkets@randomhouse.com.

AN IMPORTANT TIP & AN INVITATION

Although all prices, opening times, and other details in this book are based on information supplied to us at press time, changes occur all the time in the travel world, and Fodor's cannot accept responsibility for facts that become outdated or for inadvertent errors or omissions. So **always confirm information when it matters,** especially if you're making a detour to visit a specific place. Your experiences—positive and negative—matter to us. If we have missed or misstated something, **please write to us.** We follow up on all suggestions. Contact the France editor at editors@fodors.com or c/o Fodor's at 1745 Broadway, New York, NY 10019.

PRINTED IN CHINA

10 9 8 7 6 5 4 3 2 1

CONTENTS

Fodor's Features

MAPS

ABOUT THIS BOOK

Our Ratings

Sometimes you find terrific travel experiences and sometimes they just find you. But usually the burden is on you to select the right combination of experiences. That's where our ratings come in.

As travelers we've all discovered a place so wonderful that its worthiness is obvious. And sometimes that place is so experiential that superlatives don't do it justice: you just have to be there to know. These sights, properties, and experiences get our highest rating, **Fodor's Choice** indicated by orange stars throughout this book.

Black stars highlight sights and properties we deem **Highly Recommended** places that our writers, editors, and readers praise again and again for consistency and excellence.

By default, there's another category: any place we include in this book is by definition worth your time, unless we say otherwise. And we will.

Disagree with any of our choices? Care to nominate a place or suggest that we rate one more highly? Visit our feedback center at www.fodors.com/feedback.

Budget Well

Hotel and restaurant price categories from ¢ to $$$$ are defined in the opening pages of each chapter. For attractions, we always give standard adult admission fees; reductions are usually available for children, students, and senior citizens. Want to pay with plastic? **AE, D, DC, MC, V** following restaurant and hotel listings indicate if American Express, Discover, Diners Club, MasterCard, and Visa are accepted.

Restaurants

Unless we state otherwise, restaurants are open for lunch and dinner daily. We mention dress only when there's a specific requirement and reservations only when they're essential or not accepted—it's always best to book ahead.

Hotels

Hotels have private bath, phone, TV, and air-conditioning and operate on the European Plan (aka EP, meaning without meals), unless we specify that they use the Breakfast Plan (BP, with a full breakfast), or Modified American Plan (MAP, with breakfast and dinner daily), or Full American Plan (FAP, with three meals a day). We always list facilities but not whether you'll be charged an extra fee to use them, so when pricing accommodations, find out what's included.

Listings

- ★ Fodor's Choice
- ★ Highly recommended
- ✉ Physical address
- ✣ Directions or Map coordinates
- Mailing address
- ☎ Telephone
- Fax
- On the Web
- E-mail
- Admission fee
- ⊙ Open/closed times
- M Metro stations
- Credit cards

Hotels & Restaurants

- Hotel
- Number of rooms
- Facilities
- Meal plans
- ✕ Restaurant
- Reservations
- Dress code
- Smoking
- BYOB

Outdoors

- Golf
- Camping

Other

- Family-friendly
- ⇨ See also
- Branch address
- ☞ Take note

Experience France

1

FRANCE TODAY

It may be a cliché to say the French fret over their place in the world, but they do. Faced with the ever-dominant Anglo-American axis and hobbled by the global economic crisis, the French are rallying to protect their institutions, their language and, above all, *la vie française*—their treasured lifestyle. Still, polls show the French are optimistic about the future—and there's plenty of good news.

Tourism is thriving, with France maintaining its rank as the world's top tourist destination, with more than 80 million visitors each year. The French remain leaders in science and technology. France is the world's leading producer of luxury goods, and fashion remains the nation's birthright.

No Longer L'Américain

Once nicknamed L'Américain for his U.S.-loving ways, French President Nicolas Sarkozy isn't exactly waving the Stars and Stripes these days. Miffed that President Barack Obama has repeatedly snubbed his overtures for a close and personal relationship, Sarkozy has taken to dissing his American counterpart in private as wet behind the ears. Obama isn't the only world leader who has kept Sarkozy at arm's length. The irreverent "Sarko" has watched as European heads of state have refused to go along with the brash Frenchman's view of himself as their self-proclaimed leader.

The price at home has been steep, moreover, with the President's popularity rating sinking steadily. In the face of noisy street protests, Sarkozy has backed off from many of his promised reforms. With the first whispers of the financial crisis came a hasty retreat from the free-market restructuring Sarkozy had trumpeted when he was elected in 2007. These days, in classic Gallic fashion, he has enjoyed tweaking his "friends" across the pond, even lecturing about the need to "remoralize capitalism."

With an eye toward reelection in 2012, however, Sarkozy was looking to regain the upper hand. Among the feathers in his cap is a ground-breaking carbon tax on fossil fuels hailed by environmentalists. Once-sacred Sunday shopping rules have been eased, no small feat given France's boisterous unions.

And Sarkozy's legacy project Le Grand Paris—a €21-billion plan to remake Paris into an economic and cultural mega-capital—was creeping ahead as construction was set to begin in early 2013 on key components, including an 80-mi-long automatic subway system ringing Paris.

Captivated by Carla

Lucky for Sarkozy his best asset may be his popular wife, Carla Bruni-Sarkozy—the supermodel-turned-singer-turned–demure First Dame, whose every move is slavishly tracked by French magazines. The former bad girl has made headlines as much for her turns in the spotlight (performing for Nelson Mandela; signing on for a part in a Woody Allen film) as for her philanthropy (she's an anti-AIDS ambassador; she has her own charitable foundation). The Italian-born Carla B holds considerable influence over her lovesick husband, and isn't afraid to wield it.

Sizing Up

Despite a diet dripping in butter and fat, the French are among the world's thinnest people, with one of the world's longest life expectancies to boot. The so-called "French paradox" may help keep them skinny as éclairs, but that hasn't stopped the French from obsessing about how to stay that way.

Warning bells were sounded, furthermore, after studies showed obesity rates creeping up. French health experts declared war against junk food. Ads for everything from candy to McDonald's cheeseburgers come with warnings to indulge modestly. Fizzy sodas are not allowed, and butter on bread is frowned upon (though cheese is not).

Even the Elysée Palace has gotten into the act. Avid jogging and a crash diet are said to be behind the slimmed-down figure of Nicolas Sarkozy. Much to the dismay of guests, even the Elysée menu has been pared down to Weight Watchers proportions.

The French Model Reconsidered

And the winner of the global financial crisis was . . . France? Not quite. But long criticized for maintaining a socialist economy out of step with the modern world, France found itself on the rare receiving end of praise for an economic model that helped the country weather the worldwide downturn more gently than its Anglo-American rivals. France-bashers were caught short as the economy they love to scorn enjoyed a slightly higher rate of growth coming out of the recession than other developed countries. With banks tightly regulated, French homeowners were spared an equivalent of the U.S. subprime mortgage crisis. Experts credited France for its long-term formula of economic fairness, with a less-pronounced gap between rich and poor than in other countries. Education is inexpensive; and the health care system, often called the world's best, is available to all. President Sarkozy even floated the idea, however briefly, of adopting a happiness index to replace traditional measures of progress, taking into account quality of life factors.

Under Siege: The French Café

The 2007 anti-smoking law came as a breath of fresh air in France, making meals in cheek-to-jowl bistros far more enjoyable for those who prefer their foie gras without their neighbor's Gaulois an accompaniment. Since the rigorously observed law passed, cigarette sales have plunged to all-time lows in France, proof the French could live without their clopes. One tragic victim, however, has been that icon of French society—the neighborhood café. Many French workers who would pop in for a smoke with their morning petit café and their evening petit verre of wine simply stopped coming. Business was already declining, as modern life had chipped away at café culture, with fewer young people having the time or desire to drink during the day. Predictions that business would rebound as smokers got used to lighting up outside have not been borne out. With an average of two cafés closing each day in France, café denizens worry about the end of an era.

Paris: The City that . . . Sleeps?

Fall-out from the smoking ban has had another effect: antagonizing ordinary French trying to get a good night's sleep. With smokers sent outside to light up, many neighbors of nightclubs have groused that the new sidewalk culture is keeping them awake at night. The new battle lines have annoyed neighbors who use eggs, buckets of water, and the odd garden hose to rout merry-makers. Authorities have now slapped bars with heavy fines and shuttering repeat offenders. The situation has become so bad that music promoters launched a campaign to combat the transformation of the City of Light into what Le Monde called Europe's "capital of boredom"!

WHAT'S WHERE

2 Paris. A quayside vista that takes in the Seine, a passing boat, Notre-Dame, the Eiffel Tower, and mansard roofs all in one generous sweep is enough to convince you that Paris is indeed the most beautiful city on Earth.

3 Ile-de-France. Appearing like all France in miniature, the Ile-de-France region is the nation's heartland. Here Louis XIV built vainglorious Versailles, Chartres brings the faithful to their knees, and Monet's Giverny enchants all.

4 Loire Valley. Chenonceaux, Chambord, and Saumur—the parade of royal and near-royal châteaus magnificently captures France's golden age of monarchy in an idyllic region threaded by the Loire River.

5 Normandy. Sculpted with cliff-lined coasts, Normandy has been home to saints and sculptors, with a dramatic past marked by Mont-St-Michel's majestic abbey, Rouen's towering cathedral, and the D-Day beaches.

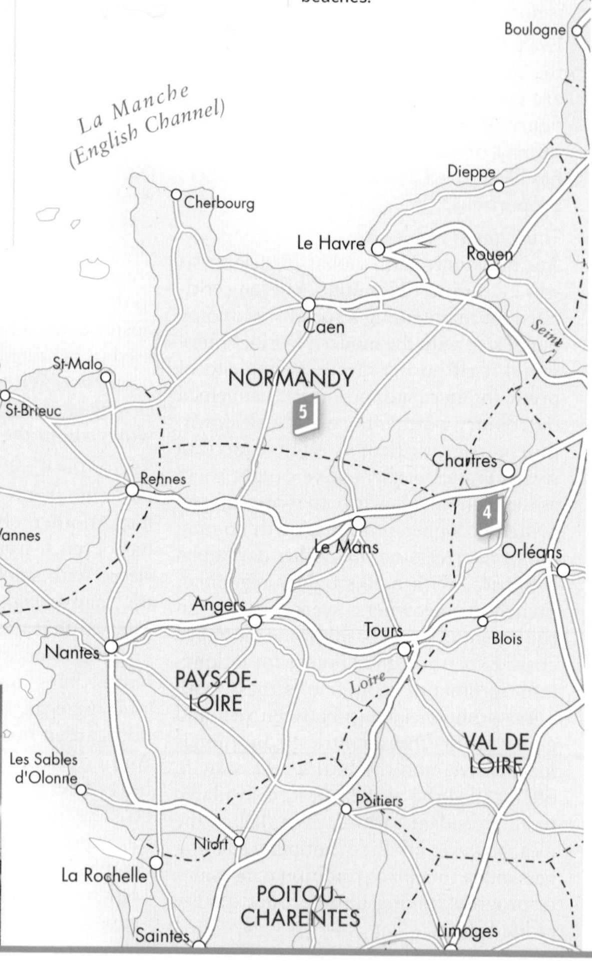

6 Brittany. A long arm of rocky land stretching into the Atlantic, Brittany is a place unto itself, with its own language and time-defying towns such as Gauguin's Pont-Aven and the pirate haven of St-Malo.

7 Champagne Country. The capital of bubbly is Reims, set near four great Gothic cathedrals.

8 Alsace-Lorraine. Although this region bordered by the Rhine often looks German and sounds German, its main sights—18th-century Nancy, medieval Strasbourg, and the lovely Route du Vin—remain proudly French.

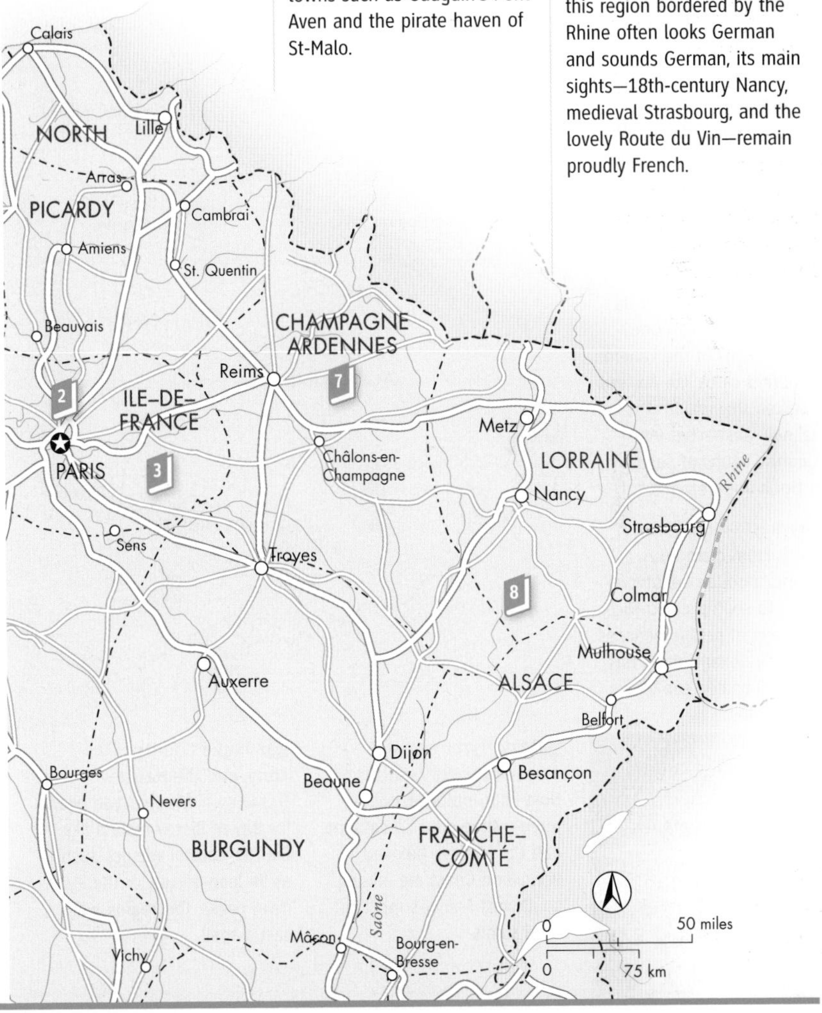

WHAT'S WHERE

9 Burgundy. Hallowed ground for wine lovers, Burgundy hardly needs to be beautiful—but it is. Around the gastronomic hub of Dijon, the region is famed for its verdant vineyards and Romanesque churches.

10 Lyon and the Alps. Local chefs rival their Parisian counterparts in treasure-filled Lyon, heart of a diverse region where you ski down Mont Blanc or take a heady trip along the Beaujolais Wine Road.

11 Provence. Famed for its Lavender Route, the honey-gold hill towns of the Luberon, and vibrant cities like Aix and Marseilles, this region was dazzlingly abstracted into geometric daubs of paint by Van Gogh and Cézanne.

12 French Riviera (*Côte D'Azur*). From glamorous St-Tropez through beauteous Antibes to sophisticated Nice, this sprawl of pebble beaches and zillion-dollar houses has always captivated sun lovers and socialites.

PAYS-DE-LOIRE
VAL DE LOIRE
Les Sables d'Olonne
Poitiers
Niort
La Rochelle
POITOU–CHARENTES
Saintes
Limoges
Royan
Angoulême
LIMOUSIN
Périgueux
Brive-la-Gaillarde
Bordeaux
16
15
Garonne
Dordogne
Langon
Cahors
AQUITAINE
Montauban
Albi
Bayonne
Biarritz
N17
Toulouse
14
MIDI-PYRÉNÉES
Pau
Tarbes
13

13 Midi-Pyrénées and Languedoc-Roussillon. Rose-hue Toulouse, once-upon-a-time-ified Carcassone, and the Matisse-beloved Vermillion Coast are among southwest France's most colorful sights.

14 Basque Country, Gascony, and the Hautes-Pyrénées. Whether you head for Bay of Biscay resorts like Biarritz, coastal villages such as St-Jean-de-Luz, or the Pyrenean peaks, this region will cast a spell.

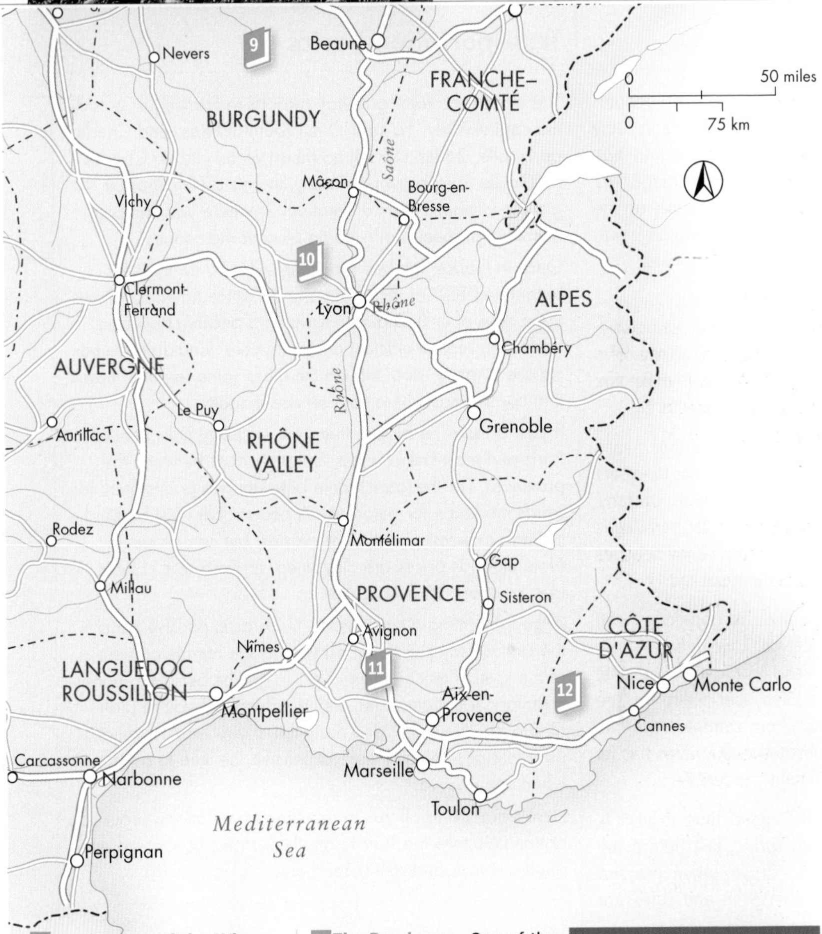

1

Beaune
Nevers
BURGUNDY
FRANCHE–COMTÉ
Saône
Mâcon
Bourg-en-Bresse
Vichy
Clermont-Ferrand
Lyon
Rhône
ALPES
Chambéry
AUVERGNE
Le Puy
Aurillac
Grenoble
RHÔNE VALLEY
Rodez
Montélimar
Gap
Millau
PROVENCE
Sisteron
Avignon
Nîmes
CÔTE D'AZUR
LANGUEDOC ROUSSILLON
Nice
Monte Carlo
Montpellier
Aix-en-Provence
Cannes
Carcassonne
Narbonne
Marseille
Toulon
Mediterranean Sea
Perpignan
0 50 miles
0 75 km

Bordeaux and the Wine Country. The wines of Bordeaux tower as a standard against which others are measured, and they made the city of Bordeaux rich and owners of its vineyards—like Château Mouton-Rothschild—even richer.

The Dordogne. One of the hottest destinations in France, the Dordogne is a stone-cottage pastorale studded with fairy-tale castles, storybook villages, and France's top prehistoric sights.

FRANCE PLANNER

When to Go

Summer is the most popular (and expensive) season. July in Paris is crowded and hot, although the Paris Plage, the "beach" on the banks of the Seine, is very popular with locals and tourists alike.

The Riviera sparkles in August—but the notorious *embouteillages* (traffic jams) on the drive south from Paris can make you wish you stayed home.

Famously fickle weather means you never know what to expect in Normandy and Brittany, where picture-postcard villages and languorous sandy beaches are never jam-packed.

September is gorgeous, with temperate weather, saner airfares, and cultural events scheduled specifically for the return from summer vacation, an institution that even has its own name: *la rentrée*.

Another good time to visit is in late spring, just before the masses arrive, when the sun sets after 9 PM and cafés are abuzz.

Unless you're skiing in the Alps, winter is the least appealing time to come, though it's the best time to find less expensive airfares and hotel deals—and escape the crowds.

Transportation Basics

There are two major gateway airports to France just outside the capital: Orly, 16 km (10 mi) south of Paris, and Charles de Gaulle, 26 km (16 mi) northeast of the city. At Charles de Gaulle, also known as Roissy, there's a TGV (*train à grande vitesse*) station at Terminal 2, where you can connect to high-speed trains going all over the country.

Once in France, the best way to travel is by train, either high-speed TGV or regional train. A France Rail Pass allows three days of unlimited train travel in a one-month period. With train service efficient and enjoyable, long-distance bus service is rarely used, though there are some regional buses that cover areas where train service is spotty.

If you're traveling by car, there are excellent links between Paris and most French cities, but poor ones between the provinces. For the fastest route between two points, look for roads marked A for *autoroute*. A *péage* (toll) must be paid on most expressways: the rate varies, but can be steep. Note that gas prices are also steep, upward of €1.30 a liter, or about $6.50 a gallon.

Although renting a car is about twice as expensive as in the United States, it's the best way to see remote corners of the lovely French countryside. To get the best rate, book a rental car at home, and well in advance if you're planning a trip in summer and early fall. If you want automatic transmission, which is more expensive, be sure to ask for it when you reserve.

Here's a good tip: If you're traveling from Paris, a practical option is to take the TGV to another large city, such as Avignon or Nice, and rent a car there.

Hours

In Paris and larger cities, store hours are generally 10 AM to 7:30 PM; smaller shops may open later. Elsewhere, expect stores to close in the afternoon, usually 2–4. Museums are closed one day a week, often Tuesday. As a general rule, shops close on Sunday, though many food stores are open in the morning.

Tips on Eating and Staying

Restaurants follow French mealtimes, serving lunch from noon to 2 or 2:30 and dinner from 7:30 or 8 on. Some cafés in larger cities serve food all day long. Always reserve a table for dinner, as top restaurants book up months in advance. You must ask for the check (it's considered rude to bring it unbidden) except in cafés, where a register slip often comes with your order. Gratuities (*servis*) are included in the bill, but leave some small change on the table: a few cents for drinks, €1 for lunch, or €3 at dinner. You can leave more at a top restaurant, but note that more than 10% is considered extremely generous.

To save money on food, take advantage of France's wonderful outdoor markets and chain supermarkets. Just about every town has its own market once or a couple times a week. Ask the people at the front desk of wherever you're staying to find out when market days are. For supermarkets, the largest chain is Monoprix.

Some of the bigger stores have cafés where you can sit down and eat whatever you buy, as well as mini department stores that sell everything from clothing to children's toys to toiletries. French cities generally have good hotel options at decent prices. There are several options in Paris, including furnished apartments, at all price levels.

In the countryside, seek out *chambres d'hôtes* (bed-and-breakfasts), which can mean anything from a modest room in a host's home to a grand suite in a Norman château or Provençal farmhouse. Or rent a *gîte rural*, a furnished apartment, often on a farm or a larger property.

For more information on accommodations, see the France Lodging Primer later in this chapter, as well as the Travel Smart chapter.

DINING AND LODGING PRICE CATEGORIES (IN EUROS)

	¢	$	$$	$$$	$$$$
Restaurants	under €13	€13–€17	€18–€24	€25–€32	over €32
Hotels	under €65	€65–€105	€106–€145	€146–€215	over €215

Restaurant prices are per person for a main course at dinner, including tax (5.5%) and service; note that if a restaurant offers only prix-fixe (set-price) meals, it has been given the price category that reflects the full prix-fixe price. Hotel prices are for a standard double room in high season, including tax (19.6%) and service charge.

Fête-ing It Up

Spring. Spot your favorite star at the Cannes Film Festival in May (🌐 *www.festival-cannes.fr*). The French Open kicks off the last week of May in Paris (🌐 *www.rolandgarros.com*).

Love *grand cru*? Head to Bordeaux for the wine festival in late June (🌐 *www.bordeaux-fete-le-vin.com*).

Summer. Avignon sparkles in July during the monthlong theater and arts festival (🌐 *www.festival-avignon.com*). French cities and towns celebrate le 14 juillet (July 14, Bastille Day), marking the start of the French Revolution (🌐 *www.14-juillet.cityvox.com*).

The popular Paris Plage transforms the Seine's banks into a "beach" in mid-July with palm trees, sand, and lounge chairs (🌐 *www.paris.fr*).

Fall. Tour France's most beautiful buildings on the Journée du Patrimoine (Patrimony Day), usually the third Sunday in September (🌐 *www.journeesdupatrimoine.culture.fr*).

Paris has cultural events throughout September for *la rentrée* (the return) from summer vacation (🌐 *www.paris.fr*).

Winter. The Carnaval de Nice rocks Lent for three weeks in February (🌐 *www.nicecarnaval.com*). Strasbourg's famous Marchés de Noël (Christmas Markets) runs from late November to early January (🌐 *www.noel-strasbourg.com*).

GETTING AROUND

Bus Travel

Because France has invested so dearly in its highly organized national rail network and well-connected highway system, nationwide bus service simply doesn't exist.

Eurolines offers only international routes, so you can get in or out of the country, but there are no routes connecting the big cities within France.

Happily, domestic bus travel is managed regionally, usually serving small rural communities or replacing SNCF train routes that are no longer commercially viable.

These bus routes, however, tend to be slow, with confusing schedules posted online (and rarely in English). Still, they can often be a cheap and direct way to travel short distances.

The Getting Around section at the start of each of our chapters has handy local information about useful bus routes.

Remember that it is always useful to visit the local tourism office or the central bus depot for schedules and tickets.

Car Travel

While the French train network is quite vast, smaller towns—especially in harder-to-reach mountainous regions—may have only limited schedules. And since many route hubs are in major cities such as Paris, there's often a lack of direct routes in between these smaller towns, requiring a circuitous trajectory to cover a relatively short distance. This isn't a big deal for visitors with plenty of extra time who are flexible in their travel plans.

But if you're seeking the maximum amount of freedom to explore France off the beaten path, then a rental car could be your best option.

France's highways, or autoroutes (A), are well maintained, and generally traffic-free outside certain holidays and metropolitan areas during rush hour, but with so much natural beauty, charming villages and interesting sights along the way, we would recommend sticking to the national trunk roads, or Routes Nationales (RN), which allow you to easily stop to see local site, pick up some fresh produce at a farm, or pull over for a picnic at a lakeside park.

Of course, driving in France requires a valid license from your home country, a bit of talent with a map (as a backup to any GPS system), and enough knowledge about the local road rules to stay out of trouble.

While there are many pluses to driving a car, there are important minuses. One of the biggest expenses of your trip can wind up being the gasoline, which has been hovering around €1.35/liter (or €5.08 gallon) at this writing. In addition, signage in France can be spotty—we've heard plenty of horror stories about half-hour trips turning into two-hour ordeals.

Finally, there is the obstacle-course that is parking, with travelers to French cities having to run the gauntlet of meters, parking-ticket machines, parking cards (*cartes de stationnements*), chaotic rush-hour traffic, and the eternal search for an overnight garage.

If you're determined to drive, however, see our Travel Smart chapter for more tips for renting and driving a car in France.

Train Travel

The next best thing to flying, and sometimes more convenient, is by France's efficient railways, from regional trains connecting small towns and villages all over the country to the high-speed TGVs serving major cities.

The best thing about the trains is that the stations are usually right in the center of town, and in the case of Paris, connected to the metro. This means that backpackers can find a hotel within walking distance of the train station without worrying about long taxi rides to and from the airport.

Traveling by train also eliminates long security checks and excess baggage fees, and you get to enjoy the scenery as you travel.

Managed by the SNCF, almost every corner of France can be reached by train, including about 60 cities by TGV, and thousands more under the regional rail lines including Téoz (Paris, Bordeaux, Nice, Perpignan, and Clermont-Ferrand), the Lunéa sleeper trains (which have 1st class, 2nd class, and reclining seat options starting at €17), iDTGV theme trains (choose "zen," "games," or "nightclub" themed atmospheres on 20 routes), and the "TER" (Transport Express Régional) medium-distance trains serving the different French regions.

For instance, the Ile-de-France département surrounding Paris is served by the Transilien network, which links to the suburban Paris commuter rail known as the "RER" (Réseau Express Régional) and the Paris Métropolitan, or Métro.

Aside from these Paris networks, which are part of the Parisian Transportation Authority known as the "RATP" (Régie Autonome des Transports Parisiens), all trains in France are managed by the French National Railway, or "SNCF" (Société Nationale des Chemins de Fer Français).

This makes it a lot easier for travelers to find the best ticket whether it's by TGV or by regional TER, either by the official French site (🌐 *www.voyages-sncf.com*) or via Rail Europe (🌐 *www.raileurope.com*), which lets you search in your home country's language and currency before you arrive in France.

If you want to remain flexible even after you've arrived in France, sign up for their "Anywhere Anytime France e-tickets" for the convenience of ordering your tickets online and printing them at any train station up to an hour before departure time.

Read our Travel Smart chapter for the different discount options when traveling by train, including Eurail Passes and student/senior rates.

Air Travel

With a land-mass about 4/5 that of Texas, France presents its own set of transporation challenges when confronting the big question: What's the best way to get around? Fact is, the quickest and often least expensive option—thanks to budget airlines and competitive rates on Air France—is flying. You can fly in one hour from Paris into Nice Airport (plus 15 minutes by bus into town) on easyJet from Orly Airport (15 minutes south of Paris) from about €40 one-way (without checked bags). But factor in the extra hour at the airport for security, the baggage restrictions, and out-of-town location of airports—budget lines use smaller airports far from city centers. An Air France flight from Paris Orly to Marseille costs €125 while a RyanAir flight starts at just €30 but flies from Beauvais Airport (an hour north of Paris by bus) plus plenty of extra fees. But flying is often the best option if you have little luggage, less time, and travel to major cities.

Word of Mouth

"I've negotiated the RER trains in and out of Paris with luggage during rush hour without trauma. Use the pull-down jump seats near the doors. They almost certainly will be available when you get on since the trains originate at CDG airport."
—Robespierre

FRANCE TOP ATTRACTIONS

Louvre, Paris

(A) Home to art's most photogenic beauties—the *Venus de Milo, the Winged Victory*, and the *Mona Lisa*—this is not only the largest palace in France but also the most important museum in the world.

Chartres, Ile-de-France

(B) Triply famous for its peerless stained-glass windows, as the resting place for an important relic of the Virgin Mary, and as the birthplace of High Gothic, Chartres is more than a cathedral—it's a nondenominational spiritual experience.

Versailles, Ile-de-France

(C) A palace and then some, this prime example of royals-gone-wild Baroque style served as backdrop for the rise to power of King Louis XIV. To escape all his bicep-flexing grandeur visit the park to see Marie-Antoinette's fairytale farm.

Monet's Garden, Giverny, Ile-de-France

(D) A 8-acre "Monet," these lush gardens were works of art the Impressionist master spent years perfecting before he began re-creating them on canvas. The colors radiate best on sunny spring days.

Chenonceau, Loire Valley

Half-bridge, half-pleasure palace, this "queen of the châteaux" was presided over by six remarkable women. It was Catherine de' Medici who brilliantly enlarged it to span the River Cher in homage to the Ponte Vecchio of her native Florence.

Lyon, Rhône-Alps

The second largest city in France, Lyon vies with Paris as the country's true gastronomic capital—gourmands flock here for its galaxy of multistar superchefs and cozy bouchon taverns.

Mont-St-Michel, Normandy

(E) Once seen, never forgotten, this Romanesque abbey rises from its bay like a shimmering apparition, becoming an island at high tide. French and English fought to dominate the "rock" until the 13th century, when it was crowned with a splendid Gothic church.

Strasbourg, Alsace-Lorraine

(F) The cosmopolitan seat of Europe's Parliament, this fascinating mix of half-timber houses and modern glass buildings was fought over by France and Germany—a battle that resulted in a rich intertwining of cultures.

Beaune, Burgundy

At the heart of some of the world's most esteemed vineyards, this atmospheric town is inextricably linked with the wine trade, especially during the annual auction at Beaune's beautiful 15th-century Hôtel-Dieu.

Eze, the French Riviera

Spectacularly perched atop a rocky promontory, this watercolor-pretty village has some of the most breathtaking views this side of a NASA space capsule.

St-Tropez, the French Riviera

(G) Singlehandedly propelled from sleepy hamlet to glamorous resort by Brigitte Bardot, St-Trop today heaves with crowds of petulant glitterati. Chill out in the quiet pastel-hued alleys of the La Ponche quarter.

Aix-en-Provence, Provence

(H) With sun-dappled squares, luxuriant fountains, and Paul Cézanne's hallowed studio, this captivating town is just the spot for those who consider café-sitting, people-watching, and boutique shopping a way of life.

TOP EXPERIENCES

How will you experience France? Will you wile away the hours in the shops and cafés of Paris? Will you dine at the temples of gastronomy in Lyon? Will you play feudal lord among the châteaux of the Loire Valley? Or will you simply throw away your map and chance upon nestled-away villages of the Côte d'Azur or fairy-tale hamlets of the Dordogne? These suggestions, and the following, await you as memorable experiences for your next trip to France.

Walk Like a Parisian

Paris was made for wandering, and the French have coined a lovely word for a person who strolls, usually without a destination in mind: *le flâneur*. In Paris, no matter how aimlessly you wander, chances are you'll end up somewhere magical. Why not first head to the most beautiful spot on the Left Bank: the Cour du Commerce St-André?

Go Glam in Paris

Break out your bling in this capital of luxury with a stroll down the Avenue Montaigne to window-shop—the French call it *lèche-vitrine* (or "licking the windows")—from Chanel to Céline. Then do some real feasting at Paris's most legendary restaurant, Le Grand Vefour (lunch main courses are around 100 euros).

Rendezvous with the Phantom

Want to feel like a Rothschild for no money at all? Promenade the fabulously opulent lobby and theater of the 19th-century Palais Garnier (🌐 *www.opera-de-paris.fr*)—haunt of the Phantom and Degas's immortal dancers—daily 10 to 4:30 for free, or get tickets for an evening performance.

Pique-Nique at Place des Vosges

No restaurant can beat the "décor" of Paris's most beautiful square, the 17th-century Place des Vosges, so pull up a bench and enjoy your own foodie fixings. Get them at the nearby Marché d'Aligre market, off Rue du Faubourg Saint-Antoine. It beats those drab *supermarchés!*

Step into a 8-Acre Monet

It doesn't matter how many posters, photos, or tee-shirts you've seen emblazoned with Monet's famous water lilies, nothing beats a visit to Giverny. Savor the impressionist painter's famous house and gardens (🌐 *www.giverny.org*) in person.

Trip the Light Fantastique at Versailles

Exquisitely choreographed pyrotechnical shows are held each summer and fall in Versailles's immense château gardens (🌐 *www.chateauversailles.fr*). Accompanied by sun-et-lumière music and dance performances, these evenings are fit for the Sun King himself.

Plan an Ascent on Heaven at Mont-St-Michel

Keep the faith with a climb to the top and get a God's View of this fabled Benedictine abbey (🌐 *mont-saint-michel.monuments-nationaux.fr*), whose fortified medieval village is the crowning glory of the Normandy coastline.

Become Scott and Zelda on the Riviera

Channel F. Scott Fitzgerald and his wife at their old haunts and discover their side of paradise: stay at their Les Belles Rives hotel in Juan-les-Pins, visit hang-outs like the Villa Eilenroc at Cap d'Antibes (🌐 *www.antibes-juanlespins.com*), or dine with superstars at the Hôtel du Cap-Eden Roc.

Rate the Best of Alsace's Würsts

As you head down Alsace's famous Wine Road, Hansel and Gretel villages pop up every few miles, and each have winstubs that cook up delicious dishes of choucroute garnie. The inns in Riquewihr and Ribeauvillé (🌐 *www.ribeauville-riquewihr.com*) are supposed to serve the best.

Pop Your Cork along the Champagne Road

The famous Route du Champagne (🌐 *www.tourisme-en-champagne.com*) leads fans of the famous bubbly to the prestigious Champagne houses of Epernay and Reims (including Mumm and Taittinger) plus smaller, family-run estates for tours and tastings.

Que la Fête Commence at Nice's Carnaval

February is festival time on the Côte d'Azur, with boisterous street processions and a celebratory bonfire for the Mardi-Gras Carnaval de Nice (🌐 *www.nicecarnaval.com*). Or march along the citrus-decked parade floats of Menton's Fête du Citron (🌐 *www.feteducitron.com*).

Go Castle-Hopping on a Loire Valley Bike Tour

From Orléans to Angers, bike with VBT Tours (🌐 *www.vbt.com*) along the meandering Loire River past royal châteaux and bountiful gardens, and discover quirky cliffside troglodyte dwellings that house wine caves and mushroom growers.

Wear Hip-Deep Purple along the Lavender Route

Join the lavender-happy crowds from June to early September and travel the Route de la Lavande (🌐 *www.routes-lavande.com*), a wide blue-purple swath that connects major sights like the Abbaye Notre-Dame de Sènaque, Coustellet's Musée de la Lavande, and Forcalquier's famous market.

Apres-Ski the Day Away in the French Alps

As home to the first Winter Olympic games in 1924, the ski station of Chamonix (🌐 *www.chamonix.com*), set at the foot of Mont Blanc, provides an ideal winter backdrop for all winter outdoor activities.

Be a Road Buddy to Picasso in St-Paul-de-Vence

Use Aix-en-Provence, Arles, or Antibes as a base for touring the Modern Art Road. Explore picture-perfect villages immortalized by Cézanne and Van Gogh and pose oh-so-casually under the Picassos on view at the Colombe d'Or inn (🌐 *www.la-colombe-dor.com*).

Play Once-Upon-a-Time in Carcassonne

Protected by a double ring of ramparts and 53 towers, this perfectly preserved fortified city (🌐 *www.carcassonne.org*) of the Languedoc-Roussillon region is considered to be one of the most romantic medieval settings in France.

Attend the Festival d'Avignon

This internationally renowned summer theater festival (🌐 *www.festival-avignon.com*) features nearly a thousand performances throughout the city, plus hundreds more in the "unofficial" "Avignon Off" festival.

Track the Tour de France

No tickets are required to watch this famed cycling competition (🌐 *www.letour.fr*) as it winds through some of the country's most dramatic scenery. Why not enjoy a picnic anywhere along the route as the riders race past?

QUINTESSENTIAL FRANCE

Café Society

Along with air, water, and wine, the café remains one of the basic necessities of life in France. You may prefer a posh perch at a renowned Paris spot such as the Deux Magots on Boulevard St-Germain or opt for a tiny *café du coin* (corner café) in Lyon or Marseilles, where you can have a quick cup of coffee at the counter. Those on Paris's major boulevards (such as Boulevard St-Michel and the Champs-Élysées) will almost always be the most expensive and the least interesting.

In effect, the more modest establishments (look for nonchalant locals) are the places to really get a feeling for French café culture.

And we do mean culture—not only the practical rituals of the experience (perusing the posted menu, choosing a table, unwrapping your sugar cube) but an intellectual spur as well.

You'll see businessmen, students, and pensive types pulling out notebooks for intent scribblings. In fact, some Paris landmarks like the Café de Flore host readings, while several years ago a trend for *cafés philos* (philosophy cafés) took off.

And there's always the frisson of history available at places like La Closerie des Lilas, where an expensive drink allows you to rest your derrière on the spots once favored by Baudelaire and Apollinaire.

Finally, there's people-watching, which goes hand in glove with the café lifestyle—what better excuse to linger over your *café crème* or Lillet? So get ready to settle in, sip your *pastis*, and pretend your travel notebook is a Hemingway story in the making.

Street Markets

Browsing through the street markets and *marchés couverts* (covered markets) of France is enough to make you regret all the tempting restaurants around.

If you want to get a sense of contemporary French culture, and indulge in some of its pleasures, start by familiarizing yourself with the rituals of daily life. These are a few highlights—things you can take part in with relative ease.

But even though their seafood, free-range poultry, olives, and produce cry out to be gathered in a basket and cooked in their purest forms, you can also enjoy them as a simple visual feast.

Over at flea and *brocante* (collectibles) markets, food plays second fiddle. With any luck, you'll find a little 18th-century engraving that makes your heart go *trottinant.*

Bistros and Brasseries

The choice of restaurants in France is a feast in itself. Of course, at least once during your trip you'll want to indulge in a luxurious meal at a great haute-cuisine restaurant—but there's no need to get knee-deep in white truffles at Paris's Alain Ducasse to savor the France the French eat. For you can discover the most delicious *French-Women-Don't-Get-Fat* food with a quick visit to a city neighborhood bistro.

History tells us that bistros served the world's first fast food—after the fall of Napoléon, the Russian soldiers who occupied Paris were known to cry *bistro* ("quickly" in Russian) when ordering.

Here, at zinc-top tables, you'll find the great delights of *cuisine traditionelle,* like *grand-mère's* lamb with white beans.

Today the bistro boom has meant that many are designer-decorated and packed with trendsetters.

If you're lucky, the food will be as witty and colorful as the clientele.

Brasseries, with few exceptions, remain unchanged—great bustling places with white-aproned waiters and hearty, mainly Alsatian, food, such as pork-based dishes, *choucroute* (sauerkraut), and beer ("brasserie" also means brewery).

Bon appétit!

IF YOU LIKE

Great Food

Forget the Louvre or the Château de Chenonceau—the real reason for a visit to France is to dine at its famous temples of gastronomy. Once you dive into Taillevent's lobster soufflé, you'll quickly realize that food in France is far more than fuel. The French regard gastronomy as essential to the art of living, so don't feel guilty if your meal at Paris's Grand Véfour takes as long as your visit to the Musée d'Orsay: two hours for a three-course menu is par, and you may, after relaxing into the routine, feel pressured at less than three. Gastronomads—those who travel to eat—won't want to miss a pilgrimage out to Mougins to witness the culinary fireworks of chef Alain Llorca, whose name reveals his Basque roots. These days, la haute cuisine in the States and England is nearly as rare as Tibetan food, so plan on treating dining as religiously as the French do—at least once.

- **Le Grand Véfour, Paris.** Guy Martin's Savoyard creations are extraordinaire, but the 18th-century decor is almost more delicious.
- **Le Moulin de Mougins, Mougins.** Master chef Alain Llorca marries grand cuisine with humble Provençal touches—don't be surprised to find octopus in your bouillabaisse.
- **Le Louis XV, Monaco.** If you're going to feast like a king, this Alain Ducasse outpost is the place to do it.

La Vie de Châteaux

From the humblest feudal ruin to the most delicate Loire Valley spires to the grandest of Sun King spreads, the châteaux of France evoke the history of Europe as no museum can. Standing on their castellated ramparts, it is easy to slip into the role of a feudal lord scrambling to protect his patchwork of holdings from kings and dukes. The lovely landscape takes on a strategic air and you find yourself role-playing thus, whether swanning aristocratically over Chenonceau's bridgelike *galerie de bal* spanning the River Cher or curling a revolutionary lip at the splendid excesses of Versailles. These are, after all, the castles that inspired Charles Perrault's Sleeping Beauty and Beauty and the Beast, and their fairy-tale magic—rich with history and Disney-free—still holds true. Better yet, enjoy a "queen-for-a-stay" night at one of France's many châteaux-hotels. Many are surprisingly affordable—even though some bathrooms look like they should be on a postcard.

- **Château de la Bourdaisière, Loire Valley.** Not one but *two* princes de Broglie welcome you to this idyllic and elegant neo-Renaissance hotel.
- **Vaux-le-Vicomte, Ile-de-France.** Louis XIV was so jealous when he saw this 17th-century Xanadu that he commissioned Versailles.
- **Chambord, Loire Valley.** This French Renaissance extravaganza—all 440 rooms and 365 chimneys—will take your breath away. Be sure to go up the down staircase designed by da Vinci.
- **Château d'Ussé, Loire Valley.** Step into a fairy tale at Sleeping Beauty's legendary home.

Beautiful Villages

Nearly everyone has a mind's-eye view of the perfect French village. Oozing half-timber houses and roses, these once-upon-a-time-ified villages have a sense of tranquillity not even tour buses can ruin. The Loire Valley's prettiest village, Saché, is so small it seems your own personal property—an eyebrow of cottages, a Romanesque church, a 17th-century auberge inn, and a modest château. Little wonder Honoré de Balzac came here to write some of his greatest novels. Auvers-sur-Oise, the pretty riverside village in the Ile-de-France, inspired some of Van Gogh's finest landscapes. In the Dordogne region, hamlets have a Walt Disney–like quality, right down to Rapunzel windows, flocks of geese, and storks'-nest towers. Along the Côte d'Azur you'll find the sky-kissing, hilltop *villages perchés*, like Èze. All in all, France has an *embarras de richesses* of nestled-away treasures—so just throw away the map. After all, no penciled itinerary is half as fun as stumbling upon some half-hidden Brigadoon.

- **Riquewihr, Alsace.** Full of storybook buildings, cul-de-sac courtyards, and stone gargoyles, this is the showpiece of the Alsatian Wine Route.
- **Haut-de-Cagnes, French Riviera.** This perfect example of the eagle's-nest village near the coast is nearly boutique-free, was once adored by Renoir, and remains ancient in atmosphere.
- **La Roque-Gageac, Dordogne.** Lorded over by its immense rock cliff, this centuries-old riverside village is the perfect backdrop for a beautiful *pique-nique*.

Monet, Manet, and Matisse

It is through the eyes of its artists that many first get to know France. No wonder people from across the globe come to search for Gauguin's bobbing boats at Pont-Aven, Monet's bridge at Giverny, and the gaslit Moulin Rouge of Toulouse-Lautrec—not hung in a museum but alive in all their three-dimensional glory. In Arles you can stand on the spot where Van Gogh painted and compare his perspective to a placard with his finished work; in Paris you can climb into the garret-atelier where Delacroix created his epic canvases, or wander the redolent streets of Montmartre, once haunted by Renoir, Utrillo, and Modigliani. Of course, an actual trip to France is not necessary to savor this country: a short visit to any major museum will probably just as effectively transport the viewer—by way of the paintings of Pisarro, Millet, Poussin, Sisley, and Matisse—to its legendary landscapes. But go beyond museums and discover the actual towns that once harbored these famed artists.

- **St-Paul-de-Vence, Côte d'Azur.** Pose oh-so-casually under the Picassos at the famed Colombe d'Or inn, once favored by Signac, Modigliani, and Bonnard.
- **Céret, Languedoc-Roussillon.** Pack your crayons for a trip to Matisse Country, for this is where the artist fell in love with the *fauve* (savage) hues found only in Mother Nature.
- **Giverny, Ile-de-France.** Replacing paint and water with earth and water, Monet transformed his 5-acre garden into a veritable live-in Impressionist painting.

Le Shopping

Although it's somewhat disconcerting to see Gap stores gracing almost every major street corner in Paris and other urban areas in France, if you take the time to peruse smaller specialty shops, you can find rare original gifts—be it an antique brooch from the 1930s or a modern vase crafted from Parisian rooftop-tile zinc. It's true that the traditional gifts of silk scarves, perfume, and wine can often be purchased for less in the shopping mall back home, but you can make an interesting twist by purchasing a vintage Hermès scarf, or a unique perfume from an artisan perfumer. Bargaining is traditional in outdoor and flea markets, antiques stores, small jewelry shops, and craft galleries, for example. If you're thinking of buying several items, or if you're simply in love with something a little bit too expensive, you've nothing to lose by cheerfully suggesting to the proprietor, "Vous me faites un prix?" ("How about a discount?") The small businessperson will immediately size you up, and you'll have some good-natured fun.

■ **Colette, Paris.** Wiggle into the ultimate little black dress at this fashionista shrine.

■ **L'Isle-sur-la-Sorgue, Provence.** This canal-laced town becomes a Marrakech of marketeers on Sunday, when dazzling brocante (antiques) dealers set up shop.

■ **Grain de Vanille, Cancale.** These sublime tastes of Brittany—salted butter caramels, rare honeys, and malouine cookies—make great gifts, *non*?

Gothic Churches and Cathedrals

Their extraordinary permanence, their everlasting relevance even in a secular world, and their transcendent beauty make the Gothic churches and cathedrals of France a lightning rod if you are in search of the essence of French culture. The product of a peculiarly Gallic mix of mysticism, exquisite taste, and high technology, France's 13th- and 14th-century "heavenly mansions" provide a thorough grounding in the history of architecture (some say there was nothing new in the art of building between France's Gothic arch and Frank Lloyd Wright's cantilevered slab). Each cathedral imparts its own monumental experience—knee-weakening grandeur, a mighty resonance that touches a chord of awe, and humility in the unbeliever. Even cynics will find satisfaction in these edifices' social history—the anonymity of the architects, the solidarity of the artisans, and the astonishing bravery of experiments in suspended stone.

■ **Notre-Dame, Paris.** Make a face back at the gargoyles high atop Quasimodo's home.

■ **Reims, Champagne.** Tally up the 34 VIPs crowned at this magnificent edifice, the age-old setting for the coronations of French kings.

■ **Chartres, Ile-de-France.** Get enlightened with France's most beautiful stained-glass windows.

■ **Mont-St-Michel, Normandy.** From its silhouette against the horizon to the abbey and gardens at the peak of the rock, you'll never forget this awe-inspiring sight.

L'Esprit Sportif

Though the physically inclined would consider walking across Scotland or bicycling across Holland, they often misconstrue France as a sedentary country where one plods from museum to château to restaurant. But it's possible to take a more active approach: imagine pedaling past barges on the Saône River or along slender poplars on a *route départementale* (provincial road); hiking over Alpine meadows near Megéve; or sailing the historic ports of Honfleur or Antibes. Experiencing this side of France will take you off the beaten path and into the countryside. As you bike along French country roads or along the extensive network of Grands Randonnées (Lengthy Trails) crisscrossing the country, you will have time to tune into the landscape—to study crumbling garden walls, smell the honeysuckle, and chat with a farmer in his *potager* (vegetable garden).

- **The VBT Loire Biking Tour.** Stunning châteaux-hotels, Pissarro-worthy riverside trails, and 20 new best friends make this a *fantastique* way to go "around the whirl."
- **Sentier des Cascades, Haute-Pyrénées.** Near Cauterets is the GR10 walk, which features stunning views of the famous waterfalls and abundant *marmottes* (Pyrenean groundhogs).
- **Tracking the Camargue Reserve, Provence.** Take an unforgettable *promenade équestre* (horseback tour) of this amazing nature park, home to bulls and birds—50,000 flamingos, that is.

Clos Encounters

Bordeaux or Burgundy, Sauternes or Sancerre, Romanée-Conti or Côte du Rhône—wherever you turn in France, you'll find famous Gallic wine regions and vineyards, born of the country's curvaceous landscape. Speckled unevenly with hills, canals, forests, vineyards, châteaux, and the occasional cow clinging to 30-degree inclines, the great wine regions of France attract hordes of travelers more interested in shoving their noses deep into wine glasses than staring high into the stratosphere of French cathedral naves. Fact is, you can buy the bottles of the fabled regions—the Côte d'Or, the Rhône Valley, or that oenophile's nirvana, Bordeaux—anywhere, so why not taste the lesser-known local crus from, say, the lovely vineyards in the Loire Valley. Explore the various *clos* (enclosures) and *côtes* (hillsides) that grow golden by October, study the *vendangeur* grape-pickers, then drive along the wine routes looking for those "Dégustation" signs, promising free sips from the local vintner. Pretty soon you'll be an expert on judging any wine's aroma, body, and backwash.

- **Mouton-Rothschild, Route de Médoc.** Baron Philippe perfected one of the great five premiers crus here—and there's a great visitor center.
- **Clos de Vougeot, Burgundy.** A historic wine-making barn, 13th-century grape presses, and its verdant vineyard make this a must-do.
- **The Alsace Route de Vin.** Between Mulhouse and Strasbourg, many picture-book villages entice with top vintners.

HISTORY YOU CAN SEE

France has long been the standard bearer of Western civilization—without her, neither English liberalism nor the American Constitution would exist today. It has given us Notre Dame, Loire châteaux, Versailles, Stendhal, Chardin, Monet, Renoir, and the most beautiful city in the world, Paris. So it is no surprise that France unfolds like a gigantic historical pop-up book. To help you understand the country's masterful mélange of old and new, here's a quick overview of La Belle France's stirring historical pageant.

Ancient France

France's own "Stonehenge"—the megalithic stone complexes at Carnac in Brittany (circa 3500 BC)—were created by the Celts, who inhabited most of northwest Europe during the last millenniums BC. In the 1st century BC Julius Caesar conquered Gaul, and the classical civilizations of the Mediterranean soon made artistic inroads. The Greek trading colonies at Marseille eventually gave way to the Roman Empire, with the result that ancient Roman aesthetics left a lasting impression: it is no accident that the most famous modern example of a Roman triumphal arch—the **Arc de Triomphe**—should have been built in Paris.

What to See: France possesses examples of ancient Roman architecture that even Italy cannot match: Provence, whose name comes from the Latin, had been one of the most popular places to holiday for the ancient Romans. The result is that you can find the best preserved **Roman arena in Nimes** (along with the **Maison Carrée**), the best preserved **Roman theater at Orange**, and the best preserved Roman bridge aqueduct, the **Pont du Gard**.

The Middle Ages: From Romanesque to Gothic

By the 7th century AD Christianity was well established throughout France. Its interaction with an inherited classical tradition produced the first great indigenous French culture, the Frankish or Merovingian, created by the Franks (who gave their name to the new nation), Germanic tribes who succeeded in expelling the Romans from French soil. Various French provinces began to unite as part of Charlemagne's new Holy Roman Empire and, as a central core of European Catholicism, France now gave rise to great monastic centers—**Tours, Auxerre, Reims, and Chartres**—that were also cultural powerhouses. After the Crusades, more settled conditions led to the flowering of the

58–51 BC	Caesar's conquest of Gaul
800 AD	Charlemagne made Holy Roman Emperor
1066	William of Normandy invades England with victory at the Battle of Hastings
12th–13th century	Cathedrals of Notre Dame and Chartres.
1431	Joan of Arc burned; from lowest point, French nation revived
1572	St. Bartholomew Massacre of Protestants
1580–87	Montaigne's *Essays*
1678	Louis XIV adds the Hall of Mirrors to Versailles
18th century	Zenith of French enlightenment and influence, thanks to Molière, Racine, Voltaire, Diderot, and Rousseau
1789–92	The French Revolution
1793	Queen Marie-Antoinette is guillotined on Paris's Place de la Concorde

Romanesque style developed by reformist monastic orders like the Benedictines at Cluny. This then gave way to the Gothic, which led to the construction of many cathedrals—perhaps the greatest architectural achievement created in France—during the biggest building spree of the Middle Ages. Under the Capetian kings, French government became more centralized. The most notable king was Louis IX (1226–70), known as Saint Louis, who left important monuments in the Gothic style, which lasted some 400 years and gained currency throughout Europe.

What to See: The Romanesque style sprang out of the forms of classical art left by the Romans and its top artistic landmarks adorn Burgundy: the giant transept of **Cluny**, the sculptures of Gislebertus at **Autun's Cathèdrale St-Lazare,** and the amazing tympanum of the **Basilique Ste-Madeleine at Vézelay.** Another top Romanesque artwork is in Normandy: the **Bayeux Tapestry** on view in Bayeux. The desire to span greater area with stone and to admit more light led to the development of the new Gothic style. This became famed for its use of the pointed arch and the rib vault, resulting in an essentially skeletal structure containing large areas of glass. First fully developed at **Notre Dame**, Paris (from 1163), **Chartres** (from 1200), **Reims** (from 1211), and **Amiens** (from 1220), the Gothic cathedral contains distinctive Gothic forms: delicate filigree-like rose windows of stained glass, tall lancet windows, elaborately sculpted portails, and "flying buttresses." King Louis IV commissioned **Paris's Sainte-Chapelle** chapel in the 1240s and it remains the most beautiful artistic creation of the Middle Ages.

The Renaissance

France nationalism came to the fore once the tensions and wars fomented by the warring clans of the Houses of Anjou and Capet climaxed in the Hundred Years' War (1328–1453). During this time, Joan of Arc helped drive English rulers from France with the Valois line of kings taking the throne. From the late 15th century into the 16th, the golden light of the Italian Renaissance then dawned over France. This was due, in large measure, to King François I (accession 1515), who returned from wars in Italy with many Italian artists and craftsmen, among them Leonardo da Vinci (who lived in Amboise from 1507). With decades of peace, fortresses soon became châteaux and the picture palaces of the Loire Valley came

1799–1804	Napoléon rules as First Consul of the Consulate
1805–12	Napoléon conquers large parts of Europe but is defeated in Russia
1815	Napoléon loses battle at Waterloo to England's Duke of Wellington
1848–70	The Second Empire, ruled by Emperor Napoléon III, with colonial expansion into Indochina, Syria, and Mexico
1863	Impressionists show at the Salon des Refusés in Paris
1870	Franco-Prussian War; France defeated, but Flaubert and Baudelaire writing
1871	Alsace-Lorraine ceded to Germany
1940	France surrenders to Germany during World War II: Paris falls
1958	General de Gaulle elected president
1969	Student riots in Paris; government is subsequently stabilized through presidents including Georges Pompidou, François Mitterand, and Nicolas Sarkozy

into being. The grandest of these, Fontainebleau and Chambord, reflected the growing centralization of the French court and were greatly influenced by the new Italian styles.

What to See: An earnest desire to rival and outdo Italy in cultural pursuits dominated French culture during the 15th and 16th centuries. For the decoration of the new **Palace of Fontainebleau** (from 1528) artists like **Cellini, Primaticcio,** and **Rosso** used rich colors, elongated forms, and a concentration upon allegory and eroticism to help cement the Mannerist style. Gothic and vernacular forms of architecture were now rejected in favor of classical models, as could be seen in the châteaux in the Loire Valley such as **Blois** (from 1498), **Chambord** (from 1519, where design elements were created by **Leonardo**), and **Chenonceau,** which was commissioned by the king's mother, Catherine de' Medici. The rebuilding of Paris's **Louvre,** begun in 1546, marked the final assimilation of Italian classical architecture into France.

Royal Absolutism and the Baroque Style

Rising out of the conflicts between Catholic and Protestant (thousands of Huguenots were murdered in the St. Bartholomew's Day massacre of 1572), King Henry IV became the first Bourbon king and fomented religious tolerance with the Edict of Nantes (1598). By the 17th century architecture still had an Italianate flavor, as seen in the Roman Baroque forms adorning Parisian churches. The new Baroque architectural taste for large-scale town planning gave rise to the many squares that formed focal points within cities. King Louis XIV, the Sun King, came to the throne in 1643, but he chose to rule from a new power base he built outside Paris: Versailles soon became a symbol of the absolutist court of the Sun King and the new insatiable national taste for glory. But with Louis XIV, XV, and XVI going for broke, a reaction against extravagance and for logic and empirical reason took over. Before long, writers like Jean-Jacques Rousseau argued for social and political reform—the need for revolution.

What to See: To create a more carefully ordered aristocratic bureaucracy, courtiers were commanded to leave their family châteaux and take up residence in the massive new **Versailles** palace. A golden age for art began, since patronage of the arts enjoyed almost equal expenditure to that lavished on Louis's continual wars. The palaces of the **Louvre** (1545–1878) and **Versailles** (1661–1756) bear witness to this in their sheer scale. "After me, the deluge," Louis XIV said, and early 18th-century France was on the verge of bankruptcy. In turn, the court turned away from the over-the-top splendor of Versailles and Paris's **Luxembourg Palace** to retreat to smaller, more domestic houses in Paris, seen in such hôtel particuliers as the **Musée Nissim de Camondo** and the charming **Hameau** farm created for Marie-Antoinette in Versailles' park. Bombastic Baroque gave way to the Rococo style, as the charming, feminine paintings of **Watteau, Boucher,** and **Fragonard** provided cultural diversions for an aristocracy withdrawn from the stage of power politics. Find their masterpieces at the Louvre, **Carnavalet,** and other museums.

Revolution and Romanticism

The end of Bourbon rule came with the execution of **Louis XVI and Marie-Antoinette.** The French Revolution ushered in the First Republic (1792–1804). After a backlash to the Terror (1793–94), in which

hundreds were guillotined, **Napoléon** rose to power from the ashes of the Revolutionary **Directoire**. With him a new intellectual force and aesthetic mode came to the fore—**Romanticism**. With lucid introspection, this new style revolved around inner emotions and the personal self, leading to the withdrawal of the artists from politics, growing industrialization, and urbanization into a more subjective world. Napoléon's First Empire (1804–14) conquered most of Europe, but after the disastrous Russian invasion the Bourbon dynasty was restored with the rule of Charles X and Louis-Philippe. The latter, known as the Citizen King, abdicated in 1848 and made way for the Second Republic and the return of Napoleonic forces with Napoléon III's Second Empire (1852–70).

What to See: As often happens, art is one step ahead of history. The design of Paris's **Panthéon** by Soufflot, Gabriel's refined **Petit Trianon** at Versailles (1762), and the paintings of **Greuze** (1725–1805) and **David** (1745–1825), on view at the Louvre, display a conceit for moral order in great contrast to the flippancies of Fragonard. A renewed taste for classicism was seen in the Empire style promulgated by Napoléon; see the emperor's Paris come alive at the Left Bank's charming **Cour du Commerce St-André** and his shrine, **Les Invalides**. But the rigidly formal Neoclassical style soon gave way to Romanticism, whose touchstones are immediacy of technique, emotionalism, and the ability to convey the uncertainties of the human condition. Go to Paris's **Musée Delacroix** to get an up-close look at this expresive, emotive master of Romanticism.

The Modern Age Begins

Napoléon's III's Second Empire lead to the vast aggrandization of France on the world stage, with colonies set up across the globe, a booming economy, and the capital city of Paris remade into Europe's showplace thanks to **Baron Haussman**. After the Prussians invaded, France was defeated and culture was shattered and reformed. Romanticism became **Realism**, often carrying strong social overtones, as seen in the works of **Courbet**. The closer reexamination of reality by the **Barbizon School** of landscape painters lead to **Impressionism**, whose masters approached their subjects with a fresh eye, using clear, bright colors to create atmospheric effects and naturalistic observation. By 1870 French rule was reinstated with the **Third Republic**, which lasted until 1940.

What to See: Thanks to Haussman, Paris became the City of Light, with new large boulevards opening up the dark urban city, an outlook culminating in the **Eiffel Tower**, built for the Paris Exposition of 1889. Taking modern life as their subject matter, great Impressionist masters like **Monet** (1840–1926), **Renoir** (1841–1919), and **Degas** (1834–1917) proceeded to break down visual perceptions in terms of light and color, culminating in the late series of *Waterlily* paintings (from 1916) done at **Monet's Giverny estate**. Along with masterpieces by **Degas, Gauguin, Van Gogh,** and **Cézanne,** the most famous Impressionist and Post-Impressionist paintings can be seen at Paris's famed **Musée d'Orsay.** These artists began the myth of the Parisian Bohemian artist, the disaffected idealist kicking at the shins of tradition, and they forged the path then boldly trod by the greatest artist of the 20th century, **Picasso**, whose works can be seen at Paris's **Musée Picasso** and **Centre Beaubourg**.

GREAT ITINERARIES

THE GOOD LIFE

Beginning in château country, head south and west, through Cognac country into wine country around Bordeaux. Then lose yourself in the Dordogne, a landscape of rolling hills peppered with medieval villages, fortresses, and prehistoric caves.

Loire Valley Châteaux

3 or 4 days. Base yourself at the crossroads of Blois, starting with its multi-era château. Then head for the huge château in Chambord. Amboise's château echoes with history, and the neighboring manor, Clos Lucé, was Leonardo da Vinci's final home—or instead of this "town" château, head west to the tiny village of Rigny-Ussé for the Sleeping Beauty castle of Ussé. Heading southeast, finish up at Chenonceau—the most magical one of all—then return to the transportation hub city of Tours. ⇨ *The Loire Valley in Chapter 4*

Bordeaux Wine Country

2 days. Pay homage to the great names of Médoc, north of the city of Bordeaux, though the hallowed villages of Margaux, St-Julien, Pauillac, and St-Estèphe aren't much to look at. East of Bordeaux, via the prettier Pomerol vineyards, the village of St-Émilion is everything you'd want a wine town to be, with ramparts and medieval streets. ⇨ *Bordeaux in Chapter 15*

Dordogne and Périgord

2 or 3 days. Follow the famous Dordogne River east to the half-timber market town of Bergerac. Wind through the green, wooded countryside into the region where humans' earliest ancestors left their mark, in the caves in Les Eyzies-de-Tayac and the famous Grotte de Lascaux. Be sure to sample the region's culinary specialties: truffles, foie gras, and preserved duck. Then travel south to the stunning and sky-high village of Rocamadour. ⇨ *Dordogne in Chapter 16*

By Public Transportation

It's easy to get to Blois and Chenonceaux by rail, but you'll need to take a bus to visit other Loire châteaux. Forays farther into Bordeaux country and the Dordogne are difficult by train, involving complex and frequent changes (Limoges is a big railway hub). Further exploration requires a rental car or sometimes unreliable bus routes.

FRANCE FROM NORTH TO SOUTH

Zoom from Paris to the heart of historic Burgundy, its rolling green hills traced with hedgerows and etched with vineyards. From here, plunge into the arid beauty of Provence and toward the spectacular coastline of the Côte d'Azur.

Burgundy Wine Country

2 to 3 days. Base yourself in the market town of Beaune and visit its famous hospices and surrounding vineyards. Make a day trip to the ancient hill town of Vézelay, with its incomparable basilica, stopping in Autun to explore Roman ruins and its celebrated Romanesque cathedral. For more vineyards, follow the Côte d'Or from Beaune to Dijon. Or make a beeline to Dijon, with its charming Vieille Ville and fine museums. From here it's a two-hour drive to Lyon, where you can feast on this city's famous earthy cuisine. Another three hours' push takes you deep into the heart of Provence. ⇨ *Burgundy in Chapter 9 and Lyon in Chapter 10*

Arles and Provence

2 to 3 days. Arles is the atmospheric, sun-drenched southern town that inspired Van Gogh and Gauguin. Make a day trip into grand old Avignon, home to the 14th-century rebel popes, to view their imposing palace. And make a pilgrimage to the Pont du Gard, the famous triple-tiered Roman aqueduct west of Avignon. From here two

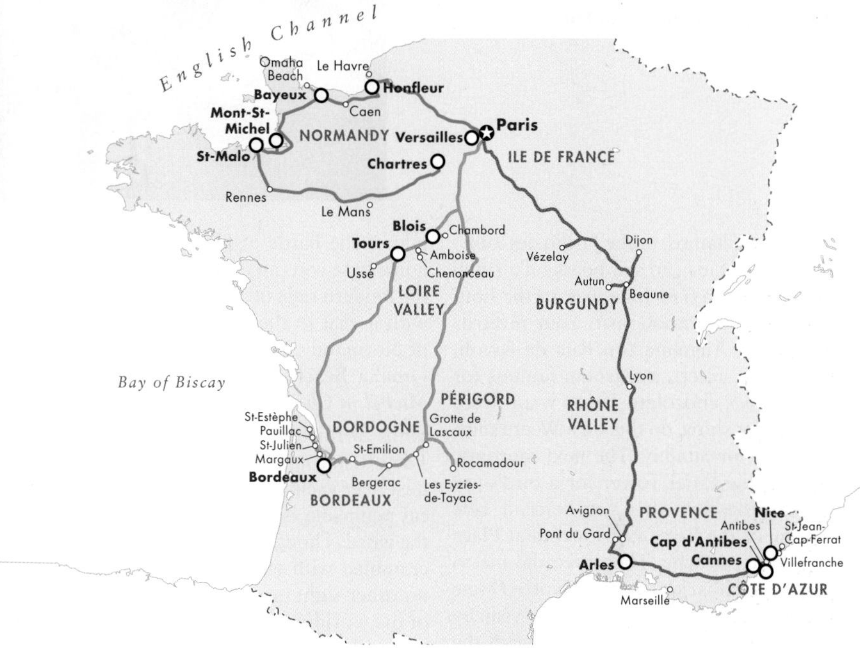

hours' drive will bring you to the glittering Côte d'Azur. ⇨ *Arles, Avignon, and Pont du Gard in Chapter 11*

Antibes and the French Riviera

2 to 3 days. This historic and atmospheric port town is well positioned for day trips. First, head west to glamorous Cannes. The next day head east into Nice, with its exotic Vieille Ville and its bounty of modern art. There are ports to explore in Villefranche and St-Jean-Cap-Ferrat, east of Nice. Allow time for a walk out onto the tropical paradise peninsula of Cap d'Antibes, or for an hour or two lolling on the coast's famous pebble beaches. ⇨ *Cannes, Nice, Villefranche-sur-Mer, St-Jean-Cap-Ferrat, and Cap d'Antibes in Chapter 12*

By Public Transportation

The high-speed TGV travels from Paris through Burgundy and Lyon, then zips through the south to Marseille. Train connections to Beaune from the TGV are easy; getting to Autun from Beaune takes up to two hours, with a change at Chagny. Vézelay can be reached by bus excursion from Dijon or Beaune. Rail connections are easy between Arles and Avignon; you'll need a bus to get to the Pont du Gard from Avignon. Antibes, Cannes, and Nice are easily reached by the scenic rail line, as are most of the resorts and ports along the coast. To squeeze the most daytime out of your trip, take a night train or a plane from Nice back to Paris.

A CHILD'S-EYE VIEW

Make your way through Normandy and Brittany, with enough wonders and evocative topics to inspire any child to put down his computer game and gawk.

Paris

2 days. Paris's major museums, like the Louvre, can be as engaging as they are educational—as long as you keep your visits short. Start out your Paris stay by giving your kids an idea of how the city was planned by climbing to the top of the Arc de Triomphe. From here work your way down the Champs-Élysées toward Place de la Concorde. Stop for a puppet show at the Marionettes des Champs-Élysées, at Avenues Matignon and Gabriel, halfway down the Champs. Continue walking

down the Champs, to the Jardin des Tuileries, where kids can sail boats on a small pond. Then taxi or hike over to the Louvre for an afternoon visit. Your reward? Stop in at Angélina (on Rue de Rivoli, across the street), a tearoom famous for its thick hot chocolate. If you want to see the puppet show, do this on a Wednesday, Saturday, or Sunday. The next morning, head to the Eiffel Tower for a bird's-eye view of the city. After you descend, ride on one of the Bateaux Mouches at Place de l'Alma, nearby. Then take the métro to the hunchback's hangout, Notre-Dame Cathedral. Finish up your Paris visit by walking several blocks over, through the center of the Ile de la Cité, to Paris's most storybook sight—the Sainte-Chapelle, a fairy-tale, stained-glass chapel that looks like a stage set for Walt Disney's *Sleeping Beauty.* ⇨ *Paris in Chapter 2*

Versailles

1 day. Here's an opportunity for a history lesson: with its amazing Baroque extravagance, no other monument so succinctly illustrates what inspired the rage of the French Revolution. Louis XIV's eye-popping château of Versailles pleases the secret monarch in most of us. ⇨ *Western Ile-de-France in Chapter 3*

Honfleur

1 day. From this picture-book seaport lined with skinny half-timber row houses and salt-dampened cobblestones, the first French explorers set sail for Canada in the 15th century. ⇨ *Honfleur to Mont-St-Michel in Chapter 5*

Bayeux

2 days. William the Conqueror's extraordinary invasion of England in 1066 was launched from the shores of Normandy. The famous Bayeux tapestry, showcased in a state-of-the-art museum, spins the tale of the Battle of Hastings. From this home base you can introduce the family to the modern saga of 1944's Allied landings with a visit to the Museum of the Battle of Normandy, then make a pilgrimage to Omaha Beach. ⇨ *Honfleur to Mont-St-Michel in Chapter 5*

Mont-St-Michel

1 day. Rising majestically in a shroud of sea mist over vacillating tidal flats, this mystical peninsula is Gothic in every sense of the word. Though its tiny, steep streets are crammed with visitors and tourist traps, no other sight gives you a stronger sense of the worldly power of medieval monasticism than Mont-St-Michel. ⇨ *Honfleur to Mont-St-Michel in Chapter 5*

St-Malo

1 day. Even in winter you'll want to brave the Channel winds to beachcomb the shores of this onetime pirate base. In summer, of course, it's mobbed with sun seekers who stroll the old streets, restored to quaintness after World War II. ⇨ *Northeast Brittany and the Channel Coast in Chapter 6*

Chartres

1 day. Making a beeline on the autoroute back to Paris, stop in Chartres to view the loveliest of all of France's cathedrals. ⇨ *Western Ile-de-France in Chapter 3*

By Public Transportation

Coordinating a sightseeing tour like this with a limited local train schedule isn't easy, and connections to Mont-St-Michel are especially complicated. Versailles, Chartres, and St-Malo are easy to reach, and Bayeux and Honfleur are doable, if inconvenient. But you'll spend a lot of vacation time waiting along train tracks.

FRANCE LODGING PRIMER

If your France fantasy involves staying in a historic hotel with the smell of fresh-baked croissants gently rousing you in the morning, here's some good news: you need not be Ritz-rich to realize it. Throughout the country, you'll find stylish lodging options—from charming hotels and intimate B&Bs to regal apartments and grand country houses—in all price ranges.

Hotels

Rates are always by room, not per person. Sometimes a hotel in a certain price category will have a few less-expensive rooms; it's worth asking about. In the off-season—usually November to Easter (except for southern France)—tariffs may be lower. Always inquire about promotional specials and weekend deals. Rates must be posted in all rooms, with extra charges clearly indicated.

Hotel rooms have telephones, television, and private bath unless otherwise noted. When making your reservation, state your preference for shower (*douche*) or tub (*baignoire*)—the latter always costs more. Also when booking, ask for a *grand lit* if you want a double bed.

Apartment and House Rentals

If you want more spacious accommodations with cooking facilities, consider a furnished rental. These can save you money, especially if you're traveling with a group.

Renting a *gîte rural*—furnished house in the country—for a week or month can also save you money. Gîtes are nearly always maintained by on-site owners, who greet you on your arrival and provide information on groceries, doctors, and nearby attractions.

The national rental network, the Fédération Nationale des Gîtes de France, rents all types of accommodations rated by ears of corn (from one to four) based on comfort and quality criteria.

You can find listings for fabulous renovated farmhouses with swimming pools or simple cottages in the heart of wine country. Besides country houses, Gîtes de France has listings for B&Bs, lodges, hostels, and campsites.

Bed-and-Breakfasts

Chambres d'hôtes (bed-and-breakfasts) range from simple lodgings with breakfast in a humble home to beautiful rooms in a château with gourmet food. Chambres d'hôtes are most common in rural France, though they are becoming more popular in Paris and other major cities.

Check with local tourist offices or private reservation agencies like Hôtes Qualité Paris. Often *table d'hôte* dinners (meals cooked by and eaten with the owners) can be arranged for a nominal fee.

Note that your hosts at B&Bs, unlike those at hotels, are more likely to speak only French.

Hostels

Hostels offer bare-bones lodging at low, low prices—often in shared dorm rooms with shared baths—to people of all ages, though the primary market is students. Most hostels serve breakfast; dinner and/or shared cooking facilities may also be available.

In some hostels you aren't allowed to be in your room during the day, and there may be a curfew at night. Nevertheless, hostels provide a sense of community, with public rooms where travelers often gather to share stories.

For resources and booking information, see the Travel Smart chapter.

WHEN TO GO

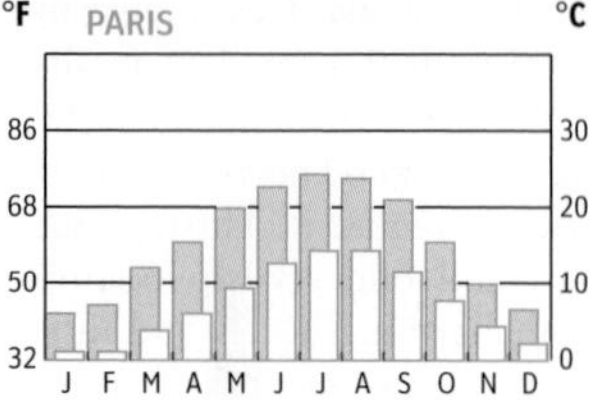

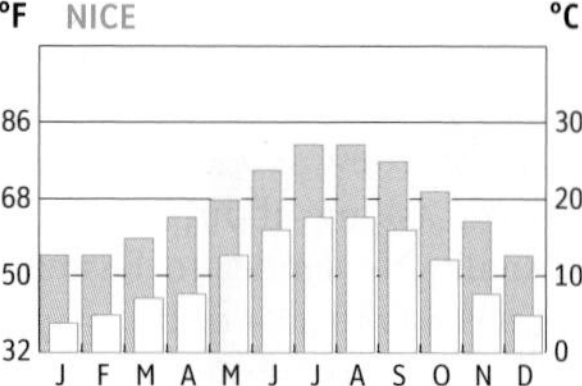

Keep in mind that French schoolchildren have *five* holidays a year: one week at the end of October, two weeks at Christmas, two weeks in February, two weeks in April, and the two full months of July and August. During these times travel in France is truly at its peak season, which means that prices are higher, highways are busier, the queues for museums are long, and transportation is at its most expensive. Your best bet for quality and calm is to travel off-season. June and September are the best months to be in France, as both are free of the midsummer crowds. Try to avoid the second half of July and all of August, when almost everyone in France goes on vacation. July and August in southern France can be stifling. Paris can be stuffy and uncomfortable in August. Many restaurants, theaters, and small shops close, but enough stay open these days to make a low-key, unhurried visit a pleasure. Anytime between March and November will offer you a good chance to soak up the sun on the Côte d'Azur. If Paris and the Loire are among your priorities, remember that the weather is unappealing before Easter. If you're dreaming of Paris in the springtime, May is your best bet, not rainy April. But the capital remains a joy during midwinter, with plenty of things to see and do.

2

Paris

WORD OF MOUTH

"The color of the Eiffel Tower was amazing, as I was standing underneath and looking up at it."

— ajkarlin, Fodors.com member, on the above photo, a finalist in Fodor's "Show Us Your France" contest

"At the Louvre, we made a beeline for the Mona Lisa. We were practically alone—she smiled, we smiled, it was magic."

— bardo

WELCOME TO PARIS

TOP REASONS TO GO

★ **Masterpiece Theater:** There will always be something new to see at the Louvre—after all, the Mona Lisa is just one of 800,000 treasures.

★ **Feasting at Le Grand Véfour:** Back when Napoléon dined here, this was the most beautiful restaurant in Paris. Guess what? It still is.

★ **Quasimodo's Notre Dame:** Get to know the stone gargoyles high atop this playground of Victor Hugo's hunchback, then savor the splendor inside this great Gothic cathedral.

★ **Café Society:** Whether you prefer a posh perch at Les Deux Magots or just the corner café *du coin*, be sure to Hemingway an afternoon away over two café filtrés.

★ **Spend Time on the Seine:** Take a leisurely stroll along the Rive Droite and the Rive Gauche, making sure to carve out time to visit the oldest part of Paris—Ile de la Cité and Ile St-Louis.

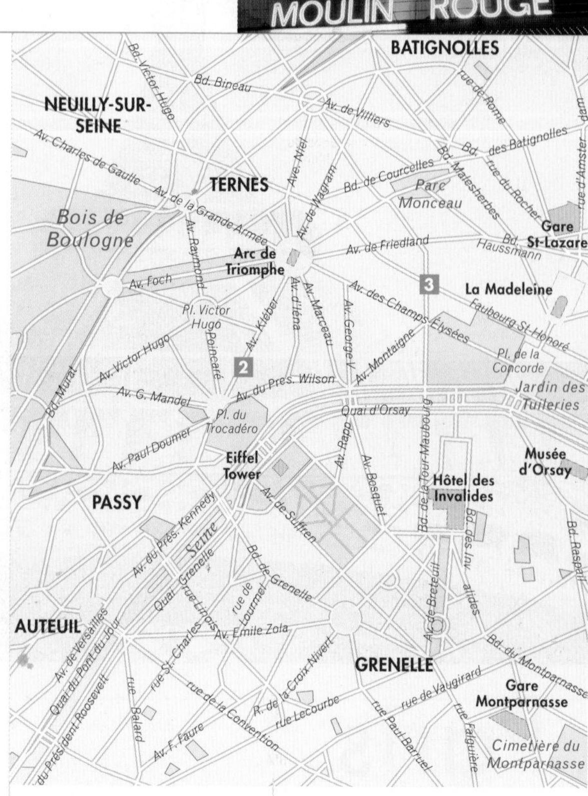

1 From Notre-Dame to the Place de la Concorde. Spend time wandering around the lovely Ile-de-la-Cité, home of Notre-Dame, and relaxing in the Tuileries before and after tackling the Louvre.

2 From the Tour Eiffel to the Arc de Triomphe. You won't be able to cover this whole area in one day, but plan lots of time for what could be called "monumental" Paris. In addition to the Eiffel Tower, the Champs Élysée, and the Arc de Triomphe, there are several excellent museums worth planning your days around.

3 The Faubourg St-Honoré. Chic spots in cities come and go, but the Faubourg's always had it and probably always will, with its well-established shops and cafés.

2

GETTING ORIENTED

Paris is divided into 20 *arrondissements* (or neighborhoods) spiraling out from the center of the city. The numbers reveal the neighborhood's location, and its age: the 1st arrondissement at the city's heart being the oldest. The arrondissements in central Paris—the 1st to 8th—are the most-visited. If you want to figure out what arrondissement something is in, check the zip code. The first three digits are always 750 for Paris, and the last two identify the arrondissement. It's worth picking up a copy of *Paris Pratique*, the essential map guide, available at bookstores and souvenir shops.

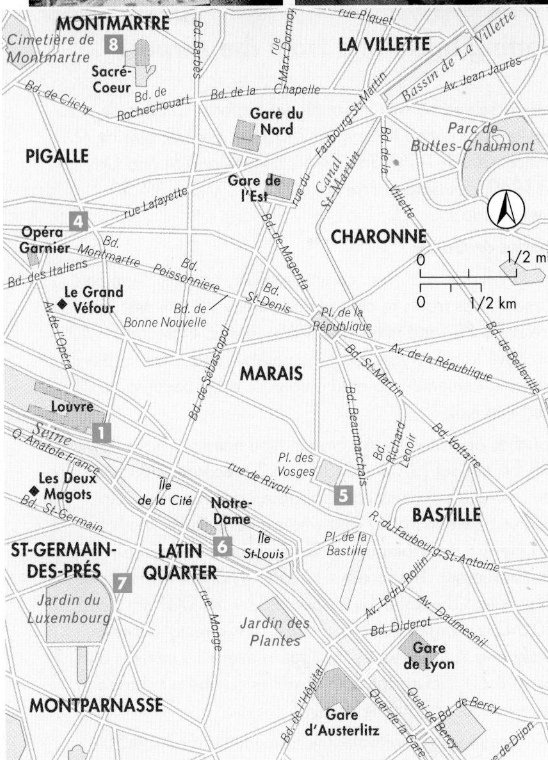

4 The Grands Boulevards. Use the Opéra Garnier as your orientation landmark and set out to do some power shopping. There are some intriguing small museums in the neighborhood, too, if you want a dose of culture.

5 The Marais, the Bastille, and the Canal St. Martin. The Marais is Paris's most popular lazy-Sunday-afternoon neighborhood, where you can while away the day at the Place des Vosges, shop to your heart's content. Or hang with the hipsters in the Bastille or along the Canal St. Martin.

6 Ile St-Louis and the Quartier Latin. Ile St-Louis is tiny, and one of the most romantic spots in Paris. Leave yourself lots of time to wander the Latin Quarter, a 'hood known for its vibrant student life.

7 From Orsay to St-Germain-des-Pres. Fabulous cafés and two of the city's most fabulous museums are found here, on the Left Bank, but make sure you also leave yourself time to wander the Jardins du Luxembourg.

8 Montmartre. Like a small village inside a big city, charming Montmartre feels distinctly separate from the rest of Paris.

PARIS PLANNER

The Big Picture

As world capitals go, Paris is surprisingly compact. The city is divided in two by the River Seine, with two islands (Ile de la Cité and Ile St-Louis) in the middle. Each bank of the Seine has its own personality; the Rive Droite (Right Bank), with its spacious boulevards and formal buildings, generally has a more genteel, dignified feel than the carefree and chic Rive Gauche (Left Bank), to the south. The east–west axis from Châtelet to the Arc de Triomphe, via the Rue de Rivoli and the Champs-Élysées, is the Right Bank's principal thoroughfare for sight-seeing and shopping

Rules of the Rue: Etiquette

Simply put, the French like to look at people, so get used to being stared at. Flirting is as natural here (at all ages) as breathing. The French don't smile at strangers, and doing so can be taken as an invitation for something more. Are the French rude? In a word: *Non.* In France, *politesse* is highly prized, as well as good manners. For example, failing to say *bonjour* (hello) when entering a shop—and *au revoir* (good-bye) on the way out—is considered rude.

Getting Into Paris from the Airport

Paris is served by two international airports: Charles de Gaulle (also called Roissy) (☎ *3950* in English; outside of France, 0033–1–70–36–39–50* 🌐 *www.adp.fr*) and Orly (☎ *3950*; outside of France, 0033–1–70–36–39–50* 🌐 *www.adp.fr*).

Charles de Gaulle

The RER-B, the suburban commuter train, beneath Terminals 2 and 3, has trains to central Paris every 20 minutes; the fare is €8.50, and takes about 45 minutes. Note that you have to carry your luggage up from and down to the platform. Remember to hold onto your ticket because you'll need it to exit.

Coaches operated by Air France (you need not have flown with the airline) (☎ *08–92–35–08–20 recorded information in English* 🌐 *www.cars-airfrance.com*) run every 20 minutes between Roissy and western Paris (Porte Maillot and the Arc de Triomphe, or Gare de Lyon and Gare Montparnasse). The fare is €15 to €19, and it takes about 60 minutes. The Roissybus, operated by the RATP (☎ *3246 [€0.34 per min]* 🌐 *www.ratp.com*), runs directly between Roissy and Rue Scribe by the Opéra every 15 minutes and costs €8.60. Tickets for both bus lines can be purchased in the terminals or from the driver.

Taxis are readily available; the fare will be around €50–€60, depending on traffic.

Orly

There are several options to get to Paris from Orly Airport. Take the free OrlyVal shuttle train, departing every 7 minutes, to the Antony station; then take the RER-B line into Paris. The fare is €9.85 and it takes about 25 minutes. Or, take the airport shuttle bus to the RER-C line station; trains leave every 15 minutes. The fare is €6.20 total (bus and train have separate tickets).

Air France buses run every 12 minutes between Orly and Montparnasse station, Les Invalides and L'Etoile/Arc de Triomphe. The fare is €11.50, and the trip can take from 30 minutes to an hour, depending on traffic. RATP also runs the Orlybus between the Denfert-Rochereau métro station and Orly every 15 minutes, and the trip costs €6.40.

2

When to Go

The City of Light is magical all year round, but it's particularly gorgeous in June, when the long days (the sun doesn't set until 10 PM) stretch sightseeing hours and make it ideal to linger in the cafés practicing the city's favorite pastime—people-watching.

Winter can be dark and chilly, but it's also the best time to find cheap airfares and hotel deals. April in Paris, despite what the song says, is often rainy. Summer is the most popular (and expensive) season, and at the height of it, in July, Paris can feel like a city under siege, bursting at the seams as crowds descend en masse.

Keep in mind that, like some other European cities, Paris somewhat shuts down in August—some restaurants are closed for the entire month, for example—though there are still plenty of fun things to do, namely, free open-air movies and concerts, and the popular Paris Plage, the "beach" on the right bank of the Seine.

September is gorgeous, with temperate weather, saner airfares, and cultural events timed for the ***rentrée*** (or return), signifying the end of summer vacation.

Tips on Dining

Generally, restaurants are open from noon to about 2:30 and from 7:30 or 8 to 10 or 10:30. It's best to make reservations, particularly in summer, although the reviews only state when reservations are absolutely essential.

Brasseries often have nonstop service; some are open 24 hours. Assume a restaurant is open every day, unless otherwise indicated. Surprisingly, many prestigious restaurants close on weekends and sometimes Monday. July and August are the most common months for annual closings, although Paris in August is no longer the wasteland it once was.

DINING AND LODGING PRICE CATEGORIES (IN EUROS)

	¢	$	$$	$$$	$$$$
Restaurants	Under €13	€13–€17	€18–€24	€25–€32	Over €32
Hotels	Under €80	€80–€120	€121–€175	€176–€250	Over €250

Restaurant prices are per person for a main course at dinner, including tax (5.5%) and service; note that if a restaurant offers only prix-fixe (set-price) meals, it has been given the price category that reflects the full prix-fixe price. Hotel prices are for a standard double room in high season, including tax (19.6%) and service charge.

Saving Time and Money

Paris is one of the world's most visited cities, so it pays to be prepared. Buy tickets online when you can. Investigate alternate entrances at popular sites and check when rates are reduced. Also, most major museums are free the first Sunday of each month. A Paris Museum Pass can save you money and allows you to bypass the lines. It's sold at the destinations it covers and at airports, major métro stations, and the tourism office in the Carrousel du Louvre (2-, 4-, or 6-day passes are €32, €48, and €64, respectively 🌐 *www.parismuseumpass.com*). Stick to the omnipresent ATMs for the best exchange rates.

Hours

Paris is by no means a 24/7 city, so planning your days beforehand can save you aggravation. Museums are closed one day a week, usually Tuesday, and most stay open late at least one night each week. Store hours are generally from 10 AM to 7:30 PM, though smaller shops may not open until 11 AM, only to close for several hours during the afternoon. Most retailers are barred by law from doing business on Sunday, but exceptions include the shops along the Champs-Élysées, the Carrousel du Louvre, and around the Marais, where most boutiques open at 2 PM.

GETTING AROUND

Taxi Travel

On weekend nights after 11 PM, and during the morning rush, it's nearly impossible to find a taxi—you're best off asking hotel or restaurant staff to call you one, but, be forewarned: you'll have to pay for them to come get you and, depending on where they are, the fare can quickly add up.

If you want to hail a cab on your own, look for the taxis with their signs lighted up (their signs will be glowing white as opposed to the taxis that are already taken whose signs will be a dull orange).

There are taxi stands on almost every major street corner but again, expect a wait if it's a busy weekend night.

Taxi stands are marked by a square dark blue sign with a white T in the middle.

There's a basic hire charge of €2.10 for all rides, and a minimum voyage charge of €5.60.

Expect a €1 supplement per bag after the second piece, and a €2.70 supplement for a fourth person.

Taxi G7 (☎ *01–47–39–47–39*) is one of the most reliable taxi companies in Paris.

Bus Travel

The Paris bus system (✉ *54 quai de la Rapée, Paris* ☎ *3246 [€0.34 per min]* 🌐 *www.ratp.com*)is user-friendly and a great way to see the city.

With dedicated lanes throughout the city allowing buses and taxis to whiz past traffic jams, taking the bus can be a pleasant way to get around. Buses are marked with the route number and destination in front and with major stopping places along the sides. The brown bus shelters contain timetables, route maps and electronic boards tell you when the next bus will arrive. Maps are also found on each bus. To get off, press one of the red buttons mounted on the silver poles that run the length of the bus and the *arrêt demandé* (stop requested) light directly above the driver will light up. Use the rear door to exit (some require you to push a silver button to open the door).

You can use your métro ticket on buses; if you have individual tickets (as opposed to weekly or monthly tickets), be prepared to punch your ticket in the gray machines on board the bus.

The best bet is to buy a *carnet* of 10 tickets for €11.60 at any métro station, or you can buy a single ticket on board for €1.60 (though the drivers may gripe about selling you one, so have exact change ready).

Car Travel

Driving is not recommended within Paris. Parisian drivers are aggressive behind the wheel and it's often very difficult to park. Should you be driving into the city from elsewhere in Ile de France, the major ring road encircling the city is called the *périférique,* with the *périférique intérieur* going counterclockwise around the city, and the *périférique extérieur,* or the outside ring, going clockwise. Five lanes wide, the périférique is a highway from which *portes* (gates) connect Paris to the major highways of France. The highway names function on the same principle as the métro, with the final destination used as the route "name."

Métro Travel

The métro is by far the quickest and most efficient way to get around and cost €1.60 each; a *carnet* (10 tickets for €11,60) is a better value. Trains run from 5:30 AM until 1 AM and 2 AM on Friday and Saturday (and be forewarned—this means the famous "last métro" can pass your station anytime after 12:30 AM on weekdays).

Stations are signaled either by a large yellow M within a circle or by their distinctive curly green Art Nouveau railings and archway entrances bearing the subway's full title (Métropolitain).

It's essential to know the name of the last station on the line you take, as this name appears on all signs. You can make as many connections as you wish on one ticket.

Keep your ticket during your journey; you'll need it to leave the RER system and to avoid being fined, as inspectors appear regularly.

In general, the métro is safe, although try to avoid the larger, mazelike stations at Châtelet-Les Halles and République if you're alone late at night.

Parisian pickpockets are famously discreet, so be aware of your surroundings.

Train Travel

Paris has five international train stations run by the SNCF: (☎ *3635; outside of France, 00338–92–35–35–35 [€0.34 per min]* 🌐 *www.sncf.fr*). Gare du Nord; Gare St-Lazare; Gare de l'Est; Gare de Lyon; and Gare d'Austerlitz. Trains heading outside of Ile-de-France are usually referred to as *Grandes Lignes*, while regional train service is referred to as *trains de banlieue*, or *Le Transilien*.

RER (☎ *3246 [€0.34 per min]* 🌐 *www.ratp.com*) trains travel between Paris and the suburbs and are operated by the RATP.

When they go through Paris, they act as a sort of baby métro—they connect with the métro network at several points—and can be great time-savers.

Access to RER platforms is through the same type of automatic ticket barrier (if you've started your journey on the métro, you can use the same ticket), but you'll need to have the same ticket handy to put through another barrier when you leave the system.

Visitor Information

Paris is without question best explored on foot and, thanks to Baron Haussmann's mid-19th-century redesign, the City of Light is a compact wonder of wide boulevards, gracious parks, and leafy squares. Happily and conveniently, there are more than five branches of the Paris tourist office located at key points in the capital:

Espace du Tourisme d'Ile-de-France (✉ *Carrousel du Louvre, 99 rue de Rivoli* ☎ *08–92–68–30–00 in English [€0.34 per min]* 🌐 *www.pidf.com* Ⓜ *Palais-Royal, Musée du Louvre*).

Office du Tourisme de la Ville de Paris Pyramides (✉ *25 rue des Pyramides* ☎ *08–92–68–30–00 [€0.34 per min]* Ⓜ *Pyramides*).

Office du Tourisme de la Ville de Paris Gare du Lyon (✉ *Arrivals, 20 bd. Diderot* Ⓜ *Gare du Lyon*).

Office du Tourisme de la Ville de Paris Gare du Nord (✉ *18 rue de Dunkerque* Ⓜ *Gare du Nord*).

Office du Tourisme de la Ville de Paris Opéra-Grands Magasins (✉ *11 rue Scribe* Ⓜ *Opéra*).

Office du Tourisme de la Ville de Paris Tour Eiffel (✉ *Between east and north legs of Eiffel Tower* Ⓜ *Champs de Mars, Tour Eiffel*).

Updated by Jennifer Ditsler-Ladonne, Linda Hervieux, Rosa Jackson, Lisa Pasold, Nicole Pritchard, and Heather Stimmler-Hall

If there's a problem with a trip to Paris, it's the embarrassment of riches that faces you. No matter which aspect of Paris you choose—touristy, historic, fashion-conscious, pretentious-bourgeois, thrifty, or the legendary bohemian arty Paris of undying attraction—one thing is certain: you will carve out your own Paris, one that is vivid, exciting, ultimately unforgettable.

Wherever you head, your itinerary will prove to be a voyage of discovery. But choosing the Paris of your dreams is a bit like choosing a perfume or cologne. Do you want something young and dashing, or elegant and worldly? How about sporty, or perhaps strictly glamorous? No matter: they are all here—perfumes, famous museums, legendary churches, or romantic cafés. Whether you spend three days or three months in this city, it will always have something new to offer you, which may explain why the most assiduous explorers of Paris are the Parisians themselves.

Veterans know that Paris is a city of vast, noble perspectives and intimate, ramshackle streets, of formal *espaces vertes* (green open spaces) and quiet squares. This combination of the pompous and the private is one of the secrets of its perennial pull. Another is its size: Paris is relatively small as capitals go, with distances between many of its major sights and museums invariably walkable.

For the first-timer there will always be several must-dos at the top of the list, but getting to know Paris will never be quite as simple as a quick look at Notre-Dame, the Louvre, and the Eiffel Tower. You'll discover that around every corner, down every *ruelle* (little street) lies a resonance-in-waiting. You can stand on the Rue du Faubourg St-Honoré at the very spot where Edmond Rostand set Ragueneau's pastry shop in *Cyrano de Bergerac*. You can read the letters of Madame de Sévigné in her actual *hôtel particulier*, or private mansion, now the Musée Carnavalet. You can hear the words of Racine resound in the ringing, hair-raising diction of the Comédie Française. You can breathe in the fumes of hubris before the extravagant onyx tomb Napoléon designed for himself. You can gaze through the gates at the school where Voltaire honed his wit, and you can add your own pink-lipstick kiss to Oscar Wilde's bedecked grave at Père-Lachaise Cemetery.

If this is your first trip, you may want to take a guided tour of the city—a good introduction that will help you get your bearings and provide you with a general impression before you return to explore the sights that particularly interest you. To help track those down, this chapter's exploration of Paris is divided into eight neighborhood walks. Each *quartier*, or neighborhood, has its own personality, which is best discovered by foot power. Ultimately, your route will be marked by your preferences, your curiosity, and your state of fatigue. You can wander for hours without getting bored—though not, perhaps, without getting lost. By the time you have seen only a few neighborhoods, drinking in the rich variety they have to offer, you should not only be culturally replete but downright exhausted—and hungry, too. Again, take your cue from Parisians and think out your next move in a sidewalk café. So you've heard stories of a friend who paid $8 for a coffee at a café. So what? What you're paying for is time, and the opportunity to watch the intricate drama of Parisian street life unfold. Hemingway knew the rules; after all, he would have remained just another unknown sportswriter if the waiters in the cafés had hovered around him impatiently.

Numbers in the text correspond to numbers in the margin and on the Paris, From the Tour Eiffel to the Arc de Triomphe, and Montmartre maps.

FROM NOTRE-DAME TO THE PLACE DE LA CONCORDE

In the center of Paris, nestled in the River Seine are the two celebrated islands, the Ile de la Cité and the Ile St-Louis. Of the two, it's the Ile de la Cité that forms the historic ground zero of Paris. It was here that the earliest inhabitants of Paris, the Gaulish tribe of the Parisii, settled in about 250 BC, calling their home Lutetia, meaning "settlement surrounded by water." Today it's famed for the great, brooding cathedral of Notre-Dame, the haunted Conciergerie, and the dazzling Sainte-Chapelle. If Notre-Dame represents Church, another major attraction of this walk—the Louvre—symbolizes State. A succession of French rulers was responsible for filling this immense structure with the world's greatest paintings and works of art. It's the largest museum in the world, as well as one of the easiest to get lost in. Beyond the Louvre lie the graceful Tuileries Gardens, the grand Place de la Concorde—the very hub of the city—and the Belle Époque splendor of the Grand Palais and the Pont Alexandre III. All in all, this area comprises some of the most historic and beautiful sights to see in Paris.

TOP ATTRACTIONS

Grand Palais. With its curved-glass roof and gorgeous restored Belle Époque ornamentation, you can't miss the Grand Palais whether you're approaching from the Seine or the Champs-Élysées. It forms a voluptuous duo with the Petit Palais across Avenue Winston-Churchill: both stone buildings, adorned with mosaics and sculpted friezes, were built

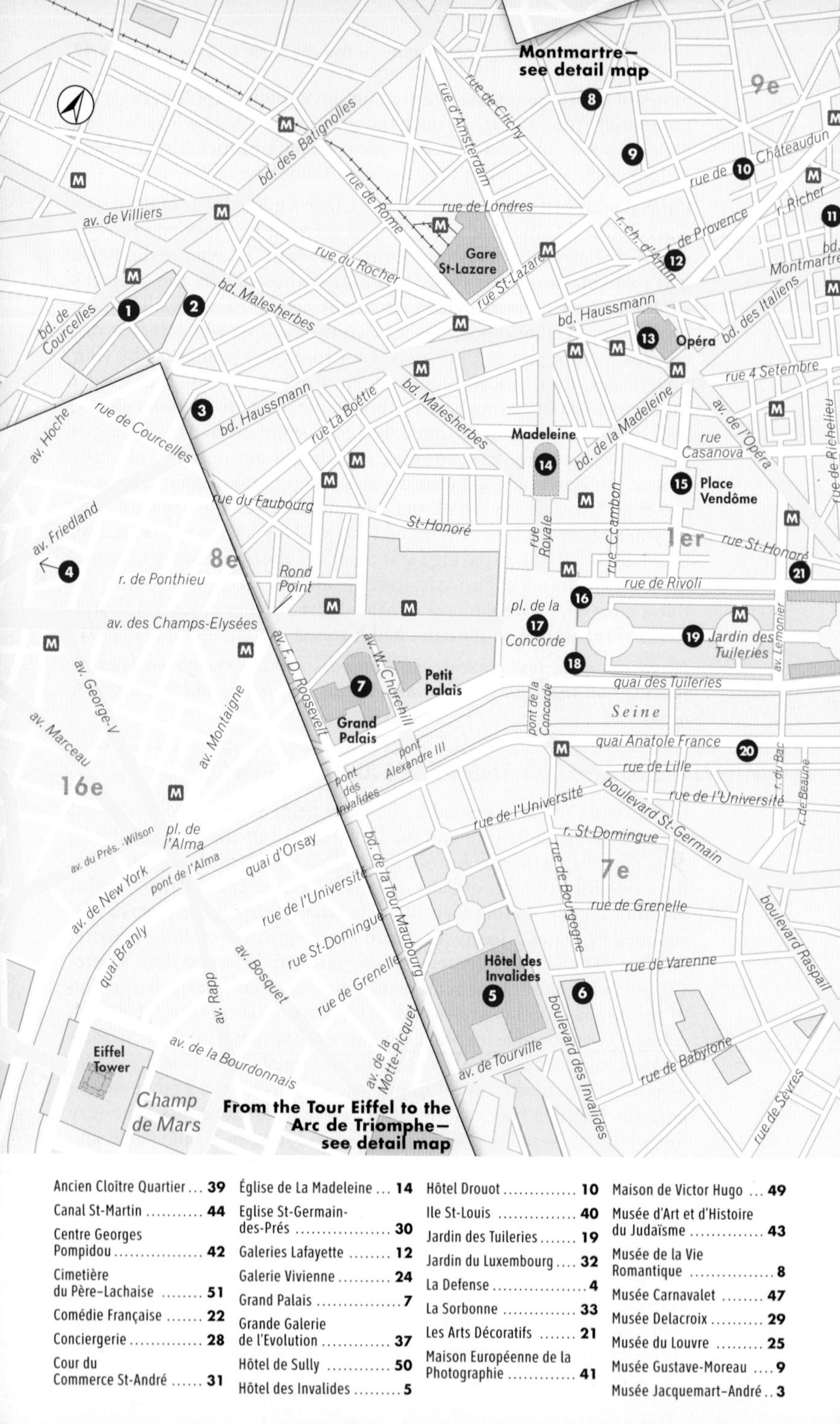

Montmartre–
see detail map
9e
rue de Clichy
rue d'Amsterdam
bd. des Batignolles
rue de Rome
rue de Londres
rue de Châteaudun
r. Richer
rue de Provence
r. ch. d'Antin
bd. Montmartre
av. de Villiers
Gare
St-Lazare
rue du Rocher
rue St-Lazare
bd. de Courcelles
bd. Malesherbes
bd. Haussmann
bd. des Italiens
Opéra
rue 4 Setembre
rue de Courcelles
av. Hoche
bd. Haussmann
rue La Boétie
bd. Malesherbes
Madeleine
bd. de la Madeleine
av. de l'Opéra
rue Casanova
rue de Richelieu
rue du Faubourg
St-Honoré
Place
Vendôme
rue Cambon
rue Royale
1er
rue St-Honoré
av. Friedland
8e
r. de Ponthieu
Rond
Point
rue de Rivoli
pl. de la
Concorde
av. des Champs-Elysées
av. W. Churchill
Petit
Palais
Jardin des
Tuileries
av. Lemonier
quai des Tuileries
Grand
Palais
av. F. D. Roosevelt
av. George-V
av. Marceau
av. Montaigne
pont de la Concorde
Seine
quai Anatole France
pont Alexandre III
pont des Invalides
rue de Lille
r. du Bac
r. de Beaune
16e
rue de l'Université
boulevard St-Germain
rue de l'Université
pl. de l'Alma
av. du Prés. Wilson
quai d'Orsay
r. St-Dominique
bd. de la Tour Maubourg
rue de Bourgogne
7e
av. de New York
pont de l'Alma
rue de l'Université
rue de Grenelle
boulevard Raspail
quai Branly
rue St-Dominique
av. Bosquet
rue de Grenelle
Hôtel des
Invalides
rue de Varenne
av. Rapp
av. de la Motte-Picquet
boulevard des Invalides
av. de la Bourdonnais
av. de Tourville
rue de Babylone
Eiffel
Tower
Champ
de Mars
From the Tour Eiffel to the
Arc de Triomphe–
see detail map
rue de Sèvres

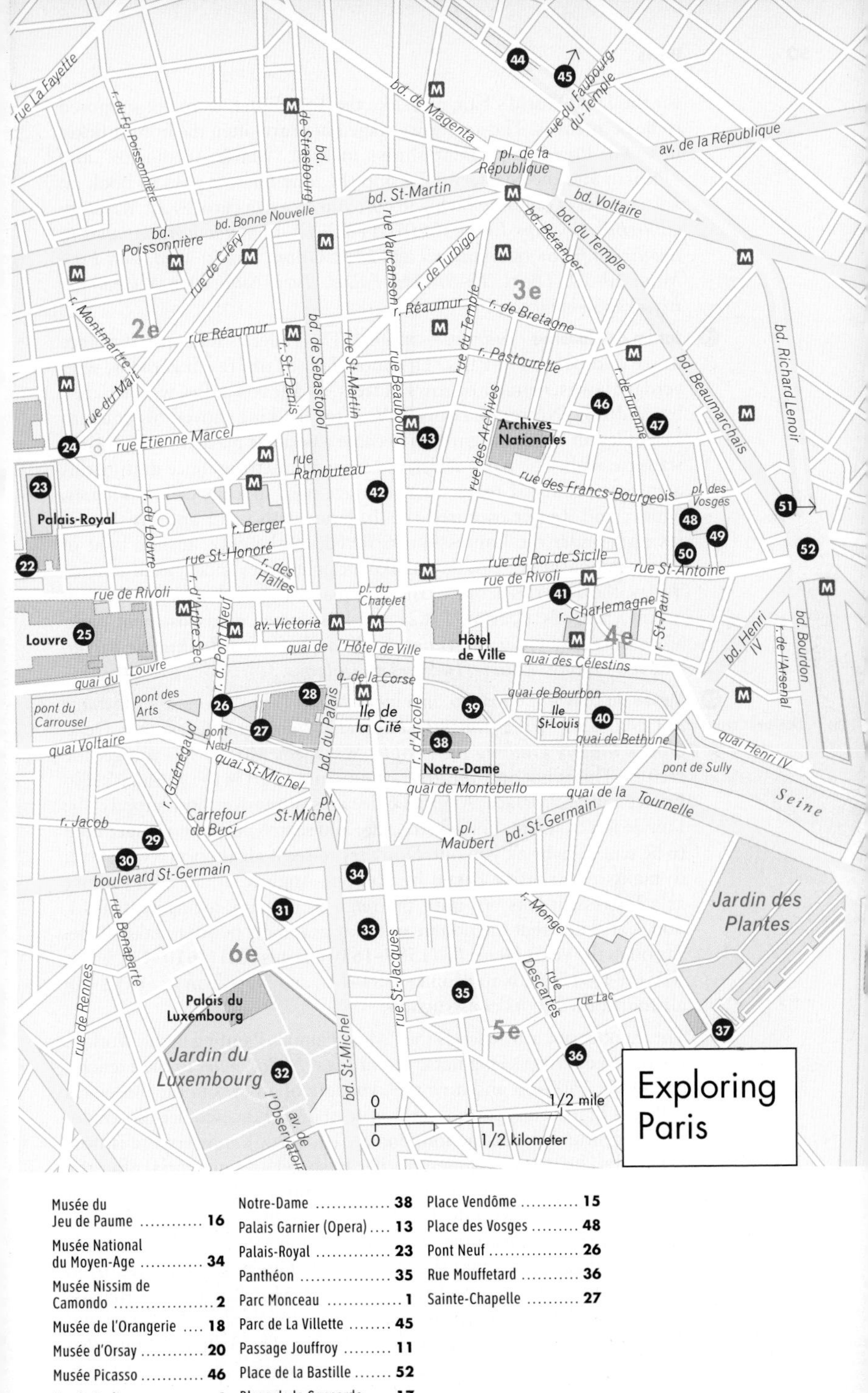

Exploring Paris
rue La Fayette
r. du Fg. Poissonnière
bd. de Strasbourg
bd. de Magenta
rue du Faubourg-du-Temple
pl. de la République
av. de la République
bd. St-Martin
bd. Bonne Nouvelle
bd. Poissonnière
rue de Cléry
rue Vaucanson
r. de Turbigo
bd. Béranger
bd. Voltaire
bd. du Temple
3e
2e
r. Montmartre
rue Réaumur
r. Réaumur
r. St-Denis
bd. de Sebastopol
rue St-Martin
rue Beaubourg
rue du Temple
r. de Bretagne
r. Pastourelle
r. de Turenne
bd. Beaumarchais
bd. Richard Lenoir
rue du Mail
rue Etienne Marcel
rue Rambuteau
rue des Archives
Archives Nationales
rue des Francs-Bourgeois
pl. des Vosges
Palais-Royal
r. du Louvre
r. Berger
rue St-Honoré
r. des Halles
rue de Roi de Sicile
rue de Rivoli
rue St-Antoine
pl. du Chatelet
r. d'Arbre Sec
r. Pont Neuf
av. Victoria
r. Charlemagne
r. St-Paul
bd. Henri IV
r. de l'Arsenal
bd. Bourdon
Louvre
quai de l'Hôtel de Ville
Hôtel de Ville
quai des Célestins
4e
quai du Louvre
q. de la Corse
pont des Arts
pont du Carrousel
Ile de la Cité
bd. du Palais
r. d'Arcole
quai de Bourbon
Ile St-Louis
quai de Bethune
quai Henri IV
pont de Sully
quai Voltaire
pont Neuf
r. Guénégaud
quai St-Michel
Notre-Dame
quai de Montebello
quai de la Tournelle
Seine
r. Jacob
Carrefour de Buci
pl. St-Michel
pl. Maubert
bd. St-Germain
boulevard St-Germain
rue Bonaparte
r. Monge
Jardin des Plantes
6e
rue St-Jacques
rue Descartes
rue Lac
rue de Rennes
Palais du Luxembourg
5e
Jardin du Luxembourg
bd. St-Michel
av. de l'Observatoire
0
1/2 mile
0
1/2 kilometer

for the 1900 World's Fair, and, like the Tour Eiffel, were not supposed to be permanent. The art shows staged here are often the hottest ticket in town. Previous popular shows include "Marie Antoinette" and "Picasso and the Masters." To skip the long lines, it pays to book an advance ticket online, which will cost you an extra euro. ✉ *Av. Winston-Churchill, Champs-Élysées* ☎ *01–44–13–17–17* 🌐 *www.grandpalais.fr, www.rmn.fr for reservations* 🎫 *€12* ⏲ *Grand Palais: Wed. and Fri.–Mon. 10–10, Thurs. 10–8. Petit Palais: Tues.–Sun. 10–6* Ⓜ *Champs-Élysées–Clemenceau.*

19 **Jardin des Tuileries** *(Tuileries Gardens).* The Tuileries was once *the* place to see and be seen in Paris. This most French of French gardens, with verdant lawns, manicured rows of trees, and gravel paths, was designed by André Le Nôtre for Louis XIV. After the king moved his court to Versailles, in 1682, the gardens became a popular place for stylish Parisians to stroll. The name is derived from the factories once dotting this area that produced *tuiles,* or roof tiles, fired in kilns called *tuileries.* Monet and Renoir captured the Tuileries with paint and brush, and it's no wonder the Impressionists loved it—the gray, austere light of Paris's famously overcast days make the green trees appear even greener. Today, the Tuileries is one of the best places to take kids itching to run around. There's a carousel (€2) and in summer, an amusement park. ✉ *Bordered by Quai des Tuileries, Pl. de la Concorde, Rue de Rivoli, and the Louvre, Louvre/Tuileries* Ⓜ *Tuileries.*

25 **Musée du Louvre.** Leonardo da Vinci's *Mona Lisa,* Veronese's *Marriage at Cana,* Giorgione's *Concert Champêtre,* Vermeer's *Lacemaker*, Delacroix's *Liberty Guiding the People,* Whistler's *Mother* . . . you get the picture. This is not only the greatest museum of art in the world, it's also France's largest palace. After two decades of renovations, happily, the Louvre is a coherent, unified structure and search parties no longer need to be sent in to bring you out. Don't try to see it all at once; try, instead, to make repeat visits. Begun by Philippe-Auguste in the 13th century as a fortress, it was not until the reign of pleasure-loving François I, 300 years later, that the Louvre of today gradually began to take shape. Through the years Henri IV (1589–1610), Louis XIII (1610–43), Louis XIV (1643–1715), Napoléon I (1804–14), and Napoléon III (1852–70) all contributed to its construction.

Fodor's Choice ★

The number one attraction is the "Most Famous Painting in the World": Leonardo da Vinci's enigmatic *Mona Lisa* (*La Joconde,* to the French), painted in 1503–06 and now the cynosure of all eyes in the museum's Salle des États. The portrait of the wife of one Francesco del Giocondo, a 15th-century Florentine millionaire, Leonardo's masterpiece is now believed to have been painted for her husband as a memorial after the lady's death (while some historians maintain that her black garb is in honor of her baby who died in 1502). If so, however, this may be at odds with the famous smile, which critics point to as a prime example of Leonardo's famous wit: the family name Giocondo is derived from the Latin word for "jocundity," or humor. More great High Renaissance masterpieces line nearby walls, including Leonardo's *Virgin and St. Anne* and Raphael's *La Belle Jardinière.* The Salle des États also contains one of the largest pictures in the Louvre: the *Feast at Cana,*

DID YOU KNOW?

The magnificent Grand Palais, with its enormous glass roof, is known for its provacaive and crowd-pleasing temporary art exhibits.

Architect I. M. Pei's pyramid entrance reaffirms the ever-old-but-always-new vitality of the Louvre's French Baroque architecture.

by Pablo Veronese (1528–88), a sumptuous painting reminiscent of the Venetian painter's *Christ in the House of Levi* (which is in Venice). These paintings, filled with partygoers, prompted a formal summons from the pope, asking Veronese to explain in person why he had scandalously included the chaos of drunken revelers, dwarves, and animals in what was purportedly a holy scene.

Some other highlights of the painting collection are Jan van Eyck's magnificent *The Madonna and Chancellor Rolin,* painted in the early 15th century; *The Lacemaker,* by Jan Vermeer (1632–75); *The Embarkation for Cythera,* by Antoine Watteau (1684–1721); *The Oath of the Horatii,* by Jacques-Louis David (1748–1825); *The Raft of the Medusa,* by Théodore Géricault (1791–1824); and *La Grande Odalisque,* by Jean-Auguste-Dominique Ingres (1780–1867). But the Louvre is packed with other legendary collections, which are divided into eight curatorial departments: Near Eastern Antiquities; Egyptian Antiquities; Greek, Etruscan, and Roman Antiquities; Islamic Art; Sculptures; Decorative Arts; Paintings; and Prints and Drawings.

As for famed sculpture, atop the marble Escalier Daru perches the Nike, or *Winged Victory of Samothrace,* which seems poised for flight over the stairs (remember Audrey Hepburn's take in *Funny Face*?). Other hightlights include Michelangelo's two *Slaves,* intended for the tomb of Pope Julius II. These can be admired in the Denon Wing, where a medieval and Renaissance sculpture section is housed partly in the former imperial stables. Perhaps the most photogenic is the legendary *Venus de Milo*, housed in Salle (Room) 12 of the Richelieu Wing, which once housed the Ministry of Finance. The lush salons here (around Salle 87) are just the ticket if you're a fan of the Napoléon III style—the apotheosis of 19th-century, red-and-gilt opulence.

To get into the Louvre, you may have to wait in two long lines: one outside the Pyramide entrance portal and another downstairs at the ticket booths. You can avoid the first by entering through the Carrousel du Louvre and buying a ticket at the machines. Your ticket (be sure to hold on to it) will get you into any and all of the wings as many times as you like during one day—and once you have your ticket you can skip the entry line. Once inside, you should stop by the information desk to pick up a free color-coded map and check which rooms are closed for the day. (Closures rotate through the week, so you can come back if something is temporarily unavailable.) Beyond this, you'll have all you need—shops, a post office, and places to eat. Café Marly may have an enviable location facing into the Cour Napoléon, but its food is decidedly lackluster. For a more soigné lunch, keep your appetite in check until you get to the museum's stylish Café Richelieu, or head outside the palace walls. There's also a full calendar of lectures, films, concerts, and special exhibits; some are part of the excellent lunch-hour series called Les Midis du Louvre. Most are not included in the basic ticket price—pick up a three-month schedule at the information desk or check online for information. Remember that the Louvre is closed on Tuesday. ✉ *Palais du Louvre, Louvre/Tuileries* ☎ *01–40–20–53–17 information* ⊕ *www.louvre.fr* 🎫 *€9.50, €6 after 6* PM *Wed. and Fri., free 1st Sun. of month; €11 for Napoléon Hall exhibitions* ⏲ *Mon., Thurs., and weekends 9–6, Wed. and Fri. 9* AM*–10* PM Ⓜ *Palais-Royal.*

18 ★ **Musée de l'Orangerie.** People line up for hours for a glimpse of Claude Monet's huge, meditative *Water Lilies* (*Nymphéas*), displayed in galleries designed in 1914 by the master himself. The museum, once a winter greenhouse for the Tuileries' citrus trees, was renovated in 2006. The small, excellent collection includes early-20th-century paintings by Renoir, Cézanne, Matisse, and Modigliani, among others. ✉ *Jardin des Tuileries at Pl. de la Concorde, Louvre/Tuileries* ☎ *01–44–77–80–07* ⊕ *www.musee-orangerie.fr* 🎫 *€7.50, €13.50 for same-day entry to Musée d'Orsay* 🎫 *Wed.–Mon., 9–6* Ⓜ *Concorde.*

16 **Musée du Jeu de Paume.** This 19th-century building at the entrance to the Jardin des Tuileries, on the Rue de Rivoli side, was once used for *jeu de paume* (or "palm game," a forerunner of tennis). It later served as a transfer point for art looted by the Germans in World War II. Today it's been given another lease on life as an ultramodern, white-walled showcase for temporary photography exhibits displaying icons such as Richard Avedon and Lee Miller as well as up-and-comers. ✉ *1 pl. de la Concorde, Louvre/Tuileries* ☎ *01–47–03–12–50* ⊕ *www.jeudepaume.org* 🎫 *€7* ⏲ *Tues. noon–9, Wed.–Fri. noon–7, weekends 10–7* Ⓜ *Concorde.*

38 **Notre-Dame.** *See highlighted listing in this chapter.*

Fodor's Choice ★

17 **Place de la Concorde.** This majestic square at the foot of the Champs-Élysées was laid out in the 1770s, but there was nothing in the way of peace or concord about its early years. Called Place de la Révolution, more than 2,500 victims, including Louis XVI and Marie-Antoinette, lost their heads to the guillotine here. Renamed Concorde in 1836, it got a new centerpiece: the 75-foot granite Obelisk of Luxor, a gift from Egypt quarried in the 8th century BC. Among the handsome 18th-century buildings facing the square is the Hôtel Crillon, originally built as a private home by Gabriel, architect of Versailles's Petit Trianon. ✉ *Champs-Élysées* Ⓜ *Concorde.*

27 Fodor's Choice ★ **Sainte-Chapelle** *(Holy Chapel).* Not to be missed and one of the most magical sights in European medieval art, this Gothic chapel was built by Louis IX (1226–70; later canonized as St. Louis) in the 1240s to house what he believed to be Christ's Crown of Thorns, purchased from Emperor Baldwin of Constantinople. A dark lower chapel is a gloomy prelude to the shimmering upper one. Here the famous beauty of Sainte-Chapelle comes alive: instead of walls, all you see are 6,458 square feet of stained glass, delicately supported by painted stonework that seems to disappear in the colorful light streaming through the windows. The lowest section of the windows was restored in the mid-1800s, but otherwise this chapel presents intact incredibly rare stained glass. Deep reds and blues dominate the background glass here, noticeably different from later, lighter medieval styles such as those in Notre-Dame's rose windows. The Sainte-Chapelle is essentially an enormous magic lantern illuminating the 1,130 figures from the Bible, to create—as one writer poetically put it—"the most marvelous colored and moving air ever held within four walls." Originally, the king's holy relics were displayed in the raised apse and shown to the faithful on Good Friday. Today the magic of the chapel comes alive during the regular concerts held here;check the schedule at www.ampconcerts.com. ✉ *4 bd. du Palais, Ile de la Cité* ☎ *01–53–40–60–80* 🌐 *sainte-chapelle.monuments-nationaux.fr* 🎟 *€8, joint ticket with Conciergerie €11* ⏲ *Mar.– Oct., daily 9:30–6; Nov.–Feb., daily 9–5* Ⓜ *Cité.*

WORTH NOTING

39 Fodor's Choice ★ **Ancien Cloître Quartier.** Hidden in the shadows of Notre-Dame, this adorable and often overlooked nook of Paris was thankfully spared when Baron Haussmann knocked down much of the Ile de la Cité in the 19th century. Enter the quarter—originally the area where seminary students boarded with the church canons—by heading north from the cathedral toward the Seine to reach Rue Chanoinesse, once the seminary's cloister walk. Here, at No. 10, is the house that was once paradise to those fabled lovers of the Middle Ages, Héloïse and Abélard. That house, unfortunately, is completely renovated, but there are other houses here that date back to the Middle Ages. Although defaced by a modern police station and garage, this tiny warren of six streets still casts a spell, particularly at the intersection of Rue des Ursins and Rue des Chantres, where a lovely medieval palace, tiny flower garden, and quayside steps form a cul-de-sac where time seems to be holding its breath. ✉ *Rue du Cloître-Notre-Dame north to Quai des Fleurs, Ile de la Cité* Ⓜ *Cité.*

Continued on page 59

NOTRE-DAME

Notre-Dame is the symbolic heart of Paris and, for many, of France itself. Napoléon was crowned here, and kings and queens exchanged marriage vows before its altar. There are a few things worth seeing inside the Gothic cathedral, but the real highlights are the exterior architectural details and the unforgettable view of Paris, framed by stone gargoyles, from the top of the south tower.

THE STONE GARGOYLES

Notre-Dame's gargoyles were designed by Eugène Viollet-le-Duc, the architect who oversaw the cathedral's 19th-century renovations. Technically they're chimeras, not gargoyles, as they're purely ornamental; a true "gargoyle" is a carved sculpture that functions as a waterspout.

OUTSIDE NOTRE-DAME

Begun in 1163, completed in 1345, badly damaged during the Revolution, and restored by the architect Eugène Viollet-le-Duc in the 19th century, Notre-Dame may not be France's oldest or largest cathedral, but in beauty and architectural harmony it has few peers. The front entranceways seem like hands joined in prayer, the sculpted kings on the facade form a noble procession, and the west (front) rose window gleams with what seems like divine light.

The most dramatic approach to Notre-Dame is from the Rive Gauche, crossing at the Pont au Double from quai de Montebello, at the St-Michel métro or RER stop. This bridge will take you to the open square, place du Parvis, in front of the cathedral. (The more direct metro stop is Cité.)

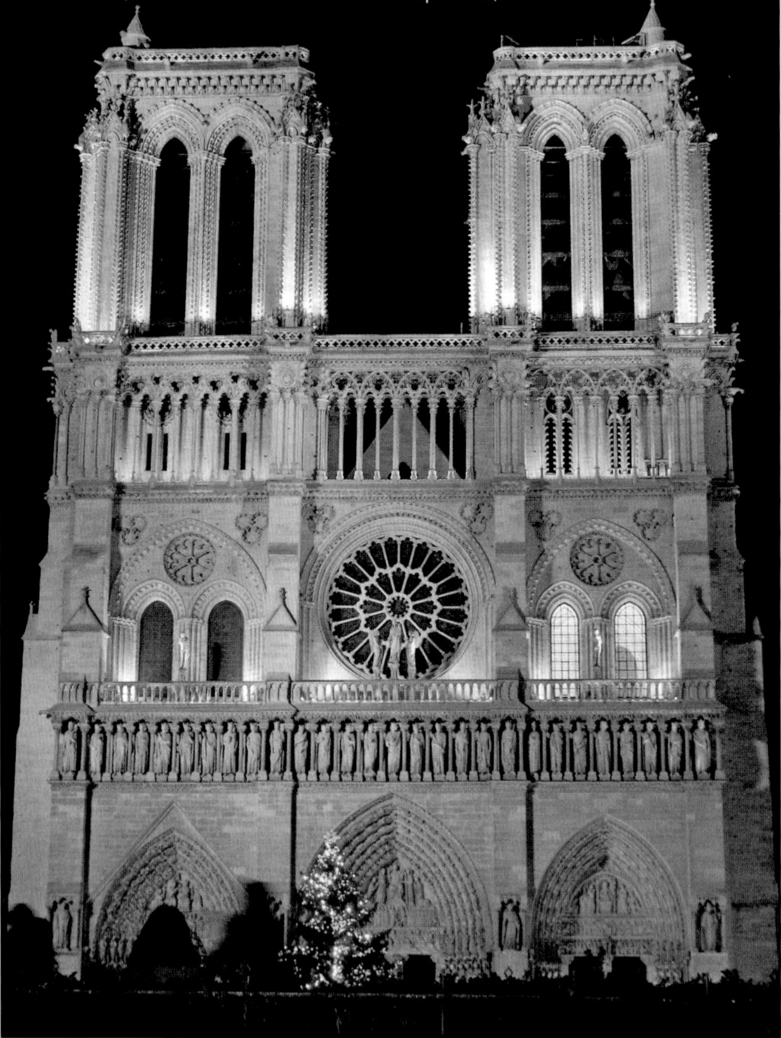

THE WEST (FRONT) FACADE

The three front entrances are, left to right: the Portal of the Virgin, the Portal of the Last Judgment (above), and the Portal of St. Anne, the oldest of the three. Above the three front entrances are the 28 restored statues of the kings of Israel, the Galerie des Rois.

INSIDE THE CATHEDRAL

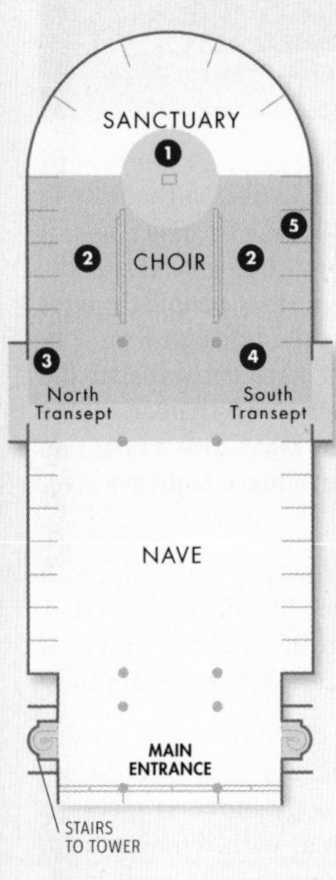

❶ **The Pietà,** behind the choir, represents the Virgin Mary mourning over the dead body of Christ.

❷ **The biblical scenes** on the north and south screens of the choir represent the life of Christ and the apparitions of Christ after the Resurrection.

❸ **The north rose window** is one of the cathedral's original stained-glass panels; at the center is an image of Mary holding a young Jesus.

❹ At the south (right) entrance to the choir, you'll glimpse the haunting 12th-century statue of **Notre-Dame de Paris,** "Our Lady of Paris," the Virgin, for whom the cathedral is named.

❺ **The treasury,** on the south side of the choir, holds a small collection of religious garments, reliquaries, and silver- and gold-plate.

MAKING THE CLIMB A separate entrance, to the left of the front facade if you're facing it, leads to the 387 stone steps of the south tower. These steps take you to the bell of Notre-Dame (as tolled by the fictional Quasimodo). Looking out from the tower, you can see how Paris—like the trunk of a tree developing new rings—has grown outward from the Ile de la Cité. To the north is Montmartre; to the west is the Arc de Triomphe, at the top of the Champs-Elysées; and to the south are the towers of St-Sulpice.

Place du Parvis

Detail of the Gallery of Kings, over the front entrance.

Notre-Dame was one of the first Gothic cathedrals in Europe and one of the first buildings to make use of **flying buttresses**—exterior supports that spread out the weight of the building and roof. At first people thought they looked like scaffolding that the builders forgot to remove. ■TIP→ **The most tranquil place to appreciate the architecture of Notre-Dame is from the lovely garden behind the cathedral, Square Jean-XXIII. By night, take a boat ride on the Seine for the best view—the lights at night are magnificent.**

Place du Parvis is *kilomètre zéro,* the spot from which all distances to and from the city are officially measured. A polished brass circle set in the ground, about 20 yards from the cathedral's main entrance, marks the exact spot.

The Crypt Archéologique (entrance down the stairs in front of the cathedral) is a quick visit but very interesting, especially for kids and archaeology buffs. It gives an "under the city" view of the area, with remains from previous churches that were built on this site, scale models charting the district's development, and artifacts dating from 2,000 years ago.

☎ 01-42-34-56-10

🌐 www.notredameparis.fr

Cathedral free. Towers: €8. Crypt €4. Treasury €2.50.

Cathedral daily 8–6:45. Towers Apr.–June and Sept., daily 10 AM–6:30; July and Aug., weekdays 10 AM–6:30, weekends 10 AM–11 PM; Oct.–Mar., daily 10–5:30. Note: towers close early when overcrowded. Treasury Mon.–Fri. 9:30–6 PM, Sat. 9:30–6:30, Sun. 1:30–6:30. Crypt Tues.–Sun. 10–6. Museum Wed. and weekends 2:30–6.

SOMETHING TO PONDER

Do Notre-Dame's hunchback and its gargoyles have anything in common other than bad posture? Quasimodo was created by Victor Hugo in the novel *Notre-Dame de Paris,* published in 1831. The incredible popularity of the book made Parisians finally take notice of the cathedral's state of disrepair and spurred Viollet-le-Duc's renovations. These included the addition of the gargoyles, among other things, and resulted in the structure we see today.

■TIP→ **The best time to visit Notre-Dame is early in the morning, when the cathedral is at its brightest and least crowded.**

■TIP→ **There are free guided tours in English on Wed. and Thurs. at 2 PM, and Sat. at 2:30 PM.**

28 **Conciergerie.** Much of Ile de la Cité's medieval buildings fell victim to wunderkind planner Baron Georges-Eugène Haussmann's ambitious rebuilding program of the 1860s. Among the rare survivors is the former city prison where Marie-Antoinette and other victims of the French Revolution spent their last days. Built by Philip IV in the 13th and 14th centuries, the Conciergerie was part of the original palace of the kings of France, before the royals moved into the Louvre, in 1358; in 1391, this palace was turned into a prison. During the French Revolution, the Conciergerie famously imprisoned Queen Marie-Antoinette as she awaited her fatal trip to the guillotine. You can visit a re-creation of Marie-Antoinette's cell, see lifelike wax figures sadly await their fate behind bars, and read letters penned by some of Paris's famous revolutionaries. The chapel's stained glass is emblazoned with the initials M. A.; it was commissioned after the queen's death by her daughter. Outside, in the courtyard, victims of the Terror spent their final days playing piquet, writing letters to loved ones, washing clothes, and waiting for the dreaded climb up the staircase to the Chamber of the Revolutionary Council to hear its final verdict. The building takes its name from the palace's *concierge,* or high-level keeper of the palace. ✉ *2 bd. du Palais, Ile de la Cité* ☎ *01–53–40–60–80* 🌐 *conciergerie.monuments-nationaux.fr* 🎫 *€7, joint ticket with Sainte-Chapelle €11* ⏲ *Mar.–Oct., daily 9:30–6; Nov.–Feb., daily 9–5* Ⓜ *Cité.*

4 **La Défense.** First conceived in 1958, this modernist suburb across the Seine from Neuilly was inspired by Le Corbusier's dream of high-rise buildings, pedestrian walkways, and sunken vehicle circulation. An experiment to keep high-rises out of the historic downtown, this Parisian business hub has survived economic uncertainty to become a surprising success, dotted with modern art, public sculptures, hundreds of corporate offices, and even 20,000 residents. Crowning the main plaza is the iconic **Grande Arche de La Défense,** an enormous open cube of a building where tubular glass elevators whisk you 360 feet to the top. ✉ *Parvis de La Défense, La Défense* ☎ *01–49–07–27–27* 🌐 *www.grandearche.com* 🌐 *www.grandearche.com* 🎫 *Grande Arche €10* ⏲ *Apr.–Aug., daily 10–8; Sept.–Mar. daily 10–7* Ⓜ *Métro; RER: Grande Arche de LaDéfense.*

26 **Pont Neuf** *(New Bridge).* Crossing the Ile de la Cité, just behind Square du Vert-Galant, is the oldest bridge in Paris, confusingly called the New Bridge—the name was given when it was completed in 1607, and it stuck. It was the first bridge in the city to be built without houses lining either side, allegedly because Henri IV wanted a clear view of Notre-Dame from his windows at the Louvre. ✉ *Ile de la Cité* Ⓜ *Pont-Neuf.*

FROM THE EIFFEL TOWER TO THE ARC DE TRIOMPHE

The Eiffel Tower (or Tour Eiffel, to use the French) lords over southwest Paris, and from nearly wherever you are on this walk you can see its jutting needle. For years many Parisians felt it was an iron eyesore and called it the Giant Asparagus, a vegetable that weighed 15 million pounds and grew 1,000 feet high. But gradually the tower became part of the Parisian landscape, entering the hearts and souls of Parisians and

BUS TOURS

For a two-hour orientation tour by bus, the standard price is about €25. The two largest bus-tour operators are Cityrama (✉ *4 pl. des Pyramides, 1er* ☎ *01–44–55–61–00* 🌐 *www.ecityrama.com*) and Paris Vision (✉ *214 rue de Rivoli, 1er* ☎ *01–42–60–30–01* 🌐 *www.parisvision.com* ✉ *53 bis, quai des Grands-Augustins, 6e* ☎ *08–92–68–41–14* ✉ *Pl. de la Madeleine, 8e*) ; for a more intimate tour of the city, Cityrama also runs several minibus excursions per day with a private multilingual tour operator for about €80. Paris Vision runs nonstop two-hour tours with multilingual commentary available via individual headphones with more than 10 languages for €24, or €38 for a 2.5 hour night tour with boat ride.

Paris L'Open Tour (✉ *13 rue Auber, 9e* ☎ *01–44–55–61–00* 🌐 *www.pariscityrama.com*) gives tours in a double-decker bus with an open top; commentary is available in French and English on individual headphones. Get on or off at one of the 50 pickup points indicated by the lime-green sign posts; tickets may be purchased on board and cost €29 for one day, €32 for unlimited use for two days.

Les Cars Rouges (☎ *01–53–95–39–53* 🌐 *www.carsrouges.com*) offer double-decker London-style buses with nine stops—a ticket for two consecutive days is available for €24.

RATP (Paris Transit Authority) also offers economical, commentary-free excursions; the Montmartrobus (€1.80) departs from métro Anvers and zips through the winding cobbled streets of Montmartre to the top of the hill for those who don't want to brave the walk. The RATP Balabus goes from Gare du Lyon to the Grande Arche at La Défense passing by all major tourist attractions on the way for the price of one to three métro tickets. The Balabus runs from mid-April to September.

visitors alike. Thanks to its stunning nighttime illumination, topped by four 6,000-watt projectors creating a lighthouse beacon visible for 80 km (50 mi) around, it continues to make Paris live up to its moniker *La Ville Lumière*—the City of Light. Water is the second highlight here: fountains playing beneath Place du Trocadéro and boat tours along the Seine on a Bateau Mouche. Museums are the third; the area around Trocadéro is full of them. Style is the fourth, and not just because the buildings here are overwhelmingly elegant—but because this is also the center of haute couture, with the top names in fashion all congregated around Avenue Montaigne, only a brief walk from the Champs-Élysées, to the north.

TOP ATTRACTIONS

6 ★ **Arc de Triomphe.** Set on Place Charles-de-Gaulle—known to Parisians as L'Étoile, or the Star (a reference to the streets that fan out from it)—the colossal, 164-foot Arc de Triomphe arch was planned by Napoléon but not finished until 1836, 20 years after the end of his rule. It's decorated with some magnificent sculptures by François Rude, such as the *Departure of the Volunteers*, better known as *La Marseillaise*, to the right of the arch when viewed from the Champs-Élysées. A small museum halfway up the arch is devoted to its history. France's Unknown Soldier

is buried beneath the archway; the flame is rekindled every evening at 6:30. ✉ *Pl. Charles-de-Gaulle, Champs-Élysées* ☎ *01–55–37–73–77* 🌐 *www.arc-de-triomphe.monuments-nationaux.fr* 🎟 *€9, under 18 free* ⏲ *Apr.–Sept., daily 10* AM*–11* PM*; Oct.–Mar., daily 10* AM*–10:30* PM Ⓜ *Métro; RER: Étoile.*

10 **Bateaux Mouches.** If you want to view Paris in slow motion, hop on one of these famous motorboats, which set off on their hour-long tours of the city waters regularly (every half hour in summer) from Place de l'Alma. Their route heads east to the Ile St-Louis and then back west, past the Tour Eiffel, as far as the Allée des Cygnes and its miniature version of the Statue of Liberty. Note that some travelers prefer to take this Seine cruise on the smaller Vedettes du Pont Neuf, which depart from Square du Vert-Galant on the Ile de la Cité, as the Vedettes have a guide giving commentary in French and English, while the Bateaux Mouches have a loud recorded spiel in several languages. For the quietest journey, take the city-run Batobus, which has no commentary and allows you to get on and off at its various quayside stops. ✉ *Pl. de l'Alma, Trocadéro/Tour Eiffel* ☎ *01–42–25–96–10* 🌐 *www.bateaux-mouches.fr* 🎟 *€10* Ⓜ *Alma-Marceau.*

5 **Champs-Élysées.** Marcel Proust lovingly described the genteel elegance of the storied Avenue des Champs-Élysées during its Belle Époque heyday, when its cobblestones resounded with the clatter of horses and carriages. Today, despite unrelenting traffic and the intrusion of chain stores and fast-food restaurants, the avenue still sparkles. There's always something happening here: the stores are open late—and many are open on Sunday (a rarity in Paris), the nightclubs remain top destinations, and the cafés offer prime people-watching—though you'll pay for the privilege: after all, this is Europe's most expensive stretch of real estate. Along the 2-km (1¼-mi) stretch, you can find the marquee names in French luxury, including Cartier, the *perfumier* Guerlain, and Louis Vuitton. Old stalwarts are still going strong, if a bit faded, like the Lido cabaret and Fouquet's, whose celebrity clientele extends from James Joyce to President Nicolas Sarkozy, who celebrated his election night victory at this restaurant in May 2007. The avenue is also the setting for the last leg of the Tour de France bicycle race (the third or fourth Sunday in July), and ceremonies on Bastille Day (July 14) and Armistice Day (November 11). The Champs-Élysées, which translates as "Elysian Fields" (the resting place of the blessed in Greek mythology), began life as a cow pasture. Ⓜ *Champs-Élysées–Clemenceau, Franklin-D.-Roosevelt, George V, Étoile.*

4 **Musée Guimet.** The excellent Guimet National Museum of Asian Arts traces its roots to the 19th-century Lyonnais industrialist Émile Guimet. The world-class collection, enriched by the state's vast holdings, is laid out geographically in airy, light-filled rooms, thanks to a top-end renovation a decade ago. The museum is home to the largest collection of Khmer sculpture outside of Cambodia, a comprehensive China collection, and treasures from across the Far East. Peek into the old library rotunda, where Mata Hari danced for the city's notables one evening in 1905. Pick up a free English-language audio guide and brochure at the entrance. If you have time, check out the Guimet's impressive

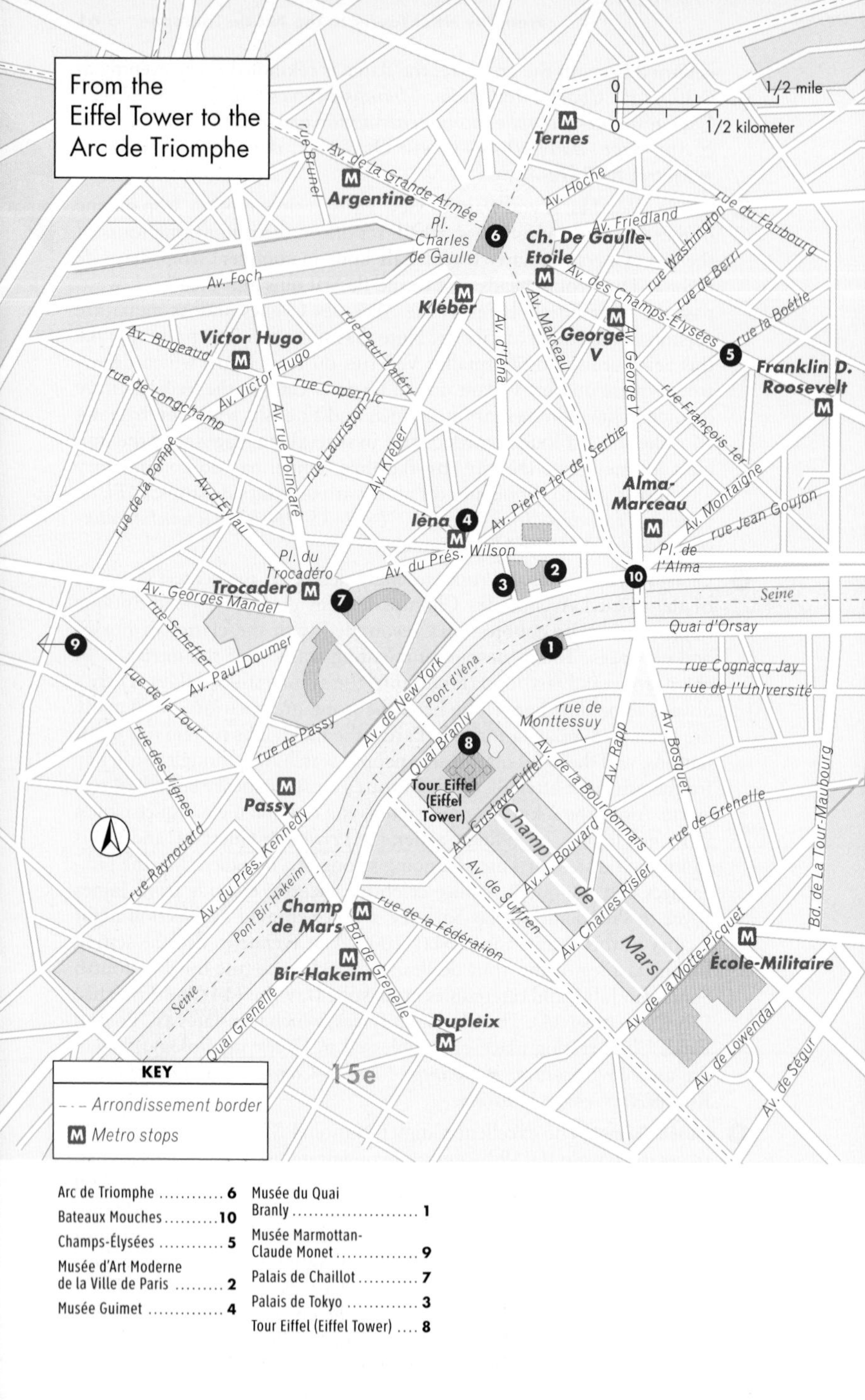

Arc de Triomphe 6
Bateaux Mouches 10
Champs-Élysées 5
Musée d'Art Moderne de la Ville de Paris 2
Musée Guimet 4
Musée du Quai Branly 1
Musée Marmottan-Claude Monet 9
Palais de Chaillot 7
Palais de Tokyo 3
Tour Eiffel (Eiffel Tower) 8

Buddhist Pantheon down the street at 19 ave. d'Iéna (admission is free). *6 pl. d'Iéna, Trocadéro/Tour Eiffel 01–56–52–53–00 www.museeguimet.fr €6.50 Wed.–Sun. 10–6 Iéna or Boissiére.*

9 **Musée Marmottan–Claude Monet.** A few years ago the underrated Marmottan tacked Claude Monet onto its official name—and justly so, as this may be the best collection of the artist's works anywhere. Monet's works occupy a specially built basement gallery in this elegant 19th-century mansion, where you can find such captivating works as the *Cathédrale de Rouen* series (1892–96) and *Impression: Soleil Levant* (*Impression–Sunrise*, 1872), the work that helped give the Impressionist movement its name. Upstairs the mansion still feels like a graciously decorated private home. *2 rue Louis-Boilly, Passy-Auteuil 01–44–96–50–33 www.marmottan.com €9 Tues. 11–9, Wed.–Sun. 11–6 La Muette.*

8 **Tour Eiffel** *(Eiffel Tower). See highlighted listing in this chapter.*

WORTH NOTING

2 **Musée d'Art Moderne de la Ville de Paris** *(Paris Museum of Modern Art).* Although the city's modern-art museum hasn't generated a buzz comparable to that of the Centre Georges Pompidou, it can be a more pleasant experience because, like many smaller museums, there are often no crowds. The building reopened after a long renovation in February 2006, and its vast, white-walled galleries make an ideal backdrop for the museum's temporary exhibitions of 20th-century art. The permanent collection on the lower floor takes over where the Musée d'Orsay leaves off, chronologically speaking: among the earliest works are Fauvist paintings by Maurice Vlaminck and André Derain, followed by Pablo Picasso's early experiments in Cubism. Other highlights include works by Robert and Sonia Delaunay, Chagall, Matisse, Rothko, and Modigliani. *11 av. du Président-Wilson, Trocadéro/Tour Eiffel 01–53–67–40–00 www.mam.paris.fr Permanent collection free, temporary exhibitions €5–€12, depending on exhibition Tues.–Sun. 10–6, Thurs. until 10 for temporary exhibits Alma Marceau or Iéna.*

3 **Palais de Tokyo.** This Art Nouveau museum reopened in 2002 after many derelict years as a trendy, stripped-down space for contemporary arts with unorthodox, ambitious programming. There is no permanent collection; instead, dynamic temporary exhibits spread over a large, open area reminiscent of a construction site, with a trailer for a ticket booth. Instead of traditional museum guards, young art students—most of whom speak at least some English—are on hand to help explain the installations. There's also an offbeat gift shop, a bookstore, and the hippest museum restaurant in town, Tokyo Eat. *13 av. du Président-Wilson, Trocadéro/Tour Eiffel 01–47–23–54–01 www.palaisdetokyo.com €6 Tues.–Sun. noon–midnight Iéna.*

1 **Musée du Quai Branly.** Paris's newest museum was built by top architect Jean Nouvel to house the state-owned collection of "non-Western" art, culled from several other museums. Despite the interminable queues after the opening in 2006, the museum drew criticism for a seemingly

Continued on page 66

New York has the Statue of Liberty, London has Big Ben—and Paris has the Eiffel Tower. This symbol of Paris, recognized the world over, did not, however, begin life as the beloved icon it is today. Engineer Gustave Eiffel's iron creation for the 1889 World's Fair was greeted with disgust by Parisians, who dubbed it the Giant Asparagus. French author Guy de Maupassant supposedly hated the tower so much that he often ate lunch there, explaining that it was the only place in the city where he could avoid seeing it. Parisians eventually warmed to the tower, an inescapable part of the landscape that has captured the minds and hearts of generations.

Total height: 1,063 feet

LA TOUR EIFFEL

■ The 250 millionth visitor went to the top of the Eiffel Tower in 2010.

■ To get to the first viewing platform, Gustave Eiffel originally used avant-garde hydraulic cable elevators designed by American Elisha Otis for two of the curved base legs of the tower. French elevators with a chain-drive system were used in the other two legs. During the 1989 renovation, all the elevators were rebuilt by the Otis company.

■ An expensive way to beat the queue is to reserve a table at **Le Jules Verne**, the restaurant on the 2nd level, which has a private elevator. Taken over by star chef Alain Ducasse, count on a dinner bill of €450 for 2 with wine, though there's an €85 prix-fine menu at lunch (without wine). www.lejulesverne-paris.com 01-45-55-61-44.

■ If you're in good shape, you can take the stairs to the 2nd level. If you want to go to the top you have to take the elevator.

■ Every 7 years the tower is repainted. The job takes 15 months and uses 60 tons of "Tour Eiffel Brown" paint in three shades—lightest on top, darkest at the bottom

■ The tower nearly became a giant heap of scrap in 1909, when its concession expired, but its use as a radio antenna saved the day.

■ The tower is most breathtaking at night, when the girders are illuminated. The light show, conceived to celebrate the turn of the millennium, was so popular that the 20,000 lights were reinstalled for permanent use in 2003. It does its electric shimmy for 5 minutes every hour on the hour (cut from 10 to save energy) until 1 am.

NEED A BITE?

58 Tour Eiffel, the restaurant on the first level, serves a good-value, self-service lunch. There is table service at dinner.

Le Café Branly, in the nearby Musée du Quai Branly, 27 Quai Branley, Trocadéro/Tour Eiffel, 01-47-53-68-01 is a good choice for lunch or a late-afternoon snack.

The base formed by the tower's feet is 410 by 410 feet.

01-44-11-23-23
www.tour-eiffel.fr
By elevator: 1st and 2nd levels €8, top €13; By stairs: 1st and 2nd levels only, €4.50
June 13–Aug. 29, daily 9AM–midnight* (11PM for summit); Aug. 30–Dec. 31, 9:30AM–11PM* (10:30PM for summit); Jan. 1–June 12, 9:30–11PM* (10:30 for summit); Stairs: June 13–Aug. 29, 9 AM–midnight; Aug.30–Dec.31, 9:30AM–6:30PM *LAST TICKET SOLD

M Bir-Hakeim, Trocadéro, Ecole Militaire; RER Champ de Mars

■ TIP→ Beat the crush by reserving your tickets online.

incoherent assemblage of artifacts, from antiquity to the modern age. Critics questioned the connection between funeral masks from Melanesia, Siberian shaman drums, Indonesian textiles, and African statuary. A corkscrew ramp leads from the lobby to a cavernous exhibition space, color-coded to designate sections from Asia, Africa, Oceania, and the Americas. The lighting is dim, sometimes too dim to read the information panels (which makes the €5 audio guide a good idea). A "living wall" of some 150 species of exotic plants grows on the exterior—an impressive sight after dark when scores of cylindrical colored lights are illuminated. If you're hungry, try pricey Les Ombres, with a commanding 5th-floor view of the Eiffel Tower, or the more down-to-earth Le Café Branly on the ground floor. ✉ *37 quai Branly, Trocadéro/Tour Eiffel* ☎ *01–56–61–70–00* 🌐 *www.quaibranly.fr* 🎫 *€8.50* ⏲ *Tues., Wed., and Sun. 11–7, Thurs.–Sat. 11–9* Ⓜ *Iéna.*

7 **Palais de Chaillot.** This honey-color Art Deco cultural center on Place du Trocadéro was built in the 1930s to replace a Moorish-style building constructed for the World's Fair of 1878. The plaza-terrace is a top draw for camera-toting visitors intent on snapping the perfect shot of the Eiffel Tower. In the building to the left is the **Cité de l'Architecture et du Patrimoine**—an excellent architecture museum—and the **Theâtre National de Chaillot,** which occasionally stages plays in English. The twin building to the right contains the **Musée de la Marine,** an excellent small museum with a nautical theme; and the **Musée de l'Homme,** which is closed for renovation and set to reopen, as the Musée de l'Humanité, in 2012 or beyond. Also here is the cozy Café de l'Homme, which has a fantastic view of the tower, but a pricey menu that is not nearly as stellar. The garden leading to the Seine has sculptures and dramatic fountains and is a dramatic staging ground for fireworks on July 14, Bastille Day. ✉ *Pl. du Trocadéro, Trocadéro/Tour Eiffel* Ⓜ *Trocadéro.*

THE FAUBOURG ST-HONORÉ AND LES HALLES

The impossibly posh Faubourg St-Honoré has been a fashionista destination for three centuries, as popular now as it was when royal mistresses shopped here. Just about every chic boutique has a branch here, and this is where you can find some of the city's best hotels. Once the stomping ground of kings and queens, today it's home to the French president and the American and British ambassadors. Stroll the historic passageways and arcaded streets to experience all that is elegant about Paris. Top-end boutiques, dressmakers, and perfume shops combined to make this faubourg (district) a symbol of luxury throughout the world. The centerpiece of the western end is ritzy Place Vendome, where you'll find, yes, the Hotel Ritz. Ambitious women play a role in the history here, with Rue de Castiglione named after a former denizen, Countess de Castiglione, sent to (successfully) plead the cause of Italian unity with Napoléon III. Coco Chanel founded her fashion house on Rue Cambon.

As you walk east, don't miss gems such as Galerie Vivienne, the exquisitely restored 19th-century shopping arcade. Nearby is the Place Colette, named after the writer Colette and home to the stately theater, the **Comédie Française**, still going strong after 400 years. Hidden just off the place is the Palais-Royal, a romantic garden ringed by arcades with boutiques selling everything from antique war medals to the latest frock by Stella McCartney. To the east, mercantile Les Halles has risen from its roots as the city's vermin-infested wholesale food market (closed in 1969) to become one of the city's trendiest neighborhoods, with expensive apartments and trendy shops, cafés, and bars centered on the pedestrian streets Montorgueil and Montmartre. At the hub of it all is Paris's most famous modern art museum, the Centre Georges Pompidou.

TOP ATTRACTIONS

42 ★ **Centre Georges Pompidou.** Love it or hate it, the Pompidou is certainly the city's most unique-looking building. Most Parisians have warmed to the industrial, Lego-like exterior that caused a scandal when it opened in 1977. Named after French president Georges Pompidou (1911–74), it was designed by then-unknowns Renzo Piano and Richard Rogers. The architects' claim to fame was putting the building's guts on the outside and color-coding them: water pipes are green, air ducts are blue, electrics are yellow, and things like elevators and escalators are red. Art from the 20th century to the present day is what you can find inside. The **Musée National d'Art Moderne** (*Modern Art Museum*, entrance on Level 4) occupies the top two levels. Level 5 is devoted to modern art, 1905–60 including major works by Matisse, Modigliani, Marcel Duchamp, and Picasso; Level 4 is dedicated to contemporary art from the '60s on, including video installations. Outside, next to the museum's sloping plaza—where throngs of teenagers hang out (and there's free Wi-Fi)—is the **Atelier Brancusi** (*Brancusi Studio*). This small, airy museum contains four rooms reconstituting Brancusi's Montparnasse studios with works from all periods of his career. On the opposite side, in the **Place Igor-Stravinsky,** is the Stravinsky Fountain, which has 16 gyrating mechanical figures in primary colors. ✉ *Pl. Georges-Pompidou, Beaubourg/Les Halles* ☎ *01–44–78–12–33* 🌐 *www.centrepompidou.fr* ⏱ *€12 May–Aug., €10 Sept.–Apr.; €8–€9 for temporary exhibits; free 1st Sun. of month* ⏱ *Wed.–Mon. 11–9, temporary exhibitions 11–10; Atelier Brancusi 2–6*

NEED A BREAK?

There are many cafés around the Centre Pompidou, but Dame Tartine (✉ *2 rue Brisemiche* ☎ *01-42-77-32-22* Ⓜ *Rambuteau*) overlooking the Stravinsky fountain, with its colorful sculptures, is a good choice. You won't go wrong with a homemade quiche, salad, or a classic *cassoulet*.

24 **Galerie Vivienne.** The grand dame of Paris's 19th-century *passages couverts,* or covered arcades, a walk through this beautifully restored galerie, with its tiled floor, will send you back to a time of gaslights and horse-drawn carriages. Parisians came to passages like this one to escape the muddy streets, and browse the boutiques under the glass-and-iron roofs—the world's first shopping malls. Today, the Galerie Vivienne still attracts top-flight shops such as Jean-Paul Gaultier (6 rue Vivienne), as well as some more affordable ones. If you need a break, A Priori Thé has been comforting travelers for more than 20 years with its teas and sweets. Or pull up a stool at the wine bar at Legrand Filles et Fils, a family-run *épicerie* (grocery) and wine shop. ✉ *Main entrance at 4 rue des Petits-Champs, Louvre/Tuileries* Ⓜ *Palais-Royal/Bourse.*

21 ★ **Les Arts Décoratifs.** *(Decorative Arts Center).* Sharing a wing of the Musée du Louvre, but with a separate entrance and admission charge, the **Musée des Arts Décoratifs** is home to a stellar collection of decorative arts. Spread across nine floors, the vast holdings include altarpieces from the Middle Ages and furnishings from the Italian Renaissance to the present day. Renovated in 2006, the museum has period rooms reflecting the ages. The arts center comprises two other museums—more aptly called departments—which play host to temporary exhibitions: the **Musée de la Mode et du Textiles** (Museum of Fashion and Textiles) and the **Musée de la Publicité,** dedicated to advertising and publicity. There is also a quiet restaurant, **Le Saut du Loup,** with an outdoor terrace that serves lunch even on Monday when the museum is closed. ✉ *107 rue de Rivoli, Louvre/Tuileries* ☎ *01–44–55–57–50* 🌐 *www.lesartsdecoratifs.fr* 🎟 *€8–€16.50* ⏲ *Tues., Wed., and Fri. 11–6, Thurs. 11–9, weekends 10–6* Ⓜ *Palais-Royal.*

NEED A BREAK?

Once patronized by Proust and Gertrude Stein (who loved the chocolate cake here) Angélina (✉ *226 rue de Rivoli, Louvre/Tuileries* ☎ *01–42–60–82–00*), founded in 1903, is an elegant *salon de thé* (tearoom), famous for its *chocolat africain*, a jug of incredibly thick hot chocolate served with whipped cream (irresistible even in summer). Although it's still among the city's best chocolate hits, finicky Proust would probably sniff at the slightly shopworn air of the place today and reserve his affections for the ever-elegant teas served at historic Ladurée, a short walk to the east at 16 rue Royale.

23 Fodor's Choice ★ **Palais-Royal** *(Royal Palace).* This most romantic and quiet of Paris gardens, enclosed within the former home of Cardinal Richelieu (1585–1642), is an ideal spot to while away an afternoon. Do like the locals and cuddle with your sweetheart on a bench under the trees, soak up the sunshine beside the fountain, or browse the 400-year-old arcades, now home to chic boutiques and quirky shops. One of the city's oldest restaurants is here, the haute-cuisine jewel box Le Grand Véfour, where brass plaques recall regulars like Napoléon and Victor Hugo. Built in 1629, the *palais* became royal when Richelieu bequeathed it to Louis XIII. Other famous residents include Jean Cocteau and Colette, who wrote of her pleasurable "country" view of the *province à Paris*. Today, the garden often plays host to giant-size temporary art installations sponsored by another tenant, the Ministry of Culture. The courtyard off Place Colette is outfitted with a strange collection of black-and-white columns created in 1986 by the artist Daniel Buren. ✉ *Pl. du Palais-Royal, Louvre/Tuileries* Ⓜ *Palais-Royal.*

15 **Place Vendôme.** Property laws have kept this refined square spare and pure. The architect Jules-Hardouin Mansart designed the perfectly proportioned plaza in 1702 as an octagon. To maintain a uniform appearance, Mansart built only the façades of the *hôtels particuliers* (mansions), and the lots behind were then sold to buyers who customized their palaces. In the square's center, a 144-foot column erected by Napoléon was toppled in 1871 by painter Gustave Courbet and his band of Revolutionaries. The Third Republic stuck the pieces back

CLOSE UP

Hemingway's Paris

There is a saying: "Everyone has two countries, his or her own—and France." For the Lost Generation after World War I, these words rang particularly true. Lured by favorable exchange rates, free-flowing alcohol, and a booming artistic scene, many American writers, composers, and painters moved to Paris in the 1920s and 1930s, Ernest Hemingway among them. He arrived in Paris with his first wife, Hadley, in December 1921 and made for the Rive Gauche—the Hôtel Jacob et d'Angleterre, to be exact (still operating at 44 rue Jacob). To celebrate their arrival the couple went to the Café de la Paix for a meal they nearly couldn't afford.

Hemingway worked as a journalist and quickly made friends with other expat writers such as Gertrude Stein and Ezra Pound. In 1922 the Hemingways moved to 74 rue du Cardinal Lemoine, a bare-bones apartment with no running water (his writing studio was around the corner, on the top floor of 39 rue Descartes). Then in early 1924 the couple and their baby son settled at 113 rue Notre-Dame des Champs. Much of *The Sun Also Rises,* Hemingway's first serious novel, was written at nearby café La Closerie des Lilas. These were the years in which he forged his writing style, paring his sentences down to the pith. As he noted in *A Moveable Feast,* "hunger was good discipline." There were some particularly hungry months when Hemingway gave up journalism and tried to publish short stories, and the family was "very poor and very happy."

They weren't happy for long. In 1926, just when *The Sun Also Rises* made him famous, Hemingway left Hadley and the next year wedded his

mistress, Pauline Pfeiffer, across town at St Honoré-d'Eylau, then moved to 6 rue Férou, near the Musée du Luxembourg, whose collection of Cézanne landscapes (now in the Musée d'Orsay) he revered.

For gossip and books, and to pick up his mail, Papa would visit Shakespeare & Co., then at 12 rue de l'Odéon, owned by Sylvia Beach, who became a trusted friend. For cash and cocktails Hemingway usually headed to the upscale Rive Droite. He collected the former at the Guaranty Trust Company, at 1 rue des Italiens. He found the latter, when he was flush, at the bar of the Hôtel Crillon, or, when poor, at the Caves Mura, at 19 rue d'Antin, or Harry's Bar, still in brisk business at 5 rue Daunou. Hemingway's legendary association with the Hotel Ritz was sealed during the Liberation in 1944, when he strode in at the head of his platoon and "liberated" the joint by ordering martinis all around. Here Hemingway asked Mary Welsh to become his fourth wife, and here also, the story goes, a trunk full of notes on his first years in Paris turned up in the 1950s, giving him the raw material to write *A Moveable Feast.*

together again and sent him the bill, though he died without paying. Chopin lived and died at No. 12, which is also where Napoléon III enjoyed trysts with his mistress; since 1902 it has been home to Chaumet, one of several high-end jewelers in the area. At No. 15, the Hotel Ritz remains a top destination where celebs can often be found quaffing some of the city's best—and priciest—cocktails in the tiny Hemingway Bar. Ⓜ *Opéra.*

ROOM WITH A VIEW

Visit the arcades of the Palais-Royal to see why the French writer Colette called the view from her window "a little corner of the country" in the heart of the city.

WORTH NOTING

22 **Comédie Française.** Mannered productions of Molière, Racine, and Corneille appear regularly on the bill here, but only in French. Founded in 1680 by Louis XIV, the theater finally opened its doors to the public in 1799. It nearly burned to the ground a hundred years later; what you're looking at dates from 1900. The *comedienne* Sarah Bernhardt began her career here. ✉ *1 pl. Colette, Louvre/Tuileries* ☎ *08–25–10–16–80* 🌐 *www.comedie-francaise.fr* Ⓜ *Palais-Royal.*

14 **Église de La Madeleine** *(Church of La Madeleine).* With its rows of uncompromising columns, this enormous neoclassical edifice in the center of the Place de la Madeleine was consecrated as a church in 1842, nearly 78 years after construction began. Initially planned as a Baroque building, it was later razed and begun anew by an architect who had the Roman Pantheon in mind. Interrupted by the Revolution, the site was razed yet again when Napoléon decided to make it into a Greek temple dedicated to the glory of his army. Those plans changed when the army was defeated and the emperor deposed. Other ideas for the building included making it into a train station, a market, and a library. Finally, Louis XVIII decided to make it a church, which it still is today. There are also concerts here. ✉ *Pl. de la Madeleine, Faubourg* 🌐 *www.eglise-lamadeleine.com* ⏲ *Daily 9–7* Ⓜ *Madeleine.*

THE GRANDS BOULEVARDS

In Belle Époque Paris, the Grand Boulevards were the place to see and be seen: in the cafés, at the opera, or in the ornate passages, the glass-covered arcades that were the world's first shopping malls. If you close your eyes, you can almost imagine the Grands Boulevards immortalized on canvas by the Impressionists: well-dressed Parisians strolling wide avenues dotted with shops, cafés, and horse-drawn carriages—all set against a backdrop of stately Haussmannian buildings. Today, despite the chain stores, sidewalk vendors, and fast-food joints, the Grands Boulevards remain the city's shopping epicenter, home to the most popular *grands magasins* (department stores), Galeries Lafayette and Au Printemps, near Place de l'Opéra at the heart of the long chain of avenues, which change names six times.

Commerce aside, the Grands Boulevards are a cultural destination anchored by the **Palais Garnier,** the magnificent opera house commissioned by Napoléon III. The neighborhood is also home to some of the city's best small museums, all former private collections housed in 19th-century *maisons particuliers* (mansions) that alone are worth the trip. The exquisite **Musée Jacquemart-André** plays host to an impressive collection of Italian Renaissance art, while the jewel box **Musée Nissim de Camondo** remembers one family's tragic end.

TOP ATTRACTIONS

51 **Cimetière du Père-Lachaise** *(Père-Lachaise Cemetery).* As far as cemeteries go, this one is a powerhouse—a veritable necropolis with 118 acres of sedate cobbled avenues and tombs competing in pomposity and originality. Rocker Jim Morrison of the Doors still draws pilgrims three decades after his death, as does the tomb of scribe Oscar Wilde, covered in lipstick kisses. If puckering up isn't your thing, bring a red rose for the "little sparrow" Edith Piaf. The famed medieval lovers Héloïse and Abélard are here, along with composer Chopin; artists Ingres and Georges Seurat; playwright Molière; writers Balzac, Proust, Colette, and Gertrude Stein, sharing a grave with lover Alice B. Toklas. Named for Pére François de la Chaise, Louis XIV's confessor, Père-Lachaise has some political history attached to it—it was the site of the Paris Commune's final battle on May 28, 1871, when 147 rebels were lined up and shot against the Mur des Fédérés (Federalists' Wall) in the southeast corner. Buy a map on the street before you enter; you'll still get lost but it's well worth it. ✉ *Entrances on Rue des Rondeaux, Bd. de Ménilmontant, Rue de la Réunion, Père Lachaise* ☎ *01–55–25–82–10* 🌐 *www.pere-lachaise.com* ⏲ *Easter–Sept., daily 8–6; Oct.–Easter, daily 8–dusk* Ⓜ *Gambetta, Philippe-Auguste, Père-Lachaise.*

12 **Galeries Lafayette.** The stunning Byzantine glass *coupole,* or dome, is not to be missed—just wander to the center of the perfume and cosmetics department on the main floor and look up. Next door, the excellent Lafayette Gourmet food hall, on the second floor of the men's store, has one of the city's best selections of delicacies. Try the apricot-pistachio bread at Eric Kayser or a green tea éclair from Japanese-French baker Sadaharu Aoki. ✉ *40 bd. Haussmann, Opéra/Grands Boulevards* ☎ *01–42–82–34–56* 🌐 *www.galerieslafayette.com* ⏲ *Mon.–Wed., Fri., and Sat. 9:30–8, Thurs. 9:30–9* Ⓜ *Chaussée d'Antin, Opéra; RER: Auber.*

3 ★ **Musée Jacquemart-André.** Perhaps the city's best small museum, the opulent Musée Jacquemart-André is home to a vast collection of art and furnishings lovingly assembled in the late 19th century by banking heir Edouard André and his artist wife, Nélie Jacquemart. Their midlife marriage in 1881 raised eyebrows—he was a dashing bachelor and a Protestant, and she, no great beauty, hailed from a modest Catholic family. Still, theirs was a happy union fused by a common passion for art. Their collection favored the Italian Renaissance, but they also amassed works by French painters Fragonard, Jacques-Louis David, and François Boucher, and Dutch masters Van Dyke and Rembrandt. Immortalized in the Oscar-winner *Gigi*, the Belle Époque mansion itself is a star attraction. You can tour the separate bedrooms—his in dusty pink, hers in pale yellow. The former dining room, now an elegant café with an outdoor terrace, has one of the mansion's several stunning ceilings by Tiepolo. Don't forget the free audio guide in English.

⊠ *158 bd. Haussmann, Parc Monceau* ☎ *01–45–62–11–59* 🌐 *www.musee-jacquemart-andre.com* 🎟 *€10* ⏲ *Daily 10–6* Ⓜ *St-Philippe-du-Roule or Miromesnil.*

NEED A BREAK?

Just steps from the Drouot auction house, J'go (⊠ *4 rue Drouot, Grands Boulevards* ☎ *01–40–22–09–09*) , one of two Paris outposts of the Toulouse wine bar and restaurant, is a perfect spot for an evening apéritif or a light dinner. The cozy bar serves an impressive menu of *grignotages* (tapas) from France's southwest, such as peppery foie gras on bread or Basque cheese with jam, either of which is nicely paired with a glass of *madiran*, a hearty red from the Pyrenees. The restaurant upstairs serves rib-sticking specialties such as lamb stuffed with foie gras. The name is a play on the French "J'y vais," or "I go there."

2 Fodor's Choice ★ **Musée Nissim de Camondo.** Perhaps the most opulent and best museum devoted to French 18th-century decorative arts, this mansion is about as glamorous as Paris gets. However, all of its splendor is steeped in tragedy, as it was created by the Camondo family whose haunting story is recorded within the walls of this superb museum. Patriarch Moïse de Camondo, born in Istanbul to a successful banking family, built this showpiece mansion in 1911 in the style of the Petit Trianon at Versailles, and stocked it with some of the most exquisite furniture, *boiseries* (wainscoting), and bibelots of the mid- to late 18th century. Despite his vast wealth and purported charm, his wife left him five years after their marriage. Then his son, Nissim, was killed in World War I. Upon Moïse's death in 1935, the house and its contents were left to the state as a museum, and named for his lost son. A few years later, daughter Irène, her husband, and two children were murdered at Auschwitz. No heirs remained. Today, the house remains an impeccable tribute to Moïse's life, from the gleaming salons to the state-of-the-art kitchen. There are background materials and an excellent free audio guide in English. ⊠ *63 rue de Monceau, Parc Monceau* ☎ *01–53–89–06–50* 🌐 *www.lesartsdecoratifs.fr* 🎟 *€6* ⏲ *Wed.–Sun. 10–5:30* Ⓜ *Villiers.*

13 Fodor's Choice ★ **Palais Garnier (Opéra).** Haunt of the Phantom of the Opera and the real-life inspiration for Edgar Degas's dancer paintings, the opulent Palais Garnier, also called the Opéra Garnier, is one of two homes of the National Opera of Paris. The building was begun in 1860 by then-unknown architect Charles Garnier, who finished his masterwork 15 long years later, way over budget. Festooned with (real) gold leaf, colored marble, paintings, and sculpture from the top artists of the day, the opera house was about as subtle as Versailles and sparked controversy in post-Revolutionary France. Treat yourself to a performance, or take a guided tour (€12; in English), which includes a stop in the lavish auditorium with a ceiling by Chagall. There is also a small ballet museum with a few works by Degas and the tutu worn by prima ballerina Anna Pavlova when she danced her epic Dying Swan in 1905. ⊠ *Pl. de l'Opéra, Opéra/Grands Boulevards* ☎ *08–92–89–90–90, 01–41–10–08–10 for tours* 🌐 *www.operadeparis.fr* 🎟 *€12 for guided visit; €8 for solo visit* ⏲ *Daily 10–5.*

The Grand Foyer proves that Paris's Palais Garnier is the most opulent theater in the world.

❶ **Parc Monceau.** This exquisitely landscaped park began in 1778 as the Duc de Chartres's private garden. Though some of the parkland was sold off under the Second Empire (creating the exclusive real estate that now borders the park), the refined atmosphere and some of the fanciful faux-ruins have survived. Immaculately dressed children play, watched by their nannies, while lovers picnic on the grassy lawns. In 1797 André Garnerin, the world's first-recorded parachutist, staged a landing in the park. The rotunda—known as the Chartres Pavilion—is surely the city's grandest public restroom; it started life as a tollhouse. ☒ *Entrances on Bd. de Courcelles, Av. Velasquez, Av. Ruysdaël, Av. van Dyck, Parc Monceau* Ⓜ *Monceau.*

⓫ **Passage Jouffroy.** Before there were the *grands magasins* (department stores), there were the passages couverts, covered arcades that offered the early-19th-century Parisian shopper a little bit of heaven: a hodge-podge of shops under one roof, and a respite from the gritty streets. East of Place de l'Opéra, three of these arcades are still standing end-to-end, with the most refined, Passage Jouffroy, in the center. Built in 1846, as its giant clock will tell you, this shop-filled passage also contains the Musée Grevin, a wax museum, and the well-regarded budget Hotel Chopin at No. 46. At the northern end, across the Rue de la Grange-Batelière, is the Passage Verdeau (Rue de la Grange-Batelière 9*e*), and on the opposite end of Jouffroy, across Grands Boulevards, is the Passage des Panoramas (2*e*). The granddaddy of the arcades, built in 1800, it was the first public space in Paris equipped with gaslights in 1817. ☒ *10 bd. Montmartre, Opéra/Grands Boulevards* Ⓜ *Richelieu Drouot.*

WORTH NOTING

10 **Hôtel Drouot.** Hidden away in a small antiques district not far from the opera house is Paris's central auction house, selling everything from bric-a-brac to old clothes to rare Chinese laquered boxes to Renoirs. You can walk in off the street and browse through the open salesrooms, which can be tons of fun depending on what's on the selling block. Mingle with a mix of art dealers, ladies who lunch, and art amateurs hoping to unearth an unidentified masterpiece. Anyone can attend the sales and viewings. ■ **TIP→ Don't miss the small galleries and antiques dealers in the Quartier Drouot, a warren of small streets around the auction house.** ✉ *9 rue Drouot, Opéra/Grands Boulevards* ☎ *01–48–00–20–00* 🌐 *www.drouot.com* ⏲ *Viewings of merchandise Mon.–Sat. 11–6. Auctions begin at 2* Ⓜ *Richelieu Drouot.*

OF OPERATIC PROPORTIONS

Over-the-top with gilt and multicolor marble both inside and out, it's no wonder the Phantom haunted the Palais Garnier. Unable to settle on any one style, Charles Garnier, the designer, chose them all: a Renaissance-inspired detail here, a Rococo frill there, Greek shields put up at random. To best appreciate the luxury of the Second Empire style, walk around the outside of the Opéra, then pause on the steps to watch the world rush by. The building is magically illuminated on performance nights—it's worth dropping by to admire the spectacle even if you're not heading inside.

9 **Musée Gustave-Moreau.** A visit to the town house and studio of painter Gustave Moreau (1826–98), a high priest of the Symbolist movement, is one of the most unique art experiences in Paris. Moreau had always planned to have his home made into a museum after his death, so he created a light-flooded gallery on the two top floors to best show off his dark paintings. The Symbolists loved objects, and Moreau was no different. His cramped private apartment on the first floor is jam-packed with bric-a-brac, and artworks cover every inch of the walls. From Galeries Lafayette (or the Chaussée D'Antin métro stop), follow Rue de la Chaussée d'Antin up to the Trinité church, turn right on Rue St-Lazare, and left on Rue de la Rochefoucauld. The museum is a block up on the right. ✉ *14 rue de la Rochefoucauld, Opéra/Grands Boulevards* ☎ *01–48–74–38–50* 🌐 *www.musee-moreau.fr* 🎫 *€5* ⏲ *Wed.–Mon. 10–12:45 and 2–5:15* Ⓜ *Trinité.*

8 **Musée de la Vie Romantique.** A visit to the charming Museum of the Romantic Life, dedicated to novelist George Sand (1804–76), will transport you to the countryside. In a pretty 1830s mansion at the end of a tree-lined courtyard, the small permanent collection includes drawings by Delacroix and Ingrès, among others, though Sand is the star. There are glass cases stuffed with her jewelry and snuff boxes, and even a mold of the hand of composer Frederic Chopin, one of her many lovers. There is usually an interesting temporary exhibition. Take a break in the charming garden café, open from Easter to late September. ✉ *16 rue Chaptal, Opéra/Grands Boulevards* ☎ *01–55–31–95–67* 🌐 *www.vie-romantique.paris.fr* 🎫 *Free; €7 for temporary exhibits* ⏲ *Tues.–Sun. 10–6* Ⓜ *Blanche, Pigalle, St. Georges.*

THE MARAIS AND THE BASTILLE

From swampy to swanky, Le Marais has a fascinating history that continues to evolve. Like an aging pop star, the *quartier* has remade itself many times, and today retains several identities: the city's epicenter of cool with hip boutiques, designer hotels, and art galleries galore; the hub of Paris's gay community; and, though fading, the nucleus of Jewish life. You could easily spend your entire visit to Paris in this neighborhood, there is that much to do.

Marais means "marsh" and that is exactly what this area was until the 12th century when it was converted to farmland. In 1605, Henri IV began building the Place Royale (today's Place des Vosges, the oldest square in Paris), which touched off a building boom, and the wealthy and fabulous moved in. Despite the odors—the area was one of the city's smelliest—it remained the chic quarter until Louis XIV moved his court to Versailles, trailed by dispirited aristocrats unhappy to decamp to the country. Here you can see the hodgepodge of narrow streets leveled by Baron Haussmann, who feared a redux of the famous *barricades* that revolutionaries threw up to thwart the monarchy. Miraculously, the Marais escaped destruction, though much of it fell victim to neglect and ruin. Thanks to restoration efforts over the past half century, the district is enjoying its latest era of greatness, and the apartments here—among the city's oldest—are also the most in demand.

To the east, the hip **Bastille**—home turf of the French Revolution—still buzzes at night, but competition has emerged from gentrifying neighborhoods farther afield, notably the **Canal St-Martin.** Once the down-and-out cousin on the city's northeastern border, the canal is now trend-spotting central, brimming with funky bars, cafés, art galleries, and boutiques.

TOP ATTRACTIONS

44 **Canal St-Martin.** The once-forgotten canal has morphed into one of the city's hippest places to wander by day—and party by night. A good time to come is Sunday afternoon, when the Quai de Valmy is closed to cars and some of the shops are open. The 2.7-mi canal opened in 1825 between the Seine at the southern end at Place de la Bastille, and the Canal de l'Ourcq to the north. Baron Haussmann later ordered a mile-long stretch of it to be covered—this is today's Boulevard Richard Lenoir—from Rue Faubourg du Temple to the Bastille. These days you can take a boat tour from end to end through the canal's nine locks.

Fodor's Choice ★

Canauxrama offers 2½-hour boat cruises through the locks (€15 adults). Check the Web site for times (🌐 *www.canauxrama.com*). ✉ *Embarkation is at each end of canal: at Bassin de la Villette, 13 quai de la Loire, La Villette or at Marina Arsenal, 50 bd. de la Bastille, Bastille* Ⓜ *Jaurès (northern end) or Bastille (southern end).*

47 ★ **Musée Carnavalet.** If it has to do with Paris history, it's here. This collection is a fascinating hodgepodge of Parisian artifacts and art, from the prehistoric canoes used by Parisii tribes to the furniture of the cork-lined bedroom where Marcel Proust labored over his evocative novels. You can get a great feel for the evolvement of the city through the ages

One of the most beautiful examples of 17th-century town planning, the Place des Vosges is a Parisian jewel constructed by King Henri IV.

thanks to scores of paintings. The museum fills two adjacent mansions, including the Hôtel Carnavalet, a Renaissance jewel that in the mid-1600s was home to the writer Madame de Sévigné, whose hundreds of frank and funny letters to her daughter offer an incomparable view of life during the time of Louis XIV. The museum gives a glimpse into her world, but the collection covers far more than just the 17th century. The exhibits on the Revolution are especially interesting, with scale models of guillotines and a replica of the Bastille prison carved from one of its stones. There is an amazing assortment of reconstructed interiors from the Middle Ages through the rococo period and into Art Nouveau—showstoppers include the Fouquet jewelry shop and the Café de Paris's original furnishings. There is some information in English. ✉ *23 rue de Sévigné, Le Marais* ☎ *01–44–59–58–58* 🌐 *www.carnavalet.paris.fr* 🎫 *Free for permanent collection, €7 for exhibits* ⏲ *Tues.–Sun. 10–6* Ⓜ *St-Paul.*

46 ★ **Musée Picasso.** This immensely popular museum closed in August 2009 for extensive renovations. Set to reopen in February 2012, the $43 million overhaul will double the museum's display space to 21,500 square feet. ✉ *5 rue de Thorigny, Le Marais* ☎ *01–42–71–25–21* 🌐 *www.musee-picasso.*

52 **Place de la Bastille.** Nothing remains of the infamous Bastille prison, destroyed more than 200 years ago, though tourists still ask bemused Parisians where to find it. Until the late 1980s, there was little more to see here than a busy traffic circle ringing the **Colonne de Juillet** (*July Column*), a memorial to the victims of later uprisings in 1830 and 1848. The opening of the Opéra Bastille in 1989 rejuvenated the area,

however, drawing art galleries, bars, and restaurants to the narrow streets, notably along Rue de Lappe—once a haunt of Edith Piaf—and Rue de la Roquette. Ⓜ *Bastille.*

48 Fodor's Choice ★ **Place des Vosges.** The oldest square in Paris and—dare we say it?—the most beautiful, the Place des Vosges is one of Europe's oldest stabs at urban planning. The precise proportions offer a placid symmetry, but things weren't always so calm. Four centuries ago this was the site of the Palais des Tournelles, home to King Henri II and Queen Catherine de' Medici. The couple staged regular jousting tournaments, and during one of them, in 1559, Henri was fatally lanced in the eye. Catherine fled for the Louvre, abandoning her palace and ordering it destroyed. At the base of the 36 redbrick-and-stone houses—nine on each side of the square—is an arcaded, covered walkway lined with art galleries, shops, and cafés. ✉ *Chemin Vert or St-Paul.*

NEED A BREAK?

"The dormouse in the teapot," Le Loir dans la Théière (✉ *3 rue des Rosiers, Le Marais* ☎ *01-42-72-90-61*) is aptly named for the dormouse who fell asleep at Alice in Wonderland's tea party. This is the perfect place to recover from museum overload—cozy into a leather chair, order a silver pot of tea, and choose a homemade cake.

WORTH NOTING

50 **Hôtel de Sully.** This early Baroque gem, built in 1624, is one of the city's loveliest hôtels particuliers;among the back courtyard's sculpted rows of hedges you can find a door that opens into the Place des Vosges. Like much of the area, it fell into ruin until the 1950s, when it was rescued by the administration of French historic monuments, **Caisse Nationale des Monuments Historiques,** which has its headquarters here. This is also one of two homes of the Jeu de Paume (the other is in the Tuileries), which stages regular photography exhibitions. Near the entrance on the Rue de Rivoli, the bookstore, which stocks many unusual guides on Paris (some in English), is worth a stop to admire the 17th-century ceiling of painted beams. The recently renovated private apartment of the Duchess de Sully—four rooms furnished with period pieces—is open for visits by reservation, for a small charge. ✉ *62 rue St-Antoine, Le Marais* ☎ *01-44-61-20-00 Hotel de Sully, 01-42-74-47-75 Jeu de Paume* ⏲ *Tues.–Sun. 10–7 Hotel de Sully, Tues.–Fri. noon–7, weekends 10–7 Jeu de Paume* Ⓜ *St-Paul.*

41 **Maison Européenne de la Photographie** (*MEP; European Photography Center*). Much of the credit for photography's current perch in the city's cultural scene can be given to MEP (whose director, Jean-Luc Monterosso, also founded Paris's hugely successful Mois de la Photographie festival held in November in even-number years). This terrific center hosts up to four exhibitions every three months, and they include photographers from around the world in their selection. A show on a Magnum photographer could overlap with an Irving Penn display or a collection of 19th-century images. Programs and guided tours are available in English. ✉ *5 rue de Fourcy, Le Marais* ☎ *01-44-78-75-00* 🌐 *www.mep-fr.org* 🎟 *€6.50, free Wed. after 5* PM ⏲ *Wed.–Sun. 11–8* Ⓜ *St-Paul.*

49 **Maison de Victor Hugo.** France's most famous scribe lived in the northeast corner of Place des Vosges between 1832 and 1848. The house's first floor is dedicated to temporary exhibits that often have modern ties to Hugo's work. In Hugo's apartment on the second floor, you can see the tall desk, next to the short bed, where he began writing his masterwork *Les Misérables* (as always, standing up). There are manuscripts and early editions of that famous work on display, as well as others such as *The Hunchback of Notre Dame.* You can see illustrations of Hugo's writings by other artists, including Bayard's rendition of the impish Cosette holding her giant broom (which has graced countless *Les Miz* T-shirts). The collection includes many of Hugo's own, sometimes macabre, ink drawings (he was a fine artist) and furniture from several of his homes. Particularly impressive is the room of carved and painted Chinese-style wooden panels that Hugo designed for Juliette Drouet's—his mistress—house on the island of Guernsey, during the writer's exile there. Try to spot the intertwined Vs and Js. (Hint: Look for the angel's trumpet in the left corner.) ⊠ *6 pl. des Vosges, Le Marais* ☎ *01–42–72–10–16* ⊕ *www.musee-hugo.paris.fr* 🎫 *Free; €7 for temporary exhibitions* ⏲ *Tues.–Sun. 10–6* Ⓜ *St-Paul.*

43 **Musée d'Art et d'Histoire du Judaïsme** *(Museum of Jewish Art and History).* This excellent museum traces the tempestuous history of French and European Jews through art and history. Opened in 1998 in the refined 17th-century Hôtel St-Aignan, exhibits have good explanatory texts in English, and the free English audio guide is a must; guided tours in English are also available upon request. Highlights include 13th-century tombstones excavated in Paris; a wooden model of a destroyed Eastern European synagogue; and a roomful of early paintings by Marc Chagall. ⊠ *71 rue du Temple, Le Marais* ☎ *01–53–01–86–53* ⊕ *www.mahj.org* 🎫 *€6.80* ⏲ *Weekdays 11–6, Sun. 10–6* Ⓜ *Rambuteau or Hôtel de Ville.*

45 **Parc de La Villette.** This 130-acre ultramodern park was once an abattoir, but don't let its history put you off: today it's the perfect place to entertain sightseeing-weary kids, with lots of green space, a submarine, and the Espace Chapiteaux, a circus tent featuring superb contemporary acrobatic theater performances. The highlight is the excellent science museum, the **Cité des Sciences et de l'Industrie** (⊠ *30 av. Corentin-Cariou, La Villette* ☎ *01–40–05–80–00* ⊕ *www.cite-sciences.fr* 🎫 *€3–€15.50* ⏲ *Tues.–Sat. 10–6, Sun. 10–7* Ⓜ *Porte de la Villette*). Nearby, **La Géode,** looks like a huge silver golf ball but it's actually an Omnimax cinema made of polished steel. The complex includes the postmodern **Cité de la Musique**, a music academy and concert hall, and the **Musée de la Musique**, with an impressive collection of some 900 musical instruments. (⊠ *221 av. Jean-Jaurès, La Villette* ☎ *01–44–84–44–84* ⊕ *www.cite-musique.fr* 🎫 *€8* ⏲ *Tues.–Thurs. noon–6, Fri–Sat. noon–10, Sun.10–6* Ⓜ *Porte de Pantin*).

THE ILE ST-LOUIS AND THE LATIN QUARTER

Set behind the Ile de la Cité is one of the most romantic spots in Paris, tiny Ile St-Louis. Of the two islands in the Seine—the Ile de la Cité is just to the west—the St-Louis best retains the romance and loveliness of *le Paris traditionnel.* It has remained in the heart of Parisians as it has remained in the heart of every tourist who came upon it by accident, and without warning—a tiny universe unto itself, shaded by trees, bordered by Seine-side quays, and overhung with ancient stone houses. Up until the 1800s it was reputed that some island residents never crossed the bridges to get to Paris proper—and once you discover the island's quiet charm, you may understand why. South of the Ile St-Louis on the Left Bank of the Seine is the bohemian **Quartier Latin** (Latin Quarter), the heart of student Paris for more than 800 years. The neighborhood takes its name from the fact that Latin was the common language of the students, who came from all over Europe. Today the area is full of cheap and cheerful cafés, bars, and shops, and even Roman ruins.

France's oldest university, *La Sorbonne,* was founded here in 1257 as a theology school; later it became the headquarters of the University of Paris. In 1968, the student revolution here had an explosive effect on French politics, resulting in major reforms in the education system. The aging *soixante-huitards* continue to influence French politics, as shown by the election of openly gay, Green Party member Bertrand Delanoë to the mayoralty of Paris.

TOP ATTRACTIONS

37 **Grande Galerie de l'Evolution** *(Great Hall of Evolution).* With a parade of taxidermied animals ranging from the tiniest dung beetle to the tallest giraffe, this museum is an excellent break for kids who have been reluctantly trudging through the Louvre. The flagship of the three natural-history museums in the Jardin des Plantes, it is easily the most impressive. The original 1889 building was renovated in 1994, and has a ceiling that changes color to suggest storms, twilight, or the hot savanna sun. Don't miss the gigantic skeleton of a blue whale, and the stuffed royal rhino—he came from the menagerie at Versailles, where he was a pet of Louis XV. Some English-language information boards are available, but not many. Be sure to hang on to your ticket; it'll get you a discount at the other museums within the Jardin des Plantes. ✉ *36 rue Geoffroy-St-Hilaire, Quartier Latin* ☎ *01–40–79–54–79* 🌐 *www.mnhn.fr* *€9* *Wed.–Mon. 10–6* Ⓜ *Pl. Monge or Jussieu.*

40 **Ile St-Louis.** One of the more fabled addresses in Paris, this tiny island has long harbored the rich and famous, including Chopin, Daumier, Helena Rubinstein, Chagall, and the Rothschild family. In fact, the entire island displays striking architectural unity, stemming from the efforts of a group of early-17th-century property speculators led by Christophe Marie. The group commissioned leading Baroque architect Louis Le Vau (1612–70) to design a series of imposing town houses. An especially somber reminder adorns 19 quai de Bourbon: "Here lived Camille Claudel, sculptor, from 1899 to 1913. Then ended her brave career as an artist and began her long night of internment." Rodin's muse, she was committed by her family to an insane asylum, where she was forbidden

Fodor's Choice ★

ICE CREAM VS. GELATO

Cafés all over sell this haute couture brand of ice cream, but the headquarters of **Berthillon** (✉ *31 rue St-Louis-en-l'Ile, Ile St-Louis* ☎ *01–43–54–31–61*) is *the* place to come for this amazing treat. It features more than 30 flavors that change with the seasons, including scrumptious *chocolat au nougat* and mouth-puckering *cassis* (black currant). Expect to wait in line. The shop and adjacent tea salon is open Wednesday to Sunday 10–8 but closed during the peak summer season, from July 20 to September 1.

Also popping up all over Paris—there were 28 outlets at this writing, including the popular spot on Ile St-Louis (✉ *47 rue St-Louis-en-l'Ile, Ile St-Louis* ☎ *01–44–07–48–08*)—and winning converts faster than you can finish a double scoop, is the **Amorino** chain of gelaterias. Popular flavors include rich *Bacio* (dark chocolate and hazelnuts) and *spécialités* such as amaretto laced with crunchy biscuits and almonds. The shop is open every day, noon to midnight.

to practice her art. Other than some elegant facades and the island's highly picturesque quays along the Seine, there are no cultural hot spots here, just a few streets that may make you think you've stumbled into a village, albeit an unusually tony one. Small hotels, restaurants, art galleries, and shops selling everything from cheese to pâté to silk scarves along the main drag, Rue St-Louis-en-l'Ile. Ⓜ *Pont-Marie.*

34 ★ **Musée National du Moyen-Age** *(National Museum of the Middle Ages, nicknamed the Musée Cluny).* Built on the ruins of Lutecia's Roman Baths, the **Hôtel de Cluny** has been a museum since medievalist Alexandre Du Sommerard established his collection here in 1844. The over-the-top mansion was a choice location for such a collection; the 15th-century building was created for the abbot of Cluny, leader of the most powerful monastery in France. Symbols of the abbot's power literally surround the building, from the crenellated walls that proclaimed his independence from the king, to the carved Burgundian grapes, symbolizing his valuable vineyards, twining up the entrance. The scallop shells *Coquilles-Saint-Jacques* covering the facade are a symbol of religious pilgrimage; the well-traveled pilgrimage route to Spain, Rue St-Jacques, once ran just around the corner. The highlight of the collection is the world-famous *Dame à la Licorne* (*Lady and the Unicorn*) tapestry series, woven in the 15th or 16th century, probably in Belgium. The tapestries are an allegorical representation of the five senses. You can also visit the remnants of the city's Roman baths—hot (*caldarium*) and cold (*frigidarium*), the latter containing the *Boatmen's Pillar,* Paris's oldest sculpture. A charming garden is laid out in the medieval style, using the flora depicted in the unicorn tapestries. ✉ *6 pl. Paul-Painlevé, Quartier Latin* ☎ *01–53–73–78–00* 🌐 *www.musee-moyenage.fr* 🎫 *€8 (includes English audio guide), free 1st Sun. of month* ⏲ *Wed.–Mon. 9:15–5:45* Ⓜ *Cluny–La Sorbonne.*

Anchoring the western end of the Ile de la Cité, the Square du Vert-Galant is a great place to picnic—you can almost dangle your feet in the Seine.

36 **Rue Mouffetard.** This winding cobblestone street is one of Paris's oldest—it was once a Roman road leading south from Lutecia (the Roman name for Paris) to Italy. The upper half of the street is dotted with restaurants that can get rather touristy; the lower half is home to a lively market, open Tuesday through Sunday, when couples are inspired to dance in the street to old Paris accordion tunes. The highlight of *le Mouffe* is the stretch in between, where, as your nose will tell you, the shops are literally spilling into the street with luscious offerings such as roasting chickens and potatoes, rustic saucisson, pâtés, and pungent cheeses, especially at Androuët (No. 134). You can find everything you'll need for a picnic as well as gifts to bring home to your favorite foodie. If you're here in the morning, Le Mouffetard Café (No. 116) is a good place to stop for breakfast (for about €8). For one of the best baguettes in Paris detour to the nearby Boulanger de Monge, which includes a scrumptious selection of organic offerings, at 123 rue Monge. Note that most of the shops are closed on Monday.

Fodor's Choice ★

WORTH NOTING

33 **La Sorbonne.** You can't get into Paris's most famous university without a student ID, although you can try to talk your way past a friendly guard. If you succeed, enter on Rue Victor Cousin, cross the cobbled courtyard where students have gathered for nine centuries, and peek into the muraled lecture halls. Today, La Sorbonne remains the heart and soul of the Quartier Latin, though it is also known as Paris IV, one of several campuses that make up the public Université de Paris. ✉ *1 rue Victor Cousin, Quartier Latin* Ⓜ *Cluny–La Sorbonne.*

35 **Panthéon.** Rome has St. Peter's, London has St. Paul's, and Paris has the Panthéon, whose enormous dome dominates the Rive Gauche. Built as a church, it has long been the resting place of a virtual who's who of France's cultural and political elite, including Voltaire, Zola, Dumas, Victor Hugo, Rousseau, and Marie Curie. Begun in 1764, the building was almost complete when the French Revolution erupted. By then, architect Jacques-German Soufflot had died, supposedly from worrying that the dome would collapse. He needn't have fretted: The dome is so perfect that Foucault used this space to test his famous pendulum to prove the rotation of the earth. The best view is had from outside, however, as the vast neoclassical interior looks more like an abandoned wine cellar than a hallowed burial ground. It's entirely empty except for the 19th-century murals lining the walls and a model of Foucault's pendulum hanging from the center of the dome. The famous residents are in the crypt. There is little info in English—and none on the people buried here, so if you're a history buff, do your homework before you come. ✉ *Pl. du Panthéon, Quartier Latin* ☎ *01–44–32–18–00* 🌐 *pantheon.monuments-nationaux.fr/en/* 🎫 *€8* 🕙 *Apr.–Sept., daily 10–6:30; Oct.–Mar., daily 10–6* Ⓜ *Cardinal Lemoine; RER: Luxembourg.*

FROM ORSAY TO ST-GERMAIN-DES-PRÉS

If you had to choose the most classically Parisien neighborhood in Paris, this would be it. St-Germain-des-Prés has it all: genteel blocks lined with upscale art galleries, storied cafés, designer boutiques, and a fine selection of museums. Cast your eyes upward after dark and you may spy a frescoed ceiling in a tony apartment. These historic streets can get quite crowded, so mind your elbows and plunge in.

This *quartier* is named for the oldest church in Paris, **St-Germain-des-Prés,** and it's become a prized address for Parisians and expats alike. Despite its pristine facade, though, this wasn't always silver-spoon territory. Claude Monet and Auguste Renoir shared a cramped studio at 20 rue Visconti, and the young Picasso barely eked out an existence in a room on the Rue de Seine. By the 1950s St-Germain bars bopped with jazz, and the likes of Albert Camus, Jean-Paul Sartre, and Simone de Beauvoir puffed away on Gaulois while discussing the meaninglessness of existence at Café Flore. At the southern end of this district is the city's poshest park, the Jardin du Luxembourg, which is also home to the **Musée du Luxembourg.** This small museum plays host to excellent temporary exhibitions. The **Musée Delacroix,** in lovely Place Furstenburg, is home to a small collection of the Romantic master's works. Not far away is the stately **Église St-Sulpice,** where you can see two impressive Delacroix frescoes.

Nearby in the 7e arrondissement, the star attraction is the Musée d'Orsay, home to a world-class collection of Impressionist paintings in a converted Belle Époque rail station on the Seine. It's famous for having some of Paris's longest lines, so a visit to d'Orsay should be planned with care. Farther along the river, the 18th-century Palais Bourbon—now home to the National Assembly—sets the tone for the 7e arrondissement. This is Edith Wharton territory, where aristocrats live in gorgeous, sprawling, apartments or *maisons particulières* (*very* private town houses). Embassies—and the Hôtel Matignon, residence of the French prime minister—line the surrounding streets, overshadowed by the Hôtel des Invalides, whose gold-leaf dome climbs heavenward above the regal tomb of Napoléon. The Rodin Museum—set in a gorgeous 18th-century mansion—is only a short walk away. Less well-known is sculptor Aristide Maillol, whose impressive private collection is housed nearby in the Musée Maillol.

TOP ATTRACTIONS

30 **Eglise St-Germain-des-Prés.** Paris's oldest church was built to shelter a simple shard of wood, said to be a relic of Jesus' cross brought back from Spain in AD 542. Vikings came down the Seine and sacked the church, and Revolutionaries used it to store gunpowder, yet the elegant building has defied history's abuses: its 11th-century Romanesque tower continues to be the central symbol of the neighborhood. The colorful 19th-century frescoes in the nave are by Hippolyte Flandrin, a pupil of the classical master Ingres. The church stages superb organ concerts and recitals. Step inside for spiritual nourishment, or pause in the square to people-watch—there's usually a street musician tucked against the church wall, out of the wind. ✉ *Pl. St-Germain-des-Prés, St-Germain-des-Prés* ⏲ *Daily 8–7:30* Ⓜ *St-Germain-des-Prés.*

NEED A BREAK?

Les Deux Magots, at 6 place St-Germain-des-Prés, and the neighboring Café de Flore, at 172 boulevard St-Germain, have been duking it out on this bustling corner in St-Germain for more than a century. Les Deux Magots, the snootier of the two, is named for the two Chinese figurines, or *magots*, inside, and has hosted the likes of Oscar Wilde, Hemingway, James Joyce, and Richard Wright. Jean-Paul Sartre and Simone du Beauvoir frequented both establishments, though they are claimed by the Flore. The two cafés remain packed, though these days you're more likely to rub shoulders with tourists than with philosophers. Still, if you're in search of that certain *je ne sais quoi* of the Rive Gauche, you can do no better than to station yourself at one of the sidewalk tables—or at a window table on a wintry day—to watch the passing parade. Stick to a croissant and an overpriced coffee or an early-evening apéritif; the food is expensive and nothing special.

5 ★ **Hôtel des Invalides.** Les Invalides, as this Baroque complex is known, is the eternal home of Napoléon Bonaparte (1769–1821), or more specifically, the little dictator's tomb, which lies under the towering golden dome. Louis XIV ordered this complex built in 1670 to house disabled soldiers, and at one time 4,000 military men lived here. Today, a portion of it remains a veterans' residence and hospital. There's also the **Musée de l'Armée,** an exhaustive collection of military artifacts from antique armor to weapons. If you see only one sight here, make it the **Église du Dome** at the back of the complex. Napoléon's tomb was moved here in 1840 from the island of Saint Helena, where the emperor died in forced exile. Napoléon's body is protected by a series of no fewer than six coffins, one inside the next (sort of like a Russian nesting doll), which is then encased in a sarcophagus of red quartzite. The bombastic tribute

is ringed by statues symbolizing Napoléon's campaigns of conquest. Also on display are the emperor's trademark gray frock coat and huge bicorne hat. For the 200th anniversary of the French Revolution, in 1989, the dome was regilded using more than half a million gold leaves, or more than 20 pounds of gold. Renovations of the church and the museum are ongoing, so parts of it may be closed. ✉ *Pl. des Invalides, Tour Eiffel* ☎ *01–44–42–38–77* 🌐 *www.invalides.org* 🎫 *€9* ⏲ *Eglise du Dôme and museums Apr.–Sept., daily 10–6; Oct.–Mar., daily 10–5; closed 1st Mon. of every month* Ⓜ *La Tour-Maubourg/Invalides.*

32 **Jardin du Luxembourg** *(Luxembourg Gardens).* Immortalized in countless paintings, the Luxembourg Gardens possess all that is unique and befuddling about Parisian parks: swarms of pigeons, cookie-cutter trees, ironed-and-pressed dirt walkways, and immaculate lawns meant for admiring, not touching. The tree- and bench-lined paths offer a reprieve from the incessant bustle of the Quartier Latin, as well as an opportunity to discover the dotty old women and smooching university students who once found their way into Doisneau photographs. The park's northern boundary is dominated by the Palais du Luxembourg, now the Senate. A sweet attraction is the **Théâtre des Marionnettes** where, on weekends at 11 and 3:15 and on Wednesday at 3:15 (hours may vary), you can catch a classic puppet show for a small charge. Kids will also love the merry-go-round, swings, pony rides, and toy sailboats for rent that ply the lake. Marie de Medici, widow of Henry IV, ordered the palace built in the style of the Florentine Medici home, the Palazzo Pitti. The **Musée du Luxembourg** (☎ *01–44–32–18–00 www.museeduluxembourg.fr*), which is part of the palace, plays host to prestigious (and crowded) temporary exhibitions. ✉ *Bordered by Bd. St-Michel and Rues de Vaugirard, de Médicis, Guynemer, and Auguste-Comte, St-Germain-des-Prés* 🎫 *Free* ⏲ *Daily until dusk* Ⓜ *Odéon; RER: Luxembourg.*

20 **Musée d'Orsay.** In a spectacularly converted Belle Époque train station, the Orsay Museum—devoted to the arts (mainly French) spanning the period 1848–1914—is one of the city's most popular, thanks to the presence of the world's greatest collection of Impressionist and Postimpressionist paintings. Here you can find Manet's *Déjeuner sur l'Herbe* (*Lunch on the Grass*), the painting that scandalized Paris in 1863 when it was shown at the Salon des Refusés, an exhibit organized by artists refused permission to show their work at the Academy's official annual salon, as well as the artist's provocative nude, *Olympia*. There's a dazzling rainbow of masterpieces by Renoir (including his beloved *Le Moulin de la Galette*), Sisley, Pissarro, and Monet. The Postimpressionists—Cézanne, Van Gogh, Gauguin, and Toulouse-Lautrec—are on the top floor. On the ground floor you can find the work of Manet, the powerful realism of Courbet, and the delicate nuances of Degas. If you prefer more academic paintings, look for Puvis de Chavannes's larger-than-life classical canvases. And if you're excited by more modern developments, look for the early-20th-century Fauves (meaning "wild beasts," the name given them by an outraged critic in 1905)—particularly Matisse, Derain, and Vlaminck.

Fodor's Choice ★

The museum is arranged on three floors. Once past the ticket booths (get your tickets in advance through the Web site to avoid the lines),

Continued on page 91

THE SEINE

No matter how you approach Paris—historically, geographically, or emotionally—the Seine flows through its heart, dividing the City of Light into two banks, the *Rive Droite* (Right Bank) and the *Rive Gauche* (Left Bank).

The Seine has long been used as a means for transportation and commerce and although there are no longer any factories along its banks, all manner of boats still ply the water. You'll see tugboats, fire and police boats, the occasional bobbing houseboat, and many kinds of tour boats; it might sound hokey, but there's really no better introduction to the City of Light than a boat cruise, and there are several options, depending on whether you want commentary on the sights or not. Many of the city's most famous attractions can be seen from the river, and are especially spectacular at dusk, as those celebrated lights of Paris glint against the sky.

FROM ILE DES CYGNES TO THE LOUVRE

Musée d'Orsay clock

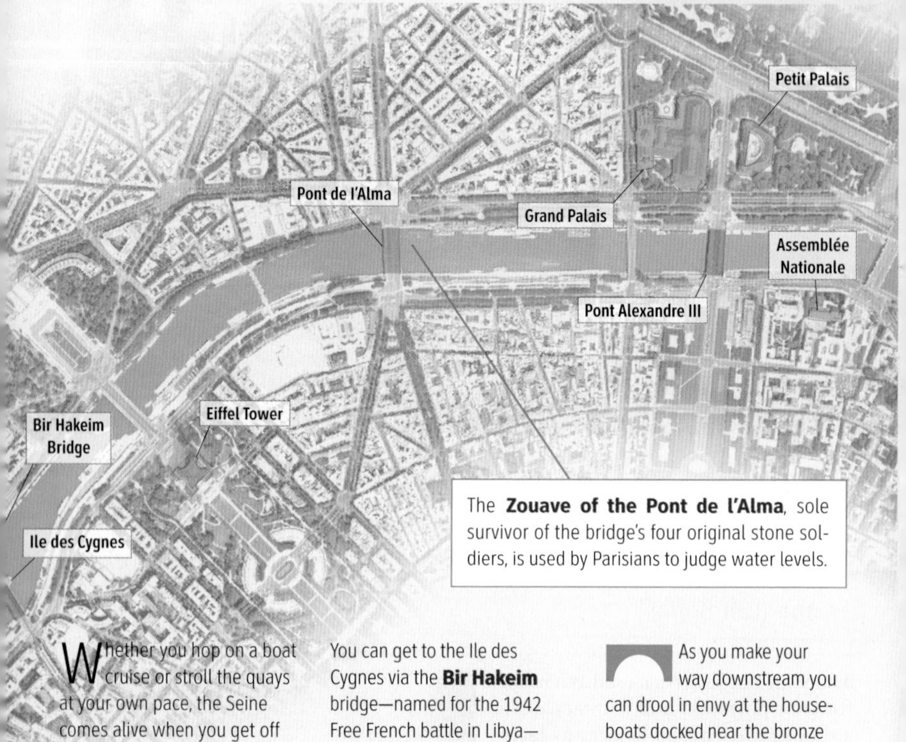

Petit Palais

Pont de l'Alma

Grand Palais

Assemblée Nationale

Pont Alexandre III

Eiffel Tower

Bir Hakeim Bridge

Ile des Cygnes

The **Zouave of the Pont de l'Alma**, sole survivor of the bridge's four original stone soldiers, is used by Parisians to judge water levels.

Whether you hop on a boat cruise or stroll the quays at your own pace, the Seine comes alive when you get off the busy streets of Paris. At the western edge of the city on the **Ile des Cygnes** (literally the Isle of Swans), a small version of the Statue of Liberty stands guard. Auguste Bartholdi designed the original statue, given as a gift from France to America in 1886, and in 1889 a group of Americans living in Paris installed this ¼ scale bronze replica—it's 37 feet, 8 inches tall.

You can get to the Ile des Cygnes via the **Bir Hakeim** bridge—named for the 1942 Free French battle in Libya—whose lacy architecture horizontally echoes the nearby **Eiffel Tower**. You might recognize the view of the bridge from the movie *Last Tango in Paris.*

As you make your way downstream you can drool in envy at the houseboats docked near the bronze lamp–lined Pont Alexandre III. No other bridge over the Seine epitomizes the fin-de-siècle frivolity of the Belle Epoque: It seems as much created of cake frosting and sugar sculptures as of stone and iron, and makes quite the backdrop for fashion shoots and weddings. The elaborate decorations include Art Nouveau lamps, cherubs, nymphs, and winged horses at either end. The bridge was built, like the Grand Palais and Petit Palais nearby, for the 1900 World's Fair.

Along the banks of the Seine

Bouquinistes (book sellers) near the Seine

The average depth of the Seine within Paris city limits is 8 m (about 26 feet).

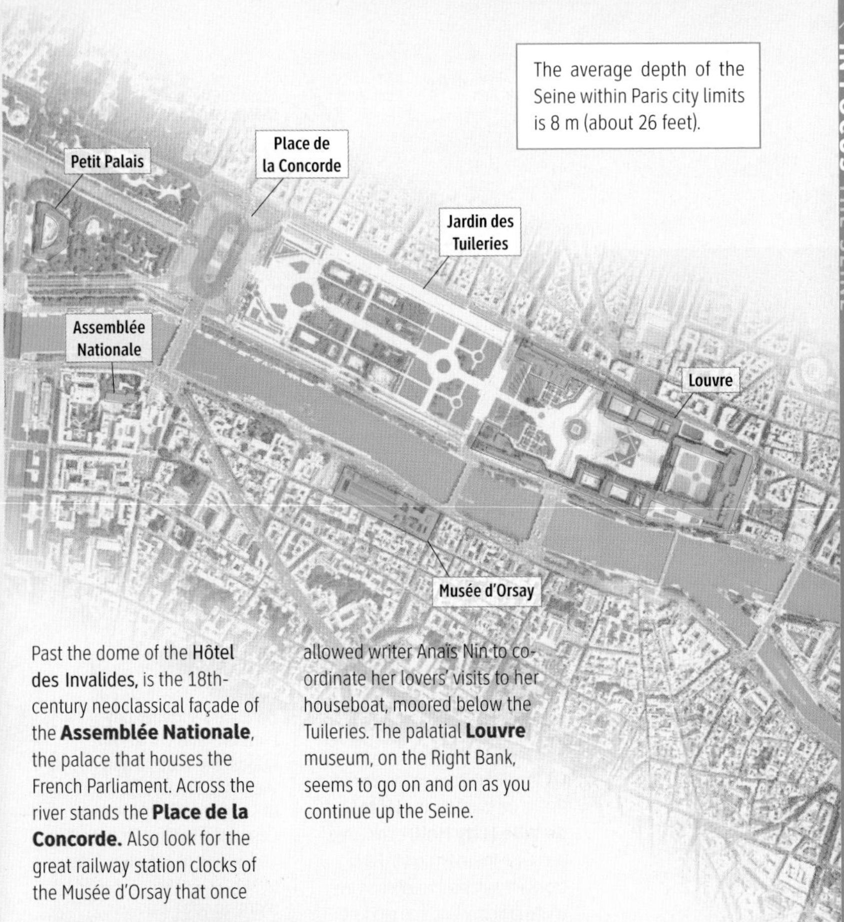

Petit Palais

Place de la Concorde

Jardin des Tuileries

Assemblée Nationale

Louvre

Musée d'Orsay

Past the dome of the **Hôtel des Invalides**, is the 18th-century neoclassical façade of the **Assemblée Nationale**, the palace that houses the French Parliament. Across the river stands the **Place de la Concorde.** Also look for the great railway station clocks of the Musée d'Orsay that once allowed writer Anaïs Nin to co-ordinate her lovers' visits to her houseboat, moored below the Tuileries. The palatial **Louvre** museum, on the Right Bank, seems to go on and on as you continue up the Seine.

PERFECT PICNIC PLACES

Paris abounds with romantic spots to pause for a picnic or a bottle of wine, but the Seine has some of the best.

Try scouting out a place on the point of Ile St-Louis; at sunset you can watch the sun slip beneath receding arches of stone bridges.

The long, low quays of the Left Bank, with its public sculpture work, are perfect for an alfresco lunch.

FROM PONT DES ARTS TO JARDIN DES PLANTES

At the water's edge.

The Institut de France

Parisians love to linger on the elegant **Pont des Arts** footbridge that streches between the palatial Louvre museum and the Institut de France. Napoléon commissioned the original cast-iron bridge with nine arches; it was rebuilt in 1984 with seven arches.

Five carved stone arches of the **Pont Neuf**—the name means "new bridge" but it actually dates from 1605 and is the oldest bridge in Paris—connect the Left Bank to the Ile de la Cité. Another seven arches connect the Ile and the Right Bank. The pale gray curving balustrades include a row of stone heads; some say they're caricatures of King Henry IV's ministers, glaring down at the river.

On the Right Bank at the end of the Ile de la Cité is the **Hôtel de Ville (City Hall)**—this area was once the main port of Paris, crowded with boats delivering everything from wood and produce to visitors and slaves.

Medieval turrets rise up from **Ile de la Cité,** part of the original royal palace; the section facing the Right Bank includes the **Conciergerie**, where Marie Antoinette was imprisoned in 1793 before her execution.

PARIS PLAGE

Paris Plage, literally Paris Beach, is Mayor Bertrand Delanoë's summer gift to Parisians and visitors. In August the roads along the Seine are closed, tons of sand are brought in and decorated with palm trees, and a slew of activities are organized, from free early-morning yoga classes to evening samba and swimming (not in the Seine, but in the fabulous Josephine Baker swimming pool). Going topless is discouraged, but hammocks, kids' playgrounds, rock-climbing, and cafés keep everyone entertained.

View of the Seine and the Pont des Arts

Paris Plage

Notre-Dame

Also on the Ile de la Cité is the cathedral of **Notre-Dame,** a stunning sight from the water. From the side it looks almost like a great boat sailing down the Seine.

As you pass the end of the island, you'll notice a small grated window: this is the evocative Deportation Memorial.

Next to the Ile de la Cite is the lovely residential **Ile St-Louis**; keep an eye out for the "proper" depth measuring stick on Ile St-Louis, near the Tour d'Argent restaurant.

Sightseeing boats turn near the public sculpture garden at the **Jardin des Plantes**, where you'll get a view of the huge national library, **Bibliothèque François Mitterrand**—the four towers look like opened books. Moored in the Seine near the bibliothèque is the Josephine Baker swimming pool with its retractable roof. Paris used to have several floating pools, including the elaborate Piscine Deligny, which was used in the Paris Olympics in 1924; it inexplicably sank in 1993.

Ile St-Louis

Jardin des Plantes

Bibliothéque Francois Mitterand

PLANNING A BOAT TOUR ON THE SEINE

■ Most boat tours last about an hour; in the winter, even the interior of the boats can be cool, so take an extra scarf or sweater.

■ It never hurts to book ahead since schedules vary with the season and the (unpredictable) height and mood of the Seine.

■ As you float along, consider that Parisians used similar boats as a form of public transportation until the 1930s. Not really like Venice; more like the Staten Island ferry.

■ For optimal Seine enjoyment, combine a boat tour with a stroll—walk around Ile St-Louis, stroll along the Left Bank quays near the Pont Neuf, or start at the quay below the Louvre and walk to the Eiffel Tower, past the fabulous private houseboats.

WHICH BOAT IS FOR YOU?

If you want...	Details	Departures
If you want... lots of information	☎ 01-42-25-96-10 🌐 www.bateaux-mouches.fr 🎫 €10 Ⓜ Alma-Marceau	
	The massive, double-decker **Bateaux Mouches,** literally "fly boats," offer prerecorded commentary in seven languages.	Departs from the Pont de l'Alma (Right Bank) daily April to September: every 20, 30, or 45 min., from 10:15 AM to 11 PM; daily: October through March approximately every hour from 11 AM to 9 PM.
If you want... to do your own thing	☎ 08-25-05-01-01 🌐 www.batobus.com 🎫 €13, €17 *for 2 consecutive days*	
	The commentary-free **Batobus** boat-bus service allows you to hop on and off at any of the eight stops along the river. (Note: there's no service early January through early February.)	Departs from 8 locations: Eiffel Tower, Champs Elysées, Musée d'Orsay, Louvre, St. Germain-des-Pres, Notre-Dame, Hotel de Ville, and Jardin des Plantes.
If you want... to impress a date or client	☎ 01-44-54-14-70 🌐 www.yachtsdeparis.fr 🎫 €198–249 *for dinner cruise* Ⓜ Bastille	
	The **Yachts de Paris** specialize in gorgeous boats—expensive, yes, but glamorous as all get-out, with surprisingly good meals.	Departs from Quai de Javel (west of the Eiffel Tower); dinner cruises leave from Port Henri IV (near Bastille).
If you want... the Seine, with music	☎ 01-43-54-50-04 🌐 www.calife.com 🎫 €49 *and up for dinner cruise* Ⓜ Louvre-Rivoli	
	Le Calife is the Aladdin's lamp of the Seine, moored across from the Louvre. Jazz, piano music, and evenings devoted to French song makes this a quirky and charming choice.	Departs from the Quai Malaquais, opposite the Louvre and just west of the Pont des Arts footbridge.

you can pick up an English-language audio guide along with a free color-coded map of the museum. Then step down the stairs into the sculpture hall. Here the vastness of the space complements a ravishing collection of French sculpture from 1840 to 1875. ✉ *1 rue de la Légion d'Honneur, St-Germain-des-Prés* ☎ *01–40–49–48–14* 🌐 *www.musee-orsay.fr* 🎫 *€9.50, €7 after 4:15 except Thurs. after 6; free 1st Sun. of every month* 🕑 *Tues.–Sun., 9:30–6, Thurs. 9:30 AM–9:45 PM* Ⓜ *Solférino; RER: Musée d'Orsay.*

2

NEED A BREAK?

If those *Déjeuner sur l'Herbe* paintings make you think about lunch, stop at the middle floor's Musée d'Orsay Restaurant (☎ *01–45–49–47–03*) in the former train station's sumptuous dining room. Train food, however, this is not: an elegant lunch is available 11:30 to 2:30, high tea from 3:30 to 5:40 (except on Thursday, when dinner is served instead, from 7 to 9:30 PM). For a simpler snack anytime, visit the top-floor Café des Hauteurs and drink in its panoramic view across the Seine toward Montmartre.

6 ★ **Musée Rodin.** Auguste Rodin (1840–1917) briefly made his home and studio in the Hôtel Biron, a grand 18th-century *hôtel particulier* (private mansion) that now houses the museum dedicated to his work. He died rich and famous, but many of the sculptures that earned him his place in history were originally greeted with contempt by a public unprepared for his powerful brand of sexuality and raw physicality. If you're pressed for time, buy a ticket (€1) for the gardens only, where most of Rodin's well-known sculptures are found, such as *The Thinker* and *The Gates of Hell*, inspired by the monumental bronze doors of Italian Renaissance churches. The museum's interior, though showing its age, still serves as an elegantly creaky setting for two floors of Rodin's work. There's also a room of impressive works by Camille Claudel (1864–1943), Rodin's student and longtime mistress. A remarkable sculptor in her own right, her torturous relationship with Rodin eventually drove her out of his studio—and out of her mind. In 1913 she was packed off to an asylum, where she remained until her death. ✉ *79 rue de Varenne, Invalides or Eiffel Tower* ☎ *01–44–18–61–10* 🎫 *www.musee-rodin.fr* Ⓜ *€6, €1 gardens only* 🕑 *Apr.–Oct., Tues.–Sun. 9:30–5:45; Nov.–Mar., Tues.–Sun. 9:30–4:45* Ⓜ *Varenne.*

WORTH NOTING

31 Fodor's Choice ★ **Cour du Commerce St-André.** Like an 18th-century engraving come to life, this charming street arcade is perhaps the prettiest nook of the Left Bank. A remnant of *ancien* Paris with its enormous uneven cobblestones and famed for its rabble-rousing inhabitants—journalist Jean-Paul Marat ran the Revolutionary newspaper *L'Ami du Peuple,* at No. 8, and the agitator Georges Danton lived at No. 20—it is also home to Le Procope, Paris's oldest café (now a very fancy restaurant). This passageway also contains a turret from the 12th-century wall of Philippe-Auguste (visible through the windows of the Catalogne tourist office). Just pass the turret is a gate leading to Paris's most beautiful cul-de-sac: the 17th-century Cour de Rohan courtyard—if the gate is open you'll recognize the setting used for Chez Mamita in Vincente

Minelli's *Gigi* film. ✉ *Linking Bd. St-Germain and Rue St-André-des-Arts, St-Germain-des-Prés* Ⓜ *Odéon.*

29 **Musée Delacroix.** The final home of artist Eugène Delacroix (1798–1863) contains only a small collection of his sketches and drawings, but you can see the studio he had built in the large and lovely garden at the back to work on the frescoes he created for St-Sulpice Church, where they remain on display today. The museum also plays host to temporary exhibitions, such as Delacroix's experiments with photography. France's foremost Romantic painter had the good luck to live on **Place Furstenberg,** one of the smallest, most romantic squares in Paris, which is worth a visit in itself. ✉ *6 rue Furstenberg, St-Germain-des-Prés* ☎ *01–44–41–86–50* 🌐 *www.musee-delacroix.fr* 🎫 *€5* 🕒 *Wed.–Mon. 9:30–5* Ⓜ *St-Germain-des-Prés.*

MONTMARTRE

Montmartre has become almost too charming for its own good. Yes, it feels like a village (if you can see through the crowds); yes, there are working artists here (though far fewer than there used to be); and, yes, the best view of Paris is yours for free from the top of the hill (if there's no haze). That's why on any weekend day, year-round, you can find hordes of visitors crowding these cobbled alleys, scaling the staircases that pass for streets, and queuing to see **Sacré-Coeur,** the "sculpted cloud," at the summit.

If you're lucky enough to have a little corner of Montmartre to yourself, you'll understand why locals love it so. Come on a weekday, or in the morning or later in the evening. Stroll around **Place des Abbesses,** where the rustic houses and narrow streets escaped the heavy hand of urban planner Baron Haussmann. Until 1860, the area was in fact a separate village, dotted with windmills. Today, there are only two windmills left as well as one quaint vineyard; you cannot visit the vineyard. Always a draw for bohemians and artists, many of whom had studios at **Bateau-Lavoir** and **Musée de Montmartre,** resident painters have included Géricault, Renoir, Suzanne Valadon, Picasso, Van Gogh, and of course Henri Toulouse-Lautrec, whose iconic paintings of the cancan dancers at the **Moulin Rouge** are now souvenir-shop fixtures from **Place du Tertre** to the Tour Eiffel. You can still see shows at the Moulin Rouge and the pocket-size cabaret **Lapin Agile,** though much of the entertainment here is on the seedier side—the area around Pigalle is the city's largest red-light district. The *quartier* is a favorite of filmmakers, and visitors still seek out Café des Deux Moulins (15 rue Lepic), the real-life café where Audrey Tautou worked in 2001's *Amélie.* Movie biz roots run deep here—the blockbuster *Moulin Rouge* took its inspiration from here.

TOP ATTRACTIONS

5 **Au Lapin Agile.** This authentic survivor from the 19th century considers itself the doyen of cabarets. Founded in 1860, it still inhabits a modest house, once a favorite subject of painter Maurice Utrillo. It became the home-away-from-home for Braque, Modigliani, Apollinaire, and Picasso—who once paid for a meal with one of his paintings, then promptly exited and painted another that he named after this place (it

Fodor's Choice ★

was purchased in 1989 for a record $40.7 million and later bequeathed to New York's Metropolitan Museum). There are no topless dancers—this is a genuine French cabaret with songs, poetry, and humor in a publike setting. ✉ *22 rue des Saules, Montmartre* ☎ *01–46–06–85–87 reservations* 🌐 *www.au-lapin-agile.com* 🎫 *€24 (includes first drink)* 🕐 *Tues.–Sun. 9* PM*–2* AM Ⓜ *Lamarck-Caulaincourt.*

4 **Moulin de la Galette.** Of the 14 windmills (*moulins*) that used to sit atop this hill, only two remain. Known collectively as Moulin de la Galette, the more storied is known as Le Blute-fin: it's on a leafy hillock across from 88 rue Lepic. In the late 1800s there was a dance hall on the site, famously painted by Renoir (you can see the painting in the Musée d'Orsay). Unfortunately, the windmill is on private land and can't be visited. Just down the street is the other moulin, Le Radet, perched atop a well-regarded restaurant (called Le Moulin de la Galette) at 83 rue Lepic. ✉ *Le Blute-fin, corner of Rue Lepic and Rue Tholozé, Montmartre* Ⓜ *Abbesses.*

2 **Place des Abbesses.** This triangular square is typical of the countrified style that has made Montmartre famous. Now a hub for shopping and people-watching, the *place* is surrounded by hip boutiques, sidewalk cafés, and shabby-chic restaurants—a prime habitat for the young, neo-bohemian crowd and a sprinkling of expats. Trendy streets like Rue Houdon and Rue des Martyrs have attracted small designers, and some shops are open on Sunday afternoon. The entrance to the Abbesses métro station, designed by the great Hector Guimard as a curving, sensuous mass of delicate iron, is one of only two original Art Nouveau métro canopies left in Paris. Ⓜ *Abbesses.*

NEED A BREAK?

There are few attractive food options around ultra-touristy Sacré-Coeur, but Le Botak is where the locals go (✉ *1 rue Paul Albert, Montmartre* ☎ *01–46–06–98–30* Ⓜ *Anvers).* Tucked on the eastern side of the basilica, this little café with outdoor tables in leafy Square Louise Marie serves a small, ever-changing menu of French home cooking like *saumon au pistou* (salmon in pesto) and *poulet botak*, roasted chicken with garlic and mashed potatoes (about €18 for two courses). Or come for a late-afternoon apéritif.

7 ★ **Sacré-Coeur.** It's hard to not feel as though you're climbing up to heaven when you visit Sacré-Coeur, the white castle in the sky, perched atop Montmartre. The French government began building this church in 1873 as a symbol of the return of self-confidence after the devastating years of the Commune and Franco-Prussian War. Critics, however, dismissed its mix of Romanesque and Byzantine architectural styles as gaudy. Construction lasted until World War I, and the church was consecrated in 1919. Many visitors come to Sacré-Coeur to admire the superlative view from the top of the 271-foot-high dome, the second-highest point in Paris after the Tour Eiffel. But don't miss spending some time inside the basilica, noted for its massive golden mosaics set high above the choir depicting Christ with a golden heart and outstretched arms. The stained-glass windows, which were installed in 1922, were destroyed by a bombing during World War II (there were miraculously no deaths), and later rebuilt in 1946. ✉ *Pl. du Parvis-du-Sacré-Coeur,*

Montmartre ☎ *01–53–41–89–00* 🎟 *Free, dome €5* 🕒 *Basilica daily 6 AM–11 PM; dome and crypt Oct.–Mar., daily 9–6; Apr.–Sept., daily 9–7* Ⓜ *Anvers plus funicular.*

WORTH NOTING

3 **Bateau-Lavoir** *(Boat Wash House).* The birthplace of Cubism isn't open to the public, but a display in the front window details this unimposing building's rich history. Montmartre poet Max Jacob coined the name for the original building here, which reminded him of the laundry boats that used to float in the Seine, and he joked that the warren of paint-splattered artists' studios needed a good hosing down (wishful thinking, since the building had only one water tap). It was in the original Bateau-Lavoir that, early in the 20th century, Pablo Picasso, Georges Braque, and Juan Gris made their first bold stabs at Cubism, and Picasso painted the groundbreaking *Les Demoiselles d'Avignon* here in 1906–07. All but the facade was rebuilt after a fire in 1970. Like the original building, the Bateau houses artists and their studios. ✉ *13 pl. Emile-Goudeau, Montmartre* Ⓜ *Abbesses.*

9 **Espace Salvador-Dalí** *(Dalí Center).* One of several museums dedicated to the Surrealist master, the collection in this black-walled exhibition space includes about 300 works, mostly etchings and lithographs (some for sale). The two dozen sculptures include several versions of Dalí's melting bronze clock and variations on the Venus de Milo. A multimedia pioneer ahead of his time, there are videos with Dalí's voice, and temporary exhibits have included the mustached man's foray into holograms. ✉ *11 rue Poulbot, Montmartre* ☎ *01–42–64–40–10* 🌐 *www.daliparis.com* 🎟 *€10* 🕒 *Daily 10–6* Ⓜ *Abbesses.*

1 **Moulin Rouge** *(Red Windmill).* When the world-famous cabaret opened in 1889, aristocrats, professionals, and the working classes all flocked to see the scandalous performers. The cancan was considerably raunchier in Toulouse-Lautrec's day—girls used to kick off their knickers—than it is today. (⇨ *See the Nightlife section.*) There's not much to see from the outside, but a decent gift shop around the corner (11 rue Lepic) sells official merchandise, from jewelry to sculpture, by reputable French makers. ✉ *82 bd. de Clichy, Montmartre* ☎ *01–53–09–82–82* 🌐 *www.moulin-rouge.fr* Ⓜ *Blanche.*

6 **Musée de Montmartre** *(Montmartre Museum).* In its turn-of-the-20th-century heyday, the building—now home to Montmartre's historical museum—was a studio block for painters, writers, and cabaret artists. Foremost among them was Renoir—he painted the *Moulin de la Galette,* an archetypal scene of sun-drenched revelers, while he lived here—and Maurice Utrillo, Montmartre painter par excellence. The museum recaps the area's history; the strong points are the many Toulouse-Lautrec posters and original Eric Satie scores. Temporary exhibitions focus on famous residents like Jean Marais, the late, dashing actor who dabbled in painting and sculpture. Check out the view from the second floor of the tiny vineyard—the only one in Paris—on Rue des Saules. There's some basic info available in English. ✉ *12 rue Cortot, Montmartre* ☎ *01–49–25–89–37* 🌐 *www.museedemontmartre.fr* 🎟 *€8* 🕒 *Wed.–Sun. 11–6* Ⓜ *Lamarck Caulaincourt.*

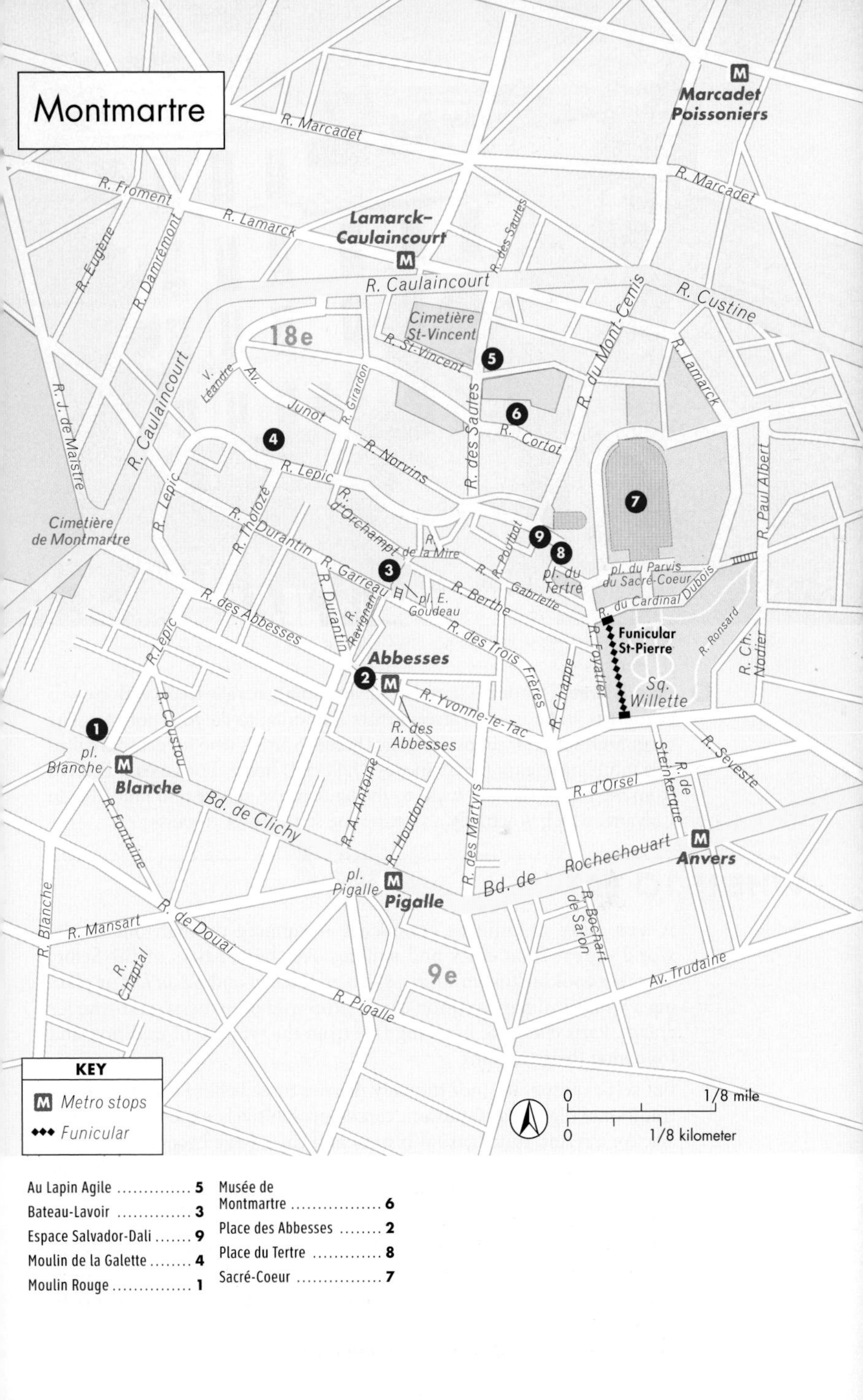
Montmartre
R. Marcadet
Marcadet Poissoniers
R. Froment
R. Lamarck
Lamarck-Caulaincourt
R. des Saules
R. Eugène
R. Damrémont
R. Caulaincourt
R. Custine
R. du Mont-Cenis
Cimetière St-Vincent
18e
R. St-Vincent
R. Lamarck
V. Léandre
Av. Junot
R. Girardon
R. Norvins
R. Cortot
R. J. de Maistre
R. Lepic
R. Tholozé
R. d'Orchampt
R. Paul Albert
Cimetière de Montmartre
R. Durantin
R. de la Mire
R. Poulbot
pl. du Parvis du Sacré-Coeur
R. Garreau
pl. du Tertre
R. Berthe
R. Gabrielle
R. du Cardinal Dubois
pl. E. Goudeau
R. des Abbesses
R. Ravignan
R. des Trois Frères
Funicular St-Pierre
R. Ronsard
R. Ch. Nodier
Abbesses
R. Foyatier
R. Chappe
Sq. Willette
R. Yvonne-le-Tac
R. Coustou
R. des Abbesses
pl. Blanche
Blanche
R. Seveste
R. de Steinkerque
R. d'Orsel
R. Fontaine
Bd. de Clichy
R. A. Antoine
R. Houdon
R. des Martyrs
Bd. de Rochechouart
Anvers
pl. Pigalle
Pigalle
R. Bochart de Saron
R. Blanche
R. Mansart
R. de Douai
R. Chaptal
9e
Av. Trudaine
R. Pigalle
KEY
Metro stops
Funicular
0 1/8 mile
0 1/8 kilometer
Au Lapin Agile 5
Bateau-Lavoir 3
Espace Salvador-Dali 9
Moulin de la Galette 4
Moulin Rouge 1
Musée de Montmartre 6
Place des Abbesses 2
Place du Tertre 8
Sacré-Coeur 7

Residents of Montmartre often talk about "going down into Paris," and after climbing the many steps to get here you'll understand why.

8 **Place du Tertre.** This once-charming square, now generally teems with crowds of tourists and hordes of street artists clamoring to do your portrait. The ubiquitous souvenir shops were once home to artists who for decades called this tumbling square (*tertre* means "hillock") home. For an easy descent from the top of the hill, walk to the back of the square and find Rue du Calvaire, which is actually a picturesque staircase. Ⓜ *Abbesses.*

WHERE TO EAT

A new wave of culinary confidence is running through one of the world's great food cities and spilling over both banks of the Seine. Whether cooking up *grand-mère's* roast chicken and *riz au lait* or placing a whimsical hat of cotton candy atop wild-strawberry-and-rose ice cream, Paris chefs are breaking free from the tyranny of tradition and following their passions.

But self-expression is not the only driving force behind the changes. A traditional high-end restaurant can be prohibitively expensive to operate. As a result, more casual bistros and cafés have become attractive businesses for even top chefs, making the cooking of geniuses such as Joël Robuchon and Pierre Gagnaire more accessible to all (even if these star chefs rarely cook in their lower-priced restaurants).

Like the chefs themselves, Paris diners are breaking away—albeit cautiously—from tradition. New restaurants and sandwich bars are multiplying rapidly. And because Parisians are more widely traveled than in the past, many ethnic restaurants are making fewer concessions to French tastes, resulting in far better food.

RESTAURANTS

(In alphabetical order)

Use the coordinate ⊕ 1:B3 at the end of each listing to locate a site on the corresponding map

$$$$ HAUTE FRENCH Champs-Élysées, 8e

✕ **Alain Ducasse au Plaza Athénée.** The dining room at Alain Ducasse's flagship Paris restaurant gleams with 10,000 crystals, confirming that this is the flashiest place in town for a blowout meal. Clementine-color tablecloths and space-age cream-and-orange chairs with pull-out plastic trays for business meetings provide an upbeat setting for the cooking of young Ducasse protégé chef Christophe Moret. Some dishes are subtle, whereas in others strong flavors overwhelm delicate ingredients. Service is also a little inconsistent, with occasional long waits between courses. Even so, a meal here is delightfully luxe, starting with a heavenly amuse-bouche of langoustine with caviar and a tangy lemon cream. You can continue with a truffle-and-caviar fest, or opt for more down-to-earth dishes like lobster in spiced wine with quince or saddle of lamb with sautéed artichokes. ✉ *Hôtel Plaza Athénée, 25 av. Montaigne, Champs-Élysées* ☎ *01–53–67–65–00* ✍ *Reservations essential; jacket required* ▭ *AE, DC, MC, V* ⊙ *Closed weekends, 2 wks in late Dec., and mid-July–mid-Aug. No lunch Mon.–Wed.* Ⓜ *Alma-Marceau* ⊕ *1:B3.*

$ BISTRO République, 11e

✕ **Astier.** There are three good reasons to go to Astier: the generous cheese platter plonked on your table atop a help-yourself wicker tray, the exceptional wine cellar with bottles dating to the 1970s, and the French bistro fare, even if portions seem to have diminished over the years. Dishes like marinated herring with warm potato salad, sausage with lentils, and baba au rhum are classics on the frequently changing set menu for €31, which doesn't allow you to order fewer than three courses. The vintage 1950s wood-panel dining room attracts plenty of locals and remains a fairly sure bet in the area, especially since it's open every day. ✉ *44 rue Jean-Pierre Timbaud* ☎ *01–43–57–16–35* ✍ *Reservations essential* ▭ *MC, V* Ⓜ *Parmentier* ⊕ *1:H3.*

$$–$$$ BISTRO Le Marais, 4e

✕ **Au Bourguignon du Marais.** The handsome, contemporary look of this Marais bistro and wine bar is the perfect backdrop for the good traditional fare and excellent Burgundies served by the glass and bottle. Unusual for Paris, food is served nonstop from noon to 11 PM. Always on the menu are Burgundian classics such as *jambon persillé* (ham in parsleyed aspic jelly), escargots, and *bœuf Bourguignon* (beef stewed in red wine). More up-to-date picks include a cèpe-mushroom velouté with poached oysters (though the fancier dishes are generally less successful). The terrace is hotly sought after in warmer months. ✉ *52 rue François-Miron* ☎ *01–48–87–15–40* ▭ *AE, MC, V* ⊙ *Closed Sun. and Mon., 3 wks in Aug., and 2 wks in Feb.* Ⓜ *St-Paul* ⊕ *1:G4.*

$$–$$$ BISTRO Opéra/Grands Boulevards, 2e Fodor's Choice ★

✕ **Aux Lyonnais.** With a passion for the old-fashioned bistro, Alain Ducasse has resurrected this 1890s gem by appointing a terrific young chef to oversee the short, frequently changing, and reliably delicious menu of Lyonnais specialties. Dandelion salad with crisp potatoes, bacon, and silky poached egg; watercress soup poured over parsleyed frogs' legs; and fluffy *quenelles de brochet* (pike-perch dumplings) show he is no bistro dilettante. The decor hews to tradition, too, with a zinc

BEST BETS FOR PARIS DINING

With thousands of restaurants to choose from, how will you decide where to eat? Fodor's writers and editors have selected their favorite restaurants by price, cuisine, and experience in the lists below. You can also search by neighborhood for excellent eating experiences—just peruse the following pages. Or find specific details about a restaurant in the full reviews, which are listed alphabetically later in the chapter.

Fodor'sChoice★

Frenchie, $$ p. 103
Guilo Guilo, $$$ p. 104
Guy Savoy, $$$$ p. 104
Hiramatsu, $$$$ p. 105
Il Vino, $$$$ p. 105
L'Adroise, $$ p. 108
L'Astrance, $$$$ p. 109
L'Epigramme, $ p. 110
La Table Lauriston, $$$ p. 109
Le Bistrot Paul Bert, $$ p. 110
Le Grand Véfour, $$$$ p. 112
Le Violon d'Ingres, $$$$ p. 113
Mon Vieil Ami, $$ p. 113
Rech, $$$ p. 114
Ribouldingue, $$$ p. 115

By Price

¢

Cantine Merci, p. 99
Higuma, p. 104
La Ferme Opéra, p. 107

$

L'As du Fallafel, p. 108
L'Epigramme, p. 110
Le Café Constant, p. 111

$$

Frenchie, p. 103
L'Ardoise, p. 108
Le Pré Verre, p. 112
Mon Vieil Ami, p. 113

$$$

Guilo Guilo, p. 104
La Table Lauriston, p. 109
Le Comptoir du Relais Saint-Germain, p. 111

$$$$

Guy Savoy, p. 104
L'Astrance, p. 109
L'Atelier de Joël Robuchon, p. 109
Le Violon d'Ingres, p. 113

By Type

BISTRO

Benoît, $$$ p. 99
Frenchie, $$ p. 103
Le Café Constant, $ p. 111

BRASSERIE

Bofinger, $$$ p. 99
La Coupole, $–$$ p. 107

CAFÉ

Café Marly, $$ p. 118
Rose Bakery, $ p. 115

MODERN FRENCH

Chez les Anges, $$$ p. 102
L'Atelier de Joël Robuchon, $$–$$$$ p. 109
Ze Kitchen Galerie, $$ p. 117

NORTH AFRICAN

Chez Omar, $–$$ p. 102

By Experience

GREAT VIEW

Lapérouse, $$$–$$$$ p. 108
La Tour d'Argent, $$$$ p. 110
Le Georges, $–$$$$ p. 111

HOT SPOT

Frenchie, $$ p. 103
L'Atelier de Joël Robuchon, $$–$$$$ p. 109
Le Violon d'Ingres, $$$–$$$$ p. 113

MOST ROMANTIC

Lapérouse, $$$–$$$$ p. 108
La Tour d'Argent, $$$$ p. 110
Le Grand Vefour, $$$$ p. 112
Restaurant du Palais-Royal, $$$ p. 114

NEWCOMERS

Cantine Merci, ¢ p. 99
Cru, $$–$$$ p. 103
Frenchie, $$ p. 103
Guilo Guilo, $$$ p. 104
Yam'Tcha, $$–$$$ p. 117

bar, an antique coffee machine, and original turn-of-the-20th-century woodwork. There is a no-choice lunch menu for €30, but the temptation is strong to splurge on the more luxurious à la carte dishes. ✉ *32 rue St-Marc* ☎ *01–42–96–65–04* ▭ *AE, MC, V* ⊙ *Closed Sun., Mon., and 2 wks in Aug. No lunch Sat.* Ⓜ *Bourse* ✣ *1:E2.*

$$$–$$$$ BISTRO Le Marais, 4e

Benoît. If you loved Benoît before it became the property of Alain Ducasse and Thierry de la Brosse—the pair that revived Aux Lyonnais—chances are you'll adore it now. Without changing the vintage 1912 setting, which needed nothing more than a minor dusting, the illustrious new owners have subtly improved the menu with dishes such as marinated salmon, frogs' legs in a morel-mushroom cream sauce, and an outstanding cassoulet served in a cast-iron pot. Hardworking young chef David Rathgeber, formerly of Aux Lyonnais, keeps the kitchen running smoothly, and the waiters are charm incarnate. It's a splurge to be here, so go all the way and top off your meal with tarte tatin that's caramelized to the core or a rum-doused baba. ✉ *20 rue St-Martin* ☎ *01–42–72–25–76* ▭ *AE, MC, V* ⊙ *Closed Aug.* Ⓜ *Châtelet* ✣ *1:F4.*

$$$–$$$$ BRASSERIE Bastille/Nation, 4e

Bofinger. One of the oldest, loveliest, and most popular brasseries in Paris has generally improved in recent years, so stake out one of the tables dressed in crisp white linen under the glowing Art Nouveau glass cupola and enjoy classic brasserie fare (stick to trademark dishes such as the seafood choucroute, lamb fillet, or smoked haddock with spinach, as the seasonal specials can be hit-or-miss). The prix-fixe for €31.50 includes a decent half bottle of red or white wine, and there is a generous children's menu. ✉ *5–7 rue de la Bastille* ☎ *01–42–72–87–82* ▭ *AE, DC, MC, V* Ⓜ *Bastille* ✣ *1:H5.*

¢ MODERN FRENCH Le Marais, 3e

Breizh Café. Eating a crepe in Paris might seem a bit clichéd, until you venture into this modern offshoot of a creperie in Cancale, Brittany. The pale-wood, almost Japanese-style decor is refreshing, but what really makes the difference are the ingredients—farmers' eggs, unpasteurized Gruyère, shiitake mushrooms, Valrhona chocolate, homemade caramel, and extraordinary butter from Breton dairy farmer Jean-Yves Bordier. You'll find all the classics among the *galettes* (buckwheat crepes), but it's worth choosing something more adventurous like the *cancalaise* (traditionally smoked herring, potato, crème fraîche, and herring roe). You might also slurp a few Cancale oysters, a rarity in Paris, and try one of the 20 artisanal ciders on offer. ✉ 109 rue Vieille du Temple, ☎ 01–42–72–13–77 ▭ *MC, V* ⊙ *Closed Mon., Tues., and 3 wks in Aug.* Ⓜ *St-Sébastien-Froissart* ✣ *1:G4.*

¢ CAFÉ Le Marais, 3e

Cantine Merci. Deep inside the city's latest concept store, whose proceeds go to charities for women in India and Madagascar, lurks the perfect spot for a quick and healthy lunch between bouts of shopping. The brief menu of soups, salads, risottos, and a daily hot dish is more than slightly reminiscent of Rose Bakery—salads such as fava beans with radish and lemon wedges or melon, cherry tomato, and arugula are bright, lively, and crunchy, and you can order a freshly squeezed juice or iced tea with fresh mint to wash it all down. Delicious homey desserts might include cherry clafoutis or raspberry and pistachio crumble. ✉ *111 blvd. Beaumarchais,* ☎ *01–42–77–78–92* 🌐 *www.merci-merci.com* ▭ *MC, V* ⊙ *Closed Sun. No dinner* Ⓜ *St-Sébastien-Froissart* ✣ *1:H4.*

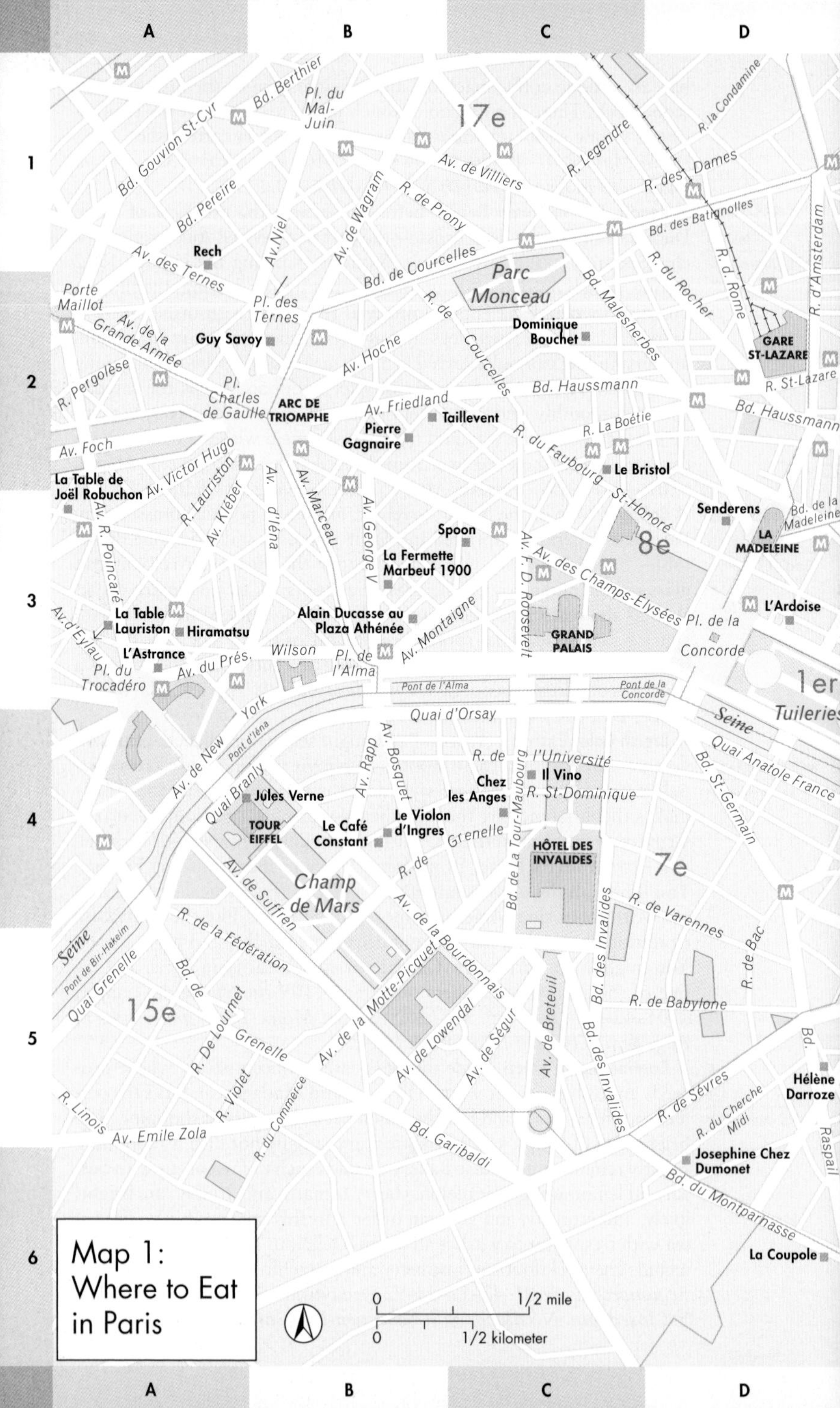

Map 1:
Where to Eat
in Paris
A
B
C
D
1
2
3
4
5
6
17e
8e
7e
15e
1er
Parc Monceau
ARC DE TRIOMPHE
GARE ST-LAZARE
LA MADELEINE
GRAND PALAIS
TOUR EIFFEL
HÔTEL DES INVALIDES
Champ de Mars
Tuileries
Seine
Rech
Guy Savoy
Dominique Bouchet
Taillevent
Pierre Gagnaire
Le Bristol
La Table de Joël Robuchon
Senderens
Spoon
La Fermette Marbeuf 1900
Alain Ducasse au Plaza Athénée
L'Ardoise
La Table Lauriston
Hiramatsu
L'Astrance
Il Vino
Chez les Anges
Jules Verne
Le Violon d'Ingres
Le Café Constant
Hélène Darroze
Josephine Chez Dumonet
La Coupole
Bd. Berthier
Pl. du Mal-Juin
Bd. Gouvion St-Cyr
Bd. Pereire
Av. des Ternes
Porte Maillot
Av. de la Grande Armée
R. Pergolèse
Pl. des Ternes
Av. Niel
Av. de Wagram
R. de Prony
Av. de Villiers
R. Legendre
R. la Condamine
R. des Dames
Bd. des Batignolles
R. d'Amsterdam
R. du Rocher
R. d. Rome
Bd. Malesherbes
Bd. de Courcelles
R. de Courcelles
Av. Hoche
Pl. Charles de Gaulle
Av. Friedland
Bd. Haussmann
R. St-Lazare
R. La Boétie
R. du Faubourg St-Honoré
Av. Foch
Av. Victor Hugo
R. Lauriston
Av. Kléber
Av. d'Iéna
Av. Marceau
Av. George V
Av. R. Poincaré
Av. d'Eylau
Av. F. D. Roosevelt
Av. des Champs-Élysées
Bd. de la Madeleine
Pl. de la Concorde
Av. Montaigne
Pl. de l'Alma
Wilson
Av. du Prés.
Pl. du Trocadéro
Pont de l'Alma
Pont de la Concorde
Quai d'Orsay
Av. de New York
Pont d'Iéna
Quai Branly
Av. Rapp
Av. Bosquet
R. de l'Université
R. St-Dominique
Quai Anatole France
Bd. St-Germain
R. de Grenelle
Bd. de La Tour-Maubourg
Av. de Suffren
Av. de la Bourdonnais
R. de Varennes
R. de Bac
Bd. des Invalides
R. de la Fédération
Pont de Bir-Hakeim
Quai Grenelle
Bd. de Grenelle
R. De Lourmel
Av. de la Motte-Picquet
Av. de Lowendal
Av. de Ségur
Av. de Breteuil
R. de Babylone
Bd. Raspail
R. de Sèvres
R. du Cherche Midi
R. Violet
R. du Commerce
R. Linois
Av. Emile Zola
Bd. Garibaldi
Bd. du Montparnasse
0
1/2 mile
0
1/2 kilometer

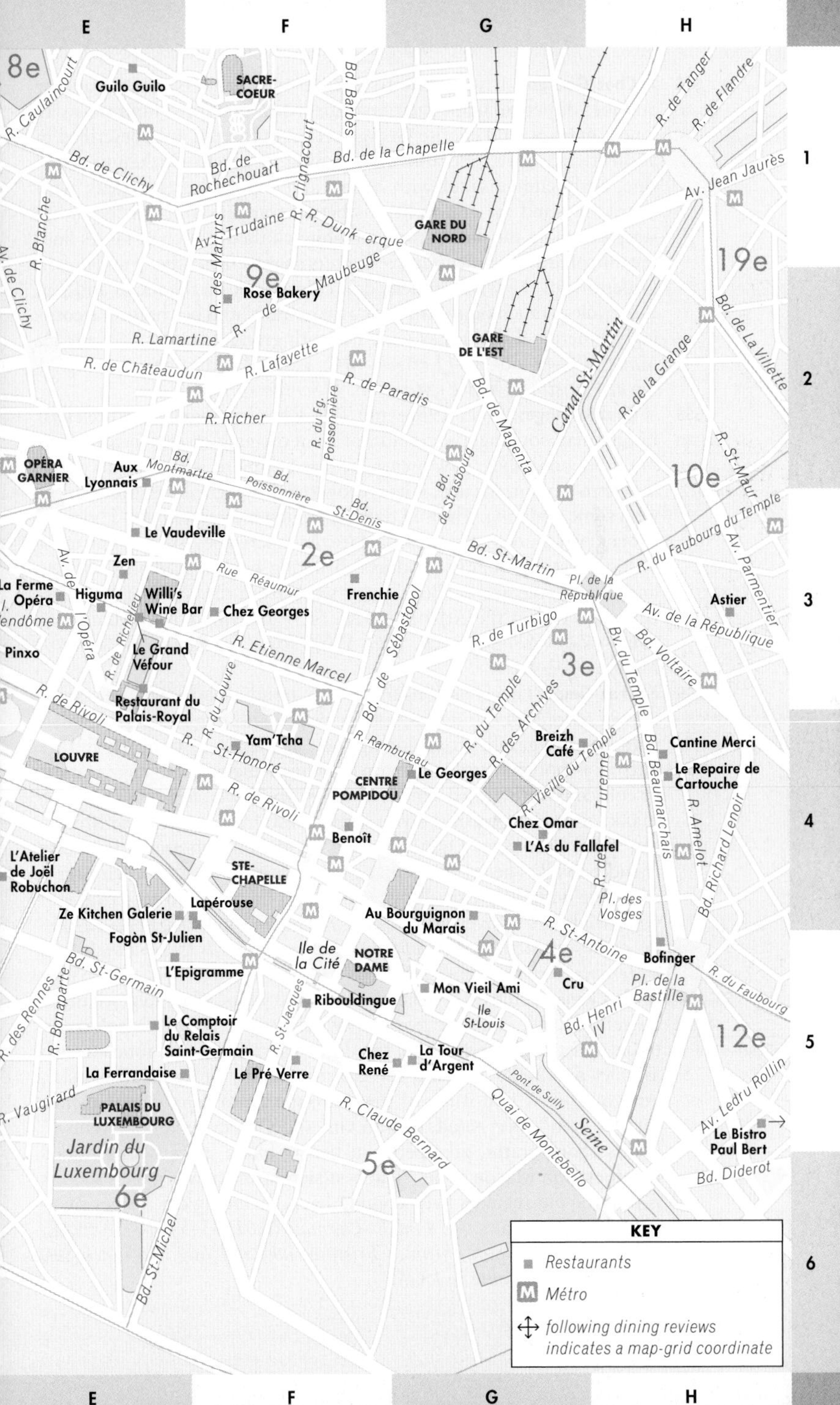

E
F
G
H
1
2
3
4
5
6
8e
9e
2e
3e
4e
5e
6e
10e
12e
19e
Guilo Guilo
SACRE-COEUR
GARE DU NORD
GARE DE L'EST
Rose Bakery
OPÉRA GARNIER
Aux Lyonnais
Le Vaudeville
Zen
La Ferme Opéra
Higuma
Willi's Wine Bar
Chez Georges
Frenchie
Astier
Pinxo
Le Grand Véfour
Restaurant du Palais-Royal
Yam'Tcha
LOUVRE
CENTRE POMPIDOU
Le Georges
Breizh Café
Cantine Merci
Le Repaire de Cartouche
Chez Omar
L'As du Fallafel
Benoît
L'Atelier de Joël Robuchon
STE-CHAPELLE
Lapérouse
Ze Kitchen Galerie
Fogòn St-Julien
Au Bourguignon du Marais
Ile de la Cité
NOTRE DAME
L'Epigramme
Ribouldingue
Mon Vieil Ami
Cru
Bofinger
Pl. de la Bastille
Ile St-Louis
Le Comptoir du Relais Saint-Germain
La Ferrandaise
Le Pré Verre
Chez René
La Tour d'Argent
PALAIS DU LUXEMBOURG
Jardin du Luxembourg
Le Bistro Paul Bert
Seine
Canal St-Martin
Pl. de la République
Pl. des Vosges
R. Caulaincourt
Bd. de Clichy
Bd. de Rochechouart
Bd. Barbès
R. Clignancourt
Bd. de la Chapelle
R. de Tanger
R. de Flandre
Av. Jean Jaurès
R. Blanche
Av. de Clichy
Av. Trudaine
R. des Martyrs
R. Dunkerque
R. de Maubeuge
R. Lamartine
R. de Châteaudun
R. Lafayette
R. de Paradis
R. Richer
R. du Fg. Poissonnière
Bd. de Magenta
Bd. de Strasbourg
R. de la Grange
Bd. de La Villette
R. St-Maur
Bd. Montmartre
Bd. Poissonnière
Bd. St-Denis
Bd. St-Martin
R. du Faubourg du Temple
Av. Parmentier
Av. de la République
Bd. Voltaire
Rue Réaumur
Av. de l'Opéra
R. de Richelieu
R. de Turbigo
R. Etienne Marcel
Bd. de Sébastopol
Bv. du Temple
R. de Rivoli
R. du Louvre
R. St-Honoré
R. Rambuteau
R. du Temple
R. des Archives
R. Vieille du Temple
R. de Turenne
Bd. Beaumarchais
R. Amelot
Bd. Richard Lenoir
R. St-Antoine
R. du Faubourg
Bd. Henri IV
Bd. St-Germain
R. des Rennes
R. Bonaparte
R. St-Jacques
R. Claude Bernard
Pont de Sully
Quai de Montebello
Av. Ledru Rollin
Bd. Diderot
R. Vaugirard
Bd. St-Michel
KEY
Restaurants
Métro
following dining reviews indicates a map-grid coordinate

$$$ BISTRO Louvre/Tuileries, 2e

Chez Georges. If you were to ask Parisian bankers, aristocrats, or antiques dealers to name their favorite bistro for a three-hour weekday lunch, many would choose Georges. The traditional fare, described in authentically indecipherable handwriting, is good—chicken-liver terrine, curly endive salad with bacon and a poached egg, steak with béarnaise—and the atmosphere is better, compensating for the rather steep prices. In the dining room, a white-clothed stretch of tables lines the mirrored walls and attentive waiters sweep efficiently up and down. Order one of the wines indicated in colored ink on the menu and you can drink as much or as little of it as you want (and be charged accordingly); there's also another wine list with grander bottles. ✉ *1 rue du Mail* ☎ *01–42–60–07–11* ▭ *AE, MC, V* ⏲ *Closed weekends, Aug., 1 wk at Christmas, and 1 wk in Feb.* Ⓜ *Sentier* ⊕ *1:F3.*

$$$ BISTRO Trocadéro/Tour Eiffel, 7e

Chez les Anges. In the 1960s and '70s, Chez les Anges served celestial Burgundian cooking; the restaurant went through several incarnations since, but now, under new owner Jacques Lacipière, who runs the popular bistro Au Bon Accueil, it has recovered the original name and spirit, with some updating. The €34 daily-changing menu from chef Hidenori Kitaguchi is a notch above bistro fare. Lacipière goes further than most in his quest for quality products, bringing back ingredients such as line-caught sole and scallops every week from the town of St-Gilles-Croix-de-Vie on the Atlantic coast. ✉ *54 bd. de la Tour-Maubourg* ☎ *01–47–05–89–86* ▭ *AE, MC, V* ⏲ *Closed weekends* Ⓜ *La Tour-Maubourg* ⊕ *1:C4.*

$$$ NORTH AFRICAN République, 3e ★

Chez Omar. This is no longer the only trendy North African restaurant in town, but during fashion week you still might see top models with legs like gazelles touching up their lipstick in front of the vintage mirrors—though that doesn't stop them from digging into huge platters of couscous with grilled skewered lamb, spicy *merguez* sausage, lamb shank, or chicken, washed down with robust, fruity Algerian or Moroccan wine. Proprietor Omar Guerida speaks English and is famously friendly to all. The setting is that of a beautifully faded French bistro, complete with elbow-to-elbow seating, so be prepared to partake of your neighbors' conversations. ✉ *47 rue de Bretagne* ☎ *01–42–72–36–26* ✍ *Reservations not accepted* ▭ *No credit cards* ⏲ *No lunch Sun.* Ⓜ *Temple, République* ⊕ *1:G4.*

$$–$$$ BISTRO Quartier Latin, 5e

Chez René. Run by the same family for 50 years, Chez René changed owners in 2007. The new team has wisely preserved the bistro's traditional spirit while brightening the decor and adding chic touches such as valet parking. The menu still consists mainly of Lyonnais classics, but you'll now find some of these grouped into color-theme menus such as "red" (beet salad, coq au vin, and Quincy wine) or "yellow" (Swiss chard gratin, pike-perch in beurre blanc sauce with steamed potatoes, and Mâcon wine). The best sign of the new regime's success is that the old regulars keep coming back, including the former owners, who live upstairs. ✉ *14 bd. St-Germain* ☎ *01–43–54–30–23* ▭ *AE, MC, V* ⏲ *Closed Sun., Mon., Christmas wk, and Aug. No lunch Sat.* Ⓜ *Maubert-Mutualité* ⊕ *1:G5.*

$$–$$$
MODERN FRENCH
Le Marais, 4e

✕ **Cru.** It's hard to imagine a raw food restaurant in a city famous for its slow-simmered dishes but, since opening in summer 2009, Cru has enjoyed instant success—the bucolic terrace in a cobbled Marais courtyard has something to do with this, as does the extensive menu's refusal to take the raw concept to extremes: a few cooked dishes are available, such as meat or fish prepared a la plancha and root vegetable "fries." If you decide to stick to the raw dishes, you won't be disappointed: the "green plate," variations on cucumber, displays the chef's well-judged creativity, while silky veal carpaccio with preserved lemon has a lively flavor. Most of the desserts depart from the raw theme, which is not necessarily a bad thing. The restaurant doubles as a wine bar, so there are plenty of interesting bottles to choose from. ✉ *7 rue Charlemagne, Le Marais* ☎ *01–40–27–81–84* 🌐 *www.restaurantcru.fr* ▬ *MC, V* ⏲ *Closed Mon. and 2 wks in Aug.* Ⓜ *St-Paul* ✣ *1:G5.*

$$$–$$$$
BISTRO
Champs-Élysées, 8e

✕ **Dominique Bouchet.** To taste the cooking of one of the city's great chefs, you no longer need pay for the sumptuous backdrop once provided by the Hotel Crillon: Dominique Bouchet has left that world behind for an elegant bistro where contemporary art brightens cream-painted walls, and he seems all the happier for it. On the menu, refined French technique meets country-style cooking, as in leg of lamb braised in wine with roasted cocoa bean and potato purée, or a chocolate éclair with black cherries and ice cream. Sometimes the dishes can get a touch too complicated, but the warm service makes up for it. If you're feeling indecisive you might treat yourself to the €98 tasting menu: a succession of six small plates followed by a dessert. ✉ *11 rue Treilhard* ☎ *01–45–61–09–46* ▬ *AE, DC, MC, V* ⏲ *Closed weekends and 3 wks in Aug.* Ⓜ *Miromesnil* ✣ *1:C2.*

$–$$
SPANISH
Quartier Latin, 6e

✕ **Fogòn St-Julien.** The most ambitious Spanish restaurant in Paris occupies an airy Seine-side space, avoiding tapas-bar clichés. The seasonal all-tapas menu, at €49 per person, is the most creative choice, but that would mean missing out on the paella: saffron with seafood (which could be a bit more generous), inky squid, or Valencia-style with rabbit, chicken, and vegetables. Finish up with custardy crème Catalan and a glass of muscatel. ✉ *45 quai des Grands-Augustins* ☎ *01–43–54–31–33* ✍ *Reservations essential* ▬ *MC, V* ⏲ *Closed Mon. No dinner weekends* Ⓜ *St-Michel* ✣ *1:F4.*

$$
BISTRO
Les Halles, 2e
Fodor's Choice ★

✕ **Frenchie.** Grégory Marchand worked in New York and with Jamie Oliver in London before opening this brick-and-stone-walled bistro on a pedestrian street near Rue Montorgueil, which explains the tongue-in-cheek name. Though it hasn't had much press, word of mouth has quickly made it one of the most packed bistros in town. Marchand owes a large part of his success to the great-value €35 three-course menu at dinner—boldly flavored dishes such as calamari gazpacho with squash blossoms, and melt-in-the-mouth braised lamb with roasted eggplant and spinach are excellent options. Desserts seem a tiny bit less stunning, but with good service and a laid-back atmosphere, this restaurant is headed for long-term success. It's prix fixe only. ✉ *5 rue de Nil, Les Halles* ☎ *01–40–39–96–19* 🌐 *www.frenchie-restaurant.com* ▬ *AE, MC, V* ⏲ *Closed Sun., Mon., 2 wks in Aug., 10 days at Christmas. No lunch Tues. or Sat.* Ⓜ *Sentier* ✣ *1:F3.*

$$$
JAPANESE
Montmartre, 18e
Fodor's Choice ★

✕ **Guilo Guilo.** Already a star in Kyoto, Eiichi Edakuni has created a sensation with his first Parisian restaurant, where 20 diners seated around the black bar can watch him at work each night. The no-choice, €45 set menu is a bargain given the quality and sophistication of the food: it changes every month, but you might come across dishes such as sea bream and wagyu beef on shiso leaves with ponzu sauce, or the chef's signature foie gras sushi, an idea that could easily fall flat but instead soars. If you can afford it, complement your meal with exceptional sakes by the glass, one of which is sparkling. This restaurant is no secret, so reserve three weeks ahead. ✉ *8 rue Garreau, Montmartre* ☎ *01–42–54–23–92* 🌐 *www.guiloguilo.com* *Reservations essential* *MC, V* ⏲ *Closed Sun. and Mon.* Ⓜ *Abbesses* ✥ *1:E1.*

$$$$
HAUTE FRENCH
Champs-Élysées, 17e
Fodor's Choice ★

✕ **Guy Savoy.** Revamped with dark African wood, rich leather, cream-color marble, and the chef's own art collection, Guy Savoy's luxury restaurant doesn't dwell on the past. Come here for a perfectly measured haute-cuisine experience, since Savoy's several bistros have not lured him away from his kitchen. The artichoke soup with black truffles, sea bass with spices, and veal kidneys in mustard-spiked jus reveal the magnitude of his talent, and his mille-feuille is an instant classic. If the waiters see you are relishing a dish, they won't hesitate to offer second helpings. Generous half portions allow you to graze your way through the menu—unless you choose a blowout feast for €275 or €345—and reasonably priced wines are available (though beware the cost of wines by the glass). Special promotions are sometimes available on the Web site (🌐 *www.guysavoy.com*). Best of all, the atmosphere is joyful, because Savoy knows that having fun is just as important as eating well. ✉ *18 rue Troyon* ☎ *01–43–80–40–61* *Reservations essential; jacket required* *AE, MC, V* ⏲ *Closed Sun., Mon., Aug., and 1 wk at Christmas. No lunch Sat.* Ⓜ *Charles-de-Gaulle–Étoile* ✥ *1:B2.*

$$$$
HAUTE FRENCH
St-Germain, 6e

✕ **Hélène Darroze.** The most celebrated female chef in Paris is now cooking at the Connaught in London, but her St-Germain dining room was revamped in 2008 to create an even more exclusive setting for her sophisticated take on southwestern French food. Darroze's intriguingly modern touch comes through in such dishes as a sublime duck foie gras confit served with an exotic-fruit chutney or a blowout of roast wild duck stuffed with foie gras and truffles. If the food, at its best, lives up to the very high prices, the service sometimes struggles to reach the same level. For a more affordable taste, try the relatively casual Salon d'Hélène downstairs, which serves dishes starting at €6.50 a plate. ✉ *4 rue d'Assas, St-Germain-des-Prés* ☎ *01–42–22–00–11* 🌐 *www.helenedarroze.com* *Reservations essential* *AE, DC, MC, V* ⏲ *Closed Sun. and Mon.* Ⓜ *Sèvres-Babylone* ✥ *1:D5.*

¢
JAPANESE
Opéra/Grands Boulevards, 9e

✕ **Higuma.** When it comes to steaming bowls of noodles, this no-frills dining room divided into three sections beats its many neighboring competitors. Behind the counter—an entertaining spot for solo diners—cooks toil over giant flames, tossing strips of meat and quick-fried vegetables, then ladling noodles and broth into giant bowls. A choice of *formules* (fixed-price menu options) allows you to pair various soups and stir-fried noodle dishes with six delicious gyoza (Japanese dumplings), and the stir-fried dishes are excellent, too. Don't expect much in the way of service, but it's hard to find a more generous meal in Paris at this price. There is a more subdued annex (without the open kitchen) at 163 rue St-Honoré, near the Louvre. ✉ *32 rue Ste-Anne, Opéra/Grands Boulevards* ☎ *01–47–03–38–59* ▭ *MC, V* Ⓜ *Pyramides* ✥ *1:E3.*

$$$$ FRENCH FUSION Trocadéro/Tour Eiffel, 7e Fodor's Choice ★

✕ **Hiramatsu.** In this Art Deco dining room near Trocadéro, Hajime Nakagawa continues his variations on the subtly Japanese-inspired French cuisine of restaurant namesake Hiroyuki Hiramatsu, who still sometimes works the kitchen. Luxury ingredients feature prominently in dishes such as thin slices of lamb with onion jam and thyme-and-truffle-spiked jus, or an unusual pot-au-feu of oysters with foie gras and black truffle. For dessert, a mille-feuille of caramelized apples comes with rosemary sorbet. Helpful sommeliers will guide you through the staggering wine list, with more than 1,000 different bottles to choose from. There's no way to get away cheaply, so save it for a special occasion, when you might be tempted to order a tasting menu for €95 or €130 (lunch menus start at €48). ✉ *52 rue de Longchamp, Trocadéro/Tour Eiffel* ☎ *01–56–81–08–80* 🌐 *www.hiramatsu.co.jp/fr* ✍ *Reservations essential* ▭ *AE, DC, MC, V* ⊙ *Closed weekends, Aug., and 1 wk at Christmas* Ⓜ *Trocadéro* ✥ *1:A3.*

$$$$ FRENCH FUSION Invalides, 7e Fodor's Choice ★

✕ **Il Vino.** It might seem audacious to present hungry diners with nothing more than a wine list, but the gamble is paying off for Enrico Bernardo at his newly opened restaurant with a branch in Courcheval. Winner of the world's best sommelier award in 2005, this charismatic Italian has left the George V to oversee a dining room where food plays second fiddle (in status, not quality). The hip decor—plum banquettes, body-hugging white chairs, a few high tables—has attracted a mostly young clientele that's happy to play the game by ordering one of the blind, multicourse tasting menus for €75 or €100. This might bring you a white Mâcon with saffron risotto, crisp Malvasia with crabmeat and black radish, a full-bodied red from Puglia with Provençal-style lamb, sherrylike *vin jaune* d'Arbois with aged Comté cheese, and sweet Jurançon with berry crumble. You can also order individual wine-food combinations à la carte or pick a bottle straight from the cellar and ask for a meal to match. ✉ *13 bd. de la Tour-Maubourg* ☎ *01–44–11–72–00* ▭ *AE, DC, MC, V* Ⓜ *Invalides* ✥ *1:C4.*

$$$ BISTRO St-Germain, 6e

✕ **Josephine Chez Dumonet.** Theater types, politicos, and well-padded locals fill the moleskin banquettes of this venerable bistro, where the frosted-glass lamps and amber walls put everyone in a good light. Unlike most bistros, Josephine caters to the indecisive, since half portions allow you to graze your way through the temptingly retro menu. Try the excellent *bœuf Bourguignon,* roasted saddle of lamb with artichokes, top-notch steak tartare prepared table-side, or anything with truffles in season. For dessert, choose between a mille-feuille big enough to serve three and a Grand Marnier soufflé that simply refuses to sink, even with prodding. The wine list, like the food, is outstanding but expensive. ✉ *117 rue du Cherche-Midi* ☎ *01–45–48–52–40* ▭ *AE, MC, V* ⊙ *Closed weekends* Ⓜ *Duroc* ✥ *1:D6.*

$$$$ HAUTE FRENCH Tour Eiffel, 7e

✕ **Jules Verne.** Alain Ducasse doesn't set his sights low, so it was no real surprise when he took over this prestigious dining room on the second floor of the Eiffel Tower, and had designer Patrick Jouin give the room a

DID YOU KNOW?

Because the Latin Quarter is Student Central it is home to many reasonably priced eateries—pull up a café seat during *l'heure bleue* (twilight) to enjoy some real Parisian magic.

neo-futuristic look in shades of brown. Sauces and pastries are prepared in a kitchen below the Champ de Mars before being whisked up the elevator to the kitchen, which is overseen by young chef Pascal Féraud. Most accessible is the €85 lunch menu (weekdays only), which brings you à la carte dishes in slightly smaller portions. Spend more (about €150–€200 per person) and you'll be entitled to more lavish dishes such as lobster with celery root and black truffle, and fricassee of Bresse chicken with crayfish. For dessert the kitchen reinterprets French classics, as in an unsinkable pink grapefruit soufflé with grapefruit sorbet. Book months ahead or try your luck at the last minute. ☒ *Tour Eiffel, south pillar, Av. Gustave Eiffel* ☎ *01–45–55–61–44* ✍ *Reservations essential; jacket required* ▭ *AE, DC, MC, V* Ⓜ *Bir-Hakeim* ✢ *1:B4.*

2

$$–$$$
BRASSERIE
Montparnasse, 14e

✕ **La Coupole.** This world-renowned cavernous spot with Art Deco murals practically defines the term *brasserie.* La Coupole might have lost its intellectual aura since the Flo group's restoration, which has put its rather commercial stamp on many historic Paris brasseries, but it's been popular since Jean-Paul Sartre and Simone de Beauvoir were regulars, and it's still great fun. Today it attracts a mix of bourgeois families, tourists, and elderly lone diners treating themselves to a dozen oysters. Recent additions to the classic brasserie menu are a tart of caramelized apple and panfried foie gras, beef fillet flambéed with cognac before your eyes, and profiteroles made with Valrhona chocolate. On most days, you can't make a reservation after 8 or 8:30, so be prepared for a wait at the bar. ☒ *102 bd. du Montparnasse* ☎ *01–43–20–14–20* 🌐 *www.flobrasseries.com* ▭ *AE, DC, MC, V* Ⓜ *Vavin* ✢ *1:D6.*

¢
CAFÉ
Opéra/Grands Boulevards, 1er

✕ **La Ferme Opéra.** If your arm aches from flagging down café waiters, take a break in this bright, friendly, self-service restaurant near the Louvre that specializes in produce from the Ile-de-France region (around Paris). Inventive salads, sandwiches, and pastas are fresh and delicious, and on the sweeter side, you can find wholesome fruit crumbles, tarts, and cheesecakes. They serve whole-wheat scones and freshly squeezed juices for breakfast, from 8 AM on weekdays and 9 AM on Saturday; breakfast is served from 10 AM on Sunday, when there is also brunch from 11 AM to 4 PM. There's free Wi-Fi access in the barnlike dining room. ☒ *55 rue St-Roch* ☎ *01–40–20–12–12* ▭ *MC, V* Ⓜ *Pyramides* ✢ *1:E3.*

$$–$$$
BRASSERIE
Champs-Élysées, 8e

✕ **La Fermette Marbeuf 1900.** Graced with one of the most mesmerizing Belle Époque rooms in town—accidentally rediscovered during renovations in the 1970s—this is a favorite haunt of French celebrities, who adore the sunflowers, peacocks, and dragonflies of the Art Nouveau mosaic. The menu rolls out solid, updated classic cuisine: try the snails in puff pastry, saddle of lamb with *choron* (a tomato-spiked béarnaise sauce), and bitter-chocolate fondant—but ignore the limited-choice €32 prix fixe (€24.50 at lunch) unless you're on a budget. Popular with tourists and businesspeople at lunch, La Fermette becomes truly animated around 9 PM. ☒ *5 rue Marbeuf* ☎ *01–53–23–08–00* 🌐 *www.fermettemarbeuf.com* ▭ *AE, DC, MC, V* Ⓜ *Franklin-D.-Roosevelt* ✢ *1:B3.*

$$$–$$$$
BISTRO
Quartier Latin, 6e

Lapérouse. Émile Zola, George Sand, and Victor Hugo were regulars, and the restaurant's mirrors still bear diamond scratches from the days when mistresses didn't take jewels at face value. All together, it's hard not to fall in love with this 17th-century Seine-side town house whose warren of intimate, woodwork-graced salons breathes history. The latest chef, Alain Hacquard, has found the right track with a daring (for Paris) spice-infused menu: his lobster, Dublin Bay prawn, and crayfish bisque is flavored with Szechuan pepper and lemon. Game is prominent in the fall, with a selection of southwestern wines to accompany dishes like Scottish grouse. For a truly intimate meal, reserve one of the legendary private *salons* where anything can happen (and probably has). You can also sample the restaurant's magic at lunch, when a bargain prix-fixe menu is served for €35–€45 in both the main dining room and the private salons. *51 quai des Grands Augustins 01–43–26–68–04 Reservations essential AE, DC, MC, V Closed Sun. No lunch Sat. St-Michel 1:F4.*

WORD OF MOUTH

"Try L'As du Fallafel. Don't be seduced by the other fallafel places on the street—find this one! And it is so cheap you'll have a little more money to splurge elsewhere!"

—RondaTravels

$$
BISTRO
Louvre/Tuileries, 1er
Fodor's Choice ★

L'Ardoise. This minuscule storefront, decorated with enlargements of old sepia postcards of Paris, is a model of the kind of contemporary bistros making waves in Paris. Chef Pierre Jay's first-rate three-course dinner menu for €34 tempts with such original dishes as mushroom and foie gras ravioli with smoked duck; farmer's pork with porcini mushrooms; and red mullet with creole sauce (you can also order à la carte, but it's less of a bargain). Just as enticing are the desserts, such as a superb *feuillantine au citron*—caramelized pastry leaves filled with lemon cream and lemon slices—and a boozy baba au rhum. With friendly waiters and a small but well-chosen wine list, L'Ardoise would be perfect if it weren't often crowded and noisy. *28 rue du Mont Thabor 01–42–96–28–18 www.lardoise-paris.com MC, V Closed Mon. and Aug. No lunch Sun. Concorde 1:D3.*

¢–$
ISRAELI
Le Marais, 4e

L'As du Fallafel. Look no further than the fantastic falafel stands on the newly pedestrian Rue de Rosiers for some of the cheapest and tastiest meals in Paris. L'As (the Ace) is widely considered the best of the bunch, which accounts for the lunchtime line that extends into the street. A falafel sandwich costs €5 to go, €7 in the dining room, and comes heaped with grilled eggplant, cabbage, hummus, tahini, and hot sauce. The *shawarma* (grilled, skewered meat) sandwich, made with chicken or lamb, is also one of the finest in town. Though takeout is popular, it can be more fun (and not as messy) to eat off a plastic plate in one of the two frenzied dining rooms. Fresh lemonade is the falafel's best match. *34 rue des Rosiers 01–48–87–63–60 MC, V Closed Sat. No dinner Fri. St-Paul 1:G4.*

$$$$ HAUTE FRENCH Trocadéro/Tour Eiffel, 16e Fodor's Choice ★

L'Astrance. Granted, Pascal Barbot rose to fame thanks to his restaurant's amazing-value food and casual atmosphere, but after the passage of several years, L'Astrance has become resolutely haute, with prices to match. With no à la carte, you can choose from a lunch menu for €70, a seasonal menu for €120, or the full tasting menu for €190 (this is what most people come for)—the latter two are available at lunch and dinner. Barbot's cooking has such an ethereal quality that it's worth the considerable effort of booking a table—you should start trying at least six weeks in advance. His dishes often draw on Asian ingredients, as in grilled lamb with miso-lacquered eggplant and a palate-cleansing white sorbet spiked with chili pepper and lemongrass. Each menu also comes at a (considerably) higher price with wines to match each course. ✉ *4 rue Beethoven* ☎ *01–40–50–84–40* *Reservations essential* *AE, DC, MC, V* *Closed Sat.–Mon. and Aug.* Ⓜ *Passy* ✣ *1:A3.*

$$$$ MODERN FRENCH Trocadéro/Tour Eiffel, 16e

La Table de Joël Robuchon. Chef David Alves keeps up the lofty standard set by star chef Joël Robuchon, with dishes like quail stuffed with foie gras, served with truffled potato purée. As at Robuchon's L'Atelier, you'll find a selection of small plates alongside more substantial dishes, but the seating arrangement is more conventional (no bar, just tables and chairs) and La Table accepts reservations—in fact, you should book weeks in advance for a seat in this small dining room that is somewhat disconcertingly decorated in gold leaf. The "menu club" set-menu for €59 at lunch is a relative bargain. ✉ *16 av. Bugeaud* ☎ *01–56–28–16–16* *Reservations essential* *MC, V* Ⓜ *Victor-Hugo* ✣ *1:A3.*

$$–$$$ BISTRO Trocadéro/Tour Eiffel, 16e Fodor's Choice ★

La Table Lauriston. Serge Barbey has developed a winning formula in his chic bistro near the Trocadéro: top-notch ingredients, simply prepared and generously served. To start, you can't go wrong with his silky foie gras au torchon—the liver is poached in a flavorful bouillon—or one of the seasonal salads, such as white asparagus in herb vinaigrette; his trademark dish, a gargantuan rib steak, is big enough to silence even the hungriest Texan. Given the neighborhood you might expect a businesslike setting, but the dining room feels cheerful, with vividly colored walls and velvet-upholstered chairs, and there is a 16-seat terrace. Don't miss the giant baba au rhum, which the waiters will douse in a choice of three rums. ✉ *129 rue de Lauriston, Trocadéro/Tour Eiffel* ☎ *01–47–27–00–07* *www.restauranttablelauriston.com* *Reservations essential* *AE, MC, V* *Closed Sun., 3 wks in Aug., and 1 wk at Christmas. No lunch Sat.* Ⓜ *Trocadéro* ✣ *1:A3.*

$$$–$$$$ MODERN FRENCH St-Germain, 7e

L'Atelier de Joël Robuchon. Famed chef Joël Robuchon retired from the restaurant business for several years before opening this red-and-black-lacquer space with a bento-box-meets-tapas aesthetic. High seats surround two U-shape bars, and this novel plan encourages neighbors to share recommendations and opinions. Robuchon's devoted kitchen staff whip up "small plates" for grazing (€10–€25) as well as full portions, which turn out to be the better bargain. Highlights from the oft-changing menu have included an intense tomato jelly topped with avocado purée and thin-crusted mackerel tart, although his inauthentic (but who's complaining?) take on carbonara with cream and Alsatian bacon, and the *merlan* Colbert (fried herb butter) remain signature dishes. Bookings are taken for the first sittings only at lunch and dinner. ✉ *5 rue Montalembert* ☎ *01–42–22–56–56* ▭ *MC, V* Ⓜ *Rue du Bac* ✣ *1:E4.*

$ BISTRO St-Germain-des-Prés, 6e Fodor's Choice ★

✕ **L'Epigramme.** Great bistro food is not so hard to find in Paris, but only rarely does it come in such a comfortable setting. At L'Epigramme, the striped orange-and-yellow chairs are softly padded, there's space between you and your neighbors, and a big glass pane lets in plenty of light from the courtyard. Service from Stéphane Marcouzzi's staff is also worthy of a much more expensive restaurant. The chef has an almost magical touch with meat: try his stuffed suckling pig with turnip choucroute, or seared slices of pink lamb with root vegetables in a glossy reduced sauce. In winter, the eleborate game dish *lièvre à la royale* (hare stuffed with goose or duck liver and cooked in wine) sometimes makes an appearance. ✉ *9 rue de l'Eperon, St-Germain-des-Prés* ☎ *01–44–41–00–09* ✍ *Reservations essential* ▭ *AE, MC, V* ⊙ *Closed Sun., Mon., 3 wks in Aug., and 1 wk at Christmas* Ⓜ *Odéon* ✣ *1:E5.*

$$ BISTRO St-Germain-des-Prés, 6e

✕ **La Ferrandaise.** Portraits of cows adorn the stone walls of this bistro near the Luxembourg gardens, hinting at the kitchen's penchant for meaty cooking (Ferrandaise is a breed of cattle). Still, there's something for every taste on the market-inspired menu, which always lists three meat and three fish mains. Dill-marinated salmon with sweet mustard sauce is a typical starter, and a thick, milk-fed veal chop might come with a squash pancake and spinach. The dining room buzzes with locals who appreciate the good-value €32 prix-fixe and the brilliant bento-box-style €15 lunch menu, in which three courses are served all at once. ✉ *8 rue de Vaugirard, St-Germain-des-Prés* ☎ *01–43–26–36–36* 🌐 *www.laferrandaise.com* ▭ *AE, MC, V* ⊙ *Closed Sun. and 3 wks in Aug. No lunch Sat.* Ⓜ *Odéon, RER: Luxembourg* ✣ *1:E5.*

$$$$ HAUTE FRENCH Quartier Latin, 5e

✕ **La Tour d'Argent.** La Tour d'Argent has had a rocky time in recent years with the loss of a Michelin star, the death of famed owner Claude Terrail, but chef Stéphane Haissant has found his footing, and there's no denying the splendor of its setting overlooking the Seine. If you don't want to splash out on dinner, treat yourself to the three-course lunch menu for a reduced price of €65; this entitles you to succulent slices of one of the restaurant's numbered ducks (the great duck slaughter began in 1919 and is now well past the millionth mallard, as your numbered certificate will attest). Don't be too daunted by the vast wine list—with the aid of the sommelier you can splurge a little (about €80) and perhaps taste a rare vintage Burgundy from the extraordinary cellars, which survived World War II. ✉ *15–17 quai de la Tournelle, Quartier Latin* ☎ *01–43–54–23–31* 🌐 *www.latourdargent.com* ✍ *Reservations essential; jacket and tie* ▭ *AE, DC, MC, V* ⊙ *Closed Sun., Mon., and Aug.* Ⓜ *Cardinal Lemoine* ✣ *1:G5.*

$$ BISTRO Bastille, 11e Fodor's Choice ★

✕ **Le Bistrot Paul Bert.** Faded 1930s decor: check. Boisterous crowd: check. Thick steak with real frites: check. Good value: check. The Paul Bert delivers everything you could want from a traditional Paris bistro, so it's no wonder its two dining rooms (one recently added) fill every night with a cosmopolitan crowd. Some are from the neighborhood, others clutch copies of the *Financial Times*, but they've all come in search of the elusive balance of ingredients that makes for a feel-good experience every time. The laid-back yet efficient staff serves up hearty dishes such as monkfish with white beans and duck with pears—the reasonable prix-fixe is three courses for €34, or you can order à la carte. ✉ *18 rue Paul Bert, Bastille* ☎ *01–43—72–24–01* *Reservations essential* ▭ *MC, V* ⏲ *Closed Sun., Mon., and Aug.* ✥ *1:H5.*

$$$$ HAUTE FRENCH Champs-Elysées, 8ᵉ

✕ **Le Bristol.** After a rapid ascent at his own new-wave bistro, which led to his renown as one of the more inventive young chefs in Paris, Eric Frechon became head chef at the Bristol, the home-away-from-home for billionaires and power brokers. Frechon creates masterworks—say, farmer's pork cooked "from head to foot" with truffle-enhanced crushed potatoes—that rarely stray far from the comfort-food tastes of bistro cooking. The €85 lunch menu makes his cooking accessible not just to the palate but to many pocketbooks. No wonder his tables are so coveted. Though the two dining rooms are impeccable—an oval oak-panel one for fall and winter and a marble-floor pavilion overlooking the courtyard garden for spring and summer—they provide few clues to help the world-weary traveler determine which city this might be. ✉ *Hôtel Bristol, 112 rue du Faubourg St-Honoré, Champs-Elysées* ☎ *01–53–43–43–00* 🌐 *www.hotel-bristol.com* *Reservations essential; jacket and tie* ▭ *AE, DC, MC, V* Ⓜ *Miromesnil* ✥ *1:C2.*

$ BISTRO Invalides, 7ᵉ

✕ **Le Café Constant.** Middle-aged Parisians are a nostalgic bunch, which explains the popularity of this down-to-earth venue from esteemed chef Christian Constant. This is a relatively humble bistro with cream-color walls, red banquettes, and wooden tables. The menu reads like a French cookbook from the 1970s—who cooks veal *cordon bleu* these days?—but with Constant overseeing the kitchen, the dishes taste even better than you remember. There's delicious and creamy lentil soup with morsels of foie gras, and the artichoke salad comes with fresh—not bottled or frozen—hearts. A towering *vacherin* (meringue layered with ice cream) might bring this delightfully retro meal to a close. On weekdays there is a bargain lunch menu for €16 (two courses) or €23 (three courses). ✉ *139 rue St-Dominique* ☎ *01–47–53–73–34* *Reservations not accepted* ▭ *MC, V* ⏲ *Closed Sun. and Mon. and school holidays* Ⓜ *École Militaire; RER: Pont de l'Alma* ✥ *1:B4.*

$$$ BISTRO St-Germain, 6ᵉ

✕ **Le Comptoir du Relais Saint-Germain.** Run by legendary bistro chef Yves Camdeborde, this tiny Art Deco hotel restaurant is booked up several months in advance for the single dinner sitting that comprises a five-course, €48 set menu of haute-cuisine-quality food. On weekends and before 6 PM during the week a brasserie menu is served and reservations are not accepted, resulting in long lineups and brisk service. Start with charcuterie or pâté, then choose from open-face sandwiches, salads, and a handful of hot dishes such as braised beef cheek, roast tuna, and Camdeborde's famed deboned and breaded pig's trotter. Sidewalk tables make for prime people-watching in summer and Le Comptoir also runs a down-to-earth snack shop next door that serves crepes and sandwiches. ✉ *9 carrefour de l'Odéon* ☎ *01–44–27–07–50* ▭ *AE, DC, MC, V* Ⓜ *Odéon* ✥ *1:E5.*

$$–$$$ MODERN FRENCH Beaubourg/Les Halles, 3ᵉ

✕ **Le Georges.** One of those rooftop showstopping venues so popular in Paris, Le Georges preens atop the Centre Georges Pompidou, accessed by its own entrance to the left of the main doors. The staff is as streamlined and angular as the furniture, and at night the terrace has distinct snob appeal. Come snappily dressed or you may be relegated to something resembling a dentist's waiting room. Part of the Costes brothers' empire, the establishment trots out fashionable dishes such as sesame-crusted tuna and coriander-spiced beef fillet flambéed with cognac. It's all considerably less dazzling than the view, except for the suitably decadent desserts (indulge in the Cracker's cheesecake with yogurt sorbet). ✉ *Centre Pompidou, 6th fl., 19 rue Rambuteau* ☎ *01–44–78–47–99* ▭ *AE, DC, MC, V* ⊙ *Closed Tues.* Ⓜ *Rambuteau* ✥ *1:G4.*

$$$$
HAUTE FRENCH
Louvre/Tuileries, 1er
Fodor's Choice ★

✕ **Le Grand Véfour.** Victor Hugo could stride in and still recognize this place—in his day, as now, a contender for the title of most beautiful restaurant in Paris. Originally built in 1784, it has welcomed everyone from Napoléon to Colette to Jean Cocteau. The mirrored ceiling and early-19th-century glass paintings of goddesses and muses create an air of restrained seduction. Foodies as well as the fashionable gather here to enjoy chef Guy Martin's unique blend of sophistication and rusticity, as seen in dishes such as frogs' legs with sorrel sauce, and oxtail parmentier (a kind of shepherd's pie) with truffles. There's an outstanding cheese trolley and for dessert, try the house specialty, *palet aux noisettes* (meringue cake with chocolate mousse, hazelnuts, and salted caramel ice cream). Prices are as extravagant—a single main course averages €100—as the decor, but there's an €88 lunch menu. ✉ *17 rue de Beaujolais* ☎ *01–42–96–56–27* 🌐 *www.grand-vefour.com* ✍ *Reservations essential ; jacket and tie* ▭ *AE, DC, MC, V* ⊙ *Closed weekends, Aug., 1 wk in Apr., and 1 wk at Christmas. No dinner Fri.* Ⓜ *Palais-Royal* ✥ *1:E3.*

$
MODERN FRENCH
Quartier Latin, 5e

✕ **Le Pré Verre.** Chef Philippe Delacourcelle knows his cassia bark from his cinnamon, thanks to a long stint in Asia, and he opened this lively bistro, with its purple-gray walls and photos of jazz musicians, to showcase his unique culinary style, rejuvenating archetypal French dishes with Asian and Mediterranean spices. So popular has it proved, especially with Japanese visitors, that the restaurant opened a branch in Tokyo in late 2007. His bargain prix-fixe menus (€13.50 at lunch for a main dish, glass of wine, and coffee; €28.50 for three courses at dinner) change constantly, but his trademark spiced suckling pig with crisp cabbage is a winner, as is his rhubarb compote with gingered white-chocolate mousse. Ask for advice in selecting wine from a list that highlights small producers. ✉ *8 rue Thénard* ☎ *01–43–54–59–47* ▭ *MC, V* ⊙ *Closed Sun., Mon., and 3 wks in Aug.* Ⓜ *Maubert-Mutualité* ✥ *1:F5.*

$$–$$$
BISTRO
Bastille/Nation, 11e

✕ **Le Repaire de Cartouche.** In this split-level, dark-wood bistro between Bastille and République, chef Rodolphe Paquin applies a disciplined creativity to earthy French regional dishes. The menu changes regularly, but typical are a salad of haricots verts (green beans) topped with tender slices of squid, scallops on a bed of diced pumpkin, juicy lamb with white beans, game dishes in winter, and old-fashioned desserts like baked custard with tiny shell-shape madeleines. In keeping with cost-conscious times, he whips up a bargain three-course lunch menu for €16that doesn't skimp on ingredients—expect the likes of homemade pâté to start, followed by fried red mullet or hanger steak with french fries, and chocolate tart. The wine list is very good, too, with some bargain wines from small producers. ✉ *8 bd. des Filles du Calvaire* ☎ *01–47–00–25–86* ✍ *Reservations essential* ▭ *MC, V* ⏲ *Closed Sun., Mon., and Aug.* Ⓜ *Filles du Calvaire* ✣ *1:H4.*

$$–$$$$
BRASSERIE
Opéra/Grands Boulevards, 2e

✕ **Le Vaudeville.** Part of the Flo group of historic brasseries, Le Vaudeville is filled with journalists, bankers, and locals *d'un certain âge* who come for the good-value assortment of prix-fixe menus (including two courses for €20.50 after 10:30 PM) and highly professional service. Shellfish, house-smoked salmon, foie gras with raisins, slow-braised lamb, and desserts such as the floating island topped with pralines are particularly enticing. Enjoy the graceful 1920s decor—almost the entire interior of this intimate dining room is done in real or faux marble—and lively dining until 1 AM daily. ✉ *29 rue Vivienne* ☎ *01–40–20–04–62* ▭ *AE, DC, MC, V* Ⓜ *Bourse* ✣ *1:E3.*

$$$–$$$$
HAUTE FRENCH
Invalides, 7e
Fodor's Choice ★

✕ **Le Violon d'Ingres.** Following in the footsteps of Joël Robuchon and Alain Senderens, Christian Constant has given up the star chase in favor of more accessible prices and a packed dining room (book at least a week ahead). And with Stéphane Schmidt in charge of the kitchen here Constant can dash between his four restaurants on this street, making sure the hordes are happy. And why wouldn't they be? The food is sophisticated and the atmosphere is lively; you can even find signature dishes like the almond-crusted sea bass with rémoulade (a buttery caper sauce), alongside game and scallops (in season), and comforting desserts like *pots de crème* and chocolate tart. The food is still heavy on the butter, but with wines starting at around €20 this is a wonderful place for a classic yet informal French meal. ✉ *135 rue St-Dominique* ☎ *01–45–55–15–05* 🌐 *www.leviolondingres.com* ✍ *Reservations essential* ▭ *AE, DC, MC, V* ⏲ *Closed Sun. and Mon.* Ⓜ *École Militaire* ✣ *1:B4.*

$–$$
MODERN FRENCH
Ile St-Louis, 4e
Fodor's Choice ★

✕ **Mon Vieil Ami.** "Modern Alsatian" might sound like an oxymoron, but once you've tasted the food here, you'll understand. The updated medieval dining room—stone walls, dark-wood tables, and small glass-panel dividers—provides a stylish milieu for the inventive cooking orchestrated by star Alsatian chef Antoine Westermann, which showcases heirloom vegetables (such as yellow carrots and pink-and-white beets) from star producer Joël Thiébault. Pâté *en croûte* (wrapped in pastry) with a knob of foie gras is hard to resist among the starters. Long-cooked, wine-marinated venison comes with succulent accompaniments of quince, prune, celery root, and chestnuts. This is not necessarily the place for a romantic dinner since seating is a little tight, but the quality of the food never falters. Call during opening hours (11:30–2:30 and 7–11) to book, since they don't answer the phone the rest of the time. ✉ *69 rue St-Louis-en-l'Ile* ☎ *01–40–46–01–35* 🌐 *www.mon-vieill-ami.com* ▭ *AE, DC, MC, V* ⏲ *Closed Mon., Tues., 3 wks in Jan., and 3 wks in Aug.* Ⓜ *Pont Marie* ✣ *1:G5.*

$$$$
HAUTE FRENCH
Champs-Élysées, 8e

✕ **Pierre Gagnaire.** If you want to venture to the frontier of luxe cooking today—and if money is truly no object—dinner here is a must. Chef Pierre Gagnaire's work is at once intellectual and poetic, often blending three or four unexpected tastes and textures in a single dish. Just taking in the menu requires concentration (ask the waiters for help), so complex are the multi-line descriptions about the dishes' six or seven ingredients. The Grand Dessert, a seven-dessert marathon, will leave you breathless, though it's not as overwhelming as it sounds. The businesslike gray-and-wood dining room feels refreshingly informal, especially at lunch, but it also lacks the grandeur expected at this level. The uninspiring prix-fixe lunch (€105) and occasional ill-judged dishes (Gagnaire is a big risk taker, but also one of France's top chefs) linger as drawbacks, and prices keep shooting skyward, which makes Pierre Gagnaire an experience best saved for the financial elite. ✉ *6 rue de Balzac* ☎ *01–58–36–12–50* 🌐 *www.pierre-gagnaire.com* ✍ *Reservations essential* 💳 *AE, DC, MC, V* ⏲ *Closed Sat. No lunch Sun.* Ⓜ *Charles-de-Gaulle–Étoile* ✣ *1:B2.*

$$–$$$
MODERN FRENCH
Louvre/Tuileries, 1er

✕ **Pinxo.** The word *pinxo* means "to pinch" in Basque, and this is how the food in this fashionable hotel restaurant is meant to be eaten—often with your fingers, and off your dining companion's plate (each dish is served in three portions for sharing). Freed from the tyranny of the *entrée-plat-dessert* cycle, you can nibble your way through such minidishes as marinated herring with Granny Smith apple and horseradish, and squid cooked *à la plancha* (on a grill) with ginger and chili peppers. Alain Dutournier, who also runs the more formal Le Carré des Feuillants and Au Trou Gascon, drew on his southwestern roots to create this welcoming modern spot; granted, some dishes work better than others, but it's hard not to love a place that serves fried Camembert croquettes with celery sticks as a cheese course. ✉ *9 rue d'Alge, or through Hôtel Plaza Paris Vendôme, at 4 rue du Mont Thabor* ☎ *01–40–20–72–00* 💳 *AE, DC, MC, V* ⏲ *Closed 2 wks in Aug.* ✣ *1:E3*

$$$
SEAFOOD
Champs Élysées, 8e
Fodor's Choice ★

✕ **Rech.** Having restored the historic Paris bistros Aux Lyonnais and Benoît to their former glory, star chef Alain Ducasse has turned his piercing attention to this seafood brasserie founded in 1925. His wisdom lies in knowing what not to change: the original Art Deco chairs in the main floor dining room; seafood shucker Malec, who has been a fixture on this chic stretch of sidewalk since 1982; and the XXL éclair (it's supersized) that's drawn in the locals for decades. Original owner Auguste Rech believed in serving a limited selection of high-quality products, a principle that suits Ducasse perfectly, and from the compact open kitchen upstairs, young chef Baptiste Peupion turns out impeccable dishes such as octopus carpaccio with Genovese pesto, lobster ravioli, and astonishingly good clam chowder. Save room for the whole farmer's Camembert, another Rech tradition. A good-value €30 menu is available at lunch. ✉ *62 av. des Ternes* ☎ *01–45–72–29–47* 🌐 *www.rech.fr* 💳 *AE, DC, MC, V* ⏲ *Closed Sun. and Mon.* ✣ *1:A1.*

$$$
BISTRO
Louvre/Tuileries, 1er

✕ **Restaurant du Palais-Royal.** This stylish modern bistro decorated in jewel tones serves food to match its stunning location under the arcades of the Palais-Royal, facing its magnificent gardens. Sole, scallops, and risotto—including a dramatic black squid-ink and lobster or an all-green vegetarian version—are beautifully prepared, but juicy beef fillet with *pommes Pont Neuf* (thick-cut frites) is also a favorite of expense-account lunchers. Finish with an airy mille-feuille that changes with the seasons—berries in summer, chestnuts in winter—or a decadent baba doused with rum from Guadeloupe. Book in advance, especially in summer, when the terrace tables are hotly sought after. ✉ *Jardins du Palais-Royal, 110 Galerie Valois* ☎ *01–40–20–00–27* 🌐 *www.*

Just across the street from famed Café de Flore, the legendary Les Deux Magots was once the favorite of Hemingway, Joyce, and Sartre.

restaurantdupalaisroyal.com ☰ *AE, DC, MC, V* ⊙ *Closed Sun.* Ⓜ *Palais-Royal* ✥ *1:E3.*

$$$
BISTRO
Quartier Latin, 5e
Fodor's Choice ★

✕ **Ribouldingue.** Find offal off-putting? Don't let that stop you from trying this new bistro near the ancient St-Julien-le-Pauvre church, where offcuts take pride of place on the compulsory €27 prix-fixe. You can avoid odd animal bits completely, if you must, and still have an excellent meal—opt for dishes like marinated salmon or veal rib with fingerling potatoes—or go out on a limb with the *tétine de vache* (thin breaded and fried slices of cow's udder) and *groin de cochon* (the tip of a pig's snout). This adventurous menu is the brainchild of Nadège Varigny, daughter of a Lyonnais butcher (*quel surpise*). She runs the front of the house while chef Caroline Moncel turns out the impeccable food—veal kidney with potato gratin is a house classic and there are always three fish dishes. Don't miss the unusual desserts, like tangy ewe's-milk ice cream. ✉ *10 rue St-Julien-le-Pauvre, Quartier Latin* ☎ *01–46–33–98–80* ☰ *MC, V* ⊙ *Closed Sun., Mon., 1 wk in spring, 3 wks in Aug., and 1 wk in winter* Ⓜ *St-Michel* ✥ *1:F5.*

$
BRITISH
Montmartre, 9e

✕ **Rose Bakery.** On a street lined with French food shops selling produce, fish, baguettes, and monastery cheeses, this British-run café-restaurant might easily go unnoticed—if it weren't for the frequent line out the door. Whitewashed walls, childlike art, and concrete floors provide the decor, and organic producers supply the ingredients for food so fresh and tasty it puts most Paris lunch spots to shame. French office workers and the area's Anglos fill the room at lunch to feast on salads, soups, and hot dishes such as delicious risotto, followed by carrot cake, sticky toffee pudding, or comically large lemon tarts. There is also a branch at

30 rue Debelleyme in Le Marais. Weekend brunch is popular, so plan to arrive early. ✉ *46 rue des Martyrs, Montmartre* ☎ *01–42–82–12–80* ✍ *Reservations not accepted* ▭ *AE, MC, V* ⊙ *Closed Mon. and 2 wks in Aug. No dinner* Ⓜ *Notre-Dame-de-Lorette* ✣ *1:F2.*

$$$–$$$$
HAUTE FRENCH
Opéra/Grands Boulevards, 8e

✕ **Senderens.** Iconic chef Alain Senderens waited until retirement age to make a rebellious statement against the all-powerful Michelin inspectors, "giving back" the three stars he had held for 28 years and renaming his restaurant (it was Lucas Carton). He also updated the decor, juxtaposing curvy, white, new furnishings and craterlike ceiling lights against the splendid Art Nouveau interior. The fusion menu spans the globe, though Senderens has also, happily for the patrons, reintroduced the occasional Lucas Carton signature dishes such as polenta with truffles in winter. Some dishes work, as in warm semi-smoked salmon with Thai spices and cucumber, and some fall flat, as in a too-rich starter of roast foie gras with fig salad and licorice powder. Upstairs, Le Passage Bar serves tapas-style dishes for less than €20 a plate, or €36 for four small courses. ✉ *9 pl. de la Madeleine* ☎ *01–42–65–22–90* ⊕ *www.senderens.fr* ▭ *AE, DC, MC, V* Ⓜ *Madeleine* ✣ *1:D3.*

$$$–$$$$
MODERN FRENCH
Champs-Élysées, 8e

✕ **Spoon.** Alain Ducasse's original fusion bistro is centered around a silver screen, a long central, communal table, and some of the superchef's most fashionable food. The mix-and-match menu hasn't changed significantly since the restaurant first opened, but you can now order the bento-style lunch for €33 or a more elaborate €80 tasting menu at dinner (€120 with matching wines). Fashion folk love this place for its many vegetable and pasta dishes and its irresistible desserts, such as the cheesecake or the chocolate pizza to share. If you've sampled the Spoon concept elsewhere in the world, don't expect the same here; each branch is tailored to a particular city's tastes, and what looks exotic in Paris (the Spoon Burger with a slice of bacon or foie gras) might seem humdrum in New York. ✉ *12 rue de Marignan, Champs-Elysées* ☎ *01–40–76–34–44* ⊕ *www.spoon-restaurants.com* ✍ *Reservations essential* ▭ *AE, DC, MC, V* ⊙ *Closed weekends and Aug.* Ⓜ *Franklin-D.-Roosevelt* ✣ *1:C3.*

$$$$
HAUTE FRENCH
Champs-Élysées, 8e

✕ **Taillevent.** Perhaps the most traditional—for many diners this is only high praise—of all Paris luxury restaurants, this *grande dame* basks in renewed freshness under brilliant chef Alain Solivérès, who draws inspiration from the Basque country, Bordeaux, and Languedoc for his daily-changing menu. Traditional dishes such as scallops meunière (with butter and lemon) are matched with contemporary choices such as a splendid spelt risotto with truffles and frogs' legs or panfried duck liver with caramelized fruits and vegetables. One of the 19th-century paneled salons has been turned into a winter garden, and contemporary paintings adorn the walls. The service is flawless, and the exceptional wine list is well priced. All in all, a meal here comes as close to the classic haute-cuisine experience as you can find in Paris. There's an €80 lunch menu, with wines by the glass starting at €10. ✉ *15 rue Lamennais* ☎ *01–44–95–15–01* ✍ *Reservations essential; jacket and tie* ▭ *AE, DC, MC, V* ⊙ *Closed weekends, last wk in July, and 1st 3 wks in Aug.* Ⓜ *Charles-de-Gaulle–Étoile* ✣ *1:B2.*

$–$$ MODERN FRENCH Louvre/Tuileries, 1er

Willi's Wine Bar. More a restaurant than a wine bar, this British-owned spot is a stylish haunt for Parisian and visiting gourmands who might stop in for a glass of wine at the oak bar or settle into the wood-beam dining room. The selection of reinvented classic dishes changes daily and might include roast cod with artichokes and asparagus in spring, venison in wine sauce with roast pears and celery-root chips in fall, and mango candied with orange and served with vanilla cream in winter. Chef François Yon has been in the kitchen for 15 years, ensuring a consistency that isn't always reflected in the service. The restaurant is prix-fixe only but at the bar you order appetizers. The list of about 250 wines reflects co-owner Mark Williamson's passion for the Rhône Valley and Spanish sherries. *13 rue des Petits-Champs 01–42–61–05–09 www.williswinebar.com MC, V Closed Sun. Bourse 1:E3.*

$$–$$$ FRENCH FUSION Les Halles, 2e

Yam'Tcha. Adeline Grattard's little bistro has become so popular that tables are snapped up weeks ahead, which is no surprise when you learn that she worked at L'Astrance before spending time in Hong Kong, where she picked up many of her techniques. Inspired by Chinese cooking, many of her dishes rely on brilliant flavor combinations and very precise cooking. A signature dish is the roasted Challans duck with Sichuan-style eggplant: two elements that create magic together. Adeline's husband Chi Wa acts as a tea sommelier, though alcohol is also available. It's prix fixe only. *4 rue Sauval, Les Halles 01–40–26–08–07 Reservations essential MC, V Closed Mon. and Tues. Louvre-Rivoli or Les Halles 1:F4.*

$$$ MODERN FRENCH Quartier Latin, 6e

Ze Kitchen Galerie. William Ledeuil made his name at the popular Les Bouquinistes (a Guy Savoy baby bistro) before opening this contemporary bistro in a loftlike space. If the name isn't exactly inspired, the cooking shows creativity and a sense of fun: from a deliberately deconstructed menu featuring raw fish, soups, pastas, and *à la plancha* (grilled) plates, consider the roast and confit duck with a tamarind-and-sesame condiment and foie gras, or lobster with mussels, white beans, and Thai herbs. A tireless experimenter, Ledeuil buys heirloom vegetables direct from farmers and tracks down herbs and spices in Asian supermarkets. The menu changes monthly and there are several different prix-fixe options at lunch, starting at €29. *4 rue des Grands-Augustins 01–44–32–00–32 www.zekitchengalerie.fr AE, DC, MC, V Closed Sun. No lunch Sat. St-Michel 1:E4.*

¢–$ JAPANESE Louvre/Tuileries 1er

Zen. There is no shortage of Japanese restaurants in this area around the Louvre, but this recent addition is a cut above much of the competition. The white-and-lime-green space feels refreshingly bright and modern, and you can perch at one of the curvy counters or settle in at a table. The menu has something for every taste, from warming ramen soups (part of a €9.90 lunch menu that includes five pork dumplings) to sushi and sashimi prepared with particular care. For a change, try the *donburi,* a bowl of rice topped with meat or fish, or Japanese curry with breaded pork or shrimp. A sign of the chef's pride in his food is that he offers cooking classes some Sundays (in French). *8 rue de l'Échelle 01–42–61–93–99 MC, www.restaurant-zen.fr V Closed 10 days in mid-Aug. Pyramides or Palais Royal 1:E3.*

CAFÉS AND SALONS DE THÉ

Along with air, water, and wine (Parisians eat fewer and fewer three-course meals), the café remains one of the basic necessities of life in Paris; following is a small selection of cafés and *salons de thé* (tearooms) to whet your appetite. **Brasserie Lipp** (✉ *151 bd. St-Germain, St-Germain-des-Prés, 6e* ☎ *01–45–48–53–91* Ⓜ *St-Germain-des-Prés*), with its turn-of-the-20th-century decor, was a favorite spot of Hemingway's; today television celebrities, journalists, and politicians come here for coffee—but not the mediocre food—on the small glassed-in terrace off the main restaurant. **Café Marly** (✉ *Cour Napoléon du Louvre, 93 rue de Rivoli, Louvre/Tuileries, 1er* ☎ *01–49–26–06–60* Ⓜ *Palais-Royal*), overlooking the main courtyard of the Louvre, is perfect for an afternoon break or a nightcap. Note that ordinary café service shuts down during meal hours, when overpriced, mediocre food is served.

★ **La Charlotte en l'Ile** (✉ *24 rue St-Louis-en-l'Ile, Ile St-Louis, 4e* ☎ *01–43–54–25–83* Ⓜ *Pont-Marie*) would be fancied by the witch who baked gingerbread children in *Hansel and Gretel*—set with fairy lights, carnival masques, and decoupaged detritus, it's a tiny, storybook spot that offers more than 30 varieties of tea along with a sinfully good hot chocolate. **Le Progrès** (✉ *7 rue Trois , Montmartre, 18e* ☎ *01–42–64–07–37* Ⓜ *Abbesses*) draws a quirky mix, from retirees sipping espresso at the counter to hipsters, artists, and discriminating tourists. **les éditeurs** (✉ *4 carrefour de l'Odéon, St-Germain-des-Prés, 6e* ☎ *01–43–26–67–76* Ⓜ *St-Germain-des-Prés*) makes for a perfect setting to sip a kir (white wine with black currant syrup) alongside the Parisian publishing set, either from a perch on the skinny sidewalk or at an inside table shadowed by book-lined walls. **Le Flore en l'Ile** (✉ *42 quai d'Orléans, Ile St-Louis, 4e* ☎ *01–43–29–88–27* Ⓜ *Pont-Marie*) is on the Ile St-Louis and has a magnificent view of the Seine. **Ladurée** (✉ *16 rue Royale, Opéra/Grands Boulevards, 8e* ☎ *01–42–60–21–79* 🌐 *www.laduree.fr* Ⓜ *Madeleine* ✉ *75 av. des Champs-Élysées, Champs-Élysées, 8e* ☎ *01–40–75–08–75* Ⓜ *Georges V*) is pretty enough to bring a tear to Proust's eye—these salons de thé have barely changed since 1862 (there's another outpost on the Left Bank at 21 rue Bonaparte). For sheer Traviata opulence, the one on the Champs-Élysées can't be beat: wait until you see the pâtisserie counter or the super-sumptuous Salon Paéva. You can dote on the signature lemon-and-caramel macaroons, or try them in a dazzling array of other flavors including hazelnut praline, rose petal, pistachio, blackcurrant violet, or salted butter caramel. Oooooh! **Ma Bourgogne** (✉ *19 pl. des Vosges, Le Marais, 4e* ☎ *01–42–78–44–64* Ⓜ *St-Paul*), on magical Place des Vosges, is a calm oasis for a coffee or a light lunch away from the noisy streets. **Mariage Frères** (✉ *30 rue du Bourg-Tibourg, Le Marais, 4e* ☎ *01–42–72–28–11* Ⓜ *Hôtel-de-Ville*) is an outstanding tea shop serving 500 kinds of tea, along with delicious tarts. **La Palette** (*43 rue de Seine, St-Germain-des-Prés7e* ☎ *01–43–26–68–15* ☎ *St-Germain-des-Prés*) is a favorite haunt of local gallery owners and Beaux Arts students. Come at sunset—or later—when the scene gets lively.

WHERE TO STAY

Updated by Heather Stimmler-Hall

Winding staircases, flower-filled window boxes, concierges who seem to have stepped out of a 19th-century novel—all of these can still be found in Paris hotels, and despite the scales being tipped in favor of the well-heeled, overall there's good news for travelers of all budgets. Increased competition means the bar for service and amenities has been raised everywhere. Many good-value establishments in the lower-to-middle price ranges have updated their funky '70s wallpaper and "Why should I care, Madame?" attitudes, while still keeping their prices in check. Virtually every hotel is now equipped with cable TV to meet the needs of international guests. Now it's not uncommon for mid-range hotels to have a no-smoking floor, for inexpensive hotels to offer air-conditioning and buffet breakfast service, and even for budget places to have wireless Internet or an Internet terminal in their little lobbies. So, whatever price you're looking for, compared to most other cities Paris is a paradise for the weary traveler tired of dreary, out-of-date, or cookie-cutter rooms. The best hotels still emanate an unmistakable Paris vibe: weathered beamed ceilings, vaulted stone breakfast crypts, tall windows overlooking zinc rooftops, and leafy courtyards where you can sit and linger over your daily croissant and café.

Use the coordinate ⊕ 2:D4 at the end of each listing to locate a site on the corresponding map

1ER ARRONDISSEMENT (LOUVRE/LES HALLES)

$$$ **Hôtel Brighton.** Many of Paris's most prestigious palace hotels face the Tuileries or Place de la Concorde, and while the Brighton breathes the same rarified air under the arcades, it does so for a fraction of the price. Smaller rooms look onto a courtyard; street-facing ones have balconies and a royal view of the gardens and Rive Gauche. Extensive renovations updated all the rooms, with the newest ones featuring flat-screen TVs and heated towel racks. First-floor rooms have high ceilings. **Pros:** great views; central location in a prestigious neighborhood; free Wi-Fi. **Cons:** the busy street can make rooms with a view a bit noisy; variable quality in decor between rooms. ✉ *218 rue de Rivoli, Louvre/Tuileries* ☎ *01–47–03–61–61* 🌐 *www.paris-hotel-brighton.com* *61 rooms* *In-room: a/c, safe, Wi-Fi. In-hotel: laundry service* 💳 *AE, DC, MC, V* Ⓜ *Tuileries* ⊕ *2:D3.*

$$$ **Hôtel Britannique.** Open since 1861 and a stone's throw from the Louvre, the Britannique blends courteous English service with old-fashioned French elegance. Take the winding staircase to rooms done in a mix of attractive repro furniture and antiques. Wi-Fi and in-room flat-screen TVs lend an air of modernity. In World War I, the hotel served as headquarters for a Quaker mission. **Pros:** one of the city's most charming hotels, on a calm side street less than a block from the métro/RER station; attentive staff. **Cons:** smallish rooms; soundproofing between rooms could be better. ✉ *20 av. Victoria Beaubourg/Les Halles* ☎ *01–42–33–74–59* 🌐 *www.hotel-britannique.fr* *38 rooms, 1 suite* *In-room: a/c, safe, Wi-Fi. In-hotel: bar, laundry service* 💳 *AE, DC, MC, V* Ⓜ *Châtelet* ⊕ *2:F4.*

BEST BETS FOR PARIS LODGING

Fodor's offers a selective listing of quality lodging experiences at every price range, from the city's best budget motel to its most sophisticated luxury hotel. Here we've compiled our top recommendations by price and experience. The very best properties—those that provide a particularly remarkable experience in a price range—are designated in the listings with a Fodor's Choice logo.

Fodor's Choice ★

Four Seasons Hôtel George V Paris, 8e, p. 139
Hôtel Bel-Ami, 6e, p. 133
Hôtel Langlois, 9e, p. 143
Hôtel Mama Shelter, 20e, p. 145
Hôtel Odéon Saint-Germain, 6e, p. 135
Hôtel Relais Saint-Sulpice, 6e, p. 135
Hôtel Saint Merry, 4e, p. 129

By Price

¢

Hôtel Henri IV, 1e, p. 124
Hôtel Tiquetonne, 2e, p. 125
Port-Royal Hôtel, 5e, p. 133

$

Hôtel de Nesle, 6e, p. 134
Hôtel Familia, 5e, p. 131
Hôtel Mama Shelter, 20^{e}, p. 145

$$

Hôtel Amour, 9^{e}, p. 141
Hôtel Eiffel Rive Gauche, 7e, p. 138
Hôtel Familia, 5e, p. 131
Hôtel Langlois, 9e, p. 143

$$$

Hôtel Relais Saint-Sulpice, 6e, p. 135
Hôtel Saint Merry, 4e, p. 129

$$$$

Four Seasons Hôtel George V Paris, 8e, p. 139
Hôtel Duc de Saint-Simon, 7e, p. 136
Hôtel Plaza Athénée, 8e, p. 140
Hôtel Odéon Saint-Germain, 6e, p. 135

By Experience

MOST CHARMING

Hôtel Britannique, 1er, p. 119
Hôtel d'Aubusson, 6e, p. 134
Hôtel des Jardins du Luxembourg, 5e, p. 131
Les Degrés de Notre-Dame, 5e, p. 132

HISTORIC

Hôtel de la Place des Vosges, 4e, p. 128
Hôtel Odéon St-Germain, 6e, p. 135
Hôtel Saint Merry, 4e, p. 129
Ritz, 1er, p. 125

BEST DESIGN

Le Bellechasse, 7e, p. 138
The Five Hotel, 5e, p. 133

MOST CENTRAL

Hôtel Henri IV, 1er, p. 124
Hôtel Meurice, 1er, p. 124
Hôtel Saint-Louis Marais, 4e, p. 129

BUSINESS TRAVEL

Four Seasons Hôtel George V Paris, 8e, p. 139
Renaissance Paris Vendôme, 1e, p. 124

BEST VIEWS

Hôtel Brighton, 1er, p. 119
Hôtel Plaza Athénée, 8er, p. 140

MOST ROMANTIC

Hôtel Bourg Tibourg, 4e, p. 127
Hôtel Caron de Beaumarchais, 4e, p. 127
Hôtel Raphael, 16e, p. 144
L'Hôtel, 6e, p. 136

WHERE SHOULD I STAY?

	NEIGHBORHOOD VIBE	PROS	CONS
St-Germain and Montparnasse (6e, 14e, 15e)	The center of café culture and the emblem of the Left Bank, the mood is leisurely, the attractions are well established, and the prices are high.	A safe, historic area with chic fashion boutiques, famous cafés and brasseries, and lovely side streets. Lively day and night.	Expensive. Noisy along the main streets. The area around the monstrous Tour Montparnasse is a soul-sucking tribute to commerce.
The Quartier Latin (5e)	The historic student quarter of the Left Bank, full of narrow, winding streets, and major parks and monuments such as the Panthéon.	Plenty of cheap eats and sleeps, discount book and music shops, and noteworthy open-air markets. Safe area for wandering walks.	Touristy. No métro stations on the hilltop around the Panthéon. Student pubs can be noisy in summer. Hotel rooms tend to be smaller.
Marais and Bastille (3e, 4e, 11e)	Cute shops, museums, and laid-back bistros line the narrow streets of the Marais, home to both the gay and Jewish communities. Farther east, ethnic eats and edgy shops.	Generally excellent shopping, sightseeing, dining, and nightlife in the super-safe Marais. Bargains aplenty at Bastille hotels. Several modern-design hotels, too.	The Marais's narrow sidewalks are always overcrowded, and rooms don't come cheap. It's noisy around the gritty boulevards of Place de la Bastille and Nation.
Montmartre and northeast Paris (18e, 19e)	The hilltop district is known for winding streets leading from the racy Pigalle district to the stark-white Sacré-Coeur Basilica.	Amazing views of Paris, romantic cobblestone streets, easy access to Roissy-Charles de Gaulle airport.	Steep staircases, few métro stations, and Pigalle can be too seedy to stomach, especially late at night, when it can also be unsafe.
Champs-Élysées and western Paris (8e, 16e, 17e)	The world-famous avenue is lively 24/7 with cinemas, high-end shops, and nightclubs, all catering to the moneyed jet set.	The home to most of the city's famous palace hotels, there's no shortage of luxurious sleeps here.	The high prices of this neighborhood, along with its Times Square tendencies, repel Parisians but lure pickpockets.
Around the Tour Eiffel (7e, 15e)	The impressive Eiffel Tower and monumental Palais de Chaillot at Trocadéro straddle the Seine River.	Safe, quiet, and relatively inexpensive area of Paris with green spaces and picture-perfect views at every turn.	With few shops and restaurants, this district is very quiet at night; long distances between métro stations.
Louvre, Les Halles, Ile de la Cité (1e, 2e, 8e)	The central Parisian district around the Tuileries gardens and Louvre museum is best known for shopping and sightseeing; Les Halles is a buzzing hub of commerce and mass transit.	Convenient for getting around Paris on foot, bus, or métro. Safe, attractive district close to the Seine and shops of all types. All the major métro and RER lines are right by Les Halles.	The main drag along Rue de Rivoli can be noisy with traffic during the day, and the restaurants cater mostly to tourists. Shops are tacky and fast food predominates around Les Halles.

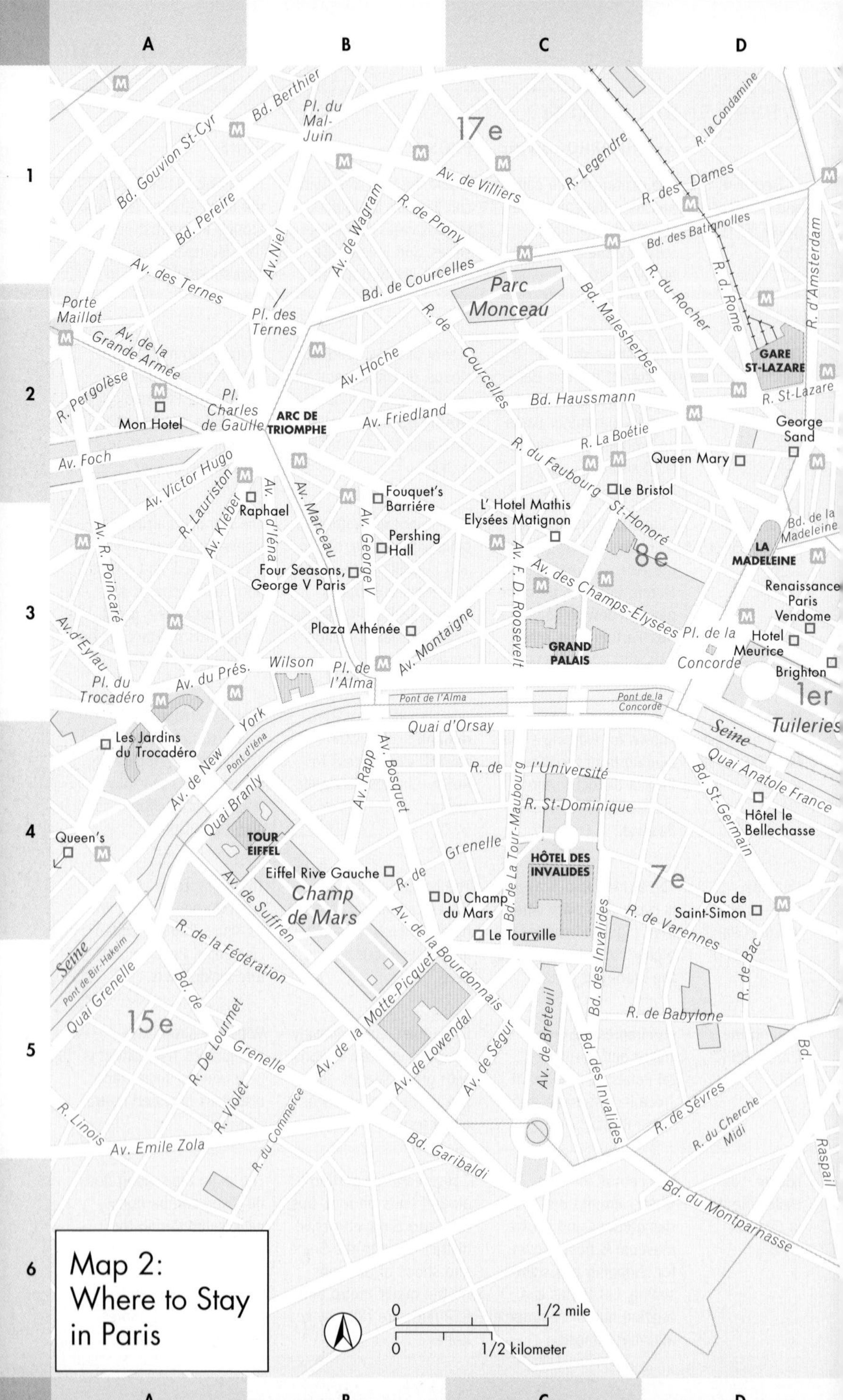

Map 2:
Where to Stay
in Paris
Mon Hotel
Raphael
Fouquet's Barriére
Pershing Hall
Four Seasons, George V Paris
Plaza Athénée
L' Hotel Mathis Elysées Matignon
Le Bristol
Queen Mary
George Sand
Renaissance Paris Vendome
Hotel Meurice
Brighton
Les Jardins du Trocadéro
Queen's
Eiffel Rive Gauche
Du Champ du Mars
Le Tourville
Hôtel le Bellechasse
Duc de Saint-Simon
ARC DE TRIOMPHE
GARE ST-LAZARE
LA MADELEINE
GRAND PALAIS
TOUR EIFFEL
HÔTEL DES INVALIDES
Parc Monceau
Champ de Mars
Tuileries
Seine
17e
8e
7e
15e
1er
1/2 mile
1/2 kilometer

E
F
G
H
1
2
3
4
5
6
18e
9e
19e
10e
2e
3e
4e
12e
5e
6e
SACRE-COEUR
GARE DU NORD
GARE DE L'EST
OPÉRA GARNIER
LOUVRE
CENTRE POMPIDOU
STE-CHAPELLE
NOTRE DAME
Ile de la Cité
Ile St-Louis
PALAIS DU LUXEMBOURG
Jardin du Luxembourg
Canal St-Martin
Seine
Utrillo
Royal Fromentin
Amour
Langlois
Chopin
Vivienne
Hôtel de Noailles
Ritz
Londres St-Honoré
Tiquetonne
Bellevue et du Chariot d'Or
Hôtel Mama Shelter
Murano Urban Resort
Résidence Alhambra
Beaumarchais
du Vieux Marais
de la Bretonnerie
Saint Merry
Duo
Britannique
Henri IV
L'Hôtel
de Nesle
D'Aubusson
Millésime
Bel-Ami
Le Relais Christine
du Lys
Bourg Tibourg
Caron de Beaumarchais
Jeanne-d'Arc
Pavillon de la Reine
de la Place des Vosges
Hotel Saint Louis
Saint-Louis Marais
Les Degrés de Notre-Dame
Bonaparte
L'Hotel Odéon Saint-Germain
Relais Saint-Sulpice
de l'Abbaye
Collège de France
Marignan
Saint-Jacques
Familia
Grandes Écoles
des Jardins du Lexembourg
Lyon-Bastille
Port-Royal
The Five
R. Caulaincourt
Bd. de Clichy
Bd. de Rochechouart
Bd. Barbès
R. Clignacourt
Bd. de la Chapelle
R. de Tanger
R. de Flandre
Av. Jean Jaurès
R. Blanche
Av. de Clichy
Av. Trudaine
R. Dunkerque
R. des Martyrs
R. de Maubeuge
R. Lamartine
R. de Châteaudun
R. Lafayette
R. de Paradis
Bd. de Magenta
Bd. de La Villette
R. de la Grange
R. Richer
Bd. Haussmann
Bd. Montmartre
Bd. Poissonnière
R. du Fg. Poissonnière
Bd. de Strasbourg
R. St-Maur
Bd. St-Denis
Bd. St-Martin
R. du Faubourg du Temple
Av. Parmentier
Pl. de la République
Rue Réaumur
Av. de l'Opéra
Pl. Vendôme
R. de Richelieu
R. Etienne Marcel
R. de Turbigo
Av. de la République
Bd. Voltaire
Bd. de Sebastopol
Bv. du Temple
R. de Rivoli
R. du Louvre
R. Berger
R. St-Honoré
R. Rambuteau
R. du Temple
R. des Archives
R. Vieille du Temple
R. de Turenne
Bd. Beaumarchais
R. Amelot
Bd. Richard Lenoir
Pl. des Vosges
R. St-Antoine
R. du Faubourg
Pl. de la Bastille
Bd. Henri IV
Bd. St-Germain
R. des Rennes
R. Bonaparte
R. St-Jacques
R. Vaugirard
R. Claude Bernard
Pont de Sully
Quai de Montebello
Av. Ledru Rollin
Bd. Diderot
Bd. St-Michel
KEY
Hotels
Métro
Following lodging reviews indicates a map-grid coordinate

¢ **Hôtel Henri IV.** When tourists think of staying on one of the islands, it's usually Ile St-Louis, not Ile de la Cité, but the overlooked isle shelters one of the city's most beloved budget-priced sleeps. The 17th-century building that once housed King Henri IV's printing presses offers few comforts: the narrow staircase (five flights, no elevator) creaks and the rooms have few amenities. Recent renovations, however, have added showers and toilets in almost every room. The payoff is a location overlooking the oasislike Place Dauphine, just a few steps from the Pont Neuf and Sainte-Chapelle. **Pros:** very quiet, central location; breakfast included. **Cons:** steep stairs and no elevator; few services or amenities; no e-mail or online reservations. ✉ *25 pl. Dauphine, Ile de la Cité* ☎ *01–43–54–44–53* 🌐 *www.henri4hotel.fr* *15 rooms, 11 with bath* *In-room: no a/c, no phone, no TV* ▭ *MC, V* *CP* Ⓜ *Cité, St-Michel, Pont Neuf* ✣ *2:F4.*

$$ **Hôtel Londres St-Honoré.** An appealing combination of character and comfort distinguishes this small, inexpensive hotel, which is a five-minute walk from the Louvre. Exposed oak beams, statues in niches, and rustic stone walls give this place an old-fashioned air. Most rooms have floral bedspreads and standard hotel furniture, though bathrooms are refreshingly modern, with real hair dryers. Note that elevator service begins on the second floor, so some stairs are guaranteed. **Pros:** within walking distance of major sites; free Wi-Fi. **Cons:** small elevator that doesn't go to ground floor; small beds; upper rooms can get very hot in summer (fans are available). ✉ *13 rue St-Roch* ☎ *01–42–60–15–62* 🌐 *www.hotellondresssthonore-paris.com* *21 rooms, 4 suites* *In-room: no a/c (some), safe, Wi-Fi. In-hotel: Internet terminal, some pets allowed* ▭ *AE, DC, MC, V* Ⓜ *Pyramides* ✣ *2:E3.*

$$$$ **Hôtel Meurice.** Since 1835, the Meurice has welcomed royalty and celebrities, from the Duchess of Windsor to Salvador Dalí. In late 2007 the lobby, bar, and restaurant were given a swanky makeover by French designer Philippe Starck. Rooms have a gilded Louis XVI or Napoleonic Empire style, with antique furnishings covered in sumptuous French and Italian brocades. Most rooms have a Tuileries/Louvre or Sacré-Coeur view, but the massive Royal Suite takes in a 360-degree panorama. Bathrooms are marble, with deep, spacious tubs. The health club includes grape-seed-based treatments, such as "cabernet sauvignon" massages; children are pampered with their own Meurice teddy bear and tot-size slippers and bathrobe. **Pros:** views over the gardens; central location; trendy public spaces. **Cons:** on a noisy street; popularity makes the public areas not very discreet. ✉ *228 rue de Rivoli, Louvre/Tuileries* ☎ *01–44–58–10–09* 🌐 *www.meuricehotel.com* *160 rooms, 36 suites* *In-room: a/c, safe, Internet. In-hotel: 2 restaurants, room service, bar, gym, Internet terminal, some pets allowed, no-smoking rooms* ▭ *AE, DC, MC, V* Ⓜ *Tuileries, Concorde* ✣ *2:D3.*

$$$$ ★ **Renaissance Paris Vendôme.** Hiding behind a classic 19th-century facade is a fresh, contemporary hotel with subtle 1930s influences. Under a huge atrium skylight, the lobby's polished black marble floors, lacquered hardwood furnishings, neutral fabrics, and decadent antiques set the mood. The small library has free Wi-Fi and a wood-burning fireplace, and the intimate Bar Chinois is decorated with elaborate Chinese

wallpaper. Imported woods and black slate accent the hotel's sauna, steam room, and countercurrent swimming pool. **Pros:** posh location; trendy restaurant; free Wi-Fi. **Cons:** as part of the Marriott group it can feel a bit lacking in character. ✉ *4 rue du Mont Thabor, Louvre/Tuileries* ☎ *01–40–20–20–00* 🌐 *www.renaissanceparisvendome.com* *82 rooms, 15 suites* *In-room: a/c, safe, DVD, Internet. In-hotel: restaurant, room service, bar, pool, gym, laundry service, Internet terminal, parking (paid)* ▭ *AE, DC, MC, V* Ⓜ *Tuileries* ✢ *2:D3.*

WORD OF MOUTH

"We always start at L'Étoile and walk up the Champs-Élysées to Ladurée—there's just something so breathtaking each time you see the Arc de Triomphe all lit up at night! But for romance you can't beat going up the beautiful marble stairs of Ladurée to the first two front salons—take a look at their Web site, which has photos and layouts of the various rooms to choose from." —Klondike

2

$$$$ **Ritz.** Ever since César Ritz opened the doors of his hotel in 1898, the mere name of this venerable institution has become synonymous with luxury. The famed Ritz Escoffier cooking school, where you can learn the finer points of *gateaux*, is here, as is the new Ritz Lounge Bar and the Hemingway Bar. There's also a Greek-temple-style subterranean spa and swimming pool. Guest rooms match this level of luxe; even the humbler spaces have every modern doodad, cleverly camouflaged with the decor of gleaming mirrors, chandeliers, and antiques. (Think marble baths with gold pull chains that summon the valet or maid.) The most palatial suites are named after famous Ritz residents: Coco Chanel, the Prince of Wales, and Elton John. **Pros:** spacious swimming pool; selection of bars and restaurants; top-notch service. **Cons:** can feel stuffy and old-fashioned; easy to get lost in the vast hotel; paparazzi magnet. ✉ *15 pl. Vendôme, Louvre/Tuileries* ☎ *01–43–16–30–30* 🌐 *www.ritzparis.com* *106 rooms, 56 suites* *In-room: a/c, safe, Wi-Fi. In-hotel: 3 restaurants, room service, bars, pool, gym, spa, children's programs (ages 6–12), laundry service, Internet terminal, parking (paid)* ▭ *AE, DC, MC, V* Ⓜ *Opéra* ✢ *2:E3.*

2E ARRONDISSEMENT (BOURSE/LES HALLES)

$$$ **Hôtel de Noailles.** With a nod to the work of postmodern designers like Putman and Starck, this style-driven boutique is both contemporary and cozy. Rooms are sleek and streamlined, with backlit, custom-built cabinets, glassed-in bathrooms, and fabric or faux-leather wall coverings. A spacious outdoor terrace is off the breakfast lounge. **Pros:** a block from the airport bus; easy walk to the Louvre and Opéra. **Cons:** small elevator; no interesting views. ✉ *9 rue de Michodière, Opéra/Grands Boulevards* ☎ *01–47–42–92–90* 🌐 *www.hoteldenoailles.com* *58 rooms* *In-room: a/c, safe, Wi-Fi. In-hotel: room service, bar, laundry service, some pets allowed* ▭ *AE, DC, MC, V* Ⓜ *Opéra* ✢ *2:E3.*

¢ **Hôtel Tiquetonne.** Just off the Montorgueil market and a short hoof from Les Halles (and slightly seedy Rue St-Denis), this is one of the least expensive hotels in the city center. The so-old-fashioned-they're-vintage-cool rooms aren't much to look at and have few amenities, but they're clean, and some are spacious. Cheaper rooms are available with just a sink (toilets and pay showers are in each hall). **Pros:** dirt-cheap rooms in the center of town; in a newly trendy shopping and nightlife area. **Cons:** minimal service and no amenities; noise from the street. ✉ *6 rue Tiquetonne, Beaubourg/Les Halles* ☎ *01–42–36–94–58* *45 rooms, 33 with bath* *In-room: no a/c, no TV. In-hotel: some pets allowed* *AE, MC, V* *Closed Aug. and last wk of Dec.* Ⓜ *Étienne Marcel* *2:F3.*

$ **Hôtel Vivienne.** The decor is a bit schizoid: some guest rooms have chandeliers, others have fuzzy brown rugs and busy bedspreads, and another is fashionably minimalist. Room Nos. 39, 40, and 41 are blessed with large rooftop balconies. The location near the Opéra Garnier and Grands Boulevards department stores and the free Internet station in the lobby make this a good bet in this price range. **Pros:** good value for central Paris; a block from the métro station; free Internet. **Cons:** a noisy street and late-night bar across the road can make it hard to keep windows open in summer; some rooms are small and ugly. ✉ *40 rue Vivienne, Opéra/Grands Boulevards* ☎ *01–42–33–13–26* *45 rooms, 35 with bath* *In-room: no a/c, Wi-Fi. In-hotel: some pets allowed* *MC, V* Ⓜ *Bourse, Richelieu Drouot* *2:F3.*

3E ARRONDISSEMENT (BEAUBOURG/MARAIS)

¢ **Hôtel Bellevue et du Chariot d'Or.** This old Belle Époque time traveler is proud to keep its dingy chandeliers and faded gold trimming. Budget groups from France and the Netherlands come for the clean, sans-frills rooms; some units sleep four. Halls are lined with stamped felt that helps muffle sounds trickling up from the marble-floor lobby and bar. There may be some quirks, but you're just a few blocks from hipper addresses in the heart of the Marais. **Pros:** large rooms great for families; Wi-Fi; easy walk to the Marais and Les Halles districts. **Cons:** on a very busy, noisy street; not the most attractive part of central Paris; drab decor. ✉ *39 rue de Turbigo, Beaubourg/Les Halles* ☎ *01–48–87–45–60* *www.hotelbellevue75.com* *59 rooms* *In-room: no a/c, Wi-Fi hotspot. In-hotel: bar* *AE, DC, MC, V* *BP* Ⓜ *Réaumur-Sébastopol, Arts et Métiers* *2:G3.*

$$$$ ★ **Murano Urban Resort.** As the epicenter of Parisian cool migrates eastward, it's no surprise that a design-conscious hotel has followed. On the trendy northern edge of the Marais, this cheeky hotel that dares to call itself a resort combines Austin Powers playfulness with serious 007-inspired gadgetry. A psychedelic elevator zooms guests to ultraviolet-light hallways, where they enter pristine white rooms via fingerprint sensor locks. Pop-art furniture and bedside control panels that change the color of the lighting keep guests amused—until it's time for cocktails. Stylish Parisians pack the hotel's vodka bar and sleek restaurant, where a live DJ holds court. Two suites have private terraces with heated, countercurrent pools. **Pros:** high-tech amenities and funky style; very trendy bar attracts stylish locals; brunch served until 5 PM on Sunday. **Cons:** on the far edge of the Marais on a noisy, busy boulevard; dark hallways can make it difficult to find your room; the white carpeting quickly shows wear and tear. ✉ *13 bd. du Temple, République* ☎ *01–42–71–20–00* *www.muranoresort.com* *43 rooms, 9 suites* *In-room: a/c, safe, DVD, Wi-Fi. In-hotel: restaurant, room service,*

bar, pool, gym, spa, laundry service, parking (paid), some pets allowed ▭ *AE, DC, MC, V* Ⓜ *Filles du Calvaire* ✥ *2:H3.*

$$$$ ★ **Pavillon de la Reine.** This enchanting countrylike château is hidden off the regal Place des Vosges behind a stunning garden courtyard. Gigantic beams, chunky stone pillars, original oils, and a weathered fireplace speak to the building's 1612 origins. The hotel has large doubles, duplexes, and suites decorated in either contemporary or 18th-century-style wall fabrics. Many rooms look out on the entry court or an interior Japanese-inspired garden. **Pros:** beautiful garden courtyard; typically Parisian historic character; proximity to the Place des Vosges without the noise. **Cons:** expensive for the Marais and the size of the rooms; the nearest métro is a few long blocks away. ✉ *28 pl. des Vosges, Le Marais* ☎ *01–40–29–19–19, 800/447–7462 in U.S.* 🌐 *www.pavillon-de-la-reine.com* *30 rooms, 26 suites* *In-room: a/c, safe, Wi-Fi. In-hotel: room service, bar, laundry service, parking (free), some pets allowed* ▭ *AE, DC, MC, V* Ⓜ *Bastille, St-Paul* ✥ *2:H4.*

4ᴱ ARRONDISSEMENT (MARAIS/ILE ST-LOUIS)

$ ★ **Grand Hôtel Jeanne-d'Arc.** You can get your money's worth at this hotel in an unbeatable location off the tranquil Place du Marché Ste-Catherine, one of the city's lesser-known pedestrian squares. The 17th-century building has been a hotel for more than a century, and although rooms are on the spartan side, they're well maintained, with spotless tiled bathrooms and cheery, if somewhat mismatched, colors (some rooms facing the back are more muted). The welcoming staff is informal and happy to recount the history of this former market quartier. **Pros:** charming street close to major sites; good value for Le Marais; lots of drinking and dining options nearby. **Cons:** late-night revelers on the square can be noisy after midnight; minimal amenities; rooms have varying quality and size. ✉ *3 rue de Jarente, Le Marais* ☎ *01–48–87–62–11* 🌐 *www.hoteljeannedarc.com* *36 rooms* *In-room: no a/c. In-hotel: Wi-Fi, some pets allowed* ▭ *MC, V* Ⓜ *St-Paul* ✥ *2:G4.*

$$$ ★ **Hôtel Bourg Tibourg.** Scented candles and subdued lighting announce designer-du-jour Jacques Garcia's mix of haremlike romance and Gothic contemplation. Royal-blue paint and red velvet line the claustrophobic halls, and Byzantine alcoves hold mosaic-tile tubs. Rooms are barely bigger than the beds, and every inch has been upholstered, tasseled, and draped in a cacophony of stripes, florals, and medieval motifs. A pocket garden has room for three tables, leafy plants, and a swath of stars above. **Pros:** quiet side street in central Paris; luxurious style at moderate prices; great nightlife district. **Cons:** rooms are small and ill equipped for those with large suitcases; no hotel restaurant. ✉ *19 rue Bourg Tibourg, Le Marais* ☎ *01–42–78–47–39* 🌐 *www.hotelbourgtibourg.com* *29 rooms, 1 suite* *In-room: a/c, safe, Wi-Fi. In-hotel: room service, laundry service* ▭ *AE, DC, MC, V* Ⓜ *Hôtel de Ville* ✥ *2:G4.*

$$ ★ **Hôtel Caron de Beaumarchais.** The theme of this intimate, romantic hotel is the work of former next-door neighbor Pierre-Augustin Caron de Beaumarchais, supplier of military aid to American revolutionaries and a playwright who penned *The Marriage of Figaro* and *The Barber of Seville*. First-edition copies of his books adorn the public spaces, and the salons reflect the taste of 18th-century French nobility—down to the

wallpaper and 1792 pianoforte. Richly decorated with floral fabrics and period furnishings, the rooms have original beams and hand-painted bathroom tiles, as well as flat-screen TVs and Wi-Fi. **Pros:** cozy, historic Parisian decor; central location within easy walking distance to major monuments. **Cons:** small rooms; busy street of bars and cafés can be noisy. ✉ *12 rue Vieille-du-Temple, Le Marais* ☎ *01–42–72–34–12* 🌐 *www.carondebeaumarchais.com* *19 rooms* *In-room: a/c, safe, Wi-Fi. In-hotel: laundry service* ▭ *AE, DC, MC, V* Ⓜ *Hôtel de Ville* ✣ *2:G4.*

$$ **Hôtel de la Bretonnerie.** This small hotel is in a 17th-century *hôtel particulier* (town house) on a tiny street in the Marais, a few minutes' walk from the Centre Pompidou and the bars and cafés of Rue Vieille du Temple. Rooms are classified as either *chambres classiques* or *chambres de charme,* the latter being more spacious, and naturally pricier, but with more elaborate furnishings, like Louis XIII–style four-poster canopy beds and marble-clad bathtubs. Overall, the establishment is spotless, and the staff is welcoming. **Pros:** central location and comfortable decor at a moderate price; typical Parisian character; Wi-Fi. **Cons:** quality and size of the rooms vary greatly; location in heart of bustling gay district may not please everyone. ✉ *22 rue Ste-Croix-de-la-Bretonnerie, Le Marais* ☎ *01–48–87–77–63* 🌐 *www.bretonnerie.com* *22 rooms, 7 suites* *In-room: no a/c, safe, Wi-Fi. In-hotel: laundry service* ▭ *MC, V* Ⓜ *Hôtel de Ville* ✣ *2:G4.*

$ **Hôtel de la Place des Vosges.** Despite a lack of some expected comforts and an elevator that doesn't serve all floors, a loyal clientele swears by this small, historic hotel on a street leading directly into Place des Vosges. The Louis XIII–style reception area and rooms with oak-beam ceilings, rough-hewn stone, and a mix of rustic finds from secondhand shops evoke the Old Marais. The lone top-floor room, the hotel's largest, has a Jacuzzi and a view over Rive Droite rooftops. Other, considerably smaller rooms are cheaper. Fans are provided in summer. **Pros:** excellent location; fans on request; historic Parisian decor; good value rates for the amenities **Cons:** no air-conditioning; most rooms are very small; street-facing rooms can be noisy. ✉ *12 rue de Birague, Le Marais* ☎ *01–42–72–60–46* 🌐 *www.hotelplacedesvosges.com* *16 rooms* *In-room: no a/c, safe, Wi-Fi* ▭ *AE, DC, MC, V* Ⓜ *Bastille* ✣ *2:H4.*

$$$ ★ **Hôtel Duo.** The former Axial Beaubourg hotel doubled in size and changed its name in 2006. It now has a fresh, contemporary style with bold colors and dramatic lighting, particularly in the newer wing, and the original 16th-century beams add character to the older rooms. Amenities include a small fitness area, a sauna, and a stylish bar and breakfast lounge that fits in perfectly with the hip design vibe of the Marais district. **Pros:** trendy Marais location; walking distance to major monuments; choice of two different room styles. **Cons:** noisy street; service not always delivered with a smile. ✉ *11 rue du Temple, Le Marais* ☎ *01–42–72–72–22* 🌐 *www.duoparis.com* *58 rooms* *In-room: safe, Wi-Fi. In-hotel: room service, bar, gym, laundry service* ▭ *AE, DC, MC, V* Ⓜ *Hôtel de Ville* ✣ *2:G4.*

$$ **Hôtel du Vieux Marais.** A great value for the money in one of the most popular neighborhoods in Paris, this pleasingly minimalist hotel with a

fin de siècle facade is on a quiet street in the heart of Le Marais. Rooms are bright and impeccably clean, with contemporary oak furnishings, burgundy-leather seating, and velour curtains. Bathrooms are immaculately tiled in Italian marble, with walk-in showers or combination shower/tubs. If you prefer a bit of extra space, ask about special rates on the triple rooms. The staff is exceptionally friendly, and the lobby has Wi-Fi. **Pros:** quiet side street location in central Paris; good value for the size and comfort. **Cons:** some rooms are very small and face a dark inner courtyard; decor lacks character. ✉ *8 rue du Plâtre, Le Marais* ☎ *01–42–78–47–22* 🌐 *www.vieuxmarais.com* *30 rooms* *In-room: a/c, safe, Wi-Fi* ▭ *MC, V* Ⓜ *Hôtel de Ville* ✣ *2:G4.*

$$ **Hôtel Saint Louis.** The location on the Ile St-Louis is the real draw of this modest hotel, which retains many of its original 17th-century stone walls and wooden beams. Tiny balconies on the upper levels have Seine views. Number 51 has a tear-shape tub and a peek at the Panthéon. Breakfast is served in the vaulted stone cellar. **Pros:** romantic location on the tiny island Ile St-Louis; ancient architectural details; air-conditioning. **Cons:** the location makes the price high; métro stations are across the bridge; small rooms. ✉ *75 rue St-Louis-en-l'Ile* ☎ *01–46–34–04–80* 🌐 *www.hotelsaintlouis.com* *19 rooms* *In-room: a/c, safe, Wi-Fi. In-hotel: some pets allowed* ▭ *MC, V* Ⓜ *Pont Marie* ✣ *2:G5*

$$ **Hôtel Saint-Louis Marais.** Once an annex to a local convent, this 18th-century hotel has retained its stone walls and beams while adding red-clay tile floors and antiques. A wooden-banister stair leads to the small but proper rooms, decorated with basic red carpet and green bedspreads. (Those with heavy luggage, beware: no elevator.) One room is equipped with a kitchenette. The hotel's in Village St-Paul, a little tangle of medieval lanes just south of the well-traveled Marais that has an excellent English-language bookstore and is not yet overrun by tourists. **Pros:** quiet area of the Marais within walking distance of the islands and Bastille; historic Parisian character; Wi-Fi. **Cons:** no elevator; small rooms with outdated decor. ✉ *1 rue Charles V, Le Marais* ☎ *01–48–87–87–04* 🌐 *www.saintlouismarais.com* *19 rooms* *In-room: no a/c, safe, Wi-Fi. In-hotel: laundry service, Internet terminal, parking (paid), some pets allowed* ▭ *DC, MC, V* Ⓜ *Sully Morland, Bastille* ✣ *2:G5.*

$$–$$$ Fodor's Choice ★ **Hôtel Saint-Merry.** Due south of the Pompidou Center is this small and stunning Gothic hideaway, once the presbytery of the adjacent Saint Merry church. In its 17th-century stone interior you can gaze through stained glass, relax on a church pew, or lean back on a headboard recycled from an old Catholic confessional. With a massive hardwood table, fireplace, and high ceiling, the suite is fit for a royal council. Room 9 is bisected by stone buttresses still supporting the church. The Saint Merry's lack of an elevator and 21st-century temptations like TV is also in keeping with its ascetic past. **Pros:** unique medieval character; central location on a pedestrian street full of cafés and shops. **Cons:** no amenities; street-facing rooms can be too noisy to open windows in summer. ✉ *78 rue de la Verrerie, Beaubourg/Les Halles* ☎ *01–42–78–14–15* 🌐 *www.hotelmarais.com* *11 rooms, 1 suite* *In-room: no a/c (some), safe, no TV (some), Wi-Fi. In-hotel: room service, laundry*

Fodor's Choice ★

Hôtel d'Aubusson.

Hôtel Langlois

Hôtel Mama Shelter

service, some pets allowed ▭ *AE, MC, V* Ⓜ *Châtelet, Hôtel de Ville* ✣ *2:F4.*

5E ARRONDISSEMENT (LATIN QUARTER)

$ **Hôtel Collège de France.** Exposed-stone walls, wooden beams, and medieval artwork echo the style of the Musée Cluny, two blocks from this small, family-run hotel. Rooms convey a less elaborate, more streamlined aesthetic than the lobby and are relatively quiet owing to the side-street location. Number 62, on the top floor, costs a bit more but has a small balcony with superb views. **Pros:** walking distance to major Rive Gauche sights and the islands; free Wi-Fi; good value. **Cons:** big difference between renovated and unrenovated rooms; no air-conditioning; thin walls between rooms. ✉ *7 rue Thénard, Quartier Latin* ☎ *01–43–26–78–36* 🌐 *www.hotel-collegedefrance.com* *29 rooms* *In-room: no a/c, safe, Wi-Fi. In-hotel: room service* ▭ *AE, DC, MC, V* Ⓜ *Maubert-Mutualité, St-Michel–Cluny–La Sorbonne* ✣ *2:F5.*

$$ ★ **Hôtel des Jardins du Luxembourg.** Blessed with a personable staff and a smart, stylish look, this hotel, on an unbelievably calm cul-de-sac just a block from the Luxembourg Gardens, is an oasis for contemplation. A cheery hardwood-floor lobby with fireplace leads to smallish rooms furnished with wrought-iron beds, puffy duvets, and contemporary bathrooms. Ask for one with a balcony, or request one of the larger ground-floor rooms with private entrance directly onto the street. **Pros:** quiet street close to gardens; nice decor; hot buffet breakfast; close to RER station to airport or Eurostar. **Cons:** extra charge to use Wi-Fi; some very small rooms; weak air-conditioning. ✉ *5 impasse Royer-Collard* ☎ *01–40–46–08–88* 🌐 *www.les-jardins-du-luxembourg.com* *26 rooms* *In-room: a/c, safe, Wi-Fi In-hotel: laundry service* ▭ *AE, DC, MC, V* Ⓜ *RER: Luxembourg* ✣ *2:E6.*

$–$$ **Hôtel Familia.** Owners Eric and Sylvie continue to update and improve their popular budget hotel without raising the prices. They've added custom-carved wooden furniture from Brittany, new carpeting, and antique tapestries and prints on the walls. The second and fifth floors have balconies (some with views of Notre-Dame) and all of the rooms are soundproofed from traffic below, though noise between rooms can be loud. **Pros:** attentive, friendly service; great value; has all the modern conveniences. **Cons:** on a busy street; some rooms are small; noise between rooms can be loud. ✉ *11 rue des Écoles* ☎ *01–43–54–55–27* 🌐 *www.hotel-paris-familia.com* *30 rooms* *In-room: a/c. In-hotel: laundry service, Wi-Fi, parking (paid)* ▭ *AE, DC, MC, V* *CP* Ⓜ *Cardinal-Lemoine* ✣ *2:F5.*

$$ **Hôtel Grandes Écoles.** Guests enter Madame Lefloch's country-style domain through two massive wooden doors. Distributed among a trio of three-story buildings, rooms have a distinct grandmotherly vibe with flowery wallpaper and lace bedspreads, but are downright spacious for this part of Paris. The Grandes Écoles is legendary for its cobbled interior courtyard and garden, which becomes the second living room and a perfect breakfast spot, weather permitting. Rooms in the "garden" wing are coolest in summer. **Pros:** large courtyard garden; close to Quartier Latin nightlife spots; good value. **Cons:** uphill walk from the métro; outdated decor; few amenities. ✉ *75 rue du Cardinal Lemoine*

☎ *01–43–26–79–23* 🌐 *www.hotel-grandes-ecoles.com* *51 rooms* *In-room: no a/c, no TV, Wi-Fi. In-hotel: room service, parking (paid), some pets allowed* ▭ *MC, V* Ⓜ *Cardinal Lemoine* ✣ *2:F6.*

¢–$ **Hôtel Marignan.** Paul Keniger, the energetic third-generation owner, has cultivated a convivial atmosphere for independent international travelers. Not to be confused with the hotel of the same name near the Champs-Elysées, this Marignan lies squarely between budget-basic and youth hostel (no TVs or elevator) and offers lots of communal conveniences—a fully stocked kitchen, free laundry machines, and copious tourist information. Rooms are modest (some sleep four or five) but generally large, and bathrooms are clean. It's a good choice for families. The least expensive rooms share toilets and/or showers. **Pros:** great value for the location; kitchen and laundry; free Wi-Fi. **Cons:** no elevator; room phones only take incoming calls; has a bit of a youth-hostel atmosphere. ✉ *13 rue du Sommerard, Quartier Latin* ☎ *01–43–54–63–81* 🌐 *www.hotel-marignan.com* *30 rooms, 12 with bath* *In-room: no a/c, no TV, Wi-Fi. In-hotel: laundry facilities* ▭ *MC, V* *CP* Ⓜ *Maubert Mutualité* ✣ *2:F5.*

$–$$ ★ **Hôtel Saint-Jacques.** Nearly every wall in this bargain hotel is bedecked with faux-marble and trompe-l'oeil murals. As in many old, independent Paris hotels, each room is unique, but a general 19th-century theme of Second Empire furnishings and paintings dominates, with a Montmartre cabaret theme in the new breakfast room. Wi-Fi is available in the lounge bar. About half the rooms have tiny step-out balconies that give a glimpse of Notre-Dame and the Panthéon. Room 25 has a long, around-the-corner balcony, and No. 16 is popular for its historic ceiling fresco and moldings. Repeat guests get souvenir knickknacks or T-shirts. **Pros:** unique Parisian decor; close to Quartier Latin sights. **Cons:** very busy street makes it too noisy to open windows in summer; thin walls between rooms. ✉ *35 rue des Écoles* ☎ *01–44–07–45–45* 🌐 *www.hotel-saintjacques.com* *38 rooms* *In-room: no a/c (some), safe, Wi-Fi. In-hotel: bar, Internet terminal* ▭ *AE, DC, MC, V* Ⓜ *Maubert-Mutualité* ✣ *2:F5.*

$$ ★ **Les Degrés de Notre Dame.** On a quiet lane a few yards from the Seine, this diminutive hotel is lovingly decorated with the owner's flea-market finds. Number 23 is the largest of the lower-price rooms, whereas the more costly No. 24 has more space, wooden floors, and particularly appealing antique furnishings. The most expensive room, No. 501, occupies the entire top floor, with views of Notre-Dame and space for four guests. There's no elevator, but colorful murals of Parisian scenes decorate the winding stairwell. The shabby-chic Parisian character of the hotel and its French-Moroccan restaurant-bar make this unique establishment charming and unforgettable. **Pros:** within walking distance of Notre-Dame and Ile St-Louis; attractive location in quiet part of Quartier Latin; popular locals' restaurant. **Cons:** no air-conditioning; outdated decor; no elevator. ✉ *10 rue des Grands Degrés* ☎ *01–55–42–88–88* 🌐 *www.lesdegreshotel.com* *10 rooms* *In-room: no a/c (some), safe. In-hotel: restaurant, bar, Wi-Fi, no kids under 12* ▭ *MC, V* *CP* Ⓜ *Maubert-Mutualité* ✣ *2:F5.*

¢ ★ **Port-Royal Hôtel.** The spotless rooms and extra-helpful staff at the Port-Royal are well above average for this price range. Just below the Rue Mouffetard market at the edge of the 13e arrondissement, it may be somewhat removed from the action, but the snug antiques-furnished lounge areas, garden courtyard, and rooms with wrought-iron beds make it worth the trip. Rooms at the lower end of the price range are equipped only with sinks (an immaculate shared shower room is in the hallway). **Pros:** excellent value for the money; attentive service; typical Parisian neighborhood close to two major markets. **Cons:** not very central; on a busy street; few amenities. ✉ *8 bd. de Port-Royal* ☎ *01–43–31–70–06* *46 rooms, 20 with bath/shower* *In-room: no a/c, no TV* *No credit cards* Ⓜ *Les Gobelins* *2:F6.*

$$ **The Five Hôtel.** Small is beautiful at this tiny design hotel on a quiet street near the Mouffetard market. Rooms combine cozy and high-tech features such as fiber-optic fairy lights above the beds and in the bathrooms, fluffy duvet comforters, original Chinese lacquer artworks, and 400 satellite channels on flat-screen TVs. All rooms have free Wi-Fi and L'Occitane toiletries; the ground-floor suite has a private Jacuzzi patio. The One by the Five apartment-hotel across the street provides a luxurious getaway for a romantic weekend. **Pros:** stylish design; personalized welcome; quiet side street. **Cons:** most rooms are too small for excessive baggage; the nearest métro is a 10-minute walk. ✉ *3 rue Flatters* ☎ *01–43–31–74–21* *www.thefivehotel.com* *24 rooms* *In-room: a/c, safe, Wi-Fi. In-hotel: room service, laundry service* *AE, DC, MC, V* Ⓜ *Gobelins* *2:F6.*

6^E^ ARRONDISSEMENT (ST-GERMAIN)

$$$$ Fodor's Choice ★ **Hôtel Bel-Ami.** Just a stroll from Café de Flore, the Bel-Ami hides its past as an 18th-century textile factory behind veneer furnishings and crisply jacketed staff. You're immediately hit by the Conran Shop–meets–espresso bar lobby, with club music and a sleek fireplace lounge to match. There's Wi-Fi throughout, and a fitness center with sauna and Tibetan massage treatment rooms. Rooms lean toward minimalist chic in soothing colors but are transformed often to keep up with the hotel's young and trendy clientele. It fills up fast when the fashion circus comes to town. **Pros:** upscale, stylish hotel; central St-Germain-des-Prés location; spacious fitness center and spa. **Cons:** some guests report loud noise between rooms; some very small rooms in lower price category. ✉ *7–11 rue St-Benoît* ☎ *01–42–61–53–53* *www.hotel-bel-ami.com* *113 rooms, 2 suites* *In-room: a/c, safe, Wi-Fi. In-hotel: room service, bar, gym, laundry service* *AE, DC, MC, V* Ⓜ *St-Germain-des-Prés* *2:E4.*

$$–$$$ **Hôtel Bonaparte.** The congenial staff makes a stay in this intimate hotel a special treat. Old-fashioned upholsteries and 19th-century furnishings make the relatively spacious rooms feel comfortable and unpretentious. Services may be basic, but the location in the heart of St-Germain is fabulous. Light sleepers should request rooms overlooking the courtyard. **Pros:** upscale shopping neighborhood; large rooms for the Rive Gauche; newly upgraded air-conditioning. **Cons:** outdated decor and some tired mattresses. ✉ *61 rue Bonaparte* ☎ *01–43–26–97–37* *www.*

hotelbonaparte.fr *29 rooms* *In-room: a/c, safe, refrigerator, Wi-Fi (some)* *MC, V* *CP* *St-Sulpice* *2:E5.*

$$$$ **Hôtel d'Aubusson.** The staff greets you warmly at this 17th-century town house and former literary salon. The showpiece is the stunning front lobby spanned by massive beams and headed by a gigantic fireplace. Decked out in rich burgundies, greens, or blues, the bedrooms are filled with Louis XV– and Regency-style antiques and Hermès toiletries; even the smallest rooms are a generous size by Paris standards. Behind the paved courtyard is a second structure with three apartments, which are ideal for families. The hotel's Café Laurent hosts jazz musicians Thursday through Saturday evenings, and piano on Wednesdays. All returning guests (and new guests who book at least three nights) get VIP treatment such as champagne and flowers on arrival. **Pros:** central location near shops and market street; live jazz on weekends; personalized welcome. **Cons:** some of the newer rooms lack character; busy street; bar can be noisy on weekends. *33 rue Dauphine, St-Germain-des-Prés* *01–43–29–43–43* *www.hoteldaubusson.com* *49 rooms* *In-room: a/c, safe, DVD (some), Wi-Fi. In-hotel: room service, bar, laundry service, parking (paid), some pets allowed* *AE, DC, MC, V* *Odéon* *2:E4.*

$$$ **Hôtel de l'Abbaye.** This hotel on a tranquil side street near St-Sulpice welcomes you with a cobblestone ante-courtyard and vaulted stone entrance. The lobby's salon bears vestiges of the original 18th-century convent and the spacious garden comes replete with a fountain. Rooms are either a mix of floral and striped fabrics with period furnishings or contemporary minimalist with wood paneling and modern art. All have flat-screen TVs, and upper floors have oak beams and sitting alcoves. Duplexes (split-level suites) have lovely private terraces. **Pros:** tranquil setting in upscale neighborhood; good value for price. **Cons:** rooms differ greatly in size and style; some are quite small. *10 rue Cassette* *01–45–44–38–11* *www.hotel-abbaye.com* *42 rooms, 4 suites* *In-room: a/c, safe, Wi-Fi. In-hotel: room service, bar, laundry service, Internet terminal* *AE, MC, V* *CP* *St-Sulpice* *2:E5.*

$ ★ **Hôtel de Nesle.** This one-of-a-kind budget hotel is like a quirky and enchanting dollhouse. Services are bare-bones—no elevator, phones, TVs, or breakfast—but the payoff is in the snug rooms cleverly decorated by theme. Sleep in Notre-Dame de Paris, lounge in an Asian-style boudoir, spend the night with writer Molière, or steam it up in Le Hammam. Decorations include colorful murals, canopy beds, and custom lamps. Most rooms overlook an interior garden, and the dead-end-street location keeps the hotel relatively quiet. If you book one of the 11 rooms without a shower, you'll have to share the one bathroom on the second floor. **Pros:** unique, fun vibe; good value for chic location; small garden. **Cons:** few amenities or services; reservations by phone only. *7 rue de Nesle* *01–43–54–62–41* *www.hoteldenesleparis.com* *20 rooms, 9 with bath* *In-room: no a/c, no phone, no TV, Wi-Fi. In-hotel: Internet terminal, some pets allowed* *MC, V* *Odéon* *2:E4.*

$–$$ **Hôtel du Lys.** To jump into an inexpensive Parisian fantasy, just climb the stairway to your room (there's no elevator) in this former 17th-century royal residence. Well maintained by Madame Steffen, the endearingly odd-shape guest rooms have tiny nooks, weathered antiques, and exposed beams. It may be modest, but it's extremely atmospheric. Breakfast is served in the lobby or in your room. **Pros:** central location on a quiet side street; historic character. **Cons:** old-fashioned decoration is decidedly outdated; perfunctory service; no air-conditioning. ✉ *23 rue Serpente* ☎ *01–43–26–97–57* 🌐 *www.hoteldulys.com* *22 rooms* *In-room: no a/c, safe. In-hotel: some pets allowed* ▭ *MC, V* *CP* Ⓜ *St-Michel, Odéon* ✥ *2:F5.*

$$$ **Hôtel Millésime.** Step through the doors of this St-Germain-des-Prés hotel and you'll feel transported to the sunny south of France. Rooms in this 17th-century city mansion are decorated in warm reds, yellows, and royal blues, with rich fabrics and sparkling tiled bathrooms. The centerpiece is the gorgeous Provençal courtyard with ocher walls and wrought-iron balconies (Room 15 has direct access). Friendly service and a bountiful buffet breakfast make this a great find. **Pros:** upscale shopping location; young, friendly staff; well-appointed rooms. **Cons:** ground floor rooms can be noisy; larger rooms are significantly more expensive. ✉ *15 rue Jacob* ☎ *01–44–07–97–97* 🌐 *www.millesimehotel.com* *20 rooms, 1 suite* *In-room: a/c, safe, Wi-Fi. In-hotel: room service, bar, laundry service, Internet terminal, some pets allowed* ▭ *AE, MC, V* *CP* Ⓜ *St-Germain-des-Prés* ✥ *2:E4.*

$$$$ Fodor's Choice ★ **Hôtel Odéon Saint-Germain.** The exposed stone walls and original wooden beams give this 16th-century building typical Left Bank character, and designer Jacques Garcia's generous use of striped taffeta curtains, velvet upholstery, and plush carpeting imbues the family-run hotel with the distinct luxury of St-Germain-des-Prés. Several small rooms decorated with comfy armchairs and Asian antiques make up the lobby, where guests can help themselves to a continental buffet breakfast in the morning and an honesty bar throughout the day. Rooms are decorated in eggplant and caramel, with flat-screen TVs and designer toiletries. The ones overlooking the street have more space and double windows for soundproofing. **Pros:** warm welcome; free Internet; luxuriously appointed, historic building in an upscale shopping district. **Cons:** small rooms aren't convenient for those with extra-large suitcases. ✉ *13 rue St-Sulpice* ☎ *01–43–25–70–11* 🌐 *www.paris-hotel-odeon.com* *22 rooms, 5 junior suites* *In-room: safe, Wi-Fi. In hotel: a/c, room service, bar, laundry service, Internet terminal, some pets allowed* ▭ *DC, MC, V* Ⓜ *Odeon* ✥ *2:E5.*

$$$ Fodor's Choice ★ **Hôtel Relais St-Sulpice.** A savvy clientele frequents this fashionable little hotel sandwiched between St-Sulpice and the Jardin du Luxembourg. Eclectic art objects and furnishings, some with an Asian theme, oddly pull off a unified look. A zebra-print stuffed armchair sits beside an Art Deco desk, and an African mud cloth hangs above a neo-Roman pillar. The rooms themselves, set around an ivy-clad courtyard, are understated, with Provençal fabrics, carved wooden furnishings, and sisal carpeting. Downstairs there's a sauna and a glass-roofed breakfast salon. Room 11 has a terrific view of St-Sulpice. **Pros:** chic location; close to two métro stations; bright breakfast room and courtyard; good value. **Cons:** smallish rooms in the lower category; noise from the street on weekend evenings. ✉ *3 rue Garancière* ☎ *01–46–33–99–00* 🌐 *www.*

relais-saint-sulpice.com 26 *rooms* *In-room: a/c, safe, Wi-Fi. In-hotel: laundry service* *AE, DC, MC, V* M *St-Germain-des-Prés, St-Sulpice* *2:E5.*

$$$$ **L'Hôtel.** Why do rock stars love this eccentric and opulent boutique hotel? Though sophisticated in every way, there's something just a bit naughty in the air. Is it its history as an 18th-century *pavillion d'amour* (inn for trysts)? Is it that Oscar Wilde permanently checked out in Room 16, back in 1900? Or is it Jacques Garcia's makeover—rooms done in yards of thick, rich fabrics in colors like deep red and emerald green? We say all of the above, plus the intimate bar and restaurant allows guests to mingle with the Parisian *beau monde.*A grotto holds a countercurrent pool and a steam room. **Pros:** luxurious decor; elegant bar and restaurant; walking distance to the Orsay and the Louvre. **Cons:** some rooms are very small for the price; closest métro station is a few blocks' walk. *13 rue des Beaux-Arts, St-Germain-des-Prés* *01–44–41–99–00* *www.l-hotel.com* *16 rooms, 4 suites* *In-room: a/c, safe, Wi-Fi. In-hotel: restaurant, room service, bar, pool, laundry service, some pets allowed* *AE, DC, MC, V* M *St-Germain-des-Prés* *2:E4.*

$$$$ ★ **Relais Christine.** This exquisite property was once a 13th-century abbey, but don't expect monkish quarters. You enter from the impressive stone courtyard into a lobby and fireside honor bar done up in rich fabrics, stone, wood paneling, and antiques. The cavernous breakfast room and adjacent fitness center flaunt their vaulted medieval stonework. The spacious, high-ceiling rooms (many spanned by massive beams) offer a variety of classical and contemporary styles: Asian-theme wall fabrics or plain stripes, rich aubergine paints or regal scarlet-and-gold. Split-level lofts house up to five people, and several ground-level rooms open onto a lush garden with private patios and heaters. **Pros:** quiet location while still close to the action; historic character; luxuriously appointed rooms. **Cons:** some guests report noise from doors on the street; no on-site restaurant. *3 rue Christine* *01–40–51–60–80, 800/525–4800 in U.S.* *www.relais-christine.com* *33 rooms, 18 suites* *In-room: a/c, safe, DVD (some), Wi-Fi. In-hotel: room service, bar, gym, spa, laundry service, Internet terminal, parking (free), some pets allowed* *AE, DC, MC, V* M *Odéon* *2:E5.*

7^E ARRONDISSEMENT (TOUR EIFFEL/INVALIDES)

$$$$ ★ **Hôtel Duc de Saint-Simon.** If it's good enough for the notoriously choosy Lauren Bacall, you'll probably fall for the Duc's charms, too. Its hidden location between Boulevard St-Germain and Rue du Bac is one plus; another is the shady courtyard entry. Rooms in pastels teem with antiques and countrified floral and striped fabrics. Four rooms have spacious terraces overlooking the courtyard. The 16th-century basement lounge is a warren of stone alcoves with a zinc bar and plush seating. To keep the peace, children aren't welcome. **Pros:** upscale neighborhood close to St-Germain-des-Prés; historic character. **Cons:** rooms in the annex are smaller and have no elevator; no air-conditioning; some worn decor. *14 rue St-Simon, St-Germain-des-Prés* *01–44–39–20–20* *www.hotelducdesaintsimon.com* *29 rooms, 5 suites* *In-room: no a/c (some), safe, Wi-Fi. In-hotel: bar, laundry service, parking (paid), no kids under 10* *AE, DC, MC, V* M *Rue du Bac* *2:D4.*

Fodor's Choice ★

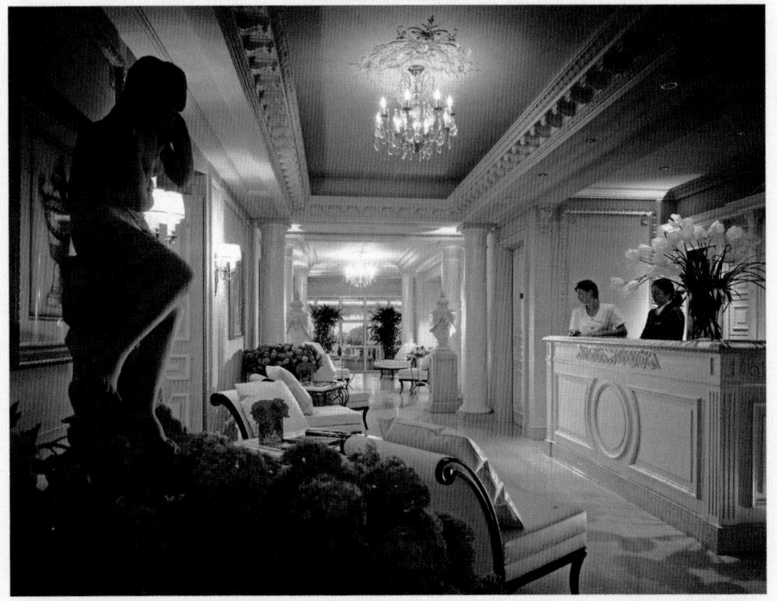

Four Seasons Hôtel George V Paris

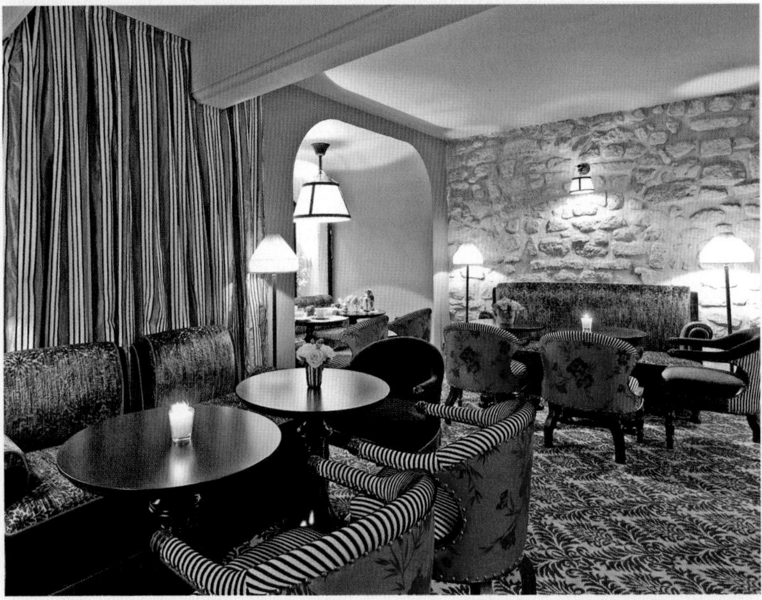

Hôtel Odéon Saint-Germain

$ **Hôtel du Champ de Mars.** This hotel just off Rue Cler has an appealing down-home feel, with a vibrant Provençal-inspired lobby and huge picture windows overlooking the street. Country-style wood furnishings and crisp fabric chair covers decorate each room. The two on the ground floor open onto a leafy private courtyard. **Pros:** cozy country decor; good value; walking distance to Eiffel Tower and Les Invalides. **Cons:** smallish rooms; no air-conditioning. ✉ *7 rue du Champ de Mars, Invalides* ☎ *01–45–51–52–30* 🌐 *www.hotelduchampdemars.com* *25 rooms* *In-room: no a/c, safe, Wi-Fi* ▭ *MC, V* Ⓜ *Ecole Militaire* ✥ *2:B4.*

$$ **Hôtel Eiffel Rive Gauche.** On a quiet street near the Tour Eiffel, this bright and welcoming hotel is a good budget find. The rooms are small but comfortable, with modern wood furnishings and orange and gold walls. Many of them open directly onto the Tuscan-style patio with its verdigris railings and terra-cotta tiles. Fans are available in summer. The owner, Monsieur Chicheportiche, is a multilingual encyclopedia of Paris. **Pros:** close to the Eiffel Tower; bright and cheery decor; fans in summer. **Cons:** no air-conditioning; some noise between rooms; big difference in room sizes. ✉ *6 rue du Gros Caillou* ☎ *01–45–51–24–56* 🌐 *www.hotel-eiffel.com* *29 rooms* *In-room: no a/c, safe, Wi-Fi. In-hotel: laundry service, Internet terminal* ▭ *MC, V* Ⓜ *École Militaire* ✥ *2:B4.*

$$$ **Hôtel Le Tourville.** Here is a rare find: a cozy upscale hotel that doesn't cost a fortune. Each room has crisp, milk-white damask upholstery set against pastel or ocher walls, a smattering of antique bureaus and lamps, original artwork, and fabulous old mirrors. The junior suites have hot tubs, whereas the Superior room has its own private garden terrace. The staff couldn't be more helpful. **Pros:** close to the Eiffel Tower and Invalides; attentive service; soundproofed windows. **Cons:** no shower curtains for the bathtubs; air-conditioning only in summer. ✉ *16 av. de Tourville* ☎ *01–47–05–62–62* 🌐 *www.hoteltourville.com* *27 rooms, 3 suites* *In-room: a/c, safe (some), Wi-Fi. In-hotel: room service, bar, laundry service, some pets allowed* ▭ *AE, DC, MC, V* Ⓜ *École Militaire* ✥ *2:C4.*

$$$$ ★ **Le Bellechasse.** French designer Christian Lacroix helped decorate all 34 rooms of Le Bellechasse, which is just around the corner from the popular Musée d'Orsay. Guests enter a refreshingly bright lobby of black slate floors, white walls, and mismatched velour and leather armchairs. Floor-to-ceiling windows overlook the elegant patio courtyard. Each room design is unique, but all have an eclectic mix of fabrics, textures, and colors, as well as Lacroix's whimsical characters screened on the walls and ceilings. Most guest rooms have an open-concept bathroom, with the bathtub and sink in a corner and a separate toilet. Four rooms have doors leading to the patio courtyard. **Pros:** central location near top Paris museums; unique style; spacious and bright; Anne Semonin toiletries. **Cons:** street-facing rooms can be a bit noisy. ✉ *8 rue de Bellechasse Invalides* ☎ *01–45–50–22–31* 🌐 *www.lebellechasse.com* *34 rooms* *In-room: a/c, safe, Internet, Wi-Fi* ▭ *AE, DC, V* Ⓜ *Solferino* ✥ *2:D4.*

2

8E ARRONDISSEMENT (CHAMPS-ÉLYSÉES)

$$$$ Fodor's Choice ★ **Four Seasons Hôtel George V Paris.** The George V is as poised and polished as the day it opened in 1928: the original Art Deco detailing and 17th-century tapestries have been restored, the bas-reliefs regilded, the marble-floor mosaics rebuilt tile by tile. Rooms are decked in fabrics and Louis XVI trimmings but have homey touches like selections of CDs and French books. Le Cinq restaurant is one of Paris's hottest tables, and the business center has six working stations with computers and printers. The low-lighted spa and fitness center pampers guests with 11 treatment rooms, walls covered in *toile de Jouy* fabrics, and an indoor swimming pool evoking Marie-Antoinette's Versailles. A relaxation room is available for guests who arrive before their rooms are ready. Even children get the four-star treatment with personalized T-shirts and portable DVD players to distract them at dinnertime. **Pros:** in the couture shopping district; courtyard dining in the summer; guest-only indoor swimming pool. **Cons:** several blocks from the nearest métro; lacks the intimacy of smaller boutique hotels. ✉ *31 av. George V* ☎ *01–49–52–70–00, 800/332–3442 in U.S.* 🌐 *www.fourseasons.com/paris* *184 rooms, 61 suites* *In-room: a/c, safe, kitchen (some), DVD, Internet, Wi-Fi. In-hotel: 2 restaurants, room service, bar, pool, gym, spa, children's programs (ages 1–12), laundry service, some pets allowed* *AE, DC, MC, V* Ⓜ *George V* ✥ *2:B3.*

$$$$ ★ **Hôtel Fouquet's Barrière.** This luxury hotel opened in 2006 above the legendary Fouquet's Brasserie at the corner of the Champs-Elysées and Avenue George V. The design, by Jacques Garcia, is more refined retro than opulent, with a rich neutral palette in silk, mahogany, velvet, and leather. The hotel competes with Parisian palaces by offering 24-hour butler service and plasma TV screens hidden behind mirrors and above bathtubs. Le Diane restaurant offers a more feminine atmosphere than the brasserie, and the teak- and red-walled spa claims to have the largest indoor pool in Paris. **Pros:** many rooms overlooking the Champs-Elysées; bathroom TVs; métro right outside. **Cons:** anonymous decor; busy street can be noisy; expensive part of town. ✉ *46 av. George V* ☎ *01–40–69–60–00* 🌐 *www.fouquets-barriere.com* *107 rooms, 40 suites* *In-room: a/c, safe, DVD, Internet, Wi-Fi. In-hotel: 2 restaurants, room service, bar, pool, gym, spa, laundry service, parking (paid), some pets allowed* *AE, DC, MC, V* Ⓜ *George V* ✥ *2:B3.*

$$$$ **Hôtel Le Bristol.** The Bristol ranks among Paris's most exclusive hotels and has the prices to prove it. Some of the spacious and elegant rooms have authentic Louis XV and Louis XVI furniture and marble bathrooms in pure 1920s Art Deco; others have a more relaxed 19th-century style. The public salons are stocked with old-master paintings and sculptures, and sumptuous carpets and tapestries. The huge interior garden restaurant and monthly fashion shows in the bar draw the posh and wealthy. A lounge bar and a casual brasserie overlook the Faubourg St-Honoré. **Pros:** large interior garden; luxury shopping street. **Cons:** a few blocks from the nearest métro, old-fashioned atmosphere may not be for everyone. ✉ *112 rue du Faubourg St-Honoré* ☎ *01–53–43–43–00* 🌐 *www.hotel-bristol.com* *162 rooms, 73 suites* *In-room: a/c, safe, DVD, Internet. In-hotel: restaurant, room service, bar, pool, gym, spa,*

laundry service, Wi-Fi, parking (free), some pets allowed ▭ *AE, DC, MC, V* Ⓜ *Miromesnil* ✥ *2:C2.*

$$$$ **Hôtel Mathis Elysées Matignon.** Each room in this boutique hotel has been lovingly decorated with antiques and artworks. Leopard-print carpets, rich aubergine, slate, and mustard walls, and Baroque mirrors make for an eclectic look. Room 43 has a sexy boudoir style, and the top-floor suite has a modern pop-art look. The Mathis's restaurant is owned separately from the hotel, but shares an entrance. **Pros:** a block from the Champs-Elysées and Faubourg St-Honoré; large choice in decor of rooms; free Wi-Fi. **Cons:** some noise from street and bar downstairs; small closets; few services. ✉ *3 rue de Ponthieu, Champs-Elysées* ☎ *01–42–25–73–01* 🌐 *www.paris-inn.com* *23 rooms* *In-room: a/c, safe, Wi-Fi. In-hotel: room service, laundry service, some pets allowed* ▭ *AE, DC, MC, V* Ⓜ *Franklin-D.-Roosevelt* ✥ *2:C3.*

$$$$ ★ **Hôtel Plaza-Athenée.** Prime-time stardom as Carrie Bradshaw's Parisian pied-à-terre in the final episodes of *Sex and the City* boosted the street cred of this 1911 palace hotel. Its revival as the city's lap of luxury, however, owes more to the meticulous attention of the renowned chef Alain Ducasse, who oversees everything from the hotel's flagship restaurant and restored 1930s Relais Plaza brasserie to the quality of the breakfast croissants. Rooms have been redone in Regency, Louis XVI, or Art Deco style, with remote-control air-conditioning, mini hi-fi/CD players, and even a pillow menu. The trendy bar has as its centerpiece an impressive Bombay glass *comptoir* (counter) glowing like an iceberg. **Pros:** on a luxury shopping street; new Dior spa; Eiffel Tower views; special attention to children. **Cons:** vast difference in style of rooms; easy to feel anonymous in such a large hotel. ✉ *25 av. Montaigne* ☎ *01–53–67–66–65, 866/732–1106 in U.S.* 🌐 *www.plaza-athenee-paris.com* *145 rooms, 43 suites* *In-room: a/c, safe, DVD, Internet. In-hotel: 3 restaurants, room service, bar, spa, laundry service, some pets allowed* ▭ *AE, DC, MC, V* Ⓜ *Alma-Marceau* ✥ *2:B3.*

$$$ **Hôtel Queen Mary.** This cheerfully cozy hotel is two blocks from Place de la Madeleine and Paris's famous department stores. Sunny yellow walls, plush carpeting, and fabrics in burgundy, gold, and royal blue soften the regal architectural detailing and high ceilings. Rooms are handsomely appointed with large beds and such thoughtful extras as trouser presses, Roger & Gallet toiletries, and decanters of sherry. Guests mingle in the bar during happy hour and, in good weather, enjoy breakfast in the garden courtyard. **Pros:** close to high-end shopping streets and department stores; large beds; extra-attentive service. **Cons:** some rooms are quite snug; ones on the ground floor can be noisy. ✉ *9 rue Greffulhe* ☎ *01–42–66–40–50* 🌐 *www.hotelqueenmary.com* *35 rooms, 1 suite* *In-room: a/c, safe, Wi-Fi. In-hotel: room service, bar, laundry service, some pets allowed* ▭ *MC, V* Ⓜ *Madeleine, St-Lazare, Havre Caumartin* ✥ *2:D2.*

$$$$ **Pershing Hall.** Formerly an American Legion hall, this circa-2001 boutique hotel quickly became a must-stay address for the dressed-in-black pack. Designed by Andrée Putman, Pershing Hall champions masculine minimalism, with muted surfaces of wood and stone and cool attitudes to match. Rooms have stark white linens, slender tubelike hanging

lamps, and tubs perched on round marble bases. The only trace of lightheartedness is the free minibars. Deluxe rooms and suites face the courtyard dining room, whose west wall is a six-story hanging garden with 300 varieties of plants. The lounge bar serves drinks, dinner, and DJ-driven music until 2 AM. **Pros:** prime shopping and nightlife district; bar and restaurant frequented by hip locals; in-room DVD players. **Cons:** bar noise can be heard in some rooms; expensive neighborhood. ✉ *49 rue Pierre-Charron, Champs-Elysées* ☎ *01–58–36–58–00* 🌐 *www.pershinghall.com* *20 rooms, 6 suites* *In-room: a/c, safe, DVD, Internet, Wi-Fi. In-hotel: restaurant, room service, bar, gym, spa, laundry service, some pets allowed* *AE, DC, MC, V* Ⓜ *George V, Franklin-D.-Roosevelt* ✛ *2:B3.*

9E ARRONDISSEMENT (OPÉRA)

$$ ★ **Hôtel Amour.** The hipster team behind this designer boutique hotel just off the trendy Rue des Martyrs already counts among its fiefdoms some of the hottest hotels, bars, and nightclubs in Paris. But despite the cool factor and the funky rooms individually decorated by Parisian avant-garde artists, the prices remain democratically bohemian. Of course, there are few amenities, but there is a 24-hour retro brasserie and garden terrace in the back where locals come to hang out in warmer weather. It's best to take the kids elsewhere; vintage nudie magazines decorate, and the sex shops of Pigalle are blocks away. **Pros:** hip clientele and locals at the brasserie; close to Montmartre; garden dining in summer. **Cons:** few amenities; a few blocks from the nearest métro; close to red-light district. ✉ *8 rue Navarin, Montmartre* ☎ *01–48–78–31–80* 🌐 *www.hotelamour.com* *20 rooms* *In-room: no a/c, no phone, no TV. In-hotel: restaurant, room service, bar, laundry service, Wi-Fi, some pets allowed* *AE, DC, MC, V* Ⓜ *Pigalle* ✛ *2:F1.*

$ **Hôtel Chopin.** The Chopin recalls its 1846 birth date with a creaky-floored lobby and aged woodwork. The basic but comfortable rooms overlook the Passage Jouffroy's quaint toy shops and bookstores or the rooftops of Paris, but none face the busy nearby streets. The best rooms end in "7" (No. 407 overlooks the Grévin Wax Museum's ateliers), whereas those ending in "2" tend to be darkest and smallest (but cheapest). **Pros:** unique location; close to major métro station; great nightlife district. **Cons:** neighborhood can be noisy; some rooms are dark and cramped; few amenities. ✉ *10 bd. Montmartre, 46 passage Jouffroy, Opéra/Grands Boulevards* ☎ *01–47–70–58–10* 🌐 *www.hotelchopin.com* *36 rooms* *In-room: no a/c, safe* *AE, MC, V* Ⓜ *Grands Boulevards* ✛ *2:F2.*

$$$ ★ **Hôtel George Sand.** This family-run boutique hotel where the 19th-century writer George Sand once lived is fresh and modern, while preserving some original architectural details. Rooms have tea/coffee-making trays and high-tech comforts such as complimentary high-speed Internet and cordless phones. Bathrooms are decked out in yacht-inspired wood flooring, with Etro toiletries. **Pros:** next door to two department stores; historic atmosphere; free Internet. **Cons:** noisy street; some rooms are quite small. ✉ *26 rue des Mathurins* ☎ *01–47–42–63–47* 🌐 *www.hotelgeorgesand.com* *20 rooms* *In-room: a/c,*

DID YOU KNOW?

The views of majestic Sacré-Coeur might be as lovely as the views from Sacre-Coeur, especially as the sun is setting or rising.

safe, Internet, Wi-Fi. In-hotel: room service, laundry service ▭ *AE, MC, V* Ⓜ *Havre Caumartin* ✣ *2:D2.*

$$ **Hôtel Langlois.** After starring in *The Truth About Charlie* (a remake of *Charade*), this darling hotel gained a reputation as one of the most atmospheric budget sleeps in the city. Rates have crept up, but the former circa-1870 bank retains its beautiful wood-panel reception area and wrought-iron elevator. The individually decorated and spacious rooms are decked out with original glazed-tile fireplaces and period art. Some rooms, such as Nos. 15, 21, and 41, have enormous retro bathrooms. Street-facing rooms can be noisy, but the top-floor views over the rooftops make up for it. **Pros:** excellent views from the top floor; close to department stores and Opéra Garnier; historic decor. **Cons:** noisy street; off the beaten path; some sagging furniture. ✉ *63 rue St-Lazare, Opéra/Grands Boulevards* ☎ *01–48–74–78–24* 🌐 *www.hotel-langlois.com* *24 rooms, 3 suites* *In-room: a/c, Wi-Fi. In-hotel: Internet terminal, some pets allowed* ▭ *AE, MC, V* Ⓜ *Trinité* ✣ *2:E2.*

Fodor's Choice ★

$$ ★ **Hôtel Royal Fromentin.** At the border of Montmartre's now tamed red-light district sits this former cabaret with much of its Art Deco wood paneling and theatrical trappings intact. Prices are at the low end of its category. The hotel has dark, rich decor, with green walls, red armchairs, an antique caged elevator, and vaudeville posters in the stained-glass-ceiling lounge. Reproduction furniture, antique prints and oils, and busy modern fabrics fill out the larger-than-average rooms. Some windows face Sacré-Coeur. Guests receive a complimentary book illustrating the history of absinthe, which is once again served in the hotel's historic bar. **Pros:** spacious rooms for the price; historic absinthe bar; close to Sacré-Coeur. **Cons:** some guests may find neighborhood peep shows and sex shops disturbing; far from the center of Paris. ✉ *11 rue Fromentin* ☎ *01–48–74–85–93* 🌐 *www.hotelroyalfromentin.com* *47 rooms* *In-room: no a/c, Wi-Fi. In-hotel: room service, bar, laundry service, some pets allowed* ▭ *AE, DC, MC, V* Ⓜ *Blanche* ✣ *2:E1.*

11^E^ ARRONDISSEMENT (BASTILLE)

$$ **Hôtel Beaumarchais.** This bold hotel straddles the fashionable Marais district in the 3^e^ and the hip student and artist neighborhood of Oberkampf in the 11^e^. Brightly colored vinyl armchairs, an industrial metal staircase, and glass tables mark the lobby, which hosts monthly art exhibitions. Out back, a small courtyard is decked in hardwood, a look you'll rarely see in Paris. The rooms hum with primary reds and yellows, some with Keith Haring prints. Kaleidoscopes of ceramic fragments tile the bathrooms. **Pros:** free Internet; popular nightlife district; bright and colorful. **Cons:** smallish rooms; off the beaten tourist track. ✉ *3 rue Oberkampf* ☎ *01–53–36–86–86* 🌐 *www.hotelbeaumarchais.com* *31 rooms* *In-room: a/c, safe, Internet, Wi-Fi. In-hotel: room service, some pets allowed* ▭ *AE, MC, V* Ⓜ *Filles du Calvaire, Oberkampf* ✣ *2:H4.*

$ **Hôtel Résidence Alhambra.** The white facade, rear garden, and flower-filled window boxes brighten this lesser-known neighborhood between the Marais and Rue Oberkampf. Rooms are smallish (splurge for a triple, just €116), with modern furnishings and run-of-the-mill bedspreads and drapes. Some overlook the flowery courtyard. There is a

2

free Internet station in the lobby, and five métro lines are around the corner. **Pros:** bright and colorful; popular nightlife district. **Cons:** small doubles; long walk to the center of town; no air-conditioning. ✉ *13 rue de Malte* ☎ *01–47–00–35–52* 🌐 *www.hotelalhambra.fr* *58 rooms* *In-room: no a/c. In-hotel: Internet terminal, some pets allowed* *AE, DC, MC, V* Ⓜ *Oberkampf* ✥ *2:H4.*

12^E ARRONDISSEMENT (BASTILLE/GARE DE LYON)

$$ **Hôtel Lyon-Bastille.** This cozy, family-run hotel is just a block from the Gare de Lyon and has been open since 1903. Its turn-of-the-20th-century pedigree shows up in its curves and alcoves, and tall French windows let in plenty of light. The rooms have been done up in pale blues and lilacs, and have satellite TV and free Wi-Fi. The Marché Aligre and Viaduc des Arts artisan boutiques are just a few blocks away. **Pros:** easy access to major métro and train lines; free Wi-Fi; friendly welcome. **Cons:** outdated decor; noisy traffic area; tiny elevator. ✉ *3 rue Parrot, Bastille/Nation* ☎ *01–43–43–41–52* 🌐 *www.hotellyonbastille.com* *47 rooms, 1 suite* *In-room: a/c, safe, Wi-Fi.* *AE, DC, MC, V* Ⓜ *Gare de Lyon* ✥ *2:H5.*

16^E ARRONDISSEMENT (ARC DE TRIOMPHE/LE BOIS)

$$$$ ★ **Hôtel Raphael.** This discreet palace hotel was built in 1925 to cater to travelers spending a season in Paris, so every space is generously sized for such long, lavish stays—the closets, for instance, have room for ball gowns and plumed hats. Guest rooms, most with king-size beds, are turned out in 18th- and early-19th-century antiques and have 6-foot windows, Oriental rugs, silk damask wallpaper, chandeliers, and ornately carved wood paneling. Bathrooms are remarkably large; most have claw-foot bathtubs and separate massage-jet showers. The roof terrace, topped with a summer restaurant, has a panoramic view of the city, with the Arc de Triomphe looming in the foreground. Parents will find a friend in the concierge, who can arrange for bilingual babysitters and priority access to amusement parks, and offers recommendations on kid-friendly restaurants and entertainment. **Pros:** a block from the Champs-Élysées and Arc de Triomphe; rooftop garden terrace; cozy hotel bar frequented by locals. **Cons:** old-fashioned Parisian decor won't impress fans of minimalism; the neighborhood can feel majestic yet cold. ✉ *17 av. Kléber* ☎ *01–53–64–32–00* 🌐 *www.raphael-hotel.com* *52 rooms, 38 suites* *In-room: a/c, safe, DVD (some), Wi-Fi. In-hotel: 2 restaurants, room service, bar, gym, laundry service, some pets allowed* *AE, DC, MC, V* Ⓜ *Kléber* ✥ *2:B2.*

$ **Hôtel Utrillo.** This very likable hotel is on a quiet side street at the foot of Montmartre, near colorful Rue Lepic. The tired old decor is slowly being replaced by a more contemporary style with bold colors and artworks. Two rooms (Nos. 61 and 63) have views of the Tour Eiffel. In the lobby are two free Internet stations, and the sauna is a luxury at this price. **Pros:** family-run feel; some Eiffel Tower views; free Internet. **Cons:** no air-conditioning; some street noise. ✉ *7 rue Aristide-Bruant* ☎ *01–42–58–13–44* 🌐 *www.hotel-paris-utrillo.com* *30 rooms* *In-room: no a/c, Wi-Fi. In-hotel: Internet terminal, some pets allowed* *MC, V* Ⓜ *Abbesses, Blanche* ✥ *2:E1.*

$$$$ **Les Jardins du Trocadéro.** This hotel near Trocadéro and the Eiffel Tower blends old-style French elegance (period antiques, Napoleonic draperies, classical plaster busts) with modern conveniences (DVDs, flat-screen TVs, free Wi-Fi). Wall paintings of genies and dressed-up monkeys add a fanciful dash. Beds are large—either kings or queens—and have hypoallergenic bedding and mattresses. Marble bathrooms have whirlpool tubs. **Pros:** hillside views over the Eiffel Tower; free Wi-Fi; upscale residential district. **Cons:** not an easy walk to the center of town; some rooms are rather small and cramped; room service doesn't always speak English. ✉ *35 rue Benjamin-Franklin* ☎ *01–53–70–17–70, 800/246–0041 in U.S.* 🌐 *www.jardintroc.com* *20 rooms* *In-room: a/c, safe, DVD (some), Wi-Fi. In-hotel: restaurant, room service, bar, laundry service, parking (paid)* *AE, DC, MC, V* Ⓜ *Trocadéro* ✥ *2:A4.*

$$$$ **Mon Hotel.** Contemporary design and modern comforts, two blocks from the Arc de Triomphe and Champs Élysées, are big draws for this stylish boutique hotel. The lobby is dramatic, whereas the rooms are more comforting with chamois wall coverings, neutral tones, and black-and-white portraits of famous personalities. High-tech amenities include MP3 docking stations and Nespresso machines, and more than 1,000 satellite TV stations. **Pros:** free Wi-Fi; unique contemporary decor; convenient for walking to the Champs-Élysées. **Cons:** some rooms have limited closet space; no extra beds for children; inconvenient for walking to the center of Paris. ✉ *1 rue Argentine, Champs-Élysées* ☎ *01–45–02–76–76* 🌐 *www.monhotel.fr* *37 rooms* *In-room: a/c, safe, Wi-Fi. In-hotel: room service, bar, spa* *AE, MC, V* Ⓜ *Argentine* ✥ *2:A2.*

$$ **Queen's Hôtel.** One of only a handful of hotels in the tony residential district near the Bois de Boulogne, the Queen's is a small, comfortable, old-fashioned place with a high standard of service. It bills itself an hôtel-musée, because it contains works by contemporary French artists such as René Julian and Maurice Friedman, whose paintings hang in the rooms and public areas. Guest rooms pair contemporary and older furnishings and have large mirrors and spotless tiled bathrooms, many with jetted tubs. **Pros:** unique artsy atmosphere; charming shopping street; friendly welcome. **Cons:** not so convenient for getting around the city on foot; vast difference in quality of room decor. ✉ *4 rue Bastien-Lepage, Passy-Auteuil* ☎ *01–42–88–89–85* 🌐 *www.queens-hotel.fr* *21 rooms, 1 suite* *In-room: a/c, safe, Wi-Fi. In-hotel: some pets allowed* *AE, DC, MC, V* Ⓜ *Michel-Ange Auteuil* ✥ *2:A4.*

20E ARRONDISSEMENT

$ Fodor's Choice ★ **Hôtel Mama Shelter.** The heir to the Club Med empire has decided to do for the hotel industry what jeans did for fashion: democratize style. Opened in fall 2008 in the up-and-coming 20e district close to Père Lachaise cemetery, this spanking new hotel is immense by Paris standards, with a fun and funky interior designed by Philippe Starck. Rooms have kitchenettes with microwave, Kiehl's toiletries, and wireless Internet via flat-screen TVs; many have huge balconies. The spacious restaurant-bar-lounge is open to the public, and guests can rent electric scooters and cars. The popular Fleche d'Or nightclub is across the street and Roissy-CDG airport just a quick drive. **Pros:** trendy design; easy access to airport; good value. **Cons:** on the edge of Paris; club across the street can be noisy. ✉ *109 rue de Bagnolet* ☎ *01–43–48–48–48* 🌐 *www.mamashelter.com* *172 rooms* *In-room: a/c, safe, kitchen, DVD, Internet, Wi-Fi. In-hotel: restaurant, bar, laundry service, Internet terminal, parking (paid), some pets allowed* ▭ *AE, MC, V* ✣ *2:H2.*

NIGHTLIFE AND THE ARTS

With a heritage that includes the cancan, the Folies-Bergère, the Moulin Rouge, Mistinguett, and Josephine Baker, Paris is one city where no one has ever had to ask, "Is there any place exciting to go to tonight?" Today the city's nightlife and arts scenes are still filled with pleasures. Hear a chansonnier belt out Piaf, take in a *Victor/Victoria* show, catch a Molière play at the Comédie Française, or perhaps spot the latest supermodel at Johnny Depp's Mandala Ray. Detailed entertainment listings in French can be found in the weekly magazines *Pariscope* (🌐 *www.pariscope.fr)* and *L'Officiel des Spectacles,* available at newsstands and in bookstores; in the Wednesday entertainment insert "Figaroscope," in *Le Figaro* newspaper (🌐 *scope.lefigaro.fr/guide)*; and in the weekly "A Nous Paris," distributed free in the métro. Also look for the Webzine *Paris Voice* (🌐 *www.parisvoice.com*). The Web site of the **Paris Tourist Office** (☎ *08–92–68–30–00 in English [€0.34min]* 🌐 *www.parisinfo.com*) has theater and music listings in English.

The best place to buy tickets is at the venue itself; try to purchase in advance, as many of the more popular performances sell out. Also try your hotel or a ticket agency, such as www.theatreonline.com. **FNAC** (🌐 *www.fnacspectacles.com*) and **Virgin** (🌐 *www.virginmega.fr*) superstores sell tickets in-store and online. The **FNAC** at Les Halles has a large board listing major concerts. ✉ *1–5 rue Pierre Lescot, Forum des Halles, 3rd level down, Beaubourg/Les Halles, 1er* ☎ *08–92–68–36–22* Ⓜ *Châtelet–Les Halles.* Half-price tickets for many same-day theater performances are available at some venues and at the **Kiosques Théâtre** (✉ *Across from 15 pl. de la Madeleine, Opéra/Grands Boulevards* Ⓜ *Madeleine* ✉ *Outside Gare Montparnasse on Pl. Raoul Dautry, Montparnasse, 15e* 🌐 *www.kiosquetheatre.com* Ⓜ *Montparnasse-Bienvenüe*); open Tuesday–Saturday 12:30 PM–8 PM and Sunday 12:30 PM–4 PM. Expect to pay a €3 commission per ticket and to wait in line. Half-price tickets are also available at many private theaters during the first week of each new show, and inexpensive tickets are often available at the last minute.

THE ARTS

EARLY AND CLASSICAL MUSIC

Classical- and world-music concerts are held at the **Cité de la Musique** (✉ *221 av. Jean-Jaurès, Parc de la Villette, 19e* ☎ *01–44–84–45–00* 🌐 *www.citedelamusique.fr* Ⓜ *Porte de Pantin*). The **Salle Cortot** (✉ *78 rue Cardinet, Parc Monceau 17e* ☎ *01–47–63–80–16* 🌐 *www.ecolenormalecortot.com* Ⓜ *Malesherbes*) is an acoustic gem hosting jazz and classical concerts; there are free student recitals at noon and 12:30 on Tuesday and Thursday. **IRCAM** (✉ *1 pl. Igor-Stravinsky, Beaubourg/Les Halles 4e* ☎ *01–44–78–48–43* 🌐 *www.ircam.fr* Ⓜ *Châtelet Les Halles, Hôtel de Ville*) organizes contemporary classical music concerts in its own theater and at the Centre Pompidou next door. The newly renovated **Salle Pleyel** (✉ *252 rue du Faubourg–St-Honoré, Champs-Élysées, 8e* ☎ *01–45–61–53–00* 🌐 *www.sallepleyel.fr* Ⓜ *Ternes*), features varied musical presentations from international stars like Lionel Hampton to repeat performances by the Orchestre de Paris. The **Théâtre des Champs-Élysées** (✉ *15 av. Montaigne, Champs-Élysées, 8e* ☎ *01–49–52–50–50* 🌐 *www.theatrechampselysees.fr* Ⓜ *Alma-Marceau*), an Art Deco temple and famed site of the premiere of Stravinsky's 1913 *Le Sacre du Printemps,* hosts concerts and ballet. Many **Churches** hold classical concerts (often free). Check weekly listings and flyers posted at the churches themselves for information. The Web site 🌐 *www.ampconcerts.com* lists the schedule at the lovely Sainte-Chapelle and other historic churches.

DANCE

The biggest news on the French dance scene is the spanking new **Centre National de la Danse** (✉ *1 rue Victor Hugo, Pantin* ☎ *01–41–83–98–98* 🌐 *www.cnd.fr* Ⓜ *Hoche; RER: Pantin*), which was sidelined by problems for a decade but finally opened in a former jail in the Pantin suburb of Paris. Dedicated to teaching dance, there's also a regular program of performances, expositions, and conferences open to the public.

★ The super-spectacular 19th-century **Opéra Garnier** (✉ *Pl. de l'Opéra, Opéra/Grands Boulevards, 9e* ☎ *08–92–89–90–90 [€0.34 min]* 🌐 *www.opera-de-paris.fr* Ⓜ *Opéra*) is home to the reputable Ballet de l'Opéra National de Paris and hosts other dance companies. Note that many of the cheaper seats have obstructed views, more of an obstacle in dance than in opera performances. At its two houses, the **Théâtre de la Ville** (✉ *2 pl. du Châtelet, Beaubourg/Les Halles, 4e* ☎ *01–42–74–22–77 for both* 🌐 *www.theatredelaville-paris.com* Ⓜ *Châtelet* ✉ *31 rue des Abbesses, Montmartre, 18e* Ⓜ *Abbesses*) is *the* place for contemporary dance. Troupes like Anne-Teresa de Keersmaeker's Rosas company are presented here and sell out quickly.

OPERA

Paris offers some of the best opera in the world—and thousands know it. Consequently, it's best to plan ahead if you'd like to attend a performance of the **Opéra National de Paris** at its two homes, the Opéra de la Bastille and the Opéra Garnier. Review a list of performances by checking the Web site 🌐 *www.opera-de-paris.fr.* For performances at either the Opéra de la Bastille or the Opéra Garnier *(for complete info on this theater, see Dance, above)*, seats go on sale at the box office two weeks before any given show or a month ahead by phone or online; you must go in person to buy the cheapest tickets. Last-minute discount tickets, when available, are offered 15 minutes before a performance for seniors and anyone under 28. The box office is open 11 to 6:30 PM daily. Prices for tickets start at €5 for standing places (at the Opéra Bastille, only) and go up to €200.

The **Opéra de la Bastille** (✉ *Pl. de la Bastille, Bastille/Nation, 12e* ☎ *08–92–89–90–90 [€0.34 min]* 🌐 *www.opera-de-paris.fr* Ⓜ *Bastille*), a modern auditorium, has taken over the role of Paris's main opera house from the Opéra Garnier. The grandest opera productions are usually mounted here, while the Garnier now presents smaller-scale operas such as Mozart's *La Clemenza di Tito* and *Così Fan Tutte*. Gorgeous though the Garnier is, its tiara-shape theater means that many seats have limited sight lines, so it's best to ask specifically what the sight lines are when booking (partial view in French is *visibilité partielle*). Needless to say, the cheaper seats are often those with partial views—of course, views of Garnier's house could easily wind up being much more spectacular than any sets on stage, so it's not really a loss. The opera season usually runs September through July; the box office is open Monday–Saturday 11–6:30.

The **Opéra Comique** (✉ *5 rue Favart, Opéra/Grands Boulevards, 2e* ☎ *08–25–00–00–58* 🌐 *www.opera-comique.com* Ⓜ *Richelieu-Drouot*) is a gem of a house that stages operettas, modern dance, classical concerts, and vocal recitals. Tickets range from €6–€50 and can be purchased at the theater, by mail, online, or by phone.

Théâtre Musical de Paris (✉ *Pl. du Châtelet, Beaubourg/Les Halles, 1er* ☎ *01–40–28–28–40* 🌐 *www.chatelet-theatre.com* Ⓜ *Châtelet*), better known as the Théâtre du Châtelet, puts on some of the finest opera productions in the city, and regularly attracts international divas like Cecilia Bartoli and Anne-Sofie von Otter. It also plays host to classical concerts, dance performances, and the occasional play.

THEATER

A number of theaters line the Grands Boulevards between Opéra and République, but there's no Paris equivalent of Broadway or the West End. Shows are mostly in French. English-language theater groups playing in venues throughout Paris include the **International Players** (🌐 *www.internationalplayers.info*). Broadway-scale singing-and-dancing musicals are generally staged at either the Palais des Sports or the Palais des Congrès.

Théâtre des Bouffes du Nord (✉ *37 bis, bd. de la Chapelle, Stalingrad/La Chapelle, 10e* ☎ *01–46–07–34–50* Ⓜ *La Chapelle*) is the wonderfully atmospheric theater that is home to English director Peter Brook. The **Comédie-Française** (✉ *Salle Richelieu, 2 rue de Richelieu, 1er* ☎ *08–25–10–16–80* Ⓜ *Palais-Royal–Musée du Louvre* ✉ *Studio Théâtre, Galerie du Carrousel du Louvre, 99 rue de Rivoli, Louvre/Tuileries, 1er* ☎ *01–44–58–98–54* Ⓜ *Palais-Royal* ✉ *Théâtre du Vieux Colombier, 21 rue Vieux Colombier, St-Germain-des-Prés, 6e* ☎ *01–44–39–87–00* Ⓜ *St-Sulpice*) dates from 1680 and is the most hallowed institution in French theater. It specializes in splendid classical French plays by the likes of Racine and Molière. Reserve in advance or line up an hour before showtime for cancellations. The legendary 19th-century **Odéon Théâtre de l'Europe** (✉ *Pl. de l'Odéon, St-Germain-des-Prés, 6e* ☎ *01–44–85–40–00* Ⓜ *Odéon*), once home to the Comédie Française, has today made pan-European theater its primary focus. **Théâtre National de Chaillot** (✉ *1 pl. du Trocadéro, Trocadéro/Tour Eiffel, 16e* ☎ *01–53–65–30–00*

The Left Bank is now home to many glittering nightclubs filled with off-duty celebs.

Ⓜ *Trocadéro*) has two theaters dedicated to drama and dance. Since 2003 it has hosted the groundbreaking duo of Deborah Warner (director) and Fiona Shaw (actress) for several excellent English-language productions. **Théâtre du Palais-Royal** (✉ *38 rue Montpensier, Louvre/Tuileries, 1er* ☎ *01–42–97–40–00* Ⓜ *Palais-Royal*) is a sumptuous 750-seat Italian theater bedecked in gold and purple.

For children, one "theatrical" experience can be a delight—the **Marionnettes du Jardin du Luxembourg** (✉ *St-Germain-des-Prés* ☎ *01–43–26–46–47* Ⓜ *Vavin*) stages the most traditional performances (in French) on most Wednesdays and weekends, including *Pinocchio* and *The Three Little Pigs*. Look for the puppet shows in Paris's other larger parks. Entrance is €3–€4.50.

NIGHTLIFE

If you prefer clinking drinks with models and celebrities, check out the Champs-Élysées area, but be prepared to shell out *beaucoup* bucks and stare down surly bouncers. Easygoing, bohemian-chic revelers can be found in the northeastern districts like Canal St-Martin and Belleville, while students tend to pour into the Bastille, St-Germain-des-Prés, and the Quartier Latin. Grands Boulevards and Rue Montorgueil, just north of Les Halles, is party central for young professionals and the fashion crowd, and the Pigalle and Montmartre areas are always hopping with plenty of theaters, cabarets, bars, and concert venues. Warmer months draw the adventurous to floating clubs and bars, moored along the Seine from Bercy to the Eiffel Tower.

BARS AND CLUBS

American Bar at La Closerie des Lilas (✉ *171 bd. du Montparnasse, Montparnasse, 6e* ☎ *01–40–51–34–50* Ⓜ *Montparnasse*) lets you drink in the swirling action of the adjacent restaurant and brasserie at a piano bar hallowed by plaques honoring such former habitués as Man Ray, Jean-Paul Sartre, Samuel Beckett, and Ernest Hemingway, who talks of "the Lilas" in *A Moveable Feast*. A cherished relic from the days of Picasso and Modigliani, **Au Lapin Agile** (✉ *22 rue des Saules, Montmartre, 18e* ☎ *01–46–06–85–87* Ⓜ *Lamarck-Caulaincourt*), the fabled artists' hangout in Montmartre, is an authentic survivor from the early 20th century. This is an authentic French cabaret of songs, poetry, and humor in a publike setting.

Bar du Marché (✉ *16 rue de Buci, 6e St-Germain/Buci* ☎ *01–43–26–55–15* Ⓜ *Mabillon/Odeon*) is a local legend where the waiters sport red overalls and revolutionary "Gavroche" hats, and seats on the outdoor terrace are hard to come by.

Barramundi (✉ *3 rue Taitbout, Opéra/Grands Boulevards, 9e* ☎ *01–47–70–21–21* Ⓜ *Richelieu Drouot*) is one of Paris's hubs of nouveau-riche chic. The lighting is dim, the copper bar is long, and the walls are artfully textured. The namesake of **Buddha Bar** (✉ *8 rue Boissy d'Anglas, Champs-Élysées, 8e* ☎ *01–53–05–90–00* Ⓜ *Concorde*), is past its prime with Parisians, but visitors can't seem to get enough of the high-camp towering gold Buddha, and a spacious mezzanine bar that, in turn, overlooks a dining room serving pan-Asian fare. **Cab** (✉ *2 pl. du Palais Royal, Louvre/Tuileries, 1er* ☎ *01–58–62–56–25* Ⓜ *Palais-Royal*) is a popular fashion-centric dance club across from the Louvre, where models, photographers, and stylists bypass the lesser beings at the velvet rope. **Le Nouveau Casino** (✉ *109 rue Oberkampf, 11e, République* ☎ *01–43–57–57–40* Ⓜ *Parmentier*) is tucked in the Belle Epoque-meets-bobo Café Charbon. Pop and rock concerts prevail during the week, with DJ spinning everything else on weekend nights from midnight until dawn.

★ **De la Ville Café** (✉ *34 bd. Bonne Nouvelle, 10e, Opéra/Grands Boulevards* ☎ *01–48–24–48–09* Ⓜ *Bonne Nouvelle, Grands Boulevards*) is a funky, industrial-baroque place, with its huge, heated sidewalk terrace, mosaic-tile bar, and swish lounge. As the anchor of the slowly reawakening Grands Boulevards scene, it requires that you arrive early on weekends for a seat.

Experimental Cocktail Club (✉ *37 rue Saint-Sauveur, 2e, Bourse* ☎ *01–45–08–88–09* Ⓜ *St-Germain*) fashioned itself as a speakeasy on a tiny brick-paved street packed with a diverse mix of locals, professionals, and fashionistas.

Harry's New York Bar (✉ *5 rue Daunou, Opéra/Grands Boulevards, 2e* ☎ *01–42–61–71–14* Ⓜ *Opéra*) is a cozy, wood-panel hangout decorated with dusty college pennants; it's popular with expatriates and American-loving French people who welcome the ghosts of Ernest Hemingway and F. Scott Fitzgerald, who drank himself unconscious here. Bartenders mix a mean Bloody Mary. The legendary spot was founded in 1911, and Gershwin composed "An American in Paris" on the piano bar downstairs. **Le Gibus** (✉ *18 rue du Faubourg du Temple, République, 11e* ☎ *01–47–00–78–88* Ⓜ *République*) is one of Paris's most famous music venues and has hosted everyone from the Police to Billy Idol. Today the Gibus's cellars are *the* place for trance, techno, hip-hop, hard-core, and jungle music. **Kong** (✉ *1 rue du Pont-Neuf, Rivoli 1er* ☎ *01–40–39–09–00* Ⓜ *Pont-Neuf*) is glorious not only for its panoramic skyline views, but for its exquisite manga-inspired decor, the top-shelf DJs for weekend dancing, and its kooky, disco-ball-and-kid-sumo-adorned bathrooms. It was featured as a chic eatery in *Sex and the City;* need we say more? **WAGG** (✉ *62 rue Mazarine, St-Germain-des-Prés, 6e* ☎ *01–55–42–22–00* Ⓜ *Odéon*) is tucked beneath the popular bar-resto Alcazar, in a vaulted stone cellar that was Jim Morrison's hangout back in its '70s incarnation as the Whiskey-a-Go-Go. It's now a welcoming dance club featuring vintage disco, funk, groove, and salsa (the latter on Sunday nights, with classes that start at 3 PM), with state-of-the-art sound, lighting, and guest DJs.

COOL PLACES IN A HOT SPOT

Once it was the Bastille area, then gritty Oberkampf; today the trendy nightlife zone is the Canal St-Martin, an old working-class neighborhood just east of Gare de l'Est and clustered around the canal built by Napoléon I. While you're likely to spot celebrity photographer Mario Testino, the neighborhood mood feels refreshingly more relaxed than poseur-ish. A top hangout is the atmospheric Hôtel du Nord (✉ *102 quai de Jemmapes* ☎ *01–40–40–78–78*), once famous as the setting for Marcel Carné's 1938 film, now transformed into a restaurant where you might see Christian Lacroix belly up to the zinc bar.

FLOOR SHOWS AND CABARET

Paris's cabarets are household names, though mostly just tourists go to them these days. Prices range from about €30 (admission plus one drink) to more than €130 (dinner plus show).

Crazy Horse (✉ *12 av. George V, Champs-Élysées, 8e* ☎ *01–47–23–32–32* 🌐 *www.lecrazyhorseparis.com* Ⓜ *Alma-Marceau*) is one of the best-known cabarets, with pretty dancers and raunchy routines characterized by lots of humor and few clothes. Burlesque artist extraordinaire Dita von Teese has been known to perform here. **Lido** (✉ *116 bis, av. des Champs-Élysées, Champs-Élysées, 8e* ☎ *01–40–76–56–10* 🌐 *www.lido.fr* Ⓜ *George V*) stars the famous Bluebell Girls; the owners claim that no show this side of Vegas rivals it for special effects. The glitzy cabaret offers a special sanitized kids' show. **Michou** (✉ *80 rue des Martyrs, Montmartre, 18e* ☎ *01–46–06–16–04* 🌐 *www.michou.fr* Ⓜ *Pigalle*) is owned by the always blue-clad Michou, famous in Paris circles. The men on stage wear extravagant drag—high camp and parody are the order of the day. That old favorite at the foot of Montmartre, **Moulin Rouge** (✉ *82 bd. de Clichy, Montmartre, 18e* ☎ *01–53–09–82–82* Ⓜ *Blanche*) offered a circuslike atmosphere when it opened in 1889; today, the famous cancan is still a popular highlight of what is now more of a Vegas-y show, starring 100 dancers, acrobats, ventriloquists, and contortionists, and more than 1,000 costumes.

HOTEL BARS

Some of Paris's best hotel bars mix historic pedigrees with hushed elegance—and others go for a modern, edgy luxe. Following are some

Fodor's Choice ★

perennial favorites. The super-chic bar at **L'Hôtel** (✉ *13 rue des Beaux-Arts, St-Germain-des-Prés, 6e* ☎ *01-44-41-99-00* Ⓜ *St-Germain-des-Prés*) gorgeously revamped by stylemeister Jacques Garcia, evokes the decadent spirit of onetime resident Oscar Wilde. **Hôtel Le Bristol** (✉ *112 rue du Faubourg-St-Honoré, Champs-Élysées, 8e* ☎ *01-53-43-43-42* Ⓜ *Miromesnil*) attracts the rich and powerful with fab cocktails, and occasional mini-runway shows at teatime. **Hôtel Costes** (✉ *239 rue Saint-Honoré, Louvre/Tuileries, 1er* ☎ *01-42-44-50-25* Ⓜ *Tuileries*) draws the big names to its exclusive red-velvet interior, and not just during fashion week. **Hôtel Plaza Athénée** (✉ *25 av. Montaigne, Champs-Élysées, 8e* ☎ *01-53-67-66-00* Ⓜ *Alma Marceau*) is Paris's perfect chill-out spot; the bar was designed by Starck protegé Patrick Jouin. Hot–cool **Pershing Hall** (✉ *49 rue Pierre Charron, Champs-Élysées, 8e* ☎ *01-58-36-58-36* Ⓜ *George V*) has a stylish lounge bar with muted colors and an enormous "wall garden" in the courtyard. Colin Field, the best

★ barman in Paris, presides at the **Hemingway Bar & The Ritz Bar** (✉ *15 pl. Vendôme, Louvre/Tuileries, 1er* ☎ *01-43-16-30-30* Ⓜ *Opéra*), but with a dress code and cognac *aux truffes* on the menu, Hemingway might raise an eyebrow. Across the hallway is the reopened Ritz Bar (formerly the Cambon), a soigné setting where Cole Porter composed "Begin the Beguine."

★ **Murano Urban Resort** (✉ *13 bd. du Temple, République, 3e* ☎ *01-42-71-20-00* Ⓜ *Filles du Calvaire*) is Paris's epitome of space-age-bachelor-pad-hipness du jour with a black-stone bar, candy-color walls, and packed nightly with beautiful art and fashion types.

SHOPPING

THE BEST SHOPPING NEIGHBORHOODS

AVENUE MONTAIGNE

Shopping doesn't come much more chic than on Avenue Montaigne, with its graceful town mansions housing some of the top names in international fashion: **Chanel, Dior, Céline, Valentino, Krizia, Ungaro, Prada, Dolce & Gabbana,** and many more. Neighboring Rue François 1er and Avenue George V are also lined with many designer boutiques: **Versace, Fendi, Givenchy,** and **Balenciaga.**

CHAMPS-ÉLYSÉES

Cafés and movie theaters keep the once-chic Champs-Élysées active 24 hours a day, but the invasion of exchange banks, car showrooms, and fast-food chains has lowered the tone. Four glitzy 20th-century arcade malls—**Galerie du Lido, Le Rond-Point, Le Claridge,** and **Élysées 26**—capture most of the retail action, not to mention the **Gap** and the **Disney Store.** Some of the big luxe chain stores—also found in cities around the globe—are here: **Sephora** has reintroduced a touch of elegance, and

South of the Champs-Elysées you'll find the posh Avenue Montaigne shopping district; to its north, the ritzy boutiques of the Faubourg St-Honoré.

the mothership **Louis Vuitton** (on the Champs-Élysées proper) has kept the cool factor soaring.

THE FAUBOURG ST-HONORÉ

This chic shopping and residential area is also quite a political hub. It's home to the Élysée Palace as well as the official residences of the American and British ambassadors. The Paris branches of **Sotheby's** and **Christie's** and renowned antiques galleries such as **Didier Aaron** add artistic flavor. Boutiques include **Hermès, Lanvin, Gucci, Chloé,** and **Christian Lacroix.**

LEFT BANK

For an array of bedazzling boutiques with hyper-picturesque goods—antique toy theaters, books on gardening—and the most fascinating antiques stores in town, be sure to head to the area around Rue Jacob, nearly lined with *antiquaires,* and the streets around super-posh Place Furstenberg. After decades of clustering on the Right Bank's venerable shopping avenues, the high-fashion houses have stormed the Rive Gauche. The first to arrive were **Sonia Rykiel** and **Yves St-Laurent** in the late '60s. Some of the more recent arrivals include **Christian Dior, Giorgio Armani,** and **Louis Vuitton.** Rue des St-Pères and Rue de Grenelle are lined with designer names.

LE MARAIS

The Marais is a mixture of many moods and many influences; its lovely, impossibly narrow cobblestone streets are filled with some of the most original, small name, nonglobal goods to be had—a true haven for the original gift—including the outposts of **Jamin Puech,** the **Red Wheelbarrow,** and **Sentou Galerie.** Avant-garde designers **Azzedine Alaïa** and **Tsumori**

Chistato have boutiques within a few blocks of stately Place des Vosges and the Picasso and Carnavalet museums. The Marais is also one of the few neighborhoods that has a lively Sunday-afternoon (usually from 2 PM) shopping scene.

LOUVRE–PALAIS ROYAL

The elegant and eclectic shops clustered in the 18th-century arcades of the Palais-Royal sell such items as antiques, toy soldiers, music boxes, some of the world's most exclusive vintage designer dresses at **Didier Ludot**, and high-end hipness at **Stella McCartney and Marc Jacobs.**

OPÉRA TO LA MADELEINE

Two major department stores—**Printemps** and **Galeries Lafayette**—dominate Boulevard Haussmann, behind Paris's ornate 19th-century Opéra Garnier. Place de la Madeleine tempts many with its two luxurious food stores, **Fauchon** and **Hédiard.**

PLACE VENDÔME AND RUE DE LA PAIX

The magnificent 17th-century Place Vendôme, home of the Ritz Hotel, and Rue de la Paix, leading north from Vendôme, are where you can find the world's most elegant jewelers: **Cartier, Boucheron, Bulgari,** and **Van Cleef and Arpels.** The most exclusive, however, is the discreet **Jar's.**

PLACE DES VICTOIRES AND RUE ÉTIENNE MARCEL

The graceful, circular Place des Victoires, near the Palais-Royal, is the playground of fashion icons such as **Kenzo,** while **Comme des Garçons** and **Yohji Yamamoto** line Rue Étienne Marcel. In the nearby oh-so-charming Galerie Vivienne shopping arcade, **Jean-Paul Gaultier** has a shop that has been renovated by Philippe Starck, and is definitely worth a stop.

RUE ST-HONORÉ

A fashionable set makes its way to Rue St-Honoré to shop at Paris's trendiest boutique, **Colette.** The street is lined with numerous designer names, while on nearby Rue Cambon you can find the wonderfully elegant **Maria Luisa** and the main **Chanel** boutique.

DEPARTMENT STORES

★ **Au Printemps** (✉ *64 bd. Haussmann, Opéra/Grands Boulevards, 9e* ☎ *01–42–82–50–00* Ⓜ *Havre-Caumartin, Opéra, or Auber*) is actually three major stores and has everything plus a whopping six floors dedicated to men's fashion. **Le Bon Marché** (✉ *24 rue de Sèvres, St-Germain-des-Prés, 7e* ☎ *01–44–39–80–00* Ⓜ *Sèvres-Babylone*) is Paris's chicest department store, with an impressive array of designers represented for both men and women, and home to **La Grande Épicerie,** one of the largest groceries in Paris and a gourmand's home away from home. **BHV** (✉ *52–64 rue de Rivoli, Beaubourg/Les Halles, 4e* ☎ *01–42–74–90–00* Ⓜ *Hôtel de Ville*), short for Bazar de l'Hôtel de Ville, has minimal fashion offerings but is noteworthy for its enormous basement hardware store and household items.

Galeries Lafayette (✉ *35–40 bd. Haussmann, Opéra/Grands Boulevards, 9e* ☎ *01–42–82–34–56* Ⓜ *Chaussée d'Antin, Opéra, or Havre-Caumartin*) is dangerous—the granddaddy of them all—everything you never even dreamt of and then some under a gorgeous Belle Époque stained-glass dome.

BUDGET

Monoprix (✉ *21 av. de l'Opéra, Opéra/Grands Boulevards, 1er* ☎ *01–42–61–78–08* Ⓜ *Opéra* ✉ *20 bd. de Charonne, Bastille/Nation, 20e* ☎ *01–43–73–17–59* Ⓜ *Nation* ✉ *50 rue de Rennes, St-Germain-des-Prés, 6e* ☎ *01–45–48–18–08* Ⓜ *St-Germain-des-Prés*), with branches throughout the city, is the French dime store par excellence, stocking everyday items like toothpaste, groceries, toys, typing paper, and bath mats—a little of everything. It also has a line of relatively inexpensive basic wearables for the whole family and isn't a bad place to stock up on French liqueurs at reasonable prices.

MARKETS

The lively atmosphere that reigns in most of Paris's open-air food markets makes them a sight worth seeing even if you don't want or need to buy anything. Every neighborhood has one, though many are open only a few days each week. Sunday morning until 1 PM is usually a good time to go. Many of the better-known markets are in areas you'd visit for sightseeing; here's a list of the top bets.**Boulevard Raspail** (✉ *Between Rue de Rennes and Rue du Cherche-Midi, Quartier Latin, 6e* Ⓜ *Rennes*) has a great organic market on Tuesday and Friday. **Rue Mouffetard** (✉ *Quartier Latin, 5e* Ⓜ *Place Monge*), near the Jardin des Plantes, is best on weekends. **Rue Montorgueuil** (✉ *Beaubourg/Les Halles, 1er* Ⓜ *Châtelet Les Halles*) is closed Sunday afternoon and Monday. **Rue Lévis** (E *Parc Monceau, 17e* m *Villiers*), near Parc Monceau, has Alsatian specialties and a terrific cheese shop. It's closed Sunday afternoon and Monday. The **Marché d'Aligre** (✉ *Rue d'Aligre, Bastille/Nation, 12e* Ⓜ *Ledru-Rollin*), open until 1 PM every day except Monday, is a bit farther out but is the cheapest and probably most locally authentic market in Paris.

On Paris's northern boundary, the **Marché aux Puces** (Ⓜ *Porte de Clignancourt*), or flea market, which takes place Saturday through Monday, is a century-old labyrinth of alleyways spreading for more than a square mile packed with antiques dealers' booths, junk stalls, and world-class pickpockets; arrive early. On the southern and eastern sides of the city—at **Porte de Vanves** (Ⓜ *Porte de Vanves*) and Porte de Montreuil—are other, smaller weekend flea markets. Vanves is a hit with the fashion set and specializes in smaller objects—mirrors, textiles, handbags, clothing, and glass. Arrive early if you want to find a bargain; the good stuff goes fast, and stalls are liable to be packed up before noon.

SHOPPING ARCADES

Paris's 19th-century commercial arcades, called *passages* or *galeries* are the forerunners of the modern mall. Glass roofs, decorative pillars, and mosaic floors give the passages character. The major arcades are on the Right Bank in central Paris. **Galerie Vivienne** (✉ *4 rue des Petits-Champs, Opéra/Grands Boulevards, 2e* Ⓜ *Bourse*) is home to a range of inter-

The eye-popping atrium of the Galeries Lafayette is the subject of this entry by Elizabeth A. Millar, a Fodors.com member, to Fodor's "Show Us Your France" contest.

esting shops, including **Jean-Paul Gaultier's** Philippe Starck–designed fantasy, an excellent tearoom, and a quality wine shop.

★ **Passage du Grand-Cerf** (✉ *Entrances on Rue Dussoubs, Rue St-Denis, Beaubourg/Les Halles, 4e* Ⓜ *Étienne-Marcel*) is a pretty, glass-roof gallery filled with crafts shops offering an innovative selection of jewelry, paintings, and ceramics. **Passage Jouffroy** (✉ *12 bd. Montmartre, Opéra/Grands Boulevards, 9e* Ⓜ *Montmartre*) is full of shops selling toys, postcards, antique canes, and perfumes. **Passage des Panoramas** (✉ *11 bd. Montmartre, Opéra/Grands Boulevards, 2e* Ⓜ *Montmartre*), built in 1800, is the oldest of them all and with a new organic wine

★ bar, enjoying a rebirth. The elegant **Galerie Véro-Dodat** (✉ *19 rue Jean-Jacques Rousseau, Louvre/Tuileries, 1er* Ⓜ *Louvre*) has painted ceilings and copper pillars with shops selling contemporary art, silks, antiques, designer cosmetics, and a boutique by shoemaker-to-the-stars Christian Louboutin.

SPECIALTY STORES

ACCESSORIES, COSMETICS, AND PERFUMES

Fodor's Choice ★ **Chantal Thomass** (✉ *211 rue St-Honoré, Louvre/Tuileries, 1er* ☎ *01–42–60–40–56* Ⓜ *Tuileries*), a legendary lingerie diva, is back with this *Pillow Talk*–meets–Louis XV–inspired boutique. This is French naughtiness at its best, striking just the right balance between playfulness and straight-on seduction. **Christian Louboutin** (✉ *19 rue Jean-Jacques Rousseau, Beaubourg/Les Halles, 1er* ☎ *01–42–36–53–66* Ⓜ *Palais-Royal* ✉ *38–40 rue de Grenelle, St-Germain-des-Prés, 7e* ☎ *01–42–22–33–07* Ⓜ *Sèvres Babylone*) shoes carry their own red carpet with them, in their trademark crimson soles and impressive client list including Catherine Deneuve and Gwyneth Paltrow. **E. Goyard** (✉ *233 rue St-Honoré, Louvre/Tuileries, 1er* ☎ *01–42–60–57–04* Ⓜ *Tuileries*) has been making the finest luggage for the jet set since 1853.

★ **Hermès** (✉ *24 rue du Faubourg St-Honoré, Louvre/Tuileries, 8e* ☎ *01–40–17–47–17* Ⓜ *Concorde* ✉ *42 av. Georges V, Champs-Élysées, 8e* ☎ *01–47–20–48–51* Ⓜ *George V*) created the eternally chic Kelly (named for Grace Kelly) and Birkin (named for Jane Birkin) handbags. The silk scarves are legendary for their intricate designs, which change yearly. Other accessories are also extremely covetable: enamel bracelets, dashing silk-twill ties, and small leather goods.

★ **Jamin Puech** (✉ *43 rue Madame, St-Germain-des-Prés, 6e* ☎ *01–45–48–14–85* Ⓜ *St-Sulpice* ✉ *68 rue Vieille-du-Temple, Le Marais, 3e* ☎ *01–48–87–84–87* Ⓜ *St-Paul*) thinks of its bags as jewelry, not just a necessity. Nothing's plain-Jane here—everything is whimsical, unusual, and fun.

★ **Louis Vuitton** (✉ *101 av. des Champs-Élysées, Champs-Élysées, 8e* ☎ *08–10–81–00–10* Ⓜ *George V* ✉ *6 pl. St-Germain-des-Prés, St-Germain-des-Prés 6e* ☎ *08–10–81–00–10* Ⓜ *St-Germain-des-Prés* ✉ *22 av. Montaigne, Champs-Élysées, 8e* ☎ *08–10–81–00–10* Ⓜ *Franklin-D.-Roosevelt*) has spawned a voracious fan base from Texas to Tokyo with its mix of classic leather goods and the saucy revamped versions orchestrated by Marc Jacobs, with collaborators such as Japanese artist Murakami. This soaring cathedral-esque paean to luxury (and consumption) is unsurpassed, notably at the opulent flagship on the Champs-Élysées.

Fodor's Choice ★ **Loulou de la Falaise** (✉ *21 rue Cambon, Louvre/Tuileries, 1er* ☎ *01–42–60–02–66* Ⓜ *Concorde*) was the original muse of Yves Saint Laurent; she was at his side for more than 30 years of collections and designed his accessories line. Now this paragon of the fashion aristocracy has her own two-floor boutique filled with the best style around. **Sabbia Rosa** (✉ *71–73 rue des Sts-Pères, St-Germain-des-Prés, 6e* ☎ *01–45–48–88–37* Ⓜ *St-Germain-des-Prés*) sells some of the world's finest lingerie favored by celebrities like Catherine Deneuve and Claudia Schiffer.

BOOKS

The scenic open-air bookstalls along the Seine sell secondhand books (mostly in French), prints, and souvenirs. Numerous French-language bookstores—specializing in a wide range of topics, including art, film, literature, and philosophy—are found in the Latin Quarter and around St-Germain-des-Prés.

UNCOMMON-SCENTS

Guerlain (✉ *68 av. des Champs-Élysées* ☎ *01–45–62–52–57* Ⓜ *Franklin-D.-Roosevelt*) reopened its historic address in 2005 after a spectacular renovation befitting the world-class perfumer. Still the only Paris outlet for legendary perfumes like Shalimar and L'Heure Bleue, they've added several new signature scents (Rose Barbare, Cuir Beluga), and the perfume "fountain" allows for personalized bottles to be filled on demand. Or, for a mere €30,000, a customized scent can be blended just for you. Also here are makeup, scented candles, and a spa.

Comptoir de l'Image (✉ *44 rue de Sévigné, Le Marais, 3e* ☎ *01–42–72–03–92* Ⓜ *St-Paul*) is where designers John Galliano, Marc Jacobs, and Emanuel Ungaro stock up on old copies of *Vogue, Harper's Bazaar,* and *The Face.*

★ **La Hune** (✉ *170 bd. St-Germain, St-Germain-des-Prés, 6e* ☎ *01–45–48–35–85* Ⓜ *St-Germain-des-Prés*), sandwiched between the Café de Flore and Les Deux Magots, is a landmark for intellectuals with a comprehensive collection of international books on art and architecture. Open until midnight. The **Red Wheelbarrow** (✉ *22 rue St-Paul, Le Marais, 4e* ☎ *01–48–04–75–08* Ⓜ *St-Paul*) is *the* anglophone bookstore—if it was written in English, they can get it. It also has a complete academic section and every literary review you can think of. **Shakespeare & Company** (✉ *37 rue de la Bûcherie, Quartier Latin, 5e* ☎ *01–43–25–40–93* Ⓜ *St-Michel*), the sentimental Left Bank favorite, is named after the bookstore whose American owner, Sylvia Beach, first published James Joyce's *Ulysses*. Nowadays it specializes in expat literature and secondhand treasures. **Taschen** (✉ *2 rue de Buci, St-Germain-des-Prés, 6e* ☎ *01–40–51–79–22* Ⓜ *Mabillon*) is perfect for night owls, as it's open until midnight on Friday and Saturday. The Starck-designed shelves and desks hold glam titles on photography, fine art, design, fashion, and fetishes.

Village Voice (✉ *6 rue Princesse, St-Germain-des-Prés, 6e* ☎ *01–46–33–36–47* Ⓜ *Mabillon*) a heavy hitter in Paris's ever-thriving expat literary scene, is known for its excellent current and classic book selections, frequent book signings, and readings by notable authors. **W. H. Smith** (✉ *248 rue de Rivoli, Louvre/Tuileries, 1er* ☎ *01–44–77–88–99* Ⓜ *Concorde*) carries a multitude of travel and language books, cookbooks, and fiction for adults and children. It also has the best selection of foreign magazines and newspapers in Paris (which you're allowed to peruse without interruption—many magazine dealers in France aren't so kind).

CLOTHING

MEN'S WEAR

Berluti (✉ *26 rue Marbeuf, Champs-Élysées, 8e* ☎ *01–53–93–97–97* Ⓜ *Franklin-D.-Roosevelt*) has been making exquisite and exclusive men's shoes for more than a century. **Charvet** (✉ *28 pl. Vendôme,Opéra/Grands Boulevards, 1er* ☎ *01–42–60–30–70* Ⓜ *Opéra*) is the Parisian equivalent of a Savile Row tailor.

WOMEN'S WEAR

It doesn't matter, say the French, that fewer and fewer of their top couture houses are still headed by compatriots. It's the chic elegance, the classic ambience, the *je ne sais quoi,* that remains undeniably Gallic. Here are some meccas for Paris chic. **Antik Batik** (✉ *113 Vielle du Temple , Le Maraiss, 3e* ☎ *01–48–87–39–46* Ⓜ *St Paul* ✉ *18 rue Turenne, Marais, 4e* ☎ *01–44–78–93–75* Ⓜ *St-Paul* ✉ *20 rue Vaugirard, St-Germain-des-Prés, 6e* ☎ *01–43–25–30–22* Ⓜ *Odéon*) has a wonderful line of ethnically inspired clothes. There are row upon row of beaded and sequined dresses, Chinese silk tunics, short fur jackets, flowing organza separates, and some of Paris's most popular handbags. **Azzedine Alaïa**

(✉ *7 rue de Moussy, Le Marais, 4e* ☎ *01–42–72–19–19* Ⓜ *Hôtel-de-Ville*) is the undisputed "king of cling" dresses, but you don't have to be under 20 to look good in one of his dresses; devotees include Tina Turner and Michelle Obama.

Catherine Malandrino (✉ *10 rue de Grenelle, 6e, St-Germain-des-Prés* ☎ *01–42–22–26–95* Ⓜ *Sèvres Babylone*) designs for the urban sophisticate, expertly combining glamor, smarts, and allure in her office-to-soirée styles. Dresses caress the body without clinging and incorporate ingenious details—cutout seams, a flattering wide bodice, transparent sleeves—for an ultrastylish look.

★ **Chanel** (✉ *42 av. Montaigne, Champs-Élysées, 8e* ☎ *01–47–23–74–12* Ⓜ *Franklin-D.-Roosevelt* ✉ *31 rue Cambon, Louvre/Tuileries, 1er* ☎ *01–42–86–26–00* Ⓜ *Tuileries*) is helmed by Karl Lagerfeld, whose collections are steadily vibrant. Great investments include all of Coco's favorites: the perfectly tailored tweed suit, a lean, soigné black dress, a quilted bag with a gold chain, or a camellia brooch.

Chloé (✉ *54–56 rue du Faubourg St-Honoré, Louvre/Tuileries, 8e* ☎ *01–44–94–33–00* Ⓜ *Concorde*) is revising its image yet again with Hannah McGibbon at the helm; less romantic and feminine than days of yore, the line still features flowing layered dresses but with an asymmetric edge. Bold colors and patterns on lovely diaphanous fabrics made a big splash recently. **Christian Dior** (✉ *30 av. Montaigne, Champs-Élysées, 8e* ☎ *01–40–73–54–44* Ⓜ *Franklin-D.-Roosevelt* ✉ *16 rue de l'Abbé, St-Germain-des-Prés, 6e* ☎ *01–56–24–90–53* Ⓜ *St-Germain-des-Prés*) features the flamboyant John Galliano . . . so what if he pairs full-length body-skimming evening dresses with high-tops and a Davy Crockett raccoon hat? It's fashion, darling.

★ **Colette** (✉ *213 rue St-Honoré, Louvre/Tuileries, 1er* ☎ *01–55–35–33–90* Ⓜ *Tuileries*) is the most fashionable, most hip, and most hyped store in Paris (and possibly the world). The ground floor, which stocks design objects, gadgets, and makeup, is generally packed with fashion victims and the simply curious. Upstairs are handpicked fashions, accessories, magazines, and books, all of which ooze trendiness. The basement has a water bar and a small restaurant that's good for a quick bite.

★ **Galliano** (✉ *384 rue St-Honoré, Louvre/Tuileries, 1er* ☎ *01–55–35–40–40* Ⓜ *Concorde*), fittingly enough, landed an address with Revolutionary history for his first namesake store. What more can be said about John Galliano, a living hyperbole? Well, the boutique pairs glass and stone, a high-tech plasma

GRAND COUTURE REDUX

Didier Ludot (✉ *Jardins du Palais-Royal, 24 Galerie Montpensier* ☎ *01–42–96–06–56* Ⓜ *Palais-Royal*) is one of the world's most famous vintage-clothing dealers—and an incredibly charming man to boot. Check out his three lovely boutiques: No. 20 houses his amazing collection of vintage couture, No. 24 the vintage ready-to-wear, and across the way at No. 125 you'll find his own vintage-inspired black dresses and his coffee-table book aptly titled *The Little Black Dress.*

screen grabs your eye. Clothes ricochet between debauchery, humor, and refinement.

★ **Jean-Paul Gaultier** (✉ *44 av. George V, Champs-Élysées, 8e* ☎ *01–44–43–00–44* Ⓜ *George V* ✉ *6 Galerie Vivienne, Opéra/Grands Boulevards, 2e* ☎ *01–42–86–05–05* Ⓜ *Bourse*) first made headlines with his celebrated corset with the ironic i-conic breasts for Madonna, but now sends fashion editors into ecstasy with his sumptuous haute-couture creations. Designer Philippe Starck spun an *Alice in Wonderland* fantasy for the boutiques, with quilted cream walls and Murano mirrors.

GIFTS FOR THE HOME

★ **Maison de Baccarat** (✉ *11 pl. des États-Unis, Trocadéro/Tour Eiffel, 16e* ☎ *01–40–22–11–00* Ⓜ *Trocadéro*) was once the home of Marie-Laure de Noailles, known as the Countess of Bizarre; now it's a museum and crystal store of the famed manufacturer. Philippe Starck revamped the space with his signature cleverness—yes, that's a chandelier floating in an aquarium and, yes, that crystal arm sprouting from the wall alludes to Jean Cocteau (a friend of Noailles).

★ **Muji** (✉ *47 rue des Francs Bourgeois, Le Marais, 4e* ☎ *01–49–96–41–41* Ⓜ *St-Paul* ✉ *27 and 30 rue St-Sulpice, St-Germain-des-Prés, 6e* ☎ *01–46–34–01–10* Ⓜ *Odéon*) runs on the concept of *kanketsu*, or simplicity. The resultant streamlined designs for sportswear, housewares, and other supplies are all the rage in Europe. Must-haves include a collection of mini-necessities—travel essentials, wee office gizmos, purse-size accoutrements—so useful and adorable you'll want them all. **Le Monde Sauvage** (✉ *11 rue de l'Odéon, Quartier Latin, 6e* ☎ *01–43–25–60–34* Ⓜ *Odéon*) is a must-visit for home accessories—reversible silk bedspreads in rich colors, velvet throws, hand-quilted bed linens, silk floor cushions, Venetian mirrors, and the best selection of hand-embroidered curtains in silk, cotton, linen, or velvet.

GOURMET GOODIES

À la Mère de Famille (✉ *35 rue du Faubourg-Montmartre, Opéra/Grands Boulevards, 9e* ☎ *01–47–70–83–69* Ⓜ *Cadet*) is an enchanting shop well versed in French regional specialties and old-fashioned bonbons, sugar candy, and more. **Fauchon** (✉ *26 pl. de la Madeleine, Opéra/Grands Boulevards, 8e* ☎ *01–70–39–38–00* Ⓜ *Madeleine*) is the most famous and iconic of all Parisian food stores and sells renowned pâté, honey, jelly, tea, and private-label champagne. There's a café for a quick bite.

3

Ile-de-France

WORD OF MOUTH

"I wouldn't buy a ticket to Versailles ahead of time. It's very easy to get there from Paris, so choose your day with good weather to fully enjoy the lovely gardens."

—TPAYT

"Weekends are supposed to be a lot more crowded at Versailles but you miss the FANTASTIC fountains. The gardens are so large, you wouldn't notice a crowd anyway."

—Connie

WELCOME TO ILE-DE-FRANCE

TOP REASONS TO GO

★ **Louis XIV's Versailles:** Famed as glorious testimony to the Sun King's megalomania, this is the world's most luxe palace and nature-tamed park.

★ **Creamy Chantilly:** Stately château, stellar art collection, fabulous forest, palatial stables . . . all within the same square mile.

★ **Van Gogh in Auvers:** The great painter spent his last, manically productive three months here—you can see where he painted, where he got drunk, where he shot himself, and where he remains.

★ **Chartres Cathedral:** A pinnacle of Gothic achievement, this 13th-century masterpiece has peerless stained glass and a hilltop silhouette visible for miles around.

★ **Monet's Water Lilies:** Come to Giverny to see his lily pond—a half-acre "Monet"—then peek around his charming home and stroll the time-warped streets to the new Musée des Impressionismes.

1 The Western Ile-de-France. Versailles to Auvers-sur-Oise. The Ile-de-France's richest frontier for you, if you want to dig into the past, is the western half of the 60-km (35-mi) circle that rings Paris. These sylvan woods are literally full of châteaux of all descriptions, the towns are charming, and no one should miss the world's grandest palace. Haunt of Louis XIV, Madame de Pompadour, and Marie-Antoinette, Versailles is a monument to splendidly wretched excess and once home to 20,000 courtiers and servants. More spiritual concerns are embodied in Chartres Cathedral, a soaring pinnacle of Gothic architecture. Thirty miles north are landscapes of lasting impressions: Giverny and Auvers, immortalized by Monet and Van Gogh, respectively.

GETTING ORIENTED

Appearing like all France in miniature, the Ile-de-France region is the heartland of the nation. The "island of France" is the poetic name for the area surrounding Paris and taking in the valleys of three rivers: the Seine, the Marne, and the Oise. Ever since the days of Julius Caesar, this has been the economic, political, and religious hub of France and, consequently, no other region boasts such a wealth of great buildings, from Chartres to Fontainebleau and Versailles. Though small, this region is so rich in treasures that a whole day of fascinating exploration may take you no more than 60 km (35 mi) from the capital.

2 The Eastern Ile-de-France. Chantilly to Fontainebleau. By traveling an eastward arc through the remainder of the Ile you can savor the icing on the cake. Begin with Chantilly, one of the most opulent châteaux in France, noted for its royal stables, art treasures, and gardens by André Le Nôtre. Northward lie medieval Senlis and the storybook castle of Pierrefonds. Heading east, Disneyland Paris is where the Mickey-smitten rejoice. Continuing south, two magnificent châteaux—Vaux-le-Vicomte and Fontainebleau—were built for some of France's most pampered monarchs and merchants.

ILE-DE-FRANCE PLANNER

Transportation Basics

A comprehensive rail network ensures that most towns in Ile-de-France can make comfortable day trips from Paris, but make sure you know the right station to head out from (Gare de Lyon for Fontainebleau, Gare St-Lazare for Vernon, Gare du Nord for Compiègne/Pierrefonds, or Gare Montparnasse for Chartres). RER (commuter) trains tunnel through central Paris en route to Versailles and Disneyland.

A handful of venues need other means of access. To reach Giverny, rail it to Vernon, then take a taxi or local bus (or bike). To reach Vaux-le-Vicomte, head first for Melun, then take a taxi or local bus (in summer a shuttle service). Senlis can be reached by bus from Chantilly. And note that Fontainebleau station is in neighboring Avon, and getting to the château means a 10-minute bus ride. The best way to crisscross the region without returning to the capital is by car. There's no shortage of expressways or fast highways. Expressways fan out from Paris in all directions: A13 northwest to Versailles and Giverny; A1 north to Senlis and Compiègne; A4 east to Disneyland; A6 southeast to Fontainebleau; and A10 southwest to Chartres.

Experiencing Impressionism

Paris's Musée d'Orsay may have some of the most fabled Monet and Van Gogh paintings in the world, but Ile-de-France has something (almost) better—the actual landscapes that were rendered into masterpieces by the brushes of many great Impressionist and Postimpressionist artists.

At Giverny, Claude Monet's house and garden are a moving visual link to his finest daubs—its famous lily-pond garden gave rise to his legendary water-lilies series (some historians feel it was the other way around).

Nearby, villages like Vétheuil still look like three-dimensional "Monets." Here, too, is the impressive Musée des Impressionismes.

In Auvers-sur-Oise, Vincent van Gogh had a final burst of creativity before ending his life; the famous wheat field where he was attacked by crows and painted his last painting is just outside town.

Back then, they called him Fou-Roux (mad redhead) and derided his art. But now, more than a century after his passionate rendering of life and landscape, the townspeople here love to pay tribute to the man who helped make their village famous.

André Derain lived in Chambourcy, Camille Pissarro in Pontoise, Alfred Sisley in Moret-sur-Loing—all were inspired by the silvery sunlight that tumbles over these hills and towns.

Earlier, Rousseau, Millet, and Corot paved the way for Impressionism with their penchant for outdoor landscape painting in the village of Barbizon, still surrounded by its romantic, quietly dramatic forest. A trip to any of these towns will provide lasting impressions.

Finding a Place to Stay

In summer, hotel rooms are at a premium, and making reservations is essential; almost all accommodations in the swankier towns—Versailles, Rambouillet, and Fontainebleau—are on the costly side. Take nothing for granted; picturesque Senlis, for instance, does not have a single hotel in its historic downtown area.

Making the Most of Your Time

Though small, the Ile-de-France is so rich in treasures that a whole day of fascinating exploration may take you no more than 60 km (35 mi) from the capital. Thus, a great advantage to exploring this region is that all its major monuments are within a half-day's drive from Paris, or less, if you take the trains that run to many of the towns in this chapter.

The catch is that most of those rail lines connect the towns of the Ile with Paris, not, in general, with neighboring towns of the region. Thus, it may be easier to plan on "touring" the Ile in a series of side trips from Paris, rather than expecting to travel through the Ile in clockwise fashion (which, of course, can be handily done if you have a car).

This chapter is broken up into two halves. Threading the western half of the Ile, the first tour heads southwest from Paris to Versailles and Chartres, turns northwest along the Seine to Monet's Giverny, and returns to Paris after visiting Vincent van Gogh's Auvers. Exploring the eastern half of the Ile, the second tour picks up east of the Oise Valley in glamorous Chantilly, then detours north to Pierrefonds, and finishes up southward by heading to Disneyland Paris, Vaux-le-Vicomte, and Fontainebleau.

For a stimulating mix of pomp, nature, and spirituality, we suggest your three priorities should be Versailles, Giverny, and Chartres.

Loosen Those Belts

Ile-de-France's fanciest restaurants can be just as pricey as their Parisian counterparts. Close to the Channel for fresh fish, to lush Normandy for beef and dairy products, and to the rich agricultural regions of Picardy and the Beauce, Ile-de-France chefs have all the ingredients they could wish for, and shop for the freshest produce early each morning at the huge food market at Rungis.

DINING AND LODGING PRICE CATEGORIES (IN EUROS)

	¢	$	$$	$$$	$$$$
Restaurants	under €12	€12–€17	€18–€24	€25–€32	over €32
Hotels	under €65	€65–€105	€106–€145	€146–€215	over €215

Restaurant prices are per person for a main course at dinner, including tax (5.5%) and service; note that if a restaurant offers only prix-fixe (set-price) meals, it has been given the price category that reflects the full prix-fixe price. Hotel prices are for a standard double room in high season, including tax (19.6%) and service charge.

When to Go

With its extensive forests, Ile-de-France is especially beautiful in fall, particularly October.

May and June are good months, too, while July through August can be sultry and crowded.

On a Saturday night in summer, however, you can make a candlelight visit to Vaux-le-Vicomte.

Be aware when making your travel plans that some places are closed one or two days a week.

The château of Versailles is closed Monday; and the châteaux of Chantilly and Fontainebleau are closed Tuesday.

In fact, as a rule, well-touristed towns make their *fermeture hebdomadaire* (weekly closing) on Monday or Tuesday.

At these times museums, shops, and markets may be closed—call ahead if in doubt.

Disneyland Paris tends to be mobbed on summer weekends.

So does Giverny (Monet's garden), which is at its best May through June and, like Vaux-le-Vicomte, is closed November to March.

During the winter months, it's always best to check and phone ahead to make sure your sightseeing stops are still open.

GETTING AROUND

Air Travel

Major airports in the Ile-de-France area are Charles de Gaulle (☎ *01–48–62–22–80* 🌐 *www.adp.fr*), commonly known as Roissy, 25 km (16 mi) northeast of Paris, and Orly (☎ *01–49–75–15–15* 🌐 *www.adp.fr*), 16 km (10 mi) south.

Shuttle buses link Disneyland to the airports at Roissy, 56 km (35 mi) away, and Orly, 50 km (31 mi) distant; buses take 45 minutes and run every 45 minutes from Roissy, every 60 minutes from Orly (less frequently in low season), and cost €17.

Visitor Information

Special *forfait* tickets, combining travel and admission, are available for several regional tourist destinations (including Versailles, Fontainebleau, and Auvers-sur-Oise).

Contact the Espace du Tourisme d'Ile-de-France (🌐 *www.pidf.com* ⏲ *Wed.–Mon. 10–7*), under the inverted pyramid in the Carrousel du Louvre, for general information on the area.

Information on Disneyland is available from the Disneyland Paris reservations office. Local tourist offices are listed throughout the chapter by town.

Bus Travel

Although many of the major sights in this chapter have train lines connecting them on direct routes with Paris, the lesser towns and destinations pose more of a problem and require taking a local bus run by SNCF (☎ *36–35 [€0.34 per min]* 🌐 *www.transilien.com*) from the train station.

For instance, to get to Senlis from the Chantilly Gare SNCF station , or Fontainebleau and Barbizon from the Avon Gare SNCF station, or Vaux-le-Vicomte from the Melun Gare SNCF station, or Giverny from the Vernon Gare SNCF staion.

Other buses travel outward from Paris's suburbs—the No. 158A bus, for instance, which goes from La Défense to St-Germain-en-Laye and Rueil-Malmaison.

Car Travel

A13 links Paris (from the Porte d'Auteuil) to Versailles. You can get to Chartres on A10 from Paris (Porte d'Orléans).

For Fontainebleau take A6 from Paris (Porte d'Orléans).

For a more attractive, although slower route through the Forest of Sénart and the northern part of the Forest of Fontainebleau, take N6 from Paris (Porte de Charenton) via Melun.

A4 runs from Paris (Porte de Bercy) to Disneyland.

Although a comprehensive rail network ensures that most towns in Ile-de-France can make comfortable day trips from Paris, the only way to crisscross the region without returning to the capital is by car.

There's no shortage of expressways or fast highways.

However, you should be prepared for delays close to Paris, especially during the morning and evening rush hours.

Train Travel

Many sights can be reached by SNCF (☎ *08–91–36–20–20 [€0.23 per min]* 🌐 *www.transilien.com*) trains from Paris.

The handiest of Versailles's three train stations is the one reached by the RER-C line.

The main Paris station for this train are at Austerlitz, St-Michel, Invalides, and Champ-de-Mars; the trip takes 30–40 minutes.

Both regional and main-line (Le Mans–bound) trains leave Gare Montparnasse for Chartres (50–70 mins).

The former also stops at Versailles and Rambouillet.

Gare Montparnasse is also the terminal for the suburban trains that stop at Montfort-L'Amaury, a helpful rail station for the northwest regions of the Ile-de-France area.

Most main-line trains from Gare St-Lazare stop at Vernon (50 mins), for Monet's House at Giverny, on their way to Rouen and Le Havre.

Chantilly is on the main northbound line from Gare du Nord (the trip takes 25–40 mins).

The lovely medieval town of Senlis can be reached by bus from Chantilly.

Fontainebleau—or, rather, neighboring Avon, 2 km (1½ mi) away (there is frequent bus service)—is 45 minutes from Gare de Lyon.

To reach Vaux-le-Vicomte, head first for Melun, then take a taxi or local bus (in summer a shuttle service).

To reach Giverny, rail it to Vernon, then use the taxi or local bus.

The RER-A also accesses the station for Disneyland Paris (called Marne-la-Vallée–Chessy).

Happily, this leaves visitors within 100 yards of the entrance to both the theme park and Disney Village.

Journey time is around 40 minutes, and trains operate every 10–30 minutes, depending on the time of day.

A main-line TGV (Trains à Grande Vitesse 🌐 *www.tgv.com*) station also links Disneyland to Lille, Lyon, Brussels, and London (via Lille and the Channel Tunnel).

Ile de France Tour Options

Cityrama (✉ *2 rue des Pyramides, Paris* ☎ *01–44–55–60–00* 🌐 *www.cityrama.fr*) organizes guided excursions to Giverny, Chartres, and Fontainebleau/Barbizon (€60–€70) from April through October. Cityrama and **Paris Vision** (✉ *214 rue de Rivoli, Paris* ☎ *01–42–60–30–01* 🌐 *www.parisvision.com*) run half- and full-day trips to Versailles (€50–€120).

Alliance Autos (✉ *149 rue de Charonne, Paris* ☎ *01–55–25–23–23*) has bilingual guides who can take you on a private tour around the Paris area in a luxury car or minibus for a minimum of four hours for about €80 an hour (call to check details and prices).

Euroscope (✉ *27 rue Taitbout, Paris* ☎ *01–56–03–56–81* 🌐 *www.euroscope.fr*) runs minibus excursions to Versailles (€80) and Giverny (€85).

Word of Mouth

"Monet's Giverny is very easy to do on your own. To get there, take a train from Paris's Gare St. Lazare to Vernon. There, a bus takes visitors to the gardens—it should be parked a half block from the station on the right. The bus times its departures with the train arrivals. Or you can rent a bike, walk, or cab it—find more info (including the bus schedule) at 🌐 *www.giverny.org*." —cls2paris

Updated by Jennifer Ditsler-Ladonne

Just what is it that makes the Ile-de-France so attractive, so comfortingly familiar? Is it its proximity to the great city of Paris—or perhaps that it's so far removed?

Had there not been the world-class cultural hub of Paris right nearby, would Monet have retreated to his Japanese gardens at Giverny? Or Paul Cézanne and Van Gogh to bucolic Auvers? Kings and courtiers to the game-rich forests of Rambouillet? Would Napoléon have truly settled at Malmaison and then abdicated at the palace at Fontainebleau? Would medieval castles and palaces have sprouted in the town of St-Germain-en-Laye? Would abbeys and cathedrals have sprung skyward in Chartres and Senlis?

If you asked Louis XIV, he wouldn't have minced his words: the city of Paris—yawn—was simply *démodée*—out of fashion. In the 17th century the new power base was going to be Versailles, once a tiny village in the heart of the Ile-de-France, now the site of a gigantic château from which the Sun King's rays (Louis XIV was known as *le roi soleil*) could radiate, unfettered by rebellious rabble and European arrivistes. Of course, later heirs kept the lines open and restored the grandiose palace as the governmental hub it was meant to be—and commuted to Paris, well before the high-speed RER.

That, indeed, is the dream of most Parisians today: to have a foot in both worlds. Paris may be small as capital cities go, with just under 2 million inhabitants, but Ile-de-France, the region around Paris, contains more than 10 million people—a sixth of France's entire population. That's why on closer inspection the once rustic villages of Ile-de-France reveal cosseted gardens, stylishly gentrified cottages, and extraordinary country restaurants no peasant farmer could afford to frequent.

The Ile-de-France is not really an *île* (island), of course. This green-forested buffer zone that enfolds Paris is only vaguely surrounded by the three rivers that meander through its periphery. But France's capital city seems to crown this genteel sprawl of an atoll, peppered with pretty villages, anchored by grandiose châteaux. In the end, Ile-de-France offers a rich and varied mini sampling of everything you expect from France—cathedrals, painters' villages, lavish palaces, along with the bubblegum-pink turrets of Disneyland Paris—and all delightfully set within easy day trips from Paris.

THE WESTERN ILE-DE-FRANCE

Not only is majestic Versailles one of the most unforgettable sights in Ile-de-France, it's also within easy reach of Paris, less than 30 minutes by either train or car (A13 expressway from Porte d'Auteuil). It's the starting point for a visit to the western half of the Ile-de-France, anchored by holy Chartres to the south and Vincent van Gogh's Auvers-sur-Oise to the north.

VERSAILLES

16 km (10 mi) west of Paris via A13.

Fodor's Choice ★ It's hard to tell which is larger at **Château de Versailles**—the world-famous château that housed Louis XIV and 20,000 of his courtiers, or the mass of tour buses and visitors standing in front of it. The grandest palace in France remains one of the marvels of the world (⇨ *Its full story is covered in the special photo feature on the château in this chapter, "Gilt Trip: A Tour of Versailles"*). But this edifice was not just home to the Sun King, it was to be the new headquarters of the French government capital (from 1682 to 1789 and again from 1871 to 1879). To accompany the palace, a new city—in fact, a new capital—had to be built from scratch. Tough-thinking town planners took no prisoners, dreaming up vast mansions and avenues broader than the Champs-Élysées.

GETTING HERE

Versailles has three train stations, all reached from different stations in Paris (journey time 25–40 mins). Versailles Rive Gauche provides the easiest access from Paris. The other two stations in Versailles are about a 10-minute walk from the château, although the municipal Bus B or a summertime shuttle service (use métro ticket or pay small fee in coins) can also deposit you at the front gates.

Visitor Information **Versailles Tourist Office** (✉ *2 bis, av. de Paris* ☎ *01–39–24–88–88* 🌐 *www.versailles-tourisme.com*).

EXPLORING

EXPLORING

If you have any energy left after exploring Louis XIV's palace and park, a tour of Versailles—a textbook 18th-century town—offers a telling contrast between the majestic and the domestic. From the front gate of Versailles' palace turn left onto the Rue de l'Independence-Américaine and walk over to Rue Carnot past the stately Écuries de la Reine—once the queen's stables, now the regional law courts—to octagonal Place Hoche. Down Rue Hoche to the left is the powerful Baroque facade of **Notre-Dame**, built from 1684 to 1686 by Jules Hardouin-Mansart as the parish church for Louis XIV's new town.

Around the back of Notre-Dame, on Boulevard de la Reine (note the regimented lines of trees), are the elegant Hôtel de Neyret and the **Musée Lambinet**, a sumptuous mansion from 1751, furnished with paintings,

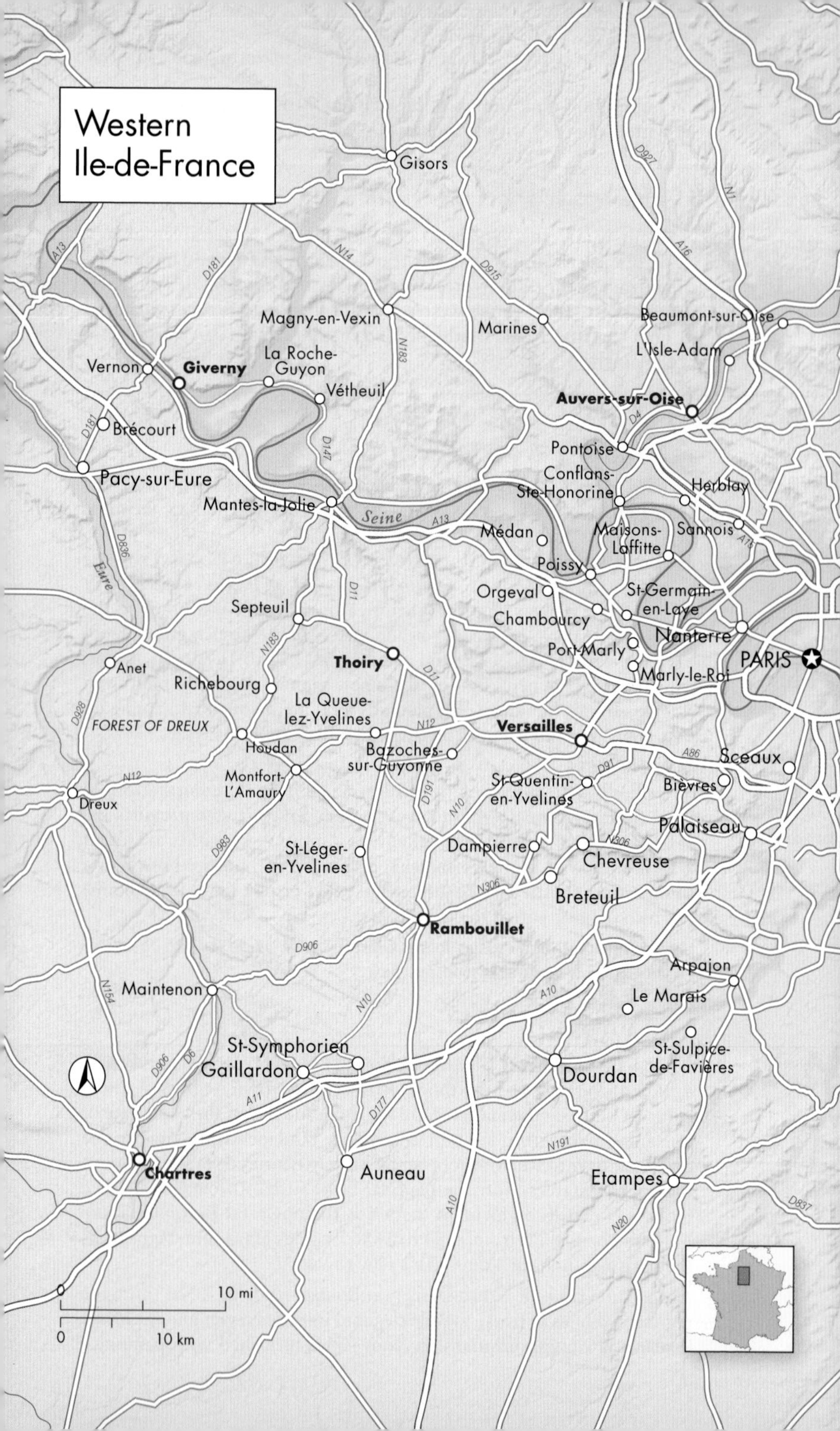

Western Ile-de-France
Gisors
Magny-en-Vexin
Marines
Beaumont-sur-Oise
L'Isle-Adam
Vernon
Giverny
La Roche-Guyon
Vétheuil
Auvers-sur-Oise
Brécourt
Pontoise
Pacy-sur-Eure
Conflans-Ste-Honorine
Herblay
Mantes-la-Jolie
Seine
Médan
Maisons-Laffitte
Sannois
Poissy
Orgeval
St-Germain-en-Laye
Septeuil
Chambourcy
Nanterre
Port-Marly
Thoiry
PARIS
Anet
Marly-le-Roi
Richebourg
La Queue-lez-Yvelines
FOREST OF DREUX
Versailles
Houdan
Bazoches-sur-Guyonne
Sceaux
Montfort-L'Amaury
St-Quentin-en-Yvelines
Bièvres
Dreux
Palaiseau
St-Léger-en-Yvelines
Dampierre
Chevreuse
Breteuil
Rambouillet
Arpajon
Maintenon
Le Marais
St-Symphorien
St-Sulpice-de-Favières
Gaillardon
Dourdan
Chartres
Auneau
Etampes
Eure
10 mi
0
10 km

weapons, fans, and porcelain (including the Madame du Barry "Rose"). ✉ *54 bd. de la Reine* ☎ *01–39–50–30–32* *€5.50* ⏲ *Tues.–Thurs. and weekends 2–6, Fri. 2–5, Wed. 1–6.*

Passage de la Geôle, a cobbled alley lined with quaint antiques shops, climbs up to **Place du Marché-Notre-Dame**, whose open-air morning market on Tuesday, Friday, and Sunday is famed throughout the region (note the four 19th-century timber-roof halls).

3

WHERE TO EAT

$$–$$$ FRENCH ✕ **Au Chapeau Gris**. This bustling wood-beam restaurant just off Avenue de St-Cloud, overlooking elegant Place Hoche, offers hearty selections of meat and fish, ranging from *bœuf Rossini* with wild mushrooms to salmon and scallops marinated in lime and the top-price lobster fricasseed in Sancerre. The wine list roams around the vineyards of Bordeaux and Burgundy, while desserts include crème brûlée with lemon zest, and apricot and caramel tart. The €21 prix-fixe menu makes a filling lunchtime option. ✉ *7 rue Hoche* ☎ *01–39–50–10–81* 🌐 *www.auchapeaugris.com* ▭ *AE, MC, V* ⏲ *Closed Wed. No dinner Tues. and daily late July–late Aug.*

$$$$ FRENCH ★ ✕ **Gordon Ramsay au Trianon**. Gordon Ramsay has finally arrived in France thanks to Westin's Trianon Palace hotel revamp. The ebullient "bad boy de la cuisine anglaise" has already amassed a string of restaurants worldwide, including three in New York, London's only Michelin three-star, and two stars for this establishment in 2009. But, although he cut his culinary teeth in the kitchens of master chefs Guy Savoy and Joël Robuchon, this is his first eatery on French soil. The delicious results—overseen by his longstanding London number two, Simone Zanoni—are predictably conversation-worthy: pigs' feet and knuckle of ham with Bellota Iberico, toasted muffin, poached egg, and Hollandaise sauce; pan-fried John Dory with tourteau crab, crushed new potatoes, caviar, and basil vinaigrette; and turbot fillet with coriander and carrot tagliolini, asparagus salad, and citrus sauce. Desserts are marvels, too, with "carpaccio" of pineapple with lychee bubbles and mascarpone ice cream vying for top honors with the raspberry soufflé with chocolate and tarragon ice cream. The Trianon's more casual, 75-seat Véranda restaurant is now also under Ramsay's sway, and in its black-and-white contemporary setting you can opt for Ramsay's "light, modern take" on such bistro banalities as chicorée risotto, sautéed lobster, scallops with shiitake, and chicken with cabbage and braised shallots. ✉ *1 bd. de la Reine* ☎ *01–30–84–55–56* 🌐 *www.gordonramsay.com/grautrianon* *Reservations essential* *Jacket required* ▭ *AE, DC, MC, V* ⏲ *Closed Sun. and Mon. Lunch on Fri. and Sat. only.*

WHERE TO STAY

$ **Home St-Louis**. This family-run, three-story stone-and-brick hotel is a good, cheap, quiet bet—close to the cathedral and a 15-minute walk from the château. The quietest rooms overlook the courtyard at the back, rather than facing the street. **Pros:** cheap; friendly. **Cons:** not in town center; rooms are small. ✉ *28 rue St-Louis* ☎ *01–39–50–23–55* *25 rooms* *In-room: no a/c, Internet, Wi-Fi. In-hotel: room service, some pets allowed* ▭ *AE, MC, V.*

Continued on page 181

GILT TRIP
A TOUR OF VERSAILLES

Louis XIV's Hall of Mirrors

A two-century spree of indulgence in the finest bling-bling of the age by the consecutive reigns of three French kings produced two of the world's most historic artifacts: gloriously, the Palace of Versailles and, momentously, the French Revolution.

Less a monument than an entire world unto itself, Versailles is the king of palaces. The end result of 380 million francs, 36,000 laborers, and enough paintings, if laid end to end, to equal 7 miles of canvas, it was conceived as the ne plus ultra expression of monarchy by Louis XIV. As a child, the king had developed a hatred for Paris (where he had been imprisoned by a group of nobles known as the Frondeurs), so, when barely out of his teens, he cast his cantankerous royal eye in search of a new power base. Marshy, inhospitable Versailles was the stuff of his dreams. Down came dad's modest royal hunting lodge and up, up, and along went the minion-crushing, Baroque palace we see today.

Between 1661 and 1710, architects Louis Le Vau and Jules Hardouin Mansart designed everything his royal acquisitiveness could want, including a throne room devoted to Apollo, god of the sun (Louis was known as *le roi soleil*). Convinced that his might depended upon dominating French nobility, Louis XIV summoned thousands of grandees from their own far-flung châteaux to reside at his new seat of government. In doing so, however, he unwittingly triggered the downfall of the monarchy. Like an 18th-century Disneyland, Versailles kept its courtiers so richly entertained they all but forgot the murmurs of discontent brewing back home.

As Louis XV chillingly foretold, "After me, the deluge." The royal commune was therefore shocked—shocked!—by the appearance, on October 5, 1789, of a revolutionary mob from Paris ready to sack Versailles and imprison Louis XVI. So as you walk through this awesome monument to splendor and excess, give a thought to its historic companion: the French Revolution. A tour of Versailles's grand salons inextricably mixes pathos with glory.

CROWNING GLORIES: TOP SIGHTS OF VERSAILLES

Versailles from the outside

Seducing their court with their self-assured approach to 17th- and 18th-century art and decoration, a trinity of French kings made Versailles into the most vainglorious of châteaux.

Detail of the ceiling

Galerie des Glaces (Hall of Mirrors). Of all the rooms at Versailles, none matches the magnificence of the Galerie des Glaces (Hall of Mirrors). Begun by Mansart in 1678, this represents the acme of the Louis Quatorze (Louis-XIV) style. Measuring 240 feet long, 33 feet wide, and 40 feet high, it is ornamented with gilded candlesticks, crystal chandeliers, and a coved ceiling painted with Charles Le Brun's homage to Louis XIV's reign.

Hall of Mirrors

In Louis's day, the Galerie was laid with priceless carpets and filled with orange trees in silver pots. Nighttime galas were illuminated by 3,000 candles, their blaze doubled in the 17 gigantic mirrors that precisely echo the banner of windows along the west front. Lavish balls were once held here, as was a later event with much greater world impact: the signing of the Treaty of Versailles, which put an end to World War I on June 28, 1919.

Inside the Apollo Chamber

The Grands Appartements (State Apartments). Virtual stages for ceremonies of court ritual and etiquette, Louis XIV's first-floor state salons were designed in the Baroque style on a biceps-flexing scale meant to one-up the lavish Vaux-le-Vicomte château recently built for Nicolas Fouquet, the king's finance minister.

Flanking the Hall of Mirrors and retaining most of their bombastic Italianate Baroque decoration, the Salon de la Guerre (Salon of War) and the Salon de la Paix (Salon of Peace) are ornately decorated with gilt stucco, painted ceilings, and marble sculpture. Perhaps the most extravagant is the Salon d'Apollon (Apollo Chamber), the former throne room.

Hall of Battles

Appartements du Roi (King's Apartments). Completed in 1701 in the Louis-XIV style, the king's state and private chambers comprise a suite of 15 rooms set in a "U" around the east facade's Marble Court. Dead center across the sprawling cobbled forecourt is Louis XIV's bedchamber—he would awake and rise (just as the sun did, from the east) attended by members of his court and the public. Holding the king's chemise when he dressed soon became a more definitive reflection of status than the possession of an entire province. Nearby is Louis XV's magnificent Cabinet Intérieur (Office of the King), shining with gold and white boiseries; in the center is the most famous piece of furniture at Versailles, Louis XV's roll-top desk, crafted by Oeben and Riesener in 1769.

Louis XIV

King's Apartments

Chambre de la Reine (Queen's Bedchamber). Probably the most opulent bedroom in the world, this was initially created for Marie Thérèse, first wife of Louis XIV, to be part of the Queen's Apartments. For Marie Antoinette, however, the entire room was glammed up with silk wall-hangings covered with Rococo motifs that reflect her love of flowers. Legend has it that the gardens directly beyond these windows were replanted daily so that the queen could enjoy a fresh assortment of blossoms each morning. The bed, decked out with white ostrich plumes *en panache*, was also redone for Louis XVI's queen. Nineteen royal children were born in this room.

VINTAGE BOURBON

Versailles was built by three great kings of the Bourbon dynasty. Louis XIV (1638–1715) began its construction in 1661. After ruling for 72 years, Louis Quatorze was succeeded by his great grandson, Louis XV (1710–74), who added the Royal Opera and the Petit Trianon to the palace. Louis XVI (1754–93) came to the throne in 1774 and was forced out of Versailles in 1789, along with Marie Antoinette, both guillotined three years later.

Queen's Bedchamber

Petits Appartements (Small Apartments). As styles of decor changed, Louis XIV's successors felt out of sync with their architectural inheritance. Louis XV exchanged the heavy red-and-gilt of Italianate Baroque for lighter, pastel-hued Rococo. On the top floor of the palace, on the right side of the central portion, are the apartments Louis XV commissioned to escape the wearisome pomp of the first-floor rooms. Here, Madame de Pompadour, mistress of Louis XV and famous patroness of the Rococo style, introduced grace notes of intimacy and refinement. In so doing, she transformed the daunting royal apartments into places to live rather than pose.

Parc de Versailles. Even Bourbon kings needed respite from Versailles's endless maze, hence the creation of one of Europe's largest parks. The sublime 250-acre grounds (☎ 01–30–83–77–88 for guided tour) is the masterpiece of André Le Nôtre, presiding genius of 17th-century classical French landscaping. Le Nôtre was famous for his "green geometries": ordered fantasies of clipped yew trees, multicolored flower beds (called *parterres*), and perspectival allées cleverly punctuated with statuary, laid out between 1661 and 1668. The spatial effect is best admired from inside the palace, views about which Le Nôtre said, "Flowers can only be walked on by the eyes."

Ultimately, at the royal command, rivers were diverted—to flow into more than 600 fountains—and entire forests were imported to ornament the park, which is centered around the mile-long Grand Canal. As for the great fountains, their operation costs a fortune in these democratic days, and so they perform only on Saturday and Sunday afternoons (⏲ 3:30–5:30) from mid-April through mid-October; admission to the park during this time is €8. The park is open daily 8 AM–8:30 PM.

LIGHTING UP THE SKY

The largest fountain in the Versailles park, the Bassin de Neptune, becomes a spectacle of rare grandeur during the Fêtes de Nuit (☎ 01–30–83–78–88 or online), a light-and-fireworks show held on ten nights (usually Saturday) between late July and early September. The spectacle begins at 10:30 PM, and also features some 200-plus actors costumed in knee-breeches wigs. The 90-minute show is well worth the ticket admission of €16 to €48.

Dauphin's Apartments

Bassin de Neptune

Chapel and Opéra Royal: In the north wing of the château are three showpieces of the palace. The solemn white-and-gold Chapelle was completed in 1710—the king and queen attended daily mass here seated in gilt boxes. The Opéra Royal (Opera House), entirely constructed of wood painted to look like marble, was designed by Jacques-Ange Gabriel for Louis XV in 1770. Connecting the two, the 17th-century Galeries have exhibits retracing the château's history.

Opéra Royal

VERSAILLES: FIRST FLOOR, GARDENS & ADJACENT PARK

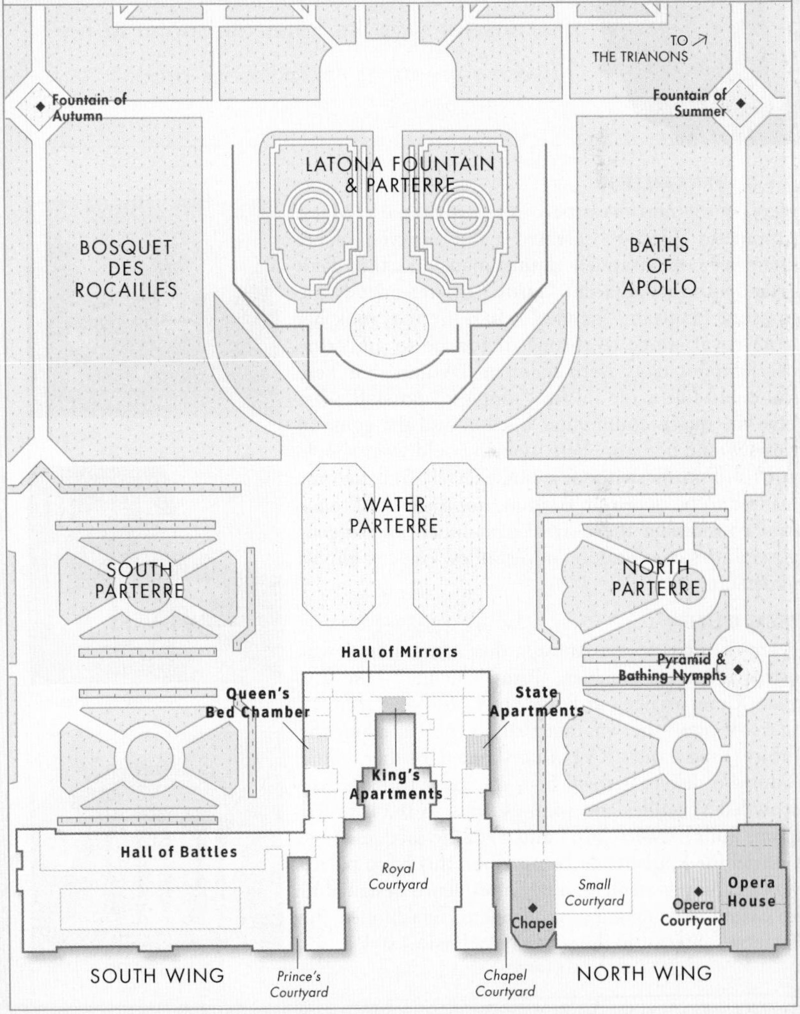

TO THE TRIANONS
Fountain of Autumn
Fountain of Summer
LATONA FOUNTAIN & PARTERRE
BOSQUET DES ROCAILLES
BATHS OF APOLLO
WATER PARTERRE
SOUTH PARTERRE
NORTH PARTERRE
Hall of Mirrors
Pyramid & Bathing Nymphs
Queen's Bed Chamber
State Apartments
King's Apartments
Hall of Battles
Royal Courtyard
Small Courtyard
Chapel
Opera Courtyard
Opera House
SOUTH WING
Prince's Courtyard
Chapel Courtyard
NORTH WING

LET THEM EAT CRÊPE: MARIE ANTOINETTE'S ROYAL LAIR

Was Marie Antoinette a luxury-mad butterfly flitting from ball to costume ball? Or was she a misunderstood queen who suffered a loveless marriage and became a prisoner of court etiquette at Versailles? Historians now believe the answer was the latter and point to her private retreats at Versailles as proof.

R.F.D. VERSAILLES?

Here, in the northwest part of the royal park, Marie Antoinette (1755–93) created a tiny universe of her own: her comparatively dainty mansion called Petit Trianon and its adjacent "farm," the relentlessly picturesque Hameau ("hamlet"). In a life that took her from royal cradle to throne of France to guillotine, her happiest days were spent at Trianon. For here she could live a life in the "simplest" possible way; here the queen could enter a salon and the game of cards would not stop; here women could wear simple gowns of muslin without a single jewel. Toinette only wanted to be queen of Trianon, not queen of France. And considering the horrible, chamber-pot-pungent, gossip-infested corridors of Versailles, you can almost understand why.

TEEN QUEEN

From the first, Maria-Antonia (her actual name) was ostracized as an outsider, "l'Autrichienne"—the Austrian. Upon arriving in France in 1770—at a mere 15 years of age—she was married to the Dauphin, the future King Louis XVI. But shamed by her initial failure to deliver a royal heir, she grew to hate overcrowded Versailles and soon escaped to the Petit Trianon. Built between 1763 and 1768 by Jacques-Ange Gabriel for Madame de Pompadour, this bijou palace was a radical statement: a royal residence designed to be casual and unassuming. Toinette refashioned the Trianon's interior in the sober Neoclassical style.

Hameau

Queen's House

Temple of Love

Petit Trianon

"THE SIMPLE LIFE"

Just beyond Petit Trianon lay the storybook Hameau, a mock-Norman village inspired by the peasant-luxe, simple-life daydreams caught by Boucher on canvas and by Rousseau in literature. With its water mill, thatched-roof houses, pigeon loft, and vegetable plots, this make-believe farm village was run by Monsieur Valy-Busard, a farmer, and his wife, who often helped the queen—outfitted as a Dresden shepherdess with a Sèvres porcelain crook—tend her flock of perfumed sheep.

As if to destroy any last link with reality, the queen built nearby a jewel-box theater (open by appointment). Here she acted in little plays, sometimes essaying the role of a servant girl. Only the immediate royal family, about seven or so friends, and her personal servants were permitted entry; disastrously, the entire officialdom of Versailles society was shut out—a move that only served to infuriate courtiers. This is how fate and destiny close the circle. For it was here at Trianon that a page sent by Monsieur de Saint-Priest found Marie-Antoinette on October 5, 1789, to tell her that Paris was marching on an already half-deserted Versailles.

Was Marie Antoinette a political traitor to France whose execution was well merited? Or was she the ultimate fashion victim? For those who feel that this tragic queen spent—and shopped—her way into a revolution, a visit to her relatively modest Petit Trianon and Hameau should prove a revelation.

Marie Antoinette

LES BEAUX TRIANONS

A mile from the château, the Grand Trianon was created by Hardouin Mansart in 1687 as a retreat for Louis XIV; it was restored in the early 19th century, with Empire-style salons. It's a memorable spot often missed by foot-weary tourists exhausted by the château, but well worth the effort. A special treat is Marie Antoinette's hideaway nearby, the Petit Trianon, presumably restored to how she left it before being forced to Paris by an angry mob of soon-to-be revolutionaries.

TAKING ON VERSAILLES (WITHOUT LOSING YOUR HEAD)

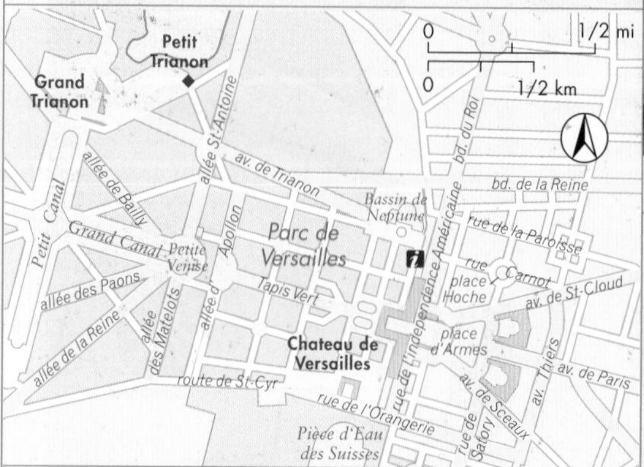

Statue of King Louis XIV

Place d'Armes, Versailles

www.chateauversailles.fr

01–30–83–78–00

A €25 day pass will get you into almost all of the sites, with audio-guide, on weekdays, €18 in low season.

Château only is €15. Petit and Grand Trianons (joint ticket) €10; Parc de Versailles free; Grand Eaux Musicale fountain show's €8; Fêtes de Nuit €16–€48.

The château is open Apr.–Oct., Tues.–Sun. 9–6:30; Nov.–Mar., Tues.–Sun, 9–5:30. Trianons Tues.—Sun. noon—6:30, Nov.–Mar. Park open daily 8–8:30.

RER Line C from Paris to Versailles–Rive Gauche station (closest to the Palace) or SNCF trains from Paris's Gare St-Lazare to Versailles–Rive Droite and Gare Montparnasse to Versailles.

Train tickets are €16. The best bargain (and a line-dodging time saver) is to buy a Forfait Loisirs Château de Versailles ticket (€22) that includes round-trip transportation from Paris and entrance to the main Versailles sights. Tickets are available at SNCF transilien train stations.

TOURING THE PALACE

The army of 20,000 noblemen, servants, and sycophants who moved into Louis XIV's huge Château de Versailles is matched today by the battalion of 3 million visitors a year. You may be able to avoid the modern-day crowds if you arrive here at 9 AM and buy your ticket in advance at FNAC or SNCF or online. The main entrance is near the top of the courtyard to the right; there are different lines depending on tour, physical ability, and group status. Frequent English guided tours visit the private royal apartments. More detailed hour-long tours explore the opera house (now reopened after a spectacular renovation; book a tour or concert ticket online) or Marie Antoinette's private parlors. You can wander the grandest rooms—including the Hall of Mirrors—without a group tour. To figure out the system, pick up a brochure at the information office for details.

TOURING THE PARK

If the grandeur of the palace begins to overwhelm, the Parc de Versailles is the best place to come back down to earth. The distances of the park are vast—the Trianons themselves are more than a mile from the château—so you might want to climb aboard the train (€6 round-trip, 01–39–54–22–00), or rent a bike from Petite-Venise (€5.20 per hr or €26 for 6 hrs, 01–39–66–97–66). You can hire a rowboat on the Grand Canal (€8.50 per hr) or drive to the Trianons and canal through the Grille de la Reine (€5.50 per car).

$–$$ **Le Cheval Rouge.** This unpretentious old hotel, built in 1676, is in a corner of the town market square, close to the château and strongly recommended if you plan to explore the town on foot. Some rooms around the old stable courtyard have their original wood beams. Several were renovated in 2007 and upholstered in pastel colors; the most spacious is Room 108, one of the few rooms with a bath rather than just a shower. **Pros:** great setting in town center; good value for Versailles. **Cons:** bland public areas; some rooms need renovating. ✉ *18 rue André-Chénier* ☎ *01–39–50–03–03* 🌐 *www.chevalrougeversailles.fr* *38 rooms* *In-room: no a/c, Wi-Fi. In-hotel: room service, bar, parking (free), some pets allowed* *AE, DC, MC, V.*

3

$$$$ ★ **Trianon Palace.** A modern-day Versailles, this deluxe hotel is in a turn-of-the-20th-century, creamy white creation of imposing size, filled with soaring rooms (including the historic Salle Clemenceau, site of the 1919 Versailles Peace Conference), palatial columns, and with a huge garden close to the château park. Once faded, the hotel, now part of the Westin chain, is aglitter once again with a health club (the pool idles beneath a glass pyramid) and a refurbished lobby glammed up with Murano chandeliers and high-back, green-leather armchairs. The hotel headliner these days is famed, foul-mouthed superchef Gordon Ramsay who has remade the luxury restaurant here (along with a more casual eaterie) with a big splash. As for the guest rooms, try to avoid the newer annex, the Pavillon Trianon, and insist on the full treatment in the main building (ask for one of the even-number rooms, which look out over the woods near the Trianons; odd-number rooms overlook the modern annex). **Pros:** palatial glamour; wonderful setting right by château park; Gordon Ramsay. **Cons:** lack of a personal touch after recent changes of ownership. ✉ *1 bd. de la Reine* ☎ *01–30–84–50–00* 🌐 *www.trianonpalace.com* *165 rooms, 27 suites* *In-room: a/c, safe, refrigerator, Wi-Fi. In-hotel: 2 restaurants, room service, bar, pool, gym, parking (free), some pets allowed* *AE, DC, MC, V* *BP.*

NIGHTLIFE AND THE ARTS

Directed by Bartabas, the **Académie du Spectacle Equestre** (☎ *01–39–02–07–14* 🌐 *www.acadequestre.fr*) stages hour-long shows on weekend afternoons of horses performing to music—sometimes with riders, sometimes without—in the converted 17th-century Manège (riding school) at the Grandes Écuries opposite the palace. The **Centre de Musique Baroque** (🌐 *www.cmbv.com*) often presents concerts of Baroque music in the château opera and chapel. The **Mois Molière** (☎ *01–30–97–84–48*) in June heralds a program of concerts, drama, and exhibits inspired by the famous playwright. The **Théâtre Montansier** (☎ *01–39–20–16–00*) has a full program of plays.

SHOPPING

Aux Colonnes (✉ *14 rue Hoche*) is a highly rated *confiserie* (candy shop) with a cornucopia of chocolates and candies; it's closed Monday. **Les Délices du Palais** (✉ *4 rue du Maréchal-Foch*) has all the makings for an impromptu picnic (cold cuts, cheese, salads); it's also closed Monday. **Legall** (✉ *Place du Marché*) has a huge choice of cheeses—including one of France's widest selections of goat cheeses; it's closed Sunday afternoon and Monday. **Passage de la Geôle**, which is open Friday–Sunday 9–7 and is close to the town's stupendous market, houses several good antiques shops.

CHÂTEAU DE RAMBOUILLET

32 km (20 mi) southwest of Versailles, 42 km (26 mi) southwest of Paris.

GETTING HERE

Trains arriving and departing from the Gare de Rambouillet (Place Prud-homme) connect often with Paris's Gare Montparnasse on a daily basis; departures are up to every 20 minutes during rush hours for the half-hour ride.

Visitor Information **Rambouillet Tourist Office** (✉ *1 pl. de la Libération* ☎ *01–34–83–21–21* 🌐 *www.ot-rambouillet.fr*).

Haughty Rambouillet, once favored by kings and dukes, is now home to affluent gentry and, occasionally, the French president.

The **Château de Rambouillet** is surrounded by a magnificent 30,000-acre forest that remains a great place for biking and walking. Most of the château dates from the early 18th century, but the brawny **Tour François-Ier** (François I Tower), named for the king who died here in 1547, was part of the fortified castle that stood on this site in the 14th century. Highlights include the wood-panel apartments, especially the **Boudoir de la Comtesse** (Countess's Dressing Room); the marble-wall **Salle de Marbre** (Marble Hall), dating from the Renaissance; and the **Salle de Bains de Napoléon** (Napoléon's Bathroom), adorned with Pompeii-style frescoes. Compared to the muscular forecourt, the château's lakeside facade is a sight of unsuspected serenity and, as flowers spill from its balconies, cheerful informality. ☎ *01–34–94–28–79* 🌐 *www.monuments-nationaux.fr* 🎫 *€7* ⏲ *Wed.–Mon. 10–11:30 and 2–5:30.*

An extensive **park**, with a lake with small islands, stretches behind the château, site of the **Laiterie de la Reine** (Queen's Dairy), built for Marie-Antoinette, who, inspired by the writings of Jean-Jacques Rousseau, came here to escape from the pressures of court life, pretending to be a simple milkmaid. It has a small marble temple and grotto and, nearby, the shell-lined Chaumière des Coquillages (Shell Pavilion). The **Bergerie Nationale** (National Sheepfold) is the site of a more serious agricultural venture: the merinos raised here, prized for the quality and yield of their wool, are descendants of sheep imported from Spain by Louis XVI in 1786. A museum alongside tells the tale and evokes shepherd life. 🎫 *Dairy and Shell Pavilion €3, Sheepfold €4* ⏲ *Dairy Apr.–Sept., Wed.–Mon. 10–noon and 2–6; Oct.–Mar., Wed.–Mon. 10–noon and 2–4:30; Sheepfold mid-Jan.–mid-Dec., Wed.–Sun. 2–5.*

WHERE TO EAT

$$–$$$ FRENCH ✕ **La Poste**. You can bank on traditional, unpretentious cooking at this lively former coaching inn in the center of town, close to the château park; ask for a table by the window overlooking the square, with the château visible beyond. Service is good, as is the selection of prix-fixe menus (€22–€38). Chef Gabriel Niort specializes in hearty Perigord

cuisine from southwest France, including foie gras, chicken fricassee with crayfish, along with game and wild mushrooms in season. ✉ *101 rue du Général-de-Gaulle* ☎ *01–34–83–03–01* ▭ *MC, V* ⊗ *Closed Mon. No dinner Sun. and Thurs.*

CHARTRES

39 km (24 mi) southwest of Rambouillet via N10 and A11, 88 km (55 mi) southwest of Paris.

If Versailles is the climax of French secular architecture, perhaps Chartres is its religious apogee. All the descriptive prose and poetry that have been lavished on this supreme cathedral can only begin to suggest the glory of its 12th- and 13th-century statuary and stained glass, somehow suffused with burning mysticism and a strange sense of the numinous. Chartres is more than a church—it's a nondenominational spiritual experience.

GETTING HERE

Both regional and main-line (Le Mans–bound) trains leave Paris's Gare Montparnasse for Chartres (50–70 mins); ticket price is around €27 round-trip. Chartres's train station on Place Pierre-Sémard puts you within walking distance of the cathedral.

Visitor Information Chartres Tourist Office (✉ *Pl. de la Cathédrale* ☎ *02–37–18–26–26* 🌐 *www.chartres-tourisme.com*).

EXPLORING

If you arrive in summer from Maintenon across the edge of the Beauce, the richest agrarian plain in France, you can see Chartres's spires rising up from oceans of wheat. The whole town—with its old houses and quaint streets—is worth a leisurely exploration. From Rue du Pont-St-Hilaire there's an intriguing view of the rooftops below the cathedral. Ancient streets tumble down from the cathedral to the river, lined most weekends with bouquinistes selling old books and prints. Each year on August 15 pilgrims and tourists flock here for the Procession du Vœu de Louis XIII, a religious procession through the streets commemorating the French monarchy's vow to serve the Virgin Mary.

Fodor's Choice ★ Worship on the site of the **Cathédrale Notre-Dame**, better known as Chartres Cathedral, goes back to before the Gallo-Roman period; the crypt contains a well that was the focus of druid ceremonies. In the late 9th century Charles II (known as the Bald) presented Chartres with what was believed to be the tunic of the Virgin Mary, a precious relic that went on to attract hordes of pilgrims. The current cathedral, the sixth church on the spot, dates mainly from the 12th and 13th centuries and was erected after the previous building, dating from the 11th century, burned down in 1194. A well-chronicled outburst of religious fervor followed the discovery that the Virgin Mary's relic had miraculously survived unsinged. Princes and paupers, barons and bourgeois gave their money and their labor to build the new cathedral. Ladies of the manor came to help monks and peasants on the scaffolding in a tremendous resurgence of religious faith that followed the Second Crusade.

Just 25 years were needed for Chartres Cathedral to rise again, and it has remained substantially unchanged since.

The lower half of the facade survives from the earlier Romanesque church: this can be seen most clearly in the use of round arches rather than the pointed Gothic type. The **Royal Portal** is richly sculpted with scenes from the life of Christ—these sculpted figures are among the greatest created during the Middle Ages. The taller of the two spires (380 feet versus 350 feet) was built at the start of the 16th century, after its predecessor was destroyed by fire; its fanciful Flamboyant intricacy contrasts sharply with the stumpy solemnity of its Romanesque counterpart (access €3, open daily 9:30–noon and 2–4:30). The **rose window** above the main portal dates from the 13th century, and the three windows below it contain some of the finest examples of 12th-century stained-glass artistry in France.

As spiritual as Chartres is, the cathedral also had its more-earthbound uses. Look closely and you can see that the main nave floor has a subtle slant. This was built to provide drainage, as this part of the church was often used as a "hostel" by thousands of overnighting pilgrims in medieval times.

Your eyes will need time to adjust to the somber interior. The reward is seeing the gemlike richness of the stained glass, with the famous deep Chartres blue predominating. The oldest window is arguably the most beautiful: **Notre-Dame de la Belle Verrière** (Our Lady of the Lovely Window), in the south choir. The cathedral's windows are being gradually cleaned—a lengthy, painstaking process—and the contrast with those still covered in the grime of centuries is staggering. It's worth taking a pair of binoculars along with you to pick out the details. If you wish to know more about stained-glass techniques and the motifs used, visit the small exhibit in the gallery opposite the north porch. For even more detail, try to arrange a tour (in English) with local institution Malcolm Miller, whose knowledge of the cathedral's history is formidable. (He leads tours twice a day Monday through Saturday; the cost is €10. You can reach him at the telephone number below.) The vast black-and-white labyrinth on the floor of the nave is one of the few to have survived from the Middle Ages; the faithful were expected to travel along its entire length (some 300 yards) on their knees. Guided tours of the **Crypte** start from the Maison de la Crypte opposite the south porch. You can also see a 4th-century Gallo-Roman wall and some 12th-century wall paintings. ✉ *16 cloître Notre-Dame* ☎ *02–37–21–75–02* 🌐 *www.chartres-tourisme.com* 🎫 *Crypt €3* ⏲ *Cathedral 8:30–7:30, guided tours of crypt Apr.–Oct., daily at 11, 2:15, 3:30, and 4:30; Nov.–Mar., daily at 11 and 4:15.*

The **Musée des Beaux-Arts** *(Fine Arts Museum)* is in a handsome 18th-century building just behind the cathedral that used to serve as the bishop's palace. Its varied collection includes Renaissance enamels, a portrait of Erasmus by Holbein, tapestries, armor, and some fine (mainly French) paintings from the 17th, 18th, and 19th centuries. There's also a room devoted to the forceful 20th-century landscapes of Maurice de Vlaminck, who lived in the region. ✉ *29 cloître Notre-Dame*

DID YOU KNOW?

Chartres's beautiful Clocher Neuf ("New Bell-tower") was completed in 1134, well before the Clocher Vieux ("Old Bell-tower"), on the right, which was built between 1145 and 1165.

☎ *02–37–90–45–80* 🎫 *€3* ⏱ *Wed.–Sat. and Mon. 10–noon and 2–5, Sun. 2–5.*

The Gothic church of **St-Pierre** (✉ *Rue St-Pierre*), near the Eure River, has magnificent medieval windows from a period (circa 1300) not represented at the cathedral. The oldest stained glass here, portraying Old Testament worthies, is to the right of the choir and dates from the late 13th century.

Exquisite 17th-century stained glass can be admired at the church of **St-Aignan** (✉ *Rue des Grenets*), around the corner from St-Pierre.

STAINED GLASS IN CHARTRES

Vitrail (stained glass) being the key to Chartres's fame, you may want to visit the **Galerie du Vitrail** (✉ *17 cloître Notre-Dame* ☎ *02–37–36–10–03* 🌐 *www.galerie-du-vitrail.com*), which specializes in the noble art. Pieces range from small plaques to entire windows, and there are books on the subject in English and French.

WHERE TO EAT AND STAY

$$$–$$$$ FRENCH ✕ **La Vieille Maison.** Just 100 yards from the cathedral, in a pretty 14th-century building with a flower-decked patio, this restaurant is a fine choice for either lunch or dinner. Chef Bruno Letartre changes his menu regularly, often including such regional specialties as asparagus, rich duck pâté, and superb homemade foie gras along with fish, seafood, and game in season. Prices, though justified, can be steep, but the €33 lunch menu served on summer weekdays is a good bet. ✉ *5 rue au Lait* ☎ *02–37–34–10–67* 🌐 *www.lavieillemaison.fr* 💳 *MC, V* ⏱ *No dinner Sun. Closed Mon.*

$$$–$$$$ FRENCH Fodor's Choice ★ ✕ **Moulin de Ponceau.** Ask for a table with a view of the River Eure, with the cathedral looming behind, at this 16th-century converted water mill. Better still, on sunny days you can eat outside, beneath a parasol on the stone terrace by the water's edge—an idyllic setting. Choose from a regularly changing menu of French stalwarts such as rabbit terrine, trout with almonds, and tarte tatin, or splurge on "la trilogie" of scallops, foie gras, and langoustine. ✉ *21 rue de la Tannerie* ☎ *02–37–35–30–05* 🌐 *www.moulindeponceau.fr* 💳 *AE, MC, V* ⏱ *Closed 2 wks in Jan. No dinner Sun. Closed Mon and Tues.*

$$$–$$$$ Fodor's Choice ★ 🏨 **Château d'Esclimont.** On the way south from Rambouillet to Chartres is the town of St-Symphorien, famed for one of France's most spectacular château-hotels. Adorned with pointed turrets, *pièces d'eau* (moated pools), and a checkerboard facade, the 19th-century Esclimont domaine—built by La Rochefoucaulds—is well worth seeking out if you wish to eat and sleep like an aristocrat in luxuriously furnished guest rooms (many are loftily dimensioned, others snug in corner turrets) adorned with reproduction 18th-century French pieces. Carved stone garlands, cordovan leathers, brocades, and period antiques grace the public salons; the superbly manicured grounds cradle a heated pool. The cuisine is sophisticated: quail, duck, lobster, and mushroom and chestnut fricassee top the menu at the restaurant, La Rochefoucauld (dinner reservations are essential, and a jacket and tie are required, as is a very fat wallet). **Pros:** the grand style of a country château; wonderful rural

setting. **Cons:** service can be pompous; off the beaten path and not easy to find. ✉ *2 rue du Château-d'Esclimont, 24 km (15 mi) northeast of Chartres via N10/D18, St-Symphorien-le-Château* ☎ *02–37–31–15–15* 🌐 *www.esclimont.com* *46 rooms, 6 suites* *In-room: no a/c, refrigerator, Wi-Fi. In-hotel: restaurant, room service, tennis courts, pool, Internet terminal, parking (free), some pets allowed* 💳 *AE, DC, MC, V* *MAP.*

$$–$$$ ★ **Le Grand Monarque.** Set on Chartres's main town square not far from the cathedral, this is a delightful option with decor that remains seductively and warmly redolent of the 19th century. Built originally as a coaching inn (and today part of the Best Western chain), the hotel has numerous rooms, many attractively outfitted with brick walls, wood antiques, lush drapes, and modern bathrooms; the best are in a separate turn-of-the-20th-century building overlooking a garden, while the most atmospheric are tucked away in the attic. Downstairs, the stylishly decorated Georges restaurant serves such delicacies as pheasant pie and scallops with lentils and has prix-fixe menus starting at €48. It's closed Monday and there's no dinner Sunday, but the hotel's La Cour brasserie is open daily. **Pros:** old-fashioned charm; restaurant earned a Michelin star in 2009. **Cons:** best rooms are in an annex; stiff uphill walk to cathedral. ✉ *22 pl. des Épars* ☎ *02–37–18–15–15* 🌐 *www.bw-grand-monarque.com* *55 rooms* *In-room: a/c (some), refrigerator, Wi-Fi. In-hotel: restaurant, bar, parking (paid), some pets allowed* 💳 *AE, DC, MC, V* *BP.*

GIVERNY

70 km (44 mi) northwest of Paris.

The small village of Giverny (pronounced jee-vair-knee), just beyond the Epte River, which marks the boundary of Ile-de-France, has become a place of pilgrimage for art lovers. It was here that Claude Monet lived for 43 years, until his death at the age of 86 in 1926. Although his house is now prized by connoisseurs of 19th-century interior decoration, it's his garden, with its Japanese-inspired water-lily pond and its bridge, that remains the high point for many—a 5-acre, three-dimensional Impressionist painting you can stroll around at leisure. Most make this a day trip, although Giverny has some jewel bed-and-breakfasts, so you should consider an overnight or two.

GETTING HERE

Take a main-line train (departures every couple of hours) from Paris's Gare St-Lazare to Vernon (50 mins) on the Rouen–Le Havre line, then a taxi, bus, or bike (which you can hire at the café opposite Vernon station—head down to the river and take the cycle path once you've crossed the Seine) to Giverny, 6 mi away. Buses, which run April through October only, meet the trains daily and whisk you away to Giverny for €5 more.

EXPLORING

Fodor's Choice ★ The **Maison et Jardin Claude-Monet** *(Monet's House and Garden)* has been lovingly restored. Monet was brought up in Normandy and, like many of the Impressionists, was captivated by the soft light of the Seine

An entry to Fodor's France contest, ShutterbugBill, a Fodors.com member, sent in this entracing view of the Japanese Footbridge in Monet's Garden.

Valley. After several years in Argenteuil, just north of Paris, he moved downriver to Giverny in 1883 along with his two sons; his mistress, Alice Hoschedé (whom he later married); and her six children. By 1890 a prospering Monet was able to buy the house outright. With its pretty pink walls and green shutters, the house has a warm feeling that may come as a welcome change after the stateliness of the French châteaux. Rooms have been restored to Monet's original designs: the kitchen with its blue tiles, the buttercup-yellow dining room, and Monet's bedroom on the second floor. The house was fully and glamorously restored only in the 1970s, thanks to the millions contributed by fans and patrons (who were often Americans). Reproductions of his works, and some of the Japanese prints he avidly collected, crowd its walls. During this era, French culture had come under the spell of Orientalism, and these framed prints were often gifts from visiting Japanese diplomats, whom Monet had befriended in Paris.

Three years after buying his house and cultivating its garden—which the family called the "Clos Normand"—the prospering Monet purchased another plot of land across the lane to continue his gardening experiments, even diverting the Epte to make a pond. The resulting garden *à la japonaise* (reached through a tunnel from the "Clos"), with flowers spilling out across the paths, contains the famous "tea-garden" bridge and water-lily pond, flanked by a mighty willow and rhododendrons. Images of the bridge and the water lilies—in French, *nymphéas*—in various seasons appear in much of Monet's later work. Looking across the pond, it's easy to conjure up the grizzled, bearded brushsmith dabbing at his canvases—capturing changes in light and pioneering a breakdown in form that was to have a major influence on 20th-century art.

The garden is a place of wonder, filled with butterflies, roosters, nearly 100,000 plants bedded every year, and more than 100,000 perennials. No matter that nearly 500,000 visitors troop through it each year; they fade into the background thanks to all the beautiful roses, purple carnations, lady's slipper, aubrieta, tulips, bearded irises, hollyhocks, poppies, daises, lambs' ears, larkspur, and azaleas, to mention just a few of the blooms (note that the water lilies flower during the latter part of July and the first two weeks of August). Even so, during the height of spring, when the gardens are particularly popular, try to visit during midweek. If you want to pay your respects, Monet is buried in the family vault in Giverny's village church. ✉ *84 rue Claude-Monet* ☎ *02–32–51–28–21* 🌐 *www.fondation-monet.com* 🎫 *Gardens and home €6, gardens only €4* ⏲ *Apr.–Oct., Tues.–Sun. 10–6.*

After touring the painterly grounds of Monet's house, you may wish to see some real paintings at the newly reconceived **Musée des Impressionnismes** (formerly the Musée Américain), farther along the road. Originally endowed by the late Chicago art patrons Daniel and Judith Terra, it featured works by the American Impressionists, including Willard Metcalf, Louis Ritter, Theodore Wendel, and John Leslie Breck, who flocked to Giverny to study at the hand of the master. As of May 2009, the museum has extended its scope with an exciting array of exhibitions that explore the origins, geographical diversity and wide-ranging influences of Impressionism, particularly in view of Giverny and the Seine Valley as essential landmarks in the history of a movement that was a major influence and transition point in 20th-century art. On-site is a restaurant and *salon de thé* (tearoom) with a fine outdoor terrace, as well as a garden "quoting" some of Monet's plant compositions. Head down the road to visit Giverny's landmark Hôtel Baudy *(see below)*, now a restaurant and once the stomping grounds and watering hole of many of these 19th-century artists. ✉ *99 rue Claude-Monet* ☎ *02–32–51–94–65* 🌐 *mdig.fr/* 🎫 *€6.50* ⏲ *May–Oct., daily 10–6.*

WHERE TO EAT AND STAY

$$ FRENCH ✕ **Hôtel Baudy**. Back in Monet's day, this pretty-in-pink villa, originally an *épicerie-buvette* (café-cum-grocer's store), was the hotel of the American painters' colony. Today, the rustic dining room and flowery patio, overlooked by a rose garden and the hut Cézanne once used as a studio, retain more historic charm than the simple cuisine (mainly warm and cold salads, large enough to count as a main course in their own right) or the busloads of tour groups (luckily channeled upstairs). ✉ *81 rue Claude-Monet* ☎ *02–32–21–10–03* 💳 *MC, V* ⏲ *Closed Nov.–Mar.*

$ 🏨 **La Musardière**. Just a short stroll from chez Monet, this 1880 manor house (the name means "Place to Idle") has a cozy lobby, guest rooms with views overlooking a leafy garden, and its own restaurant-creperie (closed November–March). **Pros:** only hotel in Giverny; surrounded by greenery. **Cons:** mediocre restaurant attracts noisy tourist crowds in midsummer. ✉ *123 rue Claude-Monet* ☎ *02–32–21–03–18* 🌐 *www.lamusardiere.fr* 🛏 *10 rooms* 🛎 *In-room: no a/c. In-hotel: restaurant* 💳 *MC, V* ⏲ *Closed Jan.* 🍽 *MAP.*

$ ★ **Le Clos Fleuri**. Giverny's dire shortage of hotels is made up for by several enticing, stylish, and affordable B&Bs set up in village homes; among the best is Le Clos Fleuri, the domaine of Danielle and Claude Fouche, a charming couple (she speaks English thanks to years spent in Australia). Set in a large garden, with Giverny's picturesque church steeple looming in the background, and just 600 yards from Monet's estate and a bit farther from the Musée des Impressionnismes, Le Clos beckons enticingly. Inside, three sweet and tranquil accommodations (all with their own entrance) welcome weary travelers: the "Poppies" and "Waterlilies" rooms have Louis Philippe–style beam ceilings and both overlook the house gardens, while "Clematis" has a very dramatic cathedral ceiling. The couple adore gardening and are fonts of information about touring the immediate area. Needless to say, book in advance. **Pros:** colorful oasis in the heart of the village; gardening is in the air. **Cons:** no a/c; no pets. ✉ *5 rue de la Dîme* ☎ *02–32–21–36–51* 🌐 *www.giverny-leclosfleuri.fr* *3 rooms* *In-room: no a/c, no TV* *No credit cards* *Closed Nov.–Mar.* *BP.*

AUVERS-SUR-OISE

Fodor's Choice ★ *74 km (46 mi) east of Giverny via D147, N14, and D4, 33 km (21 mi) northwest of Paris via N328.*

The tranquil Oise River valley, which runs northeast from Pontoise, retains much of the charm that attracted Camille Pissarro, Paul Cézanne, Camille Corot, Charles-François Daubigny, and Berthe Morisot to Auvers-sur-Oise in the second half of the 19th century. But despite this lofty company, it's the spirit of Vincent van Gogh that haunts every nook and cranny of this pretty riverside village. For while the great painter created many masterpieces here he also decided to end his life in a wheat field just outside the town. Today, thousands make a pilgrimage here to walk in his footsteps and pay their respects to his grave.

GETTING HERE

Getting to Auvers from Paris (Gare du Nord) invariably requires a change of train, either in Valmondois (suburban trains) or St-Ouen l'Aumone (RER-C). Journey time is 45–55 minutes. There is no connecting public transportation from the area around Vernon.

Visitor Information Auvers-sur-Oise Tourist Office (✉ *Rue de la Sansonne* ☎ *01–30–36–10–06* 🌐 *www.auvers-sur-oise.com*).

EXPLORING

Van Gogh moved to Auvers from Arles in May 1890 to be nearer his brother. Little has changed here since that summer of 1890, during the last 10 weeks of Van Gogh's life, when he painted no fewer than 70 pictures. You can find out about his haunts and other Impressionist sites in Auvers by stopping in at the tourist office at Les Colombières, a 14th-century manor house, set on the Rue de la Sansonne (closed from 12:30 to 2 PM every day). Short hikes outside the town center—sometimes marked with yellow trail signs—will lead you to rural landscapes once beloved by Pissarro and Cézanne, including the site of one of Van Gogh's last paintings, *Wheat Fields with Crows*.

On July 27, 1890, the great painter laid his easel against a haystack, walked behind the Château d'Auvers, shot himself, then stumbled to the Auberge Ravoux, where the owner sent to Paris for the artist's brother Theo. Van Gogh died on July 29. The next day, using a hearse from neighboring Méry (because the priest of Auvers refused to provide his for a suicide victim), Van Gogh's body was borne up the hill to the village cemetery. His heartbroken brother died the following year and, in 1914, was reburied alongside Vincent in his simple ivy-covered grave.

Set opposite the village town hall, the Auberge Ravoux, the inn where Van Gogh stayed, is now the **Maison de Van Gogh** *(Van Gogh House)*. The inn opened in 1876 and owes its name to Arthur Ravoux, the landlord from 1889 to 1891. He had seven lodgers in all, including the minor Dutch painter Anton Hirsching; they paid 3.50 francs for board and lodging, cheaper than the other inns in Auvers, where 6 francs was the going rate. A dingy staircase leads up to the tiny, spartan wood-floor attic where Van Gogh stored some of modern art's most famous pictures under his bed. A short film retraces Van Gogh's time at Auvers, and there's a well-stocked souvenir shop. Stop for a drink or for lunch in the ground-floor restaurant. ✉ *8 rue de la Sansonne* ☎ *01–30–36–60–60* 🎫 *€6* ⏲ *Mar.–Nov., Wed.–Sun. 10–6.*

A major town landmark opened to the public for the first time in 2004: the house and garden of Van Gogh's closest friend in Auvers, Dr. Paul Gachet. Documents and souvenirs at the **Maison du Dr. Gachet** evoke Van Gogh's stay in Auvers and Gachet's passion for the avant-garde art of his era. The good doctor was himself the subject of one of the artist's most famous portraits (and the world's second–most expensive painting when it sold for $82 million in the late 1980s), the actual painting of which was reenacted in the 1956 Kirk Douglas biopic, *Lust for Life*. Friend and patron to many of the artists who settled in and visited Auvers in the 1880s, among them Cézanne (who immortalized the doctor's house in a famous landscape), Gachet also taught them about engraving processes. The ivy covering Van Gogh's grave in the cemetery across town was provided by Gachet from this house's garden. ✉ *78 rue du Dr-Gachet* ☎ *01–30–36–81–27* 🎫 *€4* ⏲ *Apr.–Oct., Wed.–Sun. 10–6.*

The elegant 17th-century village château—also depicted by Van Gogh—set above split-level gardens, now houses the **Voyage au Temps des Impressionnistes** *(Journey Through the Impressionist Era)*. You'll receive a set of headphones (English available), with commentary that guides you past various

A VAN GOGH SELF-TOUR

Auvers-sur-Oise is peppered with plaques marking the spots that inspired his art. The plaques bear reproductions of his paintings, enabling you to compare his final works with the scenes as they are today. His last abode—the Auberge Ravoux—has been turned into a shrine. You can also visit the medieval village church, subject of one of Van Gogh's most famous paintings, *L'Église d'Auvers;* admire Osip Zadkine's powerful statue of Van Gogh in the village park; and visit the restored house of Dr. Gachet, Vincent's best friend.

tableaux illustrating life during the Impressionist years. Although there are no Impressionist originals—500 reproductions pop up on screens interspersed between the tableaux—this is one of France's most imaginative, enjoyable, and innovative museums. Some of the special effects—talking mirrors, computerized cabaret dancing girls, and a simulated train ride past Impressionist landscapes—are worthy of Disney. The museum restaurant, Les Canotiers—named after Renoir's famous painting of boaters—offers dishes favored by such artists as Morisot, Degas, and Manet, while more casual fare is offered at a re-creation of a 19th-century *guinguette* (riverbank café). ✉ *Rue de Léry* ☎ *01–34–48–48–40* 🌐 *www.chateau-auvers.fr* 🎫 *€12* ⏲ *Apr.–Sept., Tues.–Sun. 10–6; Oct.–mid-Dec. and mid-Jan.–Mar., Tues.–Sun. 10:30–4:30.*

The landscape artist Charles-François Daubigny, a precursor of the Impressionists, lived in Auvers from 1861 until his death in 1878. You can visit his studio, the **Maison-Atelier de Daubigny**, and admire the mural and roof paintings by Daubigny and fellow artists Camille Corot and Honoré Daumier. ✉ *61 rue Daubigny* ☎ *01–34–48–03–03* 🎫 *€5.50* ⏲ *Easter–Oct., Thurs.–Sun. 2–6.*

You may also want to visit the modest **Musée Daubigny** to admire the drawings, lithographs, and occasional oils by local 19th-century artists, some of which were collected by Daubigny himself. The museum is opposite the Maison de Van Gogh, above the tourist office, which shows a free 15-minute film (in English on request) about life in Auvers, *From Daubigny to Van Gogh.* ✉ *Manoir des Colombières, Rue de la Sansonne* ☎ *01–30–36–80–20* 🎫 *€4* ⏲ *Apr.–Oct., daily 2–6; Nov.–mid-Dec. and mid-Jan.–Mar., Wed.–Sun. 2–5.*

WHERE TO EAT AND STAY

$$$ FRENCH ★ ✕ **Auberge Ravoux.** For total Van Gogh immersion, have lunch in the restaurant he patronized regularly more than 100 years ago, in the building where he finally expired. The €38, three-course menu changes regularly, with saddle of lamb and homemade terrine among Loran Jattufo's specialties, but it's the genius loci that makes eating here special, with glasswork, lace curtains, and wall blandishments carefully modeled on the original designs. Table No. 5, the "table des habitués," is where Van Gogh used to sit. A magnificently illustrated book, *Van Gogh's Table* (published by Artisan), by culinary historian Alexandra Leaf and art historian Fred Leeman, recalls Vincent's stay at the Auberge and describes in loving detail the dishes served there at the time. ✉ *52 rue Général-de-Gaulle* ☎ *01–30–36–60–63* ✍ *Reservations essential* 💳 *AE, MC, V* ⏲ *Closed Mon. and Tues. and Nov.–Feb.*

$$–$$$ 🏨 **Hostellerie du Nord.** This sturdy white mansion began life as a coach house in the 17th century. Rubicund owner Joël Boilleaut is a noted chef and expects his diners to linger over the cheeseless three-course €49 lunch menu (coffee and a half bottle of wine thrown in) or the €59 four-course dinner banquet, when tuna carpaccio with fennel and spinach, and guinea fowl with licorice and apple, raise gastronomic eyebrows. The restaurant is closed Monday, Saturday lunch, and Sunday dinner, but no worries: a scaled-down bistro service provides a more than adequate alternative, with scallops and jugged hare among the healthy choices. Joël's wife Corinne oversees the prim hotel, whose small, white-

wall bedrooms, adorned with gilt-framed pictures, are named after artists, including Cézanne, who stayed here in 1872, and Van Gogh, commemorated by the Chambre Van Gogh, a junior suite that provides your wood-beam quaintest, if priciest, slumbertime option. **Pros:** only hotel in Auvers; great location close to river, train station, and Van Gogh's house. **Cons:** bland decor; small rooms. ✉ *6 rue du Général-de-Gaulle* ☎ *01–30–36–70–74* 🌐 *www.hostelleriedunord.fr* *8 rooms* *In-room: a/c, safe, refrigerator, Wi-Fi. In-hotel: restaurant, room service, parking (free), some pets allowed* ▭ *MC, V* ⏲ *Closed Sun. night.* *MAP.*

3

THE EASTERN ILE-DE-FRANCE

This area covers a broad arc, beginning northeast of Paris in Chantilly, one of the most popular day trips from the French capital. From the frozen-in-time medieval town of Senlis, we detour north to visit Pierrefonds, a fairy-tale 19th-century castle that may even outdo the one at Disneyland Paris, the very next stop on this tour heading south. The grand finale comprises three of the most spectacular châteaux in France: Vaux-le-Vicomte, Courances, and Fontainebleau.

CHANTILLY

37 km (23 mi) north of Paris via N16.

Celebrated for lace, cream, and the most beautiful medieval manuscript in the world—*Les Très Riches Heures du Duc de Berry*—romantic Chantilly has a host of other attractions: a faux Renaissance château with an eye-popping art collection, splendid Baroque stables, a classy racecourse, and a 16,000-acre forest.

GETTING HERE

Chantilly can be reached on both suburban (Transilien) and main-line (to Creil and beyond) trains from Paris's Gare du Nord; the trip takes 25–40 minutes and costs €8.

Visitor Information Chantilly Tourist Office (✉ *60 av. du Maréchal-Joffre* ☎ *03–44–57–08–58* 🌐 *www.ville-chantilly.fr*).

EXPLORING

Fodor's Choice ★ Although its lavish exterior may be 19th-century Renaissance pastiche, the **Château de Chantilly**, sitting snugly behind an artificial lake, houses the outstanding **Musée Condé**, with illuminated medieval manuscripts, tapestries, furniture, and paintings. The most famous room, the **Santuario** (sanctuary), contains two celebrated works by Italian painter Raphael (1483–1520)—the *Three Graces* and the *Orleans Virgin*—plus an exquisite ensemble of 15th-century miniatures by the most illustrious French painter of his time, Jean Fouquet (1420–81). Farther on, in the **Cabinet des Livres** (library), is the world-famous Book of Hours whose title translates as *The Very Rich Hours of the Duc de Berry,* which was illuminated by the Brothers Limbourg with magical pictures of early-15th-century life as lived by one of Burgundy's richest lords (unfortunately, due to their fragility, painted facsimiles of the celebrated calendar illuminations are on display, not the actual pages of the book). Other highlights of this unusual museum are the **Galerie de Psyché** (Psyche Gallery), with 16th-century stained glass and portrait drawings by Flemish artist Jean Clouet II; the **Chapelle,** with sculptures by Jean Goujon and Jacques Sarrazin; and the extensive collection of paintings by 19th-century French artists, headed by Jean-Auguste-Dominique Ingres. In addition, there are grand and smaller salons, all stuffed with palace furniture, family portraits, and Sèvres porcelains, making this a must for lovers of the decorative and applied arts. ☎ *03–44–27–31–80* 🌐 *www.domainedechantilly.com* 🎫 *€12, joint ticket with park* 🕐 *Apr.–Oct., daily 10–6; Nov.–Mar., daily 10:30–5.*

A DAY AT THE RACES

Since 1834 Chantilly's fabled racetrack, the Hippodrome des Princes de Condé (✉ *Rte. de la Plaine-des-Aigles* ☎ *03–44–62–44–00*) has come into its own each June with two of Europe's most prestigious events: the **Prix du Jockey-Club** (French Derby) on the first Sunday of the month, and the **Prix de Diane** for three-year-old fillies the Sunday after. On main race days, a free shuttle bus runs between Chantilly's train station and the racetrack.

Le Nôtre's **park** is based on that familiar French royal combination of formality (neatly planned parterres and a mighty, straight-banked canal) and romantic eccentricity (the waterfall and the Hameau, a mock-Norman village that inspired Marie-Antoinette's version at Versailles). You can explore on foot or on an electric train, and take a **hydrophile** (electric-powered boat) for a glide down the Grand Canal. ☎ *03–44–27–31–80* 🎫 *€19, joint ticket with château* and *Grand Stables; €6 park only* 🕐 *Apr.–Oct., daily 10–8; Nov.–Mar., daily 10:30–6.*

★ The palatial 18th-century **Grandes Écuries** *(Grand Stables)* by the racetrack, built by Jean Aubert in 1719 to accommodate 240 horses and 500 hounds for stag and boar hunts in the forests nearby, are the grandest stables in France. They're still in use as the home of the **Musée Vivant du Cheval** (Living Horse Museum), with 30 breeds of horses and ponies housed in straw-lined comfort—in between dressage performances in the courtyard or beneath the majestic central dome. The 31-room museum has a comprehensive collection of equine paraphernalia: everything from saddles, bridles, and stirrups to rocking horses, anatomy displays, and old postcards. There are explanations in English throughout. ✉ *7 rue du Connétable* ☎ *03–44–27–31–80* 🎫 *€10* 🕐 *Apr.–Oct., Wed.–Mon. 10–5; Nov.–Mar., Wed.–Mon. 2–5, weekends 10:30–6:30.*

WHERE TO EAT AND STAY

$$$ FRENCH ★ ✕ **La Capitainerie.** Housed in the stone-vaulted kitchens of the Château de Chantilly's legendary 17th-century chef Vorace Vatel, with an open-hearth fireplace big enough for whole lambs or oxen to sizzle on the spit, this quaint restaurant is no ordinary museum cafeteria. Reflect at leisure on your cultural peregrinations over mouthfuls of grilled turbot or roast quail, and don't forget to add a good dollop of homemade crème de Chantilly to your dessert. ✉ *In Château de Chantilly* ☎ *03–44–57–15–89* 💳 *DC, MC, V* 🕐 *Closed Tues. No dinner.*

Eastern Ile-de-France
Compiègne
Pierrefonds
Morienval
Villers-Cotterêts
Creil
Oise
St-Leu d'Esserent
N324
D335
Crépy-en-Valois
Senlis
Chantilly
D924
La Ferté-Milon
Chaalis
D136
Royaumont
Parc Astérix
Ermenonville
D936
N330
D84
D922
D909
A1
Roissy/CDG Airport
Dammartin-en-Goële
N330
Ecouen
D405
A4
N2
A104
Meaux
St-Denis
A3
Claye-Souilly
N3
A4
Bobigny
Lagny
Champs-sur-Marne
Crécy-la-Chapelle
PARIS
Vincennes
Marne-la-Vallée
N34
A4
Guermantes
Disneyland Paris
Ferrières
Coulommiers
D231
D471
N104
N4
Orly
Orly Airport
Brie-Comte-Robert
Rozay-en-Brie
N6
Evry
N36
N19
Corbeil-Essonnes
Vaux-le-Vicomte
Nangis
Provins
Seine
Melun
D408
D201
St-Loup-de-Naud
N105
N7
D132|D64
Barbizon
Fontainebleau
see detail map
Donnemarie
FOREST OF FONTAINEBLEAU
Milly-la-Forest
D210
D403
St-Mammès
Seine
D837
N6
Montereau
0
10 mi
Moret-sur-Loing
Yonne
A5
0
10 km
Loing

$$$ FRENCH ✕ **La Ferme de Condé.** At the far end of the racetrack, in a building that began life as an Anglican chapel, lost its tower, then served as a private gym, is one of the classier restaurants in Chantilly. It serves traditional French cuisine, some of it on the hearty side (andouillettes, calf's head, game stew in season). Other dishes, with a more subtle touch, include roast suckling pig, duck with honey and spices, and lobster terrine. A €25 menu makes it a suitable lunch spot. There's a good wine list and choice of wine by the jug. ✉ *42 av. du Maréchal-Joffre* ☎ *03–44–57–32–31* 🌐 *lafermedeconde.fr* *Reservations essential* 💳 *AE, DC, MC, V.*

$ **Campanile.** This functional, modern motel is in quiet Les Huit Curés, on the northern outskirts of Chantilly on the banks of the Nonette River (which compensates for the lack of interior charm). There's a grill room for straightforward meals, with a buffet for appetizers, cheese, and desserts. You can dine outside on the terrace in summer. **Pros:** cheap for Chantilly; easy-to-find parking. **Cons:** out of town; lacks character. ✉ *Rte. de Creil, on N16 toward Creil, Les Huit Curés* ☎ *03–44–57–39–24* *50 rooms* *In-room: Wi-Fi. In-hotel: restaurant, bar, some pets allowed* 💳 *AE, DC, MC, V.*

$$$–$$$$ **Dolce Chantilly.** Surrounded by forest and its own 18-hole golf course, this luxe, highly restored, and meetings-friendly hotel is set 1½ km (1 mi) northeast of the château. The marble-floor reception hall creates a glitzy impression not quite matched by the guest rooms, which are functional, modern, and a bit small. The Le Swing brasserie, in the golf clubhouse, serves lunch for €20, and the deluxe Carmontelle has formal dining under top-ranked chef Alain Montigny. **Pros:** great facilities; stylish public areas. **Cons:** rooms lack character; overall the whole place can feel impersonal. ✉ *Rte. d'Apremont, Vineuil–St-Firmin* ☎ *03–44–58–47–77* 🌐 *chantilly.dolce.com* *200 rooms, 25 suites* *In-room: a/c, refrigerator, Wi-Fi. In-hotel: 3 restaurants, room service, golf course, tennis court, pool, gym* 💳 *AE, DC, MC, V* *Closed Christmas–New Year's* *FAP.*

SENLIS

10 km (6 mi) east of Chantilly via D924, 45 km (28 mi) north of Paris via A1.

Senlis is an exceptionally well-preserved medieval town with crooked, mazelike streets dominated by the svelte, soaring spire of its Gothic cathedral. Be sure to also inspect the moss-tile church of St-Pierre, with its stumpy crocketed spire. You can enjoy a 40-minute tour of the Vieille Ville by horse and carriage, departing from in front of the cathedral, daily April–December (€35 for up to three people).

Visitor Information Senlis Tourist Office (✉ *Pl. du Parvis Notre-Dame* ☎ *03–44–53–06–40* 🌐 *www.ville-senlis.fr*).

EXPLORING

★ The **Cathédrale Notre-Dame** (✉ *Pl. du Parvis*), one of France's oldest and narrowest cathedrals, dates from the second half of the 12th century. The superb spire—arguably the most elegant in France—was added around 1240, and the majestic transept, with its ornate rose windows, in the 16th century.

The town's excellent **Musée d'Art** *(Art Museum)*, built atop an ancient Gallo-Roman residence, displays archaeological finds ranging from Gallo-Roman votive objects unearthed in the neighboring Halatte Forest to the building's own excavated foundations (uncovered in the basement), including some macabre stone heads bathed in half light. Paintings upstairs include works by Manet's teacher Thomas Couture (who lived in Senlis) and a whimsical fried-egg still life by 19th-century realist Théodule Ribot. ✉ *Palais Épiscopal, Pl. du Parvis-Notre-Dame* ☎ *03–44–32–00–83* 🎫 *€4* ⏲ *Mon., Thurs., and Fri. 10–noon and 2–6; weekends 11–1 and 2–6; Wed. 2–6.*

3

WHERE TO EAT AND STAY

$$$ SEAFOOD ✕ **Le Scaramouche.** Although perfectly comfortable inside, this quaint restaurant is best on a warm day, as the outdoor terrace, just across from the graceful Notre Dame cathedral, is one of the nicest in town. With a menu steeped in French stalwarts, there's plenty here to like: escargot in a rich garlicky cream, pressed foie gras with toast tips, veal kidney with shallot confit, and a classic entrecôte with tarragon butter. The €29 menu, including a generous cheese course, is well rounded and satisfying. ✉ *4 pl. Notre Dame, Senlis* ☎ *03–44–53–01–26* 🌐 *www.le-scaramouche.fr* 💳 *AE, DC, MC, V* ⏲ *Closed Tues. and Wed. and last 2 wks of Aug.*

$ 🏨 **L'Hostellerie de la Porte-Bellon.** This old stone house with a garden, a five-minute walk from the cathedral and close to the bus station, is the closest you can get to spending a night in the historic center of Senlis. The prettiest room is No. 14, which overlooks the garden and has sloping walls and exposed beams. Chef-owner Philippe Patenotte presides over the venerable, recently renovated restaurant (no dinner Sunday), which has light oak tables and wrought-iron chairs, and fish and game–heavy set menu at €25. **Pros:** only hotel close to historic town center; attractive old building. **Cons:** modest facilities; some rooms need renovating. ✉ *51 rue Bellon* ☎ *03–44–53–03–05* 🛏 *18 rooms* 👍 *In-room: no a/c. In-hotel: restaurant, room service, some pets allowed* 💳 *AE, V* ⏲ *Closed mid-Dec.–mid-Jan.* 🍽 *MAP.*

PIERREFONDS

38 km (24 mi) northeast of Senlis via N324, D335, and D973.

Dominating the attractive lakeside village of Pierrefonds, a former spa resort, is its immense ersatz medieval castle. Built on a huge mound in the 15th century, the **Château de Pierrefonds** was dismantled in 1620 then comprehensively restored and re-created in the 1860s to imagined former glory at the behest of Emperor Napoléon III, seeking to cash in on the craze for the Middle Ages. Architect Viollet-le-Duc left a crenelated fortress with a fairy-tale silhouette, although, like the fortified town of Carcassonne, which he also restored, Pierrefonds is more a construct of what Viollet-le-Duc thought it should have looked like than what it really was. A visit takes in the chapel, barracks, and the majestic keep holding the lord's bedchamber and reception hall, which is bordered by a spiral staircase whose lower and upper sections reveal clearly what is ancient and modern in this former fortress. Don't miss the plaster casts of tomb sculptures from all over France in the cellars, and the **Collection Monduit**—industrially produced, larger-than-life lead decorations made by the 19th-century firm that brought the Statue of Liberty to life. Buses from Compiègne run three times daily (fewer on Sunday) from the train station. Taxis are pricey but bikes are another option—this is great bicycling countryside. ✉ *Rue Viollet-le-Duc* ☎ *03–44–42–72–72* *€7* ⏲ *Tues.–Sun. 9:30–12:30 and 2–5:30.*

WHERE TO EAT AND STAY

¢–$ Fodor's Choice ★ **Le Relais Brunehaut.** Five kilometers (3 mi) north of Pierrefonds, in the hamlet of Chelles, is this adorably quaint hotel-restaurant with a view of the abbey church next door. Topped with a super-picturesque stepped gable room, this tiny ensemble of stucco-and-stone buildings is bordered by several acres of pleasant park and a small duck-populated river. An old wooden waterwheel in the dining room and the good, simple seasonal fare make eating here an added pleasure (the dining room is closed Monday and Tuesday for lunch year-round). **Pros:** bucolic setting; good restaurant. **Cons:** rooms are old-fashioned; management can be gruff. ✉ *3 rue de l'Église, 5 km (3 mi) east of Pierrefonds on D85, Chelles* ☎ *03–44–42–85–05* *11 rooms* *In-room: no a/c. In-hotel: restaurant* *MC, V* ⏲ *Closed mid-Jan.–mid-Feb.* *MAP.*

DISNEYLAND PARIS

68 km (40 mi) southwest of Pierrefonds via D335, D136, N330, and A4; 38 km (24 mi) east of Paris via A4.

Originally called Euro Disney, Disneyland Paris is probably not what you've traveled to France to experience. But if you have a child in tow, the promise of a day here may get you through an afternoon at Versailles or Fontainebleau. If you're a dyed-in-the-wool Disney fan, you'll want to make a beeline for the park to see how it has been molded to appeal to the tastes of Europeans (Disney's "Imagineers" call it their most lovingly detailed park). And if you've never experienced this particular form of Disney showmanship, you may want to put in an appearance if only to see what all the fuss is about.

GETTING HERE

Take the RER from central Paris (stations at Étoile, Auber, Les Halles, Gare de Lyon, and Nation) to Marne-la-Vallée–Chessy, 100 yards from the Disneyland entrance. Journey time is around 40 minutes, and trains operate every 10–30 minutes, depending on the time of day. Note that a TGV (Train à Grande Vitesse) station links Disneyland to Lille, Lyon, Brussels, and London (via Lille and the Channel Tunnel). Disneyland's hotel complex offers a shuttle-bus service to Orly and Charles de Gaulle airports for €21.

Visitor Information **Disneyland Paris reservations office** (*B.P. 100, cedex 4, 77777 Marne-la-Vallée* ☎ *01–60–30–60–90, 407/939–7675 in U.S.* 🌐 *www.disneylandparis.co*).

The Alice in Wonderland Labyrinth delights children—and intrigues children of all ages—at Disneyland Paris.

EXPLORING

Fodor's Choice ★

Disneyland Paris (originally called Euro Disney) is probably not what you've traveled to France to experience. But if you have a child in tow, the promise of a day here may get you through an afternoon at Versailles or Fontainebleau. If you're a dyed-in-the-wool Disney fan, you'll want to make a beeline for the park to see how it has been molded to appeal to the tastes of Europeans (Disney's "Imagineers" call it their most lovingly detailed park). And if you've never experienced this particular form of Disney showmanship, you may want to put in an appearance if only to see what all the fuss is about. When it opened, few turned up to do so; today the place is jammed with crowds, and Disneyland Paris is here to stay—and grow, with **Walt Disney Studios** opened alongside it in 2002.

Disneyland Park, as the original theme park is styled, consists of five "lands": Main Street U.S.A., Frontierland, Adventureland, Fantasyland, and Discoveryland. The central theme of each land is relentlessly echoed in every detail, from attractions to restaurant menus to souvenirs. The park is circled by a railroad, which stops three times along the perimeter. **Main Street U.S.A.** goes under the railroad and past shops and restaurants toward the main plaza; Disney parades are held here every afternoon and, during holiday periods, every evening.

Top attractions at **Frontierland** are the chilling Phantom Manor, haunted by holographic spooks, and the thrilling runaway mine train of Big Thunder Mountain, a roller coaster that plunges wildly through floods and avalanches in a setting meant to evoke Utah's Monument Valley. Whiffs of Arabia, Africa, and the West Indies give **Adventureland** its exotic cachet; the spicy meals and snacks served here rank among the best food in the park. Don't miss the Pirates of the Caribbean, an exciting mise-en-scène populated by eerily humanlike, computer-driven figures, or Indiana Jones and the Temple of Doom, a breathtaking ride that re-creates some of this luckless hero's most exciting moments.

Fantasyland charms the youngest parkgoers with familiar cartoon characters from such classic Disney films as *Snow White, Pinocchio, Dumbo,* and *Peter Pan.* The focal point of Fantasyland, and indeed Disneyland Paris, is Le Château de la Belle au Bois Dormant (Sleeping Beauty's Castle), a 140-foot, bubblegum-pink structure topped with 16 blue- and gold-tipped turrets. Its design was allegedly inspired by illustrations from a medieval *Book of Hours*—if so, it was by way of Beverly Hills. The castle's dungeon conceals a 2-ton scaly green dragon that rumbles in its sleep and occasionally rouses to roar—an impressive feat of engineering, producing an answering chorus of shrieks from younger children. **Discoveryland** is a futuristic eye-knocker for high-tech Disney entertainment. Robots on roller skates welcome you on your way to Star Tours, a pitching, plunging, sense-confounding ride based on the *Star Wars* films. In Le Visionarium, a simulated space journey is presented by 9-Eye, a staggeringly realistic robot. One of the park's newest attractions, the Jules Verne–inspired **Space Mountain Mission 2,** pretends to catapult *exploronauts* on a rocket-boosted, comet-battered journey through the Milky Way.

Disneyland Paris is peppered with places to eat, ranging from snack bars and fast-food joints to five full-service restaurants—all with a distinguishing theme. In addition, Walt Disney Studios, Disney Village, and Disney Hotels have restaurants open to the public. But since these are outside the park, it's not recommended that you waste time traveling to them for lunch. Disneyland Paris has relaxed its no-alcohol policy and now serves wine and beer in the park's sit-down restaurants, as well as in the hotels and restaurants outside the park.

Walt Disney Studios opened next to the Disneyland Park in 2002. The theme park is divided into four "production zones." Beneath imposing entrance gates and a 100-foot water tower inspired by the one erected in 1939 at Disney Studios in Burbank, California, **Front Lot** contains shops, a restaurant, and a studio re-creating the atmosphere of Sunset Boulevard. In **Animation Courtyard,** Disney artists demonstrate the various phases of character animation; Animagique brings to life scenes from *Pinocchio* and *The Lion King*; while the Genie from *Aladdin* pilots Flying Carpets over Agrabah. **Production Courtyard** hosts the Walt Disney Television Studios; Cinémagique, a special-effects tribute to U.S. and European cinema; and a behind-the-scenes Studio Tram tour of location sites, movie props, studio decor, and costuming, ending with a visit to Catastrophe Canyon in the heart of a film shoot. **Back Lot** majors in stunts. At Armageddon Special Effects you can confront a flaming meteor shower aboard the Mir space station, then complete your visit at the giant outdoor arena with a Stunt Show Spectacular involving cars, motorbikes, and Jet Skis. ☎ *01–60–30–60–90* 🌐 *www.disneylandparis.com* 🎟 *€52, €138 for 3-day Passport; includes admission to all individual attractions within Disneyland or Walt Disney*

Studios, but not meals; tickets for Walt Disney Studios are also valid for admission to Disneyland during last 3 opening hrs of same day ⏲ Disneyland mid-June–mid-Sept., daily 9 AM–10 PM; mid-Sept.–Dec. 19 and Jan. 5–mid-June, weekdays 10–8, weekends 9–8; Dec. 20–Jan. 4, daily 9–8. Walt Disney Studios daily 10–6 ▭ AE, MC, V.

WORD OF MOUTH

"The most surprising thing to me was that we had trouble getting decent food. We wanted to eat dinner about 7 before the light parade, but most of the restaurants closed before that. When we finally landed a reservation, it was simply mediocre—worse than food at WDW in Orlando or in Anaheim. I was very surprised. But the light parade was really special—lots of blacklight effects, and each float stopped while the people performed, then moved on." —WoodyVQ

WHERE TO EAT AND STAY

$$$$ **Sequoia Lodge.** Ranging from superluxe to still-a-pretty-penny, Disneyland Paris has 5,000 rooms in five hotels (plus the not-so-rustic Camp Davy Crockett). Perhaps your best mid-range bet is the Sequoia Lodge—although it's just a few minutes' walk from the theme park, the mood here is quite different from the other, glitzier big hotels at the resort. Surrounded by already towering evergreens, this hotel conjures up the ambience of an American mountain lodge; in fact, you're greeted when you arrive by an open fire crackling on a giant stone hearth in the "Redwood Bar." Guest rooms have natural wooden furniture, meant to evoke log cabins; it's best to try for one in the main Montana building, with a view of Lake Disney, rather than find yourself in one of the smaller annexes ("lodges"). For youngsters there's a children's corner, outdoor play area, and video-game room. For food, the choice is between the family-oriented, buffet-service Hunter's Grill and the more upscale Beaver Creek Tavern offering international cuisine. Free transportation to the park is available at every hotel. Note that room prices can fluctuate strongly depending on season and school vacation period—keep hunting to find lower-priced days. **Pros:** package deals include room prices and admission to theme park; cozy, secluded feel; great pools. **Cons:** restaurants a bit ho-hum, many rooms do not have lake view. *Centre de Réservations, B.P. 100, cedex 4, 77777 Marne-la-Vallée ☎ 01–60–30–60–90, 407/939–7675 in U.S. 🌐 www.disneylandparis.co ☞ In-room: a/c, refrigerator. In-hotel: 4 restaurants, bar, pools, children's programs (ages 3–12), Wi-Fi hotspot ▭ AE, MC, V FAP.*

NIGHTLIFE AND THE ARTS

Nocturnal entertainment outside the park centers on **Disney Village**, a vast pleasure mall designed by American architect Frank Gehry. Featured are American-style restaurants (crab shack, diner, deli, steak house), including **Billybob's Country Western Saloon** (☎ *01–60–45–71–00*). Also in Disney Village is **Buffalo Bill's Wild West Show** (☎ *01–60–45–71–00 for reservations*), a two-hour dinner extravaganza with a menu of sausages, spare ribs, and chili; performances by a talented troupe of stunt riders, bronco busters, tribal dancers, and musicians; plus some 50 horses, a dozen buffalo, a bull, and an Annie Oakley–style sharpshooter, with

Louis XIV was so jealous of the splendor of Vaux-le-Vicomte that he promptly went out and built Versailles.

a golden-maned "Buffalo Bill" as emcee. A re-creation of a show that dazzled Parisians 100 years ago, it's corny but great fun. There are two shows nightly, at 6:30 and 9:30; the cost is €58 for adults, €44 for children under 12.

CHÂTEAU DE VAUX-LE-VICOMTE

48 km (30 mi) south of Disneyland Paris via N36, 5 km (3 mi) northeast of Melun via N36 and D215, 56 km (35 mi) southeast of Paris via A6, N104, A5, and N36.

GETTING HERE

Get to Vaux by taking the train on a 45-minute trip to Melun, then taxi (for about €30 each way) the 7 km (4 mi) to the château. However, from mid-March to mid-November, Vaux runs a special Châteaubus shuttle, which you can get at the Melun train station and costs €7 round-trip.

Fodor's Choice ★ A manifesto for French 17th-century splendor, the **Château de Vaux-le-Vicomte** was built between 1656 and 1661 by finance minister Nicolas Fouquet. The construction program was monstrous: entire villages were razed, 18,000 workmen called in, and architect Louis Le Vau, painter Charles Le Brun, and landscape architect André Le Nôtre recruited at vast expense to prove that Fouquet's taste was as refined as his business acumen. The housewarming party was so lavish it had star guest Louis XIV, tetchy at the best of times, spitting jealous curses. He hurled Fouquet in the slammer and set about building Versailles to prove just who was top banana.

A CANDLELIGHT TOUR

Perhaps the most beautiful time to visit the château and gardens is when they are illuminated by thousands of candles during the Candlelight Evenings, held every Saturday night, from 8 to midnight, from May through mid-October (also Friday in July and August). Readers complain, however, that at night the vast and grand gardens are nearly invisible and the low candlepower doesn't really do justice to the splendor of the salons.

The high-roof château, partially surrounded by a moat, is set well back from the road behind iron railings topped with sculpted heads. A cobbled avenue stretches up to the entrance, and stone steps lead to the vestibule, which seems small given the noble scale of the exterior. Charles Le Brun's captivating decoration includes the ceiling of the **Chambre du Roi** (Royal Bedchamber), depicting *Time Bearing Truth Heavenward,* framed by stuccowork by sculptors François Girardon and André Legendre. Along the frieze you can make out small squirrels, the Fouquet family's emblem—squirrels are known as *fouquets* in local dialect. But Le Brun's masterwork is the ceiling in the **Salon des Muses** (Hall of Muses), a brilliant allegorical composition painted in glowing, sensuous colors that some feel even surpasses his work at Versailles. On the ground floor the impressive **Grand Salon** (Great Hall), with its unusual oval form and 16 caryatid pillars symbolizing the months and seasons, has harmony and style even though the ceiling decoration was never finished.

The state salons are redolent of *le style louisquartorze,* thanks to the grand state beds, Mazarin desks, and Baroque marble busts—gathered together by the current owners of the château, the Comte et Comtesse de Vogüé—that replace the original pieces, which Louis XIV trundled off as booty to Versailles. In the basement, whose cool, dim rooms were used to store food and wine and house the château's kitchens, you can find rotating exhibits about the château's past and life-size wax figures illustrating its history, including the notorious 19th-century murder-suicide of two erstwhile owners, the Duc and Duchess de Choiseul-Praslin. The house has been featured in many Hollywood films, including *Moonraker.* Le Nôtre's carefully restored **gardens** are at their best when the fountains are turned on (the second and final Saturday of each month from April through October, 3–6 PM). ☎ *01–64–14–41–90* 🌐 *www.vaux-le-vicomte.com* 🎟 *€16, candlelight château visits €19; gardens only €8.*

WHERE TO EAT

¢–$ FRENCH ✕ **L'Écureuil.** An imposing barn to the right of the château entrance has been transformed into this self-service cafeteria, where you can enjoy fine steaks (insist yours is cooked enough), salads, pastries, coffee, or a snack beneath the ancient rafters of a wood-beam roof. The restaurant is open daily for lunch and tea, and for dinner during candlelight visits. ✉ *Château de Vaux-le-Vicomte* ☎ *01–60–66–95–66* 💳 *AE, MC, V.*

BARBIZON

17 km (11 mi) southwest of Vaux-le-Vicomte via Melun and D132/ D64, 52 km (33 mi) southeast of Paris.

On the western edge of the 62,000-acre Forest of Fontainebleau, the village of Barbizon retains its time-stained allure despite the intrusion of art galleries, souvenir shops, and busloads of tourists. The group of landscape painters known as the Barbizon School—Camille Corot, Jean-François Millet, Narcisse Diaz de la Peña, and Théodore Rousseau, among others—lived here from the 1830s on. They paved the way for the Impressionists by their willingness to accept nature on its own terms rather than using it as an idealized base for carefully structured compositions. Sealed to one of the famous sandstone rocks in the forest—which starts, literally, at the far end of the main street—is a bronze medallion by sculptor Henri Chapu, paying homage to Millet and Rousseau. Threading the village is a Painters Trail (marked in yellow), which ranges from main village landmarks to natural splendors such as the rocky waterfall once painted by Corot.

Visitor Information **Barbizon Tourist Office** (✉ *41 Grande-Rue* ☎ *01-60-66-41-87* 🌐 *www.barbizon.fr*).

EXPLORING

Corot and company would often repair to the Auberge Ganne after painting to brush up on their social life; the inn is now the **Musée de l'École de Barbizon** *(Barbizon School Museum)*. Here you can find documents of the village as it was in the 19th century, as well as a few original works. The Barbizon artists painted on every available surface, and even now you can see some originals on the upstairs walls. Two of the ground-floor rooms have been reconstituted as they were in Ganne's time—note the trompe-l'oeil paintings on the buffet doors. There's also a video on the Barbizon School. ✉ *92 Grande-Rue* ☎ *01-60-66-22-27* 🎫 *€6, joint ticket with Musée-Atelier Théodore-Rousseau* ⏲ *Wed.–Mon. 10–12:30 and 2–5:30.*

Though there are no actual Millet works, the **Atelier Jean-François Millet** *(Millet's Studio)* is cluttered with photographs and mementos evoking his career. It was here that Millet painted some of his most renowned pieces, including *The Gleaners*. ✉ *27 Grande-Rue* ☎ *01-60-66-21-55* 🎫 *Free* ⏲ *Wed.–Mon. 9:30–12:30 and 2–5:30.*

By the church, beyond the extraordinary village war memorial featuring a mustached ancient Gaul in a winged helmet, is the **Musée Théodore-Rousseau** *(Rousseau's House-cum-Studio)* in a converted barn. It's crammed with personal and artistic souvenirs and also has an exhibition space for temporary shows. ✉ *55 Grande-Rue* ☎ *01-60-66-22-38* 🎫 *€6, joint ticket with Barbizon School Museum* ⏲ *Wed.–Mon. 10–12:30 and 2–5:30.*

WHERE TO EAT AND STAY

$$$$ FRENCH ✕ **Le Relais de Barbizon.** French country specialties and fish are served at this rustic restaurant with a big open fire and a large terrace shaded by lime and chestnut trees. The four-course weekday menu is a good value, but wine here is expensive and cannot be ordered by the *pichet*

(pitcher). Reservations are essential on weekends. ✉ *2 av. Charles de Gaulle* ☎ *01–60–66–40–28* ▭ *MC, V* ⊙ *Closed Tues. and Wed. and part of Aug. and part of Dec.*

¢–$ ★ **Les Alouettes.** This delightful, family-run 19th-century inn is on 2 acres of leafy parkland, which the better rooms overlook (No. 9 is the largest). The interior is '30s style, and many rooms have oak beams. Jean-Paul Karampournis's rustic restaurant (reservations essential; no dinner Sunday and Monday), with its large open terrace, serves traditional French cuisine such as hare with mushrooms and lamb with eggplant. **Pros:** verdant setting; rooms have character. **Cons:** no air-conditioning; no Internet in rooms. ✉ *4 rue Antoine-Barye* ☎ *01–60–66–41–98* *22 rooms* *In-room: no a/c. In-hotel: restaurant, bar, Internet terminal, parking (free), some pets allowed* ▭ *AE, DC, MC, V* *MAP.*

3

FONTAINEBLEAU

9 km (6 mi) southeast of Barbizon via N7, 61 km (38 mi) southeast of Paris via A6 and N7.

Like Chambord, in the Loire Valley, or Compiègne, to the north, Fontainebleau was a favorite spot for royal hunting parties long before the construction of one of France's grandest residences. Although not as celebrated as Versailles, this palace is almost as spectacular.

GETTING HERE

Fontainebleau—or, rather, neighboring Avon, 2 km (1½ mi) away (there's frequent shuttle-bus service to the château for €3 round-trip)—is a 45-minute rail ride from Paris's Gare de Lyon; tickets are €7.80 one-way.

Visitor Information **Fontainebleau Tourist Office** (✉ *4 rue Royale* ☎ *01–60–74–99–99* 🌐 *www.fontainebleau-tourisme.com*).

EXPLORING

★ The **Château de Fontainebleau** you see today dates from the 16th century, although additions were made by various royal incumbents through the next 300 years. The palace was begun under the flamboyant Renaissance king François I, the French contemporary of England's Henry VIII. The king hired Italian artists Il Rosso (a pupil of Michelangelo) and Primaticcio to embellish his château. In fact, they did much more: By introducing the pagan allegories and elegant lines of Mannerism to France, they revolutionized French decorative art. Their virtuoso frescoes and stuccowork can be admired in the **Galerie François-Ier** (Francis I Gallery) and in the jewel of the interior, the 100-foot-long **Salle de Bal** (Ballroom), with its luxuriant wood paneling, completed under Henri II, François's successor, and its gleaming parquet floor that reflects the patterns on the ceiling. Like the château as a whole, the room exudes a sense of elegance and style—but on a more intimate, human scale than at Versailles: this is Renaissance, not Baroque. **Napoléon's apartments** occupied the first floor. You can see a lock of his hair, his Légion d'Honneur medal, his imperial uniform, the hat he wore on his return from Elba in 1815, and one bed in which he definitely did spend a night (almost every town in France boasts a bed in which the

Fontainebleau

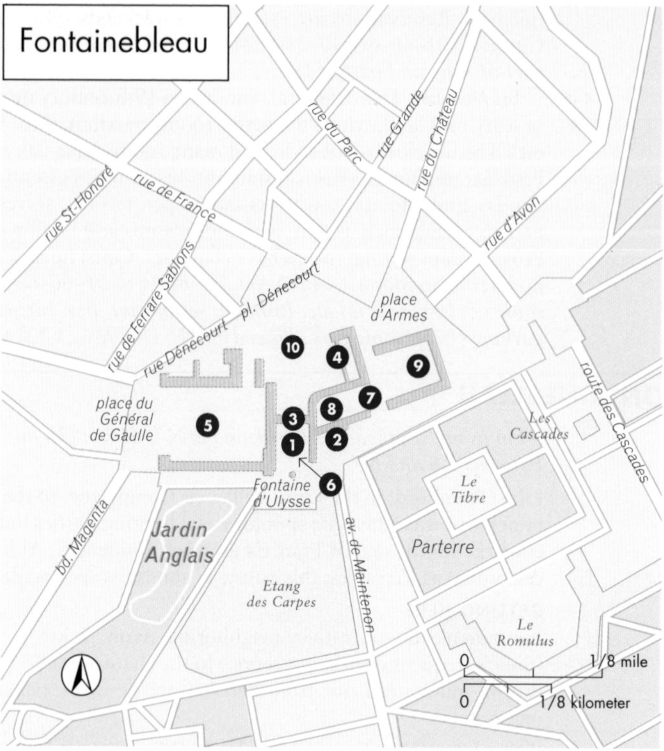

emperor supposedly snoozed). Joséphine's **Salon Jaune** (Yellow Room) is one of the best examples of the Empire style—the austere Neoclassical style promoted by the emperor. There's also a throne room—Napoléon spurned the one at Versailles, a palace he disliked, establishing his imperial seat in the former King's Bedchamber here—and the Queen's Boudoir, also known as the Room of the Six Maries (occupants included ill-fated Marie-Antoinette and Napoléon's second wife, Marie-Louise). The sweeping **Galerie de Diane,** built during the reign of Henri IV (1589–1610), was converted into a library in the 1860s. Other salons have 17th-century tapestries and paintings, and frescoes by members of the Fontainebleau School.

Although Louis XIV's architectural fancy was concentrated on Versailles, he commissioned Mansart to design new pavilions and had André Le Nôtre replant the gardens at Fontainebleau, where he and his court returned faithfully in fall for the hunting season. But it was Napoléon who spent lavishly to make a Versailles, as it were, out of Fontainebleau. He held Pope Pius VII here as a captive guest in 1812, signed the second church-state concordat here in 1813, and, in the cobbled **Cour des Adieux** (Farewell Courtyard), said good-bye to his Old Guard on April 20, 1814, as he began his brief exile on the Mediterranean island of Elba. The famous **Horseshoe Staircase** that dominates the

Cour des Adieux, once the Cour du Cheval Blanc (White Horse Courtyard), was built by Androuet du Cerceau for Louis XIII (1610–43); it was down this staircase that Napoléon made his way slowly to take a final salute from his Vieille Garde. Another courtyard—the **Cour de la Fontaine** (Fountain Courtyard)—was commissioned by Napoléon in 1812 and adjoins the Étang des Carpes (Carp Pond). Across from the pond is the formal Parterre (flower garden) and, on the other side, the leafy Jardin Anglais (English Garden).

3

The **Porte Dauphine** is the most beautiful of the various gateways that connect the complex of buildings; its name commemorates the christening of the dauphin—the heir to the throne, later Louis XIII—under its archway in 1606. The gateway fronts the **Cour Ovale** (Oval Court), shaped like a flattened egg. Opposite the courtyard is the **Cour des Offices** (Kitchen Court), a large, severe square built at the same time as Place des Vosges in Paris (1609). Around the corner is the informal **Jardin de Diane** (Diana's Garden), with peacocks and a statue of the hunting goddess surrounded by mournful hounds. ✉ *Pl. du Général-de-Gaulle* ☎ *01–60–71–50–70* 🌐 *www.musee-chateau-fontainebleau.fr* 🎫 *€8, Napoléon's Apartments €6 extra; gardens free* ⏲ *Palace Oct.–May, Wed.–Mon. 9:30–5; June–Sept., Wed.–Mon. 9:30–6; gardens May–Sept., daily 9–7; Oct. and Apr., daily 9–6; Nov.–Mar., daily 9–5.*

WHERE TO EAT AND STAY

$$ FRENCH ✕ **Arrighi.** This cozy, pink-wall, Art Deco restaurant near the château pulls in local gourmets with its three-course €19 menu that sometimes includes salmon or *bœuf bourguignon*. Jugged hare, *pavé de biche* (venison), and scallops with ginger and *roquette* salad are among seasonal specialties à la carte. ✉ *53 rue de France* ☎ *01–64–22–29–43* ▭ *AE, MC, V* ⏲ *Closed Mon. No dinner Sun.*

$$$$ FRENCH ✕ **Restaurant Croquembouche.** Bright and welcoming, with splashes of vibrant color, this popular restaurant draws enthusiastic praise from locals, who appreciate the combination of modest prices and inspired cuisine. With a menu that revolves around what's best in the market that day, the focus is on fresh, seasonal ingredients, along with a pleasing variety of seafood. Dishes are light, unfussy and original: scallops and roasted fennel in a mussel-langoustine bisque; wild sea bass with spinach and *bigorneaux* (tiny marine snails); St. Pierre etoufée in a buttered mussel bouillon, are just a few of the featured dishes. ✉ *43 rue de France, Fontainebleau* ☎ *01–64–22–01–57* 🌐 *www.restaurant-croquembouche.com* ▭ *AE, DC, MC, V* ⏲ *Closed Sun. No lunch Mon. and Sat.*

$$$ ★ **Aigle Noir.** This may be Fontainebleau's costliest hotel, but you can't go wrong if you request one of the rooms overlooking either the garden or the palace. They have late-18th- or early-19th-century reproduction furniture, creating a Napoleonic vibe. Sadly the excellent restaurant, Le Beauharnais, no longer exists. **Pros:** Napoleonic ambience; great location opposite château. **Cons:** no restaurant; no room service Friday or Saturday. ✉ *27 pl. Napoléon-Bonaparte* ☎ *01–60–74–60–00* 🌐 *www.hotelaiglenoir.com* *53 rooms* *In-room: a/c, safe, refrigerator (some), Wi-Fi. In-hotel: gym, some pets allowed* ▭ *AE, DC, MC, V* *BP.*

$$–$$$ **Londres.** Established in 1850, the Londres is a small, family-style hotel with Louis XV accents. Six rooms have balconies overlooking Fontainebleau's palace entrance and the Cour des Adieux, where Napoléon bade his troops an emotional farewell; the best views are from Rooms 10 and 11 on the top floor. The hotel's prim 19th-century facade is a registered landmark. **Pros:** château views from some rooms; cozy, family-run feel. **Cons:** no air-conditioning in some rooms; limited parking. ✉ *1 pl. du Général-de-Gaulle* ☎ *01–64–22–20–21* 🌐 *www.hoteldelondres.com* *14 rooms; 2 suites* *In-room: a/c (some), Wi-Fi. In-hotel: bar, parking (paid)* *AE, DC, MC, V* *Closed 1 wk in Aug. and Christmas–early Jan.* *BP.*

SPORTS AND THE OUTDOORS

The Forest of Fontainebleau is laced with hiking trails; for more information ask for the *Guide des Sentiers* (trail guide) at the tourist office. Bikes can be rented at the Fontainebleau-Avon train station. The forest is also famed for its quirky rock formations, where many a novice alpinist first caught the climbing bug; for more information contact the **Club Alpin Français** (✉ *24 av. Laumière, Paris* ☎ *01–53–72–87–00* 🌐 *www.ffcam.fr*).

4

The Loire Valley

WORD OF MOUTH

"Châteaux are the number one draw of the Loire valley but you can easily succumb to 'châteaux burnout.' However, as most are vastly different from each other, this really poses no problem. Especially if you be sure to also explore the neighboring villages for a bit of wine tasting, the odd troglodyte cave or two, and some lovely, elegant lunches. *Santé*!"

—WiseOwl

WELCOME TO THE LOIRE VALLEY

TOP REASONS TO GO

★ **Sleeping Beauty's Castle:** Play once-upon-a-time at Ussé—gleaming white against an emerald forest backcloth, it's so beautiful it inspired Perrault's immortal tale.

★ **Kingly Chambord:** The world's wackiest rooftop, with a forest of chimneys to match the game-rich woodlands extending in all directions, marks the Loire's grandest château.

★ **Splendor in the Grass:** The Renaissance reblooms at Villandry, whose geometric gardens have been lovingly restored to floricultural magnificence.

★ **Romantic Chenonceau:** Half bridge, half pleasure palace, this epitome of picturesque France extends across the Cher River, so why not row a boat under its arches?

★ **Medieval Magic:** Fontevraud is the majestic medieval abbey that is the resting place of English kings . . . and you can sleep on the spot.

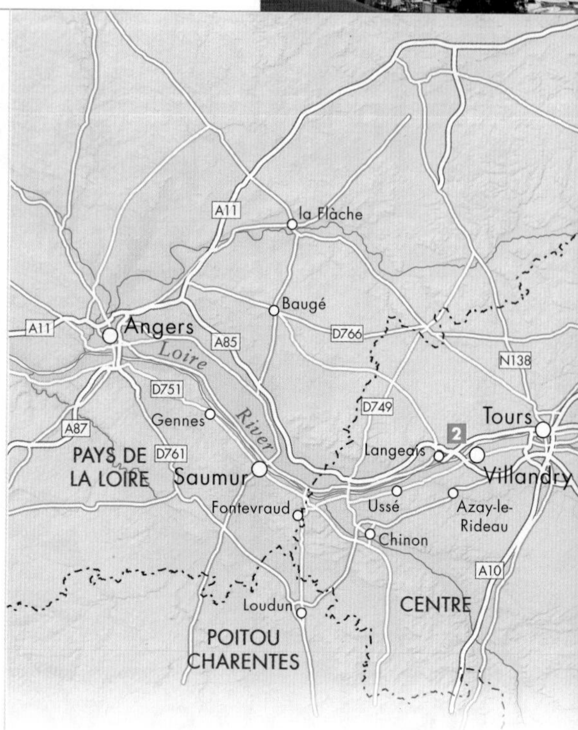

1 From Tours to Orleans. East from Tours, strung like precious gems along the peaceful Loire, the royal and near-royal châteaux are among the most fabled sights in France. From magical Chenonceau—improbably suspended above the River Cher—to mighty Chambord, with its 440 rooms, to Amboise (where Leonardo da Vinci breathed his last), this architectural conveyor belt moves up along the southern bank to deposit you at Orléans, newly burnished to old-world splendor with its pedestrianized *centre ville historique* (it was here that Joan of Arc had her most rousing successes against the English). Heading back to Tours on the northern bank, you'll discover the immense palace at Blois and some of the best hotels in the region.

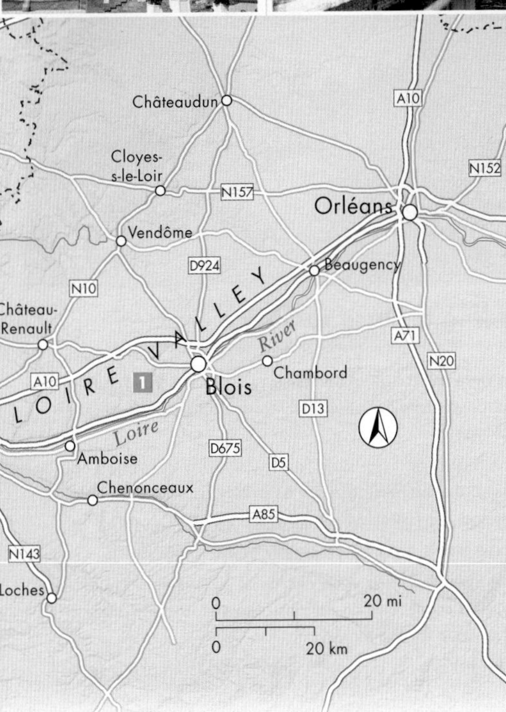

GETTING ORIENTED

The Loire Valley, which pretty much splits France in two, has been much traversed down the ages, once by Santiago pilgrims, now by Bordeaux-bound TGV trains. It retains a backwater feel that mirrors the river's sluggish, meandering waters, although trade along the river gave rise to major towns along its banks: Angers, Saumur, Blois, Orléans. But Tours remains the gateway to the region, not only for its central position but because the TGV links it with Paris in little more than an hour. From Angers you can drive northeast to explore the winding, intimate Loire Valley. Continue along the Loire as far as Nantes, the southern gateway to Brittany.

2 From Villandry to Langeais. Step into a fairy tale by castle-hopping among the most beautiful châteaux in France, from Villandry's fabled gardens to Ussé, which seems to levitate over the unicorn-haunted Forest of Chinon. From the Renaissance jewel of Azay-le-Rideau, continue west to Chinon for a dip in the Middle Ages along its Rue Haute St-Maurice—a pop-up illuminated manuscript. Continue time-traveling at the 12th-century royal abbey of Fontevraud, resting place of Richard the Lion-Hearted and Eleanor of Aquitaine. Then fast-forward to the 15th century at the storybook castle at Saumur—looming over the Loire's choicest town—and Angers's brooding fortress.

LOIRE VALLEY PLANNER

Making the Most of Your Time

More than a region in the usual sense, the Loire Valley is just that: a valley. Although most of the sites are close to the meandering river, it's a long way—140 mi—between Orléans, on the eastern edge, and Angers away to the west. If you have 10 days or so you can visit the majority of the sites we cover. Otherwise we suggest you divide the Valley into three segments and choose the base(s) as your time and tastes dictate. To cover the eastern Loire (Chambord, Cheverny, Chaumont), base yourself in or near Blois. For the central Loire (Amboise, Chenonceaux, Villandry, Azay-le-Rideau), base yourself in or around Tours. For the western Loire (Ussé, Chinon, Fontevraud, Angers), opt for pretty Saumur. There are many other scenarios, including this interesting one posted on the Talk Forums of www.fodors.com: "Angers is only about a 1.5-hour TGV ride from Paris, the train station is in the center of the city; and much is within walking distance. You might consider renting your car in Angers, if driving is your plan, and then tour the other châteaux (if you were renting a car in Paris it would save you the headache of the Paris traffic), then take the return TGV to Paris." —Randy

Finding a Place to Stay

Even before the age of the railway, the Loire Valley drew vacationers from far afield, so there are hundreds of hotels of all types.

At the higher end are sumptuously, stylishly converted châteaux, but even these are not as pricey as you might think. Note that most of these are in small villages, and that upscale hotels are in short supply in the major towns.

At the lower end is a wide choice of gîtes, bed-and-breakfasts, and small, traditional inns in towns, usually offering terrific value for the money.

The Loire Valley is a popular destination, so make reservations well in advance—in July and August, this is essential (and we're talking weeks, not days).

Beware that from November through Easter, many properties are closed.

Assume that all hotel rooms have air-conditioning, telephones, TV, and private bath, unless otherwise noted.

DINING AND LODGING PRICE CATEGORIES (IN EUROS)

	¢	$	$$	$$$	$$$$
Restaurants	under €13	€13–€17	€18–€24	€25–€32	over €32
Hotels	under €65	€65–€105	€106–€145	€146–€215	over €215

Restaurant prices are per person for a main course at dinner, including tax (5.5%) and service; note that if a restaurant offers only prix-fixe (set-price) meals, it has been given the price category that reflects the full prix-fixe price. Hotel prices are for a standard double room in high season, including tax (19.6%) and service charge.

Biking the Loire Valley: Wheel Estate

Fewer regions of France repay leisurely exploration more than the Val de Loire. And perhaps the best way to gentle meander through the Loire Valley may be by bike. As many discover, there's nothing like seeing Chenonceaux with your head pumped full of endorphins, surrounded by 20 new best friends, and knowing you'll be spending the night in a pointed turret bedroom fit for sleeping princesses.

So if you want to experience this region at its most blissful—but not blisterful!—take the **VBT** *(Vermont Biking Tours)* Loire Valley Tour. Many participants found it to be the most wonderful, truly ooooooooooo-lala travel experience they ever had in France.

Every morning, for six days, you sally forth for two to four hours of biking (about 34 to 56 km [19 to 35 mi]), with an option of either calling it quits at lunch and returning to your hotel or continuing on with the rack pack for the afternoon. The tour guide likes to joke that "real men don't ask for directions—at least not in English," but since the instructions direct you along the route virtually pebble-to-pebble, this faux pas never arises.

The itinerary reads like the pages of a Perrault fairy tale, studded as it is with such legendary abodes as Azay-le-Rideau, Chenonceau, Villandry, and Ussé. It's a good morning's work to see two châteaux, non?

You can have an even better evening of it, thanks to VBT's choice of châteaux-hotels. At the 16th-century La Bourdaisière, retreat of King François I, you'll feel a wand has been waved over you as you repair to the candle-lighted Richelieu-red dining room to enjoy a supper-lative *filet de carpe au Bourgueil.* Audrey Hepburn's favorite, the Domaine de la Tortinière, fulfills anyone's "Queen-for-a-Stay" fantasies. Your final hotel, the Château de Rochecotte, was the 19th-century Xanadu of Prince de Talleyrand-Périgord.

It's little wonder that most of the 20 bikers in the group are in a state of dumb intoxication after six days with VBT. And we're not talking about all the wine tastings. ✉ *614 Monkton Rd., Bristol, VT* ☎ *800/245–3868* 🌐 *www.vbt.com.*

Backroads (✉ *801 Cedar St., Berkeley, CA* ☎ *800/462–2848* 🌐 *www.backroads.com*) also offers the option of luxury accommodations, English-speaking guides, and travel logistics.

Tour Options

Excursion bus tours of the main châteaux leave daily in summer from the main hubs like Tours, Orléans, and Saumur: tourist offices have latest times and prices. Readers rave about Acco-Dispo van tours—usually three top châteaux are included. Their half-day trips cost €33 per person and leave from Tours or Amboise. Jet Systems makes helicopter trips over the Loire Valley on Tuesday, Thursday, and weekends from the aerodrome at Dierre, just south of Amboise; cost ranges from €65 (10 mins, flying over Chenonceau) to €275 (50 mins, from Chenonceau to Ussé) per person. Contact France Montgolfières for details of their balloon trips over the Loire; prices run €185–€225 per person. Croisières de Loire offers some unique Loire river tours. See historic Amboise from a traditional flat-bottom riverboat—cruises with commentary are offered May through September (50 mins, €8.50). Or sail the Cher River from the foot of Chenonceau April through October (€9.25).

Contacts **Acco-Dispo Tours** (✉ *18 rue des Vallees, Amboise* ☎ *06–82–00–64–51* 🌐 *www.accodispo-tours.com*). **Jet Tours** (✉ *Aérodrome d'Amboise Dierre* ☎ *02–47–30–20–21* 🌐 *www.jet-systems.fr*). **France Montgolfiéres** (☎ *02–54–32–20–48* 🌐 *www.franceballoons.com*). **Croisières de Loire** (✉ *Quai Charles Guinot, Amboise* ☎ *02–47–23–98–64* 🌐 *www.croisieresdeloire.com*).

4

GETTING AROUND

Transportation Basics

The regional rail line along the riverbank will get you to the main towns (Angers, Saumur, Tours, Blois, Orléans, along with 10 other towns), while some other châteaux are served by branch lines (Chenonceau, Azay, Langeais, Chinon, along with 20 or so other towns) or SNCF bus.

Occasionally, you may arrive at the rail station and need to invest in a taxi ride to get to the châteaux buried deep in the countryside.

The station staff can recommend the best regional taxi services, many of whom have advertisements at the stations.

The downside of train travel is having to fit your visits within the constraints of a railroad timetable.

For some, that makes a hired car a particularly practical option (although minimal signage in this rural area can turn a half-hour trip into a two-hour ordeal).

The N152, hugging the riverbank, is the region's four-wheeled backbone.

Given the region's flattish terrain, hiring a bike may well appeal. There are also local bus services and coach excursions, notably from Tours.

Train Travel

The great writer Henry James used the train system to tour Touraine back in the late 19th century and found it a most convenient way to get around. Things have only gotten better since then. Thanks to superbly organized timetables, you can whisk around from château to château with little worry or stress.

True, you may sometimes need to avail yourself of a quick taxi ride from the station to the château door, but compared to renting a car, this adds up to little bother and expense.

As gateways to the region, Tours (70 mins, €45) and Angers (95 mins, €47) are both served by the superfast TGV (Trains à Grande Vitesse) from Paris (Gare Montparnasse); note that the main-line station in Tours is in suburban St-Pierre-des-Corps.

There are also TGV trains from Charles-de-Gaulle Airport direct to the Loire Valley to Angers (2 hrs, 30 mins; €56), and St-Pierre-des-Corps (for Tours, 1 hr, 45 mins; €48). Express trains run every 2 hours from Paris (Gare d'Austerlitz) to Orléans (1 hr, 5 mins; €18.20, usually you must change at nearby Les Aubrais) and Blois (1 hr, 40 mins; €25.20).

The main train line follows the Loire from Orléans to Angers (1 hr, 50 mins; €29.30); there are trains every 2 hours or so, stopping in Blois, Tours, and Saumur; trains stop less frequently in Onzain (for Chaumont), Amboise, and Langeais.

There are branch lines with trains from Tours to Chenonceaux (30 mins, €6.30), Azay-le-Rideau (30 mins, €5.20), and Chinon (50 mins, €8.50).

Ask the SNCF for the brochure *Les Châteaux de la Loire en Train* for more detailed information. Helpful train-schedule brochures are available at most stations.

Train Information Gare SNCF Tours (✉ *Cour de la Gare* ☎ *03–80–43–16–34*). **Gare SNCF Orléans** (✉ *1 pl. François Mitterand* ☎ *03–80–43–16–34*). **Gare SNCF Angers** (✉ *Pl. de la Gare* ☎ *02–41–86–41–24*). **SNCF** (☎ *36–35 [€0.34 per min]* 🌐 *www.voyages-sncf.com*). **TGV** (🌐 *www.tgv.com*).

Bus Travel

Local bus services are extensive and reliable, providing a link between train stations and scenic areas off the river; it's possible to reach many villages and châteaux by bus (although many routes are in place to service schoolchildren, meaning service is less frequent in summer and sometimes all but nonexistent on Sunday)—most of the big towns and châteaux are more easily reached by train, however. Inquire at tourist offices about routes and timetables. The leading companies are Les Rapides du Val de Loire, based in Orléans; TLC, serving Chambord and Cheverny from Blois; Touraine Fil Vert and Fil Bleu, both of which serve the Touraine region, including out-of-the-way Loches; and Anjou Bus. The hardest place to reach is the magical Château d'Ussé, but there's one municipal bus line to Rigny-Ussé that connects with Chinon—when in doubt, taxi. For Fontevraud, catch buses from Saumur.

Bus Information Anjou Bus (✉ *Pl. Michel-Debré, Angers* ☎ *02–41–81–49–72* 🌐 *www.cg49.fr/le-conseil-general-a-votre-service/transports/transports-en-commun/reseau-anjoubus*). **Fil Bleu** (✉ *Pl. Jean-Jaurès, Tours* ☎ *02–47–66–70–70* 🌐 *www.filbleu.fr*). **Les Rapides du Val de Loire** (✉ *27-B bd. Marie-Stuart, Orléans* ☎ *02–38–61–90–00* 🌐 *www.rvl-info.com*). **TLC (Transports du Loir-et-Cher)** (✉ *9 rue Alexandre-Vézin, Blois* ☎ *02–54–58–55–44* 🌐 *tlcinfo.net*). **Touraine Fil Vert** (✉ *10 rue Alexander-Fleming, Tours* ☎ *02–47–47–17–18* 🌐 *www.touraine-filvert.com*).

Car Travel

The Loire Valley is an easy drive from Paris. A10 runs from Paris to Orléans—a distance of around 125 km (80 mi)—and on to Tours, with exits at Meung, Blois, and Amboise. After Tours, A10 veers south toward Poitiers and Bordeaux. A11 links Paris to Angers and Saumur via Le Mans. Slower but more scenic routes run from the Channel ports down through Normandy into the Loire region. The "easiest" way to visit the Loire châteaux is by car; N152 hugs the riverbank and is excellent for sightseeing. But note that signage can be few and far between once you get off the main road, and many a traveler has horror stories about a 15-minute trip lasting two hours ("Next time, by bus and train . . ."). You can rent a car in all the large towns in the region, or at train stations in Orléans, Blois, Tours, or Angers, or in Paris.

Visitor Information

The Loire region has three area tourist offices, all of which are for written inquiries only. For Chinon and points east, contact the Comité Régional du Tourisme de la Région Centre or the Comité Départemental du Tourisme de Touraine. For Fontevraud and points west, contact the Comité Départemental du Tourisme de l'Anjou. *For specific town tourist offices, see the town entries in this chapter.*

Contacts Comité Régional du Tourisme de la Région Centre (✉ *37 av. de Paris, Orléans* 🌐 *www.loirevalleytourism.com*). **Comité Départemental du Tourisme de l'Anjou** (✉ *Pl. Kennedy, Angers* ☎ *02–41–23–51–51* 🌐 *www.anjou-tourisme.com*). **Comité Départemental du Tourisme de Touraine** (✉ *30 rue de la Préfecture BP 3217 Tours Cedex* ☎ *02–47–31–47–48* 🌐 *www.tourism-touraine.com*). **Comité Départemental du Tourisme des Pays de la Loire** (✉ *1 pl. Galarne Nantes* 🌐 *www.enpaysdelaloire.com*).

Word of Mouth

"As we came close, driving up a long narrow road bordered by tall trees, I saw something that at first looked like a New York City skyline. Then I realized I was looking at the 365 towers of the immense Château de Chambord, silhouetted against the sky. All I could say was 'Oh my God . . .' I was completely overwhelmed." —drbb

EATING AND DRINKING WELL IN THE LOIRE VALLEY

Finesse rather than fireworks marks the gastronomy of this gentle, lovely region, known for exceptional white wines, delicate fish, and France's most bountiful fruits and vegetables.

Pike perch in beurre blance sauce is the Loire's most famous dish (above); goat cheeses are often paired with Loire white wines (right, top); Tartes Tatins are delicieux (right, bottom).

The serene and gentle Loire imposes its placid personality throughout this fertile valley region. The weather, too, is calm and cool, ideal for creating the Loire's diverse and memorable wines, from the elegant and refined Savennières to the mildly sweet, pretty-in-pink rosés of the Anjou. No big, bold, heavily tannic wines here. The culinary repertoire evokes a sense of the good life, with a nod to the royal legacy of châteaux living over centuries past. There is more gentility than dazzle in the cuisine; many dishes are simply presented, and they couldn't be better: a perfect pike-perch, called *sandre*, from the river, bathed in a silky beurre blanc sauce; coq au vin prepared with a fruity red Sancerre; a tender fillet of beef in a Chinon red-wine reduction sauce. It is the wines that highlight the Loire's gastronomic scene, and these alone justify a trip here, although of course, you could make time to visit a château or two while you're in the neighborhood.

OF CABBAGES AND KINGS

The great kitchens of the royal households that set up camp throughout the Loire planned menus around the magnificent produce that thrives in this fecund region, dubbed the Garden of France. Local cooks still do. There are fat white asparagus in the spring; peas, red cherries, haricots verts beans, artichokes, and lettuces in the summer; followed by apples, pears, cabbages, and pumpkins in the fall.

WHITE WINES (REDS, TOO!)

The Loire region spawns not only dazzling châteaux, but also some of the best wines in France—this is an important region for white-wine lovers, thanks to great chenin blanc and sauvignon blanc grapes. Top white appellations to imbibe, starting at the eastern end of the Loire and moving west, include flinty Sancerres, slightly smoky Pouilly-Fumés, vigorous and complex Vouvrays, distinguished Savennières, sparkling Champagne-style Saumurs, and finally the light, dry Muscadets, perfect with oysters on the half-shell.

In the realm of reds, try the raspberry-scented reds of Touraine, the heartier Chinons and Bourgueils, and the elegant rosés of the Anjou. For tastings, just follow the "Dégustation" signs, though it's always a good idea to call ahead.

Check out Vinci Cave in Amboise (☎ *02–47–23–41–52* 🌐 *www.vinci-cave.fr*); Domaine Huet in Vouvray (☎ *02–47–52–78–87* 🌐 *www.huet-echansonne.com*); Charles Joguet in Chinon (☎ *02–47–58–55–53* 🌐 *www.charlesjoguet.com*); Bouvet-Ladubay in Saumur (☎ *02–41–83–83–83* 🌐 *www.bouvet-ladubay.fr*); and the Maison du Vin d'Angers (☎ *02–41–88–81–13* 🌐 *www.vinsdeloire.fr*).

TARTE TATIN

This luscious "upside-down" apple tart is sometimes claimed by Normandy, but originated, so legend has it, at the Hotel Tatin in the Loire Valley town of Beuvron-Lamotte south of Orléans. The best tarts Tatin are made with deeply caramelized apples cooked under a buttery short-crust pastry, then inverted and served while still warm.

BEURRE BLANC

Made with a shallot, wine vinegar, and fish-stock reduction, and swirled with lots of butter, this iconic white sauce originated in the western Loire about a century ago in the kitchen of an aristocrat whose chef devised this variation on the classic béarnaise sauce. Beurre blanc is the perfect accompaniment to the Loire's delicate shad and pike.

CHÈVRE

With your glass of Pouilly Fumé, there are few things better than one of the region's tangy, herby, and assertive goat cheeses. Among the best, appellation-controlled and farmhouse-made: the squat, pyramid-shape Pouligny-Saint-Pierre; the creamy, cylindrical Sainte-Maure de Touraine; and the piquant Crottins de Chavignol from Sancerre. Try a warmed and melty Crottin atop a salad for a real treat.

4

Updated by Heather Stimmler-Hall

A fairy-tale realm par excellence, the Loire Valley is studded with storybook castles, time-burnished towns, and—*bien sûr*—the famous châteaux de la Loire, which are strung like a strand of pearls across a countryside so serene it could win the Nobel Peace Prize. With magic at every curve in the road, Cinderella's glass coach might be the optimum way to get around. If that is not available, buses and trains can beautifully ferry you to the main towns of the three Loire provinces—Anjou (to the west), Orléanais (to the east), and the center ring of the show, Touraine.

But why did the Loire become so prized for its châteaux? With the wars of the 15th century fading, the Loire Valley, long known as "the garden of France" became a showplace of new and fabulous châteaux *d'agrément,* or pleasure castles. In short order, there were boxwood gardens endlessly receding toward vanishing points, moats graced with swans, parades of delicate cone-top towers, frescoes, and fancywork ceilings. The glories of the Italian Renaissance, observed by the Valois while making war on their neighbor, were brought to bear on these mega-monuments with all the elegance and proportions characteristic of antiquity.

By the time François I took charge, extravagance knew no bounds: on a 13,000-acre forest estate, hunting parties at Chambord drew A-list crowds from the far reaches of Europe—and the availability of 430 rooms made weekend entertaining a snap. Queen Claudia hired only the most recherché Italian artisans: Chambord's famous double-helix staircase may, in fact, have been Leonardo da Vinci's design (he was a frequent houseguest there when not in residence in a manor on the Amboise grounds). From massive kennels teeming with hunting hounds at Cheverny to luxurious stables at Chaumont-sur-Loire, from endless allées of pollarded lime trees at Villandry to the fairy-tale towers of Ussé—worthy of Sleeping Beauty herself—the Loire Valley became the power base and social center for the New France, allowing the monarchy to go all out in strutting its stuff.

All for good reason. In 1519 Charles V of Spain, at the age of 19, inherited the Holy Roman Empire, leaving François and his New France out in the cold. It was perhaps no coincidence that in 1519 François, in a grand stab at face-saving one-upmanship, commenced construction on his gigantic Chambord. Centuries later, even the Revolution and the efforts of latter-day socialists have not totally erased a lingering gentility in the people of the region, characterized by an air of refined assurance far removed from the shoulder-shrugging, chest-tapping French stereotypes. Here life proceeds at a pleasingly genteel pace, and—despite the delights of a 1,001 châteaux that await—you should, too.

SO NEAR AND YET SO LOIRE: FROM TOURS TO ORLÉANS

At Orléans, halfway along the route of the Loire—the longest river in France—the river takes a wide, westward bend, gliding languidly through low, rich country known as the Val de Loire—or Loire Valley. In this temperate region—a 225-km (140-mi) stretch between Orléans and Angers—scores of châteaux built of local *tufa* (creamy white limestone) rise from the rocky banks of the Loire and its tributaries: the rivers Cher, Indre, Vienne, and Loir (with no *e*).

The Loire is liquid history. For centuries the river was the area's principal means of transportation and an effective barrier against invading armies. Towns arose at strategic bridgeheads, and fortresses—the earliest châteaux—appeared on towering slopes. The Loire Valley was hotly disputed by France and England during the Middle Ages; it belonged to England (under the Anjou Plantagenet family) between 1154 and 1216 and again during the Hundred Years' War (1337–1453). It was the example of Joan of Arc, the Maid of Orléans (so called after the site of one of her most stirring victories), that crystallized French efforts to expel the English.

The Loire Valley's golden age came under François I (ruled 1515–47)—flamboyant contemporary of England's Henry VIII—whose salamander emblem can be seen in many châteaux, including Chambord, the mightiest of them. Although the nation's power base shifted to Paris around 1600, aristocrats continued to erect luxurious palaces along the Loire until the end of the 18th century.

TOURS

240 km (150 mi) southwest of Paris.

Tours is the region's largest and most commercial city whose greatest asset is energy—the cobblestone streets in the pedestrian-only vielle ville crackle with cafés, bars, and restaurants. Students make up a quarter of the population, thanks to Tours's noted university. While much of the city was bombed in World War II, its pretty historic district remains to allure and enchant visitors to this important gateway to the Loire Valley.

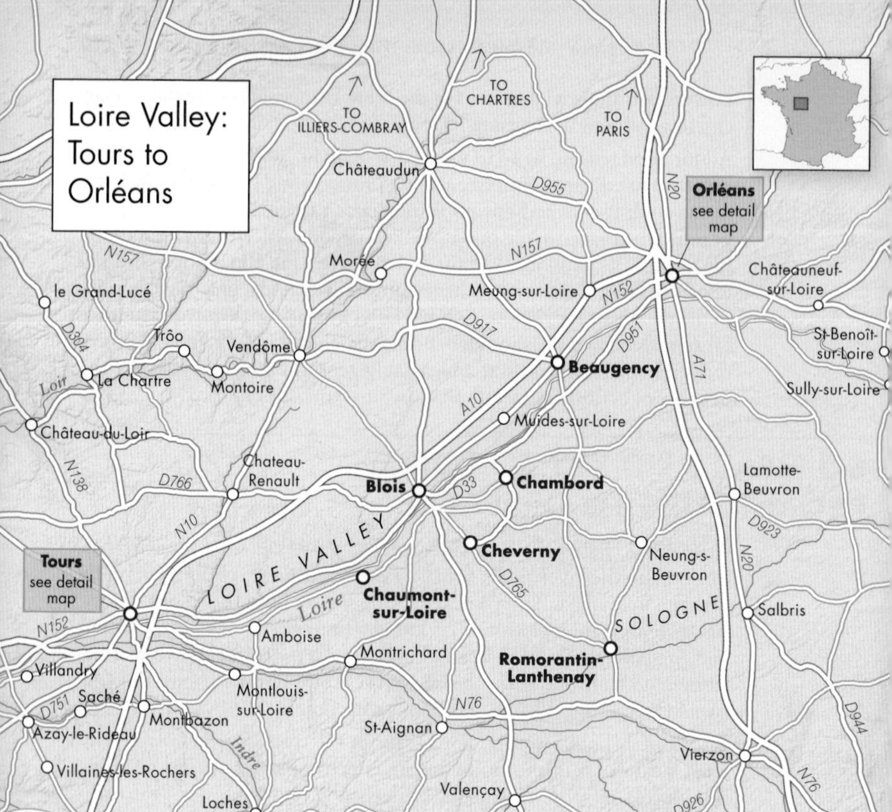

GETTING HERE

The handful of direct TGV trains from Paris (Gare Montparnasse) to Tours each day cover the 150 mi in 70 minutes; fare is €40–€55 depending on time of day. Some trains involve a change in suburban St-Pierre-des-Corps. A cheaper, slower alternative is the twice-daily traditional (non-TGV) service from Gare d'Austerlitz that takes around 2 hours, 30 minutes but costs only €30.50. Tours is the Loire Valley rail hub. Trains leave every couple of hours or so for Chinon (50 mins, €8.50); Langeais (15 mins, €4.90); Amboise (20 mins, €4.90); Saumur (40 mins, €10.50); Chenonceaux (30 mins, €6); and Blois (30–40 mins, €9.50), in addition to other towns.

Visitor Information Tours Tourist Office ✉ *78 rue Bernard-Palissy* ☎ *02–47–70–37–37* 🌐 *www.ligeris.com.*

EXPLORING

Little remains of Tours's own château—one of France's finest cathedrals more than compensates—but the city serves as the transportation hub for the Loire Valley. Trains from Tours (and from its adjacent terminal at St-Pierre-de-Corps) run along the river in both directions, and regular bus services radiate from here; in addition, the city is the starting point for organized bus excursions (many with English-speaking guides). The town has mushroomed into a city of a quarter of a million inhabitants, with an ugly modern sprawl of factories, high-rise blocks, and overhead expressway junctions cluttering up the outskirts. But the timber-frame houses in **Le Vieux Tours** (Old Tours) and the attractive medieval center around Place Plumereau were smartly restored after extensive damage in World War II.

TOP ATTRACTIONS

7 ★ **Cathédrale St-Gatien.** Built between 1239 and 1484, this noted cathedral, one of the greatest churches of the Loire Valley, reveals a mixture of architectural styles. The richly sculpted stonework of its majestic, soaring, two-tower facade betrays the Renaissance influence on local château-trained craftsmen. The stained glass dates from the 13th century (if you have binoculars, bring them). Also take a look at the little tomb with kneeling angels built in memory of Charles VIII and Anne of Brittany's two children; and the **Cloître de La Psalette** (Psalm Cloister), on the south side of the cathedral. ✉ *Rue Lavoisier* ☎ *02–47–47–05–19* ⊙ *Daily 9–7.*

9 Fodor's Choice ★ **Château de Candé.** When Edward VIII of England abdicated his throne in 1937 to marry the American divorcée Wallace Simpson, the couple chose this elegant 16th-century château (found 10 minutes south of Tours) to escape from international limelight and exchange their wedding vows. Open to the public since 2000, the lovely museum offers a video and guided tour through the rooms of the chateau. While decorated with period furnishings and Art Deco bathrooms, all eyes are drawn to the mementos from the Duke and Duchess of Windsor's stay (including the famous Cecil Beaton photographs taken on the big day) along with the haute couture wardrobe of the fashionable lady of the house, Fern Bedaux. Befitting the duchess's flawless taste (if questionable politics, as the Bedaux were known fascist sympathizers), the château is a particularly pretty example of late Gothic style—the perfect setting for the Windsors' "fairy-tale" marriage. ✉ *Rte. National 10, Monts (8 km/5 mi southwest of Tours)* ☎ *02–47–34–03–70* 🌐 *www.chateau-cande.fr* 🎫 *€4.50* ⊙ *Apr.–Oct., Wed.–Sun., 50-min guided tours only*

5 **Hôtel Gouin** *(Archaeology Museum). Still closed for a multi-year renovation, this museum* is set in Tours's most extravagant example of early Renaissance domestic architecture (too bad its immediate vicinity was among the hardest hit by German bombs), its facade covered with carvings that seemed to have grown like Topsy. Once the museum reopens, assorted oddities—ranging from ancient Roman finds to the scientific collection of Dupin de Chenonceau (owner of the great château in the 18th century)—will once again be on view ✉ *25 rue du Commerce* ☎ *02–47–66–22–32* 🌐 *www.monuments-touraine.fr.*

4 **Musée du Gemmail.** Housed in the imposing 19th-century Hôtel Raimbault, this noted museum contains an unusual collection of three-dimensional colored-glass window panels depicting patterns, figures, and portraits. The gemmail

LUSCIOUS LOIRE

If the natives of Tours are known for one thing, it's their elegant French. Paris may be the capital, but for the Tourangeaux, Parisians are the ones with the accent.

technique of nonleaded stained glass was invented in the 1950s and can also be seen in Lourdes. Incidentally, Jean Cocteau coined the word *gemmail* by combining *gemme* (gem) with *émail* (enamel). ✉ *7 rue du Mûrier* ☎ *02–47–61–01–19* 🎟 *€5.50* ⏲ *Apr.–mid-Oct., Tues.–Sun. 2–6:30.*

3 Fodor's Choice ★ **Place Plumereau.** North from the Basilique St-Martin to the river is **Le Vieux Tours,** the lovely medieval quarter centered around that postcard icon, the half-timbered Place Plumereau. A warren of quaint streets, wood-beam houses, and grand mansions once home to 15th-century merchants, Tours's Old Towns has been gentrified with chic apartments and pedestrianized streets—Tours's college students and tourists alike love to sit at the cafés lining the Place Plumereau, once the town's *carroi aux chapeaux* (hat market). Lining the square, Nos. 1 through 7 form a magnificent series of half-timber houses; note the wood carvings of royal moneylenders on Nos. 11 and 12. At the top of the square a vaulted passageway leads on to a cute medieval **Place St-Pierre-le-Puellier.** Running off the Place Plumereau are other streets adorned with historic houses, notably Rue Briçonnet—No. 16 is the **Maison de Tristan,** with a noted medieval staircase. ✉ *Bordered by Rues du Commerce, Briçonnet, de la Monnaie, and du Grand-Marché.*

WORTH NOTING

1 **Basilique St-Martin.** Only two sturdy towers—the Tour Charlemagne and the Tour de l'Horloge (Clock Tower)—remain of the great medieval abbey built over the tomb of St. Martin, the city's 4th-century bishop and patron saint. Most of the abbey, which once dominated the heart of Tours, was razed during the French Revolution. Today the site is occupied by the bombastic neo-Byzantine **Basilique St-Martin**, which was completed in 1924. There's a shrine to St. Martin in the crypt. ✉ *Rue Descartes.*

8 **Musée des Beaux-Arts** *(Fine Arts Museum).* In what was once the archbishop's palace (built into an ancient Roman wall), this museum features an eclectic selection of furniture, sculpture, wrought-iron work, and pieces by Rubens, Rembrandt, Boucher, Degas, and Calder. It even displays Fritz the Elephant, stuffed in 1902. ✉ *18 pl. François-Sicard* ☎ *02–47–05–68–73* 🎟 *€4* ⏲ *Wed.–Mon. 9–6.*

6 **Musée du Compagnonnage** *(Guild Museum). Also incorporating the city's* **Musée du Vin** (Wine Museum), these twin museums are housed in the cloisters of the 13th-century church of St-Julien. *Compagnonnage* is a sort of apprenticeship-cum–trade union system, and here you see the masterpieces of the candidates for guild membership: virtuoso craft work, some of it eccentric (an Eiffel Tower made of slate, for instance, or a château constructed of varnished noodles). ✉ *8 rue Nationale* ☎ *02–47–21–62–20* 🌐 *www.musee-du-compagnonnage.info* 🎟 *Musée du Compagnonnage €5, Musée du Vin €3; joint ticket €5.50* ⏲ *Jan.–mid-June and Sept.–Dec., Wed.–Mon. 9–noon and 2–6; mid-June–Aug., daily 9–noon and 2–6.*

2 **Musée St-Martin.** Old mosaics and Romanesque sculptures from the former abbey are on display here in this small museum. Housed in a restored 13th-century chapel that adjoined the abbey cloisters, the

Basilique St-Martin 1
Cathédrale St-Gatien 7
Château de Candé 9
Hotêl Goüin et Musée Archéologique .. 5
Musée des Beaux-Arts 8
Musée du Compagnonnage/ Musée du Vin ... 6
Musée du Gemmail 4
Musée St-Martin 2
Place Plumereau 3

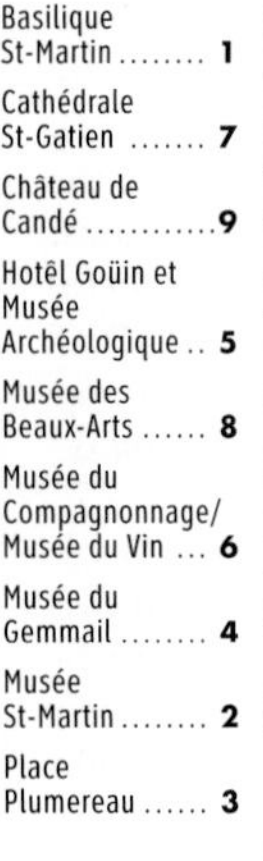

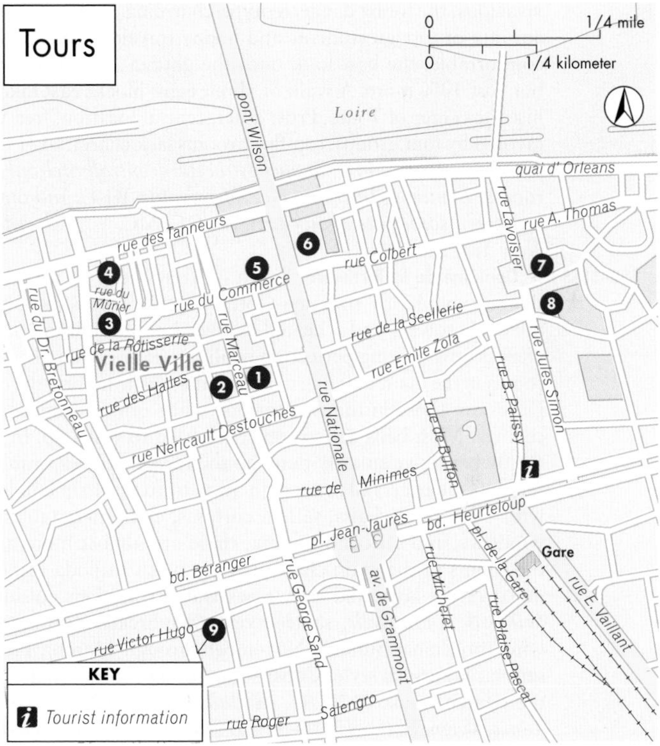

exhibits retrace the life of St. Martin, so important to Tours's history, and the abbey's long and storied saga. ✉ *3 rue Rapin* ☎ *02–47–64–48–87* €2 ⏲ *Wed.–Sun. 9:30–12:30 and 2–5:30.*

WHERE TO EAT

$$$–$$$$ FRENCH ✕ **L'Odéon.** Enjoy the best of traditional Loire Valley haute cuisine in an Art Deco setting at this popular option in the heart of Tours. The modern flair here combines surprising flavors, such as fresh lobster with crispy apples and thyme juice, beef fillet cooked with grapes and peppers, or roasted seas bass with a creamy artichoke sauce. Go for the good deals, such as lunch menus from €25 or four-course dinner menus from €34. ✉ *10 pl. du Général Leclerc* ☎ *02–47–20–12–65* 🌐 *www.restaurant-lodeon.com* ▭ *MC, V* ⏲ *Closed Sat. lunch and Sun.*

$$ FRENCH ✕ **Le Petit Patrimoine.** Locals in the know reserve well in advance to get a table at this tiny restaurant in Vieux Tours specializing in traditional regional cuisine. Don't miss Balzac's much-loved Rillons de Tours, a glazed pork dish, and the delicious St-Maure goat cheese. ✉ *58 rue Colbert* ☎ *02–47–66–05–81* ▭ *MC, V* ⏲ *Closed Sun. and Mon.*

WHERE TO STAY

$$–$$$ **Best Western Central.** A delightfully friendly city-center oasis, this Best Western hotel near the Musée du Compagnonnage is set back from the street behind a gravel court and terraced garden. Inside, the welcome is

vivacious, the lobby daguerreotype-charming, and the clientele a pleasant mix of foreign students and happy travelers. The guest rooms are comfortable; the best look onto the garden (No. 441 is the largest), but cost 40% more. A walk of about eight blocks east takes you to the historic center of Tours. **Pros:** quiet, central location, free Wi-Fi. **Cons:** favored by tour groups; top-floor rooms lack charm. ✉ *21 rue Berthelot* ☎ *02–47–05–46–44* 🌐 *www.bestwesterncentralhoteltours.com* *35 rooms, 2 suites* *In-room: a/c, refrigerator, Wi-Fi. In-hotel: bar, parking (free), some pets allowed* *AE, DC, MC, V* *Closed Christmas–New Year's* *BP.*

$$$–$$$$ ★ **Domaine de la Tortinière.** South of Tours atop a vast, sloping lawn, this storybook, toy-size, neo-Gothic château comes complete with two fairy-tale towers and a heated, terraced pool. Built in 1861, La Tortinière is now nearing perfection in all things bright and beautiful. Guest rooms in the main building convey quiet, rustic luxury; the conversation pieces are those in the two turrets, while others delight with beamed ceilings. Most beds are so comfy it's hard to wake up. In recent years the owners have smartly done up the former stables, warehouses, and servants' quarters (all just a path away from the main building). Replete with Louis XVI chairs, taffeta curtains, chiffonière tables, plate-glass windows, and air-conditioning, these are almost more alluring than the rooms in the main château. The stylish rotunda restaurant looks out over the lawn and showcases David Chartier's cuisine, including *beuchelle tourangelle,* sautéed veal sweetbreads with morels in white wine (no dinner Sunday, November through March). **Pros:** romantic setting; luxurious style. **Cons:** some rooms on the small side; a bit off the beaten track. ✉ *10 rte. de Ballan-Miré, 12 km (7 mi) south of Tours, Veigné* ☎ *02–47–34–35–00* 🌐 *www.tortiniere.com* *24 rooms, 6 suites* *In-room: a/c, safe, refrigerator, Wi-Fi (some). In-hotel: restaurant, tennis court, pool* *MC, V* *Closed mid-Dec.–Feb.* *MAP.*

$ **L'Adresse.** A charming little hotel with fresh decor in the heart of Tours's Old Town, this is located just a block from the Place Plumereau and the open-air market. Guest rooms have contemporary bathrooms with shower or bath and a neutral color palette punctuated with touches of deep red. Top-floor rooms feature whitewashed wood-beam ceilings. Breakfast is served in the rooms or in the bright dining room overlooking the pedestrian street. **Pros:** central location in Vieux Tours; flat-screen TVs and air-conditioning. **Cons:** student district can be noisy at night; decor borders on bland. ✉ *12 rue de la Rôtisserie* ☎ *02–47–20–85–76* 🌐 *www.hotel-ladresse.com* *17 rooms* *In-room: a/c. In-hotel: some pets allowed* *AE, DC, MC, V* *MAP.*

$$$–$$$$ ★ **Les Hautes Roches.** *Extraordinaire* is the word for some of the dozen luxe-troglodyte rooms at this famous hotel, set 5 km (3 mi) to the east of Tours in elegant Rochecorbon (a favored country residence for rich Parisians). Studding a towering cliff-face, these amazing accommodations come replete with elegant sash windows, gas-lantern lamps, and finished marble steps. Don't expect furnishings à la Fred Flintstone: half the guest-room walls are Ice Age, but stylish fabrics, Louis Treize seating, and carved fireplaces are the main allurements. Some prefer rooms in the regular house—no cave-dwelling drama, but exquisitely

Spend your first evening in the Loire Valley dining on gorgeous Place Plumereau, hub of the historic district of Tours, gateway to the region.

comfortable and air-conditioned. The restaurant and its enchanting terrace offer a panoply of hyper-elegant goodies and overlooks the lovely pool. Rochecorbon is a treat (once off the main traffic road), thanks to its pretty town center, vineyards, and a "Bateaux Promenade" (boat-ride) on the Loire. **Pros:** unique troglodyte setting; river views. **Cons:** apprentice-style service; busy road in front of hotel. ✉ *86 quai de la Loire, Rochecorbon* ☎ *02–47–52–88–88* 🌐 *www.leshautesroches.com* *15 rooms* *In-room: a/c (some), refrigerator, Wi-Fi. In-hotel: restaurant, pool, Wi-Fi hotspot, some pets allowed* ▭ *AE, DC, MC, V* ⏲ *Closed mid-Jan.–mid-Mar.* *MAP.*

$ **Mondial.** Tucked away in the city center on a small leafy square 300 yards from the Loire, this hotel is a five-minute walk to historic half-timber Place Plumereau. The white-wall, postwar building has recently renovated rooms in contemporary neutral tones with red or foral accents. All are on the small side—room No. 31 is the largest—but spotlessly clean and offer good value, and service is friendly. There's no restaurant, but the brasserie Bure is right next door. **Pros:** free Wi-Fi; good location. **Cons:** street noise; steep stairs and restricted reception hours. ✉ *3 pl. de la Résistance* ☎ *02–47–05–62–68* 🌐 *www.hotelmondialtours.com* *19 rooms* *In-room: no a/c, Wi-Fi* ▭ *AE, MC, V.*

MONTLOUIS-SUR-LOIRE

11 km (7 mi) east of Tours on south bank of the Loire.

Visitor Information **Montlouis-sur-Loire Tourist Office.** ✉ *Pl. François-Mitterrand* ☎ *02–47–45–00–16* 🌐 *www.tourisme-montlouis-loire.fr.*

Like Vouvray—its sister town on the north side of the Loire—Montlouis is noted for its white wines. On Place Courtemanche the **Cave Touristique** will help you learn all about the fine vintages produced by the wine growers of Montlouis. On the eastern side of town is one of the most alluring châteaux of the region, **La Bourdaisière.** Although open to day-trippers for guided tours, this once-royal retreat and birthplace of noted 17th-century courtesan Gabrielle d'Estrées is today the enchanted hotel-domain of Prince Louis-Albert de Broglie.

WHERE TO STAY

$$$–$$$$ Fodor's Choice ★ **Château de la Bourdaisière.** Few other hotels so magically distill all the grace, warmth, and élan of *la vie de château* as does this 15th-century, 100-carat jewel. Once the favored retreat of two kings, François I and Henri IV, today its presiding spirit is the Prince Louis-Albert de Broglie, scion of one of France's top families (two prime ministers and one Nobel Prize winner, at last count) andone of Paris's most famed biodiversity preservationists, who here cultivates 650 types of tomatoes in the château's *potager* (vegetable garden). It's not surprising, then, to find the three main public salons suavely done up in shades of tomato red, sumptuously offsetting such accents as an immense marble fireplace, majestic taxidermied animals, and curio cabinet objects collected by the prince. Inside the neo-Renaissance castle, guest rooms range from the grand—*François-Premier* is a timber-roof cottage blown up to ballroom dimensions—to more standard-issue, yet always stylish salons (garden-view rooms away from the gravel driveway are best). Cheaper rooms are found in the adjoining 17th-century "stables" fitted out with a gardening shop and a tiny eatery (lunch only, June–September). And don't overlook the enormous secluded pool—a gift from heaven during hot summer days. **Pros:** exquisite setting; extensive and "eco"-style gardens. **Cons:** only offers quick and casual lunches; rooms lack air-conditioning; town is a bore. ✉ *25 rue de la Bourdaisière* ☎ *02–47–45–16–31* 🌐 *www.chateaulabourdaisiere.com* *17 rooms, 3 suites* *In-room: no a/c, Internet. In-hotel: restaurant, tennis court, pool, some pets allowed* ▭ *MC, V* ⊗ *Closed mid-Nov.–Mar.* *BP.*

AMBOISE

13 km (8 mi) northeast of Montlouis via D751, 24 km (15 mi) east of Tours.

The Da Vinci trail ends here in one of the more popular towns along the river. Site of Leonardo's final home, crowned with a royal château, and jammed with bustling markets and plenty of hotels and restaurants, Amboise is one of the major hubs of the Loire. On hot summer days, however, the plethora of tour buses turns the Renaissance town into a carbon monoxide nightmare. So why come? The main château is soaked in history (and blood), while Leonardo's very pretty Clos-Lucé mansion is a must-do on any Val de Loire itinerary.

GETTING HERE

Amboise has frequent train connections with Tours (20 mins, €5.20), Blois (24 mins, €6.30), and many other towns that lie along the main train route, which follows the banks of the river; about 10 trains a day make the Tours–Blois transit. From Amboise's station, the town is across the Loire (the island in the middle of the river is the less-than-exciting Ile d'Or); follow the signs across two bridges to the centre ville and Place Richelieu.

Visitor Information **Amboise Tourist Office.** ✉ *Quai du Général-de-Gaulle* ☎ *02–47–57–09–28* 🌐 *www.amboise-valdeloire.com.*

EXPLORING

The **Château d'Amboise** became a royal palace in the 15th and 16th centuries. Charles VII stayed here, as did the unfortunate Charles VIII, best remembered for banging his head on a low doorway lintel (you will be shown it) and dying as a result. The gigantic **Tour des Minimes** drops down the side of the cliff, enclosing a massive circular ramp designed to lead horses and carriages up the steep hillside. François I, whose long nose appears in so many château paintings, based his court here, inviting Leonardo da Vinci as his guest. The castle was also the stage for the Amboise Conspiracy, an ill-fated Protestant plot against François II; you're shown where the corpses of the conspirators dangled from the castle walls. Partly due to the fact that most interior furnishings have been lost, most halls here are haunted and forlorn. In 2009 the maze of underground passages were newly opened to the public for guided visits (April–September). But don't miss the lovely grounds, adorned with a Flamboyant Gothic gem, the little chapel of St-Hubert with its carvings of the Virgin and Child, Charles VIII, and Anne of Brittany, and once graced by the tomb of Leonardo. ☎ *02–47–57–00–98* 🌐 *www.chateau-amboise.com* 🎫 *€9.50* ⏲ *Nov.–Mar., daily 9–noon and 2–4:45; Apr.–June, Sept., and Oct., daily 9–6; July and Aug., daily 9–7.*

★ If you want to see where "the 20th century was born"—as the curators here like to proclaim—head to the legendary **Clos Lucé**, about 600 yards up Rue Victor-Hugo from the château. Here, in this handsome Renaissance manor, Leonardo da Vinci (1452–1519) spent the last four years of his life, tinkering away at inventions, amusing his patron, King François I, and gazing out over a garden that was planted in the most fashionable Italian manner (which was completely restored in 2008 to contain the plants and trees found in the artist's sketches, as well as a dozen full-size renderings of machines he designed). The **Halle Interactive** contains working models, built by IBM engineers using the detailed sketches in the artist's notebooks, of some of Leonardo's extraordinary inventions; by this time Leonardo had put away his paint box because of arthritis. Mechanisms on display include three-speed gearboxes, a military tank, a clockwork car, and a flying machine complete with designs for parachutes. Cloux, the house's original name, was given to Anne of Brittany by Charles VIII, who built a chapel for her that is still here. Some of the house's furnishings are authentically 16th century—indeed, thanks to the artist's presence this house was one of the first places where the Italian Renaissance made inroads in France: Leonardo's *Mona Lisa* and *Virgin of the Rocks*, both of which graced the walls here, were bought by the king, who then moved them to the Louvre. ✉ *2 rue du Clos-Lucé* ☎ *02–47–57–00–73* 🌐 *www.vinci-closluce.com* 🎫 *€12.50* ⏲ *Sept.–Dec. and Feb.–June, daily 9–6; July and Aug., daily 9–8; Jan., daily 10–5.*

Continued on page 233

ONCE UPON A CHÂTEAU

The châteaux of the Loire Valley range in style from medieval fortresses to Renaissance country homes, and they don't skip a beat in between. Today, travelers hop their way from the fairy-tale splendor of Ussé to the imposing dungeons at Angers to the graceful spans of Chenonceau. But to truly appreciate these spectacular structures, it helps to review their evolution from warlike stronghold to Sleeping Beauty's home.

Château de Chambord

Loire and château are almost synonymous. There may be châteaux in every region of France, but nowhere are they so thickly clustered as they are in the Loire Valley. There are several reasons for this. By the early Middle Ages, prosperous towns had already evolved due to being strategically sited on the Loire, and defensive fortresses—the first châteaux—were built by warlords to control certain key points along the route. And with good reason: the riches of this wildly fertile region drew many feuding lords; in the 12th century, the medieval Plantagenet kings of France and England had installed themselves here (at Chinon and Fontevraud, to be exact).

During this time, dukes and counts began to build châteaux, from which they could watch over the king's lands and also defend themselves from each others' invasions. Spare, cold, and uninviting (that being the point), their châteaux were compartmented to house whole courts which settled in with their own furniture, pantry, and wall-sized tapestries (for insulation against the drafts). The notion of defense extended to the décor: massive high-back chairs protected the sitter from being stabbed in the back during dinner, and the *crédence* (credenza) was a table used by a noble's official taster to test for poison in the food.

These fortifications continued to come in handy during the Hundred Years' War, during which France and England quibbled over the French crown, for 116 years. When that war came to an end, in 1453, King François I went to Italy, looking for someone else to beat up on, and came back with the Renaissance (he literally brought home Leonardo da Vinci). The king promptly built a 440-room Xanadu, Chambord, in the Italianate style.

By the 15th century, under the later medieval Valois kings, the Loire was effectively functioning as the country's capital, with new châteaux springing up apace, advertising their owners' power and riches. Many were built using a chalky local stone called *tuffeau* (tufa), whose softness and whiteness made it ideal for the sculpted details which were the pride of the new architectural style. The resulting Renaissance pleasure palaces were sumptuous both inside and out—Charles Perrault found the Château de Ussé to be so peaceful and alluring it inspired him to write "Sleeping Beauty" in 1697. A few years before, Louis XIV had started building his new seat of government. It wasn't long before it was goodbye Loire Valley, hello Versailles.

FROM DEFENSE TO DECORATION

13TH CENTURY

Angers

The parade of châteaux began with the medieval fortress at Angers, a brooding, muscular fort built by St. Louis to defend the gateway to the Loire against pesky English invaders. Military architecture gave birth to this château, a perfect specimen of great, massive defensiveness. Such castles were meant to look grim, advertising horrid problems for attackers—defenders shot cross-bow arrows from the slit windows—and unpleasant conditions for prisoners in the dungeons. The most important features of these fortress-châteaux were the *châtelets* (twin turrets that frame the drawbridge), the *chemin de ronde* (the machicolated passageways between towers), and the *donjon* (fortress keep).

14TH CENTURY

Saumur

When the battle cries faded and periods of peace once more beguiled the land, the château changed its appearance and the picture palaces of the Loire came into being. Elegance arrived early at Saumur, built in 1360 by Louis I of Anjou. His heir, the luxury-loving Duc de Berri, dressed up the sturdy fort with high, pointed roofs, gilded steeples, iron weather vanes, and soaring pinnacles, creating a Gothic-style castle that Walt Disney would have been proud of. Former cross-bow apertures were replaced with good-size windows, from which love-sick princesses would gaze down on chivalric tournaments, now featuring fancy cloth-of-gold trappings, and festive banquets with blaring trumpet backup became the norm.

1214 French king **Philippe Auguste** defeats English and German armies in Anjou.

1228 1238 Constructuion of **Angers Castle.**

1270 **Death of Louis IX** (St. Louis) in Tunis during the 8th Crusade.

1300

1337 **Hundred Years' War** between France and England. begins.

1348 The **Black Death** kills one third of the French population.

1360 Louis I of Anjou tranforms **Saumur** into his elegant residence.

1400

16TH CENTURY

Azay-le-Rideau

By the Renaissance—brought to France from Italy by Charles VIII at the end of the 15th century—balance, harmony, and grace were brought to the fore. Rich officials wowed the womenfolk with châteaux that were homages to the bygone days of chivalry, such as Azay-le-Rideau. The château may look Gothic from a distance, but its moat is actually the River Indre, and its purpose is to provide a pleasing reflection, thereby emphasizing the Italianate symmetry of this architectural bijou. Funded by the royal financier Berthelot but designed by his wife, Philippe, this was a fairy-tale castle. The turrets and machicolations were just for fun, and a grand staircase was added to showcase the ladies' sweeping skirts.

16TH CENTURY

Chenonceau

Its architecture is civilized, peaceful, and feminine, aptly so since it was constructed by three ladies. Catherine Briçonnet, a tax collector's wife, built the Gothic-style château; Diane de Poitiers, the mistress of Henri II, extended it by adding a bridge across the river (for easy access to her hunting grounds), before being kicked out by Henri's wife, Catherine de Medici, who tacked galleries onto the bridge in homage to the Ponte Vecchio in Florence, her home town. Although its broad facade offers a curtsey to the virtues of Baroque style, Chenonceau is actually only two rooms deep—the château had become an exquisite stage curtain and little more.

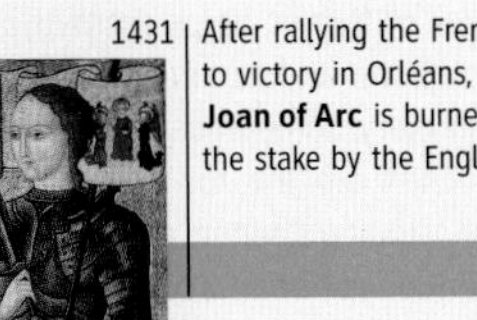

1431 After rallying the French to victory in Orléans, **Joan of Arc** is burned at the stake by the English.

1485 **Charles VIII** invades Italy, importing home the Renaissance.

1500

1518 **Azay-le-Rideau** is rebuilt with Italian influences.

1525 François I builds **Chambord.**

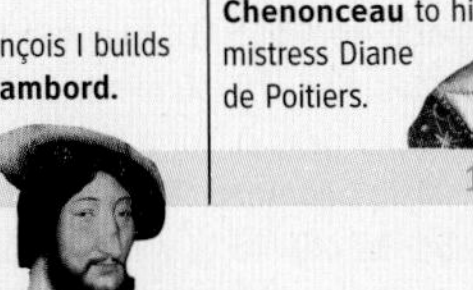

1547 King Henri II gives **Chenonceau** to his mistress Diane de Poitiers.

1600

LA VIE DE CHÂTEAUX

Inside or out, the Château de la Bourdaiserie epitomizes Loire elegance.

To truly savor the châteaux of the "Valley of the Kings," you can do more than just tour them: You can sleep in them, party in them, and helicopter-ride over them.

QUEEN FOR A STAY

Here are the crème de la crème of the Loire Valley's magical châteaux-hotels:

Château de la Bordaisière, Montlouis-sur-Loire. Not far from Chenonceau, this enchanting neo-Renaissance castle is run by prince Louis-Albert de Broglie. Royal red salons, chic bedrooms, a famous tomato potager, a vast pool, and heirloom gardens are just a few of the goodies here.

Château de Colliers, Muides-sur-Loire. Close to Chambord, this *très charmant* jewel has ravishing Rococo salons and the most beautiful hotel river terrace along the Loire.

Château de Pray, Amboise. With its storybook towers, tapestried-and-chandeliered restaurant, and 19th-century style rooms, you'll be raising your glass of Veuve Clicquot to toast La Loire in no time.

AN EYE ON HIGH

Thanks to helicopter excursions, you can get a new perspective on the grand châteaux by taking to the air—appropriately so, since Leonardo da Vinci invented the contraption while residing in Amboise. Jet Systems (☎ 02–47–30–20–21 🌐 www.jet-systems.fr) makes helicopter trips over the Loire Valley on Tuesday, Thursday, and weekends from the aerodrome at Dierre, just south of Amboise; costs range from €65 (10 minutes, flying over Chenonceau) to €275 (50 minutes, covering six châteaux) per person. For a more leisurely airborne visit, contact France Montgolfière (☎ 02–54–32–20–48 🌐 www.franceballoons.com) for details of their balloon trips over the Loire; prices run €185–€225.

LET THERE BE A LIGHT SHOW

In summer, several châteaux offer celebrated *son-et-lumière* (sound-and-light) extravaganzas after dark. Some are historical pageants—with huge casts of people dressed in period costume, all floodlit (the flicker of flames helps dramatize the French Revolution), and accompanied by music and commentary, sometimes in English; Amboise and Loches are the top examples. Other châteaux—including Chenonceau, Chambord, and Azay-le-Rideau—offer recorded commentary and magical effects created by slide projections (pictured), smoke-machines, and color spotlights.

Just 3 km (2 mi) south of Amboise on the road to Chenonceaux, the **Pagode de Chanteloup** is a remarkable sight—a 140-foot, seven-story Chinese-style lakeside pagoda built for the Duke of Choiseul in 1775. Children will adore puffing their way to the top for the vertigo-inducing views, but some adults will find the climb—and the 400-yard walk from the parking lot—a little arduous. Sadly, the adjoining lake and park have become the worse for wear. ✉ *Rte. de Bléré* ☎ *02–47–57–20–97* 🌐 *www.pagode-chanteloup.com* *€8* ⏲ *Apr.–June, and Sept., daily 10–6:30; Feb., weekdays 2–5, weekends noon–5; July and Aug., daily 9:30–7.30; Oct.–mid-Nov., weekends 10–noon and 2–5.*

WHERE TO STAY

$$–$$$ Fodor's Choice ★ **Château de Pray.** Fifty years ago Loire Valley guidebooks praised this domain and, delightfully, things have only gotten better. Like a Rolls-Royce Silver Cloud, this hotel keeps purring along, offering many delights: a romantic, twin-tower château, a Loire River vista, tranquil guest rooms (four of the less expensive are in a charming "Pavillon Renaissance"), and an excellent restaurant. The latter is set in two salons, one in Charles-Dix golds, the other lighted with chandeliers and stained-glass windows, lined with tapestries, and spectacularly centered around a neo-Gothic, sculpted-wood fireplace. Chef Ludovic Laurenty, who earned his first Michelin rosette in 2008, loves his independence: he has his own vegetable garden on the grounds, and cooks his own bread. You can sample his skill for €30 with the lunchtime menu, or by enrolling in a cooking class. **Pros:** marvelous setting; superlative good-value restaurant; open year-round. **Cons:** service can be haughty; no bar. ✉ *Rte. de Chargé, 4 km (2 mi) east of Amboise* ☎ *02–47–57–23–67* 🌐 *praycastel.online.fr* *17 rooms, 2 suites* *In-room: no a/c, refrigerator, Internet, Wi-Fi. In-hotel: restaurant, pool* *AE, DC, MC, V* *MAP.*

¢–$ **Le Blason.** Two blocks behind Château d'Amboise and a five-minute walk from the town center, this small, old hotel has enthusiastic, very welcoming, English-speaking owners and rooms of different shapes and sizes: No. 229, for example, has exposed beams and a cathedral ceiling; No. 109 is comfortably spacious with a good view of the square. The on-site restaurant, L'Alliance (under different management; no lunch Tuesday or Wednesday), offers a three-course menu for €20 and four courses for €27, with scrumptious roast lamb with garlic; tuna with sesame seeds; and salmon carpaccio with mustard dressing. But beware: you must arrive by 8:45 for dinner. **Pros:** quaint charm; families welcome. **Cons:** small bathrooms; traffic noise in some rooms. ✉ *11 pl. Richelieu* ☎ *02–47–23–22–41* 🌐 *www.leblason.fr* *26 rooms* *In-room: refrigerator, Wi-Fi (some). In-hotel: restaurant, some pets allowed* *DC, MC, V* ⏲ *Closed mid-Jan.–mid-Feb.* *MAP.*

$$–$$$ ★ **Le Manoir Les Minimes.** Picture-perfect and soigné as can be, this gorgeously stylish hotel is lucky enough to preside over a Loire riverbank under the shadow of Amboise's great cliff-side château. Set within its own compound, this quaintly shuttered late-18th-century *manoir*, or manor, looks like it's on sabbatical from a Fragonard landscape. Inside, the grand staircase, dining room, and main salon are all a-dazzle in daffodil-yellow silks and gilt-framed mirrors, with ruby accents of Louis Seize sofas and bergères. The standard guest rooms are pleasant enough,

but try to spring for the showpieces, such as the Suite Prestige (in a stunning blue toile de Jouy). **Pros:** historic style; calm oasis in town center. **Cons:** overpriced breakfasts; no outside food/drink allowed. ✉ *34 quai Charles-Guinot* ☎ *02–47–30–40–40* 🌐 *www.manoirlesminimes.com* *13 rooms, 2 suites* *In-room: a/c, safe, refrigerator. In-hotel: bar, Internet terminal* ▭ *MC, V* ⏲ *Closed mid-Nov.–mid-Mar.*

$$$ Fodor's Choice ★ **Le Vieux Manoir.** An ultimate welcome mat for anyone visiting the Loire Valley, this hotel is the creation of Gloria Belknap—a Californian whose immense style Edith Wharton would have cottoned to immediately. You'll have a hard time tearing yourself away from your guest room, as Gloria has turned loose some decorator extraordinaires on her inn: Toile de Jouy screens, gilt-framed paintings, comfy Napoléon III covered-in-jute armchairs, timeworn armoires, and tables adorned with Shaker baskets make this place *House & Garden* worthy. Each chamber is a delight: a bleached redbrick chimney and red-and-white calico accent one, while ceiling beams and a French Provincial four-poster bed warm another (and note that two separate cottages offer cooking facilities and sleep up to four). But you'll probably spend more time by the fountain in the leafy garden. **Pros:** charming rooms; scrumptious breakfasts. **Cons:** steep staircase; too many "house rules." ✉ *13 rue Rabelais* ☎ *02–47–30–41–27* 🌐 *www.le-vieux-manoir.com* *6 rooms, 2 cottages* *In-room: a/c, no TV (some), Wi-Fi. In-hotel: Internet terminal, parking (free)* ▭ *MC, V* *BP.*

CHÂTEAU DE CHENONCEAUX

12 km (8 mi) southeast of Amboise via D81, 32 km (20 mi) east of Tours.

GETTING HERE

Three to five trains run daily between Tours and Chenonceaux (30 mins, €6.30), one of the main destinations on one of the extensive branch lines of the Loire rail system. The station is especially convenient, a minute's walk from the front gates of the château; across the tracks is the one-road town.

Fodor's Choice ★ Achingly beautiful, the **Château de Chenonceau** has long been considered the "most romantic" of all the Loire châteaux, thanks in part to its showpiece—a breathtaking *galerie de bal* that spans the River Cher like a bridge. The gallery was used as an escape point for French Resistance fighters during World War II, since all other crossings had been bombed. Set in the village of Chenonceaux (spelled with an *x*) on the River Cher, this was the fabled retreat for the *dames de Chenonceau*, Diane de Poitiers, Catherine de' Medici, and Mary Queen of Scots. Happily spending at least half a day wandering through the château and grounds, you can see that this monument has an undeniable feminine touch. During the peak summer season the only drawback is the château's popularity: if you want to avoid a roomful of schoolchildren, take a stroll on the grounds and come back to the house at lunchtime.

More pleasure palace than fortress, the château was built in 1520 by Thomas Bohier, a wealthy tax collector, for his wife, Catherine Briçonnet. When he went bankrupt, it passed to François I. Later, Henri II gave it to his mistress, Diane de Poitiers. After his death, Henri's not-so-understanding widow, Catherine de' Medici, expelled Diane to nearby Chaumont and took back the château. Before this time, Diane's five-arched bridge over the River Cher was simply meant as a grand ceremonial entryway leading to a gigantic château, a building never constructed. It was to Catherine, and her architect, Philibert de l'Orme, that historians owe the audacious plan to transform the bridge itself into the most unusual château in France. Two stories were constructed over the river, including an enormous gallery that runs from one end of the château to the other. This design might seem the height of originality but, in fact, was inspired by Florence's covered Ponte Vecchio bridge, commissioned by a Medici queen homesick for her native town.

July and August are the peak months at Chenonceau: Only then can you escape the madding crowds by exiting at the far end of the gallery to walk along the opposite bank (weekends only), rent a rowboat to spend an hour just drifting in the river (where Diane used to enjoy her morning dips), and enjoy the **Promenade Nocturne,** an evocative son et lumière performed in the illuminated château gardens.

Before you go inside, pick up an English-language leaflet at the gate. Then walk around to the right of the main building to see the harmonious, delicate architecture beyond the formal garden—the southern part belonged to Diane de Poitiers, the northern was Catherine's—with the river gliding under the arches (providing superb "air-conditioning" to the rooms above). Inside the château are splendid ceilings, colossal fireplaces, scattered furnishings, and paintings by Rubens, del Sarto, and Correggio. The curatorial staff have delightfully dispensed with velvet ropes and adorned some of the rooms with bouquets designed in 17th-century style. As you tour the salons, be sure to pay your respects to former owner Madame Dupin, tellingly captured in Nattier's charming portrait: Thanks to the affection she inspired among her proletarian neighbors, the château and its treasures survived the Revolution intact (her grave is enshrined near the northern embankment). The château's history is illustrated with wax figures in the **Musée des Cires** (Waxwork Museum) in one of the château's outbuildings. A cafeteria, tearoom, and the ambitious Orangerie restaurant handle the crowds' varied appetites. ☎ *02–47–23–90–07* 🌐 *www.chenonceau.com* 🎫 *Château €10; including Musée des Cires, €12; night visit of gardens €5* ⏲ *Feb. and Mar., daily 9:30–6; Apr. and May, daily 9–7; June–Sept., daily 9–7:30; Oct., daily 9–6; Nov.–Jan., daily 9:30–5.*

HAVE THAT NIKON READY

Be sure to walk to the most distant point of Chenonceau's largest parterre garden, le Jardin de Diane de Poitiers—there you can find a tiny bridge leading to a river lookout point where you can find the most beautiful view of France's most glorious château. Sorry, no picnics allowed.

WHERE TO STAY

$–$$ ★ **La Roseraie.** The Bon Laboureur may be Chenonceaux's most famous hostelry, but this runs close for charm, thanks in part to the joyful welcome of its English-speaking hosts, Laurent and Sophie Fiorito. But let's not forget the guest rooms, many of which are designed with

DID YOU KNOW?

Catherine de' Medici commissioned Chenonceau's river-spanning design because, homesick for her hometown, she wanted to pay homage to Florence's covered Ponte Vecchio bridge.

florals, checks, and lace, or the copious meals served in the wood-beam dining room (where foie gras, duck with fruit and honey, and apple tart are among the specialties), or the pretty pool. Try to get a garden-side room, even if too many pink tablecloths and white chairs make the patio less than restful. If car traffic bothers you, be sure to avoid the rooms overlooking the main street. **Pros:** wonderful welcome; free Wi-Fi; verdant setting. **Cons:** some rooms in separate block; garish patio-pool area. ✉ *7 rue du Dr-Bretonneau* ☎ *02–47–23–90–09* 🌐 *www.hotel-chenonceau.com* *13 rooms, 2 suites* *In-room: a/c, Wi-Fi. In-hotel: restaurant, bar, pool, parking (free), some pets allowed* *AE, MC, V* ⊙ *Closed Dec.–Mar.* *BP.*

$$–$$$ Fodor's Choice ★ **Le Bon Laboureur.** In 1882 this ivy-covered inn won Henry James's praise, and the author might be even more impressed today. Thanks to four generations of the Jeudi family, this remains one of the Loire's most stylish auberges. Charm is in abundance—many guest rooms are enchantingly accented in toile de Jouy fabrics, rustic wainscoting, tiny lamps, and Redouté pink-and-blue pastels. Those in the main house are comfortably sized (a few overlook the main street—avoid these if you are a light sleeper), those in the former stables are larger (some overlook a pert vegetable garden) and more renovated, but our favorites are the quaint rooms in the separate patio house near the terrace. Bag a table in the "old" dining room (not the more modern ones), whose wood-beam ceiling, glazed terra-cotta walls, and Louis XVI chairs are almost as elegant as chef Jean-Marie Burnet's turbot with fennel. **Pros:** charming decor; outstanding food. **Cons:** small bathrooms; some rooms overlook busy road. ✉ *6 rue du Dr-Bretonneau* ☎ *02–47–23–90–02* 🌐 *www.bonlaboureur.com* *25 rooms* *In-room: a/c, safe, refrigerator, Internet. In-hotel: restaurant, bar, pool, bicycles, some pets allowed* *AE, MC, V* ⊙ *Closed mid-Nov.–mid-Dec.* *MAP.*

CHAUMONT-SUR-LOIRE

26 km (16 mi) northeast of Chenonceaux via D176/D62, 21 km (13 mi) southwest of Blois.

★ Although a favorite of Loire connoisseurs, the 16th-century **Château de Chaumont** is often overlooked by visitors who are content to ride the conveyor belt of big châteaux like Chambord and Chenonceau, and it's their loss. Set on a dramatic bluff that towers over the river, Chaumont has always cast a spell—perhaps literally so. One of its fabled owners, Catherine de' Medici, occasionally came here with her court "astrologer," the notorious Ruggieri. In one of Chaumont's bell-tower rooms, the queen reputedly practiced sorcery. Whether or not Ruggieri still haunts the place (or Nostradamus, another on Catherine's guest list), there seem to be few castles as spirit-warm as this one.

Centerpiece of a gigantic park (a stiff walk up a long path from the little village of Chaumont-sur-Loire; cars and taxis can also drop you off at the top of the hill) and built by Charles II d'Amboise between 1465 and 1510, the château greets visitors with glorious, twin-tower *châtelets*—twin turrets that frame a double drawbridge. The castle became the residence of Henri II. After his death his widow Catherine de' Medici took revenge on his mistress, the fabled beauty Diane de Poitiers, and forced her to exchange Chenonceau for Chaumont. Another "refugee" was the late-18th-century writer Madame de Staël. Exiled from Paris by Napoléon, she wrote *De l'Allemagne* (*On Germany*) here, a book that helped kick-start the Romantic movement in France. In the 19th century her descendants, the Prince and Princess de Broglie, set up regal shop, as you can still see from the stone-and-brick stables, where purebred horses (and one elephant) lived like royalty in velvet-lined stalls. The couple also renovated many rooms in the glamorous neo-Gothic style of the 1870s. Today their sense of fantasy is retained in the castle's **Festival International des Jardins** (€9.50), held May to October in the extensive park and featuring the latest in horticultural invention, and with the contemporary art installations in different rooms of the château. Chaumont is one of the more difficult locations to reach via public transportation, but you can take a five-minute cab ride from the nearest train station across the river at Onzain. *02–54–51–26–26 www.domaine-chaumont.fr €8 (€15 for combined château-festival entrance) Apr.–Sept., daily 10–6:30; Oct.–Mar., daily 10–5.*

4

WHERE TO STAY

$$$–$$$$ ★ **Domaine des Hauts-de-Loire.** Long a landmark of Loire luxe, this aristocratic outpost is across the river from Chaumont (which has a handy bridge) and some 4 km (2 mi) inland. This is no château but an 18th-century, turreted, vine-covered hunting lodge, replete with a grand salon furnished with 18th-century antiques, a lovely pool, an adorable swan lake, a helipad, and the most blissful air-conditioning in all Touraine. Guest rooms are beige and suave; those in the adjacent coach house can be considerably more spectacular—the best have exposed brick walls and timbered cathedral ceilings. The restaurant (closed Monday and Tuesday) is famous for its style and quality—an evening here glows with sumptuous white bouquets and dazzling dishes like goose Rossini with mushroom risotto. **Pros:** kingly service; luxurious style. **Cons:** no château architecture; pricey restaurant. *Rte. de Herbault, across Loire from Chaumont, Onzain 02–54–20–72–57 www.domainehautsloire.com 25 rooms, 11 suites In-room: a/c, safe, refrigerator, Wi-Fi. In-hotel: restaurant, tennis court, pool AE, DC, MC, V Closed Dec.–Feb. MAP.*

¢–$ **Hostellerie du Château.** Set on a bank of the Loire and directly opposite the road leading up to Chaumont's château, this quaint edifice was—rather unusually for these parts—built in the early 20th century as a hotel pure and simple. Four stories tall, fitted out with half-timber eaves, the hotel conjures up the grace of earlier days. Today, happily, it's purring along as a reasonably priced option. The entry hall soars, the restaurant is cozy and friendly. Rooms were renovated in 2007 with cheerfully colored walls and crisp white bed quilts. The hotel does, however, front the main road zipping through Chaumont (with loads of traffic), so be sure to bag a room away from the street, preferably on the side facing the Loire. **Pros:** handy setting; good value. **Cons:** street-facing rooms are noisy; grouchy owner. *2 rue du Mal-de-Lattre-de-Tassigny 02–54–20–98–04 www.hostellerie-du-chateau.com 15*

CLOSE UP

Which Chateau Is Right for You?

We admit it—there are almost too many châteaux in this part of France. Since it's nearly impossible to see all of them, we've noted the prime characteristics of the best to help you decide which you'd most like to visit.

■ **Amboise:** Powerful, haunted, and nearly empty, this was the birthplace of the Renaissance in France but loses out in charm to the adjacent Clos-Lucé manor, where Leonardo Da Vinci lived out his last years.

■ **Angers:** An impenetrable curtain wall and massive towers protect this muscular 13th-century fortress, home to the famed Apocalypse tapestries.

■ **Azay-le-Rideau:** With Rapunzel turrets, moat, and Italianate facade, this charming Renaissance castle is right out of a fairy tale. Toy-sized, it has pretty Gothic-style salons and nightly sound-and-light shows.

■ **Blois:** Big and bombastic, this shows the evolution from the Middle Ages to the Neo-Classic.

■ **Candé:** A storybook illustration come to life, this tiny "faux" château is where the Duke of Windsor married Wallis Simpson in 1937.

■ **Chambord:** Built for François I, the largest of the Loire Valley châteaux immediately takes your breath away. Fascinating salons, equestrian parades, and a sound-and-light show make this a wow.

■ **Chaumont-sur-Loire:** This dramatic cliff-top château combining Gothic fortifications with Renaissance style has a masculine touch despite once belonging to Catherine de Medici. Inside is ravishing neo-Gothic decor; outside, April through October, a famed garden show.

■ **Chenonceau:** Instantly recognized by its ballroom gallery spanning the Cher river, the magnificent "Château des Dames" was owned by famed chatelaines and still maintains a feminine touch with enormous bouquets, fanciful decor, and vast gardens.

■ **Cheverny:** Ornate and *tres* elegant, this 17th-century château has opulent salons for adults and hunting hounds' kennels and a Tintin exhibition for the kids.

■ **Chinon:** This brooding 12th-century fortress, perched high over the beautiful medieval town, is where Joan of Arc met with the future King Charles VII in 1429—recent renovations have brought it back to its former glory.

■ **Saché:** Set in a pretty hamlet and long-time home to writer Honoré de Balzac, this is more of a sturdy 19th-century country manor.

■ **Saumur:** Panoramic views over its eponymous river are worth a hike up to this gorgeously Gothic château (interior under renovation) set on a cliff above Saumur.

■ **Ussé:** A fairy-tale extravaganza, this is the most magical château of them all. It inspired Charles Perrault's (and Walt Disney's) "Sleeping Beauty" and the waxwork figurines in the turrets do give it the feel of a Disney set.

■ **Villandry:** A true Renaissance palace, this family-owned château is famed for its vast themed gardens, replete with stunning topiaries and Cinderella pumpkins.

rooms ♂ In-room: a/c, Wi-Fi. In-hotel: restaurant, pool, Wi-Fi hotspot ▭ MC, V ⊙ Closed Feb.

CHEVERNY

24 km (15 mi) east of Chaumont, 14 km (9 mi) southeast of Blois.

Perhaps best remembered as Capitaine Haddock's mansion in the Tintin comic books, the **Château de Cheverny** is also iconic for its restrained 17th-century elegance. One of the last in the area to be built, it was finished in 1634, at a time when the rich and famous had mostly stopped building in the Loire Valley. By then, the taste for quaintly shaped châteaux had given way to disciplined Classicism; so here a white, elegantly proportioned, horizontally coursed, single-block facade greets you across manicured lawns. To emphasize the strict symmetry of the plan, a ruler-straight drive leads to the front entrance. The Louis XIII interior with its stridently painted and gilded rooms, splendid furniture, and rich tapestries depicting the Labors of Hercules is one of the few still intact in the Loire region. Despite the priceless Delft vases and Persian embroideries, it feels lived in. That's because it's one of the rare Loire Valley houses still occupied by a noble family. You can visit a small Tintin exhibition called *Le Secret de Moulinsart* (admission extra) and are free to contemplate the antlers of 2,000 stags in the Trophy Room: hunting, called "venery" in the leaflets, continues vigorously here, with red coats, bugles, and all. In the château's kennels, hordes of hungry hounds lounge around dreaming of their next kill. Feeding times—*la soupe aux chiens*—are posted on a notice board (usually 5 PM in summer), and you are welcome to watch the "ceremony" (delicate sensibilities beware: the dogs line up like statues and are called, one by one, to wolf down their meal from the trainer). ✉ ☎ *02–54–79–96–29* 🌐 *www.chateau-cheverny.fr* 🎫 *€7.40, €12 with Tintin exhibition, €17 including boat-and-buggy rides* ⊙ *Apr.–Sept., daily 9:15–6:15; Oct.–Mar., daily 9:45–5.*

CHAMBORD

Fodor's Choice ★ *13 km (21 mi) northeast of Chaumont-sur-Loire via D33, 19 km (12 mi) east of Blois, 45 km (28 mi) southwest of Orléans.*

The "Versailles" of the 16th century and the largest of the Loire châteaux, the **Château de Chambord** is the kind of place William Randolph Hearst might have built if he'd had the money. Variously dubbed "megalomaniacal" and "an enormous film-set extravaganza," this is one of the most extraordinary structures in Europe, set in the middle of a royal game forest, with just a cluster of buildings—barely a village—across the road.

GETTING HERE

There is surprisingly little public transportation to famed Chambord (a state-owned château, to boot). There are no trains, but Transports du Loir et Cher (🌐 *tlcinfo.net*) offers a bus route from Blois (two departures daily).

The beautiful Château de Colliers is one of the most charming hotels along the Loire—it is so petite you'll almost think it is your own home.

EXPLORING

As you travel the gigantic, tree-shaded roadways that converge on Chambord, you first spot the château's incredible towers-19th-century novelist Henry James said they were "more like the spires of a city than the salient points of a single building"-rising above the forest. When the entire palace breaks into view, it is an unforgettable sight.

With a facade that is 420 feet long, 440 rooms and 365 chimneys, a wall 32 km (20 mi) long to enclose a 13,000-acre forest, the **Château de Chambord** is one of the greatest buildings in France. Under François I, building began in 1519, a job that took 12 years and required 1,800 workers. His original grandiose idea was to divert the Loire to form a moat, but someone (perhaps his adviser, Leonardo da Vinci, who some feel may have provided the inspiration behind the entire complex) persuaded him to make do with the River Cosson. François I used the château only for short stays; yet when he came, 12,000 horses were required to transport his luggage, servants, and entourage. Later kings also used Chambord as an occasional retreat, and Louis XIV, the Sun King, had Molière perform here. In the 18th century Louis XV gave the château to the Maréchal de Saxe as a reward for his victory over the English and Dutch at Fontenoy (southern Belgium) in 1745. When not indulging himself with wine, women, and song, the marshal planted himself on the roof to oversee the exercises of his personal regiment of 1,000 cavalry. Now, after long neglect—all the original furnishings vanished during the French Revolution—Chambord belongs to the state.

There's plenty to see inside. You can wander freely through the vast rooms, filled with exhibits (including a hunting museum)—not all concerned with Chambord, but interesting nonetheless—and lots of Ancien Régime furnishings. The enormous double-helix staircase (probably envisioned by Leonardo, who had a thing about spirals) looks like a single staircase, but an entire regiment could march up one spiral while a second came down the other, and never the twain would meet. But the high point here in more ways than one is the spectacular chimneyscape—the roof terrace whose forest of Italianate towers, turrets, cupolas, gables, and chimneys have been compared to everything from the minarets of Constantinople to a bizarre chessboard. The most eye-popping time to see this roof is at night, when the château is spectacularly illuminated with slide projections; the presentation, called "Rêve de Lumières," (€12; combined with château entry €17), is held nightly late June through July at 11 PM; August at 10:45 PM; until mid-September at 10:15 PM. During the year there's a packed calendar of activities on tap, from 90-minute tours of the park in a 4x4 vehicle (€18) to guided tours on bike or horseback. A soaring three-story-tall hall has been fitted out to offer lunches and dinners. ✉ ☎ *02–54–50–40–00* 🌐 *www.chambord.org* 🎟 *€9.50* ⏲ *Apr.–Sept., daily 9–6:15; Oct.–Mar., daily 9–5:15.*

WHERE TO EAT AND STAY

$$$–$$$$ FRENCH ✕ **La Maison à Côté.** Just five minutes' drive from Chambord in a tiny village, this country inn serves traditional French haute cuisine in a cozy yet contemporary dining room with a fireplace, exposed beam ceilings, and wrought-iron entry gate. Specialties vary with the seasons, including the foie gras with apricot, pear, and lemon confit, the Challans duck filet with caramelized endives and Szechuan pepper, or the lacquered cod with carrots and Orléans mustard. Save room for the surprisingly creative desserts. There's plenty of free parking in the church parking lot across the street, and a handful of tastefully modern rooms from €75 for a double. ✉ *25 Rte. de Chambord* ☎ *02–54–20–62–30* 🌐 *www.lamaisondacote.fr* 💳 *MC, V* ⏲ *May–mid-Jan., no dinner Tues., no lunch Wed; mid-Jan.–May 2, closed Tues.–Wed. Hotel closed Nov. 16–Dec. 3 and Dec. 28–Jan. 14.*

$$–$$$ Fodor's Choice ★ 🏨 **Château de Colliers.** Keep Chenonceau. You can have Chambord. For a few lucky travelers, the most unforgettable château in the Loire proves to be this tiny, overlooked treasure. Other château-hotels may have pomp, but this has something more precious—*authenticité*. The home of Christian and Marie-France de Gélis (both of whom are charming and speak English), it was sold to their family in 1779 by the Marquis de Vaudreuil, first French governor of Louisiana. At the end of a long allée, this "pavillon Mansart" embraces you in a semicircular layout (the *collier*, or necklace). Ten family descendants study you from gilded Charles-Dix frames in the gorgeous main salon, a confectionery vision of white Rococo moldings, glittering chandelier, and furniture that Madame Bovary would have loved. The breakfast room is covered with quaint 16th-century Italian frescoes, and each guest room is a bouquet of antiques and comfy furniture. Unfortunately, Monsieur and Madame de Gélis don't hold down the fort year-round any longer. While their housekeepers are friendly, they don't provide that distinctive family feeling. **Pros:** authentic antique furnishings; unique riverside setting. **Cons:**

grounds and exterior a bit worse for wear; surrounding area fairly dull. ✉ *Rue Nationale (D951), Muides-sur-Loire, 8 km (4 mi) northwest of Chambord; 17 km (10 mi) southwest of Blois* ☎ *02–54–87–50–75* 🌐 *www.chateau-colliers.com* *2 rooms, 3 suites* *In-room: no a/c, no TV, Wi-Fi. In-hotel: pool, some pets allowed* *MC, V* *BP.*

$–$$ **Grand St-Michel.** The village of Chambord is as tiny as its château is massive. Its leading landmark is this historic hotel, a revamped hunting lodge set across the lawn from the château. Guest rooms once boasted fabled views of the palace, but towering oak trees now block the view from all but two—room No. 5 has the best view. Inside you'll find a cozy lobby, solidly bourgeois guest rooms, and a 19th-century-flavored restaurant. Adorned with mounted deer heads, majolica serving platters, and thick curtains, this room is straight out of a Flaubert novel. The fare is local, hearty (including deer pâté, pumpkin soup, and game in fall), attractively priced (especially the €22 menu), and there's a delightfully leafy terrace café facing the château. **Pros:** wondrous location opposite Chambord; impressive, good-value restaurant. **Cons:** little village has some garish tourist shops; creeky hallways. ✉ *Pl. St-Louis* ☎ *02–54–20–31–31* 🌐 *www.saintmichel-chambord.com* *40 rooms* *In-room: no a/c. In-hotel: restaurant, tennis court, Internet terminal, some pets allowed* *MC, V* *Closed mid-Nov.–mid-Dec.* *BP.*

THE OUTDOORS

Hire a horse carriage (*attelage*) in the former stables, **Les Écuries du Maréchal de Saxe** (✉ *On grounds of Château de Chambord* ☎ *02–54–20–31–01* 🌐 *www.ecuries-chambord.com*), for a one-hour ride through the vast national park surrounding the château (€9.50 per person). From April through October you can hire a rowboat or join a boat tour to explore the château moat and the **Grand Canal** (☎ *02–54–33–37–54 for details*) linking it to the River Cosson.

ORLÉANS

115 km (23 mi) northeast of Chambord, 112 km (70 mi) northeast of Tours, 125 km (78 mi) south of Paris.

Orléans once had the biggest inferiority complex this side of Newark, New Jersey. The city paled pitifully in comparison with other cities of central France, so the townsfolk clung to the city's finest moment—the coming of *la pucelle d'Orléans* (the Maid of Orleans), Joan of Arc, in 1429 to liberate the city from the English during the Hundred Years' War. There's little left from Joan's time, but the city is festooned with everything from her equestrian monument to a Jeanne d'Arc Dry Cleaners. Today, however, Orléans is a thriving commercial city, and wonderfully sensitive urban renewal has added enormous charm, especially to the medieval streets between the Loire and the cathedral.

GETTING HERE

Trains from Paris (Gare d'Austerlitz) leave for Orléans every hour or so; the 85-mi trip (€18.20) takes between 1 hour, 5 minutes and 1 hour, 25 minutes with a change in suburban Les Aubrais sometimes necessary. Trains run every couple of hours from Orléans to Tours (75 mins,

€17.80) via Blois (25–40 mins, €10.40). Three trains daily continue to Angers (1 hr, 50 mins; €29.30).

Visitor Information Orléans Tourist Office. ✉ *6 rue Albert-Ier* ☎ *02-38-24-05-05* 🌐 *www.tourisme-orleans.com.*

SWEET DREAMS

The Château de Colliers has a vast river terrace over a magnificent stretch of the Loire—there's nothing like drifting off to sleep with the burbling sound of the water as your lullaby.

EXPLORING

Despite the city's lackluster neighborhoods, Orléans's wide array of lodging and restaurants, and its superb transportation connections, make it a comfy and leading base for exploring the châteaux, villages, and forests nearby. Thankfully, the vielle ville (old town) quarter has been gorgeously restored and lends a big dollop of charm to the city.

4

The story of the Hundred Years' War, Joan of Arc, and the Siege of Orléans is widely known. In 1429 France had hit rock bottom. The English and their Burgundian allies were carving up the kingdom. Besieged by the English, Orléans was one of the last towns about to yield, when a young Lorraine peasant girl, Joan of Arc, arrived to rally the troops and save the kingdom. During the Wars of Religion (1562–98), much of the cathedral was destroyed. A century ago ham-fisted town planners razed many of the city's fine old buildings. Both German and Allied bombs helped finish the job during World War II.

❶ The **Cathédrale Ste-Croix** is a riot of pinnacles and gargoyles, both Gothic and pseudo-Gothic, embellished with 18th-century wedding-cake towers. After most of the cathedral was destroyed in the 16th century during the Wars of Religion, Henry IV and his successors rebuilt it. Novelist Marcel Proust (1871–1922) called it France's ugliest church, but most find it impressive. Inside are dramatic stained glass and 18th-century wood carvings, plus the modern **Chapelle de Jeanne d'Arc** (Joan of Arc Chapel), with plaques in memory of British and American war dead. ✉ *Pl. Ste-Croix* ⏲ *Daily 9:15–noon and 2:15–6.*

❷ Fodor's Choice ★ Just across the square from the cathedral is the **Hôtel Groslot**, a Renaissance-era extravaganza (1549–55) bristling with caryatids, strap work, and Flemish columns. Inside are regal salons redolent of the city's history (this used to be the Town Hall), all done in the most sumptuous 19th-century Gothic Troubadour style and perhaps haunted by King François II (who died here in 1560 by the side of his bride, Mary Queen of Scots). ✉ *Pl. de l'Étape* ☎ *02-38-79-22-30* 🎟 *€4* ⏲ *June–Aug., Sun.–Fri. 9–6, Sept.–May, Sun.–Fri. 9–noon and 2–6.*

❸ The modern **Musée des Beaux-Arts** *(Fine Arts Museum)* is across from the cathedral. Take the elevator to the top of the five-story building; then make your way down to see works by such artists as Tintoretto, Velázquez, Watteau, Boucher, Rodin, and Gauguin. The museum's richest collection is its 17th-century French paintings, prints, and drawings, reputedly second only to the Louvre. ✉ *1 rue Fernand-Rabier* ☎ *02-38-79-21-55* 🎟 *€4, joint ticket with History Museum* ⏲ *Tues.–Sun. 10–6.*

Cathédrale Ste-Croix **1**
Hôtel Groslot **2**
Maison de Jeanne d'Arc **5**
Musée des Beaux-Arts **3**
Musée Historique **4**

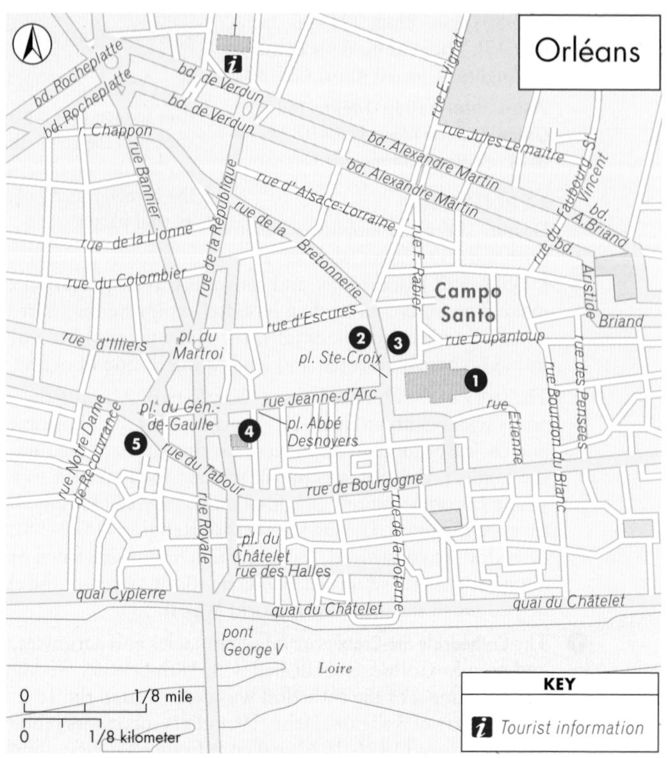

❹ The **Musée Historique et Archéologique** *(History and Archeology Museum)* is housed in the **Hôtel Cabu,** a Renaissance mansion restored after World War II. It contains works of both "fine" and "popular" art connected with the town's past, including a remarkable collection of pagan bronzes of animals and dancers. These bronzes were hidden from zealous Christian missionaries in the 4th century and discovered in a sandpit near St-Benoît in 1861. ✉ *Sq. de l'Abbé-Desnoyers* ☎ *02–38–79–25–60* 🎫 *€4, joint ticket with Fine Arts Museum* ⏲ *July and Aug., Tues.–Sat. 9:30–12:15 and 1:30–5:45, Sun. 2–6; May, June, and Sept., Tues.–Sat. 1:30–5:45, Sun. 2–6:30; Oct.–Apr., Wed. 1:30–5:45, Sun. 2–6.*

❺ During the 10-day Siege of Orléans in 1429, 17-year-old Joan of Arc stayed on the site of the **Maison de Jeanne d'Arc** *(Joan of Arc House).* This faithful reconstruction of the house she knew contains exhibits about her life and costumes and weapons of her time. Several dioramas modeled by Lucien Harmey recount the main episodes in her life, from the audience at Chinon to the coronation at Reims, her capture at Compiègne, and her burning at the stake at Rouen. ✉ *3 pl. du Général-de-Gaulle* ☎ *02–38–52–99–89* 🌐 *www.jeannedarc.com.fr* 🎫 *€2* ⏲ *May–Oct., Tues.–Sun. 10–12:30 and 1:30–6:30; Nov.–Apr., Tues.–Sun. 1:30–6.*

WHERE TO EAT AND STAY

$$$–$$$$ FRENCH ✕ **Le Lift.** Decorated with quirky contemporary statues, this is a surprisingly modern and stylish restaurant. Using only the freshest local ingredients, chef Philippe Bardeau combines textures and flavors to create a colorfully vibrant cuisine. Large windows offer views of the leafy park across the way (and, thankfully, not of the cineplex, which sits just below the restaurant); reserve a seat on the panoramic terrace overlooking the Loire River when the weather is warm. ✉ *Pl. de la Loire* ☎ *02–38–53–63–48* 🌐 *www.restaurant-le-lift.com* ▭ *MC, V.*

$$–$$$ **Château de Champvallins.** When you enter the gates of this magnificent 18th-century estate, with its vast wooded grounds and impressive historic mansion, you'll immediately feel the outside world melt away. Parisian native Jacqueline Létang, who opened this bed-and-breakfast after meticulous restoration in 2008, graciously makes her guests feel right at home with a welcoming cup of tea and a tour of the rooms and 16th-century chapel. Each guest room has a different look, but are all decked out in luxury: toile de Jouy fabrics, polished terra-cotta tiles, claw-foot tubs, and views over the gardens. In warmer months guests can enjoy the pool nestled in the orchard. **Pros:** authentic antique furnishings; peaceful forest setting; friendly welcome. **Cons:** no restaurant; only accessible by car. ✉ *1079 rue de Champvallins, 12 km (7 mi) southeast of Orléans, Sandillon* ☎ *02–38–41–16–53* 🌐 *www.chateaudechampvallins.com* *5 rooms* *In-room: no a/c, no TV (some), Wi-Fi. In-hotel: pool, parking (free)* ▭ *MC, V* *BP.*

$ Fodor's Choice ★ **L'Abeille.** Conveniently located on the main shopping street in Orléans, this charming family-run hotel is located just a block from the train and tram station. Guest rooms are bright and çozy, with fresh floral wall coverings, parquet flooring, and immaculate tiled bathrooms (many as large as the rooms). A roof-top garden terrace offers panoramic views of the city in warmer months, while the lounge decorated with Joan of Arc memorabilia is a comfy place for a coffee while perusing their collection of historic books. **Pros:** easily accessible by train; free Wi-Fi; extra-spacious rooms. **Cons:** rooms facing street can be noisy; pricey city parking. ✉ *64 rue Alsace Lorraine* ☎ *02–38–53–54–87* 🌐 *www.hoteldelabeille.com* *28 rooms* *In-room: no a/c, Wi-Fi. In-hotel: bar, bicycles, Internet terminal, parking (paid), some pets allowed* ▭ *MC, V* *MAP.*

NIGHTLIFE AND THE ARTS

The **Fêtes de Jeanne d'Arc** *(Joan of Arc Festival* 🌐 *www.fetesjeannedarc.com)*, in early May celebrates the heroic Maid of Orléans with a parade, religious procession, medieval fair, and reenactments of the famous siege of Orléans.

BLOIS

54 km (34 mi) southwest of Orléans, 58 km (36 mi) northeast of Tours.

Perched on a steep hillside overlooking the Loire, site of one of France's most historic châteaux, and birthplace of those delicious Poulain chocolates and gâteaux (check out the bakeries along Rue Denis-Papin), the

CLOSE UP

Bike Tour Options

With its nearly flat terrain, the Loire Valley is custom-built for traveling by bike, and the newly created Loire à Vélo signposted bike trails extending 800 km (500 mi) from Orléans to the Atlantic Ocean make it even easier to cycle between each town and village. Bike rental agencies and trail maps are easily found in the towns along the route for independent exploration. For stress-free planning, local bike tour companies such as Biking France and Loire à Vélo offer turnkey self-guided vacations of 2–6 days for which they arrange the hotels, restaurants, itineraries, maps, baggage transfers, and bike hire for as little as €100 per day per person. The Anjou tourism offices in Angers and Saumur also rent out "Cyclopédia" GPS gadgets that attach to your bike and guide you through the paths and sights of the Anjou region. The bigger towns all have bike rental agencies—one of the top is Loire Vélo Nature. Though based in Bréhémont, they have more than a dozen outlets along the Loire, where you can rent bikes from €15 a day or €55 a week.

Contacts Biking France(✉ *2 rue Jean Moulin, Blois* ☎ *02–54–78–62–52* 🌐 *www.biking-france.com*). **Loire à Vélo** (✉ *37 av. de Paris, Orléans* ☎ *02–38–79–95–28* 🌐 *www.loire-a-velo.fr*). **Loire Vélo Nature** (✉ *7 rue des Déportés, Bréhémont* ☎ *06–03–89–23–14* 🌐 *www.loirevelonature.com*). **Anjou Vélo** (☎ *08–20–15–00–49* 🌐 *www.anjou-velo.com*).

bustling big town of Blois is a convenient base, well served by train and highway.

GETTING HERE

Trains from Paris (Gare d'Austerlitz) leave for Blois every 1 or 2 hours; the 115-mi trip (€25.20) takes between 1 hour, 30 minutes and 1 hour, 55 minutes, according to service. There are trains every 2 hours or so from Blois to Tours (30–40 mins, €9.50) and Orléans (25–40 mins, €9.80).

Visitor Information Blois Tourist Office. ✉ *3 av. du Dr-Jean-Laigret* ☎ *02–54–90–41–41* 🌐 *www.bloispaysdechambord.com.*

EXPLORING

A signposted route leads you on a walking tour of Blois's **Vieille Ville** (Old Town)—a romantic honeycomb of twisting alleys, cobblestone streets, and half-timber houses—but it's best explored with the help of a map available from the tourist office. The historic highlight is Place St-Louis, where you can find the Maison des Acrobats (note the timbers carved with *jongleurs*, or jugglers), Cathédrale St-Louis, and unexpected Renaissance-era galleries and staircases lurking in tucked-away courtyards.

The massive **Château de Blois** spans several architectural periods and is among the valley's finest. Your ticket entitles you to a guided tour—given in English when there are enough visitors who don't understand French—but you're more than welcome to roam around without a guide. Before you enter, stand in the courtyard to admire examples of four centuries of architecture. On one side stand the 13th-century hall and tower, the latter offering a stunning view of the town and countryside. The Renaissance begins to flower in the Louis XII wing (built between 1498 and 1503), through which you enter, and comes to full bloom in the François I wing (1515–24). The masterpiece here is the openwork spiral staircase, painstakingly restored. The fourth side consists of the Classical Gaston d'Orléans wing (1635–38). Upstairs in the François I wing is a series of enormous rooms with tremendous fireplaces decorated with the gilded porcupine, emblem of Louis XII, the ermine of Anne of Brittany, and, of course, François I's salamander, breathing fire and surrounded by flickering flames. Many rooms have intricate ceilings and carved, gilt paneling. In the council room the Duke of Guise was murdered by order of Henri III in 1588. Every evening mid-April through mid-September, **son-et-lumière** shows are staged (in English on Wednesday); tickets cost €7 (joint ticket with château €13). ✉ ☎ *02–54–90–33–33* 🌐 *www.chateaudeblois.fr* 🎫 *€8* ⏲ *Apr.–Sept., daily 9–6:30; Oct.–Mar., daily 9–12:30 and 1:30–5:30.*

4

WHERE TO EAT AND STAY

$$$ SEAFOOD ★ ✕ **Au Rendez-Vous des Pêcheurs**. This friendly restaurant in an old grocery near the Loire has simple decor but impressively creative cooking. Chef Christophe Cosme was an apprentice with Burgundy's late Bernard Loiseau, and his inventive dishes range from fish and seafood specialties (try the crayfish-and-parsley flan) to succulent baby pigeon on a bed of cabbage. ✉ *27 rue du Foix* ☎ *02–54–74–67–48* 🌐 *www.rendezvousdespecheurs.com* ✍ *Reservations essential* 💳 *AE, MC, V* ⏲ *Closed Sun. and 2 wks in Aug. No lunch Mon.*

$–$$ 🏨 **16 Place Saint Louis**. Situated in the heart of Blois' Old Town across the square from the St-Louis Cathedral, this elegant bed-and-breakfast gives guests the experience of staying in a classic haute bourgeoise home in Blois. Guest rooms are decorated in pink or blue fabrics with antique furnishings, and the top-floor suite in red and gold is set under ancient wooden beams. Marie and her husband speak perfect English, and enjoy helping their guests make the most of their stay. **Pros:** convenient location in historic center; beautifully appointed, antiques-bedecked home. **Cons:** shared bathroom for the rooms; no space for large luggage. ✉ *16 pl. Saint Louis* ☎ *02–54–74–13–61* 🌐 *16placesaintlouis.free.fr* 🛏 *2 rooms, 1 suite* 👍 *In-room: a/c, no TV, Wi-Fi. In-hotel: Internet terminal, some pets allowed* 💳 No credit cards ⏲ *Closed 3 wks in Jan.* 🍴 *MAP.*

$$ 🏨 **Le Clos Pasquier**. Claire and Laurent opened their country home on the edge of the forest to guests in 2009 after lovingly converting their 16th-century manor into a cozy bed-and-breakfast. Time seems to have stood still here thanks to heavy wooden beams, well-worn terra-cotta floor tiles, and welcoming stone fireplaces. Guest rooms are simple but comfy, and have gleaming new bathrooms. Suites have their own entrances and one opens onto a private garden. **Pros:** luxurious bedding; historic building; direct bus to town center. **Cons:** no restaurant; not in town center. ✉ *10–12 impasse de l'Orée du Bois* ☎ *02–54–58–84–08* 🌐 *www.leclospasquier.fr* 🛏 *2 rooms, 2 suites* 👍 *In-room: a/c, no TV, Wi-Fi. In-hotel: parking (free)* 🍴 *MAP.*

$-$$ **Le Médicis.** Guest rooms at this smart little hotel 1 km (½ mi) from the château de Blois are comfortable, air-conditioned, and soundproof; all share a joyous color scheme but are individually decorated. Room No. 211 is the largest. The restaurant alone—done Renaissance-style with a coffered ceiling—makes a stay here worthwhile. Chef-owner Damien Garanger turns his innovative classic dishes into a presentation—*coquilles St-Jacques* (scallops) with bitter *roquette* lettuce, roast pigeon, and thin slices of roast hare with a black-currant sauce. For dessert, try the raspberry sorbet with brioche and chocolate sauce. The staff is cheerful and there are 250 wines to choose from (the restaurant does not serve Sunday dinner October–March). **Pros:** soundproof rooms; excellent restaurant. **Cons:** no views; not in town center. ✉ *2 allée François-Ier* ☎ *02–54–43–94–04* 🌐 *www.le-medicis.com* *8 rooms, 2 suites* *In-room: a/c, refrigerator, Wi-Fi. In-hotel: restaurant, some pets allowed* *AE, DC, MC, V* *Closed 3 wks in Jan.* *MAP.*

THE STORYBOOK LOIRE: VILLANDRY TO LANGEAIS

To the west of Tours, breathtaking châteaux dot the Indre Valley between the regional capital and the historic town of Chinon on the River Vienne. This is the most glamorous part of the Val de Loire, and the beauty pageant begins with the fabled gardens of the Château de Villandry. Your journey then continues on to the fairy-tale châteaux of Azay-le-Rideaux, Ussé, and Montreuil-Bellay. Farther on, no one will want to miss the towns of Chinon, Saumur, Fontevraud, and Langeais, which contain sights that remain the quintessence of romantic medievalism. Along the way, you can savor such storybook delights as Saché—perhaps the Loire's prettiest village and the historic fortress of Angers.

CHÂTEAU DE VILLANDRY

18 km (11 mi) west of Tours via D7, 48 km (30 mi) northwest of Loches.

Fodor's Choice ★ Green-thumbers get weak in the knees at the mere mention of the **Château de Villandry**, a grand estate near the Cher River, thanks to its painstakingly relaid 16th-century **gardens,** now the finest example of Renaissance garden design in France. These were originally planted in 1906 by Dr. Joachim Carvallo and Anne Coleman, his American wife, whose passion resulted in three terraces planted in styles that combine the French monastic garden with Italianate models depicted in historic Du Cerceau etchings. Seen from Villandry's cliff-side walkway, the garden terraces look like flowered chessboards blown up to the nth power—a breathtaking sight.

Beyond the water garden and an ornamental garden depicting symbols of chivalric love is the famous *potager,* or vegetable garden, which stretches on for bed after bed—the pumpkins here are *les pièces de résistance.* Flower lovers will rejoice in the main *jardin à la française* (French-style garden): framed by a canal, it's a vast carpet of rare and

DID YOU KNOW?

Almost as famed as the vegetable gardens at the Château de Villandry are its gardens à la française whose hedges are strikingly shaped into symbols of love, including hearts, fans, and daggers.

colorful blooms planted *en broderie* ("like embroidery"), set into patterns by box hedges and paths. The aromatic and medicinal garden, its plots neatly labeled in three languages, is especially appealing. Below an avenue of 1,200 precisely pruned lime trees lies an ornamental lake that is home to two swans: not a ripple is out of place. The château interior, still used by the Carvallo family, was redecorated in the mid-18th century; of particular note are the painted and gilt Moorish ceiling from Toledo and one of the finest collections of 17th-century Spanish paintings in France. Note that the quietest time to visit is usually during the two-hour French lunch break, while the most photogenic is during the **Nuits des Mille Feux** (Nights of a Thousand Lights, held the first weekend in July), when paths and pergolas are illuminated with myriad lanterns and a dance troupe offers a tableau vivant. There is a gardening weekend held in late September and a music festival in October. There is no train station at Villandry, but the Line V bus between Tours and Azay-le-Rideau stops there every Wednesday and Saturday, daily in July and August; you can also train to nearby Savonnières and taxi the rest of the 4-km (2½-mi) distance. ☎ *02–47–50–02–09* 🌐 *www.chateauvillandry.com* 🎫 *Château and gardens €9, gardens only €6* ⏲ *Château Apr.–Oct., daily 9–6; mid-Feb., Mar., and 1st half Nov., daily 9–5. Gardens Apr.–Sept., daily 9–7; Oct.–mid-Nov., daily 9–5.*

WHERE TO STAY

¢–$ **Auberge Le Colombien.** Just a few steps away from the château, this humble yet cozy family-run inn is conveniently located on the main street in the heart of Villandry village. The country-style rooms each have their own style, some with have exposed wooden beams or stone walls, floral prints or brightly painted walls, and wooden floors or carpeting. Happily, there is an on-site restaurant which serves up traditional local cuisine in a casual setting. If traffic noise is a problem, request a room in the back, as this hotel fronts the main throughfare. **Pros:** walking distance to the château; free Wi-Fi; historic building. **Cons:** small windows; right on main road; few amenities. ✉ *2 rue de la Mairie* ☎ *02–47–50–07–27* 🌐 *www.hotel-villandry.com* *14 rooms* *In-room: no a/c, Wi-Fi. In-hotel: restaurant, parking (paid)* ▭ *V, MC, AE* *MAP.*

AZAY-LE-RIDEAU

11 km (7 mi) south of Villandry via D39, 27 km (17 mi) southwest of Tours.

A largish town surrounding a sylvan dell on the banks of the River Indre, pleasant Azay-le-Rideau (located on the main train line between Tours and Chinon) is famed for its white-wall Renaissance pleasure palace, called "a faceted diamond set in the Indre Valley" by Honoré de Balzac.

★ The 16th-century **Château d'Azay-le-Rideau** was created as a literal fairytale castle. When it was constructed in the Renaissance era, the nouveau-riche treasurer Gilles Berthelot decided he wanted to add tall corner turrets, a moat, and machicolations to conjure up the distant seigneurial past when knighthood was in flower and two families, the Azays and the Ridels, ruled this terrain. It was never a serious fortress—it certainly offered no protection to its builder when a financial scandal forced him to flee France shortly after the château's completion in 1529. For centuries the château passed from one private owner to another until it was finally bought by the State in 1905. Though the interior contains an interesting blend of furniture and artwork (one room is an homage to the Marquis de Biencourt who, in the early 20th century, led the way in renovating château interiors in sumptuous fashion—sadly, many of his elegant furnishings were later sold), you may wish to spend most of your time exploring the enchanting gardens, complete with a moatlike lake. Innovative **son-et-lumière** shows are held on the grounds from 10:30 PM, July and August. ✉ ☎ *02–47–45–42–04* 🌐 *azay-le-rideau.monuments-nationaux.fr* 🎫 *€8* ⏲ *Apr.–Sept., daily 9:30–6; Oct.–Mar., daily 10–12:30 and 2–5:30.*

4

WHERE TO STAY

¢–$ ★ **Biencourt.** Charmingly set on the pedestrian street that leads to Azay's château gates, this recently renovated red-shuttered town house hides an authentic, 19th-century schoolhouse within a delightful courtyard-garden. Opt for these rooms, now fitted out in cozily traditional country school-house style (and the stray blackboard and school desk) or the main house's guest rooms done up in 19th-century neo-classic "Directoire" style. The village has quite a few restaurant selections—if you just don't want to stroll around and pick, ask the friendly owners Cédric and Emmanuelle about the best. **Pros:** families welcome; free Wi-Fi; handicap-accessible room. **Cons:** cramped public areas; thin walls. ✉ *7 rue Balzac* ☎ *02–47–45–20–75* 🌐 *www.hotelbiencourt.com* *17 rooms* *In-room: no a/c (some), Wi-Fi. In-hotel: Internet terminal* 💳 *MC, V* ⏲ *Closed mid-Nov.–mid-Mar.*

$–$$ **Le Grand Monarque.** Grand and once-elegant, this town landmark is about a three-minute walk from Azay's château. Some complain that its fame brings a captive audience, which can result in offhand service. However, rooms, which vary in size and style, have character; most are simple, with an antique or two, and many have exposed beams. The largest room is called the Monsoreau. Public salons are luxe and alluring, while the restaurant (which, from mid-October to December and mid-February to late March, is closed Monday, and does not serve dinner Sunday) serves high-style food and boasts one of the region's most extensive wine lists, with more than 700 choices. There's also a bistro for a quicker, cheaper lunch, with a menu at €15. Weekend stays must include dinner. **Pros:** fine restaurant; town-center setting. **Cons:** some rooms need redecorating; distracted staff. ✉ *3 pl. de la République* ☎ *02–47–45–40–08* 🌐 *www.legrandmonarque.com* *24 rooms* *In-room: no a/c, Wi-Fi. In-hotel: restaurant, bar, some pets allowed* 💳 *AE, MC, V* ⏲ *Closed Dec.–mid-Feb.* 🍽 *MAP.*

THE OUTDOORS

Rent bikes from **Leprovost** (✉ *13 rue Carnot* ☎ *02–47–45–40–94*) to ride along the Indre; the area around Azay-le-Rideau is among the most tranquil and scenic in Touraine.

SACHÉ

Fodor's Choice ★ *7 km (4½ mi) east of Azay-le-Rideau via D17.*

A crook in the road, a Gothic church, the centuries-old Auberge du XIIe Siècle, an Alexander Calder stabile (the great American sculptor created a modern atelier nearby), and the country retreat of novelist Honoré de Balzac (1799–1850)—these few but choice elements all add up to Saché, one of the prettiest (and most undiscovered) nooks in the Val de Loire. If you're heading in to the town from the east, you're first welcomed by the **Pont-de-Ruan**—a dream sequence of a flower-bedecked bridge, water mill, and lake that is so picturesque it will practically click your camera for you.

Two kilometers (1 mi) farther, you hit the center of Saché and the **Château de Saché**, which contains the **Musée Balzac.** If you've never read any of Balzac's "Comédie Humaine," you might find little of interest here; but if you have, and do, you can return to such novels as *Cousine Bette* and *Eugénie Grandet* with fresh enthusiasm and understanding. Much of the landscape around here, and some of the people back then, found immortality by being fictionalized in many a Balzac novel. Surrounded by six acres of gardens, the present château, built between the 16th and the 18th century, is more of a comfortable country house than a fortress. Born in Tours, Balzac came here—to stay with his friends, the Margonnes—during the 1830s, both to write such works as *Le Père Goriot* and to escape his creditors. The château houses substantial exhibits, ranging from photographs to original manuscripts to the coffee service Balzac used to enjoy the caffeine that helped to keep him writing up to 16 hours a day. A few period rooms are here and impress with 19th-century charm, including a lavish emerald-green salon and the author's writing room. Be sure to study some of the corrected author proofs on display. Balzac had to pay for corrections and additions beyond a certain limit. Painfully in debt, he made emendations filling all the margins of his proofs, causing dismay to his printers. Their legitimate bills for extra payment meant that some of his books, best sellers for nearly two centuries, failed to bring him a centime. ✉ ☎ *02–47–26–86–50* 🌐 *www.musee-balzac.fr* 🎫 *€4.50* 🕒 *Apr.–June and Sept., daily 10–6; July and Aug., daily 10–7; Oct.–Mar., Wed.–Mon. 10–12:30 and 2–5.*

WHERE TO EAT

$$$$ FRENCH ★ ✕ **Auberge du XIIe Siècle.** You half expect Balzac himself to come strolling in the door of this half-timber, delightfully historic auberge, so little has it changed since the 19th century. Still sporting a time-stained painted sign and its original exterior staircase, and nearly opposite

THE VERSAILLES OF VEGETABLES

Organized in square patterns, Villandry's world-famous *potager* (vegetable garden) is seasonally ablaze with purple cabbages, bright pumpkins, and many other heirloom veggies. In total, there are nearly 150,000 plantings, with two seasonal shows presented—the spring show is a veritable "salad." The fall show comes to fruition in late September or early October and is the one with the pumpkins. Paging Cinderella.

the great author's country retreat, this inn retains its centuries-old dining room, now warmed by a fireplace, bouquets, and rich wood tables. Beyond this room is a modern extension—all airy glass and white walls but not exactly what you're looking for in such historic surrounds. Balzac's ample girth attested to his great love of food, and he would no doubt enjoy the sautéed lobster or the nouvelle spins on his classic *géline* chicken favorites served here today, or the *aiguillettes de canard rosées en réduction de Chinon* (slices of duck flavored in Chinon wine). Dessert is excellent, and so is the coffee, a refreshment Balzac drank incessantly (little wonder he created more than 2,000 characters). ✉ *1 rue du Château* ☎ *02–47–26–88–77* ▭ *MC, V* ⏲ *Closed Mon. and 2 wks in Jan., 1 wk in June, 1 wk in Sept., and 1 wk in Nov. No dinner Sun., no lunch Tues.*

CHÂTEAU DE USSÉ

14 km (9 mi) west of Azay-le-Rideau via D17 and D7.

Fodor's Choice ★

The most beautiful castle in France is first glimpsed as you approach the **Château d'Ussé** and an astonishing array of blue-slate roofs, dormer windows, delicate towers, and Gothic turrets greets you against the flank of the Forest of Chinon. Literature describes this château, overlooking the banks of the River Indre, as the original *Sleeping Beauty* castle; Charles Perrault—author of this beloved 17th-century tale—spent time here as a guest of the Count of Saumur, and legend has it that Ussé inspired him to write the famous story. Though parts of the castle are from the 1400s, most of it was completed two centuries later. By the 17th century, the region was so secure that one fortified wing of the castle was demolished to allow for grand vistas over the valley and the castle gardens, newly designed in the style Le Nôtre had made so fashionable at Versailles.

Only Disney could have outdone this white-tufa marvel: the château is a flamboyant mix of Gothic and Renaissance styles—romantic and built for fun, not for fighting. Its history supports this playful image: it endured no bloodbaths—no political conquests or conflicts—while a tablet in the chapel indicates that even the French Revolution passed it by. Inside, a tour leads you through several sumptuous period salons, a 19th-century French fashion exhibit, and the Salle de Roi bedchamber built for a visit by King Louis XV (the red-silk, canopied four-poster bed is the stuff of dreams). At the end of the house tour, you can go up the fun spiral staircases to the *chemin de ronde* of the lofty towers; there are pleasant views of the Indre River from the battlements, and you can also find rooms filled with waxwork effigies detailing the fable of Sleeping Beauty herself. Kids will love this.

Before you leave, visit the exquisite Gothic-becomes-Renaissance chapel in the garden, built for Charles d'Espinay and his wife in 1523–35. Note the door decorated with pleasingly sinister skull-and-crossbones carvings. Just a few steps from the chapel are two towering cedars of Lebanon—a gift from the genius-poet of Romanticism, Viscount René de Chateaubriand, to the lady of the house, the Duchess of Duras. When her famous amour died in 1848, she stopped all the clocks in the house—à la Sleeping Beauty—"so as never to hear struck the hours you will not come again." The castle then was inherited by her relations, the Comte and Comtesse de la Rochejaquelin, one of the most dashing couples of the 19th century. Today, Ussé belongs to their descendant, the Duc de Blacas, who is as soigné as his castle. If you do meet him, proffer thanks, as every night his family floodlights the entire château, a vision that is one of the Loire Valley's dreamiest sights. Long regarded as a symbol of *la vieille France*, Ussé can't be topped for fairy-tale splendor, so make this a must-do. ✉ *Rigny-Ussé* ☎ *02–47–95–54–05* 🌐 *www.chateaudusse.fr* 🎫 *€13* 🕓 *Mid-Feb.–mid-Nov., daily 10–6.*

A GARDEN NAMED L'ÉLÉGANCE

Set 4 km (2½ mi) north of Azay-le-Rideau and tended by Madame Béatrice de Andia—one of the grandes dames of the Loire—and her staff are the **Jardins de la Chatonnière**, a 15-acre rose and lily garden that will make most emerald-green with envy. Framing the private, turreted Renaissance château are seven spectacular visions, each garden devoted to a theme, including L'Élégance and L'Abondance, in the extraordinary shape of a gigantic leaf. ✉ *Rte. D57, direction Lignières–Langeais* ☎ *02–47–45–40–29* 🌐 *www.lachatonniere.com* 🎫 *€7* 🕓 *Mar.–mid-Nov., daily 10–7.*

LOIRE VALLEY THROUGH THE AGES

Marauding Huns laid siege to Orléans in AD 451, just 44 years after the death of St. Martin, fabled Bishop of Tours. The next invaders were the Vikings, who pillaged their way down to Angers in the 9th century. Then came the English: in 1154—two years after wedding Eleanor of Aquitaine—Henry Plantagenet became King of England and sovereign of almost all western France, the Loire included. In 1189 he died (as Henry II) in Chinon. In 1199 his son, Richard the Lion-Hearted, died there, too; both are buried (alongside Eleanor) in Fontevraud Abbey, founded a century earlier.

But the French were having none of this foreign hegemony. Beefy castles (Langeais, Chinon) sprouted up along the valley. In 1429 Joan of Arc kicked the English out of Orléans.

Her triumph was short-lived but soon the Loire was back in French hands, and a period of peace and prosperity ensued that saw the region become the center of French culture and politics. The Renaissance arrived in the 1490s, when Charles VII hired Italian craftsmen to update his château at Amboise; then Renaissance prince François I lured Leonardo da Vinci to Amboise, where he died in 1519—the year François began building the world's most fanciful château, Chambord.

The next hundred years were the Loire's pleasure-palace golden age. The decline set in with Louis XIV and his obsession with Versailles. Tours served briefly as French capital in 1870 during the Franco-Prussian War, and the region enjoyed an unwelcome spotlight in 1940, when Petain met Hitler in Montoire-sur-Loir. When France freed itself from the Nazi yoke four years later, the Loire was briefly in the frontline, as bombarded Tours and Orléans recall. But, elsewhere, its rural tranquillity emerged untouched. You'll mostly have the impression that time has stopped still.

4

WHERE TO STAY

¢–$ ★ **Le Clos d'Ussé.** Thank heavens for this delightful inn. The best time to see the great Château d'Ussé is in early morning light or illuminated at night, and the easiest way to do that is to overnight in the village of Rigny-Ussé here at the home of the *famille* Duchemin. Eric runs the place, Muriel is in charge of the extremely cozy restaurant, while *grand-mère* offers a warm smile. Not surprisingly, families will adore this place, especially as three of the rooms are custom-built for them (and rather stylish, to boot). Three rooms have a view of the château, but best of all, a one-minute walk from the front door takes you to the castle gates. **Pros:** close to château; charming restaurant. **Cons:** basic guest-room facilities; you-get-what-you-pay-for bathrooms. ✉ 7 *rue PrincipaleRigny-Ussé* ☎ *02–47–95–55–47* *8 rooms, 4 with bath* *In-room: no a/c, no phone, Wi-Fi. In-hotel: restaurant, bar, some pets allowed* *MC, V* *Closed Nov.–mid-Feb.*

As an overnight guest, Charles Perrault was so seduced by the secluded beauty of Château d'Ussé that he was inspired to write "Sleeping Beauty."

CHINON

Fodor's Choice ★ *13 km (8 mi) southwest of Rigny-Ussé via D7 and D16, 44 km (28 mi) southwest of Tours.*

The historic town of Chinon—birthplace of author François Rabelais (1494–1553)—is dominated by the towering ruins of its medieval castle, perched high above the River Vienne. But Chinon's leading photo-op is the medieval heart of town, where one of France's most time-burnished streets, the Rue Haute St-Maurice, has block after block of storybook, half-timber houses. Little wonder that Jean Cocteau used Chinon's fairy-tale allure to effectively frame Josette Day when she appeared as Beauty in his 1949 film *La Belle et la Bête*.

GETTING HERE

SNCF trains (50 mins, €8.50) leave for Chinon from Tours' train station at least three times a day.

Visitor Information Chinon Tourist Office. ✉ *Place Hofheim* ☎ *02-47-93-17-85* 🌐 *www.chinon-valdeloire.com.*

EXPLORING

Magical, medieval, and magnificent, the main road of Chinon's historic quarter, Rue Haute St-Maurice is a virtual open-air museum as this street runs, spectacularly, for more than 15 blocks. Although there are some museums in town—the **Musée d'Art et d'Histoire** (Art and History Museum) in a medieval town house on Rue Haute St-Maurice, the **Maison de la Rivière,** devoted to Chinon's maritime trade and set along the embankment, and the **Musée du Vin** (Wine Museum) on

Rue Voltaire—the medieval quarter remains the must-do, as a walk here catapults you back to the days of Rabelais.

"DRINK ALWAYS AND NEVER DIE"

Participants in Chinon's medieval festival, the Marché à l'Ancienne (🌐 *www.chinon.com*), are fond of quoting the presiding muse of the city, Renaissance writer François Rabelais. Held on the third Saturday of August, this free wine-tasting extravaganza has stalls, displays, and costumed locals recalling rural life of a hundred years ago. For details, contact the tourist office.

Due to open completely in 2010 after many years of extensive restorations, the vast **Fortresse de Chinon** is a veritable fortress with walls 400 yards long. It dates from the time of Henry II of England, who died here in 1189 and was buried at Fontevraud. Two centuries later the castle witnessed an important historic moment: Joan of Arc's recognition of the disguised dauphin, later Charles VII; the castle was also one of the domiciles of Henry II and his warring wife, Eleanor of Aquitaine. Once little more than ruins completely open to the elements, Chinon's majestic rooftop, ramparts, and towers have been carefully restored. A new visitor center will welcome guests a few steps from the glass elevator that provides direct access to the center of Chinon's Old Town. Visitors will be able to tour the **Logis Royal** (Royal Chambers), a section of which has been transformed into an interactive museum. For a fine view of the region, climb the **Tour Coudray** (Coudray Tower), where in 1307 leading members of the crusading Knights Templar were imprisoned before being taken to Paris, tried, and burned at the stake. The **Tour de l'Horloge** (Clock Tower), whose bell has sounded the hours since 1399, contains the **Musée Jeanne d'Arc** (Joan of Arc Museum). There are sensational views from the ramparts over Chinon, the Vienne Valley, and, toward the back of the castle, the famous vineyard called Le Clos de l'Echo. ✉ ☎ *02–47–93–13–45* 🌐 *www.forteresse-chinon.fr* 🎫 *€3* ⏲ *Apr.–Sept., daily 9–7; Oct.–Mar., daily 9:30–5.*

WHERE TO EAT AND STAY

$$$ FRENCH ✕ **Les Années Trente.** Located in the heart of medieval Chinon, at the foot of the royal fortress, this spot welcomes diners with a venerable 16th-century facade. Inside, a romantic Belle Époque atmosphere continues the historic vibe, but the food, au contraire, is prepared with a light, modern touch. Stéphane and Karine Charles's delicious dishes combine fish, game, and regional specialties that melt in your mouth without weighing you down. There are three different menus, the best of which might be the hearty Terroir; at just €27, it comes perfectly paired with local wines and cheeses. ✉ *78 rue Voltaire* ☎ *02–47–93–37–18* 🌐 *www.lesannees30.com* ✍ *Reservations essential* 💳 *AE, DC, MC, V* ⏲ *Closed Tues. and Wed.*

$–$$ 🏨 **Best Western Hôtel de France.** Right on Chinon's most charming square—a picture postcard come to life with splashing fountain and a bevy of cafés—this sweetly agreeable hotel, two blocks from the medieval quarter, has been a hotel since 1577. Many regional notables lived here before the Revolution, when it became the Hôtel Lion d'Or, the first hostelry in the region. The wood-beam guest rooms are comfortable and cozy; some overlook two tiny, flowerpot-bedecked courtyards, while others take in views that include Chinon's castle ruins. The restaurant, Au Chapeau Rouge (closed Monday and no dinner Sunday), serves regional cuisine, and there's also a brasserie for cheaper snacks. **Pros:** cozy; many rooms have balconies overlooking town square. **Cons:** small guest rooms/bathrooms; poor breakfasts. ✉ *47 pl. du Général-de-Gaulle* ☎ *02–47–93–33–91* 🌐 *bestwestern.worldexecutive.com/locations/france/chinon/3974.html* *30 rooms* *In-room: a/c (some), safe, refrigerator (some), Wi-Fi. In-hotel: restaurant* *AE, DC, MC, V* *Closed Nov. and Feb.* *MAP.*

FAITH, HOPE, AND CLARITY

With its clean-cut lines, Fontevraud's Abbey Church is a gigantic monument of the French Romanesque, the solid style of simple geometric forms eschewing ornamentation. Home to the tombs of Eleanor of Aquitaine and Richard the Lion-Heart, the soaring nave was intended to elevate the soul.

¢–$ Fodor'sChoice ★ **Hôtel Diderot.** With its ivy-covered stone, white shutters, mansard roof, dormer windows, and Rococo spiral staircase, this hotel looks like it is on sabbatical from an 18th-century François Boucher painting. Inside, things get darker and a bit frumpier, but guest rooms are spacious, and, while hardly modern, are equipped with cable TV, free Wi-Fi, and plenty of closet space. Breakfast is served in the beamed dining room with roaring fireplace in winter, or on the garden terrace in summer, with over two dozen homemade preserves, fresh breads, cheese, yogurt, and fresh fruit. All in all, quite an excellent value for the money. **Pros:** lots of space; cozy bar and breakfast room; accessible ground-floor rooms. **Cons:** somewhat worn decor; outdated bathrooms. ✉ *4 rue Buffon* ☎ *02–47–93–18–87* 🌐 *www.hoteldiderot.com* *27 rooms* *In-room: no a/c, Wi-Fi. In-hotel: bar, parking (paid)* *AE, DC, MC, V* *MAP.*

FONTEVRAUD-L'ABBAYE

20 km (12 mi) northwest of Chinon via D751.

Visitor Information **Fontevraud-l'Abbaye Tourist Office.** ✉ *Pl. St-Michel* ☎ *02–41–51–79–45* 🌐 *www.ot-saumur.fr.*

A refreshing break from the worldly grandeur of châteaux, the small village of Fontevraud is crowned with the largest abbey in France, a magnificent complex of Romanesque and Renaissance buildings that were of central importance in the history of both England and France.

Fodor'sChoice ★ Founded in 1101, the **Abbaye Royale de Fontevraud** had separate churches and living quarters for nuns, monks, lepers, "repentant" female sinners, and the sick. Between 1115 and the French Revolution in 1789, a succession of 39 abbesses—among them a granddaughter of William the Conqueror—directed operations. The great 12th-century **Église Abbatiale** (Abbey Church) contains the tombs of Henry II of England, his wife Eleanor of Aquitaine, and their son, Richard Cœur de Lion (the

Lion-Hearted). Though their bones were scattered during the Revolution, their effigies still lie *en couchant* in the middle of the echoey nave. Napoléon turned the abbey church into a prison, and so it remained until 1963, when historical restoration work—still under way—began. The **Salle Capitulaire** (Chapter House), adjacent to the church, with its collection of 16th-century religious wall paintings (prominent abbesses served as models), is unmistakably Renaissance; the paving stones bear the salamander emblem of François I. Next to the long refectory is the famously octagonal **Cuisine** (Kitchen), topped by 20 scaly stone chimneys led by the **Tour d'Evrault.** ✉ *Pl. des Plantagenêts* ☎ *02–41–51–71–41* 🌐 *www.abbaye-fontevraud.com* 🎫 *€8.40* ⏲ *Apr.–Oct., daily 10–6; Nov.–Mar., daily 10–5.*

4

After touring the Abbaye Royale, head outside the gates of the complex a block to the north to discover one of the Loire Valley's most time-machine streets, the **Allée Sainte-Catherine**. Bordered by the Fontevraud park, headed by a charming medieval church, and lined with a few scattered houses (which now contain the town tourist office, a gallery that sells medieval illuminated manuscript pages, and the delightful Licorne restaurant), this street still looks like the 14th century.

WHERE TO EAT AND STAY

$$$ FRENCH ★ ✕ **La Licorne**. A hanging shop sign adorned with a painted unicorn beckons you to this pretty-as-a-picture 18th-century town-house restaurant just off Fontevraud's idyllic Allée Sainte-Catherine. Past a flowery garden and table-adorned terrace, tiny salons glow with happy folks feasting on some of the best food in the region: the chef's Loire salmon, guinea fowl in Layon wine, langoustine ravioli with wild mushrooms, colvert (duck), and lobster with fava beans make most diners purr with contentment. ✉ *31 rue Robert-d'Arbrissel* ☎ *02–41–51–72–49* 🌐 *www.la-licorne-restaurant.com* ✍ *Reservations essential* 💳 *AE, DC, MC, V* ⏲ *Closed late Dec.–mid-Jan. and Mon. and Wed. during mid-Sept.–Mar. No dinner Sun.*

$–$$ ★ 🏨 **Hôtel Abbaye Royale de Fontevraud.** One of the more unusual hotels in the Loire Valley and set right within the medieval splendor of Fontevraud, this series of outbuildings was once the abbey's lepers' hospice. The entrance gives onto the vast *salle capitulaire* (conference room), and the cloisters now house a fine restaurant, Le Saint Lazare (reservations essential, closed mid-November–April), where Anthony Vaillant's delicacies, such as duck foie-gras fillet with raspberry sauce or seared sea bass tartare with sesame seeds, entice. In a muscular side wing the erstwhile monks' cells have been transformed into small but alluring guest rooms, chic and bright in modern checks and fine wood accents. The more expensive rooms—No. 106 is the largest—have bath rather than shower. Staying here lets you explore the abbey grounds when its gates are closed to the public—an exceptional experience. **Pros:** unique historic setting; superb restaurant. **Cons:** rooms are tiny; facilities basic. ✉ *Abbaye Royale* ☎ *02–41–51–73–16* 🌐 *www.hotelfp-fontevraud.com* 🛏 *52 rooms* 👍 *In-room: no a/c, refrigerator . In-hotel: restaurant, bar, Wi-Fi hotspot, parking (free)* 💳 *AE, MC, V* ⏲ *Closed mid-Nov.–Mar.* 🍽 *MAP.*

SAUMUR

★ *15 km (9 mi) northwest of Fontevraud via D947, 68 km (43 mi) west of Tours.*

You'll find putting up with the famous *snobisme* of the Saumurois well worth it once you get a gander at Saumur's magnificent historic center. Studded with elegant 19th-century town houses and the charming Place St-Pierre, lorded over by the vast 12th-century church of St-Pierre and centerpiece of a warren of streets, cafés, and ice-cream parlors, this *centre historique* is sheer delight. Looming over it all—icon of the town and a vision right out of a fairy tale—is Saumur's mighty turreted castle high above the river. You'll be using up many of your flash cards here in a jiffy.

GETTING HERE

To reach Saumur by train from Paris (Gare Montparnasse) requires a change in either Angers (2 hrs, 20 mins; €55.60) or St-Pierre-des-Corps (3 hrs, 1 hr, 35 mins; €36.90). Regional trains link Saumur to Tours (40 mins, €11) and Angers (20–30 mins, €7.80) every 2 hours or so.

Visitor Information Saumur Tourist Office. ✉ *Pl. de la Bilange* ☎ *02-41-40-20-60* 🌐 *www.ot-saumur.fr.*

EXPLORING

A gorgeous dip into the Middle Ages, Saumur is not content to rest on former glories: today it's one of the largest towns along the Loire and a key transportation hub for Anjou, the province just to the west of Touraine. Saumur is also known for its riding school and flourishing mushroom industry, which produces 100,000 tons per year. The same cool tunnels in which the mushrooms grow provide an ideal storage place for the local *mousseux* (sparkling wines); many vineyards hereabouts are open to the public for tours.

If you arrive in the evening, the sight of the elegant, floodlighted, white 14th-century **Château de Saumur** takes your breath away. Look familiar? Probably because you've seen it in reproductions from the famous *Très Riches Heures* (Book of Hours) painted for the Duc de Berry in 1416 (now in the Musée Condé at Chantilly). Inside it's bright and cheerful, with a fairy-tale gateway and plentiful potted flowers. Owing to renovation of the castle walls, the two museums based here, the **Musée des Arts Décoratifs** (Decorative Arts Museum) and the **Musée du Cheval** (Equestrian Museum), will be closed for restoration through 2012, but visitors have access to the gardens and panoramic terrace. From April through August there are temporary expositions open in certain areas of the château. From the cliff-side promenade beyond the parking lot there's a thrilling vista of the castle on its bluff against the river backdrop. ✉ *Esplanade du Château* ☎ *02-41-40-24-40* 🌐 *www.saumur-tourisme.net/chateausaumur.html* 🎟 *€3* ⏲ *Apr.–June and Sept and Oct., Tues.–Sun. 10–1 and 2–5:30; July and Aug. 10–6.*

The **Cadre Noir de Saumur** *(Riding School)* is unique in Europe, with its 400 horses, extensive stables, five Olympic-size riding schools, and miles of specially laid tracks. Try for a morning tour, which includes a chance to admire the horses in training. The horses put on a full gala display for enthusiastic crowds during special weekends in May, July, and October. ✉ *Ave. de l'Ecole Nationale d'Equitation* ☎ *02–41–53–50–60* 🌐 *www.cadrenoir.fr* 🎫 *€7* ⏲ *Guided tours only, mid-Feb.–mid-Nov., Mon. 2–4, Tues.–Fri. 9:30–4, Sat. 9:30–11; closed during performances of Matinées.*

Saumur is the heart of one of the finest wine regions in France. To pay a call on some of the vineyards around the city, first stop into the **Maison du Vin** *(House of Wine)* for the full scoop on hours and directions; also consult the Web site for Loire wines. ✉ *Quai Lucien-Gautier* ☎ *02–41–38–45–83* 🌐 *www.vinsdeloire.fr* ⏲ *Apr.–Sept., Tues.–Sat. 9:30–1 and 2–7, Mon. 2–7; Oct.–Mar., Tues.–Fri. 10:30–12:30 and 3–6, Sat. 10:30–12:30 and 2:30–6:30.*

THE VERY RICH HOURS

Presided over by its magnificent cliff-top castle—which has a starring role in *Les Très Riches Heures du Duc de Berry,* France's most famous illuminated book—Saumur is known as one of the ritziest towns in France. Regional government offices, wealthy wine producers, and hordes of *bon chic, bon genre* shoppers means you can probably enjoy a blast of old-time French attitude (the waiters are even snobbier than the matrons). Little seems to have changed over the centuries: Honoré de Balzac famously wrote up the surly side of the Saumurois in *Eugénie Grandet.*

4

Here are some of the top vineyards of the Saumur region. Note that Loire wine is not a practical buy—except for instant consumption—but if wine-tasting tours of vineyards inspire you, enterprising winemakers will arrange shipments.

Les Caves Louis de Grenelle (✉ *20 rue Marceau* ☎ *02–41–50–17–63* 🌐 *www.caves-de-grenelle.fr* 🎫 *€2.50* ⏲ *May–Sept., daily 9:30–6:30; Oct.–Mar., weekdays 9:30–noon and 1:30–6; Apr. and Dec., daily 10–noon and 1:30–6*) are in the center of town, easily accessible on foot or by car (free parking). The fascinating 90-minute tour through the 15th-century quarry tunnels includes a tasting of their sparkling and still wines.

For sparkling Saumur wine, including a rare sparkling red, try **Ackerman** (✉ *13 rue Léopold-Palustre, St-Hilaire* ☎ *02–41–03–30–20* 🌐 *www.ackerman-remypannier.com*).

Veuve Amiot (✉ *21 rue Jean-Ackerman, St-Hilaire* ☎ *02–41–83–14–14* 🌐 *www.veuve-amiot.com*) is a long-established producer of Saumur wines.

WHERE TO STAY

$$–$$$ **Anne d'Anjou.** The spectacular setting at the foot of Saumur castle may appeal to you most about this elegant 18th-century hotel—or maybe the flower-strewn courtyard, or perhaps the views of the Loire from some of the guest rooms (although not the traffic rushing by). The finest retain their original, late-18th- and early-19th-century decoration, and one is even furbished to the designs of Percier and Fontaine, Napoléon's favorite architects. A real plus is the restaurant Les Ménestrels (closed Sunday), found in a lovingly restored 16th-century house up against

the castle cliff. **Pros:** classic architecture; serious restaurant; free Wi-Fi. **Cons:** smallish rooms; busy road close by. ✉ *32 quai Mayaud* ☎ *02–41–67–30–30* 🌐 *www.hotel-anneanjou.com* *44 rooms* *In-room: no a/c, safe, refrigerator. In-hotel: restaurant, Internet terminal, Wi-Fi hotspot, some pets allowed* *AE, MC, V* *MAP.*

$–$$ Fodor's Choice ★ **Saint-Pierre.** At the very epicenter of historic Saumur, this gorgeous little jewel is hidden beneath the medieval walls of the church of Saint-Pierre—look for the hotel's storybook entrance on one of the pedestrian *passages* that circle the vast nave. Once inside the 15th- to 17th-century house, you can find a sweet reception area and suave staff to welcome you. Up the Renaissance corkscrew staircase (or modern mini-elevator) you can find the astonishingly refined guest rooms. Designer fabrics, antique *pont* cabinets (forming a "bridge" over bed headboards), elegant wainscoting, Persian rugs, tuffeau fireplaces, and bathrooms replete with Paloma Picasso designs make this a favored home-away-from-home for Saumur's most savvy visitors. The smaller rooms face the church, but they also are quieter than those overlooking the road leading up to the castle. There's no restaurant, but steps away is lovely Place St-Pierre, lined with outdoor cafés. **Pros:** central location; sophisticated decor. **Cons:** some rooms face busy roadway. ✉ *Rue Haute-Saint-Pierre* ☎ *02–41–50–33–00* 🌐 *www.saintpierresaumur.com* *15 rooms* *In-room: a/c, refrigerator, Internet. In-hotel: bar, some pets allowed* *AE, DC, MC, V.*

ANGERS

45 km (28 mi) northwest of Saumur, 88 km (55 mi) northeast of Nantes.

The bustling city of Angers, on the banks of the Maine River, just north of the Loire, is famous for its towering castle filled with the extraordinary Apocalypse Tapestry. But it also has a fine Gothic cathedral, a selection of art galleries, and a network of pleasant, traffic-free streets around Place Ste-Croix, with its half-timber houses.

GETTING HERE

TGV trains from Paris (Gare Montparnasse) leave for Angers every hour or so; the 180-mi trip takes 90 minutes (€45.10). Trains run every 2 hours or so to Saumur (20–30 mins, €7.80) and Tours (1 hr, €17). Three regional trains daily continue to Blois (1 hr, 20 mins; €23) and Orléans (1 hr, 50 mins; €29.30).

Visitor Information **Angers Tourist Office.** ✉ *7 pl. Kennedy* ☎ *02–41–23–50–00* 🌐 *www.angersloiretourisme.com.*

EXPLORING

Angers's principal sights lie within a compact square formed by the three main boulevards and the Maine, all accessible via the new city tramway scheduled to open in late 2010.

★ The banded black-and-white **Château d'Angers**, built by St. Louis (1228–38), glowers over the town from behind turreted moats, now laid out as gardens and overrun with flowers. As you explore the grounds, note the startling contrast between the thick defensive walls, guarded by a drawbridge and 17 massive round towers in a distinctive pattern, and the formal garden, with its delicate white-tufa chapel, erected in the 15th century. For a sweeping view of the city and surrounding countryside, climb one of the castle towers. A well-integrated modern gallery on the castle grounds contains the great **Tenture de l'Apocalypse** (Apocalypse Tapestry), woven in Paris in the 1380s for the Duke of Anjou. Measuring 16 feet high and 120 yards long, its many panels show a series of 70 horrifying and humorous scenes from the Book of Revelation. In one, mountains of fire fall from heaven while boats capsize and men struggle in the water. Another has the Beast with Seven Heads. ✉ *2 promenade du Bout-du-Monde* ☎ *02–41–86–48–77* 🌐 *angers.monuments-nationaux.fr* 🎟 *€6* ⏲ *May–Aug., daily 9:30–6:30; Sept.–Apr., daily 10–5:30.*

Set within the 15th-century Logis Barrault, the **Musée des Beaux Arts** (Fine Arts Museum of Angers) houses a collection of art spanning the 14th to the 21st century, as well as a section on the history of Angers through archeological and artistic works from Neolithic period to the present. ✉ *14 rue du Museé* ☎ *02–41–05–38–00* 🌐 *www.musees.angers.fr* 🎟 *€4* ⏲ *June–Sept., daily 10–6:30; Oct.–May, Tues.–Sun. 10–noon and 2–6 (temporary exhibitions open 10–6).*

The **Cathédrale St-Maurice** (✉ *Pl. Monseigneur-Chappoulie*) is a 12th- and 13th-century Gothic cathedral noted for its curious Romanesque facade and original stained-glass windows; bring binoculars to appreciate both fully. Its medieval Treasury is open to the public Monday through Saturday in summer (every other Saturday off-season) from 2:30 to 6.

To learn about the heartwarming liqueur made in Angers since 1849, head to the **Carré Cointreau** on the east of the city. It has a museum and offers a guided visit of the distillery, which starts with an introductory film, moves past "cointreauversial" advertising posters, through the bottling plant and alembic room, with its gleaming copper-pot stills, and ends with a tasting. English tours are staged at 3 PM. The city bus No. 7 from the Angers train station stops just outside. ✉ *2 bd. des Bretonnières, St-Barthélémy d'Anjou* ☎ *02–41–31–50–50* 🌐 *www.cointreau.fr* 🎟 *€9.50* ⏲ *Tues.–Sat. 11–6 (reservations essential).*

WHERE TO STAY

$$–$$$ **Hôtel d'Anjou.** In business since 1846 (and now a member of the Best Western franchise), the Anjou has a vaguely 18th-century style, and stained-glass windows in the lobby. Rooms vary in size but most have high ceilings, double doors, and modern bathrooms where terry robes await you. There's a fine restaurant, La Salamandre (closed Sunday), where Danie Louboutin's meticulously prepared classic cuisine ranges from lamb and duck with cranberries to calamari with crab sauce. Opt for one of the reasonably priced prix-fixe menus. **Pros:** central location; stylish public areas, free Wi-Fi. **Cons:** sardine-size elevator; busy street outside. ✉ *1 bd. du Maréchal-Foch* ☎ *02–41–21–12–11, 800/528–1324 in U.S.* 🌐 *www.hoteldanjou.fr* *53 rooms* *In-room: a/c, refrigerator, Wi-Fi. In-hotel: restaurant, bar, some pets allowed, parking (paid)* 💳 *AE, DC, MC, V* *BP.*

¢–$ **Mail.** A stately lime tree stands sentinel behind wrought-iron, wisteria-framed gates outside this 17th-century mansion on a calm street between the Hôtel de Ville and the river. Inside, an extreme makeover has lent a spiffy, modern air to the interiors. The blazing red reception area, smartly adorned with modern seating, segues to the upstairs guest rooms: rather *petit*, most are decorated in sunny yellow or pastel tones. **Pros:** calm; good value. **Cons:** basic room decor; no elevator. ✉ *8 rue des Ursules* ☎ *02–41–25–05–25* 🌐 *www.hotel-du-mail.com* *26 rooms* *In-room: no a/c, refrigerator, Wi-Fi. In-hotel: some pets allowed* *AE, DC, MC, V.*

NIGHTLIFE AND THE ARTS

July and August see the **Angers Tempo'Rives** (*Angers Summer festival* ☎ *02–41–23–50–00* 🌐 *www.angers.fr/temporives*), with free concerts at the Parvis du Théâtre Le Quai.

LANGEAIS

82 km (47 mi) east of Angers via N152.

Sometimes unjustly overlooked, the **Château de Langeais**—a castle in the true sense of the word—will particularly delight those who dream of lions rampant, knights in shining armor, and the chivalric days of yore. Built in the 1460s, bearing a massive portcullis and gate, and never altered, it has an interior noted for its superb collection of medieval and Renaissance furnishings—fireplaces, tapestries, chests, and beds—which would make Guinevere and Lancelot feel right at home. An hourly waxworks and video show tells the story of the secret dawn wedding of King Charles VIII with Anne of Brittany in the room where it took place in 1491. Outside, gardens nestle behind sturdy walls and battlements; kids will make a beeline for the playgrounds and tree house added in 2009. The town itself has other sites, including a Renaissance church tower, but chances are you won't want to move from the delightful outdoor cafés that face the castle entrance. Do follow the road a bit to the right (when looking at the entrance) to discover the charming historic houses grouped around a waterfall and canal. ☎ *02–47–96–72–60* 🌐 *www.chateau-de-langeais.com* *€8.20* *Apr.–June and Sept.–mid-Nov., daily 9:30–6:30; July and Aug., daily 9–7; mid-Nov.–Mar., daily 10–5.*

5

Normandy

WORD OF MOUTH

"Shortly after 9:00 AM, we found ourselves on the long causeway to Mont-Saint-Michel, with no sight of the famed monastery. Finally, about halfway out, the Mont appeared out of the fog—a truly stunning moment. I've read that the Mont is one of France's most-visited sights: I can see why. More, we learned while touring the American D-Day sites that the power of place really trumps all the books we had read and movies we had seen."

—Rumseydog

WELCOME TO NORMANDY

TOP REASONS TO GO

★ **Mont-St-Michel:** The spire-top silhouette of this mighty offshore mound, dubbed the Marvel of the Occident, is one of the greatest sights in Europe. Get there at high tide, when the water races across the endless sands.

★ **Bayeux:** Come not just for the splendor of the tapestry telling how William conquered England, but for untouched medieval buildings and the beefy, bonnet-top cathedral.

★ **Honfleur:** From France's prettiest harbor, lined with beam-fronted houses, you can head to the ravishing wooden church of Ste-Catherine.

★ **Rouen:** Sanctified by the memory of Jeanne d'Arc, hallowed by its towering Gothic cathedral (immortalized by Monet), and lined with medieval half-timber houses, Rouen makes a great gateway city to Normandy.

★ **D-Day Beaches:** From rocky Omaha to pancake-flat Utah, muse on the stirring deeds of World War II.

1 Upper Normandy. Fascinating portal city to Normandy, Rouen still contains—despite World War II's battering—such an overwhelming number of lovely churches, chapels, towers, fountains, and old cross-beam houses that many take two full days to enjoy this commercial and cultural hub. Heading some 60 km (35 mi) northwest to the Channel shore, the Côte d'Alabâtre beckons, named for the white cliffs that stretch north, including the spectacular rock formations often painted by Monet at Étretat. Nearby seaside Fécamp regales with its noted Benedictine palace and distillery.

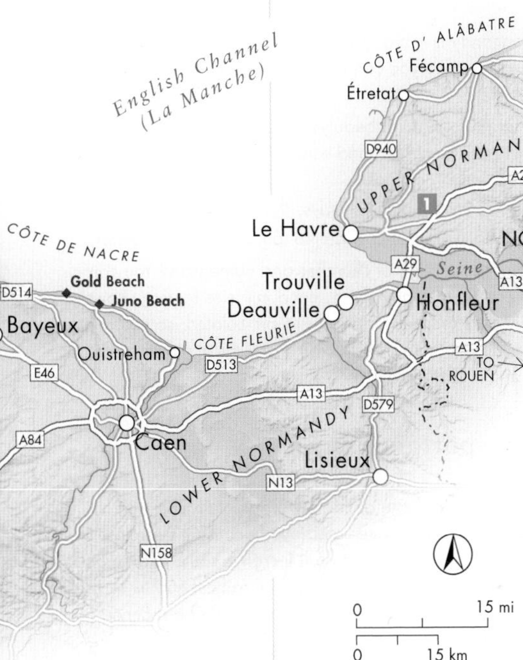

GETTING ORIENTED

The Seine Valley divides Normandy in two as it flows northwest from Paris through Rouen and into the English Channel at Le Havre. To the north lies Upper Normandy and a spectacular coastline lined with towering chalk cliffs called the Côte d'Alabâtre, or Alabaster Coast. West of the Seine lies Lower Normandy, full of lush meadows and lined with the sandy beaches of the Côte Fleurie, or Flower Coast. (These are the same beaches where the Allies landed on D-Day.) Far to the west, at the foot of the sparsely populated Cotentin Peninsula, the offshore Mont-St-Michel patrols one of the continent's biggest bays.

2 Honfleur to Mont-St-Michel. Basse (or Lower) Normandie begins with the sandy Côte Fleurie (Flower Coast), announced by seaside Honfleur, an artist's paradise full of half-timber houses. Just south, Rothschilds by the Rolls arrive in season at the Belle Époque seaside resorts of Trouville and Deauville—both beautiful if hard on the pocket. Modern and student-filled Caen is famed for its two gigantic abbey churches, one begun by William the Conqueror, who is immortalized in nearby Bayeux's legendary tapestry. This town makes a great base to explore the somber D-Day sites along Utah and Omaha beaches; bus tours and moving memorials make a fitting prelude for a drive across Normandy's Cotentin Peninsula to Mont-St-Michel, whose tiny island is crowned by one of the most beautiful Gothic abbeys in France.

NORMANDY PLANNER

Bus Tours

Cityrama and Paris-Vision run full-day bus excursions from Paris to Mont-St-Michel for €158, meals and admission included.

This is definitely not for the faint of heart—buses leave Paris at 6:45 or 7:15 AM and return around 10:30 PM.

In Caen, the Mémorial organizes four-hour English-language daily minibus tours of the D-Day landing beaches; the cost is €75, including entrance fees.

Normandy Sightseeing Tours runs a number of trips to the D-Day beaches and Mont-St-Michel. One of their full-day excursions to the D-Day beaches (8:30–6) costs €80.

Cityrama (✉ *4 pl. des Pyramides, Paris* ☎ *01–44–55–61–00* 🌐 *www.cityrama.fr*).

Mémorial (☎ *02–31–06–06–44* 🌐 *www.memorial.fr*).

Normandy Sightseeing Tours (✉ *618 rte. du Lavoir, Mosles* ☎ *02–31–51–70–52* 🌐 *www.normandywebguide.com*).

Paris-Vision (✉ *214 rue de Rivoli, Paris* ☎ *01–42–60–30–01* 🌐 *www.parisvision.com*).

Making the Most of Your Time

Normandy is a big region with lots to see. If you have 10 days or so you can do it justice. If not, you'll need to prioritize.

In search of natural beauty? Head to the coastline north of Le Havre. Prefer sea and sand? Beat it to the beaches west of Trouville.

Like city life? You'll love pretty Rouen. Are you a history buff? Base yourself in Caen to tour the D-Day beaches.

Can't get enough of churches and cathedrals? You can go pretty much anywhere, but don't miss Bayeux, Rouen, or Mont-St-Michel. (The last is a bit isolated, so you might want to get there directly from Paris, or at the start or end of a tour of Brittany.)

Transportation Basics

Although this is one of the few areas of France with no high-speed rail service—perhaps because it's so close to Paris, or because it's not on a lucrative route to a neighboring country—Normandy's regional rail network is surprisingly good, meaning that most towns can be reached by train.

Rouen is the hub for Upper Normandy, Caen for Lower Normandy. Unless you're driving, you'll need a bus to reach the coastal resorts like Étretat, Honfleur, and Houlgate.

For Mont-St-Michel, a combination of train and bus is required.

To visit the D-Day beaches, a guided minibus tour, leaving from Caen or Bayeux, is your best bet.

The A13 expressway is the gateway from Paris, running northwest to Rouen and then to Caen. From here the A84 takes you almost all the way to Mont-St-Michel, and the N13 brings you to Bayeux.

If you're arriving from England or northern Europe, the A16/A28 from Calais to Rouen is a scenic (and near-empty) delight.

Touring the D-Day Beaches

One of the great events of modern history, the D-Day invasion of June 1944, was enacted on the beaches of Normandy.

Omaha Beach (site of an eye-opening museum), Utah Beach, as well as many sites on the Cotentin Peninsula, and the memorials to Allied dead, all bear witness to the furious fighting that once raged in this now-peaceful corner of France.

Today, as seagulls sweep over the cliffs where American rangers scrambled desperately up ropes to silence murderous German batteries, visitors now wander through the blockhouses and peer into the bomb craters, the carnage of *Saving Private Ryan* thankfully now a distant, if still horrifying, memory.

Unless you have a car, the D-Day beaches are best visited on a bus tour from Bayeux. Public buses are rare, although Bus No. 75 heads to Arromanches and Bus No. 70 goes to Omaha Beach and the American cemetery (summer only). However, Bus Verts du Calvados (🌐 *www.busverts.fr*) offers a "Circuit Caen-Omaha Beach" route that connects many of the D-Day sights.

As for guided tours, Normandy Tours (☎ *02–31–92–10–70* 🌐 *www.normandy-landing-tours-hotel.com*), which carries up to eight in its minivan, leaves from Bayeux's Hotel de la Gare.

The guides are walking encyclopedias of local war lore and may be flexible about points interest to you. The half-day tours (€40) are available all year in English.

In addition, other Bayeux-based tour outfitters include D-Day Tours (☎ *02–31–51–70–52* 🌐 *www.normandywebguide.com*), with half-day tours (€50) and full-day tours (€80). Battlebus (☎ *02–31–22–28–82* 🌐 *www.battlebus.fr*) has a full-day extravaganza (€85).

Finding a Place to Stay

Accommodations to suit every taste can be found throughout Normandy, from basic bed-and-breakfasts to the most luxurious hotel.

Even in the ultraswank resorts of Deauville and Trouville it is possible to find delightful and inexpensive little vacation spots.

Prices are ratcheted up in summer along the coast, so be sure to book ahead, especially on weekends when half of Paris heads to the seaside.

Many hotels are closed in winter. In the beach resorts the season runs from the end of April to October.

The region's two largest cities, Rouen and Caen, are not among France's best-served when it comes to high-end hotels.

To stay the night on Mont-St-Michel is a memorable experience, but be sure to reserve your room weeks in advance.

DINING AND LODGING PRICE CATEGORIES (IN EUROS)

	¢	$	$$	$$$	$$$$
Restaurants	under €13	€12–€17	€18–€24	€25–€32	over €32
Hotels	under €65	€65–€105	€106–€145	€146–€215	over €215

Restaurant prices are per person for a main course at dinner, including tax (5.5%) and service; note that if a restaurant offers only prix-fixe (set-price) meals, it has been given the price category that reflects the full prix-fixe price. Hotel prices are for a standard double room in high season, including tax (19.6%) and service charge.

5

GETTING AROUND

Air Travel

Paris's Charles de Gaulle (Roissy) and Orly airports are the closest intercontinental links with the region.

There are flights in summer from London to Deauville. Year-round service between Jersey and Cherbourg, which sits at the northern tip of the Cotentin Peninsula, about 90 minutes' drive from Bayeux.

Rouen airport has direct flights to Lyon and Montpellier.

Airport Information **Caen** (☎ *02–31–71–20–10*). **Cherbourg** (☎ *02–33–88–57–60*). **Deauville** (☎ *02–31–65–65–65*). **Rouen** (☎ *02–35–79–41–00*).

CARRIERS

Air France flies to Caen from Paris.

Ryanair flies to Deauville and Dinard (in Brittany, 56 km [35 mi] west of Mont-St-Michel) from London's Stansted Airport.

Airlines and Contacts **Air France** (☎ *08–02–80–28–02 for information* 🌐 *www.air-france.com*).

Train Travel

From Paris (Gare St-Lazare), separate train lines head to Upper Normandy (Rouen and Le Havre or Dieppe) and Lower Normandy (Caen, Bayeux, and Cherbourg, via Évreux and Lisieux).

There are frequent trains from Paris to Rouen (70 mins, €19); some continue to Le Havre (2 hrs, €27). Change in Rouen for Dieppe (2 hrs from Paris, €25).

The trip from Paris to Deauville (2 hrs, €26) often requires a change at Lisieux.

There are regular trains from Paris to Caen (1 hr, 50 mins; €28), some continuing to Bayeux (2 hrs, €31).

Taking the train from Paris to Mont-St-Michel is not easy—the quickest way (3 hrs, 45 mins; €60) is to take the TGV from Gare Montparnasse to Rennes, then take the bus.

There are three trains daily, but the only one that will allow you a full day on the Mont leaves at 6:35 AM and arrives at 9:55 AM.

The other options are 11:05 (arriving 3:13 PM) and 1:05 PM (arriving 5:04). From Caen you can take either an early morning or an afternoon train to Pontorson (2 hrs, €22.20), the nearest station to the Mont; then it's another 15 minutes to the foot of the abbey by bus or taxi (buses are directly in front of the station).

Unless you're content to stick to the major towns (Rouen, Dieppe, Caen, Bayeux, Cherbourg), visiting Normandy by train may prove frustrating.

You can sometimes reach several smaller towns (Fécamp, Houlgate/Cabourg) on snail-paced branch lines, but the irregular intricacies of what is said to be Europe's most complicated regional timetable will probably have driven you nuts by the time you get here.

Other destinations, like Honfleur or Étretat, require train/bus journeys.

Train Information **Gare SNCF Rouen** (✉ *Rue Jeanne d'Arc* ☎ *08–36–35–35–39*). **SNCF** (☎ *08–36–35–35–35* 🌐 *www.ter-sncf.com/regions/basse-normandie/fr/Default.aspx*).

Visitor Information

If traveling extensively by public transportation, be sure to load up on information (Guide Regional des Transport schedules, the best taxi-for-call companies, etc.) upon arriving at the ticket counter or help desk of the bigger train and bus stations in the area, such as Rouen, Deauville, and Caen. The capital of each of Normandy's départements—Caen, Évreux, Rouen, St-Lô, and Alençon—has its own central tourist office. ⇨ *They, and numerous other tourist offices, are listed under town names below.*

Bus Travel

Cars Perier runs buses from Fécamp to Le Havre, stopping in Étretat along the way. **Bus Verts du Calvados** covers the coast, connecting with Caen and Honfleur, Bayeux, and other towns. It also runs, during July and August, the special D-Day Circuit 44, which allows you to see as many D-Day sights as you can squeeze into one day. These buses depart from the train stations in Bayeux and Caen. Bus routes connect many towns, including Rouen, Dieppe, Fécamp, Étretat, Le Havre, Caen, Honfleur, Deauville, Trouville, Cabourg, and Arromanches. To get to Honfleur, take a bus from Deauville; from Rouen, train it first to Le Havre, then continue on bus to Honfleur.

For Mont-St-Michel, hook up with buses from nearby Pontorson, St. Malo, or from Rennes in adjacent Brittany. If you are traveling from Paris to the Mont, take the high-speed TGV train from Gare Montparnasse to Rennes (in high season, five departures a day), then a **Keolis** bus transfer to the Mont. Many trains depart from Paris's Gare-St-Lazare for Rouen (70 mins). Tourist offices and train stations in Normandy will have printed schedules.

Bus Information **Bus Verts du Calvados** (☎ *08–10–21–42–14* 🌐 *www.busverts.fr*). **VTNI** (☎ *08–25–07–60–27*). **Keolis** (☎ *02–99–19–70–80* 🌐 *www.keolis-emeraude.com*). **Cars Perier** (☎ *02–32–84–12–60* 🌐 *www.cars-perier.fr*).

Bike and Moped Travel

Traveling with your bike is free on all regional trains and many national lines; be sure to ask the SNCF which ones when you're booking.

Car Travel

From Paris, A13 slices its way to Rouen in 1½ hours (toll €5.20) before forking to Caen (an additional hr, toll €7.50) or Le Havre (45 mins on A131).

N13 continues from Caen to Bayeux in another two hours.

At Caen, the A84 forks off southwest toward Mont-St-Michel and Rennes.

From Paris, scenic D915 will take you to Dieppe in about three hours.

The Pont de Normandie, between Le Havre and Honfleur, effectively unites Upper and Lower Normandy.

Boat and Ferry Travel

A number of ferry companies sail between the United Kingdom and ports in Normandy.

Brittany Ferries travels between Caen (Ouistreham) and Portsmouth and between Poole/Portsmouth and Cherbourg.

The Dieppe-Newhaven route is covered by a daily service from Transmanche.

Brittany Ferries (☎ *08–03–82–88–28* 🌐 *www.brittany-ferries.com*).

Transmanche (☎ *08–00–65–01–00* 🌐 *www.transmancheferries.com*).

EATING AND DRINKING WELL IN NORMANDY

It's the felicitous combination of the dairy farm, the apple orchard, and the sea that inspire Normandy's crème de la crème cuisine, featuring voluptuous cream sauces, tender cheeses, lavish seafood platters, and head-spinning Calvados brandy.

As befits one of France's best regional cuisines, Normandy boasts many delightful kitchens (above); fresh-this-very-hour oysters (right, top); great cheeses make great desserts (right, bottom).

Normandy's verdant landscape—a patchwork of pastures and apple orchards bordered by the sea—heralds a region of culinary delights. The apples are rendered into tarts, cakes, sauces, and *cidre bouché,* a sparkling cider sold in cork-top bottles. Brown and white cows grazing beneath the apple blossoms—the famous *vaches normandes*—each produce up to seven gallons of milk a day, destined to become golden butter, thick crème fraîche, and prized cheeses. Coastal waters from Dieppe to Granville are equally generous, yielding sole, turbot, and oysters. To fully appreciate Normandy's gastronomic wealth, stroll through a weekend markets, such as the splendid Saturday morning affair in Honfleur on the cobbled Place Sainte-Catherine, sample a seafood platter at a boardwalk café in Deauville, or meet the omelet of your dreams at La Mère Poulard at Mont-Saint-Michel.

APPLE COUNTRY

One fragrance evokes Normandy—the pungent, earthy smell of apples awaiting the press in the autumn. Normandy is apple country, where apples with quaint varietal names, such as Windmill and Donkey Snout, are celebrated in the region's gastronomy, along the Route du Cidre, or at Vimoutier's Foire de la Pomme festival in October (where they vote for the Most Beautiful Apple!).

CHEESE PLATTER

Camembert is king in the dairy realm of Normandy. This tangy, opulently creamy cow's-milk cheese with the star billing and worldwide reputation hails from the Auge region.

The best—Véritable Camembert de Normandie—with velvety white rinds and supple, sometimes oozy interiors, are produced on small farm properties, such as the esteemed Moulin de Carel.

Other members of Normandy's (cheese) board are the savory, grassy Pont L'Évêque, the impressively pungent Livarot with rust-color rind, and the Pavé d'Auge, a robust cheese with a honey-hue center.

CALVADOS

There are no wines in Normandy, but the region makes its mark in the spirits world with the apple-based Calvados, a fragrant oak-aged brandy.

Like Cognac, Calvados, which is distilled from cider, gets better and more expensive with age.

Top producers, such as Dupont in Victot-Pontfol and Pierre Huet in Cambremer, sell Calvados from "Vieux," aged a minimum of three years, to "X.O." or "Napoléon," aged from 6 to 25 years.

Many producers also offer Pommeau, an aperitif blending cider with a generous dose of Calvados.

ON THE HALF SHELL

Few places in France make an oyster lover happier than Normandy's Cotentin Peninsula.

Here, where the land juts into the sea a few miles beyond the Landing Beaches, are ports such as Blanville-sur-Mer, Granville, and particularly St-Vaast-La Hougue, where oystermen haul in tons of plump, briny oysters distinguished by a subtle note of hazelnut.

Enjoy a dozen on the half shell at many traditional restaurants in this region, accompanied by a saucer of shallot vinegar and brown bread.

OMELET EXTRAORDINAIRE

There is no more famous omelet in the world than the puffy, pillowlike confection offered at La Mère Poulard in Mont-Saint-Michel (☎ *02–33–89–68–68*).

Whipped with a balloon whisk in a large copper bowl, then cooked in a long-handled skillet over a wood fire, the omelet is delicately brown and crusted on the outside, as soft and airy as a soufflé within. Order the omelet with ham and cheese as a main course, or sugared and flambéed as a majestic dessert.

Updated by Jennifer Ladonne

The maritime Garden of Eden called Normandy sprawls out over France's northwestern corner in a shape roughly resembling a segment of a jigsaw puzzle. Due to its geographic position, this region is blessed with a stunning natural beauty, one that once inspired Maupassant and Monet. Little wonder today's sightseers pack into colorful Rouen, seaside Honfleur, and magnificent and magical Mont-St-Michel.

Happily, it is easy to escape all those travelers. Simply lose yourself along Normandy's spectacular cliff-lined coast and in the green spaces inland, where the closest thing to a crowd is a farmer with his herd of brown-and-white cows. But whatever road you turn down the region's time-stained history is there to enchant and fascinate. Say the name "Normandy," and which Channel-side scenario comes to mind?

Are you reminded of the dramatic silhouette of Mont-St-Michel looming above the tidal flats, its cobbles echoing with the footfalls of medieval scholars? Or do you think of iron-gray convoys massing silently at dawn, lowering tailgates to pour troops of young Allied infantrymen into the line of German machine-gun fire? At Omaha Beach you may marvel at the odds faced by the handful of soldiers who in June 1944 were able to rise above the waterfront carnage to capture the cliff-top battery, paving the way for the Allies' reconquest of Europe.

Perhaps you think of Joan of Arc—imprisoned by the English yet burned at the Rouen stake by the Church she believed in? In a modern church you may light a candle on the very spot where, in 1431, the Maiden Warrior sizzled into history at the hands of panicky politicians and time-serving clerics: a dark deed that marked a turning point in the Hundred Years' War. The destinies of England and Normandy have been intertwined ever since William, Duke of Normandy, insisted that King Edward the Confessor had promised him the succession to the English crown. When a royal council instead anointed the Anglo-Saxon Harold Godwinsson, the irate William stormed across the Channel with 7,000 well-equipped archers, well-mounted knights, and well-paid Frankish mercenaries. They landed at Pevensey Bay on September 28, 1066, and two weeks later, conquered at Hastings.

There followed nearly 400 years of Norman sovereignty in England. For generations England and Normandie (as the French spell it) blurred, merged, and diverged. Today you can still feel the strong flow of English culture over the Channel, from the Deauville horse races frequented by high-born ladies in gloves, to silver spoons mounded high with teatime cream; from the bowfront, slope-roof shops along the harbor at Honfleur to the black-and-white row houses of Rouen, which would seem just as much at home in the setting of *David Copperfield* as they are in *Madame Bovary.*

The French divide Normandy into two: Haute-Normandie and Basse-Normandie. Upper (Haute) Normandy is delineated by the Seine as it meanders northwest from Ile-de-France between chalky cliffs and verdant hills to Rouen—the region's cultural and commercial capital—and on to the port of Le Havre. Pebbly beaches and even more impressive chalk cliffs line the Côte d'Alabâtre (Alabaster Coast) from Le Havre to Dieppe. Lower (Basse) Normandy encompasses the sandy Côte Fleurie (Flower Coast), stretching from the resort towns of Trouville and Deauville to the D-Day landing beaches and the Cotentin Peninsula, jutting out into the English Channel. After the World War II D-Day landings, some of the fiercest fighting took place around Caen and Bayeux, as many monuments and memorials testify. Rising to the west is the fabled Mont-St-Michel. Our tour starts in Rouen, then heads north to the Channel Coast, which we follow all the way from Honfleur to Mont-St-Michel.

5

UPPER NORMANDY

From Rouen to the coast—the area known as Upper Normandy—medieval castles and abbeys stand guard above rolling countryside, while resort and fishing towns line the white cliffs of the Côte d'Alabâtre. In the 19th century, the dramatic scenery and bathing resorts along the coast attracted and inspired writers and artists like Maupassant, Monet, and Braque—and today it has the same effect on thousands of visitors.

ROUEN

Fodor's Choice ★ *32 km (20 mi) north of Louviers, 130 km (80 mi) northwest of Paris, 86 km (53 mi) east of Le Havre.*

"O Rouen, art thou then to be my final abode!" was the agonized cry of Joan of Arc as the English dragged her out to be burned alive on May 30, 1431. The exact spot of the pyre is marked by a concrete-and-metal cross in front of the Église Jeanne-d'Arc, an eye-catching modern church on Place du Vieux-Marché, just one of the many landmarks that make Rouen a fascinating destination. Known as the City of a Hundred Spires, Rouen is famed for its many important churches.

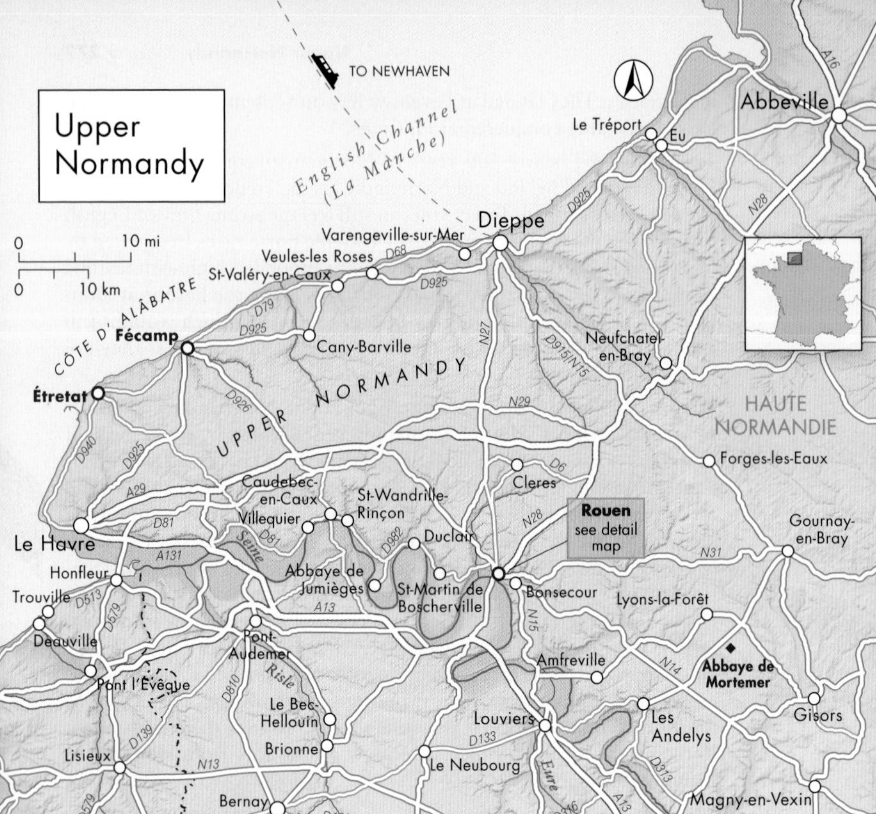

GETTING HERE

Trains from Paris (Gare St-Lazare) leave for Rouen every two hours or so (€19.50); the 85-mi trip takes 70 minutes. Change in Rouen for Dieppe (2 hrs from Paris, €26). Several trains daily link Rouen to Caen (90 mins, €22) and Fécamp (90 mins, €12.50), sometimes requiring a change to a bus at Bréauté-Beuzeville.

Visitor Information Rouen Tourist Office (✉ *25 pl. de la Cathédrale* ☎ *02-32-08-32-40* 🌐 *www.rouentourisme.com*).

EXPLORING

Once the capital of the duchy of Normandy, Rouen overflows with monuments, medieval streets, and churches. Today a busy industrial port city of about a half-million people, it has inspired many along the way, including Gustave Flaubert and Claude Monet, who immortalized Rouen's great cathedral in a famous series of paintings. Although much of Rouen was destroyed during World War II, a wealth of medieval half-timber houses happily still lines the cobblestone streets, many of which are pedestrian-only—most famously Rue du Gros-Horloge between Place du Vieux-Marché and the cathedral, suitably embellished halfway along with a giant Renaissance clock. This landmark, the Gros-Horloge, is featured on ninety-nine percent of the postcards sold in Rouen, so be sure to peer up at the real thing, especially as it lies at the heart of **Vieux Rouen** (Old Rouen), a district of tiny streets lined with hundreds of enchanting half-timber houses.

MONET IN 3-D

If you're familiar with the works of Impressionist artist Claude Monet, you'll immediately recognize Rouen cathedral's immense west front, rendered in an increasingly hazy fashion in his series *Cathédrales de Rouen*—you can enjoy a ringside view and a coffee at the Brasserie Paul, just opposite. The facade is illuminated by a free light show, based on Monet's canvases, for an hour every evening from June through mid-September.

5

TOP ATTRACTIONS

4 **Abbaye St-Ouen.** Next to the imposing Neoclassical City Hall, this stupendous example of high Gothic architecture is noted for its stained-glass windows, dating from the 14th to the 16th century. They are the most spectacular grace notes of the spare interior along with the 19th-century pipe organ, among the finest in France. ✉ *Pl. du Général-de-Gaulle, Hôtel de Ville* ☎ *02–32–08–32–40* ⏲ *Apr.–Oct., Wed.–Mon. 10–12:30 and 2–5:30; Nov.–Mar., Tues.–Thur. and weekends 10–12:30 and 2–4:30.*

1 **Cathédrale Notre-Dame.** Lording it over Rouen's "Hundred Spires" this cathedral is crowned with the highest spire in France, erected in 1876, a cast-iron tour-de-force rising 490 feet above the crossing. The original 12th-century construction was replaced after a devastating fire in 1200; only the left-hand spire, the **Tour St-Romain** (St. Romanus Tower), survived the flames. Construction on the imposing 250-foot steeple on the right, known as the **Tour de Beurre** (Butter Tower), was begun in the 15th century and completed in the 17th, when a group of wealthy citizens donated large sums of money for the privilege of continuing to eat butter during Lent. Interior highlights include the 13th-century choir, with its pointed arcades; vibrant stained glass depicting the crucified Christ (restored after heavy damage during World War II); and massive stone columns topped by some intriguing carved faces. The first flight of the famous **Escalier de la Librairie** (Library Stairway), attributed to Guillaume Pontifs (also responsible for most of the 15th-century work seen in the cathedral), rises from a tiny balcony just to the left of the transept. ✉ *Pl. de la Cathédrale, St-Maclou* ☎ *02–32–08–32–40* ⏲ *Daily 8–6.*

11 **Gros-Horloge.** The name of the pedestrian Rue du Gros-Horloge, Rouen's most popular street, comes from the Gros-Horloge itself, a giant Renaissance clock. In 1527 the Rouennais had a splendid arch built especially for it, and today its golden face looks out over the street. You can see the clock's inner workings from the 15th-century belfry. Though the street is crammed with stores, a few old houses, dating from the 16th century, remain. Wander through the surrounding **Vieux Rouen** (Old Rouen), a warren of tiny streets lined with more than 700 half-timber houses, many artfully transformed into fashionable shops. ✉ *Rue du Gros-Horloge, Vieux-Marché* 🎫 *€6* ⏲ *Apr.–Oct., Tues.–Sun. 10–7; Nov.–Mar., Tues.–Sun. 2–6.*

Abbaye St-Ouen 4
Aître St-Maclou 3
Cathédrale Notre-Dame 1
Église Jeanne d'Arc .. 10
Gros-Horloge 11
Musée des Antiquités 5
Musée des Beaux-Arts 6
Musée de la Céramique 8
Musée Le Secq des Tournelles 7
St-Maclou 2
Tour Jeanne-d'Arc 9

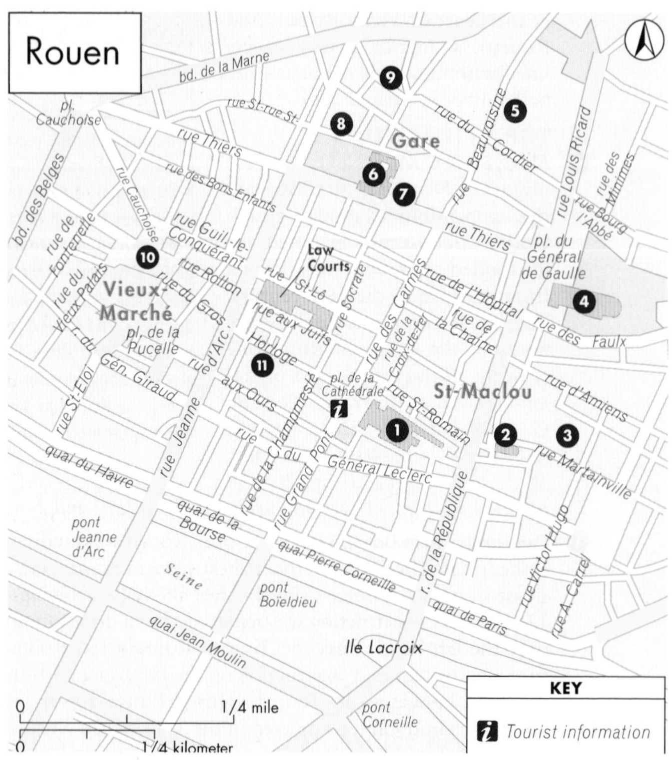

6 **Musée des Beaux-Arts** *(Fine Arts Museum)*. One of Rouen's cultural mainstays, this museum is famed for its scintillating collection of paintings and sculptures from the 16th to the 20th century, including works by native son Géricault as well as by David, Rubens, Caravaggio, Velasquez, Poussin, Delacroix, Chassériau, Degas, and Modigliani. Most popular of all, however, is the impressive Impressionist gallery, with Monet, Renoir, and Sisley, and the Postimpressionist School of Rouen headed by Albert Lebourg and Gustave Loiseau. ✉ *Square Verdrel, Gare* ☎ *02–35–71–28–40* 🌐 *www.rouen-musees.com* 🎟 *€5, €8 includes Musée Le Secq des Tournelles and Musée de la Céramique* ⏲ *Wed.–Mon. 10–6.*

2 **St-Maclou.** A late-Gothic masterpiece, this church sits across Rue de la République behind the cathedral and bears testimony to the wild excesses of Flamboyant architecture. Take time to examine the central and left-hand portals of the main facade, covered with little bronze lion heads and pagan engravings. Inside, note the 16th-century organ, with its Renaissance wood carving, and the fine marble columns. ✉ *Pl. St-Maclou, St-Maclou* ☎ *02–32–08–32–40* ⏲ *Mon.–Sat. 10–noon and 2–6, Sun. 3–5:30.*

9 **Tour Jeanne-d'Arc.** Sole remnant of the early-13th-century castle built by French king Philippe-Auguste, this beefy, pointed-top circular tower is

a fine photo-op. Inside you'll find a small exhibit of documents and models charting the history of the castle where Joan of Arc was tried and held prisoner in 1430. ✉ *Rue Bouvreuil, Gare* ☎ *02–35–98–16–21* 🎫 *€1.50* ⏲ *Mon. and Wed.–Sat. 10–12:30 and 2–6, Sun. 2–6:30.*

WORTH NOTING

3 **Aître St-Maclou.** A former ossuary (a charnel house used for the bodies of plague victims), this is a reminder of the plague that devastated Europe during the Middle Ages; these days it holds Rouen's Fine Art Academy. French composer Camille Saint-Saëns (1835–1921) is said to have been inspired by the ossuary when he was working on his *Danse Macabre*. The half-timber courtyard, where you can wander at leisure and maybe visit a picture exhibition, contains graphic carvings of skulls, bones, and grave diggers' tools. ✉ *186 rue Martainville, St-Maclou.*

10 **Église Jeanne d'Arc** *(Joan of Arc Church)*. Dedicated to Joan of Arc, this church was built in the 1970s on the spot where she was burned to death in 1431. The aesthetic merit of its odd cement-and-wood design is debatable—the shape of the roof is *supposed* to evoke the flames of Joan's fire. Not all is new, however: the church showcases some remarkable 16th-century stained-glass windows taken from the former Église St-Vincent, bombed out in 1944. The adjacent **Musée Jeanne-d'Arc** evokes Joan's history with waxworks and documents. ✉ *33 pl. du Vieux-Marché, Vieux-Marché* ☎ *02–35–88–02–70* 🌐 *www.jeanne-darc.com* 🎫 *Museum €4* ⏲ *Museum mid-Apr.–mid-Sept., daily 9:30–7; mid-Sept.–mid-Apr., daily 10–noon and 2–6:30.*

8 **Musée de la Céramique** *(Ceramics Museum)*. A superb array of local pottery and European porcelain can be admired at this museum, housed in an elegant mansion near the Musée des Beaux-Arts. ✉ *1 rue Faucon, Gare* ☎ *02–35–07–31–74* 🎫 *€3, €8 includes Musée Le Secq des Tournelles and Musée des Beaux-Arts* ⏲ *Wed.–Mon. 10–1 and 2–6.*

5 **Musée des Antiquités.** Gallo-Roman glassware and mosaics, medieval tapestries and enamels, and Moorish ceramics vie for attention at this collection, an extensive antiquities museum housed in a former monastery dating from the 17th century. A new display devoted to natural history, which includes some skeletons dating to prehistoric times, opened in February 2007. ✉ *198 rue Beauvoisine, Gare* ☎ *02–35–98–55–10* 🎫 *€3* ⏲ *Tues.–Sat. 10–12:15 and 1:30–5:30, Sun. 2–6.*

7 **Musée Le Secq des Tournelles** *(Wrought-Iron Museum). Set* near the Musée des Beaux-Arts, this claims to have the world's finest collection of wrought iron, with exhibits spanning from the 4th through the 19th century. The displays, imaginatively housed in a converted medieval church, include the professional instruments of surgeons, barbers, carpenters, clockmakers, and gardeners. ✉ *2 rue Jacques-Villon, Gare* ☎ *02–35–88–42–92* 🎫 *€3, €8 includes Musée des Beaux-Arts and Musée de la Céramique* ⏲ *Wed.–Mon. 10–1 and 2–6.*

NEED A BREAK?

The friendly Maison Hardy (✉ *Pl. du Vieux-Marché, Vieux-Marché* ☎ *02–35–71–81–55*) offers zestful service and a splendid view of the picturesque market square, scene of the burning of Joan of Arc, whose story is retraced in colorful frescoes on the café wall.

WHERE TO EAT

$$–$$$ FRENCH Fodor's Choice ★ **Gill Côté Bistro.** With two Michelin stars under his toque for his tony gastronomic restaurant Gill, chef Gilles Tournadre jumped at the chance to open a contemporary bistro on Rouen's storied Place du Vieux-Marché. The atmosphere is sleek and modern, and the updated bistro fare, which has the distinct advantage of being served up seven days a week, consists of inspired versions of much-loved French classics, like tête de veau with sauce gribich (a caper, parsley, and cornichon Hollandaise) and andoillette, along with more contemporary dishes, like a piquant Caesar salad. Portions are ample and the small but choice menu—with a great-value €22 fixed-price option—changes monthly. *14 pl. du Vieux-Marché, Vieux-Marché 02–35–89–88–72 DC, MC, V.*

> **THE MESSENGER**
>
> Before Joan of Arc was torched on Rouen's Place du Vieux-Marché, she asked a friar to hold a crucifix high in the air and to shout out assurances of her salvation so that she could hear him above the roar of the fire.

$$$$ FRENCH Fodor's Choice ★ **La Couronne.** If P.T. Barnum, Florenz Ziegfeld, and Cecil B. DeMille had put together a spot distilling all the charm and glamour of Normandy, this would be it. Behind a half-timber facade gushing geraniums, the "oldest inn in France," dating from 1345, is a sometimes-ersatz extravaganza crammed with stained leaded glass, sculpted wood beams, marble Norman chimneys, leather-upholstered chairs, and damasked curtains. The Salon Jeanne d'Arc is the largest room and has a wonderful wall-wide sash window and quaint paintings, but the only place to sit is the adorably cozy, wood-lined Salon des Rôtisseurs, an antiquarian's delight. The star attractions on Vincent Taillefer's €33 menu—lobster soufflé, sheeps' feet, duck in blood sauce—make few modern concessions. Dine at La Couronne and you'll be adding your name to a list that includes Sophia Loren, John Wayne, Jean-Paul Sartre, Salvador Dalí, and Princess Grace of Monaco. *31 pl. du Vieux-Marché, Vieux-Marché 02–35–71–40–90 www.lacouronne.com AE, DC, MC, V.*

$$ FRENCH **La Toque d'Or.** Overlooking the Église Jeanne d'Arc, this large, bustling restaurant has been renowned since time immemorial for Normandy classics such as veal with Camembert flamed in Calvados, breast of duck glazed in cider, or spicy braised turbot. Try the excellent house-smoked salmon (they'll give you a tour of the smokehouse if you wish) and the Norman apple *tarte soufflée. 11 pl. du Vieux-Marché, Vieux-Marché 02–35–71–46–29 AE, MC, V.*

WHERE TO STAY

$ ★ **Cathédrale.** There are enough half-timbered walls and beams here to fill a super-luxe hotel, but the happy news is that this is a budget option—even better, it is found on a narrow pedestrian street just behind the cathedral. Ensconsced in a 17th-century building, the pretty Normand decor begins in the lobby, extends to the large dining room—fitted out with grand 17th-century-style chairs and a historic fireplace—and crescendos in the flower-laden patio, a green oasis oh-so-picturesquely framed with walls of timber and stucco. Done largely in pastel patterns, guest rooms are petite but neat and comfortable; No. 7 is the largest.

DID YOU KNOW?

Dating from the 14th century, the Gros-Horloge clock is the heart of Vieux Rouen, a warren of tiny streets lined with more than 700 half-timber houses, many gorgeously transformed into shops.

Breakfast is served in the beamed tearoom. **Pros:** storybook decor; can't-be-beat location. **Cons:** small rooms; no car access. ✉ *12 rue St-Romain, St-Maclou* ☎ *02–35–71–57–95* 🌐 *www.hotel-de-la-cathedrale.fr* *26 rooms* *In-room: no a/c, Wi-Fi. In-hotel: bar, parking (paid), some pets allowed* *AE, MC, V.*

$–$$ **Dieppe.** Established in 1880, the Dieppe remains up-to-date thanks to resolute management by five generations of the Guéret family. Staff members also are helpful, and they speak English. The compact rooms are cheerful and modern (No. 22 is the largest); street noise can be a problem, however, despite double-glazed windows. The restaurant, Les Quatre Saisons (no lunch Saturday), serves seasonal dishes with an emphasis on fish, such as the sole Michèle (poached in a light wine sauce), but is best known for its pressed duckling. **Pros:** personal service; handy for train station. **Cons:** lacks character; a bit away from city center. ✉ *Pl. Bernard-Tissot, Gare* ☎ *02–35–71–96–00* 🌐 *www.hotel-dieppe.fr* *41 rooms* *In-room: no a/c, Wi-Fi. In-hotel: restaurant, bar, some pets allowed* *AE, MC, V* *MAP.*

$$–$$$ **Mercure Centre.** In the jumble of streets near the cathedral—a navigational challenge if you arrive by car—this modern chain hotel has small, comfortable guest rooms done in breezy pastels. The hotel is handy for exploring the old streets of the city center. **Pros:** functional; central. **Cons:** featureless decor; hard to find. ✉ *7 rue de la Croix-de-Fer, St-Maclou* ☎ *02–35–52–69–52* 🌐 *www.mercure.com* *125 rooms* *In-room: a/c, safe, refrigerator, Wi-Fi. In-hotel: bar, parking (paid), some pets allowed* *AE, DC, MC, V* *BP.*

¢–$ **Vieux Carré.** In the heart of Old Rouen, this cute hotel has small, practical, and comfortable rooms furnished with a taste for the exotic: lamps from Egypt, tables from Morocco, and 1940s English armoires. Ask for one of the rooms on the third floor for a view of the cathedral; No. 23 is the prettiest. Breakfast and lunch are served in the leafy courtyard, weather permitting, or in the cozy little bistro (closed Sunday) off the reception area. Lunches are light and simple. **Pros:** charming; central. **Cons:** small rooms; hard to park. ✉ *34 rue Ganterie, Gare,* ☎ *02–35–71–67–70* *14 rooms* *In-room: no a/c, Wi-Fi. In-hotel: restaurant, some pets allowed* *AE, DC, MC, V.*

NIGHTLIFE AND THE ARTS

The **Fête Jeanne d'Arc** *(Joan of Arc Festival)* takes place on the Sunday nearest to May 30, with parades, street plays, concerts, exhibitions, and a medieval market.Operas, plays, and concerts are staged at the **Théâtre des Arts** (✉ *7 rue du Dr-Rambert, Vieux-Marché* ☎ *02–35–71–41–36* 🌐 *www.operaderouen.com*). Visit the popular local haunt **Bar de la Crosse** (✉ *53 rue de l'Hôpital, St-Maclou* ☎ *02–35–70–16–68*) for an aperitif and a good chat with some friendly Rouennais.

FÉCAMP

Visitor Information Fécamp Tourist Office. ✉ *113 rue Alexandre-le-Grand* ☎ *02–35–28–51–01* 🌐 *www.fecamptourisme.com.*

The ancient cod-fishing port of Fécamp was once a major pilgrimage site. The magnificent abbey church, **Abbaye de La Trinité** (✉ *Rue Leroux*

), bears witness to Fécamp's religious past. The Benedictine abbey was founded by the Duke of Normandy in the 11th century and became the home of the monastic order of the Précieux Sang de la Trinité (Precious Blood of the Trinity—referring to Christ's blood, which supposedly arrived here in the 7th century in a reliquary from the Holy Land).

Fécamp is also the home of Benedictine liqueur. The **Palais de la Bénédictine** *(Benedictine Palace)*, across from the tourist office, is a florid building dating from 1892 that mixes neo-Gothic and Renaissance styles. Watery pastiche or taste-tingling architectural cocktail? Whether you're shaken or stirred, this remains one of Normandy's most popular attractions. The interior is just as exhausting as the facade. Paintings, sculptures, ivories, advertising posters, and fake bottles of Benedictine compete for attention with a display of the ingredients used for the liqueur, and a chance to sample it. There's also a shop selling Benedictine products and souvenirs. ⊠ *110 rue Alexandre-le-Grand* ☎ *02–35–10–26–10* 🌐 *www.benedictine.fr* 🎫 *€6* ⏲ *July and Aug., daily 10–7; Sept.–Dec. and Feb.–June, daily 10–12:45 and 2–6.*

5

WHERE TO EAT

$$ FRENCH ★ ✕ **La Marée.** Overlooking Fécamp's lively harbor, this popular seafood restaurant makes up in conviviality what it lacks in charm. Considering the number of seafood *plateaux* that breeze by, it seems no one pays much attention to decor anyway. For sheer volume, the dishes will please even the most insatiable gourmand, then factor in variety and freshness (most everything is caught locally) and you've got a winning combo. Gigantic langoustine, plump crabs, and the renowned Fécamp herring are standouts, along with a nice variety of warm dishes, including a sensational whole grilled sole and a hearty local specialty: salt cod poached in Normandy cream. At €22, the lunch *formule* is a good bargain. ⊠ *77 quai Bérigny* ☎ *02–35–29–39–15* 🌐 *www.fecamp-restaurant-la-maree.com* 💳 *AE, DC, MC, V* ⏲ *Closed Mon. No dinner Sun. and Thurs.*

$ SEAFOOD ✕ **L'Escalier.** This delightfully simple little restaurant, right by the bustling, mast-peppered harbor, serves traditional Norman cuisine with, as you might expect in the region's foremost port, fish, and seafood at the top of the menu. Try the homemade fish soup or mussels in Calvados with French fries. Portions are generous. Desserts don't always measure up to the rest of the meal—the tarte tatin (overturned apple tart) has been known to be a shade limp—but the cozy ambience and great-value €14 set menu make this the perfect quayside spot for a quick, nourishing meal. ⊠ *101 quai Bérigny* ☎ *02–35–28–26–79* ✍ *Reservations essential* 💳 *AE, MC, V* ⏲ *Closed Dec. and Thurs. out of season.*

THE ALABASTER COAST

Named for the white cliffs that stretch between Dieppe and Le Havre, the scenic Côte d'Alabâtre attracted writers and artists like Maupassant, Proust, and Monet in the 19th century. Perhaps they were inspired by the area's châteaux and rock formations, but they probably didn't spend time sunbathing in their Speedos; the coast is known for its *galets*—large pebbles that cover the beaches.

WHERE TO STAY

$ **Auberge de la Rouge.** The Enderlins welcome you to this little inn just south of Fécamp. Guest rooms overlook the garden and are actually good-size lofts—quaint ladders lead you to balcony beds—that sleep four. The restaurant (closed Monday; no dinner Sunday) showcases modern classics by chef Paul Durel, such as scallops with ham and leek shoots, and local specialties like roast turbot, veal and mushrooms in wine, or beef with toasted thyme. Top it off, if you can, with a local favorite, soufflé *à la Bénédictine*. **Pros:** spacious rooms; family feel. **Cons:** away from town center; busy road outside. ✉ *1 rue du Bois-de-Boclon, 1 km (½ mi) south of Fécamp, St-Léonard* ☎ *02–35–28–07–59* 🌐 *www.auberge-rouge.com* *8 rooms* *In-room: no a/c, refrigerator. In-hotel: restaurant, Internet terminal, Wi-Fi hotspot, some pets allowed* *AE, MC, V* *BP.*

$ **La Ferme de la Chapelle.** The charm of this former priory lies neither in the simple, comfortable guest rooms around the courtyard nor in the restaurant with its no-frills €24 menu, but rather in its outstanding location high atop the cliffs overlooking Fécamp. There's a breathtaking, dramatic view over the entire coastline—explore it on an invigorating hike along the nearby coastal footpath. The €140 split-level family room can accommodate up to five people. **Pros:** spectacular setting; good-value meals. **Cons:** not central; often fully booked for conferences. ✉ *Côte de la Vierge* ☎ *02–35–10–12–12* 🌐 *www.fermedelachapelle.fr* *17 rooms, 5 studios* *In-room: no a/c. In-hotel: restaurant, room service, pool, some pets allowed* *AE, DC, MC, V* *MAP.*

ÉTRETAT

17 km (11 mi) southwest of Fécamp via D940, 88 km (55 mi) northwest of Rouen.

The plunging chalk cliffs of Etretat are so gorgeous and strange that they seem surreal at first. The crowds of camera-toting visitors, however, will bring you back to reality very quickly. But if you head for the cliffs in early morning or late evening, you'll see what drew artists like Monet, Boudin, and Maupassant here. Chances are you'll be just as inspired by this natural beauty as old Claude was.

GETTING HERE

There are no trains to Étretat. Your best bet is to take the bus from either Fécamp (30 mins) or Le Havre (60 mins). Occasional trains from Paris (Gare St-Lazare) are met at Bréauté-Beuzeville station, between Rouen and Le Havre, by a bus that reaches Étretat in 30 minutes. For further train information, contact SNCF (☎ *08–36–35–35–35*).

Visitor Information **Étretat Tourist Office.** ✉ *Place Maurice Guillard* ☎ *02–35–27–05–21* 🌐 *www.etretat.net.*

EXPLORING

Fodor's Choice ★ This large village, with its promenade running the length of the pebble beach, is renowned for the magnificent tall rock formations that extend out into the sea. The **Falaises d'Étretat** are white cliffs that are as famous in France as Dover's are in England—and have been painted by many artists, Claude Monet chief among them. At low tide it's possible to walk through the huge archways formed by the rocks to neighboring beaches. The biggest arch is at the **Falaise d'Aval,** to the south. For a breathtaking view of the whole bay, take the path up to the top of the Falaise d'Aval. From here you can hike for miles across the Manneporte Hills.or play a round of golf on one of Europe's windiest and most scenic courses, overlooking **L'Aiguille** (The Needle), a 300-foot spike of rock jutting out of the sea just off the coast. To the north towers the **Falaise d'Amont,** topped by the chapel of Notre-Dame de la Garde.

WHERE TO EAT AND STAY

$$$ SEAFOOD **Les Roches Blanches.** The exterior of this family-owned restaurant off the beach is a post–World War II concrete eyesore. But take a table by the window with a view of the cliffs, order the superb fresh seafood (try the tuna steak or the sea bass roasted in Calvados or champagne), and you'll be glad you came. Reservations are essential for Sunday lunch. *Rue de l'Abbé-Cochet* *02–35–27–07–34* *MC, V* *Closed Wed. and Nov.–Feb.*

$$$–$$$$ ★ **Domaine Saint Clair Le Donjon.** From the looks of this charming ivy-covered, Anglo-Norman château, it is easy to understand why Monet, Proust, Offenbach, and other greats accepted invitations here. Built overlooking Étretat by a rich Parisian couple in 1862, the Belle Époque house, replete with storybook tower, was built in a private park and affords lovely sea views. Guest rooms are spacious, comfortable, quiet, and individually furnished, with the emphasis on "individual"—vast swaths of red fabric, decorator mirrors, and antique gramophones are some flamboyant accents, while other rooms are stylish enough for *Maison Française*. For a spectacular view, request the Oriental Suite, the Horizon Room, or the Marjorie Room. Thomas Sakic's dramatic cuisine, ranging from warm hare terrine to scallops and salmon in cider, is dished up in a cozy, romantic restaurant. Rooms are reserved on a half-board basis on weekends. **Pros:** grand architecture; gorgeous setting. **Cons:** pricey; strident decor in some rooms. *Chemin de St-Clair* *02–35–27–08–23* *www.hoteletretat.com* *21 rooms* *In-room: no a/c, Wi-Fi. In-hotel: restaurant, bar, pool, parking (free), some pets allowed* *AE, DC, MC, V* *MAP.*

¢–$ **Résidence.** The cheapest rooms in this picturesque 16th-century house in the heart of Étretat are pretty basic—both the bathroom and the shower are in the hallway—but the more expensive have in-room bathrooms, and one even has a hot tub. The service is friendly; the staff is young and energetic. The brasserie-type restaurant on the ground floor, La Salamandre, is rather cutting-edge for the region; all products are certified organic, farm-raised, and homemade, from the vegetable terrine to the nougat ice cream. In winter a fire crackles in the hearth. **Pros:** great value; eco-friendly restaurant. **Cons:** spartan facilities; unsavvy staff. *4 bd. du Président-René-Coty* *02–35–27–02–87* *www.hotellaresidenceetretat.com* *15 rooms* *In-room: no a/c. In-hotel: restaurant* *MC, V* *BP.*

5

SPORTS

Don't miss the chance to play at **Golf d'Étretat** (✉ *Rte. du Havre* ☎ *02–35–27–04–89*), where the breathtaking 6,580-yard, par-72 course drapes across the cliff tops of the Falaise d'Aval; it's closed Tuesday.

HONFLEUR TO MONT-ST-MICHEL

Basse Normandy (Lower Normandy) begins to the west of the Seine Estuary, near the Belle Époque resort towns of Trouville and Deauville, extending out to the sandy Côte Fleurie (Flower Coast), stretching northwest from the D-Day landing sites past Omaha Beach and on to Utah Beach and the Cotentin Peninsula, which juts out into the English Channel. After the World War II D-Day landings, some of the fiercest fighting took place around Caen and Bayeux, as many monuments and memorials testify. Heading south, in the prosperous Pays d'Auge, dairy farms produce the region's famous cheeses. Rising to the west is the fabled Mont-St-Michel. Inland, heading back toward central France, lush green meadows and apple orchards cover the countryside starting west of the market town of Lisieux—the heart of Calvados country.

HONFLEUR

Fodor's Choice ★ *35 km (22 mi) southwest of Etretat via D940, A131, and D579, 80 km (50 mi) west of Rouen.*

Honfleur is the most interesting of the Côte Fleurie's little seaside towns. Much of the city's Renaissance architecture remains intact, especially around the 17th-century Vieux Bassin harbor, which is almost as supremely colorful as in the days when the great Impressionist masters often painted it. The town has become increasingly crowded since the opening of the elegant Pont de Normandie, providing a direct link with Le Havre and Upper Normandy. (The world's largest cable-stayed bridge, it's supported by two concrete pylons taller than the Eiffel Tower and is designed to resist winds of 160 mph.) Honfleur, full of half-timber houses and cobbled streets, and once an important departure point for maritime expeditions, including the first voyages to Canada in the 15th and 16th centuries, remains a time-burnished place.

GETTING HERE

To get to Honfleur, take the bus from Deauville (30 mins, €2.05); from Caen (1 hr, 45 mins; €7.20); or from Le Havre (30 mins, €4.10). Buses run every two hours or so and are operated by **Bus Verts du Calvados** (☎ *08–10–21–42–14* 🌐 *www.busverts.fr*).

Visitor Information **Honfleur Tourist Office.** ✉ *9 rue de la Ville* ☎ *02–31–89–23–30* 🌐 *en.ot-honfleur.fr.*

EXPLORING

Honfleur is beloved as one of France's most picturesque ports. Its 17th-century harbor is fronted on one side by two-story stone houses with low, sloping roofs and on the other by tall, narrow houses whose wooden facades are topped by slate roofs. Note that parking can be a

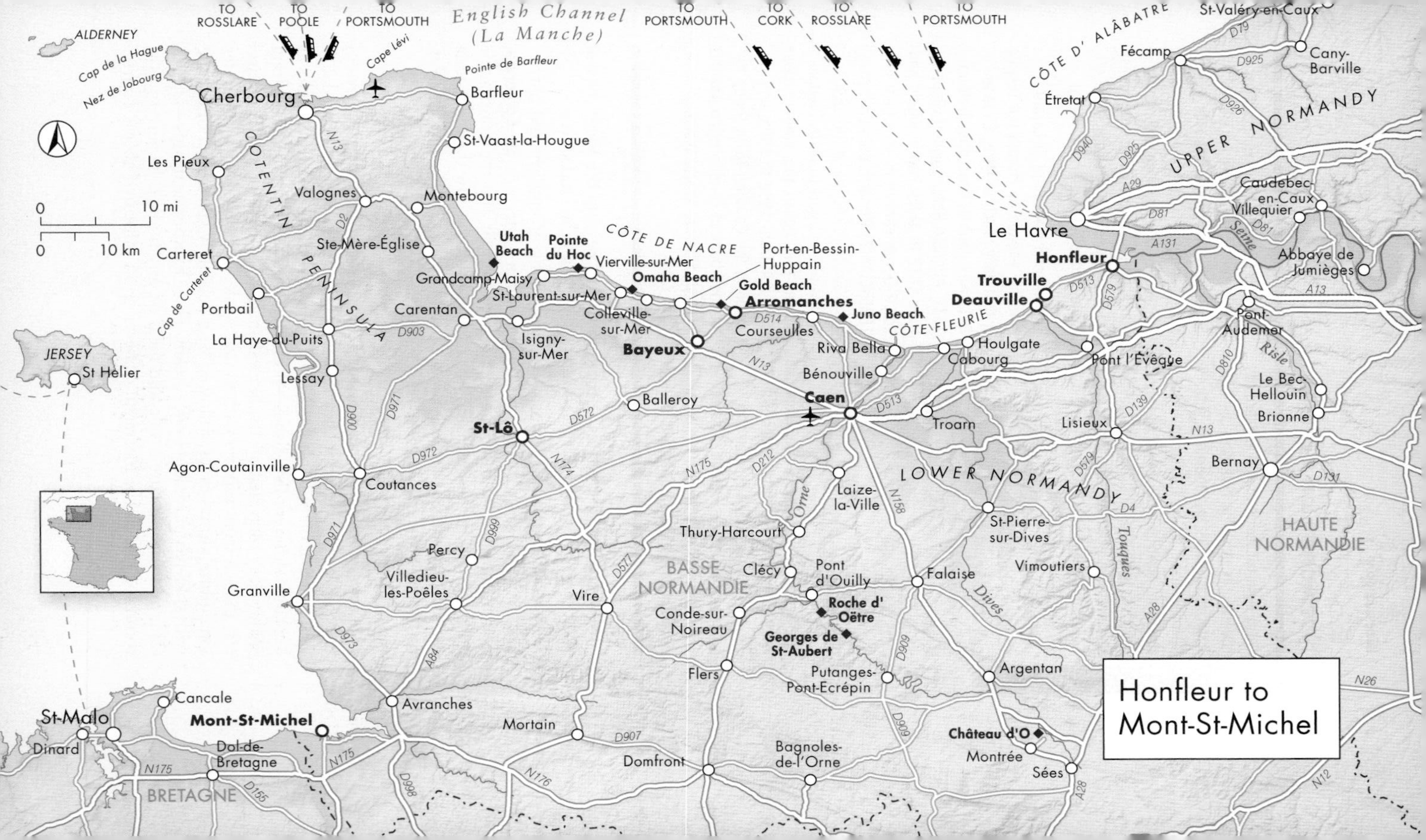

Honfleur to Mont-St-Michel
English Channel (La Manche)
TO ROSSLARE
TO POOLE
TO PORTSMOUTH
TO PORTSMOUTH
TO CORK
TO ROSSLARE
TO PORTSMOUTH
ALDERNEY
Cap de la Hague
Nez de Jobourg
Cape Lévi
Pointe de Barfleur
Cherbourg
Barfleur
St-Vaast-la-Hougue
Les Pieux
COTENTIN PENINSULA
Valognes
Montebourg
Ste-Mère-Église
Carteret
Cap de Carteret
Portbail
La Haye-du-Puits
Lessay
JERSEY
St Helier
Utah Beach
Pointe du Hoc
Grandcamp-Maisy
St-Laurent-sur-Mer
Vierville-sur-Mer
Omaha Beach
Colleville-sur-Mer
Carentan
Isigny-sur-Mer
CÔTE DE NACRE
Port-en-Bessin-Huppain
Gold Beach
Arromanches
Juno Beach
Courseulles
Riva Bella
Bénouville
Bayeux
Balleroy
St-Lô
Caen
CÔTE FLEURIE
Cabourg
Houlgate
Deauville
Trouville
Honfleur
Troarn
Le Havre
Étretat
Fécamp
CÔTE D' ALÂBATRE
St-Valéry-en-Caux
Cany-Barville
UPPER NORMANDY
Caudebec-en-Caux
Villequier
Seine
Abbaye de Jumièges
Pont-Audemer
Risle
Pont l'Évêque
Le Bec-Hellouin
Brionne
Lisieux
Bernay
LOWER NORMANDY
HAUTE NORMANDIE
Agon-Coutainville
Coutances
Laize-la-Ville
Orne
Thury-Harcourt
St-Pierre-sur-Dives
Touques
Percy
Villedieu-les-Poêles
BASSE NORMANDIE
Clécy
Pont d'Ouilly
Falaise
Vimoutiers
Dives
Granville
Vire
Conde-sur-Noireau
Roche d' Oëtre
Georges de St-Aubert
Flers
Putanges-Pont-Ecrépin
Argentan
Cancale
St-Malo
Dinard
Mont-St-Michel
Avranches
Mortain
Dol-de-Bretagne
BRETAGNE
Domfront
Bagnoles-de-l'Orne
Château d'O
Montrée
Sées
N13
D2
D903
D900
D971
D972
D572
N174
D999
D973
A84
D577
N175
D212
N158
D514
D513
D579
D139
D810
D131
D4
A28
N26
N12
D909
D907
N176
D998
D155
D79
D925
D926
D940
A29
D81
A131
A13
0
10 mi
0
10 km

CLOSE UP

Normandy on Canvas

Long before Claude Monet created his Giverny lily pond by diverting the Epte River that marks the boundary with Ile-de-France, artists had been scudding into Normandy. For two watery reasons: the Seine and the sea. Just downstream from Vernon, where the Epte joins the Seine, Richard the Lion-Hearted's ruined castle at Les Andelys, immortalized by Paul Signac and Félix Vallotton, heralds the soft-lighted, cliff-lined Seine Valley, impressionistically evoked by Albert Lebourg and Gustave Loiseau in the Arts Museum in Rouen—where Camille Corot once studied, and whose mighty cathedral Monet painted until he was pink, purple, and blue in the face.

The Seine joins the sea at Le Havre, where Monet grew up, a protégé of Eugène Boudin, often termed the precursor of Impressionism. Boudin would boat across the estuary from Honfleur, where he hobnobbed with Gustave Courbet, Charles Daubigny, and Alfred Sisley at the Ferme St-Siméon. Le Havre in the 1860s was base camp for Monet and his pals Frédéric Bazille and Johan Barthold Jongkind to explore the rugged coast up to Dieppe, with easels opened en route beneath the cliffs of Étretat.

The railroad from Gare St-Lazare (smokily evoked by Monet) put Dieppe within easy reach of Paris. Eugène Delacroix daubed seascapes here in 1852. Auguste Renoir visited Dieppe from 1878 to 1885; Paul Gauguin and Edgar Degas clinked glasses here in 1885; Camille Pissarro painted his way from Gisors to Dieppe in the 1890s. As the nearest port to Paris, Dieppe wowed the English, too. Walter Sickert moved in from 1898 to 1905, and artists from the Camden Town Group he founded back in London often painted in Dieppe before World War I.

problem. Your best bet is the parking lot just beyond the Vieux-Bassin (Old Harbor) on the left as you approach from the land side.

★ Soak up the seafaring atmosphere by strolling around the old harbor and paying a visit to the ravishing wooden church of **Ste-Catherine,** which dominates a tumbling square. The church and the ramshackle belfry across the way were built by townspeople to show their gratitude for the departure of the English at the end of the Hundred Years' War, in 1453. ✉ *Rue des Logettes* ☎ *02-31-89-11-83.*

WHERE TO EAT

$$$–$$$$ FRENCH ✕ **Le Fleur de Sel.** A low-beamed 16th-century fisherman's house provides the cozy atmosphere for chef Vincent's Guyon's locally influenced cuisine centered on the daily catch. The ambitious menu usually includes at least five different fish dishes—presented with artistic panache—along with plenty of grilled meats, like salt-marsh lamb or pigeon. For starters, the sea trout tartare, with oyster, apple, and lime with a coriander vinaigrette, draws raves, followed by a delicately spiced filet of dorade with split-pea puree and oyster cream. Three fixed-price menus—at €28, €38, and €58—assure a splendid meal on any budget. Be sure to save room for one of the masterful desserts or an informed cheese course.

Relentlessly picturesque Honfleur has been immortalized by many painters, most famously by J. M. W. Turner and Eugène Boudin.

✉ 17 rue Haute ☎ 02–31–89–01–92 ⊕ www.lafleurdesel-honfleur.com ▭ AE, MC, V ⊙ Closed Tues. and Wed. and Jan.

$$$$ FRENCH ✕ **Sa.Qua.Na.** Chef Alexandre Bourdas earned his first Michelin star in 2008, a mere nine months after opening, and single-handedly put Honfleur on the gastronomic map. From the small but ravishing dining room to the impeccable presentation, his restaurant is a study in getting it right down to the smallest detail. Surprising combinations—dorade with pigs' feet and edamame beans; roast chicken with blood orange and juniper—attest to Bourdas's far-flung influences: his native Aveyron, Japan (where he cooked for three years), and the regional fare he seeks out daily from local farmers and fishermen. Having also worked as a pastry chef, Bourdas creates all of his own desserts, like the glorious *feuille de nougatine cacao* with white chocolate and black truffles. Along with two sublime tasting menus, the chef has thoughtfully provided an €18 menu for kids under 10. Bien sûr, reserve well in advance. *✉ 22 Pl. Hamelin ☎ 02–31–89–40–80 ⊕ www.alexandre-bourdas.com ▭ MC, V ⊙ Closed Sun. and Mon. and Jan. and Feb. No lunch weekdays.*

WHERE TO STAY

$$$$ ★ **Ferme St-Siméon.** The story goes that this 19th-century manor house was the birthplace of Impressionism, and that its park inspired Monet and Sisley. Inside, the decor is a rich mix of 19th-century elegance—rich fabrics, grand paintings, Louis Seize chairs—and down-home Norman delights, with rustic antiques, ancient beams, and half-timbered walls casting a deliciously cozy spell. Guest rooms are opulent, with pastel colors, floral wallpaper, antiques, and period accents. Those in the

converted stables are quieter but have less character. Be aware, however, that the high prices have more to do with the hotel's reputation than with the amenities it offers (although spa treatments are among them). Under chef Patrick Ogheard, the sophisticated restaurant specializes in fish; the cheese board does justice to the region, as does the €129 gastronomic menu. A second (slightly) more modest restaurant, La Table Toutain, opened in 2007. **Pros:** famed historic charm. **Cons:** expensive; bland annex rooms. ✉ *Rue Adolphe-Marais on D513 to Trouville* ☎ *02–31–81–78–00* 🌐 *www.fermesaintsimeon.fr* *32 rooms, 3 suites* *In-room: no a/c, refrigerator, Wi-Fi. In-hotel: 2 restaurants, tennis court, pool, some pets allowed* *AE, MC, V* *MAP.*

$$–$$$ ★ **La Petite Folie.** Charming simply doesn't suffice to describe this beautifully renovated 1830s town house a stone's throw from Honfleur's old port (nearby landmark: the birthplace of composer Eric Satie). No luxury was spared in appointing the main house's five rooms, whose design credits read like an A-list of Paris notables, including fabrics by Pierre Frey and Porthault linens. Although lavished with antiques, the rooms feel surprisingly contemporary (flat-screen TVs), and the sleek, modern bathrooms are equipped with glassed-in showers, except for the roomy La Directoire, which sports a capacious claw-foot tub. For those seeking a bit more space or privacy, the half-timbered 14th-century sea captain's house next door (complete with 400-year-old sailor's graffiti) offers three apartments, one more lovely than the next; the giant windows in the all-white top-floor suite affords a view to the water and gives the feel of an artist's loft. Add to all this a delightful garden and "folie" terrace out back, and the magic's complete. **Pros:** gracious welcome; a good value, with generous breakfast included. **Cons:** no-children-under-10 policy. ✉ *44 rue Haute* ☎ *02–35–52–69–52* 🌐 *www.lapetitefolie-honfleur.com* *5 rooms, 3 apartments* *In-room: a/c, Wi-Fi. In-hotel: parking (paid)* *MC, V* *BP.*

$$$–$$$$ ★ **Le Manoir du Butin.** An archetypal fin-de-siècle villa, this gorgeous half-timber, dormer-roof manor welcomes you with a pretty green-and-white facade in the Anglo-Norman style. Perched on top of a small wooded hill 200 yards from the sea, the hotel offers guest rooms with appetizing views, all traditionally and tastefully furnished, and with modern marble bathrooms. The room on the first floor has a four-poster bed and its own balcony. The atmospheric restaurant (closed Wednesday; no lunch Tuesday and Thursday) specializes in seasonal fish dishes such as a light lobster consommé and braised freshwater cod. **Pros:** exquisite decor; sea views; stylish bathrooms. **Cons:** away from town center; no elevator. ✉ *Phare du Butin* ☎ *02–31–81–63–00* 🌐 *www.hotel-lemanoir.fr* *10 rooms* *In-room: no a/c. In-hotel: restaurant, Internet terminal, Wi-Fi hotspot, some pets allowed* *AE, MC, V* *Closed Dec.–mid-Feb.* *MAP.*

NIGHTLIFE AND THE ARTS

The two-day **Fête des Marins** *(Marine Festival)* is held on Pentecost Sunday and Monday. On Sunday all the boats in the harbor are decked out in flags and paper roses, and a priest bestows his blessing at high tide. The next day, model boats and local children head a musical procession. There's also a five-day **Fête du Jazz** (Jazz Festival) in August.

DEAUVILLE-TROUVILLE

Fodor's Choice ★ *16 km (10 mi) southwest of Honfleur via D513, 92 km (57 mi) west of Rouen.*

Twin towns on the beach, divided only by the River Touques, Deauville and Trouville compete for the title of Most Extravagant Norman Town.

GETTING HERE

Trains to Deauville-Trouville (the station is between the two towns) from Gare St-Lazare in Paris (2 hrs, €29) often require a change at Lisieux. There are also buses to Deauville from Le Havre (1 hr, €6); Honfleur (30 mins, €2); and Caen (75 mins, €5). Buses run every two hours or so and are operated by **Bus Verts du Calvados** (☎ *08–10–21–42–14* 🌐 *www.busverts.fr*).

Visitor Information Deauville-Trouville Tourist Office ✉ *Pl. de la Mairie* ☎ *02–31–14–40–00* 🌐 *www.deauville.org.*

5

EXPLORING

Deauville and Trouville have distinctly different atmospheres, but it's easy (and common) to shuttle between them. Trouville—whose beaches were immortalized in the 19th-century paintings of Eugène Boudin (and *Gigi,* Vincente Minnelli's 1958 Oscar-winner)—is the oldest seaside resort in France. In the days of Louis-Philippe, it was discovered by artists and the upper crust; by the end of the Second Empire it was the beach à la mode. Then the Duc de Mornay, half brother of Napoléon III, and other aristocrats who were looking for something more exclusive, built their villas along the deserted beach across the Touques (more than a few of these were built simply as love-shacks for their mistresses).

Thus was launched Deauville, a vigorous grande dame who started kicking up her heels during the Second Empire, kept swinging through the Belle Époque, and is still frequented by a fair share of Rothschilds, princes, and movie stars. Few of them ever actually get in the water here, since other attractions—casino, theater, music hall, polo, galas, racecourses (some of the world's most fabled horse farms are here), marina and regattas, palaces and gardens, and extravagant shops along the Rue Eugène-Colas—compete for their attention. Fashionable avenues like Rue des Villas and Place Morny also entice. But perhaps Deauville is known best for its **Promenade des Planches**—the boardwalk extending along the seafront and lined with deck chairs, bars, striped cabanas, and an array of lovely half-timber Norman villas—*the* place for celebrity-spotting. With its high-price hotels, designer boutiques, and one of the smartest gilt-edge casinos in Europe, Deauville is often jokingly called Paris's 21st arrondissement.

HOOFBEATS YOU CAN BET ON

If you can't catch up with a Rothschild bidding on a new colt at Deauville's famous August yearling sales, aim for the Grand Prix de Deauville race held on the last Sunday in August. Throughout the summer, Deauville's Toques and Clairefontaine hippodromes hold horse races (or polo matches) nearly every afternoon.

Trouville—a short drive or five-minute boat trip across the Touques River from its more prestigious neighbor—remains more of a family resort, harboring few pretensions. If you'd like to see a typical French holiday spot rather than look for glamour, stay in Trouville. It, too, has a casino and boardwalk, an aquarium and bustling fishing port, a lively Sunday morning market, plus a native population that makes it a livelier spot out of season than Deauville.

WHERE TO EAT AND STAY

$$–$$$ FRENCH Fodor's Choice ★ **L'Essentiel.** A nice change from the grand, overly formal hotel dining rooms that dominate Deauville, the relaxed atmosphere and sensational cuisine at this contemporary eatery have made extremely popular. Chef Charles Thuillant, whose pedigree includes stints at two top Paris restaurants, focuses on a lighter, Asian-inspired cuisine, with Italian influences. Brimming with fresh, seasonal ingredients, the menu changes almost weekly. Dishes like lightly cooked salmon with paper-thin slices of green mango and a hint of lemon and pumpkin ravioli in a creamy parmesan broth bring this talented chef's mastery to the forefront. A capacious terrace, a choice selection of excellent wines by the glass, and a €18 midday prix-fixe menu on weekdays make this the perfect place to linger. ⊠ *29–31 rue Mirabeau* ☎ *02–31–87–22–11* ⊕ *www.lessentieldeauville.com* ▭ *AE, MC, V* ⊗ *Closed Mon. and Tues.*

$$$–$$$$ **81 L'Hôtel.** Reopened in 2007 after an extensive renovation, this compact boutique hotel pours on the gloss. Happily, the nicer original features of the 1906 mansion remain—parquet floors, magnificent fireplace, stained glass windows, impossibly high ceilings—while the usual postmodern touches (faux crocodile chairs, silver furniture, shrouded chandeliers, ersatz-Baroque beds) were added. Although on a main road, 81 is set back enough so that the guest rooms are quiet. The top-floor suite, No. 132, offers a nice view of the famous racetrack and others sport a terrace. Eight beautifully appointed and spacious studios next door feel like you've snagged your very own designer apartment. **Pros:** catering facilities available for take-out meals; easy parking. **Cons:** a bit of a walk to beach. ⊠ *81 av. de la République* ☎ *02–31–14–01–50* ⊕ *www.81lhotel.com* *21 rooms* *In-room: a/c, Wi-Fi. In-hotel: parking (free)* ▭ *AE, MC, V* *BP.*

¢–$ **Continental.** Vintage daguerrotypes prove that this is one of Deauville's oldest establisments (opened 1866) and its once-picturesque building—shoehorned into a triangle plot and topped with an elegant mansard roof—was painted by Eugène Boudin himself. The famed Impressionist wouldn't appreciate the modern signs that now blemish the exterior, but inside renovations have created an inviting hotel: flowering plants, comfy new chairs, and snug but tranquil guest rooms make this a good bet, especially because it's close to the train station yet within easy walking distance of the town center. In pricey Deauville, this is a real find. **Pros:** cheap; handy for train station. **Cons:** far from the beach; lacks character. ⊠ *1 rue Désiré-Le-Hoc* ☎ *02–31–88–21–06* ⊕ *www.hotel-continental-deauville.com* *42 rooms* *In-room: no a/c, Wi-Fi. In-hotel: bar* ▭ *AE, DC, MC, V* ⊗ *Closed mid-Nov.–mid-Dec.*

$$$–$$$$ **Normandy-Barrière.** With a facade that is a riot of pastel-green timbering, checkerboard walls, and Anglo-Norman balconies, the Normandy has been one of the town's landmarks since it opened in 1912. From the beginning it attracted well-heeled Parisians (many of whom appreciated the underground passage to the casino), but it has kept them coming as its grand salons have been transformed by Jacques Garcia—France's self-styled chicest and most aristo decorator—and now overflow with needlepointed sofas, fin-de-siècle chandeliers, and opulent silks. The lobby is a Belle Époque blowout, with soaring oak walls, a forest of columns, and islands of comfy, 19th-century-style armchairs. The courtyard is its outdoor version, with a grassy patio surrounded by a spectacular panoply of turrets and balconies. Request a room with a sea view, and don't forget to ask about the special thalassotherapy rates with full or half days of mud baths, salt massages, and soothing heated-seawater swims. Creamy sauces swamp the Norman dishes served up in the L'Étrier restaurant, set in a grand hall which, on a bright night, after a couple of bottles of Dom Pérignon, glitters like the salons of Versailles. **Pros:** spectacular decor; luxurious amenities; Deauville's place to be seen. **Cons:** some elements of kitschy bombast; patronizing service. ✉ *38 rue Jean-Mermoz* ☎ *02–31–98–66–22, 800/223–5652 for U.S. reservations* 🌐 *www.normandy-barriere.com* *290 rooms, 31 suites* *In-room: no a/c, safe, refrigerator, Internet, Wi-Fi. In-hotel: 2 restaurants, bar, pool, some pets allowed* 💳 *AE, DC, MC, V* *BP.*

Fodor's Choice ★

NIGHTLIFE AND THE ARTS

One of the biggest cultural events on the Norman calendar is the week-long **American Film Festival**, held in Deauville in early September. Formal attire is required at the **Casino de Deauville** (✉ *2 rue Edmond-Blanc* ☎ *02–31–14–31–14*). Trouville's **Casino de Trouville** (✉ *Pl. du Maréchal-Foch* ☎ *02–31–87–75–00*) is slightly less highbrow than Deauville's. Night owls enjoy **Le Privé** (✉ *13 rue Albert-Fracasse, Deauville*); it's open until 5 AM. The **Y Club** (✉ *14 bis, rue Désiré-le-Hoc, Deauville*) is the place to go out dancing.

SPORTS AND THE OUTDOORS

Deauville becomes Europe's horse capital in August, when breeders jet in from around the world for its yearling auctions and the races at its two attractive *hippodromes* (racetracks). Afternoon horse races are held in the heart of Deauville at the **Hippodrome de Deauville–La Toques** (✉ *Blvd. Mauger* ☎ *02–31–14–20–00*). Horse races and polo can be seen most summer afternoons at the **Hippodrome de Deauville Clairefontaine** (✉ *Rte. de Clairefontaine* ☎ *02–31–14–69–00*). Head for the **Poney Club** (✉ *Rue Reynoldo-Hahn* ☎ *02–31–98–56–24*) for a wonderful horseback ride on the beach. (The sunsets can be spectacular.) It's open weekends and holidays, but be sure to call early to reserve a horse, or a pony for your little one. Sailing boats large and small can be rented from the **Club Nautique de Trouville** (✉ *Digue des Roches Noires* ☎ *02–31–88–13–59*).

Even in the 19th century, elegant Parisians loved to flock to Deauville to enjoy a promenade along its beautiful beach.

CAEN

Fodor's Choice ★

54 km (35 mi) southwest of Deauville-Trouville, 28 km (17 mi) southeast of Bayeux, 120 km (75 mi) west of Rouen.

With its abbeys and castle, Caen, a busy administrative city and the capital of Lower Normandy, is very different from the coastal resorts. William of Normandy ruled from Caen in the 11th century before he conquered England. Nine hundred years later, during the two-month Battle of Caen in 1944, a fire raged for 11 days, devastating much of the town. Today the city is basically modern and commercial, with a vibrant student scene. The Caen Memorial, an impressive museum devoted to World War II, is considered a must-do by travelers interested in 20th-century history (many avail themselves of the excellent bus tours the museum sponsors to the D-Day beaches). But Caen's former grandeur can be seen in its extant historic monuments and along scenically restored Rue Ecuyère and Place St-Sauveur.

GETTING HERE

Trains from Paris (Gare St-Lazare) leave for Caen every two hours or so (€29); the 150-mi trip takes less than two hours. Some trains continue to Bayeux (2 hrs, €43). Several trains daily link Caen to Rouen (90 mins, €25) and St-Lô (45 mins, €13.50). Bus Verts du Calvados (☎ *08–10–21–42–14* 🌐 *www.busverts.fr*) operates buses every two hours or so from the Caen train station to Le Havre (2 hrs, 15 mins; €10.20) via Deauville (75 mins, €5.10) and Honfleur (1 hr, 45 mins; €7.20).

Visitor Information Caen Tourist Office. ✉ *Pl. du Canada* ☎ *02–31–27–90–30* 🌐 *www.tourisme.caen.fr.*

EXPLORING

A good place to begin exploring Caen is the **Hôtel d'Escoville**, a stately mansion in the city center built by wealthy merchant Nicolas Le Valois d'Escoville in the 1530s. The building was badly damaged during the war but has since been restored; the austere facade conceals an elaborate inner courtyard, reflecting the Italian influence on early Renaissance Norman architecture. The on-site city **tourist office** is an excellent resource. ✉ *Pl. St-Pierre* ☎ *02–31–27–14–14* 🌐 *www.tourisme.caen.fr.*

Across the square, beneath a 240-foot spire, is the late-Gothic church of **St-Pierre**, a riot of ornamental stonework.

Looming on a mound ahead of the church is the **château**—the ruins of William the Conqueror's fortress, built in 1060 and sensitively restored after the war. The castle gardens are a perfect spot for strolling, and the ramparts afford good views of the city. The citadel also contains two museums and the medieval church of **St-Georges**, used for exhibitions.

5

The **Musée des Beaux-Arts**, within the castle's walls, is a heavyweight among France's provincial fine-arts museums. Its old masters collection includes works by Poussin, Perugino, Rembrandt, Titian, Tintoretto, van der Weyden, and Paolo Veronese; there's also a wide range of 20th-century art. ✉ *Entrance by castle gateway* ☎ *02–31–30–47–70* 🌐 *www.ville-caen.fr/mba* 🎫 *Free* 🕐 *Wed.–Mon. 9:30–6.*

The **Musée de Normandie** *(Normandy Museum)*, in the mansion built for the castle governor, is dedicated to regional arts, such as ceramics and sculpture, plus some local archaeological finds. ✉ *Entrance by castle gateway* ☎ *02–31–30–47–60* 🌐 *www.ville-caen.fr/mdn* 🎫 *Free; €3 for exhibitions* 🕐 *June–Sept., daily 9:30–6; Oct.–May, Wed.–Mon. 9:30–6.*

Fodor's Choice ★ Caen's finest church, of cathedral proportions, is part of the **Abbaye aux Hommes** *(Men's Abbey)*, built by William the Conqueror from local Caen stone (also used for Canterbury Cathedral, Westminster Abbey, and the Tower of London). The abbey was begun in Romanesque style in 1066 and expanded in the 18th century; its elegant buildings are now part of City Hall and some rooms are brightened by the city's fine collection of paintings. Note the magnificent yet spare facade of the abbey church of **St-Étienne,** enhanced by two 11th-century towers topped by octagonal spires. Inside, what had been William the Conqueror's tomb was destroyed by 16th-century Huguenots during the Wars of Religion. However, the choir still stands; it was the first to be built in Norman Gothic style, and many subsequent choirs were modeled after it. ✉ *Pl. Louis-Guillouard* ☎ *02–31–30–42–81* 🎫 *Tours €3* 🕐 *Tours daily at 9:30, 11, 2:30, and 4.*

The **Abbaye aux Dames** *(Ladies' Abbey)* was founded by William the Conqueror's wife, Matilda, in 1063. Once a hospital, the abbey—rebuilt in the 18th century—was restored in the 1980s by the Regional Council, which then promptly requisitioned it for office space; however, its elegant arcaded courtyard and ground-floor reception rooms can be admired during a free guided tour. You can also visit the squat **Église de la Trinité** (Trinity Church), a fine example of 11th-century Romanesque architecture, though its original spires were replaced by timid balustrades in the early 18th century. Note the intricate carvings on columns and arches in the chapel; the 11th-century crypt; and, in the choir, the marble slab commemorating Queen Matilda, buried here in 1083. ✉ *Pl. de la Reine-Mathilde* ☎ *02–31–06–98–98* *Free* ⏲ *Tours daily at 2:30 and 4.*

FROM WAR TO PEACE

Normandy war museums are legion, but the Mémorial, its one and only *peace* museum, is special. Even better, readers rave about the museum's four-hour minibus tours of the D-Day beaches, run daily April to September. You can even make a day trip from Paris for this by catching the 8:40 AM train out of Gare St-Lazare to Caen and returning on the 7:55 PM train. Besides the tour, this €100 trip includes pickup at the station and lunch.

★ The **Mémorial**, an imaginative museum erected in 1988 on the north side of the city, is a must-see if you're interested in World War II history. The stark, flat facade, with a narrow doorway symbolizing the Allies' breach in the Nazi's supposedly impregnable Atlantic Wall, opens onto an immense foyer containing a café, brasserie, shop, and British Typhoon aircraft suspended overhead. The museum itself is down a spiral ramp, lined with photos and documents charting the Nazi's rise to power in the 1930s. The idea—hardly subtle but visually effective—is to suggest a descent into the hell of war. The extensive displays range from wartime plastic jewelry to scale models of battleships, with scholarly sections on how the Nazis tracked down radios used by the French Resistance and on the development of the atomic bomb. A room commemorating the Holocaust, with flickering candles and twinkling overhead lights, sounds a jarring, somewhat tacky note. The D-Day landings are evoked by a tabletop Allied map of the theater of war and by a spectacular split-screen presentation of the D-Day invasion from both the Allied and Nazi standpoints. Softening the effect of the modern 1988 museum structure are tranquil gardens; the newest is the British Garden, inaugurated by Prince Charles in 2004. The museum itself is fittingly set 10 minutes away from the Pegasus Bridge and 15 minutes from the D-Day beaches. ✉ *Esplanade Dwight-D.-Eisenhower* ☎ *02–31–06–06–44* 🌐 *www.memorial.fr* *€16* ⏲ *Mid-Feb.–Oct., daily 9–7; Nov., Dec., and late Jan.–mid-Feb., Tues.–Sun. 9:30–6.*

WHERE TO EAT AND STAY

$$$ FRENCH ✕ **Le P'tit B.** On one of Caen's oldest pedestrian streets near the castle, this typically Norman, half-timber 17th-century dining room—stone walls, beam ceilings, and large fireplace—showcases the good-value regional cuisine of David Schiebold. The three-course €28 menu is a good value, and highlights include the grilled duck, cannelloni with goat cheese, king-prawn risotto, and, to finish, red berries in flaky pastry with coconut milk. ✉ *15 rue de Vaugueux* ☎ *02–31–93–50–76* *Reservations essential* *AE, MC, V.*

$–$$ **Best Western Dauphin.** Despite being in the heart of the city, this hotel, in a heavily restored 12th-century priory, is surprisingly quiet. Some of the smallish guest rooms have exposed beams; those overlooking the street are soundproof; the ones in back look out on the courtyard. Service is friendly and efficient in the hotel and in the excellent though expensive restaurant. **Pros:** quiet; historic building. **Cons:** small rooms; overpriced restaurant. ✉ *29 rue Gémare* ☎ *02–31–86–22–26* 🌐 *www.le-dauphin-normandie.com* *32 rooms, 5 suites* *In-room: no a/c, refrigerator. In-hotel: restaurant, bar, gym, Wi-Fi hotspot* 💳 *AE, DC, MC, V* *MAP.*

SHOPPING

A **marché aux puces** *(flea market)* is held on Friday morning on Place St-Saveur and on Sunday morning on Place Courtonne. In June collectors and dealers flock to Caen's bric-a-brac and **antiques fair.**

THE OUTDOORS

Take a barge trip along the canal that leads from Caen to the sea on the **Boëdic** (✉ *Quai Vendeuvre* ☎ *02–31–43–86–12*); there is a daily departure at 3 PM, except on Saturday and Monday, from April 15–October 15.

5

EN ROUTE

Early on June 6, 1944, the British 6th Airborne Division landed by glider and captured **Pegasus Bridge** (named for the division's emblem, showing Bellerophon astride his winged horse, Pegasus). This proved the first step toward the liberation of France from Nazi occupation. To see this symbol of the Allied invasion, from Caen take D514 north and turn right at Bénouville. The original bridge—erected in 1935—has been replaced by a similar but slightly wider bridge; but the actual original can still be seen at the adjacent **Mémorial Pegasus** visitor center (*€6* *Feb.–Nov., daily*). Café Gondrée by the bridge—the first building recaptured on French soil—is still standing, still serving coffee, and houses a small museum. A 40-minute son-et-lumière show lights up the bridge and the café at nightfall between June and September.

BAYEUX

28 km (17 mi) northwest of Caen.

Bayeux, the first town to be liberated during the Battle of Normandy, was already steeped in history—as home to a Norman Gothic cathedral and the world's most celebrated piece of needlework: the Bayeux Tapestry. Bayeux's medieval backcloth makes it a popular base, especially among British travelers, for day trips to other towns in Normandy. Since Bayeux had nothing strategically useful like factories or military bases, it was never bombed by either side, leaving its beautiful cathedral and old town intact.

Visitor Information **Bayeux Tourist Office.** ✉ *Pointe Saint-Jean* ☎ *02–31–51–28–28* 🌐 *www.bessin-normandie.fr.*

EXPLORING

Bayeux offers both sides of the coin, old and new. The Old-World mood is at its most boisterous during its Fêtes Médiévales, a market-cum-carnival held in the streets around the cathedral on the first weekend of July. A more traditional market is held every Saturday morning. But more modern sights await if you use Bayeux as a fine starting point for visits to Normandy's stirring World War II sites; there are many custom-tour guides, but Taxis du Bessin (☎ *02–31–92–92–40*) is one of the best.

Fodor's Choice ★ Really a 225-foot-long embroidered scroll stitched in 1067, the **Bayeux Tapestry**, known in French as the *Tapisserie de la Reine Mathilde* (Queen Matilda's Tapestry), depicts, in 58 comic strip–type scenes, the epic story of William of Normandy's conquest of England in 1066, narrating Will's trials and victory over his cousin Harold, culminating in the Battle of Hastings on October 14, 1066. The tapestry was probably commissioned from Saxon embroiderers by the count of Kent—who was also the bishop of Bayeux—to be displayed in his newly built cathedral, the Cathédrale Notre-Dame. Despite its age, the tapestry is in remarkably good condition; the extremely detailed, often homey scenes provide an unequaled record of the clothes, weapons, ships, and lifestyles of the day. It's showcased in the **Musée de la Tapisserie** (Tapestry Museum; free headphones let you to listen to an English commentary about the tapestry). ✉ *Centre Guillaume-le-Conquérant, 13 bis, rue de Nesmond* ☎ *02–31–51–25–50* 🌐 *www.tapisserie-bayeux.fr* 🎫 *€7.80, includes admission to Musée Baron-Gérard* ⏲ *May–Aug., daily 9–7; Sept.–Apr., daily 9:30–12:30 and 2–6.*

Housed in the Bishop's Palace beneath the cathedral, and fronted by a majestic plane tree planted in March 1797 and known as the Tree of Liberty, the **Musée Baron-Gérard** contains a fine collection of Bayeux porcelain and lace, ceramics from Rouen, a marvelous collection of pharmaceutical jars from the 17th and 18th centuries, and 16th- to 19th-century furniture and paintings by local artists. ✉ *1 pl. de la Liberté* ☎ *02–31–92–14–21* 🎫 *€3.50 (€7.80 with Tapestry Museum)* ⏲ *Daily 10–12:30 and 2–6.*

Bayeux's mightiest edifice, the **Cathédrale Notre-Dame**, is a harmonious mixture of Norman and Gothic architecture. Note the portal on the south side of the transept that depicts the assassination of English archbishop Thomas à Becket in Canterbury Cathedral in 1170, following his courageous opposition to King Henry II's attempts to control the church. ✉ *Rue du Bienvenu* ☎ *02–31–92–01–85* ⏲ *Daily 9–6.*

Handmade lace is a specialty of Bayeux. The best place to learn about it and to buy some is the **Conservatoire de la Dentelle** near the cathedral, which has a good display. ✉ *6 rue du Bienvenu* ☎ *02–31–92–73–80* 🎫 *Free* ⏲ *Mon.–Sat. 10–12:30 and 2:30–6.*

At the **Musée de la Bataille de Normandie** *(Battle of Normandy Museum)*, exhibits trace the story of the struggle from June 7 to August 22, 1944. This modern museum near the moving British War Cemetery, sunk partly beneath the level of its surrounding lawns, contains some impressive war paraphernalia. ✉ *Bd. du Général-Fabian-Ware* ☎ *02–31–51–46–90* 🌐 *www.normandiememoire.com* 🎫 *€6.50* ⏲ *May–Sept., daily 9:30–6:30; Oct.–Apr., daily 10–12:30 and 2–6.*

HOW WILL GOT HERE

Kind of like the world's longest cartoon, the Bayeux Tapestry features 58 gloriously hand-embroidered scenes, some amusing but also including gory battles and the hand of God reaching down from the sky to meddle in human activities and help Will out. If you know nothing of the conqueror, read the history blurb in the museum before seeing the tapestry—you'll enjoy it more that way.

WHERE TO EAT AND STAY

$$$–$$$$ ★ **Château d'Audrieu.** Princely opulence, overstuffed chairs, wall sconces, antiques: this family-owned château with an elegant 18th-century facade fulfills a Hollywood notion of a palatial property. Guest rooms 50 and 51 have peaked ceilings with exposed-wood beams. The enchanting restaurant (closed Monday; no lunch weekdays)—all white wainscoting, crystal chandeliers, gilt accents—has an extensive wine list. Chef Olivier Barbarin explores an exotic repertoire of dishes, like scallops with chestnuts and cranberry juice. **Pros:** grandiose building; magnificent gardens. **Cons:** out of the way; bland decor in some rooms, food too nouvelle-ish. ✉ *13 km (8 mi) southeast of Bayeux off N13, Audrieu* ☎ *02–31–80–21–52* 🌐 *www.chateaudaudrieu.com* *25 rooms, 4 suites* *In-room: a/c, safe, refrigerator. In-hotel: restaurant, bar, pool, Internet terminal, Wi-Fi hotspot, some pets allowed* 💳 *AE, MC, V* ⏲ *Closed Dec. and Jan.* *MAP.*

$–$$ **Grand Hôtel du Luxembourg.** The Luxembourg has small but adequate guest rooms, fully renovated with bland modern furniture but with chic color schemes; all but two face a courtyard garden. Happily, it has one of the town's best restaurants, Les Quatre Saisons (closed January), set in a bright-red salon, with a seasonal menu and regular favorites like sole with vanilla and regional tripe. Depending on the time of year, choose the honey-roast ham with melted apples, or braised turbot with sage. **Pros:** quiet; central, fine restaurant. **Cons:** unprepossessing lobby; some rooms are on the dark side. ✉ *25 rue des Bouchers* ☎ *02–31–92–00–04* 🌐 *www.hotel-luxembourg-bayeux.com* *25 rooms, 3 suites* *In-room: no a/c, Wi-Fi. In-hotel: restaurant, bar, some pets allowed* 💳 *AE, DC, MC, V* *MAP.*

THE D-DAY BEACHES

History focused its sights along the coasts of Normandy at 6:30 AM on June 6, 1944, as the 135,000 men and 20,000 vehicles of the Allied troops made land in their first incursion in Europe in World War II. The entire operation on this "Longest Day" was called Operation Overlord—the code name for the invasion of Normandy. Five beachheads (dubbed Utah, Omaha, Gold, Juno, and Sword) were established along the coast to either side of Arromanches. Preparations started in mid-1943, and British shipyards worked furiously through the following winter and spring building two artificial harbors (called "mulberries"), boats, and landing equipment. The British and Canadian troops that landed on Sword, Juno, and Gold on June 6, 1944, quickly pushed inland and joined with parachute regiments previously dropped behind German lines, before encountering fierce resistance at Caen, which did not fall until July 9. Today the best way to tour this region is by car. Or—since public buses from Bayeux are infrequent—opt for one of the guided bus tours leaving from Caen.

OÙ EST PRIVATE RYAN?

The American Cemetery is a moving tribute to the fallen, with its Wall of the Missing, drum-like chapel, and avenues of holly oaks trimmed to resemble open parachutes. The crisply mowed lawns are studded with 9,386 marble tombstones; this is where Stephen Spielberg's fictional hero Captain John Miller was supposed to have been buried in *Saving Private Ryan.*

BUS TOURS

In Caen, the Mémorial organizes four-hour English-language daily minibus tours of the D-Day landing beaches; the cost is €69, including entrance fees. Normandy Sightseeing Tours runs a number of trips to the D-Day beaches; a full-day excursion to the D-Day beaches (8:30–6) costs €75.

Fees and Schedules Mémorial (☎ *02–31–06–06–44* 🌐 *www.memorial.fr*). **Normandy Sightseeing Tours** (✉ *618 rte. du Lavoir, Mosles* ☎ *02–31–51–70–52* 🌐 *www.normandywebguide.com*).

★ You won't be disappointed by the rugged terrain and windswept sand of **Omaha Beach**, 16 km (10 mi) northwest of Bayeux. Here you can find the **Monument du Débarquement** (Monument to the Normandy Landings) and the **Musée-Mémorial d'Omaha Beach,** a large shedlike structure packed with tanks, dioramas, and archival photographs which stand silent witness to "Bloody Omaha." Nearby, in Vierville-sur-Mer, is the **U.S. National Guard Monument.** Throughout June 6, Allied forces battled a hailstorm of German bullets and bombs, but by the end of the day they had taken the Omaha Beach sector, although they had suffered grievous losses. In Colleville-sur-Mer, overlooking Omaha Beach, is the hilltop **American Cemetery and Memorial,** designed by the landscape architect Markley Stevenson. You can look out to sea across the landing beach from a platform on the north side of the cemetery. ✉ *Musée-Mémorial d'Omaha Beach, Les Moulins on ave. de la Libération, Saint-Laurent-sur-Mer* ☎ *02–31–21–97–44* 🌐 *www.musee-memorial-omaha.com* 🎫 *€5.90* ⏲ *Daily Feb. 15–Mar. 15, 10–noon and 2:30–6; Mar. 16–May 15, 9:30–6:30; May 16–Sept. 15, 9:30–7; Sept. 16–Nov. 15, 9:30–6:30.*

★ The most spectacular scenery along the coast is at the **Pointe du Hoc**, 13 km (8 mi) west of St-Laurent. Wildly undulating grassland leads past ruined blockhouses to a cliff-top observatory and a German machine-gun post whose intimidating mass of reinforced concrete merits chilly exploration. Despite Spielberg's cinematic genius, it remains hard to imagine just how Colonel Rudder and his 225 Rangers—only 90 survived—managed to scale the jagged cliffs with rope ladders and capture the German defenses in one of the most heroic and dramatic episodes of the war. A granite memorial pillar now stands on top of a concrete bunker, but the site otherwise remains as the Rangers left it—look down through the barbed wire at the jutting cliffs the troops ascended and see the huge craters left by exploded shells.

Head west around the coast on N13, pause in the town of **Carentan** to admire its modern marina and the mighty octagonal spire of the Église Notre-Dame, and continue northwest to **Sainte-Mère Église**. At 2:30 AM on June 6, 1944, the 82nd Airborne Division was dropped over Ste-Mère, heralding the start of D-Day operations. After securing their position at Ste-Mère, U.S. forces pushed north, then west, cutting off the Cotentin Peninsula on June 18 and taking Cherbourg on June 26. German defenses proved fiercer farther south, and St-Lô was not liberated until July 19. Ste-Mère's symbolic importance as the first French village to be liberated from the Nazis is commemorated by the Borne 0 (Zero) outside the town hall—a large, dome milestone marking the start of the Voie de la Liberté (Freedom Way), charting the Allies' progress across France.

The **Musée Airborne** *(Airborne Museum)*, built behind the church in 1964 in the form of an open parachute, houses documents, maps, mementos, and one of the Waco CG4A gliders used to drop troops. ✉ *Pl. du 6-juin-1944* ☎ *02–33–41–41–35* 🌐 *www.musee-airborne.com* €7 ⏲ *Apr.–Sept. 9–6:45; Feb and Mar. and Oct. and Nov., daily 9:30–noon and 2–6.*

★ Head east on D67 from Ste-Mère to **Utah Beach**, which, being sheltered from the Atlantic winds by the Cotentin Peninsula and surveyed by lowly sand dunes rather than rocky cliffs, proved easier to attack than Omaha. Allied troops stormed the beach at dawn, and just a few hours later had managed to conquer the German defenses, heading inland to join up with the airborne troops.

In **La Madeleine** (✉ *Plage de La Madeleine* ☎ *02–33–71–53–35*) inspect the glitteringly modern **Utah Beach Landing Museum** (✉ *Ste-Marie-du-Mont* ☎ *02–33–71–53–35*), whose exhibits include a W5 Utah scale model detailing the German defenses; it's open April–June, September, and October, daily 9:30–noon and 2–6, and July and August, daily 9:30–6:30; it's closed in January. Continue north to the **Dunes de Varreville,** set with a monument to French hero General Leclerc, who landed here. Offshore you can see the fortified **Iles St-Marcouf.** Continue to **Quinéville,** at the far end of Utah Beach, with its **museum** (✉ *Rue de la Plage* ☎ *02–33–95–95–95*) evoking life during the German Occupation; the museum is open April through mid-November, daily 10–7.

WHERE TO EAT AND STAY

$ **Casino.** You can't get closer to the action than this. The handsome, postwar, triangular-gabled stone hotel, run by the same family since it was built in the 1950s, looks directly onto Omaha Beach. The bar is made from an old lifeboat, and it's no surprise that seafood and regional cuisine with creamy sauces predominate in Bruno Clemençon's airy sea-view restaurant, where set-price menus start at €26 and hotel guests are reserved a table by the window. **Pros:** calm; right by the beach. **Cons:** small bathrooms; slow service in restaurant. ✉ *Rue de la*

Percée, Vierville-sur-Mer ☎ *02–31–22–41–02* 🌐 *www.logis-de-france.fr* 🛏 *12 rooms* 👍 *In-room: no a/c. In-hotel: restaurant, bar, Wi-Fi hotspot, some pets allowed* 💳 *AE, MC, V* ⏲ *Closed mid-Nov.–mid-Mar.* 🍽 *MAP.*

> **THE LONGEST NIGHT**
>
> Famously, one parachutist—his name was John Steele—got stuck on the church tower of Sainte-Mère Église (an episode memorably re-created in the 1960 film *The Longest Day*) one evening; a dummy is strung up each summer to recall the event, and a stained-glass window inside the church honors American paratroopers.

$$$$ ★ **La Chenevière.** Topped by an impressive mansard roof, set in an elegant 18th-century château mansion, and surrounded by adorable gardens, this is a true oasis of peace a few kilometers down the road—and yet a million miles away—from the nearby World War II sites like Omaha Beach. Found inland from Port-en-Bessin, the hotel allures with super-stylish guest rooms, which comprise a fetching mix of Louis Seize chairs, gilded ormolu objects, modern photographs, and very chic fabrics. Overlooking the grand pool is La Chenevière's showpiece: a stunning, glassed-in modern conservatory set with wicker furniture and abstract art. The restaurant serves cuisine appropriate to its surroundings: Dover sole with artichokes, lobster with wild-mushroom risotto, or roast veal with truffles. **Pros:** magnificent architecture; luxurious rooms. **Cons:** three different buildings; no a/c in the château. ✉ *Les Escures, Commes* ☎ *02–31–51–25–25* 🌐 *www.lacheneviere.com* 🛏 *26 rooms, 3 suites* 👍 *In-room: a/c (some), safe, refrigerator, Internet, Wi-Fi. In-hotel: restaurant, bar, pool, some pets allowed* 💳 *AE, DC, MC, V* ⏲ *Closed Dec.– Feb.* 🍽 *MAP.*

ST-LÔ

78 km (49 mi) southeast of Cherbourg, 36 km (22 mi) southwest of Bayeux.

St-Lô, perched dramatically on a rocky spur above the Vire Valley, was a key communications center that suffered so badly in World War II that it became known as the "capital of ruins." The medieval **Église Notre-Dame** bears mournful witness to those dark days: its imposing, spire-top west front was never rebuilt, merely shored up with a wall of greenish stone. Reconstruction elsewhere, though, was wholesale. Some of it was spectacular, like the slender, spiral-staircase tower outside Town Hall; the circular theater; or the openwork belfry of the church of Ste-Croix. The town was freed by American troops, and its rebuilding was financed with U.S. support, notably from the city of Baltimore. The **Hôpital Mémorial France–États-Unis** (France–United States Memorial Hospital), designed by Paul Nelson and featuring a giant mosaic by Fernand Léger, was named to honor those links.

Visitor Information St-Lô Tourist Office. ✉ *Place General de Gaulle* ☎ *02–33–77–60–35* 🌐 *www.tourisme.fr/office-de-tourisme/saint-lo.htm.*

EXPLORING

St-Lô is capital of the Manche *département* (province) and, less prosaically, likes to consider itself France's horse capital. Hundreds of breeders are based in its environs, and the **Haras National** *(National Stud)* was established here in 1886. ✉ *Av. du Maréchal-Juin* ☎ *02–33–77–60–35* 🌐 *www.haras-nationaux.fr* 🎫 *€5* ⏲ *Guided tours only, June and Sept. at 3:30, July and Aug. at 11, 2:30, 3:30, and 4:30.*

★ St-Lô's art museum, the **Musée des Beaux-Arts**, is the perfect French provincial museum. Its halls are airy, seldom busy, not too big, yet full of varied exhibits—including an unexpected masterpiece: *Gombault et Macée,* a set of nine silk-and-wool tapestries woven in Bruges around 1600 relating a tale about a shepherd couple, exquisitely showcased in a special circular room. Other highlights include brash modern tapestries by Jean Lurçat; paintings by Corot, Boudin, and Géricault; court miniatures by Daniel Saint (1778–1847); and the Art Deco pictures of Slovenian-born Jaro Hilbert (1897–1995), inspired by ancient Egypt. Photographs, models, and documents evoke St-Lô's wartime devastation. ✉ *Centre Culturel, Pl. du Champ-de-Mars* ☎ *02–33–72–52–55* 🎫 *€2.80* ⏲ *Wed.–Sun. 2–6.*

5

MONT-ST-MICHEL

Fodor's Choice ★ *61 km (39 mi) southwest of St-Lô via D999 and N175; 123 km (77 mi) southwest of Caen; 67 km (42 mi) north of Rennes; 325 km (202 mi) west of Paris.*

GETTING HERE

There are two routes to Mont-St-Michel, depending on whether you arrive from Caen or from Paris. From Caen you can take either an early-morning or an afternoon train to Pontorson (2 hrs, €23.40), the nearest station; then it's another 15 minutes to the foot of the abbey by bus or taxi. (Both leave from in front of the station.) From Paris, take the TGV from Gare Montparnasse to Rennes, then take a Courriers Bretons bus (☎ *02–99–19–70–80*). The total journey takes 3 hours, 20 minutes (€40). There are three trains daily, but the only one that allows you a full day on the Mont leaves at 6:35 AM and arrives at 9:55 AM. The other options are 11:05 (arriving 3:13 PM) and 1:05 PM (arriving 5:04 PM).

Visitor Information Mont-St-Michel Tourist Office. ✉ *Corps de Garde* ☎ *02–33–60–14–30* 🌐 *www.ot-montsaintmichel.com.*

EXPLORING

Mont-St-Michel is the most-visited sight in France after the Eiffel Tower and the Louvre. This beached mass of granite, rising some 400 feet, was begun in 709 and is crowned with the "Marvel," or great monastery, that was built during the 13th century. ⇨ *For information about this spectacular sight, see "A Spire to Greatness: Mont-St-Michel" below.*

A Spire to Greatness:

MONT-ST-MICHEL

A magnetic beacon to millions of travelers each year, this "Wonder of the Western World" —a 264-foot mound of rock topped by a history-shrouded abbey—remains the crowning glory of medieval France.

Wrought by nature and centuries of tireless human toil, this mass of granite surmounted by the soul-lifting silhouette of the **Abbaye du Mont-St-Michel** is Normandy's most enduring image. Its fame stems not just from the majesty of its geographical situation but even more from its impressive history. Perched on the border between Normandy and Brittany, the medieval Mont (or Mount) was a political football between English conquerors and French kings for centuries. Mont-St-Michel was designed to be as much a fortress as it was a shrine, so it looks as tough as it is beautiful.

Legend has it that the Archangel Michael appeared in 709 to Aubert, Bishop of Avranches, inspiring him to build an oratory on what was then called Mont Tombe. The original church was completed in 1144, but further buildings were added in the 13th century to accommodate the hordes of pilgrims—known as *miquelots*—who flocked here even during the Hundred Years' War (1337–1453), when the region was in English hands.

Out of the French rulers' desire to protect Brittany from subjugation by the Normans (whose leader, William the Conqueror, had assumed the English throne in 1066) came the clever strategy of what we would call propaganda. Because of St. Michel's legendary role as dragon slayer and leader of the Heavenly Army, the French lords transformed him, and the Mont, into a major rallying force. During this period the abbey remained a symbol, both physical and emotional, of French independence.

By 1203, King Philippe-Auguste of France had succeeded in wresting the Mont back from the Normans and to shore up French popularity in Normandy he provided funds to restore the abbey. The resulting, greatly expanded, three-level Gothic abbey (1203–1228) became known as *La Merveille* (The Marvel).

During the French Revolution, the abbey was converted into a prison, but shortly after Victor Hugo (of *Hunchback of Notre Dame* fame) declaimed "A toad in a reliquary! When will we understand in France the sanctity of monuments?," the prison was converted into a museum in 1874 and, fittingly, Emmanuel Frémiet's great gilt statute of St. Michael was added to the spire in 1897.

Only at high tide is the Mont transformed into an island.

CLIMB EVERY MONT

Mont-St-Michel is the result of more than 500 years of construction, from 1017 to 1521, and traces the history of French medieval architecture, from earliest Romanesque to its last flowering, Flamboyant Gothic.

HOW TO TOUR THE MONT

There are two basic options for touring the abbey of Mont-St-Michel: guided tours and exploring on your own (which you can do with the aid of an excellent audioguide tour in English). Realistically, a visit to Mont-St-Michel's abbey and village needs a half a day but an entire day at least is needed if you do several of the museums, go on one of the abbey's guided tours, and fit in a walk on the surrounding expanses of sand.

General admission to the abbey includes an optional hour-long guided tour in English, offered twice a day and night in high season. A more extensive, two-hour-long guided tour in French costs an extra 4 euros. The English-language tour takes you throughout the spectacular **Église Abbatiale,** the abbey church that crowns the rock, as well as the **Merveille,** a 13th-century, three-story

collection of rooms and passageways built by King Philippe-Auguste. The French tour also includes the celebrated **Escalier de Dentelle** (Lace Staircase) and other highlights. Invest in at least one tour while you are here—each of them gets you on top of or into things you can't see alone.

If you do go it alone, stop halfway up Grande-Rue at the church of St-Pierre to admire its richly carved side chapel with its dramatic statue of St. Michael slaying the dragon. The famous **Grand Degré** staircase leads to the abbey entrance, from which a wider flight of steps climbs to the **Saut Gautier Terrace** outside the sober, dignified church. After visiting the arcaded cloisters alongside, you can wander at leisure, and probably get lost, among the maze of vaulted halls.

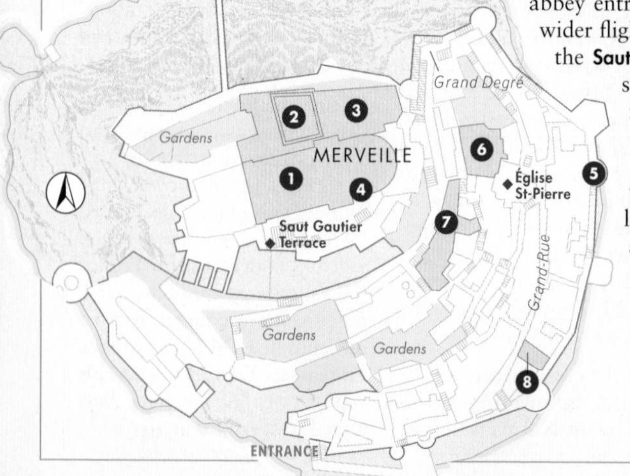

(above) Watchtower at Mont-Saint-Michel

DON'T MISS

❶ **Église Abbatiale** (above). Crowning the mount, the Abbey Church is in two different styles. The main nave and transepts (1020–1135) were built in the Norman Romanesque style; after the collapse of the original chancel in 1421, it was rebuilt in Flamboyant Gothic with seven Rayonnant-style chapels.

❷ **La Cloitre de l'Abbatiale** (above). The main cloister was the only part of the abbey complex open to "heaven"—the sky. Its southern gallery contains the lavabos (washing stands) of the monks. Look for the column capitals beautifully chiseled with flower and vine motifs.

❸ **Salle des Chevaliers** (above). Part of the triple-tiered "La Merveille"—the complex of state chambers, refectory, and cloister that surrounds the main church—the Knights' Hall was originally a scriptorium for copying manuscripts. It was the only heated room on the Mont.

❹ **Escalier de Dentelle** Set atop one of the "flying buttresses" (top right) of the main church, the famous perforated Lace Staircase is a bravura Gothic showpiece of carved stone. It leads to a parapet—adorned with stone gargoyles—390 feet above the sea.

MUSEUMS

Scattered through the Mont are four mini-museums. The most popular is the ❺ **Archéoscope** (Chemin de la Ronde, 02-33-89-01-85) whose sound-and-light show, *L'Eau et La Lumiere* (Water and Light), offers the best introduction to the Mont. Some exhibits use wax figures garbed in the most elegant 15th-century-style clothes. ❻ **The Logis Tiphaine** (02-33-60-23-34) is the home that Bertrand Duguesclin, a general fierce in his allegiance to the cause of French independence, built for his wife Tiphaine in 1365. ❼ **The Musée Historique** (Chemin de la Ronde, 02-33-60-07-01) traces the 1,000-year history of the Mont in one of its former prisons. ❽ **The Musée Maritime** (Grande Rue, 02-33-60-14-09) explores the science of the Mont's tidal bay and has a vast collection of model ships.

INFORMATION

☎ 02-33-89-80-00. 🌐 www.monum.fr; http://mont-saint-michel.monuments-nationaux.fr 🎫 €8.50, with audioguide €12.50. Guided tour in French: €4. Museums: single ticket, €8, combined ticket €16. The abbey is open May–Aug., daily 9–7; Sept.–Apr., daily 9:30–6. The tourist office (☎ 02-33-60-14-30, 🌐 www.au-mont-saint-michel.com) is in the Corps de Garde, left of the island gates.

WHERE TO EAT AND STAY

When day-trippers depart, Mont-St-Michel becomes a completely different experience, and a stay overnight—when the island is spectacularly floodlit—is especially memorable. But if you want to save money—and perhaps your sanity—during the very crowded peak months consider staying nearby at Pontorson, Avranches, Courtils, or day-trip it from St-Malo or Rennes.

LA MÈRE POULARD

With walls plastered with photographs of illustrious guests, Mont-St-Michel's most famous hostelry can be tough to book, thanks to its historic restaurant, birthplace of Mère Poulard's legendary soufflé-like omelet. Chef Michel Bruneau also offers an array of tempting Norman dishes (reservations are essential in summer). Set in adjoining houses, the hotel itself is linked by three steep and narrow stairways. Room prices start low but ratchet upward according to size; the smallest rooms are bearable for an overnight stay, not longer. You are usually requested to book two meals with the room. The hotel's location, right by the main gateway, is most convenient—just don't come expecting any views from atop the Mont.

(above) Winner of Fodor's France photo contest is this beauty by fanotravel.

$$$-$$$$ ✉ Grande-Rue, 50116 ☎ 02-33-89-68-68 🌐 www.mere-poulard.fr 27 rooms In-room: no a/c, refrigerator. In-hotel: restaurant, bar ▭ AE, DC, MC, V

AUBERGE ST-PIERRE

This inn is a popular spot thanks to the fact that it's in a half-timber 15th-century building adjacent to the ramparts and has its own garden restaurant and interesting half-board rates. If you're lucky, you'll wind up in No. 16, which has a view of the abbey. The hotel annex, La Croix Blanche, has another nine rooms and dining patio with awesome view.

$$-$$$ ✉ Grande-Rue, 50170 ☎ 02-33-60-14-03 🌐 www.auberge-saint-pierre.fr 21 rooms In-room: no a/c, Wi-Fi. In-hotel: restaurant, Internet terminal ▭ AE, MC, V

FOOD WITH A VIEW

Many Mont restaurants don't have views (other than of rooms crammed with diners), so another option is to enjoy a picnic along the *promenade des remparts*, where the vistas will spice up the blandest sandwich.

LES TERRASSES POULARD

Run by the folks who own the noted Mère Poulard hotel, this charming ensemble of buildings is clustered around a small garden in the middle of the Mount. Rooms at this hotel are some of the best—with views of the bay and rustic-style furnishings—and most spacious on the Mount, although many require you to negotiate a labyrinth of steep stairways. It's a long way to the car park.

$$–$$$ ✉ Grande-Rue, opposite parish church, 50170 ☎ 02–33–89–02–02 🌐 www.terrasses-poulard.com 30 rooms In-room: no a/c, refrigerator. In-hotel: restaurant ▭ AE, DC, MC, V

MANOIR DE LA ROCHE TORIN

Run by the Barraux family, this pretty, slate-roofed, stone-walled manor set in 4 acres of parkland is a delightful alternative to crowded Mont-St-Michel. Rooms are pleasantly old-fashioned, and the bathrooms modern. With walls of Normand stonework and its open fireplace, the restaurant (closed Tuesday, Wednesday, and Saturday lunch) has superb seafood and char-grilled *pré-salé* (salt-meadow lamb). In summer, apéritifs are served in the garden, with a view of Mont-St-Michel.

$$–$$$ ✉ 34 rte. de la Roche-Torin, 9 km (5 mi) from Mont-St-Michel, 50220 Courtils ☎ 02–33–70–96–55 🌐 www.manoir-rochetorin.com 15 rooms In-room: no a/c, refrigerator, Wi-Fi. In-hotel: restaurant, bar, some pets allowed (fee), Internet ▭ AE, DC, MC, V ⏲ Closed mid-Nov.–mid-Feb.

DU GUESCLIN

The courtesy of the staff, the comfy and stylish guest rooms, and a choice of two restaurants make this great value hotel a most pleasant option. Downstairs try the casual brasserie for salads and sandwiches; upstairs the panoramic full-service restaurant has a wonderful view of the bay, shared by a few guest rooms.

$ ✉ Grande-Rue, 50170 ☎ 02–33–60–14–10 🌐 www.hotelduguesclin.com 10 rooms In-room: no a/c. In-hotel: 2 restaurants ▭ MC, V ⏲ Closed Nov.–Mar.

NOW YOU SEE IT . . .

The Mont's choir was rebuilt during the 15th century and it was only then that the heaven-thrusting Gothic spire was added. To step back several centuries, place your hand to block your view of the spire and see the abbey return to its original Romanesque squatness.

TIME AND TIDE WAIT FOR NO MAN

Most visitors to the Mont see it "beached" by its sandy strands.

Mont-St-Michel can be washed by the highest tides in Europe, rising up to a crest of 45 feet at times. Dangerously unpredictable, the sea here runs out as far as nine miles before rushing back in—more than a few ill-prepared tourists over the years have drowned. Even when the tide is out, the sandy strand is treacherous because of dangerous quicksands (guided hikes over the strand are available). A 2 km (1 mi) causeway links Mont-St-Michel to the mainland.

Note that the Mont is surrounded by water only at very high tides (99% of visitors see the island "beached" by sand). ■ TIP→ **To see the rare occurrence of the Mont washed by tides, plan a visit when the moon is full.** Occuring only twice a month, the highest tides occur 36 to 48 hours after the full and new moons, with the most dramatic ones during the spring and fall equinoxes (around March 21 and September 23). Experts say the best time to visit is six hours after full or new moons. Time tidetables (posted on the board outside the tourist office) can be accessed on the internet at www.ot-montsaintmichel.com.

TO AND FROM

Set across from the mainland village of La Digue, Mont-St-Michel is 44 km (27 mi) south of Granville via D973, N175, and D43; 67 km (42 mi) north of Rennes 123 km (77mi) southwest of Caen; and 325 km (202 mi) west of Paris.

BY CAR Parking lots (€5) at either end of the causeway. The one just outside the Mont's main gate is reserved for hotel users, who access the lot through a pass-key issued by their hotel. The larger parking lot during very high tides is closed to the public, who can then park on the causeway or, if no room is left, in a car park on the mainland about one mile away (a shuttle bus connects the two).

BY TRAIN & BUS Taking the train from Paris to Mont-St-Michel is not easy—the quickest way (3 hrs, 45 mins, €64) is to take the high-speed TGV train from Gare Montparnasse to Rennes (in high season, five departures a day), then a SNCF (02–99–19–70—70) one-hour bus transfer to the Mont. The only train that will allow you a full day on the Mont leaves at 7 am and arrives at 10:50 am. The other options are 8 (arriving 1 pm) and 2 pm (arriving 7). From Caen you can take either an early morning or late afternoon train to Pontorson (2 hrs, €24), the nearest station to the Mont; then it is another 15 minutes to the foot of the abbey by bus or taxi.

6

Brittany

WORD OF MOUTH

" If you are looking for Brittany's 'atmosphere,' head to its Western part—a place full of Celtic legends and tales, beautiful scenery, and old parish closes, where many people still speak Breton."

—Slartibartfast3

"With such a variety of coastline, Brittany's Côte de Granit Rose, around Ploumanac'h, was like stepping into modern sculpture. The rock formations were spectacular."

—DeborahAnn

WELCOME TO BRITTANY

TOP REASONS TO GO

★ **Waterworld:** Will you prefer the coastal drama of the Granite Coast, with its crazy-shape outcrops, or the rippling waters of the Bay of Morbihan, snuggling in the Gulf Stream behind the angry Atlantic?

★ **The Isle Has It:** Venture down the untamed Quiberon Peninsula to boat across to the rugged, unspoiled beauty of Belle-Ile-en-Mer, Brittany's wildest island.

★ **Gauguin's Pont-Aven:** A *cité des artistes,* its colorful folkloric ways helped ignite the painter's interest in Tahiti.

★ **Unidentical Twins:** A ferry ride across the Rance River links two delightfully contrasting towns: ancient, once pirate-ridden St-Malo and grand, genteel, Edwardian Dinard.

★ **Stone Me!:** Muse upon the solemn majesty of row-upon-row of *anciens menhirs* at Carnac, the "French Stonehenge."

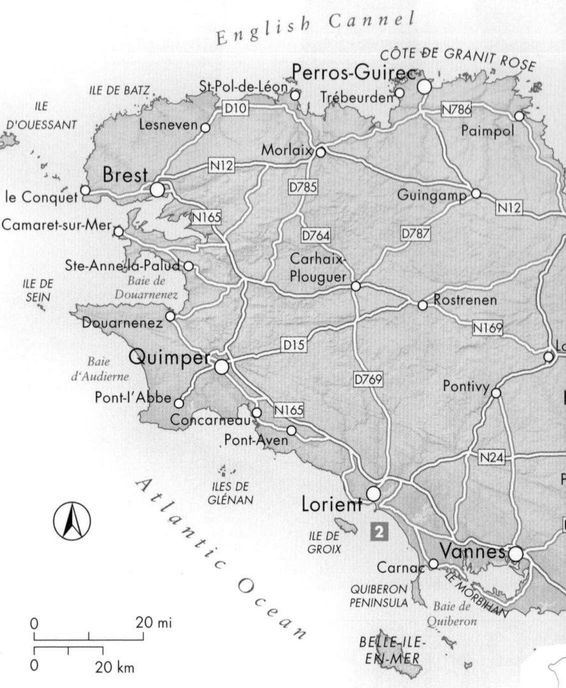

1 Northeast Brittany and the Channel Coast. The northern half of Brittany is demarcated by its 240-km (150-mi) Channel Coast, which stretches from Cancale, just west of Mont-St-Michel, to Morlaix, and can be loosely divided into two parts: the Côte d'Emeraude (Emerald Coast), with cliffs punctuated by golden, curving beaches; and the Côte de Granit Rose (Pink Granite Coast), including the stupefying area around Trébeurden, where Brittany's granite takes amazing forms glowing an otherworldly pink. On the road heading there are the gateway city of Rennes; Vitré, a beautifully preserved historic town; the oyster mecca that is Cancale; and the great port of St-Malo, whose stone ramparts conjure up the days of the great marauding corsairs.

GETTING ORIENTED

Bretons like to say they are Celtic, not Gallic, and other French people sometimes feel they are in a foreign land when they visit this jagged triangle perched on the northwest tip of mainland Europe. Two sides of the triangle are defined by the sea. Brittany's northern coast faces the English Channel; its western coast defies the Atlantic Ocean. The north of Brittany tends to be wilder than the south, or Basse Bretagne, where the countryside becomes softer as it descends toward Nantes and the Loire. But wherever you go, "maritime Armor"—the Land of the Sea—is never too far away.

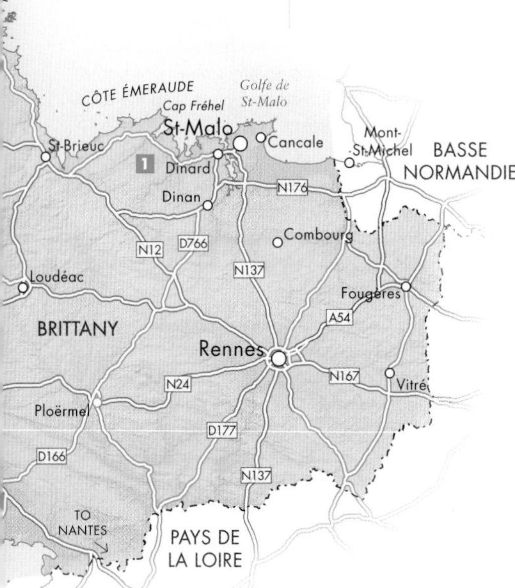

2 The Atlantic Coast. Bypassing the lobster-claw of Brittany's Finistère ("World's End"), this westernmost region allures with folkloric treasures like Ste-Anne-la-Palud (famed for its *pardon* festival); Quimper, noted for its signature ceramics; and cheerful, riverside villages like Pont-Aven, which Gauguin immortalized in many sketches and paintings. Here, the 320-km (200-mi) Atlantic coast zigzags its way southeast, with frenzied, cliff-bashing surf alternating with sprawling beaches and bustling harbors. Belle-Ile island is a jewel off the Morbihan coast, another beautiful stretch of shoreline. Enjoy its away-from-it-all atmosphere, because the bustling city of Nantes lies just to the southeast.

BRITTANY PLANNER

Parlez-Vous Breton?

Most place names in Brittany are Breton; the popular *plou* means "parish"—this is where the French got the word *plouc,* meaning "hick."

Other common geographical names are *coat* (forest), *mor* (sea), *aber* or *aven* (estuary), *ster* (river), and *enez* (island). *Ty* and *ti*, like the French *chez,* mean "at the house of."

While under the radar screen for the most part during the past decade, the Breton Revolutionary Army is a nationalist group committed to preserving Breton culture against French efforts to repress it. Now that everyone agrees that traditional Breton folkways are a priceless boost to tourism and cultural patrimony, this is a common goal shared by many.

Pardons and Festivals

It has been said that there are as many Breton saints as there are stones in the ground. One of the great attractions of Brittany, therefore, remains its many festivals, pardons, and folklore events: Banners and saintly statues are borne in colorful parades, accompanied by hymns, and the entire event is often capped by a feast.

In February, the great Pardon of Terre-Neuve takes place at St-Malo, and in March, Nantes celebrates with a pre-Lenten carnival procession. In mid-May there is a notable pardon of Saint-Yves, patron saint of lawyers, at Tréguier. June is the month of St. John, honored by the ceremonial Feux de Saint-Jean at Locronan and Nantes.

July sees Quimper's Celtic Festival de Cornouaille and the famed pardon in Ste-Anne-d'Auray. August has Lorient's Festival Interceltique, Pont-Aven's Festival of the Golden Gorse, Brest's bagpipe festival, and a big pardon in Ste-Anne-la-Palud. Another pardon held in Le Folgoët during September is one of the most extraordinary, with flocks of bishops, Bretons in traditional costumes, and devout pilgrims.

Making the Most of Your Time

If you have just a few days here, choose your coast—Channel or Atlantic! Cliffs and beaches, boat trips, culture and history. both shorelines offer all these and more. St-Malo makes a good base if you're Channel-bound, handily placed for medieval Dinan; Chateaubriand's home at Combourg; Dinard, the elegant Belle Époque resort once favored by British aristocrats; and the lively city of Rennes, the gateway to Brittany set 354 km (220 mi) west of Paris. Pretty Vannes is a good base for exploring the Atlantic coast. Highlights hereabouts include lively Quimper, with its fine cathedral and pottery; the painters' village of Pont-Aven, made famous by Gauguin; the prehistoric menhirs of Carnac; the rugged island of Belle-Ile; and the picturesque Bay of Morbihan. The third side of the Brittany triangle is its verdant, unhurried hinterland. Charming—but forget it unless you're here for the month.

When to Go

The tourist season is short in Brittany (late June through early September).

Long, damp winters keep visitors away, and many hotels are closed until Eastertime.

Brittany is particularly crowded in July and August.

During these months, most French people are on vacation, so why not opt to choose crowd-free June or September?

Some say early October, with autumnal colors and crisp evenings, is even better and truly makes for an invigorating visit.

But if you want to sample local folklore, late summer is the most festive time to come.

Finding a Place to Stay

Outside the main cities (Rennes and Nantes), Brittany has plenty of small, appealing family-run hotels which cater essentially to seasonal visitors.

Note that many close for one or several months between October and March.

Booking ahead is strongly advised for the Easter period.

In addition, this is the case during the midsummer period, when it is routine for prices to be ratcheted up by 30% to 50%.

For luxury hotels Dinard, on the English Channel, and La Baule, on the Atlantic, are the area's two most expensive resorts.

Assume that all hotel rooms have TV, telephones, and private bath, unless otherwise noted.

DINING AND LODGING PRICE CATEGORIES (IN EUROS)

	¢	$	$$	$$$	$$$$
Restaurants	under €13	€13–€17	€18–€24	€25–€32	over €32
Hotels	under €65	€65–€105	€106–€145	€146–€215	over €215

Restaurant prices are per person for a main course at dinner, including tax (5.5%) and service; note that if a restaurant offers only prix-fixe (set-price) meals, it has been given the price category that reflects the full prix-fixe price. Hotel prices are for a standard double room in high season, including tax (19.6%) and service charge.

Transportation Basics

In just over two hours the TGV train from Paris whisks you to Rennes, the region's hub. From Rennes you can continue to distant outpoints like Quimper or take a branch line to St-Malo or Dinan. You need to use buses, or a car, to explore the coast between Dinard and Rostoff, and the smaller towns along the Atlantic coast, like Concarneau, and Pont-Aven. The A11 expressway leads from Paris to Rennes, continuing as the N12 dual-carriageway to Brest, where the N165 dual-carriageway heads down the coast toward Nantes.

Visitor Information

In addition to the Regional Tourist Boards, try the very helpful Maison de la Bretagne in Paris.

Comité Départemental du Tourisme des Côtes-d'Armor (✉ *7 rue St-Benoît, St-Brieuc* ☎ *02–96–62–72–00* 🌐 *www.cotesdarmor.com*). **Comité Départemental du Tourisme de Finistère** (✉ *11 rue Théodore-Le Hars, Quimper* ☎ *02–98–76–20–70* 🌐 *www.finisteretourisme.com*). **Comité Départemental du Tourisme de Loire-Atlantique** (✉ *2 allée Baco, Nantes* ☎ *02–51–72–95–30* 🌐 *www.cdt44.com*). **Maison de la Bretagne** (✉ *203 bd. St-Germain, Paris* ☎ *01–53–63–11–50*).

6

GETTING AROUND

Bus Travel

Brittany is serviced by a bewildering number of companies. While the region is nicely threaded by train lines, some towns are bus-only. These include Carnac (90 mins) and Quiberon (2 hrs), on a **Keolis Atlantique** bus from Vannes; Dinard (30 mins) with a Keolis Emeraude bus from St-Malo; and Cancale (40 mins, €2), also from St-Malo.

As for Mont-St-Michel, buses connect with St-Malo (1 hr, 50 mins via Dol, €4.50) and with Rennes (80 mins, €10.30). Use **Transports Caoudal** from Quimper to reach Pont-Aven.

Bus Information

Keolis Atlantique (☎ *02–97–47–29–64* ⊕ *morbihan.fr*).

Cars du Kreisker (☎ *02–98–69–00–93* ⊕ *www.cars-kreisker.com*).

CAT (☎ *02–96–39–21–05* ⊕ *tibus.fr*).

Keolis Emeraude (☎ *02–99–19–70–80* ⊕ *www.keolis-emeraude.com*).

TIV (☎ *02–99–26–11–11*).

Transports Caoudal (☎ *02–98–90–88–89*).

Transports Le Bayon (☎ *02–97–24–26–20 or 02–99–29–60–00* ⊕ *www.rennes.aeroport.fr*).

Train Travel

Most towns in this region are accessible by train, though you need a car to get to some of the more secluded spots. The high-speed TGV (Train à Grande Vitesse) departs 15 times daily from Paris (Gare Montparnasse) for Rennes, making this region easily accessible. The trip takes about 2¼ hours (€55).

Some trains from Paris branch in Rennes to either Brest or Quimper (4 hrs, 45 mins from Paris; €83), stopping in Vannes (3 hrs, 20 mins from Paris; €63.80). From Rennes there are frequent regional trains via Dol to St-Malo (55–80 mins, €16).

You can reach Dinan from Dol (20 mins, €6). Change at Auray for Quiberon (train service July and August only; otherwise, bus links, 1 hr; €6.30).

Train Information SNCF (☎ *36–35 [€0.34 per min]* ⊕ *www.voyages-sncf.com*). **TGV** (⊕ *www.tgv.com*).

Car Travel

Rennes, the gateway to Brittany, is 310 km (195 mi) west of Paris. It can be reached in about three hours via Le Mans using A81 and A11 (A11 continues southwest from Le Mans to Nantes). Rennes is linked by good roads to Morlaix (E50), Quimper (N24/N165), and Vannes (N24/N166). A car is pretty much essential if you want to see out-of-the-way places.

Air Travel

Aéroport de Rennes has domestic flights to and from both Paris airports and Bordeaux, Lyon, Toulouse, Marseille, Strasbourg, and Basle-Mulhouse. **Aéroport de Nantes** also hosts Ryanair flights to and from London Stansted.

Air Travel Information Aéroport de Nantes (✉ *Bouguenais, southwest of city* ☎ *02–40–84–80–00* ⊕ *www.nantes-aeroport.fr*). **Aéroport de Rennes** (✉ *St-Jacques de la Lande, southwest of city* ☎ *02–99–29–60–00* ⊕ *www.rennes.aeroport.fr*).

DID YOU KNOW?

Elaborately half-timbered houses (called *colombage* in French) are everywhere in Brittany, relics of the medieval days when this region, along with Normandy, was colonized by the English.

EATING AND DRINKING WELL IN BRITTANY

Brittany is a land of the sea. Surrounded on three sides by water, it's a veritable trove of fish and shellfish. These aquatic delights, not surprisingly, dominate Breton cuisine, but crêpes, lamb, and butter also play starring roles.

One taste and you'll know why Cancale oysters are so prized (above); who can resist those Breton dessert crêpes? (right, top); Plougastel strawberries are red as rubies (right, bottom).

Maritime headliners include *coquilles St-Jacques* (scallops); langoustines, which are something between a large shrimp and a lobster; and oysters, prized for their balance of briny and sweet. Perhaps the most famous regional seafood dishes are *homard à l'armoricaine*, lobster with cream, and *cotriade*, fish soup with potatoes, onions, garlic, and butter.

Beyond the sea, the lamb that hails from the farms on the little island of Ouessant, off the coast of Brest, is well known. Called *pré-salé*, or "salt meadow," they feed on sea-salted grass, which tenderizes their meat while their hearts are still pumping. Try the regional *ragout de mouton* and you can taste the difference. Of all its culinary treasures, however, Brittany is best known as home of the humble crêpe—a large, delicate pancake served warm with a variety of sweet or savory fillings.

—Jennifer Ladonne

CELTIC ELIXIR

Chouchen, Brittany's classic mead-like beverage made from honey, dates back to Celtic times, when it was considered an aphrodisiac and an *elixir d'immortalité*. Artisanal chouchen is often blended with luscious Breton honeys. This delicious drink is traditionally served cold as an aperitif to highlight its refreshing qualities and its soft, earthy flavor.

CRÊPES

Brittany's most illustrious contribution to French cuisine is the crêpe and its heartier sibling the *galette*. What's the difference between the two? The darker galette is made with tender buckwheat called blé noir or blé sarrasin, and has a deeper flavor best paired with savory fillings—like lobster, mushrooms, or the traditional ham and cheese. A crêpe is wafer-thin and made with a lighter batter. It is typically served with sweet fillings like strawberries and cream, apples in brandy, or chocolate. Accompanied by a glass of local cider, galettes and crêpes make an ideal light, inexpensive meal. Traditionally, crêpes are eaten from the tails toward the center point to save the most flavorful, buttery part for last.

CANCALE OYSTER

At seven dollars a dozen, you simply can't do better than a plate of freshly shucked Cancale oysters and half a lemon from a seafood stand along the quay. Best enjoyed atop the breezy sea wall overlooking the Mont Saint-Michel bay, the shells are simply tossed seaward after slurping the succulent insides. Cancale's oyster beds benefit from some of the world's highest tides and strongest currents, which keep the oysters oxygen- and plankton-rich, resulting in a large, firm, yet tender specimen.

PLOUGASTEL STRAWBERRY AND CAMUS DE BRETAGNE ARTICHOKE

Together, the four regions of Brittany make up France's highest yielding farmland. Among the more prosaic crops grown here are two standouts: the large, fleshy camus artichoke and the plump Plougastel strawberry. Come spring, the markets of Brittany (and Paris, for that matter) are teeming with enthusiastic cooks just itching to get their hands on the first produce of the season. The juicy Plougastel strawberry season lasts for only a few weeks in June, while artichoke season runs into the fall.

LE BUERRE

Temperate Brittany's lush grazing lands make for exceptional milk products and, like wine, they are discussed in terms of *élévages* and *terroir*. Butter your roll at a four-star Paris restaurant and you're likely getting a taste of Brittany's finest—*le buerre Bordier*. Jacques Bordier, headquartered in St. Malo's Vieille Ville, sets the gold standard for butter, and his luscious sweet cream version is imported daily to top restaurants throughout France. Other flavors include a pungent purple- and green-flecked algae butter (best slathered on sourdough and eaten with oysters), and the *buerre fleur de sel de Guérande*, laced with crunchy grains of the prized grey-hued salt hand-harvested in the salt marshes of Guérande, near La Baule.

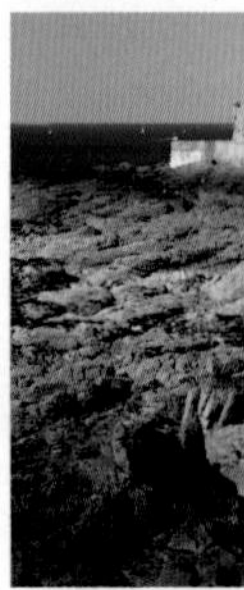

Updated by Jennifer Ladonne

Wherever you wander in Brittany—along jagged coastal cliffs, through cobbled seaport streets, into burnished-oak cider pubs—you'll hear the primal pulse of Celtic music. Made up of bagpipes, drums, and the thin, haunting filigree of a tin-whistle tune, these folkloric notes tell you that you are in the land of the Bretons, where Celtic bloodlines run deep as a druid's roots into the rocky, sea-swept soil.

France's most fiercely and determinedly ethnic people, the Bretons delight in celebrating their primeval culture—circle dancing at street fairs, the women donning starched lace-bonnet *coiffes,* and the men in striped fishermen's shirts at the least sign of a regional celebration. They name their children Erwan and Edwige, carry sacred statues in ceremonial religious processions called *pardons,* pray in hobbit-scale stone churches decked with elfin, moonfaced gargoyles. And scattered over the mossy hillsides stand Stonehenge-like dolmens and menhirs (prehistoric standing stones), eerie testimony to a primordial culture that predated and has long outlived Frankish France.

Similarities in character, situation, or culture to certain islands across the Channel are by no means coincidental. Indeed, the Celts that migrated to this westernmost outcrop of the French landmass spent much of the Iron Age on the British Isles, where they introduced the indigenes to innovations like the potter's wheel, the rotary millstone, and the compass. This first influx of Continental culture to Great Britain was greeted with typically mixed feelings, and by the late 5th century AD the Saxon hordes had sent these Celtic "Brits" packing southward, to the peninsula that became Brittany. So completely did they dominate their new, Cornwall-like peninsula (appropriately named Finistère, from *finis terrae,* or "land's end") that when in 496 they allied themselves with Clovis, the king of the Franks, he felt as if he'd just claimed a little bit of England.

Needless to say, the cultural exchange flowed both ways over the Channel. From their days on the British Isles the Britons brought a folklore that shares with England the bittersweet legend of Tristan and Iseult, and that weaves mystical tales of the Cornwall–Cornouaille of King Arthur and Merlin. They brought a language that still renders village names unpronounceable: Aber-Wrac'h, Tronoën, Locmariaquer, Poldreuzic, Kerhornaouen. And, too, they brought a way of life with them: half-timber seaside cider bars, their blackened-oak tables softened with prim bits of lace; stone cottages fringed with clumps of hollyhock, hydrangea, and foxglove; bearded fishermen in yellow oilskins heaving the day's catch into weather-beaten boats, terns and seagulls wheeling in their wake. It's a way of life that feels deliciously exotic to the Frenchman and—like the ancient drone of the bagpipes—comfortably, delightfully, even primally familiar to the Anglo-Saxon.

NORTHEAST BRITTANY AND THE CHANNEL COAST

It's useful to know that Brittany is divided into two nearly equal parts—Upper Brittany, along the Channel coast, and Lower Brittany. The latter (called in French Basse-Bretagne or Bretagne Bretonnante) is, generally speaking, the more interesting. But the Channel coast of Upper Brittany has its share of marvels. The rolling farmland around Rennes is strewn with mighty castles, such as the one in Vitré—remnants of Brittany's ceaseless efforts to repel invaders during the Middle Ages and a testimony to the wealth derived from pirate and merchant ships. The beautiful Côte d'Émeraude (Emerald Coast) stretches west from Cancale to St-Brieuc, and the dramatic Côte de Granit Rose (Pink Granite Coast) extends from Paimpol to Trébeurden and the Corniche Bretonne. Follow the coastal routes D786 and D34—winding, narrow roads that total less than 100 km (62 mi) but can take five hours to drive; the spectacular views that unfold en route make the journey worthwhile.

VITRÉ

32 km (20 mi) south of Fougères via D798 and D178.

There's still a feel of the Middle Ages about the formidable castle, tightly packed half-timber houses, remaining ramparts, and dark alleyways of Vitré (pronounced vee-*tray*). Built high above the Vilaine Valley, the medieval walled town that spreads out from the castle's gates, though small, is the best-preserved in Brittany, and utterly beguiling. The Disney-esque castle stands at the west end of town, facing narrow, cobbled streets as picturesque as any in Brittany—Rue Poterie, Rue d'Embas, and Rue Beaudrairie, originally the home of tanners (the name comes from *baudoyers*, or leather workers).

GETTING HERE

Several trains traveling between Paris and Rennes stop daily in Vitré. The trip from Rennes takes 30 minutes. Both SNCF and TIV run a couple of daily buses between Vitré and Fougères (35 mins) but only one round-trip on Sunday.

Visitor Information Vitré Tourist Office. ✉ *Pl. St-Yves* ☎ *02–99–75–04–46* 🌐 *www.ot-vitre.fr.*

EXPLORING

★ Rebuilt in the 14th and 15th centuries to protect Brittany from invasion, the fairy-tale, 11th-century **Château de Vitré**—shaped in an imposing triangle with fat, round towers—proved to be one of the province's most successful fortresses: during the Hundred Years' War (1337–1453) the English repeatedly failed to take it, even when they occupied the rest of the town.

It's a splendid sight, especially from the vantage point of Rue de Fougères across the river valley below. Time, not foreigners, came closest to ravaging the castle, which has been heavily though tastefully restored during the past century.

The **Hôtel de Ville** (town hall), however, is an unfortunate 1913 accretion to the castle courtyard. Visit the wing to the left of the entrance, beginning with the **Tour St-Laurent** and its museum, which contains 15th- and 16th-century sculptures, Aubusson tapestries, and engravings.

Continue along the walls via the **Tour de l'Argenterie**—which contains a macabre collection of stuffed frogs and reptiles preserved in glass jars—to the **Tour de l'Oratoire** (Oratory Tower). ☎ *02–99–75–04–54* 🌐 *www.mairie-vitre.com* 🎫 *€4* ⏲ *May–Sept., Wed.–Mon. 10–12:45 and 2–6; Oct.–Apr., Mon. and Wed.–Sat. 10–12:15 and 2–5:30, Sun. 2–5:30.*

Fragments of the town's medieval ramparts include the 15th-century **Tour de la Bridolle** (✉ *Pl. de la République*), five blocks up from the castle.

The church of **Notre-Dame** (✉ *Pl. Notre-Dame*), with its fine, pinnacled south front, was built in the 15th and 16th centuries. There are at least 10 other picturesque historical sites, from medieval postern gateways to the 14th-century Saint Nicolas hospital chapel (now a museum of religious art) within town; other jewels, such as Madame de Sévigné's Château-Musée des Roches-Sévigné, are set in the nearby countryside. Inquire at the tourist office for details.

WHERE TO STAY

¢ **Le Petit Billot.** Carved paneling in the breakfast room and faded pastel tones give this small family-run hotel a delightful French provincial air. Rooms may not be spacious but are spic-and-span, and a steal at the price. The hotel has an informal relationship with Le Potager, the restaurant right next door, which serves reliable, though rather unexciting, Breton cuisine (closed Monday, no lunch Saturday, no dinner Sunday). **Pros:** family ambience; great value. **Cons:** rooms are small; most have only shower not bath. ✉ *5 bis, pl. du Général-Leclerc* ☎ *02–99–75–02–10* 🌐 *www.petit-billot.com* *21 rooms, 4 with bath* *In-room: no a/c. In-hotel: some pets allowed* 💳 *AE, MC, V* *EP.*

RENNES

36 km (22 mi) west of Vitré via D857 and N157, 345 km (215 mi) west of Paris, 107 km (66 mi) north of Nantes.

Packed with students during the school year, studded with sterile 18th-century granite buildings, and yet graced with medieval houses, Rennes (pronounced *wren*) is the traditional gateway to Brittany. Since the

Northeast Brittany & the Channel Coast
0
15 mi
0
15 km
CÔTE DE GRANIT ROSE
Perros-Guirec
Ile de Brehat
Trébeurden
Treguier
Paimpol
Pointe de Bilfot
Lannion
Plougasnou
GORROIS
Plouha
Morlaix
Guingamp
St-Brieuc
Golfe de St-Malo
TO PLYMOUTH
TO ST HELIER
TO PORTSMOUTH
CÔTE ÉMERAUDE
Cap Fréhel
Cap d'Erquy
Baie de St-Brieuc
St-Malo
Dinard
Cancale
Baie du Mont St-Michel
Mont-St-Michel
Avranches
Matignon
Pontorson
Dol-de-Bretagne
Lamballe
Plaintel
Dinan
Bazouges
Combourg
Moncontour
Corlay
Evran
Carhaix-Plouguer
Tinténiac
Bécherel
Fougères
St Gondran
Loudéac
Merdrignac
St-Méen-le-Grand
Coray
Montort-sur-Meu
Guemene-sur-Scorft
Pontivy
Rennes
Vitré
Vilaine
Oust
Josselin
Ploërmel
TO PARIS
la Guerche-de-Bretagne
Lorient
D788
D786
D767
N12-E50
D787
D764
D786
D768
D266
D210
N176
N137
D795
A34
D973
N12-E50
N164
D700
D2
D27
N175
N137
N12
D178
D15
D1
N164
D769
D1
D3
D768
N24
N12-E50
D177
N137
D178
N166
D767
N165
D126

province was joined to Paris in 1532, Rennes has been the site of squabbles with the national capital, many taking place in the Rennes's Palais de Justice, long the political center of Brittany and the one building that survived a terrible fire in 1720 that lasted a week and destroyed half the city. The remaining cobbled streets and 15th-century half-timber houses form an interesting contrast to the classical feel of the cathedral and Jacques Gabriel's disciplined granite buildings, broad avenues, and spacious squares. Many of the 15th- and 16th-century houses in the streets surrounding the cathedral have been converted into shops, boutiques, restaurants, and crêperies. The cavalier manner in which the French go about running a bar out of a 500-year-old building can be disarming to New Worlders.

GETTING HERE

The TGV Atlantique travels faster than a speeding bullet from Paris's Gare Montparnasse to Rennes (2¼ hrs, €55), leaving every two hours or so, and through to Brest, while a branch line heads to St-Malo. Rennes's Gare SNCF (Place de la Gare) is about a 20-minute walk from the heart of the city. Trains leave for Paris (2¼ hrs), Nantes (2 hrs), St-Malo (55 mins), and Bordeaux (6 hrs). The Gare Routière is next to the train station, but it's not the safest place to hang out. Buses go to Nantes (2 hrs), St-Malo (2 hrs), Dinan (1 hr), and Mont-St-Michel (85 mins). Rennes's city bus system, STAR, will deliver you to almost any destination in town. There are also Ryanair flights to Rennes from England (London Stansted).

Visitor Information Rennes Tourist Office. ✉ *11 rue St-Yves* ☎ *02–99–67–11–11* 🌐 *en.tourisme-rennes.com.*

EXPLORING

The capital of Brittany, Rennes is one of the liveliest cities in the region. During the school year, the town rhythm is set by some 40,000 students. Although summer seems to happen elsewhere for most Rennais, it is still a pleasant time to wander the city's cafés and bookstores.

The **Parlement de Bretagne** (✉ *Rue Nationale* 🌐 *www.parlement-bretagne.com*), the palatial original home of the Breton Parliament and now of the Rennes law courts, was designed in 1618 by Salomon de Brosse, architect of the Luxembourg Palace in Paris. It was the most important building in Rennes to escape the 1720 flames, but in 1994, following a massive demonstration by Breton fishermen demanding state subsidies, a disastrous fire broke out at the building, leaving it a charred shell. Fortunately, much of the artwork—though damaged—was saved by firefighters, who arrived at the scene after the building was already engulfed in flames. It was a case of the alarm that cried "fire" once too often; a faulty bell, which rang regularly for no reason, had led the man on duty to ignore the signal. Restoration has now been completed. Call the tourist office (☎ *02–99–67–11–66* to book a 90-minute guided tour [€6.80]).

The **Musée de Bretagne** *(Museum of Brittany)* reopened in 2006 in brand-new headquarters designed by superstar architect Christian de Portzamparc and now occupies a vast three-part space that it shares with the Rennes municipal library and Espaces des Sciences. Portzamparc's layout harmonizes nicely with the organization of the museum's extensive ethnographic and archaeological collection, which, chronologically ordered, depicts the everyday life of Bretons from prehistoric times up to the present. There's also a space devoted to the famous Dreyfus Affair; Alfred Dreyfus, an army captain who was wrongly accused of espionage and whose case was championed by Émile Zola, was tried a second time in Rennes in 1899. ✉ *10 cours des Allies* ☎ *02–23–40–66–70* 🌐 *www.musee-bretagne.fr* 🎫 *€4 museum, €7 including exhibitions* ⏲ *Tues. noon–9, Wed.–Fri. noon–7, weekends 2–7.*

The **Musée des Beaux-Arts** *(Fine Arts Museum)* contains works by Georges de La Tour, Jean-Baptiste Chardin, Camille Corot, Paul Gauguin, and Maurice Utrillo, to name a few. The museum is particularly strong in French 17th-century paintings and drawings, and has an interesting collection of modern French artists. Please note that the second floor was closed for renovation of unspecified duration at this writing. ✉ *20 quai Émile-Zola* ☎ *02–23–62–17–45* 🌐 *www.mbar.org* 🎫 *€4.58* ⏲ *Tues.–Sun. 10–noon and 2–6.*

6

A late-18th-century building in Classical style that took 57 years to construct, the **Cathédrale St-Pierre** looms above Rue de la Monnaie at the west end of the Vieille Ville (Old Town), bordered by the Rance River. Stop in to admire its richly decorated interior and outstanding 16th-century Flemish altarpiece. ✉ *Pl. St-Pierre* ⏲ *Mon.–Sat. 8:30–noon and 2–5, Sun. 8:30–noon.*

★ Take care to stroll through the lovely **Parc du Thabor** (✉ *Pl. St-Melaine*), east of the Palais des Musées. It's a large, formal French garden with regimented rows of trees, shrubs, and flowers, and a notable view of the church of **Notre-Dame-en-St-Melaine.**

WHERE TO EAT AND STAY

$$ FRENCH ✕ **Picca.** Around the corner from the Palais de Justice and next to the municipal theater is this oddly named brasserie that serves Patrick Pochic's traditional Breton cuisine, ranging from scallops to entrecôte steaks. Its huge, sunny terrace is the perfect place to people-watch while downing a half dozen fresh oysters and an aperitif. The prix-fixe menu is €13.50. ✉ *15 Galeries du Théâtre* ☎ *02–99–78–17–17* 💳 *MC, V.*

¢–$ ★ 🏨 **Garden.** With all rooms overlooking a picturesque, stone-lined, trelliage-bedecked garden, this hotel likes to welcome visitors to "silent nights"—restful, too, thanks to the guest room decor. As *charmant* as they come, they are stylishly wrought in cheery pink and orange pastels, wicker-wood headboards, and fetching wood-trim furniture. Breakfast is served in the garden when possible, and its age-old wooden gallery makes this sunny inner courtyard a sweet place to reboot yourself. Room 202 is the most spacious. **Pros:** pretty architecture; handy for sites. **Cons:** rooms small; parking difficult. ✉ *3 rue Jean-Marie-Duhamel* ☎ *02–99–65–45–06* 🌐 *www.hotel-garden.fr* 🛏 *25 rooms* 🛎 *In-room: no a/c, Wi-Fi. In-hotel: some pets allowed* 💳 *AE, MC, V.*

$$$–$$$$ ★ 🏨 **LeCoq-Gadby.** A 19th-century mansion with huge fireplaces and antiques sets the stage for this cozy retreat. Homey guest rooms have four-poster beds and floral covers, while hydrotherapy facilities, a hammam (steam room), a Jacuzzi, and a sauna are all available if you want

One delightful lunch on a Rennes square and you'll forget all about those headlines back home.

to be pampered. Pierre Le Grand's cuisine must be good—French presidents have dined here on such delicacies as *pigeonneau en cocotte au beurre salé* (pigeon casserole with salted butter). Book way in advance for this popular hotel and restaurant (closed Sunday). **Pros:** manorial ambience; great cuisine. **Cons:** hotel rooms often booked solid; small portions in restaurant. ✉ *156 rue d'Antrain* ☎ *02–99–38–05–55* 🌐 *www.lecoq-gadby.com* *14 rooms* *In-room: no a/c, refrigerator, Internet, Wi-Fi. In-hotel: restaurant, room service, bar, some pets allowed* ▭ *AE, DC, MC, V* 🍽 *MAP.*

$$–$$$ **Mercure Rennes Place de Bretagne.** Ranging in style from Rococo revisited to severe Neoclassical, these three side-by-side stately 19th-century buildings add up to one centrally located good option. On a quiet, narrow backstreet close to the cathedral—and a few blocks away from the town's main museums, opera, and theaters—the hotel offers a sleek, minimal-meets-trad interior. In the lobby, clocks toll the hours in countries around the world, while modern, clean-as-a-pin guest rooms, all in beiges and maroons, offer tranquil havens for businesspeople and weary travelers. **Pros:** city-center location; quiet rooms. **Cons:** bland decor; no restaurant. ✉ *6 rue Lanjuinais* ☎ *02–99–79–12–36* 🌐 *www.mercure.com* *48 rooms* *In-room: a/c, Wi-Fi. In-hotel: room service, bar, some pets allowed* ▭ *AE, DC, MC, V* 🍽 *BP.*

NIGHTLIFE AND THE ARTS

The streets around Place Ste-Anne are jammed with popular student bars, most of them housed in fantastic medieval buildings with character to spare.

If you feel like dancing the night away, head to **L'Espace** (✉ *45 bd. de la Tour d'Auvergne* ☎ *02–99–30–21–95*). For the night owl, **Pym's Club** (✉ *27 pl. du Colombier* ☎ *02–99–67–30–00*), with three dance floors, stays open all night, every night.

Brittany's top classical music venue is the **Opéra de Rennes** (✉ *Pl. de l'Hôtel de Ville* ☎ *02–99–78–48–78* 🌐 *www.opera-rennes.fr*). All kinds of performances are staged at the **Théâtre National de Bretagne** (✉ *10 av. Louis-Barthou* ☎ *02–99–35–27–74*). The famous annual international rock-and-roll festival, **Les Transmusicales** (☎ *02–99–31–12–10 for information*), happens the second week of December in bars around town and at the Théâtre National de Bretagne.

WORD OF MOUTH

"The Richeux—a gem of a place—has a sailboat anchored in St-Malo and a three-hour ride on it is included in the room rate (May-September)! Seeing St-Malo from the sea was a bonus, beautiful and very like Québec city—perhaps not surprising since Jacques Cartier sailed from St-Malo to found Québec." —JuliePA

★ The first week of July sees **Les Tombées de la Nuit** (☎ *02–99–32–56–56* 🌐 *www.lestombeesdelanuit.com*), the "Nightfalls" Festival, featuring crowds, Celtic music, dance, and theater performances staged in old historic streets and churches around town.

SHOPPING

A lively **market** is held on Place des Lices on Saturday morning.

6

CANCALE

86 km (54 mi) northwest of Rennes via N137 and D210.

Nothing says Brittany like seafood and nothing says seafood like this village, one of the most picturesque fishing village in Brittany. Head here using buses from St-Malo and then make for the countless stalls or restaurants along the quay, where you can enjoy the bounty of Cancale, renowned for its offshore *bancs d'huîtres* (oyster beds). You can sample the little brutes here or have a real seafood feast at the culinary mecca not far from town, the Château Richeux.

The **Musée de la Ferme Marine** *(Sea Farm Museum)* just south of town explains everything you ever wanted to know about farming oysters and has a display of 1,500 different types of shells. ✉ *L'Aurore* ☎ *02–99–89–69–99* 🌐 *www.ferme-marine.com* 🎫 *€6.80* ⏲ *Guided 1-hr tours in English, July–mid-Sept., daily at 2.*

WHERE TO STAY

$$$$ Fodor's Choice ★ **Château Richeux.** *Hélas!* The famed Breton gastronomic shrine known as the Maisons de Bricourt shrine is no more—superstar chef Olivier Roellinger hung up his toque because of health problems in 2008. Happily, his family still presides over their beautiful hotel empire, including the castellated 1920s waterfront Château Richeux. Even better, readers rave about Le Coquillage, the hotel's small bistro, which specializes in local oysters and seafood platters served up in a relaxed, cozy atmosphere. As the only eatery left under the master's own hand, it

provides some consolation (with a menu at €26) for those who'll miss the now-defunct Maison de Bricourt. The Richeux is built on the ruins of the Du Guesclin family's 11th-century château, 5 km (3 mi) south of Cancale, and is surrounded by a "Celtic garden." Request one of the rooms with large bay windows, which have stunning views of Mont-St-Michel. Several miles away are two other, more private hotel options, Les Rimains, four guest rooms set in a very handsome Breton stone house, perched over Cancale's harbor, along with Gîtes Marins, two airy, almost Cape Cod—style seaside vacation houses fit for several people. **Pros:** famous cuisine; picturesque setting. **Cons:** isolated site. ✉ *Le Point du Jour, St-Méloir des Ondes* ☎ *02–99–89–64–76* 🌐 *www.maisons-de-bricourt.com* *13 rooms* *In-room: no a/c, refrigerator, Wi-Fi. In-hotel: restaurant* ▭ *AE, DC, MC, V* *BP.*

SHOPPING

Sublime tastes of Brittany—salted butter caramels, fruity sorbets, rare honeys, and heirloom breads—are sold in upper Cancale at the Roellingers's **Grain de Vanille** (✉ *12 pl. de la Victoire* ☎ *02–23–15–12–70*). Tables beckon, so why not sit a spell and enjoy a cup of "Mariage" tea and—Brittany in a bite—some cinnamon-orange-flavor *malouine* cookies? Mr. Roellinger's newest addition to his culinary empire, **Les Entrepôts Épices-Roellinger** (✉ *1 rue Duguesclin* ☎ *02–99–89–64–76*), is dedicated to the exotic spices he personally searched the world to find. A treasure trove of single spices, along with his signature spice blends—such as Poudre Curry Corsaire, for mussels and shellfish; and Poudre du Vent, for squab or cream sauces—exotic peppers, *fleur de sel*, and choice vanillas.

ST-MALO

Fodor's Choice ★

23 km (14 mi) west of Cancale via coastal D201.

Thrust out into the sea, bound to the mainland only by tenuous man-made causeways, romantic St-Malo—"the pirates' city"—has built a reputation as a breeding ground for phenomenal sailors. Many were fishermen, but St-Malo's most famous sea dogs were corsairs, pirates paid by the French crown to harass the Limeys across the Channel. Robert Surcouf and Duguay-Trouin were just two of these privateers who helped make this town rich through piratical pillages. Today, the town has plenty of picturesque coastal sights.

GETTING HERE

The train station (Square Jean-Coquelin) is a 15-minute walk from the walled town—walk straight up Avenue Louis-Martin. Half a dozen trains daily make the 45-mi trip from Rennes to St-Malo (55–80 mins, €16); a TGV express from Paris's Gare Montparnassse arrives several times a day in Rennes, where you can transfer. Trains also connect St-Malo to Dol (15 mins) and Dinan via Dol (65 mins), but the bus is cheaper and faster. TIV runs buses to Rennes (1¾ hrs), Dinard (40 mins), and Cancale (30 mins). CAT makes the trip to Dinan (35 mins) and Les Courriers Bretons makes the 1¼-hour journey to Mont-St-Michel. Buses leave from the Gare Routière, immediately outside the *intra-muros* (within the walls) Old Town. You can also ferry from here to Dinan and Dinard via Emeraude Lines.

Visitor Information **St-Malo Tourist Office.** ✉ *Esplanade St-Vincent* ☎ *02–99–56–64–48* 🌐 *www.saint-malo-tourisme.com.*

EXPLORING

Facing Dinard across the Rance Estuary, the stone ramparts of St-Malo have withstood the pounding of the Atlantic since the 12th century, the founding date of the town's main church, the **Cathédrale St-Vincent** (on Rue St-Benoît). The ramparts were considerably enlarged and modified in the 18th century, and now extend from the castle for more than 1½ km (1 mi) around the Vieille Ville—known as *intra-muros*. The views are stupendous, especially at high tide. The town itself has proved less resistant: a weeklong fire in 1944, kindled by retreating Nazis, wiped out nearly all the old buildings. Restoration work was more painstaking than brilliant, but the narrow streets and granite houses of the Vieille Ville were satisfactorily re-created, enabling St-Malo to regain its role as a busy fishing port, seaside resort, and tourist destination. The ramparts themselves are authentic and the flames also spared houses along Rue de Pelicot in the Vieille Ville. Battalions of tourists invade this quaint part of town in summer, so if you want to avoid crowds, don't come then. 6

At the edge of the ramparts is the 15th-century **château** *(Town History Museum)* , whose great keep and watchtowers command an impressive view of the harbor and coastline. It houses the **Musée d'Histoire de la Ville,** devoted to the great figures—from Jacques Cartier to Chateaubriand, "Father of Romanticism"—who have touched local history, and the **Galerie Quic-en-Grogne,** a museum in a tower, where various episodes and celebrities from St-Malo's past are recalled by way of waxworks. ✉ *Hôtel de Ville* ☎ *02–99–40–71–57* 🌐 *www.st-malo.fr/decouvrir/musee-histoire.html* 🎫 *€5.40* ⏲ *Apr.–Sept., daily 10–12:30 and 2–6; Oct.–Mar., Tues.–Sun. 10–noon and 2–6.*

Five hundred yards offshore is the **Ile du Grand Bé**, a small island housing the somber military tomb of the great Romantic writer Viscount René de Chateaubriand, who was born in St-Malo. The islet can be reached by a causeway at low tide *only.*

The "Bastille of Brittany," the **Fort National**, also offshore and accessible by causeway at low tide only, is a massive fortress with a dungeon constructed in 1689 by that military-engineering genius Sébastien de Vauban. ☎ *02–99–85–34–33* 🌐 *www.fortnational.com* 🎫 *€4* ⏲ *June–Sept., daily 10:30–6 depending on tides (see Web site).*

You can pay homage to Jacques Cartier, who set sail from St-Malo in 1535 on a voyage in which he would discover the St. Lawrence River and found Québec, at his tomb in the church of **St-Vincent** (✉ *Grand-Rue*). His statue looks out over the town ramparts, four blocks away, along with that of swashbuckling corsair Robert Surcouf (hero of many daring 18th-century raids on the British navy), eternally wagging an angry finger over the waves at England.

WHERE TO EAT AND STAY

$$$ FRENCH ✕ **Chalut.** The reputation of this small restaurant with nautical decor has grown since chef Jean-Philippe Foucat decided to emphasize fresh seafood. The succinct menus change as frequently as the catch of the day. Try the sautéed John Dory with fresh coriander or the fresh lobster in lime. ✉ *8 rue de la Corne-de-Cerf* ☎ *02–99–56–71–58* ▭ *MC, V* ⊙ *Closed Mon. and Tues.*

$$$$ FRENCH ✕ **Le Saint-Placide.** This sleek, modern dining room is garnering serious accolades in a town where talent is in no short supply. Chef Luc Mobihan's impeccable cuisine, with a soft spot for local seafood, brilliantly harmonizes flavors to draw out the intrinsic qualities of the fish or meat without overpowering. Lobster risotto is both rich and light, and tender lamb rolled in a buttery phylo literally melts in the mouth. With four prix-fixe menus to choose from, including the "Mélanosporum" all-truffle *formule*, diners have the pleasure of sampling a range of dishes from this talented chef. ✉ *6 Place du Poncel* ☎ *02–99–81–70–73* ▭ *AE, MC, V* ⊙ *Closed Tues., Wed., Feb., and last 2 wks in June.*

$$–$$$ **Beaufort.** A gracious welcome and infinite sea views are first to greet you at this beachfront hotel, handsomely accented with a terra-cotta facade and stylish mansard roof. Tastefully decorated in pale earth tones, the guest rooms are bright, comfortable, and meant to harmonize with the sea and sky just outside your window or private terrace, should you be lucky enough to nab one of the six on offer. Bathrooms are petite but modern and well equipped. Although meals are limited to a bountiful continental breakfast, a lovely café-bar area, overlooking an expanse of beach and sea, offers wines, teas, and coffees throughout the day. For sports lovers, the famed La Digue promenade just in front is ideal for an early morning jog along the beach. **Pros:** few minutes' ride to the *intra-muros* Old Town and walking distance from good restaurants and shops. **Cons:** rooms are on the small side and not all face the water. ✉ *25 Chaussée du Sillon* ☎ *02–99–40–99–99* 🌐 *www.hotel-beaufort.com* *22 rooms* *In-room: a/c, refrigerator, Wi-Fi. In-hotel: bar, parking (paid)* ▭ *AE, DC, MC, V* *BP.*

$–$$ ★ **Elizabeth.** Done up with impressive style, this 17th-century town house, built into the ancient city walls and near the Porte St-Louise, is a little gem of sophistication in touristy St-Malo. The lobby welcomes with large sash windows, 400-year-old wood beams, and comfy mod furniture. Downstairs, breakfast is served in a majestic cellar with ancient stone walls and beams; upstairs, five floors of guest rooms in "Les Armateurs" attempt to channel the spirit of the fabled privateer Robert Surcouf with the use of Breton antiques. The most spacious rooms are on the top floor: No. 509 has a fine view of the harbor, No. 510 of the *intra-muros* Old Town. Next door, "Les Skippers" is a smaller abode with north-facing rooms with handsome but more modern decors. **Pros:** central; good value. **Cons:** hard to park; big difference between bland rooms and stylish suites. ✉ *2 rue des Cordiers,* ☎ *02–99–56–24–98* 🌐 *www.st-malo-hotel-elizabeth.com* *17 rooms* *In-room: no a/c, refrigerator, Wi-Fi. In-hotel: some pets allowed* ▭ *MC, V* *BP.*

NIGHTLIFE AND THE ARTS

Bar de l'Univers (✉ *12 pl. Chateaubriand*) is a nice spot to enjoy sipping a drink in a pirate's-lair setting. **La Belle Époque** (✉ *11 rue de Dinan*) is a popular hangout for all ages until the wee hours. **L'Éscalier** (✉ *La Buzardière, Rue de la Tour-du-Bonheur*) is the place for dancing the night away.In summer, performances are held at the **Théâtre Chateaubriand** (✉ *6 rue du Grout-de-St-Georges* ☎ *02–99–40–98–05*). Bastille Day (July 14) sees the **Fête du Clos Poulet**, a town festival with traditional dancing. July and August bring a monthlong religious music festival, the **Festival de la Musique Sacrée**.

SHOPPING

A lively outdoor **market** is held in the streets of Old St-Malo every Tuesday and Friday.

DINARD

Fodor's Choice ★

13 km (8 mi) west of St-Malo via Rance Bridge.

Dinard is the most elegant resort town on this stretch of the Brittany coast. Its picture-book perch on the Rance Estuary opposite the walled town of St-Malo lured the English aristocracy here in droves toward the end of the 19th century. What started out as a small fishing port soon became a seaside mecca of lavish Belle Époque villas (more than 400 still dot the town and shoreline), grand hotels, and a bustling casino.

GETTING HERE

No trains head here, so you have to train to St-Malo, then transfer to a bus (frequent departures, €3) for the 15-minute ride to Dinard. From April to September a ferryboat links the two towns (10 minutes, €6). Buses arrive here from Rennes and other towns in Brittany.

Visitor Information Dinard Tourist Office (✉ *2 bd. Féart* ☎ *02–99–46–94–12* 🌐 *www.ot-dinard.com*).

EXPLORING

While a number of modern establishments punctuate the landscape, Dinard still retains something of an Edwardian tone. To make the most of Dinard's beauty, head down to the Pointe de la Vicomté, at the town's southern tip, where the cliffs offer panoramic views across the Baie du Prieuré and Rance Estuary, or stroll along the narrow promenade.

★ The **Promenade Clair de Lune** hugs the seacoast on its way toward the English Channel and passes in front of the small jetty used by boats crossing to St-Malo. In Dinard, the road weaves along the shore and is adorned with luxuriant palm trees and mimosa blooms, which, from July to the end of September, are illuminated at dusk with spotlights; strollers are serenaded with recorded music. The promenade really hits its stride as it rounds the **Pointe du Moulinet** and heads toward the sandy **Plage du Prieuré,** named after a priory that once stood here. River meets sea in a foaming mass of rock-pounding surf: use caution as you walk along the slippery path to the calm shelter of the **Plage de l'Écluse,** an inviting sandy beach bordered by the casino and numerous stylish hotels. The coastal path picks up on the west side of Plage de l'Écluse, ringing the

Pointe de la Malouine and the Pointe des Étêtés before arriving at the **Plage de St-Énogat.**

WHERE TO EAT AND STAY

$$$–$$$$ FRENCH ✕ **Didier Méril.** Nudging right up to the beach in Dinard's historic center, this chic restaurant serves up gourmet fare along with breathtaking sea views. Chef Méril takes his inspiration from the local bounty, with seafood front and center. Fresh-from-the-sea dishes, such as salty-sweet Cancale oysters, *ricassée de langoustines,* and *Trilogie de poisson* with lobster coulis vie with Breton specialties, like terrine *paysanne au sanglier* (wild boar), on four fixed-price menus. An impressive pages-long wine list, boasting 450 wines from every region imaginable, satisfies the most discerning wine snob. In warm weather, the seaside terrace is a fine place to enjoy a frosty glass of champagne or a cigar from the *cave à cigars,* if so inclined. For lodging, six stylish rooms come with some endearing quirks. For example, the top floor's room No. 6 offers spectacular ocean vistas from the bed or the bathtub, as it's smack in the center of the room. ✉ *1 pl. du Général de Gaulle* ☎ *02–99–46–95–74* 🌐 *www.restaurant-didier-meril.com* ▭ *AE, MC, V* 🍽 *BP.*

$–$$ 🏨 **Printania.** Replete with verandas, charmingly folkloric Breton wood carvings, and a low-key Napoléon III vibe, Le Printania enjoys a sweet perch right on Dinan's Clair de Lune promenade. Many of the guest rooms face the water with "le cité corsaire"—St-Malo—looming in the distance; they're furnished with regional touches, with fine wood chairs and original paintings, rather than prints, of local scenes. The best ones have a balcony and sea view (ask for Nos. 101, 102, 211, or 311). Seafood and regional dishes are served in the riotously colorful waterfront dining room by waitresses in regional costume. **Pros:** friendly, tasteful room decor; full board plan entices thanks to tempting food. **Cons:** sturdy recent price hikes; some rooms lack a view. ✉ *5 av. George-V* ☎ *02–99–46–13–07* 🌐 *www.printaniahotel.com* 🛏 *55 rooms* 🛎 *In-room: no a/c. In-hotel: restaurant, bar, Internet terminal* ▭ *MC, V* ⏲ *Closed mid-Nov.–mid-Mar.* 🍽 *FAP.*

$$$–$$$$ ★ 🏨 **Villa Reine-Hortense.** All the Napoléon-III glamour of 19th-century-resort France is yours when you stay at this *folie*—a villa built by the Russian Prince Vlassov in homage to his "queen," Hortense de Beauharnais (daughter of Napoléon's beloved Joséphine and mother to Emperor Napoléon III). A magical grand salon topped with a trompe-l'oeil *treillage,* guest rooms with soaring, fairy-tale beds crowned with Empire-style canopies, and glamorous beach views are just some of the delights on tap here. The lucky guest who lands Room 4 will even get to bathe in Queen Hortense's own silver-plated bathtub. **Pros:** high-style paradise; intimate; quirky. **Cons:** a bit "de trop"; *une folie.* ✉ *19 rue de la Malouine* ☎ *02–99–46–54–31* 🌐 *www.villa-reine-hortense.com* 🛏 *8 rooms* 🛎 *In-room: no a/c, refrigerator, Internet. In-hotel: bar, some pets allowed* ▭ *AE, MC, V* ⏲ *Closed Oct.–Mar.* 🍽 *FAP.*

NIGHTLIFE

During July and August, stretches of the **Clair de Lune** promenade become a nighttime son-et-lumière wonderland, thanks to spotlights and recorded music.The main nightlife activity in town is at the **casino** (✉ *4 bd. du Président-Wilson* ☎ *02–99–16–30–30*).

A Belle Epoque beauty, Dinard adds a big dollop of 19th-century elegance to the natural splendor of the Breton coast.

SPORTS AND THE OUTDOORS

For windsurfing, wander over to the **Wishbone Club** (✉ *Digue de l'Écluse* ☎ *02–99–88–15–20*). Boats can be rented from the **Yacht Club** (✉ *Promenade Clair de Lune* ☎ *02–99–46–14–32*).

PAIMPOL

92 km (57 mi) west of Cap Fréhel via D786, 45 km (28 mi) northwest of St-Brieuc.

Paimpol is one of the liveliest fishing ports in the area and a good base for exploring this part of the coast. The town is a maze of narrow streets lined with shops, restaurants, and souvenir boutiques. The harbor, where fishermen used to unload their catch from far-off seas, is its main focal point; today most fish are caught in the Channel. From the sharp cliffs you can see the coast's famous pink-granite rocks. For centuries, but now no longer, Breton fishermen sailed to Newfoundland each spring to harvest cod—a long and perilous journey. The **Fête des Terres-Neuves** is a celebration of the traditional return from Newfoundland of the Breton fishing fleets; it's held on the third Sunday in July. From Paimpol, trains go to Guingamp, and CAT buses go to St-Brieuc; both towns are on the Paris–Brest TGV line.

WHERE TO STAY

$–$$ ★ **Le K'Loys.** Built in the late 19th century for a prominent ship owner, this picturesque stone house nestles right up to Paimpol's main quay, with a view over a yacht and sailboat-stocked marina. Most of the 17 rooms have harbor views, and, if you're lucky enough to nab No.

6, breakfast can be had on your own flower-bedecked balcony. Or if you prefer to catch some moonbeams, the Capitaine room offers a glass ceiling and splendid views from the bed. Although this family-run hotel focuses mostly on comfort and coziness rather than all-out luxury, the rooms—many with fireplaces and asian rugs—are quaintly decorated with traditional Breton touches, includingclassic armoires. The L'Islandais restaurant-creperie, in an old cod fisherman's house, offers traditional Breton fare, including a bargain €18.50 menu. **Pros:** afternoon tea in the glassed-in tearoom is a delight; easy walk to the beach and the old town. **Cons:** some rooms lack a view. ✉ *21 Quai Morand* ☎ *02–96–20–40–01* 🌐 *www.hotel-restaurant-soiree-vrp-paimpol-cotes-d-armor.k-loys.com* *17 rooms* *In-room: no a/c, Wi-Fi. In-hotel: restaurant, bar, some pets allowed, parking (paid)* *AE, MC, V* *BP.*

TRÉBEURDEN

Fodor's Choice ★ *46 km (27 mi) west of Paimpol via D786 and D65, 9 km (6 mi) northwest of Lannion.*

Trébeurden is just one of the scenic highlights of the Côtes d'Armor, the long stretch of Brittany's northern coast, loosely divided into two parts, the Côte d'Emeraude (Emerald Coast) and the peaceful Côte de Granit Rose (Pink Granite Coasta). A small, pleasant fishing village that is now a summer resort town, it makes a good base for exploring the rosy-hue cliffs of the Corniche Bretonne, starting with the rocky point at nearby Le Castel.

GETTING HERE

To get to Trébeurden or Perros-Guirec you must first take the train to Plouraret-Trégor, which is found on the main Paris-Brest train line. From there, take the train to Lannion, a town 12 km (7 mi) inland. From Lanion CAT runs several buses a day to Trébeurden, along with five buses a day to Perros-Guirec, with stops at Trestraou beach and neighboring Ploumanac'h (35 mins).

Visitor Information Trébeurden Tourist Office ✉ *Pl. de Crec'h Hery* ☎ *02–96–23–51–64* 🌐 *www.trebeurden.fr.*

EXPLORING

Trébeurden is near the center of the most picturesque stretches of the Breton coastline. Take a look at the profile of the dramatic rocks off the coast near Trégastel and Perros-Guirec and use your imagination to see La Tête de Mort (Death's Head), La Tortoise, Le Sentinel, and Le Chapeau de Wellington (Wellington's Hat). The coastal scene changes with the sunlight and the sweep and retreat of the tide, whose caprices can strand fishing boats among islands that were, only hours before, hidden beneath the sea.

★ The famous seaside footpath, the **Sentier des Douaniers** (🌐 *www.perros-guirec.com*), starts up at the west end of the Trestraou beach in the resort town of **Perros-Guirec,** 3 km (2 mi) east of Trébeurden; from there this beautifully manicured, fence-lined, and gorgeously scenic path provides a two-hour walk eastward, through fern forests, past cliffs and pink granite boulders to the pretty beach at Ploumanac'h. If you keep your eye out, you might even spot one of the mythical, 900-year-old Korrigans—native sprites with pointed ears, beards, and hoof feet, who come out at night from seaside grottoes to dance around fires. From Perros-Guirec you can take a boat trip out to the Sept Iles, a group of seven islets that are bird sanctuaries. On a hillside perch above **Ploumanac'h** is the village of La Clarté, home to the little Chapelle Notre Dame de la Clarté (✉ *Pl. de la Chapelle*), built of local pink granite and decorated with 14 stations of the cross painted by the master of the Pont-Aven school, Maurice Denis. During the **Pardon of la Clarté** (August 15), a bishop preaches an outdoor mass for the Virgin Mary, village girls wear Trégor costumes, and the statue of the Virgin Mary wears a gold crown (she wears a fake one for the rest of the year). On Ploumanac'h's pleasant beach, Plage de la Bastille, you'll find the Oratoire de St-Guirec, a rose-granite chapel lodged in the sand with other rocks; facing the beach is the neo-medieval, 19th-century **Château de Costaeres**, where Henryk Sienkiewicz wrote *Quo Vadis*. Unfortunately, the magical castle-by-the-sea—whose image graces many postcards of the region—was partly destroyed by a fire and remains private property.

WHERE TO STAY

$$$$ ★ **Manoir de Lan-Kerellec.** The beauty of the Breton coastline is embraced by this Relais & Châteaux hotel, where guest rooms are far more than just comfortable. Set long and cruise-liner-low, this renovated 19th-century Breton manor house has now been outfitted with dramatic windows—plate-glass, round, panoramic—so as to frame stirring vistas of the endless sea and the cliffs of the Côte de Granit Rose (all rooms have sea views). The restaurant, with a wood-beam ceiling inspired by a ship's hull, has a delightful model of the *St-Yves* ship suspended from its ceiling. It mostly serves seafood, but the roast lamb is also good; it does not serve lunch Monday through Thursday. **Pros:** great views; comfy rooms. **Cons:** pricey; restaurant only serves lunch three days a week. ✉ *11 allée Centrale* ☎ *02–96–15–00–00* 🌐 *www.lankerellec.com* *19 rooms* *In-room: no a/c (some), safe, refrigerator, Internet. In-hotel: restaurant, tennis court, some pets allowed* *AE, DC, MC, V* *Closed mid-Nov.–mid-Mar.* *MAP.*

THE ATLANTIC COAST

What Brittany offers in the way of the sea handsomely makes up for its shortage of mountain peaks and passes. Its hundreds of miles of saw-tooth coastline reveal the Atlantic Ocean in its every mood and form—from the peaceful cove where waders poke about hunting seashells to the treacherous bay whose waters swirl over quicksands in unpredictable crosscurrents; from the majestic serenity of the breakers rolling across La Baule's miles of golden-sand beaches to the savage fury of the gigantic waves that fling their force against jagged rocks 340 dizzy feet below the cliffs of Pointe du Raz.

Consisting of the territory lying west of Saint-Brieuc to the Atlantic coast a short distance east of Vannes, Lower Brittany contains in abundance all things Breton, including many of the pardons and other colorful religious ceremonies that take place hereabouts. As for bright lights, Rennes, the student-fueled mind of Brittany, gives way to poets and painters, bringing a refreshing breeze to the historical heaviness of the region. On the Atlantic coast, Nantes, the working-class heart of Brittany, pumps the economy of the region and provides a bracing swig of daily Breton life. Head inland to find a landscape studded with bent trees and craggy rocks that look like they've been bewitched by Merlin in a bad mood.

STE-ANNE-LA-PALUD

Fodor's Choice ★ *136 km (82 mi) southwest of Frébeurden via D767 and D787.*

One of the great attractions of the Brittany calendar is the celebration of a religious festival known as a village **pardon,** replete with banners, saintly statues, a parade, bishops in attendance, women in folk costume, a feast, and hundreds of attendees. The seaside village of Ste-Anne-la-Palud has one of the finest and most authentic age-old pardons in Brittany, held on the last Sunday in August.

Another celebrated *pardon* is held in early September some 40 km (25 mi) north of Ste-Anne. Pilgrims come from afar to Le Folgoët, 24 km (15 mi) northeast of Brest, to attend the town's ceremonial procession. Many also drink from the Fontaine de Salaün, a fountain behind the church, whose water comes from a spring beneath the altar. The splendid church, known as the Basilique, has a sturdy north tower that serves as a beacon for miles around and, inside, a rare, intricately carved granite rood screen separating the choir and nave.

WHERE TO STAY

$$$$ **Hôtel de la Plage.** This former private mansion, with its sturdy round tower, nestles in a cove on a quiet strip of sandy beach on the Bay of Douarnenez—a remote retreat perfect for long, restorative walks. Some of the comfortably furnished guest rooms face the water, as does the glass-front restaurant, where reservations are essential. After a seafood starter (scallops, oysters, or langoustines), try the sea bass with cress and asparagus, the turbot with marrow, or the duck and foie gras with maple syrup and celery. **Pros:** waterfront setting; top-rank restaurant. **Cons:** very expensive; rather formal. ✉ ☎ *02–98–92–50–12* 🌐 *www.plage.com* *24 rooms, 4 suites* *In-room: Internet. In-hotel: restaurant, tennis court, pool, beachfront, Internet terminal, some pets allowed* *AE, DC, MC, V* *Closed Nov.–Apr.* *MAP.*

DOUARNENEZ

14 km (8 mi) south of Ste-Anne-la-Palud.

Douarnenez is a quaint old fishing town of quayside paths and zigzagging narrow streets. Boats come in from the Atlantic to unload their catches of mackerel, sardines, and tuna. Just offshore is the Ile Tristan, accessible on foot at low tide (guided tours only organized by the tourist office, €6), and across the Port-Rhu channel is Tréboul, a seaside resort town favored by French families.

One of the three town harbors is fitted out with a unique **Port-Musée** *(Port Museum)*, which reopened in May 2006 after an extensive

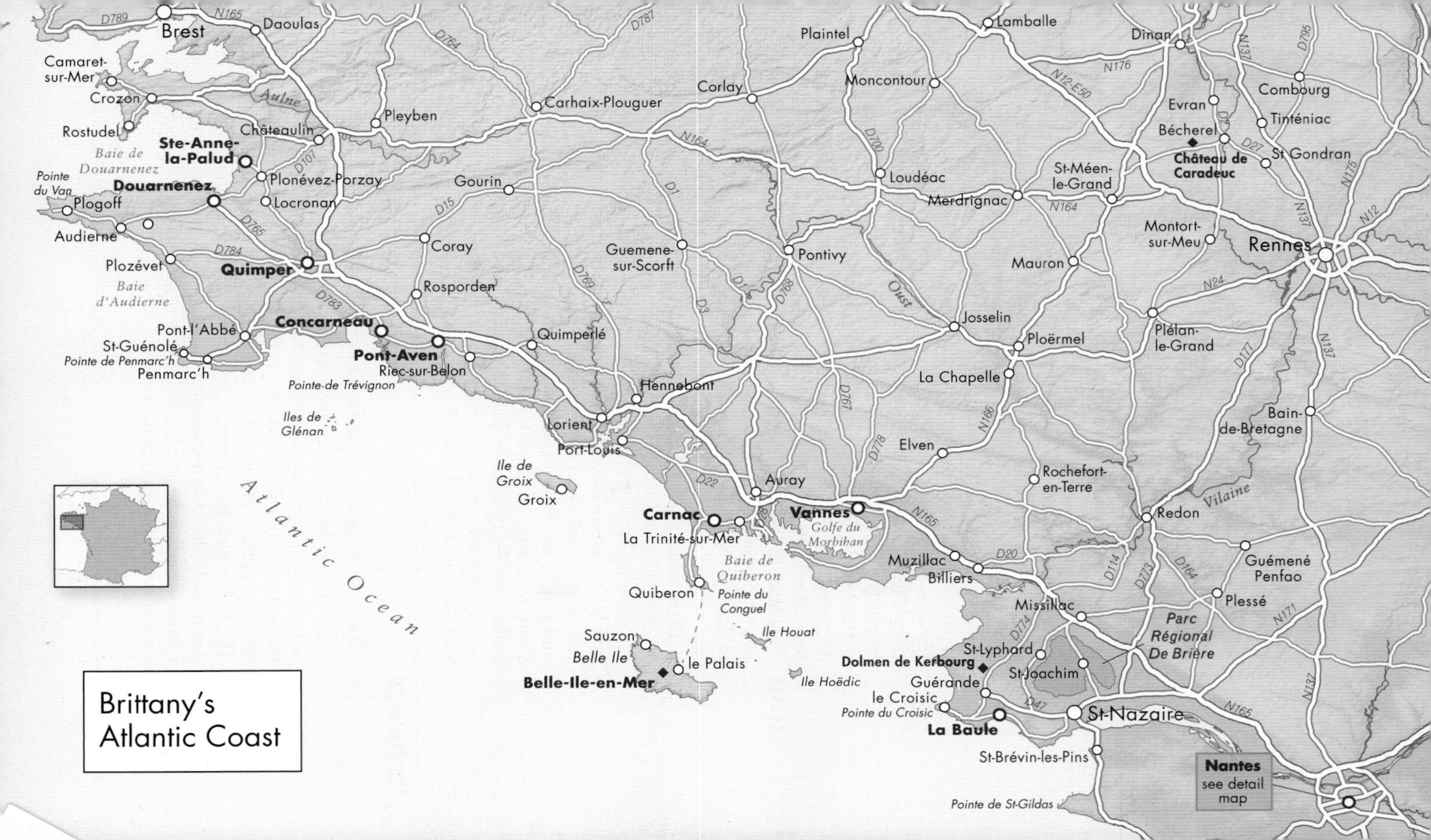
Brittany's
Atlantic Coast
Brest
Daoulas
Camaret-sur-Mer
Crozon
Rostudel
Aulne
Châteaulin
Ste-Anne-la-Palud
Baie de Douarnenez
Pointe du Van
Plogoff
Douarnenez
Plonévez-Porzay
Locronan
Audierne
Plozévet
Quimper
Baie d'Audierne
Pont-l'Abbé
St-Guénolé
Pointe de Penmarc'h
Penmarc'h
Concarneau
Pont-Aven
Riec-sur-Belon
Pointe de Trévignon
Iles de Glénan
Pleyben
Carhaix-Plouguer
Gourin
Coray
Rosporden
Quimperlé
Lorient
Port-Louis
Hennebont
Ile de Groix
Groix
Atlantic Ocean
Guemene-sur-Scorft
Corlay
Plaintel
Moncontour
Lamballe
Loudéac
Pontivy
Oust
Josselin
Ploërmel
La Chapelle
Merdrignac
St-Méen-le-Grand
Mauron
Elven
Auray
Vannes
Golfe du Morbihan
Carnac
La Trinité-sur-Mer
Baie de Quiberon
Quiberon
Pointe du Conguel
Ile Houat
Sauzon
Belle Ile
le Palais
Belle-Ile-en-Mer
Ile Hoëdic
Muzillac
Billiers
Rochefort-en-Terre
Redon
Vilaine
Dinan
Evran
Bécherel
Château de Caradeuc
Combourg
Tinténiac
St Gondran
Montort-sur-Meu
Rennes
Plélan-le-Grand
Bain-de-Bretagne
Guémené Penfao
Plessé
Missillac
Parc Régional De Brière
St-Lyphard
St-Joachim
Dolmen de Kerbourg
Guérande
le Croisic
Pointe du Croisic
La Baule
St-Nazaire
St-Brévin-les-Pins
Pointe de St-Gildas
Nantes
see detail map
D789
N165
D764
D787
D107
D765
D784
D783
D15
D769
N164
D1
D3
D768
D700
D767
D778
D22
D28
N12-E50
N176
N137
D795
D2
D27
N175
N12
N24
D177
N166
D20
D114
D773
D164
N171
D774
D47

renovation program. Along the wharves you can visit the workshops of boat wrights, sailmakers, and other old-time craftspeople, then go aboard the historic trawlers, lobster boats, Thames barges, and a former lightship anchored alongside. On the first weekend in May you can sail on an antique fishing boat. ✉ *Pl. de l'Enfer* ☎ *02–98–92–65–20* 🌐 *www.port-musee.org* 🎟 *€7.50* ⏲ *Mid-June–mid-Sept., daily 10–7; Apr.–mid-June and Oct., Tues.–Sun. 10–12:30 and 2–6; Nov.–Mar., Sun. 10–12:30 and 2–6.*

WHERE TO STAY

$–$$ ★ **Manoir de Moëllien.** Surrounded by extensive forested grounds, this textbook 17th-century granite Breton manor house, landmarked by a sturdy tower and filled with precious antiques, makes an enviable choice. Another plus is the fine restaurant (open to residents only), famous for its local seafood dishes. Sample Bruno Garet's *terrine de poisson chaud* (warm seafood terrine) or the *duo de truites de mer* (poached sea trout). Guest rooms vary greatly in size, but most have terraces overlooking the peaceful country garden. **Pros:** charming setting; historic atmosphere. **Cons:** out of the way; restaurant service can be offhand. ✉ *12 km (7 mi) northeast of Douarnenez, Plonévez-Porzay* ☎ *02–98–92–50–40* 🌐 *www.moellien.com* *18 rooms* *In-room: no a/c, refrigerator (some), Internet, Wi-Fi. In-hotel: restaurant, bar, some pets allowed* 💳 *AE, DC, MC, V* ⏲ *Closed mid-Nov.–Mar.* *FAP.*

$$–$$$ **Ty Mad.** In the 1920s artists and writers such as Picasso and Breton native Max Jacob frequented this small hotel in a quiet cove with beach in Tréboul. Since 2005 this landmark has been completely renovated and refitted with cool, light modern furnishings that blend perfectly with the white and exposed stone walls. Guest rooms are not large, but 11 of them have great sea views. A garden now adorns the property, and the separate house has been outfitted with a kitchen for larger groups and longer stays. Vincent Jugeau's menu, served in the glass-enclosed restaurant, focuses on fresh produce sourced from neighboring farms and fish boats. **Pros:** delightful seaside setting; stylish modern decor. **Cons:** rooms are small and modestly equipped. ✉ *Plage St-Jean, Treboul* ☎ *02–98–74–00–53* 🌐 *www.hoteltymad.com* *15 rooms* *In-room: no a/c. In-hotel: restaurant, bar, some pets allowed* 💳 *MC, V* ⏲ *Closed mid-Nov.–mid-Mar.* *MAP.*

QUIMPER

22 km (14 mi) southeast of Douarnenez via D765.

A traditional crowd-puller, the twisting streets and tottering medieval houses of Quimper furnish rich postcard material, but lovers of decorative arts head here because this is the home of Quimperware, one of the more famous variants of French hand-painted earthenware pottery. The techniques were brought to Quimper by Normands in the 17th century, but the Quimpérois customized them by painting typical local Breton scenes on the pottery. Today they remain some of the most prizes French collectibles and gifts.

GETTING HERE

The twice-daily direct TGV travels 350 mi from Paris's Gare Montparnasse to reach Quimper's train station, on the Avenue de la Gare, in 4 hours, 45 minutes (€90.60). Four trains each day make the 70-minute trip from Quimper to Brest (€15) and the 2-hour, 30-minute trip to Nantes (€31.40). Buses from the Gare Routière on Place Louis-Armand make infrequent connections to such destinations as Concarneau and Pont-Aven.

Visitor Information Quimper Tourist Office (✉ *7 rue Déesse* ☎ *02-98-53-04-05* 🌐 *www.quimper-tourisme.com*).

EXPLORING

Quimper's lively and commercial town began life as the ancient capital of the Cornouaille province, founded, it's said, by King Gradlon 1,500 years ago. It owes its strange name (pronounced cam-*pair*) to its site at the confluence (*kemper* in Breton) of the Odet and Steir rivers. Stroll along the banks of the Odet and through the **Vieille Ville,** with its cathedral. Then walk along the lively shopping street, Rue Kéréon, and down narrow medieval Rue du Guéodet (note the house with caryatids), Rue St-Mathieu, and Rue du Sallé. Have your Nikon handy.

6

The **Cathédrale St-Corentin** (✉ *Pl. St-Corentin*) is a masterpiece of Gothic architecture and the second-largest cathedral in Brittany (after Dol-de-Bretagne's). Legendary King Gradlon is represented on horseback just below the base of the spires, harmonious mid-19th-century additions to the medieval ensemble. The church interior remains very much in use by fervent Quimperois, giving the candlelighted vaults a meditative air. The 15th-century stained glass is luminous. Behind the cathedral is the stately **Jardin de l'Évêché** (Bishop's Garden).

More than 400 works by such masters as Rubens, Corot, and Picasso mingle with pretty landscapes from the local Gauguin-inspired Pont-Aven school in the **Musée des Beaux-Arts** *(Fine Arts Museum)*, next to the cathedral. Of particular note is a fascinating series of paintings depicting traditional life in Breton villages. ✉ *40 pl. St-Corentin* ☎ *02-98-95-45-20* 🌐 *www.musee-beauxarts.quimper.fr* 🎫 *€4.50* ⏲ *July and Aug., daily 10-7; Sept.-June, Wed.-Mon. 10-noon and 2-6.*

In the mid-18th century Quimper sprang to nationwide attention as a pottery manufacturing center, when it began producing second-rate imitations of Rouen faïence, or ceramics with blue motifs. Today's more colorful designs, based on floral arrangements and marine fauna, are still often hand-painted. To understand Quimper's pottery past with the help of more than 500 examples of "style Quimper," take one of the guided tours at the **Musée de la Faïence** *(Earthenware Museum).* ✉ *14 rue Jean-Baptiste-Bousquet* ☎ *02-98-90-12-72* 🌐 *www.quimper-faiences.com* 🎫 *€4* ⏲ *Mid-Apr.-mid-Oct., Mon.-Sat. 10-6.*

Local furniture, ceramics, and folklore top the bill at the **Musée Départemental Breton** *(Brittany Regional Museum).* ✉ *1 rue du Roi-Gradlon* ☎ *02-98-95-21-60* 🎫 *€4* ⏲ *June-Sept., daily 9-6; Oct.-May, Tues.-Sun. 9-noon and 2-5.*

Quimper hosts many parades but the largest is reserved for the nine-day Celtic extravaganza known as the Festival de Cornouaille.

WHERE TO EAT AND STAY

$$ SEAFOOD ✕ **Chez Armande.** Concarneau—22 km (14 mi) southwest of Quimper—is a busy town known for sardine-packaging, but its Vaubau-designed fortress-islet called the Ville Close is one of the most stunning sites in Brittany. The waterfront has some fine seafood restaurants; this is the oldest and one of the best. Specialties include *pot-au-feu de la mer au gingembre* (seafood in a clear ginger broth), *St-Pierre à la fricassée de champignons* (John Dory with fried mushrooms), and *homard rôti en beurre de corail* (roast lobster in coral butter). Try the *tarte de grand-mère aux pommes* (grandma's homemade apple pie) for dessert. ✉ *15 bis, av. du Dr-Nicolas* ☎ *02–98–97–00–76* 💳 *AE, DC, MC, V* ⏲ *Closed Tues. and Wed., mid-Nov.–early Dec.*

$$$ FRENCH ✕ **L'Ambroisie.** This cozy little restaurant has soft-yellow walls, huge contemporary paintings, and different settings at every table. Chef Gilbert Guyon's traditional yet nouvelle menu is seasonal; local products are chosen by hand. Try the buckwheat *galette* crêpe stuffed with egg and salmon; the fresh cod, mullet, or sole; the steamed sçlops with mushrooms and lemon juice; the sautéed crawfish with buckwheat; or the pigeon roasted in apple liqueur with whipped potatoes and mushrooms. The homemade desserts, like the omelet *norvégienne* with warm chocolate and nougat ice cream in meringue, are delicious. ✉ *49 rue Élie-Fréron* ☎ *02–98–95–00–02* 🌐 *www.ambroisie-quimper.com* ✍ *Reservations essential* 💳 *MC, V* ⏲ *Closed Mon. No dinner Sun.*

$$$–$$$$ 🏨 **Les Sables Blancs.** The sea is backdrop and motif for this spare, modern hotel, strongly reminiscent of a cruise ship. Each of the 20 bright, modern rooms offers a terrace or balcony facing the sea, where guests can indulge in an ample Breton breakfast or simply enjoy a bracing sea

breeze. One of the two large suites sports enormous windows and a wraparound terrace that seems to jut out over the sea. Smaller guest rooms are in earth tones with every high-tech convenience, and many of the sleek, serviceable bathrooms boast their own sea views. A plus here is the fine dining—with, what else, plenty of fresh seafood—offered either in the handsome dining room or, weather permitting, on a large sea-facing terrace outside the bar area. Just out front is a fine example of the white sand beaches that distinguish the Morbihan coast. **Pros:** miles of paths on the cliffs overlooking the sea make for lovely walks; open year-round. **Cons:** the relentless crashing of waves can annoy light sleepers. ✉ *20 km (12 mi) from Quimper 45 rue Sables Blancs* ☎ *02–98–50–10–12* ⊕ *www.hotel-les-sables-blancs.com* *20 rooms* *In-room: no a/c, refrigerator, Wi-Fi, In-hotel: 2 restaurants, bar, Wi-Fi hotspot, some pets allowed* *AE, MC, V.*

ANCIENT EVENINGS

During the second half of July, Quimper hosts the nine-day Festival de Cornouaille (☎ *02–98–55–53–53* ⊕ *www.festival-cornouaille.com*), a Celtic extravaganza. More than 250 artists, dancers, and musicians fill streets already packed with the 4,000 people who come each year to enjoy the traditional street fair.

SHOPPING

Keep an eye out for such typical Breton products as woven and embroidered cloth, woolen goods, brass and wood objects, puppets, dolls, and locally designed jewelry. When it comes to distinctive Breton folk costumes, Quimper is the best place to look. The streets around the cathedral, especially **Rue du Parc**, are full of shops selling woolen goods (notably thick marine sweaters). Faïence and a wide selection of hand-painted pottery can be purchased at the **Faïencerie d'Art Breton** (✉ *16 bis, rue du Parc* ☎ *02–98–95–34–13* ⊕ *www.bretagne-faience.com*).

6

CONCARNEAU

22 km (14 mi) southeast of Quimper via D783.

Concarneau is a industrial town known for its sardine-packaging but its Vaubau-designed Ville Close is one of the most picturesque sites in Brittany.

GETTING HERE

No trains arrive in Concarneau, so you'll have to come by car or bus. Buses run almost every hour until 7 PM from Quimper (40 mins, €6) and Pont-Aven (30 mins).

Visitor Information **Concarneau Tourist Office.** ✉ *Quai d'Aiguillon* ☎ *02–98–97–01–44* ⊕ *www.tourismeconcarneau.fr*

EXPLORING

Fodor's Choice ★ Sitting in the middle of Concarneau's harbor, topped by a cupola-clock-tower, and entered by way of a quaint drawbridge, the fortress-islet of the **Ville Close** is a particularly photogenic relic of medieval days. Its fortifications were further strengthened by the English under John de Montfort during the War of Succession (1341–64). Three hundred years later Sébastien de Vauban remodeled the ramparts into what you see today: 1 km (½ mi) long, with splendid views across the two harbors on either side. Held here during the second half of August is the Fête des Filets Bleus (Blue Net Festival), a weeklong folk celebration in which Bretons in costume swirl and dance to the wail of bagpipes. ✉ *Ramparts* 🎟 *€4* ⏲ *Easter–Sept., daily 10–7:30; Oct.–Easter, daily 10–noon and 2–5.*

Fodor's Choice ★ Five miles away from Concarneau is the village of Beuzec-Conq, home to the **Château de Keriolet.** Walt Disney would have loved this fairy-tale, neogothic extravaganza dating from the 19th century. Replete with gargoyles, storybook towers, and Flamboyant Gothic-style windows, this showpiece was constructed by the Comtesse de Chauveau, born Zenaide Narishkine Youssoupov, an imperial Russian princess who was niece to Czar Nicholas II and related to Prince Youssoupov, famed assassin of Rasputin. Hour-long tours guide you through the Arms Room, folkloric kitchen, and other grand salons. ✉ *Beuzec-Conq* ☎ *02–98–97–36–50* 🌐 *www.chateaudekeriolet.com* 🎟 *€5* ⏲ *June–Sept., daily 10:30–1 and 3–7; closed Sat. afternoons.*

PONT-AVEN

Fodor's Choice ★ *37 km (23 mi) east of Quimper via D783.*

Long beloved by artists, this lovely village sits astride the Aven River as it descends from the Montagnes Noires to the sea, turning the town's mills along the way (there were once 14; now just a handful remain). Surrounded by one of Brittany's most beautiful stretches of countryside, Pont-Aven (🌐 *www.pontaven.com*) is a former artists' colony where, most famously, Paul Gauguin lived before he headed off to the South Seas.

GETTING HERE

There are no direct trains, so take the rails to nearby Quimperlé and transfer to a bus (30 mins, €3). Buses make the 20-km (12-mi) run from Quimper (1¼ hrs) and Concarneau (30 mins) several times a day. The last buses leave early in the evening, and service is limited on Sunday.

Visitor Information Pont-Aven Tourist Office. ✉ *5 pl. de l'Hôtel de Ville* ☎ *02–98–06–04–70* 🌐 *www.pontaven.com.*

EXPLORING

Wanting to break with traditional Western culture and values, in 1888 lawyer-turned-painter Paul Gauguin headed to Brittany, a destination almost as foreign to Parisians as Tahiti. Economy was another lure: the Paris stock market had just crashed and, with it, Gauguin's livelihood, so cheap lodgings were also at the top of his list. Shortly after settling in to Pont-Aven Gauguin took to wearing Breton sweaters, berets, and wooden clogs; in his art he began to leave dewy, sunlighted Impressionism behind for a stronger, more linear style. The town museum captures some of the history of the Pont-Aven School, whose adherents painted Breton landscapes in a bold yet dreamy style called syntheticism.

One glance at the **Bois d'Amour** forest, set just to the north of town (from the tourist office, go left and walk along the river for five minutes), will make you realize why artists continue to come here. Past some meadows, you can find Gauguin's inspiration for his famous painting *The Yellow Christ*—a wooden crucifix inside the secluded **Chapelle de Trémalo** (usually open, per private owners, from 9 to 7) just outside the Bois d'Amour woods. While in Brittany, Gauguin painted many of his earliest masterpieces, now given pride of place in great museums around the world.

BE GAUGUIN

If the spirit of Gauguin inspires you in his former hangout of Pont-Aven, the Maison de la Presse, right next to the bridge at 5 place Paul Gauguin, has boxes of 12 colored pencils and sketchbooks for sale.

The **Musée de Beaux-Arts** has a photography exhibition documenting the Pont-Aven School, and works by its participants, such as Paul Sérusier, Maurice Denis, and Émile Bernard. After Gauguin departed for Tahiti, a group of Americans came here to paint, attracted by the light, the landscape, and the reputation. ✉ *Pl. de l'Hôtel-de-Ville* ☎ *02–98–06–14–43* 🌐 *www.pontaven.com* 🎫 *€4.50* ⏲ *July and Aug., daily 10–7; Feb.–June and Sept.–Dec., daily 10–12:30 and 2–6.*

The creperies and pizzerias that surround **Place de l'Hôtel-de-Ville** cater to the lazy visitor, just emerging from the tourist office at **No. 5** (☎ *02–98–06–04–70*); note the office's helpful list of *chambers d'hôte* accommodations offered by the residents in town.

Head to the **Moulin du Grand Poulguin** (✉ *2 quai Théodore-Botrel* ☎ *02–98–06–02–67*), a delightful setting in which to eat a crêpe or pizza on a terrace directly on the flowing waters of the Aven River in view of the footbridge.

Those with a sweet tooth can just fill up on the buttery Traou Mad cookies at the **Biscuiterie Traou Mad** (✉ *10 pl. Gauguin* ☎ *02–98–06–01–94*); they're baked with the local wheat of the last running windmill in Pont-Aven.After exploring the village, cool off (in summer) with a boat trip down the estuary.

WHERE TO EAT AND STAY

$$$$ FRENCH ✕ **La Taupinière.** On the road from Concarneau, 3 km (2 mi) west of Pont-Aven, is this roadside inn with an attractive garden. Chef Guy Guilloux's open kitchen (with the large hearth he uses to grill all langoustine, but also crab and fish) turns out local delicacies such as galette crêpes stuffed with spider crab and Breton ham specialties. Splurge without guilt on the light homemade rhubarb and strawberry compote. ✉ *Croissant St-André* ☎ *02–98–06–03–12* 🌐 *www.la-taupiniere.com* ✍ *Reservations essential* 👔 *Jacket required* 💳 *AE, MC, V* ⏲ *Closed Mon. and Tues., last 2 wks in Mar. and mid-Sept.–mid-Oct.*

$$$–$$$$ Fodor's Choice ★ 🏨 **Domaine de Kerbastic.** Exquisite and extraordinary, this lovely gated estate—a hotel only since 2008—served as the country getaway for generations of Princesses de Polignacs and their eminent friends, including Stravinsky, Colette, and Proust. Each of the 17 rooms, decorated in flawless taste, mix family antiques with a modern aesthetic and make playful reference to some of the more prominent guests and family members, including the Cocteau room, with murals in the artist's antic

CLOSE UP

Gaugin and the Pont-Aven School

Surrounded by one of Brittany's most beautiful countrysides, Pont-Aven was a natural to become a "cité des artistes" in the heady days of Impressionism and Postimpressionism. It was actually the introduction of the railroad in the 19th century that put travel to Brittany in vogue, and it was here that Gauguin and other like-minded artists founded the noted Pont-Aven School. Inspired by the vibrant colors and lovely vistas to be found here, they created *synthétisme*, a painting style characterized by broad patches of pure color and strong symbolism, in revolt against the dominant Impressionist school back in Paris. Gauguin arrived in the summer of 1886, happy to find a place "where you can live on nothing" (Paris's stock market had crashed and cost Gauguin his job). At Madame Gloanec's boardinghouse he welcomed a circle of painters to join him in his artistic quest for monumental simplicity and striking color.

Today Pont-Aven seems content to rest on its laurels. Although it's labeled a "city of artists," the galleries that line its streets display paintings that lack the unifying theme and common creative energy of the earlier works of art. The first Pont-Aven painters were American students who came here in the 1850s. Though Gauguin is not-surprisingly absent (his paintings now go for millions), except for a few of his early zincographs, the exhibit *Hommage à Gauguin* is an interesting sketch of his turbulent life. Also on view in the museum are works by other near-great Pont-Aven artists: Maurice Denis, Émile Bernard, Émile Jordan, and Emmanuel Sérusier.

style, or the ravishing India-themed Marquise de Polignac room, with inlaid black-lacquer furnishings and sisal rugs. On chilly evenings a fire is laid in a charming salon downstairs, where one might sip an *apéro*before an all-organic gourmet dinner, complete with greens from the estate's kitchen garden. The extensive grounds are perfect for a country promenade, with splendid box-hedge-lined gardens, ancient trees, and endless fields of wildflowers. **Pros:** enormous marble bathrooms, with both tub and shower, all have fetching views over the grounds or gardens. **Cons:** somewhat off the beaten path; you can't stay forever. ✉ *28 km (17 mi) southeast of Pont-Aven, off major route E60, Rue de Kerbastic, Guidel* ☎ *02–97–65–98–01* 🌐 *www.domaine-de-kerbastic.com* *15 deluxe rooms* *In-room: no a/c, safe, Wi-Fi. In-hotel: restaurant, pets allowed* ▭ *AE, MC, V, DC.*

¢–$ **La Chaumière Roz-Aven.** Partly built into a rock face on the bank of the Aven, this efficiently run hotel, renovated in 2006 by new owners Valérie and Alain Bodolec, has simple, clean rooms with 18th- and 19th-century-style furnishings. You can choose from three locations: the 16th-century enchanting thatched "chaumière" house, the modern annex, or the *maison bourgeoise* with a river or garden view. There's no restaurant, but there's a tearoom and the bar serves tapas and snacks. **Pros:** families welcome; rooms tastefully modernized. **Cons:** rooms small; mattresses can be lumpy; rooms in annex lack character. ✉ *11 quai Théodore-Botrel* ☎ *02–98–06–13–06* 🌐 *www.hotelpontaven.com*

14 rooms In-room: no a/c, Wi-Fi. In-hotel: bar AE, MC, V Closed Jan. and Feb. MAP.

$ **Le Moulin de Rosmadec.** You'll want to set up your easel in a second once you spot this pretty-as-a-picture, 15th-century stone water mill. Set at the end of a quiet street, the Sébilleaus's beloved hostelry sits in the middle of the rushing, rocky Aven River. Inside, atmospheric beam ceilings, Breton stone fireplaces, and water views (you can hear the sound of water gently splashing over the stones beneath your window) cast their spell—but who can resist dining on the "island" terrace? Outside or inside, feast on the creations of a serious kitchen: the *sauté de langoustines,* duck in cassis, and lobster *grillé Rosmadec* are all winners. Reservations are essential; the restaurant does not serve dinner Sunday and is closed Thursday. Demand for one of the four gently priced guest rooms is high—book early. **Pros:** great setting; great value. **Cons:** distracted, unhelpful staff; attic rooms can be stuffy in midsummer. *Venelle de Rosmadec 02–98–06–00–22 www.moulinderosmadec.com 4 rooms, 1 suite In-room: no a/c. In-hotel: restaurant, some pets allowed AE, MC, V.*

Fodor's Choice ★

BELLE-ILE-EN-MER

Fodor's Choice ★

45 mins by boat from Quiberon, 78 km (52 mi) southeast of Pont-Aven.

At 18 km (11 mi) long, Belle-Ile is the largest of Brittany's islands. It also lives up to its name: it's indeed beautiful, and less commercialized than its mainland harbor town, Quiberon. Monet created several famous paintings here, and you'll also be tempted to set up your easel and canvases yourself.

GETTING HERE

Take the 45-minute ferry trip (hourly July–August) to Belle-Ile's Le Palais from Quiberon's Gare Maritime, which can be reached in one hour by bus from Auray train station (on the Quimper–Vannes line) that runs several times daily in summer (€7).

Visitor Information **Belle-Ile-en-Mer Tourist Office.** *Quai Bonnelle, Le Palais 02–97–31–81–93 www.belle-ile.com.*

EXPLORING

Because of the cost and inconvenience of reserving car berths on the ferry, cross over to Belle-Ile as a pedestrian and rent a car—or, if you don't mind the hilly terrain, a bicycle. Departing from Quiberon—a spa town with pearl-like beaches on the eastern side of the 16-km-long (10-mi-long) Presqu'île de Quiberon (Quiberon Peninsula), a stretch of coastal cliffs and beaches whose dramatic western coast, the Côte Sauvage (Wild Coast), is a mix of crevices and coves lashed by the sea—the ferry lands at **Le Palais,** crushed beneath a monumental Vauban citadel built in the 1680s.

From Le Palais head northwest to **Sauzon**, the prettiest fishing harbor on the island; from here you can see across to the Quiberon Peninsula and the Gulf of Morbihan.

6

Continue on to the **Grotte de l'Apothicairerie**, which derives its name from the local cormorants' nests, said to resemble apothecary bottles.

At Port Goulphar is the **Grand Phare** *(Great Lighthouse)*. Built in 1835, it rises 275 feet above sea level and has one of the most powerful beacons in Europe, visible from 120 km (75 mi) across the Atlantic. If the keeper is available and you are feeling well rested, you may be able to climb to the top.

WHERE TO STAY

$$$$ ★ **Castel Clara**. Perched on a cliff overlooking the surf and the narrow Anse de Goulphar Bay, this '70s-era hotel was François Mitterrand's address when he vacationed on Belle-Ile. The hotel still retains its presidential glamour, with its renowned spa, saltwater pool, and spectacular room views. In the bright, airy restaurant, chef Christophe Hardouin specializes in seafood, caught just offshore. The John Dory baked in sea salt and the grilled sea bream are simple but delicious. Castel Clara's expansive wooden-deck terrace is the perfect lounging spot for cocktails at sundown. **Pros:** great facilities; spectacular setting. **Cons:** impersonal service; hard to get to. ✉ *Port-Goulphar, Bangor* ☎ *02–97–31–84–21* 🌐 *www.castel-clara.com* *59 rooms, 4 suites* *In-room: a/c, refrigerator, Internet. In-hotel: restaurant, tennis court, pool, spa, some pets allowed* *AE, DC, MC, V* *Closed Dec.–mid-Feb.* *MAP.*

NIGHTLIFE AND THE ARTS

Every year, from mid-July to mid-August, Belle-Ile hosts **Lyrique-en-Mer** (☎ *02–97–31–59–59* 🌐 *www.belle-ile.net*), an ambitious little festival whose heart is opera (the festival was founded by the American bass baritone, Richard Cowan) but which offers up a generous lyric menu of sacred music concerts, gospel, jazz, even the occasional sea chantey and Broadway musical number. Operas and concerts are performed by rising talents from around the world at various romantic locations around the island.

THE OUTDOORS

The ideal way to get around to the island's 90 spectacular beaches is by bike. The best place to rent two-wheelers (and cars—this is also the island's Avis outlet) is at **Roue Libre** (✉ *Pont Orgo* ☎ *02–97–31–49–81*) in Le Palais.

CARNAC

Fodor's Choice ★

19 km (12 mi) northeast of Quiberon via D768/D781.

Visitor Information Carnac Tourist Office. ✉ *74 av. des Druides* ☎ *02–97–52–13–52* 🌐 *www.ot-carnac.fr.*

At the north end of Quiberon Bay, Carnac is known for its expansive beaches and its ancient stone monuments. Dating from around 4500 BC, Carnac's **menhirs** remain as mysterious in origin as their English contemporary, Stonehenge, although religious beliefs and astronomy were doubtless an influence. The 2,395 megalithic monuments that make up the three *alignements*—Kermario, Kerlescan, and Ménec—form the largest megalithic site in the world, and are positioned with

One of France's prettiest islands, Belle-Ile-en-Mer casts an especially potent spell at sunset.

astounding astronomical accuracy in semicircles and parallel lines over about 1 km (½ mi). The site, just north of the town, is fenced off for protection, and you can examine the menhirs up close only October through March; in summer you must join a guided tour; some tours are in English (€4.50). More can be learned at the **Maison des Mégalithes**, a visitor center explaining the menhirs' history and significance. ✉ *Alignements du Ménec* ☎ *02–97–52–29–81* 🌐 *carnac.monuments-nationaux.fr* ⏲ *Sept.–Apr., daily 10–5; May–Aug., daily 9–7.*

Carnac also has smaller-scale dolmen ensembles and three *tumuli* (mounds or barrows), including the 130-yard-long, 38-foot-high **Tumulus de St-Michel**, topped by a small chapel with views of the rock-strewn countryside.

WHERE TO EAT AND STAY

$$$–$$$$ Fodor's Choice ★ **Château de Locguénolé**. According to local legend, Saint Guénolé (from whom the château takes its name) took refuge on this scenic spot while fleeing the devil. Nowadays, a 19th-century château and part of the original 18th-century edifice overlook a sweeping 250-acre estate, where guests can indulge in every worldly delight. On the château's ground floor, four stately salons remain exactly as they were when the family—who still maintains the hotel—lived here. Damask wallpaper, elegant antiques, marble fireplaces, and plenty of crystal and porcelain adorn each of the 22 guest rooms, along with stunning views over water, lush gardens, and woods. Two gorgeous suites on the first floor offer panoramic views. Superb gourmet meals can be had from several outdoor terraces but the candlelit, tapestried, and Michelin-starred dining room is hard to beat. For guests seeking a more virtuous itinerary,

Brittany's version of Stonehenge, this stone *menhir* at Carnac is just one of the area's impressive megalithic sights.

a "fasting" package offers every possible diversion, including walks through the estate's ancient forests, sailing, mountain biking, swimming in a lovely outdoor pool surrounded by rose gardens, tennis, and a full range of spa treatments. **Pros:** peace and quiet reign; copious bathrooms are all in marble. **Cons:** out of the way, but well worth the detour. ✉ *Rte. de Port-Louis, 25 km (16 mi) south of Carnac, direction Hennebont* Kervignac ☎ *02–97–76–76–76* 🌐 *www.chateau-de-locguenole.com* *22 rooms, 8 suites* *In-room: no a/c, refrigerator, Wi-Fi, safe. In-hotel: restaurant, Wi-Fi hotspot, pool, spa, some pets allowed* *AE, DC, MC, V* *FAP.*

$$–$$$ ★ **Hôtel Tumulus.** Dramatic views over Carnac and the Quiberon Bay have been a draw for this family-run hotel from its inception in the 1930s, along with its prime location just beneath the famous Tumulus Saint-Michel and its 16th-century chapel. Many of the modest but comfortable and well-equipped rooms have views to the bay, and those in back overlook the chapel. A small spa offers a surprising number of treatments—from thalasso therapy to seaweed wraps and massage, with good-value packages. Weary travelers can steep in the outdoor hot tub or take an invigorating swim in the pool. An airy dining room with lovely views offers excellent fare, with several reasonable prix-fixe menus, replete with fresh-caught seafood and a sophisticated wine list. **Pros:** close to Carnac's famous menhirs; tasteful decors. **Cons:** some rooms on the small side; some with less-than-pristine carpets. ✉ *Chemin de Tumulus* ☎ *02–97–52–08–21* 🌐 *www.hotel-tumulus.com* *23 rooms* *In-room: no a/c, Wi-Fi, safe. In-hotel: restaurant, bar, Wi-Fi hotspot, pool, spa, some pets allowed* *AE, MC, V* *BP.*

VANNES

★ *35 km (20 mi) east of Carnac via D768, 108 km (67 mi) southwest of Rennes.*

Scene of the declaration of unity between France and Brittany in 1532, historic Vannes is one of the few towns in Brittany to have been spared damage during World War II. Though it draws visitors in droves to its wonderful vielle ville (Old Town), Vannes remains relatively untainted.

GETTING HERE

TGVs from Paris (Gare Montparnasse) leave for Vannes twice daily (3 hrs, 20 mins; €63.80). Six trains daily (some with a change at Redon) link Vannes to Nantes (1 hr, 15 mins; €19) and trains run every hour or so between Vannes and Quimper (1 hr, €17.40). The two most useful bus companies are Cariane Atlantique and Transports Le Bayon, with frequent buses to Quiberon and Nantes (3 hrs).

Visitor Information Vannes Tourist Office. ✉ *1 rue Thiers* ☎ *02–97–47–24–34* 🌐 *www.mairie-vannes.fr.*

EXPLORING

The true appeal of Vannes is walking through the winding pedestrian streets, shopping at the lively outdoor market, or sipping coffee outdoors near the sedate harbor. Be sure to saunter through the Promenade de la Garenne, a colorful park, and admire the magnificent gardens nestled beneath the adjacent ramparts. Many of the prettiest sights are concentrated in the Old Town, hemmed in by Rue Thiers on the west and ramparts and gates to the east and south. The ramparts crumble prettily under ivy blankets and each gateway has a character all its own. Also visit the medieval wash houses and the cathedral; browse in the antiques shops in the pedestrian streets around pretty Place Henri-IV; check out the Cohue, the medieval market hall now used as an exhibition center; and take a boat trip around the scenic Golfe du Morbihan.

The **Cathédrale St-Pierre** boasts a 1537 Renaissance chapel, a Flamboyant Gothic transept portal, and a treasury. ✉ *Pl. de la Cathédrale* ⏲ *Treasury mid-June–mid-Sept., Mon.–Sat. 2–6.*

WHERE TO EAT AND STAY

$$$ SEAFOOD ✕ **Régis Mahé.** Step off the train and right into this popular spot, a haven of refinement where seafood reigns. Chef Régis Mahé prefers a small, seasonal menu with local handpicked produce and fish (especially mullet) so fresh they nearly swim to the plate. For a local specialty with a twist, try the buckwheat galette crêpe filled with lobster and pigeon and served with caramelized leeks. Attention chocolate lovers: save room for the warm chocolate tart with homemade salty caramel ice cream. ✉ *24 pl. de la Gare* ☎ *02–97–42–61–41* 💳 *MC, V* ⏲ *Closed Sun. and Mon., and part of Feb., part of Nov., and part of June.*

$$$$ Fodor's Choice ★ **Domaine de Rochevilaine.** Set on the magical Pen Lan peninsula, this enchanting collection of 15th- and 16th-century Breton stone buildings resembles a tiny village; one, however, that is surrounded by terraced gardens, has a spectacular spa, and offers grand vistas of the Bay of Vilaine. Once you step through the the grand "Portail de la Verité" 13th-century entryway, the interior allures with Baroque ex-votos,

Louis Treize chairs, rock-face fireplaces, and plate-glass windows. Chef Patrice Caillaut (formerly of Ledoyen and Troisgros) rules the restaurant which has a somewhat boring menu. Guest rooms sparkle with checked fabrics, veneered woods, and modern furnishings. To get your toes in the water, head to the alluring spa, the Aqua Phénica, replete with a full spectrum of seawater hydrotherapy facilities and gigantic indoor pool. **Pros:** stylish decor; ocean views; superb spa facilities. **Cons:** the staff seems to favor French guests; tons of steps from one house to another. ✉ *Pointe de Pen-Lan, 30 km (19 mi) southeast of Vannes, at tip of Pointe de Pen-Lan, Billiers* ☎ *02–97–41–61–61* 🌐 *www.domainerochevilaine.com* *35 rooms, 3 suites* *In-room: no a/c, refrigerator, Internet. In-hotel: restaurant, pools, some pets allowed* ▭ *AE, DC, MC, V* 🍽 *FAP.*

$ **Kyriad.** In an old, but thoroughly modernized, building, this hotel attracts a varied foreign clientele, drawn by the homey guest rooms—clean, bright, and simple, with check-pattern quilts and warm yellow walls—and the friendly and efficient staff. Claude Le Lausque serves a traditional menu in the long-established Image Sainte-Anne restaurant, stylishly refurbished with plush red carpet, gold and red wallpaper, and round-back designer chairs. You can't go wrong with straightforward seasonal specialties like crab in phyllo pastry, grilled sole, and kidneys flambéed in Calvados. **Pros:** tastefully modernized; fine restaurant. **Cons:** some rooms on the small side; some a bit noisy. ✉ *8 pl. de la Libération* ☎ *02–97–63–27–36* 🌐 *www.kyriad-vannes.fr* *33 rooms* *In-room: no a/c, refrigerator, Wi-Fi. In-hotel: restaurant, Internet terminal* ▭ *AE, MC, V* 🍽 *BP.*

LA BAULE

72 km (45 mi) southeast of Vannes via N165 and D774.

Star of the Côte d'Amour coast and gifted with a breathtaking 5-km (3-mi) beach, La Baule is a popular resort town that can make you pay dearly for your coastal frolics. Though it once rivaled Biarritz, today tackiness has replaced sophistication, but you still can't beat that sandy beach, or the lovely, miles-long seafront promenade lined with hotels. Like Le Touquet and Dinard, La Baule is a 19th-century creation, founded in 1879 to make the most of the excellent sandy beaches that extend around the broad, sheltered bay between Pornichet and Le Pouliguen. A pine forest, planted in 1840, keeps the shifting local sand dunes firmly at bay. All in all, this can offer an idyllic stay for those who will enjoy a day on the beach, an afternoon at the shops on Avenue du Général-de-Gaulle and Avenue Louis-Lajarrige, and an evening at the casino.

WHERE TO EAT AND STAY

$ FRENCH ★ ✕ **La Ferme du Grand Clos.** At this lively restaurant in an old farmhouse, 200 yards from the sea, you should understand the difference between crêpe and galette to order correctly, since the menus showcase both in all their forms (try the galette with scallops and leaks). Or you can opt for the simple, straightforward menu featuring food the owner Christophe Mercy likes to call *la cuisine de grand-mère* (grandma's cooking).

Come early for a table; it's a very friendly and popular place. ✉ *52 av. du Maréchal-de-Lattre-de-Tassigny* ☎ *02–40–60–03–30* ▭ *MC, V* ⊙ *Closed Mon. and mid-Nov.–mid-Dec.*

$–$$ **Concorde.** This bright-blue-shuttered, white-wall establishment numbers among the least expensive good hotels in pricey La Baule. Once past the formica-clad front desk, the lobby reassures with its elegant, solid Louis Treize–style chairs, antique armoires, and solid wood beams. Upstairs, guest rooms are calm, comfortable, and modernized—faux Louis XV furniture lends a nice grace note. The Concorde is but a short block from the beach (ask for a room with a sea view). **Pros:** close to beach; good value. **Cons:** no restaurant; lengthy annual closure. ✉ *1 bis, av. de la Concorde* ☎ *02–40–60–23–09* 🌐 *www.hotel-la-concorde.com* *47 rooms* *In-room: no a/c, Internet. In-hotel: bar* ▭ *AE, DC, MC, V* ⊙ *Closed Oct.–mid-Apr.*

$$–$$$ ★ **Hôtel de la Plage.** One of the few hotels on the beach in St-Marc-sur-Mer, southeast of La Baule, this comfortable lodging was the setting for Jacques Tati's classic comedy *Mr. Hulot's Holiday.* It has been updated since and, *hélas,* the swinging door to the dining room is no longer there. But the view of the sea and the sound of the surf remain. The restaurant—reserve a beachfront table in advance—serves seasonal fish specialties like the *choucroute de la mer* (sauerkraut with fish). There's also a brasserie for more casual dining. **Pros:** silver-screen claim to fame; beachside setting. **Cons:** old-fashioned; overrun by French families in midsummer. ✉ *37 rue du Commandant-Charcot, 10 km (6 mi) southeast of La Baule, St-Marc-sur-Mer* ☎ *02–40–91–99–01* 🌐 *www.hotel-delaplage.fr* *30 rooms* *In-room: no a/c, Internet. In-hotel: restaurant, bar* ▭ *AE, MC, V* *FAP.*

NIGHTLIFE

Occasionally you see high stakes on the tables at La Baule's **casino** (✉ *6 av. Pierre-Loti* ☎ *02–40–11–48–28*).

6

NANTES

72 km (45 mi) east of La Baule via N171 and N165, 108 km (67 mi) south of Rennes.

The writer Stendhal remarked of 19th-century Nantes, "I hadn't taken twenty steps before I recognized a great city." Since then, the river that flowed around the upper-crust Ile Feydeau neighborhood has been filled in and replaced with a rushing torrent of traffic, and now major highways cut through the heart of town. Still, Nantes is more than the sum of its traffic jams. Stay a spell to discover its many charms.

GETTING HERE

TGV trains leave Paris's Gare Montparnasse for Nantes every hour, covering the 387 km (240 mi) in just 2 hours 10 minutes (€72). Trains make the 2-hour, 30-minute run up the coast from Nantes to Quimper (€31.40) twice daily, stopping at Vannes (1hr, 15 mins; €19). Nantes's train station, at 27 boulevard Stalingrad, is across the street from the Jardin des Plantes and a 10-minute walk from the Vieille Ville. Cariane Atlantique runs four daily buses to Rennes (2 hrs), as well as to other nearby towns.

Visitor Information **Nantes Tourist Office.** ✉ *7 rue de Valmy* ☎ *08–92–46–40–44* 🌐 *www.nantes-tourisme.com.*

EXPLORING

Nantes's 15th-century château is still in relatively good shape, despite having lost an entire tower during a gunpowder explosion in 1800. The 15th-century cathedral floats heavenward as well. Its white stones, immense height, and airy interior make it one of France's best. Across the broad boulevard, Cours des 50-Otages, is the 19th-century city. The unlucky Ile Feydeau, surrounded and bisected by highways, still preserves the tottering 18th-century mansion built with wealth from Nantes's huge slave trade. The Loire River flows along the southern edge of the Vieille Ville, making Nantes officially part of the Loire region, although historically it belongs to Brittany. In town you can see many references to Anne de Bretagne, the last independent ruler of Brittany, who married the region away to King Charles VIII of France in 1491. Bretons have never quite recovered from the shock.

TOP ATTRACTIONS

1 **Château des Ducs de Bretagne.** Built by the dukes of Brittany, who had no doubt that Nantes belonged in their domain, this château is a massive, well-preserved 15th-century fortress with a moat. François II, the duke responsible for building most of it, led a hedonistic life here, surrounded by ministers, chamberlains, and an army of servants. Numerous monarchs later stayed in the castle, where in 1598 Henri IV signed the famous Edict of Nantes advocating religious tolerance. The castle reopened in February 2007 after extensive renovations. ✉ *4 pl. Marc-Elder* ☎ *02–51–17–49–00* 🌐 *www.chateau-nantes.fr* 🎫 *€5* 🕒 *Wed.–Mon. 10–6.*

2 **Cathédrale St-Pierre–St-Paul.** One of France's last Gothic cathedrals, this was begun in 1434, well after most other medieval cathedrals had been completed. The facade is ponderous and austere, in contrast to the light, wide, limestone interior, whose vaults rise higher (120 feet) than those of Notre-Dame in Paris. ✉ *Pl. St-Pierre* ☎ *02–40–47–84–64* 🎫 *Free* 🕒 *Crypt Mon.–Sat. 10–12:30 and 2–6, Sun. 2–6:30.*

3 **Musée des Beaux-Arts** *(Museum of Fine Arts).* Designed by Clément-Marie Josso, this noted museum was opened in 1900. Inside, skylights cast their glow over a fine array of paintings, extending from the Renaissance period onward, including works by Jacopo Tintoretto, Georges de La Tour, Jean-Auguste-Dominique Ingres, and Gustave Courbet. To go from the sublime to the ridiculous, look for the famous late-19th-century painting of a gorilla running amuck with a maiden. ✉ *10 rue Georges-Clemenceau* ☎ *02–51–17–45–00* 🎫 *€3.50* 🕒 *Mon., Wed., Fri., and weekends 10–6, Thurs. 10–8.*

7 ★ **Musée Thomas-Dobrée.** Set across the way from the medieval Manoir de la Touche, this mansion was originally built by arts connoisseur Thomas Dobrée in the 19th century. On the mock-Romanesque facade he had chiseled the old Breton saying, ANN DIANAF A ROG AC'HANOUN ("The Unknown devours me"), and his vast collection offers proof, as it ranges from old-master paintings to tapestries, from medieval manuscripts to Gothic goldwork, including the *coffret* reliquary of the heart of Anne

Nantes

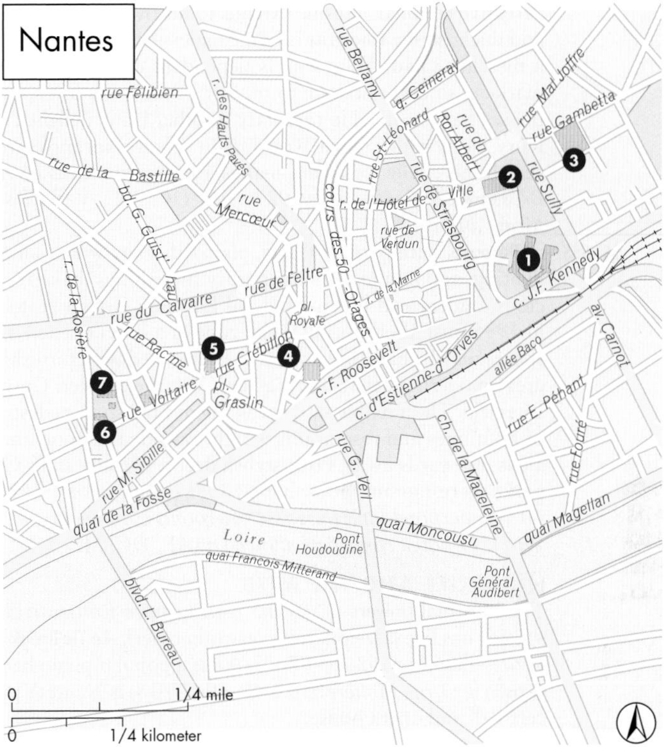

de Bretagne; one room is devoted to the Revolutionary War in Vendée. ✉ *18 rue Voltaire* ☎ *02–40–71–03–50* 🎫 *€3* ⏲ *Tues.–Sun. 2:30–5:30.*

WORTH NOTING

5 **Grand Théâtre.** Down the block from the Passage Pommeraye, this noted town landmark was built in 1783. ✉ *Pl. Graslin.*

6 **Manoir de la Touche.** This 15th-century house was once the abode of the bishops of Nantes. ✉ *Rue Voltaire.*

4 **Passage de la Pommeraye.** Erected in 1843, this is an elegant shopping gallery in the 19th-century part of town. ✉ *Rue Crébillon.*

WHERE TO EAT AND STAY

$$ FRENCH ✕ **La Cigale.** Miniature palm trees, gleaming woodwork, colorful enamel tiles, and painted ceilings have led to the official recognition of La Cigale brasserie (built in 1895) as a *monument historique.* You can savor its Belle Époque blandishments without spending a fortune—the prix-fixe lunch menus are a good value. But the banks of fresh oysters and well-stacked dessert cart may tempt you to order à la carte. ✉ *4 pl. Graslin* ☎ *02–51–84–94–94* 🌐 *www.lacigale.com* ✍ *Reservations essential* 💳 *MC, V.*

$$ FRENCH ✕ **L'Embellie.** Sweet and simple, this spot lures diners with its modern, inventive attitude and friendly service. Chef François Proquin's

"creative regional" cuisine extends to his own smokehouse for salmon and duck, so the foie gras is homemade—he likes to serve it light, atop a mesclun salad. The menu is dependent on Proquin's daily trips to markets, so don't hesitate to try any of the fresh fish specials, such as the sea bass steamed in rosemary or other briny delights, such as John Dory laced with French West Indian spices. Pineapple *croquant* with rum-laced creole ice cream makes a fitting finale. ✉ *14 rue Armand-Brossard* ☎ *02–40–48–20–02* ▭ *AE, DC, MC, V* ⏲ *Closed Sun. and Mon., and Aug.*

$$–$$$ **Pérouse.** Bare parquet floors, plain off-white walls, simple high-tech lighting, and minimal contemporary furnishings make rooms feel spacious, and earned the accolade of Europe's Design Hotel of the Year in 1995, just after this big white cube of a hotel opened its doors. The spaces may be bare, but at least they are filled with furnishings by some great modern masters, such as Le Corbusier, Eileen Gray, and Gerrit Rietvield. The amiable staff speak fluent English. A pedestrian zone full of boutiques and restaurants is right outside the door, and Place Royale is 300 yards away. **Pros:** stylish decor; friendly staff. **Cons:** hard to park; no restaurant; noisy bar. ✉ *3 allée Dusquesne* ☎ *02–40–89–75–00* 🌐 *www.hotel-laperouse.fr* *46 rooms* *In-room: a/c, refrigerator, Wi-Fi. In-hotel: some pets allowed* ▭ *AE, DC, MC, V* *BP.*

NIGHTLIFE AND THE ARTS

The informal **Univers** (✉ *16 rue Jean-Jacques-Rousseau* ☎ *02–40–73–49–55*) has live jazz concerts every other week. **Le Tie Break** (✉ *1 rue des Petites-Écuries* ☎ *02–40–47–77–00*) is a popular piano bar. The **Théâtre Graslin** (✉ *1 rue Molière* ☎ *02–40–69–77–18*) is Nantes's principal concert hall and opera house.

THE OUTDOORS

You can take a 100-minute cruise along the pretty Erdre River, past a string of gardens and châteaux, with the **Bateaux Nantais**. There are also four-course lunch and dinner cruises that last about 2½ hours (€54–€89). ✉ *Quai de la Motte Rouge* ☎ *02–40–14–51–14* 🌐 *www.bateaux-nantais.fr* *€10* ⏲ *June–Aug., daily at 3:30 and 5; May and Sept., daily at 3:30; Mar., Apr., Oct., and Nov., Sun. at 3:30.*

SHOPPING

The commercial quarter of Nantes stretches from Place Royale to Place Graslin. Various antiques shops can be found on Rue Voltaire. The Devineau family has been selling wax fruit and vegetables at **Devineau** (✉ *2 pl. Ste-Croix*) since 1803, as well as handmade candles and wildflower honey. For chocolate, head to **Gautier-Debotté** (✉ *9 rue de la Fosse* 🌐 *gautier-debotte.com*); try the local Muscadet grapes dipped in brandy and covered with chocolate.

7

Champagne Country

WORD OF MOUTH

"Touring the Champagne houses? The Reims firms are a few miles from the train, while Épernay's gaggle are a short walk. So if your goal is to see two or even three Champagne houses Épernay is more manageable."

—Palenque

"We also love visiting the great Gothic cathedrals. And even after seeing so many, my jaw still drops when I enter. Such beauty!"

—Swisshiker

WELCOME TO CHAMPAGNE COUNTRY

TOP REASONS TO GO

★ **Champagne—what else!:** Drink it, see the vineyards, visit the cavernous chalk cellars where bottles are stored by the million.

★ **Gothic Glory:** No fewer than 10 Gothic cathedrals dot the region—check out the rivalry between the biggest of them (Amiens) and the tallest (neighboring Beauvais).

★ **Tiny L'Épine:** Set on the Route du Champagne, this cozy village has the superlative Aux Armes de Champagne restaurant, set across from its pretty stone-lacework church.

★ **Laon, "Crowned Mountain":** With its cathedral towers patrolling the hilly horizon, Laon has a site whose grandeur rivals Mont-St-Michel (and just as exciting in close-up, with mighty stone oxen guarding the church towers).

★ **The Capital of Bubbly:** Drink now, pray later in Reims, the "Champagne City" and also home to France's great coronation cathedral.

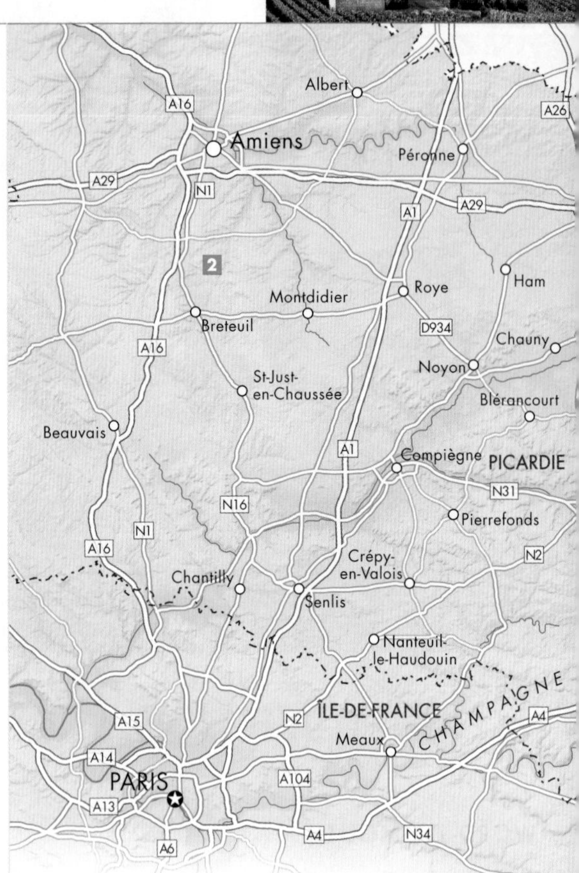

1 Champagne. The region's obsession with Champagne is especially evident in Reims, the region's hub, home to the great Champagne houses and site of one of the most historically important cathedrals in France. Once you tally up the 34 VIPs who have been crowned here and toured some Champagne cellars to bone up on the history of this noble beverage, you can head south. Smack-dab in the middle of the 28,000 hectares that make up the entire Champagne-producing region, Épernay lives and dies for the bubbly brew. Continue on the Route du Champagne to other wine villages.

2 The Cathedral Cities. To the west of Champagne lies a region where the popping of Champagne corks is only a distant murmur, and not just because Reims is 160 km (100 mi) away. For here are some of the most gargantuan Gothic hulks of architectural harmony: the cathedrals of Beauvais, Amiens, Laon, and Soissons. Beauvais is positively dizzying from within: with the highest choir in France, you nearly keel over craning your neck back. Laon is still a town with a contemplative air. Amiens is the most colossal church in the land, in places fantastically ornate, while Soissons shows Gothic at its most restrained.

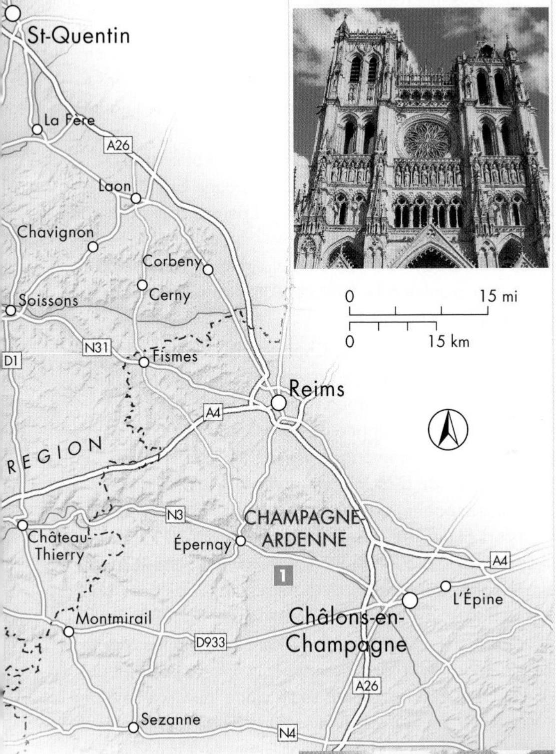

St-Quentin
La Fère
A26
Laon
Chavignon
Corbeny
Cerny
Soissons
N31
D1
Fismes
Reims
A4
REGION
N3
CHAMPAGNE-ARDENNE
Château-Thierry
Épernay
1
A4
L'Épine
Montmirail
Châlons-en-Champagne
D933
A26
Sezanne
N4
0 15 mi
0 15 km

GETTING ORIENTED

Few drinks in the world have such a pull on the imagination as Champagne, yet surprisingly few tourists visit the pretty vineyards south of Reims. Perhaps it's because the Champagne region is a bit of a backwater, halfway between Paris and Luxembourg. The 2007 arrival of the TGV line serving eastern France and Germany is helping to change all this. Northwest of Laon, the hills of Champagne give way to the plains of Picardy, where only giant cathedrals and giant pyramids of sugar beets in fall break up the skyline.

CHAMPAGNE COUNTRY PLANNER

Visitor Information

If traveling extensively by public transportation, be sure to load up on information ("Guide Régional des Transports" schedules, the best taxi-for-call companies, etc.) upon arriving at the ticket counter or help desk of the bigger train and bus stations in the area, such as Reims and Amiens.

In addition to the main tourist offices in these two cities, other smaller towns have their own tourist bureaux, *which are listed in this chapter under the town names.*

The **Marne Regional Tourist Office** (✉ *13 bis, rue Carnot, Châlons-en-Champagne* ☎ *03–26–68–37–52* 🌐 *www.tourisme-en-champagne.com*) is a mine of information about the Champagne region.

Two main Web sites for the region (🌐 *www.tourisme-champagne-ardenne.com, www.picardietourisme.com*) are packed with data and suggestions for Champagne-bound travelers.

Amiens Tourist Office (✉ *6 bis, rue Dusevel, Amiens* ☎ *03–22–71–60–50* 🌐 *www.visit-amiens.com*).

Reims Tourist Office (✉ *2 rue Guillaume-de-Machault, Reims* ☎ *03–26–77–45–25* 🌐 *www.reims-tourisme.com*).

Traveling "Les Routes de Champagne"

Threading the triangle between Reims, Épernay, and Château-Thierry are the famous Routes Touristique de Champagne (Champagne Roads), which divvy up the region into four fabulous itineraries. These follow the main four côtes of the Champagne vineyards. Northwest of Reims (use the Tinqueux exit) is the Massif de Saint-Thierry—a vineyard-rich region once hallowed by kings. Heading south of Reims to Épernay, travel west along the Vallée de la Marne through the Hauteurs d'Épernay, traveling west on the right bank of the river and east on the left. To the east of Épernay lies the most beautiful stretch of Champagne Country: the Montagne de Reims. To the south of Épernay is the Côte de Blancs, the "cradle of Chardonnay." More than 80 producers of Champagne are scattered along these roads, and you can guarantee a better reception if you call the ones you'd like to visit in advance.

The two main centers to the Champagne Wine Road are Reims and Épernay, which are about 64 km (40 mi) apart if you work your way through the wine villages that dot the slopes of the Montagne de Reims. Start in Reims, with its host of major Champagne houses, then go south on N51 and east on D26 through pretty Rilly-la-Montagne, Mailly-Champagne, and Verzy, where you can visit local producers Étienne and Anne-Laure Lefevre at 30 rue de Villers (☎ *03–26–97–96–99* 🌐 *www.champagne-etienne-lefevre.com*). Continue south to Ambonnay, then track back west to Bouzy, Ay, and Hautvillers—where Dom Pérignon is buried in the village church—before crossing the Marne River to Épernay, whose main street is home to several producers. From Épernay, spear south along the Côte de Blanc to Vertus, 19 km (12 mi) away, where Pierre and Sophie Lamandier will sell and tell you all about their organic bio-Champagne at 19 avenue du General-de-Gaulle (☎ *03–26–52–13–24* 🌐 *www.larmandier.fr*). If you're headed back to Paris, take D1 from Épernay west along the banks of the Marne to Château-Thierry 50 km (30 mi) away. The steep-climbing vineyards hugging the river are the most scenic in Champagne. For maps on the four Routes Touristique de Champagne, see 🌐 *www.ville-reims.fr/index.php?id=934*.

Transportation Basics

As always in France, intercity buses are less frequent than trains, and much slower.

There are trains to all the towns and cities mentioned in this chapter.

The natural hub remains Reims—especially now that it's just 45 minutes from Paris by TGV.

Reims is linked to Laon by the A26 expressway, and to Châlons-en-Champagne by the A4 expressway arriving from Paris.

The west, Amiens and Beauvais, are connected by the A16.

Épernay, south of Reims, can be reached from Reims by the twisting wine road or quicker N51.

Only Soissons, 20 mi southwest of Laon, is a bit off the beaten track.

Finding a Place to Stay

The Champagne Region has a mix of old, rambling hotels, often simple rather than pretentious.

In addition, there are a handful of stylish hostelries catering to those with more discerning tastes, including a large contingent of staffers who work in the vast Champagne industry.

Be warned, though, that few of the destinations mentioned in this chapter have much in the way of upscale choice.

Many of the region's most characterful establishments, to boot, are in the countryside and require a car to reach.

DINING AND LODGING PRICE CATEGORIES (IN EUROS)

	¢	$	$$	$$$	$$$$
Restaurants	under €13	€13–€17	€18–€24	€25–€32	over €32
Hotels	under €65	€65–€105	€106–€145	€146–€215	over €215

Restaurant prices are per person for a main course at dinner, including tax (5.5%) and service; note that if a restaurant offers only prix-fixe (set-price) meals, it has been given the price category that reflects the full prix-fixe price. Hotel prices are for a standard double room in high season, including tax (19.6%) and service charge.

Eating Well

This region is less dependent on tourism than many in France, and most restaurants are open year-round. However, in the largest cities, Reims and Amiens, many restaurants close for two to three weeks in July and August.

Smoked ham, pigs' feet, gingerbread, and Champagne-based mustard are specialties of the Reims area, along with sautéed chicken, kidneys, stuffed trout, pike, and snails.

One particularly hearty dish is *potée champenoise*, consisting of smoked ham, bacon, sausage, and cabbage. Rabbit (often cooked with prunes) is common, while boar and venison are specialties in fall and winter, when vegetable soups are high on the menu.

In Picardy, the popular *ficelle picarde* is a pancake stuffed with cheese, mushrooms, and ham.

Apart from Champagne, try drinking the region's *hydromel* (mead, made from honey) and ratafia, a sweet aperitif made from grape juice and brandy.

7

GETTING AROUND

Bus Travel

The main bus operator in Picardy is **Courriers Automobiles Picards**; their main hub is the Gare Routière in Amiens. In the Champagne region, services are run by **STDM Trans-Champagne**; the main hub is Châlons-en-Champagne. Their main routes are: Reims to Troyes (line 14; 2 hrs, 15 mins; €14.75) by way of Châlons-en-Champagne (50 mins, €13.50), and Épernay to Châlons (line 52; 1 hr, €6.60); **RTA** has one daily bus between Reims and Laon (Bus 510; 2 hrs). In Reims, municipal buses run by **Transports Urbains de Reims** depart from the train station (ticket prices vary on route, from €1-€3). The best way to navigate the confusing bus system is to contact the tourism office at the city you're leaving from.

Bus Information Courriers Automobiles Picards (✉ *B.P. 59, ZAC La Haute Borne, Rivéry* ☎ *03–22–70–70–70* 🌐 *www.courriersautomobilespicards.com*). **RTA** (✉ *97 rue Semard,Gauchy* ☎ *03–23–50–68–50* 🌐 *www.rta02.com*). **STDM** (✉ *86 rue des Fagnières, Châlons-en-Champagne* ☎ *03–26–65–17–07* 🌐 *www.stdmarne.fr*). **Transports Urbains de Reims** (✉ *6 rue Chanzy, Reims* ☎ *03–26–88–25–38* 🌐 *www.transdev-champagne.fr*).

Car Travel

The A4 heads east from Paris to Reims; allow 90 minutes to two hours, depending on traffic.

The A16 leads from L'Isle-Adam, north of Paris, up to Beauvais and Amiens.

If you're arriving by car via the Channel Tunnel, you'll disembark at Coquelles, near Calais, and join A16 not far from its junction with A26, which heads to Reims (2½ hrs).

Air Travel

If you're coming from the United States and most other destinations, count on arriving at Paris's Charles de Gaulle or Orly airport.

Charles de Gaulle offers easy access to the northbound A16 and A1 for Beauvais and Amiens, and the eastbound A4 for Reims.

If coming from the United Kingdom, consider the direct flights to Beauvais from Prestwick, near Glasgow.

Train Travel

It's easy to get around the region by train. Most sites can be reached by regular train service, except for the Champagne vineyards, which require a car.

There are frequent daily services from Paris (Gare du Nord) to Beauvais; Amiens; and Laon (taking up to two leisurely hours to cover 140 km [87 mi]).

The TGV service, introduced in 2007, covers the 170 km (105 mi) from Paris (Gare de l'Est) to Reims in 45 minutes.

Cross-country services connect Reims to Épernay (20 mins), Châlons (40 mins), and Amiens (2 hrs) via Laon (35 mins).

Train Information Gare SNCF Reims (✉ *Blvd. Joffre* ☎ *03–26–65–17–07*). **SNCF** (☎ *36–35 [€0.34 per min]* 🌐 *www.voyages-sncf.com*). **TGV** (🌐 *www.tgv.com*).

Updated by Heather Stimmler-Hall

As you head toward Reims, the landscape loosens and undulates, and the hills tantalize with vineyards that—thanks to *la méthode champenoise*—produce the world's antidote to gloom. Each year, millions of bottles of bubbly mature in hundreds of kilometers of chalk tunnels carved under the streets of Reims and Épernay, both of which fight for the title "The Champagne City."

Champagne, a place-name that has become a universal synonym for joy and festivity, actually began as a word of humble origin. Like *campagna*, its Italian counterpart, it's derived from the Latin *campus*, which means "open field." In French *campus* became *champ*, with the old language extending this to *champaign*, for "battlefield," and *champaine*, for "district of plains." Today this vast, endless plain—in the 19th century the famed writer Stendahl bemoaned "the atrocious flat wretchedness of Champagne"—has been the center of Champagne production for more than two centuries, stocking the cellars of its many conquerors (Napoléon, Czar Nicholas I, the Duke of Wellington) as well as those of contemporary case-toting bubblyphiles. Yet long before a drink put it on the map, this area of northern France was marked by great architecture and bloodstained history.

Picardy's monotonous chalk plains are home, in fact, to many of France's greatest medieval cathedrals, including those of Amiens, Reims, and Laon. These great structures testify to the wealth this region enjoyed thanks to its prime location between Paris and northern Europe. The "flying buttresses" and heaven-seeking spires of these cathedrals remind us that medieval stoneworkers sought to raise radically new Gothic arches to improbable heights, running for cover when the naves failed to stand. Happily, most have stood the test of time (though you might want to hover near the exits at Beauvais, the tallest cathedral in France—it still makes some engineers nervous).

But the region's crossroads status also exacted a heavy toll, and it paid heavily for its role as a battleground for the bickering British, German, and French. From pre-Roman times to the armistice of 1945, some of Europe's costliest wars were fought on northern French soil. World War I and World War II were especially unkind: epic cemeteries cover the plains of Picardy, and you can still see bullet-pocked buildings in Amiens. These days, happily, the vineyards of Champagne attract tourists interested in less sobering events.

CHAMPAGNE

An uplifting landscape tumbles about Reims and Épernay, perhaps because its inhabitants treat themselves to a regular infusion of the local, world-prized elixir. But unlike the great vineyards of Bordeaux and Burgundy, there are few country châteaux to go with the fabled names of this region—Mumm, Taittinger, Pommery, and Veuve-Clicquot. Most of the glory is to be found in *caves* (wine cellars), not to mention the fascinating guided tours offered by the most famous producers.

Despite its glamorous image as the home of Champagne, the region in fact has a laid-back rustic charm where "life in the fast lane" refers strictly to the Paris-bound A4 expressway. On the map, Champagne encompasses Reims and the surrounding vineyards and chalky plains. The province starts just beyond Château-Thierry, 96 km (60 mi) northeast of Paris, and continues along the towering Marne Valley to Épernay. Cheerful villages line the Route du Champagne (Champagne Road; for details, see our chapter Planner section), which twines north to Reims, the capital of bubbly and the largest city in Champagne. To the southeast the grapes of Champagne flourish on the steep slopes of the Marne Valley and the Montagne de Reims, really more of a mighty hill than a mountain. For a handy Web source for many of the great Champagne houses of the region, log on to 🌐 *www.maisons-champagne.com*.

REIMS

161 km (100 mi) northeast of Paris.

Reims is the largest city in Champagne. Behind a facade of austerity, it remains one of France's richest tourist sites, thanks especially to the fact that it sparkles with some of the biggest names in Champagne production. This thriving industry has conferred wealth and sometimes an arrogant reserve on the region's inhabitants. The maze of Champagne cellars constitutes a leading attraction of the city. ⇨ *See the special "Champagne Uncorked" photo-feature in this chapter for details about visiting Taittinger, Mumm, and other fabled Champagne houses.* Several of these producers organize visits to their cellars, combining video presentations with guided tours of their cavernous, hewn-chalk underground warehouses.

GETTING HERE

Since 2007 a new TGV (🌐 *www.tgv.com*) express train covers the 170 km (105 mi) from Paris (Gare de l'Est) to Reims in 45 minutes. Trains depart from Paris eight times daily and cost €12–€50. Several SNCF trains daily connect Reims to Épernay (20–30 mins, €6), and there are four trains a day from Châlons-en-Champagne (40 mins, €12–€50).

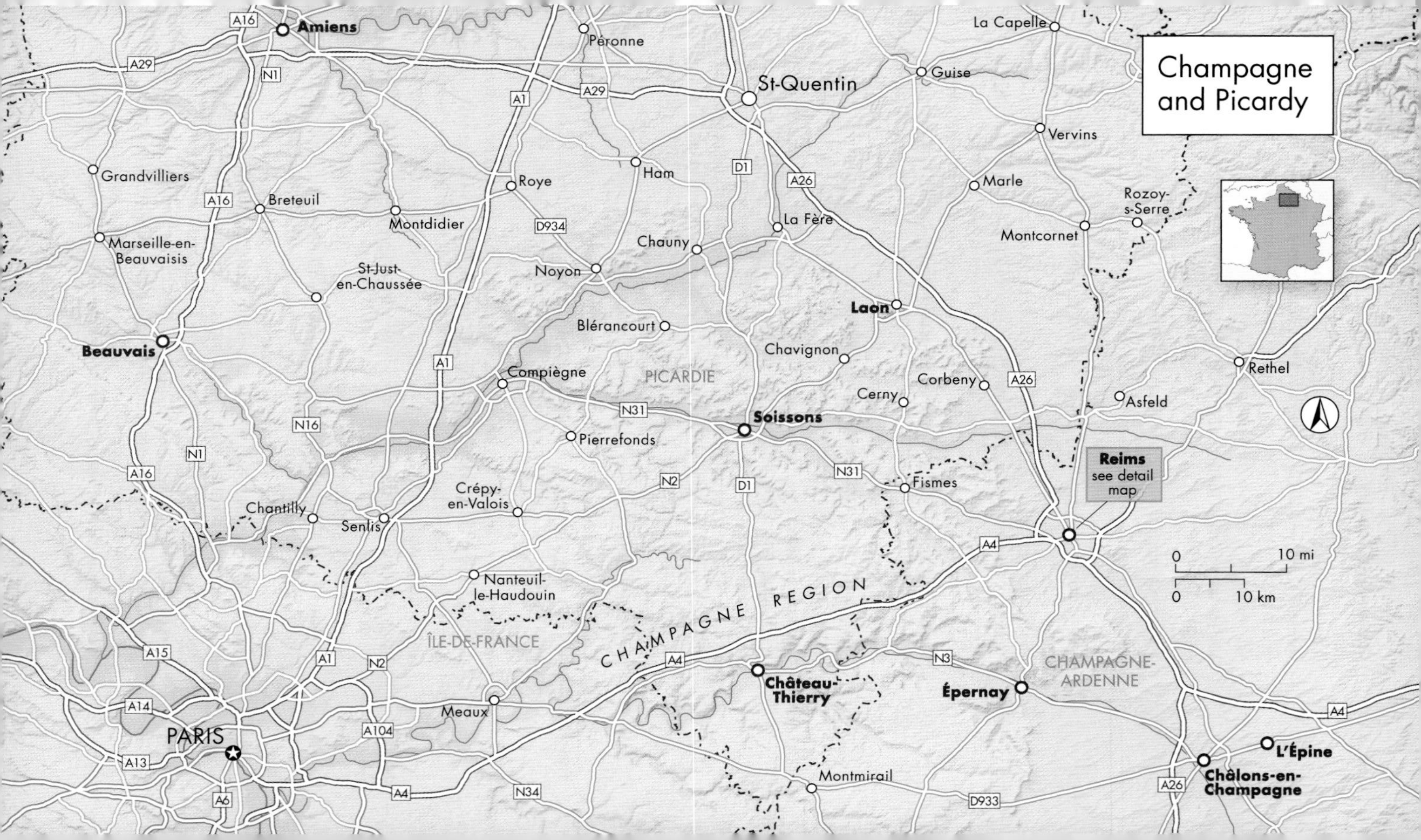
Champagne and Picardy
Amiens
Péronne
La Capelle
Guise
St-Quentin
Vervins
Grandvilliers
Ham
Roye
Breteuil
Montdidier
Marle
Rozoy-s-Serre
Montcornet
La Fère
Marseille-en-Beauvaisis
Chauny
Noyon
St-Just-en-Chaussée
Laon
Blérancourt
Beauvais
Chavignon
Rethel
Compiègne
PICARDIE
Corbeny
Cerny
Asfeld
Soissons
Pierrefonds
Reims
see detail map
Fismes
Crépy-en-Valois
Chantilly
Senlis
Nanteuil-le-Haudouin
CHAMPAGNE REGION
ÎLE-DE-FRANCE
Château-Thierry
CHAMPAGNE-ARDENNE
Épernay
Meaux
PARIS
L'Épine
Châlons-en-Champagne
Montmirail
0
10 mi
0
10 km
A16
A29
N1
A1
D1
A26
D934
N16
N31
N2
A4
A15
A14
A104
N3
A13
A6
N34
D933

There's one direct train each day from Amiens to Reims (2 hrs, 30 mins; €21.60) via Laon. STDM Trans-Champagne (☎ *03–26–65–17–07* 🌐 *www.stdmarne.fr*) runs three daily buses to Reims from Châlons-en-Champagne (line 15; 50 mins, €8.75).

Visitor Information Reims Tourist Office (✉ *2 rue Guillaume-de-Machault* ☎ *08–92–70–13–51[€0.34/min]* 🌐 *www.reims-tourisme.com*).

EXPLORING

Although many of Reims's historic buildings were flattened in World War I and replaced by drab, modern architecture, those that do remain are of royal magnitude. Top of the list goes to the city's magnificent cathedral, in which the kings of France were crowned until 1825, while the Musée des Beaux-Arts has a stellar collection of paintings, and the Le Vergeur Museum is home to a complete edition of Dürer prints. The new tramway, set to open in 2012, will make it even easier to get around the compact town and its many sites from the train station. For a complete list of Champagne cellars, head to the **tourist office** (✉ *2 rue Guillaume-de-Machault* ☎ *08–92–70–13–51 [€0.34/min]*) near the cathedral. A handy Web site that can help with planning Champagne cellar visits throughout the region is: 🌐 *www.tourisme-en-champagne.com*.

TOP ATTRACTIONS

❶ **Basilique St-Rémi.** This 11th-century basilica honors the 5th-century saint who baptized Clovis, the first French king, and who gave his name to the city. Its interior seems to stretch into the endless distance, an impression created by its relative murk and lowness. The airy four-story Gothic choir contains some fine original 12th-century stained glass. There is also a museum (open daily 2–6:30, admission €3) in the Abbaye Royale alongside the basilica, housing some of its most precious relics. ✉ *53 rue St-Rémi* ☎ *03–26–85–23–26* ⏲ *Daily 8–7.*

❹ Fodor's Choice ★ **Cathédrale Notre-Dame.** The age-old setting for the coronations of the French kings, this is one of the most magnificent Gothic cathedrals in the world. The great historical saga begins with Clovis, king of the Franks, who was baptized in an early structure on this site in the 6th century; Joan of Arc led her recalcitrant Dauphin here to be crowned King Charles VII; Charles X's coronation, in 1825, was the last. The east-end windows have stained glass by Marc Chagall. Admire the vista toward the west end, with an interplay of narrow pointed arches. The glory of Reims's cathedral is its facade: it's so skillfully proportioned that initially you have little idea of its monumental size. Above the north (left) door hovers the *Laughing Angel,* a delightful statue whose famous smile threatens to melt into an acid-rain scowl; pollution has succeeded war as the ravager of the building's fabric. With the exception of the 15th-century towers, most of the original building went up in the 100 years after 1211. You can climb to the top of the towers, and peek inside the breathtaking timber-and-concrete roof (reconstructed in the 1920s with Rockefeller money), for €7. A stroll around the outside reinforces the impression of harmony, discipline, and decorative richness. The east end presents an idyllic sight across well-tended lawns. An optical-fiber lighting system illuminates the cathedral exterior every day from dusk until midnight. ✉ *Pl. du Cardinal-Luçon* 🌐 *cathedrale-reims.*

Tally up the 34 kings who were crowned at Notre-Dame de Reims, one of the largest and greatest of French cathedrals.

monuments-nationaux.fr ⏲ Cathedral daily 7:30–7:30. Towers May–Sept., Tues.–Sun. 10–noon and 2–5; Apr. and Oct., weekends 2–4.

3 ★ **Musée des Beaux-Arts** *(Museum of Fine Arts). Located* two blocks southwest of Reims's massive cathedral, this noted museum has an outstanding collection of paintings: no fewer than 27 Corots are here, as well as Jacques-Louis David's unforgettable "Death of Marat," a portrait of the revolutionary polemicist Jean-Paul Marat shown stabbed to death in his bath, a deed done by Charlotte Corday, in 1793. One floor is devoted to 20th-century art, with significant collections in Art Deco, Surrealism, and post-1945 Abstraction. ✉ *8 rue Chanzy* ☎ *03–26–47–28–44* 🌐 *www.ville-reims.fr* 🎟 *€3* ⏲ *Wed.–Mon. 10–noon and 2–6.*

WORTH NOTING

5 **Cryptoportique.** A Gallo-Roman underground gallery and crypt, now a semisubterranean passageway, this was initially constructed around AD 200 under the forum of what was Reims's predecessor, the Roman town of Durocortorum. ✉ *Pl. du Forum* ☎ *03–26–35–34–70* 🎟 *Free* ⏲ *June–mid-Oct., Tues.–Sun. 2–6.*

6 **Hôtel Le Vergeur Museum.** One of the best examples of late medieval and early Renaissance architecture in Reims, this was built during the 13th century. Originally overlooking the historic linen and wheat market in the center of town, the noble townhouse changed hands between aristocrats, Champagne traders, and, finally, Hugues Kraft in 1910, a man whose sole passion was preserving the city's historic buildings. It was completely restored after the WWI bombings and today houses an impressive collection of historical prints, paintings, and furnishings from the region, as well as an original, complete series of 15th-century

Albert Dürer prints of the "Apocalypse" and "Large Passion." ✉ *36 pl. du Forum* ☎ *03–26–47–20–75* 🌐 *www.museelevergeur.com* 🎫 *€3.90* ⏲ *June–Aug., Tues.–Sun. 10–noon.*

7 **Musée de la Reddition** *(Museum of the Surrender).* Near the train station, this museum—also known as the Salle du 8-Mai-1945 or the "little red school house"—is a well-preserved map-covered room used by General Eisenhower as Allied headquarters at the end of World War II. It was here that General Alfred Jodl signed the German surrender at 2:41 AM on May 7, 1945. Fighting officially ceased at midnight the next day. The museum also presents a collection of local photos, documents, uniforms, and artifacts recounting the fighting, occupation, and liberation of Reims. Guided tours begin with a short documentary film in English and French. ✉ *12 rue Franklin-Roosevelt* ☎ *03–26–47–84–19* 🎫 *€3* ⏲ *Wed.–Mon. 10–noon and 2–6.*

2 ★ **Palais du Tau.** Formerly the Archbishop's Palace (alongside the cathedral), this museum now houses an impressive display of tapestries and coronation robes, as well as several statues rescued from the cathedral facade before they fell off. The second-floor views of the cathedral are terrific. ✉ *2 pl. du Cardinal-Luçon* ☎ *03–26–47–81–79* 🌐 *www.palais-du-tau.fr* 🎫 *€7* ⏲ *May–Aug., Tues.–Sun. 9:30–6:30; Sept.–Apr., Tues.–Sun. 9:30–12:30 and 2–5:30.*

WHERE TO EAT AND STAY

$$$ SEAFOOD ✕ **Le Bocal.** Freshness is guaranteed: this tiny treasure is hidden at the back of a fishmonger's shop across from the old food court, les Halles du Boulingrin. Everything is just off the boat, but most of the dozen lucky diners automatically go with the catch of the day. Tempting as that is no one should pass up the divine cooked oysters in season. Tables in this bright, contemporary room are in demand so it is best to reserve. ✉ *27 rue de Mars* ☎ *03–26–47–02–51* 💳 *MC, V* ⏲ *Closed Sun. and Mon. No lunch Wed.*

$$$$ FRENCH ★ ✕ **Le Millénaire.** Appearances deceive at this sturdy traditional town house just off Place Royale, a few feet from the cathedral, "au coeur de Reims": inside, it has an Art Deco feel with plush red carpets and sleek wooden chairs, while the designer lighting and contemporary art on the pale yellow walls ooze as much chic as does trim hostess Corinne Laplaige. Her husband Laurent's own decorative artistry finds an outlet in colorful food presentations on square glass plates, with stunning specialties ranging from sardines with gazpacho and pike-perch cooked in Champagne, to lamb with aubergine and girolle mushrooms and dessert dazzlers like apricot with caramel ice. The five-course €47 set menu is a feast, the three-course €30 menu a wiser lunchtime option. ✉ *4 rue Bertin* ☎ *03–03–26–08–26–62* 🌐 *www.lemillenaire.com* 💳 *MC, V* ⏲ *Closed Sun., no lunch Sat.*

$$ FRENCH ✕ **L'Opera.** Centrally located in Reims's historic district, this traditional "Champenoise" restaurant specializes in local dishes such as filet mignon à la moutard de Reims, *andouillette marnaise* (sausage), and *la ficelle Picardie* (Picardy-style crepes). The copious plat du jour is always a sure bet, made with the market fresh ingredients chosen daily by chef Cédric Guyot. The setting is contemporary and stylish,

Basilique St-Rémi 1
Cathédrale Notre-Dame 4
Crypto-portique 5
Hotel Le Vergeur Museum 6
Musée des Beaux-Arts 3
Musée de la Reddition 7
Palais du Tau 2

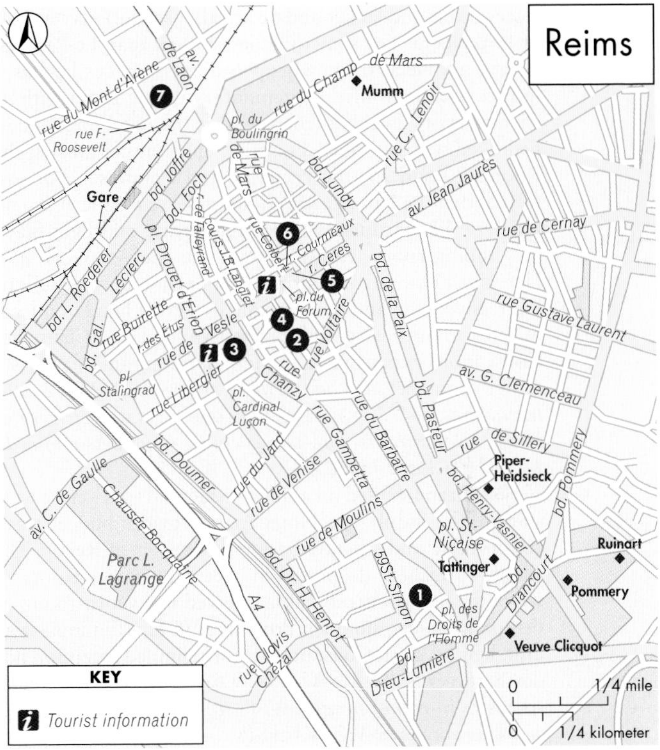

Reims

KEY

Tourist information

yet laid back. Outdoor seating faces the pedestrian street. Two-course *formules* (set menus) from €18 and three-course menus €22 are available weekdays, with a special "organic" menu on tap for the weekends at €35. ✉ *4 rue Thillois* ☎ *03–03–26–02–68–43* 🌐 *www.loperareims.com* 💳 *MC, V* ⏲ *Closed Mon., no dinner Sun.*

$$$$ ★ **Château Les Crayères.** In a grand park, romantic with towering trees planted by Champagne legend Madame Pommery, this celebrated hotel remains the top showplace of Reims. Not far from the city center (on the A26, take the Saint Rémi exit), the garden estate is centered around its stylish, late-19th-century château, replete with glorious, gilt-trimmed, bouquet-laden salons. The legendary chef Gérard Boyer made Le Parc the most famous haute gastronomic restaurant in Reims. Since his retirement, Didier Elena, who forged his international reputation as head chef at Alain Ducasse's Essex House in New York, has maintained the restaurant's gastronomic flair for contemporary Champenois cuisine. Prepared with precision pairings, the fish and game dishes really shine, including the young rabbit with Granny Smith apples, the lacquered eel with celery rémoulade, or the cod and black truffles with a peppered artichoke sauce. The extensive wine list pays homage to Reims's Champagne heritage, while the formally attentive silver service ensures that guests feel properly pampered at every moment. No matter that the restaurant (closed Monday, and no lunch is offered Tuesday;

reservations and jacket and tie are all essential) may not hit the heights of Boyer's era. For something less formal than Le Parc, guests should reserve a table at the newly opened brasserie Les Jardins, with a large terrace and light-filled contemporary dining room with a view of the chefs at work in the kitchen. As for the hotel, most guest rooms are bedecked with antiques, boiseries, and couture fabrics; the largest are Rooms 20 and 25 (the Princesse and Comtesse). For something less formal than Le Parc, guests should reserve a table at the newly opened brasserie Les Jardins, with a large terrace and light-filled contemporary dining room with a view of the chefs at work in the kitchen. Here diners can savor gourmet Champenois cuisine built up around an impressive wine and Champagne list. **Pros:** hotel and two restaurants in same luxurious setting; innovative food and Champagne pairings. **Cons:** more expensive than similar restaurants in Paris; outside the center of town. ✉ *64 bd. Henry-Vasnier* ☎ *03–26–82–80–80* 🌐 *www.lescrayeres.fr* *20 rooms* *In-room: a/c, safe, refrigerator, Wi-Fi. In-hotel: 2 restaurants, bar, tennis court, some pets allowed* ▭ *AE, DC, MC, V* ⊙ *Closed Jan.* 🍴 *BP.*

¢–$ **Hôtel Azur.** Located on a quiet residential street close to Reims's train station, the family-run Hotel Azur provides budget travelers with a comfortable and friendly base in the center of Reims. The rooms are simply furnished, decorated in cheerful primary colors with modern white tile bathrooms. Breakfast served in a sunny room, or in the garden patio during summer. **Pros:** free Wi-Fi, 10-minute walk to Cathedral, helpful staff; **Cons:** no bathtubs; limited reception hours. ✉ 9 rue des Ecrevées ☎ 03–26–47–43–39 🌐 *www.hotel-azur-reims.com* *18 rooms* *In-room: no a/c, Wi-Fi. In-hotel: Wi-Fi, parking (paid), no-smoking rooms* ▭ *MC, V* 🍴 *EP.*

$$$ **La Paix.** A modern eight-story hotel run by the same family since 1911, La Paix is a Best Western-branded property 10 minutes on foot from the cathedral. It has a cozy contemporary style with modern furnishings, dramatic artworks, and rich colors of mustard, aubergine, red, or chocolate. A heated indoor pool with jacuzzi and hammam can be found at the back of a pretty garden. Its brasserie-style restaurant serves mainly grilled meats and seafood. **Pros:** central location; stylish hotel bar; free Wi-Fi. **Cons:** often hosts corporate groups. ✉ *9 rue Buirette* ☎ *03–26–40–04–08* 🌐 *www.hotel-lapaix.fr* *169 rooms* *In-room: a/c, safe, refrigerator, Wi-Fi. In-hotel: restaurant, bar, pool, gym, some pets allowed* ▭ *AE, DC, MC, V* 🍴 *BP.*

L'ÉPINE

56 km (35 mi) southeast of Reims via N44/N3, 7 km (4½ mi) east of Châlons via N3.

The tiny village of L'Épine is dominated by its church, the twin-tower Flamboyant Gothic **Basilique de Notre-Dame de l'Épine.** The church's facade is a magnificent creation of intricate patterns and spires, and the interior exudes elegance and restraint.

WHERE TO STAY

$$$–$$$$ ★ **Aux Armes de Champagne.** The highlight of this cozy former coaching inn (just up the street from the town church, so ask for a table with a view) is the restaurant, with its renowned Champagne list and imaginative cuisine. Among the specialties are grilled scallops with cabbage and chestnuts, grilled venison with prunes, wild boar with chestnuts, and artichokes with local goat cheese. (The restaurant is closed Monday, and no dinner is served Sunday year-round.) Guest rooms are divided into three buildings, furnished with solid, traditional reproductions, wall hangings, and thick carpets. No. 21, with wood beams, is the most atmospheric. **Pros:** great restaurant (especially local game); friendly service. **Cons:** out-of-the-way location; rooms can be pricey. ✉ *31 av. du Luxembourg* ☎ *03–26–69–30–30* 🌐 *www.aux-armes-de-champagne.com* *37 rooms, 2 suites* *In-room: no a/c, refrigerator, Internet. In-hotel: restaurant, bar, tennis court* 💳 *AE, DC, MC, V* ⏲ *Closed Jan.–mid-Feb.* *BP.*

> **WORD OF MOUTH**
>
> "We spent one afternoon and evening in Reims, and only had time for two Champagne houses, so we visited Pommery and Veuve Cliquot—'the Widow Cliquot.' As you can tell by my screen name, I discovered a new and expensive love! I think the story of La Cliquot, as told in 'her cave,' is very interesting and enlightening. Maybe it's another reason I love her Champagne!" —Cliquot1

7

CHÂLONS-EN-CHAMPAGNE

7 km (4½ mi) west of L'Épine via N3, 34 km (21 mi) southeast of Épernay via N3.

Several major churches bear eloquent testimony to Châlons's medieval importance. It is also one of the few towns in Champagne that has good bus and train service.

GETTING HERE

Trains from Paris (Gare de l'Est) leave for Châlons every 2 hours or so (€25); the 174-km (108-mi) trip takes around 1 hour, 30 minutes. There's also limited TGV service from Paris: one train in the afternoon, one in the evening (1 hr, €29.30). There are four direct trains a day from Reims to Châlons-en-Champagne (36 mi, 45 mins; €9.70). STDM Trans-Champagne (☎ *03–26–65–17–07* 🌐 *www.stdmarne.fr*) runs three buses Monday through Saturday from Reims to Châlons-en-Champagne (50 mins, €8) and several buses each day from Épernay (1 hr, €6.60).

EXPLORING

★ With its twin spires, Romanesque nave, and early Gothic choir and vaults, the church of **Notre-Dame-en-Vaux** is one of the most imposing in Champagne. The small **museum** beside the excavated cloister contains outstanding medieval statuary. ✉ *Rue Nicolas-Durand* ☎ *03–26–69–38–53* *€3, free under 18* ⏲ *Apr.–Sept., Wed.–Mon. 10–noon and 2–6; Oct.–Mar., Wed.–Fri. 10–noon and 2–5, weekends 10–noon and 2–6.*

The 13th-century **Cathédrale St-Étienne** (✉ *Rue de la Marne*) is a harmonious structure with large nave windows and tidy flying buttresses; the

Continued on page 378

Champagne Uncorked

Dom Pierre Pérignon was the first to discover the secret of Champagne's production by combining the still wines of the region and storing the beverage in bottles. Today, the world's most famous sparkling wine comes from the very same vineyards, along the towering Marne Valley between Épernay and Château-Thierry and on the slopes of the Montagne de Reims between Épernay and Reims.

When you take a Champagne tasting tour, you won't be at the vineyards—it's all done inside the various houses, miles away from where the grapes are grown. Champagne firms—Veuve-Clicquot, Mumm, Pommery, Taittinger, and others—welcome travelers into their chalky, mazelike cellars. Most of the big houses give tours of their *caves* (cellars). The quality of the tours is inconsistent, ranging from hilarious to despairingly tedious, though a glass of Champagne at the end makes even the most mediocre worth it (some would say). On the tours, you'll discover that Champagne is not made so differently from the way the Dom did it three centuries ago.

A view along the Routes du Champagne; for details on the Champagne Roads see this chapter's Planner section.

BUBBLY BASICS

ALL ABOUT GRAPES

Three types of grape are used to make Champagne: pinot noir, chardonnay, and pinot meunier. The two pinots, which account for 75% of production, are black grapes with white juice. Rosé Champagne is made either by leaving pinot noir juice in contact with the grape skins just long enough to turn it pink, or by mixing local red wine with Champagne prior to bottling. Blanc de Blancs is Champagne made exclusively from white grapes. Blanc de Noirs is made exclusively from black grapes.

HOW SWEET IT IS

The amount of residual sugar determines the category—ranging from Demi-Sec (literally half-dry, actually sweet) with 33–55 grams of residual sugar per liter, to Extra-Brut (very dry) at less than 6 grams of residual sugar per liter. Classifications in between include Sec at 17 to 35 grams, Extra Dry at 12–20 grams, and Brut, under 15 grams.

VINTAGE VS. NONVINTAGE

Vintage Champagne is named for a specific year, on the premise that the grapes harvested in that year were of extraordinary quality to produce a Champagne by themselves without being blended with wine from other years. Cuvées de Prestige are the finest and most expensive Champagnes that a firm has to offer.

LABEL KNOW-HOW

Along with specific descriptors—such as Blanc de Blancs, Blanc de Noirs, Vintage, etc.—the label carries the following information:

1. The Champagne appellation
2. The brand or name of the producer
3. The level of alcohol volume. Champagne is permitted to vary between 10 and 13%; 12% is common, resulting in classifications like Brut, and Demi-Sec.

THE MERRY WIDOW & THE STARSTRUCK MONK

MADAME CLICQUOT (1777–1866)

WHY THE NICKNAME? Born Nicole-Barbe Ponsardin and married into the Clicquot family, Madame Clicquot was widowed just seven years after she married François Clicquot (in French, *veuve* means widow).

I'M A HOTSHOT BECAUSE . . . : After her husband's death, she took over the firm and was one of France's earliest female entrepreneurs and the smartest marketer of the Napoléonic era. During her 60 years in control of the firm, business soared.

GREATEST CONTRIBUTION: She invented the *table de remuage*—the slanted rack used for "riddling," a method for capturing and releasing sediment that collects in the wine—a process that is still used today.

BRAGGING RIGHTS: She persuaded Czar Alexander I to toast Napoléon's demise with Champagne rather than vodka, and other royal courts were soon in bubbly pursuit.

DOM PIERRE PÉRIGNON (1638–1715)

WHY THE NICKNAME? When Dom Pierre first tasted his creation, he is quoted as saying that he was drinking stars.

I'M A HOTSHOT BECAUSE . . . : He discovered Champagne when he was about 30 years old while he was the cellarmaster at the Abbey of Hautvillers, just north of Épernay.

GREATEST CONTRIBUTION: He blended wines from different vats and vineyards (now a common practice but then a novelty), reintroduced corks—forgotten since Roman times—and used thicker glass bottles to prevent them from exploding during fermentation.

BRAGGING RIGHTS: Who else can claim the title Father of Champagne?

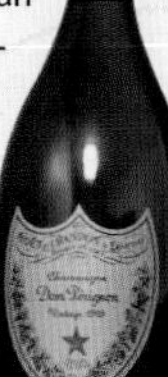

"Brother, come quickly! I'm drinking stars!"

–Dom Pierre Pérignon

WHAT YOU'LL PAY

Champagne relentlessly markets itself as a luxury product—the sippable equivalent of perfume and haute couture—so it's no surprise that two of the top Champagne brands, Krug and Dom Pérignon, are owned by a luxury goods conglomerate (Louis Vuitton-Moët Hennessy). Sure, at small local producers, or in giant French hypermarkets, you can find a bottle of nonvintage bubbly for $15. But it's more likely to be nearer $40 and, if you fancy something special—say a bottle of vintage Dom Perignon Rose—be prepared to fork out $350. One of the priciest Blanc de Noirs is Bollinger's Vieilles Vignes—tagged at around $400. At the very top of the line is Krug's single-vineyard Clos du Mesnil, with the stellar 1995 vintage retailing at around $750. Just 12,624 bottles were ever produced of this golden elixir.

TOURING THE CELLARS

Experiencing the underground *crayères* is a must for any visit to Champagne. Many firms welcome visitors; for some you need to book in advance (by phone or via Web sites). All tours end with a tasting or three. Don't forget a jacket or sweater—it's chilly down there.

REIMS

CLOSEST TO CITY CENTER

Mumm. Not the most spectacular cellars but a practical option if you have little time: You can walk it from the cathedral and the train station. Mumm was confiscated by the French state in World War I because it had always remained in German ownership. Visit starts with 10-minute film and ends with choice of three dégustations: the €20 option includes a rosé and a vintage grand cru.

✉ 29 rue du Champ-de-Mars ☎ 03–26–49–59–69 🌐 www.mumm.com 🎟 €10 🕓 Mar.–Oct., Sat.–Fri., 9–11, 2–5 PM; Nov.–Feb., Sat., 9–11, 2–5

FANCIEST ARCHITECTURE

Pommery. This turreted wedding-cake extravaganza on the city outskirts, was designed by Jeanne-Alexandrine Pommery (1819–90), another formidable Champagne widow. The 11 miles of cellars (about a hundred feet underground) are reached by a grandiose 116-step staircase. They include no fewer than 120 chalk pits, several lined with bas-reliefs carved into the rock.

✉ 5 pl. du General-Gouraud ☎ 03–26–61–62–55 🌐 www.pommery.fr 🎟 €10 🕓 Apr.–Nov., daily 9:30–7; Dec.–Mar., daily 10–6.

MOST EXPENSIVE VISIT

Ruinart. Founded back in 1729, just a year after Louis XV's decision to allow wine to be transported by bottle (previously it could only be moved by cask) effectively kick-started the Champagne industry. Four of its huge, church-sized 24 chalk galleries are listed historic monuments. This is the costliest visit on offer—and, if you shell out €38, you can taste the Blanc de Blancs.

✉ 4 rue des Crayères ☎ 03-26-77-51-21 🌐 www.champagne-ruinart.fr 🎫 €14.50 ⏲ Open by appointment.

BEST FOR HISTORY BUFFS

Taittinger. Cavernous chalk cellars, first used by monks for wine storage, house 15 million bottles and partly occupy the crypt of the 13th century abbey that used to stand on the spot. You can see a model of the abbey and its elegant church, both demolished at the Revolution.

✉ 9 pl. St-Nicaise ☎ 03-26-85-84-33 🌐 www.tattinger.com 🎫 €8 ⏲ By appointment only: Mid-Mar.–mid-Nov., daily 9:30–1 & 2–5:30; mid-Nov.–mid-Mar. weekdays only.

ÉPERNAY

BEST MUSEUM

Castellane. Some of the region's deepest cellars—down to 130 feet—and, above ground, a museum with an intriguing display of old tools, bottles, labels and posters. There's also the chance to see the bottling and labeling plant, and climb to the top of a 200-foot tower for a great view over Épernay and the surrounding Marne vineyards.

✉ 57 rue de Verdun ☎ 03-26-51-19-19 🌐 www.castellane.com 🎫 €8 (incl. museum) ⏲ Apr.–Dec., daily 10–noon and 2–6; Jan.–Mar., by appointment only.

"Cellar-brate" with a guided tour.

LADIES' CHOICE

Veuve-Clicquot. The 15-mile chalk galleries here were first excavated in Gallo-Roman times—back in the 3rd century AD! You can see and talk to cellar workers during the visit, and the souvenir shop has the most extensive range of gift ideas of any champagne house. This is Champagne's most feminist firm—named for a woman, and still headed up by a woman today.

✉ 12 rue du Temple ☎ 03-26-89-53-90 🌐 www.veuve-clicquot.com 🎫 €9 ⏲ Open by appointment Apr.–Oct., 10–6, Mon.–Sat.; Nov.–Mar., 10–6 Mon.–Fri.

Veuve Clicquot's President Cecile Bonnefond

BEST HIGH-TECH VISIT

Mercier. Ride an electric train and admire the giant 200,000-bottle oak barrel it took 24 oxen three weeks to cart to the Exposition Universelle in Paris in 1889. An elevator down to (and up from) the cellars is a welcome plus.

✉ 75 av. de Champagne ☎ 03-26-51-22-22 🌐 www.champagne-mercier.fr 🎫 €8.50 ⏲ Mid-Mar.–mid-Nov., Thurs.–Mon. 9:30–11:30 and 2–4:30; closed mid-Nov.–mid-Mar.

LONGEST CELLAR WALK

Moët & Chandon. Foreign royalty, from Czar Alexander I to Queen Elizabeth II, have visited this most prestigious of all Champagne houses, founded by Charles Moët in 1743. The chalk-cellar galleries run for a mind-blowing 17 miles. The visit includes a glass of Brut Imperial; for €27 you can also taste a couple of vintages.

✉ 18 av. de Champagne ☎ 03-26-51-20-20 🌐 www.moet.com 🎫 €14.50 ⏲ Mid-Nov.–Dec., Feb.–Mar. Mon.–Fri. 9:30–11:30 and 2:30–4:30; Apr.–mid-Nov., daily 9:30–11:30 and 2:30–4:30.

exterior effect is marred only by the bulky 17th-century Baroque west front. Recently, the cathedral reopened after many years of renovations, including restoration of its famed 19th-century organ.

WHERE TO STAY

$$–$$$ **Hôtel d'Angleterre.** Guest rooms at this stylish spot in central Châlons have modern furniture, gaily patterned curtains, and either wooden floors or plush red carpets; all have marble bathrooms. Those in the back are quietest, while those on the upper floor have the most atmosphere. In the outstanding restaurant, with its starched white tablecloths (closed Sunday; no lunch Monday or Saturday), chef Jacky Michel's creations include quail with foie gras and red mullet with artichokes, as well as the seasonal dessert *tout-pommes,* featuring five variations on the humble apple. Cheaper fare (main courses start at €12) is offered in the brasserie, Les Temps Changent. Breakfast is a superb buffet. **Pros:** beautifully modernized rooms; inventive cuisine offered at different price points. **Cons:** booming business is detracting from the family feel; restaurant doesn't serve dinner past 8:45 PM. ✉ *19 pl. Monseigneur-Tissier* ☎ *03–26–68–21–51* 🌐 *www.hotel-dangleterre.fr* *25 rooms* *In-room: a/c, refrigerator, Internet, Wi-Fi. In-hotel: restaurant, bar, some pets allowed* ▭ *AE, DC, MC, V* ⏲ *Closed mid-July–early Aug. and late Dec.–early Jan.* *BP.*

ÉPERNAY

28 km (18 mi) south of Reims via N51, 35 km (24 mi) west of Châlons-en-Champagne via N3, 50 km (31 mi) east of Château-Thierry via D3/N3.

Although Reims loudly proclaims itself to be the last word in Champagne production, Épernay—set on the south bank of the Marne—is really the center of the bubbly drink's spirit. It was here in 1741 that the first full-blown Champagne house, Moët (now Moët et Chandon), took the lifetime passion of Dom Pérignon and turned it into an industry.

GETTING HERE

Trains from Paris (Gare de l'Est) leave for Épernay every hour or so (€20.60); the 145-km (90-mi) trip takes around 1 hour, 15 minutes. Several trains daily link Épernay to Reims (20 mi, 30 mins; €6) and Châlons (15 mi, 15 mins; €5.50). STDM Trans-Champagne runs several buses each day to Épernay from Châlons (1 hr, €8).

Visitor Information Épernay Tourist Office. ✉ *7 ave. Champagne* ☎ *03–26–53–33–00* 🌐 *www.ot-epernay.fr.*

EXPLORING

Unfortunately, no relation exists between the fabulous wealth of Épernay's illustrious wine houses and the drab, dreary appearance of the town as a whole. Most Champagne firms—Moët et Chandon (✉ *20 av. de Champagne*); Mercier (✉ *70 av. de Champagne*); and De Castellane (✉ *57 rue de Verdun*)—are spaced out along the long, straight Avenue de Champagne, and although their names may provoke sighs of wonder, their facades are either functional or overdressy. ⇨ *The attractions are underground—see "Champagne Uncorked" in this chapter for details on guided tours.*

CLOSE UP

Hiking Champagne: Lift Your Spirits!

There's nothing like getting out into Mother Nature to send the spirits soaring and, as it turns out, the region of Champagne is custom-made for easy and scenic hiking.

Just south of Reims rises the Montagne de Reims, a vast forested plateau on whose slopes grow the Pinot Noir and Pinot Meunier grapes used to make Champagne.

Several *sentiers de Grandes Randonnées* (long hiking trails; also known as GRs) run across the top of the plateau, burrowing through dense forest and looping around the edges.

For example, the GR141 and the GR14 form a loop more than 50 km (30 mi) long around the plateau's eastern half, passing by several train stations en route.

You can access some of these hiking trails from the Rilly-la-Montagne, Avenay, and Ay stops on the Reims-Épernay rail line.

If you're a serious hiker, make for the Ardennes region, which lies just to the northeast of Champagne.

To understand how the region's still wine became sparkling Champagne, head across the Marne to **Hautvillers**. Here the monk Dom Pérignon (1638–1715)—upon whom, legend has it, blindness conferred the gifts of exceptional taste buds and sense of smell—invented Champagne as everyone knows it by using corks for stoppers and blending wines from different vineyards. Dom Pérignon's simple tomb, in a damp, dreary Benedictine abbey church (now owned by Moët et Chandon), is a forlorn memorial to the hero of one of the world's most lucrative drink industries.

7

WHERE TO STAY

$$$–$$$$ **La Briqueterie.** Épernay is short on good hotels, so it's worth driving south to Vinay to find this luxurious manor. The spacious guest rooms are individually decorated in lilac, blue floral, yellow and chocolate, all with carpeting; ask for one overlooking the extensive gardens. Chef Gilles Goess, who trained at the Paris Ritz, adds an inventive touch to the menu of regional cuisine, with gourmet six-course menus from €80. An indoor pool and spa overlooking the gardens include sauna and hammam facilities. **Pros:** wonderful garden; great chef; luxurious spa treatments. **Cons:** rooms can be small; corporate feel (frequent business seminars). ✉ *4 rte. de Sézanne, 6 km (4 mi) south of Épernay, Vinay* ☎ *03–26–59–99–99* 🌐 *www.labriqueterie.com* *40 rooms, 2 suites* *In-room: a/c, refrigerator, Wi-Fi. In-hotel: restaurant, bar, pool, gym, some pets allowed* 💳 *AE, MC, V* ⏲ *Closed late Dec.* *BP.*

CHÂTEAU-THIERRY

37 km (23 mi) east of Épernay via N3.

Built along the Marne River beneath the ruins of a hilltop castle that dates from the time of Joan of Arc, and within sight of the American **Belleau Wood** War Cemetery (open daily 9–5), commemorating the

Rumor has it that even the air is 30-proof in Champagne—discover whether this is true or not on the many hiking trails in the region.

2,300 American soldiers slain here in 1918, Château-Thierry is best known as the birthplace of the French fabulist Jean de La Fontaine (1621–95). Recently restored, the 16th-century mansion where La Fontaine was born and lived until 1676 is now a museum, the **Musée Jean de La Fontaine,** furnished in the style of the 17th century. It contains La Fontaine's bust, portrait, and baptism certificate, plus editions of his fables magnificently illustrated by Jean-Baptiste Oudry (1755) and Gustave Doré (1868). ✉ *12 rue Jean-de-La-Fontaine* ☎ *03–23–69–05–60* 🌐 *www.la-fontaine-ch-thierry.net* 🎫 *€3.60* 🕐 *Tues.–Sun. 9:30–noon and 2–5:30.*

EXCURSION: THE CATHEDRAL CITIES

Champagne's eastern neighbor, the province of Picardy, located to the northeast of the region, is traversed by the Aisne and Oise rivers, and remains home to some of France's greatest cathedrals. The hundreds of kilometers of chalk tunnels throughout northern France, some dug by the ancient Romans as quarries, may serve as the damp and moldy berth for millions of bottles of Champagne, but they also gave up tons of blocks to create other treasures of the region: the magical and magnificent Gothic cathedrals of the region.

Here, in the wake of regal Reims, we visit four more of the most superlative: Amiens, the largest; Beauvais, the tallest; Laon, with the most towers and fantastic hilltop setting; and Soissons, beloved by Rodin. Add in those at St-Omer, St-Quentin, and Châlons-en-Champagne, along with the bijou churches in Rue, St-Riquier, and L'Épine (⇨ *above*), and aficionados of medieval architecture may wish to explore the region more extensively, to follow the development of Gothic architecture from its debut at Noyon to its flamboyant finale at Abbeville, where, according to the 19th-century English essayist John Ruskin, Gothic "lay down and died."

LAON

66 km (41 mi) north of Château-Thierry via D1/N2, 52 km (32 mi) northwest of Reims.

Thanks to its awesome hilltop site and the forest of towers sprouting from its ancient cathedral, lofty Laon basks in the title of the "crowned mountain." The medieval ramparts, virtually undisturbed by passing traffic, provide a ready-made itinerary for a tour of old Laon. Panoramic views, sturdy gateways, and intriguing glimpses of the cathedral lurk around every bend. There's even a funicular, which makes frequent trips (except on Sunday in winter) up and down the hillside between the station and the Vieille Ville (Old Town).

GETTING HERE

Trains from Paris (Gare du Nord) chug up to Laon, via Soissons, every 2 or 3 hours (€20.50); the 145-km (90-mi) trip takes around 1 hour, 35 minutes. There are four trains a day from Reims to Laon (40 mins, €8.90) and five trains daily from Amiens (65 mi; 1 hr, 45 mins; €16.10).

Visitor Information Laon Tourist Office ✉ *Pl. du Parvis* ☎ *03-23-20-28-62* 🌐 *www.tourisme-paysdelaon.com.*

7

EXPLORING

Fodor's Choice ★ The **Cathédrale Notre-Dame**, constructed between 1150 and 1230, is a superb example of early Gothic. The light interior gives the impression of order and immense length, and the first flourishing of Gothic architecture is reflected in the harmony of the four-tier nave: from the bottom up, observe the wide arcades, the double windows of the tribune, the squat windows of the triforium, and, finally, the upper windows of the clerestory. The majestic towers can be explored during the guided visits that leave from the tourist office, housed in a 12th-century hospital on the cathedral square. Medieval stained glass includes the rose window dedicated to the liberal arts in the left transept, and the windows in the flat east end, an unusual feature for France although common in England. ✉ *Pl. du Parvis* 🎫 *Guided tours of the towers €4, audio guide €4* ⏲ *Daily 8:30–6:30; guided tours Apr.–Sept., 11* AM *and 3* PM.

The **Musée Municipal** *(Town Museum)* has some fine antique pottery and work by the local-born Le Nain brothers, Antoine, Louis, and Mathieu, active in the 17th century and abundantly represented in the Louvre. But its chief draw is the **Chapelle des Templiers** in the garden—a small, octagonal 12th-century chapel topped by a shallow dome. It houses fragments of the cathedral's gable and the chilling effigy of Guillaume de Harcigny, doctor to the insane king Charles VI, whose death from natural causes in 1393 did not prevent his memorializers from chiseling a skeletal portrait that recalls the Black Death. ✉ *32* *rue Georges-Ermant* ☎ *03–23–22–87–01* 🌐 *www.ville-laon.fr* 🎫 *€4* ⏱ *June–Sept., Tues.–Sun. 11–6; Oct.–May, Tues.–Sun. 2–6.*

NO STONE LEFT UNTURNED

The filigreed elegance of Laon's five towers is audacious and rare. Look for the 16 stone oxen protruding from the tops, a tribute to the stalwart 12th-century beasts who carted up blocks of stone from quarries far below.

WHERE TO STAY

$ **Bannière de France.** In business since 1685, this old-fashioned, uneven-floor hostelry is five minutes from the cathedral. Lieselotte Lefèvre, the German patronne, speaks fluent English. Rooms are cozy and quaint but on the small side; Room 15 is by far the largest. The restaurant's venerable dining room showcases sturdy cuisine (trout, lemon sole, guinea fowl) and good-value prix-fixe menus. **Pros:** quaint; short walk to cathedral; free Wi-Fi. **Cons:** some rooms need modernizing; short on parking space. ✉ *11 rue Franklin-Roosevelt* ☎ *03–23–23–21–44* 🌐 *www.hoteldelabannieredefrance.com* *18 rooms* *In-room: no a/c, Wi-Fi (some). In-hotel: restaurant, bar* 💳 *AE, DC, MC, V* ⏱ *Closed mid-Dec.–mid-Jan and 2 wks end of July* 🍽 *MAP.*

SOISSONS

38 km (22 mi) southwest of Laon.

Visitor Information **Soissons Tourist Office.** ✉ *16 pl. Fernand-Marquigny* ☎ *03–23–53–17–37* 🌐 *www.tourisme-soissons.fr.*

Although much damaged in World War I, Soissons commands attention for its two huge churches, one intact, one in ruins. The Gothic **Cathédrale Saint-Gervais Saint-Protais** was appreciated by Rodin, who famously declared that "there are no hours in this cathedral, but rather eternity." The interior, with its pure lines and restrained ornamentation, creates a more harmonious impression than the asymmetrical, one-tower facade. The most remarkable feature, however, is the rounded two-story transept, an element more frequently found in the German Rhineland than in France. Rubens's freshly restored *Adoration of the Shepherds* hangs on the other side of the transept. ✉ *Pl. Fernand-Marquigny* ⏱ *Daily 9:30–noon and 2:30–5:30.*

The twin-spire facade, arcaded cloister, and airy refectory, constructed from the 14th to the 16th century, are all that is left of the hilltop abbey church of **St-Jean-des-Vignes**, which was largely dismantled just after the Revolution. Its fallen stones were used to restore the cathedral and neighboring homes. But the church remains the most impressive sight in Soissons, its hollow rose window peering out over the town like the eye of some giant Cyclops. The Musée de Soissons hosts temporary expositions in the abbey's Arsenal building. ✉ *Cours St-Jean-des-Vignes* 🌐 *www.musee-soissons.org* 🎫 *Free* ⏱ *Weekdays 9–noon and 2–6, weekends 2–6.*

Partly housed in the medieval abbey of St-Léger, the **Musée de Soissons**, the town museum, has a varied collection of local archaeological finds and paintings, with fine 19th-century works by Gustave Courbet and Eugène Boudin. ✉ *6 rue de la Congrégation* ☎ *03–23–93–30–50* 🌐 *www.musee-soissons.org* 🎫 *Free* ⏲ *Weekdays 9–noon and 2–5, weekends 2–6.*

WHERE TO STAY

$$$$ ★ **Château de Courcelles.** This refined château by the Vesles River is run by easygoing Frédéric Nouhaud. Its pure, classical Louis XIV facade harmonizes oddly with the sweeping brass main staircase attributed to Jean Cocteau. Rooms vary in size and grandeur; the former outbuildings have been converted into large family-size suites. Wind down in the bar while anticipating excellent fare, including seasonal game, prepared by chef Thibaut Serin-Moulin and served up in the stately, 18th-century-style dining room. A formal garden and pool are the gateway to 40 acres of parkland and a tree-shaded canal. **Pros:** verdant setting; historic charm. **Cons:** room sizes vary, with the larger rooms in a separate block. ✉ *8 rue du Château, 20 km (12 mi) east of Soissons via N31, Courcelles-sur-Vesles* ☎ *03–23–74–13–53* 🌐 *www.chateau-de-courcelles.fr* *10 rooms, 8 suites* *In-room: no a/c, safe, refrigerator, Wi-Fi. In-hotel: restaurant, bar, tennis court, pool, some pets allowed* *AE, DC, MC, V* *MAP.*

AMIENS

112 km (70 mi) northwest of Soissons via N31/D935, 58 km (36 mi) north of Beauvais via N1 or A16.

Although Amiens showcases some pretty brazen postwar reconstruction, epitomized by Auguste Perret's 340-foot Tour Perret, a soaring concrete stump by the train station, the city is well worth exploring. It has lovely Art Deco buildings in its traffic-free city center, as well as elegant, older stone buildings like the 18th-century Beffroi (Belfry) and Neoclassical prefecture. Crowning the city is its great Gothic cathedral, which has survived the ages intact. Nearby is the waterfront quarter of St-Leu—with its small, colorful houses—rivaling the squares of Arras and streets of old Lille as the cutest city district north of Paris.

GETTING HERE

Trains from Paris (Gare du Nord) leave for Amiens every hour or so (€19.40); the 129-km (80-mi) trip takes 1 hour, 5 minutes. There's one direct train each day from Reims to Amiens (2 hrs, 30 mins; €22) via Laon; five trains daily connect Laon to Amiens (1 hr, 45 mins; €16.10). Buses run by the CAB'ARO line (☎ *03–44–48–08–47* 🌐 *www.cabaro.info*) run between Beauvais and Amiens (line 30E) six times daily (50 mi; 1 hr, 20 mins; €12).

Visitor Information Amiens Tourist Office ✉ *6 bis, rue Dusevel* ☎ *03–22–71–60–50* 🌐 *www.amiens-tourisme.com.*

EXPLORING

Fodor's Choice ★ By far the largest church in France, the **Cathédrale Notre-Dame** could enclose Paris's Notre-Dame twice. It may lack the stained glass of Chartres or the sculpture of Reims, but for architectural harmony, engineering proficiency, and sheer size, it's without peer. The soaring, asymmetrical

CLOSE UP

Medieval Architecture's Building Blocks

Consider these architectural terms before passing through Amiens's main medieval portal (front door):

CHANCEL: The space around the altar that's off-limits to everyone but the clergy. It's at the east end of the church and sometimes blocked off by a rail.

CHOIR: The section of the church set off to seat the choir. It's in the chancel.

CLERESTORY: The upper part of the church walls, typically lined with windows (often the stained-glass variety) to bathe the nave with light.

CROCKET: Usually adorning a spire, pinnacle, or gable, this carved ornament often takes the form of foliage, such as acanthus leaves.

CRYPT: An underground chamber usually used as a burial site and often found directly below a church's nave.

GABLE: The triangular upper portion of a wall comprising the area of a pitched roof.

NARTHEX: A hall leading from the main entrance to the nave.

NAVE: The main section of the church that stretches from the chancel to the main door. This is where worshippers sit during services.

PIER: As opposed to a column, this is a solid masonry support, ranging from a simple square shape to a compound pier often comprised of several distinct sub-shafts.

RIBBED VAULT: A distinct form of Gothic architecture made up of diagonal arches, called ribs, that spring from column to column to create an overhead framework. By transferring the weight of the building from the roof directly to the columns, they reduced the masonry needed for the exterior walls, enabling these to be filled with large (usually stained-glass) windows.

TRANSEPT: The part of the church that extends outward at a right angle from the main body, creating a cruciform (cross-shape) plan.

TYMPANUM: A recessed triangular or semicircular space above the portal, often decorated with sculpture.

facade has a notable Flamboyant Gothic rose window, and is brought to life on summer evenings when a sophisticated 45-minute light show re-creates its original color scheme. Inside, there's no stylistic disunity to mar the perspective, creating an overwhelming sensation of pure space. Construction took place between 1220 and 1264, a remarkably short period in cathedral-building spans. One of the highlights of a visit here is hidden from the eye, at least until you lift up some of the 110 choir-stall seats and admire the humorous, skillful misericord seat carvings executed between 1508 and 1518. ✉ *Pl. Notre-Dame* ☎ *03–22–92–03–32* 🌐 *cathedrale-amiens.monuments-nationaux.fr* 🎟 *Free* ⏲ *Apr.–Sept. 8:30–6:30; Oct.–Mar. 8:30–5:30. Access to towers (€7) Apr., May, June, and Sept., weekdays at 3 and 4:30; unaccompanied tour Wed.–Sun. 2:30–5:15; access July and Aug., Wed.–Sun. tour at 11, unaccompanied 2:30–5:15; tour Oct.–Mar. at 3:45.*

DID YOU KNOW?

Lift your eyes to discover why Amiens is the most architecturally successful cathedral in France—it may not have Chartres's stained glass or Reims's sculpture but for sheer size and harmony, it can't be beat.

★ Behind an opulent columned facade, the **Musée de Picardie**, built 1855–67, looks like a pompous offering from the Second Empire. Initial impressions are hardly challenged by its grand staircase lined with monumental frescoes by local-born Puvis de Chavannes, or its central hall with huge canvases, like Gérôme's 1855 *Siècle d'Auguste* and Maignon's 1892 *Mort de Carpeaux*. One step beyond, though, and you're in a rotunda painted top to bottom in modern minimalist fashion by Sol LeWitt. The basement is filled with subtly lighted archaeological finds and Egyptian artifacts beneath masterly brick vaulting. The ground floor reopened in 2009 after extensive renovation; the upper floor is scheduled to reopen in late 2010. ✉ *48 rue de la République* ☎ *03–22–97–14–00* 🌐 *www.amiens.fr/musees* 🎫 *€5* ⏲ *Tues.–Sun. 10–12:30 and 2–6.*

BEAM ME UP

If you're a true Verne fan, you might want to visit his last resting place in the Cimetière de la Madeleine (✉ *2 rue de la Poudrière*), where he is melodramatically portrayed pushing up his tombstone as if enacting his own sci-fi resurrection.

Jules Verne (1828–1905) lived in Amiens for the last 35 years of his life, and his former home, renovated in 2005 to mark the centenary of his death, is now the **Maison Jules-Verne** (✉ *2 rue Charles-Dubois* ☎ *03–22–45–45–75* 🌐 *www.jules-verne.net* 🎫 *€7* ⏲ *Mid-Apr.–mid-Oct., weekdays 10–12:30 and 2–6:30, weekends 11–6:30; mid-Oct.–mid-Apr., Wed.–Mon. 2–6*). It contains some 15,000 documents about Verne's life as well as original furniture and a reconstruction of the writing studio where he created his science-fiction classics.

The **Hortillonnages**, on the east side of town, are commercial water gardens—covering more than 700 acres—where vegetables have been grown since Roman times. There's a 45-minute boat tour of these aquatic jewels. ✉ *Boats leave from 54 bd. de Beauvillé* ☎ *03–22–92–12–18* 🎫 *€6* ⏲ *Apr.–Oct., daily 2–5.*

WHERE TO EAT AND STAY

$$$ FRENCH ★ ✕ **Les Marissons.** In the scenic St-Leu section of Amiens, beneath the cathedral, is this picturesque waterside restaurant in an elegantly transformed boatbuilding shed. Chef Antoine Benoit offers creative takes on foie gras and regional ingredients: eel, duck pâté with figs in pastry, rabbit with mint and goat cheese, and pigeon with black currants. His turbot with apricots has been a house favorite since the restaurant opened in the 1980s. To avoid pricey dining à la carte, order from the prix-fixe menus. ✉ *Pont de la Dodone, 68 rue des Marissons* ☎ *03–22–92–96–66* 🌐 *www.les-marissons.fr* 💳 *AE, DC, MC, V* ⏲ *Closed Sun. and 3 wks in May. No lunch Wed. or Sat.*

$ 🏨 **Carlton.** This hotel near the train station has a stylish Belle Époque facade. In contrast, rooms are sober and functional, though light and airy, with spacious marble bathrooms; the largest room, with a view of the city skyline, is No. 403. Foreign guests are common, and English is spoken. The restaurant, La Brasserie des Capucines, serves regional, mainly meat dishes. **Pros:** central location; free Wi-Fi; friendly staff. **Cons:** some rooms lack charm; used for corporate seminars. ✉ *42 rue* *de Noyon* ☎ *03–22–97–72–22* 🌐 *www.lecarlton.fr* ⇨ *24 rooms* 👍 *In-room: a/c, Wi-Fi. In-hotel: restaurant, parking (paid), some pets allowed* 💳 *AE, DC, MC, V* 🍴 *BP.*

THE ARTS

The **Théâtre de Marionnettes** (✉ *31 rue Edouard-David* ☎ *03–22–22–30–90* 🌐 *www.ches-cabotans-damiens.com*) presents a rare glimpse of the traditional Picardy marionettes, known locally as Chés Cabotans d'Amiens. Free shows are performed (in French), usually on Friday evening and Sunday afternoon (daily in August), with plot synopses printed in English.

BEAUVAIS

56 km (35 mi) south of Amiens via A16, 96 km (60 mi) west of Soissons.

Beauvais and its neighbor Amiens have been rivals since the 13th century, when they locked horns over who could build the bigger cathedral. Beauvais lost—gloriously.

GETTING HERE

Trains from Paris (Gare du Nord) leave for Beauvais every hour (€12.40); the 80-km (50-mi) trip takes around 1 hour, 15 minutes. Buses run by the CAB'ARO line (☎ *03–44–48–08–47* 🌐 *www.cabaro.info*) run between Amiens and Beauvais six times daily (50 mi; 1 hr, 20 mins; €12). The Beauvais airport shuttle stops in the town center and train station daily (20 mins; €4 for 48-hour ticket).

7

Visitor Information Beauvais Tourist Office. ✉ *1 rue Beauregard* ☎ *03–44–15–30–30* 🌐 *www.beauvaistourisme.fr.*

EXPLORING

Fodor's Choice ★

Soaring above the town center is the tallest cathedral in France: the **Cathédrale St-Pierre**. You may have an attack of vertigo just gazing up at its vaults, 153 feet above the ground. Paid for by the riches of Beauvais's wool industry, the choir collapsed in 1284, shortly after completion, and was rebuilt with extra pillars. This engineering fiasco proved so costly that the transept was not attempted until the 16th century. It was worth the wait: an outstanding example of Flamboyant Gothic, with ornate rose windows flanked by pinnacles and turrets. It's also still standing—which is more than can be said for the megalomaniacal 450-foot spire erected at the same time. This lasted precisely four years; when it came crashing down, all remaining funds were hurled at an emergency consolidation program, and Beauvais's dream of having the largest church in Christendom vanished forever. Now the cathedral is starting to lean, and cracks have appeared in the choir vaults because of shifting water levels in the soil. No such problems bedevil the **Basse Oeuvre** (Lower Edifice; closed to the public), which juts out impertinently where the nave should have been. It has been there for 1,000 years. Fittingly donated to the cathedral by the canon Étienne Musique, the oldest surviving **chiming clock** in the world—a 1302 model with a 15th-century painted wooden face and most of its original clockwork—is built into the wall of the cathedral. Perhaps Auguste Vérité drew his inspiration from this humbler timepiece when, in 1868, he made a gift to his hometown of the gilded, templelike **astrological clock** (*€4 Displays at 10:40, 11:40, 2:40, 3:40, and 4:40; English audio guide available*), which features animated religious figurines that emerge for short presentations. *Rue St-Pierre www.cathedrale-beauvais.fr May–Oct., daily 9–12:15 and 2–6:15; Nov.–Apr., daily 9–12:15 and 2–5:30.*

From 1664 to 1939 Beauvais was one of France's leading tapestry centers; it reached its zenith in the mid-18th century under the gifted artist Jean-Baptiste Oudry, known for his hunting scenes. Examples from all periods are in the modern **Galerie Nationale de la Tapisserie** *(National Tapestry Museum)* located next to the cathedral. *22 rue St-Pierre 03–44–15–39–10 Free Apr.–Sept., Tues.–Sun. 9:30–noon and 2–6; Oct.–Mar., Tues.–Sun. 10–noon and 2–5.*

One of the few remaining testaments to Beauvais's glorious past, the old Bishop's Palace is now the **Musée Départemental de l'Oise** *(Regional Museum)*. Don't miss the beautifully proportioned attic story, Thomas Couture's epic canvas of the French Revolution, the 14th-century frescoes of instrument-playing sirens on a section of the palace's vaults, or the 1st-century brass *Guerrier Gaulois* (Gallic Warrior). *1 rue du Musée 03–44–11–43–83 www.cg60.fr Free Wed.–Mon. 10–noon and 2–6.*

WHERE TO EAT AND STAY

$ FRENCH **Le Zinc Bleu.** This lively brasserie opposite Beauvais cathedral (ask for a table under the glass veranda, or on the sidewalk terrace if the weather's good) offers a choice between sturdy if unadventurous fare (salmon with tagliatelli, duck, various types of steak) and a wide choice of fresh seafood (crab, lobster, Normandy oysters). The Picardy Salada (warm beef with raw vegetables) makes a copious starter. The dining room has light wooden tables and bright modern pictures, but the openwork metal chairs can be a bit tough on the back, so mark this down as a lunch spot more than a place to linger over dinner. *61 rue St-Pierre 03–44–45–18–30 MC, V.*

¢ FRENCH **L'Ecume du Jour.** Half community-run café, half art gallery (and fair-trade products boutique), this is a great place to stop for a cool drink or a simple meal. Near the train station, the spot has a friendly, bohemian vibe. After enjoying your repas on the pretty mosaic tiled tables, head past the outdoor patio to the covered barn for the ever-changing art exhibitions. *5 rue du Faubourg St-Jacques 03–44–02–07–37 www.ecumedujour.org No credit cards Closed Sun. and Mon.*

$–$$ **Chenal Hotel.** There are few hotels in central Beauvais and this four-square street-corner establishment is perhaps the most convenient of them, close to the train station, a 10-minute walk from the cathedral, and served by a shuttle bus from the Beauvais airport. Rooms are light and soberly decorated, if on the small side. **Pros:** free Wi-Fi; convenient location. **Cons:** small rooms; lacks charm. *63 bd. Général-de-Gaulle 03–44–06–04–60 chenalhotel.fr 29 rooms In-room: no a/c, Wi-Fi. In-hotel: bar, parking (paid), some pets allowed AE, DC, MC, V BP.*

8

Alsace-Lorraine

WORD OF MOUTH

"Alsace has gobbled up more of my film per square mile than almost anywhere else in France. It's kinda like Vermont with vineyards—dozens of picture-postcard villages with church steeples sticking up above the houses, surrounded by vineyards, and backdropped by the Vosges mountains. Stay in the Riquewihr/Ribeauvillé region and day-trip from there—these villages are very close together and the area around the villages is stunning."

—StuDudley

WELCOME TO ALSACE-LORRAINE

TOP REASONS TO GO

★ **The Wine Road:** Ribeauvillé and Riquewihr are at the heart of the Alsatian wine route—two medieval villages filled with Hansel and Gretel houses, cellars bursting with bottles, and wine festivities.

★ **Reborn Colmar:** Although hit by two world wars, Colmar rebuilt itself, and the atmospheric maze of cobblestone streets and Petite Venise waterways of the Vieille Ville are pure enchantment.

★ **Nancy's Art Nouveau:** The Art Nouveau capital of France as well as home to Place Stanislas—the most beautiful royal square in Europe—make the hub city of Lorraine an art lover's paradise.

★ **Joan of Arc Country:** If you're a fan of Jeanne d'Arc, then a pilgrimage to her birthplace in Domrémy-la-Pucelle is a must.

★ **Strasbourg, Capital of Alsace:** The symbolic capital of Europe is a cosmopolitan French city rivaled only by Paris in its medieval charms, history, and haute cuisine.

1 Nancy. When Stanislas Leszczynski, ex-king of Poland, succeeded in marrying his daughter to Louis XIV, he paid homage to the Sun King by transforming Nancy into another Versailles, embellishing the city with elegant showstoppers like Place Stanislas. Elsewhere in the city, you can sate your appetite for the best Art Nouveau at the Musée École de Nancy and the Villa Majorelle—after all, the style was born here.

2 Lorraine. In long-neglected Lorraine, many make the historical pilgrimage to Joan of Arc Country. France's patron saint was born in Domrémy in 1411 and in nearby Vaucouleurs, the Maid of Orléans arrived to ask the help of the governor. If you listen carefully, you might hear the church bells in which Joan discerned voices challenging her to save France.

3 Strasbourg. An appealing combination of medieval alleys, international think tanks, and the European Parliament, this central hub of Alsace is best loved for the villagelike atmosphere of La Petite France, the looming presence of the Cathédrale de Notre-Dame, the rich museums, and the pints of beer sloshing around in the winstubs (wine-bistros).

4 Alsace. Tinged with a German flavor, Alsace is a never-ending procession of colorful towns and villages, many fitted out with spires, gabled houses, and storks' nests in chimney pots. Here you can find the Route du Vin, the famous Alsatian Wine Road, with its vineyards of Riesling and Traminer. This conveniently heads south to Colmar, where the half-timber yellow-and pink-buildings of the *centre ville* seem cut out of a child's coloring book. The town's main treasure is Grünewald's unforgettable 16th-century Issenheim Altarpiece.

LUXEMBOURG
Luxembourg
A31
Thionville
Saarbrücken
A4
Metz
GERMANY
N74
Bitche
D955
LORRAINE
2
A4
ALSACE
4
Hagenau
N4
Saverne
A35
3
N4
Strasbourg
A5
Lunéville
N420
N59
N83
A35
Route de Vin
N57
St Dié
Sélestat
River
Épinal
Ribeauvillé
GERMANY
Riquewihr
VOSGES
Colmar
Freiburg
N57
N83
Rhin
N66
A35
FRANCHE COMTE
Mulhouse
A36
Basel
SWITZERLAND
0 20 mi
0 20 km

GETTING ORIENTED

Bordered by Germany, Alsace-Lorraine has often changed hands between the two countries in the last 350 years. This back-and-forth has left a mark—you'll find that Germanic half-timber houses sometimes clash with a very French café scene. Art also pays homage to both nations, as you can see in the museums of Strasbourg, Alsace's main hub. Eastward lies Lorraine, birthplace of Joan of Arc (and the famous quiche). Due west of Strasbourg on the other side of the Vosges Mountains, the main city of Nancy allures with Art Nouveau and elegant 18th-century architecture.

ALSACE-LORRAINE PLANNER

Transportation Basics

Alsace is a small region and is fairly well interconnected with bus routes and train stations, making it possible to travel extensively by public transportation.

Be sure to load up on information (schedules, the best taxi-for-call companies, etc.) upon arriving at the ticket counter or help desk of the bigger train and bus stations in the area, such as Nancy, Strasbourg, and Colmar.

In Alsace, trains are the way to go. In Lorraine you may need to take short bus jaunts to the smaller towns.

To find out which towns are on the rail lines, pick up the *Guide Régional des Transports,* a free train and bus guide for both Alsace and Lorraine, at stations and *tabacs* (tobacco shops). You can also download the handy widgets from the TER Web site at 🌐 *www.ter-e-services.com/widget_itineraires/index.html.*

It is best to keep on top of your plans if you want to use buses hereabouts. Unfortunately, schedules change rather frequently in Alsace-Lorraine.

Making the Most of Your Time

If an overall experience is what you're after, setting up headquarters in Strasbourg or Colmar will give you the best access to the greatest number of sites, either by public transport or car, while also residing in one.

If wine tasting and vineyards are your priority, setting up in either Riquewihr or Ribeauvillé will put you at the heart of the action.

Remember that many of the region's towns and villages stage summer festivals.

The most notable are the spectacular pagan-inspired burning of the three pine trees in Thann (late June), the Flower Carnival in Sélestat (mid-August), and the wine fair in Colmar (first half of August).

And although Lorraine is a lusterless place in winter, Strasbourg pays tribute to the Germanic tradition with a Christmas fair.

Finding a Place to Stay

Alsace-Lorraine is well served in terms of accommodations.

From the picturesque villages of the Route du Vin, the "Fermes Auberges" of the Vosges to four-star palaces or international-style hotels in the main cities of Nancy and Strasbourg, the range is vast.

Since much of Alsace is in the "countryside" there's also a range of *gîtes,* self-catering cottages or houses that provide a base for longer stays (🌐 *www.gites-de-france.com*).

DINING AND LODGING PRICE CATEGORIES (IN EUROS)

	¢	$	$$	$$$	$$$$
Restaurants	under €13	€13–€17	€18–€24	€25–€32	over €32
Hotels	under €65	€65–€105	€106–€145	€146–€215	over €215

Restaurant prices are per person for a main course at dinner, including tax (5.5%) and service; note that if a restaurant offers only prix-fixe (set-price) meals, it has been given the price category that reflects the full prix-fixe price. Hotel prices are for a standard double room in high season, including tax (19.6%) and service charge.

A Tippler's Guide to Alsace

Winding south along the eastern foothills of the Vosges from Marienheim to Thann, the Alsatian Wine Road is home to delicious wines and beautiful vineyards. The 121-km (75-mi) Route du Vin passes through small towns, and footpaths interspersed throughout the region afford the opportunity to wander through the vineyards. Buses from Colmar head out to the surrounding towns of Riquewihr, St-Hippolyte, Ribeauvillé, and Eguisheim; pick up brochures on the Wine Route from Colmar's tourist office. Although the route is hilly, bicycling is a great way to take in the countryside and avoid the parking hassle in the towns along this heavily traveled route.

Wine is an object of worship in Alsace, and any traveler down the region's Route du Vin will want to become part of the cult. Just because Alsatian vintners use German grapes, don't expect their wines to taste like their counterparts across the Rhine. German vintners aim for sweetness, creating wines that are best appreciated as an aperitif. Alsatian vintners, on the other hand, eschew sweetness in favor of strength, and their wines go wonderfully with knock-down, drag-out meals.

The main wines you need to know about are Gewürztraminer, Riesling, muscat, pinot gris, and sylvaner, all white wines. The only red wine produced in the region is the light and delicious pinot noir. Gewürztraminer, which in Germany is an ultrasweet dessert wine, has a much cleaner, drier taste in Alsace, despite its fragrant bouquet. It's best served with the richest of Alsace dishes, such as goose. Riesling is the premier wine of Alsace, balancing a hard flavor with certain gentleness. With a grapy bouquet and clean finish, dry muscat does best as an aperitif. Pinot gris, also called tokay, is probably the most full-bodied of Alsatian wines. Sylvaner falls below those grapes in general acclaim, tending to be lighter and a bit dull. You can discover many of these wines as you drive along the Route du Vin.

Touring Alsace

For Colmar and its enchanting environs, take a highly recommended van tour with Les Circuits d'Alsace—castles, villages, and vineyards make for an exhilarating itinerary.

Les Circuits d'Alsace (✉ *8 pl. de la Gare, Colmar* ☎ *03–89–41–90–88* 🌐 *www.alsace-travel.com*).

It's Pronounced Veen-Shtoob

Strasbourg and Nancy may be two of France's more expensive cities, but you wouldn't know it by all their down-to-earth eating spots with down-to-earth prices. Most notably, the regional *winstubs* (veen-shtoob), cozier and more wine-oriented than the usual French brasserie, are found in most Alsace towns and villages.

In Strasbourg and Nancy, as well as the villages along Alsace's wine road, you'll need to arrive early (soon after noon for lunch, before 8 for dinner) to be sure of a restaurant table in July and August. Out of season is a different matter throughout.

When to Go

Alsace is blessed with four distinct seasons and one of the lowest rainfalls in all of France—so anytime at all is the right time to visit, as each season attests.

Snow in winter adds magic to the Christmas markets; spring brings forth the scent of burgeoning grape flowers as the world turns green with life; summer can be warm, which rhymes with swarm; autumn is nature's symphony of color as the leaves of tree and vine become a riot of golden yellows and oranges, as the grapes are being bountifully harvested.

GETTING AROUND

Bus Travel

The two main bus companies are **Les Rapides de Lorraine,** based in Nancy, and **Compagnie des Transports Strasbourgeois,** based in Strasbourg. Nancy, Strasbourg, and Colmar all have city buses. In Strasbourg, most of the 15 lines leave from the train station; bus tickets are good on city trams. Nancy's central area is manageable on foot but **Allô Bus** has routes to help, most stopping on Rue St-Jean.

Compagnie des Transports Strasbourgeois (*CTS* ✉ *Strasbourg* ☎ *03–88–77–70–70* 🌐 *www.cts-strasbourg.fr*). **Les Rapides de Lorraine** (✉ *Nancy* ☎ *03–83–34–09–99, 03–83–36–41–14 Agence Ted for ticket information and tariffs* 🌐 *www.rapidesdelorraine.fr*).

Air Travel

International flights connect with Entzheim, near Strasbourg. The airport shuttle bus Navette Routière leaves the city center every half hour from Place de la Gare.

Aéroport International Strasbourg (✉ *Rte. de Strasbourg, 15 km [9½ mi] southwest of city, Entzheim* ☎ *03–88–64–67–67* 🌐 *www.strasbourg.aeroport.fr*).

Train Travel

Sixteen TGV trains leave Paris (Gare de l'Est) every hour for the 140-mins, 500-km (315-mi) journey to Strasbourg. Nancy is only 90 mins away on one of the 10 direct TGVs also leaving every hour, where there are connections for Toul and Épinal.

Several local trains a day run between Strasbourg and Colmar (40 mins distant), stopping in Sélestat (bus link to Ribeauvillé).

There's also a snail-pace daily service from Strasbourg to Obernai, Barr, and Dambach-la-Ville. But you'll need a car to visit smaller villages.

Train Information **Gare SNCF Colmar** (✉ *Rue de la Gare* ☎ *36–35*). **Gare SNCF Nancy** (✉ *3 pl. Thiers* ☎ *36–35*). **Gare SNCF Strasbourg** (✉ *20 pl. de la Gare* ☎ *36–35*). **SNCF** (☎ *36–35 [€0.34 per min]* 🌐 *www.voyages-sncf.com*). **TGV** (🌐 *www.tgv.com*).

Car Travel

A4 heads east from Paris to Strasbourg, via Verdun, Metz, and Saverne. It's met by A26, descending from the English Channel, at Reims.

A31 links Metz to Nancy, continuing south to Burgundy and Lyon. N83/A35 connects Strasbourg, Colmar, and Mulhouse.

A36 continues to Belfort and Besançon. A4, linking Paris to Strasbourg, passes through Lorraine via Metz, linking Lorraine and Alsace.

Picturesque secondary roads lead from Nancy and Toul through Joan of Arc country.

Several scenic roads climb switchbacks over forested mountain passes through the Vosges, connecting Lorraine to Alsace.

A quicker alternative is the tunnel *under* the Vosges at Ste-Marie-aux-Mines, linking Sélestat to Lunévillel.

Alsace's Route du Vin, winding from Marlenheim, in the north, all the way south to Thann, is the ultimate in scenic driving.

DID YOU KNOW?

As this fountain on Place Stanislas proves, the city of Nancy is a spectacular showcase of the 18th-century Rococo style.

EATING AND DRINKING WELL IN ALSACE-LORRAINE

Quiches on parade in Obernai in a photo submitted by Klondike for Fodor's France contest (above); luxurious fois gras (right, top); the best of the würsts (right, bottom).

Bountiful is the watchword of this gastronomic region where lush vineyards flourish, rustic winstubs serve heaping platters of *choucroute garnie*, and restaurants with top chefs boast more Michelin stars than anywhere else in France.

A visit to the proud and bountiful region of Alsace promises sensory overload: gorgeous vistas, antique walled towns, satisfying meals—from farm-style to richly gastronomic—and, most notably, an array of superb wines to discover. The predominantly white varietals, such as Riesling and Pinot Gris, complement the region's rich and varied traditional cooking. It's not for nouvelle-style cooking or fusion dishes that you come to Alsace: no, tradition is king here, and copious is an understatement. When it comes to rustic regional fare, you have hearty stews, custardy quiches, sauerkraut platters, and the thin-crusted onion tarts known as Flammekeuche. Also to be savored are some of the best restaurants in France, including the noble, romantic Auberge de L'Ill in Illhausern, where a salmon mousse with a Riesling reduction sauce might catch your fancy.

FOLLOW THE WINES

Alsace is one of France's most important but least-known wine-producing regions, where vintners designate wines by grape varietals not by town or château. Look for distinctive whites, like full-bodied pinot gris; delicately fruity Sylvaner; citrus-y Riesling; and spicy Gewürztraminer. In reds, pinot noir stands alone. Top producers include: Hugel et Fils, Riquewihr; F.E. Trimbach, Ribeauvillé; and Léon Beyer, Eguisheim.

KOUGELHOPH

This tall, fluted, crown-shape cake, dusted with sugar and studded with raisins and almonds, beckons invitingly from every pastry-shop window in the region. You won't resist.

The delicately sweet, yeast-based dough is kneaded and proofed, baked in a bundt-style mold, and traditionally served, sometimes sprinkled with kirsch, at Sunday breakfast.

Locals say it's even better on the second day, when it achieves a perfect, slightly dry texture.

CHOUCROUTE GARNIE

Daunting in its copious generosity, a heaping platter of choucroute garnie, laden with fermented sauerkraut, smoked bacon, ham, pork shoulder, sausages and potatoes, is the signature dish of the region.

The best places serving it, usually bistro-like winstubs such as the atmospheric Wistub Zum Pfifferhus in Ribeauvillé (☎ *03–89–73–62–28*), are worth a detour.

You've never had sauerkraut like this, tender and delicate, dotted with juniper berries and often cooked with a splash of Riesling or Sylvaner white wine. Savor your choucroute with the region's own sweet white mustard.

FOIE GRAS

The production sure ain't pretty, but the product is sublime—satiny, opulent goose foie gras. Many gastronomes believe that Alsace produces the best in the world.

The meltingly tender fattened livers of plump Alsatian geese are prepared in a number of luscious ways: wrapped in a towel and gently poached—the classic *à la torchon* method; pan-fried and served on a slice of toasted gingerbread; wrapped in puff pastry and baked; then pressed into terrines and pâtés.

BAECKEOFFE

You can't get much heartier or homier than this baked casserole of pork, lamb, and beef marinated in white wine and slow-cooked in a terra-cotta pot with potatoes, onions, garlic, and herbs.

The name—pronounced "bake-eh oaf-eh"—means "baker's oven" in the Germanic Alsatian dialect.

It was so named because this was a dish traditionally assembled at home, then carried to the local baker to cook in his hot ovens.

It's a soul-warming dish for a chilly evening.

Updated by Christopher Mooney

Only the Rhine separates Germany from Alsace-Lorraine, a region that often looks German and even sounds German. But its heart—just to prove how deceptive appearances can be—is passionately French. One has only to recall that Strasbourg was the birthplace of the Marseillaise national anthem to appreciate why Alsace and Lorraine remain among the most intensely French of all France's provinces.

Yet no matter how forcefully the French tout its Frenchness, Alsace also has German roots that go deep, as one look at its storybook medieval architecture will attest. Its gabled, half-timber houses, ornate wells and fountains, oriels (upstairs bay windows), storks' nests, and carved-wood balustrades would serve well as a stage set for the tale of William Tell and satisfy a visitor's deepest craving for well-preserved old-world atmosphere. Strasbourg, perhaps France's most fascinating city outside Paris, offers all this, and urban sophistication as well.

Lorraine, on the other hand, has suffered a decline in its northern industry and the miseries of its small farmers have left much of it tarnished and neglected—or, as others might say, kept it unspoiled. Yet Lorraine's rich caches of verdure, its rolling countryside dotted with *mirabelle* (plum) orchards and crumbling-stucco villages, abbeys, fortresses, and historic cities, such as Art Nouveau-ed Nancy, offer a truly French view of life in the north. Its borders flank Belgium, Luxembourg, and Germany's mellow Mosel (Moselle in French). Home of Baccarat and St-Louis crystal (thanks to limitless supplies of firewood from the Vosges Forest), the birthplace of Gregorian chant, Art Nouveau and Joan of Arc, Lorraine-the-underdog has much of its own to contribute.

The question remains: who put the hyphen in Alsace-Lorraine? Alsace's strip of vine-covered hills squeezed between the Rhine and the Vosges Mountains started out being called Prima Germania by the Romans, and belonged to the fiercely Germanic Holy Roman Empire for more than 700 years. Yet west of the Vosges, Lorraine served under French and Burgundian lords as well as the Holy Roman Empire, coming into its own under the powerful and influential dukes of Lorraine in the Middle Ages and Renaissance. Stanislas, the duke of Lorraine who transformed Nancy into a cosmopolitan Paris of the East, was Louis XV's father-in-law. Thus Lorraine's culture evolved as decidedly less German than its neighbor to the southeast.

But then, in the late 19th century, Kaiser Wilhelm sliced off the Moselle chunk of Lorraine and sutured it, à la Dr. Frankenstein, to Alsace, claiming the unfortunate graft as German turf—as a concession after France's surrender in 1871. At that point the region was systematically Teutonized—architecturally, linguistically, culinarily ("Ve haff our own vays of cookink sauerkraut!")—and the next two generations grew up culturally torn. Until 1918, that is, when France undid its defeat and reclaimed its turf. Until 1940, when Hitler snatched it back and reinstated German textbooks in the primary schools. Until 1945, when France once again triumphantly raised the *bleu-blanc-rouge* over Strasbourg. Today, the regions remain both officially and proudly French.

NANCY

For architectural variety, few French cities match Nancy, which is in the heart of Lorraine, 300 km (190 mi) east of Paris. Medieval ornamentation, 18th-century grandeur, and Belle Époque fluidity rub shoulders in the town center, where the bustle of commerce mingles with stately elegance. Its majesty derives from a long history as domain to the powerful dukes of Lorraine, whose double-barred crosses figure prominently on local statues and buildings. Never having fallen under the rule of the Holy Roman Empire or the Germans, this Lorraine city retains an eminently Gallic charm.

8

GETTING HERE

The jewel in Lorraine's tourism crown, Nancy, has benefited greatly from the introduction of the record-breaking **TGV Est European** (🌐 *www.tgv.com/en*) with 10 direct TGVs daily (one leaving almost every hour) from Paris's Gare de l'Est, 7:12 AM to 8:12 PM, all making the run in 90 minutes. The 12:12 and 6:12 also service Épinal, 45 minutes farther on. Two others, 10:39 and 8:39, take a little longer and involve a change in Metz. Fares vary from €52.30 to €70.70 depending on the train type. Nancy's **train station** (✉ *3 pl. Thiers*), a 15-minute walk down Rue Stanislas from the town center, is open 24 hours. Fourteen direct trains to Strasbourg (€21.30) leave every 45 minutes from Nancy, and roughly every 10 minutes a train leaves for Metz (€9.30). There are frequent (every 20 minutes) daily TER services to Luneville (€6.30). The 45 lines of the **TED bus service** (☎ *03–83–36–41–14* 🌐 *www.ted.cg54.fr*) cover the entire *département*, leaving from Place de la République, for a €1.70 flat rate.

Visitor Information **Nancy Tourist Office** ✉ *14 pl. Stanislas* ☎ *03–83–35–22–41* 🌐 *www.ot-nancy.fr.*

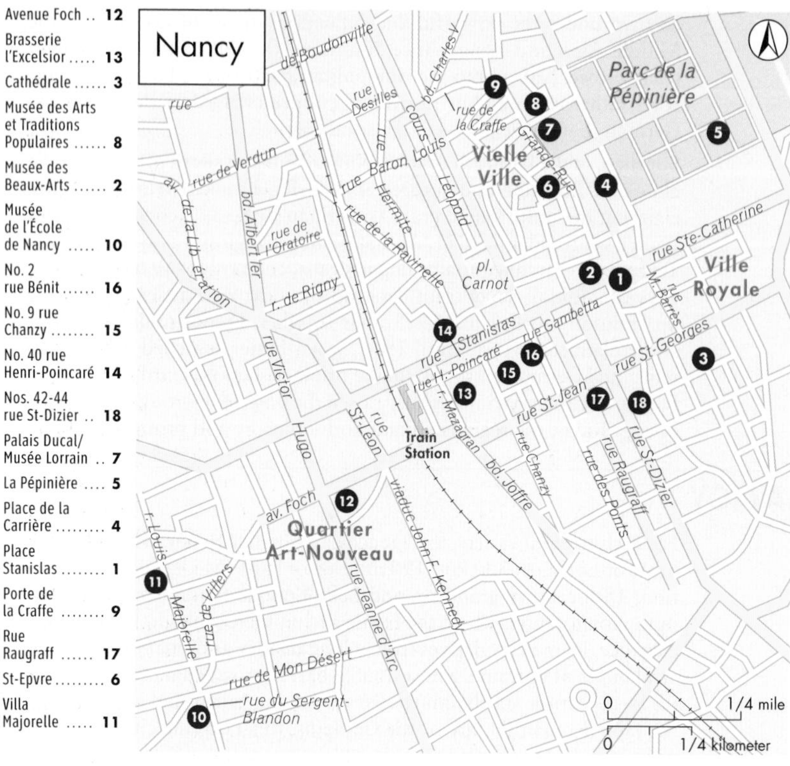

EXPLORING

Nancy is at its most sublimely French in its harmoniously constructed squares and buildings, which, as vestiges of the 18th century, have the quiet refinement associated with the best in French architecture. Curiously enough, it was a Pole, and not a Frenchman, who was responsible for much of what is beautiful in Nancy. Stanislas Leszczynski, ex-king of Poland and father of Maria Leszczynska (who married Louis XV of France) was given the Duchy of Lorraine by his royal son-in-law on the understanding that on his death it would revert to France. Stanislas installed himself in Nancy and devoted himself to the glorious embellishment of the city. Today Place Stanislas remains one of the loveliest and most perfectly proportioned squares in the world, with Place de la Carrière—reached through Stanislas's Arc de Triomphe—with its elegant, homogeneous 18th-century houses, its close rival for this honor.

THE HISTORIC CENTER

Concentrated northeast of the train station, this neighborhood—rich in architectural treasures as well as museums—includes classical Place Stanislas and the shuttered, medieval *Vieille Ville*.

TOP ATTRACTIONS

3 **Cathédrale.** This vast, frigid edifice was built in the 1740s in a ponderous Baroque style, eased in part by the florid ironwork of Jean Lamour. Its most notable interior feature is a murky 19th-century fresco in the dome. The **Trésor** (Treasury) contains minute 10th-century splendors carved of ivory and gold. ✉ *Rue St-Georges, Ville Neuve.*

8 **Musée des Arts et Traditions Populaires** *(Museum of Folk Arts and Traditions).* Just up the street from the Palais Ducal, this quirky, appealing museum is housed in the **Couvent des Cordeliers** (Convent of the Franciscans), who were known as Cordeliers until the Revolution. It re-creates how local people lived in preindustrial times, using a series of evocative rural interiors. Craftsmen's tools, colorful crockery, somber stone fireplaces, and dark waxed-oak furniture accent the tableaulike settings. The dukes of Lorraine are buried in the crypt of the adjoining **Église des Cordeliers,** a Flamboyant Gothic church; the *gisant* (reclining statue) of Philippa de Gueldra, second wife of René II, executed in limestone in flowing detail, is a moving example of Renaissance portraiture. The octagonal Ducal Chapel was begun in 1607 in the Renaissance style, modeled on the Medici Chapel in Florence. ✉ *64 Grande-Rue, Vieille Ville* ☎ *03–83–32–18–74* 🌐 *www1.nancy.fr* 🎫 *€3.50, €5.50 joint ticket with Musée Lorrain* ⏲ *Tues.–Sun. 10–12:30 and 2–6.*

2 **Musée des Beaux-Arts** *(Fine Arts Museum).* In a splendid building that now spills over into a spectacular modern wing, a broad and varied collection of art treasures lives up to the noble white facade designed by Emmanuel Héré. Among the most striking are the freeze-the-moment realist tableaux painted by native son Émile Friant at the turn of the 20th century. A sizable collection of Lipschitz sculptures includes portrait busts of Gertrude Stein, Jean Cocteau, and Coco Chanel. You'll also find 19th- and 20th-century paintings by Monet, Manet, Utrillo, and Modigliani; a Caravaggio *Annunciation* and a wealth of old masters from the Italian, Dutch, Flemish, and French schools; and impressive glassworks by Nancy native Antonin Daum. The showpiece is Rubens's massive *Transfiguration.* Good commentary cards in English are available in every hall. ✉ *3 pl. Stanislas, Ville Royale* ☎ *03–83–85–30–72* 🌐 *www.mairie-nancy.fr/culturelle/musee/html/beaux_arts.php* 🎫 *€6, €7.50 joint ticket with Musée de l'École de Nancy* ⏲ *Wed.–Mon. 10–6.*

7 ★ **Palais Ducal** *(Ducal Palace).* This palace was built in the 13th century and completely restored at the end of the 15th century and again after a fire at the end of the 19th century. The main entrance to the palace, and the **Musée Lorrain** (Lorraine History Museum), which it now houses, is 80 yards down the street from the spectacularly Flamboyant Renaissance portal. A spiral stone staircase leads up to the palace's most impressive room, the **Galerie des Cerfs** (Stags Gallery). Exhibits here (including pictures, armor, and books) recapture the Renaissance mood of the 16th century—one of elegance and merrymaking, with an undercurrent of stern morality: an elaborate series of huge tapestries, *La Condemnation du Banquet* (Condemnation of the Banquet), expounds on the evils of drunkenness and gluttony. Exhibits showcase Stanislas and his court, including "his" oft-portrayed dwarf; a section on Nancy

CLOSE UP

Nancy 1900

History has a curious way of having similar events take place at the same time in different places. The creation of the Art Nouveau (New Art) movement is one such event. Simultaneously emerging from Pre-Raphaelite, High Victorian, and the Arts and Crafts movement in England, it was also a synthesis of the Jugenstil (Youth style) movement in Germany; the Skonvirke movement in Denmark; the Mloda Polska (Young Poland) style in Poland; Secessionism in Vienna; Modernism in Spain centered in Barcelona and the wild organic architectural flourishes of Gaudi; and the florid poster art of Alfons Mucha in Prague. Its fluid, undulating organic forms drawn from nature, seaweed forms, grasses, flowers, birds, and insects also drew inspiration from Symbolism and Japanese woodcuts.

One of its founding centers was Nancy, which at the time was drawing the wealthy French bourgeoisie of Alsace, recently invaded by Germany, who refused to become German. Proud of their opulence, they had sublime houses built that were entirely furnished, from simple vases and wrought-iron beds to bathtubs in the shape of lily pads, all in the pure Art Nouveau style. All of Nancy paid homage to this style.

Everywhere stylized flowers became the preferred motif. The tree and its leaves, and plants with their flowers, were modified, folded and curled to the artist's demand. Among the main Art Nouveau emblems figure the lily, the iris, morning glory, bracken fern, poppies, peacocks, birds that feed on flowers, ivy, dragonflies, butterflies, and anything that evokes the immense poetry of the seasons. It

reveals a world that is as fragile as it is precious.

By giving an artistic quality to manufactured objects, the creators of the École de Nancy accomplished a dream that had been growing since the romantic generation of Victorian England of making an alliance between art and industry. This was a major advance on the bourgeois bad taste for mass-produced imitations inspired by styles of the past. Nancy's great strength was in this collaboration of art and industry.

Among the École de Nancy's most outstanding contributors was Émile Gallé, who worked primarily in glass inventing new, patented techniques, and who brought luxury craftsmanship to a whole range of everyday products, thus reestablishing the link between the ordinary and the exceptional.

As a meeting point for the hopes and interests of artists, intellectuals, industrials, and merchants, the École de Nancy was a thoroughly global phenomenon. From Chicago to Turin, Munich to Brussels, and on to London, the industries of Nancy went on to conquer the world.

in the revolutionary era; and works of Lorraine native sons, including a collection of Jacques Callot engravings and a handful of works by Georges de La Tour. ✉ *64 Grande-Rue, Vieille Ville* ☎ *03–83–32–18–74* 🌐 *www1.nancy.fr* 🎫 *€4, €5.50 joint ticket with Musée des Arts et Traditions Populaires* ⏲ *Tues.–Sun. 10–12:30 and 2–6.*

EVERYONE LOVES A LAMOUR

Fitting showpiece of the southern flank of the square is the 18th-century Hôtel de Ville, Nancy's Town Hall, where the handiwork of Jean Lamour can also be seen to stunning effect on the wrought-iron handrail of the *grand escalier* (grand staircase) leading off the lobby. You can get a closer view when the building is open to the public on summer evenings (July and August, 9:30 to 10 PM) and it's possible to mount the staircase to the Salle des Fêtes and survey the full beauty of Place Stanislas.

1 ★ **Place Stanislas.** With its severe, gleaming-white Classical facades given a touch of Rococo jollity by fanciful wrought gilt-iron railings, this perfectly proportioned square, stylishly repaved in honor of its 250th anniversary in 2005, may remind you of Versailles. The square is named for Stanislas Leszczynski, twice dethroned as king of Poland but offered the Duchy of Lorraine by Louis XV (his son-in-law) in 1736. Stanislas left a legacy of spectacular buildings, undertaken between 1751 and 1760 by architect Emmanuel Héré and ironwork genius Jean Lamour. The sculpture of Stanislas dominating the square went up in the 1830s, when the square was named after him. Framing the exit, and marking the divide between the Vieille Ville and the Ville Neuve (New Town), is the **Arc de Triomphe,** erected in the 1750s to honor Louis XV. The facade trumpets the gods of war and peace; Louis's portrait is here. ✉ *Ville Royale.* 8

WORTH NOTING

5 **La Pépinière.** This picturesque, landscaped city park has labeled ancient trees, a rose garden, playgrounds, a carousel, and a small zoo. ✉ *Entrance off Pl. de la Carrière, Vieille Ville.*

4 ★ **Place de la Carrière.** Spectacularly lined with pollarded trees and handsome 18th-century mansions (another successful collaboration between King Stanislas and Emmanuel Héré), this UNESCO World Heritage Site's elegant rectangle leads from Place Stanislas to the colonnaded facade of the **Palais du Gouvernement** (Government Palace), former home of the governors of Lorraine. ✉ *Vieille Ville.*

9 **Porte de la Craffe.** A fairy-tale vision out of the late Middle Ages, this gate is all that remains of Nancy's medieval fortifications. With its twin turrets looming at one end of the Grande-Rue, built in the 14th and 15th centuries, this arch served as a prison through the Revolution. Above the main portal is the Lorraine Cross, comprising a thistle and cross. ✉ *Vieille Ville.*

6 **St-Epvre.** A 275-foot spire towers over this splendid neo-Gothic church rebuilt in the 1860s. Most of the 2,800 square yards of stained glass were created by the Geyling workshop in Vienna; the chandeliers were made in Liège, Belgium; many carvings are the work of Margraff of

Munich; the heaviest of the eight bells was cast in Budapest; and the organ, though manufactured by Merklin of Paris, was inaugurated in 1869 by Austrian composer Anton Bruckner. ✉ *Pl. du Général-de-Gaulle, Vieille Ville* ⏲ *Daily 3:30–6.*

ART NOUVEAU NANCY

Fodor's Choice ★ Think *Art Nouveau*, and many will conjure up the rich salons of Paris's Maxim's restaurant, the lavender-hue Prague posters of Alphonse Mucha, and the stained-glass dragonflies and opalescent vases that, to this day, remain the darlings of such collectors as Barbra Streisand. All of that beauty was born, to a great extent, in 19th-century Nancy. Inspired and coordinated by the glass master Émile Gallé, the local movement was formalized in 1901 as L'École de Nancy—from here, it spread like wildfire through Europe, from Naples to Monte-Carlo to Prague. The ensuing flourish encompassed the floral *pâte de verre* (literally, "glass dough") works of Antonin Daum and Gallé; the Tiffany-esque stained-glass windows of Jacques Gruber; the fluidity of Louis Majorelle's furniture designs; and the sinuous architecture of Lucien Weissenburger, Émile André, and Eugène Vallin. Thanks to these artists, Nancy's downtown architecture gives the impression of a living garden suspended above the sidewalks. ⇨ *For more on Art Nouveau's birthplace, see our Close-Up box in this chapter, "Nancy 1900."*

TOP ATTRACTIONS

10 ★ **Musée de l'École de Nancy** *(School of Nancy Museum)*. The only museum in France devoted to Art Nouveau is housed in an airy turn-of-the-last-century garden–town house. It was built by Eugène Corbin, an early patron of the School of Nancy. Re-created rooms and original works of art by local Art Nouveau stars Gallé, Daum, Muller, and Walter all allure. Gallé (1846–1904) was the engine that drove the whole Art Nouveau movement. He called upon artists to resist the imperialism of Paris, follow examples in nature (not those of Greece or Rome), and use a variety of techniques and materials. Many of their gorgeous artifacts are on view here. ✉ *36 rue du Sergent-Blandan, Quartier Art-Nouveau* ☎ *03–83–40–14–86* 🌐 *www.ecole-de-nancy.com* 🎫 *€6, €7.50 joint ticket with Musée des Beaux-Arts* ⏲ *Wed.–Sun. 10–6.*

11 ★ **Villa Majorelle**. This villa was built in 1902 by Paris architect Henri Sauvage for Majorelle himself. Sinuous metal supports seem to sneak up on the unsuspecting balcony like swaying cobras, and there are two grand windows by Gruber: one lighting the staircase (visible from the street) and the other set in the dining room on the south side of the villa (peek around from the garden side). ✉ *1 rue Louis-Majorelle, Quartier Art-Nouveau.*

WORTH NOTING

12 **Avenue Foch**. This busy boulevard lined with mansions was built for Nancy's affluent 19th-century middle class. At No. 69, the occasional pinnacle suggests Gothic influence on a house built in 1902 by Émile André, who designed the neighboring No. 71 two years later. No. 41, built by Paul Charbonnier in 1905, bears ironwork by Majorelle. ✉ *Quartier Art-Nouveau.*

The centerpiece of Nancy's Ville Royale is elegant Place Stanislas, named in honor of Stanislas Leszczynski, brother-in-law to King Louis XIV.

8

⓭ **Brasserie l'Excelsior.** This bustling brasserie *(⇨ see Where to Eat, below)* has a severely rhythmic facade that is invitingly illuminated at night. Inside, the popular restaurant's fin-de-siècle decor continues to evoke the Belle Époque. ✉ *Corner of Rue Mazagran and Rue Henri-Poincaré, Quartier Art-Nouveau.*

⓰ **No. 2 rue Bénit.** This elaborately worked metal exoskeleton, the first in Nancy (1901), exudes functional beauty. The fluid decoration reminds you of the building's past as a seed supply store. Windows were worked by Gruber; the building was designed by Henry-Barthélemy Gutton, while Victor Schertzer conceived the metal frame. ✉ *Quartier Art-Nouveau.*

⓯ **No. 9 rue Chanzy.** Designed by architect Émile André, this lovely structure—now a bank—can be visited during business hours. You can still see the cabinetry of Majorelle, the decor of Paul Charbonnier, and the stained-glass windows of Gruber. ✉ *Quartier Art-Nouveau.*

⓮ **No. 40 rue Henri-Poincaré.** The Lorraine thistle and brewing hops weave through this undulating exterior, designed by architects Émile Toussaint and Louis Marchal. Victor Schertzer conceived this metal structure in 1908, after the success of No. 2 rue Bénit. Gruber's windows are enhanced by the curving metalwork of Majorelle. ✉ *Quartier Art-Nouveau.*

⓲ **Nos. 42–44 rue St-Dizier.** Eugène Vallin and Georges Biet left their mark on this graceful 1903 bank. ✉ *Quartier Art-Nouveau* ⏲ *Weekdays 8:30–5:30.*

17 **Rue Raugraff.** Once there were two stores here, both built in 1901. The bay windows are the last vestiges of the work of Charles Vallin, Émile André, and Eugène Vallin. ✉ *Corner of Rue St-Jean, Quartier Art-Nouveau.*

WHERE TO EAT

$$ FRENCH ✕ **Brasserie l'Excelsior.** Above all, you'll want to eat in this 1911 restaurant, part of the dependable Flo group, for its sensational Art Nouveau stained glass, mosaics, Daum lamps, and sinuous Majorelle furniture. But the food is stylish, too, with succulent choices ranging from local goat cheese wrapped in bacon to a cod-and–roasted pepper crumble—and don't miss out on the regional desserts like bergamot crème brûlée and French-toast style kougelhopf with caramel sauce. The white-aproned waiters are attentive and exude Parisian chic. ✉ *50 rue Henri-Poincaré, Quartier Art-Nouveau* ☎ *03–83–35–24–57* 🌐 *www.brasserie-excelsior.com* 💳 *MC, V.*

$$$ FRENCH ★ ✕ **Le Capucin Gourmand.** Barely a stone's throw from Place Stanislas and making the most of Nancy's Art Nouveau pâte *de verre,* including a giant chandelier and glowing mushroom lamps on the tables, this chic landmark puts its best foot forward under chef Hervé Fourrière. The three-course lunch menu at €29 includes crayfish tails in a lavender-cream minestrone or a veal roulade with morels and polenta. Desserts are also noteworthy, with signature sweets including *cherry-licorice soup, iced soufflé,* and *apricot tartlet.* The choice of Toul wines is extensive. ✉ *31 rue Gambetta, Ville Royale* ☎ *03–83–35–26–98* 🌐 *www.lecapu.com* ✍ *Reservations essential* 💳 *AE, DC, MC, V* ⊗ *No lunch Sat. No dinner Sun.*

$ FRENCH ✕ **Le P'tit Cuny.** If you were inspired by the rustic exhibits of the Musée des Arts et Traditions Populaires, cross the street and sink your teeth into authentic Lorraine cuisine in the form of mouthwatering choucroutes, *tête de veau* (calf's head), or foie gras–stuffed pig's trotter. Tables inside are tight, creating a bustling, canteenlike atmosphere, and the quality of the service seems to vary with the weather, but the hearty food is irreproachable. ✉ *95 Grande-Rue, Vieille Ville* ☎ *03–83–32–85–94* 🌐 *www.petitcuny.fr* 💳 *AE, MC, V.*

WHERE TO STAY

$$$–$$$$ ★ 🏨 **Grand Hôtel de la Reine.** This hotel is every bit as grand as Place Stanislas, on which it stands; the magnificent 18th-century building is officially classified as a historic monument. Guest rooms are in a suitably regal Louis XV style; the most luxurious overlook the square. The hotel's spectacular restaurant, Le Stanislas (closed Sunday November–end of March; no lunch Saturday), aglitter with chandeliers and carved-wood boiseries is closed for renovations but expected to reopen in 2011. **Pros:** sumptuous location; old-world atmosphere. **Cons:** rooms get street noise; indifferent staff. ✉ *2 pl. Stanislas, Ville Royale* ☎ *03–83–35–03–01* 🌐 *www.hoteldelareine.com* ⇐ *42 rooms* ☝ *In-room: a/c, refrigerator, Wi-Fi. In-hotel: restaurant, bar, some pets allowed* 💳 *AE, DC, MC, V* 🍽 *BP.*

¢–$ **Guise.** Deep in the shuttered Vieille Ville, this quiet and convivial hotel is in an 18th-century nobleman's mansion with a magnificent stone-floor entry and a delightful walled garden. The newly renovated rooms are furnished with period pieces and charmingly incongruous floral patterns. Breakfast on the once-grand main floor and an excellent location make this a good choice if you're a bargain-hunting romantic—and you can splurge on a suite for affordable luxury and an extra bed. Some self-catering accommodation is also available. **Pros:** tidy rooms; central location; helpful staff. **Cons:** no air-conditioning; heady decor. ✉ *18 rue de Guise, Vieille Ville* ☎ *03–83–32–24–68* 🌐 *www.hoteldeguise.com* *48 rooms, 6 suites, 2 studios* *In-room: no a/c, Wi-Fi. In-hotel: some pets allowed* *AE, MC, V* *BP.*

NIGHTLIFE AND THE ARTS

Nancy has a rich cultural life that includes ballet, opera, and a highly renowned symphonic orchestra. The **Orchestre Symphonique and Lyrique** (☎ *03–83–85–33–11* 🌐 *www.mairie-nancy.fr*) organizes concerts from fall through spring. The **Opéra National de Lorraine** (☎ *03–83–85–33–20* 🌐 *www.opera-national-lorraine.fr*) is the fifth-ranked national regional opera of France, with a repertoire ranging from ancient to contemporary music. The **Ballet de Lorraine** (☎ *03–83–85–69–01* 🌐 *www.ballet-de-lorraine.com*) was created in 1978 to assume the mission of a national ballet; performances are staged in the Opéra de Nancy in the Place Stanislas.

Les Caves du Roy (✉ *9 pl. Stanislas, Ville Royale* ☎ *03–83–35–24–14*) attracts a young upscale crowd that comes to dance. **Le Chat Noir** (✉ *63 rue Jeanne-d'Arc, Ville Neuve* ☎ *03–83–28–49–29* 🌐 *www.lechatnoir.fr*) draws a thirtysomething crowd to retro-theme dance parties. **HW** (✉ *1 ter rue du Général-Hoche, Ville Neuve* ☎ *03–83–27–07–16*) is a popular dance club.

SHOPPING

Ancienne Librairie Dornier (✉ *74 Grande-Rue, Vieille Ville* ☎ *03–83–36–50–62*), near the Musée des Arts et Traditions Populaires, is an excellent bookstore that sells engravings as well as old and new books devoted to local history. **Daum Boutique** (✉ *14 pl. Stanislas, Vieille Ville* ☎ *03–83–32–21–65* 🌐 *www.daum.fr*) sells deluxe crystal and examples of the city's traditional Art Nouveau pâté de verre.

LORRAINE: JOAN OF ARC COUNTRY

Lorraine is the country of France's patron saint, Joan of Arc. Follow D64 that winds between Contrexéville and Void, and you will be on Joan's native soil, almost unchanged since the Middle Ages. In fact, she would probably find much of the countryside today familiar. Various towns bear witness. At Neufchâteau, then a fortified town guarding the region, the inhabitants of Domrémy sought refuge in 1428 from the English armies that menaced their village. It was in Domrémy that

Joan was born in 1411, or a year later. Moving on, Vaucouleurs recalls Joan's arrival in May 1428 to ask the help of the governor to see the king to plead for France's cause—and achieve her destiny.

VAUCOULEURS

73 km (41 mi) southwest of Nancy on N4 and D964.

Above the modest main street in the market town of Vaucouleurs, you can see ruins of Robert de Baudricourt's ancient medieval castle and the Porte de France, through which Joan of Arc led her armed soldiers to Orléans. The barefoot Maid of Orléans spent a year within these walls, arriving on May 13, 1428, to ask the help of the governor Baudricourt. After wheedling an audience with Baudricourt, she then convinced him of the necessity of her mission, learning to ride and to sword-fight. Won over finally by her conviction and popular sentiment, he offered to give her an escort to seek out the king. On February 23, 1429, clad in page's garb and with her hair cut short, Jeanne d'Arc rode out through the Porte de France. A train route runs to Vaucouleurs from Toul and Nancy.

WHERE TO STAY

$$ **Hostellerie de l'Isle en Bray**. Romantic and secluded, a night in the fine Renaissance-style Château de Montbras is ideal for indulging in Joan-of-Arc related medieval musings. With a history extending back five centuries, the château has an array of historical goodies—four grand stone bastion towers, an elegant wing graced with sculpted goddesses and ornament à la Androuet du Cerceau, and some rare Baroque paintings of Indian tribes of the Americas. Upstairs, guest rooms are spacious and tastefully appointed with authentic period furniture elegantly offset against bright fabrics or airy, soaring ceilings. The ambitious restaurant has stylish menus running about 35 euros. **Pros:** timeless charm and luxury; marvelous museum atmosphere; gentle prices. **Cons:** car indispensable. ✉ *3 rue des Erables, 10 km (6 mi) south of Vaucouleurs on the D964* ☎ *03–29–90–86–36* 🌐 *www.chateau-montbras.com* *5 rooms, 2 suites* *In-room: no a/c, Wi-Fi. In-hotel: restaurant, bar, tennis court, parking (free)* ▭ *DC, MC, V* ⊗ *Closed Nov.–Mar.*

DOMRÉMY-LA-PUCELLE

19 km (12 mi) south of Vaucouleurs on D964.

Joan of Arc was born in Domrémy-la-Pucelle in a stone hut in either 1411 or 1412. You can see it as well as the church where she was baptized, the actual statue of St. Marguerite before which she prayed, and the hillside where she tended sheep and first heard voices telling her to take up arms and save France from the English.

GETTING HERE

From Nancy, 15 trains connect with Toul (€6.10); change for Neufchâteau, 39 km (24 mi) southwest of Nancy, for the twice-daily bus connection to Domrémy-la-Pucelle (€2.50), 10 km (6 mi) to the north of Neufchâteau, on the Vaucouleurs line.

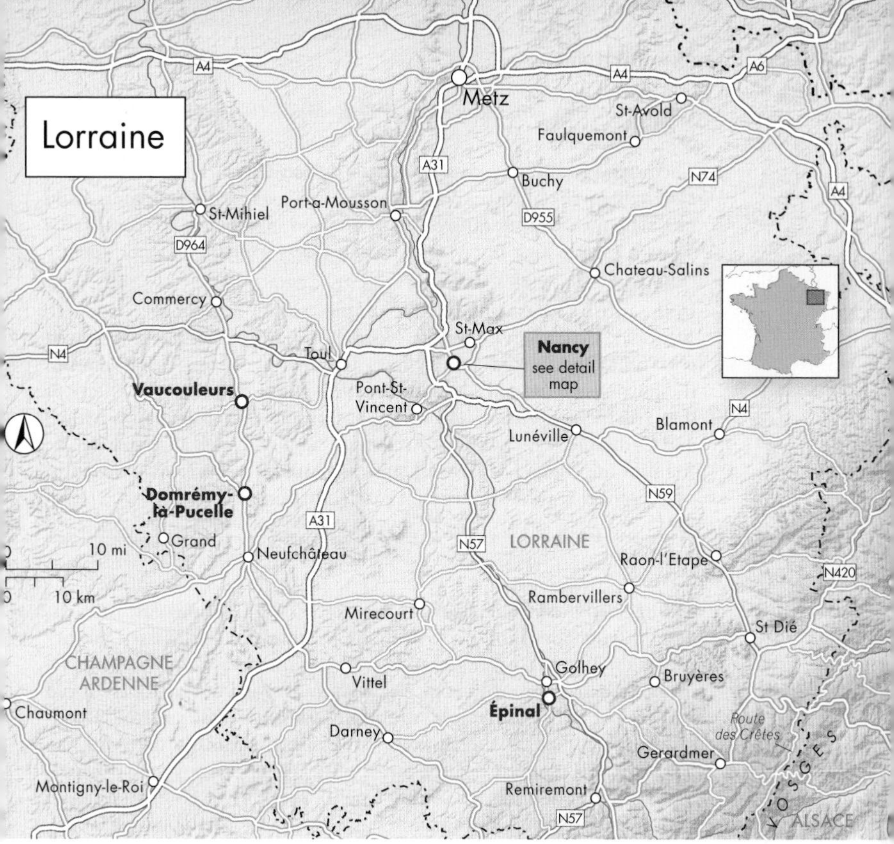

EXPLORING

Fodor's Choice ★ The humble stone-and-stucco **Maison Natale Jeanne d'Arc** *(Joan of Arc's Birthplace)*—an irregular, slope-roof, two-story cottage—has been preserved with style and reverence. The modern museum alongside, the **Centre Johannique,** shows a film (French only), while mannequins in period costume present Joan of Arc's amazing story. After she heard mystical voices, Joan walked 19 km (12 mi) to Vaucouleurs. Dressed and mounted like a man, she led her forces to lift the siege of Orléans, defeated the English, and escorted the unseated Charles VII to Reims, to be crowned king of France. Military missions after Orléans failed—including an attempt to retake Paris—and she was captured at Compiègne. The English turned her over to the Church, which sent her to be tried by the Inquisition for witchcraft and heresy. She was convicted and burned at the stake in Rouen. One of the latest theories is that Jeanne d'Arc was no mere peasant but was distantly connected to France's royal family—a controversial proposal that many historians now discount. ✉ *2 rue de la Basilique* ☎ *03–29–06–95–86*

A MODERN DAY HERO

As a figure, Joan of Arc remains pivotal to her *époque de transformation*: thanks to her and other leaders, civilization began to evolve from the medieval to the modern.

€3 ⊙ Closed Jan., Nov.–Mar., Wed.–Mon. 10–noon and 2–5; Apr.–Sept., daily 10–6.

The ornate late-19th-century **Basilique du Bois-Chenu** *(Bois Chenu Basilica)*, high up the hillside above Domrémy, boasts enormous painted and mosaic panels expounding on Joan's legend in glowing Pre-Raphaelite tones. Outside lurk serene panoramic views over the emerald, gently rolling Meuse Valley.

In the nearby forest of Bois-Chenu, perhaps an ancient sacred wood, Jeanne d'Arc gathered flowers. Near the village of Coussy, she danced with other children at country fairs attended by Pierre de Bourlémont, the local seigneur, and his wife Beatrice—the Château of Bourlémont may still be seen. Associated with Coussey and Brixey are Saints Mihiel and Catherine, who, with the Archangel Saint-Michael, appeared before Joan. In the Chapel of Notre-Dame at Bermont, where Joan vowed to save France, are the statues that existed in her time.

STRASBOURG

Though centered in the heart of Alsace 490 km (304 mi) east of Paris, and drawing appealingly on Alsatian Gemütlichkeit (coziness), the city of Strasbourg is a cosmopolitan French cultural center and the symbolic if unofficial capital of Europe. Against an irresistible backdrop of old half-timber houses, waterways, and the colossal single spire of its red-sandstone cathedral, which seems to insist imperiously that you pay homage to its majestic beauty, Strasbourg is an incongruously sophisticated mix of museums, charming neighborhoods like La Petite France, elite schools (including that notorious hothouse for blooming politicos, the École Nationale d'Administration, or National Administration School), international think tanks, and the European Parliament. The *strasbourgeoisie* have a lot to be proud of.

GETTING HERE AND AROUND

With the advent, in June 2007, of the TGV Est Européen (⊕ *www.tgv.com*), Strasbourg is now only 2 hours, 20 minutes away with any one of the 16 direct TGV trains from Paris, with fares ranging from €65.90 to €86. In addition to the extra-regional links to Nancy, Metz, Saarbrucken, Lyon, and Geneva, Strasbourg's train station (✉ 20 pl. de la Gare) is at the heart of the regional TER train system and has direct trains at least every 30 minutes to Colmar (€10.40) and Sélestat (€7.50), where you can change for omnibus services to Ribeauvillé (€2.10) and Rosheim/Molseim (for Dambach la Ville, €7.60, and Obernai, €5.30). Call the "on demand" service (☎ *08–00–10–09–48*) in Sélestat to arrange

BIRD'S-EYE VIEW

Strasbourg's center is an eye-shape island created by the River Ill and canals that connect it to the Rhine. The Cathédrale Notre-Dame lies at the east end of the island, and La Petite France lies at the west end, about 0.2 km (¼ mi) away. Narrow pedestrian streets lined with shops and restaurants connect the two, so that the whole island is just one mesh of Alsatian fare.

A finalist by Mary Jane Glauber, a Fodors.com member, in Fodor's "Show Us Your France" contest, this image shows Strasbourg's famous cathedral.

transport to Orschwiller (short walk to Haut-Koenigsbourg) for €1. Buses head out to Obernai and Wangenbourg (connection at Wasselonne for Saverne) from the Gare Routière (☎ *03–88–43–23-43*) in Place des Halles. Strasbourg's main train station is across the river from the city center, three-quarters of a mile from the cathedral, in the far west corner of the city.

Strasbourg has an extensive tram and bus network; most of the efficient lines of Companie des Transports Strasbourgeois (🌐 *www.cts-strasbourg.fr*) leave from the train station at 20 place de la Gare, travel down Rue du Vieux Marché aux Vins, and part ways at Place de la République. Tickets are good for one hour and can also be used on Strasbourg's sleek tram that travels from the train station to Place de l'Homme and out to the burbs.

Visitor Information Strasbourg Tourist Office (✉ *17 pl. de la Cathédrale* ☎ *03–88–52–28–28* 🌐 *www.ot-strasbourg.fr* ✉ *4 pl. de la Gare* ☎ *03–88–32–51–49*); there's also a city tourist office at the train station.

EXPLORING

The Romans knew Strasbourg as Argentoratum before it came to be known as Strateburgum, or City of (Cross) Roads. After centuries as part of the Germanic Holy Roman Empire, the city was united with France in 1681, but retained independence regarding legislation, education, and religion under the honorific title Free Royal City. Since World War II Strasbourg has become a symbolic city, embodying Franco-German reconciliation and the wider idea of a united Europe. The city center is effectively an island within two arms of the River Ill; most major sites are found here, but the northern districts also contain some

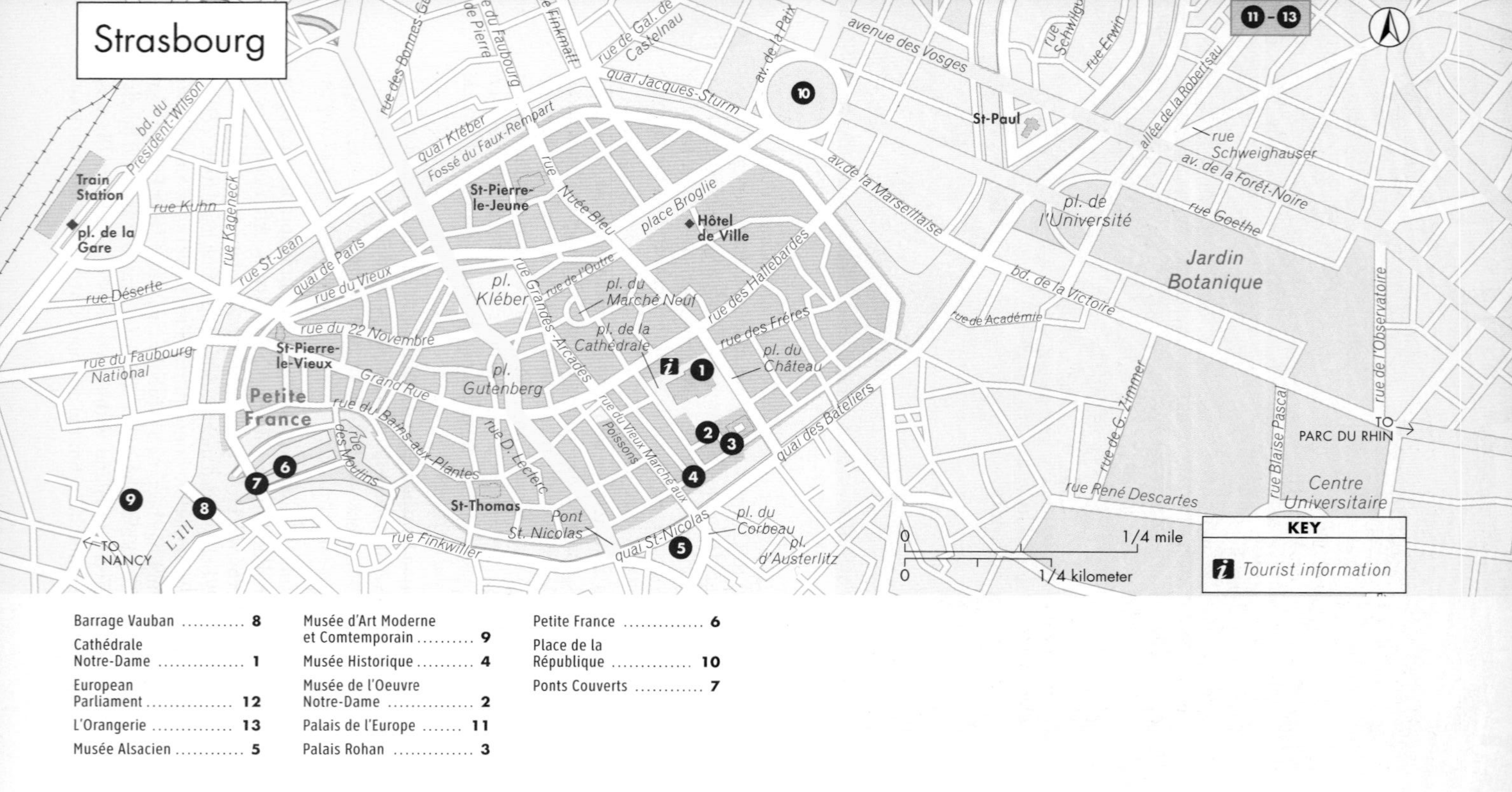

- Barrage Vauban 8
- Cathédrale Notre-Dame 1
- European Parliament 12
- L'Orangerie 13
- Musée Alsacien 5
- Musée d'Art Moderne et Comtemporain 9
- Musée Historique 4
- Musée de l'Oeuvre Notre-Dame 2
- Palais de l'Europe 11
- Palais Rohan 3
- Petite France 6
- Place de la République 10
- Ponts Couverts 7

fine buildings erected over the last 100 years, culminating in the Palais de l'Europe. You can buy a one-day pass for all the city museums for €8 or a three-day pass for €10.

Note to drivers: the configuration of downtown streets makes it difficult to approach the center via the autoroute exit marked STRASBOURG CENTRE. Instead, hold out for the exit marked PLACE DE L'ÉTOILE and follow signs to CATHÉDRALE/CENTRE VILLE. At Place du Corbeau, veer left across the Ill, and go straight to the Place Gutenberg parking garage, a block from the cathedral.

STRASBOURG STEP-BY-STEP

Walking tours of Strasbourg's Vieille Ville are directed by the tourist office for €6.80 and depart at 2:30 every Saturday afternoon in low season, daily at 10:15 in July and August; many enjoy taking the Strasbourg minitram tours (☎ *03-88-77-70-03* ✉ *€5.20*); they leave from Place du Château, by the cathedral.

THE HISTORIC HEART

This central area, from the cathedral to picturesque Petite France, concentrates the best of Old Strasbourg, with its twisting backstreets, flower-lined courts, tempting shops, and inviting *winstubs* (wine taverns).

TOP ATTRACTIONS

❶ ★ **Cathédrale Notre-Dame** *(Astronomical Clock)*. Dark pink, ornately carved Vosges sandstone masonry covers the facade of this most novel and Germanic of French cathedrals, a triumph of Gothic art begun in 1176. Not content with the outlines of the walls themselves, medieval builders lacily encased them with slender stone shafts. The off-center **spire,** finished in 1439, looks absurdly fragile as it tapers skyward some 466 feet; you can climb 330 steps to the base of the spire to take in sweeping views of the city, the Vosges Mountains, and the Black Forest.

The interior presents a stark contrast to the facade: it's older (mostly finished by 1275), and the nave's broad windows emphasize the horizontal rather than the vertical. Note Hans Hammer's ornately sculpted pulpit (1484–86) and the richly painted 14th- to 15th-century organ loft that rises from pillar to ceiling. The left side of the nave is flanked with richly colored Gothic windows honoring the early leaders of the Holy Roman Empire—Otto I and II, and Heinrich I and II. The **choir** is not ablaze with stained glass but framed by chunky Romanesque masonry. The elaborate 16th-century **Chapelle St-Laurent,** to the left of the choir, merits a visit; turn to the right to admire the **Pilier des Anges** (Angels' Pillar), an intricate column dating from 1230.

Just beyond the pillar, the Renaissance machinery of the 16th-century **Horloge Astronomique** whirs into action daily at 12:30 PM (but the line starts at the south door at 11:45 AM): macabre clockwork figures enact the story of Christ's Passion. One of the highlights: when the apostles walk past, a likeness of Christ as a rooster crows three times. ✉ *Pl. de la Cathédrale* 🌐 *www.cathedrale-strasbourg.fr* ✉ *Clock €2, spire platform €4.60* ⏲ *Cathedral daily 7–11:30 and 12:30–7.*

8

5 **Musée Alsacien** *(Alsatian Museum)*. In this labyrinthine half-timber home, with layers of carved balconies sagging over a cobbled inner courtyard, local interiors have been faithfully reconstituted. The diverse activities of blacksmiths, clog makers, saddlers, and makers of artificial flowers are explained with the help of old-time craftsmen's tools and equipment. ✉ *23 quai St-Nicolas* ☎ *03–88–52–50–01* 🌐 *www.musees-strasbourg.org* 🎫 *€5* ⏲ *Mon. and Wed.–Fri. noon–6, weekends 10–6.*

9 **Musée d'Art Moderne et Contemporain** *(Modern and Contemporary Art Museum)*. A magnificent sculpture of a building (designed by architect Adrien Faiensilber) that sometimes dwarfs its contents, this spectacular museum frames a relatively thin collection of new, esoteric, and unsung 20th-century art. Downstairs, a permanent collection of Impressionists and Modernists up to 1950 is heavily padded with local heroes but happily fleshed out with some striking furniture; all are juxtaposed for contrasting and comparing, with little to no chronological flow. Upstairs, harsh, spare works must work hard to live up to their setting; few contemporary masters are featured. Drawings, watercolors, and paintings by Gustave Doré, a native of Alsace, are enshrined in a separate room. ✉ *1 pl. Hans-Jean Arp* ☎ *03–88–23–31–31* 🌐 *www.musees-strasbourg.org* 🎫 *€6* ⏲ *Tues., Wed., and Fri. noon–7, Thurs. noon–9, weekends 10–6.*

2 ★ **Musée de l'Œuvre Notre-Dame** *(Cathedral Museum)*. There's more to this museum than the usual assembly of dilapidated statues rescued from the cathedral before they fell off (you'll find *those* rotting in the Barrage Vauban). Sacred sculptures stand in churchlike settings, and secular exhibits are enhanced by the building's fine old architecture. Subjects include a wealth of Flemish and Upper Rhine paintings, stained glass, gold objects, and massive, heavily carved furniture. ✉ *3 pl. du Château* ☎ *03–88–32–88–17* 🌐 *www.musees-strasbourg.org* 🎫 *€5* ⏲ *Tues.–Fri. noon–6, weekends 10–6.*

3 ★ **Palais Rohan** *(Rohan Palace)*. The exterior of Robert de Cotte's massive neoclassical palace (1732–42) may be starkly austere, but there's plenty of glamour inside. Decorator Robert le Lorrain's magnificent ground-floor rooms are led by the great **Salon d'Assemblée** (Assembly Room) and the book- and tapestry-lined **Bibliothèque des Cardinaux** (Cardinals' Library). The library leads to a series of less august rooms that house the **Musée des Arts Décoratifs** (Decorative Arts Museum) and its elaborate display of ceramics. This is a comprehensive presentation of works by Hannong, a porcelain manufacturer active in Strasbourg from 1721 to 1782; dinner services by other local kilns reveal the influence of Chinese porcelain. The **Musée des Beaux-Arts** (Fine Arts Museum), also in the château, includes masterworks of European painting from Giotto and Memling to El Greco, Rubens, and Goya. Downstairs, the **Musée Archéologique** (Archaeology Museum) displays regional archaeological finds, including gorgeous Merovingian treasures. ✉ *2 pl. du Château* ☎ *03–88–52–50–00* 🌐 *www.musees-strasbourg.org* 🎫 *€5 each museum* ⏲ *Mon. and Wed.–Fri. noon–6, weekends 10–6.*

6 Fodor's Choice ★ **Petite France**. With its gingerbread half-timber houses that seem to lean precariously over the canals of the Ill, its shops, and inviting little

restaurants, this is the most magical neighborhood in Strasbourg. Historically Alsatian in style, "Little France"—the district is just southwest of the center—is filled with Renaissance buildings that have survived plenty of wars. Wander up and down the tiny streets that connect Rue du Bain-aux-Plantes and Rue des Dentelles to Grand-Rue, and stroll the waterfront promenade.

WORTH NOTING

8 **Barrage Vauban** *(Vauban Dam)*. Just beyond the Ponts Couverts is the grass-roof Vauban Dam, built by its namesake in 1682. Climb to the top for wide-angle views of the Ponts Couverts and, on the other side, the Museum of Modern Art. Then stroll through its echoing galleries, where magnificent cathedral statuary lies scattered among pigeon droppings. The dam was closed for renovations in early 2010 but slated for reopening by 2011 ✉ *Ponts Couverts* 🎟 *Free* ⏲ *Daily 9–7:30.*

4 **Musée Historique** *(Local History Museum)*. This museum, in a step-gabled slaughterhouse dating from 1588, contains a collection of maps, armor, arms, bells, uniforms, traditional dress, printing paraphernalia, and two huge relief models of Strasbourg. ✉ *3 pl. de la Grande-Boucherie* ☎ *03–88–52–50–00* 🌐 *www.musees-strasbourg.org* 🎟 *€5* ⏲ *Mon. and Wed.–Fri. noon–6, weekends 10–6.*

7 **Ponts Couverts** *(Covered Bridges)*. These three bridges, distinguished by their four stone towers, were once covered with wooden shelters. Part of the 14th-century ramparts that framed Old Strasbourg, they span the Ill as it branches into four fingerlike canals.

BEYOND THE ILL

If you've seen the center and have time to strike out in new directions, head across the Ill to view two architectural landmarks unrelated to Strasbourg's famous medieval past: Place de la République and the Palais de l'Europe.

SIGHTS TO SEE

12 **European Parliament**. This sleek building testifies to the growing importance of the governing body of the European Union, which used to make do with rental offices in the Palais de l'Europe. Eurocrats continue to commute between Brussels, Luxembourg, and Strasbourg, hauling their staff and files with them. One week per month, visitors can slip into the hemicycle and witness the tribune in debate, complete with simultaneous translation. Note: You must obtain a written appointment beforehand and provide a *pièce d'identité* (ID) before entering. ✉ *Behind Palais de l'Europe* ☎ *03–88–17–52–85* 🎟 *Free* ⏲ *Call or write ahead for appointment.*

13 **L'Orangerie**. Like a private backyard for the Eurocrats in the Palais de l'Europe, this delightful park is laden with flowers and punctuated by noble copper beeches. It contains a lake and, close by, a small reserve of rare birds, including flamingos and noisy local storks. ✉ *Av. de l'Europe.*

11 **Palais de l'Europe**. Designed by Paris architect Henri Bernard in 1977, this continental landmark is headquarters to the Council of Europe,

founded in 1949 and independent of the European Union. A guided tour introduces you to the intricacies of its workings and may allow you to eavesdrop on a session. Arrange your tour by telephone in advance; appointments are fixed according to language demands and usually take place in the afternoon. Note: You must provide a *pièce d'identité* (ID) before entering. ✉ *Av. de l'Europe* ☎ *03–90–21–49–40 for appointment* 🎫 *Free* ⏲ *Guided tours by appointment weekdays.*

STRASBOURG BY WATER

Strasbourg is a big town, but the center is easily explored on foot, or, more romantically, by boat. **Fluvial Strasbourg** (☎ *03–88–84–13–13* 🌐 *www.strasbourg.port.fr*) organizes 70-minute boat tours along the Ill four times a day in winter and up to every half hour starting at 10:30 during the day from April through October (plus nocturnal tours until 10 PM May–September). Boats leave from behind the Palais Rohan; the cost is €8.

10 **Place de la République.** The spacious layout and ponderous architecture of this monumental *cirque* (circle) have nothing in common with the Vieille Ville except for the local red sandstone. A different hand was at work here—that of occupying Germans, who erected the former Ministry (1902), the Academy of Music (1882–92), and the Palais du Rhin (1883–88). The handsome neo-Gothic church of **St-Paul** and the pseudo-Renaissance **Palais de l'Université** (University Palace), constructed between 1875 and 1885, also bear the German stamp. Heavy turn-of-the-20th-century houses, some reflecting the whimsical curves of the Art Nouveau style, frame **Allée de la Robertsau,** a tree-lined boulevard that would not look out of place in Berlin.

WHERE TO EAT

$$$$ FRENCH ★ ✕ **Au Crocodile.** As one of the temples of Alsatian-French haute cuisine, this has the expected grand salon— renovated in 2009, and still asparkle with skylights and a spectacular 19th-century mural showing the *strasbourgeoisie* at a country fair—an exhaustive wine list, and some of the most dazzling dishes around, courtesy of new chef Philippe Bohrer, who formerly worked privately for French presidents Giscard d'Estaing and François Mitterand. Fittingly at a restaurant founded in the early 1800s, you get a real taste of the-way-Alsace-was here, but given a nouvelle spin. Delights include foie gras with spicy relish and green anise, caramelized monkfish, lobster with cep mushrooms, and iced meringue with warm fruit and lychee sorbet. Even more urban finesse is given to the theme menus that are occasionally offered (homages have included those to Europa, Mozart, and the TGV Est). As for Au Crocodile's name, it refers to a stuffed specimen brought back by a Strasbourg general from Napoléon's Egyptian campaign! ✉ *10 rue de l'Outre* ☎ *03–88–32–13–02* 🌐 *www.au-crocodile.com* ✍ *Reservations essential* 👔 *Jacket and tie* 💳 *AE, DC, MC, V* ⏲ *Closed Sun. and Mon., late Dec.–early Jan., and 3 wks in July.*

$ FRENCH ★ **Chez Yvonne.** Just around the corner from the cathedral is an eatery that is almost as exalted. Behind red-checked curtains you can find artists, tourists, lovers, and heads of state sitting elbow-to-elbow in this classic winstub, founded in 1873. All come to savor steaming platters of local specialties: watch for duck confit on choucroute, braised ham hocks, and quails stuffed with foie gras. Warm Alsatian fabrics dress tables and lamps, the china is regional, the photos historic—all making for chic, not kitsch. *10 rue du Sanglier 03–88–32–84–15 www.chez-yvonne.net Reservations essential AE, DC, MC, V.*

$$$ FRENCH Fodor's Choice ★ **Le Buerehiesel.** This lovely Alsatian farmhouse, reconstructed in the Orangerie park, warrants a pilgrimage if you're willing to pay for the finest cooking in Alsace. New chef Eric Westermann (son of the former chef) focuses on the freshest of local-terroir specialities, supplemented by the best seafood of Brittany. The seasonal desserts are a standout. Two smaller salons are cozy, but most tables are set in a modern annex that is mostly glass and steel. In any event, plump European *parlementaires* come on foot; others might come on their knees. *4 parc de l'Orangerie 03–88–45–56–65 www.buerehiesel.fr Reservations essential AE, DC, MC, V Closed Sun. and Mon., 3 wks in Jan., and 3 wks in Aug.*

$$ FRENCH **Maison Kammerzell.** This restaurant, probably the most familiar house in Strasbourg, glories in its richly carved, half-timber 15th-century building and sumptuous allegorical frescoes by the aptly monikered Leo Schnug. Fight your way through the tourist hordes on the terrace and ground floor to one of the atmospheric rooms above, with their gleaming wooden furniture, stained-glass windows, and unrivaled views of the cathedral. Foie gras and choucroute are best bets, though you may want to try the chef's pet discovery, choucroute with freshwater fish. *16 pl. de la Cathédrale 03–88–32–42–14 www.maison-kammerzell.com AE, DC, MC, V.*

$ FRENCH **Strissel.** This cozy, rustic winstub near the cathedral, in business since the 16th century, is now owned by Jean-Louis De Valmigere, the force behind Chez Yvonne. Happily, he has not changed anything of the charming decor, but only added lights. It has a good choice of Alsace wines and some of the finest choucroute in town (the chef is still the same), often served with pike-perch as a specialty. Menus run from €21.70 to €26.90 and the plat du jour is €6.90. Try for a room upstairs to admire the stained-glass windows with their tales of life in the vines. *5 pl. de la Grande-Boucherie 03–88–32–14–73 www.strissel.fr AE, MC, V.*

8

WHERE TO STAY

$$–$$$ **Cathédrale.** A sleek marble lobby abuts lounges, a bar, and a breakfast room that are rich with ancient beams and sandstone. Rooms feature dark timbers, and most have windows framing a view of the 16th-century half-timber Maison Kammerzell or the cathedral. The location is to die for, but if you prefer absolute silence in the evening, ask for a room that doesn't face the square (though you'll miss out on the view). **Pros:** comfortable, clean rooms; across from the cathedral. **Cons:** some rooms are small; rooms with view of cathedral get some street noise.

✉ 13 pl. de la Cathédrale ☎ 03–88–22–12–12 🌐 www.hotel-cathedrale.fr *47 rooms* *In-room: a/c, refrigerator, Wi-Fi . In-hotel: bar, some pets allowed* *AE, DC, MC, V* *BP.*

$–$$ **Hôtel Gutenberg.** In a 250-year-old mansion just off Place Gutenberg, this sturdy urban hotel, ideal for those on a tight budget, has rooms with fresh, old-fashioned wallpaper, chandeliers, and built-in wood cabinetry. Charming little fifth-floor lofts reveal roof timbers, and air-conditioning allows you to close the windows if the street noise gets too much. The skylighted breakfast room is inviting but sometimes a little crowded, so consider an early start or be prepared to wait for or share a table. The English-speaking staff is friendly, and the quaint location is only a few blocks from the cathedral. **Pros:** excellent value; old-world style with modern conveniences. **Cons:** some street noise; elevator doesn't reach the top floor. *✉ 31 rue des Serruriers ☎ 03–88–32–17–15 🌐 www.hotel-gutenberg.com* *42 rooms* *In-room: a/c, Internet* *AE, MC, V* *BP.*

$$$ **Hôtel Rohan.** Across from the cathedral on a picturesque pedestrian street, this modest little hotel has a welcoming air and a marvelous sense of French style, from the Louis XV furniture to the gilt mirrors. Though swagged in rich fabrics, rooms are fully modern, with impeccable all-tile showers (but only the "superieur" rooms come with tubs). Breakfast costs extra, so an early spin around the surrounding streets might bring richer and less pricey pickings. **Pros:** great location; air-conditioned. **Cons:** small standard rooms; pricey breakfast. *✉ 17 rue Maroquin ☎ 03–88–32–85–11 🌐 www.hotel-rohan.com* *36 rooms* *In-room: a/c, refrigerator, Wi-Fi. In-hotel: parking (paid), some pets allowed* *AE, DC, MC, V.*

$$$–$$$$ ★ **Régent-Petite France.** Opposite the Ponts Couverts and surrounded by canals, this centuries-old former ice factory—replete with noble pediment and mansard roofs—has been transformed into a boldly modern luxury hotel. Delightfully set in the heart of Strasbourg's quaintest quarter, La Petite France, the hotel welcomes you with a spacious marble vestibule, vivid graffiti art, and Le Pont Tournant, an eye-popping modernistic restaurant done up in white, pinks, and reds (enjoy its summer tables over the torrent). Upstairs, Philippe Starck–inspired sculptural room furnishings contrast sharply with the half-timber houses and roaring river viewed from nearly every room. There's no skimping on the amenities—both the beds and the bathrooms are divine. **Pros:** beautiful rooms; ideal location; great service. **Cons:** disappointing breakfast; restaurant closed Sunday and Monday. *✉ 5 rue des Moulins ☎ 03–88–76–43–43 🌐 www.regent-petite-france.com* *72 rooms* *In-room: a/c, refrigerator, Wi-Fi. In-hotel: restaurant, bar, some pets allowed* *AE, DC, MC, V* *MAP.*

NIGHTLIFE AND THE ARTS

The annual **Festival Musica** (*Contemporary Music Festival ✉ Cité de la Musique et de la Danse, 1 pl. Dauphine ☎ 03–88–23–46–46 🌐 www.festival-musica.org*) is held in September and October. The **Opéra National du Rhin** (*✉ 19 pl. Broglie ☎ 03–88–75–48–23 🌐 www.operanationaldurhin.fr*) has a sizable repertoire.Classical concerts are

Strasbourg is studded with medieval buildings that look air-lifted in from Germany and stunningly ornament the city's squares.

staged by the **Orchestre Philharmonique** (✉ *Palais des Congrès* ☎ *03–88–15–09–09* 🌐 *www.philharmonique-strasbourg.com*).

The Vieille Ville neighborhood east of the cathedral, along Rue des Frères, is the nightlife hangout for university students and twenty-somethings; among its handful of heavily frequented bars is **La Laiterie** (✉ *13 rue Hohwald* ☎ *03–88–23–72–37* 🌐 *www.laiterie.artefact.org*), a multiplex concert hall showcasing art, workshops, and music ranging from electronic to post-rock and reggae. **Le Chalet Club**(✉ *376 rte. de la Wantzenau* ☎ *03–88–31–18–31* 🌐 *www.strasbourg-by-night.com*) is the biggest and most popular disco, but it's some 10 km (6 mi) northeast of the city center.

SHOPPING

The lively city center is full of boutiques, including chocolate shops and delicatessens selling locally made foie gras. Look for warm paisley linens and rustic homespun fabrics, Alsatian pottery, and local wines. Forming the city's commercial heart are **Rue des Hallebardes,** next to the cathedral; **Rue des Grandes Arcades,** with its shopping mall; and **Place Kléber.** An **antiques market** takes place behind the cathedral on Rue du Vieil-Hôpital, Rue des Bouchers, and Place de la Grande Boucherie every Wednesday and Saturday morning.

ALSACE

The Rhine River forms the eastern boundary of both Alsace and France. But the best of Alsace is not found along the Rhine's industrial waterfront. Instead it's in the Ill Valley at the base of the Vosges, southwest of cosmopolitan Strasbourg. Northwest is Saverne and the beginning of the **Route du Vin,** the great Alsace Wine Road, which winds its way south through the Vosges foothills, fruitful vineyards, and medieval villages that would serve well as stage sets for Rossini's *William Tell.* Signs for the road help you keep your bearings on the twisting way south, and you'll find limitless opportunities to stop at wineries and sample the local wares. The Wine Road stretches 170 km (100 mi) between Thann and Marienheim, and is easily accessible from Strasbourg or Colmar. Many of the towns and villages have designated "vineyard trails" winding between towns (a bicycle will help you cover a lot of territory). Riquewihr and Ribeauvillé—accessible by bus from Colmar and Sélestat rail stations—are connected by an especially picturesque route. Along the way, stop at any *"Dégustation"* sign for a free tasting and pick up brochures on the Alsace Wine Road at any tourist office.

WAIFS-TO-GO

The illustrator Waltz Hansi, popular at the turn of the 20th century, created the ubiquitous wide-eyed waifs in Alsatian folk costume that adorn souvenir mugs, dish towels, coasters, and ashtrays on sale around the region; his original work was less clichéd.

OBERNAI

30 km (19 mi) southwest of Strasbourg via A35/N422.

Many visitors begin their saunter down the Route du Vin at Obernai, a thriving, colorful Renaissance market town named for the patron saint of Alsace. Head to the central town enclosed by the ramparts to find some particularly Nikon-friendly sites, including a medieval belfry, Renaissance well, and late-19th-century church.

GETTING HERE

Strasbourg's **train station** (✉ *20 pl. de la Gare*) is at the heart of the regional TER train system and has trains via Sélestat (€7.50) every 30 minutes to Colmar (€10.40)—the city at the southern end of Alsace's Route du Vin. Change in Sélestat for omnibus services to Rosheim/Molsheim (via Obernai, €5.30). Strasbourg also has an extensive tram and bus network that includes buses to Obernai from its Gare Routière in Place des Halles.

Visitor Information **Obernai Tourist Office** ✉ *Pl. du Beffroi* ☎ *03–88–95–64–13* 🌐 *www.obernai.fr.*

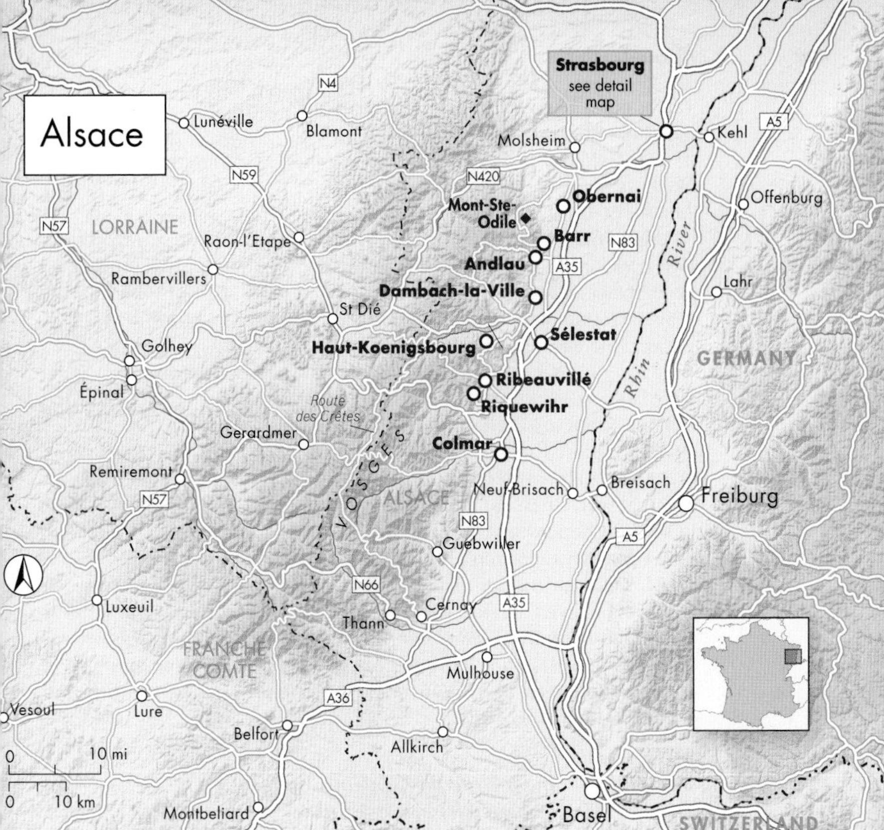

EXPLORING

Place du Marché, in the heart of town, is dominated by the stout, square 13th-century **Kapelturm Beffroi** *(Chapel Tower Belfry)*, topped by a pointed steeple flanked at each corner by frilly openwork turrets added in 1597.

An elaborate Renaissance well near the belfry, the **Puits à Six-Seaux** *(Well of Six Buckets)* was constructed in 1579; its name recalls the six buckets suspended from its metal chains.

The twin spires of the parish church of **St-Pierre–St-Paul** compete with the belfry for skyline preeminence. They date, like the rest of the church, from the 1860s, although the 1504 Holy Sepulchre altarpiece in the north transept is a survivor from the previous church. Other points of interest include the flower-bedecked **Place de l'Étoile** and the **Hôtel de Ville,** whose council chamber and historic balcony can be viewed.

WHERE TO STAY

¢ **La Cloche**. Stained glass, dark oak, and Hansi-like murals set the tone in this sturdy half-timber 14th-century landmark on Obernai's market square. Rooms are well equipped and country-pretty; two double-decker duplex rooms accommodate four. In the adjoining restaurant, the excellent-value menus (€15–€21), comprising regional dishes and blackboard specials, draw locals on market days. **Pros:** good value; good restaurant; very friendly staff. **Cons:** spotty Wi-Fi coverage; doesn't accept American Express. ✉ *90 rue du Général-Gouraud* ☎ *03–88–95–52–89* 🌐 *www.la-cloche.com* *20 rooms* *In-room: a/c, Wi-Fi (some). In-hotel: restaurant, bar* ▭ *MC, V* ⊗ *Closed 2 wks in Jan.* *MAP.*

$–$$ **L'Ami Fritz.** White-shuttered, flower-bedecked, with sunny yellow walls, this welcoming inn combines style, rustic warmth, and three generations of family tradition. Set several miles west of Obernai, the reader-recommended, picture-perfect 18th-century stone house has impeccable guest rooms decked in toile de Jouy and homespun checks (opt for rooms in the main hotel, not in the adjacent annex). Some suites can sleep three, making them good for families, and the heated outdoor pool also comes in handy. The fine restaurant (reservations essential; closed to nonguests Wednesday) is one of the region's top attractions. Here you can feast on Patrick Fritz's sophisticated twists on regional specialties, including feather-light blood sausage in flaky pastry, a delicate choucroute of grated turnips, or the gratinéed freshwater fish braised in Sylvaner. Don't miss the fruity red wine, an Ottrott exclusive. **Pros:** beautiful location; friendly staff. **Cons:** a car is needed to reach property; uneven service. ✉ *8 rue des Châteaux, 5 km (3 mi) west of Obernai Ottrott* ☎ *03–88–95–80–81* 🌐 *www.amifritz.com* *22 rooms* *In-room: a/c (some), refrigerator, Wi-Fi. In-hotel: restaurant, pool, some pets allowed* ▭ *AE, DC, MC, V* ⊗ *Closed 1st 2 wks in July and 2 wks mid-Jan.* *MAP.*

Fodor's Choice ★

SHOPPING

Dietrich (✉ *58 and 74 rue du Général-Gouraud* ☎ *03–88–95–57–58* 🌐 *www.dietrich-obernai.fr*) has a varied selection of Beauvillé linens, locally handblown Alsatian wineglasses, and Obernai-pattern china.

ANDLAU

3 km (2 mi) southwest of Barr on Rte. du Vin.

Andlau has long been known for its magnificent abbey. Built in the 12th century, the **Abbaye d'Andlau** has the richest ensemble of Romanesque sculpture in Alsace. Sculpted vines wind their way around the doorway as a reminder of wine's time-honored importance to the local economy. A statue of a female bear, the abbey mascot—bears used to roam local forests and were bred at the abbey until the 16th century—can be seen in the north transept. Legend has it that Queen Richarde, spurned by her husband, Charles the Fat, founded the abbey in AD 887 when an angel enjoined her to construct a church on a site to be shown to her by a female bear.

WHERE TO STAY

$–$$ **Arnold.** This yellow-wall, half-timber hillside hotel overlooks the cute wine village of Itterswiller; most rooms have views across the vines. The cheapest rooms, on the top floor, have a shower and no balcony; the priciest have a bath and a balcony facing south. The wood-beam lobby with its wrought-iron staircase has the same quaint charm as the hotel's winstub-style restaurant (no dinner Sunday, closed Monday, May to November) across the street, with its old winepress and local

Alsace wines served by the jug; homemade foie gras and venison in cranberry sauce top the menu, along with sauerkraut and *baeckeoffe* (meat-and-potato casserole). **Pros:** all-around excellence; good half-board meal plan. **Cons:** no air-conditioning; inconsistent service. ✉ *98 rte. des Vins, 3 km (2 mi) south of Andlau on D253, Itterswiller* ☎ *03–88–85–50–58* 🌐 *www.hotel-arnold.com* *29 rooms* *In-room: no a/c, refrigerator, Wi-Fi. In-hotel: restaurant, some pets allowed* 💳 *AE, MC, V* 🍽 *MAP.*

DAMBACH-LA-VILLE

8 km (5 mi) southeast of Andlau via Itterswiller.

GETTING HERE

Strasbourg's **train station** (✉ *20 pl. de la Gare*) is at the heart of the regional TER train system and has trains via Sélestat (€7.50) every 30 minutes to Colmar (€10.40)—the city at the southern end of Alsace's Route du Vin. Change in Sélestat for omnibus services to Rosheim/Molsheim (for Dambach la Ville, €7.60).

EXPLORING

One of the prettiest villages along the Alsace Wine Road, Dambach-la-Ville is a fortified medieval town protected by ramparts and three powerful 13th-century gateways. It's particularly rich in half-timber, high-roof houses from the 17th and 18th centuries, clustered mainly around **Place du Marché** (Market Square). Also on the square is the 16th-century **Hôtel de Ville** (Town Hall). As you walk the charming streets, notice the wrought-iron signs and rooftop oriels.

WHERE TO STAY

¢ **Le Vignoble.** Set in a beautifully restored 18th-century barn next to the village church, this unpretentious hotel offers real, rustic Alsatian charm. The guest rooms are quiet and comfy. In good weather, take advantage of the pleasant garden and courtyard. Although some are on the small side, guest rooms are quiet and comfy, with functional dark-wood furnishings; the best have balconies overlooking the street. **Pros:** wine-route location; warm Alsatian welcome. **Cons:** no air-conditioning; no restaurant. ✉ *1 rue de l'Eglise* ☎ *03–88–92–62–21* 🌐 *www.hotel-vignoble-alsace.fr* *7 rooms* *In-room: no a/c, Internet* 💳 *DC, MC, V* *Closed mid-Dec.–early Jan.* 🍽 *MAP.*

SÉLESTAT

9 km (5½ mi) southeast of Dambach via D210 and N422, 47 km (29 mi) southwest of Strasbourg.

Sélestat, midway between Strasbourg and Colmar, is a lively, historic town with a Romanesque church and a library of medieval manuscripts (and, important to note, a railway station with trains to and from Strasbourg). Head directly to the Vieille Ville and explore the quarter on foot.

8

Alsace's Wine Road passes a parade of Hansel and Gretel villages, each more picturesque than the last.

GETTING HERE

Strasbourg's **train station** (✉ *20 pl. de la Gare*) is at the heart of the regional TER train system and has trains every 30 minutes to Sélestat, €7.50.

Visitor Information Sélestat Tourist Office. ✉ *10 bd. du Mal-Leclerc* ☎ *03–88–58–87–20* 🌐 *www.selestat-tourisme.com.*

EXPLORING

The church of **St-Foy** (✉ *Pl. du Marché-Vert*) dates from between 1155 and 1190; its Romanesque facade remains largely intact (the spires were added in the 19th century), as does the 140-foot octagonal tower over the crossing. Sadly, the interior was mangled over the centuries, chiefly by the Jesuits; their most inspired legacy is the Baroque pulpit of 1733 depicting the life of St. Francis Xavier. Note the Romanesque bas-relief next to the baptistery, originally the lid of a sarcophagus.

Among the precious medieval and Renaissance manuscripts on display at the **Bibliothèque Humaniste** *(Humanist Library)*, a major library founded in 1452 and installed in the former Halle aux Blés, are a 7th-century lectionary and a 12th-century Book of Miracles. There's also a town register from 1521, with the first-ever recorded reference to a Christmas tree! ✉ *1 rue de la Bibliothèque* ☎ *03–88–58–07–20* 🌐 *www.bh-selestat.fr* 🎫 *€3.90* ⏲ *Sept.–June, Mon. and Wed.–Fri. 9–noon and 2–6, Sat. 9–noon; July and Aug., Mon. and Wed.–Fri. 9–noon and 2–6, weekends 2–5.*

HAUT-KOENIGSBOURG

11 km (7 mi) west of Sélestat via D159.

One of the most popular spots in Alsace is the romantic, crag-top castle of Haut-Koenigsbourg, originally built as a fortress in the 12th century.

FLOWER POWERED

The colorful Corso Fleuri Flower Carnival takes place on the second Sunday in August, when Sélestat decks itself—and the floats in its vivid parade—with a magnificent display of dahlias.

Fodor's Choice ★ The ruins of the **Château du Haut-Koenigsbourg** were presented by the town of Sélestat to German emperor Wilhelm II in 1901. The château looked just as a kaiser thought one should, and he restored it with some diligence and no lack of imagination—squaring the main tower's original circle, for instance. The site, panorama, drawbridge, and amply furnished imperial chambers may lack authenticity, but they are undeniably dramatic. Call the "on demand" service (☎ *08–00–10–09–48)* in Sélestat to arrange transport to Orschwiller (Haut-Koenigsbourg). ☎ *03–88–82–50–60* 🌐 *www.haut-koenigsbourg.fr* *€7.50* *Nov.–Feb., daily 9:45–noon and 1–4:30; Mar. and Oct., daily 9:45–4:30; Apr., May, and Sept., daily 9:30–5; June–Aug., daily 9:30–6.*

RIBEAUVILLÉ

Fodor's Choice ★ *13 km (8 mi) south of Haut-Koenigsbourg via St-Hippolyte, 16 km (10 mi) southwest of Sélestat.*

The beautiful half-timber town of Ribeauvillé, surrounded by rolling vineyards and three imposing châteaux, produces some of the best wines in Alsace. (The Trimbach family has made Riesling and superb Gewürztraminer here since 1626.) The town's narrow main street, crowded with winstubs, pottery shops, bakeries, and wine sellers, is bisected by the 13th-century **Tour des Bouchers,** a clock-belfry completed (gargoyles and all) in the 15th century.

GETTING HERE

Strasbourg's **train station** (✉ *20 pl. de la Gare*) is at the heart of the regional TER train system and has trains every 30 minutes to Colmar (€10.40) via Sélestat (€7.50), where you can change for omnibus services to Ribeauvillé (€2.10).

Visitor Information Ribeauvillé Tourist Office. ✉ *1 Grand Rue* ☎ *03–89–73–23–23* 🌐 *www.ribeauville-riquewihr.com.*

EXPLORING

Storks' nests crown several towers in Ribeauvillé, while streets are adorned with quaint shop signs, fairy-tale turrets, and tour guides herding the crowds with directions in French and German. Head for the Place de la Marie and its Hôtel de Ville to see its famous collection of silver-gilt 16th-century tankards and chalices.

Place de la Marie is a great place to perch come every first Sunday in September, when the town hosts a grand parade to celebrate the Fête des Ménétriers (Fête of the Minstrels), a day when at least one fountain here spouts free Riesling. Headlined by medieval musicians, the party begins mid-afternoon, while the best street seats go for €10 each. Contact the tourist office early for information.

WHERE TO EAT

$$$$ FRENCH Fodor's Choice ★ **L'Auberge de l'Ill.** England's late Queen Mother, Marlene Dietrich, and Montserrat Caballé are just a few of the famous who have feasted at this culinary temple, but, oddly, the place has never been as famous as it should be, the long trek from Paris to the half-timber village of Illhaeusern perhaps the reason. Still, you need to book weeks in advance (closed Monday and Tuesday) to snare a table in this classic yet casual dining room. Master chef Paul Haeberlin died in 2008, but his son Marc continues to marry grand and Alsatian cuisine with Asian nuances (a second Auberge de l'Ill opened in Japan in 2007). The results are impressive: salmon soufflé, lamb chops in dainty strudel, and showstoppers like *le homard Prince Vladimir,* or lobster with shallots braised in champagne and crème fraîche. Germanic-Alsatian flair is particularly apparent in such dishes as the truffled *baeckeoffe* (baker's oven), a casserole-terrine of lamb and pork with leeks. The kitchen's touch is incredibly light, so you'll have room to savor such master desserts as white peaches served in a chocolate "butterfly" with champagne sabayon sauce. The prix-fixe lunch, at €117, is the closest thing you'll find to a bargain. *2 rue de Collonges-au Mont d'Or 10 km (6 mi) east of Ribeauvillé, Illhaeusern* *03–89–71–89–00* *www.auberge-de-l-ill.com* *AE, DC, MC, V* *Closed Mon. and Tues. and Feb.–early Mar.*

$ GERMAN **Zum Pfifferhüs.** This is a true-blue winstub, with yellowed murals, glowing lighting, and great local wines available by the glass. The cooking is pure Alsace, with German-scale portions of choucroute, ham hock, and fruit tarts. Book ahead. *14 Grand-Rue* *03–89–73–62–28* *Reservations essential* *MC, V* *Closed Thurs. Nov.–July, Wed., mid-Feb.–mid-Mar., and 1st 2 wks in July.*

WHERE TO STAY

$ **Hôtel de la Tour.** In the center of Ribeauvillé and across from the Tour des Bouchers, this erstwhile family winery, with an ornate Renaissance fountain outside its front door, is a good choice for experiencing the atmospheric town by night. Rooms and amenities are modern and surprisingly spacious; those on the top floor have exposed timbers and wonderful views of ramshackle rooftops. As you would expect, given the history of the hotel, the owners can give expert advice when it comes to wine tours. **Pros:** family run; good amenities, including a sauna and Jacuzzi. **Cons:** no air-conditioning; possible language-barrier problems. *1 rue de la Mairie* *03–89–73–72–73* *www.hotel-la-tour.com* *31 rooms* *In-room: no a/c, Wi-Fi. In-hotel: bar, gym, parking (free)* *AE, DC, MC, V* *Closed Jan.–mid-Mar.*

$$$$ **Hôtel des Berges.** If you want to enjoy the pleasant surroundings of the Auberge, with its terraced lawns and romantic trees beside the River Ill, opt for an overnight in one of the guest rooms in the new **Hôtel des Berges,** set behind L'Auberge de l'Ill restaurant and designed to evoke an Alsatian tobacco barn, replete with Havanese woods, rooms

named after famous cigars, and a lulling and lovely country-luxe decor. For that quintessentially romantic moment, opt for breakfast afloat in a cane-trunk boat, complete with wicker basket, white tablecloth, and personal punter. Special "youth" rates are available to those under 35. **Pros:** romantic and opulent; close to excellent restaurant. **Cons:** pricey. ✉ *2 rue de Collonges-au Mont d'Or, 10 km (6 mi) east of Ribeauvillé, Illhaeusern* ☎ *03–89–71–87–87* 🌐 *www.hotel-des-berges.fr* *13 rooms* *In-room: a/c, refrigerator, Wi-Fi. In-hotel: restaurant, some pets allowed* *AE, DC, MC, V* *Closed Mon. and Tues. and Feb.*

THE BUTLER DID IT

At the restaurant Au Tire-Bouchon, the famous "Choucroute Royale" is garnished with seven different kinds of meats and served with a half bottle of mulled champagne plopped in the center of a mound of sauerkraut. The contents of the bottle are then poured by the waitress, with great flourish, over the entire dish.

$$–$$$ **Seigneurs de Ribeaupierre.** On the edge of Ribeauvillé's old quarter, this gracious half-timber, restored 18th-century inn offers a warm regional welcome with a touch of flair. It has exposed timbers in pastel tones, sumptuous fabrics, and slick bathrooms upstairs, as well as a fire crackling downstairs on your way to the generous breakfast. The two "Maries," owners for more than two decades, bring an unpretentious, sisterly vibe to this intimate address where, relaxing with a glass beside the hearth and gentle conversation more than compensates for the absence of a dining room. **Pros:** tasteful and cozy; central location; gracious hosts. **Cons:** stuffy in summer (no air-conditioning). ✉ *11 rue du Château* ☎ *03–89–73–70–31* 🌐 *www.ribeaupierre.com* *10 rooms* *In-room: no a/c, no TV. In-hotel: bar, parking (paid)* *AE, MC, V* *Closed Jan. and Feb.* *BP.*

8

RIQUEWIHR

Fodor's Choice ★ *5 km (3 mi) south of Ribeauvillé.*

With its dormer windows fit for a Rapunzel, hidden cul-de-sacs home to Rumpelstiltskins, and unique once-upon-a-timeliness, Riquewihr is the showpiece of the Wine Route and a living museum of the quaint architecture of old Alsace. Its steep main street, ramparts, and winding back alleys have scarcely changed since the 16th century, and could easily serve as a film set. Merchants cater to the sizable influx of tourists with a plethora of kitschy souvenir shops; bypass them to peep into courtyards with massive wine presses, to study the woodwork and ornately decorated houses, to stand in the narrow old courtyard that was once the Jewish quarter, or to climb up a narrow wooden stair to the ramparts. You would also do well to settle into a winstub to sample some of Riquewihr's famous wines. Just strolling at will down the heavenly romantic streets will reward your eye with bright blue, half-timber houses, storybook gables, and storks'-nest towers. The facades of certain houses dating from the late Gothic period take pride of place, including the Maison Kiener (1574), the Maison Priess

CLOSE UP

Sauerkraut and Choucroute

To embark on a full gastronomic excursion into the hearty, artery-clogging terrain of Alsatian cuisine, your tour should probably start with *flammekueche*—a flat tart stuffed with bacon, onions, cream cheese, and heavy cream. The next stop is *baecke-offe,* marinated pork, mutton, and beef simmered in wine with potatoes and onions, sometimes with a round of creamy Muenster cheese melted on top. And to finish up, land with a thud on a hefty slice of *Kougelhopf,* a butter-rich ring-shape brioche cake with almonds and raisins.

If, however, you have neither the constitution nor the inclination for such culinary heft, there is one dish that sums up the whole of Alsatian cuisine: *choucroute garnie.* Borrowed from the Germans, who call it sauerkraut, the base definition of choucroute is cabbage pickled in brine. In more elaborate terms, this means *quintal d'Alsace,* a substantial variety of local white cabbage, shredded and packed into crockery and left to ferment with salt and juniper berries for at least two months. Beyond this, any unanimity regarding the composition of choucroute garnie breaks down. The essential ingredients, however, seem to be sauerkraut, salted bacon, pork sausages, juniper berries, white wine, onions, cloves, black peppercorns, garlic, lard or goose fat, potatoes, and salt pork—pigs' knuckles, cheeks, loin, shanks, feet, shoulder, and who knows what else? No matter—the taste is unforgettable.

(1686), and the Maison Liebrich (1535), but the Tower of Thieves and the Postal Museum, ensconced in the château of the duke of Württemberg, are also fascinating.

WHERE TO EAT AND STAY

$–$$ GERMAN ★ **Au Tire-Bouchon.** "The Corkscrew," with its sky-blue walls and red-and-white checkered tablecloths, is the best winstub in town to feast on Alsatian varieties of choucroute garni, including some rare delights like the *verte* ("green," flavored with parsley) version and the blowout "Choucroute Royale." There are also some adventurous innovations on the menu, which changes seasonally, and a fine selection of Muscats and in-house fruit brandies. With communal tables and friendly service, this is heartily recommended for that guaranteed touch of authenticity. If booked up, try the nearby Auberge du Schoenebourg. ✉ *29 rue du Général-de-Gaulle* ☎ *03–89–47–91–61* 🌐 *www.riquewihr-zimmer.com* 💳 *AE, MC, V* ⏲ *Jan.–Mar., closed Mon., no dinner Sun. or Wed.*

$–$$ ★ **Hôtel de la Couronne.** Like an illustration out of the Brothers Grimm, this hotel is set in a 16th-century house with central tower and side wings. Its steep mansard roof, country shutters, and rusticated stone trim beautifully blend into the heart of medieval Riquewihr—the only modern note will be your car (allowed to drive to the hotel even though the town center is pedestrianized). Inside, several rooms have grand timber beams and folkloric wall stencils, making this a truly charming base for touring a truly charming town. **Pros:** good location; outdoor dining in summer, old-world charm. **Cons:** no elevator; service is inconsistent. ✉ *5 rue de la Couronne* ☎ *03–89–49–03–03* 🌐 *www.*

hoteldelacouronne.com 41 *rooms* *In-room: no a/c, Wi-Fi. In-hotel: restaurant, some pets allowed* *AE, DC, MC, V.*

¢–$ **Sarment d'Or.** This cozy little family-run hotel by the city walls, near the Dolder belfry, blends irreproachable modern comforts with bare-stone walls and dark-timber ceilings. Rooms are pleasant, bright, and clean, and despite Riquewihr's being car-free, you can drive your vehicle up to the door for a luggage drop-off. The top-floor duplex suite is an exceptional value. The restaurant downstairs offers firelight romance and delicious cuisine—foie gras, frogs' legs in garlic cream, and breast of duck in pinot noir; it's closed Monday and does not serve dinner Sunday or lunch Tuesday. **Pros:** pleasant rooms; good food. **Cons:** no elevator; no air-conditioning. *4 rue du Cerf* *03–89–86–02–86* *www.riquewihr-sarment-dor.com* *9 rooms* *In-room: no a/c, Internet. In-hotel: restaurant, parking (paid)* *MC, V* *Closed Jan.–mid-Feb. and 1st wk in July* *MAP.*

COLMAR

★ *13 km (8 mi) southeast of Riquewihr via D3/D10, 71 km (44 mi) southwest of Strasbourg.*

Forget that much of Colmar's architecture is modern (because of the destruction wrought by World Wars I and II): its Vieille Ville (Old Town) heart—an atmospheric maze of narrow streets lined with candy-color, half-timber Renaissance houses hanging over cobblestone lanes in a disarmingly ramshackle way—out-charms Strasbourg.

GETTING HERE

The three daily direct TGV high-speed return trips from Paris, Gare de l'Est, to Colmar (€72.10), taking 2 hours 50 minutes each way, are perfectly complemented by 10 semi-direct, hourly TGV/TER combos from the same station. They all require a change at either Strasbourg or Mulhouse but barely 10 minutes is added to the trip. The last of the five Sélestat-bound (€4.20) trains/buses from Colmar to stop at Ribeauvillé (€2.80) is at 1:06. The LK Groupe (*www.l-k.fr*) has regular bus services from the Gare SNCF to towns throughout the region, including Ribeauvillé (seven daily). Colmar's train station on Rue de la Gare is in the far southwestern corner of town; from here, walk 15 minutes down Avenue de la République for the tourist office, or take municipal TRACE buses (buy ticket from driver).

Visitor Information Colmar Tourist Office. *4 rue Unterlinden* *03–89–20–68–92* *www.ot-colmar.fr.*

EXPLORING

To find Colmar at its most charming, wander along the calm canals that wind through **La Petite Venise** *(Little Venice)*, an area of bright Alsatian houses with colorful shutters and window boxes that's south of the center of town. Here, amid weeping willow trees that shed their tears into the eddies of the Lauch River and half-timber houses gaily bedecked with geraniums and carnations, you have the sense of being in a tiny village. Elsewhere, the Vieille Ville streets fan out from the beefy towered church of **St-Martin.** Each shop-lined backstreet winds its way

8

DID YOU KNOW?

Colmar may be mostly modern but its heart is an Old Town that out-charms Strasbourg—head to the Lauch River to find La Petite Venise, a gorgeous district lined with candycolor, half-timber houses.

to the 15th-century customs house, the **Ancienne Douane,** and the square and canals that surround it.

The **Maison Pfister** (✉ *11 rue Mercière*), built in 1537, is the most striking of Colmar's many old dwellings. Note its decorative frescoes and medallions, carved balcony, and ground-floor arcades.

Up the street from the Ancienne Douane on the Grand Rue, the **Maison aux Arcades** *(Arcades House)* was built in 1609 in High Renaissance style with a series of arched porches (arcades) anchored by two octagonal towers.

COLMAR TOURS

For Colmar and its enchanting environs, take a highly recommended van tour with **Les Circuits d'Alsace** (✉ *8 pl. de la Gare* ☎ *03-89-41-90-88* 🌐 *www.alsace-travel.com*)—castles, villages, and vineyards make for an exhilarating itinerary.

Fodor's Choice ★ The cultural highlight of Colmar is the **Musée d'Unterlinden,** once a medieval Dominican convent and hotbed of Rhenish mysticism, and now an important museum. Its star attraction is one of the greatest altarpieces of the 16th century, the *Retable Issenheim* (1512–16), by Matthias Grünewald, majestically displayed in the convent's Gothic chapel. Originally painted for the convent at Issenheim, 22 km (14 mi) south of Colmar, the world-famous, multipanel altarpiece is either the last gasp of medievalism or a breathtaking preview of modernism and all its neuroses. Framed with two-sided wings which unfold to reveal the Crucifixion and Incarnation, the multipaneled masterpiece includes depictions of the Annunciation, the Resurrection, and scenes from the life of St. Anthony, including a Temptation rioting with monsters that even outdo those of Hieronymous Bosch. Grünewald's altarpiece, replete with its raw realism (note the chamber pots, boil-covered bellies, and dirty linen), was believed to have miraculous healing powers over ergotism, a widespread disease in the Middle Ages. Produced by the ingestion of fungus-ridden grains, the malady caused its victims—many of whom were being nursed at the Issenheim convent—to experience delusional, nearly hallucinogenic, fantasies. Other museum treasures can be found exhibited around the enchanting 13th-century cloister, including arms and armor. Upstairs are fine regional furnishings and a collection of Rhine Valley paintings from the Renaissance, including Martin Schongauer's opulent 1470 altarpiece painted for Jean d'Orlier. ✉ *1 rue Unterlinden* ☎ *03-89-20-15-50* 🌐 *www.musee-unterlinden.com* 🎫 €7 ⏲ *May–Oct., daily 9–6; Nov.–Apr., Wed.–Mon. 9–noon and 2–5.*

★ The **Église des Dominicains** *(Dominican Church)* houses the Flemish-influenced *Madonna of the Rosebush* (1473), by Martin Schongauer (1445–91), the most celebrated painting by the noted 15th-century German artist. This work, stolen from St-Martin's in 1972 and later recovered and hung here, has almost certainly been reduced in size from its original state but retains enormous impact. The grace and intensity of the Virgin match that of the Christ Child; yet her slender fingers dent the child's soft flesh (and his fingers entwine her curls) with immediate intimacy. Schongauer's text for her crown is: ME CARPES GENITO TUO O SANTISSIMA VIRGO ("Choose me also for your child, O holiest Virgin").

✉ *Pl. des Dominicains* ☎ *03–89–24–46–57* 🎟 *€1.50* ⏲ *Mid-Mar.–Dec., daily 10–1 and 3–6.*

The **Musée Bartholdi** *(Bartholdi Museum)* is the birthplace of Frédéric-Auguste Bartholdi (1834–1904), the local sculptor who designed the Statue of Liberty. Exhibits of Bartholdi's works claim the ground floor; a reconstruction of the artist's Paris apartments and furniture are upstairs; and, in adjoining rooms, the creation of Lady Liberty is explored. ✉ *30 rue des Marchands* ☎ *03–89–41–90–60* 🌐 *www.musee-bartholdi.com* 🎟 *€4.50* ⏲ *Dec. and Jan., Wed.–Mon. 10–noon and 2–6.*

"HALLUCINOGENIC"

That's the adjective often used by art historians to describe the proto-Expressionist power of Grünewald's tortured faces, which made a direct appeal to the pain-racked victims dying at the convent, often from their illness brought on by the ingestion of fungus-ridden grains.

WHERE TO EAT

$ FRENCH ✕ **Au Koïfhus.** Not to be confused with the shabby little Koïfhus winstub on Rue des Marchands, this popular landmark (the name means "customs-house") serves huge portions of regional standards, plus changing specialties: roast quail and foie gras on salad, game stews with spaetzle (tiny dumplings), and freshwater fish. Appreciative tourists and canny locals contribute to the lively atmosphere. If you can cut a swath through this enthusiastic horde, choose between the big, open dining room, glowing with wood and warm fabric, and a shaded table on the broad, lovely square. ✉ *2 pl. de l'Ancienne-Douane* ☎ *03–89–23–04–90* 💳 *MC, V.*

$$ FRENCH ✕ **Chez Hansi.** Named after the Rockwell-like illustrator whose beclogged folk children adorn most of the souvenirs of Alsace, this hyper-traditional beamed tavern in the Vieille Ville serves excellent down-home classics such as quiche Lorraine, choucroute, and pot-au-feu, prepared and served with a sophisticated touch, despite the friendly waitresses' folksy dirndls. Prices are surprisingly reasonable, given the quality of the food and the eatery's location in a heavily touristed part of town, though the wine list is limited to the Bestheim selection. ✉ *23 rue des Marchands* ☎ *03–89–41–37–84* 💳 *MC, V* ⏲ *Closed Wed. and Thurs., and Jan.*

$$$$ FRENCH ✕ **Le Rendez-vous de Chasse.** Brimming with confidence gained at the hallowed halls of Auberge de L'Ill, the stellar cuisine of Mickaela Peters is as refined, elegant, and chic as the decor of this opulent Renaissance mansion. It's well worth the wrangle to secure a table here, where some of the region's finest dishes are prepared with aplomb, and a memorable three courses will set you back a paltry €48. An extensive cellar accents perfectly dishes like foie gras and veal sweetbread terrine, and langoustine ravioli with asparagus and morel fricassee. ✉ *7 pl. de la Gare* ☎ *03–89–41–10–10* *Reservations essential* 💳 *AE, DC, MC, V.*

WHERE TO STAY

$$–$$$ Fodor's Choice ★ **Le Maréchal.** A maze of narrow, creaky corridors connects the series of Renaissance houses that make up this romantic riverside inn. Built in 1565 in the fortified walls that encircle the Vieille Ville, the Maréchal

has rooms that are small but lavished with extravagant detail, from glossy rafters to rich brocades to four-poster beds (and even Jacuzzis)—ask for the Wagner or Bach rooms. A vivid color scheme—scarlet, sapphire, candy pink—adds to the Vermeer atmosphere. This is not a high-tech luxury hotel: it's an endearing, quirky, lovely old place hanging over a Petite Venise canal. The hotel's gastronomic restaurant, À l'Échevin, offers such dishes as terrine of rouget, leeks, truffles, and pigeon breast and foie gras crisped in pastry. Dine in salons or on the terrace perched over the river. **Pros:** pretty location; good food; amiable staff. **Cons:** some rooms are unimpressive; parking is difficult to find. ✉ *4 pl. des Six-Montagnes-Noires* ☎ *03–89–41–60–32* 🌐 *www.hotel-le-marechal.com* *30 rooms* *In-room: a/c, refrigerator, Wi-Fi. In-hotel: restaurant, parking (paid), some pets allowed* *AE, DC, MC, V* *MAP.*

DESIGNATED DRINKING

During the first half of August, Colmar celebrates with its annual Foire Régionale des Vins d'Alsace, an Alsatian wine fair in the Parc des Expositions. Events include folk music and theater performances and, above all, the tasting and selling of wine.

$–$$ **Rapp.** In the Vieille Ville, just off the Champ de Mars, this solid, modern hotel has business-class comforts, a professional and welcoming staff, and a good German-scale breakfast. There's even an extensive indoor pool complex, including sauna, steam bath, and workout equipment—all included in the low price. All rooms have been recently and tastefully "refreshed." The restaurant serves dependable regional fare (including vegetarian dishes), is closed Friday, and does not serve dinner Thursday or lunch Saturday. **Pros:** good value; modern amenities; helpful staff. **Cons:** difficult to find. ✉ *1–3–5 rue Weinemer* ☎ *03–89–41–62–10* 🌐 *www.rapp-hotel.com* *38 rooms* *In-room: a/c, Internet, Wi-Fi. In-hotel: restaurant, bar, pool, gym* *AE, DC, MC, V.*

SPORTS AND THE OUTDOORS

A guide to bicycling in the Lorraine is available from the Comité Départemental de Cyclisme. For a list of signposted trails in the Vosges foothills, contact the Sélestat Tourist Office. **Loisirs Accueil Haut-Rin** (✉ *1 rue SchlumbergerColmar* ☎ *03–89–20–10–62* 🌐 *www.tourisme-alsace.com*) is a helpful association for bicyclists in the Colmar area.

Burgundy

9

WORD OF MOUTH

"I expected Dijon to be a regular provincial French city. What we found was more of a small gem—sort of a mini-Paris—a beautiful and walkable city that captivated us."

—KidstoLondon

"Rent a car and drive along the Côte de Nuits towns that sound like the wine list at a fine restaurant. And in October the vineyard leaves are in their autumn colors."

—smueller

WELCOME TO BURGUNDY

TOP REASONS TO GO

★ **Wine Is a Wonderful Thing:** Burgundy vineyards are among the world's best, so take the time to stroll through Clos de Vougeot and really get a feel for the "terroir."

★ **Dijon, Burgundy's Hub:** One of France's prettiest cities, with colorful banners and polished storefronts along narrow medieval streets, Dijon is perpetually being dolled up for a street fair.

★ **Relish the Romanesque:** Burgundy is home to a knee-weakening concentration of Romanesque churches, and Vézelay's Basilique has the region's greatest 12th-century sculptures.

★ **Beaune, Capital of Caves:** Famed for its wine caves and its 15th-century, Flemish-style Hospices, Beaune lets you get both your cultural and viticultural fill.

★ **Cluny, "Light of the World":** Once center of a vast Christian empire and today a ruin, this Romanesque abbey still inspires by the sheer volume of what it once was.

1 Northwest Burgundy. The northern part of Burgundy came under the sway of the medieval Paris-based Capetian kings, and the mighty Gothic cathedrals they built are still much in evidence, notably St-Étienne at Sens. Twenty miles to the east is Troyes, its charming half-timber houses adding to the appeal of a town overlooked by most air-conditioned bus tours. Southeast lies Auxerre, beloved for its steep, crooked streets and magnificent churches; the wine village of Chablis; and two great Renaissance châteaux, Tanlay and Ancy-le-Franc. Closer to Dijon are the great Cistercian abbey at Fontenay and the noted Romanesque basilica at Vézelay, with a delightful hilltop setting.

2 Dijon. Burgundy's only real city, Dijon became the capital of the duchy of Burgundy in the 11th century, and acquired most of its important architecture and art treasures during the 14th and 15th centuries under four Burgundian dukes. The churches, the ducal palace, and one of the finest art museums in France are evidence of the dukes' patronage of the arts. Other treasures are culinary, including the world's best *bœuf bourguignon.*

3 Wine Country. South of Dijon, follow the Côte d'Or, one of the most famous wine routes, south as it heads past the great wine villages of Clos de Vougeot and Nuits-St-Georges to Beaune, the hub of Burgundy's wine region. At the Hospices take in the great Rogier van der Weyden *Last Judgment* and the intimate Cour d'Honneur, the perfect postcard setting. Continuing south you'll find Autun, with famous Roman ruins, and the Romanesque landmark of Cluny, once the largest Christian church until Rome's St. Peter's was built.

A5
Troyes
D77
N71
0 20 mi
0 20 km
Pontigny
Tonnerre
Tanlay
Chablis
D965
Ancy-le-Franc
BURGUNDY
N6
Montbard
N71
Avallon
D905
Vézelay
A6
D958
2
Dijon
A31
D70
Saulieu
A38
N6
Clos de Vougeot
A39
BURGUNDY
Arnay-le-Duc
Nuits-St-Georges
3
D978
N81
Beaune
A36
Autun
Meursault
D978
N81
Chalon-sur-Saône
D994
A6
Montceau-les-Mines
D981
N70
Tournus
A39
Paray-le Monial
N78
Cluny
Mâcon

GETTING ORIENTED

As Burgundy is on the main Paris to the Riviera and Switzerland/Italy routes it has always had an excellent service of fast trains that connect with Paris and other major rail centers of France. All roads lead to Dijon, the Grand Central Station of Burgundy. This lively city makes the best hub to enable travelers to discover the region's many spokes, often with the help of local bus stations (which often conveniently hook up with the majority of train stations). All roads, indeed, lead to Dijon.

BURGUNDY PLANNER

Transportation Basics

Burgundy, whose northern perimeter begins 75 km (50 mi) from Paris, is one of the largest regions in France. It's sliced in half by the north–south A6. (As all roads lead to Paris, it's generally quicker to move in this direction than from west to east or vice versa.) But a vast network of secondary roads makes travel from city to city or even village to village both practical and picturesque.

While the area has a highly advanced network of roads, its public trains and buses do not have a wide network—you'll have to plan accordingly when visiting some notable villages or historic sites.

Finding a Place to Stay

Burgundy is perhaps one of the best-served regions of France in terms of accommodations. The vast range has everything from simple *gîtes d'étape* (bed-and-breakfasts) to four-star châteaux. Especially in summer, Burgundy is often overrun with tourists, so finding accommodations can be a problem. It's wise to make advance reservations, especially in the wine country (from Dijon to Beaune).

Making the Most of Your Time

France's prime preoccupations with food and wine are nowhere better celebrated than in Burgundy.

Though it might sound glib, the best way to see Burgundy is to stay for as long as possible.

If you're simply passing through, there's entirely too much to see and do in one trip.

If you want to go bike riding, the obvious place to set up is Beaune.

If, on the other hand, you're an amateur medieval art historian or are interested in the lesser-known wines of Irancy, Chitry, and Tonnerre, base yourself at Auxerre or Vézelay in northern Burgundy.

This would allow you to focus on these pursuits while also visiting vineyards, the cathedral of Sens, and a northward detour to the elegant and delightful town of Troyes.

If the conveniences of modern cities are your preference but you also want a taste of medieval Burgundy, then Dijon, Burgundy's capital, offers you the best of both worlds.

Dijon has all the charm of another era and all the functionality of a major metropolis.

It's the gateway to the Côte d'Or, as well as being the perfect place to set off for exploring the back roads of Burgundy.

DINING AND LODGING PRICE CATEGORIES (IN EUROS)

	¢	$	$$	$$$	$$$$
Restaurants	under €13	€13–€17	€18–€24	€25–€32	over €32
Hotels	under €65	€65–€105	€106–€145	€146–€215	over €215

Restaurant prices are per person for a main course at dinner, including tax (5.5%) and service; note that if a restaurant offers only prix-fixe (set-price) meals, it has been given the price category that reflects the full prix-fixe price. Hotel prices are for a standard double room in high season, including tax (19.6%) and service charge.

Give Your Regards to Uncle Mustard

Tonton Moutarde (Uncle Mustard) is what one young Parisian sophisticate affectionately used to call her Dijon relative, who was actually in the mustard business.

For many French people, mention of Burgundy's capital conjures up images of round, rosy, merry men enjoying large suppers of bœuf à la Bourguignonne and red wine. And admittedly, chances are that in any decent restaurant you can find at least one Dijonnais true to the stereotype.

These days, however, Dijon is not quite the wine-mustard capital of the world it used to be, but the happy fact remains that mustard finds its way into many regional specialties, including the sauce that usually accompanies andouillettes (chitterling sausages).

Dijon ranks with Lyon as the gastronomic capital of France, and Burgundy's hearty traditions help explain why.

It all began in the early 15th century when Jean, Duc de Berry, arrived here, built a string of castles, and proceeded to make food, wine, and art top priorities for his courtiers.

Today, Parisian gourmands consider a three-hour drive a small price to pay for the cuisine of Joigny's Jean Michel Lorain or Vézelay's Marc Meneau.

Game, freshwater trout, coq au vin, *poulet au Meursault* (chicken in white wine sauce), snails, and, of course, *bœuf à la Bourguignonne* (incidentally, this dish is only called *bœuf bourguignon* when you are *not* in Burgundy) number among the region's specialties.

The queen of chickens is the *poulet de Bresse,* which hails from east of the Côte d'Or and can be as pricey as a bottle of fine wine. Sausages—notably the *rosette du Morvan* and others served with a potato purée—are great favorites.

Ham is a big item, especially around Easter, when garlicky *jambon persillé*—ham boiled with pig's trotters and served cold in jellied white wine and parsley (no wonder it's now found throughout the summer months) often tops the menu.

Also look for *saupiquet des Amognes*—a Morvan delight of hot braised ham served with a spicy cream sauce. *Pain d'épices* (gingerbread) is the dessert staple of the region.

Like every other part of France, Burgundy has its own cheeses. The Abbaye de Cîteaux, birthplace of Cistercian monasticism, has produced its mild cheese for centuries. Chaource and hearty Époisses also melt in your mouth—as do Bleu de Bresse and Meursault.

When to Go

Whenever it's gray and cloudy in Paris, chances are the sun is shining in Burgundy. Situated in the heart of France, Burgundy has warm and dry summers. The climate in spring and fall isn't quite as idyllic, with a mixture of sun and scattered showers. The winter months vary from year to year, and although snow is not common, freezing temperatures mean the bare vines and trees are covered with a soft white hue. Layers of clothing are always advisable, so you're ready for cooler mornings and hotter afternoons. Waterproof outer layers are wise on longer day trips if the weather forecast is changeable. May in Burgundy is lovely, as are September and October, when the sun is still warm on the shimmering golden trees, and the grapes, now ready for harvesting, are scenting the air with anticipation. This is when the vines are colorful and the *caves* (cellars) are open for business. Many festivals also take place around this time.

GETTING AROUND

Train Travel

The TGV zips out of Paris (Gare de Lyon) to Dijon (1½ hrs, to €57) 15 times a day, Mâcon (1½ hrs, €36 to €74), and on to Lyon (2 hrs, €65 to €86). Trains run frequently, though the fastest Paris-Lyon trains do not stop at Dijon or go anywhere near it.

Some TGVs stop at Le Creusot, between Chalon and Autun, 90 minutes from Paris—from here, you can hop on a bus for a 45-minute ride to Autun.

There's also TGV service directly from Roissy Airport to Dijon (1 hr, 50 mins). Beaune is well serviced by trains arriving from Dijon, Lyon, and Paris. Sens is on a main-line route from Paris (45 mins).

The region has two local train routes: one linking Sens, Dijon, Beaune, Chalon, Tournus, and Mâcon and the other connecting Auxerre, Saulieu, and Autun.

If you want to get to smaller towns or to vineyards, use bus routes or a car.

Train Information SNCF (☎ *36–35 [€0.34 per min]* 🌐 *www.voyages-sncf.com*). **TGV** (🌐 *www.tgv.com*).

Bus Travel

Local bus services are extensive; where the biggest private companies, **Les Rapides de Bourgogne** and **TRANSCO,** do not venture, the national SNCF routes often do. TRANSCO's No. 44 bus travels through the Côte d'Or wine region, connecting Dijon to Beaune (1 hr) via Vougeot (40 mins) and Nuits-St-Georges (47 mins), all trips costing €1.50. The buses of Les Rapides de Bourgogne connect Auxerre to Chablis (20 mins), Pontigny (20 mins), and Sens (90 mins), all trips costing €2.50. The No. 7 bus from Chalon-sur-Saône's train station takes you over to Cluny.

It's hard to reach Vézelay: the best bet may be to train to nearby Sermizelles, then catch the one bus on Saturday at noon. To get to Avallon and Saulieu, take a train to Montbard, a TGV station stop, and then get a bus to either town. Always inquire at the local tourist office for timetables and ask your hotel concierge for information.

Bus Information Les Rapides de Bourgogne (✉ *3 rue des FontenottesAuxerre* ☎ *03–86–94–95–00* 🌐 *www.rapidesdebourgogne.com*). **TRANSCO** (✉ *Gare Routière, Cour de la Gare Dijon* ☎ *08–00–10–20–04*).

Car Travel

Although bus lines do service smaller towns, traveling through Burgundy by car allows you to explore its meandering country roads at leisure. A6 is the main route through the region; it heads southeast from Paris through Burgundy, past Sens, Auxerre, Chablis, Saulieu, and Beaune, continuing on to Lyon and the south. A38 links A6 to Dijon, 290 km (180 mi) from Paris; the trip takes around three hours.

A31 heads down from Dijon to Beaune, a distance of 45 km (27 mi). N74 is the slower, more scenic route of the two, but if it's scenery you want, D122 is the Route des Grands Crus, which reads like a wine list as it meanders through every wine village. The uncluttered A5 links Paris to Troyes, where the A31 segues south to Dijon.

DID YOU KNOW?

Burgundy at its best is during harvest time, so many head to such hallowed landmarks as the Château du Clos de Vougeot during late October so they can witness the famous vendages (harvests).

EATING AND DRINKING WELL IN BURGUNDY

In a land where glorious wines define both lifestyle and cuisine, you'll find savory, soul-warming dishes, from garlicky escargots to coq au vin rouge, both of which pair beautifully with the local vintages.

Boeuf Bourguignon is the ne plus ultra of Burgundian cuisine (above); wake up those tastebuds with a Kir (right, top); escargots are regional delights (right, bottom).

While Burgundy's glittering wine trade imparts a sophisticated image to the region, Burgundy itself is basically prosperous farm country. Traditional cuisine here reflects the area's farm-centric soul, with lots of slow-cooked, wine-laced dishes. Distinctive farm-produced cheeses, such as the magnificent, odiferous Époisses, and the mild Cîteaux, made by Trappist monks, cap meals with rustic flourish. During a day of wine tasting in the Côte d'Or, dine at a traditional bistro to savor the jambon persillé, chunks of ham enrobed in a parslied aspic jelly, or a rich bœuf bourguignon. In the summer, be sure to spend a morning at one of the region's bountiful weekend markets—Saulieu on Saturday, perhaps. Afterward, enjoy a Charolais steak *à la moutarde* at a local café and raise a glass to the good life.

SOME LIKE IT HOT

Visit the famed Maille mustard emporium, founded in 1747, at 32 rue de la Liberté to savor Dijon's world-famous mustards. Produced from stone-ground dried black or brown seeds macerated in *verjus*, the juice of unripe white grapes, these mustards accompany savory beef dishes, bind vinaigrettes, and heat up *lapin à la moutarde*, rabbit in mustard sauce. There is coarse-grained *à l'ancienne* or the classic, creamy, much hotter variety.

ESCARGOTS

Burgundy's plump snails, which grow wild in the vineyards, star on menus throughout the region. The signature preparation is *à la Bourguignonne*—simmered in white wine, stuffed with a garlicky parsley-shallot butter and baked until bubbling. The delicacy is served in portions of six or eight on ceramic escargot dishes called *escargotières,* accompanied by tongs and a little fork.

Those immune to the true snail's charms may succumb to the luscious imposters made of solid chocolate and available at local candy shops and pâtisseries.

ÉPOISSES CHEESE

The greatest of Burgundian cheeses, the rich, earthy, cow's-milk Époisses is not for the faint of heart.

This assertive—yes, even odorous—cheese with the russet-hue rind develops its character from a daily scrubbing with marc-de-Bourgogne brandy as it ripens, a process that inhibits mold but encourages the growth of a particular bacteria necessary for the development of its creamy interior and distinctive flavor.

Go to the modest village of Époisses and buy your cheese from top producer Robert Berthaut. Caveat: Transport in a tightly sealed container.

BŒUF À LA BOURGUIGNONNE

Burgundy is the birthplace of this beloved beef stew, aka bœuf bourguignon, and no place on earth makes it better.

One to two bottles of hearty red wine cooked down in the sauce is one secret to its success; the other is the region's prime Charolais beef.

The beef is braised with wine, onions, bacon and mushrooms, turning tender as the sauce reduces and intensifies.

Other wine-soaked specialties here include coq au vin and *œufs en meurette*—eggs poached in red wine.

KIR APERITIF

This rosy and refreshing aperitif, combining an inexpensive white wine called *aligoté* with a dose of crème de cassis black-currant liqueur, was dubbed a "Kir" during World War II when the Resistance hero and mayor of Dijon, Canon Félix Kir, began promoting the drink to boost local sales of cassis liqueur.

Traditionally made, the Kir has four to five parts dry white wine to one part crème de cassis. In the Kir's aristocratic cousin, the Kir Royale, Champagne replaces the wine.

Updated by Christopher Mooney

Having done its duty by producing a wealth of what many consider the world's greatest wines, Burgundy—Bourgogne to the French—deserves to be rolled on the palate and savored like a glass filled with Clos de Vougeot. Surrounded by hedge-rowed countryside, fabled vineyards, and magnificent Romanesque abbeys, all the sights here—from the medieval sanctuary of Cluny to the charming wine village of Beaune—invite the wanderer to partake of their mellow splendor.

Although you may often fall under the influence of extraordinary wine during a sojourn in Burgundy the beauty surrounding you will be no boozy illusion. Passed over by revolutions, left unscarred by world wars, and relatively inaccessible thanks to circuitous country roads, the region still reflects the pastoral prosperity it enjoyed under the Capetian kings.

Those were the glory days, when self-sufficient Burgundy held its own against the creeping spread of France and the mighty Holy Roman Empire. This grand period was characterized by the expanding role of the dukes of Bourgogne. Consider these Capetians, history-book celebrities all: there was Philippe le Hardi (the Bold), with his power-brokered marriage to Marguerite of Flanders. There was Jean sans Peur (the Fearless), who murdered Louis d'Orléans in a cloak-and-dagger affair in 1407 and was in turn murdered, in 1419. And then there was Philippe le Bon (the Good), who threw in with the English against Joan of Arc.

Yet the Capetians couldn't hold a candle to the "light of the world": the great Abbaye de Cluny, founded in 910, grew to such overweening ecclesiastical power that it dominated the European Church on a papal scale for some four centuries. It was Urban II himself who dubbed it "*la Lumière du Monde.*" But the stark geometry of Burgundy's Cistercian abbeys, such as Clairvaux and Cîteaux, stands in silent rebuke to

Cluny's excess. The basilicas at Autun and Vézelay remain today in all their noble simplicity, yet manifest some of the finest Romanesque sculpture ever created; the tympanum at Autun rejects all time frames in its visionary daring.

It's almost unfair to the rest of France that all this history, all this art, all this natural beauty comes with delicious refreshments. As if to live up to the extraordinary quality of its Chablis, its Chassagne-Montrachet, its Nuits-St-Georges, its Gevrey-Chambertin, Burgundy flaunts some of the best good, plain food in the world. Once you taste a licensed and diploma'd *poulet de Bresse* (Bresse chicken) embellished by the poetry of one perfect glass of Burgundian pinot noir, you won't be surprised to see that food and drink entries will take up as much space in your travel diary as the sights you see.

NORTHWEST BURGUNDY

Arriving in Burgundy from Paris by car, we suggest you grand-tour it from Sens to Autun. In northern Burgundy, the accents are thinner than around Dijon, and sunflowers cover the countryside instead of vineyards. Near Auxerre, many small, unheard-of villages boast a château or a once-famous abbey; they happily see few tourists, partly because public transportation is more than a bit spotty. Highlights of northern Burgundy include Sens's great medieval cathedral, historic Troyes, Auxerre's Flamboyant Gothic cathedral, the great Romanesque sculptures of the basilica at Vézelay and the cathedral at Autun. Outside these major centers of northwest Burgundy, countryside villages are largely preserved in a rural landscape that seems to have remained the same for centuries. If you're driving down from Paris, we suggest you take the A6 into Burgundy (or alternatively the A5 direct to Troyes) before making a scenic clockwise loop around the Parc du Morvan.

SENS

112 km (70 mi) southeast of Paris on N6.

Sens may be world-famous for its spectacular cathedral but it also has a reputation as a very pretty town. It enjoys a "four-leaf" ranking as a *ville fleurie,* or floral city. This finds happy and full botanical expression in the excellently manicured city parks (the Moulin à Tan and the Square Jean-Cousin) and municipal greenhouses, as well as during the Fête de la Saint-Fiacre, named after the patron saint of gardeners. For the latter, on the second Sunday in September, everything and everyone are festooned with flowers as entertainment fills the streets. But anytime during the year, the great **Cathédrale St-Étienne makes a trip here worth-while.**

GETTING HERE

It makes sense for Sens to be your first stop in Burgundy, since it's only 90 minutes by car from Paris on the N6, a fast road that hugs the pretty Yonne Valley south of Fontainebleau. Training in and out of Sens is a breeze as it's on a major route with 28 direct TER trains (€17.20) leaving the Paris Gare de Bercy train station weekdays and

23 on weekends. TER trains from Paris Gare de Bercy can take you to Auxerre (€24.70), Dijon (€39.20), Beaune (€42.50), and many points between. Avallon (€30.30) can be reached directly twice daily, leaving Paris at 8:20 AM and 12:20 PM. The regional TransYonne bus network, in conjunction with Les Rapides de Bourgogne (☎ *03–86–64–83–91* 🌐 *www.rapidesdebourgogne.com*), runs a noon link from the SNCF station in Sens to Auxerre on Wednesday and on demand on Saturday (☎ *0800–303–309 for information and to reserve*).

Visitor Information Sens Tourist Office. ✉ *Pl. Jean-Jaurès* ☎ *03–86–65–19–49* 🌐 *www.office-de-tourisme-sens.com.*

EXPLORING

Fodor's Choice ★ Historically linked more with Paris than with Burgundy, Sens was for centuries the ecclesiastical center of France and is still dominated by its **Cathédrale St-Étienne**, once the French sanctuary for Thomas à Becket and a model for England's Canterbury Cathedral. You can see the cathedral's 240-foot south tower from way off; the highway forges straight past it. The pompous 19th-century buildings lining the narrow main street—notably the meringuelike Hôtel de Ville—can give you a false impression if you're in a hurry: the streets leading off it near the cathedral (notably Rue Abelard and Rue Jean-Cousin) are full of half-timber medieval houses. On Monday the cathedral square is crowded with merchants' stalls, and the beautiful late-19th-century market hall—a distant cousin of Baltard's former iron-and-glass Halles in Paris—throbs with people buying meat and produce. A smaller market is held on Friday morning.

Begun around 1140, the cathedral once had two towers; one was topped in 1532 by an elegant though somewhat incongruous Renaissance campanile that contains two monster bells; the other collapsed in the 19th century. Note the trefoil arches decorating the exterior of the remaining tower. The gallery, with statues of former archbishops of Sens, is a 19th-century addition, but the statue of St. Stephen, between the doors of the central portal, is thought to date from late in the 12th century. The vast, harmonious interior is justly renowned for its stained-glass windows; the oldest (circa 1200) are in the north transept and include the stories of the Good Samaritan and the Prodigal Son; those in the south transept were manufactured in 1500 in Troyes and include a much-admired *Tree of Jesse*. Stained-glass windows in the north of the chancel retrace the story of Thomas à Becket: Becket fled to Sens from England to escape the wrath of Henry II before returning to his cathedral in Canterbury, where he was murdered in 1170. Below the window (which shows him embarking on his journey in a boat, and also at the moment of his death) is a medieval statue of an archbishop said to have come from the site of Becket's home in Sens. Years of restoration work have permitted the display of Becket's *aube* (vestment) in the annex to the Palais Synodal. ✉ *Pl. de la République* ☎ *03–86–83–06–29*.

The roof of the 13th-century **Palais Synodal** *(Synodal Palace)*, alongside Sens's cathedral, is notable for its yellow, green, and red diamond-tile motif—incongruously added in the mid-19th century by medieval monument restorer Viollet-le-Duc. Its six grand windows and vaulted

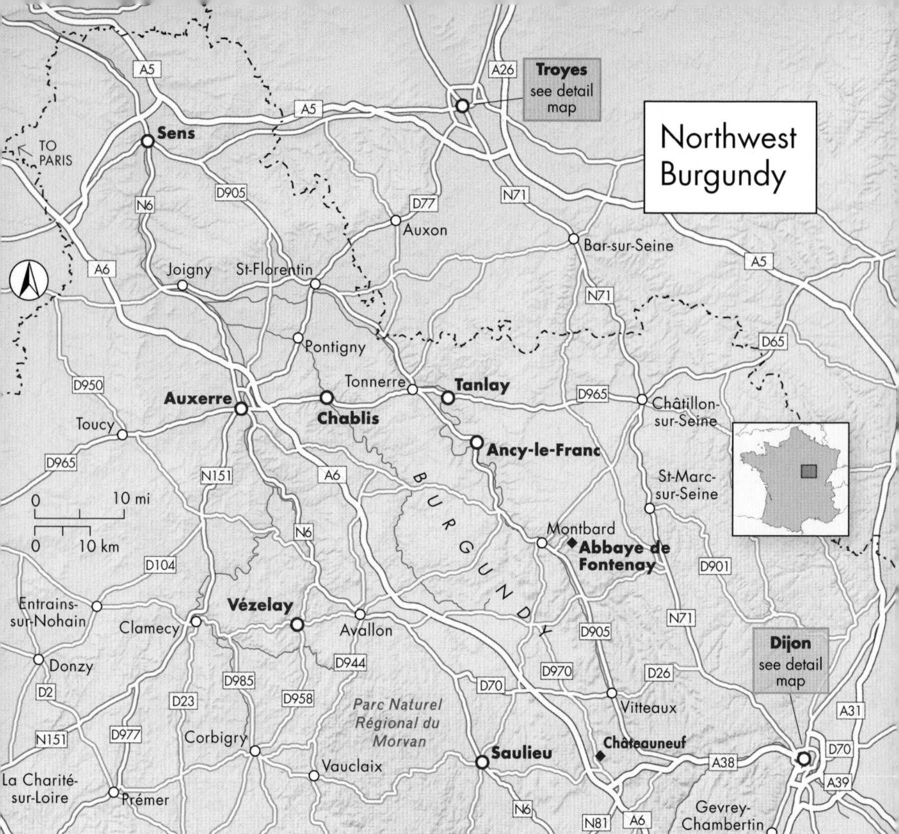

Synodal Hall are outstanding architectural features; the building now functions as an exhibition space. Annexed to the Palais Synodal is an ensemble of Renaissance buildings with a courtyard offering a fine view of the cathedral's Flamboyant Gothic south transept, constructed by master stonemason Martin Chambiges at the start of the 16th century (rose windows were his specialty, as you can appreciate here). Inside is a museum with archaeological finds from the Gallo-Roman period. The cathedral treasury, now on the museum's second floor, is one of the richest in France, comparable to that of Conques. It contains a collection of miters, ivories, the shrouds of St. Sivard and St. Loup, and sumptuous reliquaries. But the star of the collection is Thomas à Becket's restored brown-and-silver-edged linen robe. His chasuble, stole, and sandals are too fragile to display. ☎ *03–86–64–46–22* 🌐 *www.portaildusenonais.com/cathedrale* 🎫 *€4* ⏲ *June and Sept., Wed.– Mon. 10–noon and 2–6; July and Aug., Wed.–Mon. 10–6; Oct.–May, Wed. and weekends 10–noon and 2–6, Mon., Thurs., and Fri. 2–6.*

WHERE TO EAT AND STAY

$$$ SEAFOOD ✕ **Clos des Jacobins.** A modernizing face-lift in shades of chocolate and taupe can only serve to boost the popularity of this restaurant in the center of town, where the happy balance between elegant and casual finds expression in the wide choice of dishes on offer. The upscale à

la carte menu is replete with exceptional fish specialties while the €29 La Tradition menu includes a *joue de porc aux pruneaux et raisins* (pig cheeks with prunes and grapes) and *magret de canard grillé sauce au poivre* (grilled duck breast with pepper sauce). ✉ *49 Grande-Rue* ☎ *03–86–95–29–70* 🌐 *www.restaurantlesjacobins.com* ✍ *Reservations essential* 💳 *AE, MC, V* ⊗ *Closed Wed. No dinner Sun. or Tues.*

STOP TO SMELL THE ROSES

Sens has a four-leaf ranking as a *ville fleurie*, or floral city. This finds full botanical expression in the excellently manicured city parks (the Moulin à Tan and the Square Jean-Cousin) and municipal greenhouses, as well as during the Fête de la Saint-Fiacre, named after the patron saint of gardeners. For the latter, on the second Sunday in September, everything and everyone are festooned with flowers as entertainment fills the streets.

$$–$$$ ★ **La Lucarne aux Chouettes.** There's nothing Hollywood-esque about actress Leslie Caron's charmingly rustic riverside hotel and restaurant, the Owl's Nest, set in four 17th-century buildings. The lovely whitewash-brick dining room, with its ingenious twisted rope chandeliers, has a homey-meets-elegant feel, as do the rooms: the "Loft" is an enormous wood-beam aerie atop the house (the bathroom is in the room itself, just as it was in the rip-roaring days of the 1680s), while "The Suite" glows with a portrait of Sarah Bernhardt. The legendary hostess (the beloved Lili-Gigi-Fanny of everyone's memories) is often on hand to extend a warm greeting, although she does still depart for rare film shoots. In summer enjoy the terrace over the Yonne. The town itself, a *bastide* (fortified town, built on a grid pattern), is entered and exited via sturdy, angular 13th- and 14th-century gateways. **Pros:** stunning location; fabled owner-hostess. **Cons:** restaurant can be inconsistent. ✉ *7 quai Bretoche, 12 km (7 mi) south of Sens on N6 Villeneuve-sur-Yonne* ☎ *03–86–87–18–26* 🌐 *www.lesliecaron-auberge.com* *4 rooms* *In-room: no a/c. In-hotel: restaurant* 💳 *MC, V.*

TROYES

★ *64 km (40 mi) east of Sens, 150 km (95 mi) southeast of Paris.*

The inhabitants of Troyes would be dismayed if you mistook them for Burgundians. Troyes is the historic capital of the counts of Champagne but is, as the crow—if not the book—flies, some 50 miles south of the heart of Champagne province, so we retain it here, closer to Burgundy's treasures. Troyes was also the home of the late-12th-century writer Chrétien (or Chrestien) de Troyes who, in seeking to please his patrons, Count Henry the Liberal and Marie de Champagne, penned the first Arthurian legends. Few, if any, other French town centers contain so much to see. In the Vauluisant and St-Jean districts, a web of enchanting pedestrian streets with timber-frame houses, magnificent churches, fine museums, and a wide choice of restaurants makes the Old Town—Vieux Troyes—especially appealing.

Home to a famous cathedral, Sens also has many streets leading to atmospheric half-timber houses.

GETTING HERE

With the first train at 6:42, and then around one every hour until 19:11 at night, you can get to Troyes in around 90 minutes from Paris Gare de l'Est for the princely sum of €23.70. Sens to Troyes is a little harder with only one train at 14:15, which involves changing in Saint Florentin. The 3-hour plus journey costs €16.70.

Visitor Information Troyes Tourist Office. ✉ *16 bd. Carnot* ☎ *03–25–82–62–70* 🌐 *www.ot-troyes.fr* ✉ *Rue Mignard* ☎ *03–25–73–36–88.*

EXPLORING

Troyes is divided by the Quai Dampierre, a broad, busy thoroughfare. On one side is the quiet cathedral quarter, on the other the more upbeat commercial part. Keep your eyes peeled, instead, for the delightful architectural accents that make Troyes unique: *essentes,* geometric chestnut tiles that keep out humidity and are fire resistant; and sculpted *poteaux* (in Troyes they are called *montjoies*), carvings at the joint of corner structural beams. There's a lovely one of Adam and Eve next door to the Comtes de Champagne hotel. Along with its neighbors Provins and Bar-sur-Aube, Troyes was one of Champagne's major fair towns in the Middle Ages. The wool trade gave way to cotton in the 18th century when Troyes became the heartland of hosiery, and today Troyes draws millions of shoppers from all over Europe to scour for bargains at its outlet clothing stores.

The dynamic **tourist office** (✉ *16 bd. Carnot* ☎ *03–25–82–62–70* 🌐 *www.tourism-troyes.com*) has information and sells €15 passes that admit you to the town's major museums, with several theme-based state-of-the-art GPS audio guides (€5.50) and a champagne tasting thrown in.

⇨ *See the tourism Web site for further information on all the museums listed below.*

TOP ATTRACTIONS

7 ★ **Basilique St-Urbain.** Built between 1262 and 1286 by Pope Urban IV (who was born in Troyes), St-Urbain is one of the most remarkable churches in France, a perfect culmination of the Gothic quest to replace stone walls with stained glass. Its narrow porch frames a 13th-century *Last Judgment* tympanum, whose highly worked elements include a frieze of the dead rising out of their coffins (note the grimacing skeleton) and an enormous crayfish, a testament to the local river culture. Inside, a chapel on the south side houses the *Vièrge au Raisin* (*Virgin with Grapes*), clutching Jesus with one hand and a bunch of champagne grapes in the other. ✉ *Pl. Vernie* ☎ *03–25–73–37–13* 🎫 *Free* ⏲ *Tues.–Sat. 9:30–12:30 and 2–5:30, Sun. 2–5:30.*

4 **Cathédrale St-Pierre–St-Paul.** Noted monument of Flamboyant Gothic—a style regarded as the last gasp of the Middle Ages—this remarkable cathedral dominates the heart of Troyes; note the incomplete single-tower west front, the small Renaissance campaniles on top of the tower, and the artistry of Martin Chambiges, who worked on Troyes's facade (with its characteristic large rose window and flamboyant flames) around the same time as he did the transept of Sens. At night the floodlighted features burst into dramatic relief. The cathedral's vast five-aisle interior, refreshingly light thanks to large windows and the near-whiteness of the local stone, dates mainly from the 13th century. It has fine examples of 13th-century stained glass in the choir, such as the *Tree of Jesse* (a popular regional theme), and richly colored 16th-century glass in the nave and west front rose window. ✉ *Pl. St-Pierre* ☎ *03–25–76–98–18* 🎫 *Free* ⏲ *July–mid-Sept., daily 10:15–1 and 2–6; mid-Sept.–June, Tues.–Sat. 9:15–noon and 1–5:45, Sun. 2:15–4:45.*

3 ★ **Musée d'Art Moderne** *(Modern Art Museum).* Housed in the 16th- to 17th-century bishop's palace, this museum allures with its magnificent interior, with a wreath-and-cornucopia carved oak fireplace, ceilings with carved wood beams, and a Renaissance staircase. The jewel of the museum is the Lévy Collection, one of the finest provincial collections in France, including Art Deco glassware, tribal art, and an important group of Fauve paintings by André Derain and others. ✉ *Palais Épiscopal, Pl. St-Pierre* ☎ *03–25–76–26–80* 🎫 *€5* ⏲ *Tues.–Sun. 10–1 and 2–6.*

5 ★ **Musée St-Loup.** The former 18th-century abbey of St-Loup to the side of the cathedral now houses this arts and antiquities museum noted for its superlative collection of old-master paintings. Exhibits are devoted to natural history, with impressive collections of birds and meteorites; local archaeological finds, especially gold-mounted 5th-century jewelry and a Gallo-Roman bronze statue of Apollo; medieval statuary and gargoyles; and paintings from the 15th to the 19th century, including works by Rubens, Anthony Van Dyck, Antoine Watteau, François Boucher, and Jacques-Louis David. ✉ *1 rue Chrestien-de-Troyes* ☎ *03–25–76–21–68* 🎫 *€4* ⏲ *Tues.–Sun. 9–noon and 1–5.*

10 **Ste-Madeleine.** The oldest church in Troyes, Ste-Madeleine is best known for its elaborate triple-arch stone rood screen separating the nave and

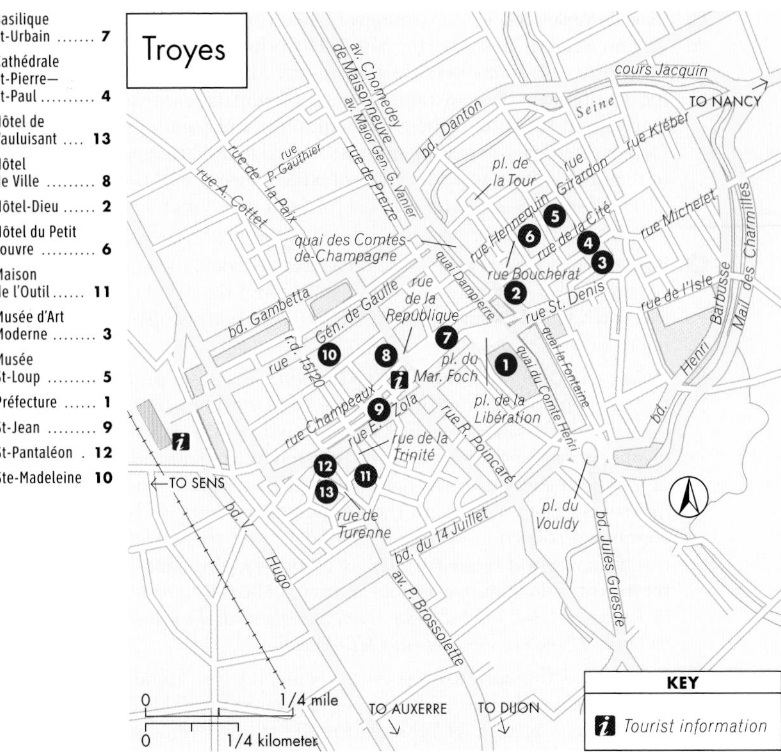

the choir. Only six other such screens still remain in France—most were dismantled during the French Revolution. This filigreed Flamboyant Gothic beauty was carved with panache by Jean Gailde between 1508 and 1517. The superbly tranquil Garden of the Innocents, newly established on the ancient "children's graveyard," symbolizes medieval spirituality. ✉ *Rue de la Madeleine* ☎ *03–25–73–82–90* 🎫 *Free* ⏲ *Tues.–Sat. 9:30–12:30 and 2–5:30, Sun. 2–5:30.*

WORTH NOTING

❷ **Hôtel-Dieu** *(hospital).* Across the Bassin de la Préfecture, an arm of the Seine, is this historic hospital, fronted by superb 18th-century wrought-iron gates topped with the blue-and-gold fleurs-de-lis emblems of the French monarchy. Around the corner is the entrance to the **Apothicairerie de l'Hôtel-Dieu,** a former medical laboratory, the only part of the Hôtel-Dieu open to visitors. Inside, time has been suspended: floral-painted boxes and ceramic jars containing medicinal plants line the antique shelves. ✉ *Quai des Comtes-de-Champagne* ☎ *03–25–80–98–97* 🎫 *€2* ⏲ *July and Aug., Tues.–Sun. 9–5; Sept.–June, Tues.–Sun. 9–noon and 1–5.*

❻ **Hôtel du Petit Louvre.** A former coaching inn, this is a handsome example of 16th-century architecture. ✉ *Pl. du Préau*

13 ★ **Hôtel de Vauluisant.** This charmingly turreted 16th- to 17th-century mansion houses two museums: the **Musée Historique** (History Museum) and the **Musée de la Bonneterie** (Textile-Hosiery Museum). The former traces the development of Troyes and southern Champagne, with a particularly magnificent selection of religious sculptures and paintings of the late-Gothic era; the latter outlines the history and manufacturing procedures of the town's 18th- to 19th-century textile industry. ✉ *4 rue Vauluisant* ☎ *03–25–43–43–20* 🎫 *Joint ticket for both museums €3* ⏲ *Tues.–Sun. 9–noon and 1–5.*

8 **Hôtel de Ville** *(Town Hall).* Place du Maréchal-Foch, the main square of central Troyes, is flanked by cafés, shops, and the delightful facade of this town hall. In summer the square is filled with people from morning to night.

11 **Maison de l'Outil** *(Tool and Craft Museum).* There's a practical reason why the windows of this mansion are filled with bizarre and beautiful outsize models—like a winding staircase and a globe on a swivel. It's the display venue for the "showpieces" created by apprentice Compagnons de Devoir, members of the national craftsmen's guild whose school is in Troyes. The museum, in the 16th-century Hôtel de Mauroy, also contains a collection of carvings, models, and tools relevant to such traditional wood-related trades as carpentry, clog making, and barrel making—including a medieval anvil, called a *bigorne.* ✉ *7 rue de la Trinité* ☎ *03–25–73–28–26* 🌐 *www.maison-de-l-outil.com* 🎫 *€6.50* ⏲ *Daily 10–6; closed Tues. in Oct.–Mar.*

1 **Préfecture.** Although Troyes is on the Seine, it's the capital of the Aube *département* (province), which is administered from this elegant mansion, a pretty picture set behind gleaming gilt-iron railings.

9 **Saint-Jean-au-Marché.** The clock tower of this church is an unmistakable landmark. England's warrior king Henry V married Catherine of France here in 1420. The church's tall 16th-century choir contrasts with the low nave, constructed earlier. The church's recent 10-year-long renovation has brought a healthy sheen to the stone gargoyles. ✉ *Pl. du Marché au Pain* 🎫 *Free.*

12 **St-Pantaléon.** This 16th- to 18th-century church of primarily serves the local Polish community. A number of fine canopied stone statues, many of them the work of the Troyen Dominique Florentin, decorator to François I, are clustered around its pillars. ✉ *Rue de Turenne* ☎ *03–25–73–06–99* 🎫 *Free* ⏲ *Tues.–Sat. 9:30–12:30 and 2–5:30, Sun. 2–5:30.*

WHERE TO EAT AND STAY

$ FRENCH ✕ **Le Bistroquet.** Everything here is authentic, from the splendid Belle Epoque decor to the rustic home-made cuisine. The two- and three-course menus, €18.60 and €29.40, give access to a choice of brasserie classics, including homemade pâté, slow-cooked lamb shanks with beans, and—a departure—wok-fried Chinese noodles with scallops. The local delicacy, andouillette, is an acquired taste well worth acquiring, and is made especially well here. Desserts are equally imposing, including the all-you-can-eat chocolate mousse. ✉ *Pl. Langevin* ☎ *03–25–73–65–65* 🌐 *www.bistroquet-troyes.fr* 💳 *AE, MC, V* ⏲ *No dinner Sun. Closed Sun. end of June–Aug.*

¢–$ **Comtes de Champagne.** In Vieux Troyes's former mint, a topsy-turvy 16th-century building, this bargain hotel has a quaint inner courtyard with large vines, a philodendron, and refurbished rooms with iron bedsteads. Ask for the largest room, on the second floor, one of the few with its own bath. The two couples who co-manage, the Guibourets and the Picards, are friendly folks. **Pros:** good value; old-fashioned charm; central location. **Cons:** bathrooms are a bit spartan and most are shared; no air-conditioning. ✉ *54–56 rue de la Monnaie* ☎ *03–25–73–11–70* 🌐 *www.comtesdechampagne.com* *35 rooms, 8 with bath* *In-room no a/c, Wi-Fi. In-hotel: bicycles, parking (paid)* *AE, MC, V.*

A TOWN MADE FOR WALKERS

The tourist literature is quick to tell you that Troyes's Old Town resembles a champagne cork: the Seine flows around what would be the top half and the train station is at the bottom. Though large for a cork, Troyes is small for a town; everything is accessible by foot—although you can hop on Le Bus to get around if you wish.

$$$–$$$$ Fodor's Choice ★ **Le Champ des Oiseaux.** Idyllically situated in ancient Troyes and named after the city's centuries-old roosting haunts of storks, this ensemble of three vine-clad pink-and-yellow 15th- and 16th-century houses (their bright colors are part of a town campaign to "medievalize" half-timber facades) seems ready to receive Manon Lescaut on the run. A daub-and-wattle facade abuzz with the pattern of timbered logs and a storybook courtyard, graced with a fairy-tale staircase, overhanging porch, and cobblestone patio, all set the scene for the charm within. Tin chandeliers, Nantes silks and calico hangings, 15th-century scrollwork panels, beamed roofs right out of the *Return of Martin Guerre,* and more traditional luxe touches make the interiors a joy. The guest salon is set in a vaulted cave-wine cellar fitted out with the latest in soigné furniture. The biggest guest room, the Suite Médiévale, is under the oak-beam eaves, while the Salle Bleue (Blue Room) looks worthy of the cover of *Maison Française.* **Pros:** quiet, comfortable rooms; friendly service; kid friendly. **Cons:** breakfast and parking cost extra. ✉ *20 rue Linard-Gonthier* ☎ *03–25–80–58–50* 🌐 *www.champdesoiseaux.com* *9 rooms, 3 suites* *In-room: no a/c, Wi-Fi. In-hotel: room service, parking (paid)* *AE, DC, MC, V.*

$–$$ **Relais St-Jean.** This half-timber hotel, in the pedestrian zone near the church of St-Jean, has changed hands recently and the good-size rooms and modern decor have undergone a refreshing and colorful transformation, the white-and-pastel-color walls contrasting tastefully with multihue furnishings. Some rooms are connected by a path running through the second floor's tree-filled atrium. The new powder-pink velvet upholstery in the predominantly dark-wall bar is worth sinking into for a pre-dinner cocktail. **Pros:** good-size rooms; friendly service; interesting bar. **Cons:** rooms sometimes feel overheated and some get street noise. ✉ *51 rue Paillot-de-Montabert* ☎ *03–25–73–89–90* 🌐 *www.relais-st-jean.com* *25 rooms* *In-room: a/c, refrigerator, Wi-Fi. In-hotel: bar, parking (paid)* *AE, DC, MC, V.*

SHOPPING

If there's an ideal place for a shopping spree, it's Troyes. Many clothing manufacturers are just outside town, clustered together in two large suburban malls: **Marques Avenue,** in St-Julien-les-Villas (take N71 toward Dijon); and **Marques City** and the American outlet store **McArthur Glen,** in Pont-Ste-Marie (take N77 toward Chalons-sur-Marne). Ralph Lauren and Calvin Klein at McArthur Glen face off with Laura Ashley at Marques Avenue and Doc Martens at Marques City, to name a few of the shops. The malls are open Monday 2–7, Tuesday–Friday 10–7, and Saturday 9:30–7.

AUXERRE

Fodor's Choice ★ *21 km (13 mi) southwest of Pontigny, 58 km (36 mi) southeast of Sens.*

Auxerre is a beautifully evocative town with three imposing and elegant churches perched above the Yonne River. Its steep, undulating streets are full of massively photogenic, half-timber houses in every imaginable style and shape. Yet this harmonious, architecturally interesting town is underappreciated, perhaps because of its location, midway between Paris and Dijon.

GETTING HERE

Auxerre is quite easily reached by rail from Gare Paris-Bercy by one of eight direct trains from Paris-Bercy daily (leaving every 2 hours from 6:20 AM to 8:20 PM). The fare is €24.70. Five trains a day put Sermizelles-Vézelay (€7.40) just one hour away, where you can take either a taxi (☎ *03–86–32–31–88*) during the week or the noon-only Saturday bus service to connect to Vézelay proper. Next stop Avallon provides six daily connections to Saulieu (€7.50) and Autun (€13.50). Twelve daily trains link Auxerre to Montbard (€15.70), mostly via Laroche-Migennes, with Dijon at the end of the line (€25.00). The TransYonne bus network (Les Rapides de Bourgogne) links Auxerre to Sens, Avallon, and Tonnerre with a daily service. Chablis can be reached daily at 11:40 AM, 4:10 PM (both on request only), and 5:58 PM by bus from the SNCF station. If you're driving, Auxerre is served by several major arteries including the A6 autoroute (Autoroute of the Sun) and the N6 (National 6).

Visitor Information Auxerre Tourist Office. ✉ *1 quai de la République* ☎ *03–86–51–03–26* 🌐 *www.ot-auxerre.fr.*

EXPLORING

Fanning out from Auxerre's main square, **Place des Cordeliers** (just up from the cathedral), are a number of venerable, crooked, steep streets lined with half-timber and stone houses. The best way to see them is to start from the riverside on the Quai de la République, where you find the tourist office (and can pick up a handy local map), and continue along the Quai de la Marine. The medieval arcaded gallery of the **Ancien Evêché** (Old Bishop's Palace), now an administrative building, is just visible on the hillside beside the tourist office. At **9 rue de la Marine** (which leads off one of several riverside squares) are the two oldest houses in Auxerre, dating from the end of the 14th century. Continue up the hill to Rue de l'Yonne, which leads into the **Rue Cochois.** Here, at No. 23, is the appropriately topsy-turvy home and shop of a *maître verrier* (lead-glass maker). Closer to the center of town, the most beautiful of Auxerre's many *poteaux* (the carved tops of wooden corner posts) can be seen at **8 rue Joubert**: The building dates from the late 15th century, and its Gothic tracery windows, acorns, and oak leaves are an open-air masterpiece.

A MAP IS A MUST

Get a map from the tourist office because Auxerre's layout is confusing. The main part of the Old Town is west of the Yonne River and ripples out from Place des Cordeliers.

The town's dominant feature is the ascending line of three magnificent churches—St-Pierre, St-Étienne, and St-Germain—and the **Cathédrale St-Étienne**, in the middle, rising majestically above the squat houses around it. The 13th-century choir, the oldest part of the edifice, contains its original stained glass, dominated by brilliant reds and blues. Beneath the choir, the frescoed 11th-century Romanesque crypt keeps company with the treasury, which has a panoply of medieval enamels, manuscripts, and miniatures. A 75-minute son-et-lumière show focusing on Roman Gaul is presented every evening from June to September. ✉ *Pl. St-Étienne* ☎ *03–86–52–23–29* 🎫 *Crypt €3, treasury €1.90* ⏲ *Easter–Nov., Mon.–Sat. 9–6, Sun. 2–6; Nov.–Easter, Mon.–Sat. 10–5, Sun. 2–5.*

North of Place des Cordeliers is the former **Abbaye de St-Germain**, which stands parallel to the cathedral some 300 yards away. The church's earliest aboveground section is the 12th-century Romanesque bell tower, but the extensive underground crypt was inaugurated by Charles the Bald in 859 and contains its original Carolingian frescoes and Ionic capitals. It's the only monument of its kind in Europe—a labyrinth retaining the plan of the long-gone church built above it—and was a place of pilgrimage until Huguenots burned the remains of its namesake, a Gallo-Roman governor and bishop of Auxerre, in the 16th century. ✉ *Pl. St-Germain* ☎ *03–86–18–05–50* 🎫 *€4.80* ⏲ *As the abbey is undergoing significant restructuring in 2010, it is advisable to call ahead before visiting.*

9

WHERE TO EAT AND STAY

$$$$ FRENCH ✕ **Le Jardin Gourmand.** As its name implies, this restaurant in a former manor house has a pretty garden (*jardin*) where you can dine on summer evenings. There's also an organic vegetable garden producing fresh herbs, gorgeous greens, and other foods that wind up on the table. The interior is accented by sea-green and yellow panels and is equally congenial and elegant. The menu, which changes eight times a year, shows both flair and invention. The staff is discreet and friendly. ✉ *56 bd. Vauban* ☎ *03–86–51–53–52* 🌐 *www.lejardingourmand.com* 💳 *MC, V* ⏲ *Closed 1 wk in mid-Mar., mid-June–July 1, 1st wk in Sept., Nov., and Tues. and Wed. year-round.*

$ ★ 🏨 **Château de Ribourdin.** Retired farmer Claude Brodard began building his *chambres d'hôte* (bed-and-breakfast) in an old stable, bucolically enshrined just south of Auxerre, 13 years ago, and the result is cozy, comfortable, and reasonably priced. Château de Laborde is

Presided over by the Cathédrale St-Etienne, Auxerre is a medieval beauty filled with historic churches.

the smallest, sunniest, and most intimate room, but they all overlook Monsieur Brodard's fields. Homemade preserves—cassis, quince, and carrot—are served at breakfast. **Pros:** tasteful rooms; beautiful location; great breakfast, swimming pool. **Cons:** can feel a little isolated; no credit cards. ✉ *8 rte. de Ribourdin, 8 km (5 mi) southwest of Auxerre on D1 Chevannes* ☎ *03–86–41–23–16* 🌐 *www.chateauderibourdin.com* *5 rooms* *In-room: no a/c, no phone, no TV, Wi-Fi. In-hotel: pool* *No credit cards* *BP.*

$ **Normandie.** A rather grand 19th-century mansion, the vine-covered Normandie is close to the center of Auxerre and just a short walk from the cathedral. Rooms are unpretentious and clean. There's a billiard room, gym with sauna, and terrace that is a nice place to relax after a long day of sightseeing. **Pros:** tidy rooms with nice bathrooms; helpful staff; games room and gym. **Cons:** overall, a little lackluster; not in town center. ✉ *41 bd. Vauban* ☎ *03–86–52–57–80* 🌐 *www.hotelnormandie.fr* *47 rooms* *In-room: a/c, Wi-Fi. In-hotel: bar, gym, parking (paid), some pets allowed* *AE, DC, MC, V.*

CHABLIS

16 km (10 mi) east of Auxerre.

EXPLORING

The pretty village of Chablis nestles amid the towering vineyards that produce its famous white wine on the banks of the River Serein and is protected, perhaps from an ill wind, by the massive, round, turreted towers of the Porte Noël gateway. Although in America Chablis has become a generic name for cheap white wine, it's not so in France: here it's a bone-dry, slightly acacia-tasting wine of tremendous character, with the premier cru and grand cru wines standing head to head with the best French whites. Prices in the local shops tend to be inflated, so your best bet is to buy directly from a vineyard; keep in mind that most are closed Sunday. Check out *www.chablis-the-french-chic.com* for more information on Chablis and the region's vineyards.

The town's **Bureau Interprofessionnel des Vins de Bourgogne** can provide information on nearby cellars where you can take tours, taste wine, and learn all you need to know about the region's illustrious wine tradition. *1 rue de Chichae 03–86–42–42–22 www.vins-bourgogne.fr Sat.–Thurs. 8:30–12:30 and 1:30–5:30; Fri. 1:30–5:30.*

WHERE TO EAT AND STAY

$ ★ **Hostellerie des Clos.** The simple yet comfortable rooms at this moderately priced inn have cheerful floral curtains, but most of all, people come for chef Vincent Grassin's cooking, some of the best in the region. Try the pan-fried scallops served with caramelized cauliflower purée and truffle cream and you'll see why. **Pros:** newer rooms are large and well appointed; stellar food; great location. **Cons:** older rooms are a bit small; hot in summer (no a/c). *18 rue Jules-Rathier 03–86–42–10–63 www.hostellerie-des-clos.fr 26 rooms, 10 suites In-room: no a/c, refrigerator, Wi-Fi. In-hotel: restaurant, parking (free) AE, MC, V Closed late Dec.–late Jan. MAP.*

TANLAY

26 km (16 mi) east of Chablis.

Fodor's Choice ★ A masterpiece of the French early Baroque, the **Château de Tanlay**, built around 1550, is a miraculous survivor due to the fact that, unlike most aristos who fled the countryside to take up the royal summons to live at Versailles, the Marquis and Marquise de Tanlay opted to live here among their village retainers. Spectacularly adorned with rusticated obelisks, pagodalike towers, the finest in French Classicist ornament, and a "grand canal," the château is centered around a typical *cour d'honneur.* Inside, the Hall of Caesars vestibule, framed by wrought-iron railings, leads to a wood-panel salon and dining room filled with period furniture. A graceful staircase climbs to the second floor, which has the showstopper—a gigantic gallery frescoed in Italianate trompe l'oeil. A small room in the tower above was used as a secret meeting place by Huguenot Protestants during the 1562–98 Wars of Religion; note the cupola with its fresco of scantily

FLIGHT CRU

If Burgundy looks sublime from the ground, have you ever wondered what it looks like from the air? Wonder no longer: put a little wind beneath your wine-soaked wings. The **France Montgolfières Balloon Flights** (*02–54–32–20–48) www.franceballoons.com*) can float you for hours over Chablis and the Morvan region. **Montgolfières Air Escargot** (*03–85–87–12–30 www.air-escargot.com*) features some dandy flights over the châteaux of Burgundy. The price may be stratospheric, but so is the experience.

clad 16th-century religious personalities. ☎ *03–86–75–70–61* 🌐 *www.chateaux-france.com/tanlay* 🎟 *€2.50, guided tours €8.50* ⏲ *Apr.–Nov., tours Wed.–Mon. at 10, 11:30, 2:15, 3:15, 4:15, and 5:15.*

ANCY-LE-FRANC

14 km (9 mi) southeast of Tanlay.

It may be strange to find a textbook example of the Italian Renaissance in Ancy-le-Franc, but in mid-16th-century France the court had taken up this import as the latest rage. So, quick to follow the fashion and gain kingly favor, the Comte de Tonnerre decided to create a family seat using all the artists François I (1515–47) had summoned from Italy to his court at Fontainebleau.

Fodor's Choice ★ Built from Sebastiano Serlio's designs, with interior blandishments by Primaticcio, the **Château d'Ancy-le-Franc** is an important example of Italianism, less for its plain, heavy exterior than for its sumptuous rooms and apartments, many—particularly the magnificent Chambre des Arts (Art Gallery)—with carved or painted walls and ceilings and original furnishings. Here Niccolò dell'Abate and other court artists created rooms filled with murals depicting the signs of the zodiac, the Battle of Pharsala, and the motif of Diana in Her Bath (much favored by Diane de Poitiers, sister of the Comtesse de Tonnerre). Such grandeur won the approval of the Sun King, Louis XIV, no less, who once stayed in the Salon Bleu (Blue Room). ✉ *Pl. Clermont-Tonnerre* ☎ *03–86–75–14–63* 🌐 *www.chateau-ancy.com* 🎟 *€9* ⏲ *Apr.–mid-Nov., tours Tues.–Sun. at 10:30, 11:30, 2, 3, 4, and 5; Oct.–mid-Nov., tours Tues.–Sun. at 10:30, 11:30, 2, 3, and 4.*

ABBAYE DE FONTENAY

32 km (20 mi) southeast of Ancy-le-Franc.

Fodor's Choice ★ The best-preserved of the Cistercian abbeys, the Abbaye de Fontenay was founded in 1118 by St. Bernard. The same Cistercian criteria applied to Fontenay as to Pontigny: no-frills architecture and an isolated site—the spot was especially remote, for it had been decreed that these monasteries could not be established anywhere near "cities, feudal manors, or villages." The monks were required to live a completely self-sufficient existence, with no contact whatsoever with the outside world. By the end of the 12th century the buildings were finished, and the abbey's community grew to some 300 monks. Under the protection of Pope Gregory IX and Hughes IV, duke of Burgundy, the monastery soon controlled huge land holdings, vineyards, and timberlands. It prospered until the 16th century, when religious wars and administrative mayhem hastened its decline. Dissolved during the French Revolution, the abbey was used as a paper factory until 1906. Fortunately, the historic buildings emerged unscathed. The abbey is surrounded by extensive, immaculately tended gardens dotted with the fountains that gave it its name. The church's solemn interior is lightened by windows in the facade and by a double row of three narrow windows, representing the Trinity, in the choir. A staircase in the south transept leads to the

Continued on page 464

GRAPE EXPECTATIONS

A BURGUNDY WINE PRIMER

From the steely brilliance of *Premier Cru Chablis* in the north to the refined *Pouilly-Fuissés* in the south, Burgundy—*Bourgogne* to the French—is where you can sample deep-colored reds and full-flavored whites as you amble from one fabled vineyard to another along the **Route des Grands Crus**.

An oenophile's nirvana, Burgundy is accorded almost religious reverence, and with good reason: its famous chardonnays and pinot noirs, and the "second-tier" gamays and aligotés, were perfected in the Middle Ages by the great monasteries of the region.

The specific character of a Burgundy wine is often dependent on the individual grower or négociant's style. There are hundreds of vintners and merchants in this region, many of them producing top wines from surprisingly small parcels of land.

Adding to the complexity is France's century-old *appellation controllée*, or AOC, wine classification system. In Burgundy, it specifies vineyard, region, and quality. The most expensive, top-tiered wines are called *monopole* and *grand cru*, followed by *premier cru*, *village*, and generic *Bourgogne*. Although there are 100 different AOC wines in the area, the thicket of labels and names is navigable once you learn how to read the road signs; and the payoff is tremendous, with palate-pleasing choices for all budgets.

GEOGRAPHY + CLIMATE = *TERROIR*

Soil, weather conditions, grapes, and savoir-faire are the basic building blocks of all great wines, but this is particularly true in Burgundy, where grapes of the same variety, grown a few feet apart, might have different names and personalities, as well as varying prices.

CHABLIS

Chablis' famous chardonnays are produced along both banks of the Serein River. The four appellations, in ascending order of excellence, are Petit Chablis AOC, Chablis AOC, Chablis Premier Cru AOC, and Chablis Grand Cru AOC. Flinty and slightly acidic, with citrus, pineapple, and green apple flavors and aromas, they age well (except the Petit Chablis, which are best drunk young) and are typically less intense than other burgundy whites, due to their colder northern climate.

CÔTE DE NUITS

The northernmost area, the Côte de Nuits, sometimes called the "Champs-Elysées of Burgundy," is the land of the unparalleled Grand Cru. Deep and ruby rich in color, full of flesh coupled with a great "nose," the powerful pinot noir reds develop wonderfully with age, and are perfect matches for hearty Burgundian beef and game dishes.

CÔTE D'OR

The 30-mile long Côte d'Or contains two of the most gorgeous and distinguished wine regions. The best wines here come from Gevrey-Chambertin, Morey-St-Denis, Vougeot, Echézeaux, Vosne-Romanée, Romanée-Conti, Nuits-St-Georges, and Prémeaux. Marsannay produces a pale pink, mouth-watering rosé, by far the best in Burgundy.

CÔTE DE BEAUNE

The Côte de Beaune, just to the south, is known for both full-bodied reds and some of the world's best dry whites. Delicately flavored, the reds mature faster than those to the north and are best in Aloxe-Corton, Beaune, Pommard, Volnay, and Santenay. Whites are dry, crisp, and pale, with a delicate bouquet and a "fat" buttery quality. Search out Corton-Charlamagne in Aloxe-Corton, then head south for the storied Montrachets. Green-gold in color and aromatically complex, they are the universal standard for dry whites.

CÔTE CHALONNAISE

Farther south is the Côte Chalonnaise. Although not as famous, it produces chardonnays almost as rich as its northern neighbors. Pinot noirs with *villages* appellations Rully, Givry, and Mercurey are well-structured, with body, bouquet, and a distinction very similar to Côte de Beaune reds. Montagny and Rully whites are dry, light, well balanced, and fruity—much ends up in sparkling Crémant de Bourgogne. Bourgogne Aligoté de Bouzeron are worth a stop, too. Named after its grape, it is the fresh and lively white wine traditionally mixed with Crème de Cassis to make a Kir, but is just as delicious on its own.

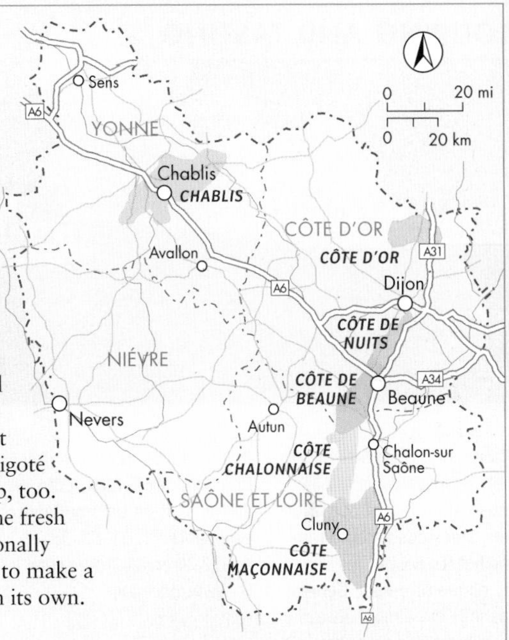

CÔTE MAÇONNAISE

Next is the Côte Maçonnaise, the largest of the four Côtes, which brings its own quality dry whites to the market, particularly the distinctive and refined Saint Vérans, Virés and the more famous Pouilly-Fuissés. With lightly oaked aromas of toast and hazelnuts, these are three of France's best wines for seafood. Macon *villages* light and fruity reds are drinkable but hardly worth a detour. The best are found between Hurigny and Viré and, like the whites, should be drunk young while they still have their freshness.

LABEL KNOW–HOW

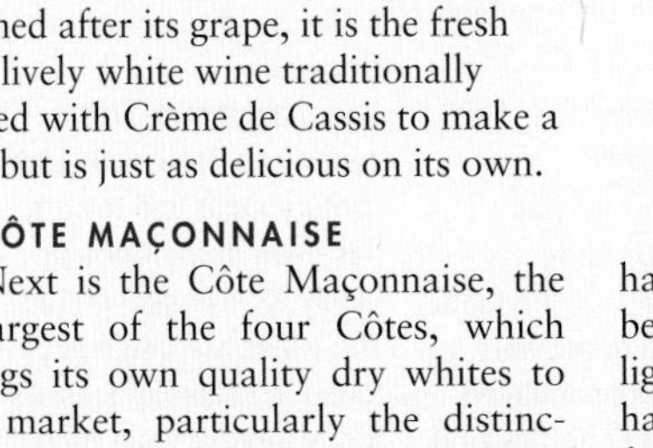

❶ The name and address of the proprietor.
❷ This wine was produced in the Montrachet region
❸ Number of bottles made
❹ Bottle number 1,201 and Vintage
❺ 'Made and bottled on the estate'—a great signifier of quality

FOR THE VINE INSPIRED

If you're going to spend a fortune on a bottle of Romanée-Conti and want to know how to savor it, sign up for one of the wine classes offered by Beaune's Ecole des Vins de Bourgogne, sponsored by the Bureau Interprofessionel des Vins de Bourgogne (✉ B.I.V.B.; 6 rue du 16éme Chasseur, 21200, Beaune ☎ 03–80–26–35–10 🌐 www.bivb.com, www.ecoledesvins-bourgogne.com). They offer several choices, ranging from a two-hour intro to a full weekend jammed with trips to vineyards and cellars in Maçon and Chablis.

TOURING AND TASTING

Cote de Nuits, Burgundy

There are a countless number of vineyards here, but these are a few of our favorites. Vineyards accept drop-ins but it's best to reserve by phone or e-mail. General tastings are almost always free, but buying a bottle is in good form. By-appointment tour prices vary with number of attendees and wines tasted. If you're not up for a drive you can taste many of these wines in town cellars or local restaurants.

Antonin Rodet

Makers of fine wines since 1875, Antonin Rodet's delivers a complete range of high quality but reasonably priced Burgundies. Six house-labeled wines can be tasted. Rodet has acquired a number of château wineries all over the region, but a visit to Château de Rully (Hautes Côtes de Beaune) or Domaine des Perdrix (Côte de Nuits), is an unforgettable experience. ☎ *03–85–98–12–12* ✉ *rodet@rodet.com* 🌐 *www.rodet.com*

Bouchard Père et Fils Château de Beaune

Bouchard is one of the major domaines and négociants in Beaune. Its unparalleled legacy of 50,000 bottles from the Côte de Beaune and Côte de Nuits appellations includes a unique collection of rare vintages dating back to the 19th century. The museum and 15th-century cellar is accessible year round (8–12; 2–6) but the personalized tour and extensive tasting is by appointment only. ☎ *03–80–24–80–24* ✉ *bpf@bouchard-pereetfils.com* 🌐 *http://www.bouchard-pereetfils.com*

Château De Chorey Les Beaune

This magnificent 17th-century château, with 13th-century moat and towers, has been in the Germain family for five generations. The wines are frequently found in cellars of France's top restaurants and though drop-in tastings are possible, a stay in one of the chambres d'hôtes, combined with the cellar visit and comprehensive tasting (3 reds and 3 whites) of the estate's wines, is a rare and exceptional experience. The château is open from Easter to end of October, up to 16 people can be accommodated overall in the luxurious five bedrooms (€185–€220) overlooking the vineyard, park or tower. English is spoken and pets are welcome. ☎ *03–80–22–06–05* ✉ *Contact@Chateau-De-Chorey-Les-Beaune.fr* 🌐 *www.chateau-de-chorey-les-beaune.fr*

■ **TIP→** Late summer is the most popular time to visit—which is reason enough to avoid it. Visit in spring, or the fall, just before the October harvests. Harvest time is exciting, but with everyone out in the fields, you're less likely to find anyone in the cellars to open a bottle for you to sample—unless you pitch in and help bring in the crop.

Château de Meursault

This elegant well-visited château has been producing a miraculous Meursault since the 7th century. Walk up the recently opened Allée des Maronniers, through the vines to the château's *cour d'honneur.* Cellars dating from the 14th and 16th centuries and an art gallery are included in the twice-daily guided tour, 9:30–12; 2:30–6, with a sommelier-aided tasting. €15 per person. English is spoken. ☎ *03–80–26–22–75* ✉ *www.meursault.com*

Château de Santenay

This majestic 9th–16th century castle is also the former residence (1302–1404) of Philippe le Hardi, son of the king of France. The estate has a total of 237 acres of vines, one of the largest in Burgundy. The château is open year round, seven days a week, a visit to the gardens and surrounding park culminates in a wine-tasting with bottles available for purchase. The award-wining Saint-Aubin 'En Vesvau', matured and aged in wooden casks, is a must-try as is the Château Philippe le Hardi AOC Aloxe-Corton "Les Brunettes et Planchots". The tour and wine tasting is €6 per person. English is spoken. ☎ *03–80–20–61–87* ✉ *contact@chateau-de-santenay.com* 🌐 *www.chateau-de-santenay.com*

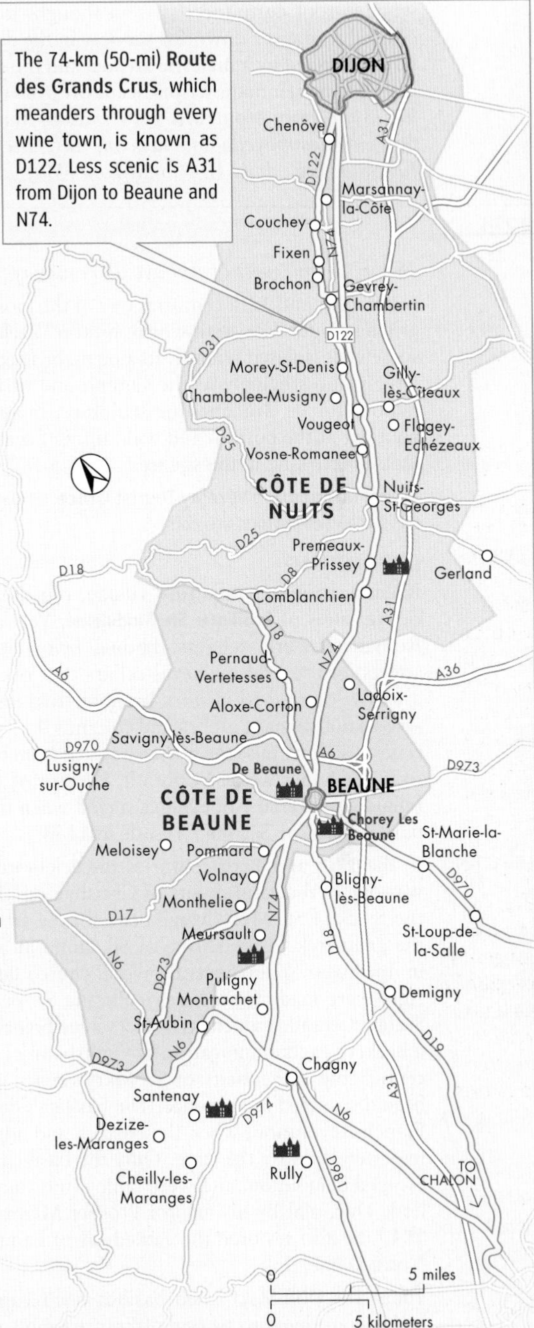

wooden-roof dormitory (spare a thought for the bleary-eyed monks, obliged to stagger down for services in the dead of night). The chapter house, flanked by a majestic arcade, and the scriptorium, where monks worked on their manuscripts, leads off from the adjoining cloisters. ✉ *6 km (3 mi) from Montbard TGV station, Marmagne* ☎ *03–80–92–15–00* 🌐 *www.abbayedefontenay.com* 🎫 *€8.90* 🕓 *Apr.–June, daily 10–6; July and Aug., daily 10–7; mid-Nov.–May, daily 10–noon and 2–5.*

VÉZELAY

48 km (30 mi) west of Abbaye de Fontenay.

In the 11th and 12th centuries one of the most important places of pilgrimage in the Christian world, hilltop Vézelay is today a picturesque, somewhat isolated, village. Its one main street, Rue St-Étienne, climbs steeply and stirringly to the summit and its medieval basilica, world-famous for its Romanesque sculpture. In summer you have to leave your car at the bottom and walk up. Off-season you can drive up and look for parking in the square.

Visitor Information Vézelay Tourist Office. ✉ *Rue St-Pierre* ☎ *03–86–33–23–69* 🌐 *www.vezelaytourisme.com.*

EXPLORING

It's easy to ignore this tiny village, but don't: other than the artistic treasures of **Basilique Ste-Madeleine,** Vézelay has an array of other Romanesque-era delights. Hiding below its narrow *ruelles* (small streets) are several medieval cellars that once sheltered pilgrims and are now opened to visitors by home owners in summer. Sections of several houses have arches and columns dating from the 12th and 13th centuries: don't miss the hostelry across from the tourist office and, next to it, the house where Louis VII, Eleanor of Aquitaine, and the king's religious supremo Abbé Suger stayed when they came to hear St. Bernard preach the Second Crusade in 1146.

Fodor's Choice ★

In the 11th and 12th centuries the celebrated **Basilique Ste-Madeleine** was one of the focal points of Christendom. Pilgrims poured in to see the relics of St. Mary Magdalene (in the crypt) before setting off on the great trek to the shrine of St. James at Santiago de Compostela, in northwest Spain. Several pivotal church declarations of the Middle Ages were made from here, including St. Bernard's preaching of the Second Crusade (which attracted a huge French following) and Thomas à Becket's excommunication of English king Henry II. By the mid-13th century the authenticity of St. Mary's relics was in doubt; others had been discovered in Provence. The basilica's decline continued until the French Revolution, when the basilica and adjoining monastery buildings were sold by the state. Only the basilica, cloister, and dormitory escaped demolition, and were falling into ruin when ace restorer Viollet-le-Duc, sent by his mentor Prosper Merimée, rode to the rescue in 1840 (he also restored the cathedrals of Laon and Amiens and Paris's Notre-Dame).

Today the UNESCO-listed basilica has recaptured much of its glory and is considered to be one of France's most prestigious Romanesque showcases. The exterior tympanum was redone by Viollet-le-Duc (have a look at the eroded original as you exit the cloister), but the narthex (circa 1150) is a Romanesque masterpiece. Note the interwoven zodiac signs and depictions of seasonal crafts along its rim, similar to those at both Troyes and Autun. The pilgrims' route around the building is indicated by the majestic flowers, which metamorphose into full-blown blooms, over the left-hand entrance on the right; an annual procession is still held on July 22. The basilica's exterior is best seen from the leafy terrace to the right of the facade. Opposite, a vast, verdant panorama encompasses vines, lush valleys, and rolling hills. In the foreground is the Flamboyant Gothic spire of St-Père-sous-Vézelay, a tiny village 3 km (2 mi) away that is the site of Marc Meneau's famed restaurant. ✉ *Pl. de la Basilique* ☎ *03–86–33–39–50* 🌐 *www.vezelaytourisme.com* 🎫 *Free, €3.20 for guided tour (phone for reservations)* 🕓 *Tues.–Sat. 9:30–noon and 2:45–4:45.*

FEAST THE EYES AND THE SOUL

The faithful have been making the pilgrimage to Vézelay since the 12th century, when it was the departure point for the Second and Third Crusades. All marvel at the feast of sculptural details of the Basilique Ste-Madeleine, complete with biblical scenes, Christ figures, and a tongue-flailing demon bearing a strange resemblance to Jim Morrison in concert. Just behind the basilica is a park that's great for picnics and views of the Parc du Morvan.

WHERE TO EAT AND STAY

$$$ FRENCH ✕ **Bougainville.** One of the few affordable restaurants in this well-heeled town is in an old house with a fireplace in the dining room and the requisite Burgundian color scheme of brown, yellow, and ocher. Philippe Guillemard presides in the kitchen, turning out such regional favorites as hare stew, crayfish, escargot ragout in chardonnay sauce, and venison with chestnuts. He has also devised a vegetarian menu—a rarity in Burgundy—with deeply satisfying dishes like terrine of Époisses cheese and artichokes. ✉ *26 rue St-Étienne* ☎ *03–86–33–27–57* ✍ *Reservations essential* 💳 *MC, V* 🕓 *Closed Tues. and Wed., and mid-Nov.–Feb.*

$$$–$$$$ ★ **L'Espérance.** Heading one of the greatest kitchens in Burgundy, chef Marc Meneau is justly renowned for his original creations, such as roast veal in a bitter caramel-based sauce and turbot in a salt *croûte.* The setting—by a stream and a large, statue-filled garden with Vézelay in the background—is exquisite. Note that the restaurant is closed Tuesday and there's no lunch Monday or Wednesday. Accommodations, which vary in price, come in a trinity of delights: charming rooms overlooking the garden; full suites in a renovated mill by the trout stream; and rooms in the annex, the Pré des Marguerites, done up in a cozy *style anglais.* **Pros:** spectacular restaurant; charming, bucolic setting. **Cons:** uneven service; some rooms are uninspiring. ✉ *St-Père-sous-Vézelay, St-Père* ☎ *03–86–33–39–10* 🌐 *www.marc-meneau.com* ✍ *Reservations essential* 🛏 *34 rooms* 👍 *In-room: a/c (some), refrigerator, Wi-Fi. In-hotel: restaurant, pool* 💳 *AE, DC, MC, V* 🕓 *Closed mid-Jan.–Feb.* 🍽 *MAP.*

9

$–$$ **Poste & Lion d'Or.** On a small square in the lower part of town is this rambling hotel, completely renovated in a traditional style in 2006. A terrace out front welcomes you; the good-size rooms have traditional chintzes. The comfortable restaurant is a popular spot with locals, who come for the regional fare, where the three-course, €26 menu includes rich pumpkin soup and cod in a chorizo crust with lobster coulis. **Pros:** big rooms with balconies; good food; friendly staff; great location. **Cons:** some rooms get street noise. ✉ *Pl. du Champ de Foire* ☎ *03–86–33–21–23* 🌐 *www.laposte-liondor.com* *37 rooms, 1 suite* *In-room: a/c, Wi-Fi. In-hotel: restaurant, bar* *AE, DC, MC, V* *Closed Jan. and Feb.* *MAP.*

$ **Val en Sel.** The four classically decorated, color-coded rooms, all with private entrances and en suite bathrooms, belie the bed-and-breakfast tag of this picturesque 18th-century country residence. The spectacular walled flower garden, hailed as one of the world's finest, is a fragrant haven of calm. Within walking distance of Vézelay itself and on the edge of the Morvan, it's an ideal base for touring the region. **Pros:** beautiful gardens; comfortable, spacious rooms. **Cons:** car essential; no credit cards. ✉ *1 Chemin de la Fontaine, St-Père-sous-Vézelay, 2 km east of Vézelay* ☎ *03–86–33–26–95* 🌐 *valensel.vezelay.free.fr* *3 rooms, 2 suites* *In-room: no a/c, no TV, Wi-Fi* *No credit cards* *Closed mid-Nov.–Easter.*

SAULIEU

48 km (30 mi) southeast of Vézelay.

Saulieu's reputation belies its size: it's renowned for good food (Rabelais, that roly-poly 16th-century man of letters, extolled its gargantuan hospitality) and Christmas trees (a staggering million are packed and sent off from the area each year).

The town's **Basilique St-Andoche** (✉ *Pl. du Docteur Roclore* *Closed Mon.*) is almost as old as that of Vézelay, though less imposing and much restored. Note the impressive Romanesque capitals.

The **Musée François-Pompon**, adjoining the basilica, is a museum partly devoted to the work of animal-bronze sculptor Pompon (1855–1933), whose smooth, stylized creations seem contemporary but predate World War II. The museum also contains Gallo-Roman funeral stones, sacred art, and a room devoted to local gastronomic lore. ✉ *Rue Sallier* ☎ *03–80–64–19–51* *€3* *Apr.–Sept., Mon.–Sat. 10–12:30 and 2–6; Oct.–Dec. and Mar., Mon.–Sat. 10–12:30 and 2–5:30, Sun. 10:30–noon and 2:30–5.*

WHERE TO EAT AND STAY

$ **Chez Camille.** Small, quiet, and friendly sum up this hotel in a 16th-century house with an exterior so ordinary you might easily pass it by. But within, rooms have period furniture and original wooden beams. Ask for No. 22, or No. 23, the most dramatic, with a beamed ceiling that looks like spokes in a wheel. Traditional Burgundian fare—fowl and fish in abundance—makes up the menu in the glass-roof restaurant with its green wicker chairs. **Pros:** good value; traditional decor and food. **Cons:** restaurant and hotel both need updating. ✉ *1 pl. Édouard-Herriot, on N6 between Saulieu and Beaune, Arnay-le-Duc* ☎ *03–80–90–01–38* 🌐 *www.chez-camille.fr* *11 rooms* *In-room: no a/c, Internet, Wi-Fi. In-hotel: restaurant, Internet terminal* *AE, DC, MC, V* *MAP.*

$$$$ Fodor's Choice ★ **Relais Bernard Loiseau.** Originally a historic coaching auberge, this is now one of the region's finest hotels and restaurants. The setting is exquisite: a chapel-like wood-beam dining room with a lush flower garden radiating around it, with a spectacular exterior spiral staircase the cynosure of all eyes. Guest rooms combine exposed beams and glass panels with cheerful traditional furnishings; a newer annex has the most comfortable (and air-conditioned) rooms, while the more stylish accommodations (styles range from Louis XVI to Empire) are in the main house. Some are tiny (one is complete with porthole window), some are luxurious (one has a comfy balcony overlooking the countryside)—no matter which you book, try to get a room facing the gorgeous garden courtyard. In the restaurant, chef Patrick Bertron continues to turn out a feather-light nouvelle version of rich Burgundian fare pioneered by Bernard Loiseau, one of France's culinary superstars, who died in 2003. Beware: the prices are stratospheric. **Pros:** first-class facilities; stellar food. **Cons:** service in hotel and restaurant can be uneven. ✉ *2 rue d'Argentine, off N6, Saulieu* ☎ *03–80–90–53–53* 🌐 *www.bernard-loiseau.com* *33 rooms* *In-room: a/c (some). In-hotel: restaurant, gym, spa, Internet terminal* *AE, DC, MC, V* *Closed early Jan.–early Feb., and Tues. and Wed. until June* *BP.*

DIJON

38 km (23 mi) northeast of Châteauneuf, 315 km (195 mi) southeast of Paris.

You may never have been to Dijon but you've certainly tasted it. Many of the gastronomic specialties that originated here are known worldwide. They include snails (many now imported from the Czech Republic), mustard (although the handmade variety is becoming a lost art), and cassis (a black-currant liqueur often mixed with white wine—preferably Burgundy Aligoté—to make Kir, the popular aperitif). The city itself is a feast for the eyes, with charming streets, chic shops, and a panopy of medieval art. It has magnificent half-timber houses and *hôtels particuliers,* some rivaling those in Paris. There's also a striking trio of central churches, built one following the other for three distinct parishes—St-Bénigne, its facade distinguished by Gothic galleries; St-Philibert, Dijon's only Romanesque church (with Merovingian vestiges); and St-Jean, an asymmetrical building now used as a theater. Dijon scores as high artistically as it does gastronmically.

GETTING HERE

As the administrative capital of Burgundy, Dijon has most everything a city has to offer, including fast TGV train service. There are 15 TGV trains leaving Paris daily and 12 on weekends (€54.40), so getting to Dijon by train is perhaps the most efficient way of arriving on Burgundy's doorstep. Once here, the extensive TER network (Express Regional

Transport) can take you almost anywhere within the region, with frequent connections to Sens (€27), Nevers (€28), Beaune (€6.80), and Auxerre (€25). Right next to the Dijon Ville train station is the Gare Routière from which the regional TRANSCO (☎ *08–00–10–20–04* 🌐 *www.cotedor.fr*) bus company operates 32 regular shared school/public bus routes that crisscross the Côte d'Or. For wine lovers the No. 44 (Dijon–Beaune) represents the logical choice, with an itinerary that reads like an oenologist's wish list. The 12:25 PM will get you to the cellar(s) of your choice in time for an early afternoon tasting. Price is based on the number of sections traveled, and at €1.50 per section the trip to Beaune will cost you €3.

Visitor Information Dijon Tourist Office ✉ *11 rue des Forges* ☎ *03–80–44–11–44* 🌐 *www.dijon-tourism.com.*

EXPLORING

The erstwhile wine-mustard center of the world, site of an important university, and studded with medieval art treasures, Dijon is the age-old capital of Burgundy. It is a fun city to explore—it has the liveliness of a capital city without being too large and crowded, as well as impressive art and architecture. Many travelers feel it is the perfect French city, possessing the charm of a village as well as the sophistication of an urbane town.

Dijon was a major player in the history of Burgundy. Throughout the Middle Ages Burgundy was a duchy that led a separate existence from the rest of France, culminating in the rule of the four "Grand Dukes of the West" between 1364 and 1477—Philippe le Hardi (the Bold), Jean Sans Peur (the Fearless), Philippe le Bon (the Good), and the unfortunate Charles le Téméraire (the Foolhardy, whose defeat by French king Louis XI at Nancy spelled the end of Burgundian independence). A number of monuments date from this period, including the Palais des Ducs (Ducal Palace), now largely converted into an art museum. Dijon's fame and fortune outlasted its dukes, and the city continued to flourish under French rule from the 17th century on. It has remained the major city of Burgundy—and the only one with more than 150,000 inhabitants. Its site, on the major European north–south trade route and within striking distance of the Swiss and German borders, has helped maintain its economic importance. It's also a cultural center—*just a portion of its museums are mentioned below.*

THE HISTORIC CENTER

TOP ATTRACTIONS

8 **Cathédrale St-Bénigne.** The chief glory of this comparatively austere cathedral is its atmospheric 11th-century crypt, restored in 2008—a forest of pillars surmounted by a rotunda. ✉ *Rue du Dr. Maret.*

12 ★ **Chartreuse de Champmol.** All that remains of this former charterhouse—a half-hour walk from Dijon's center and now surrounded by a psychiatric hospital—are the exuberant 15th-century gateway and the *Puits de Moïse* (*Well of Moses*), one of the greatest examples of late-medieval sculpture. The well was designed by Flemish master Claus Sluter, who

also created several other masterpieces during the late 14th and early 15th centuries, including the tombs of the dukes of Burgundy. If you closely study Sluter's six large sculptures, you will discover the Middle Ages becoming the Renaissance right before your eyes. Representing Moses and five other prophets, they are set on a hexagonal base in the center of a basin and remain the most compellingly realistic figures ever crafted by a medieval sculptor. ✉ *Centre Hospitalier Spécialisé de la Chartreuse* 🎫 *€6 (Well of Moses).*

7 **Hôtel de Vogüé.** This stately 17th-century mansion has a characteristic red, yellow, and green Burgundian tile roof—a tradition whose disputed origins lie either with the Crusades and the adoption of Arabic tiles or with Philip the Bold's wife, Marguerite of Flanders. ✉ *8 rue de la Chouette.*

10 **Musée de la Vie Bourguignonne et d'Art Sacré** *(Museum of Burgundian Traditions and Religious Art).* Housed in the former Cistercian convent, one museum contains religious art and sculpture; the other has crafts and artifacts from Burgundy, including old storefronts saved from the streets of Dijon that have been reconstituted, in Hollywood moviemaking style, to form an imaginary street. ✉ *17 rue Ste-Anne* ☎ *03–80–48–80–90* 🎫 *Free* ⏲ *May–Sept., Wed.–Mon. 9–12:30 and 1:30–6; Oct.–Apr., Wed.–Mon. 9–noon and 2–6.*

2 **Musée Magnin.** In a 17th-century mansion, this museum showcases a private collection of original furnishings and paintings from the 16th to the 19th century. ✉ *4 rue des Bons-Enfants* ☎ *03–80–67–11–10* 🌐 *www.musee-magnin.fr* 🎫 *€3.50* ⏲ *Tues.–Sun. 10–noon and 2–6.*

6 **Notre-Dame.** One of the city's oldest churches, Notre-Dame stands out with its spindlelike towers, delicate arches gracing its facade, and 13th-century stained glass. Note the windows in the north transept tracing the lives of five saints, as well as the 11th-century Byzantine cedar Black Virgin. Local tradition has it that stroking the small owl sculpted in the adjoining chapel with your left hand brings good luck. ✉ *Rue de la Préfecture.*

1 **Palais des Ducs** *(Ducal Palace).* The elegant, classical exterior of the former palace can best be admired from the half-moon Place de la Libération and the Cour d'Honneur. The **kitchens** (circa 1450), with their six huge fireplaces and (for its time) state-of-the-art aeration funnel in the ceiling, and the 14th-century **chapter house** catch the eye, as does the 15th-century **Salle des Gardes** (Guard Room), with its richly carved and colored tombs and late-14th-century altarpieces. The palace now houses one of France's major art museums, the **Musée des Beaux-Arts** (Fine Arts Museum). Here are displayed the magnificent tombs sculpted by celebrated artist Claus Sluter for dukes Philip the Bold and his son John the Fearless—note their dramatically moving mourners, hidden in shrouds. These are just two of the highlights of a rich collection of medieval objects and Renaissance furniture gathered here as testimony to Marguerite of Flanders, wife of Philip the Bold, who brought to Burgundy not only her dowry, the rich province of Flanders (modern-day Belgium), but also a host of distinguished artists—including Rogier van der Weyden, Jan van Eyck, and Claus Sluter. Their artistic legacy can be

Fodor's Choice ★

9

seen in this collection, as well as at several of Burgundy's other museums and monuments. Among the paintings are works by Italian old masters and French 19th-century artists, such as Théodore Géricault and Gustave Courbet, and their Impressionist successors, notably Édouard Manet and Claude Monet. ✉ *Cour de Bar de l'Hotel de Ville* ☎ *03–80–74–52–70* *Free* *May–Oct., Wed.–Mon. 9:30–6; Nov.–Apr., Wed.–Mon. 10–5.*

DO YOU GREY POUPON?

Dijon's legendary Maille mustard shop at 32 rue de la Liberté (*www.maille.com*), established in 1777, still sells Grey Poupon in painted ceramic pots at outrageous prices, along with a huge selection of oils, vinegars, and spices.

WORTH NOTING

8 **Chambre des Métiers.** This stately mansion with Gallo-Roman stelae incorporated into the walls (a remaining section of Dijon's 5th-century "Castrum" wall) was built in the 19th century. ✉ *Rue Philippe-Pot.*

9 **Musée Archéologique** *(Antiquities Museum).* This museum, in the former abbey buildings of the church of St-Bénigne, traces the history of the region through archaeological finds. ✉ *5 rue du Dr. Maret* ☎ *03–80–30–88–54* *Free* *Mid-May–Oct., Wed.–Mon. 9–12:30 and 1:30–6; Oct.–mid-May, Wed.–Sun. 9–12:30 and 1:30–6.*

11 **Musée d'Histoire Naturelle** *(Natural History Museum).* The museum is in the impressive botanical garden, the **Jardin de l'Arquebuse,** a pleasant place to stroll amid the wide variety of trees and tropical flowers. ✉ *14 rue Jehan de Marville* ☎ *03–80–48–82–00 museum* *Free* *Museum Mon. and Wed.–Fri. 9–noon and 2–6, weekends 2–6; garden daily 7:30–6; until 8 in summer.*

4 **Palais de Justice.** The meeting place for the old regional Parliament of Burgundy serves as a reminder that Louis XI incorporated the province into France in the late 15th century. ✉ *Rue du Palais.*

5 **St-Michel.** This church, with its chunky Renaissance facade, fast-forwards 300 years from Notre-Dame. ✉ *Pl. St-Michel.*

WHERE TO EAT

As a culinary capital of France, Dijon has many superb restaurants, with three areas popular for casual dining. One is around Place Darcy, a square catering to all tastes and budgets: choose from the bustling Concorde brasserie, the quiet bar of the Hôtel de la Cloche, the underground Caveau de la Porte Guillaume wine-and-snack bar, or—for your sweet tooth—the Pâtisserie Darcy. For a really inexpensive meal, try the cafeteria Le Flunch on Boulevard de Brosses (near Place Darcy). Two other areas for casual dining in the evening are Place Émile-Zola and the old market (Les Halles), along Rue Bannelier.

$ FRENCH **Le Bistrot des Halles.** Of the many restaurants in the area, this atmospheric, 1930s-style bistrot, frequented by savvy locals eager to gain reasonably priced access to Jean-Pierre Billoux's cuisine, is the best value. Well-prepared dishes range from escargots to bœuf bourguignon with braised endive—be sure to check the ardoise for daily specials.

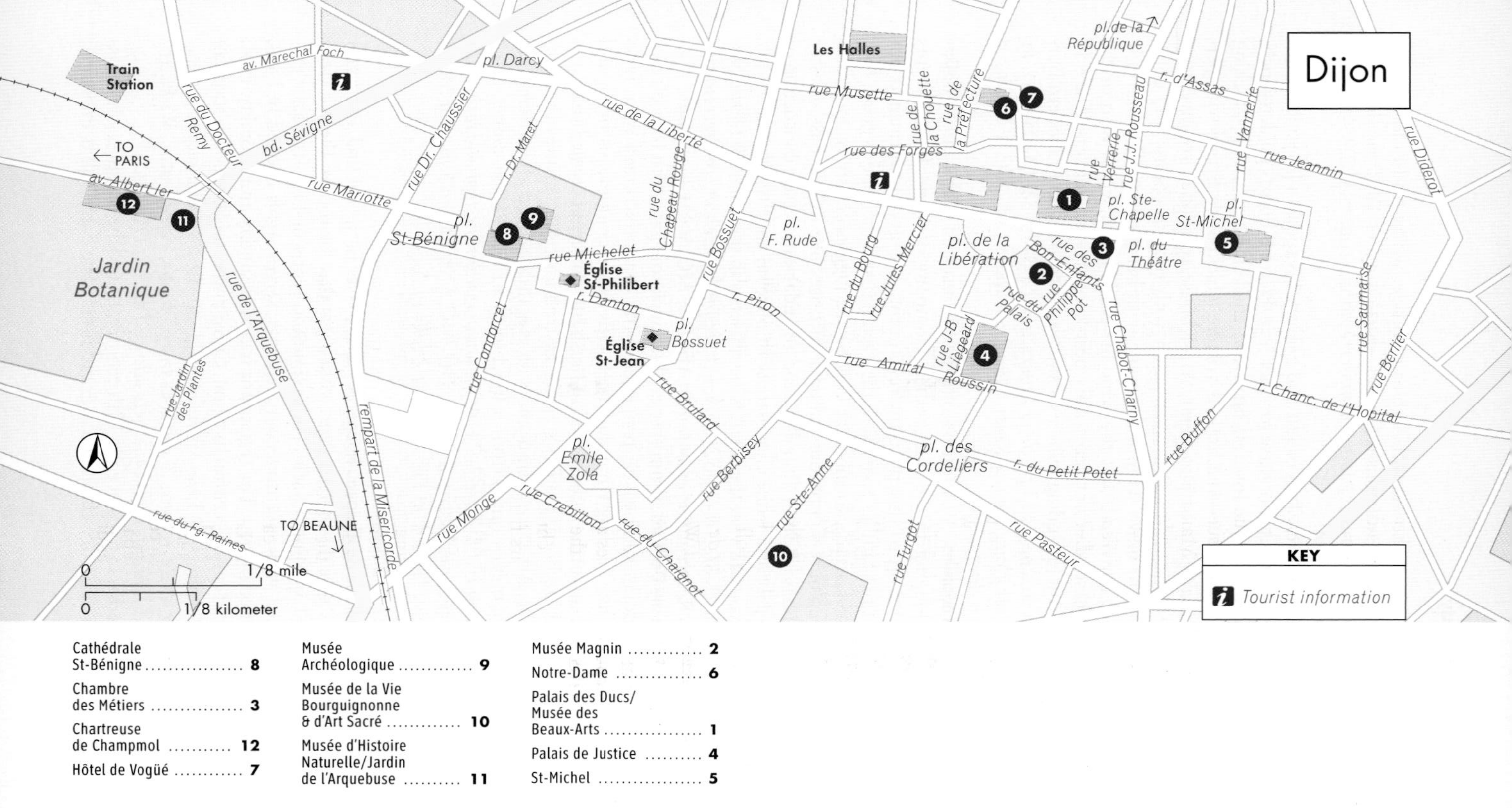
Dijon
KEY
Tourist information
Train Station
TO PARIS
TO BEAUNE
Les Halles
Jardin Botanique
pl. Darcy
pl. de la République
pl. St-Bénigne
pl. F. Rude
pl. de la Libération
pl. Ste-Chapelle
pl. St-Michel
pl. du Théâtre
pl. Bossuet
pl. Emile Zola
pl. des Cordeliers
Église St-Philibert
Église St-Jean
av. Maréchal Foch
bd. Sévigne
rue du Docteur Remy
av. Albert Ier
rue de l'Arquebuse
rue Jardin des Plantes
rue du Fg. Raines
rue Mariotte
rue Dr. Chaussier
r. Dr. Maret
rue Michelet
rue Condorcet
rue de la Liberté
rue du Chapeau Rouge
rue Bossuet
r. Danton
r. Piron
rue Brulard
rue Berbisey
rue Ste-Anne
rue Monge
rue Crebillon
rue du Chaignot
rempart de la Misericorde
rue Musette
rue de la Chouette
rue de la Préfecture
rue des Forges
rue du Bourg
rue Jules Mercier
rue Verrerie
rue J.J. Rousseau
r. d'Assas
rue Vannerie
rue Jeannin
rue Diderot
rue des Bon-Enfants
rue du Palais
rue Philippe Pot
rue J-B Liégeard
rue Amiral Roussin
rue Chabot-Charny
rue Saumaise
rue Berlier
r. Chanc. de l'Hopital
rue Buffon
r. du Petit Potet
rue Turgot
rue Pasteur
0 1/8 mile
0 1/8 kilometer
Cathédrale St-Bénigne 8
Chambre des Métiers 3
Chartreuse de Champmol 12
Hôtel de Vogüé 7
Musée Archéologique 9
Musée de la Vie Bourguignonne & d'Art Sacré 10
Musée d'Histoire Naturelle/Jardin de l'Arquebuse 11
Musée Magnin 2
Notre-Dame 6
Palais des Ducs/Musée des Beaux-Arts 1
Palais de Justice 4
St-Michel 5

Dine either at the sidewalk tables or inside, where traditional French decor—mirrors and polished wood—predominates. ✉ *10 rue Bannelier* ☎ *03–80–49–94–15* 🌐 *www.jeanpierrebilloux.com* ▭ *MC, V* ⏲ *Closed Sun. and Mon.*

$$$$ FRENCH ★ ✕ **Le Pré aux Clercs.** This bright and beautiful Napoléon III–style restaurant is the perfect showcase for chef Jean-Pierre Billoux's golden touch, which can turn the lowliest farmyard chicken into a palate-plucking pièce de résistance—the braised volaille (chicken) de Bresse with perfect vegetables, a case in point. Most house specialties are inventive, like the delicate smoked river perch with tomato confite and chive cream, or, to finish with, a meringue with berry coulis. The welcome is always convivial, and the wine list reads like a who's who of the region's best—but not necessarily best-known—winemakers. The €35 lunch menu (including wine) is a startling introduction to modern Burgundian cuisine. ✉ *13 pl. de la Libération* ☎ *03–80–38–05–05* 🌐 *www.jeanpierrebilloux.com* ✍ *Reservations essential* ▭ *AE, MC, V* ⏲ *Closed Mon. No dinner Sun.*

$$$ FRENCH ✕ **Les Œnophiles.** A collection of superbly restored 17th-century buildings belonging to the Burgundian Company of Wine Tasters forms the backdrop to this pleasant restaurant. It's lavishly furnished but also quaint (candles sparkle in the evening) and the food is good, too. Stéphane Cattane, formerly at Guy Savoy, juggles creativity and tradition to conjure sumptuous culinary surprises like his sea bass, lobster and gambas (shrimp) "bundle"; and an audacious dessert concoction of tomato jelly and white chocolate with olive oil and strawberries. After dinner you can visit the small wine museum in the cellar. ✉ *18 rue Ste-Anne* ☎ *03–80–30–73–52* 🌐 *www.hotelphilippelebon.com/restaurant.html* ✍ *Reservations essential* ▭ *AE, DC, MC, V* ⏲ *Closed Sun.*

$$$$ FRENCH ★ ✕ **Stéphane Derbord.** From starters like duck foie-gras with pain d'epice (Burgundian spice cake), prune jelly, and orange-accented brioche to entrées like sizzling Charolais beef with onion chutney, jus brun, and organic carrot tagliatelle, and, to finish off, butternut crème brulée, the talented Derbord, the city's rising gastronomic star, ensures that dinner in this Art Deco restaurant is an elegantly refined affair. Tempting prix-fixe menus range from a lunch-only €25 to €88 at dinner. ✉ *10 pl. Wilson* ☎ *03–80–67–74–64* 🌐 *www.restaurantstephanederbord.fr* ✍ *Reservations essential* ▭ *AE, DC, MC, V* ⏲ *Closed Sun. and Mon., early Jan., last wk in Feb. and 1st 2 wks in Aug.*

WHERE TO STAY

$$$ 🏨 **Hostellerie du Chapeau Rouge.** A piano player in the bar and an elegant staircase give this hotel a degree of charm that the rooms, though clean and well appointed, lack. The restaurant, renowned for its classic cuisine laced with inventive counterpoints, serves snails cooked in basil, and stuffed pigeon. The restaurant is closed Sunday and Monday. **Pros:** celebrated cuisine; central location. **Cons:** unspectacular rooms; staff can be gruff at times. ✉ *5 rue Michelet* ☎ *03–80–50–88–88* 🌐 *www.chapeau-rouge.fr* 🛏 *28 rooms, 2 suites* 👍 *In-room: a/c, refrigerator, Wi-Fi. In-hotel: restaurant, bar, some pets allowed* ▭ *AE, DC, MC, V.*

$$$ 🏨 **La Cloche.** In use since the 19th century, La Cloche is a successful cross between a luxury chain and a grand hotel. The entry hall is imposing,

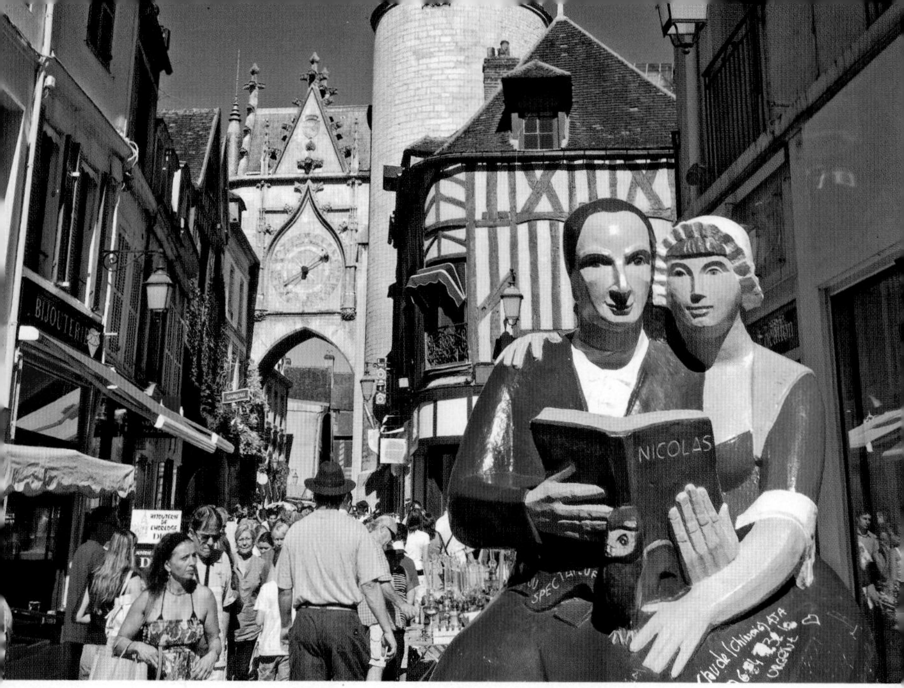

Even the streets are works of art in Dijon, treasurehouse of Burgundian art, one of the glories of 15th-century painting and sculpture.

and the gleaming bar has smart leather chairs. Rooms are large and plush; try to get one overlooking the tiny, tranquil back garden and its reflecting pool. The garden is also the backdrop for the stylish restaurant, Les Jardins de la Cloche. **Pros:** very comfortable beds; attentive staff. **Cons:** bad soundproofing; ostentatious lobby. ✉ *14 pl. Darcy* ☎ *03–80–30–12–32* 🌐 *www.hotel-lacloche.com* *53 rooms, 15 suites* *In-room: a/c, refrigerator. In-hotel: restaurant, bar, gym, Internet terminal* 💳 *AE, DC, MC, V.*

¢ **Le Jacquemart.** In old Dijon, in a neighborhood known for its antiques shops, the recently refurbished Jacquemart is housed in an 18th-century building with a steep staircase, high-ceiling rooms of variable comfort, and rustic furniture. It's a quiet, restful spot and thus very popular, so make sure you book well in advance. **Pros:** cheerful; good value; nice bathrooms. **Cons:** far from the train station; no elevator or a/c. ✉ *32 rue Verrerie* ☎ *03–80–60–09–60* 🌐 *www.hotel-lejacquemart.fr* *31 rooms* *In-room: no a/c, Internet. In-hotel: parking (paid)* 💳 *AE, MC, V.*

$ **Wilson.** This hotel's "bones" are 17th century, set as it is in a fetching timber-frame post house, but inside, rooms are modern, airy, light, and accented with wooden beams and Louis Treize chairs. Ask for one on the inner courtyard, where it's quieter. Another plus: the hotel is near Stéphane Derbord's noted restaurant. **Pros:** central location. **Cons:** some bathrooms are lackluster; rooms overlooking main road get street noise. ✉ *Pl. Wilson* ☎ *03–80–66–82–50* 🌐 *www.wilson-hotel.com* *27 rooms* *In-room: a/c (some), Wi-Fi. In-hotel: Internet terminal, parking (paid), some pets allowed* 💳 *AE, MC, V.*

NIGHTLIFE AND THE ARTS

Dijon stages **L'Été Musical** *(Musical Summer)*, a predominantly classical music festival in June; the tourist office can supply the details. For three days in June the city hosts **Arts in the Streets** (☎ *03–80–65–91–00 for information*), an event at which dozens of painters exhibit their works. Check with the Dijon tourist office for summer **music and film festivals** held at the region's prestigious wineries. During the **Bell-Ringing Festival**, in mid-August, St-Bénigne's bells chime and chime. In the first week of September, Dijon holds its own picturesque **Flea Market**. In September Dijon puts on the **Festival International de Folklore**. November in Dijon is the time for the **International Gastronomy Fair**.

Bar Messire (✉ *3 rue Jules-Mercier* ☎ *03–80–30–16–40*) attracts an older crowd. **Le Chat Noir** (✉ *20 av. Garibaldi* ☎ *03–80–73–39–57*) is a popular disco and draws a huge crowd of dedicated groovers. **Eden Bar** (✉ *12 rue des Perrieres* ☎ *03–80–41–48–64*) caters to a broad clientele and features live sports coverage.

WINE COUNTRY

Burgundy—Bourgogne to the French—has given its name to one of the world's great wines. Although many people will allow a preference for Bordeaux, others for Alsace, Loire, or Rhône wines, some of the leading French gourmets insist that the precious red nectars of Burgundy have no rivals, and treat them with reverence. So, for some travelers a trip to Burgundy's Wine Country takes on the feel of a spiritual pilgrimage. East of the Parc du Morvan, the low hills and woodland gradually open up, and vineyards, clothing the contour of the land in orderly beauty, appear on all sides. The vineyards' steeply banked hills stand in contrast to the region's characteristic gentle slopes. Burgundy's most famous vineyards run south from Dijon through Beaune to Mâcon along what has become known as the Côte d'Or (*or* doesn't mean "gold" here, but is an abbreviation of *orient*, or east). Here you can go from vineyard to vineyard tasting the various samples (both the powerfully tannic young reds and the mellower older ones). Purists will remind you that you're not supposed to drink them but simply taste them, then spit them into the little buckets discreetly provided. But who wants to be a purist?

The Côte d'Or is truly golden for wine lovers, branching out over the countryside in four great vineyard-*côtes* (slopes or hillsides) in southern Burgundy. The northernmost, the Côte de Nuits, sometimes called the "Champs-Élysées of Burgundy," is the land of the unparalleled grand-cru reds from the pinot noir grape. The Côte de Beaune, just to the south, is known for both full-bodied reds and some of the best dry whites in the world. Even farther south is the Côte Chalonnaise. Although not as famous, it produces bottle after bottle of chardonnay almost as rich as its northern neighbors. Finally, the Côte Mâconnaise, the largest of the four côtes, brings its own quality whites to the market. There are hundreds of vintners in this region, many of them producing top wines from surprisingly small parcels of land. *To connect these dots, consult the regional tourist offices for full information of the noted wine routes of the region and see our photo-feature, "Grape Expectations," in this chapter.* The 74-km (50-mi) Route des Grands Crus ranges from Dijon to Beaune and Santenay. You can extend this route southward by the Route Touristique des Grands Vins, which travels some 98 km (60 mi) in and around Chalon-sur-Saône. Coming from the north, you can tour the areas *(covered above)* around Auxerre and Chablis on the Route des Vignobles de l'Yonne. Wherever you go in this killer countryside, you'll find that small towns with big wine names draw many travelers to their cellars.

CLOS DE VOUGEOT

16 km (10 mi) south of Dijon.

The reason to come to Vougeot is to see its *grange viticole* (wine-making barn) surrounded by its famous vineyard—a symbolic spot for all Burgundy aficionados.

Fodor's Choice ★ The **Château du Clos de Vougeot** was constructed in the 12th century by Cistercian monks from neighboring Cîteaux—who were in need of wine for Mass and also wanted to make a diplomatic offering—and completed during the Renaissance. It's best known as the seat of Burgundy's elite company of wine lovers, the Confrérie des Chevaliers du Tastevin, who gather here in November at the start of an annual three-day festival, Les Trois Glorieuses. Josephine Baker slurped here once. You can admire the château's cellars, where ceremonies are held, and ogle the huge 13th-century grape presses, uncertain marvels of medieval engineering. ☎ *03–80–62–86–09* 🌐 *www.tastevin-bourgogne.com* 🎟 *€3.90* ⏲ *Apr.–Sept., daily 9–6:30; Oct.–Mar., daily 9–11:30 and 2–5:30.*

Near Clos de Vougeot at St-Nicolas-lès-Cîteaux is the **Abbaye de Cîteaux**, where the austere Cistercian order was founded in 1098 by Robert de Molesmes. The abbey has housed monks for more than 900 years. From D996, follow signs that point the way along a short country road that breaks off from the road to Château de Gilly, a four-star hotel. ✉ *Off D996* ☎ *03–80–61–32–58* 🌐 *www.citeaux-abbaye.com* 🎟 *€7 guided tour* ⏲ *May–Sept., Wed.–Sat. 9:45–12:45 and 2:15–6, Sun. noon–6:30; see Web site for tour times.*

WHERE TO STAY

$$$–$$$$ **Château de Gilly**. Considered by some an obligatory stop on their tour of Burgundy's vineyards, this château, 3 km (2 mi) from Vougeot, has almost become too popular for its own good (an on-site conference center doesn't help things). Formerly an abbey and a government-run avant-garde theater, the château does show some glorious vestiges worthy of its Relais & Châteaux parentage: painted ceilings, a gigantic vaulted crypt-cellar (now the dining room), suits of armor. Guest rooms have magnificent beamed ceilings and lovely views, though the least expensive have standard-issue fabrics, reproduction furniture, and ordinary bathrooms. The restaurant's menu includes pastries made with Cîteaux's famous handmade cheese. An "elegant form of dress" is requested for dinner. **Pros:** beautiful location; friendly staff. **Cons:** pricey; heavily touristed. ✉ *Gilly-lès-Cîteaux* ☎ *03–80–62–89–98* 🌐 *www.chateau-gilly.com* *37 rooms, 11 suites* *In-room: no a/c,*

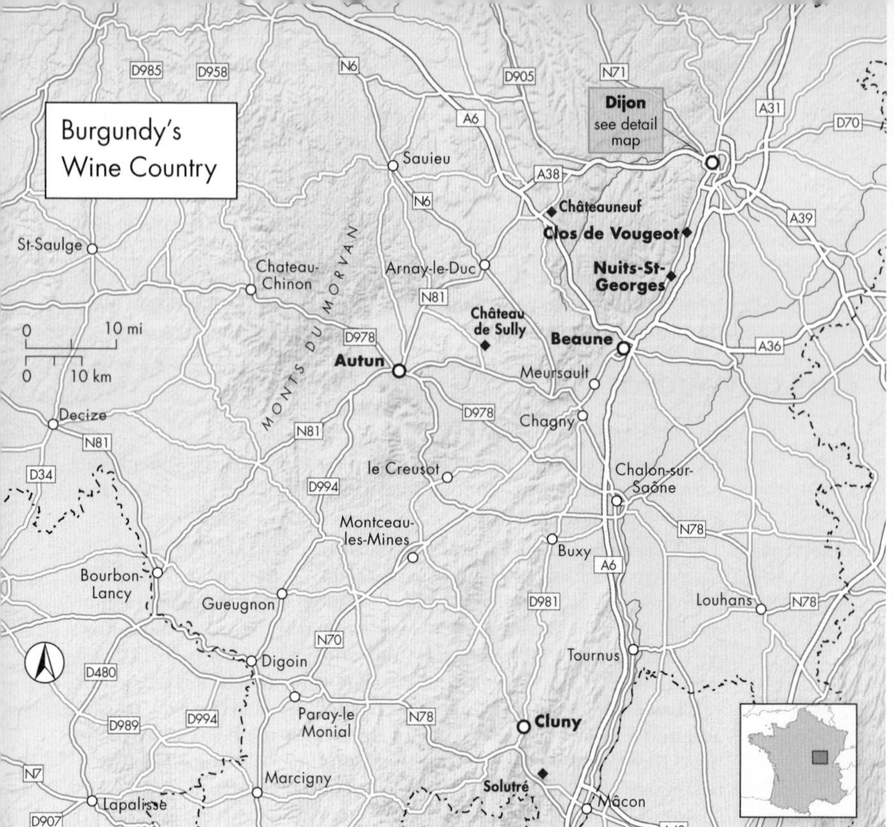

Wi-Fi. In-hotel: restaurant, tennis court, pool, Internet terminal ▭ *AE, DC, MC, V* 🍽 *MAP.*

NUITS-ST-GEORGES

21 km (13 mi) south of Dijon, 5 km (3 mi) south of Clos de Vougeot.

Wine has been made in Nuits-St-Georges since Roman times; its "dry, tonic, and generous qualities" were recommended to Louis XIV for medicinal use. But this is also the heart of currant country, where crops yield up the wonderfully delicious ingredient known as cassis (the signature taste of the famous Kir cocktail). The **Cassissium**, in a sparkling glass and steel building, explores the world of cassis using films, interactive displays, guided tours of Védrenne's liqueur production, and even a "slot" fruit machine. A cassis tasting is the final stop. ✉ *Rue des Frères Montgolfier* ☎ *03–80–62–49–70* 🌐 *www.cassissium.com* 🎟 *€7* ⏲ *Apr.–late Nov., daily 10–11:30, 2–5:30; late Nov.–Mar., Mon.–Sat. 10:30–11:30, 2–4.*

WHERE TO EAT AND STAY

$$ FRENCH ✕ **Au Bois de Charmois.** About 3 km (2 mi) out of Nuits-St-Georges, on the way toward Meuilley, is this fabulous little inn serving local fare at tasty prices—a three-course lunch (sample the huge plate of garlicky

frogs' legs) is a finger-lickin' €12. An even less expensive menu is available at lunch on weekdays. It's especially pleasant to sit in the courtyard under the ancient trees, though on chilly, gray days the small dining room is full of good cheer. ✉ *Rte. de la Serrée* ☎ *03–80–61–04–79* ▭ *MC, V* ⊗ *Closed Wed.*

$ FRENCH **La Toute Petite Auberge.** Vosne-Romanée, the greatest wine village on the côte, also entices with one of the most charming restaurants in Burgundy. No surprises on the menu (jambon persillé, coq au vin, crème brûlée), but everything is excellent and prices are more than reasonable. As you would expect, the wine list is top-notch. ✉ *Vosne-Romanée, on the N74, 2 km (1 mi) north of Nuits-St-Georges* ☎ *03–80–61–02–03* *Reservations essential* ▭ *MC, V* ⊗ *Closed Wed. No dinner Tues.*

$ **Château de la Berchère.** Originally a medieval fortification and a battlefield during the Franco-Prussian wars, this majestic chateau was transformed into a elegant hotel in the 1980s. In general, the rooms are simply but tastefully furnished, though some of the rooms, especially No. 29, are in a grander vein. Bathrooms are basic, but some are equipped with sauna and whirlpool. The grounds are impeccable, and even include a private runway. **Pros:** good value; steeped in French history. **Cons:** no air-conditioning; no restaurant; some rooms need renovating. ✉ *Boncourt-le-Bois, 4 km (2½ mi) west of Nuits-St-Georges Boncourt-le-Bois* ☎ *03–80–61–01–40* ⊕ *www.hotelchateauberchere.com* *22 rooms* *In-room: no a/c. In-hotel: bar, pool, parking (free)* ▭ *MC, V* ⊗ *Closed Dec.–Feb.* *BP.*

$–$$ ★ **Domaine Comtesse Michel de Loisy.** Comtesse Christine de Loisy is an institution unto herself in the Nuits-St-Georges area: an internationally traveled, erudite *dame d'un certain âge,* who is also a well-known oenologist and local historian. Rooms in her eclectic *hôtel particulier* are furnished with fine antiques, tapestries, chintz-covered walls, and Oriental carpets and memorably temper grandeur with old-fashioned charm. Four of the five have a view of the flower-filled courtyard or the magnificent winter garden. Happily, the domain offers an optional two-day program of wine tastings, Burgundy-focused meals, and vineyard excursions. **Pros:** the cultured Comtesse; large, comfortable rooms. **Cons:** no elevator; no air-conditioning in some rooms. ✉ *28 rue du Général-de-Gaulle* ☎ *03–80–61–02–72* ⊕ *www.domaine-de-loisy.com* *3 rooms, 2 suites* *In-room: a/c (some), no TV, Internet. In-hotel: Internet terminal* ▭ *AE, MC, V* ⊗ *Closed late Dec.–early Jan.* *BP.*

9

BEAUNE

Fodor's Choice ★ *19 km (12 mi) south of Nuits-St-Georges, 40 km (25 mi) south of Dijon, 315 km (197 mi) southeast of Paris.*

Beaune is sometimes considered the wine capital of Burgundy because it is at the heart of the region's vineyards, with the Côte de Nuits to the north and the Côte de Beaune to the south. In late November, Les Trois Glorieuses, a three-day wine auction and fête at the Hospices de Beaune, pulls in connoisseurs and the curious from France and abroad. Despite the hordes, Beaune remains one of France's most attractive provincial towns, teeming with art above ground and wine barrels down below.

GETTING HERE

The wine capital of Burgundy is also one of the most-visited towns in the region. Though there is only one direct TGV train leaving Paris's Gare de Lyon daily (at 4:58 PM), there are 14 in all, with changes at Dijon, and 12 on weekends. Travel time is under three hours and the peak fare is €65.50. Beaune is only 20 minutes from Dijon (€6.80) and gets plenty of train traffic from the through lines to Lyon (€23.10) and Nevers (€25.10). For those heading farther north, trains to Laroche Migennes (Auxerre €27.50) and the 9:05 to Sens (€31.20) are available. Beaune also benefits from the broad regional TRANSCO bus network and buses, which depart from the SNCF station, run to Dijon via Nuits-St-Georges (60 mins on the No. 44 wine-lovers line), and to Saulieu (weekdays at 6 PM) with the No. 72.

Visitor Information **Beaune Tourist Office** (✉ *6 bd. Perpreuil* ☎ *03–80–26–21–30* 🌐 *www.ot-beaune.fr*).

EXPLORING

The star attraction of Beaune is its famed **Hospices de Beaune** (better known to some as the Hôtel-Dieu). Set across from the tourist office, this building has become one of the icons of Burgundy thanks to its spectacular tile roof and Flemish architecture—the same glowing colors and intricate patterns are seen throughout the region. It was founded in 1443 as a hospital to provide free care for men who had fought in the Hundred Years' War. The interior looks medieval but was repainted by 19th-century Gothic restorer Viollet-le-Duc. Of special note are the **Grand' Salle,** more than 160 feet long, with the original furniture, a great wooden roof, and the super-picturesque **Cour d'Honneur.** The Hospices carried on its medical activities until 1971—its nurses still wearing their habitlike uniforms—and the hospital's history is retraced in the museum, whose wide-ranging collections contain some weird medical instruments from the 15th century. You can also see a collection of tapestries that belonged to the repentant founder of the Hospices, ducal chancellor Nicolas Rolin, who hoped charity would relieve him of his sins—one of which was collecting wives. Outstanding are both the tapestry he had made for Madame Rolin III, with its repeated motif of "my only star," and one relating the legend of St. Eloi and his miraculous restoration of a horse's leg.

But the showstopper at the Hôtel-Dieu is Rogier Van der Weyden's stirring, gigantic 15th-century masterpiece *The Last Judgment,* commissioned for the hospital by Rolin. The intense colors and mind-tripping imagery were meant to scare the illiterate patients into religious submission. Notice the touch of misogyny; more women are going to hell than to heaven, while Christ, the judge, remains completely unmoved. A sound and light show is presented every evening April through October. Note that some of the region's finest vineyards are owned by the Hospices. ✉ *Rue de l'Hôtel-Dieu* ☎ *03–80–24–45–00* 🌐 *www.hospices-de-beaune.com/gb/hospices* 🎫 *€6.50* ⏲ *Late Mar.–mid-Nov., daily 9–6:30; mid-Nov.–late Mar., daily 9–11:30 and 2–5:30.*

Showing off its colorfully patterned roof tiles, medieval courtyard, and Rogier van der Weyden altarpiece, the Hôtel Dieu is Beaune's showstopper.

A series of tapestries relating the life of the Virgin hangs in Beaune's main church, the 12th-century Romanesque **Collégiale Notre-Dame.** ✉ *Pl. du General Leclerc, just off Av. de la République* ☎ *03–80–24–77–95*.

9

★ To many, the liquid highlight of a visit to Burgundy is a visit to the **Marché aux Vins** *(Wine Market)*, where, in flickering candlelight, and armed with your own *tastevin* (which you get to keep as a souvenir), you can taste a tongue-tingling, mind-spinning array of regional wines in the atmospheric setting of barrel-strewn cellars and vaulted passages. The selection runs from young Beaujolais to famous old Burgundies, and there's no limit on how much you drink. Other Beaune tasting houses include Cordelier on the Rue de l'Hôtel-Dieu and the Caves Patriarche on the Rue du Collège. ✉ *2 rue Nicolas-Rolin* ☎ *03–80–25–08–20* 🌐 *www.marcheauxvins.com* 🎫 *€10* ⏲ *Sept.–June, daily 9:30–11:30 and 2–5:30; July and Aug. 9:30–5:30.*

WHERE TO EAT

$$$ FRENCH ✕ **L'Écusson.** Don't be put off by its unprepossessing exterior: this is a comfortable, friendly, thick-carpeted restaurant with good-value (€25–€55) prix-fixe menus. Showcased is chef Jean-Pierre Senelet's sure-footed culinary mastery with dishes like duck foie gras in a mustard-seed crust, and olive-roast crayfish with zucchini and almond salsa courgettes. ✉ *2 rue du Lieutenant-Dupuis* ☎ *03–80–24–03–82* 🌐 *www.ecusson.fr* ✍ *Reservations essential* 💳 *AE, DC, MC, V* ⏲ *Closed Wed., Sun., and Feb.*

$ FRENCH Fodor's Choice ★ ✕ **Le P'tit Paradis.** It's well worth squeezing into this tiny corner of paradise to experience the generous and modern bistrot fare of Beaune's most capable culinary couple. Grilled langoustine with orange butter

Wine tastings abound in and around Beaune—check in with the tourist office to get a full list of vineyards and wine caves.

and Charolais beef with an Époisses sauce grace a menu fit for a stint with the angels. Excellent value menus range from €20 to €32. ✉ 2 *rue du Paradis, Beaune* ☎ *03–80–24–91–00* ✍ *Reservations essential* ▭ *MC, V* ⏲ *Closed Sun. and Feb. 22–Mar. 10, Aug., and Dec. No lunch Sat.*

$$$$ FRENCH ★ ✕ **Loiseau des Vignes.** Where else would you expect one of Burgundy's leading culinary establishments to open a wine bar? A massive range of 70 wines, all available by the glass, is the perfect accompaniment to a selection of Bernard Loiseau's famous regional dishes (along with some old-fashioned essentials). Lunch menus start at €23 and dinner at €45, with such delights as *œufs en meurette Bernard Loiseau* (poached eggs in red-wine sauce) and spoon-fashioned pike-perch patties in a crustacean sauce—and wines from €2 to €38 a glass. ✉ *31 rue Maufoux* ☎ *03–80–24–12–06* 🌐 *www.bernard-loiseau.com* ✍ *Reservations essential* ▭ *AE, DC, MC, V* ⏲ *Closed Mon., Sun., and Feb.*

WHERE TO STAY

$$$ **Château de Chorey.** To really soak up the flavor of the vineyards, stay at this family winery about 2 km (1 mi) north of Beaune. Guest rooms are up a circular stone staircase; furnishings are from the attic. Though it's a bit rustic and casual, it's the kind of place where you can open the windows and let the country air, perfumed by grapes, waft in. A good breakfast is served and a lunch/wine tasting is available by reservation Monday through Saturday, but no other meals; try their wine before going out to eat in Beaune. **Pros:** traditional charm; winery on-site; sumptuous breakfast. **Cons:** bells from nearby church can disturb the peace; beds are on the small side. ✉ *2 rue Jacques-GermainChorey-les-*

Beaune ☎ *03–80–22–06–05* 🌐 *www.chateau-de-chorey-les-beaune.fr* *3 rooms, 2 suites* *In-room: no a/c, Internet* ☰ *MC, V* ⏲ *Closed Nov.–Easter* *BP.*

$$$–$$$$ ★ **Hostellerie de Levernois.** An idyllically elegant and gracious country manor, this Relais & Châteaux property, smartly run by Jean-Louis and Susanne Bottigliero, gleams with light from its large picture windows. The cuisine, under new chef Philippe Augé, is of the highest standard and immediately earned the restaurant its first Michelin star just last year. The lodgings in the modern annex overlooking the landscaped garden are the most up-to-date. Meals are occasions to be savored; prix-fixe menus begin at €65 and may highlight Charolais beef with a confit of shallots in cassis. The bistro offers more reasonably priced menus at €28 and €32, but is open for lunch weekdays and dinners Wednesday, Friday, and Saturday. **Pros:** lovely, spacious rooms; personable staff; great food. **Cons:** pricey; no elevator. ✉ *Rte. de Verdun-sur-le-Doubs, 3 km (2 mi) east of Beaune, Levernois* ☎ *03–80–24–73–58* 🌐 *www.levernois.com* *22 rooms, 1 suite, 3 apartments* *In-room: a/c, refrigerator, Wi-Fi. In-hotel: 2 restaurants, Internet terminal* ☰ *AE, DC, MC, V* ⏲ *Closed Feb.–mid-Mar.* *MAP.*

$ **Hôtel Central.** This well-run establishment with modern rooms, 100 yards from the Hospices de Beaune, lives up to its name. The stone-wall restaurant (closed late November to late January) is cozy—some might say cramped—and the consistently good cuisine is popular with locals, who come to enjoy œufs en meurette and coq au vin. Service is efficient, if a little hurried. **Pros:** central location; clean, comfortable rooms. **Cons:** street-facing rooms are noisy; property needs updating. ✉ *2 rue Victor-Millot* ☎ *03–80–24–77–24* 🌐 *www.hotelcentral-beaune.com* *20 rooms, 10 with bath* *In-room: a/c (some), refrigerator. In-hotel: restaurant, bar, parking (paid), Wi-Fi hotspot, some pets allowed* ☰ *AE, MC, V.*

$$$ ★ **Hôtel Le Cep.** This venerable town-center hotel might be considered the shining showpiece among Beaune's myriad hostelries. It's actually an ensemble of buildings spanning the 14th to the 16th century, oozing history from every arcade of its Renaissance courtyard, yet all rooms—named for different Burgundy wines—have been luxuriously modernized, and decorated with crystal chandeliers and individual panache; some have wood beams, others canopied or four-poster beds. Those on the top story offer views over Beaune's famed multicolor tile roofs. Breakfast is served in a vaulted cellar; there's no hotel restaurant as such, but the excellent Loiseau des Vignes operates right next door. **Pros:** luxurious rooms; historical location; friendly staff. **Cons:** thin walls; pricey breakfast. ✉ *27 rue Maufoux* ☎ *03–80–22–35–48* 🌐 *www.hotel-cep-beaune.com* *40 rooms, 22 suites* *In-room: a/c, refrigerator, Wi-Fi. In-hotel: bar, Internet terminal, parking (paid)* ☰ *AE, DC, MC, V.*

9

THE ARTS

In July Beaune celebrates its annual **International Festival of Baroque Music** (🌐 *www.festivalbeaune.com*), which draws big stars of the music world. On the third weekend in November at the Hospices is Beaune's famous wine festival, **Les Trois Glorieuses**, which closes with an auction on that

Sunday. For both festivals, contact **Beaune's Office de Tourisme** (✉ *1 rue de l'Hôtel-Dieu* ☎ *03–80–26–21–30* 🌐 *www.ot-beaune.fr*).

CHÂTEAU DE SULLY

35 km (19 mi) west of Beaune.

"The Fontainebleau of Burgundy" was how Madame de Sévigné described this turreted Renaissance château, proclaiming the inner court, whose Italianate design was inspired by Sebastiano Serlio, as the latest in chic. The building is magnificent, landmarked by four lantern-top corner towers that loom over a romantic moat filled with the waters of the River Drée. Originally constructed by the de Rabutin family and once owned by Gaspard de Saulx-Tavannes—an instigator of the St. Bartholomew's Day Massacre, August 24, 1572, he reputedly ran through Paris's streets yelling, "Blood, blood! The doctors say that bleeding is as good for the health in August as in May!"—the château was partly reconstructed in elegant Régence style in the 18th century. Maurice de MacMahon, the Irish-origin president of France from 1873 to 1879, was born here in 1808. ☎ *03–85–82–09–86* 🌐 *www.chateaudesully.com* 🎟 *€3.50 (gardens only), €7.50 for guided tour* ⏲ *Apr.–June and Sept.–Nov., daily 10–6; July and Aug., 10–7.*

AUTUN

Fodor's Choice ★ *20 km (12 mi) southwest of Sully, 48 km (30 mi) west of Beaune.*

One of the most richly endowed *villes d'art* in Burgundy, Autun is a great draw for fans of both Gallo-Roman and Romanesque art. It is unfortunate that people don't often think of Autun when creating their Burgundian itineraries. Once the second city of Burgundy, it has a host of visual delights from its ancient Roman theater to its medieval cathedral to its **Musée Rolin, one of the best in Burgundy.**

Visitor Information **Autun Tourist Office.** ✉ *2 av. Charles-de-Gaulle* ☎ *03–85–86–80–38* 🌐 *www.autun-tourisme.com.*

EXPLORING

Imposing arched gateways and a theater remain as Rome's legacy to Autun, which kicks off the town's great panoply of artistic treasures. Today, major roads and railways bypass Autun, enabling its ancient remains, medieval streets, and magnificent cathedral to be admired amid calm and serenity.

Autun's name derives from Augustodonum—city of Augustus—and it was Augustus Caesar who called it "the sister and rival of Rome itself." You can still see traces of the Roman occupation—dating from when Autun was much larger and more important than it is today—in its well-preserved archways, Porte St-André and Porte d'Arroux, and the Théâtre Romain, once the largest arena in Gaul. Parts of the Roman walls surrounding the town also remain and give a fair indication of its size in those days. The significance of the curious Pierre (stone) de Couhard, a pyramidlike Roman construction, baffles archaeologists. Logically enough, this Roman outpost became a center for the new

11th-century style based on Roman precedent, the Romanesque, and its greatest sculptor, Gislebertus, left his precocious mark on the town cathedral. Several centuries later, Napoléon and his brother Joseph studied here at the military academy.

CIRCLING THE WAGONS À LA FRANÇAISE

On Friday and Saturday nights from late July to early August, Augustodunum comes to life. Unique in France, Augustodunum draws 600 people to Autun's ancient Roman theater where they bring Celtic and Gallo-Roman times to life in a Busby Berkeley–esque extravaganza featuring Celtic fairies, Roman gladiators, and chariot races. Log on to 🌐 *www.autun.com/distraire/augustodunum.php* for all the details.

★ Autun's principal monument is the **Cathédrale St-Lazare**, a Gothic cathedral in Classical clothing. It was built between 1120 and 1146 to house the relics of St. Lazarus; the main tower, spire, and upper reaches of the chancel were added in the late 15th century. Lazarus's tricolor tomb was dismantled in 1766 by canons: vestiges of exquisite workmanship can be seen in the neighboring Musée Rolin. The same canons also did their best to transform the Romanesque-Gothic cathedral into a Classical temple, adding pilasters and other ornaments willy-nilly. Fortunately, the lacy Flamboyant Gothic organ tribune and some of the best Romanesque stonework, including the inspired nave capitals and the tympanum above the main door, emerged unscathed. Jean-Auguste-Dominique Ingres's painting *The Martyrdom of St. Symphorien* has been relegated to a dingy chapel in the north aisle of the nave. The *Last Judgment* carved in stone above the main door was plastered over in the 18th century, which preserved not only the stylized Christ and elongated apostles but also the inscription GISLEBERTUS HOC FECIT (Gislebertus did this). Christ's head, which had disappeared, was found by a local canon shortly after World War II. Make sure to visit the cathedral's **Salle Capitulaire,** which houses Gislebertus's original capitals, distinguished by their relief carvings. The cathedral provides a stunning setting for **Musique en Morvan** (🌐 *www.musique-en-morvan.com*), a festival of classical music held in late July. ✉ *Pl. St-Louis* ☎ *03–85–52–12–37.*

The **Musée Rolin**, across from the cathedral, was built by Chancellor Nicolas Rolin, an important Burgundian administrator and famous art patron (he's immortalized in one of the Louvre's greatest paintings, Jan van Eyck's *Madonna and the Chancellor Rolin*). The museum is noteworthy for its early Flemish paintings and sculpture, including the magisterial *Nativity* painted by the Maître de Moulins in the 15th century. But the collection's star is a Gislebertus masterpiece, the *Temptation of Eve,* which originally topped one of the side doors of the cathedral. Try to imagine the missing elements of the scene: Adam on the left and the devil on the right. ✉ *5 rue des Bancs* ☎ *03–85–52–09–76* 🎫 *€3.40* 🕘 *Oct.–Mar., Wed.–Sat. 10–noon and 2–5, Sun. 10–noon and 2:30–5; Apr.–Sept., Wed.–Mon. 9:30–noon and 1:30–6.*

The **Théâtre Romain**, at the edge of town on the road to Chalon-sur-Saône, is a historic spot for lunch. Pick up the makings for a picnic in town and eat it on the stepped seats, where as many as 15,000 Gallo-Roman spectators perched during performances 2 millennia ago. In August a Gallo-Roman performance—the only one of its kind—is put on by locals wearing period costumes. The peak of a Gallo-Roman pyramid can be seen in the foreground. Elsewhere on the outskirts of town are the remains of an ancient Roman Temple of Janus.

WHERE TO STAY

¢–$ **Hostellerie du Vieux Moulin.** In a calm setting near the center of town, this former mill sits in a tree-lined garden with a pond. The spacious rooms—some with views of the river, others looking out over the countryside—are done in a cozy country style. The restaurant has a rustic feel with a great stone fireplace, wooden beams, wrought-iron trim, and well-chosen antiques. The theme is carried over into the kitchen, where the refined and innovative dishes are inspired by traditional Burgundian specialties like œufs en meurette (eggs poached in red wine). Pastries are the chef's specialty, so don't forget dessert. Lunch and dinner are served in the garden in the warmer months. **Pros:** calm and charming surroundings; good restaurant. **Cons:** 15-minute walk from town center; no elevator. ✉ *Porte d'Arroux, rte. de Saulieu* ☎ *03–85–52–10–90* *16 rooms* *In-room: a/c, Wi-Fi. In-hotel: restaurant, bar* *AE, MC, V.*

$–$$ **Les Ursulines.** Placed above the Roman ramparts of the old city, this converted 17th-century convent offers spacious, well-kept rooms overlooking a geometric, French-style garden. The restaurant, adorned with plush green carpets, floral-pattern curtains, and cane-back Louis XV–style chairs, is worth a trip in itself, especially for the escargots with dried tomatoes and garlic confit. Some guest rooms have fine views of the surrounding Morvan hills, and breakfast is served in the historic chapel area. **Pros:** historical setting; fine views. **Cons:** spartan furnishings; restaurant requires discretion. ✉ *14 rue Rivault* ☎ *03–85–86–58–58* *www.hotelursulines.fr* *36 rooms, 7 suites* *In-room: a/c (some), refrigerator, Internet, Wi-Fi (some). In-hotel: parking (paid)* *AE, DC, MC, V.*

CLUNY

77 km (46 mi) southeast of Autun.

The village of Cluny is legendary for its medieval abbey, once the center of a vast Christian empire. Although most of the complex was destroyed in the French Revolution, one soaring transept of this church remains standing, today one of the most magnificent sights of Romanesque architecture.

GETTING HERE

Getting to Cluny is quite easy as there are six TGV trains leaving Paris's Gare de Lyon daily (€72) that require only a 30-minute bus liaison from Mâcon. There is also a TGV that can take you to Chalon-sur-Saône (at 4:58 PM) with Dijon en route. TRANSDEV (*Les Rapides de Saône et Loire* *www.r-s-l.fr*) has regular buses that link Cluny to Chalon-sur-Saône, where you can connect to Mâcon, Autun, and Le Creusot TGV railway station. Driving to Cluny is a delight, as the surrounding countryside of the Mâconnais is among the most beautiful of France,

The basilica of the Abbaye de Cluny was built between 1088 and 1130 and was the world's largest church before St. Peter's was built in Rome.

with rolling fields and picturesque villages reminding one of why it is so easy to fall in love with France.

Visitor Information Cluny Tourist Office. ✉ *6 rue Mercière* ☎ *03–85–59–05–34* 🌐 *www.cluny-tourisme.com.*

EXPLORING

Fodor's Choice ★ Looming as large as Cluny does, art historians have written themselves into knots tracing the fundamental influence of its architecture in the development of early Gothic style. Founded in the 10th century, the **Ancienne Abbaye** was the largest church in Europe until the 16th century, when Michelangelo built St. Peter's in Rome. Cluny's medieval abbots were as powerful as popes; in 1098 Pope Urban II (himself a Cluniac) assured the head of his old abbey that Cluny was the "light of the world." That assertion, of dubious religious validity, has not stood the test of time—after the Revolution the abbey was sold as national property and much of it used as a stone quarry. Today Cluny stands in ruins, a reminder of the vanity of human grandeur. The ruins, however, suggest the size and gorgeous super-romantic glory of the abbey at its zenith, and piecing it back together in your mind is part of the attraction.

In order to get a clear sense of what you're looking at, start at the **Porte d'Honneur,** the entrance to the abbey from the village, whose classical architecture is reflected in the pilasters and Corinthian columns of the **Clocher de l'Eau-Bénite** (a majestic bell tower), crowning the only remaining part of the abbey church, the south transept. Between the two is the reconstructed monumental staircase, which led to the portal of the abbey church, and the excavated column bases of the vast narthex. The entire nave is gone. On one side of the transept is a national horse-breeding center (*haras*) founded in 1806 by Napoléon and constructed with materials from the destroyed abbey; on the other is an elegant pavilion built as new monks' lodgings in the 18th century. The gardens in front of it once contained an ancient lime tree (destroyed by a 1982 storm) named after Abélard, the controversial philosopher who sought shelter at the abbey in 1142. Off to the right is the 13th-century *farinier* (flour mill), with its fine oak-and-chestnut roof and collection of exquisite Romanesque capitals from the vanished choir. The **Musée Ochier,** in the abbatial palace, contains Europe's foremost Romanesque lapidary museum. Vestiges of both the abbey and the village constructed around it are conserved here, as well as part of the Bibliothèque des Moines (Monks' Library). ☎ *03–85–59–15–93* 🌐 *www.cluny.monuments-nationaux.fr* 🎟 *€7.50* ⏱ *Sept.–Apr., daily 9:30–noon and 1:30–5; May–Aug., daily 9:30–6:30.*

The village of Cluny was built to serve the abbey's more practical needs, and several fine Romanesque houses around the Rue d'Avril and the Rue de la République, including the so-called **Hôtel de la Monnaie** (*Abbey Mint* ✉ *6 rue d'Avril* ☎ *03–85–59–25–66*), are prime examples of the period's different architectural styles.

Parts of the town ramparts, the much-restored 11th-century defensive **Tour des Fromages** (✉ *6 rue Mercière* ☎ *03–85–59–05–34* 🎟 *€2* ⏱ *Oct.–Mar., Mon.–Sat. 10–12:30 and 2:30–5; Apr.–June and Sept., Mon.–Sat. 10–12:30 and 2:30–6:45; July and Aug., daily 10–6:45*), now home to the tourist office, and several noteworthy medieval churches also remain.

WHERE TO STAY

$–$$ **Hôtel de Bourgogne.** This old-fashioned hotel was built in 1817, where parts of the abbey once stood. It has a small garden and a restaurant with a sober pink palette and comfort cuisine, such as *sandre cuit à la plancha* (grilled pike-perch). The restaurant is closed Tuesday and Wednesday, and the first week of July. **Pros:** historic setting; good value; helpful staff. **Cons:** no elevator. ✉ *Pl. de l'Abbaye* ☎ *03–85–59–00–58* 🌐 *www.hotel-cluny.com* *13 rooms, 3 suites* *In-room: a/c (some), Internet. In-hotel: restaurant, bar, parking (paid), some pets allowed* 💳 *AE, DC, MC, V* ⏱ *Closed Dec. and Jan., and Tues. and Wed. in Feb.* 🍽 *MAP.*

THE ARTS

The ruined abbey of Cluny forms the backdrop of the **Grandes Heures de Cluny** (☎ *03–85–59–23–83 for details*), a classical music festival held late July to early August.

Lyon and the Alps

10

WORD OF MOUTH

"Annecy has such a wonderful feel to it. The beauty of the place just takes your breath away, yet it is so welcoming and relaxing, and small enough to be absolutely charming. The town is made for strolling around—the beautiful old buildings we expected but the gardens and flowers everywhere were an unexpected pleasure. Like walking around in a Disney movie."

— AJ Kersten, Fodors.com member, on the photo submitted above.

WELCOME TO LYON AND THE ALPS

TOP REASONS TO GO

★ **Vieux Lyon:** Lyon's Old Town *traboules,* or passageways, and 16th-century courtyards reveal a hidden trove of Renaissance architecture.

★ **Le Beaujolais Nouveau est arrivé!:** The third Thursday of November is a party like no other in France, when celebrations in honor of the new Beaujolais wine go around the clock.

★ **The Mont Blanc Resorts:** Whether you brave the vertiginous slopes at Chamonix or enjoy the gentler skiing and high life of Megève, you'll be singing "Ain't No Mountain High Enough" once you see France's tallest peak.

★ **Grenoble's Market Day:** Sunday morning offers a chance to walk miles through half a dozen different markets selling everything from herbs to haberdashery.

★ **Epic Epicureanism:** There is no possible way to cite Lyon-Rhône Alps without mentioning Paul Bocuse and all the other resident superstar chefs.

1 Lyon. The city is most famous for its Vieux Lyon district with its Renaissance traboules and the bustling Presqu'île peninsula between the two rivers. The city's historic industrial power has generated ample cultural resources and the energy to create first-rate music, cinema, theater, opera, dance, and cuisine.

2 Beaujolais. Follow the Saône River north from Lyon to the area around Villefranche and you will find the vineyards of Beaujolais, a moving pilgrimage for any wine lover. Diminutive villages with poetic names such as St-Amour, Fleurie, or Juliénas are surrounded by rolling hillsides bristling with grape vines. To the east lies Bourg-en-Bresse, famed for its church and its chickens.

GETTING ORIENTED

Lyon is France's natural hub, where the rivers Rhône and Saône meet and the mountainous wilderness of the Massif Central leans toward the lofty Alps. Lyon—France's "second city"—is a magnet for the surrounding region, including the vineyards of Beaujolais. South of Lyon is the quaint Rhône Valley. Along the southeastern border of France rises a mighty barrier of mountains that provides some of the most spectacular scenery in Europe: the French Alps, soaring to their climax in Europe's highest peak, Mont Blanc.

3 The Rhône Valley. Like predestined lovers, the masculine Rhône joins the feminine Saône to form a fluvial force rolling south to the Mediterranean. Their bounty includes hundreds of steep vineyards and small-town winemakers tempting you with samples. The ancient Roman ruins of Vienne and the Romanesque relics of Valence reflect the Rhône's importance as an early trade route.

4 Grenoble and the Alps. Grenoble, in the Dauphiné, is the gateway to the Alps at the nexus of rivers and highways connecting Marseille, Valence, Lyon, Geneva, and Turin. Literati will love its Stendahl itinerary and its art-filled Musée. To the east, rustic towns announce the Alps, none more idyllic than Annecy, thanks to its blue lake, covered lanes, and quiet canals. The region's natural Alpine splendors are showcased at Chamonix and Megève, ski resorts that buzz with life from December to April.

LYON AND THE ALPS PLANNER

When to Go

Lyon and the Rhône-Alpes are so diverse in altitude and climate that the weather will depend mostly on where you are and when, and which way the wind blows. Freezing gales have been known to turn Lyon's late September dance festival into a winter carnival, with icy blasts from the Massif Central sweeping down the Saône. As a rule, however, Lyon may be rainy and misty, but not especially cold, whereas Grenoble and the Alps can be bitter cold any time of year, though especially from December to April. The Beaujolais wine region is generally temperate, though a recent third-Thursday-in-November Nouveau Beaujolais fest froze vines and revelers alike. South of Lyon along the Rhône the sun beats down on the vineyards in full summer, but the winds howl in winter.

A Votre Santé

The Beaujolais region has hundreds of village wine caves-cellars. Opt for those with signs that state DÉGUSTATION, VENTE EN DIRECT (sold directly from the property), or VENTE AU DÉTAIL (sold by the bottle). And also look for the town's co-op *caveau* (wine cellar), where you can pay a few euros to taste all the wine you want.

Getting Here and Around

Lyon is best explored on foot, with the occasional tramway or subway connection to get you across town in a hurry. Boat tours around the Presqu'île give you another perspective on this riverine metropolis, while bike rentals can also be handy. Consider taking advantage of the Lyon City Card, a one-, two-, or three-day pass to museums with discounts at boutiques, restaurants, and cultural events costing, respectively, €18, €27, and €36. Lyon is an important rail hub, with two in-town train stations and a third at Lyon-Saint-Exupéry airport. Trains from the Part-Dieu train station connect easily with Villefranche-sur-Saône in the middle of the Beaujolais country, while the Gare de Perrache serves points south such as Valence and Vienne.

The main train stations *in this chapter* are in Lyon, Annecy, and Grenoble, but most small towns along the way have train stations, too, or, more accurately, a building with a few wooden seats along the tracks. So one of the best ways to explore the Alps is to keep your eye out for a stop that looks interesting and abandon ship.

A car is the best way to get around the Beaujolais wine country and the rest of Rhône-Alpes. Regional roads are fast and well maintained, though smaller mountain routes are slower, and passes may be closed in winter.

Visitor Information

Contact the **Comité Régional du Tourisme Rhône-Alpes** (✉ *78 rte. de Paris, Charbonnières-les-Bains* ☎ *04–72–59–21–59* 🌐 *www.rhonealpes-tourisme.com*) for information.

The **Maison du Tourisme** (✉ *14 rue de la République, B.P. 227, Grenoble* ☎ *04–76–42–41–41* 🌐 *www.grenoble-isere-tourisme.com*) deals with the Isère département and the area around Grenoble.

Local tourist offices are listed under their respective towns in this chapter.

Tour Options

Boat Tours: Navig-Inter (✉ *13 bis, quai Rambaud, Lyon* ☎ *04–78–42–96–81*) arranges daily boat trips from Lyon along the Saône and Rhône rivers.

Bus Tours: Philibert (✉ *24 av. Barthélémy-Thimonier, B.P. 16, Caluire* ☎ *04–72–23–10–56*) runs bus tours of the region from April to October starting in Lyon.

Walking Tours: The **Lyon tourist office** (✉ *Pl. Bellecour* ☎ *04–72–77–69–69*) organizes walking tours of the city in English.

Eating and Staying

The food you'll find in the Rhône-Alps region is some of France's best, as it's considered the birthplace of the country's traditional cuisine. In Lyon's countless *bouchons*, (taverns or eating houses), you'll find everything from *gras double* (tripe) to *boudin noir* (black sausage) to *paillasson* (fried hashed potatoes). If it's a light or vegetarian meal you're after, you'll be hard-pressed to find one here. Hotels, inns, bed-and-breakfasts, *gîtes d'étapes* (hikers' way stations), and *tables d'hôte* run the gamut from grande luxe to spartanly rustic in this multifaceted region embracing ultra-urban chic in Lyon as well as ski huts in the Alps.

Lyon accommodations range from *péniches* (riverboats) to panoramic guest rooms high in the hilltop Croix Rousse district. The Alps, of course, are well furnished with top hotels, especially in Grenoble and the time-honored ski resorts such as Chamonix and Megève. Many hotels expect you to have at least your evening meal there, especially in summer; in winter they up the ante and hope travelers will take all three meals.

DINING AND LODGING PRICE CATEGORIES (IN EUROS)

	¢	$	$$	$$$	$$$$
Restaurants	under €13	€12–€17	€18–€24	€25–€32	over €32
Hotels	under €65	€65–€105	€106–€145	€146–€215	over €215

Restaurant prices are per person for a main course at dinner, including tax (5.5%) and service; note that if a restaurant offers only prix-fixe (set-price) meals, it has been given the price category that reflects the full prix-fixe price. Hotel prices are for a standard double room in high season, including tax (19.6%) and service charge.

Making the Most of Your Time

Lyon merits an exploration of several days, at least two, for its ample range of architecture, food, and culture. The wine country of the Beaujolais up the river Saône is another two-day visit, unless a drive-through directly to Bourg-en-Bresse is the best solution that time constraints will allow.

Medieval Pérouges is another good day's browse with time for a late afternoon and evening drive into the Alps to Annecy, where the Vieille Ville is an eyeful by day or night. Talloires and other pretty towns around the lake are other lovely visits to plan time for.

The mountain resort of Megève is a place to either settle in for a few days or blow through on your way to Chambéry and the abbey of Grande Chartreuse. Grenoble offers opportunities for perusing masterpieces in its superb museum or following Stendhal's footsteps through the old quarter.

From Grenoble, Valence via the autoroute is a quick transfer to admire the cathedral and the art museum. From here, see the limestone wonder of the Ardèche Gorge on your way to Provence or, if you're headed back to Lyon, stop at Vienne for its Roman sites.

GETTING AROUND

Air Travel

The region's international gateway airport is Aéroport-Lyon-Saint-Exupéry (☎ *08–26–80–08–26 from within France, 33–426–007–007 from abroad*), 26 km (16 mi) east of Lyon, in Satolas. There are domestic airports at Grenoble, Valence, Annecy, Chambéry, and Aix-les-Bains.

Car Travel

Regional roads are fast and well maintained, though smaller mountainous routes can be difficult to navigate and high passes may be closed in winter. A6 speeds south from Paris to Lyon (463 km [287 mi]). The Tunnel de Fourvière, which cuts through Lyon, is a classic hazard, and at peak times you may sit idling for hours. Lyon is 313 km (194 mi) north of Marseille on A7.

To get to Grenoble (105 km [63 mi] southeast) from Lyon, take A43 to A48. Coming from the south, take A7 to Valence and then swing east on A49 to A48 to Grenoble. From Grenoble to Megève and Chamonix through Annecy take A41–E712 to Annecy (direction Geneva), and then A-40 direction Montblanc-Chamonix. Turn off A-40 at Sallanches for the 17 km on the N212 to Megève.

Bus Travel

Buses from Lyon and Grenoble thoroughly and efficiently serve the region's smaller towns. Many ski centers, such as Chamonix, have shuttle buses connecting them with surrounding villages. Tourist destinations, such as Annecy, have convenient bus links with Grenoble. Grenoble's Gare Routière (✉ *11 pl. de la Gare* ☎ *04–76–87–90–31* 🌐 *www.transisere.fr*), is the place to catch buses to Annecy (1 hr, 40 mins; €11.40), Alpe d'Huez (1 hr, 30 mins; €9.60), Chamrousse (1 hr, 15 mins; €8.80), and Megève (2 hrs, 25 mins; €22.20). As for Alpine villages, regional buses head out from the main train stations at Annecy, Chambéry, Megève, and Grenoble.

Train Travel

The high-speed TGV (Train à Grande Vitesse) SNCF (☎ *36–35 [€0.34 per min]* 🌐 *www.voyages-sncf.com*). TGV (🌐 *www.tgv.com*) to Lyon leaves Paris (from Gare de Lyon) hourly and arrives in just two hours. There are also six TGVs daily between Paris's Charles de Gaulle Airport and Lyon. Two in-town train stations and a third at the airport (Lyon-Saint-Exupéry) make Lyon a major transportation hub. The Gare de La Part-Dieu (✉ *Bd. Vivier-Merle*) is used for the TGV routes and links Lyon with many other cities, including Montpellier and Marseilles, along with Grenoble (1 hr, 26 mins; €19.10) and Bordeaux, with four trains a day taking 6 (TGV) to 8½ hours. On the other side of town, the centre-ville station at Gare de Perrache (✉ *Cours de Verdun, Pl. Carnot* ☎ *04–72–56–95–30*) is the more crowded option and serves all the sights of the centre ville—many trains stop at both stations. The TGV station at Aéroport-Lyon-Saint-Exupéry serves, as well as Paris, Grenoble, Avignon, Arles, Valence, Annecy, Aix-les-Bains, and Chambéry. The TGV also has less frequent service to Grenoble, where you can connect to local SNCF trains headed for villages in the Alps. For the Beaujolais wine country, most people train to Villefranche-sur-Saône's station on the Place de la Gare; trains run to smaller towns from here.

Updated by George Semler

Lyon and the Alps are as alike as chocolate and broccoli. Lyon is fast, congested, and saturated with culture (and smog). In the bustling city—often called the gateway to the Alps—it's hard to believe that those pristine peaks are only an hour's train ride away. Likewise, when you're in a small Alpine village you could almost forget France has any large cities at all, because everything you imagined about the Alps—soaring snowcaps, jagged ridges, crystalline lakes—is true. Culturally, Lyon and the Alps could well be on different continents but geographically they make for a great vacation combo.

Cheek-by-jowl, they share a patch of earth sculpted by the noble Rhône as it courses down from Switzerland, flowing out of Lake Geneva. And this soil, or as the French call it, the *terroir,* provides many treasures to savor, beginning with the region's saucy Beaujolais wines. Glinting purple against red-checked linens in a Lyonnais *bouchon* tavern, pink-cheeked Beaujolais vintages flatter every delight listed on those famous blackboard menus: a fat *boudin noir* bursting from its casing, a tangle of country greens in a tangy mustard vinaigrette, or a taste of crackling roast chicken.

If you are what you eat, then Lyon itself is real and hearty, as straightforward and unabashedly simple as a *poulet de Bresse.* Yet the refinements of world-class opera, theater, and classical music also happily thrive in Lyon's gently patinated urban milieu, one strangely reminiscent of 1930s Paris—lace curtains in painted-over storefronts, elegant bourgeois town houses, deep-shaded parks, and low-slung bridges lacing back and forth over the broad, lazy Saône and Rhône rivers.

When you've had your fill of this, pack a picnic of victuals to tide you over and take to the hills—the Alps, to be exact. Here is a land of green-velvet slopes and icy mists, ranging from the modern urban hub of Grenoble and the crystalline lake of Annecy to the state-of-the-art ski resorts of Chamonix and Megève. Let your grand finale be Mont-Blanc, at 15,700 feet Western Europe's highest peak.

LYON

The city's setting at the confluence of the Saône and the Rhône is a spectacular riverine landscape overlooked from the heights to the west by the imposing Notre-Dame de Fourvière church and from the north by the hilltop neighborhood of La Croix Rousse. Meanwhile, the La Confluence Project at the southern tip of the Presqu'île, or peninsula, the land between the Saône and the Rhône, has reclaimed (from the rivers) nearly a square mile of center-city real estate that has become a neighborhood of parks, shops, restaurants, and cultural sites. Another attraction is Lyon's extraordinary dining scene—the city has more good restaurants per square mile than any other European city except Paris.

GETTING HERE

To get between the Aéroport-Lyon-Saint-Exupéry and downtown Lyon take the Satobus (☎ *04–72–68–72–17*), a shuttle bus that goes to the city center between 5 AM and 9 PM and to the train station between 6 AM and 11 PM; journey time is 35–45 minutes, and the fare is €9.20.

Lyon has three major train stations—two in town and a third at the Lyon-Saint-Exupéry airport, making it a major hub for transportation in the region. To get here by car, take A6 south from Paris 463 km [287 mi]).

The city's squeaky-clean and efficient subway gets you from one end of town to another in 5 to 10 minutes. Four métro lines and three tramway lines crisscross the city. A single ticket costs €1.60, and a 10-ticket book is €13.30. Both 2-hr and evening passes cost €2.30. A day "Liberté" pass for bus and métro is €4.50 (available from bus drivers and the automated machines in the métro).

Visitor Information Lyon Tourist Information (✉ *Pl. Bellecour* ☎ *04–72–77–69–69* 🌐 *www.lyon-france.com* ✉ *Av. Adolphe Max near cathedral* ☎ *04–72–77–69–69* ✉ *Perrache train station*)

EXPLORING

Lyon and Marseille both claim to be France's "second city." In terms of size and industrial importance, Marseille probably deserves that title. But for tourist appeal, Lyon is the clear winner. The city's speed and scale are human in ways that Paris may have lost forever. Lyon has its share of historic buildings and quaint *traboules*, which are the passageways under and through town houses dating from the Renaissance (in Vieux Lyon) and the 19th century (in La Croix Rousse). Originally designed as dry, high-speed shortcuts for silk weavers delivering their wares, these passageways were used by the French Resistance during World War II to elude German street patrols.

Lyon's development owes much to its riverside site halfway between Paris and the Mediterranean, and within striking distance of Switzerland, Italy, and the Alps. Lyonnais are proud that their city has been important for more than 2,000 years: Romans made their Lugdunum (the name means "hill or fortress of Lug," the supreme deity of Celtic mythology), the second largest Roman city after Rome itself, capital of Gaul around 43 BC. The remains of the Roman theater and the Odéon, the Gallo-Roman music hall, are among the most spectacular Roman ruins in the world.

In the middle of the city is the Presqu'île, a fingerlike peninsula between the rivers where modern Lyon throbs with shops, restaurants, museums, theaters, and a postmodern Jean Nouvel–designed opera house. West of the Saône is Vieux Lyon (Old Lyon), with its peaceful Renaissance charm and lovely traboules and patios; above it is the old Roman district of Fourvière. To the north is the hilltop Croix Rousse District, where Lyon's silk weavers once operated their looms in lofts designed as workshop dwellings, while across the Rhône to the east are a mix of older residential areas, the famous Halles de Lyon market, and the ultramodern Part-Dieu business and office district with its landmark *gratte-ciel* (skyscraper) beyond.

VIEUX LYON AND FOURVIÈRE

Vieux Lyon—one of the richest groups of urban Renaissance dwellings in Europe—has narrow cobblestone streets, 15th- and 16th-century mansions, small museums, and the cathedral. When Lyon became an important silk weaving town in the 15th century, Italian merchants and bankers built dozens of Renaissance-style town houses. Officially cataloged as national monuments, the courtyards and passageways are open to the public during the morning. The excellent Renaissance Quarter map of the traboules and courtyards of Vieux Lyon, available at the tourist office and in most hotel lobbies, offers the city's most gratifying exploring. Above Vieux Lyon, in hilly Fourvière, are the remains of two Roman theaters and the Basilique de Notre-Dame, visible from all over the city.

TOP ATTRACTIONS

10 **Basilique de Notre-Dame-de-Fourvière.** The rather pompous late-19th-century basilica, at the top of the *ficelle* (funicular railway), is—for better or worse—the symbol of Lyon. Its mock-Byzantine architecture and hilltop site make it a close relative of Paris's Sacré-Coeur. Both were built to underline the might of the Roman Catholic Church after the Prussian defeat of France in 1870 gave rise to the birth of the anticlerical Third Republic. The excessive gilt, marble, and mosaics in the interior underscore the Church's wealth, although they masked its lack of political clout at that time. One of the few places in Lyon where you can't see the basilica is the adjacent terrace, whose panorama reveals the city—with the cathedral of St-Jean in the foreground and the glass towers of the reconstructed Part-Dieu business complex glistening behind. For a yet more sweeping view, climb the 287 steps to the basilica observatory. ✉ *Pl. de Fourvière, Fourvière* 🎫 *Observatory €3* ⏲ *Observatory Easter–Oct., daily 10–noon and 2–6; Nov.–Easter, weekends 2–6. Basilica daily 8–noon and 2–6.*

7 **Cathédrale St-Jean.** Solid and determined—having withstood the sieges of time, revolution, and war—the cathedral's stumpy facade is stuck almost bashfully onto the nave. Although the mishmash inside has its moments—the fabulous 13th-century stained-glass windows in the choir and the varied window tracery and vaulting in the side chapels—the interior lacks drama and harmony. Still, it's an architectural history lesson. The cathedral dates from the 12th century, and the chancel is Romanesque, but construction on the whole continued over three centuries. The 14th-century astronomical clock, in the north transept, is a marvel of technology very much worth seeing. It chimes a hymn to St. John on the hour at noon, 2, 3, and 4 as a screeching rooster and other automatons enact the Annunciation. To the right of the Cathédrale St-Jean stands the 12th-century **Manécanterie** (choir school). ⊠ *70 rue St-Jean, Vieux Lyon* ☎ *04–78–92–82–29.*

13 **Hôtel Bullioud.** This superb Renaissance mansion, close to the Hôtel Paterin, is noted for its courtyard, with an ingenious gallery built in 1536 by Philibert Delorme (1510–1570), one of France's earliest and most accomplished exponents of classical architecture. Delorme also worked on several spectacular châteaux in central France, including those at Fontainebleau and Chenonceaux. ⊠ *8 rue Juiverie, off Pl. St-Paul, Vieux Lyon* 🎫 *Free* ⏲ *Daily 10–noon and 2–6.*

5 **Maison du Crible.** This 17th-century mansion is one of Lyon's oldest. In the courtyard you can glimpse a charming garden and the original Tour Rose—an elegant pink tower. The higher the tower in those days, the greater the prestige—this one was owned by the tax collector—and it's not so different today. ⊠ *16 rue du Bœuf, off Pl. du Petit-Collège, Vieux Lyon* 🎫 *Free* ⏲ *Daily 10–noon and 2–6.*

9 **Musée Gallo-Romain de Fourvière** *(Gallo-Roman Museum).* Since 1933, systematic excavations have unearthed vestiges of Lyon's opulent Roman precursor. The statues, mosaics, vases, coins, and tombstones are excellently displayed in this partially subterranean museum next to the Roman theaters. The large, bronze Table Claudienne is inscribed with part of Emperor Claudius's address to the Roman Senate in AD 48, conferring senatorial rights on the Roman citizens of Gaul. ⊠ *17 rue Clébert, Fourvière* ☎ *04–72–38–81–90* 🌐 *www.musees-gallo-romains.com* 🎫 *€5* ⏲ *Tues.–Sun. 10–6.*

3 **Musées Gadagne** *(Lyon Historical Museum and Puppet Museum).* These two museums are housed in the city's largest ensemble of Renaissance buildings, the Hôtel de Gadagne, built between the 14th and 16th centuries. The **Musée d'Histoire de Lyon** traces the city's history from before it became capital of Roman Gaul. Medieval sculpture, furniture, pottery, paintings, and engravings are on display. The **Musée de la Marionnette** (Puppet Museum), displays the history of marionettes, beginning with Guignol and Madelon, Lyon's Punch and Judy, created by Laurent Mourguet in 1795. After extensive restoration and reform, the museum reopened in spring 2009 with doubled exhibition space distributed over 39 rooms, two workshops, an auditorium, a documentation center, two hanging gardens, a café, and a museum shop. ⊠ *1 pl. du Petit-Collège,*

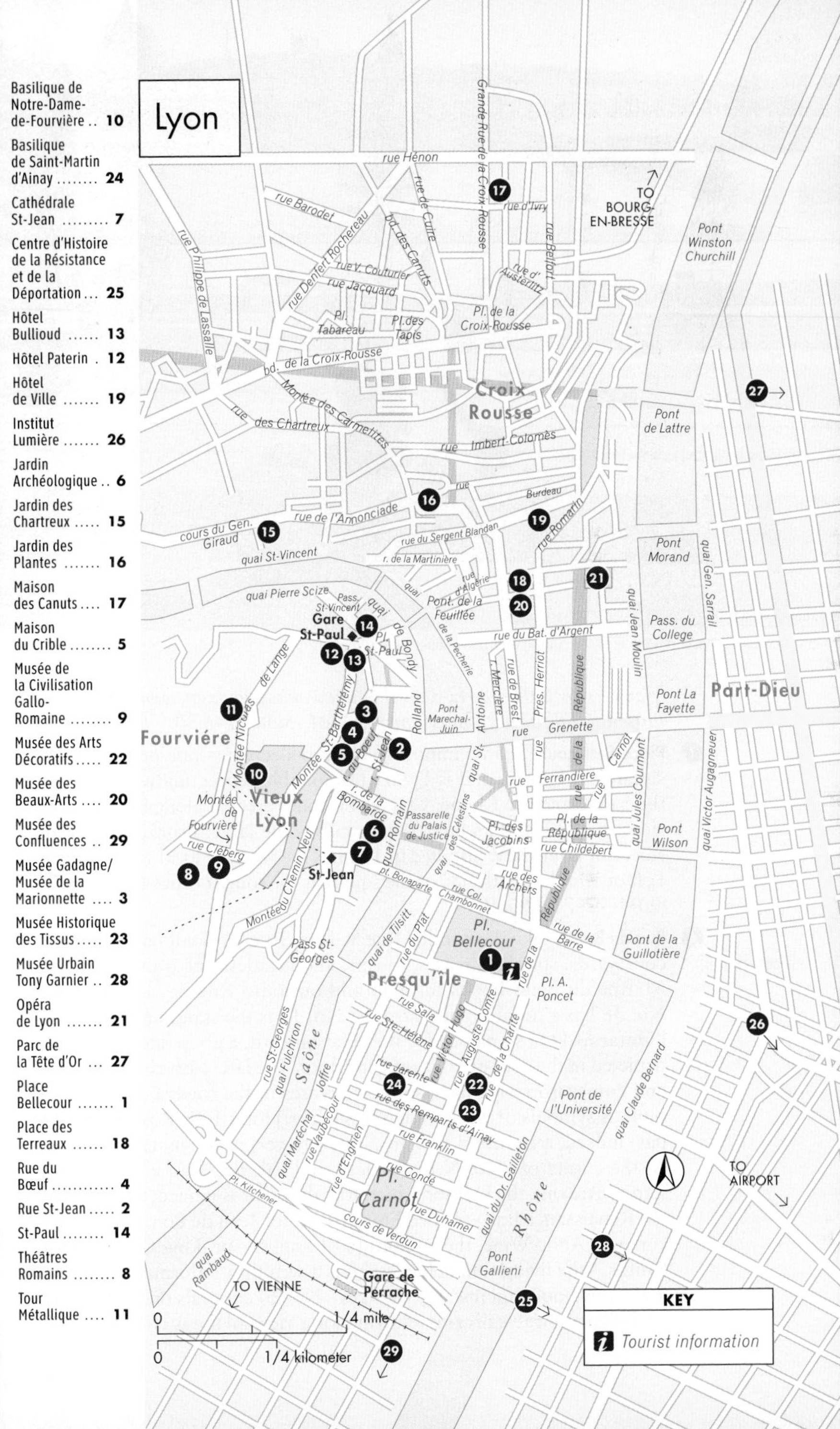

Lyon
Basilique de Notre-Dame-de-Fourvière .. 10
Basilique de Saint-Martin d'Ainay 24
Cathédrale St-Jean 7
Centre d'Histoire de la Résistance et de la Déportation ... 25
Hôtel Bullioud 13
Hôtel Paterin . 12
Hôtel de Ville 19
Institut Lumière 26
Jardin Archéologique .. 6
Jardin des Chartreux 15
Jardin des Plantes 16
Maison des Canuts 17
Maison du Crible 5
Musée de la Civilisation Gallo-Romaine 9
Musée des Arts Décoratifs 22
Musée des Beaux-Arts 20
Musée des Confluences .. 29
Musée Gadagne/ Musée de la Marionnette 3
Musée Historique des Tissus 23
Musée Urbain Tony Garnier .. 28
Opéra de Lyon 21
Parc de la Tête d'Or ... 27
Place Bellecour 1
Place des Terreaux 18
Rue du Bœuf 4
Rue St-Jean 2
St-Paul 14
Théâtres Romains 8
Tour Métallique 11
rue Hénon
Grande Rue de la Croix-Rousse
rue Barodet
rue de Cuire
rue d'Ivry
TO BOURG-EN-BRESSE
Pont Winston Churchill
rue Philippe de Lassalle
rue Denfert Rochereau
bd. des Canuts
rue Belfort
rue d'Austerlitz
rue V. Couturier
rue Jacquard
Pl. Tabareau
Pl. des Tapis
Pl. de la Croix-Rousse
bd. de la Croix-Rousse
Montée des Carmelites
Croix Rousse
rue des Chartreux
rue Imbert-Colomès
Pont de Lattre
rue Burdeau
rue de l'Annonciade
cours du Gen. Giraud
rue du Sergent Blandan
rue Romarin
quai St-Vincent
r. de la Martinière
Pont Morand
quai Gen. Sarrail
rue d'Algérie
quai Pierre Scize
Pass. St-Vincent
quai de Bondy
Pont. de la Feuillée
Gare St-Paul
Pl. St-Paul
quai Jean Moulin
Pass. du College
rue du Bat. d'Argent
de la Pecherie
r. Mercière
rue de Brest
Pres. Herriot
République
Pont La Fayette
Part-Dieu
Montée Nicolas de Lange
Montée St-Barthélemy
Rolland
Pont Marechal-Juin
quai St-Antoine
rue Grenette
Fourviére
r. du Boeuf
r. St-Jean
rue de la République
rue Carnot
quai Jules Courmont
quai Victor Augagneur
rue Ferrandière
Montée de Fourvière
Vieux Lyon
r. de la Bombarde
quai Romain
Passarelle du Palais de Justice
quai des Célestins
Pl. des Jacobins
Pl. de la République
Pont Wilson
rue Childebert
rue Cléberg
Montée du Chemin Neuf
St-Jean
pt. Bonaparte
rue Col. Chambonnet
rue des Archers
Pl. Bellecour
rue de la Barre
Pont de la Guillotière
Pass St-Georges
quai de Tilsitt
rue du Plat
rue de la Charité
Pl. A. Poncet
Presqu'île
rue Sala
rue Ste-Hélène
rue Victor Hugo
rue Auguste Comte
rue St-Georges
quai Fulchiron
Saône
Joffre
rue Jarente
rue des Remparts d'Ainay
Pont de l'Université
quai Claude Bernard
quai Maréchal
rue Vaubecour
rue Franklin
rue d'Enghien
rue Condé
Pl. Carnot
Pl. Kitchener
rue Duhamel
cours de Verdun
quai du Dr. Gailleton
Rhône
TO AIRPORT
quai Rambaud
Pont Gallieni
TO VIENNE
Gare de Perrache
0
1/4 mile
1/4 kilometer
KEY
Tourist information

Located at the confluence of the Saône and the Rhône, Lyon offers visitors a spectacular riverine landscape.

Vieux Lyon ☎ *04–78–42–03–61* 🌐 *www.museegadagne.com* 🎫 *€6 (one museum, €8 for both museums)* 🕓 *Wed.–Sun. 11–6:30.*

❶ **Place Bellecour.** Shady, imposing Place Bellecour is one of the largest squares in France, and is Lyon's fashionable center, midway between the Saône and the Rhône. Classical facades erected along its narrower sides in 1800 lend architectural interest. The large, bronze equestrian statue of Louis XIV, installed in 1828, is the work of local sculptor Jean Lemot. On the south side of the square is the **tourist office** ✉ *Presqu'île* ☎ *04–72–77–69–69.*

❹ **Rue du Bœuf.** Like the parallel Rue St-Jean, Rue du Bœuf has traboules, courtyards, spiral staircases, towers, and facades. The traboule at No. 31 Rue du Bœuf hooks through and out onto Rue de la Bombarde. No. 36 has a notable courtyard. At No. 19 is the standout Maison de l'Outarde d'Or, so named for the great bustard, a gooselike game bird, depicted in the coat of arms over the door. The late-15th-century house and courtyard inside have spiral staircases in the towers, which were built as symbols of wealth and power. The Hotel Tour Rose at No. 22 has, indeed, a beautiful *tour rose* (pink tower) in the inner courtyard. At the corner of Place Neuve St-Jean and Rue du Bœuf is the famous sign portraying the bull for which Rue du Bœuf is named, the work of the Renaissance Italy–trained French sculptor Jean de Bologne. No. 18 contains Antic Wine, the emporium of English-speaking Georges Dos Santos, "the flying sommelier," who is a wealth of information (throw away this book and just ask Georges). No. 20 conceals one of the rare open-shaft spiral staircases allowing for a view all the way up the core.

Fodor's Choice ★

At No. 16 is the Maison du Crible, and No. 14 has another splendid patio. ✉ *Vieux Lyon.*

> **WORD OF MOUTH**
>
> "Lyon—small city, great food, lots of atmosphere. Archaeological Park of Fourvière (theatre and Gallo-Roman amphitheater (Roman ruins).... If you like walking you can cover Lyon on foot—lots of steep hills and steeper hillside staircases." —meath1

2 **Rue St-Jean.** Once Vieux Lyon's major thoroughfare, this street leads north from Place St-Jean to Place du Change, where money changers operated during medieval trade fairs. Many area streets were named for their shops, still heralded by intricate iron signs. The elegant houses along the street were built for illustrious Lyonnais bankers and Italian silk merchants during the French Renaissance. The traboule at No. 54 leads all the way through to Rue du Bœuf No. 27. Beautiful Renaissance courtyards can be visited at No. 50, No. 52, and No. 42. At No. 27 rue St-Jean, an especially nice traboule winds through to No. 6 rue des 3 Maries. No. 28 has a pretty courtyard; No. 24, the Maison Laurencin, has another; Maison Le Viste at No. 21 has a splendid facade. The courtyard at No. 18 merits a close look. The houses at No. 5 place du Gouvernement and No. 7 and No. 1 rue St-Jean also have facades you won't want to miss. ✉ *Vieux Lyon.*

8 **Théâtres Romains** *(Roman Theaters).* Two ruined, semicircular Roman-built theaters are tucked into the hillside, just down from the summit of Fourvière. The **Grand Théâtre,** the oldest Roman theater in France, was built in 15 BC to seat 10,000. The smaller **Odéon,** with its geometric flooring, was designed for music and poetry performances. Lyon International Arts Festival performances are held here each September. ✉ *Colline Fourvière, Fourvière* 🎫 *Free* ⏲ *Daily 9–dusk.*

WORTH NOTING

12 **Hôtel Paterin.** This is a particularly fine example of the type of splendid Renaissance mansion found in the area. ✉ *4 rue Juiverie, off Pl. St-Paul, Vieux Lyon.*

6 **Jardin Archéologique** *(Archaeological Garden).* There are the excavated ruins of two churches that succeeded one another inside this garden. The foundations of the churches were unearthed during a time when apartment buildings—constructed here after churches had been destroyed during the Revolution—were being demolished. One arch still remains and forms part of the ornamentation in the garden. ✉ *Entrance on Rue de la Bombarde, Vieux Lyon.*

15 **Jardin des Chartreux.** One of several of Lyon's small, leafy parks in Lyon, this one is a peaceful place to take a break while admiring the splendid view of the river and Fourvière Hill. ✉ *Entrance on Quai St-Vincent, Presqu'île.*

16 **Jardin des Plantes** *(Botanical Garden).* In these luxurious Botanical Gardens you'll find remnants of the once-huge **Amphithéâtre des Trois Gauls** (Three Gauls Amphitheater), built in AD 19. ✉ *Entrance on Rue de la Tourette, Vieux Lyon* ⏲ *Daily, dawn–dusk.*

14 **St-Paul.** The 12th-century church of St-Paul is noted for its octagonal lantern, its frieze of animal heads in the chancel, and its Flamboyant-Gothic chapel. ✉ *Pl. St-Paul, Vieux Lyon* ☎ *04–78–29–69–58* .

11 **Tour Métallique** *(Metal Tower).* Beyond Fourvière Basilica is this skeletal metal tower built in 1893 and now a television transmitter. The stone staircase, the **Montée Nicolas-de-Lange,** at the foot of the tower, is a direct but steep route from the basilica to the St-Paul train station. ✉ *Colline Fourvière, Fourvière.*

PRESQU'ÎLE AND THE CROIX ROUSSE DISTRICT

Presqu'île, the peninsula flanked by the Saône and the Rhône, is Lyon's modern center, with fashionable shops, a trove of restaurants and museums, and squares graced by fountains and 19th-century buildings. This is the core of Lyon, where you'll be tempted to wander the streets from one riverbank to the other and to explore the entire stretch from the southern point of the peninsula at La Confluence, up past the Gare de Perrache railroad station to Place Bellecour and all the way up to Place des Terreaux.

The hillside and hilltop district north of Place des Terreaux, the Croix Rousse District, has the Jardin des Plantes on the west and the Rhône on the east. It once resounded to the clanking of looms churning out the exquisite silks and other cloth that made Lyon famous. By the 19th century more than 30,000 *canuts* (weavers) worked on looms on the upper floors of the houses. So tightly packed were the buildings that the only way to transport fabrics was through the traboules, which had the additional advantage of protecting the fine cloth in poor weather.

TOP ATTRACTIONS

19 **Hôtel de Ville** *(Town Hall).* Architects Jules Hardouin-Mansart and Robert de Cotte redesigned the very impressive facade of the Town Hall after a 1674 fire. The rest of the building dates from the early 17th century. ✉ *Pl. des Terreaux, Presqu'île.*

26 **Institut Lumière.** On the site where the Lumière brothers, Auguste et Louis, invented cinematography in their family home, this museum has daily showings of early film classics and contemporary movies as well as a permanent exhibit about the Lumières. Researchers may access the archives, which contain numerous films, books, periodicals, director and actor information, photo files, posters, and more. ✉ *25 rue du premier Filme , Part-Dieu* ☎ *04–78–78–18–95* 🌐 *www.institut-lumiere.org* 🎫 *€6* 🕒 *Tues.–Sun. 11–6:30.*

20 ★ **Musée des Beaux-Arts** *(Fine Arts Museum).* In the elegant 17th-century Palais St-Pierre, once a Benedictine abbey, this museum has one of France's largest collections of art after that of the Louvre, including Rodin's *Walker,* Byzantine ivories, Etruscan statues, and Egyptian artifacts. Amid old master, Impressionist, and modern paintings are works by the tight-knit Lyon School, characterized by exquisitely rendered flowers and overbearing religious sentimentality. Note Louis Janmot's *Poem of the Soul,* immaculately painted visions that are by turns heavenly, hellish, and downright spooky. A recent legacy has endowed the

LYON: A STEP-BY-STEP WALK

Start your walk armed with free maps from the Lyon tourist office on Presqu'île's Place Bellecour ❶.

Cross the square and head north along lively Rue du Président-Herriot; turn left onto Place des Jacobins and explore Rue Mercière and the small streets off it.

Cross the Saône on the Passerelle du Palais de Justice (Palace of Justice Footbridge); now you are in Vieux Lyon.

Facing you is the old Palais de Justice. Turn right and then walk 200 yards along Quai Romain Rolland to No. 17, where there's a traboule that leads to No. 9 rue des Trois Maries.

Take another right to get to small Place de la Baleine. Exit the square on the left (north) side and then go right on historic Rue St-Jean ❷.

All along Rue St-Jean are traboules and patios leading into lovely courtyards with spiral staircases and mullioned windows.

Head up to cobblestoned Place du Change; on your left is the Loge du Change church.

Take Rue Soufflot and turn left onto Rue de Gadagne. The Hôtel de Gadagne now houses two museums: the Musée Historique de Lyon, with medieval sculpture and local artifacts, and the Musée de la Marionnette ❸, a puppet museum.

Walk south along Rue du Boeuf ❹, parallel to Rue St-Jean, with its many traboules, courtyards, and spiral staircases.

Just off tiny Place du Petit-Collège, at No. 16, is the Maison du Crible ❺, with its pink tower.

Cut through the traboule at 31 rue du Boeuf into Rue de la Bombarde and go left to get to the Jardin Archéologique ❻, a small garden with two excavated churches.

Alongside the gardens is the solid Cathédrale St-Jean ❼, itself an architectural history lesson. The ficelle (funicular railway) runs from the cathedral to the top of Colline de Fourvière (Fourvière Hill).

Take the Montée de Fourvière to the Théâtres Romains ❽, the well-preserved remnants of two Roman theaters.

Overlooking the theaters is the semi-subterranean Musée de la Civilisation Gallo-Romaine ❾, a repository for Roman finds.

Continue up the hill and take the first right to the mock-Byzantine Basilique de Notre-Dame-de-Fourvière ❿.

Return to Vieux Lyon via the Montée Nicolas-de-Lange, the stone stairway at the foot of the metal tower, the Tour Métallique ⓫.

You will emerge alongside the St-Paul train station. Venture onto Rue Juiverie, off Place St-Paul, to see two splendid Renaissance mansions, the Hôtel Paterin ⓬, at No. 4, and the Hôtel Bullioud ⓭, at No. 8.

museum with a new trove of treasures including works by Manet, Monet, Degas, Bacon, Braque, and Picasso. ✉ *Palais St-Pierre, 20 pl. des Terreaux, Presqu'île* ☎ *04–72–10–17–40* 🌐 *www.mba-lyon.fr* 🎫 *€10 for combined ticket to permanent and temporary exhibits, €6 for permanent only* ⏲ *Wed.–Mon. 10:30–6.*

29 ★ **Musée des Confluences** *(Confluence Museum).* A spanking-new architectural extravaganza, the Frank Gehry–redolent glass and titanium museum designed by the Austrian Coop Himmelblau firm proposes a sweeping three-part overview of scientific knowledge and social science. Scheduled to open fully in 2013, the museum now offers tours and temporary exhibitions. Initial questions such as "Where do we come from?", "Who are we?", and "What are we doing?" are developed from the big bang theory, the history of the universe, and the concept of death in different cultures. The second question takes on mankind and biodiversity, evolution, man as animal, and the brain. The third section addresses society: cooperation, competition, and the creative process. ✉ *Centre d'Information, 86 quai Perrache, Presqu'île* ☎ *04–78–37–30–00* 🌐 *www.museedesconfluences.fr* 🎫 *Free* ⏲ *Wed.–Sat. 1–6, Sun. 10–12, 1–6.*

23 **Musée Historique des Tissus** *(Textile Arts Museum).* A sister museum to the Arts Décoratifs collection, this is a fascinating exhibition of the woven-arts industries that were so crucial to Lyon's fame and fortune. Highlights include Asian tapestries from as early as the 4th century, Turkish and Persian carpets from the 16th to the 18th century, and 18th-century Lyon silks, so lovingly depicted in many portraits of the time and still the stars of many costume exhibits mounted throughout the world today. ✉ *34 rue de la Charité, Presqu'île* ☎ *04–78–38–42–00* 🌐 *www.musee-des-tissus.com* 🎫 *€6, joint ticket with the nearby Musée des Arts Décoratifs* ⏲ *Tues.–Sun. 10–5:30.*

28 **Musée Urbain Tony Garnier** *(Tony Garnier Urban Museum).* Known also as the Cité de la Création (City of Creation), this project was France's first attempt at low-income housing. Over the years, tenants have tried to bring some art and cheerfulness to their environment: 22 giant murals depicting the work of Tony Garnier, the turn-of-the-20th-century Lyon architect, were painted on the walls of these huge housing projects, built between 1920 and 1933. Artists from around the world, with the support of UNESCO, have added their vision to the creation of the ideal housing project. To get here, take the métro from Place Bellecour to Monplaisir-Lumière and walk 10 minutes south along Rue Antoine. ✉ *4 rue des Serpollières, Quartier des États-Unis* ☎ *04–78–75–16–75* 🌐 *www.museeurbaintonygarnier.com* 🎫 *6* ⏲ *Tues.– Sun. 2– 6; Sat. 11–7 Mar.–Sept.*

21 **Opéra de Lyon.** The barrel-vaulted Lyon Opera, a reincarnation of a moribund 1831 building, was designed by star French architect Jean Nouvel and built in the early 1990s. It incorporates a columned exterior, soaring glass vaulting, neoclassical public spaces, an all-black interior down to and including the bathrooms and toilets, and the latest backstage magic. High above, looking out between the heroic statues lined up along the parapet, is a small but excellent restaurant, Les

Continued on page 508

LYON: FRANCE'S CULINARY CAULDRON

No other city in France teases the taste buds like Lyon, birthplace of traditional French cuisine. Home to the workingman's *bouchons* and celebrity chefs, the capital of the Rhône-Alpes region has become the engine room for France's modern cooking canon.

Lyon owes much of its success as a gastronomic center to its auspicious location at the crossroads of several regional cuisines—the hearty cooking traditions and smoked meats of the mountainous east; the Massif Central cattle farms and Auvergne's lambs to the west; the tomato- and olive oil-kissed Mediterranean dishes to the south; and the excellent butters and cheeses of the north. Not to mention the Rhône-Alpes' own natural riches—fish from local lakes and rivers, apricots and cherries from hillside orchards, and dairy and pork products from valley farms.

Restaurants here offer a compelling juxtaposition between simple workingman's fare and sophisticated *haute* cuisine. Casual restaurants called *bouchons* offer classic everyday dishes like *gratineé lyonnaise* (onion soup) and *boudin noir* (pork blood) sausages. At the other end of the spectrum, überchef Paul Bocuse—the original master of Nouvelle Cuisine—serves elevated preparations like black-truffle soup encased in pastry. And a coterie of creative young chefs like Nicolas Le Bec have emerged, making it hard to go wrong in this food-focused city.

Dining alfresco on Lyon's rue Saint-Jean, a cobbled pedestrian street

THE ORIGINAL CELEBRITY CHEF: PAUL BOCUSE

Born: February 11, 1926, in Collonges-au-Mont d'Or, outside Lyon, France

Personality Profile: Perfectionist, polygamous, public relations genius

Trademark: Towering white toque

Favorite pastime: *L'Amour*—with a happy 60-year marriage, and mistresses of 50 and 35 years duration, Monsieur is a busy man in the kitchen and *d'ailleurs*

Claim to Fame: Leader of the Nouvelle Cuisine movement

Bocuse at his Best: Based since 1960 at L'Auberge du Pont de Collonges restaurant outside Lyon in Collonges-au-Mont d'Or, he also owns four brasseries in town—Le Nord, L'Est, L'Ouest, and Le Sud

Best-Known Dish: *Soupe aux truffes noires VGE* (black-truffle soup in pastry, named for former French president Valéry Giscard d'Estaing)

Quote: "Food and sex have much in common. We consummate a union, devour a lover with our eyes, hunger for one another."

For forty years, Paul Bocuse has reigned as Lyon's culinary lion. Not only did he daringly remake French cooking in one of its most tradition-bound centers, he also ascended to become one of the first great male chefs in a city long famous for its *cuisine des femmes*, or women's cuisine.

As an apprentice under legendary Fernand Point at La Pyramide in Vienne, just south of Lyon, Bocuse moved away from the richness of *la grande cuisine* and introduced a lighter, fresher way of cooking that emphasized natural sauces, barely cooked baby vegetables, the parsimonious use of sauces and dressings, and artful yet simple presentation. This new style of cooking came to be known as Nouvelle Cuisine.

By the early 1970s, Bocuse had become the leading ambassador for Nouvelle Cuisine. He often traveled the world as a Nouvelle evangelist while his 60-cook staff back home cooked under his eagled-eyed wife.

These days, Bocuse's once-revolutionary cooking style has matured into the country's *cuisine classique*. "It's not nouvelle cuisine anymore," he has said, "it's now *ancienne* cuisine." But because Bocuse's touch remains so sublime, foodies from around the world still make culinary pilgrimages to L'Auberge du Pont de Collonges to experience the birthplace of modern French cooking.

Bocuse at L'Auberge du Pont de Collonges

THE NEW GUARD: MARKET-DRIVEN CREATIVITY

(far left) chef Nicolas Le Bec, (left) caviar-topped potato with sour cream, (above) sea urchin with coconut cream

A Michelin road map of the region's top dining establishments reveals a Rhône-Alpes galaxy totaling more than 60 stars, a full third of which are grouped around the city of Lyon. A new generation of chefs is shaking up Lyon's culinary scene, developing a cooking style that is even lighter and more inventive than Nouvelle Cuisine. The most important player is Nicolas Le Bec, followed by talents like Jean-Christophe Ansanay-Alex, Christian Têtedoie, and Mathieu Viannay.

NICOLAS LE BEC

This Breton chef is known for his devotion to colorful produce and exotic spices, which he layers into modern versions of classic dishes. Recent offerings include foie gras torchon hidden under a tower of herbs and greens, surrounded by colorful fruit syrups and toasted brioche; poached lobster atop curried cauliflower with chestnuts and onion confit; and steamed sea bass with shrimp won tons and dried seaweed. In addition to his modern, fine-dining flagship **Nicolas Le Bec** (✉ *14 rue Grolée, Presqu'île* ☎ *04–78–42–15–00* 🌐 *www.nicolaslebec.com*), he also has two casual places in Lyon, Espace Le Bec and Rue Le Bec.

JEAN-CHRISTOPHE ANSANAY-ALEX

For a quick escape from the city, walk up the Saône and over the bridge to **Auberge de l'Ile** (✉ *L'Ile Barbe, Collonges au Mont-D'Or* ☎ *04–78–83–99–49* 🌐 *www.jc-aa.com*), located in a 17th-century monastery, where Ansanay-Alex cooks up modern French fare.

CHRISTIAN TÊTEDOIE

Located on the quai Piere-Scize in Lyon, restaurant **Christian Têtedoie** (✉ *54 Quai Pierre-Scize, Vieux Lyon* ☎ *04–78–29–40–10* 🌐 *www.tetedoie.com*) is an elegant, classically decorated restaurant that features a market-driven menu with daring flavor pairings.

MATHIEU VIANNAY

At the formal **La Mère Brazier** (✉ *12 rue Royal, Presqu'île* ☎ *04–78–23–17–20*), Mathieu Viannay is celebrated for his creative signature dishes, such as pâté en croûte of Bresse chicken and foie gras with black cherry jam.

THE BOUCHON TRADITION

(top) Bouchons on Rue Merciere, (bottom) Ives Rivoiron, owner of Café des Fédérations

Lyon's iconic bouchons are casual bistro-like restaurants with modest décor along the lines of tiled walls, wooden benches, and zinc counters. In the late 19th-century, these informal eateries dished out hearty fare for working-class customers like pony express riders, stagecoach drivers, silk workers, and field laborers.

The term bouchon originated as a description for the bundles of straw that hung over the entrance of early bouchons, indicating the availability of food and drink for horses as well as humans. These friendly, family-run taverns were customarily run by female chefs, serving cuisine that relied heavily on humble pork and beef cuts, such as stomachs, brains, trotters, ears, cheeks, and livers.

Today many restaurants call themselves bouchons that would not fit the traditional definition. For the real thing, look for a little plaque at the door showing Gnafron, a drunken marionette with red nose and wine glass in hand. He signifies that the establishment is part of the official bouchon association. Bouchons are still a frugal dining choice: in many establishments, $25 will buy an appetizer, main course, salad, and dessert or cheese plate.

Lyon's best bouchons are located around Place des Terreaux and include **Chez Hugon** (✉ *12 rue Pizay, Presqu'île* ☎ *04–78–28–10–94* ⏲ *closed weekends*) and **Café des Fédérations** (✉ *8 rue du Major-Martin, Presqu'île* ☎ *04–78–28–26–00* ⏲ *closed weekends*) to the west toward the River Saône.

CLASSIC LYONNAIS FARE

At bouchons around the city, look for these traditional dishes:

Andouillette à la lyonnaise tripe sausages stuffed with veal and traditionally served with fried onions

Bavette skirt steak with shallots

Blanquette de veau veal stewed in cream, egg yolks, onions, and mushrooms

Boudin blanc sausage made from pork, onion, and eggs, without the blood

Boudin noir pork-blood sausage

Bresse chicken à la lyonnaise poached and stuffed chicken with truffles

Bugnes beignets of fried pork fat

Cervelas Lyonnais brioche filled with smoked sausage, truffles, and pistachio nuts

Frisée aux lardons curly leafed salad with bacon and eggs

Galette lyonnaise mashed potatoes with onions, browned in the oven and served in a gratin dish

Gâteau de foies blonds de volaille chicken liver mousse

Boudin noir sausages, the dark links at right, are just one of the area's famed pork products

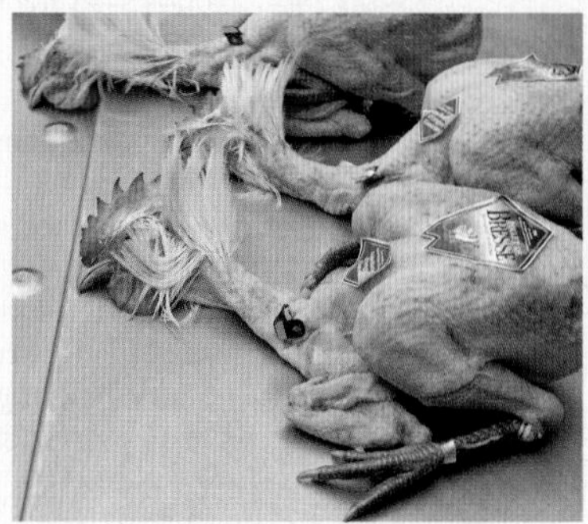

Lyon's famous blue-footed chickens, poulet de Bresse

Gras double breaded, fried tripe with onions and butter

Gratinee lyonnaise onion soup topped with bread and cheese

Paillasson fried hashed potatoes

Pot-au-feu vegetable and meat stew, a winter favorite

Pots de Lyon wine flagons, heavy-bottomed bottles originally conceived to satirize government attempts to limit silk workers' wine consumption in favor of increased labor productivity

Poularde demi-deuil chicken with black truffles sliced thinly under the skin

Quenelle de brochet velvety dumplings made from pike fish, flour, butter, and eggs, served with béchamel sauce

Rosette a garlicky pork sausage

Sabodet pig's-head sausage

Saucissons chauds slices of warm sausage with potatoes drizzled with oil and vinegar

Saucisson en brioche sausage encased in brioche

Tablier de sapeur breaded, fried tripe

Muses de l'Opéra. ✉ *1 pl. de la Comédie, Presqu'île* ☎ *04–72–00–45–00, 04–72–00–45–45 for tickets* 🌐 *www.opera-lyon.com.*

> **WORD OF MOUTH**
>
> "Places des Terreaux is a beautiful square, nice cafés, and surrounded by old classic buildings."
>
> —Michel_Paris

18 **Place des Terreaux.** The four majestic horses rearing up from a monumental 19th-century fountain in the middle of this large square are an allegory of the river Saône by Frédéric-Auguste Bartholdi, who sculpted New York Harbor's Statue of Liberty. The 69 fountains embedded in the wide expanse of the square are illuminated by fiber-optic technology at night. The notable buildings on either side are the Hôtel de Ville and the Musée des Beaux-Arts. ✉ *Presqu'île.*

WORTH NOTING

24 **Basilique de Saint-Martin d'Ainay.** The abbey church of one of Lyon's most ancient monasteries, this fortified church dates to a 10th-century Benedictine abbey and a 9th-century sanctuary before that. The millenary, circa-1,000-year energy field is palpable around this hulking structure, especially near the rear of the apse where the stained-glass windows glow richly in the twilight. It was one of the earliest buildings in France to be classified a national monument, in 1844; its interior murals and frescoes are disappointingly plain and austere compared to the quirky, rough exterior. ✉ *Pl. de l'Abbaye d'Ainay, Presqu'île* ☎ *04–78–72–10–03* 🎫 *Free* 🕒 *Daily 9–1 and 4–7.*

25 **Centre d'Histoire de la Résistance et de la Déportation** *(Museum of the History of the Resistance and the Deportation).* During World War II, especially after 1942, Lyon played an important role in the Resistance movement against the German occupation of France. Displays include equipment, such as radios and printing presses, photographs, and exhibits re-creating the clandestine lives and heroic exploits of Resistance fighters. ✉ *14 av. Berthelot, Part-Dieu* ☎ *04–78–72–23–11* 🎫 *€4, guided tour €7 on reservation* 🕒 *Wed.–Fri. 9–5:30, Sat.–Sun. 9:30–6.*

17 **Maison des Canuts** *(Silk Weavers' Museum).* Despite the industrialization of silk and textile production, old-time Jacquard looms are still in action at this historic house in the Croix Rousse. The weavers are happy to show children how to operate a miniature loom. ✉ *10–12 rue d'Ivry, La Croix Rousse* ☎ *04–78–28–62–04* 🎫 *€6* 🕒 *Tues.–Sat. 10–6:30; guided tours by appointment at 11 and 3:30.*

22 **Musée des Arts Décoratifs** *(Decorative Arts Museum).* Housed in an 18th-century mansion, the museum has fine collections of silverware, furniture, objets d'art, porcelain, and tapestries. ✉ *34 rue de la Charité, Presqu'île* ☎ *04–78–38–42–00* 🌐 *www.lesartsdecoratifs.fr* 🎫 *€6, joint ticket with the nearby Musée Historique des Tissus* 🕒 *Tues.–Sun. 10–5:30.*

27 **Parc de la Tête d'Or** *(Golden Head Park).* On the bank of the Rhône, this 300-acre park encompasses a lake, pony rides, and a small zoo. It's ideal for an afternoon's outing with children. Take the métro from Perrache train station to Masséna. ✉ *Pl. du Général-Leclerc, Quai Charles-de-Gaulle, Cité Internationale* 🎫 *Free* 🕒 *Daily, dawn–dusk.*

WHERE TO EAT

$$$$ FRENCH ★ ✕ **Auberge de l'Île.** For a pretty one-hour walk up the river Saône's right bank and a return down the other, the Ile Barbe is a lush and leafy enclave to keep in mind. Chef Jean-Christophe Ansanay-Alex is famous for his oral daily menu performance. This luscious hideaway, whether outside on the terrace or inside the graceful former 17th-century monastery refectory, serves smart, contemporary cuisine based on fresh market products prepared with originality. Look for game in fall and winter. The wine list is strong in local Condrieu and Côte-Rotie selections. ✉ *L'Ile Barbe, Collonges au Mont-D'Or* ☎ *04–78–83–99–49* 🌐 *www.aubergedelile.com* ✍ *Reservations essential* ▭ *AE, MC, V* ⏲ *Closed Sun., Mon., and Aug. 1–24.*

$ FRENCH ✕ **Brasserie Georges.** This inexpensive brasserie at the south end of Rue de la Charité next to the Perrache train station is one of the city's largest and oldest, founded in 1836 but now in a palatial 1925 Art Deco building. Meals range from hearty veal stew or sauerkraut and sausage to more refined fare. The fare is less than creative and, like the setting, a bit impersonal—stick with the great standards, such as *saucisson brioché* (sausage in brioche stuffed with truffled foie gras)—but the ambience is as delicious as it comes. ✉ *30 cours Verdun, Perrache* ☎ *04–72–56–54–54* 🌐 *www.brasseriegeorges.com* ▭ *AE, DC, MC, V.*

$ FRENCH ✕ **Café des Fédérations.** For 80 years this sawdust-strewn café with homey red-check tablecloths has reigned as one of the city's leading bouchons. It may have overextended its stay, however, by trading on past glory. Some readers report a desultory hand in the kitchen, and native Lyonnais seem to head elsewhere since the legendary Raymond Fulchiron's recent retirement. Still, for a historic setting and a taste of classic Lyon gastronomy, the deftly prepared local classics like *boudin blanc* (white-meat sausage), *boudin noir* (black sausage), or andouillettes (veal and pork tripe sausage) continue to be about as good as they get here. ✉ *8 rue du Major-Martin, Presqu'île* ☎ *04–78–28–26–00* 🌐 *www.lesfedeslyon.com* ▭ *AE, DC, MC, V* ⏲ *Closed weekends and July 23–Aug. 23.*

$ FRENCH ★ ✕ **Café 203/Café 100 Tabac.** These two clever sister bistros near the opera are young, hot, and happening. One is named for the Peugeot 203 (an antique model of which is parked outside), and the other is a play on "100/sans" (100% without) tobacco—yes, smoke-free. It is open from dawn to after midnight (but no Sunday breakfast), and the Italianate cuisine is fresh and original, fast, inexpensive, and delicious. For a quick pre- or post-opera meal, this is the spot. ✉ *9 rue du Garet, Presqu'île* ✉ *23 rue de l'Arbre Sec, Presqu'île* ☎ *04–78–28–65–66* 🌐 *www.cafe203.com* ▭ *AE, DC, MC, V.*

$$ FRENCH ✕ **Chez Hugon.** This typical bouchon-tavern with the de rigueur red-check tablecloths is behind the Musée des Beaux-Arts and is one of the city's top-rated insider spots. Practically a club, it's crowded with regulars, who keep busy trading quips with the owner while Madame prepares the best *tablier de sapeur* (tripe marinated in wine and fried in bread crumbs) in town. Whether you order the hunks of homemade pâté, the stewed chicken in wine vinegar sauce, or the plate of *ris de veau* (sweetbreads), your dinner will add up to good, inexpensive food and plenty of

10

it. ✉ *12 rue Pizay, Presqu'île* ☎ *04–78–28–10–94* ▭ *MC, V* ⊙ *Closed weekends and Aug.*

> **WORD OF MOUTH**
>
> "In 1997, an organization—L'Association de Défense des Bouchons Lyonnais—was started to protect Lyon's historic bouchon taverns. The last I heard there were 21 bouchons certified. Stay away from the ones who have huge 'BOUCHON' signs—those are touristy places. Stick to the famed landmarks like Café des Fédérations." —cigalechanta

$$ FRENCH Fodor's Choice ★ ✕ **Comptoir Abel.** About 400-years-old, this charming house is one of Lyon's most frequently filmed and photographed taverns. Simple wooden tables in wood-panel dining rooms, quirky art on every wall, heavy-bottom *pot lyonnais* wine bottles—every detail is obviously pampered and lovingly produced. The *salade lyonnaise* (green salad with homemade croutons and sautéed bacon, topped with a poached egg) or the *rognons madère* (kidneys in a madeira sauce) are standouts. ✉ *25 rue Guynemer, Presqu'île* ☎ *04–78–37–46–18* ⊕ *www.cafecomptoirabel.com* ▭ *AE, DC, MC, V* ⊙ *Closed Sat., Sun., and Dec. 22–Jan. 2.*

✕ **Jura.** Founded in 1864, the rows of tables, the 1934 mosaic-tile floor, and the absence of anything pretty gives this place the feel of a men's club. The *gateau de foies de volaille aux raviolis* (chicken liver raviolis) is a masterpiece. The game and steak dishes are robust, as is the *cassoulet des escargots* (stew of beans, mutton, and snails). For dessert, stick with the terrific cheese selection. ✉ *25 rue Tupin, Presqu'île* ☎ *04–78–42–20–57* ⊕ *www.lejura.cartesurtables.com* ▭ *MC, V* ⊙ *Closed weekends May–Sept., Sun. and Mon. Sept.–Apr.*

$ FRENCH Fodor's Choice ★ ✕ **La Famille.** True to the name of this low-key, low-cost bistro high on the Croix-Rousse hillside, photographs of the clan adorn the walls here, while the simple cuisine tends toward traditional recipes and authentic Lyon fare. From the poulet *fermier* (farm or free range chicken) to the grilled trout, the daily chalkboard announces the market specialties chef Gilles Mozziconacci has managed to cobble together on his early morning marketing tour through Les Halles de Lyon. In summer, the terrace is the place to be. ✉ *18 rue Duviard, Croix Rousse* ☎ *04–72–98–83–90* ⊕ *www.la-famille-croix-rousse.fr* ✍ *Reservations essential* ▭ *AE, DC, MC, V* ⊙ *Closed Sun., Mon., 1st 2 wks in Aug., Dec. 21–Jan 4.*

$ FRENCH ★ ✕ **La Mâchonnerie.** The verb *mâchonner* (to bite, gnaw, or chew) comes from the morning snack of Lyon's iconic silk weaver (or *canut*) and has come to mean the typical food of the Lyon region. This is one of Lyon's most respected popular bistros, under the *ficelle,* the funicular up to the Fourvière hill. Try the *pot au feu* (meat and vegetable stew) *or the blanquette de veau* (stewed veal). ✉ *36 rue Tramassac, Vieux Lyon* ☎ *04–78–42–24–62* ⊕ *www.lamachonnerie.com* ▭ *AE, DC, MC, V* ⊙ *Closed Sun. No lunch weekdays.*

$$$$ FRENCH Fodor's Choice ★ ✕ **La Mère Brazier.** The house of Eugénie Brazier is a legendary location in Lyon, and even more so now that Mathieu Viannay, one of the top representatives of the city's contemporary cuisine, has honored one of the founding forces behind the city's culinary fame by opening a restaurant in her former space. Winner of the coveted 2004 Meilleur

Lyon's Place des Terreaux is a true spectacle, thanks to 69 Daniel Buren fountains and Bartholdi's centerpiece watery marvel.

Ouvrier de France (top chef) prize, Viannay continues to experiment with taste, textures, and ingredients in this carefully restored space built into a traditional house. Mathieu Viannay describes the menu as "mixed" between completely modern cuisine and "Mère Brazier recipes revisited" such as the *volaille de Bresse demi-deuil* (Bresse poultry in "half mourning," that is with black truffles under the breast skin). ✉ *12 rue Royale, Presqu'île* ☎ *04–78–23–17–20* 🌐 *www.lamerebrazier.fr* ✍ *Reservations essential* ▭ *AE, DC, MC, V* ⏲ *Closed Sun., Mon., and 1st 2 wks in Aug.*

$$ FRENCH Fodor's Choice ★ ✕ **Le Garet.** From quenelles (pike dumplings) to the house favorite andouillettes (pork sausage), this is the perfect primer course in bouchon fare celebrated in a cozy and joyful atmosphere that is, perhaps even more than the food itself, what makes Lyon's version of the French bistro so irresistible. The salade lyonnaise (frisée lettuce, pork lardons, croutons, and a poached egg with a Dijon vinaigrette) is an institution at this famous dining room near the Hôtel de Ville while the roast veal chop and ratatouille provides a welcome break from the standard porcine bouchon lineup. ✉ *7 rue Garet, Presqu'île* ☎ *04–78–28–16–94* ✍ *Reservations essential* ▭ *AE, DC, MC, V* ⏲ *Closed Sat., Sun., Feb. 22 –Mar. 1, July 24–Aug. 24.*

$$ FRENCH ✕ **Le Nord.** Should you want to keep some change in your pocket and still sample cooking by Paul Bocuse–trained-and-supervised chefs, four Bocuse bistros are distributed around Lyon's cardinal points. Le Nord specializes in Eastern cuisine, with specialties including dishes cooked over coals and excellent fish and seafood. The decor is classical turn-of-the-20th-century brasserie with wooden benches and panel walls. For cooking from around the Mediterranean amid bright sun-

drenched colors, **Le Sud**(✉ *11 pl. Antonin-Poncet, Presqu'île* ☎ *04–72–77–80–00*) is the Bocusian homage to southern Europe. The rollicking **L'Est**(✉ *Gare des Brotteaux 14, Les Brotteaux* ☎ *04–37–24–25–26*) is set in the old 19th-century Brotteaux train station and cooks up a travel theme, thanks to a menu that includes dishes from all over the planet and a decor flavored with railroad memorabilia, paraphernalia, and a soupçon of nostalgia. **L'Ouest**(✉ *Quai du Commerce 1, Villefranche* ☎ *04–37–64 –64–64*) exults in a postmodern wood-and-steel design, a fitting setting for Bocuse's maritime culinary adventures in the islands of the Atlantic, Caribbean, and the South Seas. ✉ *18 rue Neuve, Presqu'île* ☎ *04–72–10–69–69* 🌐 *www.nordsudbrasseries.com* 💳 *AE, DC, MC, V.*

$$$$ FRENCH ✕ **Les Loges.** This lovely dining room, lavishly appointed with mahogany chairs, modern art, and a giant medieval hearth, serves a range of culinary delights that deliciously represent the New Lyon cooking. Chef Anthony Bonnet's *poitrine de veau* (breast of veal) with asparagus and essence of almonds or his *foie gras poèlé au coing* (sautéed duck or goose liver with quince) are two specialties to look for, though the menu is in constant flux according to markets and seasons. ✉ *6 rue du Bœuf, Vieux Lyon* ☎ *04–72–77–44–44* 🌐 *www.courdesloges.com* 💳 *AE, DC, MC, V* ⏲ *Closed Aug. 4–26. No dinner Sun.*

$$ FRENCH ✕ **Les Lyonnais.** Decorated with photographs of local celebrities, this popular bistro is particularly animated. The simple food—chicken simmered for hours in wine, meat stews, and grilled fish—is served on bare wood tables. A blackboard announces plats du jour, which are usually less expensive than items on the printed menu. Try the *caille aux petits legumes* (quail with baby vegetables) for a change from heavier bouchon fare such as *la quenelle* (pike dumpling) or *bugnes* (beignets of fried pork fat). ✉ *1 rue Tramassac, Vieux Lyon* ☎ *04–78–37–64–82* 🌐 *www.restaurantlyonnais.com* 💳 *AE, DC, MC, V* ⏲ *Closed Aug. and 1st wk in Jan.*

$$ FRENCH ★ ✕ **Les Muses de l'Opéra.** High up under the glass vault of the Opéra de Lyon designed by Jean Nouvel, this small restaurant looks out past the backs of sculptures of the eight Muses over the Hôtel de Ville. The quality and variety of the creative contemporary cuisine make it hard to decide between the choices offered, but the salmon in butter sauce with watercress mousse is a winner. ✉ *Pl. Comédie, Opéra de Lyon, 7th fl., Presqu'île* ☎ *04–72–00–45–58* 🌐 *www.trivago.fr* ✍ *Reservations essential* 💳 *AE, MC, V* ⏲ *No dinner Sun.*

$$ FRENCH ★ ✕ **L'Étage.** Hidden over Place des Terreaux, this semisecret upstairs dining room in a former silkweaving loft prepares some of Lyon's finest and most daring new cuisine. A place at the window (admittedly hard to come by), overlooking the facade of the Beaux Arts academy across the square, is a moment to remember, especially if it's during the December 8 Festival of Lights. With limited space, reservations are a must. ✉ *4 pl. des Terreaux (3rd fl.), Presqu'île* ☎ *04–78–28–19–59* 💳 *AE, DC, MC, V* ⏲ *Closed Sun., Mon., and July 19–Aug. 21.*

$$ FRENCH ✕ **Le Vivarais.** Robert Duffard's simple, tidy restaurant is an outstanding culinary value. Don't expect napkins folded into flower shapes—the excitement is on your plate, with dishes like *lièvre royale* (hare rolled

and stuffed with foie gras and a hint of truffles). ✉ *1 pl. du Dr-Gailleton, Presqu'île* ☎ *04–78–37–85–15* ✍ *Reservations essential* ▭ *AE, MC, V* ⊙ *Closed Sun., and July 24–Aug. 22.*

$$ FRENCH ★ ✕ **M Restaurant.** When Matthieu Viannay moved to his new restaurant La Mère Brazier in October of 2008, his former gastronomical sanctuary in the upper Brotteaux district east of the Rhône became a creative but non-wallet-busting bistrot under the direction of former Léon de Lyon chef Julien Gautier. Market cuisine, new good-value wines, and sleek contemporary design and cuisine are the rules of thumb at this popular new operation at a well known culinary corner. ✉ *47 av. Foch, Les Brotteaux* ☎ *04–78–89–55–19* ✍ *Reservations essential* ▭ *AE, MC, V* ⊙ *Closed weekends except holidays; Aug.; and Dec. 29–Jan. 5.*

$$$$ FRENCH Fodor's Choice ★ ✕ **Nicolas Le Bec.** Despite opening his new L'Espace Le Bec in the Aéroport-Lyon-Saint-Exupéry in July 2008 and, in April 2009, his Rue le Bec in the Quartier de Confluence at the southern tip of Lyon's Presqu'île, Nicolas Le Bec maintains his now-traditional hideaway near Place Bellecour. With a constantly changing menu responding to the seasons, the market, and the chef's abundant curiosity, there's always a new take on anything from artichokes to risotto in this postmodern culinary antithesis of traditional Lyonnais bouchon cooking. Le Bec's past triumphs include his duck foie gras with black figs and his roast crayfish with purple artichokes, and fans keep packing this place to see what new wonders he has up his sleeve. ✉ *14 rue Grolée, Presqu'île* ☎ *04–78–42–15–00* 🌐 *www.nicolaslebec.com* ✍ *Reservations essential* ▭ *AE, MC, V* ⊙ *Closed Sun., Mon., and 1st 3 wks in Aug.*

$$$$ FRENCH Fodor's Choice ★ ✕ **Paul Bocuse.** Parisians hop the TGV to dine at this culinary shrine in Collonges-au-Mont-d'Or, then snooze back to the capital. Whether Bocuse—who kick-started the "new" French cooking back in the 1970s and became a superstar in the process—is here or not, the legendary black-truffle soup in pastry crust he created in 1975 to honor President Giscard d'Estaing will be. So will the frogs'-leg soup with watercress, the green bean–and-artichoke salad with foie gras, or the Bresse wood-pigeon "tripled": drumstick in puff pastry with young cabbage, breast roasted and glazed in cognac, and an aromatic dark pâté of the innards. For a mere €160 for two, the *volaille de Bresse truffée en vessie "Mère Fillioux"* (Bresse hen cooked in a pig bladder with truffles) comes to the table looking something like a basketball—the bladder is removed and discarded revealing a poached chicken within. Like the desserts, the grand dining room is done in traditional style. Call ahead if you want to find out whether Bocuse will be cooking, and book far in advance. ⇨ *For more on Bocuse, see "Lyon: France's Culinary Cauldron" in this chapter.* ✉ *40 quai de la Plage, Collonges-au-Mont-d'Or, Pont de Collonges Nord* ☎ *04–72–42–90–90* 🌐 *www.bocuse.fr* ✍ *Reservations essential, jacket required* ▭ *AE, DC, MC, V.*

WHERE TO STAY

$$$–$$$$ **Boscolo Grand Hôtel.** This Belle Époque hotel off Place de la République has a courteous and efficient staff. Guest rooms have high ceilings, mostly modern furnishings, and one special piece such as an armoire or writing desk. Erté prints try hard to set a stylish tone in the guest

10

rooms, the Rhône is just across the street, and tour groups are kept happy and content. **Pros:** central location on Presqu'île good for shopping and exploring; adequately appointed and comfortable. **Cons:** a little impersonal; not an intimate hideaway. ✉ *11 rue Grôlée, Presqu'île* ☎ *04–72–40–45–45* 🌐 *www.boscolohotels.com* *140 rooms* *In-room: a/c, Wi-Fi. In-hotel: restaurant, bar, parking (paid), some pets allowed* *AE, DC, MC, V* *BP.*

$ **Citôtel Dubost.** This little gem is a lot better than a first glance might indicate. Rooms are small but impeccable; the art hanging around the walls is generic but interesting; the breakfast bread, croissant, and coffee are uniformly excellent, and the staff is friendly and helpful. The one-minute walk to Lyon's slick subway line at Gare Perrache can be handy in rain or in haste, though the walk to the other end of Presqu'île is an entertaining 45-minute gallop not to miss. Meanwhile, La Confluence Quarter is at your doorstep. **Pros:** Perrache station can get you anywhere in a hurry; neighborhood is untouristy and real. **Cons:** light to flimsy furnishings; square can be noisy on weekend nights. ✉ *19 pl. Carnot, Presqu'île* ☎ *04–78–42–00–46* 🌐 *www.hotel-dubost.com* *56 rooms* *In-room: a/c, Wi-Fi. In-hotel: Wi-Fi hotspot, some pets allowed* *AE, DC, MC, V.*

$$–$$$ Fodor's Choice ★ **Collège.** A faithful reproduction of the owner Laurent Phelip's schoolboy days in Vieux Lyon, this charmingly nostalgic theme hotel ("taking us back to our dreams," as the owner puts it) offers public spaces decorated as antique classrooms, complete with polished wooden desks with inkwells and geography maps. The breakfast room is a study hall. Guest rooms range from simple "undergraduate" quarters to "postgraduate" suites—they are challenging in their stark-white minimal decor but most of them come with splendid views over the Saône and Lyon. **Pros:** in the middle of Vieux Lyon at a reasonable price; schoolboy theme pervasive and funny. **Cons:** spartan decor; rooms a bit short on space. ✉ *5 pl. St-Paul, Vieux Lyon* ☎ *04–72–10–05–05* 🌐 *www.college-hotel.com* *39 rooms* *In-room: a/c, Wi-Fi. In-hotel: bar, Wi-Fi hotspot, parking (paid), some pets allowed* *AE, DC, MC, V* *BP.*

$$ **Hôtel des Artistes.** This intimate hotel on an elegant square opposite the Théâtre des Célestins has long been popular among stage and screen artists; black-and-white photographs of actors and actresses adorn lobby walls. Rooms are smallish but modern and comfortable, and the friendly reception and great location appeal to all comers. **Pros:** a sense of traditional theatrical chic pervades; good central location for Presqu'île; pretty view over square. **Cons:** slightly cluttered spaces; a few clicks behind cutting-edge technology. ✉ *8 rue Gaspard-André, Presqu'île* ☎ *04–78–42–04–88* 🌐 *www.hotel-des-artistes.fr* *45 rooms* *In-room: no a/c, Wi-Fi, refrigerator. In-hotel: Wi-Fi hotspot, some pets allowed* *AE, DC, MC, V.*

$ ★ **Hôtel du Théâtre.** The friendly and enthusiastic owner is sufficient reason to recommend this small hotel. But its location and reasonable prices make it even more commendable. Rooms are simple but clean; those overlooking Place des Célestins not only have a theatrical view but also a bathroom with a tub. Those facing the side have a shower only. Breakfast is included. **Pros:** sense of being at the center of the action; wallet friendly. **Cons:** small to tiny spaces in and around the hotel; street-side rooms can be noisy at night. ✉ *10 rue de Savoie, Presqu'île* ☎ *04–78–42–33–32* 🌐 *www.hotel-du-theatre.fr* *24 rooms* *In-room: no a/c, Wi-Fi. In-hotel: bar, Wi-Fi hotspot, parking (paid), some pets allowed* ▭ *AE, DC, MC, V.*

$$$$ Fodor's Choice ★ **La Cour des Loges.** King Juan Carlos of Spain, Celine Dion, and the Rolling Stones have all graced this most eye-popping of Lyon hotels. Spectacularly renovated around an arcaded and glassed-in Renaissance courtyard, this former Jesuit convent is now an extravaganza of glowing fireplaces, Florentine crystal chandeliers, Baroque credenzas, high beamed ceilings, mullioned windows, guest rooms swathed in Venetian red and antique Lyon silks, suites that are like artists' ateliers, and Philipe Starck bathrooms. The restaurant, **Les Loges,** is one of Lyon's most graceful dining rooms, with, in addition, a cellar-level wine bar and a separate café-épicerie restaurant with a lovely vaulted ceiling. **Pros:** top Vieux Lyon location; cheerful and patient service; excellent restaurant. **Cons:** hard on the budget; difficult to get an automobile to the door in a pedestrianized section. ✉ *6 rue du Bœuf, Vieux Lyon* ☎ *04–72–77–44–44* 🌐 *www.courdesloges.com* *57 rooms, 4 suites* *In-room: a/c, refrigerator, Wi-Fi. In-hotel: restaurant, bar, pool, gym, Wi-Fi hotspot, parking (paid)* ▭ *AE, DC, MC, V.*

$$$$ ★ **La Tour Rose.** A silk-swathed Vieux Lyon classic in a Renaissance-period convent, La Tour Rose is set around a gorgeous Florentine-style courtyard under a cylindrical rose-washed tower. The glass-roof restaurant occupies a former chapel and offers views of the hanging garden overhead. Each guest room is named for a famous silk-weaving concern and decorated in its goods; taffetas, plissés, and velvets cover walls, windows, and beds in daring, even startling styles. The signature specials here—grilled duck breast, scallops roasted over coals, Charlotte au Chocolat—are well worth all the extra louis d'or. Six apartments with kitchenettes in an adjacent annex provide excellent value for longer stays. **Pros:** a master class in traditional Lyonnnais silks and textiles; surrounded by some of Vieux Lyon's prettiest traboules, lovely patio, and tower. **Cons:** somewhat cramped spaces in rooms and public areas; so much drapery and textiles: claustrophobes beware! ✉ *22 rue du Bœuf, Vieux Lyon* ☎ *04–78–92–69–10* 🌐 *www.latourrose.fr* *11 rooms, 8 suites* *In-room: a/c, refrigerator, Wi-Fi. In-hotel: restaurant, bar, Wi-Fi hotspot, parking (paid), some pets allowed* ▭ *AE, DC, MC, V.*

¢–$ ★ **Lyon GuestHouse.** This spectacular location overlooking all of Lyon from atop the promontory of La Croix Rousse is an art gallery and bed-and-breakfast run by an enterprising art historian, Françoise Besson. Ninety-two stairs are the only way up to this fourth-floor crow's nest, so travel light and stay fit! **Pros:** intimate and personal; terrific views. **Cons:** minimal privacy; hot climb in summer. ✉ *6 montée du Lieutenant Aliouche, La Croix Rousse* ☎ *04–78–29–62–05* 🌐 *www.lyonguesthouse.com* *3 rooms* *In-room: no a/c* ▭ *AE, DC, MC, V.*

$$$ Fodor's Choice ★ **Phénix Hôtel.** This little hotel in Vieux Lyon is a winning combination of location, charming staff, tastefully decorated rooms, and moderate prices. Overlooking the Saône at the upstream edge of Vieux Lyon, the hotel's modern design and decor is gracefully juxtaposed with its

10

DID YOU KNOW?

On December 8th Lyon is the place to be, thanks to the Fête de la Lumiere (Festival of Light), when light shows and concerts transform city landmarks into dazzling marvels.

16th-century ceiling beams and Renaissance façade. Some rooms have fireplaces, and the smallish upper-floor rooms are charmingly built into the eaves and rooftop dormers. **Pros:** walking distance (45 mins up the Saône) from Île Barbe and Bocuse; cozy dormers over the river; handy to but not in the middle of Vieux Lyon. **Cons:** interior rooms on the air shaft can be noisy; a long walk to the middle of the Presqu'île. ✉ *7 quai Bondy, Vieux Lyon* ☎ *04–78–28–24–24* 🌐 *www.hotel-le-phenix.fr* *36 rooms* *In-room: a/c, Wi-Fi. In-hotel: restaurant, bar, Wi-Fi hotspot, parking (paid), some pets allowed* 💳 *AE, DC, MC, V* 🍽 *BP.*

$$$$ ★ **Villa Florentine.** High above the *Vieille Ville* (Old Town), near the Roman theaters and the basilica, this pristine hotel was once a 17th-century convent—and everyone knows the sisters always enjoyed the best real estate in town. Glowing in its ocher-yellow exterior, it has beamed and vaulted ceilings, terraces, and particularly marvelous views, which are seen to best advantage from the pool and the excellent restaurant, Les Terrasses de Lyon—an extravaganza complete with glassed-in winter garden and tomato-red salons. Throughout, in time-warp fashion, 17th-century Italianate architectural details are contrasted with the latest in bright postmodern Italian furnishings. The clientele tends to more senior travelers seeking peace and quiet. **Pros:** panoramic location above the Saône; good access to Fourvière and Roman Lyon. **Cons:** a hot climb up to the hotel in summer; tricky automobile access around upper Vieux Lyon; somewhat removed from the action. ✉ *25–27 montée St-Barthélémy, Fourvière* ☎ *04–72–56–56–56* 🌐 *www.villaflorentine.com* *20 rooms, 8 suites* *In-room: a/c, refrigerator, Internet, Wi-Fi. In-hotel: restaurant, bar, pool, Wi-Fi hotspot, parking (paid), some pets allowed* 💳 *AE, DC, MC, V.*

NIGHTLIFE AND THE ARTS

Lyon is the region's liveliest arts center; check the weekly *Lyon-Poche*, published on Wednesday and sold at newsstands, for cultural events and goings-on at the dozens of discos, bars, and clubs.

The low-key chic **L'Alibi** (✉ *13 quai Romain-Roland, Vieux Lyon* ☎ *04–78–42–04–66*) has a laser show along with the music. Romantics rendezvous at the **Bar de la Tour Rose** (✉ *22 rue du Bœuf, Vieux Lyon* ☎ *04–78–37–25–90*). **Le Boudoir** (✉ *13 pl. Jules Ferry, Les Brotteaux* ☎ *04–72–74–04–41*) is a popular saloon in the old Brotteaux train station. **Bouchon aux Vin** (✉ *64 rue Mercière, Presqu'île* ☎ *04–78–42–88–90*) is a wine bar with 30-plus vintages.

Café Cuba (✉ *19 pl. Tolozan, Presqu'île* ☎ *04–78–28–35–77*) provides interesting tapas, cocktails, and Havana cigars until 1 AM near the Jean Nouvel opera house. **Café Sevilla**(✉ *7 rue Ste-Catherine, Presqu'île* ☎ *04–78–30–12–98*)is salsa city on the Pentes de la Croix Rousse hillside. **Café-Théâtre de L'Accessoire** (✉ *26 rue de l'Annonciade, Presqu'île* ☎ *04–78–27–84–84*) is a leading café-theater where you can eat and drink while watching a review. **La Cave des Voyageurs** (✉ *7 pl. St-Paul–St-Barthélémy, Vieux Lyon* ☎ *04–78–28–92–28*), just below the St-Paul train station, is a cozy place to try some carefully selected wines.

Multiple bars, a terrace, and dance spaces await at gay-friendly **La Chapelle** (✉ *Impasse de Choulans, Vieux Lyon* ☎ *04–78–37–23–95*).

10

Aprhrodisiac cocktails and tentations sexy make **Le Claks** (✉ *3 rue de Cronstadt, La Guillotière* ☎ *04–78–39–05–56*) a rager east of the Rhône.

Le Complexe du Rire (✉ *7 rue des Capucins, Presqu'île* ☎ *04–78–27–23–59*), also known as the Minette Theatre, is a lively satirical café-theater above Place des Terreaux. **Edyn's Club** (✉ *3 rue Terme, Presqu'île* ☎ *04–78–30–02–01*) rocks on weekends and holiday eves. The café-theater **Espace Gerson** (✉ *1 pl. Gerson, Vieux Lyon* ☎ *04–78–27–96–99*) presents revues in conjunction with dinner.

In the old Les Brotteaux train station, **Le First Tendency** (✉ *13–14 pl. Jules Ferry, Les Brotteaux* ☎ *04–37–24–19–46*) is a popular macro-disco with capacity for 600 miscreants. Live jazz is played in the stone-vault basement of **Hot Club** (✉ *26 rue Lanterne, Presqu'île* ☎ *04–78–39–54–74*). For a student vibe and bachelor/bachelorette send-offs have a look at **Le Loft** (✉ *7 rue Renan, La Guillotière* ☎ *04–78–43–35–42*).

Live music from Blackrain to hip-hop rules at **Le Marché Gare** (✉ *34 rue Casimir Périer, Presqu'île* ☎ *04–72–77–50–25*). For the young, 30 and under, **Quai Ouest** (✉ *40 quai Pierre Scize, Presqu'île* ☎ *04–78–28–20–40*) offers surefire nocturnal action on the banks of the Saône. A gay crowd is found among the 1930s blandishments at **La Ruche** (✉ *22 rue Gentil, Presqu'île* ☎ *04–78–39–03–82*). For the hottest English pub in Lyon, the **Smoking Dog** (✉ *16 rue Lainerie, Vieux Lyon* ☎ *04–78–37–25–90*) is the place to head. **Villa Florentine** (✉ *25 Montée St-Barthélémy, Fourvière* ☎ *04–72–56–56–56*) is a quiet spot for sipping a drink to the strains of a harpist, who plays on Friday and Saturday.

Center stage for Lyon's amazing arts scene, the **Opéra de Lyon** (✉ *1 pl. de la Comédie, Presqu'île* ☎ *04–72–00–45–45* 🌐 *www.opera-lyon.org*) presents plays, concerts, ballets, and opera from October to June. Lyon's Société de Musique de Chambre performs at **Salle Molière** (✉ *18 quai Bondy, Vieux Lyon* ☎ *04–78–28–03–11*).

Early fall sees the unforgettably spectacular **Biennale de la Danse** (*Dance Biennial* 🌐 *www.biennale-de-lyon.org*), which takes place in even-number years. September is the time for the **Foire aux Tupiniers** (☎ *04–78–37–00–68*), a pottery fair. October brings the **Festival Bach** (☎ *04–78–72–75–31*). The **Biennale d'Art Contemporain** (*Contemporary Art Biennial* ☎ *04–78–30–50–66*) is held in even-number years in late September. The **Festival du Vieux Lyon** (☎ *04–78–42–39–04*) is a music festival in November and December. On December 8—the Fête de La Immaculée Conception (Feast of the Immaculate Conception)—startling lighting creations transform the city into a fantasy for the marvelous **Fête de Lumière**, Lyon's Festival of Lights.

SHOPPING

Lyon remains France's silk-and-textile capital, and all big-name designers have shops here. The 19th-century **Passage de l'Argue** (between Rue du Président Édouard-Herriot and Rue de la République in the center of town) is lined with traditional shops. The **Carré d'Or** district has more than 70 luxury shops between Place Bellecour and Cordeliers. **Passage Thiaffait** on the Croix Rousse hillside is home to the Creators' Village, with young designers offering original one-of-a-kind creations.

Lyon's biggest shopping mall is the **Part-Dieu Shopping Center** (✉ *Rue du Dr-Bouchut, Part-Dieu* ☎ *04–72–60–60–62*), where there are 14 movie theaters and 250 shops. France's major department stores are well represented in Lyon. **Galeries Lafayette** (✉ *In Part-Dieu Shopping Center, Part-Dieu* ☎ *04–72–61–44–44* ✉ *6 pl. des Cordeliers, Presqu'île* ☎ *04–72–40–48–00* ✉ *200 bd. Pinel, Villeurbanne* ☎ *04–78–77–82–12*) has always brought Parisian flair to its outlying branches. **Printemps** (✉ *42 rue de la République, Presqu'île* ☎ *04–72–41–29–29*) is the Lyon outpost of the big Paris store.

Captiva (✉ *10 rue de la Charité, Perrache* ☎ *04–78–37–96–15*) is the boutique of a young designer who works mainly in silk. **Georges Rech**(✉ *59 rue du Président-Herriot, Part-Dieu* ☎ *04–78–37–82–90*) displays top European fashions for women. **Zilli** (✉ *4 President Carnot, Presqu'île* ☎ *04–78–42–10–27*) designs and sells exclusively men's clothing. **Nicolas Faffiotte** (✉ *4 rue E. Herriot, Presqu'île* ☎ *04–78–37–36–25*) specializes in wedding dresses and high-end evening wear. **Les Gones** (✉ *33 rue Leynaud, La Croix Rousse* ☎ *04–78–28–40–78*), in the Croix Rousse, is a boutique carrying the work of several young designers.

The workshop of **Monsieur Georges Mattelon** (✉ *Rue d'Ivry, Presqu'île* ☎ *04–78–28–62–04*) is one of the oldest silk-weaving shops in Lyon. Lyonnais designer **Clémentine** (✉ *18 rue Émile-Zola, Presqu'île*) is good for well-cut, tailored clothing. **Étincelle** (✉ *34 rue St-Jean, Vieux Lyon*) has trendy outfits for youngsters.

For antiques, wander down **Rue Auguste-Comte** (✉ *From Pl. Bellecour to Perrache*). **Cité des Antiquaires** (✉ *117 bd. Stalingrad, Vieux Lyon* ☎ *04–72–69–00–00*) in the eastern Villeurbanne suburb amasses more than 100 antiques dealers Thursday through Sunday. **Image en Cours** (✉ *26 rue du Bœuf, Vieux Lyon*) sells superb engravings. **La Maison des Canuts** (✉ *10–12 rue d'Ivry, La Croix Rousse*) carries local textiles. Silks and eclectic fabrics can also be found at the **Boutique des Soyeux Lyonnais** (✉ *3 rue du Bœuf, Vieux Lyon*). To see how silk prints are made and take home a piece of Lyon visit **L'Atelier de Soierie** (✉ *33 rue Romarin, Presqu'île*).

For arts and crafts there are several places you will find irresistible. Look for Lyonnais puppets on **Place du Change**. For new art, try the **Marché des Artistes** (*Artists' Market* ✉ *Quai Romain-Rolland, Vieux Lyon*) every Sunday morning from 7 to 1. Held on Sunday morning is another **Marché des Artisans** (*Crafts Market* ✉ *Quai Fulchiron, Vieux Lyon*). A **Marché aux Puces** (*Flea Market* ✉ *Take Bus 37, 1 rue du Canal, Villeurbanne*) takes place on Thursday and Saturday mornings 8–noon and on Sunday 6–1.

For **secondhand books** try the market along Quai de la Pêcherie near Place Bellecour, held every weekend 10–6. **Diogène** (✉ *29 rue St-Jean, Vieux Lyon* ☎ *04–78–42-29–41*) smells of old leather and ancient paper and sells rare and antique books. **Food markets** are held from Tuesday through Sunday on Boulevard de la Croix-Rousse, at Les Halles on Cours Lafayette, on Quai Victor Augagneur, and on Quai St-Antoine.

For up-to-the-minute information on food, restaurants, and great wines, don't miss the (prize-winning and English-speaking) "flying sommelier,"

CLOSE UP

Lyon's Biennale de la Dance

France's second city is thrown into perpetual motion for nearly three weeks every other September (on even-number years). Brainchild of Lyon choreographer Guy Darmet, each year celebrates a different theme. The result, no matter which even year you choose, is a dance blowout at the confluence of the Saône and Rhône rivers. At each *biennale*, in addition to the more than 100 performances scheduled in the city's finest venues such as the Jean Nouvel opera house, the Maison de la Danse, and the cookie box–like Théâtre des Célestins, popular highlights include the tumultuous 4,500-dancer street parade that roars down the left bank of the Rhône on the festival's first Sunday, and the three Saturday night dance galas held in the graceful Brotteaux train station, the Halle Tony Garnier, or the Place des Terreaux. Collective dance classes for thousands and spontaneous outbursts of tango, salsa, or nearly any other genre of rhythmic movement, pop up all over town, while newspaper front pages feature little else. For details: 🌐 *www.biennale-de-lyon.org.*

Georges Dos Santos at **Antic Wine** (✉ *18 rue du Bœuf, Vieux Lyon* ☎ *04–78–37–08–96*). A wineshop with an excellent selection is **À Ma Vigne** (✉ *18 rue Vaubecour, Presqu'île* ☎ *04–78–37–05–29*). **La Cave d'à Côté** (✉ *5 rue Pleney, Presqu'île* ☎ *04–78–28 –31–46*) specializes in Côte du Rhône wines.

For chocolates, head to **Bernachon** (✉ *42 cours Franklin-Roosevelt, Les Brotteaux*); some say it's the best *chocolaterie* in France. Another top chocolate paradise is **Bouillet** (✉ *15 pl. de la Croix Rousse, Croix Rousse*), with a stunning selection of artisanal chocolate. For the famous chocolate *coussins* (pillows), check out **Voisin** (✉ *28 rue de la République, Presqu'île*).

For fragrances, photos, furniture, philosophy, and comprehensive Oriental tea culture, **Cha Yuan** (✉ *7–9 rue des Remparts d'Ainay, Presqu'île*) is the best boutique in Lyon, with more than 300 varieties of tea on sale from all over the world. **Eléphant des Montagnes** (✉ *43 rue Auguste Comte, Presqu'île*), not far from Perrache station, has treasures from Nepal, Afghanistan, India, and the Himalayas, lovingly retrieved by Pierre Chavanne.

La Boîte à Dessert (✉ *1 rue de l'Ancienne-Préfecture, Presqu'île*) makes luscious peach turnovers. For culinary variety, shop **Les Halles** (✉ *102 cours Lafayette, Part-Dieu*). **Pignol** (✉ *17 rue Émile-Zola, Presqu'île*) is good for meats and sandwich makings. **Reynon** (✉ *13 rue des Archers, Presqu'île*) is the place for charcuterie.

BEAUJOLAIS

North of Lyon along the Saône are the vineyards of Beaujolais, a thrill for any oenophile. In the area around Villefranche, small villages—perhaps comprising a church, a bar, and a boulangerie—pop up here

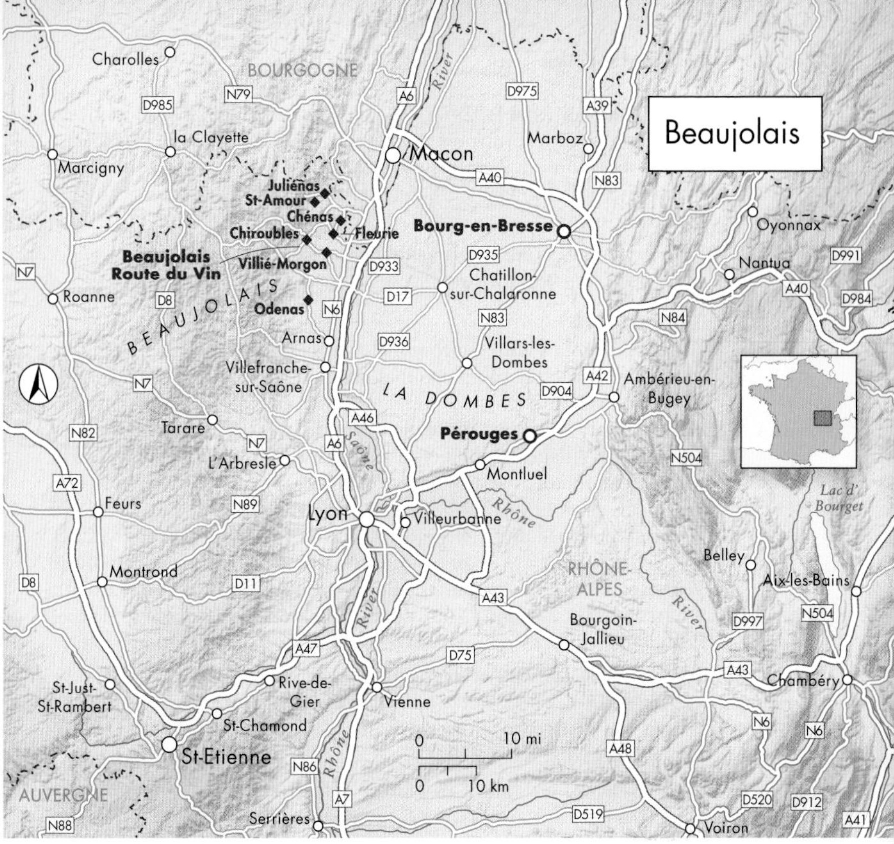

and there out of the rolling vine-covered hillsides. Beaujolais wine is made exclusively from the *gamay noir à jus blanc* grape. The region's best wines are all labeled "Grands Crus," a more complex version of the otherwise light, fruity Beaujolais. Although the region's wines get better with age, many Beaujolais wines are drunk nearly fresh off the vine; every third Thursday in November marks the arrival of the Beaujolais Nouveau, a bacchanalian festival that also showcases regional cuisine. North of La Dombes region and east of the Beaujolais wine villages is Bourg-en-Bresse, famous for its marvelous church and a breed of poultry that impassions gourmands; it makes a good base after Lyon. South toward the Rhône, the great river of southern France, is the well-preserved medieval village of Pérouges.

BEAUJOLAIS ROUTE DU VIN

Fodor's Choice ★ *16 km (10 mi) north of Villefranche-sur-Saône, 49 km (30 mi) north of Lyon.*

GETTING HERE AND AROUND

For the Beaujolais wine country, most people train to the station on the Place de la Gare in Villefranche-sur-Saône, 31 km (19 mi) north of Lyon, where trains to smaller towns are available. **SNCF** (🌐 *www.sncf.fr*) trains link Lyon Part-Dieu with Villefranche-sur-Saône (26 mins,

€6.45). **Satobus** (☎ *04–72–68–72–17* 🌐 *www.satobus.com*) connects Lyon-Saint-Exupéry airport with Villefranche-sur-Saône (25 mins, €7.65). In addition, **Autocars du Rhône** (lines 161 and 164) connects Lyon with Villefranche-sur-Saône with multiple connections to surrounding towns.

Visitor Information **Beaujolais Tourist Office** (✉ *96 rue de la sous-préfecture* ☎ *04–74–07–27–40* 🌐 *www.villefranche-beaujolais.fr*).

EXPLORING

Not all Beaujolais wine is promoted as *vin nouveau,* despite the highly successful marketing campaign that has made Beaujolais Nouveau synonymous with French wine and celebrated in full force on the third Thursday of November annually around the world. Wine classed as "Beaujolais Villages" is higher in alcohol and produced from a clearly defined region northwest of Villefranche. Beaujolais is made from one single variety of grape, the *gamay noir à jus blanc.* However, there are 12 different appellations: Beaujolais, Beaujolais Villages, Brouilly, Chénas, Chiroubles, Côte de Brouilly, Fleurie, Juliénas, Morgon, Moulin à Vent, Régnié, and St-Amour. The Beaujolais Route du Vin (Wine Road), a narrow strip 23 km (14 mi) long, is home to nine of these deluxe Beaujolais wines, also known as *grands crus.*

The **École Beaujolaise des Vins** (*Beaujolais School of Wine* ✉ *Villefranche* ☎ *04–74–02–22–18* 🌐 *www.beaujolais.com*) organizes lessons in wine tasting and on creating your own cellar.

In the southernmost and largest *vignoble* (vineyard) of the Beaujolais crus is **Odenas**, producing Brouilly, a soft, fruity wine best consumed young. In the vineyard's center is towering Mont Brouilly, a hill whose vines produce a tougher, firmer wine classified as Côte de Brouilly.

From Odenas take D68 via St-Lager to **Villié-Morgon**, in the heart of the Morgon vineyard; robust wines that age well are produced here.

At Monternot, east of Villié-Morgon, you can find the 15th-century **Château de Corcelles**, noted for its Renaissance galleries, canopied courtyard well, and medieval carvings in its chapel. The guardroom is now an atmospheric tasting cellar. ✉ *Off D9 from Villié-Morgon* ☎ *04–74–66–00–24* 🌐 *www.chateaudecorcelles.fr* ⏲ *Mon.–Sat.10–noon and 2:30–6:30.*

From Villié-Morgon D68 wiggles north through several more wine villages, including **Chiroubles**, where a rare, light wine best drunk young is produced. The wines from **Fleurie** are elegant and flowery. Well-known **Chénas** is favored for its two crus: the robust, velvety, and expensive Moulin à Vent and the fruity and underestimated Chénas. The wines of **Juliénas** are sturdy and a deep color; sample them in the cellar of the town church (closed Tuesday and lunchtime), amid bacchanalian decor. **St-Amour**, west of Juliénas, produces light but firm reds and a limited quantity of whites.

WHERE TO EAT AND STAY

$$$$ Fodor's Choice ★ **Château de Bagnols.** A destination in itself, Lady Hamlyn's celebrated (and very pricey) castle-hotel is one of the glories of the Beaujolais region. Don't be put off by the severe and fortresslike exterior: inside, all

For a true Beaujolais blow-out book a stay at Lady Hamlyn's Château de Bagnols, where even Louis XIV would feel right at home.

is trompe-l'oeil frescoes, colored marbles, and sumptuous fabrics. The Grand Salon matches the grandest of Paris's 17th-century showpieces, while guest rooms in the main château evoke the 18th century—many are covered with historic frescoes done by a Baroque school of artists inspired by the "Grand Fabrique," Lyon's famed brocade makers. Elsewhere, rooms in La Résidence—the converted stables and carriage houses—are rustic-contemporary, some with amazing wood-beam trim and calico drapes. Set with silver candelabra, giant bouquets, and a wall-wide fireplace, the massive Salle des Gardes is now the setting for the award-winning gourmet restaurant, while wine tastings are occasionally held in the beautiful stone *cuvage* (wine-pressing room). **Pros:** dazzlingly elegant; panoramic views; nonpareil dining. **Cons:** a little like living in a museum; hyper-expensive. ✉ *15 km (9 mi) southwest of Villefranche on D38 to Tarare, Bagnols* ☎ *04–74–71–40–00* 🌐 *www.chateaudebagnols.fr* *16 rooms, 5 apartments* *In-room: a/c, refrigerator, Wi-Fi. In-hotel: restaurant, bar, pool, Wi-Fi* *AE, DC, MC, V* *Closed Jan.–Mar.*

10

BOURG-EN-BRESSE

30 km (18 mi) east of St-Amour on N79, 81 km (49 mi) northeast of Lyon.

GETTING HERE

SNCF (🌐 *www.sncf.fr*) trains link Lyon Perrache station with Bourg-en-Bresse (1 hr–1 hr, 22 mins; €10.75). In addition, **Satobus** (☎ *04–72–68–72–17* 🌐 *www.satobus.com*) connects Lyon-Saint-Exupéry airport with Bourg-en-Bresse four times daily (1 hr, 20 mins; €25).

Visitor Information Bourg-en-Bresse Tourist Office (✉ *6 av. Alsace Lorraine* ☎ *04–74–22–49–40* 🌐 *www.bourg-en-bresse.org*)

EXPLORING

Cheerful, flower-festooned Bourg-en-Bresse is esteemed among gastronomes for its fowl—striking-looking chickens, the *poulet de Bresse,* with plump white bodies, bright blue feet, and red combs (adding up to France's *tricolore,* or national colors). The town's southeasternmost district, Brou, is its most interesting and the site of a singular church. This is a good place to stay before or after a trip along the Beaujolais Wine Road.

The **Église de Brou**, a marvel of the Flamboyant Gothic style, is no longer in religious use. The church was built between 1513 and 1532 by Margaret of Austria in memory of her husband, Philibert le Beau, Duke of Savoy, and their finely sculpted tombs highlight the rich interior. **Son-et-lumière** shows—on Easter and Pentecost Sunday and Monday, and on Thursday, Saturday, and Sunday from May through September—are magical. A massive restoration of the roof has brought it back to its 16th-century state, with the same gorgeous, multicolor, intricate patterns found throughout Burgundy. The museum in the nearby **cloister** stands out for its paintings: 16th- and 17th-century Flemish and Dutch artists keep company with 17th- and 18th-century French and Italian masters, 19th-century artists of the Lyon School, Gustave Doré, and contemporary local painters. ✉ *63 bd. de Brou* ☎ *04–74–22–83–83* 🎟 *€4.50 (Sun. free)* ⏲ *Apr.–Sept., daily 9–12:30 and 2–6:30; Oct.–Mar., daily 9–noon and 2–5.*

WHERE TO EAT AND STAY

$$$$ FRENCH Fodor's Choice ★

✕ **Georges Blanc.** Set in the village of Vonnas and one of the great culinary addresses in all Gaul, this simple 19th-century inn full of antique country furniture and home to 30 guest rooms makes a fine setting for poulet de Bresse, truffles, and lobster, all featured on its legendary menu. The wizard here is Monsieur Blanc, whose culinary DNA extends back to innkeepers dating from the French Revolution. He made his mark in the 1980s with a series of cookbooks, notably *The Natural Cuisine of Georges Blanc.* Today, he serves up his traditional-yet-nouvelle delights in a vast dining room (closed Monday and Tuesday; no lunch Wednesday), renovated—overly so, some might say—in a stately manner replete with Louis Treize–style chairs, fireplace, and floral tapestries. Wine connoisseurs will go weak in the knees at the cellar here, overflowing with 130,000 bottles. The guest rooms range from (relatively) simple to luxurious. It's worth the trip from Bourg-en-Bresse, but be sure you bring deep pockets. However, a block south you can also repair to Blanc's cheaper and more casual restaurant, **L'Ancienne Auberge,** most delightfully set in a 1900s "Fabrique de Limonade" soda-water plant and now festooned with antique bicycles and daguerrotypes. **Pros:** gorgeous village; the warm and accessible Blanc family. **Cons:** slightly over-commercial Bocuse-like grandeur; almost too expensive to fulfill expectations. ✉ *Pl. du Marché, 23 km (14 mi) from Bourg-en-Bresse, Vonnas* ☎ *04–74–50–90–90* 🌐 *www.georgesblanc.com* ✍ *Reservations essential* 💳 *AE, DC, MC, V* ⏲ *Closed Jan.*

$ **Hôtel de France.** This centrally located and impeccably renovated hotel offers comfortable rooms equipped with the full range of the most modern amenities, from hair dryers to refrigerator and Wi-Fi. The adjoining restaurant, Chez Blanc, has been taken over by Georges Blanc and, as expected, is rising to the top of local gastronomical charts. **Pros:** convenient location for exploring the town; good combination of traditional shell with contemporary infrastructure and equipment; handy to Georges Blanc cuisine. **Cons:** in the midst of the hustle and bustle of a provincial town. ✉ *19 pl. Bernard* ☎ *04–74–23–30–24* 🌐 *www.grand-hoteldefrance.com* *42 rooms, 2 suites* *In-room: a/c, refrigerator, Wi-Fi. In-hotel: restaurant, Wi-Fi hotspot, some pets allowed* *AE, DC, MC, V.*

PÉROUGES

★ *21 km (13 mi) southeast of Villars-les-Dombes, 36 km (22 mi) northeast of Lyon.*

Wonderfully preserved (though a little too precious), hilltop Pérouges, with its medieval houses and narrow cobbled streets surrounded by ramparts, is 200 yards across. Hand-weavers first brought it prosperity; the Industrial Revolution meant their downfall, and by the late 19th century the population had dwindled from 1,500 to 12. Now the government has restored the most interesting houses, and a potter, bookbinder, cabinetmaker, and weaver have given the town a new lease on life. A number of restaurants make Pérouges a good lunch stop.

Encircling the town is **Rue des Rondes**; from this road you can get fine views of the countryside and, on clear days, the Alps. Park your car by the main gateway, **Porte d'En-Haut,** alongside the 15th-century fortress-church. Rue du Prince, the town's main street, leads to the **Maison des Princes de Savoie** (Palace of the Princes of Savoie), formerly the home of the influential Savoie family that once controlled the eastern part of France. Note the fine watchtower. **Place de la Halle,** a pretty square with great charm, around the corner from the Maison des Princes de Savoie, is the site of a lime tree planted in 1792.

10

The **Musée du Vieux Pérouges** *(Old Pérouges Museum)*, to one side of the Place de la Halle, contains local artifacts and a reconstructed weaver's workshop. The medieval **garden** is noted for its array of rare medicinal plants. ✉ *Pl. du Tilleul* ☎ *04–74–61–00–88* *€7* *May–Sept., daily 10–noon and 2–6.*

WHERE TO EAT AND STAY

$$$–$$$$ ★ **L'Ostellerie du Vieux Pérouges.** "The Old Man of Pérouges" is uniquely comprised of four medieval stone residences set around its main showpiece—an extraordinary corbelled, 14th-century timber-frame house now home to the inn's restaurant. Here regional delights are served up on pewter plates by waitresses in folk costumes, recipes handed down from the days of Charles VII inspire the cook, and everybody partakes of the famous *galette pérugienne à la crème* (the "pancake of Pérouges") dessert. The sweet taste will linger in your guest room, thanks to time-burnished antiques, gigantic stone hearths, and glossy wood floors and

tables. Rooms in the geranium-decked 15th-century Au St-Georges et Manoir manor are more spacious than—but also nearly twice the cost of—those in Le Pavillon (aka "L'Annexe"). At the lower end of the scale, however, the rooms are fairly simple. **Pros:** a sense of stepping back into medieval France; graceful manor-house surroundings; cheerful service. **Cons:** sans a/c it can be hot during the *canicule* (the, literally, "dog days of summer"); some bathrooms lack modern showers. ✉ *Pl. du Tilleul, Pérouges* ☎ *04–74–61–00–88* 🌐 *www.hostelleriedeperouges.com* *13 rooms, 2 suites* *In-room: no a/c, refrigerator, Wi-Fi. In-hotel: restaurant, bar, some pets allowed* 💳 *AE, DC, MC, V.*

THE RHÔNE VALLEY

At Lyon, the Rhône, joined by the Saône, truly comes into its own, plummeting south in search of the Mediterranean. The river's progress is often spectacular, as steep vineyards conjure up vistas that are more readily associated with the river's Germanic cousin, the Rhine. All along the way, small-town vintners invite you to sample their wines. Early Roman towns like Vienne and Valence reflect the Rhône's importance as a trading route. To the west is the rugged, rustic Ardèche *département* (province), where time seems to have slowed to a standstill.

VIENNE

Fodor's Choice ★

27 km (17 mi) south of Lyon via A7.

If you do nothing but head up to this town's famed Roman Theater and look out over the red-tile roofs of the Rhône Valley, you'll be happy you made the 20-minute trip to Vienne from Lyon. Vienne is an historian's Candyland, and every street seems to take you to yet another ancient church, another stoic Roman ruin, and another postcard-perfect view of crumbling walls and sloped roofs.

GETTING HERE

SNCF trains (🌐 *www.sncf.fr*) link Lyon Perrache or Lyon Part-Dieu stations with Vienne (18–32 mins, €6.20). From Lyon-Saint-Exupéry, the best connection to Vienne is to take the shuttle to Lyon Part-Dieu and the train to Vienne.

Visitor Information **Vienne Tourist Office** (✉ *Cours Brillier* ☎ *04–74–53–80–30* 🌐 *www.vienne-tourisme.com*).

EXPLORING

One of Roman Gaul's most important towns,Vienne retains considerable historic charm despite its being a major road and train junction. It saw its second renaissance during the Middle Ages when it became a major religious and cultural center under its count-archbishops. Today, the tourist office anchors Cours Brillier in the leafy shadow of the Jardin Public (Public Garden). The €7 Billet Intermusée admits you to all local monuments and museums over 48 hours. Even better, the €5 Billet-Pass admits you to three museums and the Théâtre Roman. Both are available at the tourist office or at the first site that you visit.

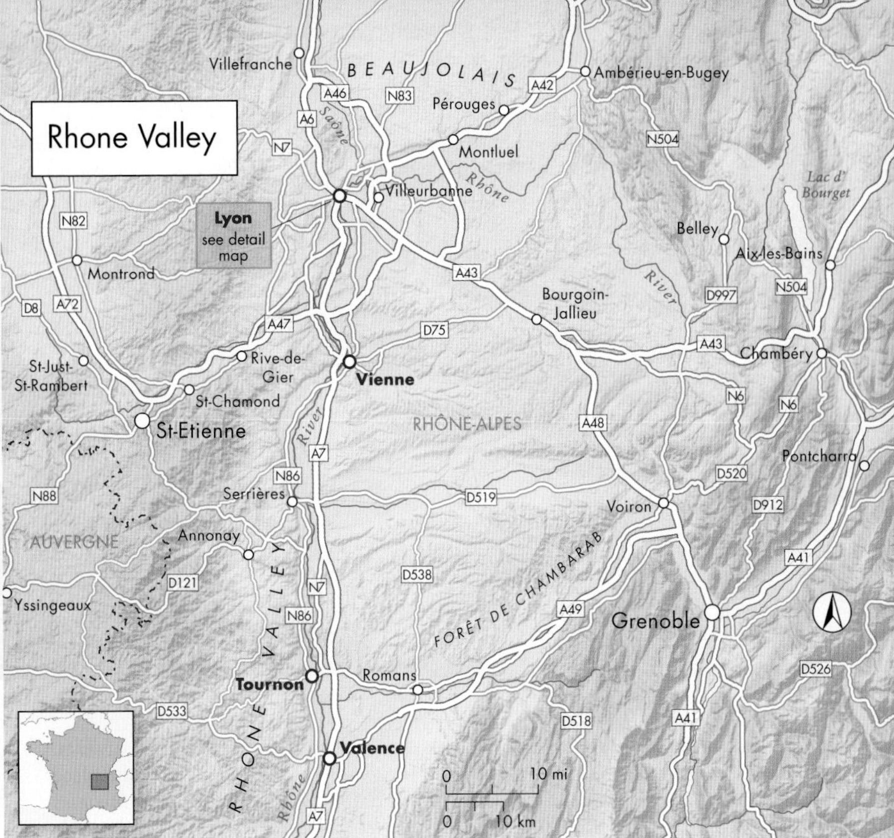

On Quai Jean-Jaurès, beside the Rhône, is the church of **St-Pierre**. Note the rectangular 12th-century Romanesque bell tower with its arcaded tiers. The lower church walls date from the 6th century.

Although religious wars deprived the cathedral of **St-Maurice** of many of its statues, much original decoration is intact; the portals on the 15th-century façade are carved with Old Testament scenes. The cathedral was built between the 12th and 16th centuries, with later additions, such as the splendid 18th-century mausoleum to the right of the altar. A frieze of the zodiac adorns the entrance to the vaulted passage that once led to the cloisters but now opens onto Place St-Paul.

★ Place du Palais is the site of the remains of the **Temple d'Auguste et de Livie** *(Temple of Augustus and Livia)*, accessible via Place St-Paul and Rue Clémentine; they probably date in part from Vienne's earliest Roman settlements (1st century BC). The Corinthian columns were walled in during the 11th century, when the temple was used as a church; in 1833 Prosper Mérimée intervened to have the temple restored.

The last vestige of the city's sizable Roman baths is a **Roman gateway** (⊠ *Rue Chantelouve*) decorated with delicate friezes.

★ The **Théâtre Romain** *(Roman Theater)*, on Rue de la Charité, is one of the largest in Gaul (143 yards across). It held 13,000 spectators and is only slightly smaller than Rome's Theater of Marcellus. Rubble buried

One of the most important towns of Roman Gaul, Vienne is an historian's Candyland and famed for its ancient theater.

Vienne's theater until 1922; excavation has uncovered 46 rows of seats, some marble flooring, and the frieze on the stage. Concerts take place here in summer. ✉ *7 rue du Cirque* ☎ *04–74–85–39–23* 🎫 *€7, includes Cité Gallo-Romaine and St-André-le-Bas museums* ⏲ *Apr.–Aug., daily 9–12:30 and 2–6; Sept.–mid-Oct., Tues.–Sun. 9–12:30 and 2–6; mid-Oct.–Mar., Tues.–Sat. 9:30–12:30 and 2–5, Sun. 1:30–5:30.*

Rue des Orfèvres (off Rue de la Charité) is lined with Renaissance facades and distinguished by the church of **St-André-le-Bas**, once part of a powerful abbey. If possible, venture past the restoration now in progress to see the finely sculpted 12th-century capitals (made of Roman stone) and the 17th-century wood statue of St. Andrew. It's best to see the cloisters during the music festival held here and at the cathedral from June through August. ✉ *Cour St-André* ☎ *04–74–85–18–49* 🎫 *€7, includes Cité Gallo-Romaine and Théâtre Romain museums* ⏲ *Apr.–mid-Oct., Tues.–Sun. 9:30–1 and 2–6; mid-Oct.–Mar., Tues.–Sat. 9:30–12:30 and 2–5, Sun. 2–6.*

Across the Rhône from the town center is the excavated **Cité Gallo-Romaine** *(Gallo-Roman City)*, covering several acres. Here you can find villas, houses, workshops, public baths, and roads, all built by the Romans. 🎫 *€7, includes Théâtre Romain and St-André-le-Bas museums* ⏲ *Daily 9–6.*

WHERE TO EAT

$$$$ FRENCH ★ ✕ **La Pyramide.** Back when your grandmother's grandmother was making the grand tour, La Pyramide was *le must.* Fernand Point had perfected haute cuisine for a generation and became the first superstar chef, teaching a regiment of students—Bocuse, Chapel, and the brothers Troisgros

among them—who went on to streamline and glamorize French dining the world over. Many decades later, La Pyramide has dropped its museum status and now offers contemporary classics by acclaimed chef Patrick Henriroux, accompanied by a peerless selection of wines featuring local stars from the nearby Côte Rôtie and Condrieu vineyards. Both classical and avant-garde dishes triumph here, from *crème soufflée de crabe au croquant d'artichaut* (cream crab soufflé with crunchy artichoke) to the *veau de lait aux légumes de la vallée* (suckling veal with vegetables from the Drôme Valley). For those who wish to sleep off the feast, there are graceful guest rooms at hand, but the mysterious Relais & Chateaux fatigue syndrome may have had a cooling effect on this previously exciting establishment. ✉ *14 bd. Fernand-Point* ☎ *04–74–53–01–96* 🌐 *www.lapyramide.com* ▭ *AE, DC, MC, V* ⏲ *Closed Feb. 3–Mar. 5, Aug. 11–19.*

$$$ FRENCH ✗ **Le Bec Fin.** With its understatedly elegant dining room and an inexpensive weekday menu, this unpretentious enclave opposite the cathedral is a good choice for lunch or dinner. Red meat, seafood, and both fresh and saltwater fish are well prepared here. Try the turbot cooked with saffron. ✉ *7 pl. St-Maurice* ☎ *04–74–85–76–72* ✍ *Reservations essential* ▭ *AE, DC, MC, V* ⏲ *Closed Mon. and Dec. 24–Jan. 12. No dinner Sun. or Wed.*

TOURNON-SUR-RHÔNE

36 km (20 mi) south of Serrières, 59 km (37 mi) south of Vienne.

Tournon is on the Rhône at the foot of granite hills. Its hefty **Château**, dating from the 15th and 16th centuries, is the chief attraction. The castle's twin terraces have wonderful views of the Vieille Ville, the river, and—towering above Tain-l'Hermitage across the Rhône—the steep vineyards that produce Hermitage wine, one of the region's most refined—and costly—reds. In the château is a museum of local history, the **Musée Rhodanien** (or du Rhône). ✉ *Pl. Auguste-Faure* ☎ *04–75–08–10–23* 🎟 *€5.50* ⏲ *June–Aug., Wed.–Mon. 10–noon and 2–6; Apr., May, Sept., and Oct., Wed.–Mon. 2–6.*

A ride on one of France's last steam trains, the **Chemin de Fer du Vivarais,** makes an adventurous two-hour trip 33 km (21 mi) along the narrow, rocky Doux Gorges to Lamastre and back to Tournon. ✉ *Departs from Tournon station* ☎ *04–78–28–83–34* 🎟 *Round-trip €22 (families €65)* ⏲ *June–Aug., daily at 10; May and Sept., weekends at 10.*

10

WHERE TO EAT AND STAY

$$$–$$$$ FRENCH **Michel Chabran.** This modern interpretation of Drôme-style stone-and-wood design has floral displays, airy picture windows over the garden, and guest rooms with a touch of contemporary Danish influence. Next to the main road, sleeping with the windows open can make for a noisy night—though the air-conditioning largely solves that. The restaurant is known for its truffle menu served from December to March and imaginative and light fare such as mille-feuille de foie gras with artichokes and lamb from Rémuzat. **Pros:** bright and cheerful; flowers everywhere; friendly receptionists. **Cons:** close to main road; touristy; steep staircase; $35 breakfast. ✉ *29 av. du 45e Parallèle, on left (east)* *bank of Rhône, 10 km (6 mi) south of Tournon via N7 and 7 km (4½ mi) north of Valence, Pont de l'Isère* ☎ *04–75–84–60–09* 🌐 *www.chateauxhotels.com/chabran* *11 rooms* *In-room: a/c, refrigerator, Wi-Fi. In-hotel: restaurant, pool, Wi-Fi hotspot, some pets allowed* *AE, DC, MC, V* *Closed Wed. No lunch Thurs. No dinner Sun. Oct.–Mar.* *MAP.*

VALENCE

17 km (11 mi) south of Tournon, 92 km (57 mi) west of Grenoble, 127 km (79 mi) north of Avignon.

GETTING HERE

SNCF trains (🌐 *www.sncf.fr*) link Lyon Part-Dieu station with Valence (1 hr, 12 mins; €16). Lyon Perrache also connects with Valence on the local train (1 hr, 12 mins; €15.80). The high-speed TGV also connects Lyon Part-Dieu to Valence (35 min; €22) once daily at 7:37 AM. From Lyon-Saint-Exupéry airport, the best connection to Valence is by shuttle to Lyon Part-Dieu station and train to Valence.

Visitor Information **Valence Tourist Office** (✉ *Parvis de la Gare* ☎ *08–92–70–70–99* 🌐 *www.tourisme-valence.com*).

EXPLORING

Valence, the Drôme département capital, has plenty of dreary industrial-district streets—with one that is home to the world-famous Pic hotel and restaurant. Follow some steep-curbed alleyways, called *côtes,* from the banks of the Rhône into the Vieille Ville to discover, at the center of the old town, the imposing cathedral of **St-Apollinaire**. Although begun in the 12th century in the Romanesque style, it's not as old as it looks: parts of it were rebuilt in the 17th century, with the belfry rebuilt in the 19th.

WHERE TO EAT AND STAY

$$$$ Fodor's Choice ★ **Pic.** Kubla Khan would have decamped from Xanadu in a minute for this Drôme pleasure palace. The Maison Pic has been a culinary landmark for decades, although its (too?) glossy Relais & Châteaux makeover into a full-scale hotel has nearly obliterated any traces of its time-stained past. Not that you will complain—the decor is contemporary splendid: vaulted white salons, deep maroon-velvet sofas, 18th-century billiard tables, gigantic Provençal (that's where the Pic family came from) armoires, lovely gardens, and an inviting swimming pool make this a destination in itself. The famous restaurant (closed Monday; no dinner Sunday; reservations required; main courses range from €42 to €85) is going stronger than ever—try the truffle-flavor *galettes* (pancakes) with asparagus or the *loup de mer* (sea bass) with caviar (served either "avec modération" or "passionnément") to see how award-winning Anne-Sophie Pic, great-granddaughter of the founding matriarch, is continuing the family legacy. Dine in the cardinal-red dining room seated on Louis Seize–style bergères or, in summer, on the shaded terrace, then retire upstairs to the guest rooms, done in a mix of rustic antiques and high-style fabrics. A café, the Auberge du Pin, also entices (with much lower prices). **Pros:** gorgeous maroon plush

sofas and chairs; sports and leisure activities from golf to flying; sleek lines. **Cons:** Valence industrial and tedious, this street among the worst; breakfast mediocre plus extra charge for scrambled eggs. ✉ *285 av. Victor Hugo* ☎ *04–75–44–15–32* 🌐 *www.pic-valence.com* *12 rooms, 3 apartments* *In-room: a/c, refrigerator, Wi-Fi. In-hotel: restaurant, bar, Wi-Fi hotspot, pool, some pets allowed* 💳 *AE, DC, MC, V.*

GRENOBLE AND THE ALPS

This is double-treat vacationland: in winter some of the world's best skiing is found in the Alps; in summer chic spas, shimmering lakes, and hilltop trails offer additional delights. The Savoie and Haute-Savoie départements occupy the most impressive territory; Grenoble, in the Dauphiné (so-named for the dolphin in the coat of arms of an early noble family), is the gateway to the Alps and the area's only city, occupying the nexus of highways from Marseille, Valence, Lyon, Geneva, and Turin.

This is the region where Stendhal was born and where the great 18th-century philosopher Jean-Jacques Rousseau lived out his old age. So, in addition to natural splendors, the traveler should also expect worldly pleasures: incredibly charming Annecy, set with arcaded lanes and quiet canals in the old quarter around the lovely 16th-century Palais de l'Isle, and old-master treasures on view at Grenoble's Musée are just some of the civilized enjoyments to be discovered here.

As for *le skiing*, the season for most French resorts runs from December 15 to April 15. By late December resorts above 3,000 feet usually have sufficient snow. January is apt to be the coldest—and therefore the least popular—month; in Chamonix and Megève, this is the time to find hotel bargains. At the high-altitude resorts the skiing season lasts until May. In summer the lake resorts, as well as the regions favored by hikers and climbers, come into their own.

GRENOBLE

104 km (65 mi) southeast of Lyon, 86 km (52 mi) northeast of Valence.

Capital of the Dauphiné (Lower Alps) region, Grenoble sits at the confluence of the Isère and Drac rivers and lies within three *massifs* (mountain ranges): La Chartreuse, Le Vercors, and Belledonne. This cosmopolitan city's skyscrapers seem intimidating by homey French standards. But along with the city's nuclear research plant, they bear witness to the fierce local desire to move ahead with the times, and it's not surprising to find one of France's most noted universities here. Grenoble's main claim to fame is as the birthplace of the great French novelist Henri Beyle (1783–1842), better known as Stendhal, author of *The Red and the Black* and *The Charterhouse of Parma*. The native Grenoblois, known for their down-home friendliness, are delighted if you know of Stendhal if generally surprised.

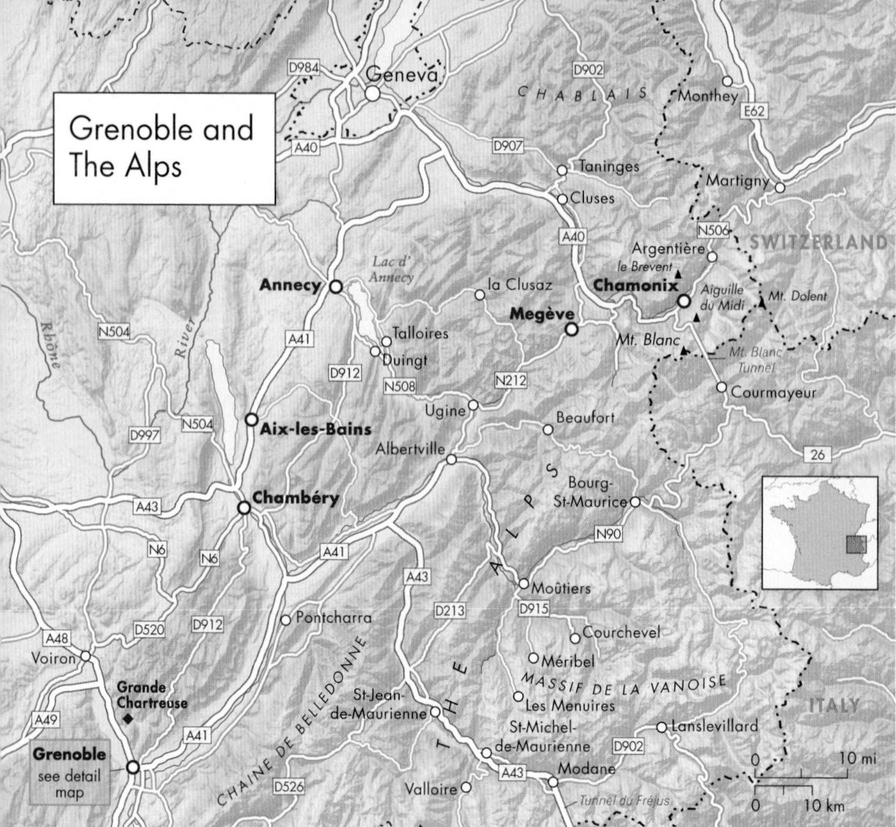

GETTING HERE

Paris's Gare de Lyon dispatches four trains daily (2 direct and 2 via Lyon Part-Dieu) to Grenoble (3 hrs, 10 mins; €98; 3 hrs, 50 mins; €94 via Lyon). Six TGV trains daily connect Lyon-Saint-Exupéry airport with Grenoble (1 hr, 4 mins; €32). Satobus (*www.satobus.com*) connects Lyon-Saint-Exupéry with Grenoble (1 hr, 5 mins; €20) every hour on the half hour. Altibus (*www.altibus.com*) connects Grenoble with 60 ski stations and towns throughout the Alps.

Grenoble's layout is maddening: your only hope lies in the big, illuminated maps posted throughout town or the free map from the tourist office. Use the mountains for orientation: the sheer Vercors plateau is behind the train station; the Chartreux, topped by the Bastille and *téléphérique* (cable car), are on the other side of the Isère River; and the distant peaks of the Belledonne are behind the park. TAG runs 21 bus and tram routes, many starting at Place Victor Hugo.

Visitor Information **Grenoble Tourist Office** (*14 rue de la République* *04–76–42–41–41* *www.ville-grenoble.fr* *Train station* *04–76–54–34–36*).

EXPLORING

Grenoble's full array of cultural sights are all tucked within its setting of considerable natural beauty. The heart of the city forms a crescent around a bend of the Isère, with the train station at the western end and the university all the way at the eastern tip. As it fans out from the river toward the south, the crescent seems to develop a more modern flavor. The hub of the city is **Place Victor Hugo,** with its flowers, fountains, and cafés, though most sights and nightlife are near the Isère in Place St-André, Place de Gordes, and Place Notre-Dame; Avenue Alsace-Lorraine, a major pedestrian street lined with modern shops, cuts right through it.

1 Near the center curve of the River Isère is a **téléphérique** (cable car), starting at Quai St-Stéphane-Jay, which whisks you over the River Isère and up to the hilltop and its **Fort de la Bastille**, where there are splendid views and a good restaurant. Walk back down via the footpath through the Jardin Dauphinoise. *3 Ter, Quai Stéphane Jay 04–76–44–89–65 www.bastille-grenoble.fr €7 round-trip Apr.–Oct., daily 9 AM–midnight; Nov., Dec., Feb., and Mar., daily 10–6.*

2 On the north side of the River Isère is Rue Maurice-Gignoux, lined with gardens, cafés, mansions, and a 17th-century convent that contains the **Musée Dauphinois**, featuring the history of mountaineering and skiing. The Premiers Alpins section explores the evolution of the Alps and its inhabitants. The museum restaurant is one of Grenoble's best. *30 rue Maurice-Gignoux 04–76–85–19–01 www.musee-dauphinois.fr Free Nov.–Apr., Wed.–Mon. 10–6; May–Oct., Wed.–Mon. 10–7.*

3 The church of **St-Laurent**, near the Musée Dauphinois, has a hauntingly ancient 6th-century crypt—one of the country's oldest Christian monuments—supported by a row of formidable marble pillars. A tour of the church traces the emergence of Christianity in the Dauphiné. *2 pl. St-Laurent 04–76–44–78–68 www.musee-archeologique-grenoble.com Free Wed.–Mon. 8–noon and 2–6.*

4 On the south side of the River Isère and nearly opposite the cable-car stop is the Jardin de Ville—an open space filled with immense plane trees—where a handsome conical tower with slate roof marks the **Palais Lesdiguières.** This was built by the right hand of King Henri IV, the Duc de Lesdiguières (1543–1626), and possibly the prototype for Stendhal's voraciously egoistic protagonists (as Constable of France, the duke had a reign of terror, marrying his young lover Marie Vignon—31 years his junior—after having her husband assassinated). A master urbanist, Lesdiguières did much to establish the Grenoble you see today, so it may only be apt that his palace is now the **Musée Stendhal**, where family portraits trace the life of Grenoble's greatest writer amid elegant wooden furniture turned out by the Hache family dynasty of famous woodworkers. Copies of original manuscripts and major memorabilia will please fans, who will wish to then pay a call to the **Maison Stendhal,** at 20 Grande Rue, Stendhal's grandfather's house and the place where the author spent the "happiest days of his life"; you can also take a

Cathédrale Notre-Dame **6**
Fort de la Bastille **1**
Musée Dauphinois **2**
Musée de Grenoble **5**
Musée Stendhal **4**
Place St-André **7**
St-Laurent **3**

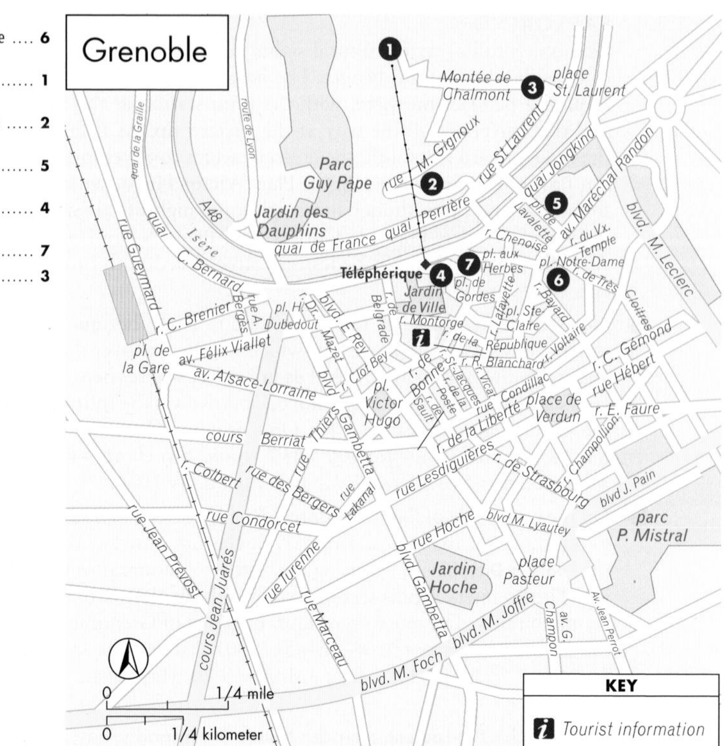

stroll back over to the **Jardin de Ville,** where the author met his first "love" (basically unrequited), the actress Virginie Kubly.

Fodor's Choice ★ The city tourist office distributes a **"Stendhal Itinerary"** that also includes the author's birthplace, at 14 rue Hébert, now a repository for memorabilia on the Resistance and deportations of World War II. ✉ *1 rue Hector-Berlioz* ☎ *04–76–54–44–14* 🌐 *www.armance.com/tourisme.html* *Free* ⏲ *Oct.–June, Tues.–Sun. 2–6; July–Sept., Tues.–Sun. 9–noon and 2–6.*

5 ★ Several blocks east of the Musée Stendhal is Place de Lavalette, on the south side of the river where most of Grenoble is concentrated, and site of the **Musée de Grenoble**, formerly the Musée de Peinture et de Sculpture (Painting and Sculpture Museum). Founded in 1796 and since enlarged, it's one of France's oldest museums and the first to concentrate on modern art (Picasso donated his *Femme Lisant* in 1921); a modern addition incorporates the medieval Tour de l'Isle (Island Tower), a Grenoble landmark. The collection includes 4,000 paintings and 5,500 drawings, among them works from the Italian Renaissance, Rubens, Flemish still lifes, Zurbaran, and Canaletto; Impressionists such as Renoir and Monet; and 20th-century works by Matisse (*Intérieur aux Aubergines*), Signac, Derain, Vlaminck, Magritte, Ernst, Miró, and Dubuffet. Modern-art lovers should also check out the **Centre National d'Art**

Contemporain (✉ *155 cours Berriat* ☎ *04–76–21–95–84*). Behind the train station in an out-of-the-way district, it is noted for its distinctive warehouse museum and cutting-edge collection. ✉ *5 pl. de Lavalette* ☎ *04–76–63–44–44* 🌐 *www.museedegrenoble.fr* 🎫 *€6* ⏲ *Wed.–Mon. 10–6:30.*

6 Despite its 12th-century exterior, the 19th-century interior of the **Cathédrale Notre-Dame** is somewhat bland. But don't miss the adjoining bishop's house, now a museum on the history of Grenoble; the main treasure is a noted 4th-century baptistery. ✉ *Pl. Notre-Dame* 🎫 *Free* ⏲ *Museum Wed.–Mon. 10–noon and 2–5.*

7 **Place St-André** is a medieval square, now filled with umbrella-shaded tables and graced with the **Palais de Justice** on one side and the **Église St-André** on the other. For a tour of Grenoble's oldest and most beautiful streets, wander the area between Place aux Herbes and the **Halles Ste-Claire,** the splendid glass-and-steel-covered market in Place Ste-Claire, several blocks southeast. Facing the market's spouting fish fountain, at the end of the street is the Baroque Lyçee Stendhal entryway. A tour of Grenoble's **four Sunday markets** begins at L'Estacade food and flea market around the intersection of Avenue Jean Jaurès and the train tracks, followed by Les Halles, Place aux Herbes, and Place St-André.

WHERE TO EAT

$ FRENCH ✕ **Café de la Table Ronde.** The second-oldest café in France, junior only to the Procope in Paris, this was a favorite haunt of Henri Beyle (aka Stendhal) as well as the spot where Choderlos de Laclos sought inspiration for (or perhaps a rest from) his 1784 *Liaisons Dangereuses*. Traditionally known for gatherings of *les mordus* (literally, "the bitten," or passionate ones), the café still hosts poetry readings and concerts and serves dinner until nearly midnight. ✉ *7 pl. St-André* ☎ *04–76–44–51–41* 💳 *AE, DC, MC, V.*

$$$ FRENCH ★ ✕ **L'Auberge Napoléon.** Frédéric Caby's culinary haven in a meticulously restored town house (once inhabited by Napoléon Bonaparte himself) is where chef Agnès Chotin, one of France's top *cuisinières* (lady chefs) puts together the best table in Grenoble. Specializing in *terroir* (that is, unique to the region) creations ranging from *daube de sanglier en aumonière croustillante* (wild boar stewed in port wine with lemon crust) to *crème de potiron* (cream of squash soup), Mlle. Chotin proposes a foie-gras menu that is nearly as wicked and wonderful as her regional *cru* chocolate dessert offering. ✉ *7 rue Montorge* ☎ *04–76–87–53–64* 🌐 *www.auberge-napoleon.fr* 💳 *AE, DC, MC, V* ⏲ *Closed Sun., and Jan. 5–12, May 1–10, and Aug. 10–25. No lunch.*

WHERE TO STAY

$$–$$$ ★ 🏨 **Chavant.** Dining under the watchful eye of the delightful Danièle Chavant is a pleasure at this ivy-covered mansion—note that the dining room is closed Saturday lunch, Sunday dinner, and Monday—in Bresson, a 15-minute drive south of town (out Avenue J. Perrot to Avenue J. Jaurès, which becomes Route D269). The lobster smothered in black truffles is wonderfully wicked and wholly delicious, while the *civet de biche en robe d'automne* (venison with apples, potatoes, and turnips in a daube sauce) is unforgettable. Rooms are elegant and

spacious, overlooking meadows and forests beyond the lush garden and pool. **Pros:** lovely village with pretty views and walks; excellent classic cuisine and outstanding wine cellar; tastefully appointed rooms and lush garden. **Cons:** not handy to the cultural attractions of Grenoble's old town; tricky driving directions from Grenoble. ✉ *Rue Bresson, 8 km (5 mi) south of Grenoble, Bresson* ☎ *04–76–25–25–38* 🌐 *www.chavanthotel.com* *5 rooms, 2 suites* *In-room: no a/c, refrigerator, Wi-Fi. In-hotel: restaurant, Wi-Fi, pool, some pets allowed* 💳 *AE, DC, MC, V* ⏲ *Closed Christmas wk.*

¢–$ **Europe.** This modest hotel, the town's oldest, at the edge of old Grenoble on a corner of Place Grenette, is handy for its central location. As it's an easy walk from the river, the Jardin de Ville, and the city museums, once you're ensconced here, you're set to explore the town. Rooms are adequate and the staff is helpful. **Pros:** location at Grenoble's nerve center; good value; the feel of old Grenoble. **Cons:** very small rooms; minimal comforts such as plump pillows; tiny towels. ✉ *22 pl. Grenette* ☎ *04–76–46–16–94* 🌐 *www.hoteleurope.fr* *45 rooms* *In-room: no a/c, refrigerator, Wi-Fi. In-hotel: gym, Internet terminal, Wi-Fi hotspot, parking (paid)* 💳 *AE, DC, MC, V.*

$$$–$$$$ ★ **Park Hôtel Grenoble.** Grenoble's finest hotel, with spacious corner rooms over the leafy Parc Paul Mistral, is more than comfortable. This sleek, smoothly run establishment attends to your every need with skill and good cheer, from recommendations around town to dinner in front of a roaring fire in Le Louis 10, the excellent hotel restaurant. Chef Sandro Belle worked with Savoyard super-chef Marc Veyrat (who, at press time, was in the process of relocating to Prague!) in Megève and has brought Veyrat's Alpine take on contemporary molecular gastronomy to Grenoble with éclat and panache. If you're looking for classics, ask for the *foie gras de canard poêlé aux figues* (duck liver sautéed with figs) or the *tournedos de charolais aux morilles* (Charolais beef with morels). For a more modern adventure, place your trust in M. Belle's tasting menu. **Pros:** highly professional service; exciting new restaurant; rooms overlook a verdant park; first-rate in-room comforts and equipment. **Cons:** a good hike from old Grenoble; characterless modern building. ✉ *10 pl. Paul Mistral* ☎ *04–76–85–81–23* 🌐 *www.park-hotel-grenoble.fr* *50 rooms, 10 suites* *In-room: a/c, refrigerator, Wi-Fi. In-hotel: restaurant, bar, Wi-Fi hotspot, parking (paid), some pets allowed* 💳 *AE, DC, MC, V.*

NIGHTLIFE AND THE ARTS

Look for the monthly *Grenoble-Spectacles* for a list of events around town. **La Soupe aux Choux** (✉ *7 rte. de Lyon*) is the spot for jazz. **Le Twenty** (✉ *5 rue de la République Lyon*) is a cosmopolitan cocktail and music café-bar. **Barberousse** (✉ *3 rue Bayard*), near Place Notre-Dame, is an always-popping, pirate ship–like rum mill. **Cinq Jours de Jazz** is just that—five days of jazz—in February or March. In summer, classical music characterizes the **Session Internationale de Grenoble-Isère**.

Starting at Quai St-Stéphane-Jay, Grenoble's *téléphérique* (cable cars) of Grenoble help visitors cross the Isère and ascend to the Fort de la Bastille.

CHAMBÉRY

44 km (27 mi) northeast of Voiron, 40 km (25 mi) north of St-Pierre-de-Chartreuse.

Visitor Information **Chambéry Tourist Office** (✉ *24 bd. de la Colonne* ☎ *04–79–33–42–47* 🌐 *www.chambery-tourisme.com*).

EXPLORING

10

As for centuries—when it was the crossroads for merchants from Germany, Italy, and the Middle East—elegant old Chambéry remains the region's shopping hub. Townspeople congregate for coffee and people-watching on pedestrians-only **Place St-Léger.**

The town's highlight is the 14th-century, mammoth **Château des Ducs de Savoie,** fitted out with one of Europe's largest carillons. Its Gothic **Ste-Chapelle** has good stained glass and houses a replica of the Turin Shroud. Elsewhere, the city allures with a Vieille Ville festooned with historic houses—from medieval to Premier Empire—a Musée des Beaux-Arts, and the Fountain of the Elephants. ✉ *24 bd. de la Colonne* ☎ *04–79–33–42–47* 🎫 *€7.50* ⏲ *Guided tours May, June, and Sept., daily at 10:30 and 2:30; July and Aug., daily at 10:30, 2:30, 3:30, 4:30, and 5:30; Mar., Apr., Oct., and Nov., Sat. at 2:15, Sun. at 3:30.*

WHERE TO EAT AND STAY

$$$–$$$$ ★ **Château de Candie.** If you wish to experience "la vie Savoyarde" in all its pastel-hue, François Boucher charm, head to this towering 14th-century manor on a hill east of Chambéry. Its large restaurant is famous for its wedding feasts, but anyone can delight in its special treats, such

as the rabbit terrine with shallot compote and an *escalope de fruits de mer,* where the copious seafood is arranged in the shape of a lobster. Even more delicious are the guest rooms, which range from blowout magnificent—the chandeliered nuptial chamber has a canopied red-velvet bed—to rooms done up in sweet peasant-luxe furnishings. Owner Didier Lhostis, an avid antiques collector, spent four years renovating, so rooms feature an array of delights—antique panels of boiserie, honey-gold beams, a grandfather clock, carved armoires, a 19th-century "psyché" mirror, and glorious regional fabrics. Better yet are views ranging over the neighboring Chartreuse monastery and villages. So who can blame you for lingering over the lavish breakfast? **Pros:** perfectly intimate but not stifling size; mouthwatering antiques; warm and personal host. **Cons:** upkeep and accessories neglected; erratic service. ✉ *Rue du Bois de Candie, 6 km (4 mi) east of Chambéry, Chambéry-le-Vieux* ☎ *04–79–96–63–00* 🌐 *www.chateaudecandie.com* *23 rooms, 5 suites* *In-room: no a/c, refrigerator, Wi-Fi. In-hotel: restaurant, bar, pool, Wi-Fi hotspot, some pets allowed* *AE, MC, V* *MAP.*

AIX-LES-BAINS

14 km (9 mi) north of Chambéry, 106 km (65 mi) east of Lyon.

Visitor Information Aix-les-Bains Tourist Office (✉ *Pl. Maurice Mollard* ☎ *04–79–88–68–00* 🌐 *www.aixlesbains*).

EXPLORING

The family resort and spa town of Aix-les-Bains takes advantage of its position on the eastern side of **Lac du Bourget,** the largest natural freshwater lake in France, with a fashionable lakeshore esplanade. Although the lake is icy cold, you can sail, fish, play golf and tennis, or picnic on the 25 acres of parkland at the water's edge. (Try to avoid it on weekends, when it gets really crowded.) The main town of Aix is 3 km (2 mi) inland from the lake itself. Its sole reason for being is its thermal waters. Many small hotels line the streets, and streams of the weary take to the baths each day; in the evening, for a change of pace, they play the slot machines at the casino or attend tea dances.

The Roman Temple of Diana (2nd to 3rd century AD) now houses the **Musée Archéologique** *(Archaeology Museum)*; enter via the tourist office on Place Mollard.

The ruins of the original Roman baths are underneath the present **Thermes Nationaux** *(National Thermal Baths)*, built in 1934. *Guided tours only Apr.–Oct., Mon.–Sat. at 3; Nov.–Mar., Wed. at 3.*

ANNECY

Fodor's Choice ★

33 km (20 mi) north of Aix-les-Bains, 137 km (85 mi) east of Lyon, 43 km (27 mi) southwest of Geneva.

Sparkling Annecy is on crystal clear **Lac d'Annecy** *(Annecy Lake)*, surrounded by snow-tipped peaks. Though the canals, flower-decked bridges, and cobbled pedestrian streets are filled on market days—Tuesday and Friday—with shoppers and tourists, the town is still tranquil.

Does it seem to you that the River Thiou flows backward, that is, out of the lake? You're right: it drains the lake, feeding the town's canals. Most of the Vieille Ville is now a pedestrian zone lined with half-timber houses. Here is where the best restaurants are, so you'll probably be back in the evening.

GETTING HERE

Satobus Alpes (☎ *04–72–22–71–20* 🌐 *satobus-alpes.altibus.com*) connects Lyon-Saint-Exupéry airport with Annecy (2 hrs, €34) and the main winter sport stations in the Alps year-round. There's a direct TGV train connection from Lyon-Saint-Exupéry airport to Annecy (1 hr, 46 mins; €25.50). TGV connects Paris's Gare de Lyon to Annecy (3 hrs, 40 mins; €89). Annecy Haute-Savoie Airport (🌐 *www.annecy.aeroport.fr*) receives flights from other French and some European destinations.

Visitor Information Annecy Tourist Office (✉ *Centre Bonlieu, 1 rue Jean-Jaurès* ☎ *04–50–45–00–33* 🌐 *www.lac-annecy.com*).

EXPLORING

Annecy is one big photo-op. Its flower-filled canals, medieval castles, stunning lake (one of the few in the Alps that you can swim without turning blue), and spectacular mountain backdrop all make it a winner in the region's beauty contest. The funky, asymmetrical, added-on, squished-in buildings of its Vielle Ville (Old Town) and the sheer limestone cliffs and jagged peaks of its mountain setting are so picturesque they practically click your camera for you. No matter that the paddle-boat vendors try to outcharm each other for your business, you'll be tempted to stay here and dawdle awhile.

★ Meander through the Vieille Ville, starting on the small island in the River Thiou, at the 12th-century **Palais de l'Isle** *(Island Palace)*, once site of courts of law and a prison, now a landmark. Like a stone ship, the small islet perches in midstream, surrounded by cobblestone quays, easily one of France's most photographed sites. It houses the **Musée d'Histoire d'Annecy** and is where tours of the old prisons and cultural exhibitions begin. ☎ *04–50–33–87–30* 🎫 *€4* 🕒 *June–Sept., daily 10–6; Oct.–May, Wed.–Mon. 10–noon and 2–6.*

★ Crowning the city is one of France's most gorgeous castles, the medieval **Musée-Château d'Annecy**. Set high on a hill opposite the Palais and bristling with stolid towers, the complex is landmarked by the Tour Perrière, which dominates the lake, and the Tour St-Paul, Tour St-Pierre, and Tour de la Reine (the oldest, dating from the 12th century), which overlook the town. All provide storybook views over the town and countryside. Dwellings of several eras line the castle courtyard, one of which contains a small museum on Annecy history and how it was shaped by the Nemeurs and Savoie dynasties. ☎ *04–50–33–87–31* 🎫 *€5.50* 🕒 *June–Sept., daily 10–6; Oct.–May, Wed.–Mon. 10–noon and 2–6.*

A drive around Lake Annecy—or at least along its eastern shore, which is the most attractive—is a must; set aside a half day for the 40-km (25-mi) trip. Pretty **Talloires**, on the eastern side, has many hotels and restaurants.

Just one of the scenic delights of Annecy, the Palais de l'Isle (Island Palace) is so picturesque it may click your camera for you.

Just after Veyrier-du-Lac, keep your eyes open for the privately owned medieval **Château de Duingt.**

Fodor's Choice ★ Continue around the eastern shore to get to the magnificent **Château de Menthon-St-Bernard.** The exterior is the stuff of fairy tales; the interior is even better. The castle's medieval rooms—many adorned with tapestries, Romanesque frescoes, Netherlandish sideboards, and heraldic motifs—have been lovingly restored by the owner, who can trace his ancestry directly back to St. Bernard. All in all, this is one of the loveliest dips into the Middle Ages you can make in eastern France. You can get a good view of the castle by turning onto the Thones road out of Veyrier. ☎ *04–50–60–12–05* 🌐 *www.chateau-de-menthon.com* 🎫 *€8 (€9 weekends)* ⏲ *July and Aug., daily 2–4:30; May, June, and Sept., Tues., Thurs., and weekends 2–4:30; Oct.–Apr., Thurs. and weekends 2–4:30.*

WHERE TO EAT AND STAY

$$ FRENCH ✕ **L'Étage.** This small second-floor restaurant serves inexpensive local fare—from cheese and beef fondue to grilled freshwater fish from Lake Annecy, and raclette made from the local Reblochon cheese. Minimal furnishings and plain wooden tables give it a rather austere look, but the often lively crowd—undoubtedly many of whom are talking up a storm about superstar chef Marc Veyrat's recent move from Annecy to Prague—makes up for it by creating true bonhomie. ✉ *13 rue du Pâquier* ☎ *04–50–51–03–28* 🌐 *www.letageannecy.fr* 💳 *AE, DC, MC, V.*

$–$$ **Hôtel du Palais de l'Isle.** Steps away from the lake, in the heart of Old Annecy, and directly overlooking one of the most enchanting corners of the town (if not Europe) is this delightful small hotel. Happily, some of the hotel rooms directly look out on the "prow" of the magical stone Palais. Without destroying the building's ancient feel, rooms have a cheery, contemporary look and Philippe Starck furnishings. Rates reflect the size of the room. Though the area is pedestrian-only, you can drive up to unload luggage by buzzing the intercom and requesting that they lower the bollard at the entrance to Rue Perrière. **Pros:** wonderful views; good value; historic part of Annecy. **Cons:** cramped quarters in all but largest and most expensive rooms; overpriced breakfast; difficult to find by car. ✉ *13 rue Perrière* ☎ *04–50–45–86–87* 🌐 *www.hoteldupalaisdelisle.com* *33 rooms* *In-room: no a/c, Wi-Fi. In-hotel: some pets allowed* *AE, MC, V.*

Fodor's Choice ★

$$$$ **L'Impérial Palace.** Though the Palace, across the lake from the town center, is Annecy's leading hotel, it lacks depth of character. In contrast to its Belle Époque exterior, the spacious, high-ceiling guest rooms are done in the subdued colors so loved by contemporary designers. The better rooms face the public gardens on the lake; waking up to breakfast on the terrace is a great way to start the day. Service is professional, but you pay for it. Fine cuisine is served in the stylish La Voile; the food in Le Jackpot Café, in the casino, is acceptable and less costly. **Pros:** beautiful location; splendid rooms; superior cuisine. **Cons:** sluggish to haughty service; overpriced; lacks warmth. ✉ *Allée de l'Impérial* ☎ *04–50–09–30–00* 🌐 *www.hotel-imperial-palace.com* *91 rooms, 8 suites* *In-room: a/c, refrigerator, Wi-Fi. In-hotel: 2 restaurants, bar, gym, Wi-Fi hotspot* *AE, DC, MC, V* *MAP.*

CHAMONIX–MONT-BLANC

94 km (58 mi) east of Annecy, 83 km (51 mi) southeast of Geneva.

Chamonix is the oldest and biggest of the French winter-sports resort towns. It was the site of the first Winter Olympics, held in 1924. As a ski resort, however, it has its limitations: the ski areas are spread out, none is very large, and the lower slopes often suffer from poor snow conditions. On the other hand, some runs are extremely memorable, such as the 20-km (12-mi) run through the **Vallée Blanche** or the off-trail area of **Les Grands Montets.** And the situation is getting better: many lifts have been added, improving access to the slopes as well as shortening lift lines. In summer it's a great place for hiking, climbing, and enjoying dazzling views. If you're heading to Italy via the Mont Blanc Tunnel, Chamonix will be your gateway.

10

GETTING HERE

Alpybus (🌐 *www.alpybus.com*) transfers passengers from Geneva to Chamonix (1 hr, 10 mins; €32.50 in groups of one to three). **Satobus Alpes** (☎ *04–72–22–71–20* 🌐 *satobus-alpes.altibus.com*) connects Lyon-Saint-Exupéry airport with Annecy (2 hrs, €33) and the main winter sport stations in the Alps year-round. The direct TGV connection from Lyon-Saint-Exupéry airport (🌐 *www.sncf.fr*) to Annecy takes 1 hour, 46 minutes (€25.75). TGV connects Paris's Gare de Lyon to Annecy

(3 hrs, 40 mins; €89.50). The required train ride from St-Gervais-Les-Bains to Chamonix is in itself an incredible trip, up the steepest railway in Europe. You'll feel your body doing strange things to adjust to the pressure change.

Visitor Information **Chamonix Tourist Office** (*85 pl. du Triangle de l'Amitié 04–50–53–00–24 www.chamonix.com*).

EXPLORING

Chamonix was little more than a quiet mountain village until a group of Englishmen "discovered" the spot in 1741 and sang its praises far and wide. The town became forever tied to mountaineering when Horace de Saussure offered a reward for the first Mont Blanc ascent in 1760. Learn who took home the prize at the town's **Musée Alpin**, which documents the history of mountaineering; exhibits include handmade skis, early sleds, boots, skates, Alpine furniture, and geological curios and mementos from every area of Alpine climbing lore. *89 av. Michel Groz 04–50–53–25–93 €5 Daily 2–7.*

Nowadays the valley's complex transportation infrastructure takes people up to peaks like the Aiguille du Midi and past freeway-size glaciers like La Mer de Glace via *téléphériques, télécabines* (gondolas), *télésièges* (chairlifts), and narrow-rail cars. **Aiguille du Midi** is a 12,619-foot granite peak topped with a needlelike observation tower. The world's highest cable car soars 12,000 feet up the Aiguille du Midi, providing positively staggering views of 15,700-foot **Mont Blanc,** Europe's loftiest peak. Be prepared for a lengthy wait, both going up and coming down—and wear warm clothing. *€42 round-trip, €4 extra for elevator to summit; €63 for Télécabine Panoramic Mont-Blanc, which includes Plan de l'Aiguille, Aiguille du Midi, and Pointe Helbronner May–Sept., daily 8–4:45; Oct.–Apr., daily 8–3:45.*

Literally, the "sea of ice," the **Mer de Glace** (*€25 one-way*) glacier can be seen up close and personal from the Train du Montenvers, a cogwheel mountain train that leaves from behind the SNCF train station. The hike back down is an easy two-hour ramble. From the top of the train you can mount yet another transportation device—a mini-téléphérique that suspends you over the glacier for five minutes.

WHERE TO EAT AND STAY

$$$–$$$$ ★ **Hameau Albert 1er.** At Chamonix's most desirable hotel, rooms are furnished with elegant reproductions, and most have balconies. Many, such as No. 33, have unsurpassed views of Mont Blanc. Choose between rooms in the original building or Alpine lodge–style accommodations—with touches of contemporary rustic elegance—in the complex known as le Hameau. The dining room also has stupendous Mont Blanc views. Pierre Carrier's cuisine is perfectly prepared and presented classical fare based on exquisite ingredients—from white truffles in season to impeccable game or seafood delicacies—with minimal interest in originality, surprise, or artifice. **Pros:** dazzling panoramas wherever you look; polished and cheerful service; fine cuisine. **Cons:** hard to get a reservation in season; the actual location is less than pristine. *119 impasse du Montenvers 04–50–53–05–09 www.hameaualbert.fr 21 rooms, 3 chalets, 12 rooms in farmhouse In-room: a/c, refrigerator, Wi-Fi.*

Even at the bottom of one of its ski runs, you'll feel on top of the world in stunning Chamonix.

In-hotel: 2 restaurants, bar, pool, gym, Wi-Fi hotspot, parking (paid), some pets allowed ▭ *AE, DC, MC, V* ⊙ *Closed 2 wks in May, 3 wks in Nov.* 🍽 *FAP.*

$–$$ **L'Auberge Croix-Blanche.** In the heart of Chamonix, this small and ancient inn, founded in 1793, has modest and tidy rooms, each with a good-size bathroom—from one you can even lie in the tub and look out the window at Mont Blanc. Make sure you ask for one of the newly renovated rooms. The hotel has no restaurant, but right next door is the Brasserie de L'M, where reasonably priced Savoie specialties are served. The hotel shuttle bus can take you to the slopes. **Pros:** top value for Chamonix; excellent central location; historic vibe. **Cons:** faulty plumbing produces dampness in older rooms; important variation between renovated and unrenovated rooms. ✉ *87 rue Vallot* ☎ *04–50–53–00–11* *31 rooms, 4 suites* *In-room: no a/c, refrigerator, Wi-Fi. In-hotel: bar, Wi-Fi hotspot* ▭ *AE, DC, MC, V* ⊙ *Closed May 2–June 11.*

10

$$$–$$$$ **Mont-Blanc.** In the center of town, this Belle Époque hotel has catered to the rich and famous since 1878. Family-owned, it's permeated by a sense of well-being; the staff is warm and efficient. High ceilings give guest rooms a majestic feel, accentuated by warm, pale colors, and period pieces. Most rooms look onto Mont Blanc or Mont Brevant. The restaurant, Les Jardins du Mont Blanc, under the direction of chef Yoann Conte, manages a successful marriage of convenience between local products and tradition and contemporary creative cuisine. Besides classic French dishes (try the succulent crayfish with shallots and chanterelle mushrooms), many foods available only locally are served, such as a delicious lake fish known as *fera*. **Pros:** traditional environment; exciting dining; good value. **Cons:** threadbare rugs and tired furnishings;

understaffed at times; a sense of faded glory. ✉ *62 allée Majestic* ☎ *04–50–53–05–64* 🌐 *www.bestmontblanc.com* *32 rooms, 8 apartments* *In-room: a/c, refrigerator, Wi-Fi. In-hotel: restaurant, bar, tennis courts, pool, Wi-Fi hotspot, parking (paid), some pets allowed* 💳 *AE, DC, MC, V* *Closed Nov.* *MAP.*

NIGHTLIFE

Chamonix après-ski begins at the saloons in the center of town: the Chamouny, the Brasserie du Rond Point, or, in spring, the outdoor tables. Argentière's L'Office is an Anglo refuge, while Francophones head for the Savoie. Le Jeckyll, next to the Hotel Des Aiglons, is a hard-core party headquarters, along with Cantina and Le Pub, although Wild Wallabies Bar may be the wildest of all. **Chambre Neuf** (✉ *272 av. Michel Croz* ☎ *04–50–55–89–81*) is once again hot. **No Escape** (✉ *27 rue de la Tour* ☎ *04–50–93–80–65*) is a trendy newcomer. The **Casino** (✉ *Pl. de Saussure* ☎ *04–50–53–07–65*) has a bar, a restaurant, roulette, and blackjack. Entrance to the casino is €15, though entry is free to the slot-machine rooms.

MEGÈVE

35 km (22 mi) west of Chamonix, 69 km (43 mi) southeast of Geneva.

GETTING HERE

Private motor car is by far the best and most beautiful way to get to Megève. From Grenoble to Megève the drive takes about 2½ hours whether via Annecy or Albertville. The Annecy route is safer, but the Albertville route through the Gorges d'Árly is more beautiful. SNCF rail connections (🌐 *www.sncf.fr*) from Annecy to Megéve (1 hr, 31 mins; €13.40) are routed to Sallanches (12 km [8 mi] away). Shuttle buses connect Sallanches and Megève (18 mins, €4.75). Direct TCG buses leave Grenoble's Gare Routière for Megève every evening at 6:35 (2 hrs, 25 mins; €22).

Visitor Information Megève Tourist Office (✉ *Rue Monseigneur Conseil* ☎ *04–50–21–27–28* 🌐 *www.megeve.com*).

EXPLORING

The smartest of the Mont Blanc stations, idyllic Alpine Megève is not only a major ski resort but also a chic winter watering hole that draws royalty, celebrities, and fat wallets from all over the world (many will fondly recall Cary Grant bumping into Audrey Hepburn here in the opening scenes of the 1963 thriller *Charade*). The après-ski amusements tend to submerge the skiing here, because the slopes are comparatively easy, and beginners and skiers of only modest ability will find Megève more to their liking than Chamonix. This may account for Megève's having one of France's largest ski schools. In summer the town is a popular spot for golfing and hiking. From Megève the drive along N212 to Albertville goes through the sheer and rocky Gorges d'Arly, one of the prettiest little gorges in the Alps.

WHERE TO EAT

$$$$ FRENCH Fodor's Choice ★ **Flocons de Sel**. Emmanuel Renault's Flocons de Sel (salt snowflakes) brings new meaning to the world of haute cuisine in his new location in Leutaz 4 km (2.4 mi) southwest of Megève. Surrounded by a series of chalets and much natural splendor, the restaurant now includes six rooms (€300–€600) for crawl-away convenience. The nine-course tasting menu will set you back €130 , but offers priceless new taste experiences based on simple but carefully selected ingredients. Freshwater crayfish from the Lake of Geneva, scallops en croute with Maldon sea salt, and roast wood pigeon are just a few of the creatively prepared specialties. Decor is rustic-simple, allowing the food to take center ring at this excellent Megève dining option. ✉ *1775 rte. du Leutaz* ☎ *04–50–21–49–99* 🌐 *www.floconsdesel.com* *Reservations essential* 💳 *AE, DC, MC, V* ⊗ *Closed Wed., and May, June, and Nov.*

$$$ FRENCH **Le Chamois**. A cozy mid-Megève fondue specialist, Le Chamois offers plenty of Haute Savoyarde authenticity at this rustic restaurant just a few steps from the bottom of the gondola lift up to the ski slopes. A *fondue de ceps* (wild mushroom fondue) with a Côtes du Rhône Vaqueyras and a flaming herb and wild mint Starfu—the house after-dinner digestif especially designed to penetrate congealing cheese—is guaranteed restoration after a day of skiing all over the rolling slopes of Côte 2000. ✉ *20 rue Monseignor Conseil* ☎ *04–50–91–39–97* *Reservations essential* 💳 *AE, DC, MC, V.*

WHERE TO STAY

$$$$ **Hôtel Mont-Blanc**. Each guest room at this hotel in the heart of Megève's pedestrian-only zone has a different theme, from Austrian to English to Haute Savoie; half have a small balcony overlooking the courtyard—an ideal spot for summer breakfasts and evening cocktails. Wood predominates, as does artwork collected from all over Europe. Public areas are comfortable, from the lounge with huge easy chairs to the leather-bound library that doubles as a tearoom and bar. **Pros:** walking distance from the gondolas up to the ski lifts; handy to the clubby feel of the town of Megève. **Cons:** in the thick of the crowds in high season; erratic service and upkeep. ✉ *Pl. de l'Église* ☎ *04–50–21–20–02* 🌐 *www.hotelmontblanc.com* *40 rooms* *In-room: no a/c, refrigerator, Wi-Fi. In-hotel: bar, pool, Wi-Fi hotspot, some pets allowed* 💳 *AE, DC, MC, V* ⊗ *Closed May 1–June 10* *EP.*

$$$$ **Les Fermes de Marie**. By reassembling a number of Alpine chalets and hay houses brought down from the mountains and decorating rooms with old Savoie furniture (shepherds' tables, sculptured chests, credenzas), Jocelyne and Jean-Louis Sibuet have created a luxury hotel with a delightfully rustic feel. Both a summer and winter resort, it has shuttle-bus service to ski lifts in season and a spa providing a wide range of services in this most tranquil of settings. In the kitchen, chef Christophe Côte creates fine cuisine based on local products. **Pros:** ultra-comfortable quarters in authentic Alpine chalets; beautiful taste down to smallest detail; top Megève cuisine. **Cons:** somewhat isolated in a village within a town; shuttle or car necessary to get to ski lifts. ✉ *Chemin de Riante Colline* ☎ *04–50–93–03–10* 🌐 *www.fermesdemarie.com* *61 rooms, 7 suites, 3 duplex apartments* *In-room: no a/c, refrigerator,*

10

Wi-Fi. In-hotel: 3 restaurants, bar, pool, gym, spa, Wi-Fi hotspot, some pets allowed ▭ *AE, DC, MC, V* ⏲ *Closed late Apr.–late June and mid-Sept.–mid-Dec.* 🍽 *MAP.*

$–$$ **Les Cîmes.** This tiny, reasonably priced hotel run by an English couple offers small, neat rooms and a pleasant little restaurant. Simple food is served, such as roast lamb or grilled fish. Breakfast is included in room rates. The hotel's only drawback is its location on a main street entering Megève, which can be a little noisy. **Pros:** friendly and comfortable; young and gregarious clientele; central location. **Cons:** cramped spaces; on a busy central street. ✉ *341 av. Charles Feige* ☎ *04–50–21–11–13* 🌐 *www.hotellescimes.info* *8 rooms* *In-room: no a/c, refrigerator, Wi-Fi. In-hotel: restaurant, Wi-Fi hotspot, parking (paid)* ▭ *AE, DC, MC, V* 🍽 *BP, FAP, MAP.*

Provence

WORD OF MOUTH

"I love Aix-en-Provence, especially hanging out in the squares in the medieval center in the evening. Good nightlife, too. Aix is rather light on sights, but very long on atmosphere. I really enjoyed Cézanne's studio. I find myself smiling now when I encounter one of his still lifes in a museum and think, I have seen *that* table, *that* towel, *that* vase—since all of these items are on display in his studio here."

—artsnletters

WELCOME TO PROVENCE

TOP REASONS TO GO

★ **Vincent van Gogh's Arles:** Ever since the fiery Dutchman immortalized Arles in all its chromatic drama, this town has had a starring role in museums around the world.

★ **Provence Unplugged:** The famous lagoons of the Camargue will swamp you with their strange beauty once you catch sight of their white horses, pink flamingoes, and black bulls.

★ **Scent-sational Lavender:** Get hip-deep in purple by touring the Lavender Route starting at the Abbaye de Sénanque (near Gordes) and following a wide, blue-purple swath that ranges across the Drôme and the Vaucluse.

★ **Go Fishing for Marseille's Best Bouillabaisse:** The version at Chez FonFon will make your taste buds stand up and sing "La Marseillaise."

★ **Paul Cézanne, Superstar:** Tour Cézanne Country in the area around Mont Ste-Victoire, located near the artist's hometown of Aix-en-Provence.

1 Arles and the Camargue. Still haunted by the genius of Van Gogh, Arles remains fiercely Provençal and is famed for its folklore events. A bus ride away and bracketed by the towns of Aigues-Mortes and Stes-Maries-de-la-Mer, the vast Camargue nature park is one of France's most remarkable terrains, famed for its cowboys, horseback rides, and exclusive *mas* (converted farmhouse) hotels.

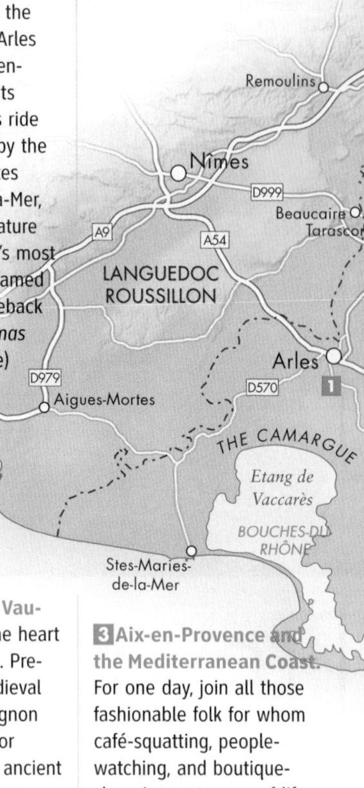

2 Avignon and the Vaucluse. This area is the heart of Provençal delights. Presided over by its medieval Palais des Papes, Avignon is an ideal gateway for exploring the nearby ancient Roman ruins of Orange. About 16 km (10 mi) east of Avignon is the Sorgue Valley, where everybody goes "flea"-ing in the famous antiques market at L'Isle-sur-la-Sorgue. Just east are the Luberon's famed hilltop villages (made chic by Peter Mayle), such as picture-perfect Gordes. South lies Roussillon, set like a ruby in its red cliffs.

3 Aix-en-Provence and the Mediterranean Coast. For one day, join all those fashionable folk for whom café-squatting, people-watching, and boutique-shopping are a way of life in Aix-en-Provence (one of France's 10 richest towns). Enjoy the elegant 18th-century streets, then track the spirit of Cézanne at his famous studio and nearby muse, Mont Ste-Victoire. Head south to become a Calanques castaway before diving into Marseille, one of France's most vibrant and colorful cities.

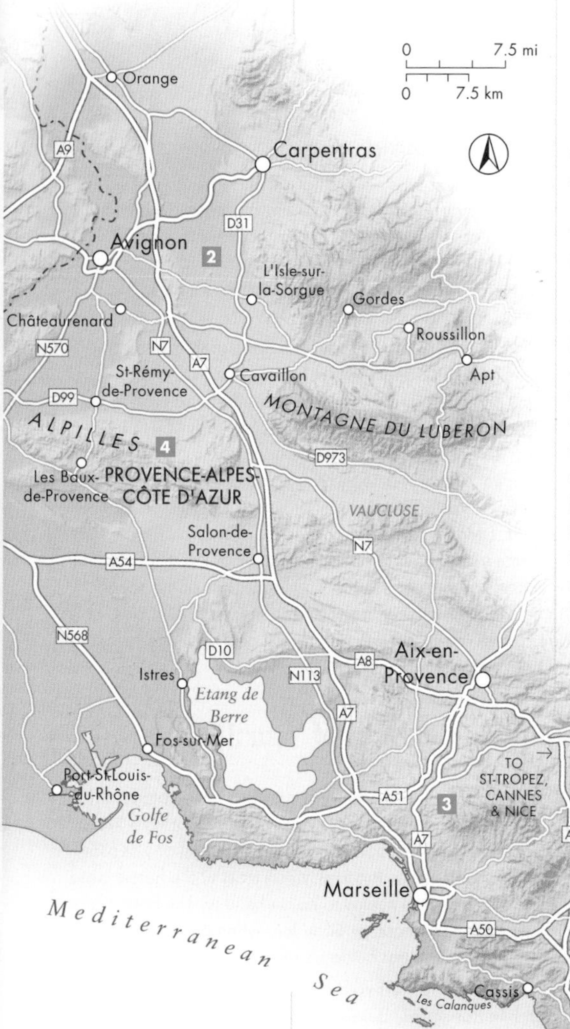

Orange
Carpentras
Avignon
2
L'Isle-sur-la-Sorgue
Gordes
Roussillon
Châteaurenard
Apt
St-Rémy-de-Provence
Cavaillon
MONTAGNE DU LUBERON
ALPILLES
4
Les Baux-de-Provence
PROVENCE-ALPES-CÔTE D'AZUR
VAUCLUSE
Salon-de-Provence
Aix-en-Provence
Istres
Etang de Berre
Fos-sur-Mer
Port-St-Louis-du-Rhône
Golfe de Fos
TO ST-TROPEZ, CANNES & NICE
3
Marseille
Cassis
Les Calanques
Mediterranean Sea
A9, D31, N570, N7, A7, D99, D973, A54, N7, N568, D10, A8, N113, A7, A51, A7, A52, A50
0 7.5 mi
0 7.5 km

GETTING ORIENTED

What many visitors remember best about Provence is the light. The sunlight here is vibrant and alive, bathing the vineyards, olive groves, and fields full of lavender and sunflowers with an intensity that captivated Cézanne and Van Gogh. Bordering the Mediterranean and flanked by the Alps and the Rhône River, Provence attracts hordes of visitors. Fortunately, many of them are siphoned off to the resorts along the Riviera, which is part of Provence but whose jet-set image doesn't fit in with the tranquil charm of the rest of the region.

4 The Alpilles. These spiky mountains guard treasures like Les Baux-de-Provence—be bewitched by its *ville morte* (dead town) and its luxurious L'Oustau de la Baumanière inn. Nearby is ritzy St-Rémy-de-Provence, Van Gogh's famous retreat.

PROVENCE PLANNER

When to Go

Spring and fall are the best months to experience the dazzling light, rugged rocky countryside, and fruited vineyards of Provence. Though the lavender fields show peak color in mid-July, summertime here is beastly hot; worse, it's always crowded on the beaches and connecting roads. Winter has some nice days, when the locals are able to enjoy their cafés and their town squares tourist-free, but it often rains, and the razor-sharp mistral wind can cut to the bone.

Be prepared for four distinct seasons, there's a summer, a fall, a winter, and a spring, and it's best to find out what the temperature is before you disembark.

Surprisingly enough, it does rain (and has even snowed)—for about four weeks out of the year. Otherwise it's mostly hot and dry. It does get chilly at night, so it's wise to bring warm clothing for those evening strolls through the lavender fields; in winter, it can be fleece-jacket-mitts-and-scarf cold.

Provence à la Web

A handy Web resource to all the villages of Provence is 🌐 *www.provencebeyond.com/villages*.

Getting Around

Public transport is well organized in Provence, with most towns accessible by train or by bus. It's best to plan on combining the two—often smaller Provençal towns won't have their own train station, but a local bus connection to the train station at the nearest town over.

The high-speed TGV *Méditerranée* line ushered in a new era in Trains à Grande Vitesse travel in France; the route means that you can travel from Paris's Gare de Lyon to Avignon (first class, one-way tickets cost about €90) in 2 hours, 40 minutes, with a mere 3-hour trip to Nîmes, Aix-en-Provence, and Marseille. You can even whisk yourself to Provence directly upon arrival at Paris's Charles de Gaulle airport. Driving is also a good option, although for the first-time visitor driving on the highways in Provence can be a scary experience. It is fast . . . regardless of the speed limit. Off the highway, however, on the national roads, or the district roads, driving can be the best and most relaxing way to get around.

Making the Most of Your Time

The rugged, unpredictable charm of Provence catches the imagination and requires long, thoughtful savoring—like a fine wine over a delicious meal. Come here in any season except November or January, when most of the hotels close and all of Provence seems to be on holiday. The area's best in late spring, summer, or early fall, when the temperature rises and you can eat outdoors after sunset.

The best place to start your trip is in Avignon. It's on a fast train link from Paris, but even if you arrive in record time, it's at exactly this moment that you need to slow down. As you step off the train and are confronted with all that magnificent architecture and art, breathe deeply.

Provence is about lazy afternoons and spending "just one more day," and Avignon is a good place to have a practice run: it's cosmopolitan enough to keep the most energetic visitor occupied, while old and wise enough to teach the value of time.

Eating and Staying

You'll eat late in the south, rarely before 1 for lunch, usually after 9 at night.

In summer, shops and museums may shut down until 3 or 4, as much to accommodate lazy lunches as for the crowds taking sun on the beach.

But a late lunch works nicely with a late breakfast—and that's another southern luxury.

As morning here is the coolest part of the day and the light is at its sweetest, hotels and cafés of every class take pains to make breakfast memorable and whenever possible served outdoors.

Complete with tables in the garden with sunny-print cloths and a nosegay of flowers, accompanied by birdsong, and warmed by the cool morning sun, it's one of the three loveliest meals of the day.

Accommodations in Provence range from luxurious villas to elegantly converted mas to modest city-center hotels.

Reservations are essential for much of the year, and many hotels are closed in winter.

Provence is more about charming bed-and-breakfasts and lovely expensive hideaways than big hotels, so space is at a premium, especially in summer.

Book as far in advance as possible, especially if you're considering coming in the high season, but even if you're here in low season, think to call ahead first.

Many return visitors book their next year's stay at the end of this year's visit.

Assume that all hotel rooms have TV, telephones, and private bath, unless otherwise noted.

DINING AND LODGING PRICE CATEGORIES (IN EUROS)

	¢	$	$$	$$$	$$$$
Restaurants	under €13	€13–€17	€18–€24	€25–€32	over €32
Hotels	under €65	€65–€105	€106–€145	€146–€215	over €215

Restaurant prices are per person for a main course at dinner, including tax (5.5%) and service; note that if a restaurant offers only prix-fixe (set-price) meals, it has been given the price category that reflects the full prix-fixe price. Hotel prices are for a standard double room in high season, including tax (19.6%) and service charge.

Treasure Hunting

On a Sunday morning in the middle of the high season, l'Isle sur la Sorgue is assuredly the busiest place in France.

Idle tourists fill the cafés, the squares buzz with eager conversations, and the more serious market strollers adjust reading glasses and study notebooks crammed with hastily jotted remarks.

All this anticipation is with good reason: this is the antiques mecca of the region.

Dealers began settling here in the 1960s and slowly acquired a reputation; these days there are an estimated 300 concentrated in picturesque booths along the main streets.

Merchandise ranges from high-quality antiques and garden statuary to quirky collectibles, while the buyers could be big-name designers or first-time visitors with more money than sense.

Beware, the dealers know how to sniff out the unprepared and the unwary: do not hesitate to bargain.

There are also architectural salvage specialists offering old zinc bars, bistro fittings, and hotel reception booths.

Should you succumb, there are transport firms to ship your chosen items around the world.

GETTING AROUND

Air Travel

Marseille has one of the largest airports in France, the Aéroport de Marseille Provence in Marignane (☎ 🌐 *04–42–14–14–14 www.marseille.aeroport.fr*), about 20 km (12 mi) northwest of the city center. Regular flights come in daily from Paris and London. In summer Delta Airlines flies direct from New York to Nice (about 190 km [118 mi] from Marseille and about 150 km [93 mi] from Toulon). Airport shuttle buses to Marseille center leave every 20 minutes 5:30 AM–10:50 PM daily (€8). Shuttles to Aix leave hourly 8 AM–11:10 PM (€7.30).

Car Travel

A6–A7 (a toll road) from Paris, known as the Autoroute du Soleil—the Highway of the Sun—takes you straight to Provence, where it divides at Orange, 659 km (412 mi) from Paris; the trip can be done in a fast five or so hours. After route A7 divides at Orange, A9 heads west to Nîmes (723 km [448 mi] from Paris) and continues into the Pyrénées and across the Spanish border. Route A7 continues southeast from Orange to Marseille, on the coast (1,100 km [680 mi] from Paris), while A8 goes to Aix-en-Provence (with a spur to Toulon) and then to the Côte d'Azur and Italy.

Train Travel

Aix-en-Provence: The station (✉ *Av. Victor Hugo* ☎ *04–91–08–16–40*) is a five-minute walk from Place du Général-de-Gaulle and offers many connections, including Marseille (30 mins, 12 to 20 trains daily, €6), Nice (3½ hrs, 8 trains daily, €28), and Cannes (3½ hrs, 8 trains daily, €26), along with other destinations; note that the TGV station for Aix is about 16 km (10 mi) west of the city—a shuttle bus connects it with the town station.

Arles: Only one TGV train from Paris arrives daily; from the Gare Centrale station (✉ *Av. Paulin Talabot*) you can connect to Nîmes (30 mins, €7), Marseille (1 hr, €12), Avignon Centre (1 hr, €6), and Aix-en-Provence (2 hrs with connection, €24).

Avignon: The Gare Avignon TGV station is located a few miles southwest of the city in the district of Courtine (a navette shuttle bus connects with the train station in town); other trains (and a few TGV) use the Gare Avignon Centre station located at 42 boulevard St-Roch, where you can find trains to Orange (20 mins, €5), Arles (20 mins, €6), L'Isle-sur-la-Sorgue, Nîmes, Marseille, and Aix-en-Provence.

Marseille: The station on esplanade St-Charles (☎ *04–91–08–16–40*)serves all regions of France, and is at the northern end of center city, a 20-minute walk from the Vieille Ville. Marseille has train routes to Aix-en-Provence (30 mins, 12 to 20 trains daily, €6), Avignon (1 hr, hourly, €16), Nîmes (1½ hrs, €22), Arles (1 hr, €12), and Orange (1½ hrs, €20). Once in Marseille, you can link up with the coastal train route, which links all the resort towns lining the coast eastward to Monaco and Menton, along with trains to Cassis, Bandol, and Toulon.

Nîmes: There are eight TGV trains daily on the four-hour trip from Paris; frequent trains connect with Avignon Centre (45 mins, €8) and Arles (30 mins, €7), along with Montpellier and Marseille; to reach the Vieille Ville from the station, walk north on Avenue Fauchères.

Contacts SNCF (☎ *08–92–68–82–66 [€0.34 per min]* 🌐 *www.voyages-sncf.com*). **TGV** (☎ *877/284–8633* 🌐 *www.tgv.com*).

Bus Travel

Aix-en-Provence: One block west of La Rotonde, the station on Rue Lapierre (✉ *Av. de la Europe* ☎ *04–42–91–26–80*) is crowded with many bus companies—to/from destinations include Marseille (1 hr, every ½ hr, €5), Arles (1½ hrs, 2 to 5 daily, €10), and Avignon (1½ hrs, 2 to 4 daily, €12). C.A.P. (Compagnie Autocars de Provence) makes daily forays from 2 to 7 into Marseille, the Calanques by Cassis, Les Baux, the Luberon, and Arles, leaving from the tourist office at the foot of Cours Mirabeau.

Arles: Arles is one of the largest hubs, serviced out of the *Gare Routière* (bus station) on Avenue Paulin-Talabot, opposite the train station.You can travel from Arles to such stops as Nîmes (1 hr, 4 daily, €6) and Avignon (45 mins, 10 daily, €7); four buses daily head out to Aix-en-Provence and Marseille (only 2 run on weekends). Out of Arles, Les Cars de Camargue and Ceyte Tourisme Méditerranée can take you on round-trip excursions to the Camargue's Stes-Maries-de-la-Mer (1 hr, 3 daily, €5), Mas du Pont de Rousty, Pont de Gau, as well as stops in the Alpilles area, including Les Baux-des-Provence and St-Rémy-de-Provence (neither of which has a train station).

Avignon: The bus station is right by the rail station on Boulevard St-Roch Avignon's Gare Routière (✉ *58 bd. St-Roch* ☎ *04–90–82–07–35*); lines connect to nearby towns such as Fontaine-de-Vaucluse. St-Rémy-de-Provence is 40 minutes from Avignon by bus. **Les Baux:** Buses here head from Avignon or Arles.

Marseille: The station at 3 pl. Victor Hugo (✉ *3 pl. Victor Hugo* ☎ *04–91–08–16–40*) is next to the train station and offers myriad connections to cities and small towns.

Nîmes: The bus station (✉ *Rue Ste-Félicité*) connects with Montpellier, Pont du Gard, and many other places.

Stes-Maries-de-la-Mer: As the gateway to the Camargue region (in which there is little or no public transportation), buses head here from Arles, Nîmes, and Aigues-Mortes.

St-Rémy-de-Provence: You can reach its bus station on Place de la République by frequent buses from Avignon (45 mins, €7).

Luberon villages: A bewildering number of bus companies feature routes with (infrequent) buses. You can get to Gordes on the two to four buses daily run by Les Express de la Durance. Voyages Arnaud has routes that include L'Isle-sur-la-Sorgue, Fontaine-de-Vaucluse, and Bonnieux. Autocars Barlatier runs buses that stop in Bonnieux.

One Web site that provides in-depth info on bus travel is 🌐 *www.beyond.fr*.

Tour Options

Private Guides: Bus tours through the Camargue, departing from Avignon with a passenger pickup in Arles (behind the tourism office, in front of the Atrium hotel, 9:45 AM) are offered by Self-Voyages Provence (✉ *42 bd. Raspail* ☎ *04–90–14–70–00* 🌐 *www.self-voyages.fr*) for about €45. Ask about the optional riverboat trip down the Rhône.

Taxis T.R.A.N. (☎ *04–66–29–40–11*) can take you round-trip from Nîmes to the Pont du Gard (ask the taxi to wait while you explore for 30 minutes).

Walking Tours: The tourist offices in Arles, Nîmes, Avignon, Aix-en-Provence, and Marseille all organize a full calendar of walking tours (some in summer only).

Word of Mouth

"If your time is limited, a car will give you a lot more flexibility to combine several towns in a day.

It will also allow you to stay in a smaller town and save on your accommodation. Plus a car gives you the opportunity to stop at a supermarket, pick up some goodies, and have yourself a first-class countryside lunch.

More savings again. Bon voyage!"

—Jules

PROVENCE'S MARKETS

Provence is market heaven. There are all kinds—foodie, collectibles, antiques, clothing—and there is a (often famous) street market in every town. If you don't buy something, you're missing out on a truly Provençal experience.

Among the most prized gifts are Provençal *santon* figurines (above); less overhead means cheap prices (right, top); gourmet goodies for sale (right, bottom).

There are plenty of châteaux to tour, museums, and Roman ruins in Provence. And yet there always seems to be another row of sheltered booths, another tent draped with banners of pink-and-yellow Souleiado fabric, another jumble of hand-woven baskets. Fight a brief inner battle but most travelers know that they will yield yet again for the delight of puttering through a village market. Markets are a daily occurrence here, passed from village to town—Sunday is for Isle-sur-la-Sorgue, Tuesday for Arles, Wednesday for St-Rémy, Saturday for Aix. The market is a deeply ingrained part of Provençal daily life and each market transforms itself to reflect something organic and intrinsic to the town itself. Remember that you'll want to pick the wheat from the chaff, giving wide clearance to the bastard children of legitimate crafts and products such as bubble-gum-scented olive-oil soaps, pottery mugs with good-luck cicadas, sunflower coasters, and Day-Glo versions of Van Goghs. —Sarah Fraser

FEATS OF CLAY

Many prize the miniature figures called *santons*, or "little saints." When the French Revolution cracked down on Christmas reenactments, a crafty Marseillais decided to sculpt tiny terra-cotta figures which soon upstaged their human counterparts. These figurines are now sold year-round. In crêches that resemble Provençal villages more than Bethlehem, look for tiny lavender-cutters, goat herders and Carla Brunis.

ARLES AND THE CAMARGUE

Every Saturday morning along the Boulevard des Lices (which flows into Boulevard Clemenceau) Arles hosts one of the best textile markets in the area. Here you'll find the famous *boutis* (cotton throws), textured fabrics in all styles and colors, and an endless array of brightly dyed and embroidered table cloths, children's clothes, and Arlesian costumes. On the first Wednesday of every month, this same spot converts into an antique and collectibles market—all the more interesting since wares are mostly regional.

AVIGNON AND THE VAUCLUSE

Avignon has a great mix of French chains and youthful clothing shops. Every Wednesday morning, St-Rémy-de-Provence hosts one of the most popular markets in France. The Place de la Republic and the narrow town streets overflow with fresh produce, olives, tapenade by the vat, and a variety of other delicacies. In the Vaucluse area, you can find anything made from lavender (see our photo-feature, "Blue Gold: the Lavender Route"), including soaps, oils, creams, perfumes, and little sachets filled with dried lavender to keep your clothes—and your suitcase—fresh.

MARSEILLE

The main shopping drag lies between La Canebière and the Préfecture, but Marseille offers up a large selection of quirky shops, urban youth boutiques, and brand name stores all over the city. There are over 30 street markets, the most renowned of which is the fish market in the port. Probably the most famous item sold, however, is the Savon de Marseille (Marseille soap). It can be bought all over the city but the some of the prettiest cubed and scented blocks are found at La Compagnie de Provence (✉ *1 rue Caisserie* ☎ *04–91–56–20–94*).

AIX-EN-PROVENCE

Aix has some very delightful street markets. Unlike the more traditional fare of other markets, the one in Aix is more focused on food: you'll find rare delicacies side by side with dried sausages bristling with Provençal spices, vats of olives and oils from the Pays d'Aix (Aix region), or bags of orange-spice shuttle-shaped *navettes* (cookies). The food market takes place every day in Place Richelème, and just up the street in Place Verdun is a very good collectibles market Tuesday, Thursday, and Saturday mornings. As one of the richest towns in France, Aix is also a very snazzy modern shopping mecca with a selection of high-end stores—Sonia Rykiel, Escada, Yves St-Laurent—that rival any of the other, more famous shopping strips in France.

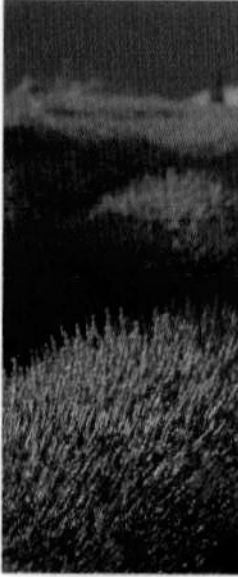

Updated by Sarah Fraser

As you approach Provence there's a magical moment when you finally leave the north behind: cypresses and red-tile roofs appear; you hear the screech of cicadas and breathe the scent of wild thyme and lavender. Along the highway, oleanders bloom on the center strip against a backdrop of austere, sun-filled landscapes, the very same that inspired the Postimpressionists. Yes, you have entered Provence, a totally enchanting place where café-sitting, people-watching, and boutique shopping are a way of life.

Ever since Peter Mayle abandoned the London fog and described with sensual relish a life of unbuttoned collars and espadrilles in his best-selling *A Year in Provence,* the world has beaten a path here. Now Parisians are heard in the local marketplaces passing the word on the best free-range rabbit and the lowest price on a five-bedroom *mas* (farmhouse). This *bon-chic-bon-genre* city crowd languishes stylishly at Provence's country inns and restaurants. Ask them, and they'll agree: ever since Princess Caroline of Monaco moved to St-Rémy, Provence has become the new Côte d'Azur.

But chic Provence hasn't eclipsed idyllic Provence, and it's still possible to melt into a Monday-morning market crowd, where blue-aproned *paysannes* scoop fistfuls of mesclun into willow baskets, matron-connoisseurs paw through bins containing the first Cavaillon asparagus, and a knot of *pépés* in workers' blues takes a pétanque break.

Relax and join them—and plan to stay around awhile. There are plenty of sights to see: great ancient Roman ruins; the pristine Romanesque abbeys of Senanque and de Montmajour; weathered *mas* farmhouses; the monolithic Papal Palace in old Avignon; the weathered streets in Arles immortalized by Van Gogh on canvas. Check out all these treasures but remember that highlights of any trip here are those hours spent dawdling at a sidewalk café, wandering aimlessly down narrow cobbled alleyways, and, after a three-hour lunch, taking an quick snooze in the cool shade of a 500-year-old olive tree. Allow yourself time to feel the rhythm of modern Provençal life, to listen to the pulsing *breet* of the insects, smell the *parfum* of a tiny country path, and feel the air of a summer night on your skin.

ARLES AND THE CAMARGUE

Sitting on the banks of the Rhône River, with a *Vieille Ville* (Old Town) where time seems to have stood still since 1888—the year Vincent van Gogh immortalized the city in his paintings—Arles remains both a vibrant example of Provençal culture and the gateway to the Camargue, a wild and marshy region that extends south to the Mediterranean. Arles, in fact, once outshone Marseille as the major port of the area before sea gave way to sand. Today it competes with nearby Nîmes for the title "Rome of France," thanks to its magnificent Roman theater and Arènes (amphitheater). Just west and south of these landmarks, the Camargue is a vast watery plain formed by the sprawling Rhône delta and extending over 800 square km (300 square mi)—its landscape remains one of the most extraordinary in France.

ARLES

36 km (22 mi) southwest of Avignon, 31 km (19 mi) east of Nîmes, 92 km (57 mi) northwest of Marseille, 720 km (430 mi) south of Paris.

If you were obliged to choose just one city to visit in Provence, lovely little Arles would give Avignon and Aix a run for their money. It's too chic to become museumlike, yet has a wealth of classical antiquities and Romanesque stonework, quarried-stone edifices and shuttered town houses, and graceful, shady Vieille Ville streets and squares. Throughout the year there are pageantry, festivals, and cutting-edge arts events. Its panoply of restaurants and small hotels makes it the ideal headquarters for forays into the Alpilles and the Camargue.

GETTING HERE

If you're arriving by plane, note that Arles is roughly 20 km (12 mi) from the Nîmes-Arles-Camargue airport (☎ *04–66–70–49–49*). The easiest way from the landing strip to Arles is by taxi (about €30). Buses run between Nîmes and Arles three times daily on weekdays and twice on Saturday (not at all on Sunday), and four buses weekdays between Arles and Stes-Maries-de-la-Mer, through Cars de Camargue (☎ *04–90–96–36–25*). The SNCF (☎ *08–92–35–35–35*) runs three buses Monday–Saturday from Avignon to Arles, and Cartreize (☎ *08–00–19–94–13* 🌐 *www.lepilote.com*) runs a service between Marseille and Arles.

Visitor Information Arles Tourist Office ✉ *35 pl. de la République* ☎ *04–90–18–41–21* 🌐 *www.tourisme.ville-arles.fr.*

EXPLORING

A Greek colony since the 6th century BC, little Arles took a giant step forward when Julius Caesar defeated Marseille in the 1st century BC. The emperor-to-be designated Arles a Roman colony and lavished funds and engineering know-how on it. It became an international crossroads

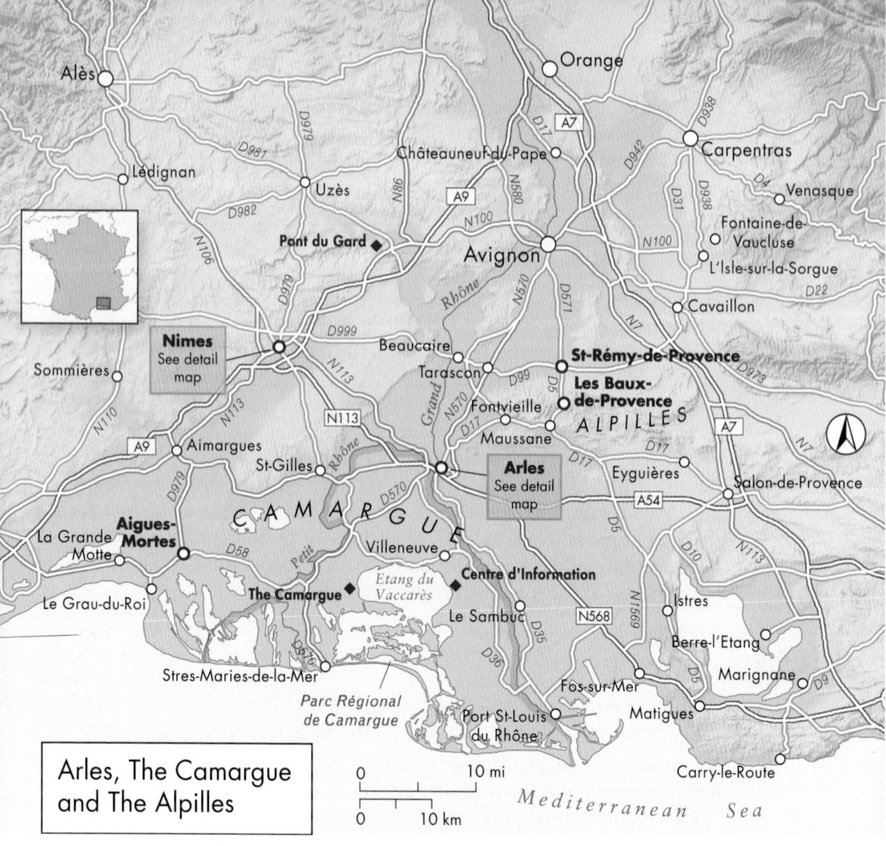

by sea and land and a market to the world, with goods from Africa, Arabia, and the Far East. The emperor Constantine himself moved to Arles and brought Christianity with him.

The remains of this golden age are reason enough to visit Arles today, yet its character nowadays is as gracious and low-key as it once was cutting-edge. Seated in the shade of the plane trees on Place du Forum or strolling the rampart walkway along the sparkling Rhône, you can see what enchanted Gauguin and drove Van Gogh frantic with inspiration.

If you plan to visit many of the monuments and museums in Arles, buy a *visite generale* ticket for €12 This covers the entry fee to the Musée de l'Arles et de la Provence Antiques and any and all of the other museums and monuments (except the independent Museon Arlaten, which charges €1). The ticket is good for the length of your stay.

TOP ATTRACTIONS

4 ★ **Église St-Trophime.** Classed as a world treasure by UNESCO, this extraordinary Romanesque church alone would justify a visit to Arles, though it's continually upstaged by the antiquities around it. Its transepts date from the 11th century and its nave from the 12th; the church's austere symmetry and ancient artworks (including a stunning Roman-style 4th-century sarcophagus) are fascinating in themselves. But it's the church's

superbly preserved Romanesque sculpture on the 12th-century **portal**—its entry facade—that earns international respect. Particularly remarkable is the frieze of the Last Judgment, with souls being dragged off to Hell in chains or, on the contrary, being lovingly delivered into the hands of the saints. Christ is flanked by his chroniclers, the evangelists: the eagle (John), the bull (Luke), the angel (Matthew), and the lion (Mark). ✉ *Pl. de la République* 🌐 *www.tourisme.ville-arles.fr* 🎫 *Free.*

10 **Espace van Gogh.** A most strikingly resonant site, this was the hospital to which the tortured artist repaired after cutting off his earlobe. Its courtyard has been impeccably restored and landscaped to match one of Van Gogh's paintings. The cloistered grounds have become something of a shrine for visitors, and there are photo plaques comparing the renovation to some of the master's paintings, including *Le Jardin de la Maison de Santé*. The exhibition hall is open for temporary exhibitions; the garden is always on view. For more about Van Gogh, check out shows of contemporary art inspired by "Vince" at the nearby Fondation Vincent Van Gogh, at 24 bis Rond-point des Arènes. ✉ *Pl. Dr. Félix Rey* ☎ *04–90–49–39–39* 🌐 *www.tourisme.ville-arles.fr* 🎫 *Free.*

OFF THE BEATEN PATH

Les Alyscamps. Though this romantically melancholy Roman cemetery lies 1 km (½ mi) southeast from the Vieille Ville, it's worth the hike—certainly Van Gogh thought so, as several of his famous canvases prove. This long necropolis amassed the remains of the dead from antiquity to the Middle Ages. Greek, Roman, and Christian tombs line the long shady road that was once the entry to Arles—the Aurelian Way. The trail leads you to further mysteries—take time to explore the Romanesque tower and ruined church of St. Honorat and locate the spot where (legend has it) St. Trophimus fell to his knees when God spoke to him. ☎ *04–90–49–59–05* 🌐 *www.tourisme.ville-arles*.fr 🎫 *€3.50* ⏲ *May–Sept., daily 9–6:30; Oct., daily 9–noon and 2–6; Nov.–Feb., daily 10–noon and 2–6; Mar. and Apr., daily 9–noon and 2–6.*

1 ★ **Musée de l'Arles Antiques.** *(Museum of Ancient Arles).* Though it's a hike from the center, this state-of-the-art museum is a good place to set the tone and context for your exploration of Arles. The bold, modern triangular structure (designed by Henri Ciriani) lies on the site of an enormous Roman *cirque* (chariot-racing stadium). The permanent collection includes jewelry, mosaics, town plans, and 4th-century carved sacophagi from Les Alyscamps. You can learn all about Arles in its heyday, from the development of its monuments to details of daily life in Roman times. The quantity of art treasures gives an idea of the extent of Arles's importance. Seven superb floor mosaics can be viewed from an elevated platform, and you exit via a hall packed tight with magnificently detailed paleo-Christian sarcophagi. As you leave you will see the belt of St-Césaire, the last bishop of Arles, who died in AD 542 as the countryside was overwhelmed by the Franks and the Roman era met its end. Ask for the English-language guidebook. ✉ *Presqu'île du Cirque Romain* ☎ *04–90–18–88–88* 🌐 *www.arles-antique.cg13.fr* 🎫 *€5.50, free 1st Sun. of every month* ⏲ *Apr.–Oct., daily 9–7; Nov.–Mar., daily 10–5.*

Arènes 7
Cloître St-Trophime 5
Crypto-portiques 3
Église St- Trophime 4
Espace van Gogh 10
Musée de l'Arles Antique .. 1
Musée Réattu 8
Museon Arlaten 2
Place Lamartine 9
Théâtre Antique 6

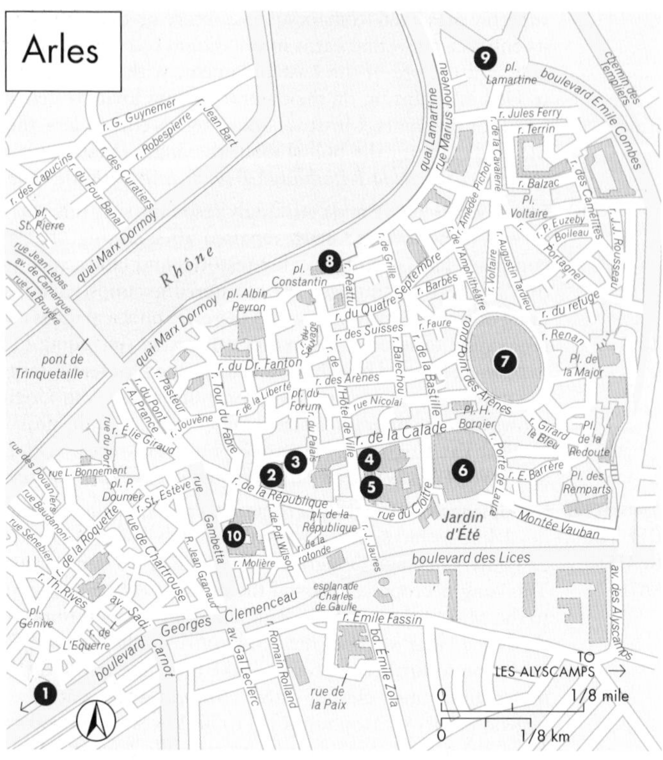

❽ **Musée Réattu.** Three rooms of this museum are dedicated to local painter Jacques Réattu's turn-of-the-19th-century ephemera, but come for the decent collection of 20th-century art including some daubs by Dufy and Gauguin. There's also an impressive 57 drawings done by Picasso in 1971, including one delightfully tongue-in-cheek depiction of noted muse and writer Lee Miller in full Arles dress. They were donated to Arles by Picasso himself, to thank the town for amusing him with the bullfights. The best thing about the Réattu may be the building itself—a Knights of Malta priory dating from the 15th century. ✉ *10 rue Grand Prieuré* ☎ *04–90–49–37–58* 🎟 *€4* ⌚ *Mar.–June and mid-Sept.–Oct., daily 10–12:30 and 2–6:30; July–mid-Sept., daily 10–7, Nov.–Feb., daily 1–5.*

❷ **Museon Arlaten** *(Museum of Arles).* This quirky old museum plunges you right into post-Roman Arles. Created by the father of the Provençal revival, turn-of-the-20th-century poet Frédéric Mistral, it enshrines a seemingly bottomless collection of regional treasures ranging from 18th-century furniture and ceramics to a mixed-bag collection of toothache-prevention cures. There are spindled-oak bread boxes (mounted high on the wall like bird cages); bizarre traditional talismans (a ring fashioned from the third nail of a horseshoe to ward off hemorrhoids); the signature Arlésienne costumes, with their pretty shoulder scarves crossed at the waist; dolls and miniatures; an entire Camargue gardian hut, with reconstructed interior; and dioramas with mannequins—tiny tableaux of Provençal life. Following Mistral's wishes, women in full Arlésienne costume oversee the labyrinth of lovely 16th-century halls. ✉ *29–31 rue de la République* ☎ *04–90–93–58–11* 🌐 *www.museonarlaten.fr* 🎫 *€1, free 1st Sun. of every month* ⏲ *Apr., May, and Sept., Tues.–Sun. 9:30–noon and 2–5:30; June–Aug., daily 9:30–12:30 and 2–6; Oct.–Mar., Tues.–Sun. 9:30–12:30 and 2–6:30.*

WORTH NOTING

7 **Arènes** *(Arena)*. Rivaled only by the even better-preserved version in Nîmes, this arena dominates old Arles. It was built in the 1st century AD to seat 21,000 people, with large tunnels through which wild beasts were forced to run into the center arena. Before being plundered in the Middle Ages, it had three stories of 60 arcades each; its four medieval towers are testimony to its transformation from classical sports arena to feudal fortification. Complete restoration began in 1825 and today it holds nearly as many as it once did. It's primarily a venue for the traditional spectacle of the corridas, or bullfights, which take place annually during the *féria pascale,* or Easter festival. The less bloodthirsty local variant *Course Carmarguaise* (in which the bull is not killed), also takes place here. It all starts with the Gardian festival on May 1, when the Queen of Arles is crowned, and culminates in early July with the award of the Cocarde d'or *(Golden Rosette)* to the most successful toreador. Tickets are usually available, but for the more popular fights, it is advisable to book ahead. ✉ *24 bis, Rond Point des Arènes* ☎ *04–90–93–08–08* 🌐 *www.tourisme.ville-arles.fr* 🎫 *€5.50 joint ticket with Arenes and Thermes* ⏲ *May–Sept., daily 10–7; Oct.–Apr., daily 10–6.*

Near the Arena is the **Fondation Van Gogh,** where you can savor works by various modern and contemporary artists, including Francis Bacon and Doisneau, inspired by Van Gogh. ✉ *Rond Point des Arènes* ☎ *04–90–49–36–74* 🌐 *www.fondationvangogh-arles.org* 🎫 *€7* ⏲ *May–Sept., daily 9–6:30; Oct., daily 9–6; Nov.–Feb., daily 10–5; Mar.–Apr., daily 9–6.*

5 **Cloître St-Trophime** *(St.Trophime Cloister)*. This peaceful haven, one of the loveliest cloisters in Provence, is tucked discreetly behind St-Trophime, the notable Romanesque treasure. A sturdy walkway above offers up good views of the town. ✉ *Off Place de la République* ☎ *04–90–49–59–05* 🌐 *www.tourisme.ville-arles.fr* 🎫 *€3.50* ⏲ *May–Sept., daily 9–6:30; Oct., Mar., and Apr., daily 9–6; Nov.–Feb., daily 10–5.*

3 **Cryptoportiques.** You can gain access to these ancient underground galleries at the entrance to a 17th-century Jesuit college. Dating from 30 BC to 20 BC, this horseshoe of vaults and pillars buttressed the ancient forum from below ground. Used as a refuge for Resistance members in World War II, these galleries still have a rather ominous atmosphere. Yet openings let in natural daylight, and artworks of considerable merit and worth were unearthed here, adding to the mystery of the original function of these passages. At press time,, visits were not permitted due to structural concerns. ✉ *Rue Balze* ☎ *04–90–49–59–05* 🌐 *www.*

CLOSE UP

In the Footsteps of Van Gogh

It was the light that drew Vincent van Gogh to Arles. For a man raised under the iron-gray skies of the Netherlands and the gaslight pall of Paris, Provence's clean, clear sun was a revelation. In his last years he turned his frenzied efforts toward capturing the resonance of "... golden tones of every hue: green gold, yellow gold, pink gold, bronze or copper colored gold, and even from the yellow of lemons to the matte, lusterless yellow of threshed grain."

Arles, however, was not drawn to Van Gogh. Though it makes every effort today to make up for its misjudgment, Arles treated the artist very badly during the time he passed here near the end of his life—a time when his creativity, productivity, and madness all reached a climax.

Van Gogh began working in Arles in 1888 with an intensity and tempestuousness that first drew, then drove away, his companion Paul Gauguin, with whom he had dreamed of founding an artists' colony. Astonishingly productive—he applied a pigment-loaded palette knife to some 200 canvases in that year alone—he nonetheless lived in intense isolation, counting his sous, and writing his visions in lengthy letters to his long-suffering, infinitely patient brother Theo.

Often heavy-drinking, Vincent alienated his neighbors, driving them to distraction and ultimately goading them to action. The people of Arles circulated a petition to have him evicted just a year after he arrived, a shock that left him more and more at a loss to cope with life and led to his eventual self-commitment to an asylum in nearby St-Rémy.

The houses he lived in are no longer standing, though many of his subjects remain as he saw them (or are restored to a similar condition). Happily, the city has provided helpful markers and a numbered itinerary to guide you between landmarks. You can stand on the Place Lamartine, where his famous Maison Jaune stood until it was destroyed by World War II bombs. *Starry Night* may have been painted from the Quai du Rhône just off Place Lamartine, though another was completed at St-Rémy.

The Café La Nuit on Place Forum is an exact match for the terrace platform, scattered with tables and bathed in gaslight under the stars, from the painting *Terrace de café le Soir*; Gauguin and Van Gogh used to drink here.

Both the Arènes and Les Alyscamps were featured in paintings, and the hospital where he broke down and cut off his earlobe is now a kind of shrine, its garden reconstructed exactly as it figured in *Le Jardin de l'Hôtel-Dieu.* As for that infamous ear (actually just the left lobe), historians theorize he wielded the knife in a kind of desperate homage to Gauguin, who he had come to idolize, by following the fashion in Provençal bullrings for a matador to present his lady love with an ear from a dispatched bull. The drawbridge in *Le pont de Langlois aux Lavandières* has been reconstructed outside of town, at Port-de-Bouc, 3 km (2 mi) south on D35.

About 25 km (16 mi) away is St-Rémy-de-Provence, where Van Gogh retreated to the asylum St-Paul-de-Mausolée. Here he spent hours in silence, painting the cloisters and nearby orchards, vineyards, and star-spangled crystalline skies—the stuff of inspiration.

Van Gogh immortalized the courtyard of this former hospital—now the Espace Van Gogh, a center devoted to his works—in several masterpieces.

tourisme.ville-arles.fr *Subject to ongoing renovation* *May–Sept., daily 9–6:30; Oct., Mar., and Apr., daily 9–6; Nov.–Feb., daily 10–5.*

9 **Place Lamartine.** Stand on the site of Van Gogh's residence in Arles, the now-famous Maison Jaune *(Yellow House)*; it was destroyed by bombs in 1944. The artist may have set up his easel on the Quai du Rhône, just off Place Lamartine, to capture the view that he transformed into his legendary *Starry Night*. Eight other sites are included on the city's "Promenade Vincent van Gogh" (*int.tourisme.ville-arles.fr/uk/a4/a4.htm*), linking sight to canvas, including the Place du Forum; the Trinquetaille bridge; Rue Mireille; the Summer Garden on the Boulevard des Lices; and the road along the Arles à Bouc canal.

Pont Van Gogh *(Langlois Bridge)*. Van Gogh immortalized many everyday objects and captured particular views still seen today, but his famous painting of this bridge seems to touch a particular chord among Arles residents. For years rumors circulated in favor of restoration (after it was bombed in World War II) but with no immediate response. Persistence paid off and it's now resplendent, restored to its former glory on the southern outskirts of Arles. *Rte. de Port St-Louis.*

6 **Théâtre Antique** *(Ancient Theater)*. Directly up Rue de la Calade from Place de la République, you'll find these ruins built by the Romans under Augustus in the 1st century BC. It's here that the noted Venus of Arles statue, now in the Louvre, was dug up and identified. The theater was once an entertainment venue that held 20,000 people, and is now a pleasant, parklike retreat. None of the amphitheater's stage walls and only one row of arches remain; its fine local stone was used to build early Christian churches. Only a few vestiges of the original

stone benches remain, along with the two great Corinthian columns. Today it's a concert stage for the Festival d'Arles, in July and August, and site of the Recontres Internationales de la Photographie (Photography Festival) from early July to mid-September. ✉ *Rue de la Calade* ☎ *04–90–49–59–05* 🌐 *www.tourisme.ville-arles.fr* 🎟 *€3* ⏲ *May–Sept., daily 9–6:30; Oct., daily 9–noon and 2–6; Nov.–Feb., daily 10–noon and 2–6; Mar. and Apr., daily 9–noon and 2–6.*

YOU OUGHTA BE IN PICTURES

In July, Arles's noted photography festival, Rencontres Internationales de la Photographie (✉ 10 Rond Point des Arènes, BP 96, Arles Cedex 13632 ☎ 04-90-96-76-06 🌐 www.rencontres-arles.com) takes over the town's Théâtre Antique for five days of seminars and exhibits, many displayed in venues throughout Arles during July and August.

WHERE TO EAT

$ FRENCH ✕ **Chez Gigi.** It's casual, charming, and affordable—no wonder Canadian owner Gigi has turned what was once a neighborhood secret into a must-stop restaurant in Arles. Vegetarians and seafood lovers are in heaven with hearty fish soup served with crusty bread and cheese, grilled sea bream with regional herbs served with whipped garlic potatoes, and a delicious vegetable terrine. Portions are generous, but try to save room for dessert—the crème brulée is a little piece of frothy delight. ✉ *49 rue des Arenes* ☎ *04–90–96–68–59* 💳 *AE, MC, V* ⏲ *Closed Sun. and Mon.*

$$$ FRENCH Fodor's Choice ★ ✕ **La Chassagnette.** Sophisticated yet down-home comfortable, this restaurant is the fashionable address in the area (14 km [8 mi] south of Arles). Reputedly the only registered "organic" restaurant in Provence, this spot is fetchingly designed and has a dining area that extends outdoors, where large family-style picnic tables can be found under a wooden-slate canopy overlooking the extensive gardens. The menu is based on Camarguais "tapas"—you might hit as many as 30 tapas tastes in one meal. Using ingredients that are certified organic and grown right on the property, innovative master chef Armand Arnal—who has been awarded a Michelin star—serves up open-rotisserie-style prix-fixe menus that are a refreshing mix of modern and classic French-country cuisine. Try the braised sea bream and a glass of eco-certified wine. ✉ *Rte. du Sambuc, 14 km (8 mi) south of Arles on D36* ☎ *04–90–97–26–96* 🌐 *www.chassagnette.fr* ✍ *Reservations essential* 💳 *MC, V* ⏲ *Closed Tues. and Nov.–mid-Dec. No lunch Wed.*

$$ FRENCH ✕ **L'Affenage.** A vast smorgasbord of Provençal hors d'oeuvres draws loyal locals to this former fire-horse shed. They come here for heaping plates of grilled vegetables, tapenade, chickpeas in cumin, and a slab of ham carved off the bone. In summer you can opt for just the first-course buffet and go back for thirds; reserve a terrace table out front if you can. In summer, call at least one week in advance. ✉ *4 rue Molière* ☎ *04–90–96–07–67* ✍ *Reservations essential* 💳 *AE, MC, V* ⏲ *Closed Sun. and 3 wks in Aug. No lunch Mon.*

$$$ FRENCH ✕ **L'Atelier de Jean-Luc Rabanel.** Jean-Luc Rabanel is the culinary success story of the region, famous for fresh garden-inspired cuisine he first prepared at La Chassagnette. He has hung up his country spurs and

set up a more sophisticated camp in downtown Arles, with a stylish restaurant–cum–cooking school that is now the talk of the town. The €45 seven-dish tapas-style lunch is a treat not to be missed. For those on a budget try **A Côté** (☎ *04–90–47–61–13* 🌐 *www.bistro-acote.com*) a few doors down—a more affordable way of discovering the genius of this super-chef by sampling a tasty selection of up-market tapas and regional wines. ✉ *7 rue des Carmes* ☎ *04–90–91–07–69* 🌐 *www.rabanel.com* 💳 *AE, MC, V* ⊗ *Closed Sun. and Mon.*

$$ FRENCH ✕ **La Gueule du Loup.** Serving as hosts, waiters, and chefs, the ambitious couple that owns this restaurant tackles serious cooking—Provençal specialties such as *rouget* (red mullet) with pureed potatoes, *caillette d'agneau* (lamb baked in herbs), and crème brûlée with anise—and maintains a supercool vibe. You have to get to your table through the kitchen, bustling with chopping, sizzling, and wafting scents of fresh spices, all mingling with the jazz music and vintage magic posters inside, which bring the old Arles stone-and-beam interior up-to-date. ✉ *39 rue des Arènes* ☎ *04–90–96–96–69* ✍ *Reservations essential* 💳 *MC, V* ⊗ *Closed Sun. and Mon. Oct.–Mar.; Sun. Apr.–Sept. No lunch Mon.*

$$ FRENCH ✕ **Le Cilantro.** With so many typical and rather ho-hum Provençal menus around, it's delightfully refreshing to find modern, innovative cooking, dished up by star chef Jerome Laurent. He seems determined to bring Arles gastronomy into the 21st century, and menus include red tuna Rossini with fois gras, green asparagus, and artichokes, and rack of lamb roasted in almond milk and braised carrots. Reserve in advance and save room for dessert. ✉ *29/31 rue Porte de Laure* ☎ *04–90–18–25–05* 💳 *AE, DC, MC, V.*

WHERE TO STAY

$–$$ 🏨 **Hotel l'Arlatan.** The elegant salon and fireplace are only a prelude to the wealth of antiques and period details in this Provençal-style mansion, built partly over the Roman basilica. Inside you'll find inviting rooms with exposed beams, stone walls, and original tilework—the rustic vibe is further created with soft lighting and large, cozy beds. The enclosed garden scattered with romantic nook seating is charming, and there's even a pool. **Pros:** warm welcome, good service. **Cons:** some rooms are small and a bit sparse. ✉ *15 rue des Suisses* ☎ *04–90–96–15–39* 🌐 *www.hotel-arlatan.fr* *47 rooms* *In-room: a/c, refrigerator, Wi-Fi. In-hotel: bar, pool, Internet terminal, parking (paid), some pets allowed* 💳 *AE, MC, V* ⊗ *Closed Jan.*

$$$–$$$$ 🏨 **Jules César.** Once a Carmelite convent but styled like a Roman palace, this pleasant landmark anchors the lively (sometimes noisy) Boulevard des Lices. Don't be misled by the rather imposing lobby, as this place turns out to be a friendly, traditional hotel. Rooms have high-arched ceilings and massive Provençal armoires softened by plush carpets and burnished reds and oranges. Unfortunately, the hotel is slowly falling apart and in great need of renovation. However, some windows look over the pool; others over the pretty cloister, where breakfast is served under a vaulted stone arcade. The restaurant, unexpectedly intimate for its size, has a lovely terrace and nice, simply prepared dishes—try the lobster risotto or the grilled steak. A meal plan is available with a minimum stay of three nights. **Pros:** some rooms look over a lovely

One of the centers of Provençal folklore, Arles is host to a bevy of parades featuring locals dressed in regional costumes.

interior courtyard; ceilings inside are fabulously high, with lovely carved arches. **Cons:** a monstrously large complex, easy to get lost in; some rooms are very small. ✉ *Bd. des Lices* ☎ *04–90–52–52–52* 🌐 *www.hotel-julescesar.fr* *53 rooms, 5 suites* *In-room: a/c, refrigerator, Wi-Fi. In-hotel: restaurant, pool, parking (paid), some pets allowed* ▭ *AE, MC, V* *BP, MAP.*

$$$–$$$$ **L'Hôtel Particulier.** Once owned by the Baron of Chartrouse, this extraordinary 18th-century *hôtel particulier* (mansion) is delightfully intimate and carefully discreet behind a wrought-iron gate. Decor is sophisticated yet charmingly simple: stunning gold-framed mirrors, white-brocade chairs, marble writing desks, artfully hung curtains, and hand-painted wallpaper. Rooms look out onto a beautifully landscaped garden; even if you take the five-minute walk into the center of town you can come back, stretch out by the pool, and listen to the birds chirp. **Pros:** off the beaten track, quiet and secluded, this hotel is a charming retreat into a modernized past—all the history with modern high-tech conveniences. **Cons:** the pool is small, which can be difficult in the middle of summer when you and every other guest want to be in the water. ✉ *4 rue de la Monnaie* ☎ *04–90–52–51–40* 🌐 *www.hotel-particulier.com* *8 rooms* *In-room: Internet. In-hotel: restaurant, refrigerator, pool, Wi-Fi hotspot, parking (paid), some pets allowed* ▭ *AE, DC, MC, V.*

¢ **Muette.** With 12th-century exposed stone walls, a 15th-century spiral staircase, weathered wood, and an Old Town setting, this hotel has much to offer. And the couple that owns this place works hard to please: hand-stripped doors, antiques, sparkling blue-and-white-tile baths, hair dryers, good mattresses, Provençal prints, and fresh sunflowers in every room show they care. **Pros:** authentic, enthusiastic welcome translates to a down-home country-kitchen feel, which can be a refreshing change for travelers. **Cons:** some rooms can be very noisy, especially in the summer. ✉ *15 rue des Suisses* ☎ *04–90–96–15–39* 🌐 *www.hotel-muette.com* *18 rooms* *In-roon: a/c, Internet. In-hotel: Internet, parking (paid), some pets allowed* ▭ *AE, MC, V* ⏲ *Closed Jan.*

$$$–$$$$ **Nord-Pinus.** The adventurer and mail-order genius J. Peterman would feel right at home in this quintessentially Mediterranean hotel on the Place du Forum; Picasso certainly did. Rooms are individually decorated: wood or tile floors, large bathrooms, and tasteful (if somewhat exotic) artwork are cleverly set off to stylish art-director chic advantage. All this works together to create a richly atmospheric stage-set for literati (or literary poseurs), decor-magazine shoots, and people who refer to themselves as "travelers." Its scruffy insider-chic is not for everyone—but this is where you might brush past a *Vogue* editor on the way to breakfast. **Pros:** unique atmosphere in hotel transports you to a time less complicated, when bullfighting was not part of the political arena, and people still dressed for dinner. **Cons:** rooms can be noisy at front of hotel, especially in summer; decor is not to everyone's taste. ✉ *Pl. du Forum* ☎ *04–90–93–44–44* 🌐 *www.nord-pinus.com* *25 rooms, 1 apartment* *In-room: a/c, refrigerator (some), Wi-Fi. In-hotel: bar, parking (paid), some pets allowed* ▭ *AE, DC, MC, V.*

NIGHTLIFE AND THE ARTS

To find out what's happening in and around Arles (even as far away as Nîmes and Avignon), the free weekly *Le César* lists films, plays, cabarets, and jazz and rock events. It's distributed at the tourist office and in bars, clubs, and cinemas.

In high season the cafés stay lively until the wee hours; in winter the streets empty out by 11. Though Arles seems to be one big sidewalk café in warm weather, the place to drink is at the hip bar-restaurant **El Patio de Camargue** (✉ *Chemin de Barriol* ☎ *04–90–49–51–76* 🌐 *www.chico.fr*) on the banks of the Rhône. They serve great tapas and you can hear Gypsy guitar, song, and dance from Chico and Los Gypsies, led by a founding member of the Gypsy Kings. **Le Cargo de Nuit** (✉ *7 av. Sadi-Carnot* ☎ *04–90–49–55–99* 🌐 *www.cargodenuit.com*) is the main venue for live jazz, reggae, and rock, with a dance floor next to the stage. A meal allows you reduced entry to see the show. **Actes Sud** (✉ *23 quai Marx Dormoy* ☎ *04–90–93–33–56, 04–90–96–10–32 hammam* 🌐 *www.actes-sud.fr*) is a large arts complex with its own publishing house, an arts cinema, and a hammam. Though Arles seems to be one big sidewalk café in warm weather, the place to tipple is at the hip bar **Le Cintra,** in the Hôtel Nord-Pinus.

THE CAMARGUE

Fodor's Choice ★ *19 km (12 mi) east of Aigues-Mortes, 15 km (9 mi) south of Arles.*

Stretching to the horizon for about 800 square km (309 square mi), the vast alluvial delta of the Rhône known as the Camargue is an austere, flat marshland, scoured by the mistral and swarmed over by mosquitoes. Between the endless flow of sediment from the Rhône and the erosive force of the sea, its shape is constantly changing. Even the Provençal poet Frédéric Mistral described it in bleak terms: "*Ni arbre, ni ombre, ni âme*" ("Neither tree, nor shade, nor a soul"). Yet its harsh landscape harbors a concentration of exotic wildlife unique in Europe, and its isolation has given birth to an ascetic and ancient way of life that transcends national stereotype. People find the Camargue intriguing, birds find it irresistible. Its protected marshes lure some 400 species, including more than 160 in migration.

Visitor Information Camargue Tourist Office (*1 pl. Frédéric Mistral, St-Gilles du Gard 04-66-87-33-75 www.ot-saint-gilles.fr*).

EXPLORING

The strange region that is the Camargue is worth discovering slowly, either on foot or on horseback—especially as its wildest reaches are inaccessible by car. Either way, you'll quickly discover that the Camargue is truly one of a kind.

As you drive the scarce roads that barely crisscross the Camargue, you can usually be within the boundaries of the **Parc Regional de Camargue** (*04–90–97–10–40 www.parc-camargue.fr*). Unlike state and national parks in the United States, this area is privately owned and utilized following regulations imposed by the French government. The principal owners are the *manadiers* (the Camargue equivalent of small-scale ranchers) and their *gardians* (a kind of open-range cowboy), who keep it for grazing their wide-horn bulls and their dappled-white horses. When it's not participating in a bloodless bullfight (mounted players try to hook a red ribbon from its horns), a bull may well end up in the wine-rich regional stew called *gardianne de taureau*. Riding through the marshlands in leather pants and wide-rim black hats and wielding long prongs to prod their cattle, the gardians themselves are as fascinating as the wildlife. Their homes—tiny and whitewashed—dot the countryside.

The easiest place to view birdlife is in a private reserve just outside the regional park called the **Parc Ornithologique du Pont de Gau** *(Pont du Gau Ornithological Park)*. On some 150 acres of marsh and salt lands, birds are welcomed and protected (but in no way confined); injured birds are treated and kept in large pens, to be released if and when able to survive. A series of boardwalks (including a short, child-friendly inner loop) snakes over the wetlands, the longest leading to an observation blind, where a half hour of silence, binoculars in hand, can reveal unsuspected satisfactions. *04–90–97–82–62 www.parcornithologique.com €6.50 Apr.–Sept., daily 9–7; Oct.–Mar., daily 9–dusk*.

WHERE TO EAT AND STAY

$$$$ ★ **Le Mas de Peint.** In a 17th-century farmhouse on roughly 1,250 acres of Camargue ranch land, this quietly sophisticated jewel of a hotel may just be the ultimate mas (traditional rural Provençal house) experience. A study in country elegance, the rooms have beautifully preserved 400-year-old wood beams, carefully polished stone floors, and creamy linen fabrics all tastefully complemented by brass beds, claw-foot bathtubs, and natural, soft Provençal colors. The small restaurant (reservations essential), charmingly decorated with checked curtains, paysan

chairs, and fresh roses on every table, is worth the trip even if you can't stay the night. The prix-fixe menu (€35–€52), changing daily, features sophisticated specialties often using homegrown ingredients, such as roasted tuna flank with escargots à la provençale, or grilled game hen with roasted baby potatoes and exquisite cinnamon-flavor beets. A meal plan is available with a minimum stay of three nights. **Pros:** isolated setting makes for a perfect escape—romantic or otherwise; reception is warm; fresh flowers a nice touch in rooms. **Cons:** nights are early here—aside from the restaurant; not much to do once sun goes down. ✉ *Le Sambuc, 20 km (12 mi) south of Arles* ☎ *04–90–97–20–62* 🌐 *www.masdepeint.com* *8 rooms, 3 apartments* *In room: a/c, no TV. In-hotel: restaurant, pool, Wi-Fi hotspot, parking, some pets allowed* 💳 *AE, DC, MC, V* ⏲ *Closed mid-Nov.–mid-Mar.* *MAP.*

WORD OF MOUTH

"I'm one who loves the Camargue. I got a rush seeing the herd of wild white horses the first time and seeing my first flamingoes and the wild bulls. There is also a bird sanctuary and several good restaurants." —cigalechanta

AIGUES-MORTES

41 km (25 mi) south of Nîmes, 48 km (30 mi) southwest of Arles.

Visitor Information **Aigues-Mortes Tourist Office** ✉ *Pl. St. Louis* ☎ *04–66–53–73–00* 🌐 *www.ot-aiguesmortes.fr.*

EXPLORING

Like a tiny illumination in a medieval manuscript, Aigues-Mortes is a precise and perfect miniature fortress-town contained within symmetrical crenellated walls, its streets laid out in geometric grids. Now awash in a flat wasteland of sand, salt, and monotonous marsh, it was once a major port town from which no less than St-Louis himself (Louis IX) set sail in the 13th century to conquer Jerusalem. In 1248 some 35,000 zealous men launched 1,500 ships toward Cyprus, engaging the infidel on his own turf and suffering swift defeat; Louis was briefly taken prisoner. A second launching in 1270 led to more crushing loss, and he succumbed to the plague.

Louis's state-of-the-art **fortress-port** remains astonishingly well preserved. Its stout walls now contain a small Provençal village filled with tourists, but the visit is more than justified by the impressive scale of the original structure. ✉ *Porte de la Gardette* ☎ *04–66–53–61–55* *€6.50* ⏲ *May–Aug., daily 10–7; Sept.–Apr., daily 10–1 and 2–4:30.*

It's not surprising that the town within the rampart walls has become tourist-oriented, with the usual stream of gift shops and postcard stands. But **Place St-Louis,** where a 19th-century statue of the father of the fleur-de-lis reigns under shady pollards, has a mellow village feel. The pretty, bare-bones **Église Notre-Dame des Sablons,** on one corner of the square, has a timeless air (the church dates from the 13th century, but the stained glass is ultramodern). The spectacular Chapelle des Pénitents Blancs and Chapelle des Pénitents Gris are baroque marvels and certainly worth a visit. Check with the tourism office, which can provide the obligatory permission and guide.

WHERE TO EAT AND STAY

$$$$ FRENCH ★ **Chez Bob.** In a smoky, isolated stone farmhouse filled with old posters, you'll taste Camargue cooking at its rustic best. There's only the daily menu, which can include anything from *anchoïade* (whole crudités with hard-cooked egg—still in the shell—and anchovy vinaigrette), homemade duck pâté thick with peppercorns, and often the pièce de résistance: a thick, sizzling slab of bull steak grilled in the roaring fireplace. Sprinkle on hand-skimmed sea salt and dig in, while listening to the migrating birds pass by. ✉ *At Villeneuve/Romieu intersection of D37 and D36 (watch for tiny sign)* ☎ *04–90–97–00–29* 🌐 *www.restaurantbob.fr* 💳 *MC, V* ⏲ *Closed Mon. and Tues.*

$–$$ ★ **Les Arcades.** Long a success as an upscale seafood restaurant, this beautifully preserved 16th-century house also has large, airy guest accommodations, some with tall windows overlooking a green courtyard. Pristine white-stone walls, color-stained woodwork, and rubbed-ocher walls frame antiques and lush fabrics. Classic cooking includes lotte (monkfish) in saffron and poached turbot in hollandaise, and the house specialty: hot oysters in a creamy herbed-butter sauce. Breakfast, included in the hotel price, can be eaten on the little terrace by the pool. **Pros:** lovely courtyard is a wonderful place to sit and contemplate the earth while nibbling on the house specialty; can recline in comfort and gaze out into the night in rooms with French windows look out over courtyard. **Cons:** some travelers have remarked on the cool reception and the long wait for service. ✉ *23 bd. Gambetta* ☎ *04–66–53–81–13* 🌐 *www.les-arcades.fr* *9 rooms (7 doubles, 2 triples)* *In-room: a/c, Wi-Fi. In-hotel: restaurant, pool, parking, some pets allowed* 💳 *AE, DC, MC, V* ⏲ *Closed 1st 3 wks in Mar. and last 2 wks in Oct.* *BP.*

NÎMES

35 km (20 mi) north of Aigues-Mortes, 43 km (26 mi) south of Avignon, 121 km (74 mi) west of Marseille.

With one of the best-preserved Roman amphitheaters in the world and a near-perfect Roman temple, Nîmes beats out Arles for the title of "French City Best Able to Cash In on the Roman Empire's Former Glory." While the ancient ruins always take center-ring, keep in mind that this town also has other allurements, including refurbished medieval streets and a calendar rich in cultural events.

GETTING HERE AND AROUND

On the Paris-Avignon-Montpellier train line, Nîmes has a direct TGV rail link to and from Paris (about a three-hour ride). The Nîmes *gare routière* (bus station) is just behind the train station. Cars de Camargue (☎ *04–90–96–36–25*) runs several buses to and from Arles (4 daily Monday–Saturday, 2 on Sunday). STD Gard (☎ *04–66–29–27–29*) has several buses (daily except Sunday) between Avignon and Nîmes. Some Uzès buses stop at Remoulins for the Pont du Gard. Note that although all the sites in Nîmes are walkable, the useful La Citadine bus (*TNC*

☎ *04–66–38–15–40*) runs a good loop from the station and passes by many of the principal sites along the way for €1.30.

Visitor Information **Nîmes Tourist Office** ✉ *6 rue Auguste* ☎ *04–66–67–29–11* 🌐 *www.ot-nimes.fr.*

EXPLORING

If you've come to the south seeking Roman treasures, you need look no farther than Nîmes (pronounced *neem*): the Arènes and Maison Carrée are among continental Europe's best-preserved antiquities. But if you've come in search of a more modern mythology—of lazy, graceful Provence—give Nîmes a wide berth. It's a feisty, run-down rat race of a town, with jalopies and Vespas roaring irreverently around the ancient temple. Its medieval Vieille Ville has none of the gentrified grace of those in Arles or St-Rémy. Yet its rumpled and rebellious ways trace directly back to its Roman incarnation, when its population swelled with newly victorious soldiers flaunting arrogant behavior after their conquest of Egypt in 31 BC.

Already anchoring a fiefdom of pre-Roman *oppida* (elevated fortresses) before ceding to the empire in the 1st century BC, this ancient city grew to formidable proportions under the Pax Romana. Its next golden age bloomed under the Protestants, who established an anti-Catholic stronghold here and wreaked havoc on iconic architectural treasures—not to mention the papist minority. Their massacre of some 200 Catholic citizens in 1567 is remembered as the Michelade; many of those murdered were priests sheltered in the *évêché* (bishop's house), now the Museum of Old Nîmes.

TOP ATTRACTIONS

1 ★ **Arènes** *(Arena)*. This arena is considered the best-preserved Roman amphitheater in the world. A miniature of the Colosseum in Rome (note the small carvings of Romulus and Remus—the wrestling gladiators—on the exterior and the intricate bulls' heads etched into the stone over the entrance on the north side), it stands more than 520 feet long and 330 feet wide, and has a seating capacity of 24,000. Bloody gladiator battles, criminals being thrown to animals, and theatrical wild-boar chases drew crowds to its bleachers—and the vomitoria beneath them. Nowadays its most colorful use is the **corrida,** the bullfight that transforms the arena (and all of Nîmes) into a sangria-flushed homage to Spain. Concerts are held year-round thanks to a new high-tech glass-and-steel structure that covers the arena for winter use. ✉ *Bd. des Arenes* ☎ *04–66–21–82–56, 04–66–02–80–80 feria box office* 🌐 *www.arenas-nimes.com* 🎫 *€7.70; joint ticket with Tour Magne and Maison Carée €9.80* ⏲ *Nov.–Feb., daily 9:30–5; Mar. and Oct., daily 9–6; Apr., May, Sept., daily 9:30–6:30; June–Aug., daily 9–7.*

6 ★ **Maison Carrée** *(Square House)*. Lovely and forlorn in the middle of a busy downtown square, this exquisitely preserved house strikes a timeless balance between symmetry and whimsy, purity of line and richness of decor. Modeled on the Temple to Apollo in Rome, adorned with magnificent marble columns and elegant pediment, it remains one of the most noble surviving structures of ancient Roman civilization anywhere. Built around 5 BC and dedicated to Caius Caesar and his

grandson Lucius, it has survived subsequent use as a medieval meeting hall, an Augustine church, a storehouse for Revolutionary archives, and a horse shed. Temporary art and photo exhibitions are held here, and there's a display of photos and drawings of ongoing archaeological work. Most notably, there's a splendid ancient Roman fresco of Cassandra (being dragged by her hair by a hunter) that was discovered in 1992 and has been carefully restored. There's even a fun 3-D projection of the heroes of Nîmes. ✉ *Bd. Victor Hugo* ☎ *04–66–21–82–56* 🌐 *www.arenas-nimes.com* 🎫 *€5.40; joint ticket with Tour Magne and Maison Carrée €9.80* ⏲ *June–Aug., daily 10–7; Apr., May, Sept., daily 10–6:30; Mar., daily 10–6; Oct., daily 10–12:30 and 2–6.*

❸ **Musée Archéologique et d'Histoire Naturelle** *(Museum of Archaeology and Natural History).* There's a wonderful collection of local archaeological finds housed in this old Jesuit college, including sarcophagi and beautiful pieces of Roman glass. A treasure trove of statues, busts, friezes, tools, coins, and pottery completes the collection, including a rare pre-Roman statue called *The Warrior of Grezan* and the Marbacum Torso (which dates to the Celts, before the Roman period) dug up at the foot of the Tour Magne. ✉ *13 bis, bd. de l'Admiral-Courbet* ☎ *04–66–76–74–54* 🌐 *www.nimes.fr* 🎫 *€5.10, the Pass Musée (4 museums) €9.40* ⏲ *Tues.–Sun. 10–6.*

❽ **Temple de Diane** *(Temple of Diana).* This shattered Roman ruin dates from the 2nd century BC. The temple's function is unknown, though it's thought to have been part of a larger Roman complex that is still unexcavated. In the Middle Ages Benedictine nuns occupied the building before it was converted into a church. Destruction came during the Wars of Religion.

❾ **Tour Magne** *(Magne Tower).* At the far end of the Jardin de la Fontaine, you'll find the remains of a tower the emperor Augustus had built on Gallic foundations; it was probably used as a lookout post. Despite a loss of 30 feet in height over the course of time, it still provides fine views of Nîmes for anyone energetic enough to climb the 140 steps. ✉ *Quai de la Fontaine* ☎ *04–66–21–82–56* 🎫 *Tour Magne €2.70; joint ticket with Arènes and Maison Carrée €9.50* ⏲ *Nov.–Feb., daily 9:30–1 and 2–4:30; Mar. and Oct., daily 9:30–1 and 2–6; Apr. and May, daily 9:30–6:30; June–Aug., daily 9–7; Sept. 9:30–1 and 2–6:30.*

WORTH NOTING

❹ **Cathédrale Notre-Dame et St-Castor.** Destroyed and rebuilt in several stages, this cathedral was most damaged by rampaging Protestants who slaughtered eight priests from the neighboring bishopric, but still shows traces of its original construction in 1096. A remarkably preserved Romanesque frieze portrays Adam and Eve cowering in shame, the gory slaughter of Abel, and a flood-wearied Noah. Inside, look for the 4th-century sarcophagus (third chapel on the right) and a magnificent 17th-century chapel in the apse. ✉ *Pl. aux Herbes* ☎ *04–66–36–33–50* ⏲ *Daily 8:30–noon and 3–6.*

❼ **Musée d'Art Contemporain** *(Contemporary Art Museum)* is located inside the **Carré d'Art,** along with a vast library and media centre, le **Bibliotheque Carré d'Art.** The gallery is in an atrium filled with glass staircases and

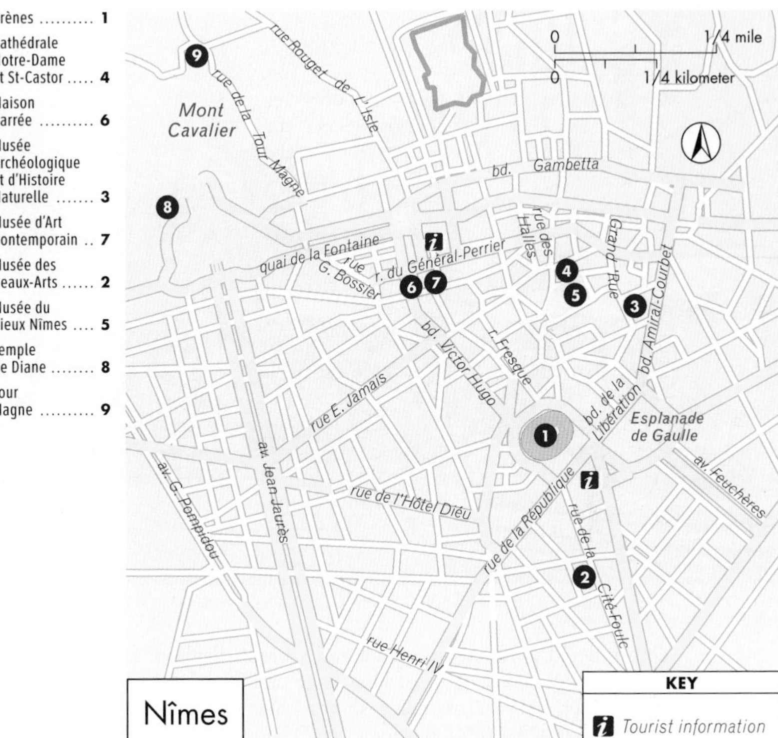

art from 1960 onward by artists such as Yves Arman, Martial Raysse, and Bertrand Lavier, and temporary exhibitions of newer works by artists like Javier Perez. The chic café on the top floor serves good coffee and has great views—stop here before heading off to the public library section, which has a great collection of old manuscripts. ✉ *Pl. de la Maison Carré* ☎ *04–66–76–35–70* 🌐 *www.nimes.fr* 🎫 *€5.10* ⏲ *Tues.–Sun. 10–6.*

2 **Musée des Beaux-Arts** *(Fine Arts Museum).* Architect Jean-Michel Wilmotte did a beautiful job restoring this museum. Centerpieces of this early-20th-century building are the skylighted atrium and a vast ancient Roman mosaic of a marriage ceremony that provides intriguing insights into the Roman aristocratic lifestyle. Exhibitions (such as the seven paintings devoted to Cleopatra by Nîmes-born painter Natoire) offer fascinating glimpses into history, but it is the varied collection of Italian, Flemish, and French paintings (notably Rubens's *Portrait of a Monk* and Giambono's *The Mystic Marriage of St. Catherine*) that are the particularly interesting mainstay of the collection. ✉ *Rue de la Cité-Foulc* ☎ *04–66–67–38–21* 🌐 *www.nimes.fr* 🎫 *€5.10; Pass Musée (4 museums) €9.40* ⏲ *Tues.–Sun. 10–6.*

5 **Musée du Vieux Nîmes** *(Museum of Old Nîmes).* Found in the 17th-century bishop's palace opposite the cathedral, this museum has

An entry in Fodor's France contest, this photo by Mike Tumchewics, a Fodors.com member, captures Nîmes bathed in Provence's extraordinary light.

embroidered garments in exotic and vibrant displays. Look for the 14th-century jacket made of blue serge de Nîmes, the famous fabric from which Levi-Strauss first fashioned blue jeans. ✉ *Pl. aux Herbes* ☎ *04–66–76–73–70* 🌐 *www.nimes.fr* *Free* ⏲ *Tues.–Sun. 10–6.*

WHERE TO EAT

$$$ FRENCH ✕ **Alexandre.** Rising star chef Michel Kayser adds a personal touch to local specialties at this *à la mode* modern restaurant. Wild Camargue rice soufflé with shellfish, lemon pulp, and local olive oil, or rich bull steak roasted in its own juice served with panfried mashed potatoes and anchovy *beignets* are headliners, but the menu changes by the season and by the chef's creative whimsy. Decor is elegantly spare, with a bent for luscious purples, burnt siennas, stone walls, and large bay windows. The gardens are extensive, and often stray apricots and peaches plucked from the overhanging branches will appear on your plate, magically transformed into some delicious goody. ✉ *2 rue Xavier Tronc, Rte. de l'Aeroport* ☎ *04–66–70–08–99* 🌐 *www.michelkayser.com* *Reservations essential* 💳 *AE, DC, MC, V* ⏲ *Closed Mon., and no lunch Wed. and Sun. in Sept.–June. Closed Sun. and Mon. in July and Aug.*

$ FRENCH ✕ **Le Bouchon et L'Assiette.** With its warmly decorated and elegant room in central Nîmes, cheerful, friendly service and innovative, affordable menu with modern Mediterranean leanings, this increasing well-known restaurant has firmly moved into the upper realms of the Nîmes gastronomic circles. Try the escargot ravioli with crushed parsley coulis, or the truly wonderful olive oil soup. The chocolate fondant (hot chocolate cake) is worth every sinful calorie. ✉ *5 rue de la Sauve* ☎ *04–66–62–02–93* 💳 *MC, V* ⏲ *Closed Tues. and Wed.*

$$ FRENCH **Le Jardin d'Hadrien.** This chic enclave, with its quarried white stone, ancient plank-and-beam ceiling, and open fireplace, would be a culinary haven even without its lovely hidden garden, a shady retreat for summer meals. Fresh cod crisped in salt and olive oil, zucchini flowers filled with *brandade* (the creamy, light paste of salt cod and olive oil), and a frozen parfait perfumed with licorice all show chef Alain Vinouze's subtle skills. Prix-fixe menus are €18 and €28. *11 rue Enclos Rey 04–66–22–07–01 Reservations essential AE, MC, V Closed Wed. No dinner Tues. Closed Sun. and no lunch Mon. in July and Aug.*

$$ FRENCH **Marché Sur la Table.** The menu changes daily depending on what the chef considers the best local produce at the morning market, and specials—always scrumptious—are scribbled on the well-worn blackboard brought to the table by cheerful servers. Marché is always jammed with devoted locals who won't consider eating anywhere else, so book well in advance. *10 rue Littré 04–66–67–22–50 AE, MC, V Closed Mon. and Tues. No dinner.*

WHERE TO STAY

$$$–$$$$ **Hotel Imperator.** Near the Jardins de la Fontaine, this luxurious hotel is a longtime favorite of toreadors. It's ideally situated and smartly decorated with a quirky bar called Hemingway's in the downstairs lobby, which opens up to a delicious flower garden and attracts all sorts of interesting literary and bullfighting fans, locals and visitors alike. The gourmet Enclos de la Fontaine is one of the best tables in Nîmes—do not miss the lacquered duck served with peaches or the fish *escabeche*—although the dining room is over-elaborate for some tastes. **Pros:** richly atmospheric; a true taste of Nîmes's bullfighting culture, both with the decor and the flavorful restaurant. **Cons:** rooms can be small and a little noisy, especially in the summertime. *15 rue Gaston Boissieruai de la Fontsain 04–66–21–90–30 www.hotel-imperator.com 62 rooms In-room: a/c, refrigerator. In-hotel: restaurant, bar, Wi-Fi hotspot, parking (paid), some pets allowed AE, DC, MC, V.*

$$$–$$$$ **La Maison de Sophie.** Far from the hustle of town and yet just five minutes from the Arena, this luxurious *hôtel particulier* has all the charm that the city itself often lacks. Rooms are elegant, large, and airy, with a sense of tranquility rarely found in Nîmes. The drifting scents of jasmine lead you out to the garden, where colorful bougainvilleas gently mix with the deep blue of the pool. Drift back to the lovely sitting room in the early evening for a cup of tea or a glass of wine, and curl up with one of the many good books thoughtfully provided by your hosts. **Pros:** big-city elegance mixes nicely with country charm and quiet nights; warm welcome. **Cons:** often fully booked long in advance; pool is quite small. *31 av. Carnot 04–66–70–96–10 www.hotel-lamaisondesophie.com 5 suites In room: a/c, Wi-Fi. In hotel: pool, parking (paid), some pets allowed MC, V.*

$–$$ **New Hotel La Baume.** In the heart of scruffy Vieux Nîmes, this noble 17th-century hôtel particulier has been reincarnated as a stylish hotel with an architect's eye for mixing ancient detail with modern design. The balustraded stone staircase is a protected historic monument, and stenciled beamed ceilings, cross vaults, and archways counterbalance hot ocher tones, swags of raw cotton, leather, and halogen lighting.

Pros: genuine welcome makes for an inviting stay; interior decor is lovely. **Cons:** neighborhood is a little suspect; walking out alone at night should be done with precaution. ✉ *21 rue Nationale* ☎ *04–66–76–28–42* 🌐 *www.new-hotel.com* *34 rooms* *In-room: a/c, refrigerator, Internet. In-hotel: parking (paid), some pets allowed* 💳 *AE, DC, MC, V* *CP.*

THE ALPILLES

The low mountain range called the Alpilles (pronounced ahl-*pee*-yuh) forms a rough-hewn, rocky landscape that rises into nearly barren limestone hills, the surrounding fields silvered with ranks of twisted olive trees and alleys of gnarled *amandiers* (almond trees). There are superb antiquities in St-Rémy and feudal ruins in Les Baux.

ABBAYE DE MONTMAJOUR

35 km (20 mi) southeast of Nîmes, 5 km (3 mi) northeast of Arles.

This magnificent Romanesque abbey looming over the marshlands north of Arles stands in partial ruin. Begun in the 12th century by a handful of Benedictine monks, it grew according to an ambitious plan of church, crypt, and cloister. Under the management of corrupt lay monks in the 17th century, it grew more sumptuous; when those lay monks were ejected by the Church, they sacked the place. After the Revolution it was sold to a junkman, and he tried to pay the mortgage by stripping off and selling its goods. A 19th-century medieval revival spurred its partial restoration, but its 18th-century portions are still in ruins. Ironically, because of this mercenary history, what remains is a spare and beautiful piece of Romanesque architecture. The **cloister** rivals that of St-Trophime in Arles for its balance, elegance, and air of mystical peace: Van Gogh was drawn to its womblike isolation and came often to the abbey to paint and reflect. The interior, renovated by Rudi Ricciotti, is now used for temporary art exhibitions, and the Chapelle St Croix is open for visits—you just need to ask for the keys. ✉ *On D17 northeast of Arles, Rte. De Fontvielle, direction Fontvieille* ☎ *04–90–54–64–17* 🌐 *montmajour.monuments-nationaux.fr* *€6.50* *May–Sept., daily 10–6:30; Oct.–Apr., Wed.–Mon. 10–5.*

LES BAUX-DE-PROVENCE

★ *17 km (10 mi) west of Montmajour, 18 km (11 mi) northeast of Arles, 29 km (18 mi) south of Avignon.*

When you first search the craggy hilltops for signs of Les Baux-de-Provence (pronounced lay-*bo-duh-pro-vance*), you may not quite be able to distinguish between bedrock and building, so naturally does the ragged skyline of towers and crenellations blend into the sawtooth jags of stone. This tiny château-village ranks as one of the most visited tourist sites in France with its natural scenery and medieval buildings of astonishing beauty. From this intimidating vantage point, the lords of Les Baux ruled throughout the 11th and 12th centuries over one of the largest fiefdoms in the south. In the 19th century Les Baux found new purpose: the mineral bauxite, valued as an alloy in aluminum production, was discovered in its hills and named for its source. A profitable industry sprang up that lasted into the 20th century before fading into history.

Visitor Information Les Baux-de-Provence Tourist Office ✉ *Maison du Roi* ☎ *04–90–54–34–39* 🌐 *www.lesbauxdeprovence.com.*

EXPLORING

Today Les Baux offers two world-famous faces to the world: its beautifully preserved medieval village and the ghostly ruins of its fortress, once referred to as the *ville morte* (dead town). In the village, lovely 12th-century stone houses, even their window frames still intact, shelter the shops, cafés, and galleries that line the steep cobbled streets. At the edge of the village is a cliff that offers up a stunning view over the Val d'Enfer (Hell's Valley), said to have inspired Dante's *Inferno.* Farther along is the **Cathédrale d'Images**. The milieu is a vast old bauxite quarry, with 66-foot-high stone walls, which makes a dramatic setting for the thousands of images projected onto its walls. ✉ *Cathédrale d'Images, Val d'Enfer, Petite Rte. de Mailliane* ☎ *04–90–54–38–65* 🎫 *€7, €12 joint ticket with Château des Baux* ⏲ *Mar., daily 10–6; Apr.–Sept., daily 10–7; Oct.–mid-Jan., daily 10–6.*

Up above, the 17-acre cliff-top sprawl of ruins is contained under the umbrella name the **Château des Baux.** At the entry, the Tour du Brau contains the **Musée d'Histoire des Baux,** a small collection of relics and models. Its exit gives access to the wide and varied grounds, where Romanesque chapels and towers mingle with skeletal ruins. The tiny **Chapelle St-Blaise** shelters a permanent music-and-slide show called *Van Gogh, Gauguin, Cézanne au Pays de l'Olivier,* which features artworks depicting olive orchards in their infinite variety. In July and August there are fascinating medieval exhibitions: people dressed up in authentic costumes, displays of medieval crafts, and even a few jousting tournaments with handsome knights carrying fluttering silk tokens of their beloved ladies. ✉ *Rue du Trencat* ☎ *04–90–54–55–56* 🌐 *www.chateau-baux-provence.com* 🎫 *€7.60 with audio guide* ⏲ *Mar.–May, Sept., and Oct., daily 9–6:30; June–Aug., daily 9–8; Nov.–Feb., daily 9–5.*

WHERE TO EAT AND STAY

¢–$ **La Reine Jeanne.** Sartre and de Beauvoir had separate rooms but a shared balcony—and what a balcony. Jacques Brel and Winston Churchill were also happy guests at this modest but majestically placed inn and stood looking over rugged views worthy of the châteaux up the street. The inn is right at the entrance to the village and offers rooms that are small, simple, and—despite the white, vinyl-padded furniture—fondly decorated with terra-cotta tiles and stencil prints. Good home-style cooking (try *l'aïoli*—a garlic mayonnaise fish dish) and a fine plat du jour are served in the restaurant, which offers views from both the panoramic dining room and a pretty terrace; it's one of the best settings for a meal in Les Baux. **Pros:** familial atmosphere allows for a relaxed stay; warm welcome makes for instant appeal; views are lovely. **Cons:** some rooms are tiny; only two smaller balconies. ✉ *Grande Rue Baux*

☎ *04–90–54–32–06* 🌐 *www.la-reinejeanne.com* ⇨ *10 rooms, 1 apartment* 👍 *In-room: a/c, Internet. In-hotel: restaurant, some pets allowed* 💳 *MC, V* ⊗ *Closed mid-Jan.–mid-Feb.*

$$$–$$$$ Fodor's Choice ★ **L'Oustau de la Baumanière.** Sheltered by rocky cliffs below the village of Les Baux, this long-famous hotel, with its formal landscaped terrace and broad swimming pool, has a guest book studded with illustrious names such as Winston Churchill, Elizabeth Taylor, and Picasso. The interior is luxe-Provençal chic, thanks to arched stone ceilings, and brocaded settees done up in Canovas and Halard fabrics. Guest rooms—breezy, private, and beautifully furnished with antiques—have a contemporary flair. As for the famed Baumanière restaurant (reservations essential), chef Jean-André Charial's hallowed reputation continues to attract culinary pilgrims who delight in the varied menu—lobster cooked in Châteauneuf-du-Pape and set on a bed of polenta is a typical dazzler. ✉ *Val d'Enfer* ☎ *04–90–54–33–07* 🌐 *www.oustaudebaumaniere.com* ⇨ *16 rooms, 14 suites* 👍 *In-room: a/c, refrigerator. In-hotel: restaurant, tennis courts, pool, Wi-Fi hotspot, parking (paid), some pets allowed* 💳 *AE, DC, MC, V* ⊗ *Hotel and restaurant closed Jan. and Feb. Restaurant closed Wed. and for Thurs. lunch Nov. and Dec.* 🍽 *MAP.*

ST-RÉMY-DE-PROVENCE

Fodor's Choice ★ *8 km (5 mi) north of Les Baux, 24 km (15 mi) northeast of Arles, 19 km (12 mi) south of Avignon.*

There are other towns as pretty as St-Rémy-de-Provence, and others in more dramatic or picturesque settings. Ruins can be found throughout the south, and so can authentic village life. Yet something felicitous has happened in this market town in the heart of the Alpilles—a steady infusion of style, of art, of imagination—all brought by people with a respect for local traditions and a love of Provençal ways. As many of them have been gossip-column names or off-duty celebs, it is easy to understand why this pretty town has earned its nickname, the Hamptons of Provence

GETTING HERE AND AROUND

For such a popular town, St-Rémy has surprisingly few public transportation links. There is a bus run by Cartreize (☎ *08–00–19–94–13* 🌐 *www.lepilote.com*) that runs a service (daily except Sunday) between Avignon and Les Baux via Chateaurenard and St-Rémy (€5.40) or Arles-St-Rémy-Les Baux (daily except Sun., €5.40). Local trains stop at Tarascon (🌐 *www.voyages-sncf.com*) and from here you can take a Cartrieze bus to St- Rémy (20 minutes, €2.60). As with Les Baux-de-Provence, the easiest way to get to St-Rémy is by car. Take the A7 until you reach exit 25, then the D99 between Tarascon and Cavaillon, direction St-Rémy on the D5.

Visitor Information St-Rémy-de-Provence Tourist Office ✉ *Pl. Jean-Jaurès* ☎ *04–90–92–05–22* 🌐 *www.saintremy-de-provence.com.*

EXPLORING

St-Rémy, more than anywhere, allows you to meditate quietly on antiquity, browse redolent markets with basket in hand, peer down the very row of plane trees you remember from a Van Gogh, and also enjoy urbane galleries, cosmopolitan shops, and specialty food boutiques. An abundance of chic choices in restaurants, mas, and even châteaux awaits you; the almond and olive groves conceal dozens of stone-and-terra-cotta gîtes, many with pools. In short, St-Rémy has been gentrified through and through, and is now a sort of arid, southern Martha's Vineyard.

> **WORD OF MOUTH**
>
> "St. Remy's highlight was visiting the cloister/asylum where Van Gogh spent a year and painted prolifically."
>
> —Hilda_Bell

First established by an indigenous Celtic-Ligurian people who worshipped the god Glan, the village Glanum was adopted and gentrified by the Greeks of Marseille in the 2nd and 3rd centuries BC. Under the Pax Romana there developed a veritable city, with temples and forum, luxurious villas, and baths. The Romans (and Glanum) eventually fell, but a village grew up next to their ruins, taking its name from their protectorate, the Abbey St-Remi, which was based in Reims. St-Rémy de Provence grew to be an important market town, and wealthy families built fine mansions in its center—among them the de Sade family (whose black-sheep relation held forth in the Luberon at Lacoste). Another famous native son was the eccentric doctor, scholar, and astrologer Michel Nostradamus (1503–66), who is credited by some as having predicted much of the modern age. Perhaps the best known of St-Rémy's residents was the ill-fated Vincent van Gogh. Shipped unceremoniously out of Arles at the height of his madness (and creativity), he committed himself to the asylum St-Paul-de-Mausolée.

A visit to St-Rémy should start from the outskirts inward. To visit Glanum you must park in a dusty roadside lot on D5 south of town (toward Les Baux).

But before crossing into town, you'll be confronted with two of the most miraculously preserved classical monuments in France, simply called **Les Antiques.** Dating from 30 BC, the **Mausolée** (mausoleum), a wedding-cake stack of arches and columns, lacks nothing but its finial on top, yet it's dedicated to a Julian (as in Julius Caesar), probably Caesar Augustus. A few yards away stands another marvel: the **Arc Triomphal,** dating from AD 20.

Across the street from Les Antiques and set back from D5, a slick visitor center prepares you for entry into the ancient village of **Glanum** with scale models of the site in its various heydays. A good map and an English brochure guide you stone by stone through the maze of foundations, walls, towers, and columns that spread across a broad field; helpfully, Greek sites are noted by numbers, Roman ones by letters. ✉ *Rte. Des Baux de Provence, off the D5, direction Les Baux* ☎ *04–90–92–64–04 info phone at Hôtel de Sade* 🌐 *www.glanum.monuments-nationaux.fr*

€7; €7.50 joint ticket with Hôtel de Sade Apr.–Sept., Tues.–Sun. 9–6:30; Oct.–Mar., Tues.–Sun. 9–5.

★ You can cut across the fields from Glanum to **St-Paul-de-Mausolée,** the lovely, isolated asylum where Van Gogh spent the last year of his life (1889–90). But enter it quietly: it shelters psychiatric patients to this day—all of them women. You're free to walk up the beautifully manicured garden path to the church and its jewel-box Romanesque **cloister,** where the artist found womblike peace. *04–90–92–77–00 www.cloitresaintpaul-valetudo.com €4 Apr.–Sept., daily 9:30–7; Oct.–Dec., and Feb. and Mar. daily 10:30–5.*

Within St-Rémy's fast-moving traffic loop, a labyrinth of narrow streets leads you away from the action and into the slow-moving inner sanctum of the **Vieille Ville.** Here trendy, high-end shops mingle pleasantly with local life, and the buildings, if gentrified, blend in unobtrusively.

Make your way to the **Hôtel de Sade,** a 15th- and 16th-century private manor now housing the treasures unearthed from the ruins of Glanum. The de Sade family built the house around remains of 4th-century baths and a 5th-century baptistery, now nestled in its courtyard. At this writing, it was closed indefinitely for restoration; call for details. *Rue du Parage 04–90–92–64–04.*

WHERE TO EAT

$$ FRENCH **Bistrot Découverte.** Wine lovers at heart, Claude and Dana Douard were happy to collaborate with some of the greatest chefs of our time—Joël Robuchon, Marco Pierre White—before getting away from the big city lights to open this boutique-bistro hotspot in the center of St-Rémy. The wine selection is magnificent, as is the tour through their cave, and the simple food is based on top-notch ingredients. Try the braised veal in wild-lemon sauce served on fresh tagliatelle pasta or made-to-order beef tartare. Already word has spread, so book ahead. *19 bd. Victor Hugo 04–90–92–34–49 www.bistrotdecouverte.com Reservations essential MC, V Closed Mon. No dinner Sun.*

$$ FRENCH **La Gousse d'Ail.** It may have moved to larger premises around the corner, but thankfully, this intimate, indoor Vieille Ville hideaway and family-run bistro remains fundamentally the same. It continues to live up to its name (the Garlic Clove), serving robust, highly flavored southern dishes in hearty portions. Try the house specialties: grilled bull steak with creamed garlic or a powerful garlic-almond pesto. Aim for Wednesday night, when there's Gypsy music and jazz. *6 bd. Marceau 04–90–92–16–87 www.la-goussedail.com AE, DC, MC, V Closed mid-Jan.–mid-Feb. No lunch Thurs. and Sat.*

$$ FRENCH **La Maison Jaune.** This modern retreat in the Vieille Ville draws crowds of summer people to its pretty roof terrace, with accents of sober stone and lively contemporary furniture both indoors and out. The look reflects the cuisine: with vivid flavors and a cool, contained touch, chef François Perraud prepares grilled sardines with crunchy fennel and lemon confit, and veal lightly flavored with olives, capers, and celery. *15 rue Carnot 04–90–92–56–14 Reservations essential AE, MC, V Closed Mon., and Jan. and Feb. No dinner Sun. No lunch Tues.*

DID YOU KNOW?

No matter that St-Rémy-de-Provence is called the "Hamptons of Provence" (due to its chic shops and restaurants); the town has succeeded in remaining true to its Provençal roots.

WHERE TO STAY

$$$–$$$$ **Château de Roussan.** New owner Philippe Roussel, a direct descendant of the 17th-century owners, arrived at the château in 2008 and took on the challenge of dragging the hotel out of the mire of badly aging eccentricity to embrace modern times. After beautiful renovations, the château has finally been returned to its former glory. There are lovingly polished antique family furniture and red clay floors buffed to their original shine, as well as crafted artistic mosaics whose colors reflect the eye of turn-of-the-century masters. Guest rooms are light and airy, and the bathrooms equipped with all the modern trinkets. There is still, however, an unfortunate penchant for floral. The kitchen dishes out simple but varied organic cuisine, served on the terrace or in the flower-filled garden. **Pros:** eager-to-please and house-proud staff are happy to recount the history of the hotel; rooms are very quiet. **Cons:** some rooms are small; food service can be slow. ✉ *D99, Rte. de Tarascon* ☎ *04–90–90–79–00* 🌐 *www.chateauderoussan.com* *16 rooms, 4 suites* *In-room: a/c, refrigerator, Wi-Fi. In-hotel: restaurant, parking (paid), some pets allowed* ▭ *AE, DC, MC, V* *MAP.*

$$$–$$$$ Fodor's Choice ★ **Chez Bru.** Belgian chef Wout Bru has gained a reputation (and Michelin stars) for his understated, light, and subtly balanced cuisine as has his wife Suzy for her equally savvy sense of style. After making a success of the Bistrot d'Eygalieres in Eygalieres' village center, they expanded their empire in 2009 to open this wonderful haven of peace and tranquillity 4 km (2 mi) outside of the village. And, although the beautiful scenery and deluxe comfort may distract guests, don't doubt the focus or magical talent of this extraordinary chef at his new restaurant here (closed Monday; no dinner Sunday in October and November; no lunch Tuesday in May through September)—try the sole with goat cheese or the lobster with candied tomatoes. The hotel is beautifully chic, offering up well-appointed rooms and sleek decor. Nostalgic regulars of the Bistrot may mourn the loss of village location, but not to worry, you can still stay in one of the four guestrooms in the old village house. In either of two places, book well ahead. **Pros:** an elegant stay in the country; lovely decor. **Cons:** some visitors have found the reception a little cool; restaurant a short distance away from inn. ✉ *Rte. D'Orgon, 4 km (2.5 mi) from Eygalieres which is 10 km (6 mi) southeast of St-Rémy on D99 then D24, Eygalières* ☎ *04–90–90–60–34* 🌐 *www.chezbru.com* *2 rooms, 2 suites* *In-room: a/c, refrigerator, Wi-Fi. In-hotel: parking (free), some pets allowed* ▭ *AE, DC, MC, V* *Closed 2 wks in Nov. and 2 wks. in Feb.*

$$$–$$$$ **Domaine de Valmouriane.** In this genteel mas-cum-resort, peacefully isolated within a broad park, overstuffed English-country furniture mixes cozily with cool Provençal stone and timber. The grounds are impressive, with picture-perfect cypress trees; inside, much has been restored, so all is comfort and ease, if not the height of authenticity. The restaurant offers up fresh game, herbs from the garden, seafood, local oils, and truffles, but it's the personal welcome from Philippe and Martin Capel that makes you feel like an honored guest. The pool, surrounded by a slate walk and delightful gardens, is most inviting. **Pros:** location is superb, elegantly snug in the middle of a huge cypress park;

rooms are large and very comfortably furnished. **Cons:** some rooms are hot in summer and cold in winter. ✉ *Petite Rte. des Baux, D27* ☎ *0490–92–44–62* 🌐 *www.valmouriane.com* *13 rooms* *In-room: a/c, Internet. In-hotel: restaurant, tennis court, pool, parking (free), some pets allowed* 💳 *AE, DC, MC, V* *Closed mid-Dec.–mid-Jan.* *FAP, MAP.*

$$–$$$ **Mas des Carassins.** A textbook example of a Provençal mas, this rambling 19th-century farmhouse is done with an impressive amount of style. Guest rooms have stonework walls and wrought-iron canopy beds, but you may wish to sleep under the stars because the mas is beautifully surrounded with thyme bushes, pots of lemon and orange trees, fountains, pools, and centuries-old olive trees. *Bien sûr,* you'll want to enjoy the copious lunch outside at a shady and intimate table. Breakfast is included in the price. **Pros:** friendly atmosphere makes for an easy, stress-free stay; breakfast is good and substantial. **Cons:** some rooms are a little dark, with heavy furniture. ✉ *1 chemin Gaulois* ☎ *04–90–92–15–48* 🌐 *www.hoteldescarassins.com* *14 rooms* *In-room: a/c, refrigerator, Wi-Fi. In-hotel: restaurant, pool, parking, some pets allowed* 💳 *MC, V* *Closed Jan. and Feb.* *BP.*

SHOPPING

Every Wednesday morning St-Rémy hosts one of the most popular **markets** in Provence, during which Place de la République and narrow Vieille Ville streets overflow with fresh produce and herbs, as well as fabrics and brocantes (antiques). With all the summer people, it's little wonder that food shops and *traiteurs* (take-out caterers) do the biggest business in St-Rémy. Olive oils are sold like fine old wines, and the breads heaped in boulangerie windows are as knobby and rough-hewn as they should be. The best food shops are concentrated in the Vieille Ville. Local goat cheeses are displayed like jewels and wrapped like fine pastries at **La Cave aux Fromages** (✉ *1 pl. Joseph-Hilaire* ☎ *04–90–92–32–45*). At **Chocolaterie Joel Durand** (✉ *3 bd. Victor Hugo* ☎ *04–90–92–38–25*) the chocolates are numbered to indicate the various flavors, from rose petal to Camargue saffron.

AVIGNON AND THE VAUCLUSE

Anchored by the magnificent papal stronghold of Avignon, the Vaucluse spreads luxuriantly east of the Rhône. Its famous vineyards—Gigondas, Vacqueyras, Beaumes-de-Venise—seduce connoisseurs, and its Roman ruins in Orange and Vaison-la-Romaine draw scholars and arts lovers. Arid lowlands with orchards of olives, apricots, and almonds give way to a rich and wild mountain terrain around the formidable Mont Ventoux and flow into the primeval Luberon, made a household name by Peter Mayle. The hill villages around the Luberon—Gordes, Roussillon, Oppède, Bonnieux—are as lovely as any you'll find in the south of France.

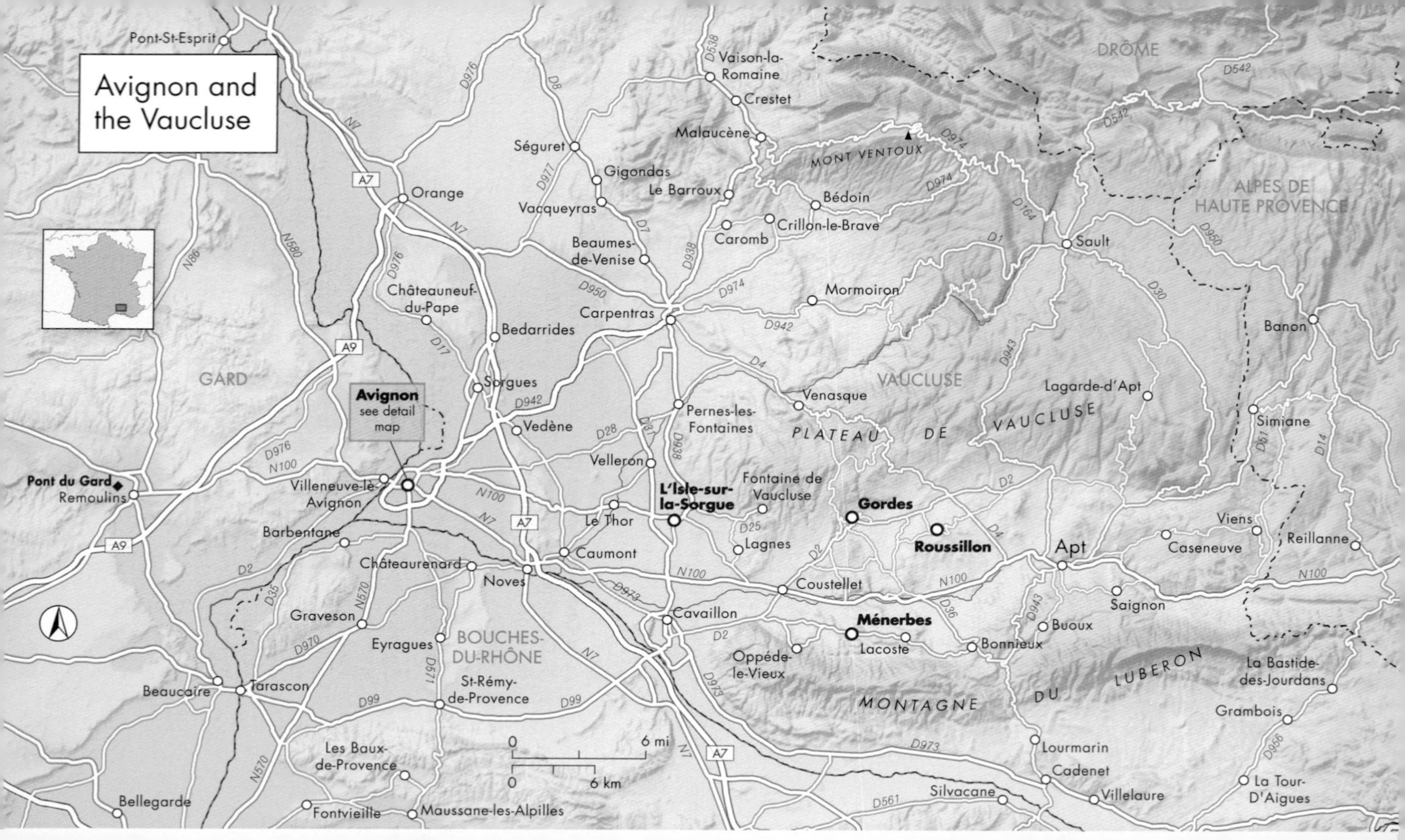
Avignon and the Vaucluse
Pont-St-Esprit
Vaison-la-Romaine
Crestet
Malaucène
Séguret
Gigondas
Vacqueyras
Le Barroux
Orange
MONT VENTOUX
Bédoin
Crillon-le-Brave
Caromb
Beaumes-de-Venise
Sault
Châteauneuf-du-Pape
Mormoiron
Carpentras
Bedarrides
Sorgues
GARD
VAUCLUSE
DRÔME
ALPES DE HAUTE PROVENCE
Banon
Lagarde-d'Apt
Simiane
Venasque
Avignon
see detail map
Pernes-les-Fontaines
Vedène
PLATEAU DE VAUCLUSE
Velleron
Fontaine de Vaucluse
Pont du Gard
Remoulins
Villeneuve-lè-Avignon
L'Isle-sur-la-Sorgue
Gordes
Le Thor
Roussillon
Viens
Caseneuve
Reillanne
Apt
Barbentane
Lagnes
Caumont
Châteaurenard
Noves
Coustellet
Saignon
Cavaillon
Graveson
Ménerbes
Buoux
Eyragues
BOUCHES-DU-RHÔNE
Oppéde-le-Vieux
Lacoste
Bonnieux
LUBERON
La Bastide-des-Jourdans
Beaucaire
Tarascon
St-Rémy-de-Provence
MONTAGNE DU LUBERON
Grambois
Les Baux-de-Provence
Lourmarin
Cadenet
La Tour-D'Aigues
Bellegarde
Silvacane
Villelaure
Fontvieille
Maussane-les-Alpilles
0 6 mi
0 6 km
A7
A9
N7
N86
N100
N570
N580
D2
D4
D7
D8
D14
D17
D25
D28
D30
D31
D35
D36
D51
D99
D164
D542
D538
D571
D561
D938
D942
D943
D950
D956
D970
D973
D974
D976
D977
D1

AVIGNON

82 km (51 mi) northwest of Aix-en-Provence, 95 km (59 mi) northwest of Marseille, 224 km (140 mi) south of Lyon.

Avignon is anything but a museum; it surges with modern ideas and energy and thrives within its ramparts as it did in the heyday of the popes—and, like those radical church lords, it's sensual, cultivated, and cosmopolitan, with a taste for worldly pleasures. Avignon remained papal property until 1791, and elegant mansions bear witness to the town's 18th-century prosperity. From its famous Palais des Papes *(Papal Palace)*, where seven exiled popes camped between 1309 and 1377 after fleeing from the corruption and civil strife of Rome, to the long, low bridge of childhood-song fame stretching over the river, you can beam yourself briefly into 14th-century Avignon, so complete is the context, so evocative the setting.

GETTING HERE AND AROUND

The main bus station is on Avenue Monteclar (☎ *04–90–82–07–35*) next to the train station. Buses run to and from Avignon, Arles (45 mins, €6), Carpentras (45 mins, €5), Nîmes (1½ hrs, €9), or farther afield to Orange, Isle-sur-la-Sorgue, Marseille, Nice, and Cannes. Town buses and services connecting the Centre Ville station with the TGV station (several times an hour) are run by TCRA (☎ 🌐 *04–32–74–18–32 www.tcra.fr*). Avignon is at the junction of the Paris–Marseille and Paris–Montpellier lines. The Gare Centre Ville has frequent links to Arles, Nîmes, Orange, Toulon, and Carcassonne. Taxi Radio Avignonnais (✉ *Pl. Pie* ☎ *04–90–82–20–20*) is one easy way to get around town.

Visitor Information Avignon Tourist Office ✉ *41 cours Jean-Jaurès* ☎ *04–90–82–65–11* 🌐 *www.ot-avignon.fr.*

EXPLORING

Everything worth seeing (except the *St. Bénézet Bridge)* is confined within the medieval city walls. Most sights cluster around Place du Palais, with signs pointing the way. This is the Avignon of the visitors. To see Avignonnais leading their daily lives, however, turn off these tourist paths and get lost among the city's cobblestone streets. Note that the free Avignon-Villeneuve PASSion (available at the tourist office) gives 20% to 50% reductions on most museums and sights after you buy the first ticket.

TOP ATTRACTIONS

8 **Musée Calvet.** Worth a visit for the beauty and balance of its architecture alone, this fine old museum contains a rich collection of antiquities and classically inspired works. Acquisitions include Neoclassical and Romantic and are almost entirely French, including works by Manet, Daumier, and David. There's also a good modern section, with works by Bonnard and Duffy, and Camille Claudet's head of her brother Paul, who incarcerated her in an insane asylum when her relationship with Rodin caused too much scandalous talk. The main building itself is a Palladian-style jewel in pale Gard stone dating from the 1740s; the garden is so lovely that it may distract you from the paintings. ✉ *65 rue Joseph-Vernet* ☎ *04–90–86–33–84* 🎫 €6 🕙 *Wed.–Mon. 10–1 and 2–6.*

1 ★ **Palais des Papes.** This colossal palace creates a disconcertingly fortress-like impression, underlined by the austerity of its interior. Most of the original furnishings were returned to Rome with the papacy, others were lost during the French Revolution. Some imagination is required to picture its earlier medieval splendor, awash with color and with worldly clerics enjoying what the 14th-century Italian poet Petrarch called "licentious banquets." On close inspection, two different styles of building emerge at the palace: the severe **Palais Vieux** *(Old Palace)*, built between 1334 and 1342 by Pope Benedict XII, a member of the Cistercian order, which frowned on frivolity, and the more decorative **Palais Nouveau** *(New Palace)*, built in the following decade by the artsy, lavish-living Pope Clement VI. The Great Court, entryway to the complex, links the two.

The main rooms of the Palais Vieux are the **Consistory** *(Council Hall)*, decorated with some excellent 14th-century frescoes by Simone Martini; the **Chapelle St-Jean** (original frescoes by Matteo Giovanetti); the **Grand Tinel,** or Salle des Festins *(Feast Hall)*, with a majestic vaulted roof and a series of 18th-century Gobelin tapestries; the **Chapelle St-Martial** (more Giovanetti frescoes); and the **Chambre du Cerf,** with a richly decorated ceiling, murals featuring a stag hunt, and a delightful view of Avignon. The principal attractions of the Palais Nouveau are the **Grande Audience,** a magnificent two-nave hall on the ground floor, and, upstairs, the **Chapelle Clémentine,** where the college of cardinals once gathered to elect the new pope. ✉ *Pl. du Palais, 6 rue Pente Rapide* ☎ *04–90–27–50–00* 🌐 *www.palais-des-papes.com* 🎟 *€9.50 entry includes choice of guided tour or individual audio guide; €11.50 includes audio-guided tour to pont St-Bénézet* 🕒 *Oct.–Mar., daily 9:30–5:45; Apr.–Nov., daily 9–7; July, during theater festival until end of Aug., daily 9–9.*

4 ★ **Pont St-Bénézet** *(St. Bénézet Bridge)*. This bridge is the subject of the famous children's song: "*Sur le pont d'Avignon on y danse, on y danse* . . " ("On the bridge of Avignon one dances, one dances . . ."). Unlike London Bridge, this one still stretches its arches across the river, but only partway: half was washed away in the 17th century. Its first stones allegedly laid with the miraculous strength granted St-Bénézet in the 12th century, it once reached all the way to Villeneuve. ✉ *Port du Rochre* 🌐 *www.palais-des-papes.com* 🎟 *€4.50* 🕒 *Apr.–Oct., daily 9–8; Nov.–Mar., daily 9–5:45.*

5 Fodor's Choice ★ **Rocher des Doms** *(Rock of the Domes)*. Walk from the entrance to the Pont St-Bénézet along the ramparts to a spiral staircase leading to these hilltop gardens. Set with grand Mediterranean pines, this park on a bluff above town offers extraordinary views of the palace, the rooftops of Old Avignon, the Pont St-Bénézet, and formidable Villeneuve across the Rhône. On the horizon loom Mont Ventoux, the Luberon, and Les Alpilles. Often called the "cradle of Avignon," the rock's grottoes were among the first human habitations in the area. Today, the park also has a fake lake, home to some swans. ✉ *Montée du Moulin off Pl. du Palais* ☎ *04–90–86–81–01* 🌐 *www.avignon-et-provence.com.*

Avignon

Cathédrale Notre-Dame-des-Doms **2**
Musée Calvet **8**
Musée Lapidaire **7**
Palais des Papes **1**
Petit Palais **3**
Place de l'Horloge **6**
Pont St-Bénézet **4**
Rocher des Doms **5**

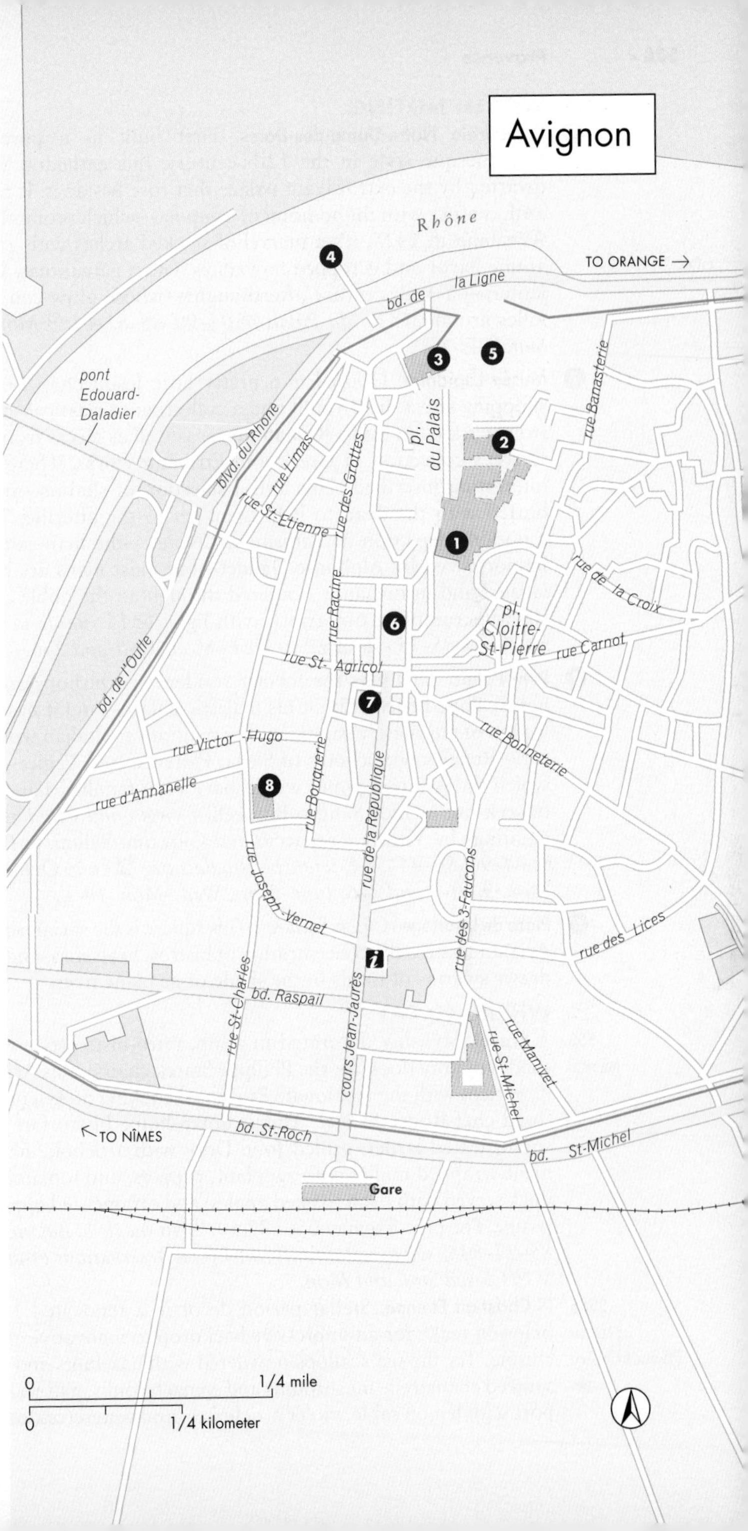

WORTH NOTING

❷ **Cathédrale Notre-Dame-des-Doms.** First built in a pure Provençal Romanesque style in the 12th century, this cathedral was quickly dwarfed by the extravagant palace that rose beside it. It rallied in the 14th century with the addition of a cupola—which promptly collapsed. As rebuilt in 1425, it's a marvel of stacked arches with a strong Byzantine flavor and is topped nowadays with a gargantuan Virgin Mary lantern—a 19th-century afterthought—whose glow can be seen for miles around. ✉ *Pl. du Palais* ☎ *04–90–86–81–01* ⏲ *Mon.–Sat. 8–6, Sun. 9–7.*

❼ **Musée Lapidaire.** Housed in a pretty little Jesuit chapel on the main shopping street, here you'll find a collection of classical sculpture and stonework from Gallo-Roman times, as well as pieces from the Musée Calvet's collection of Greek and Etruscan works. There are several interesting inscribed slabs and a selection of shabtis—small statues buried with the dead to help them get to the afterlife. There's also a notable depiction of *Tarasque of Noves*—the man-eating monster immortalized by Alphonse Daudet—but most items are haphazardly labeled and insouciantly scattered throughout the noble chapel, itself slightly crumbling but awash with light. ✉ *18 rue de la République* ☎ *04–90–85–75–38* 🎫 *€2* ⏲ *Wed.–Mon. 10–1 and 2–6.*

❸ **Petit Palais.** This was the former residence of bishops and cardinals before Pope Benedict built his majestic palace—and it has a large collection of old-master paintings. The majority are Italian works from the early-Renaissance schools of Siena, Florence, and Venice—styles with which the Avignon popes would have been familiar. Later key works to seek out include Sandro Botticelli's *Virgin and Child* and Venetian paintings by Vittore Carpaccio and Giovanni Bellini. ✉ *Pl. du Palais* ☎ *04–90–86–44–58* 🌐 *www.petit-palais.org* 🎫 *€6* ⏲ *Oct.–May, Wed.–Mon. 9:30–1 and 2–6; June–Sept., Wed.–Mon. 10–6.*

❻ **Place de l'Horloge** *(Clock Square).* This square is the social nerve center of Avignon, where the concentration of bistros, brasseries, and restaurants draws swarms of locals to the shade of its plane trees.

WHERE TO EAT

$$$ FRENCH ✕ **Brunel.** Stylishly decorated in a hip, retro-bistro style with urbane shades of gray (look for the Philippe Starck chairs), this Avignon favorite entices with the passionate Provençal cooking of Avignon-born and -bred chef Roger Brunel. This is down-home bistro fare based on a sophisticated larder: grilled John Dory with artichoke hearts; parchment-wrapped mullet with eggplant, peppers, and tomatoes; breast of duck served with oven roasted apples; and caramelized apples in tender pastry. The prix-fixe menu is €32.50. ✉ *46 rue de la Balance* ☎ *04–90–85–24–83* 🌐 *www.restaurantbrunel.fr* ✍ *Reservations essential* 💳 *MC, V* ⏲ *Closed Sun. and Mon.*

$$$$ FRENCH Fodor's Choice ★ ✕ **Christian Étienne.** Stellar period decor in a renovated 12th-century mansion make for an impressive backdrop to innovative and delicious cuisine. Try the sea scallops powdered with hazelnuts and served with sautéed chanterelle mushrooms and spinach coulis, pan-roasted Iberian port with lemon sable, violet artichokes, and watercress; or splurge for

Beautiful town squares form the hub of Avignon's historic heart, as seen in this view from the roof of the famed Palais des Papes.

the whole lobster sautéed in olive oil, muscat grapes, and beurre blanc with verjuice. If you are on a budget try the more affordable €35 lunch menu. ✉ *10 rue Mons* ☎ *04–90–86–16–50* 🌐 *www.christian-etienne.fr* ✍ *Reservations essential* 💳 *AE, MC, V* ⏲ *Closed Sun. and Mon.*

$$$ FRENCH Fodor's Choice ★ ✕ **La Fourchette.** The food here is some of the best in town, as the bevy of locals clamoring daily to get in will attest. It all smells so good that you may be tempted to rip one of the decorative forks or large ladles off the wall and attack your neighbor's plate. Don't worry, service is prompt and friendly and you, too, can soon dig in to heaping portions of fresh sardines with citrus, *caillettes* (finely minced pork with spinach and *blette*—similar to Swiss chard—and baked), or what is likely the best Provençal daube (meat stew) served with macaroni gratin in France. ✉ *7 rue Racine* ☎ *04–90–85–20–93* ✍ *Reservations essential* 💳 *AE, MC, V* ⏲ *Closed Sun. and Mon. Oct.–Apr.*

$$ FRENCH ★ ✕ **Le Grand Café.** Behind the Papal Palace and set in a massive former army supply depot—note the carefully preserved industrial decay—this urban-chic entertainment complex combines an international cinema, a bar, and this popular bistro. Gigantic 18th-century mirrors and dance-festival posters hang against crumbling plaster and brick, and votive candles half-light the raw metal framework—an inspiring environment for intense film talk and a late supper of apricot lamb on a bed of semoule, goat cheese, or marinated artichokes. The prix-fixe dinner menu is just €28. ✉ *La Manutention, Cours Maria Casares* ☎ *04–90–86–86–77* 🌐 *www.legrandcafe.com* 💳 *AE, MC, V* ⏲ *Closed Sun. and Mon., and Jan.*

$$ FRENCH ✕ **Maison Nani.** Crowded inside and out with trendy young professionals, this pretty lunch spot serves stylish home cooking in generous

portions without the fuss of multiple courses. Choose from heaping salads sizzling with fresh meat, enormous kebabs, and a creative quiche du jour. It's just off Rue de la République. ✉ *29 rue Théodore Aubanel* ☎ *04–90–14–07–30* ▭ *No credit cards* ⊙ *Closed Sun. No dinner Mon.–Thurs.*

$$ FRENCH ★ ✕ **Piedoie.** With excellent cuisine and fair prices, this local treasure has a die-hard following of locals. In a cluttered and intimate setting, ardent regulars argue vehemently with their neighbors about whether the succulent white truffle salad is better than the fresh vegetable farcis (stuffed vegetables) or the sea bass grilled to perfection. In the end, every last bite gets eaten, and everyone goes home more than satisfied. Reserve at least a few days in advance. ✉ *26 rue des Trios Faucons* ☎ *04–90–86–51–53* *Reservations essential* ▭ *AE, MC, V.*

WHERE TO STAY

$$$$ ★ **Hôtel de la Mirande.** A designer's dream of a hotel, this *petit palais* permits you to step into 18th-century Avignon, thanks to painted coffered ceilings, sumptuous antiques, and other superb *grand siècle* touches (those rough sisal mats on the floors were the height of chic back in the Baroque era). The central lounge is a skylighted and jazz-warmed haven. Upstairs, guest rooms are both gorgeous and comfy, with extraordinary baths and even more extraordinary handmade wall coverings. The costume-drama dining room is the perfect setting for the restaurant's sophisticated cuisine, one of the best in Avignon under chef Julien Allano. Look for friendly Tuesday- and Wednesday-night cooking classes (€85) from guest chefs in the massive downstairs "country" kitchen. **Pros:** convivial atmosphere of the cooking classes and the spectacular setting of the hotel, with the backdrop of the beautiful rooms, makes a heady combination. **Cons:** service can be slow, with a touch of snobbery; some rooms are small. ✉ *Pl. de la Mirande* ☎ *04–90–14–20–20* 🌐 *www.la-mirande.fr* *19 rooms, 1 suite* *In-room: a/c, refrigerator, Wi-Fi. In-hotel: restaurant, bar, parking (paid), some pets allowed* ▭ *AE, DC, MC, V.*

$$$–$$$$ **Hôtel d'Europe.** Once host to Victor Hugo, Napoléon Bonaparte, and Emperor Maximilian, this vine-covered 16th-century home is regally discreet and classic. Beyond the walled court shaded by trees, the splendor continues inside with Aubusson tapestries, porcelains, and Provençal antiques. Guest rooms are mostly emperor-size, with two suites overlooking the Papal Palace. The highly acclaimed restaurant, La Vieille Fontaine, is certainly one of Avignon's finest; during the festival period, tables in the courtyard are highly coveted and are top places to preen while enjoying such delights as hot duck foie gras with peaches. **Pros:** authentic historical setting is perfect for a visit to Avignon; perfect as a secluded romantic hideaway. **Cons:** service can be slow; high season can make for some noisy evenings. ✉ *12 pl. Crillon* ☎ *04–90–14–76–76* 🌐 *www.hotel-d-europe.fr* *41 rooms, 3 suites* *In-room: a/c, refrigerator, Wi-Fi. In-hotel: restaurant, parking (paid), some pets allowed* ▭ *AE, DC, MC, V.*

$ **Hotel du Palais des Papes.** Despite its mere two-star rating, this is a remarkably solid, comfortable hotel, just off the Place du Palais. With chic ironwork furniture and rich fabrics, the exposed-stone-and-beam decor fulfills fantasies of a medieval city—but one with good tile baths. **Pros:** richly atmospheric setting is a perfectly inexpensive way to make the most out of the city; rooms are large and airy. **Cons:** rooms with no air-conditioning can be stuffy in summertime; rooms facing the street can be a little noisy. ✉ *1 rue Gérard-Philippe* ☎ *04–90–86–04–13* 🌐 *www.hotel-avignon.com* *26 rooms, 2 suites* *In-room: a/c (some), Internet. In-hotel: restaurant, bar, some pets allowed* ▭ *AE, MC, V.*

$$–$$$ **La Banasterie.** Hidden away on a side street by the Palais des Papes, this up-market B&B offers up one of the most warmly elegant welcomes in Avignon. The Parisian couple who own it ask for little more than to share their passion: *chocolat.* The handful of warmly and luxuriously decorated bedrooms all bear the names of different kinds of chocolate; the gracious hosts offer you a hot cup of sinfully rich cocoa before bed, and the most scrumptious chocolates appear nightly on your pillow. **Pros:** on a quiet side street in the center of town; warm welcome; very comfortable rooms; a hard-to beat-place. **Cons:** if you are unfamiliar with Avignon, it can be hard to find. ✉ *11 rue de la Banasterie* ☎ *04–32–76–30–78* 🌐 *www.labanasterie.com* *2 rooms, 3 suites* *In-room: a/c, refrigerator, Wi-Fi* ▭ *MC, V.*

NIGHTLIFE AND THE ARTS

Held annually in July, the Avignon festival, known officially as the **Festival Annuel d'Art Dramatique** (*Annual Festival of Dramatic Art* ☎ *04–90–27–66–50 tickets and information*), has brought the best of world theater to this ancient city since 1947. Some 300 productions take place every year; the main performances are at the Palais des Papes.

Within its fusty old medieval walls, Avignon teems with modern nightlife well into the wee hours. Having recently joined the masses near Place Pie, the **Red Lion** (✉ *21 rue St-Jean-les-Vieux* ☎ *04–90–86–40–25*) serves Guinness, Stella, and Beck on tap and is hugely popular with students and the English-speaking crowd. At **AJMI** *(Association Pour le Jazz et la Musique Improvisée* ✉ *4 rue Escaliers Ste-Anne* ☎ *04–90–86–08–61*), in La Manutention, you can hear live jazz acts of some renown. Avignon's trendy twenty- and thirtysomethings come to dance at the **Red Zone** (✉ *25 rue Carnot* ☎ *04–90–27–02–44*). Just beyond the Ramparts by the Rhone lies the converted barn and full-blooded disco **Le Bokao's** (✉ *9 bis, quai St Lazare* ☎ *04–90–82–47–95*), playing pumping disco, house, and techno. On Wednesday, the ladies are invited to run the bar. At the cabaret **Dolphin Blues** (✉ *Chemin de L'île Piot* ☎ *04–90–82–46–96*), a hip mix of comedy and music dominates the repertoire, and there's children's theater as well. **Le Rouge Gorge** (✉ *10 bis, rue Peyrollerie, behind palace* ☎ *04–90–14–02–54*) presents a dinner show and after-dinner dancing every Friday and Saturday night.

SHOPPING

Avignon has a cosmopolitan mix of French chains, youthful clothing shops (it's a college town), and a few plummy shops. **Rue St-Agricole** is where to find Parisian designers Lacroix and Hermès, and **Rue des Marchands** off Place Carnot is another, more mainstream shopping stretch. But **Rue de la République** is the main artery, with chic street fashion names like Zara.

Stradding the Gardon River, and built during the rule of Emperor Claudius, the Pont du Gard was an aqueduct to bring waters to nearby Nîmes.

PONT DU GARD

Fodor's Choice ★ *22 km (13 mi) southwest of Avignon, 37 km (23 mi) southwest of Orange, 48 km (30 mi) north of Arles.*

No other architectural sight in Provence rivals the Pont du Gard, a mighty, three-tier aqueduct nearly midway between Nîmes and Avignon. Erected some 2,000 years ago as part of a 48-km (30-mi) canal supplying water to the Roman settlement of Nîmes, it's astonishingly well preserved. In the early morning the site offers an amazing blend of natural and classical beauty—the rhythmic repetition of arches resonates with strength, bearing testimony to an engineering concept relatively new in the 1st century AD, when it was built under Emperor Claudius. Later in the day crowds become a problem, even off-season. At the **Public Information Centre** (☎ *04–66–37–50–99* 🎫 *€10* ⏲ *May–Sept., daily 9:30–6:30; Oct.–Dec. and Feb.–Apr., daily 10–5*), a film and a multimedia display detail the history of the aqueduct; in addition, there is a nifty children's area and an interactive exhibition about life in Roman times, archaeology, nature, and water. You can approach the aqueduct from either side of the Gardon River. If you choose the south side (Rive Droite), the walk to the *pont* (bridge) is shorter and the views arguably better (and the tour buses seem to stay on the Rive Gauche). Note there have been reports of break-ins in the parking area, so get a spot close to the booth. Although access to the spectacular walkway along the top of the aqueduct is now off-limits, the bridge itself is still a breathtaking experience. If you're only interested in taking a look at the bridge, it'll only cost €5 to park. ✉ *Concession Pont-du-Gard*

☏ *08–20–90–33–30* ⊕ *www.pontdugard.fr* *€12, including parking* ⊙ *Mar., Apr., and Oct., daily 10–6; May–Sept., daily 9:30–7, Nov.–Feb. 9:30–5.*

WHERE TO EAT

$$ ★ **La Sommellerie.** This inspired regional restaurant serves local ingredients in deliciously inventive ways. Arguably the best in the area, it's often full with locals and tourists alike (book ahead). There are some extremely comfortable rooms available to sleep off all that great wine, too. ✉ *Rte. de Roquemaure, 1 km (2½ mi) down D17* ☏ *04–90–83–50–00* ⊕ *www.la-sommellerie.fr* ▭ *AE, MC, V.*

L'ISLE-SUR-LA-SORGUE

Fodor's Choice ★ *26 km (16 mi) east of Avignon, 41 km (25 mi) southeast of Orange.*

GETTING HERE

There's a 40-minute bus from the Avignon train station that stops at Place Robert Vasse in Isle-sur-la-Sorgue (where the large Caisse d'Epargne bank is). It's €3 one-way or if you return on the same day, it's €2. You could also take a train from Avignon to Fontaine du Vaucluse (€5) and then take the €2 bus to Isle-sur-la-Sorgue (about 15 mins). By car the distance is only 3 mi (5 km), but it's worth noting that you can no longer rent cars here.

Visitor Information L'Isle-sur-la-Sorgue Tourist Office ✉ *Pl. de l'Église* ☏ *04–90–38–04–78* ⊕ *www.oti-delasorgue.fr.*

EXPLORING

Crisscrossed with lazy canals and alive with moss-covered waterwheels that once drove its silk, wool, and paper mills, this old valley town retains a gentle appeal—except, that is, on Sunday, when it transforms itself into a Marrakech of marketeers, its streets crammed with antiques and brocantes, its cafés swelling with crowds of bargain seekers making a day of it. There are also street musicians, food stands groaning under mounds of rustic breads, vats of tapenade, and cloth-lined baskets of spices, and miles of café tables offering ringside seats to the spectacle. On a nonmarket day life returns to its mellow pace, with plenty of antiques dealers open year-round, as well as fabric and interior design shops, bookstores, and food stores for you to explore.

The token sight to see is L'Isle's 17th-century church, the **Collégiale Notre-Dame-des-Anges,** extravagantly decorated with gilt, faux marble, and sentimental frescoes. Its double-colonnade facade commands the center of the Vieille Ville.

WHERE TO EAT AND STAY

¢–$ **La Gueulardière.** After a Sunday glut of antiquing along the canals, you can dine and sleep just up the street in a hotel full of collectible finds, from the school posters in the restaurant to the oak armoires and brass beds that furnish the simple lodgings. Each room has French windows that open onto the enclosed garden courtyard, a nice spot to enjoy a private breakfast in the shade. **Pros:** ideal location makes it a perfect place to stay for antique hunters; rooms are bright and cheerful. **Cons:** some rooms are noisy; can be stuffy and hot in summer. ✉ *1 cours René Char*

☎ 04–90–38–10–52 ⊕ *www.gueulardiere.com* ⇨ *5 rooms* ♨ *In-room: no a/c. In-hotel: restaurant, parking (free), some pets allowed* ▭ *MC, V* ⊗ *Closed mid-Dec.–mid-Jan. Restaurant closed Wed.*

$$–$$$ Fodor's Choice ★ **La Prévôté.** With all the money you saved bargaining on that chipped Quimper vase, splurge on lunch at this pristine spot hidden off a backstreet courtyard. This hotel is lucky enough to have a restaurant that has won top awards, thanks to chef Roland Mercier—his cannelloni stuffed with salmon and goat cheese, or lobster and mango salad, or tender duckling with lavender honey are all heavenly. The prix-fixe menus start at €25 and top out at €65. Happily, there are five rooms to spend the night, each lovingly styled with exquisite taste in soft pastels and wrought-iron fixings. **Pros:** top dining; antiques-bedecked decor. **Cons:** a little tricky to find. ✉ *4 bis, rue Jean-Jacques-Rousseau* ☎ *04–90–38–57–29* ⊕ *www.la-prevote.fr* ⚠ *Reservations essential* ⇨ *5 rooms* ♨ *In-room: a/c. In-hotel: restaurant, pool, Wi-Fi hotspot, parking (free), some pets allowed* ▭ *MC, V* ⊗ *Closed Tues. and Wed. Dec.–June, Tues. in July and Aug.*

$–$$ **Le Mas de Cure-Bourse.** This graceful old 18th-century post-coach stop is well outside the fray, snugly hedge-bound in the countryside amid 6 acres of fruit trees and fields. Rooms are freshly done in Provençal prints and painted country furniture, and you can be served sophisticated home cooking with a local touch. Half-pension is strongly encouraged, although the restaurant is closed for the month of November and on Monday, and lunch is not served Tuesday. **Pros:** convivial atmosphere makes for a true Provençal escape; restaurant's fine selection of wine eases all your troubles away. **Cons:** not as easy to find as one might think; a fair distance outside of town. ✉ *120 chemin de la Serre* ☎ *04–90–38–16–58* ⊕ *www.masdecurebourse.com* ⇨ *13 rooms* ♨ *In-room: a/c. In-hotel: restaurant, pool, Wi-Fi hotspot, parking (free), some pets allowed* ▭ *MC, V* 🍽 *MAP.*

SHOPPING

The famous **L'Isle-sur-la-Sorgue Sunday morning flea market** takes place from the Place Gambetta up the length of Avenue des Quatre Otages. Of the dozens of antiques shops in L'Isle, one conglomerate concentrates some 40 dealers under the same roof: **L'Isle aux Brocantes** (✉ *7 av. des Quatre Otages* ☎ *04–90–20–69–93*); it's open Saturday–Monday. Higher-end antiques are concentrated next door at the twin shops of **Xavier Nicod et Gérard Nicod** (✉ *9 av. des Quatre Otages* ☎ *04–90–38–35–50 or 04–90–38–07–20*). **Maria Giancatarina** (✉ *4 av. Julien Guigue, across from train station* ☎ *04–90–38–58–02*) showcases beautifully restored linens, including *boutis* (Provençal quilts). A major group of antiquaires is found at **Hôtel Dongler** (✉ *9 esplanade Robert Vasse* ☎ *04–90–38–63–63*). A tempting selection is on view at **Le Quai de la Gare** (✉ *4 av. Julien Guigue* ☎ *04–90–20–73–42*). A popular source is **Village des Antiquaires de la Gare** (✉ *2 bis, av. de l'Égalité* ☎ *04–90–38–04–57*).

Continued on page 603

Van Gogh may have made the sunflower into the icon of Provence, but it is another flower —one that is unprepossessing, fragrant, and tiny—that draws thousands of travelers every year to Provence. They come to journey the famous "Route de la Lavande " (the Lavender Route), a wide blue-purple swath that connects over 2,000 producers across the south of France.

BLUE GOLD: THE LAVENDER ROUTE

Once described as the "soul of Haute-Provence," lavender has colored Provence's plains since the days of the ancient Romans. Today it brings prosperity, as consumers are madly buying hundreds of beauty products that use lavender essence. Nostrils flared, they are following this route every summer. To help sate their lavender lust, the following pages present a detail-rich tour of the Lavender Route.

TOURING THE LAVENDER ROUTE

❶ Have your Nikon ready for the beautifully preserved Cistercian simplicity of the **Abbaye Notre-Dame de Sénanque**, a perfect foil for the famous waving fields of purple around it.

❷ No shrinking violet, the hilltop village of **Gordes** is famous for its luxe hotels, restaurants, and lavender-stocked shops.

❸ Get a fascinating A to Z tour—from harvesting to distilling to production—at the **Musée de la Lavande** near Coustellet.

❹ If you want to have a peak lavender experience—literally—detour 18 km (10 mi) to the northwest and take a spectacular day's drive up the winding road to the **summit of Mont Ventoux** (follow signs from Sault to see the lavender-filled valleys below).

❺ Even if you miss the biggest blow-out of the year, the Fête de la Lavande in **Sault** (usually on August 15), take in the charming *vieille ville* boutiques or the fabulous lavender fields that surround the hillside town.

❻ The awe-inspiring lavender fields around **Forcalquier** are one step away from perfection, and the Monday morning market is a treasure trove of local products.

❼ **Distillerie "Le Coulets"** on the outskirts of Apt has been a lavender farm for generations and offers free tours and products for sale at its boutique.

❽ You've bought the famous lavender products of L'Occitane everywhere, so how can you resist a tour of their **Manosque** factory?

Provence is threaded by the "Routes de la Lavande" (the Lavender Routes), a wide blue-purple swath that connects over 2,000 producers across the Drôme, the plateau du Vaucluse, and the Alpes-de-Haute-Provence, but our itinerary is lined with some of the prettiest sights—and smells—of the region. Whether you're shopping for artisanal bottles of the stuff (as with wine, the finest lavender carries its own Appellation d'Origine Contrôlée), spending a session at a lavender spa, or simply wearing hip-deep purple as you walk the

Forcalquier Market

Purple haze

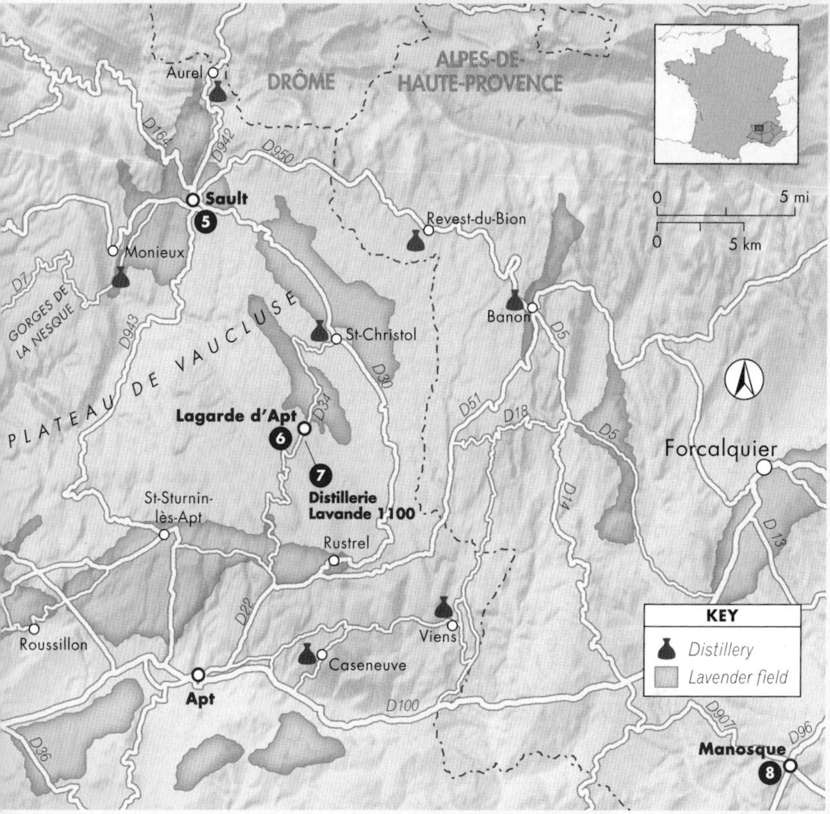

fields, the most essential aspect on this trip is savoring a magical world of blue, one we usually only encounter on picture postcards.

To join the lavender-happy crowds, you have to go in season, which runs from June to early September. Like Holland's May tulips, the lavender of Haute-Provence is in its true glory only once a year: the last two weeks of July, when the harvesting begins—but fields bloom throughout the summer months for the most part. Below, we wind through the most generous patches of lavender. Drive the colorful gambit southeastward (Coustellet, Gordes, Sault, Forcalquier, and Manosque), which will give you good visiting (and shopping) time in a number of the villages that are *fou de la lavande* (crazy for lavender). And for the complete scoop on the hundreds of sights to see in lavender land, contact **Les Routes de la Lavande** through the association La Grande Traversée des Alpes in Grenoble (☎ *04–76–42–08–31* 🌐 *www.grande-traversee-alpes.com*).

Abbaye Notre-Dame de Sénanque

DAY 1

SÉNANQUE

A Picture-Perfect Abbey

An invisible Master of Ceremonies for the Lavender Route would surely send you first to the greatest spot for lavender worship in the world: the 12th-century Cistercian **Abbaye Notre-Dame de Sénanque**, which in July and August seems to float above a sea of lavender, a setting immortalized in a thousand travel posters. Happily, you'll find it via the D177 only 4 km (2½ mi) north of Gordes, among the most beautiful of Provence's celebrated perched villages. An architecture student's dream of neat cubes, cylinders, and pyramids, its pure Romanesque form alone is worth contemplating in any context. But in this arid, rocky setting the gray stone building seems to have special resonance—ancient, organic, with a bit of the borie about it. Along with the abbeys of Le Thornet and Silvacane, this is one of the trio of "Three Sisters" built by the Cistercian order in this area. Sénanque's **church** is a model of symmetry and balance. Begun in 1150, it has no decoration but still touches the soul with its chaste beauty.

The adjoining **cloister,** from the 12th century, is almost as pure, with barrel-vaulted galleries framing double rows of discreet, abstract pillars. Next door, the enormous vaulted dormitory and the refectory shelter a display on the history of Cistercian abbeys. The few remaining monks here now preside over a cultural center that presents concerts and exhibitions. The bookshop is one of the best in Provence, with a huge collection of Provençaliana (lots in English). ☎ *04–90–72–17–92* ⊕ *www.abbayedesenananque.com, www.senanque.fr* 🎫 *€7* 🕑 *Guided tours of the abbey in French only by reservation. Bookshop open Feb.–Nov., Mon.–Sat. 10–6, Sun. 2–6; Nov.–Jan., daily 2–6.*

THE ESSENCE OF THE MATTER

Provence and lavender go hand in hand—but why? The flower is native to the Mediterranean, and grows so well because the pH balance in the soil is naturally perfect for it (pH 6–8). But lavender was really put on the map here when ancient Romans arrived to colonize Provence and used the flower to disinfect their baths and perfume their laundry (the word comes from Latin *lavare*, "to wash"). From a small grass-roots industry, lavender proliferated over the centuries until the first professional distillery opened in Provence in the 1880s to supply oils for southern French apothecaries. After World War I, production boomed to meet the demand of the perfumers of Grasse (the perfume center of the world). Once described as the "soul of Haute-Provence," lavender is now farmed in England, India, and the States, but the harvest in the South of France remains the world's largest.

After spending the morning getting acquainted with the little purple flower at Sénanque, drive south along the D2 (or D177) back to **Gordes**, through a dry, rocky region mixed with deep valleys and far-reaching plains.

Wild lavender is already omnipresent, growing in large tracts as you reach the entrance of the small, unspoiled hilltop village, making for a patchwork landscape as finely drawn as a medieval illumination. A cluster of houses rises above the valley in painterly hues of honey gold, with cobbled streets winding up to the village's picturesque Renaissance château, making it one of the most beautiful towns in Provence.

Gordes has a great selection of hotels, restaurants, and B&Bs to choose from (see our listings under Gordes). Spend the early afternoon among tasteful shops that sell lovely Provençal crafts and produce, much of it lavender-based, and then after lunch, head out to Coustellet.

COUSTELLET

A Great Lavender Museum

Set 2 mi south of Gordes, Coustellet is noted for its **Musée de la Lavande** (take the D2 southeast to the outskirts of Coustellet). Owned by one of the original lavender families, who have cultivated and distilled the flower here for over five generations, this museum lies on the outskirts of more than 80 acres of prime lavender-cultivated land.

ON THE CALENDAR

If you plan to be at the Musée de la Lavande between July 1 and August 25 you can work up a sweat cutting your own swath of lavender with a copper scythe, then make your own distillation in the museum's lab.

Not only can you visit the well-organized and interesting museum (note the impressive collection of scythes and distilling apparatus), you can buy up a storm in the boutique, which offers a great selection of lavender-based products at very reasonable prices. ☎ *04–90–76–91–23* 🌐 *www.museedelalavande.com* €6 🕓 *Daily, Feb.–Mar., and Dec., 9–12:15 and 2–6; Apr. and Oct., 9–1 and 2–6; May–Sept., 9–7.*

There are four main species. True lavender (*Lavandula angustifolia*) produces the most subtle essential oil and is often used by perfume makers and laboratories. Spike lavender (*Lavandula latifolia*) has wide leaves and long floral stems with several flower spikes. Hybrid lavender (*lavandin*) is obtained from pollination of true lavender and spike lavender, making a hybrid that forms a highly developed large round cluster. French lavender (*Lavendula stoechas*) is wild lavender that grows throughout the region and is collected for the perfume industry. True lavender thrives in the chalky soils and hot, dry climate of higher altitudes of Provence. It was picked systematically until the end of the 19th century and used for most lavender-based products. But as the demand for this remarkable flower grew, so did the need for a larger production base. By the beginning of the 20th century, the demand for the flower was so great that producers planted fields of lavender at lower altitudes, creating the need for a tougher, more resistant plant: the hybrid *lavandin*.

In many towns, Provence's lavender harvest is celebrated with charming folkloric festivals.

DAY 2

LAGARDE D'APT

A Top Distillerie

On the second day of your lavender adventure, begin by enjoying the winding drive 25 km (15 mi) east to the town of **Apt**. Aside from its Provençal market, busy with all the finest food products of the Luberon and Haute Provence, Apt itself is unremarkable (even actively ugly from a distance) but is a perfect place from which to organize your visits to the lavender fields of Caseneuve, Viens, and Lagarde d'Apt.

Caseneuve (east exit from Apt onto the D900 and then northwest on the D35) and Viens (16 km/10 mi east from Apt on the D209) are small but charming places to stop for a quick bite along the magnificent drive through the rows upon rows of lavender, but if you have to choose between the three, go to the minuscule village of Lagarde d'Apt (12 km/7 mi east from Apt on the D209).

Or for a closer look, take the D22 (direction Rustrel) a few kilometres outside of Apt to **Distillerie "Les Coulets."** From June to September, you can take a free tour of the distillery, visit the farm and browse the gift shop. ✉ *Hameau Les Coulets* ☎ *04–90–74–07–55* ⏲ *July and Aug. 9–noon and 1:30–7.*

SAULT

The Biggest Festival

To enjoy a festive overnight, continue northwest from Lagarde d'Apt to the village of **Sault**, 15 km (9 mi) to the northeast. Beautifully perched on a rocky outcrop overlooking the valley that bears its name, Sault is one of the key stops along the Lavender Route.

There are any number of individual distilleries, producers, and fields to visit—to make the most of your visit, ask the Office du Tourisme (☎ *04–90–64–01–21* 🌐 *www.saultenprovence.com*) for a list of events. Make sure to pop into the **Centre de Découverte de la Nature et du Patrimoine Cynégétique** (✉ *Av. de l'Oratoire* ☎ *04–90–64–13–96* 🎫 *€3*) to see the exhibitions on the natural history of the region, including some on lavender. Aim to be in Sault for the not-to-be-missed **Fête de la Lavande** (✉ *along the D950 at the Hippodrome le Defends* 🌐 *www.saultenprovence.com*), a day-long festival entirely dedicated to lavender, the best in the region, and usually held around August 15.

Village folk dress in traditional Provençal garb and parade on bicycles, horses leap over barrels of fragrant bundles of hay, and local producers display their wares at the market—all of which culminates in a communal Provençal dinner (€20) served with lavender-based products.

DAY 3

FORCALQUIER

The Liveliest Market

On your third day, the drive from Sault over 53 km (33 mi) east to Forcalquier is truly spectacular.

As you approach the village in late July, you will see endless fields of *Lavandula vera* (true wild lavender) broken only by charming stone farmhouses or discreet distilleries.

The epicenter of Haute-Provence's lavender cultivation, **Forcalquier** boasts a lively Monday morning market with a large emphasis on lavender-based products, and it is a great departure point for walks, bike rides, horse rides, or drives into the lavender world that surrounds the town.

In the 12th century, Forcalquier was known as the capital city of Haute-Provence and was called the *Cité des Quatre Reines* (City of the Four Queens) because the four daughters (Eleanor of Aquitaine among them) of the ruler of this region, Raimond Béranger V, all married royals.

Relics of this former glory can be glimpsed in the Vieille Ville of Forcalquier, notably its Cathédrale Notre-Dame and the Couvent des Cordeliers.

MAKING SCENTS

BLOOMING

Lavender fields begin blooming in late June, depending on the area and the weather, with fields reaching their peak from the first of July to mid-October. The last two weeks in July are considered the best time to catch the fields in all their glory.

HARVESTING

Lavender is harvested from July to September, when the hot summer sun brings the essence up into the flower. Harvesting is becoming more and more automated; make an effort to visit some of the older fields with narrow rows—these are still picked by hand. Lavender is then dried for two to three days before being transported to the distillery.

DISTILLING

Distillation is done in a steam alembic, with the dry lavender steamed in a double boiler. Essential oils are extracted from the lavender by water vapor, which is then passed through the cooling coils of a retort.

However, everyone heads here to marvel at the lavender fields outside town. Contact Forcalquier's Office du Tourisme (✉ *13 pl. Bourguet* ☎ *04–92–75–10–02* 🌐 *www.forcalquier.com*) for information on the lavender calendar, then get saddled up on a bicycle for a trip into the countryside at the town's Moulin de Sarret.

Plan on enjoying a fine meal and an overnight stay (reserve way in advance) at the town's most historic establishment, the **Hostellerie des Deux Lions** (✉ *11 pl. du Bourguet* ☎ *04–92–75–25–30*).

MANOSQUE

Love That L'Occitane

Fifteen mi (25 km) south of Forcalquier is Manosque, home to the **L'Occitane** factory.

You can get a glimpse of what the Luberon was like before it became so hip—Manosque is certainly not a tourist epicenter—but a trip here is worth it for a visit to the phenomenally successful cosmetics and skin care company that is now the town's main employer.

Once you make a reservation through the Manosque Tourist Office (✉ *Pl. du Docteur Joubert* ☎ *04–92–72–16–00* 🌐 *www.manosque-tourisme.com*) you can take a two-hour tour of the production site, view a documentary film, get a massage with oils, then rush into the shop where you can stock up on L'Occitane products for very reasonable prices.

From Manosque you can head back to Apt and the Grand Luberon area or turn south about 52 km (30 mi) to Aix-en-Provence. ✉ *Z. I. St-Maurice* ☎ *04–92–70–19–00* 🌐 *www.loccitane.com* ⏲ *Mon.–Sat. 10–7.*

BRINGING IT HOME

Yes, you've already walked in the pungent-sweet fields, breathing in the ephemeral scent that is uniquely a part of Provence. Visually, there is nothing like the waving fields rising up in a haze of bees. But now it's time to shop! Here are some top places to head to stop and smell the lavender element in local wines, honey, vinegar, soaps, and creams. A fine place to start is 8 km (5 mi) east of Sault at the **Ho! Bouquet de Lavande** (✉ follow signs on the D189, Ferrassières ☎ 04–75–28–87–52). Take a free guided visit and cut your own lavender bouquet before buying up all the inventory available in the shop.

In Gordes and Sault there are lovely Provençal markets that have a wide range of lavender-based products, from honey to vinegar to creams. A great selection of the finest essential oils is available at **Distillerie du Vallon** (✉ Rte. des Michouilles, Sault ☎ 04–90–64–14–83). **L'Occitane** (✉ Z.I. St-Maurice, Manosque ☎ 04–92–70–19–00) is the mother store. In nearby Volx you can hit the **Maison aux Huiles Essentiels** (✉ Z.I. La Carretière, Volx ☎ 04–92–78–46–77) for aromatherapy in all its glory.

SCENT-SATIONAL

GORDES

Fodor's Choice ★ *16 km (10 mi) southeast of Fontaine-de-Vaucluse, 35 km (22 mi) east of Avignon.*

Gordes was once merely an unspoiled hilltop village; it's now a famous unspoiled hilltop village surrounded by luxury vacation homes, modern hotels, restaurants, and B&Bs. No matter: the ancient stone village still rises above the valley in painterly hues of honey gold, and its cobbled streets—lined with boutiques, galleries, and real-estate offices—still wind steep and narrow to its Renaissance château—making this certainly one of the most beautiful towns in Provence.

GETTING HERE

There is only one bus that stops at the Place du Château in Gordes and that's the Cavaillon-Roussillon. It runs twice a day, morning and night and costs €5. Otherwise you'll need a car or take a taxi: to Avignon it's about €85 or to Fontaine du Vaucluse €50.

Visitor Information **Gordes Tourist Office** ✉ *Le Chateau* ☎ *04–90–72–02–75* 🌐 *www.gordes-village.com.*

EXPLORING

The only way to see the interior of Gordes's town **château** is to view its ghastly collection of photo paintings by pop artist Pol Mara, who lived in Gordes. It's worth the price of admission just to look at the fabulously decorated stone fireplace, created in 1541. ☎ *04–90–72–02–75* 🎫 *€4* ⏲ *Daily 10–noon and 2–6.*

Just outside Gordes, on a lane heading north from D2, follow signs to the **Village des Bories.** Found throughout this region of Provence, the bizarre and fascinating little stone hovels called *bories* are concentrated some 20 strong in an ancient community. Their origins are provocatively vague: built as shepherds' shelters with tight-fitting, mortarless stone in a hivelike form, they may date to the Celts, the Ligurians, even the Iron Age—and were inhabited or used for sheep through the 18th century. A photo exhibition shows other structures, similar to bories, in countries around the world ☎ *04–90–72–03–48* 🎫 *€5.50* ⏲ *Daily 9–dusk or 8, whichever comes earlier.*

If you've dreamed of Provence's famed lavender fields, head to a wild valley some 4 km (2½ mi) north of Gordes (via D177) to find the beautiful 12th-century Romanesque **Abbaye de Sénanque,** which floats above a redolent sea of lavender (in full bloom in July and August; ⇨ *for more information, see the special photo feature, "Blue Gold—The Lavender Route," in this chapter*). Begun in 1150 and completed at the dawn of the 13th century, the **church** and adjoining **cloister** are without decoration, but still touch the soul with their chaste beauty. In this orbit, the gray-stone buildings seem to have special resonance—ancient, organic, with a bit of the *borie* (stone hut) about them. Next door, the enormous vaulted **dormitory** contains an exhibition on the abbey's construction, and the **refectory** shelters a display on the history of Cistercian abbeys. ☎ *04–90–72–05–72* 🌐 *www.senanque.fr* 🎫 *€6* ⏲ *Mar.–Oct., Mon.–Sat. 10–6, Sun. 2–6; Nov.–Feb., daily 2–6; call ahead for reservations.*

Fodor's Choice ★

WHERE TO EAT AND STAY

$$ FRENCH ✕ **Les Cuisines du Château.** Across from the château, this tiny but deluxe bistro has daily *aioli,* a smorgasbord of fresh cod and lightly steamed vegetables crowned with the garlic mayonnaise. Evenings are reserved for intimate, formal indoor meals à la carte—roast Luberon lamb, beef with truffle sauce. The '30s-style bistro tables and architectural lines are a relief from Gordes's ubiquitous rustic-chic. There is a revolving array of paintings by local artists, many of which are for sale. There are only 26 seats, so book well in advance—especially since the square was recently used as one of the locations for the Ridley Scott adaptation of Peter Mayle's A Year in Provence, and there are now twice as many people clamoring for a seat. ✉ *Pl. du Château* ☎ *04–90–72–01–31* *Reservations essential* ▭ *MC, V* ⊙ *Closed Wed., no dinner Tues., Sept.–May and mid-Jan.–mid-Mar. Closed Nov.–mid-Dec. and mid-Jan. to Easter.*

$$$–$$$$ ★ **La Bastide de Gordes.** Spectacularly perched on Gordes's hilltop, the smartly renovated Bastide is big, yet intimately scaled, with architectural origins going back to the 16th century. The hotel, with its superb restaurant (and impressive 20,000-bottle wine cellar), is surrounded by manicured lawns and a broad, elegantly appointed shaded terrace. Guest rooms are traditional and comfortable, with a few *haut-Provençal* accents. The clientele is increasingly upscale and international, attracted by the luxe three-level Daniel Jouvance spa, which includes a Roman-style steam room, Japanese baths, and a chromatic pool with breathtaking views of the Vallée de Gordes. **Pros:** views are unmatched in the area; wine cellar is a little piece of heaven. **Cons:** dress code has become increasingly select; service can be correspondingly pretentious. ✉ *Le Village* ☎ *04–90–72–12–12* 🌐 *www.bastide-de-gordes.com* *39 rooms, 6 suites* *In-room: a/c, refrigerator. In-hotel: restaurant, bar, pools, spa, Wi-Fi hotspot, parking (paid)* ▭ *AE, MC, V* ⊙ *Closed Jan. and 1st 2 wks of Feb.*

$$–$$$ **La Ferme de la Huppe.** This 17th-century stone farmhouse just outside Gordes has several sweet touches, including a courtyard and rooms furnished with secondhand finds. Dine poolside on three styles of roast lamb, prepared by the proprietors' son, Gerald Konings, but reserve ahead: the restaurant (closed Thursday) is as popular as the hotel. Breakfast is included in the price, and meal plans are available with a minimum stay of three nights. **Pros:** warm familial welcome makes you feel right at home; food is a delight. **Cons:** service can be slow on busy nights; wine list is small. ✉ *Les Pourquiers, 3 km (2 mi) east of Gordes, R. D. 156* ☎ *04–90–72–12–25* 🌐 *www.lafermedelahuppe.com* *9 rooms* *In-room: a/c, refrigerator, Wi-Fi. In-hotel: restaurant, pool, parking , some pets allowed* ▭ *AE, MC, V* ⊙ *Closed Nov.–Mar.* *MAP.*

$–$$ **Les Romarins.** At this small hilltop inn on the outskirts of Gordes you can gaze at the town across the valley while having breakfast on a sheltered terrace in the morning sun. Rooms are clean, well lighted, and feel spacious—ask for either No. 1, in the main building, which has a seemingly limitless view, or the room with a terrace in the atelier. Oriental rugs, antique furniture, and a pool add to your contentment.

Pros: views are lovely; nights are so quiet you can hear the buzzing of insects in the fields. **Cons:** can be difficult to find; far from the village. ✉ *Rte. de Sénanque* ☎ *04–90–72–12–13* 🌐 *www.masromarins.com* *13 rooms* *In-room: refrigerator. In-hotel: pool, Wi-Fi, parking, some pets allowed* ▭ *MC, V* ⏲ *Closed mid–Nov.–mid–Dec. and Jan.–mid–Mar.*

ROUSSILLON

Fodor's Choice ★ *10 km (6 mi) east of Gordes, 45 km (28 mi) east of Avignon.*

In shades of deep rose and russet, this quintessential and gorgeous hilltop cluster of houses blends into the red-ocher cliffs from which its stone was quarried. The ensemble of buildings and jagged, hand-cut slopes is equally dramatic, and views from the top look out over a landscape of artfully eroded bluffs that Georgia O'Keeffe would have loved. Roussillon is definitely one of the top winners in Provence's beauty contest.

GETTING HERE

The Cavaillon-Roussillon bus runs twice a day, morning and night, and costs €5.30. The only other way to arrive in Roussillon is by car from the D4. There's also a daily bus from Cavaillon to Bonnieux (€3), with stops at Lacoste and Menerbes (€2).

Visitor Information Roussillon Tourist Office ✉ *2 pl. de la Poste* ☎ *04-90-05-60-25* 🌐 *www.roussillon-provence.com.*

EXPLORING

Unlike neighboring hill villages, Roussillon offers little of historic architectural detail here; the pleasure of a visit lies in the richly varied colors that change with the light of day, and in the views of the contrasting countryside, where dense-shadowed greenery sets off the red stone with Cézanne-esque severity. There are pleasant *placettes* (tiny squares) to linger in nonetheless, and a Renaissance fortress tower crowned with a clock in the 19th century; just past it, you can take in expansive panoramas of forest and ocher cliffs. Unfortunately it can get overcrowded with tourists in summer—the best time to visit is in spring or early fall. A **Sentier des Ocres** *(Ocher Trail)* starts out from the town cemetery and takes 45 minutes to wend its way through a magical, multicolor "palette de pierres" (palette of rocks) replete with eroded red cliffs and chestnut groves. *€2, €6 joint ticket with Usine Mathieu Roussillon* ⏲ *July and Aug., daily 10–5:30; Sept.–mid-Nov. and Mar.–June, daily 9–noon and 1–5; mid-Nov.–Feb., Wed.–Mon. 9–noon and 1–5.*

The area's famous vein of natural ocher, which spreads some 25 km (16 mi) along the foot of the Vaucluse plateau, has been mined for centuries, beginning with the ancient Romans, who used it for their pottery. You can visit the old **Usine Mathieu de Roussillon** *(Roussillon's Mathieu Ocher Works)* to learn more about ocher's extraction and its modern uses. There are explanatory exhibits, ocher powders for sale, and guided tours in English on advance request. ✉ *On D104 southeast of town* ☎ *04–90–05–66–69* 🌐 *www.okhra.com* *€5 for guided tour, €6 joint ticket with Sentier des Ocres* ⏲ *Mar.–Nov., Wed.–Mon. 10–7.*

WHERE TO EAT AND STAY

$–$$ **La Fontaine de Faucon.** A restored vine-covered 18th-century mas surrounded by an enclosed, south-facing courtyard spells "idyllic weekend getaway." With gardens by the celebrated designer Nicole de Verian filled with cherry and olive trees, a beautiful pool, and the warm welcome of British couple Nick and Maggie Denny, this gorgeous old farmhouse 10 minutes from Roussillon is hard to beat. **Pros:** friendly, efficient service; lovingly decorated rooms add to the charm of an idyllic weekend spot. **Cons:** a little difficult to find; nights are early and very quiet. ✉ *Chemin de la Fontain de Faucon, Quartier Ste-Anne, Goult* ☎ *04–90–09–90–16* 🌐 *www.fontainedefaucon.com* *5 rooms, 1 suite* *In-room: a/c, Wi-Fi. In-hotel: pool, parking (paid), some pets allowed* 💳 *MC, V* *Closed Nov.*

$$ **Ma Maison.** In the valley 4 km (2½ mi) below Roussillon, this isolated 1850 mas has been infused with a laid-back, cosmopolitan style by its artist-owners. Wicker-back chairs mix with Oriental rugs, wrought iron, and fluffy white bedspreads. There's a big saltwater pool, a massive country kitchen, and a garden with lovely breakfast tables romantically set under sprawling, shady branches. Breakfast is included. **Pros:** friendly welcome makes you feel right at home; kitchen acts as a gathering place at mealtime. **Cons:** quite far from Roussillon; nights can be very quiet. ✉ *Quartier Les Devens* ☎ *04–90–05–74–17* *3 rooms, 2 suites* *In-room: a/c. In-hotel: pool, Wi-Fi hotspot, some pets allowed* 💳 *MC, V* *Closed mid-Oct.–mid-Mar.* *BP.*

$$$ **Mas de Garrigon.** An exquisite hotel, tastefully decorated in classic Provençal style, the Garrigon has spacious rooms, a cozy library, and views of the surrounding ocher cliffs. It also has the best restaurant (by far) in Roussillon—which is a good thing, as the management takes it very personally if you pass on their demi-pension offer. So don't: the food is superb—monkfish in salt crust, straw-baked lamb with rosemary jus, inventive vegetable courses, plus wonderful desserts. Note that the restaurant is closed on Monday and Tuesday. And the family welcome is warm and genuine. **Pros:** location is ideal; rooms are large; food is excellent. **Cons:** service can be slow; rooms warm in summer. ✉ *Rte. de St-Saturnin-d'Apt, 3 km (2 mi) north on D2* ☎ *04–90–05–63–22* 🌐 *www.masdegarrigon-provence.com* *8 rooms, 1 suite* *In-room: a/c, refrigerator, Wi-Fi. In-hotel: pool, parking (paid)* 💳 *AE, DC, MC, V* *MAP.*

MÉNERBES

30 km (19 mi) southeast of Avignon.

Famous as the former home base of *A Year in Provence* author Peter Mayle (he has since moved on to another town in the Luberon), the town of Ménerbes clings to a long, thin hilltop over this sought-after valley, looming over the surrounding forests like a great stone ship. At its prow juts the **Castellet,** a 15th-century fortress. At its stern looms the 13th-century **Citadelle.** These redoubtable fortifications served the Protestants well during the 16th-century Wars of Religion—until the Catholics wore them down with a 15-month siege. Artists Picasso, Nicholas

Uniting natural and man-made beauty, ochre quarried from the surrounding painted-desert cliffs is applied directly to many roofs and facades in Roussillon.

de Stael, and Dora Maar all lived here at one time, attracted by the remarkable views and eccentric character of the town. Don't miss the quirky **Musée du Tire-Bouchon** *(Corkscrew museum)*, which has an enormous selection of corkscrews on display and interesting historical detail on various wine-related subjects. ✉ *Domaine de la Citadelle, chemin de Cavaillon* ☎ *04–90–72–41–58* 🎫 *€4* ⏲ *Apr.–Sept., daily 9–noon and 2–7; Oct.–Mar., Mon.–Sat. 9–noon and 2–7.*

A campanile tops the Hôtel de Ville *(Town Hall)* on pretty **Place de l'Horloge** *(Clock Square)*, where you can admire the delicate stonework on the arched portal and mullioned windows of a Renaissance house. Just past the tower on the right is an overlook taking in views toward Gordes, Roussillon, and Mont Ventoux.

Fodor's Choice ★

Seven kilometers (4 mi) east of Ménerbes is the eagle's-nest village of Lacoste, presided over by the once-magnificent Château de Sade, erstwhile retreat to the notorious Marquis de Sade (1740–1814) when he wasn't on the run from authorities. For some years, the wealthy Paris couturier Pierre Cardin has been restoring the castle wall by wall, and under his generous patronage the **Festival Lacoste** takes place here throughout the months of July and August. A lyric, musical, and theatrical extravaganza, events (and their dates) change yearly, ranging from outdoor poetry recitals to ballet to colorful operettas. ✉ *Carrières du Château, Lacoste* ☎ *04–90–75–93–12* 🌐 *www.lacoste-84.com* 🎫 *€20–€140.*

WHERE TO EAT AND STAY

$$$ **Hostellerie Le Roy Soleil.** In the imposing shadow of the Luberon, this luxurious country inn has pulled out all stops on comfort and decor: marble and granite bathrooms, wrought-iron beds, and coordinated Provençal fabrics. But the integrity of its 17th-century building, with thick stone walls and groin vaults and beams, keeps it just short of pretentiousness and makes it a lovely place to escape to. **Pros:** warm welcome of the proud owners makes you feel right at home; softer-than-clouds beds are simply marvelous. **Cons:** some say the reception area is a little too sleek; food sometimes rather ordinary for such a seductive setting. ✉ *Rte. des Beaumettes* ☎ *04–90–72–25–61* 🌐 *www.roy-soleil.com* *10 rooms, 9 suites, 3 apartments* *In-room: a/c. In-hotel: restaurant, bar, pool, Wi-Fi hotspot, parking (free), some pets allowed* *AE, MC, V* *Closed last 3 wks of Jan.–late Feb.* *FAP.*

AIX-EN-PROVENCE AND THE MEDITERRANEAN COAST

The southeastern part of this area of Provence, on the edge of the Côte d'Azur, is dominated by two major towns: Aix-en-Provence, considered the main hub of Provence and the most cultural town in the region; and Marseille, a vibrant port town that combines seediness with fashion and metropolitan feistiness with classical grace. For a breathtaking experience of the dramatic contrast between the azure Mediterranean Sea and the rocky, olive tree–filled hills, take a trip along the coast east of Marseille and make an excursion to the Iles d'Hyères.

AIX-EN-PROVENCE

★ *82 km (51 mi) southeast of Avignon, 176 km (109 mi) west of Nice, 759 km (474 mi) south of Paris.*

Gracious, posh, cultivated, and made all the more cosmopolitan by the presence of some 30,000 international university students, the lovely old town of Aix (pronounced *ex*) was once the capital of Provence. The vestiges of that influence and power—fine art, noble architecture, and graceful urban design—remain beautifully preserved today. That and its thriving market, vibrant café life, and world-class music festival make Aix vie with Arles and Avignon as one of the towns in Provence that shouldn't be missed.

GETTING HERE

The Aix TGV station is 10 km (6 mi) west of the city and is served by regular shuttle buses. The old Aix station is on the slow Marseille–Sisteron line, with trains arriving roughly every hour from Marseille St-Charles. The center of Aix is best explored on foot, but there's a municipal bus service that serves the entire town and the outlying suburbs. Most leave from La Rotonde in front of the tourism office (☎ *04–42–16–11–61* 🌐 *www.aixenprovencetourism.com*), where you can also buy tickets (€1.30 one-way) and ask for a bus route map.

Visitor Information **Aix-en-Provence Tourist Office** ✉ *2 pl. du Général-de-Gaulle, B.P. 160, Cedex 1* ☎ *04–42–16–11–61* 🌐 *www.aixenprovencetourism.com.*

EXPLORING

The museums and churches in Aix are overshadowed by the city itself, with its beautiful fountains, elegant hôtels particuliers, and time-burnished streets. Aix's centre ville is a maze of narrow roadways and it is difficult to keep your sense of direction. Happily, the main drag, the tree-lined and gorgeous Cours Mirabeau, neatly divides old Aix in half, with the Quartier Ancien's narrow medieval streets to the north and the 18th-century houses and fancy restaurants of the Quartier Mazarin to the south. At the very center, and always photo-ready, are Place Richelme and Place de l'Hôtel de Ville, the main squares. You can't go wrong either ending up or beginning with them.

Romans were first drawn here by mild thermal baths, naming the town Aquae Sextiae *(Waters of Sextius)* in honor of the consul who founded a camp near the source in 123 BC. Just 20 years later some 200,000 Germanic invaders besieged Aix, but the great Roman general Marius pinned them against the mountain known ever since as Ste-Victoire. Marius remains a popular local first name to this day. Under the wise and generous guidance of Roi René (King René) in the 15th century, Aix became a center of Renaissance arts and letters. At the height of its political, judicial, and ecclesiastic power in the 17th and 18th centuries, Aix profited from a surge of private building, each grand *hôtel particulier* (mansion) vying to outdo its neighbor. Its signature *cours* (courtyards) and *places* (squares), punctuated by grand fountains and intriguing passageways, date from this time.

It was into this exalting elegance that artist Paul Cézanne (1839–1906) was born, though he drew much of his inspiration from the raw countryside around the city and often painted Ste-Victoire. A schoolmate of Cézanne's made equal inroads: the journalist and novelist Émile Zola (1840–1902) attended the Collège Bourbon with Cézanne and described their friendship as well as Aix itself in several of his works. You can still sense something of the ambience that nurtured these two geniuses in the streets of modern Aix.

TOP ATTRACTIONS

❻ ★ **Atelier Cézanne** *(Cézanne Studio)*. Just north of the Vieille Ville loop you'll find this painting master's studio. After the death of his mother forced the sale of the painter's beloved country retreat, known as Jas de Bouffan, he had this studio built just above the town center. In the upstairs work space Cézanne created some of his finest paintings, including *Les Grandes Baigneuses* (*The Large Bathers*). But what is most striking is its collection of simple objects that once featured prominently in the portraits and still lifes he created—redingote, bowler hat, ginger jar—all displayed as if awaiting his return. The atelier is behind an obscure garden gate on the left as you climb the Avenue Paul-Cézanne. Be sure not to miss the after-dark Nuit des Toiles shows that take place in July and August, or the literary and gastronomic evenings also held in July. It's advisable to book these in advance through the tourist office. ✉ *9 av. Paul-Cézanne* ☎ *04–42–21–06–53* 🌐 *www.*

Aix-en-Provence

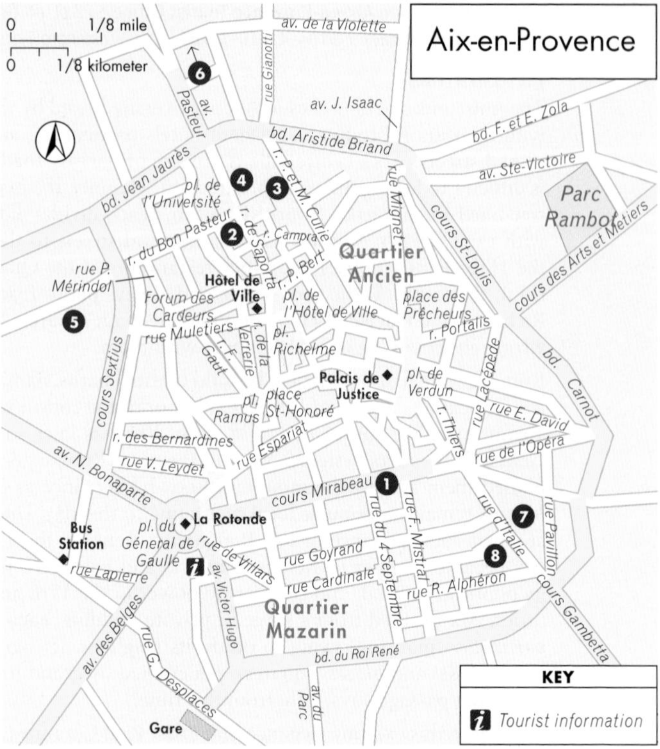

atelier-cezanne.com 🎫 *€5.50* ⏲ *Apr.–Sept., daily 10–noon and 2–6; Oct.–Mar., daily 10–noon and 2–5.*

4 ★ **Cathédrale St-Sauveur.** This cathedral juxtaposes so many eras of architectural history, all clearly delineated and preserved, it's like a survey course in itself. It has a double nave—Romanesque and Gothic side by side—and a Merovingian (5th-century) **baptistery,** its colonnade mostly recovered from Roman temples built to honor pagan deities. The deep bath on the floor is remnant of total-immersion baptism. Shutters hide the ornate 16th-century carvings on the **portals,** opened by a guide on request. The guide can also lead you into the tranquil Romanesque **cloister** next door, so that you can admire its carved pillars and slender columns. As if these treasures weren't enough, the cathedral also has an extraordinary 15th-century triptych painted by Nicolas Froment in the heat of inspiration following his travels in Italy and Flanders. Called the *Triptyque du Buisson Ardent* (*Mary and the Burning Bush*), it depicts the generous art patrons King René and Queen Jeanne kneeling on either side of the Virgin, who is poised above a burning bush. These days, to avoid light damage, it's only opened for viewing on Tuesday from 3 to 4. ✉ *Pl. des Martyrs de la Résistance* ☎ *04–42–23–45–65* 🌐 *www.cathedrale-aix.net.*

1 **Cours Mirabeau.** Found under the deep shade of tall plane trees whose branches interlace over the street (when not seasonally pollarded back) this street prevails as the city's social nerve center. One side is lined with dignified 18th-century hôtels particuliers; you can view them from a comfortable seat in one of the dozen or so cafés and restaurants that spill onto the sidewalk on the other side.

WORD OF MOUTH

"There's no shortage of natural beauty in this area with the vineyards, mountains and perched villages. There's some industrial sprawl around several towns but when you get out into the countryside lovely drives abound." —crazyfortravel

8 **Musée Granet.** Found in the graceful Quartier Mazarin, this museum is set below the Cours Mirabeau. Once the École de Dessin (Art School) that granted Cézanne a second-place prize in 1856, this former priory of the Église St-Jean-de-Malte is now an art museum. Its entry in the history books is a bit inglorious, as it once granted Cézanne a *second* prize in 1856. The academic teacher in charge poo-pooed the young Paul and, in fact, wouldn't allow any Cézannes to enter the museum collection while he was alive (surprisingly, this philistine attitude is still shared by a large number of Aixois). The museum was beautifully renovated and now has a complete selection showcasing more than 600 paintings. There are eight of Cézanne's paintings upstairs as well as a nice collection of his watercolors and drawings, bestowed on the museum by the government, as the locals still have mixed feelings about their resident master. In the same room are the recent Philippe Meyer donations: Bonnard, Picasso, Klee, and Tal Coat have pride of place. You can also find works by Rubens, David, Giacometti, and a group of sentimental works by the museum's founder, François Granet. ⊠ *Pl. St-Jean-de-Malte* ☎ *04–42–26–88–32* 🌐 *www.museegranet-aixenprovence.fr* 🎫 *€4* ⏲ *June–Sept., Tues.–Sun., 11–7; Oct.–May, Tues.–Sun. noon–6.*

Fodor's Choice ★

5 **Pavillon de Vendôme.** This extravagant Baroque villa was first built in 1665 as a "country" house for the Duke of Vendome; its position just outside the city's inner circle allowed the duke to commute discreetly from his official home on the Cours Mirabeau to this love nest, where his mistress, La Belle du Canet, was comfortably installed. Though never officially inhabited, it was expanded and heightened in the 18th century to draw attention to the classical orders—Ionic, Doric, and Corinthian—in its parade of neo-Grecian columns. Inside its cool, broad chambers you can find a collection of Provençal furniture and artwork. Note the curious two giant Atlantes that hold up the interior balcony. ⊠ *34 rue Celony* ☎ *04–42–21–05–78* 🎫 *€2.50* ⏲ *Mar.–mid-Sept., Wed.–Mon. 10–6; mid-Sept.–Dec. and Feb., Wed.–Mon. 1:30–5.*

Fodor's Choice ★

WORTH NOTING

7 **Église St-Jean-de-Malte.** Built in the 12th-century, this church served as a chapel of the Knights of Malta, a medieval order of friars devoted to hospital care. It was Aix's first attempt at the Gothic style. It was here that the counts of Provence were buried throughout the 18th century; their tombs (in the upper left) were attacked during the Revolution

and have been only partially repaired. ✉ *Intersection of Rue Cardinale and Rue d'Italie.*

NEED A BREAK?

For an excellent cup of more than 50 choices of flavored tea, wander into Orienthé (✉ *5 rue du Félibre Gaut*). Comfy pillows, low tables, and lively student patronage make this place super-casual, and the light snacks are just the thing.

3 **Musée des Tapisseries.** Housed in the 17th-century **Palais de l'Archevêché** *(Archbishop's Palace)*, this museum showcases a sumptuous collection of tapestries that once decorated the walls of the bishops' quarters. Their taste was excellent: there are 17 magnificent hangings from Beauvais and a series on the life of Don Quixote from Compiègne. Temporary exhibitions offer interesting sneak peeks into contemporary textile art. The main opera productions of the Festival International d'Art Lyrique take place in the broad courtyard here. ✉ *Pl. de l'Ancien-Archevêché* ☎ *04–42–23–09–91* *€2.50* *Oct.–Dec. and Feb.–Apr., Wed.–Mon. 1:30–5; Apr.–Oct., Wed.–Mon. 10–6.*

2 **Musée du Vieil Aix** *(Museum of Old Aix)*. There's an eclectic assortment of local treasures inside this 17th-century mansion, from faïence to *santons* (terra-cotta figurines) to ornately painted furniture. The building itself is lovely, too. ✉ *17 rue Gaston-de-Saporta* ☎ *04–42–21–43–55* *€4* *Apr.–Oct., Tues.–Sun. 10–noon and 2:30–6; Nov.–Mar., Tues.–Sun. 10–noon and 2–5.*

OFF THE BEATEN PATH

Jas de Bouffon. Cézanne's father bought this lovely estate-whose name translates as "the sheepfold" in 1859 to celebrate his rise from hat-maker to banker. The budding artist lived here until 1899 and painted his first images of Mont Ste-Victoire-the founding seeds of 20th-century art-from here. Today its salons are empty but the grounds are full of his spirit, especially the Allée des Marronniers out front. The Jas is a mile south of the center of town and can only be visited on tour by booking a minibus seat through the town's central tourist office. ☎ *04–42–16–10–91* *www.aixenprovencetourism.com* *€7* *Daily 10–6 for reserved tours.*

WHERE TO EAT

$$ FRENCH **Antoine Coté Cour.** Filled with trendy insiders and fashion-conscious Aixois, this lively Italian restaurant has floor-to-ceiling windows that give almost every table a view of the plant-filled courtyard. Delicious smells wafting out from the open kitchen make this place literally hum in hungry anticipation. Pastas are superb; try the mushroom and prosciutto fettuccine or the gnocchi à la Provençal. And get your taste buds ready to bow—all hail the tiramisu. ✉ *19 cours Mirabeau* ☎ *04–42–93–12–51* *DC, MC, V* *Closed Sun. No lunch Mon.*

$–$$ FRENCH **Brasserie Les Deux Garçons.** Cézanne and Émile Zola used to chow down here back when, so who cares if the food is rather ordinary. Eating isn't what you came for. Instead, revel in the exquisite gold-ivory *style Consulate* decor, which dates from the restaurant's founding in 1792. It's not so hard to picture the greats—Mistinguett, Churchill, Sartre, Picasso, Delon, Belmondo, and Cocteau—enjoying their demitasse under these mirrors. Better, savor the linen-decked sidewalk tables that look out to the Cours Mirabeau, the fresh flowers, and the white-swathed waiters serving espressos in tiny gilt-edge cups. In winter at night the upstairs turns into a cozy, dimly lighted piano bar buzzing with an interesting mix of local jazz lovers, tourists, and students. ✉ *53 cours Mirabeau* ☎ *04–42–26–00–51* ▭ *AE, MC, V.*

$$ FRENCH ✕ **Café La Chimère.** Although the decor in this artists' hangout is a bit overdone, the food is excellent. Not only are the plates balanced creations, but the presentation of each is distinctly impressive. There's a sense of playful whimsy in the vertically arranged concoctions of fresh, local ingredients garnished with shaved fennel, spun sugar, or drizzled sauces. The prices are fantastic and the atmosphere lively, making this an altogether fun place to spend an evening. ✉ *15 rue Brueys* ☎ *04–42–38–30–00* ▭ *V* ⊗ *Closed Sun. No lunch.*

$$ FRENCH ✕ **La Rotonde.** Trendy, young, and cool, this hotter-than-hot spot is the place to hit before heading out for a night on the town. The trappings are funky, service is fun, and the food is very good. Chef Philippe Sublet comes up with easy-to-eat, fresh, and inexpensive cuisine while the house DJ plays soft Buddha Bar–style music in the background—a combination that is a sure recipe for a convivial evening. Try the dual salmon lasagne with spinach and ricotta, or the risotto with marinated artichokes and pancetta bacon. And don't forget the lemon tart with orange shavings—it is exactly the right way to finish off the meal. ✉ *Place Jeanne D'Arc* ☎ *04–42–91–61–41* ⊕ *www.larotonde-aix.com* ▭ *MC, V.*

$$$$ FRENCH ✕ **Le Clos de la Violette.** Whether you dine under the chestnut trees or in the airy, pastel dining room, you can experience the cuisine of one of the south's top chefs, Jean-Marc Banzo. He spins tradition into gold, from panfried tuna with crushed basil, smoked bacon, and crystallized shallots or poached crab set atop a humble white-bean-and-shrimp salad to grilled red mullet with squid-stuffed cabbage. The restaurant isn't far from the Atelier Cézanne, outside the Vieille Ville ring. Some feel that the service can be erratic, but the welcome is warm. ✉ *10 av. de la Violette* ☎ *04–42–23–30–71* ⊕ *www.closdelaviolette.fr* ✍ *Reservations essential; jacket required* ▭ *AE, MC, V* ⊗ *Closed Sun. and Mon.*

$$ FRENCH ✕ **Le Passage.** This is an edgy, urban brasserie from chef Reine Sammut, who has created a wildly popular setting for good, affordable food. In a sleekly converted former candy factory in the center of town, the complex also has a bookstore, cooking workshop, and a small wine store and épicerie all arranged around a sunny atrium. Its New York vibe runs from the Andy Warhol reproductions in the main dining room to the trio of young chefs that maintain Sammut's mod-Med vision: roasted beef fillet with thick-cut fries and a terrific raspberry crème brûlée with fig chutney. ✉ *10 rue Villars* ☎ *04–42–37–09–00* ⊕ *www.le-passage.fr* ✍ *Reservations essential* ▭ *AE, MC, V.*

WHERE TO STAY

$$$–$$$$ **Hotel Cézanne.** Carefully thought out and beautifully orchestrated, the extensive face-lift for this old favorite has made it the newest and hippest boutique hotel in town. Rooms are modern and individually decorated—look for life-size red cutouts holding up shelving units, curling vine sculptures back-lit and embedded in the walls, stainless-steel

four-poster beds, and gold or pink accents. And the downstairs bar, a mecca for young BCBG's, features scarlet velvet, fun abstract art, and cool people. **Pros:** rooms have excellent beds and great showers. **Cons:** some rooms are a little too over-the-top for some tastes, service can be snooty. ✉ *40 av. Victor Hugo* ☎ *04–42–91–11–11* 🌐 *www.hotelaix.com* *55 rooms* *In-room: a/c, Wi-Fi. In-hotel: restaurant, Wi-Fi hotspot, parking (paid), some pets allowed* ▭ *AE, DC, MC, V* *BP.*

$$$–$$$$ Fodor's Choice ★ **Le Pigonnet.** Cézanne painted Ste-Victoire from what is now the large flower-filled garden terrace of this enchanting abode, and the likes of Princess Caroline, Iggy Pop, and Clint Eastwood have spent a few nights under the luxurious roof of the family-owned, old-world, country-style hotel. Spacious and filled with light, each room is a marvel of decoration: baby-soft plush rugs, beautifully preserved antique furniture, rich colors of burnt reds, autumn yellows, and delicate oranges. The restaurant's terrace spills out onto a sculpted green, but the inside dining salon is equally pleasant on a rainy day, thanks to its softly draped yellow curtains and large picture windows. For sheerest Provençal luxe, this place can't be beat. **Pros:** unique garden setting in the center of Aix; welcome is friendly; decor soft and elegant; rooms all have large French windows. **Cons:** reception area has been called stuffy and old-fashioned; some of the antiques are a little threadbare. ✉ *5 av. du Pigonnet* ☎ *04–42–59–02–90* 🌐 *www.hotelpigonnet.com* *49 rooms, 2 villas* *In-room: a/c, refrigerator, Wi-Fi. In-hotel: restaurant, pool, parking (paid)* ▭ *AE, MC, V.*

$–$$ **Nègre-Coste.** Its prominent Cours Mirabeau position and its lavish public areas make this 18th-century town house a popular hotel. Provençal decor and newly tiled bathrooms live up to the lovely ground-floor salons. Large windows open up to the Cours Mirabeau, perfect for people-watching with a morning cup of coffee; quieter ones at the back look over the rooftops to the cathedral. **Pros:** a perfect location for visiting Aix and all its sights; the welcome is warm and friendly; affordable price. **Cons:** rooms can be noisy; some rooms are quite small. ✉ *33 cours Mirabeau* ☎ *04–42–27–74–22* 🌐 *www.hotelnegrecoste.com* *36 rooms, 1 suite* *In-room: a/c, refrigerator. In-hotel: Wi-Fi hotspot, parking (paid)* ▭ *AE, MC, V.*

$–$$ **Quatre Dauphins.** In the quiet Mazarin quarter, this modest but impeccable lodging inhabits a noble hôtel particulier. The pretty, comfortable little rooms have been spruced up with *boutis* (Provençal quilts), Les Olivades fabrics, quarry tiles, jute carpets, and hand-painted furniture. The house-proud but unassuming owner-host bends over backward to please. **Pros:** ideal center-of-town location; super-friendly staff. **Cons:** rooms are small; in summer it is impossible to get a room. ✉ *55 rue Roux-Alphéran* ☎ *04–42–38–16–39* 🌐 *www.lesquatredauphins.fr* *13 rooms* *In-room: a/c. In-hotel: Wi-Fi hotspot, some pets allowed* ▭ *MC, V.*

$$$$ **Villa Gallici.** Perched on a hill overlooking the pink roofs of Aix, this former archbishop's palace was transformed into an homage to *le style provençal* thanks to the wizardry of three designers, Gilles Dez, Charles de Montemarco, and Daniel Jouvre. Hued in the lavenders and blues, ochers and oranges of Aix, rooms swim in the most gorgeous Souleiado

Crammed with elegant shops, chic cafes, and 18th-century houses, Aix-en-Provence is one of France's most charming towns.

and Rubelli fabrics and trim. This hilltop garden retreat stands serenely apart from the city center on the outskirts of town (offering great views), and that means the shops of Cours Mirabeau are a 15-minute walk away. **Pros:** rich fabrics and decor create a harmonious look that translates to genuine harmony in the feel of the rooms and space. **Cons:** some visitors say that the restaurant is not as good as it should be, and that service can be haughty. ✉ *Av. de la Violette* ☎ *04–42–23–29–23* 🌐 *www.villagallici.com* *18 rooms, 4 suites, 3 duplexes* *In-room: a/c, refrigerator, Wi-Fi. In-hotel: restaurant, pool, parking (free)* *AE, DC, MC, V* *Closed Jan.*

NIGHTLIFE AND THE ARTS

To find out what's going on in town, pick up a copy of the events calendar *Le Mois à Aix* or the bilingual city guide *Aix la Vivante* at the tourist office. **Le Scat Club** (✉ *11 rue de la Verrerie* ☎ *04–42–23–00–23*) is the place for live soul, funk, reggae, rock, blues, and jazz. **Le Divino** (✉ *Mas des Auberes, Rte. de Venelles, 5 km [3 mi], from town* ☎ *04–42–99–37–08*) is New York stylish and draws the hip, young, and beautiful people. The **Bistrot Aixois** (✉ *37 cours Sextius* ☎ *04–42–27–50–10*) is still the hottest student nightspot, with young yuppies lining up to get in. The **Red Clover** (✉ *30 rue de la Verrerie* ☎ *04–42–23–44–61*) is a friendly, boisterous Irish pub. Don't expect to speak any French here. For a night of playing roulette and the slot machines, head for the **Casino Municipal** (✉ *2 bis, av. N.-Bonaparte* ☎ *04–42–26–30–33*).

Every July during the **Festival International d'Art Lyrique** *(International Opera Festival* ☎ *04–42–17–34–00 for information*), you can see world-class opera productions in the spectacular courtyard of the Palais de l'Archevêché.

SHOPPING

Aix is a market town, and a sophisticated **food and produce market** sets up every morning on Place Richelme; just up the street, on Place Verdun, is a good high-end *brocante* (collectibles market) Tuesday, Thursday, and Saturday mornings. A famous Aixois delicacy is *calissons*, a blend of almond paste and glazed melon in almond shapes. The most picturesque shop specializing in calissons is **Bechard** (⊠ *12 cours Mirabeau*). **Leonard Parli** (⊠ *35 av. Victor Hugo*), near the train station, also offers a lovely selection of calissons.

In addition to its old-style markets and jewel-box candy shops, Aix is a modern shopping town—perhaps the best in Provence. The winding streets of the Vieille Ville above Cours Mirabeau—centered around **Rue Clemenceau, Rue Marius Reinaud, Rue Espariat, Rue Aude,** and **Rue Maréchal Foch**—have a head-turning parade of goods.

MARSEILLE

31 km (19 mi) south of Aix-en-Provence, 188 km (117 mi) west of Nice, 772 km (483 mi) south of Paris.

Marseille may sometimes be given a wide berth by travelers in search of a Provençal idyll, but it's their loss. Miss it and you miss one of the more vibrant, exciting cities in France. With its Cubist jumbles of white stone rising up over a picture-book seaport, bathed in light of blinding clarity and crowned by larger-than-life neo-Byzantine churches, the city's neighborhoods teem with multiethnic life, its souklike African markets reek deliciously of spices and coffees, and its labyrinthine Vieille Ville is painted in broad strokes of saffron, cinnamon, and robin's-egg blue. Feisty and fond of broad gestures, Marseille is a dynamic city, as cosmopolitan now as when the Phoenicians first founded it, and with all the exoticism of the international shipping port it has been for 2,600 years. Vital to the Crusades in the Middle Ages and crucial to Louis XIV as a military port, Marseille flourished as France's market to the world—and still does today.

GETTING HERE

The main train station is the Gare St-Charles on the TGV line, with frequent trains from Paris, the main coast route (Nice/Italy), and Arles. Note that inside the train station, SOS Voyageurs (☎ *04–91–62–12–80* ⌚ *Mon.–Sat. 9–7*) helps with children, senior citizens, and lost luggage. The Gare Routière (bus station) is on Place Victor Hugo (☎ *04–91–08–16–40*). Here you will find Cartrieze (☎ *08–00–19–94–13* 🌐 *www.lepilote.com*) controlling the routes into and from the Bouches du Rhone; Eurolines (☎ *04–91–50–57–55* 🌐 *www.eurolines.fr*) operating coaches between Marseille, Avignon, and Nice via Aix-en-Provence. Marseille also has a local bus, tram, and métro system. Most of the lines service the suburbs, but several stop in the city center (including Gare St-Charles, Colbert, Vieux Port, and Notre Dame; tickets €1.70 for trips up to an hour, or €4.50 for day passes) and can help you get

Abbaye St-Victor **11**
Cathédrale de la Nouvelle Major **7**
Centre de la Vielle Charité **6**
Ferry Boat **10**
Fort St-Nicolas/ Fort St-Jean ... **12**
Jardin des Vestiges **4**
Le Panier **5**
Musée des Docks Romains **9**
Musée d'Histoire de Marseille **3**
Musée de la Marine et de l'Economie de Marseille **1**
Musée de la Mode de Marseille **2**
Musée du Vieux Marseille **8**
Notre-Dame-de-la-Garde ... **13**

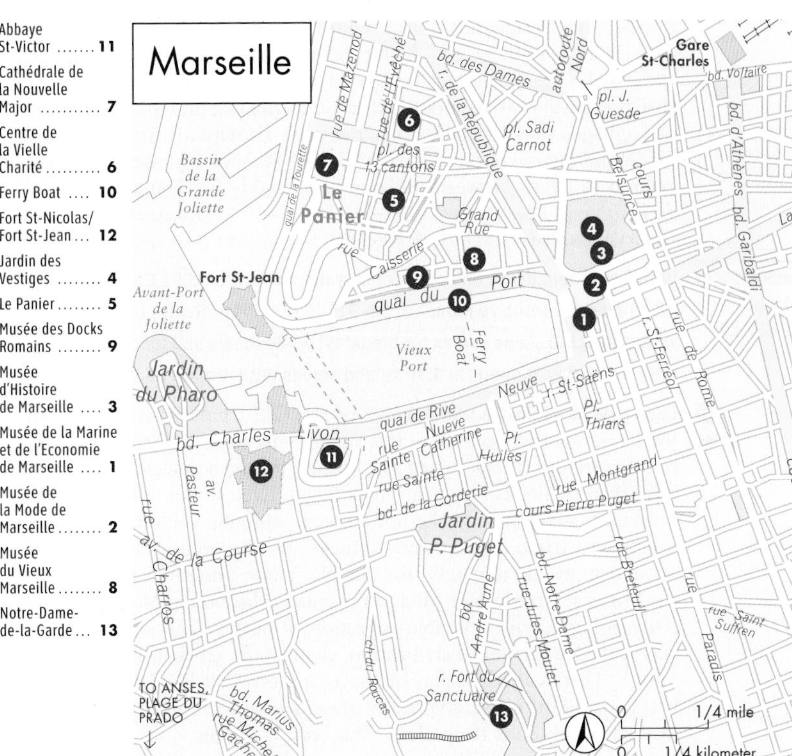

around quickly. At night, a network of buses runs between Canebiére and the outer districts.

Visitor Information Marseille Tourist Office ✉ *4 la Canebière* ☎ *04–91–13–89–00* 🌐 *www.destination-marseille.com.*

EXPLORING

The heart of Marseille is clustered around the Vieux Port—immortalized in all its briny charm in the 1961 Leslie Caron film version of *Fanny.* The hills to the south of the port are crowned with mega-monuments, such as Notre-Dame de la Garde and Fort St-Jean. To the north lies the ramshackle hilltop Vieille Ville known as Le Panier. East of the port you can find the North African neighborhood and, to its left, the famous thoroughfare called La Canebière. South of the city, the cliff-top waterfront highway leads to obscure and colorful ports and coves.

If you plan on visiting many of the museums in Marseille, buy a museum "passport" for €16 (2 days €23) at the tourism office. It covers the entry fee into all the museums in Marseille.

TOP ATTRACTIONS

11 ★ **Abbaye St-Victor.** Founded in the 4th century by St-Cassien, who sailed into Marseille's port full of fresh ideas on monasticism acquired in Palestine and Egypt, this church grew to formidable proportions. With its

Romanesque design, this church would be as much at home in the Middle East as its founder was. By far the best reason to come is the **crypt,** St-Cassien's original, which lay buried under the medieval church's new structure. In evocative nooks and crannies you can find the 5th-century sarcophagus that allegedly holds the martyr's remains. Upstairs, look for the reliquary containing what's left of St. Victor himself, who was ground to death between millstones, probably by Romans. ✉ *3 rue de l'Abbaye, Rive Neuve* ☎ *04–96–11–22–60* 🌐 *www.saintvictor.net* 🎫 *Crypt entry €2* 🕓 *Daily 8:30–6:30.*

NEED A BREAK?

With handsome decor and pale green walls, the pretty 1901 Café Parisien (✉ *1 pl. Sadi Carnot, Le Panier* ☎ *04-91-90-05-77*) is always buzzing. It's where the club scene comes for breakfast while locals and tourists stop by later in the day. It opens at 4:30 AM and serves until around midnight.

6 ★ **Centre de la Vieille Charité** *(Center of the Old Charity)*. At the top of the Panier district you'll find this superb ensemble of 17th- and 18th-century architecture designed as a hospice for the homeless by Marseillais artist-architects Pierre and Jean Puget. Even if you don't enter the museums, walk around the inner court, studying the retreating perspective of triple arcades and admiring the Baroque chapel with its novel egg-peaked dome. Of the complex's two museums, the larger is the **Musée d'Archéologie Méditerranéenne** *(Museum of Mediterranean Archaeology)*, with a sizable collection of pottery and statuary from classical Mediterranean civilization, elementally labeled (for example, "pot"). There's also a display on the mysterious Celt-like Ligurians who first peopled the coast, cryptically presented with emphasis on the digs instead of the finds themselves. The best of the lot is the evocatively mounted Egyptian collection, the second-largest in France after the Louvre's. There are mummies, hieroglyphs, and gorgeous sarcophagi in a tomblike setting. Upstairs, the **Musée d'Arts Africains, Océaniens, et Amérindiens** *(Museum of African, Oceanic, and American Indian Art)* creates a theatrical foil for the works' intrinsic drama: the spectacular masks and sculptures are mounted along a pure black wall, lighted indirectly, with labels across the aisle. ✉ *2 rue de la Charité, Le Panier* ☎ *04–91–14–58–80* 🎫 *€2 per museum* 🕓 *May–Sept., Tues.–Sun. 11–6; Oct.–Apr., Tues.–Sun. 10–5.*

OFF THE BEATEN PATH

★ **Château d'If.** François I, in the 16th century, recognized the strategic advantage of an island fortress surveying the mouth of Marseille's vast harbor, so he had one built. Its effect as a deterrent was so successful that it never saw combat, and was eventually converted into a prison. It was here that Alexandre Dumas locked up his most famous character, the Count of Monte Cristo. Though he was fictional, the hole Dumas had him escape through is real enough, and is visible in the cells today. Video monitors playing relevant scenes from dozens of Monte Cristo films bring each tower and cell to life. On the other hand, the real-life Man in the Iron Mask, whose cell is still being shown, was not actually imprisoned here. The GACM boat ride (from the Quai des Belges, €10, for information call ☎ *04–91–55–50–09*) and the views from the broad terrace alone are worth the trip. ☎ *04–91–55–50–09* *www.monuments-france.fr* *€8* *No credit cards* *Apr.–Sept., daily 9:30–6:30; Oct.–Mar., Tues.–Sun. 9:30–5.*

10 Fodor's Choice ★ **Ferry Boat.** This Marseille treasure departs from the Quai below the Hôtel de Ville. To hear the natives pronounce "fer-ry bo-at" (they've adopted the English) is one of the joys of a visit here. For a pittance (although technically free, it is appropriate to tip the crew) you can file onto this little wooden barge and chug across the Vieux Port. *Pl. des Huiles on Quai de Rive Neuve side and Hôtel de Ville on Quai du Port, Vieux Port* *Free.*

5 ★ **Le Panier.** This is the old heart of Marseille, a maze of high-shuttered houses looming over narrow cobbled streets, *montées* (stone stairways), and tiny squares. Long decayed and neglected, it's the principal focus of the city's efforts at urban renewal. Wander this neighborhood at will, making sure to stroll along Rue du Panier, the montée des Accoules, Rue du Petit-Puits, and Rue des Muettes.

3 ★ **Musée d'Histoire de Marseille** *(Marseille Museum of History)*. A modern and open space, this museum illuminates Massalia's history by mounting its treasure of archaeological finds in didactic displays and miniature models of the city as it appeared in various stages of history. Best by far is the presentation of Marseille's Classical halcyon days. There's a recovered wreck of a Roman cargo boat, its 3rd-century wood amazingly preserved, and the hull of a Greek boat dating from the 4th century BC. And that model of the Greek city should be authentic—it's based on the eyewitness description of Aristotle. *Centre Bourse, entrance on Rue de Bir-Hakeim, Vieux Port* *04–91–90–42–22* *€3 joint ticket with Jardin des Vestiges* *June–Sept., Mon.–Sat. noon–7; Oct.–May., Tues.–Sun. 10–5.*

WORTH NOTING

7 **Cathédrale de la Nouvelle Major.** This gargantuan, neo-Byzantine 19th-century fantasy was built under Napoléon III—but not before he'd ordered the partial destruction of the lovely 11th-century original, once a perfect example of the Provençal Romanesque style. You can view the flashy decor—marble and rich red porphyry inlay—in the newer of the two churches; the medieval one is being restored. *Pl. de la Major, Le Panier.*

12 **Fort St-Nicolas and Fort St-Jean.** At the entrance to the Vieux Port, you'll find these two twin forts. In order to keep the feisty, rebellious Marseillais under his thumb, Louis XIV had the fortresses built with the guns pointing *toward* the city. The Marseillais, whose local identity has always been mixed with a healthy dose of irony, are quite proud of this display of the king's (later justified) doubts about their allegiance. To view them, climb up to the Jardin du Pharo. Sometime in 2012 the Fort St-Jean will open under the banner of the Musée National des Civilisations de L'Europe et de la Mediterranée, exposing the folk-art collection of the former Musée des Arts et Traditions Populaires in Paris. *Quai du Port Vieux Port* *04–96–13–80–90* *www.musee-europemediterranee.org* *€2* *Mon., Wed., and Sun. 10–noon and 2–7.*

4 **Jardin des Vestiges** *(Garden of Remains)*. Found just behind the Marseille History Museum, these gardens stand on the site of Marseille's classical

The heart of Marseille is its Vieux Port (Old Port), with its small boats and port-side cafés, while the city's soul is hilltop Notre-Dame-de-la-Garde.

waterfront and includes remains of the Greek fortifications and loading docks. It was discovered in 1967 when roadwork was being done next to the Bourse *(Stock Exchange)*. ✉ *Centre Bourse, Vieux Port* ☎ *04–91–90–42–22* 🎟 *€3 joint ticket with Marseille Museum of History* ⏲ *Mon.–Sat. noon–7.*

9 **Musée des Docks Romains** *(Roman Docks Museum)*. In 1943 Hitler destroyed the neighborhood along the Quai du Port—some 2,000 houses—displacing 20,000 citizens. This act of brutal urban renewal, ironically, laid the ground open for new discoveries. When Marseille began to rebuild in 1947, they dug up remains of a Roman shipping warehouse full of the terra-cotta jars and amphorae that once lay in the bellies of low-slung ships. This museum, created around it all, demonstrates the scale of Massalia's shipping prowess. ✉ *2 pl. de Vivaux, Vieux Port* ☎ *04–91–91–24–62* 🎟 *€2* ⏲ *Oct.–May, Tues.–Sun. 10–5; June–mid-Sept., Tues.–Sun. 11–6.*

1 **Musée de la Marine et de l'Economie de Marseille** *(Marine and Economy Museum)*. This is one of the many museums here devoted to Marseille's history as a shipping port. Inaugurated by Napoléon III in 1860, this impressive building houses both the museum and the city's Chamber of Commerce. The front entrance and hallway are lined with medallions celebrating the ports of the world with which the city has traded, or trades still. The museum charts the maritime history of Marseille from the 17th century onward with paintings and engravings. It's a model-lover's dream, with hundreds of steamboats and schooners, all in miniature. ✉ *Palais de la Bourse, 7 La Canebière* ☎ *04–91–39–33–33* 🎟 *€2* ⏲ *Weekdays 10–6.*

2 **Musée de la Mode de Marseille** *(Marseille Fashion Museum)*. There are more than 3,000 outfits and accessories here, as well as ever-changing exhibitions about fashion, dating from the 1920s to the present. Thematic shows also highlight new and cutting-edge designers like Fred Sathel. ✉ *11 La Canebière La Canebière* ☎ *04–96–17–06–00* 🌐 *www.espacemodemediterranee.com* 🎫 *€2* ⏲ *June–Sept., Tues.–Sun. 11–6; Oct.–May, Tues.–Sun. 10–5.*

8 **Musée du Vieux Marseille** *(Museum of Old Marseille)*. This museum is found in the 16th-century **Maison Diamantée** *(Diamond House)*—so named for its diamond-faceted Renaissance facade—built in 1570 by a rich merchant. Focusing on the history of Marseille, the newly reopened, painstakingly renovated museum features santons, crèches, and furniture, offering a glimpse into 18th-century Marseille life. ✉ *Rue de la Prison, Vieux Port* ☎ *04–91–55–28–69* 🎫 *€2* ⏲ *June–Sept., Tues.–Sun. 10–6; Oct.–May, Tues.–Sun. 10–5.*

13 **Notre-Dame-de-la-Garde.** Towering above the city and visible for miles around, this preposterously overscaled neo-Byzantine monument was erected in 1853 by the ever-tasteful Napoléon III. Its interior is a Technicolor bonanza of red-and-beige stripes and glittering mosaics. The gargantuan *Madonna and Child* on the steeple (almost 30 feet high) is covered in real gold leaf. The boggling panoply of naive ex-votos, mostly thanking the Virgin for deathbed interventions and shipwreck survivals, makes the pilgrimage worth it. ✣ *On foot, climb up Cours Pierre Puget, cross Jardin Pierre Puget, cross bridge to Rue Vauvenargues, and hike up to Pl. Edon. Or catch Bus 60 from Cours Jean-Ballard* ☎ *04–91–13–40–80* ⏲ *May–Sept., daily 7 AM–8 PM; Oct.–Apr., daily 7–7.*

WHERE TO EAT

¢ PIZZA ✕ **Au Petit Naples.** With huge portions, a convivial atmosphere, and a small, busy beachfront location, this restaurant is jammed with locals and savvy tourists from every walk of life. Some connoisseurs say that the pizza here is even better than at Marseille's noted Étienne. ✉ *14 plage de l'Estaque L'Estaque* ☎ *04–91–46–05–11* 💳 *No credit cards* ⏲ *Closed Sun. No lunch Sat.*

$$$ SEAFOOD ✕ **Baie des Singes.** On a tiny rock-ringed lagoon as isolated from the nearby city as if it were a desert island, this cinematic corner of paradise was once a customs house under Napoléon III. You can rent a mattress and lounge chair, dive into the turquoise water, and shower off for the only kind of food worthy of such a locale: fresh fish. It's all served at terrace tables overlooking the water. ✉ *Anse des Croisettes, Les Goudes* ☎ *04–91–73–68–87* 💳 *MC, V* ⏲ *Closed Oct.–Mar.*

$$$ SEAFOOD ✕ **Chez Fonfon.** Tucked into the filmlike tiny fishing port Vallon des Auffes, this Marseillais landmark has one of the loveliest settings in greater Marseille. Once presided over by cult chef "Fonfon," it used to be a favorite movie-star hangout. A variety of fresh seafood, impeccably grilled, steamed, or roasted in salt crust are served in two pretty dining rooms with picture windows overlooking the fishing boats that supply your dinner. Try classic bouillabaisse served with all the bells and whistles—broth, hot-chili rouille, and flamboyant table-side filleting. ✉ *140 rue du Vallon des Auffes, Vallon des Auffes* ☎ *04–91–52–14–38*

www.chez-fonfon.com *Reservations essential* *AE, DC, MC, V* *Closed Sun. and 1st 2 wks in Jan. No lunch Mon.*

$ FRENCH **Étienne.** A historic Le Panier hole-in-the-wall, this small pizzeria is filled daily with politicos and young professionals who enjoy the personality of the chef Stéphane Cassero, who was famous at one time for having no printed menu and announcing the price of the meal only after he'd had the chance to look you over. Remarkably little has changed over the years, except now there is a posted menu (with prices). Brace yourself for an epic meal, starting with a large anchovy pizza from the wood-burning oven, then dig into fried squid, eggplant gratin, and a slab of rare grilled beef all served with a background of laughter, rich patois, and abuse from the chef. *43 rue de la Lorette, Le Panier* *No phone* *No credit cards.*

$$$$ SEAFOOD **L'Epuisette.** Artfully placed on a rocky, fingerlike jetty surrounded by the sea, this seafood restaurant offers gorgeous views of crashing surf on one side and the port of Vallon des Auffes on the other. Chef Guillaume Sourrieu has acquired a big reputation (and Michelin stars) for sophisticated cooking—shellfish risotto with violet and coriander fritter, or sea bass baked in a salt crust, are some top delights—all matched with a superb wine list. Save room for dessert—the chocolate brownie with bananas and pepper ice cream is amazing. *Anse du Vallon des Auffes, Vallon des Auffes* *04–91–52–17–82* *www.l-epuisette.com* *AE, MC, V* *Closed Sun. and Mon.*

$$$$ FRENCH **Le Restaurant Peron.** Chic and stylishly modern with its dark-wood interior and large windows overlooking the sea, this restaurant is a magnet for hip young professionals. The staff are efficient and friendly; meals are well presented and tasty, despite several recent changes in chefs—try the delicious bouillabaisse (€48 per person), the catch of the day (price by the weight), or a bargain prix-fixe price of €58 which includes three courses. Highly recommended is the fois gras with kumquat marmalade and the fresh scallops panfried with lime confit polenta. The view is one of the best in the city. *56 corniche J.-F.-Kennedy, Endoume* *04–91–52–15–22* *www.restaurant-peron.com* *AE, DC, MC, V.*

$$ FRENCH **Les Arcenaulx.** At this book-lined, red-wall haven in the stylish book-and-boutique complex of a renovated arsenal, you can have a sophisticated regional lunch—and read while you're waiting. Look for mussels in saffron with buckwheat crepes, carpaccio of cod coriander and tempura vegetables, or sardines with ginger. The terrace (on the Italian-scale Cours d'Estienne d'Orves) is as pleasant as the interior. *25 cours d'Estienne d'Orves, Vieux Port* *04–91–59–80–30* *www.les-arcenaulx.com* *AE, DC, MC, V* *Closed Sun. and 1 wk in Aug.*

$$$$ FRENCH **Mets de Provence.** Climb the oddly slanted wharf-side stairs and enter a cosseted Provençal world. With boats bobbing out the window and a landlubbing country decor, this romantic restaurant makes the most of Marseille's split personality. Classic Provençal hors d'oeuvres—tapenade, brandade, aioli—lead into seafood (sea bass roasted with fennel and licorice) and meats (rack of lamb in herb pastry). The four-course lunch (€40, including wine) is marvelous. *18 quai de Rive-Neuve, Vieux Port* *04–91–33–35–38* *MC, V* *Closed Sun. No lunch Sat. No dinner Mon.*

WHERE TO STAY

$ **Alizé.** On the Vieux Port, its front rooms taking in postcard views, this straightforward lodging has been modernized to include tight double-pane windows, slick modular baths, and a laminate-and-all-weather carpeted look. Public spaces have exposed stone and historic details, and a glass elevator whisks you to your floor. It's an excellent value and location for the price. **Pros:** ideal location on the waterfront gives access to all shops and sights to see. **Cons:** decor is badly in need of some tender love and care. ✉ *35 quai des Belges, Vieux Port* ☎ *04–91–33–66–97* 🌐 *www.alize-hotel.com* *39 rooms* *In-room: a/c, Wi-Fi. In-hotel: Wi-Fi hotspot, some pets allowed* 💳 *AE, DC, MC, V.*

$$$$ **Le Petit Nice.** On a rocky promontory overlooking the sea, this fantasy villa was bought from a countess in 1917 and converted to a hotel-restaurant. The Passédat family has been getting it right ever since, with father and son manning the exceptional kitchen (one of the coast's best), creating truffle brandade, sea-anemone beignets, fresh fish roasted whole, and licorice soufflé (the restaurant is closed Sunday and Monday in winter, and dinner-only Sunday and Monday in summer; prix-fixe menus are €110 and €139). Most rooms are sleek and minimalist, with some Art Deco–cum–postmodern touches, while outside the fetching heated pool is illuminated at night by antique gaslight fixtures. **Pros:** a true complete hotel experience, with lovely rooms, breathtaking views, and good service. **Cons:** some of the decor needs freshening up; pool is smaller than expected. ✉ *Anse de la Maldormé, Corniche J.-F.-Kennedy, Endoume* ☎ *04–91–59–25–92* 🌐 *www.petitnice-passedat.com* *13 rooms, 3 suites* *In-room: a/c, refrigerator. In-hotel: restaurant, pool, Wi-Fi hotspot, parking (free), some pets allowed* 💳 *AE, DC, MC, V* 🍽 *MAP.*

$$$–$$$$ **Mercure Grand Hotel Beauvau Vieux Port.** Chopin spent the night and George Sand kept a suite in this historic hotel overlooking the Vieux Port. Public rooms still have real antiques, burnished woodwork, Provençal-style decor, and plush carpets, all comprising a convincing part of this intimate urban hotel's genuine old-world charm. Guest rooms are in the same style but have been updated to include all the modern comforts. Harbor-view rooms, with balconies high over the fish market, more than justify the splurge and the duplex is particularly good for families. **Pros:** filled with special charm from years past, hotel is a historical landmark made new with modern amenities. **Cons:** service can be cool; some rooms are a bit dark. ✉ *4 rue Beauvau, Vieux Port* ☎ *04–91–54–91–00, 800/637–2873 for U.S. reservations* 🌐 *www.mercure.com* *70 rooms, 2 suites* *In-room: a/c, refrigerator. In-hotel: bar, Wi-Fi hotspot, some pets allowed* 💳 *AE, DC, MC, V.*

NIGHTLIFE AND THE ARTS

With a population of more than 800,000, Marseille is a big city by French standards, with all the nightlife that entails. Arm yourself with *Marseille Poche,* a glossy monthly events minimagazine; the monthly *In Situ,* a free guide to music, theater, and galleries; *Sortir,* a weekly about film, art, and concerts in southern Provence; or *TakTik,* a hip weekly on theater and art. They're all in French. Rock, jazz, and reggae concerts are held at the **Espace Julien** (✉ *39 cours Julien Préfecture*

From Cassis be sure to take an excursion boat to the Calanques, the rocky finger-coves washed by emerald and blue waters.

☎ *04–91–24–34–10*). **Le Trolleybus** (✉ *24 quai de Rive Neuve, Bompard* ☎ *04–91–54–30–45*) is the most popular disco in town, with a young, *branché* (hip) crowd. **Le Warm'Up** (✉ *8 blvd. Mireille Jourdan BarryPrado* ☎ *04–96–14–06–30*) is the newest super-club complex with everything from a booming sound system and heaving dance floor to an Oriental tearoom terrace. The **Red Lion** (✉ *231 av. Pierre Mendès France, Vieux Port* ☎ *04–91–25–17–17*) is a mecca for English speakers; they even pour onto the sidewalk, pints in hand, pub-style. There's happy hour daily (5 to 8) and live music Wednesday. **Le Moulin** (✉ *47 bd. Perrin, St-Just* ☎ *04–91–06–33–94*) is a converted cinema that has become one of Marseille's best live-music venues for visiting French and international music stars.

Classical music concerts are given in the **Abbaye St-Victor** (☎ *04–91–05–84–48 for information*). Operas and orchestral concerts are held at the **Opéra Municipal** (✉ *2 rue Molière, Vieux Port* ☎ *04–91–55–21–24*).

SHOPPING

Savon de Marseille (Marseille soap) is a household standard in France, often sold as a satisfyingly crude and hefty block in odorless olive-oil green. But its chichi offspring are dainty pastel guest soaps in almond, lemon, vanilla, and other scents.

The locally famous bakery **Four des Navettes** (✉ *136 rue Sainte, Garde Hill* ☎ *04–91–33–32–12*), up the street from Notre-Dame-de-la-Garde, makes orange-spice, shuttle-shape navettes. These cookies are modeled on the little boat in which Mary Magdalene and Lazarus washed up onto Europe's shores.

CASSIS

Fodor's Choice ★ *30 km (19 mi) southeast of Marseille, 42 km (26 mi) west of Toulon.*

Surrounded by vineyards and monumental cliffs, guarded by the ruins of a medieval castle, and nestled around a picture-perfect fishing port, Cassis is the prettiest coastal town in Provence. Way back in the 19th century, famed author Colette raved about this town. Today, many visitors still do the same.

Visitor Information Cassis Tourist Office ✉ *Quai des Moulins* ☎ *04–08–92–25–98–92* 🌐 *www.cassis.fr.*

EXPLORING

Stylish without being too recherché, Cassis is where pleasure-boaters come to spend the night, restock their galleys at its market, replenish their nautical duds in its boutiques, and relax with a bottle of cassis and a platter of sea urchins in one of its numerous waterfront cafés. Pastel houses set at Cubist angles frame the port, and the mild rash of parking-garage architecture that scars its outer neighborhoods doesn't spoil the general effect, one of pure and unadulterated charm. The **Château de Cassis** has loomed over the harbor since the invasions of the Saracens in the 7th century, evolving over the centuries into a walled enclosure crowned with stout watchtowers. It's private property today and best viewed from a port-side café.

From Cassis, head east out of town and cut sharply right up the **Route des Crêtes.** This road takes you along a magnificent crest over the water and up to the very top of **Cap Canaille.** Venture out on the vertiginous trails to the edge, where the whole coast stretches below.

You can't visit Cassis without touring the **calanques,** the fjordlike finger bays that probe the rocky coastline. Either take a sightseeing cruise or hike across the cliff tops, clambering down the steep sides to these barely accessible retreats. Or you can combine the two, going in by boat and hiking back; make arrangements at the port. The calanque closest to Cassis is the least attractive: **Port Miou** was a stone quarry until 1982, when the calanques became protected sites. Now this calanque is an active leisure and fishing port. **Calanque Port Pin** is prettier, with wind-twisted pines growing at angles from the white-rock cliffs. But ★ it's the third calanque that's the showstopper: the **Calanque En Vau** is a castaway's dream, with a tiny beach at its root and jagged cliffs looming overhead. The series of massive cliffs and calanques stretches all the way to Marseille. Note that boats make round-trips several times a day to the Calanques de Cassis from Marseille's Quai des Belges. Here, boat tours to the Calanques are organized by the **Groupement des Armateurs Côtiers Marseillais** (✉ *1 quai des Belges, Marseille* ☎ *04–91–55–50–09* 🌐 *www.answeb.net/gacm*) and a four-hour round-trip will cost around Û25; otherwise, contact the tourism office and they will give the right numbers to call, or they will help you organize a tour.

WHERE TO EAT AND STAY

$$$ SEAFOOD ✕ **Chez Nino.** This is the best of the many restaurants lining the harbor, with top-notch Provençal food and wine and a spectacular terrace view. The owners, Claudie and Bruno, are extremely hospitable as long as

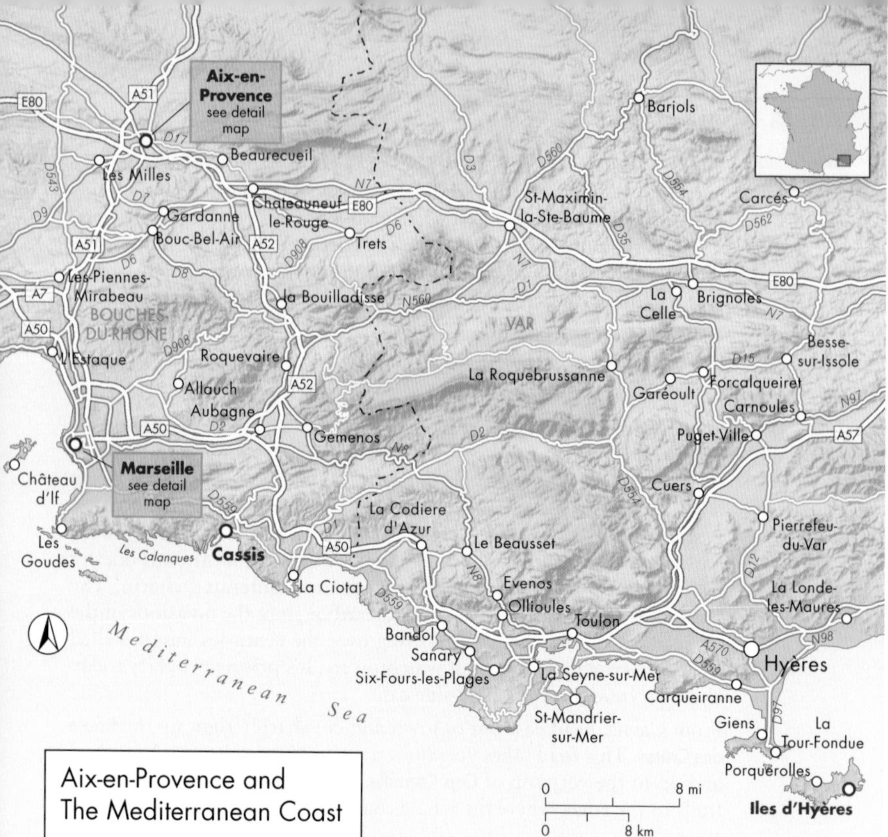

you stick to the menu—don't ask for sauce on the side—and you're as passionate about fish and seafood as they are. The sardines in *escabeche* are textbook perfect, as are the grilled fish and the bouillabaisse. And if you want to indulge, there are now two suites (€700) and one room (€300) available for the night, beautifully decorated with views of the sea. ✉ *2 quai Barthélémy* ☎ *04–42–01–74–32* 🌐 *www.nino-cassis.com* 💳 *AE, DC, MC, V* ⊙ *Closed Mon. No dinner Sun. off-season.*

$$ 🏨 **Les Roches Blanches.** First built as a private home in 1887, this cliff-side villa takes in smashing views of the port and the Cap Canaille, both from the best rooms and from the panoramic dining hall. The beautifully landscaped terrace is shaded by massive pines, and the horizon pool appears to spill into the sea. Yet the aura is far from snooty or deluxe; it's friendly, low-key, and pleasantly mainstream. **Pros:** sweeping vistas are captivating; service is quick and friendly. **Cons:** even if views are inspired, the food is not. ✉ *Rte. des Calanques* ☎ *04–42–01–09–30* 🌐 *www.roches-blanches-cassis.com* *19 rooms, 5 suites* *In-room: a/c, refrigerator. In-hotel: 2 restaurants, bar, pool, Wi-Fi hotspot, parking (paid), some pets allowed* 💳 *AE, MC, V* ⊙ *Closed Nov.–Mar.* 🍽 *MAP.*

SPORTS AND THE OUTDOORS

To go on a **boat ride** to Les Calanques, get to the port around 10 AM or 2 PM and look for a boat that's loading passengers. Round-trips should include visits to at least three calanques and average €25. To **hike** the calanques, gauge your skills: the GR98 (marked with red-and-white bands) is the most scenic, but requires scrambling to get down the sheer walls of En Vau. The alternative is to follow the green markers and approach En Vau from behind. If you're ambitious, you can hike the length of the GR98 between Marseille and Cassis, following the coastline.

ILES D'HYÈRES

32 km (20 mi) off coast south of Hyères. To get to islands, follow narrow Giens Peninsula to La Tour-Fondue, at its tip. Boats (leaving every half-hr in summer, every 60 or 90 mins rest of year, for €15 round-trip) make a 20-min beeline to Porquerolles. For Port-Cros and Levant, depart from Port d'Hyères at Hyères-Plages.

Off the southeastern point of France's star and spanning some 32 km (20 mi), this archipelago of islands could be a set for a pirate movie; in fact, it has been featured in several, thanks to a soothing microclimate and a wild and rocky coastline dotted with palms. And not only film pirates made their appearance: in the 16th century the islands were seeded with convicts to work the land. They soon ran amok and used their adopted base to ambush ships heading into Toulon. A more wholesome population claims the islands today, which are made up of three main areas. **Port-Cros** is a national park, with both its surface and underwater environs protected. **Levant** has been taken over, for the most part, by nudists.

★ **Porquerolles** is the largest and best of the lot—and a popular escape from the modern world. Off-season, it's a castaway delight of pine forests, sandy beaches, and vertiginous cliffs above rocky coastline. Inland, its preserved pine forests and orchards of olives and figs are crisscrossed with dirt roads to be explored on foot or on bikes; except for the occasional jeep or work truck, the island is car-free. In high season (April to October), day-trippers pour off the ferries and surge to the beaches. For information on the islands, contact the tourism office of Hyères.

WHERE TO EAT AND STAY

$–$$ **Les Glycines.** In soft shades of yellow-ocher and sky-blue, this sleekly modernized little bastide has an idyllic enclosed courtyard. Back rooms look over a jungle of mimosa and eucalyptus. Public salons have Provençal chairs and fabrics. The restaurant, where food is served on the terrace or in the garden, proffers port-fresh tuna and sardines. The inn is just back from the port in the village center. Prices include breakfast and dinner. **Pros:** quiet and simply elegant, this little hotel is a gem on an island paradise. **Cons:** some rooms are small; beds are creaky. ✉ *Pl. d'Armes, Ile de Porquerolles* ☎ *04–94–58–30–36* 🌐 *www.auberge-glycines.com* *8 rooms, 3 suites* *In-room: a/c, Wi-Fi. In-hotel: restaurant, bar* *AE, MC, V* *MAP.*

$$$–$$$$ **Mas du Langoustier.** A fabled forgetaway, the Langoustier comes with a lobster-orange building, pink bougainvillea, and a secluded spot at the westernmost point of the Ile de Porquerolles, 3 km (2 mi) from the harbor. Manager Madame Richard—who may pick you up at the port in her Dodge—knows a thing or two about the island: her grandmother was given the island as a wedding gift. Choose between big California-modern rooms and charming old-style Provençal. Chef Joël Guillet creates inspired, spectacular southern French cuisine, to be accompanied by the rare island rosé (note that prices include breakfast and dinner). **Pros:** a bastion of taste and culinary pleasure, there are few places that can so completely meet the critics' criteria, as this one does. **Cons:** a hike to get here; a bit pricey. ✉ *Pointe du Langoustier, Ile de Porquerolles* ☎ *04–94–58–30–09* 🌐 *www.langoustier.com* *45 rooms, 4 suites, 1 apartment* *In-room: a/c, refrigerator. In-hotel: restaurant, tennis court, pool, beachfront, Wi-Fi hotspot* *DC, MC, V* *Closed Nov.–Apr.* *MAP.*

The French Riviera

WORD OF MOUTH

"Now this is a vacation spot! While on a Mediterranean cruise, this was my favorite view from our balcony room. What a way to wake up in the morning on the French Riviera!"

—mkinct, Fodors.com member, on the above photo

"Eze is in the hills above Monaco, and IMO is the best hill town on the Riviera. The views are outstanding."

—TPAYT

WELCOME TO THE FRENCH RIVIERA

TOP REASONS TO GO

★ **Monaco, Toy Kingdom:** Yes, Virginia, you can afford to visit Monte Carlo—that is, if you avoid its casinos and head for its tropical gardens.

★ **Picasso and Company:** Because artists have long loved the Côte d'Azur, it's blessed with superb art museums, including the Fondation Maeght in St-Paul and the Musée Picasso in Antibes.

★ **Èze, Island in the Sky:** The most perfectly perched of the coast's villages perchés, Èze has some of the most breathtaking views this side of a NASA space capsule.

★ **St-Tropez à Go-Go:** Brave the world's most outlandish fishing port in high summer and soak up the scene. Just don't forget the fake tan lotion.

★ **Nice, Queen of the Riviera:** With its bonbon-color palaces, blue Baie des Anges, time-stained Old Town, and Musée Matisse, this is one of France's most colorful cities.

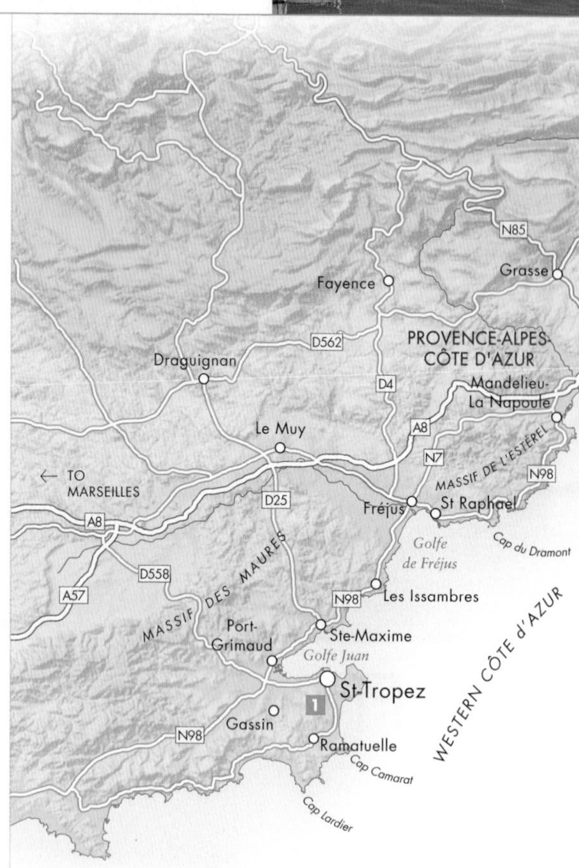

1 St-Tropez to Antibes. Put on the map by Brigitte Bardot, St-Tropez remains one of France's ritziest vacation spots. Happily, the town has managed to stay small and laid-back, thanks to the lack of train service and chain hotels. Conspicuous consumption characterizes the celluloid city of Cannes when its May film fest turns it into Oscar-goes-to-the-Mediterranean but the Louis Vuitton set enjoys this city year-round. For the utmost in Riviera charm, head up the coast to Antibes: once Picasso's home, it's set with a harbor and Old Town so dreamy it will have you reaching for your paintbrush.

2 The Hill Towns. High in the hills overlooking Nice are the medieval walled villages of St-Paul-de-Vence and Vence, invaded by waves of artists in the 20th century. Today, you can hardly turn around without bumping into a Calder mobile, and top sights include the famous inn La Colombe d'Or, Matisse's sublime Chapelle du Rosaire, and the Fondation Maeght—probably the best museum this side of the Louvre.

3 Nice. Walking along the seaside Promenade des Anglais is one of the iconic Riviera experiences. Add in top-notch museums, a charming old quarter, scads of ethnic restaurants, and a raging nightlife, and Nice is a must-do.

4 The Eastern Côte d'Azur. The 24-karat sun shines most brightly on the fabled glamour ports of Villefranche-sur-Mer and St-Jean-Cap-Ferrat. If you want to kiss the sky, head up to the charming, mountaintop village of Èze. To the east of glittering Monaco—looking more like Manhattan every day—lies Menton, an enchanting Italianate resort where winters are so mild that lemon trees bloom in January.

GETTING ORIENTED

The French Riviera can supply the visitor with everything his heart desires—and his purse can stand. Home to sophisticated resorts beloved by billionaires, remote hill villages colonized by artists, Mediterranean beaches, and magnificent views, the Côte d'Azur (to use the French name) stretches from Marseille to Menton. Thrust out like two gigantic arms, divided by the Valley of the Var at Nice, the Alpes-Maritimes peaks throw their massive protection, east and west, the length of that favored coast from St-Tropez to the Italian frontier.

FRENCH RIVIERA PLANNER

When to Go

Unless you enjoy jacked-up prices, traffic jams, and sardine-style beach crowds, avoid the coast like the plague in July and August. Many of the better restaurants simply shut down to avoid the coconut-oil crowd, and the Estérel, the rocky hillside that overlooks the Mediterranean, is closed to hikers during this flash-fire season.

Cannes books up early for the film festival in May, so aim for another month (April, June, September, or October). Between Cannes and Menton, the Côte d'Azur's gentle microclimate usually provides moderate winters; it's protected by the Estérel from the mistral wind that razors through places like Fréjus and St-Raphaèl.

Sexy south of France may be reputed for many steamy things, but it's not at all humid. It is, in fact, hot and dry for most of the year. Recent high-season temperatures have gone up to 105° F, while spring and fall still see highs of 68°F. Summer wear usually boils down to a bikini and light wrap.

Rainfall between March and October cools things off. According to the locals, winter (November–early March) is cold, rainy, miserable—which may be relative, as the area's famous for having more than 340 days of sunshine per year.

Getting Around

The less budget-conscious can consider jetting around by helicopter (heliports in Monaco, Nice, Cannes, St-Tropez, and some of the hill towns) or speedboat (access to all resort towns), but affordable public transport along the Riviera translates to the train, the bus, or renting a car. The train accesses all major coastal towns, and most of the *gares* (train stations) are in town centers. Note that only a handful of hill towns have train stations. The bus network between towns is fantastic. Renting a car is a good option, and the network of roads here is well marked and divided nicely into slow and very curvy (Bord de Mer Coast Road), faster and curvy (Route National 98), and fast and almost straight (Autoroute A8). Make sure you leave extra time if you're driving or taking the bus, as traffic is always heavy.

Making the Most of Your Time

If you're settling into one town and making day trips, it's best to divide your time by visiting west and then east of Nice. Parallel roads along the Corniches allow for access into towns with different personalities.

The A8 main *autoroute* (keep spare change at the ready, as there's a toll to use different parts of this road—€2.60 between Cannes and Nice, for example) makes zipping up and down from Monaco to Fréjus-St-Raphael a breeze. The coastal train is equally efficient.

Visit different resort towns, but make sure you tear yourself away from the coastal *plages* (beaches) to visit the perched villages that the region is famed for. Venture farther north to reach these villages, east or west, either by the Route Napoléon (RN 98), the D995, or on the Corniche roads, and plan on at least one overnight.

Food plays a crucial role here, and some of the best restaurants aren't so easy to access; make sure to include taxi money in your budget to get to some of the more remote restaurants, or plan on renting a car. Try to come in truffle, lavender, or olive season.

Eating and Staying

It's up in the hills above the coast that you'll find the charm you expect from France, both in sophisticated hotels with gastronomic restaurants and in friendly mom-and-pop auberges (inns); the farther north you drive, the lower the prices.

Even in tiny villages some haute cuisine places can be as dressy as those in Monaco, if not more so, but in general, restaurants on the Côte d'Azur are quite relaxed.

At lunchtime, a T-shirt and shorts are just fine in all but the fanciest places; bathing suits, however, should be kept for the beach.

Nighttime wear is casual, too—but be aware that for after-dinner drinks, many clubs and discos draw the line at running shoes and jeans.

Certain areas of the Riviera book up faster than others, but all hit overload from June to September.

It's essential to book in advance; up to half a year for the summer season is not unheard of, and is, in fact, much appreciated.

Festivals and good weather will also affect your chances. If you arrive without a reservation, try the tourist information centers, which can usually be of help.

Smaller villages often have tiny, charming hotels or bed-and-breakfasts, which translates to fewer than 10 rooms, and which also means they fill up fast, even out of season in some places.

If you're really out of luck, don't try sleeping on the beach; as romantic as it sounds, it is not tolerated and strictly controlled.

Worst-case scenario is a string of cheap motels on the outskirts of most major city centers, which cost €25–€65.

DINING AND LODGING PRICE CATEGORIES (IN EUROS)

	¢	$	$$	$$$	$$$$
Restaurants	Under €13	€13–€17	€18–€24	€25–€32	Over €32
Hotels	Under €65	€65–€105	€106–€145	€146–€215	Over €215

Restaurant prices are per person for a main course at dinner, including tax (5.5%) and service; note that if a restaurant offers only prix-fixe (set-price) meals, it has been given the price category that reflects the full prix-fixe price. Hotel prices are for a standard double room in high season, including tax (19.6%) and service charge.

Riviera Festivals

Every month of the year there's a festival somewhere on the Riviera, catering to all manner of tastes and pastimes. The queen of all festivals is of course the International Film Festival in Cannes, where all the stars of today and yesterday play for 10 jam-packed days in May, but there's every other type of festival imaginable, too. To give you a small taste: in May there's the Monaco Grand Prix; in June there's the Advertising festival in Cannes, as well as both the Nice and Juan-les-Pins jazz festivals; in July, the lavender festivals; in August, the fireworks festivals; in February, the Fête du Citron *(Citrus festival)* in Menton, and Carnival in Nice. Check with the local tourism office to see what's happening during your stay. Information is also available online at *www.cr-paca.fr*. Tickets can be bought at local tourist offices, FNAC branches (*www.fnac.fr*), or through agencies like France Billet (*08–92–69–26–94* *www.francebillet.com*) or Globaltickets (*01–42–81–88–98* *www.globaltickets.com*).

12

GETTING AROUND

Air Travel

Nice is the main point of entry into the French Riviera region. It's home to the second-largest airport in France, which sits on a peninsula between Antibes and Nice, the Aéroport Nice-Côte d'Azur (☎ *08–20–42–33–33* 🌐 *www.nice.aeroport.fr*), which is 7 km (4 mi) south of the city.

French Riviera Tour Options

Bus Tours: Santa Azur (✉ *11 av. Jean-Médecin* ☎ *04–93–85–46–81*) organizes all-day or half-day bus excursions to sights near Nice, including Monaco, Cannes, and nearby hill towns, either leaving from its offices or from several stops along the Promenade des Anglais, mainly in front of the big hotels.

In Antibes, Phocéens Voyages (✉ *8 pl. de Gaulle* ☎ *04–93–34–15–98*) organizes similar bus explorations of the region.

Private Tours: The city of Nice arranges individual guided tours on an à la carte basis according to your needs. For information contact the Bureau d'Accueil (☎ *04–93–14–48–00*) and specify your dates and language preferences.

Bus Travel

Note that the quickest way to get around by public transportation is the great coastal train line that connects the main cities and a lot of villages from Cannes to Menton, but if you want to explore more remote villages, you can take a bus out of Cannes, Nice, Antibes, or Menton. Rapides Côte d'Azur (☎ *04–93–85–64–44* 🌐 *www.rca.tm.fr*) runs Bus No. 100, which departs every 15 minutes, €1 one way (between 6 AM and 8 PM) making stops from Nice to Menton. For the villages on the Moyenne Corniche, take Bus No. 112, which departs from Nice six times a day (three times on Sunday). Ligne Azur (🌐 *www.lignedazur.com*) runs buses to 24 different communes in the Alpes Maritimes for the bargain price of €1 one way (except the express Nice airport bus 99 or 98, which costs €4). You can catch one from the Antibes bus station by Rue de la République, connecting with Nice (express bus every half hour, regular bus every 20 minutes), Cagnes-sur-Mer (20 mins), Biot (25 mins), and Cannes (30 mins). You can also take a bus from Antibes to Vallauris (every 30 mins). The new Envibus line (☎ 04–89–87–72–00 🌐 www.envibus.fr), which originates in Antibes, covers Antibes, Biot, and heads into the hills. The €2 pass is good for 2 hours and 40 minutes of travel time. Cagnes-sur-Mer is one of the coastal towns served by train, but you can easily connect with nearby St-Paul-de-Vence and Vence using Bus. No. 400, with departures every 30 minutes from Cagnes Ville's bus station on Place du Général de Gaulle. St-Tropez's Gare Routière is on Avenue du Général de Gaulle and has bus routes run by Sodetrav (☎ *0825/000–650* 🌐 *www.sodetrav.fr*) to and from to St-Raphaël (1½ hrs, 10 daily, €9), the town with the nearest railway station, with stops in Port Grimaud and Fréjus (1 hr, €9). In high season traffic can lead to two-plus-hour bus rides, so if you arrive in St-Raphaël, it may be best to hop on the shuttle boats that connect the two ports. In Monaco, CAM (☎ *377/97–70–22–22* 🌐 *www.cam.mc*) runs six bus lines with service throughout the principality and to Eze and Beaulieu. You can purchase the €1 ticket or €3 all-day pass from the driver or at the main station on 3 av. du President J.F. Kennedy. CAM's bateau (boat) bus (€1) crosses the port 8 AM–8 PM and connects with their bus line.

12

Car Travel

The best way to explore the secondary sights in this region is by car. It also allows you the freedom to zip along A8 between the coastal resorts and to enjoy the views from the three corniches that trace the coast from Nice to the Italian border. N98, which connects you to coastal resorts in between, can be slow, though scenic. A8 parallels the coast from above St-Tropez to Nice to the resorts on the Grand Corniche; N98 follows the coast more closely. From Paris the main southbound artery is A6/A7, known as the Autoroute du Soleil; it passes through Provence and joins the eastbound A8 at Aix-en-Provence.

Train Travel

Nice is the rail crossroads for trains arriving from Paris and other northern cities and from Italy, too. To get from Paris to Nice (with stops along the coast), you can take the TGV (☎ *877/284–8633* 🌐 *www.tgv.com*), though it only maintains high speeds to Valence. Night trains arrive at Nice in the morning from Paris, Metz, and Strasbourg.

You can easily move along the coast between Cannes, Nice, and Ventimiglia by train on the slick double-decker Côte d'Azur line, a dramatic and highly tourist-pleasing branch of the SNCF (☎ *08–92–68–82–66 [€0.34 per min]* 🌐 *www.voyages-sncf.com*) that offers panoramic views as it rolls from one famous resort to the next, with more than two dozen trains running a day. This line is also called Marseille–Vintimille (Ventimiglia, in Italy) heading east to Italy and Vintimille–Marseille in the west direction. Some main stops on this line are: Antibes (every 30 mins, €4), Cannes (40 mins, €6), Menton (30 mins, €4), and Monaco (25 mins, €3); other stops include Villefranche-sur-Mer, Beaulieu, Cap-Martin, St-Jean-Cap-Ferrat, and Èze-sur-Mer. However, to reach St-Paul, Vence, Peillon, and other back-country villages, you must take a bus or car.

As for the western parts of the French Riviera, catch trains at Fréjus's main station on Rue Martin-Bidoure and St-Raphaël's Gare de St-Raphaël on Rue Waldeck-Rousseau, where the rail route begins its scenic crawl along the coast. St-Raphaël is the main hub on the line between Menton and Marseille (it's about 2 hrs from the latter by rail, with hourly trains costing €20). The resort port of Mandelieu-La Napoule is on the main rail line between St-Raphaël and Cannes. There's no rail access to St-Tropez; St-Raphaël and Fréjus are the nearest stops.

Boat Travel

Considering the congestion on the road to St-Tropez, the best way to get to that resort is to train to St-Raphaël, then hop on one of the four boats each day (Apr.–Oct.) that leave from Gare Maritime de St-Raphaël on Rue Pierre-Auble. The trip takes an hour (€9). Transports Maritimes MMG (✉ *Quai L.-Condroyer, Ste-Maxime* ☎ *04–94–96–51–00*) also offers a shuttle boat linking St-Tropez and Ste-Maxime (Apr.–Oct.; €6) and the ride is a half-hour. Once in St-Tropez, do the one-hour boat ride tour offered by MMG of the Baie des Cannebiers (nicknamed the "Bay of Stars") to see some celebrity villas.

Bus and Train Info

Cannes Gare Routière ✉ *Pl. Bernard Cornut Gentille*

Menton Gare Routière ✉ *12 promenade Maréchal Leclerc*

Nice Gare Routière ✉ *5 bd. Jean Jaurès*

Compagnie des Autobus de Monaco 🌐 *wwww.cam.mc*

Phocéens Santa Azur (Voyages) ☎ *04–93–13–18–20*

Rapides Côte d'Azur 🌐 *www.rca.tm.fr*

Société des Cars Alpes-Littoral ☎ *04–92–51–06–05*

Transports Alpes-Maritimes (TAM) 🌐 *www.lignedazur.com*

Updated by Sarah Fraser

You may build castles in Spain or picture yourself on a South Sea island, but when it comes to serious speculation about how to spend that first $10 million and slip easily into the life of the idle rich, most people head for the French Riviera—or, to use the French term for the region, the Côte d'Azur.

This is where the dreamland of azure waters and indigo sky begins, where balustraded white villas edge the blue horizon, the evening air is perfumed with jasmine, and parasol pines are silhouetted against sunsets of ripe apricot. As emblematic as the sheet-music cover for a Jazz Age tune, the French Riviera seems to epitomize happiness, a state of being the world pursues with a vengeance.

But the Jazz Age dream confronts modern reality: on the hills that undulate along the blue water, every cliff bristles with cubes of hot-pink cement and balconies of ironwork, each skewed to catch a glimpse of the sea and the sun. Like a rosy rash, these crawl and spread, outnumbering the trees and blocking each other's views. But the Côte d'Azur (or Azure Coast) has always been exceedingly popular, starting with the ancient Greeks, who were drawn eastward from Marseille to market their goods to the natives. From the 18th-century English aristocrats who claimed it as one vast spa, to the 19th-century Russian nobles who transformed Nice into a tropical St. Petersburg, to the 20th-century American tycoons who cast themselves as romantic sheiks, the beckoning coast became a blank slate for their whims. Like the modern vacationers who followed, they all left their mark—villas, shrines, Moroccan-fantasy castles-in-the-air—temples all to the sensual pleasures of the sun and the sultry sea breezes. Artists, too, made the French Riviera their own, as museumgoers who have studied the sunny legacy of Picasso, Renoir, Matisse, and Chagall will attest.

Today's admirers can take this all in, along with the Riviera's textbook points of interest: animated St-Tropez; the Belle Époque aura of Cannes; the towns made famous by Picasso—Antibes, Vallauris, Mougins; the urban charms of Nice; and a number of spots where the per-capita population of billionaires must be among the highest on the planet: Cap d'Antibes, Villefranche-sur-Mer, and Monaco. The latter, once a Belle Époque fairyland, now has enough skyscrapers to earn it the nickname of the Hong Kong of the Riviera The ghosts of Grace Kelly and Cary Grant must have long since gone elsewhere.

But with just a little luck and a bus ride or two, you can find towns and villages far from the madding crowd, especially if you head to the low-lying mountains known as the *arriére-pays* (backcountry). Here, medieval stone villages cap rocky hills and play out scenes of Provençal life,with games of boules andslowly savored drinks of pastis (the anise-and-licorice-flavor spirit). Some of them—Èze, St-Paul, Vence—may have become virtual Provençal theme parks but even so you'll probably find a gorgeous and deserted Riviera alleyway hidden in one of their cobblestone mazes.

THE WESTERN FRENCH RIVIERA

Flanked at each end by subtropical capes and crowned by the red-rock Estérel, this stretch of the coast has a variety of waterfront landmarks. St-Tropez first blazed into fame when it was discovered by painters like Paul Signac and writers like Colette, and since then it has never looked back. It remains one of the most animated stretches of territory on the French Riviera, getting flooded at high season with people who like to roost at waterfront cafés to take in the passing parade. St-Tropez vies with Cannes for name recognition and glamour, but the more modest resorts—Ste-Maxime, Fréjus, and St-Raphaël—offer a more affordable Riviera experience. Historic Antibes and jazzy Juan-les-Pins straddle the subtropical peninsula of Cap d'Antibes.

ST-TROPEZ

35 km (22 mi) southwest of Fréjus, 66 km (41 mi) northeast of Toulon.

At first glance, St-Tropez really doesn't look all that lovely: there's a moderately pretty port full of bobbing boats, a picturesque Vieille Ville *(Old Town)* in candied-almond hues, sandy beaches, and old-fashioned squares with plane trees and *pétanque* (lawn bowling) players. So what made St-Tropez a household name? In two words: Brigitte Bardot. When this *pulpeuse* (voluptuous) teenager showed up in St-Tropez on the arm of the late Roger Vadim in 1956 to film *And God Created Woman,* the world snapped to attention. Neither the gentle descriptions of writer Guy de Maupassant (1850–93) nor the watercolor tones of Impressionist Paul Signac (1863–1935), nor even the stream of painters who followed him (including Matisse and Bonnard), could focus the world's attention on this seaside hamlet as could this one luscious female, in head scarf, Ray-Bans, and capri pants. With the film world following in her steps, St-Tropez became the hot spot it—to some extent—remains.

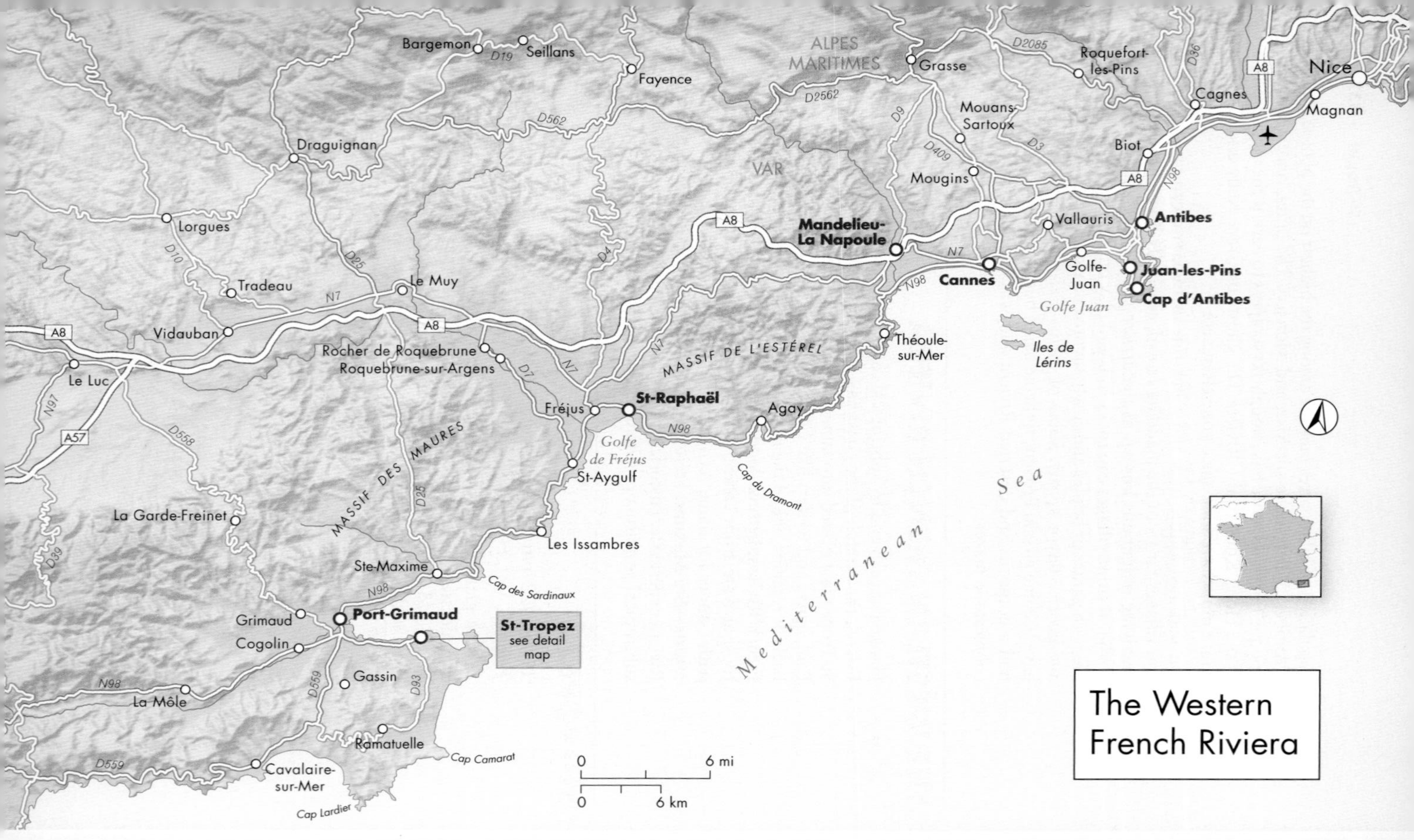

The Western French Riviera
Nice
Magnan
Cagnes
Roquefort-les-Pins
Biot
Antibes
Juan-les-Pins
Cap d'Antibes
Golfe-Juan
Golfe Juan
Vallauris
Iles de Lérins
Cannes
Mougins
Mouans-Sartoux
Grasse
ALPES MARITIMES
VAR
Mandelieu-La Napoule
Théoule-sur-Mer
MASSIF DE L'ESTÉREL
Agay
Cap du Dramont
St-Raphaël
Fréjus
Golfe de Fréjus
St-Aygulf
Les Issambres
Cap des Sardinaux
Ste-Maxime
Port-Grimaud
St-Tropez see detail map
Grimaud
Cogolin
Gassin
Ramatuelle
Cap Camarat
Cavalaire-sur-Mer
Cap Lardier
La Môle
La Garde-Freinet
MASSIF DES MAURES
Rocher de Roquebrune
Roquebrune-sur-Argens
Le Muy
Tradeau
Vidauban
Le Luc
Lorgues
Draguignan
Bargemon
Seillans
Fayence
Mediterranean Sea
A8
A57
N7
N97
N98
D3
D4
D7
D9
D10
D19
D25
D36
D39
D409
D558
D559
D562
D2085
D2562
0
6 mi
0
6 km

GETTING HERE

You can only get to St-Trop by car, bus, or boat (from nearby ports like St-Raphaël). If you decide to drive, take the N98 coast road (the longest route but also the prettiest, with great picnic stops along the way). Note that the Parking du Port parking lot (opposite the bus station on Avenue du Général de Gaulle, with shuttle bus into town mid-March to October) and the Parc des Lices (beneath the Place des Lices) in the center of town are a staggering €5 an hour in peak season. A train-bus connection can be made from Nice; the train runs to St-Raphaël, where you can take a bus on to St-Tropez. Total travel time is 1½ hours. The other option is to take a boat from the Nice harbor with Trans Côte d'Azur (☎ *04–92–00–42–30* 🌐 *www.trans-cote-azur.com*), which has daily trips from June to September.

Visitor Information St-Tropez Tourist Office ✉ *Quai Jean-Jaurès, B. P. 183* ☎ *04–94–97–45–21* 🌐 *www.ot-saint-tropez.com.*

EXPLORING

Anything associated with the distant past seems almost absurd in St-Tropez. Still, the place has a history that predates the invention of the string bikini, and people have been finding reasons to come here since AD 68, when a Roman soldier from Pisa named Torpes was beheaded for professing his Christian faith in front of Emperor Nero, transforming this spot into a place of pilgrimage.

Since then people have come for the sun, the sea, and, more recently, the celebrities. The latter—ever since St-Tropez became "hot" again, there have been Elton, Barbra, Oprah, Jack, and Uma sightings—stay hidden in villas, so the people you'll see are mere mortals, lots of them, many intent on displaying the best, and often the most, of their youth, beauty, and wealth.

Get up early (before the 11 AM breakfast rush at Le Gorille Café and other port-side spots lining Quai Suffern and Quai Jean-Jaurès) and wander the narrow medieval backstreets and waterfront by yourself—the rest of the town will still be sleeping off the Night Before. At this hour, you can experience what the artists found to love: its soft light, warm pastels, and the scent of the sea wafting in from the waterfront. Later, when you're tired, you can sit under a colored awning at a cute café and watch the spectacle that is St-Trop (*trop* in French means "too much") saunter by.

Start your St-Trop tour at the *nouveau bassin* (new harbor) for private pleasure boats. There's a large parking lot and the bus station here. With the sea on your left, walk around to the Vieux Port (old harbor), enjoying the life of the quays and the views around the bay as you go.

4 **Citadelle.** Head up Rue de la Citadelle to these 16th-century ramparts, which stand in a lovely hilltop park offering a fantastic view of the town and the sea. Although it's hard to imagine St-Tropez as a military outpost amid today's bikini-clad sun worshippers, inside the Citadelle's donjon the **Musée Naval** *(Naval Museum)* displays ship models, cannons, maps, and pictures of St-Tropez from its days as a naval port. At this writing the museum was closed for renovations, expected to reopen in late 2011. It's likely that the theme of the museum will change, but

until that decision is made you can still see some of the navy models in the Citadelle, as well as a series of temporary art exhibitions. ✉ *Rue de la Citadelle* ☎ *04–94–97–59–43* 🎟 *Citadelle €2.50* ⏲ *Oct.–Mar., daily 10–noon and 1:30–5; Apr.–Sept., daily 10–12:30 and 1–6:30.*

❷ ★ **Musée de l'Annonciade** *(Annunciation Museum).* Just inland from the southwest corner of the Vieux Port stands this extraordinary museum, where the legacy of the artists who loved St-Tropez has been lovingly preserved. This 14th-century chapel, converted to an art museum, alone merits a visit to St-Tropez. Cutting-edge temporary exhibitions keep visitors on their toes while works stretching from Pointillists to Fauves to Cubists line the walls of the permanent collection. Signac, Matisse, Signard, Braque, Dufy, Vuillard, Rouault: many of them painted in (and about) St-Tropez, tracing the evolution of painting from Impressionism to Expressionism. The museum also hosts temporary exhibitions every summer, from local talent to up-and-coming international artists like Georges Rouault, whose specialty is landscapes. ✉ *Quai de l'Épi/Pl., Georges Grammont* ☎ *04–94–17–84–10* 🎟 *€5* ⏲ *June–Sept., Wed.–Mon. 10–1 and 3–7; Oct. and Dec.–May, Wed.–Mon. 10–noon and 2–6.*

❺ **Place des Lices.** Also called the Place Carnot, you'll find this social center of the Old Town as you descend from the Citadelle using the Montée G.-Ringrave. Here, you can hear pétanque balls—a southern version of boules—clicking in the sand square. The square's symmetrical forest of plane trees (what's left of them) provides shade to rows of cafés and restaurants, skateboarders, children, and the grandfatherly pétanque players. Enjoy a time-out in the town "living room"—Le Café (not to be confused with the nearby Café des Arts). The square becomes a moveable feast (for both eyes and palate) on market days—Tuesday and Saturday—while at night a café seat is as hotly contested as a quayside seat during the day. Just as Deborah Kerr and David Niven once did in *Bonjour Tristesse,* watch the boule players under the glow of hundreds of electric bulbs. Heading back to the Vieux Port area, take in the boutiques lining Rues Sibilli, Clemenceau, or Gambetta to help accessorize your evening look—you never know when that photographer from *Elle* will be snapping away at the trendoisie.

❸ **Quartier de la Ponche.** This old town maze of backstreets and ramparts is daubed in shades of gold, pink, ocher, and sky-blue. Trellised jasmine and wrought-iron birdcages hang from the shuttered windows, and many of the tiny streets dead-end at the sea. Here you can find the **Port des Pécheurs** *(Fishermen's Port),* on whose beach Bardot did a star-turn in *And God Created Woman.* Twisting, narrow streets, designed to break the impact of the mistral, open to tiny squares with fountains. The main drag here, Rue de la Ponche, leads into Place l'Hôtel de Ville, landmarked by a **mairie** (town hall) marked out in typical Tropezienne hues of pink and green.

❶ **Vieux Port.** Bordered by Quai de l'Épi, Quai Bouchard, Quai Peri, Quai Suffren, and Quai Jean-Jaurès, Vieux Port is the nerve center of this famous yachting spot, a place for strolling and looking over the shoulders of artists daubing their versions of the view on easels set up along

Citadelle 4
Musée de l'Annonciade 2
Place des Lices ..5
Quartier de la Ponche 3
Vieux Port 1

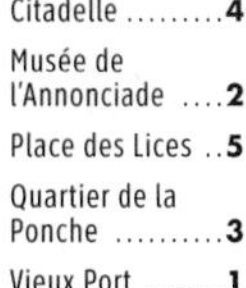

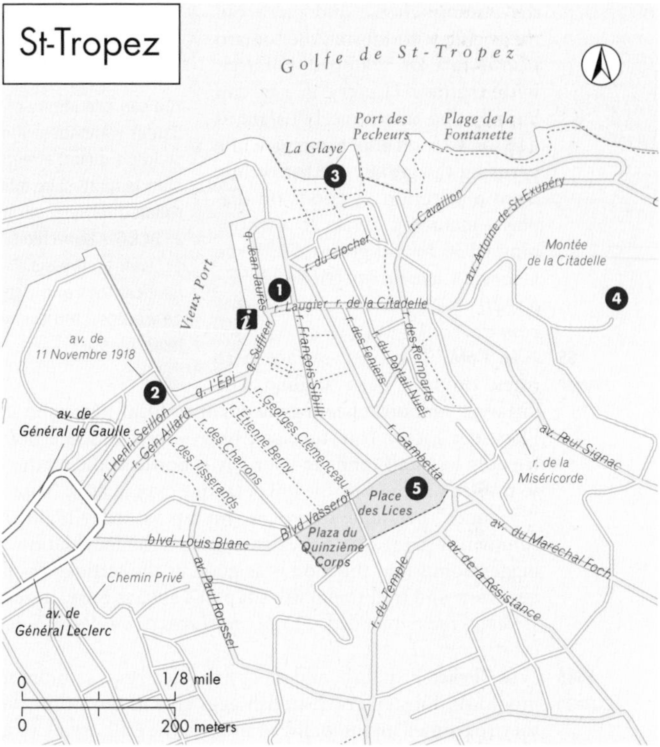

the water's edge, surreptitiously looking out for any off-duty celebs. For it's here, from folding director's chairs at the famous port-side cafés Le Gorille (named for its late exceptionally hirsute manager), Café de Paris, and Sénéquier's—which line Quai Suffren and Quai Jean-Jaurès—that the cast of St-Tropez's living theater plays out its colorful roles.

WHERE TO EAT

$$$ FRENCH ✕ **Au Caprice des Deux.** After overdosing on the high-octane jet set people—and prices—that pepper the popular spots of St-Trop, it is a wonderful surprise to come across this charmingly authentic restaurant in a picturesque village house tucked behind the port. Filled with happy, relaxed regulars, the menu offers up tasty French delicacies like spicy beef salad, egg cocotte with truffles, crab cannelloni with shrimp sauce or grilled scallops with truffle risotto. There are only two wines on the list—but, no matter, the extensive dessert menu compensates. ✉ *40 rue Portail Neuf* ☎ *04–94–97–76–78* 🌐 *www.aucapricedesdeux.com* 💳 *AE, MC, V.*

$$$ FRENCH ✕ **La Table du Marché.** With an afternoon tearoom and deli bar, this charming bistro from celebrity chef Christophe Leroy offers up a mouthwatering spread of regional specialties in a surprisingly casual atmosphere. Although the burgundy couches and black wicker chairs set against pristine white walls are a little severe, the service adds warmth, as does

the yummy cheese and macaroni made chic with lobster, the tomato *pistou* tart or whipped potatoes with truffles. Hungry guests can happily dive into a nicely balanced €18 or €26 set lunch menu while perusing the good wine list or buy from a selection of goods on display—including caviar at a whopping €130 for 30 grams. ✉ *38 rue Georges Clemenceau* ☎ *04–94–97–85–20* 🌐 *www.christophe-leroy.com* 💳 *AE, D, MC, V.*

YOU CAN NEVER BE TOO RICH, TOO THIN, OR TOO TAN

You can see plenty of Brigitte Bardot wannabes who strut along St-Trop's quaint streets in skin-tight leopard skin, toting leopard-collared terriers, mixing in with a "BCBG"-"bon-chic-bon-genre," or "well-bred yuppie"–crowd in nautical togs and Gap shirts, with only golden retrievers or dalmatians, please.

$$ FRENCH ✕ **Le Café.** The busy terrace here often doubles as a stadium for different factions cheering on favorite local pétanque players in the Place des Lices. You, too, can play—borrow some boules from the friendly bar staff (and get your pastis bottle at the ready: you'll need it to properly appreciate the full pétanque experience). Note that hilarious "beginner" pétanque soirees are on tap Saturday nights in spring and summer. A great way to really sink into the local culture, it's an even bigger bonus that the food is as good as the setting. Try the Provençal beef stew and traditional fish soup. It's always busy, so reservations are strongly recommended. ✉ *5 pl. des Lices* ☎ *04–94–97–44–69* 🌐 *www.lecafe.fr* 💳 *AE, MC, V.*

$$$$ SEAFOOD ✕ **Le Girelier.** Fish, fish, and more fish—sea bass, salmon, sole, sardines, monkfish, lobster, crayfish, fish eggs spread on a thin slice of toast—they're painted on the walls, sizzling on the grill, trying to jump for their lives as the boats come into the Old Port. Will they make it? Not if chef Yves Rouet gets to them first, with a little thyme or perhaps a whisper of olive oil and garlic. Like his father before him, chef Yves makes an effort to prepare Mediterranean-only fish for his buffed and bronzed clientele, who enjoy the casual sea-shanty space and the highly visible Vieux Port terrace tables. Grilling is the order of the day, with most fish sold by weight (beware the check), but this is also a stronghold for bouillabaisse. There's beef on the menu, too, in case you're a fish-phobe. The €38 set menu is one of the best bargains in town. ✉ *Quai Jean-Jaurès* ☎ *04–94–97–03–87* 🌐 *www.legirelier.fr* 💳 *AE, DC, MC, V* ⏲ *Closed Mon. and Nov.–Mar. No lunch July and Aug.*

WHERE TO STAY

$$–$$$ 🏨 **Ermitage.** Surrounded by mimosas and lemon trees, this big, old-fashioned, tangerine-hue hotel is on a hill above town and from its back rooms commands striking sea views. Once a 19th-century private villa, it still has some of its former glory: the beautiful walled garden is a lovely summer retreat and the wood-burning fireplace and cozy "colonial"-rattan bar make for solid elegance. The guest rooms are simply decorated, light-bathed in soft pastels. Owner Annie Bolloreis's friendly welcome makes this a real charmer. **Pros:** service is excellent; strength of the decor is its comfort and easy accessibility—shower taps are easy to use, light switches are easy to find, and comforters are

Problems in paradise? St-Tropez may be a beaut but it is outrageously priced, has hard-to-get-to beaches, and doesn't have much public transportation.

down-filled and soft. **Cons:** rooms facing the street can be noisy; some of the rooms are a little small. ✉ *Av. Paul-Signac* ☎ *04–94–97–52–33* 🌐 *www.ermitagehotel.fr* 27 *rooms* *In-room: a/c. In-hotel: bar, Wi-Fi hotspot, parking (free), some pets allowed* 💳 *MC, V* ⏲ *Closed mid-Nov.–Mar.*

$$$$ **La Bastide de St Tropez.** With a private terrace or garden or Jacuzzi for each room, clean lines and tasteful decor, elegant colors and the softest pillows imaginable, this luxe hotel has hit the ground running. The large pool beckons from a magnificent garden setting, and the service is prompt and discreet. A further plus? The hotel restaurant, aptly named L'Olivier, serves up tasty dishes, like sea bass wrapped in rock salt with seasonal vegetables, grilled beef with crunchy homemade fires and béarnaise sauce, or green asparagus with black truffle dressing and parmesan chips, under the gentle swaying olive trees that pepper the terrace. **Pros:** free shuttle into the town center is a nice touch, as is the surprisingly warm welcome. **Cons:** a bit far from the center of town, and some of the rooms seem small. ✉ *Route des Carles* ☎ *04–94–55–82–55* 🌐 *www.bastide-saint-tropez.com* *26 rooms* *In-room: a/c, refrigerator. In-hotel: restaurant, pool, gym, spa, Wi-Fi hotspot, parking (free), some pets allowed* 💳 *AE, DC, MC, V.*

$$$$ **La Résidence de la Pinède.** Perhaps the most opulent of St-Tropez's luxe hangouts, this balustraded white villa and its broad annex sprawl elegantly along a private waterfront, wrapped around an isolated courtyard and a pool shaded by parasol pines. Louis XVI bérgères, a beam here and there, gilt frames, indirect spots, and oh-so-comfy beds make for an alluring if somewhat homogenized interior. Pay extra for a seaside room, where you can lean over the balcony and take in broad coastal views and the large seafront restaurant; chef Arnaud Donckele has a celebrated reputation, and you'll understand why after one taste of his truffle ravioli. Rates (beware: they start at €700) including half board are available. **Pros:** discreet elegance at its best; stunning views; nicely decorated rooms (note the very plump and fluffy pillows, which smell delightfully of lavender). **Cons:** for the price, some rooms are a little small; staff sometime take themselves way too seriously. ✉ *Plage de la Bouillabaisse* ☎ *04–94–55–91–00* 🌐 *www.residencepinede.com* *35 rooms, 4 suites* *In-room: a/c, refrigerator, Wi-Fi. In-hotel: restaurant, bar, pool, parking (free), some pets allowed* *AE, DC, MC, V* *Closed mid-Oct.–mid-Apr.* *MAP.*

$$$$ **Le Byblos.** Arranged like a toy Mediterranean village, fronted with stunning red, rust, and yellow facades, and complete with ocher-stucco cottagelike suites grouped around courtyards landscaped with palms, olive trees, and lavender, this longtime fave of the glitterati began life as a "Phoenician-style" resort (the name means Bible) dreamed up by a Lebanese millionaire. Decades later, it has seen the jet set *jet, jet, jet.* Guest rooms are *à la provençale,* but modern in comfort. Chef Vincent Maillard creates artful dinner classics in the Bayader restaurant: sea bass roasted with salsify and garlic chips or rib-sticking beef tournedos with foie gras.As evening falls, all head to the hotel's Caves du Roy—a gigantic disco extravaganza where squillionaires have been seen buying champagne by the carton for the crowd. Paparazzi-free, it's virtually impossible to get in unless you get there early or reserve a table in advance (be aware that very impressive-looking security guards will turn away anyone not dressed appropriately). **Pros:** everything and anything . . . all in one place—like having a little bit of Las Vegas in the South of France: the glitter, the rhinestones, the stars; even better, the champagne flows like water. **Cons:** level of service depends on the size of your bankbook; glitz wears thin after too many days; and does one really have to take one's yappy little dog everywhere? ✉ *Av. Paul-Signac* ☎ *04–94–56–68–00* 🌐 *www.byblos.com* *52 rooms, 43 suites* *In-room: a/c, refrigerator. In-hotel: 2 restaurants, pool, gym, spa, Wi-Fi hotspot, parking (free), some pets allowed* *AE, DC, MC, V* *Closed mid-Oct.–Easter.*

NIGHTLIFE AND THE ARTS

Costing the devil and often jammed to the scuppers, **Les Caves du Roy** (✉ *Av. Paul-Signac* ☎ *04–94–97–16–02*), a disco in the Byblos Hotel, is *the* place to see and be seen; it's filled with svelte model types and their wealthy, silver-haired fans. You, too, may be sprayed with Moët during one of those champagne-spraying parties (so many bottles are set off, waiters are given football helmets). Virtually impossible to get into unless you book long in advance, there's a horrific door policy during high season; don't worry, it's *not* you. Every July and August, classical music concerts are given in the gardens of the **Château de la Moutte** (✉ *Rte. des Salins* ☎ *04–94–97–45–21 information* 🌐 *www.music-lamoutte.com* *€30*). For ticket information, inquire at the tourist office. Swanky **Octave Café** (✉ *Rue Garonne* ☎ *04–94–97–22–56*) is a piano bar (obligatory drinks) with soft seating and sleek black tables. Although not a bar listed among the "big players," stars like

Liza Minnelli and Johnny Hallyday have been known to get up and sing a song or two here. The **VIP Room** (✉ *Residence du Nouveau Port* ☎ *04–94–97–14–70* 🌐 *www.viproom.fr*) draws flashy, gilded youths with deep pockets—although more and more question the "VIP" in the club's name.

SHOPPING

Designer boutiques may be spreading like wild mushrooms all over St-Tropez, but the main fashionista strutting platform is along **Rue Gambetta** or **Rue Allard.** For those who balk at spending a small fortune on the latest strappy sandal, **Rue Sibilli,** behind the Quai Suffren, is lined with all kinds of trendy, more affordable boutiques. The **Place des Lices** overflows with produce, regional foods, clothing, and *brocantes* (collectibles) on Tuesday and Saturday mornings. Don't miss the picturesque little fish market that fills up **Place aux Herbes** every morning.

PORT-GRIMAUD

7 km (4½ mi) west of St-Tropez.

Although much of the coast has been targeted with new construction of extraordinary ugliness, this modern architect's version of a Provençal fishing village works. A true operetta set and only begun in 1966, it has grown gracefully over the years, and offers hope for the pink concrete–scarred coastal landscape. It's worth parking and wandering up the village's Venice-like canals to admire its Old Mediterranean canal-tile roofs and pastel facades, already patinaed with age. Even the church, though resolutely modern, feels Romanesque. There is, however, one modern touch some might appreciate: small electric tour boats (get them at Place du Marché) that carry you for a small charge from bar to shop to restaurant throughout the complex of pretty squares and bridges.

ST-RAPHAËL

38 km (24 mi) northeast of St-Tropez, 41 km (25½ mi) southwest of Cannes.

Right next door to Fréjus, with almost no division between, is St-Raphaël, a sprawling resort town with a busy downtown anchored by a casino. It's also a major sailing center, has five golf courses nearby, and draws the weary and indulgent to its seawater-based thalassotherapy. It serves as a major rail crossroads, the closest stop to St-Tropez

GETTING HERE

St-Raphaël is the western terminus of SNCF's regional TER line that runs along the Riviera. To get to towns farther west, you have to take a bus from just behind the St-Raphaël-Valescure train station (✉ *Pl. de la Gare*); various companies connect with Cannes, Fréjus, and St-Tropez. Popular ferries leave from St-Raphaël's Vieux Port from St-Tropez, the Iles-de-Lérins, and the Calanques de l'Esterel.

Visitor Information **St-Raphaël Tourist Office** ✉ *Rue Waldeck-Rousseau* ☎ *04–94–19–52–52* 🌐 *www.saint-raphael.com.*

EXPLORING

Worth the bother of penetrating dense city traffic and cutting inland past the train station is St-Raphaël's **Vieille Ville** *(Old Town)*, a tiny enclave of charm crowned by the 12th-century **Église St-Pierre-des-Templiers,** a miniature-scale Romanesque church, and the intimate little **Musée Archéologique Marin** *(Marine Archaeology Museum)*, both located on Rue des Templiers.

St-Raphaël's port has a rich history: Napoléon landed here on his triumphant return from Egypt in 1799; it was also from here in 1814 that he cast off for Elba in disgrace. F. Scott Fitzgerald and his wife Zelda had a hidden hideaway here, reputably throwing some very wild parties; Dumas, Maupassant, and Berlioz also settled in for a time.

WHERE TO EAT AND STAY

$$$ SEAFOOD **L'Arbousier.** Philippe Troncy is one of St. Raphael's most respected up and coming chefs. Menus change according to the season, with market-fresh produce and simple recipes made nouveau with original twists. Try the sinfully smooth fois gras baked with cracked black pepper. His bouillabaisse is a delight of fresh fish and steaming broth (one of the best on the coast) and the garden terrace is a shady oasis filled with magnolia and lemon trees. *6 av. Valescure 04–94–95–25–00 www.arbousier.net AE, MC, V Closed Mon. and Tues.*

$ ★ **Le Thimothée.** The owners of this bargain lodging are throwing themselves wholeheartedly into improving an already attractive 19th-century villa. They've also restored the garden, with its grand palms and pines shading the walk leading to a pretty little swimming pool. Though it's tucked away in a neighborhood far from the waterfront, the two top-floor rooms have poster-perfect sea views. **Pros:** familial atmosphere and gentle hospitality make for a very pleasant stay; lovely garden. **Cons:** distance to the beach is significant on a hot summer day, which also means a bit of a walk for nighttime excursions to the waterfront cafés. *375 bd. Christian-Lafon 04–94–40–49–49 www.thimothee.com 12 rooms In-room: a/c, refrigerator. In-hotel: pool, Wi-Fi hotspot, parking (free), some pets allowed AE, MC, V Closed Jan.*

EN ROUTE

The rugged **Massif de l'Estérel,** between St-Raphaël and Cannes, is a hiker's dream. Made up of rust-red volcanic rocks (porphyry) carved by the sea into dreamlike shapes, the harsh landscape is softened by patches of lavender, scrub pine, and gorse. By car, take N7, the mountain route to the north, and lose yourself in the desert landscape far from the sea.

Or keep on N98, the **Corniche de l'Estérel** (the coastal road along the dramatic corniche), and drive past sheer rocks faces plunging down to the waves, tiny calanques, and little coves dotted with sunbathers. Try to leave early in the morning, as tempers tend to fray when the route gets congested with afternoon traffic.

MANDELIEU–LA NAPOULE

32 km (20 mi) northeast of St-Raphaël, 8 km (5 mi) southwest of Cannes.

12

La Napoule is the small, old-fashioned port village, Mandelieu the big-fish resort town that devoured it. You can visit Mandelieu for a golf-and-sailing retreat—the town is replete with many sporting facilities and hosts a bevy of sporting events, including sailing regattas, windsurfing contests, and golf championships (there are two major golf courses in Mandelieu right in the center of town overlooking the water). By the sea, a yacht-crammed harbor sits under the shadow of some high-rise resort hotels. La Napoule, on the other hand, offers the requisite quaintness, ideal for a port-side stroll, casual meal, beach siesta, or visit to its peculiar castle. Mandelieu-La Napoule's train and bus stations offer frequent connections between Cannes and St-Raphaël.

★ Set on Pointe des Pendus *(Hanged Man's Point)*, the **Château de la Napoule,** looming over the sea and the port, is a spectacularly bizarre hybrid of Romanesque, Gothic, Moroccan, and Hollywood cooked up by the eccentric American sculptor Henry Clews (1876–1937). Working with his architect-wife, he transformed the 14th-century bastion into something that suited his personal expectations and then filled the place with his own fantastical sculptures. The couple reside in their tombs in the tower crypt, its windows left slightly ajar to permit their souls to escape and allow them to "return at eventide as sprites and dance upon the windowsill." Today the château's foundation hosts visiting writers and artists, who set to work surrounded by Clews's gargoyle-ish sculptures. ✉ *Av. Henry Clews* ☎ *04–93–49–95–05* 🌐 *www.chateau-lanapoule.com* 🎫 *€6, gardens only €3.50* ⏲ *Feb.–Oct., daily 10–6; guided visits at 11:30, 2:30, 3:30, and 4:30; Nov.–Jan., daily 2–5; guided visits at 2:30, 3:30, and 4:30.*

WHERE TO EAT AND STAY

$$$ SEAFOOD ★ ✕ **Le Boucanier.** The low-ceiling dining room is upstaged by wraparound plate-glass views of the marina and château at this waterfront favorite. Locals gather here for mountains of oysters and whole fish, grilled simply and served with a drizzle of fruity olive oil, a pinch of rock salt, or a brief flambé in pastis. ✉ *Port de La Napoule* ☎ *04–93–49–80–51* 🌐 *www.boucanier.fr* 💳 *AE, DC, MC, V* ⏲ *Closed Thurs. Nov.–Mar.*

$$$$ FRENCH ✕ **L'Oasis.** Long famed as a culinary landmark, this Gothic villa by the sea is home to Stéphane Raimbault, a master of Provençal cuisine and a great connoisseur of Asian techniques and flavorings. The combination creates unexpected collisions—Pan-fried duck liver with oriental flavors and wok vegetables, risotto with black truffles, or Thai-spiced crayfish with squid-ink ravioli—most but not all entirely successful. Still, few can quibble with the beauty of the famous garden terrace shadowed by gorgeous palm trees. ✉ *Rue J. H. Carle* ☎ *04–93–49–95–52* 🌐 *www.oasis-raimbault.com* 💳 *AE, MC, V* ⏲ *Closed mid-Dec.–mid-Jan. No dinner Sun. No lunch Mon. May–Sept.*

$$$ 🏨 **L'Ermitage du Riou.** A smart Florentine-style hotel, with elegant marble columns and lovely ceiling frescoes, this dainty treasure also has a deeply atmospheric restaurant where you can sit out on the dock over

the water and eat lobster salad with mixed citrus fruits followed by a scrumptious mushroom risotto. Meal plans are available with a minimum three-night stay. **Pros:** ideal location, looking out over the waterfront; service is friendly without being presuming; Italian frescoes are a treat, beautifully restored to their original splendor. **Cons:** some rooms are noisy, especially in high summer months; service can be a little slow if you are still on New York time. ✉ *Av. Henri Clews* ☎ *04–93–49–95–56* 🌐 *www.ermitage-du-riou.fr* *41 rooms, 4 suites* *In-room: a/c, refrigerator. In-hotel: pool, Wi-Fi hotspot, parking (free), some pets allowed* ▭ *AE, DC, MC, V.*

SPORTS

The **Golf Club de Cannes-Mandelieu** (✉ *Rte. du Golf* ☎ *04–92–97–32–00* 🌐 *www.golfoldcourse.com*) is one of the most beautiful in the south of France; it's bliss to play on English turf, under Mediterranean pines with mimosa blooming here and there in spring. The club has two courses—one with 18 holes (par 71) and one with 9 (par 33).

CANNES

6 km (4 mi) east of Mandelieu-La Napoule, 73 km (45 mi) northeast of St-Tropez, 33 km (20 mi) southwest of Nice.

A tasteful and expensive breeding ground for the upscale, Cannes is a sybaritic heaven for those who believe that life is short and sin has something to do with the absence of a tan. Backed by gentle hills and flanked to the southwest by the Estérel, warmed by dependable sun but kept bearable in summer by the cool Mediterranean breeze, Cannes is pampered with the luxurious climate that has made it one of the most popular and glamorous resorts in Europe. The cynosure of sun worshippers since the 1860s, it has been further glamorized by the modern success of its film festival.

GETTING HERE

Cannes has one central train station, the *Gare SNCF* (✉ *Rue Jean Jaures* 🌐 *www.voyages-sncf.com*). All major trains pass through here—check out the SNCF Web site for times and prices—but many of the trains run the St-Raphaël–Ventimiglia route. You can also take the TGV directly from Paris (6½ hrs). Cannes's main bus station, which is on Place de l'Hôtel-de-Ville by the port, serves all coastal destinations. Rapides Côtes d'Azur runs most of the routes out of the central bus station on Place Bernard Gentille, including Nice (1½ hrs, €6), Mougins (20 mins, €3), Grasse (45 mins, €5), and Vallauris (30 mins, €4). Within Cannes, Bus Azur runs the routes, with a ticket costing €1. The bus line RCA (☎ *04–93–85–64–44* 🌐 *wwww.rca.tm.fr*) goes to Nice along the coast road, stopping in all villages along the way, and to the Nice airport, every 30 minutes, Monday–Saturday, for a maximum ticket price of €13.70 round-trip.

Visitor Information Cannes Tourist Office ✉ *Palais des Festivals, Esplanade G. Pompidou, B. P. 272* ☎ *04–93–39–24–53* 🌐 *www.cannes-on-line.com.*

EXPLORING

With the democratization of modern travel, Cannes has become a tourist and convention town; there are now 20 compact Twingos for every Rolls-Royce. But it didn't start life that way for, up to 1834, its bay served as nothing more than a fishing port. But when an English aristocrat, Lord Brougham, fell in love with the site that year during an emergency stopover with a sick daughter, he had a home built here and returned every winter for a sun cure—a ritual quickly picked up by his peers. Today, glamour—and the perception of glamour—is self-perpetuating, and as long as Cannes enjoys its ravishing climate and setting, it will maintain its incomparable panache. If you're a culture-lover of art of the non-celluloid type, however, you should look elsewhere—there is only one museum here, devoted to history. Still, as his lordship instantly understood, this is a great place to pass the winter.

Pick up a map at the tourist office in the **Palais des Festivals,** the scene of the famous Festival International du Film, otherwise known as the Cannes Film Festival. As you leave the information center, follow the Palais to your right to see the red-carpeted stairs where the stars ascend every year. Set into the surrounding pavement, the **Allée des Étoiles** (Stars' Walk) enshrines some 300 autographed imprints of film stars' hands—of Départdieu, Streep, and Stallone, among others.

Head to the famous mile-long waterfront promenade, **La Croisette,** which starts at the western end by the Palais des Festivals, and allow the *esprit de Cannes* to take over. This is precisely the sort of place for which the verb *flâner* (to dawdle, saunter) was invented, so stroll among the palm trees and flowers and crowds of poseurs (fur coats in tropical weather, cell phones on Rollerblades, and sunglasses at night). Head east past the broad expanse of private beaches, glamorous shops, and luxurious hotels (such as the wedding-cake Carlton, famed for its see-and-be-seen terrace-level brasserie). The beaches along here are almost all private, though open for a fee—each beach is marked with from one to four little life buoys, rating their quality and expense.

If you need a culture fix, check out the modern art and photography exhibitions (varying admission prices) held at the **Malmaison,** a 19th-century mansion that was once part of the Grand Hotel. ✉ *47 bd. La Croisette, La Croisette* ☎ *04–93–06–44–90* 🎫 *€3* ⏲ *Oct.–Mar., Tues.–Sun. 10–noon and 2–6; Apr. and May, Tues.–Sun. 10–1 and 2:30–6:30; June–Aug., Tues.–Sun. 10–1 and 3–8; Sept. 10–1 and 2:30–6:30.*

NEED A BREAK?

Head down the Croisette and fight for a spot at Le 72 Croisette (✉ *71 La Croisette* ☎ *04–93–94–18–30*), the most feistily French of all the Croisette bars. It offers great ringside seats for watching the rich and famous enter the Martinez hotel next door, and it's open 24 hours a day (open summer 7 AM to 3 AM and winter 7 AM to 8 PM.

Two blocks behind La Croisette lies **Rue d'Antibes,** Cannes's main high-end shopping street. At its western end is **Rue Meynadier,** packed tight with trendy clothing boutiques and fine food shops. Not far away is the covered **Marché Forville,** the scene of the animated morning food market.

Climb up Rue St-Antoine into the picturesque Vieille Ville neighborhood known as **Le Suquet,** on the site of the original Roman *castrum.* Shops proffer Provençal goods, and the atmospheric cafés give you a chance to catch your breath; the pretty pastel shutters, Gothic stonework, and narrow passageways are lovely distractions.

The hill is crowned by the 11th-century château, housing the **Musée de la Castre,** with its mismatched collection of weaponry, ethnic artifacts and ceramics amassed by a 19th century aristocrat. The imposing four-sided **Tour du Suquet** *(Suquet Tower)* was built in 1385 as a lookout against Saracen-led invasions. ✉ *Pl. de la Castre, Le Suquet* ☎ *04–93–38–55–26* 🎟 *€3* ⏲ *Apr.–June, Tues.–Sun. 10–1 and 2–6; July and Aug., daily 10–7; Sept., Tues.–Sun. 10–1 and 2–6; Oct.–Mar., Tues.–Sun. 10–1 and 2–5.*

WHERE TO EAT

$$$ SEAFOOD ✕ **Astoux et Brun.** Deserving of its reputation for impeccably fresh *fruits de mer,* this restaurant is a beacon to all fish lovers. Well-trained staff negotiate cramped quarters to lay down heaping seafood platters, shrimp casseroles, or piles of oysters shucked to order. Astoux is noisy, cheerful, and always busy, so arrive early to get a table and avoid the line, especially since they do not accept reservations. ✉ *27 rue Felix Faure, La Croisette* ☎ *04–93–39–21–87* 🌐 *www.astouxbrun.com* 💳 *MC, V.*

$ ITALIAN ✕ **Dell'Arte.** Don't be misled by the jumble of mismatched chairs and vintage advertising: the food at this new Italian eatery is anything but out of date. The symphony of flavors begins even before you've picked up the menu: crumbly chunks of parmesan, fresh Italian bread and imported olive oil tide you over while you peruse the impeccable—although short—menu. Try the spaghetti with clams or the gnocchi with gorgonzola and nuts, and save room for the lighter-than-air tiramisu. ✉ *6 rue Marechal Joffre, La Croisette* ☎ *04–93–38–72–79* 🌐 *www.ristorantedellarte.com* 💳 *AE, MC, V* ⏲ *Closed Sun.*

$$$ FRENCH ✕ **L'Affable.** Cannes is often criticized for not having the same gastronomic punch as Mougins, so when Chef Battaglia decided to sell the Feu Follet and set up shop in Cannes, gastronomes were delighted. And, from one food-lover to another, the chef does not disappoint. The curried lobster is fantastic, the lamb rack succulent, and the risotto all that is creamy. Jammed daily since its opening, reservations are essential. ✉ *5 rue de la Fontaine, La Croisette* ☎ *04–93–68–02–09* 🌐 *www.restaurant-laffable.fr* 💳 *AE, MC, V.*

$ PIZZA ✕ **La Pizza.** Sprawling up over two floors and right in front of the old port, this busy Italian restaurant serves steaks, fish, and salads, but go there for what they're famous for: gloriously good right-out-of-the-wood-fire-oven pizza in hungry-man-size portions. ✉ *3 quai St-Pierre, La Croisette* ☎ *04–93–39–22–56* 💳 *AE, MC, V.*

$$ FRENCH ✕ **Le Petit Lardon.** Popular and unpretentious, this tiny bistro is feisty and fun. Watch for a great mix of seasonal Provençal and Burgundian flavors: escargots served with butter and garlic, roast rabbit au jus stuffed with raisins, and melt-in-your-mouth lavender crème brûlée. Busy, bustling, and friendly, it's ideal for a casual meal, but it's tiny, so reserve

DID YOU KNOW?

Europe's upper crust flocked to Cannes' La Croisette beach because they believed that lying on its white sands (instead of the beach pebbles of Nice) was enough to cure most ailments.

well in advance. ✉ *3 rue de Batéguier, La Croisette* ☎ *04–93–39–06–28* ▭ *AE, MC, V* ⊙ *Closed Sun.*

$$ FRENCH ✕ **Pastis.** With its sleek milk-bar decor and reasonable prices, this busy lunch hot spot is a must in Cannes. Just off the Croisette, the service is remarkably friendly and the food good. There are nice American touches—the grilled-chicken Caesar salad, the club sandwich and home-cut fries, pizza—which can make for a comfortable day off from your gourmet voyage through Provençal cuisine. ✉ *28 rue Commandant André, La Croisette* ☎ *04–92–98–95–40* ⊕ *www.pastis-cannes.com* ▭ *AE, MC, V.*

WHERE TO STAY

$$$$ ★ **Carlton InterContinental.** As one of the turn-of-the-19th-century pioneers of this resort town, this deliciously pompous Neoclassical landmark quickly staked out the best position: La Croisette seems to radiate symmetrically from its figurehead waterfront site. Almost sharing star billing with Grace Kelly and Cary Grant in Alfred Hitchcock's *To Catch a Thief,* the Carlton still hosts many film-festival banquets in its gilt-and-marble Grand Salon (along with, alas, business conferences year-round). Seven deluxe suites on the top floor, each with unsurpassed sea views and every comfort imaginable, as well as snazzy seafront rooms add to its cachet; those at the back compensate for the lack of a sea view with cheery Provençal prints. The top-floor suites have been recently renovated and are a glory of burnished wood and rich creams, and the health and fitness center, although small, has every luxe item imaginable. The restaurant is good, the brasserie swank, and the Bar des Célébrités lives up to its name during the film festival. **Pros:** with the best location in Cannes, this iconic hotel has all the cliché and style that the rich and famous look for; service is remarkably unpretentious. **Cons:** some rooms are tiny; avoid back rooms that look out over the back parking/delivery area (very noisy early in the morning). ✉ *58 bd. de la Croisette, La Croisette* ☎ *04–93–06–40–06* ⊕ *www.ichotelsgroup.com/interncontinental* *346 rooms, 42 suites* *In-room: a/c, refrigerator. In-hotel: 2 restaurants, bars, gym, Wi-Fi hotspot, parking (paid), some pets allowed* ▭ *AE, DC, MC, V.*

$$$ ★ **Le Cavendish Boutique Hotel.** Lovingly restored by friendly owners Christine and Guy Welter, this giddily opulent former residence of English Lord Cavendish is a true delight. Guest rooms are done in bright swaths of color ("wintergarden" greens, "incensed" reds) that play up both contemporary decor and 19th-century elegance. Beauty, conviviality, even smells—sheets are scented with lavender water, and fresh flowers line the entryway—all work together in genuine harmony. The downstairs bar is cozy for a nightcap and the copious buffet breakfast is simply excellent. **Pros:** genuine welcome at this out-of-the-way hotel is a refreshing change from the notoriously frosty reception at other Cannes palace hotels. **Cons:** even though the rooms all have double-pane windows, the hotel is located on the busiest street in Cannes, which means an inevitable amount of noise; a 15-minute walk from the beach. ✉ *11 bd. Carnot, St-Nicolas* ☎ *04–97–06–26–00* ⊕ *www.cavendish-cannes.com* *34 rooms* *In-room: a/c, refrigerator. In-hotel: bar, Wi-Fi hotspot, parking (paid)* ▭ *AE, DC, MC, V.*

12

$–$$ **Le Romanesque.** If it's not the hand-painted, intricately carved antique bed and free-standing bath in one room, or the romantic private terrace and sinfully soft pillows in another, the genuine charm of this gorgeous new boutique hotel will quickly seduce all but the most world-weary. **Pros:** steps from the Croisette and the beaches, it still retains its sophisticated country house charm; the breakfast is remarkable. **Cons:** some rooms can be noisy in summer; although undergoing significant renovations, the neighborhood is still run-down. ✉ *10 rue du Bateguier, La Croisette* ☎ *04–93–68–04–20* 🌐 *www.hotelleromanesque.com* *8 rooms* *In-room: a/c refrigerator. In-hotel: Wi-Fi hotspot, parking (paid), some pets allowed* *AE, DC, MC, V.*

$$$ **Molière.** Plush, intimate, and low-key, this hotel, a short stroll from the Croisette, has pretty tile baths and small rooms in cool shades of peach, indigo, and white-waxed oak. Nearly all overlook the vast, enclosed front garden, where palms and cypresses shade terrace tables, and where breakfast, included in the price, is served most of the year. **Pros:** charm of paying a low price for excellent service never wears thin; when beach becomes tiresome, the lovely garden is a real refuge. **Cons:** nights can be noisy as high season brings a lot of party vacationers, who see the garden as a perfect place to have one last nightcap. ✉ *5 rue Molière, La Croisette* ☎ *04–93–38–16–16* 🌐 *www.hotel-moliere.com* *24 rooms* *In-room: a/c. In-hotel: bar, Wi-Fi hotspot, some pets allowed* *AE, MC, V* *Closed late Nov.–late Dec.* *BP.*

NIGHTLIFE AND THE ARTS

The Riviera's cultural calendar is splashy and star-studded, and never more so than during the **International Film Festival** in May. The film screenings are not open to the public, so unless you have a pass, your stargazing will be on the streets or in restaurants (though if you hang around in a tux, a stray ticket might come your way).

As befits a glamorous seaside resort, Cannes has two casinos. The famous **Casino Croisette** (✉ *In Palais des Festivals, La Croisette* ☎ *04–92–98–78–00* 🌐 *www.lucienbarriere.com*) draws more crowds to its slot machines than any other casino in France. The **Palm Beach Casino Club** (✉ *Pl. Franklin-Roosevelt, Point de la Croisette, La Croisette* ☎ *04–97–06–36–90*) manages to retain an exclusive atmosphere even though you can show up in jeans. The biggest player to date in the Cannes nightlife scene is **Le Baoli** (✉ *Port Pierre Canto, La Croisette* ☎ *04–93–43–03–43* 🌐 *www.lebaoli.com*), where the likes of Leonardo DiCaprio and Ivana Trump have been known to stop by; it's usually packed until dawn even outside of festival time.

If you're craving something a little less French, the most English of pubs in Cannes, **Morrison's Irish Pub** (✉ *10 rue Teisseire, La Croisette* ☎ *04–92–98–16–17* 🌐 *www.morrisonspub.com*), has live music every Wednesday and Thursday and plenty of Irish-English staff. The stylish and the beautiful flock to sushi specialists **Tantra** (✉ *13 rue Doctor Gerard Monod, La Croisette* ☎ *04–93–39–40–39* 🌐 *www.tantra-cannes.com*) before moving upstairs to their sexy and fun offshoot, aptly named **Upstairs** (☎ *04–93–39–40–39* 🌐 *www.upstairs-cannes.com*) to dance the night away. The hip Latin bar **Caliente** (✉ *84 bd. de la*

Croisette, La Croisette ☎ *04–93–94–49–59*) is jammed in summer until dawn with salsa-dancing regulars.

THE OUTDOORS

Most of the beaches along La Croisette are owned by hotels and/or restaurants, though this doesn't necessarily mean the hotels or restaurants front the beach. It does mean they own a patch of beachfront bearing their name, where they rent out chaise longues, mats, and umbrellas to the public and hotel guests (who also have to pay). Public beaches are between the color-coordinated private beach umbrellas and offer simple open showers and basic toilets. Sailboats can be rented at either port or at some of the beachfront hotels.

JUAN-LES-PINS

5 km (3 mi) southwest of Antibes.

If Antibes is the elderly, historic parent, then Juan-les-Pins is the jazzy younger-sister resort town that, with Antibes, bracelets the wrist of the Cap d'Antibes. The scene along Juan's waterfront is something to behold, with thousands of international sunseekers flowing up and down the promenade or lying flank to flank on its endless stretch of sand. The **Plage de Juan-les-Pins** is made up of sand, not pebbles, and ranks among the Riviera's best (rent a beach chair from the nearby hotel concessions, the best of which is Les Belles Rives). Along with these white-powder wonders, Juan is famous for the quality—some pundits say quantity—of its nightlife. There are numerous nightclubs where you can do everything but sleep, ranging from casinos to discos to strip clubs. If all this sounds like too much hard work, wait for July's jazz festival—one of Europe's most prestigious—or simply repair to the Juana or Les Belles Rives (same owners); if you're lucky enough to be a guest at either hotel, you'll understand why F. Scott Fitzgerald set his *Tender Is the Night* in "Juantibes," as both places retain the golden glamour of the Riviera of yore. These hotels are surrounded by the last remnants of the pine forests that gave Juan its name. Elsewhere, Juan-les-Pins suffers from a plastic feel and you might get more out of Antibes.

WHERE TO EAT AND STAY

$–$$ **Hotel des Mimosas.** The fabulous setting, in an enclosed hilltop garden studded with tall palms, mimosas, and tropical greenery, makes up for the hike down to the beach. Guest rooms are small and modestly decorated in Victorian florals; ask for one with a balcony: many look over the garden and sizable pool. Rates can include half board. **Pros:** quiet buzzing of cicadas is the only interruption to completely silent nights; a perfect pool for a hot summer day. **Cons:** some rooms are noisy; nowhere to eat (aside from in hotel) that's within easy walking distance. ✉ *Rue Pauline* ☎ *04–93–61–04–16* 🌐 *www.hotelmimosas.com* *34 rooms* *In-room: a/c, refrigerator. In-hotel: 2 restaurants, bar, pool, Wi-Fi hotspot, parking (free), some pets allowed* 💳 *AE, MC, V* *MAP.*

$$$$ ★ **Les Belles Rives.** If "living well is the best revenge," then vacationers at this landmark hotel should know. Not far from the onetime villa of Gerald and Sara Murphy—those Roaring Twenties millionaires who

devoted their lives to proving this maxim—the Belles Rives became the home-away-from-home for literary giant F. Scott Fitzgerald and his wife Zelda (chums of the Murphys). Lovingly restored to 1930s glamour, the public salons and piano bar prove that what's old is new again: France's stylish young set now make this endearingly *neoclassique* place one of their favorites. The gastronomic restaurant's cuisine is innovative; the fixed menu is good value. Dine on the terrace on a fine summer night, with the sea lapping below and stars twinkling in the velvety Mediterranean sky. There's no pool, but happily the private beach is just steps away. **Pros:** the views really are quite spectacular; looking out over the bay and the private beach at your doorstep is a seductive way to spend the day. **Cons:** some dishes in the gastronomic restaurant can be a little too innovative (and service can also be slow on busier nights). ✉ *33 bd. Baudoin* ☎ *04–93–61–02–79* 🌐 *www.bellesrives.com* *43 rooms* *In-room: a/c, refrigerator. In-hotel: 2 restaurants, bar, beachfront, Wi-Fi hotspot, parking (free), some pets allowed* 💳 *AE, DC, MC, V* ⏲ *Closed Jan. and Feb.*

NIGHTLIFE AND THE ARTS

The glassed-in complex of the **Eden Casino** (✉ *Bd. Baudoin, Juan-les-Pins* ☎ *04–92–93–71–71*) houses restaurants, bars, dance clubs, and a casino. By far the most popular club in the town—and rumored to be the favorite haunt of Oasis's Noel Gallagher—is the **Village** (✉ *Pl. de la Nouvelle Orléans, 1 bd. de la Pinède, Juan-les-Pins* ☎ *04–92–93–90–00* ⏲ *Closed Sun.–Thurs.*). Every July the **Festival International Jazz à Juan** (☎ *04–97–23–11–10*) challenges Montreux for its stellar lineup and romantic venue under ancient pines. This place hosted the European debut performances of such stars as Meels Dah-*vees* (Miles Davis) and Ray Charles.

CAP D'ANTIBES

2 km (1 mi) south of Antibes.

This extravagantly beautiful peninsula, protected from the concrete plague infecting the mainland coast, has been carved up into luxurious estates shaded by thick, tall pines. Since the 19th century its wild greenery and isolation have drawn a glittering guest list of aristocrats, artists, literati, and the merely fabulously wealthy: Guy de Maupassant, Anatole France, Claude Monet, the Duke and Duchess of Windsor, the Greek shipping tycoon Stavros Niarchos, and the cream of the Lost Generation, including Ernest Hemingway, Gertrude Stein, and Scottie and Zelda Fitzgerald. Now the most publicized focal point is the Hotel Eden Roc, rendezvous and weekend getaway of film stars. The Cap is about 6 km (4 mi) long, so don't consider it a gentle stroll from downtown Antibes. Happily, the 2A or 2A bis municipal bus (🌐 *www.envibus.fr* *€1.30*) often connects the two. You can sample a little of what draws famous people to the site by walking up the Chemin de Calvaire from the Plage de la Salis in Antibes (about 1 km [½ mi]) and taking in the extraordinary views (spectacular at night) from the hill that supports the old lighthouse, the **Phare de la Garoupe** *(Garoupe Lighthouse)*. Next to the lighthouse, the 16th-century double chapel

This street scene in Antibes only hints at the extraordinary beauty hidden in the back alleys of the quarter surrounding the Musée Picasso.

of **Notre-Dame-de-la-Garoupe** contains ex-votos and statues of the Virgin, all in memory and for the protection of sailors. ☎ *04–93–67–36–01* ⏲ *Easter–Sept., daily 9:30–noon and 2:30–7; Oct.–Easter, daily 10–noon and 2:30–5.*

★ To fully experience the Riviera's heady hothouse exoticism, visit the glorious **Jardin Thuret** *(Thuret Garden)*, established by botanist Gustave Thuret in 1856 as a testing ground for subtropical plants and trees. Thuret was responsible for the introduction of the palm tree, forever changing the profile of the French Riviera. On his death the property was left to the Ministry of Agriculture, which continues to dabble in the introduction of exotic species. The Jardin is in the middle of the Cap; from the Port du Croûton, head up Chemin de l'Aureto, then Chemin du Tamisier, and turn right on the Boulevard du Cap. ✉ *90 chemin Raymond* ☎ *04–97–21–25–00* 🌐 *jardin-thuret.antibes.inra.fr* 🎫 *Free* ⏲ *Oct.–May, weekdays 8:30–5:30; June–Sept., weekdays 8–6.*

Fodor's Choice ★ Bordering the Cap's zillion-dollar hotels and fabled estates runs one of the most spectacular footpaths in the world: the **Sentier Tirepoil,** which stretches about 1½ km (1 mi) along the outermost tip of the peninsula. It begins gently enough at the pretty Plage de la Garoupe (where Cole Porter and Gerard Murphy used to hang out), with a paved walkway and dazzling views over the Baie de la Garoupe and the faraway Alps. Round the far end of the cap, however, and the paved promenade soon gives way to a boulder-studded pathway that picks its way along 50-foot cliffs, dizzying switchbacks, and thundering breakers (*Attention Mort*—"Beware: Death"—read the signs, reminding you this path can be very dangerous in stormy weather). On sunny days, with exhilarating winds and spectacular breakers coming in from the sea, you'll have company (families, even), although for most stretches all signs of civilization completely disappear—except for a yacht or two. The walk is long, and takes about two hours to complete, but it may prove to be two of the more unforgettable hours of your trip (especially if you tackle it at sunset).

Fodor's Choice ★ The Sentier Tirepoil passes below (but unfortunately does not access) the **Villa Eilenroc,** designed by Charles Garnier, who created the Paris Opéra—which should give you some idea of its style. It commands the tip of the peninsula from a grand and glamorous garden. On Wednesdays from September to June, visitors are allowed to wander through the reception salons, which retain the Louis Seize-Trianon feel of the noble facade. The Winter Salon still has its 1,001 Nights ceiling mural painted by Jean Dunand, the famed Art Deco designer; display cases are filled with memorabilia donated by Caroline Groult-Flaubert (Antibes resident and goddaughter of the great author); while the boudoir has boiseries from the Marquis de Sévigné's Paris mansion. As you leave, be sure to detour to La Rosaerie, the rose garden of the estate—in the distance you can spot the white portico of the Château de la Cröe, another legendary villa (now reputedly owned by a syndicate of Russian billionaires). Whether or not the Eilenroc is haunted by Helene Beaumont, the rich singer who built it, or King Leopold II of Belgium, King Farouk of Egypt, Aristotle Onassis, or Greta Garbo—who all rented here—only you will be able to tell. ✉ *At peninsula's tip* ☎ *04–93–67–74–33* 🌐 *www.antibes-juanlespins.com* 🎟 *Free* ⏲ *House mid-Sept.–June, Wed. 9–noon and 1:30–5; gardens mid-Sept.–June, Tues. and Wed. 9–5.*

Across the Bay of Millionaires from the Villa Eilenroc (and just down the road from the posh Hôtel du Cap–Eden Roc) is a picturesque mini-peninsula, landmarked by an ancient battery tower that now contains the **Musée Napoléonien** *(Napoleonic Museum).* Here, you can peruse a collection of watercolors of Antibes, platoons of lead soldiers, and scale models of military ships. Head here, if only to savor one of the most coveted pieces of real estate on the entire Riviera. ✉ *Batterie du Grillon, bd. J. F. Kennedy* ☎ *04–93–61–45–32* 🎟 *€3* ⏲ *Mid-Sept.–mid-June, Tues.–Sat. 10–4:30; mid-June–mid-Sept., Tues.–Sat. 10–6.*

WHERE TO EAT AND STAY

$$$$ SEAFOOD ★ ✕ **Restaurant de Bacon.** Since 1948, under the careful watch of the Sordello brothers, this has been *the* spot for seafood on the French Riviera. The catch of the day may be minced in lemon ceviche, floating in a top-of-the-line bouillabaisse, or simply grilled with fennel, crisped with hillside herbs. The warm welcome, discreet service, sunny dining room, and dreamy terrace over the Baie des Anges, with views of the Antibes ramparts, justify extravagance. Many of the à la carte fish dishes are pricey, with many going for €60 or €70 apiece (the luxe lobster version of their bouillabaisse soars to €145) but, happily, fixed-menu prices are €49 and €79. ✉ *Bd. de Bacon* ☎ *04–93–61–50–02* 🌐 *www.restaurantdebacon.com* ✍ *Reservations essential* 💳 *MC, V* ⏲ *Closed Mon. and Nov.–Jan. No lunch Tues.*

$$$$ ★ 🏨 **Hôtel du Cap–Eden Roc.** In demand by celebrities from De Niro to Madonna (perhaps understandably, since their bills are picked up by

film companies when they fly in for the Cannes film festival—don't even try to book a room in early May), this extravagantly expensive hotel has long catered to the world's fantasy of a subtropical idyll on the French Riviera. First opened in 1879, the Villa Soleiljoined forces with the neighboring Eden Roc tearoom in 1914, and expanded its luxuries to include a swimming pool blasted into seaside bedrock. After the Great War, two stylish American intellectuals, Sara and Gerald Murphy, rented the entire complex and invited all their friends, a stellar lot ranging from the Windsors to Rudolf Valentino and Marlene Dietrich. Their most frequent guests were Zelda and F. Scott Fitzgerald, who used it as the model for Hôtel des Etrangers in his *Tender Is the Night*. Today its broad, sun-drenched rooms, thickly carpeted and furnished with antiques in the main Second Empire mansion, look out on 22 acres of immaculate tropical gardens bordered by rocky shoreline. Down by the water is the Pavillon Eden Roc wing, more modern but with sheer-horizon views. Everyone dresses stylishly for dinner. Credit cards are now finally accepted. And if you're not a celebrity, tip big to keep the staff interested. **Pros:** it's the Hotel du Cap; no other hotel in Southern France has the same reputation or style. **Cons:** even tipping big doesn't mean the staff stay interested; there *are* prettier hotels on the coast. ⊠ *Bd. J.F. Kennedy* ☎ *04–93–61–39–01* 🌐 *www.edenroc-hotel.fr* *121 rooms, 9 suites* *In-room: a/c. In-hotel: restaurant, bar, tennis courts, pool, gym, Wi-Fi hotspot* ▭ *AE, MC, V* ⊗ *Closed mid-Oct.–mid-Apr.*

$$ **Hôtel La Jabotte.** A few steps from a sandy beach, this adorable guesthouse is built around a central courtyard, where guests relax over a breakfast (included in the room price) of croissants, baguette, fresh juice, and homemade jam. Rooms are tastefully decorated with motifs of birds, flowers, or calligraphy, and the owner is as charming as the setting. **Pros:** very warm welcome is completely unexpected after stints in some of the other, better-known hotels; breakfast with homemade wild strawberry jam is simply delicious. **Cons:** it's difficult to find, so bring a good map or drive with a GPS; hotel is often full. ⊠ *13 av. Max-Maurey* ☎ *04–93–61–45–89* 🌐 *www.jabotte.com* *10 rooms* *In-room: no a/c. In-hotel: bar, Wi-Fi hotspot, some pets allowed* ▭ *AE, MC, V* 🍴 *BP.*

$$–$$$ **Hôtels La Garoupe and La Gardiole.** Cool, simple, and accessible to non–movie stars, this pair of partnered hotels offers a chance to sleep on the hallowed peninsula and bike or walk to the pretty Garoupe beach. A sizable pool, framed by high walls and tall pines, offers cool-down time. Rooms are comfortably furnished in both buildings, the Garoupe offering modern decor and the Gardiole rustic Provençal design. **Pros:** these hotels provide accessible luxury on the Cap, without making a fuss; the rooms are large and comfortable, and the service is correct. **Cons:** a fair walk to the beach; limited choices for restaurants within an easy distance. ⊠ *60–74 chemin de la Garoupe* ☎ *04–92–93–33–33* 🌐 *www.hotel-lagaroupe-gardiole.com* *40 rooms* *In-room: a/c, refrigerator. In-hotel: restaurant, bar, pool, Wi-Fi hotspot, parking (free), some pets allowed* ▭ *AE, MC, V* ⊗ *Closed Nov.–Mar.*

ANTIBES

Fodor's Choice ★ *11 km (7 mi) east of Cannes, 15 km (9 mi) southeast of Nice.*

No wonder Picasso once called this home—Antibes (pronounced Awn-*teeb*) is a stunner. With its broad stone ramparts scalloping in and out over the waves and backed by blunt medieval towers and a skew of tile roofs, it remains one of the most enchantingly romantic old towns on the Mediterranean coast.

12

GETTING HERE

Antibes has one central train station, the *Gare SNCF* (✉ *Pl. Pierre-Semard* 🌐 *www.voyages-sncf.com*), which is at the far end of town but still within walking distance of the Vieille Ville and only a block or so from the beach. Local trains are frequent, coming from Nice (20 mins, €4), Juan-les-Pins, Biot, Cannes (10 mins, €3), and almost all other coastal towns. There are also high-speed TGVs that depart from Antibes. Bus service, available at Antibes's Gare Routière (bus station) (✉ *1 pl. Guynemer*) is supplied by both the RCA lines (☎ *04–93–85–64–44* 🌐 *www.rca.tm.fr*) and the TAM lines (☎ *08–92–70–17–06* 🌐 *www.lignedazur.com*). One example is the No. 200 RCA bus between Cannes and Antibes, which runs every 15–20 minutes and costs €1.

Visitor Information Antibes Tourist Office ✉ *11 pl. de Gaulle, Antibes* ☎ *04–92–90–53–00* 🌐 *www.antibesjuanlespins.com.*

EXPLORING

As gateway to the Cap d'Antibes, Antibes's Port Vauban harbor has some of the largest yachts in the world tied up at its berths—their millionaire owners won't find a more dramatic spot to anchor, with the tableau of the snowy Alps looming in the distance and the formidable medieval block towers of the Fort Carré guarding entry to the port. Stroll Promenade Amiral-de-Grasse along the crest of Vauban's sea walls, and you can understand why the views inspired Picasso to paint on a panoramic scale. Yet a few steps inland you can enter a souklike maze of old streets that are relentlessly picturesque and joyously beautiful—this district is perhaps the most enchanting along the entire Riviera coast, so miss it at your own peril. Think about stopping off at the tourist office to buy a *billet combiné* (combined ticket) for €10, which gives prepaid access to all museums over a period of seven days.

To visit Old Antibes, pass through the **Porte Marine,** an arched gateway in the rampart wall. Follow Rue Aubernon to **Cours Masséna,** where the little sheltered market sells lemons, olives, and hand-stuffed sausages, and the vendors take breaks in the shoe-box cafés flanking one side. Along the way, wander back alleys, check out the adorable shops, and chill out at one of the dawdle-and-dine cafés. But perhaps the most beguiling street in all Antibes is Rue St-Esprit, located just a block or two from the Musée Picasso (if you head past the Eglise de l'Immaculée-Conception). Continue further on and just follow your nose to discover other magical cul-de-sacs.

★ From Cours Masséna head up to the **Eglise de l'Immaculée-Conception** (✉ *Pl. de la Cathédrale*), which served as the region's cathedral until the bishopric was transferred to Grasse in 1244. The church's 18th-century facade, a marvelously Latin mix of classical symmetry and fantasy, has been restored in stunning shades of ocher and cream. Its stout medieval watchtower was built in the 11th century with stones "mined" from Roman structures. Inside is a Baroque altarpiece painted by the Niçois artist Louis Bréa in 1515.

★ Next door to the cathedral, the famed **Musée Picasso** rises high over the water in its stunning home, the medieval Château Grimaldi. Famed as rulers of Monaco, the Grimaldi family lived here until the Revolution, but this fine old castle was little more than a monument until in 1946 its curator offered use of its vast chambers to Picasso, at a time when that extraordinary genius was enjoying a period of intense creative energy. The result was a bounty of exhilarating paintings, ceramics, and lithographs inspired by the sea and by Greek mythology—all very Mediterranean. The **château**, which became the **Musée Picasso** in 1966, houses more than 300 works by the artist, as well as pieces by Miró, Calder, and Léger; the first floor displays over 100 paintings of Russian-born artist Nicholas de Stael. Even those who are not great Picasso fans should enjoy his vast paintings on wood, canvas, paper, and walls, alive with nymphs, fauns, and centaurs. ✉ *Pl. du Château* ☎ *04–92–90–54–20* 🌐 *www.antibes-juanlespins.com/eng/culture/musees/Picasso/index.html* 🎫 *€6* 🕙 *Mid-June–mid-Sept., Tues.–Sun. 10–6; July and Aug., Wed. and Fri. until 8; mid-Sept.–mid-June, Tues.–Sun. 10–noon and 2–6 (may change).*

Fodor's Choice ★ A few blocks south of the Château Grimaldi is the **Commune Libre du Safranier** *(Free Commune of Safranier)*, a magical little 'hood with a character all its own. Here, not far off the seaside promenade and focused around the Place du Safranier, tiny houses hang heavy with flowers and vines and neighbors carry on conversations from window to window across the stone-stepped Rue du Bas-Castelet. It's said that Place du Safranier was once a tiny fishing port; now it's the scene of this subvillage's festivals.

The Bastion St-André, a squat Vauban fortress, now contains the **Musée d'Histoire et d'Archéologie** *(History and Archaeology Museum)*. Its collection focuses on Antibes's classical history, displaying amphorae and sculptures found in local digs as well as salvaged from shipwrecks from the harbor. ✉ *Bastion Saint-Andre* ☎ *04–92–90–54–35* 🎫 *€3* 🕙 *Mid-Sept.–mid-June, Tues.–Sun. 10–1 and 2–6; mid-June–mid-Sept., Tues.–Sun. 10–noon and 2–8; July and Aug., Wed. and Fri. until 8.*

WHERE TO EAT AND STAY

$$ FRENCH Fodor's Choice ★ ✕ **La Taverne du Safranier.** At this bastion of local cuisine, sit on the lively terrace jammed with locals and dig in to mountains of sardine fritters, *petit farcis* (stuffed vegetables), or a mini-bouillabaisse that is not mini at all. The servers know everybody, and friendly banter wafts over the crowds; don't be surprised if they treat you like a long-lost old friend—including taking liberal license to tease. Reserve well in advance. ✉ *1 pl. du Safranier* ☎ *04–93–34–80–50* 💳 *AE, MC, V* 🕙 *Closed mid-Nov.–Dec.*

Vauban's Fort Carré and the sea walls he designed guard Antibes's harbor, home to some of the most glamorous yachts in the world.

$$$ FRENCH ★ ✕ **Le Brûlot.** Set one street back from the market, this bistro remains one of the most popular in Antibes. Burly chef Christian Blancheri hoists anything from pigs to apple pies in and out of his roaring wood oven, and it's all delicious. Watch for the duck and crispy chips, sardines *à l'escabèche* (in a tangy sweet-sour marinade), sizzling lamb chops, or grilled fresh fish. ✉ *3 rue Frédéric Isnard* ☎ *04–93–34–17–76* 🌐 *www.brulot.com* ▭ *MC, V* ⏲ *Closed Sun. No lunch Tues. and Wed.*

$$ **L'Auberge Provençale.** Overlooking the largest square in Antibes's Old Town, this onetime abbey now has seven rooms complete with exposed beams, canopy beds, and lovely antique furniture. The dining room and the arbor garden are informed with the same impeccable taste; the menu allures with fresh seafood inventions such as *rascasse* (rock fish) sausage with mint, as well as bouillabaisse and duck grilled over wood coals. The restaurant is closed Monday and for Tuesday lunch. **Pros:** lovely decor and friendly service. **Cons:** nights in summer can be a little noisy. ✉ *61 pl. Nationale* ☎ *04–93–34–13–24* 🌐 *www.aubergeprovencale.com* *7 rooms* *In-room: a/c (some). In-hotel: restaurant, bar, Wi-Fi hotspot, some pets allowed* ▭ *MC, V* ⏲ *Closed 2 wks in Jan.*

NIGHTLIFE

La Siesta (✉ *Rte. du Bord de Mer, Antibes* ☎ *04–93–33–31–31* 🌐 *www.lasiesta.fr*) is an enormous summer entertainment center with seven dance floors (some on the beach), bars, slot machines, and roulette.

THE OUTDOORS

Antibes and Juan together claim 25 km (15½ mi) of coastline and 48 **beaches** (including Cap d'Antibes). In Antibes you can choose between small sandy inlets—such as **La Gravette,** below the port; the central **Place de Ponteil;** and **Plage de la Salis,** toward the Cap; rocky escarpments around the Vieille Ville; or the vast stretch of sand above the Fort Carré.

THE HILL TOWNS

The hills that back the French Riviera are often called the *arrière-pays,* or backcountry. This particular wedge of backcountry—behind the coast between Cannes and Antibes—has a character all its own: deeply, unselfconsciously Provençal, with undulating fields of lavender watched over by villages perched on golden stone. Many of these villages look as if they do not belong to the last century—but they do, since they played the muse to some of modern art's most famous exemplars, notably Pablo Picasso and Henri Matisse. A highlight here is the Maeght Foundation, in St-Paul de Vence (also home to the incomparable inn, La Colombe d'Or), one of France's leading museums of modern art. The town's neighbor, Vence, has the Chapelle du Rosaire, entirely designed and decorated by Matisse. It's possible to get a small taste of this backcountry on a day trip out of Fréjus, Cannes, or Antibes; even if you're vacationing on the coast, you may want to settle in for a night or two for this is when the scent of the boutiques' strawberry potpourri is washed away by the natural perfume of bougainvillea and jasmine wafting from terra-cotta jars.

VALLAURIS

6 km (4 mi) northeast of Cannes, 6 km (4 mi) northwest of Antibes.

In the low hills over the coast, dominated by a blocky Renaissance château, this ancient village was ravaged by waves of the plague in the 14th century, then rebuilt in the 16th century by 70 Genoese families imported to repopulate the abandoned site. They brought with them a taste for Roman planning—hence the grid format in the Old Town—but, more important in the long run, a knack for pottery making, as well. Their skills and the fine clay of Vallauris proved to be a marriage made in heaven, and the village thrived as a pottery center for hundreds of years.

In the 1940s Picasso found inspiration in the malleable soil and settled here in a simple stone house, creating pottery art with a single-minded passion. But he returned to painting in 1952 to create one of his masterworks in the château's Romanesque chapel, the vast multipanel oil-on-wood composition called *La Guerre et la Paix* (*War and* ★ *Peace*). The chapel is part of the **Musée National Picasso** today, where several of Picasso's ceramic pieces are displayed. ✉ *Pl. de la Libération* ☎ *04–93–64–71–83* 🌐 *www.musee-picasso-vallauris.fr* 🎫 *€3.50* ⏲ *Mid-June–mid-Sept., Wed.–Mon. 10–12:15 and 2–6; mid-Sept.–mid-June, Wed.–Mon. 10–12:15 and 2–5.*

MOUGINS

6 km (4 mi) northwest of Valluris, 8 km (5 mi) north of Cannes, 11 km (7 mi) northwest of Antibes.

> **WORD OF MOUTH**
>
> "Head for the hilltowns for an unbelievable change of scenery and serious shopping. These medieval villages, some perched at the edge of a cliff, are something to see." —carolandbob

Passing through Mougins, a popular summerhouse community convenient to Cannes and Nice and famously home to a group of excellent restaurants, you may perceive little more than suburban sprawl. But in 1961 Picasso found much to admire and settled into a *mas* (farmhouse) that verily became a pilgrimage spot for artists and art lovers; he died here in 1973.

You can find Picasso's final home and see why, of all spots in the world, he chose this one, by following D35 2 km (1 mi) south of Mougins to the ancient ecclesiastical site of **Notre-Dame-de-Vie** (✉ *Chemin de la Chapelle*). This was the hermitage, or monastic retreat, of the Abbey of Lérins, and its 13th-century bell tower and arcaded chapel form a pretty ensemble. Approached through an allée of ancient cypresses, the house Picasso shared with his wife, Jacqueline, overlooks the broad bowl of the countryside (now blighted with modern construction). Unfortunately, the residence—the former priory—is closed to the public. The chapel is only open during Sunday Mass at 9 AM. Elsewhere in town are a small **Musée Municipal,** set in the 17th-century St-Bernardin Chapel, and a huge **Musée de l'Automobile,** with 100 vintage cars, in a modern structure on the Aire des Bréguières.

WHERE TO EAT AND STAY

$$ FRENCH ✕ **Le Bistrot de Mougins.** In a 15th-century stable with high, curved brick ceilings, this restaurant plays up to its historic past. Rustic chairs and flowered tablecloths offer a real picnic-in-the-country feel. Simple, Provençal-style dishes are hard to beat: escargots in butter and herbs, steak with a green peppercorn sauce, or sea bass grilled with fennel are top choices. Reservations are recommended in the summer months. ✉ *Pl. du Village* ☎ *04–93–75–78–34* ▭ *MC, V* ⊗ *Closed Tues. and Wed.*

$$$ FRENCH ★ ✕ **Le Feu Follet.** In a beautiful period-house set right in the center of the village, chef Didier Chouteau is causing quite a stir: from the homemade foie gras to the hand-smoked salmon to mouthwatering basics like roasted scampi with lemon and basil. The best seats are on the enclosed terrace by the quietly tinkling fountain looking out into the mayor's flower garden, but the cozy rooms inside are atmospheric, too. Try to save room for dessert—the lighter-than-the-clouds crème brûlée is truly outstanding. ✉ *Pl. du Commandant Lamy* ☎ *04–93–90–15–78* ⊕ *www.feu-follet.fr* ▭ *AE, MC, V* ⊗ *Closed Sun. dinner–Mon. lunch.*

$$$$ **Le Mas Candille.** Nestled in a huge private park, this 19th-century *mas* (farmhouse) has been cleverly transformed into an ultraluxurious hotel. Rooms—all cool colors and country chic—are very refined, with a profusion of pillows, heated towels, and all the hidden electrical hookups you could possibly need. Antique wallpapers, "reissued" vintage furniture, and too many other high-gloss touches make this

place *Elle Decor*–worthy, if not really authentic to the locale. The opulent, saffron-hue restaurant is the well-ordered domain of chef Serge Gouloumes, whose impressive résumé includes stints at Ma Maison in Beverly Hills and the Poisson d'Or in Saint Martin. His succulent menus are causing quite a stir in gastronomic circles; watch for items like wild bass in a rosemary tempura clay crust or foie gras tartin with Armagnac. In addition to the main house and the gourmet restaurant, there's a *bastide* (villa) and a Shiseido spa. **Pros:** friendly service and beautiful views. **Cons:** the location makes this place hard to find. ✉ *Bd. Clément-Rebuffel* ☎ *04–92–28–43–43* 🌐 *www.lemascandille.com* *39 rooms, 7 suites* *In-room: a/c, refrigerator. In-hotel: 2 restaurants, room service, pools, spa, Wi-Fi hotspot, some pets allowed* ▭ *AE, DC, MC, V.*

$$$$ ★ **Le Moulin de Mougins.** Housed in a 16th-century olive mill on a hill above the coastal fray, this sophisticated inn houses one of the most famous restaurants in the region (reservations essential). When brilliant but temperamental chef Alain Llorca left in 2009, food aficionados waited with mixed feelings for the arrival of Sebastien Chambru. Although impossible not to be intimidated by the ghosts of previous kitchen chiefdoms (Roger Verge and Alain Llorca), this newest bright star—with much panache and seemingly little effort—has wrought tasty little miracles. Try the pan-fried fois gras with crisp banana French toast, followed by sole stuffed with prawns, shellfish jus, lemon confit, and apple mousse; and finished off with candied tomatoes, local strawberries and olive oil ice cream. And, if all this good food is just a bit too much indulgence, you can sleep it off in one of the 11 beautifully and individually decorated rooms. Much sought after are the "Zen" and "Papillion" (butterfly) rooms, which put a new, luxurious spin on the idea of cocooning. **Pros:** the garden setting is a lovely summer escape from the busy coast; even non-food-focused travelers should try the excellent cuisine. **Cons:** rooms are luxe but small; service can be snooty. ✉ *Av. Notre-Dame-de-Vie* ☎ *04–93–75–78–24* 🌐 *www.moulindemougins.com* *11 rooms, 1 suite, 2 junior suites, 2 apartments* *In-room: a/c, refrigerator. In-hotel: restaurant, bar, Wi-Fi hotspot, parking (free), some pets allowed* ▭ *AE, DC, MC, V* *Closed mid-Jan.–early Apr.*

GRASSE

10 km (6 mi) northwest of Mougins, 17 km (10½ mi) north of Cannes, 22 km (14 mi) northwest of Antibes, 42 km (26 mi) west of Nice.

High on a plateau over the coast, this busy, modern town is usually given a wide berth by anyone who isn't interested in its prime tourist industry, the making of perfume. But its unusual art museum features works of the 18th-century artist Fragonard, its famed perfume museum, and the picturesque backstreets of its very Mediterranean Vieille Ville round out a pleasant day trip from the coast. You can't visit the laboratories where the great blends of Chanel, Dior, and Guerlain are produced, but to accommodate the crowds of tourists who come here wanting to know more, Grasse has three functioning perfume factories that create simple blends and demonstrate production techniques

Continued on page 670

CUISINE OF THE SUN

Don't be surprised if colors and flavors seem more intense in Provence. It could be the hot, dry climate, which concentrates the essence of fruit and vegetables, or the sun beaming down on market tables overflowing with produce. Or maybe you're seeing the world anew through rosé-tinted wine glasses. Whatever the reason, here's how to savor Provence's *incroyable* flavors and culinary favorites.

Provence's rustic cuisine, based on local tomatoes, garlic, olive oil, anchovies, olives, and native wild herbs—including basil, lavender, mint, rosemary, thyme, and sage—has more in common with other Mediterranean cuisines than it does with most regional French fare. Everywhere you'll find sun-ripened fruit dripping with nectar and vegetables so flavor-packed that meat may seem like a mere accessory.

The natural bounty of the region is ample, united by climate—brilliant sunshine and fierce winds—and divided by dramatically changing landscapes. In the Vaucluse, scorched plains give way to lush, orchard-lined hills and gently sloped vineyards. The wild Calanques of Marseille, source of spiky sea urchins, ease into the tranquil waters of St-Tropez, home to gleaming bream and sea bass. Provence's pantry is overflowing with culinary treasures.

Simple preparations, like grilled vegetables with crusty bread, are best enjoyed with the region's famous rosé wine

RUSTIC FARE: NATURE AS MUSE AND MASTER

(top left) Provence's markets have bountiful produce, (top right) *soupe au pistou*, a version of minestrone

As you bite into a honey-ripe Cavaillon melon or a fennel-perfumed sea bass fillet, you might think that nature has always been kind to Provence. Not so.

On the wind-battered coast of Marseille, fishermen salvaged the boniest rock fish to create a restorative soup—bouillabaisse—that would become legendary worldwide.

In the sun-blasted mountains north of Nice, impoverished farmers developed a repertoire of dishes found nowhere else in France, using hardy Swiss chard, chickpea flour, and salt cod.

Fish are filleted tableside for the bouillabaisse presentation at some restaurants

Olive oil, the very symbol of Provençal food, is only now overcoming a 1950s frost that entirely wiped out France's olive groves. Even the tomato has a relatively short history here, having been introduced in the 1820s and at first used only in cooked dishes.

The best Provençal chefs remain fiercely proud of the dishes that define their region or their village, even while injecting their own identities and ideas into the food. Thanks to its ports, Provence has always been open to outside influences, yet the wealth of readily available ingredients prevents chefs from straying too far from their roots—when the local basil is so headily perfumed, why use lemongrass?

If menus at first seem repetitive, go beyond the words (tapenade, ratatouille, pistou) to notice how each chef interprets the dish: this is not a land of printed recipes but of spontaneity inspired by the seasons and the markets. Don't expect perfect food every time, but seek out those who love what they do enough to make *la cuisine de soleil* dazzle.

TASTEMAKERS AND THEIR RESTAURANTS

While Provence is best-known for its rustic fare, the region also has a sophisticated side. It was here—outside of Cannes—that the founding father of French haute cuisine, **Auguste Escoffier** (1846–1935), was born and raised. His former villa has been transformed into a culinary museum, Musee Escoffier de l'Art Culinare (✉ *3 rue Auguste Escoffier, Villenueve-Loubet Village* ☎ *04–93–20–80–51*), displaying Escoffier's kitchen and collection of cookware, along with artwork and reproductions of his famous feasts.

These days, upscale culinary creations are best experienced at the "new Mediterranean" restaurants of the region's star chefs. Former Moulin de Mougins Michelin-starred super chef **Alain Llorca** has found the perfect setting for his Spanish-influenced style at **La Passagère** located in the glamorous Hotel Belles Rives (✉ *33 blvd. Baudoin, Juan-les-Pins* ☎ *04–93–61–02–79*). At this beachside property, he brings the ocean's bounty to life in upscale riffs on famous regional dishes like bouillaisse. For a taste of Llorca's creative cooking in a less formal atmosphere, try **Café Juana** at the Belles Rives' sister property Hotel Juana (✉ *Ave. Gallice, Juan-les-Pins* ☎ *04–93–61–08–70*).

Everyone from antique dealers to fashionable hipsters feel at home at **Le Jardin du Quai** (✉ *91 av. Julien Guidue, L'Isle-sur-la-Sorgue* ☎ *04–90–20–14–98*), where jovial young chef **Daniel Hébet** runs the restaurant like an open house. In summer, regulars linger on the garden patio, while in winter the high-ceiling bistro-style dining room exudes the same welcoming vibe. Shrugging off the constraints of haute cuisine with a no-choice set menu at lunch and dinner, Hébet makes creative presentations like an open-faced tart filled with baby fava beans, cherry tomatoes, and chorizo-stuffed baby squid.

Dining on the terrace of Le Jardin du Quai

Chef Alain Llorca is known for his fanciful presentations

At **Restaurant Christian Etienne** (✉ *10 rue de Mons, Avignon* ☎ *04–90–86–16–50*), the summer tomato menu has become a much-anticipated annual tradition, where each year chef Etienne celebrates the versatility of this vegetable with a tasting extravaganza that might include tartare of three tomato varieties with olive oil from the Bleu Argent mill in Provence, foie gras with Roma tomato petals, and tomato macaroon with lime sorbet. Etienne is one of the long-established masters of Provençal cooking, and if his cooking sometimes makes generous use of butter (rather than the area's renowned olive oil), his customers aren't complaining.

PROVENCE'S TOP REGIONAL DISHES

Ratatouille

Fougasse

AÏOLI

The name for a deliciously pungent mayonnaise made with generous helpings of garlic, *aïoli* is a popular accompaniment for fish, meat, and vegetable dishes. The mayonnaise version shares its name with "grand aïoli," a recipe featuring salt cod, potatoes, hard-boiled eggs, and vegetables. Both types of aïoli pop up all over Provence, but they seems most beloved in Marseille. In keeping with Catholic practice, some restaurants serve grand aïoli only on Fridays. And it's a good sign if they ask you to place your order at least a day in advance. A grand aïoli is also a traditional component of the Niçois Christmas feast.

BOUILLABAISSE

Originally a humble fisherman's soup made with the part of the catch that nobody else wanted, bouillabaisse—the famous fish stew—consists of four or five kinds of fish: the villainous-looking *rascasse* (red scorpion fish), *grondin* (sea robin), *baudroie* (monkfish), *congre* (conger eel), and *rouget* (mullet). The fish are simmered in a stock of onions, tomatoes, garlic, olive oil, and saffron, which gives the dish its golden color. When presented properly, the broth is served first, with croutons and *rouille*, a creamy garlic sauce that you spoon in to suit your taste. The fish comes separately, and the ritual is to place pieces into the soup to enjoy after slurping up some of the broth.

BOURRIDE

This poached fish dish owes its anise kick to pastis and its garlic punch to aïoli. The name comes from the Provençal bourrido, which translates less poetically as "boiled." Monkfish—known as baudroie in Provence and lotte in the rest of France—is a must, but chefs occasionally dress up their bourride with other species and shellfish.

DAUBE DE BOEUF

To distinguish their prized beef stew from *boeuf bourguignon*, Provençal chefs make a point of not marinating the meat, instead cooking it very slowly in tannic red wine that is often flavored with orange zest. In the Camargue, daube is made with the local taureau (bull's meat), while the Avignon variation uses lamb.

Bourride

Bouillabaisse

FOUGASSE

The Provençal answer to Italian focaccia, this soft flatbread is distinguished by holes that give it the appearance of a lacy leaf. It can be made savory—flavored with olives, anchovy, bacon, cheese, or anything else the baker has on hand—or sweet, enriched with olive oil and dusted with icing sugar. When in Menton, don't miss the sugary *fougasse mentonnaise*.

LES PETITS FARCIS

The Niçois specialty called *les petits farcis* are prepared with tiny summer vegetables (usually zucchini, tomatoes, peppers, and onions) that are traditionally stuffed with veal or leftover *daube* (beef stew). Like so many Niçois dishes, they make great picnic food.

RATATOUILLE

At its best, *ratatouille* is a glorious thing—a riot of eggplant, zucchini, bell peppers, and onions, each sautéed separately in olive oil and then gently combined with sweet summer tomatoes. A well-made ratatouille, to which a pinch of saffron has been added to heighten its flavor, is also delicious served chilled.

SOUPE AU PISTOU

The Provençal answer to pesto, *pistou* consists of the simplest ingredients—garlic, olive oil, fresh basil, and Parmesan—ideally pounded together by hand in a stone mortar with an olive-wood pestle. Most traditionally it delivers a potent kick to *soupe au pistou*, a kind of French minestrone made with green beans, white beans, potatoes, and zucchini.

SOCCA

You'll find *socca* vendors from Nice to Menton, but this chickpea pancake cooked on a giant iron platter in a wood-fired oven is really a Niçois phenomenon, born of sheer poverty at a time when wheat flour was scarce. After cooking, it is sliced into finger-lickin' portions with an oyster knife. Enjoy it with a glass of chilled rosé.

TIAN DE LÉGUMES

A *tian* is both a beautiful earthenware dish and one of many vegetable gratins that might be cooked in it. This thrifty dish makes a complete meal of seasonal vegetables, eggs, and a little cheese.

for free: **Fragonard** (✉ *20 bd. Fragonard* ☎ *04–93–36–44–65* 🌐 *www.fragonard.com*) operates in a factory built in 1782 that is open daily to the public. **Galimard** (✉ *73 rte. de Cannes* ☎ *04–93–09–20–00* 🌐 *www.galimard.com*) traces its pedigree back to 1747, and is open daily. **Molinard** (✉ *60 bd. Victor Hugo* ☎ *04–93–36–01–62* 🌐 *www.molinard.com*) was established in 1849, and is open weekdays.

★ Thanks to a 2008 renovation and expansion, the **Musée International de la Parfumerie** *(International Museum of Perfume)* is now one of the more sleekly spectacular museums along the coast. Now housed in soaring steel, glass, and teak woods, the museum trace the 3,000-year history of perfume making, with one highlight being its fascinating collection of some 4,000 antique perfume bottles. In the rooftop greenhouse you can breathe in the heady smells of different herbs and flowers, while the expert and amusing guide crushes delicate petals under your nose to better release the scents. ✉ *8 pl. du Cours Honore Cresp* ☎ *04–93–36–80–20* 🎫 *€4* ⏲ *June–Sept., daily 10–7; Oct.–May, Wed.–Sun. 10–12:30 and 2–5:30.*

The **Musée Fragonard** headlines the work of Grasse's most famous son, Jean-Honoré Fragonard (1732–1806), one of the great French chocolate-box artists of his day. The lovely villa contains a collection of drawings, engravings, and paintings by the artist. Other rooms in the mansion display works by Fragonard's son Alexandre-Evariste and his grandson, Théophile. ✉ *23 bd. Fragonard* ☎ *04–93–36–93–10* 🎫 *€3.50* ⏲ *June–Sept., daily 10–12:30 and 1:30–6:30; Oct. and Dec.–May, Wed.–Sun. 10–12:30 and 2–5:30.*

The **Musée d'Art et d'Histoire de Provence** *(Museum of the Art and History of Provence)*, just down from the Fragonard perfumery, has a large collection of faïence from the region, including works from Moustiers, Biot, and Vallauris. ✉ *2 rue Mirabeau* ☎ *04–93–36–80–20* 🎫 *€3* ⏲ *June–Sept., daily 10–12:30 and 2–6:30; Oct. and Dec.–May, Wed.–Sun. 10–12:30 and 2–5:30.*

Continue down Rue Mirabeau and lose yourself in the dense labyrinth of the **Vieille Ville** *(Old Town)*, its steep, narrow streets thrown into shadow by shuttered houses five and six stories tall.

WHERE TO EAT AND STAY

$ FRENCH ✕ **Arnaud.** Just off Place aux Aires, and unfortunately close to the bus station, this easygoing corner bistro is one of the oldest in Grasse and serves up inventive home cooking under a vaulted ceiling decorated with stenciled grapevines. Choose from an ambitious and sophisticated menu of à la carte specialties—grilled kebab with lemon and curry sauce, *tête de veau* (calf's head), or a hearty *homemade fois gras*. ✉ *10 pl. de la Foux* ☎ *04–93–36–44–88* 💳 *AE, DC, MC, V.*

$$ FRENCH ✕ **Le Gazan.** A local institution, this cozy and crowded restaurant serves consistently good food. Try the succulent house specialty: steak fillet grilled to a nice turn with a violet-infused *jus* served with seasonal vegetables. For a lighter snack, indulge in delicious *girolles* (wild mushrooms) panfried with garlic, parsley, and butter. ✉ *3 rue Gazan* ☎ *04–93–36–22–88* 💳 *AE, DC, MC, V.*

$$$$ FRENCH ★ **La Bastide Saint-Antoine.** The cicadas live better than most humans at this picture-perfect 18th-century estate overlooking the Estéval. Once the home of an industrialist who hosted Kennedys and the Rolling Stones, now the domain of celebrated chef Jacques Chibois, it welcomes you with old stone walls, shaded walkways, an enormous pool, and a mouthwatering ocher-hue and blue-shutter mansion draped with red trumpet-flower begonia and purple bougainvillea. The guest rooms glossily mix Louis Seize–style chairs, Provençal embroidered bedspreads, and high-tech delights (massaging showers). The restaurant is exceedingly excellent and expensive—try the extraordinary truffle, cream, and foie gras soup or the lobster with a black-olive fondue and beet juice. Happily, lunch is a bargain €55. Reserve well in advance. **Pros:** truly a bastion of culinary excellence; every visitor should try the sun-drenched cuisine; cooking classes are of interest, too. **Cons:** the undeniable fact that dinner can only last four hours—five, max—otherwise one moves into sheer gourmandise; rooms are a touch too Provençal for some. ✉ *48 av. Henri-Dunant* ☎ *04–93–70–94–94* 🌐 *www.jacques-chibois.com* *9 rooms, 7 suites* *In-room: a/c, refrigerator. In-hotel: restaurant, pool, Wi-Fi hotspot* *AE, DC, MC, V.*

VENCE

20 km (12 mi) east of Grasse, 4 km (2½ mi) north of St-Paul, 22 km (14 mi) northwest of Nice.

Encased behind stone walls inside a thriving modern market town is **la Vieille Ville,** the historic part of Vence, which dates from the 15th century. Though crowded with boutiques and souvenir shops, it's slightly more conscious of its history than St-Paul—plaques guide you through its historic squares and *portes* (gates).

GETTING HERE

No trains run to Vence or St-Paul-de-Vence. Nos. 400 or 94 buses of Compagnie SAP frequently make the hour-long run to and from Nice for about €5 a ticket; frequent buses also connect Vence and St-Paul-de-Vence with Cagnes-sur-Mer's train station, about 10 km (6 mi) from Vence. Or inquire at that station about taxi service—and don't be surprised to have a Mercedes pull up and your female chauffeur garbed in a pink Chanel suit!

Visitor Information Vence Tourist Office ✉ *Pl. du Grand Jardin* ☎ *04–93–58–06–38* 🌐 *www.ville-vence.fr.*

EXPLORING

Leave your car on Place du Grand Jardin and head to the gate to the Vieille Ville, passing Place du Frêne, with its ancient ash tree planted in the 16th century, and then through the Portail du Peyra to the Place du Peyra, with its fountains. Ahead lies the former cathedral on Place Clemenceau, adjacent to the ocher-color Hôtel de Ville (town hall). A flea market is held on the square on Wednesday; backstreets and alleys hereabouts have been colonized by craft stores and "art galleries."

In the center of the Vieille Ville, the **Cathédrale de la Nativité de la Vierge** *(Cathedral of the Birth of the Virgin, on Place Godeau)* was built on the

Romans' military drilling field and traces bits and pieces to Carolingian and even Roman times. It's a hybrid of Romanesque and Baroque styles, expanded and altered over the centuries. Note the rostrum added in 1499—its choir stalls are carved with particularly vibrant and amusing scenes of daily life back when. In the baptistery is a ceramic mosaic of Moses in the bulrushes by Chagall.

Fodor's Choice ★ On the outskirts of "new" Vence, toward St-Jeannet is the **Chapelle du Rosaire** *(Chapel of the Rosary)*, better known to the world-at-large as the Matisse Chapel. Matisse decorated it with beguiling simplicity and clarity between 1947 and 1951—the chapel was the artist's gift to nuns who had nursed him through illness. It reflects the reductivist style of the era: walls, floor, and ceiling are gleaming white, and the small stained-glass windows are cool greens and blues. "Despite its imperfections I think it is my masterpiece . . . the result of a lifetime devoted to the search for truth," wrote Matisse, who designed and dedicated the chapel when he was in his eighties and nearly blind. ✉ *446 Av. Henri-Matisse* ☎ *04–93–58–03–26* *€3* *Mid-Dec.–mid-Nov., Tues. and Thurs. 10–11:30 and 2–5:30, Mon., Wed., Fri., and Sat. 2–5:30; Sun Mass at 10.*

WHERE TO EAT AND STAY

$$$ FRENCH ★ ✕ **La Farigoule.** A long, beamed dining room that opens onto a shady terrace casts an easygoing spell and serves as an hors d'oeuvre for some sophisticated Provençal cooking. Watch for tangy *pissaladières* (pizza-like tarts) with sardines marinated in ginger and lemon, salt-cod ravioli, lamb with olive polenta, and a crunchy parfait of honey and hazelnuts. Fixed-menu dinners are €30 and €40. Reservations are recommended. ✉ *15 rue Henri-Isnard* ☎ *04–93–58–01–27* *www.lafarigoule-vence.fr* *MC, V* *Closed Tues.*

$$$$ FRENCH ★ ✕ **Les Bacchanales.** The opening of this much-anticipated restaurant has set new standards for its already high gastronomic expectations. Under the innovative but steady hand of star chef Christophe Dufau, the daily changing menu puts an inventive spin on traditional local ingredients; the sea bass served with white cabbage, green onion, thyme, coriander, and mullet caviar is a must. It's all served in a sun-filled and beautifully decorated garden villa, a mere 10 minutes walk from Vence. ✉ *247 av. de Provence* ☎ *04–93–24–19–19* *www.lesbacchanales.com* *MC, V* *Closed Tues. and Wed.*

$$$$ ★ **Château du Domaine St. Martin.** Exuding an expensive charm, this famous domain occupies the ancient site of a fortress of the Knights Templars. Sitting on a hilltop perch and surrounded by acres of greenery designed by Jean Mus, the mansion welcomes you with public salons that are light, airy, and a bit too sleek for some tastes. All guest rooms are, luxuriously, junior suites, except for six *bastides* (two- and three-bedroom villas) accented with beautiful antiques. **La Commanderie** restaurant is perhaps the best reason to come here, thanks to its stunning walls adorned with china, chef Yannick Franques's superb creations, and one of the most panoramic terraces around—the views over Old Vence to the Baie des Anges are eye-popping. **Pros:** stunning views stretching out over the valley to the sea; famous guests often stay here (Brad Pitt and Angelina Jolie, among others), so servers are used to

discreet excellence. **Cons:** restaurant decor has been labeled fussy and old-fashioned; reception can be cool. ✉ *Av. des Templiers* ☎ *04–93–58–02–02* 🌐 *www.chateau-st-martin.com* *38 rooms* *In-room: a/c, refrigerator. In-hotel: 2 restaurants, bar, tennis courts, pool, spa, Wi-Fi hotspot, parking (free), some pets allowed* *AE, MC, V* ⏲ *Closed mid-Oct.–mid-Feb.* *MAP.*

$–$$ ★ **L'Auberge des Seigneurs et du Lion d'Or.** Dating to the 15th century and the only hotel set within Vence's ancient walls, this time-stained inn has rustic, medieval charm. Downstairs is the restaurant, all copper pots, wood trim, and *ambience à la François Premier.* Upstairs, surprisingly, guest rooms are airy and bright; drapes, bedspreads, and bureau runners are all in matching hues—*de provence.* Some rooms have great views. The kitchen here specializes in roast meats—the chicken prepared on a spit of vines instead of wood is *magnifique*; the restaurant is very popular so be sure to book well in advance. **Pros:** lovely family atmosphere makes for an easy stay; nice touches (fresh flowers in the rooms). **Cons:** rooms can be noisy, especially facing street; the smell of cooking can waft up into the rooms. ✉ *Pl. du Frêne* ☎ *04–93–58–04–24* 🌐 *www.auberge-seigneurs.com* *6 rooms* *In-room: a/c, refrigerator. In-hotel: restaurant, Internet terminal, some pets allowed* *AE, MC, V.*

ST-PAUL-DE-VENCE

Fodor's Choice ★ *4 km (2½ mi) south of Vence, 18 km (11 mi) northwest of Nice.*

Visitor Information St-Paul-de-Vence Tourist Office ✉ *2 Rue Grande* ☎ *04–93–32–86–95* 🌐 *www.saint-pauldevence.com.*

The famous medieval village of St-Paul-de-Vence can be seen from afar, standing out like its companion, Vence, against the skyline. In the Middle Ages St-Paul was basically a city-state, and it controlled its own political destiny for centuries. But by the early 20th century St-Paul had faded to oblivion, overshadowed by the growth of Vence and Cagnes—until it was rediscovered in the 1920s when a few penniless artists began paying for their drinks at the local auberge with paintings. Those artists turned out to be Signac, Modigliani, and Bonnard, who met at the Auberge de la Colombe d'Or, now a sumptuous inn, where the walls are still covered with their ink sketches and daubs. Nowadays art of a sort still dominates in the myriad tourist traps that take your eyes off the beauty of St-Paul's old stone houses and its rampart views. The most commercially developed of Provence's hilltop villages, St-Paul is nonetheless a magical place when the tourist crowds thin. Artists are still drawn to St-Paul's light, its pure air, its wraparound views, and its honey-color stone walls, soothingly cool on a hot Provençal afternoon. Film stars continue to love its lazy yet genteel ways, lingering on the garden-bower terrace of the Colombe d'Or and challenging the locals to a game of pétanque under the shade of the plane trees. Even so, you have to work hard to find the timeless aura of St-Paul; get here early in the day to get a jump on the cars and tour buses, which can clog the main D36 highway here by noon, or plan on a stay-over. Either way, do consider a luncheon or dinner beneath the Picassos at the Colombe d'Or, even if the menu prices seem almost as fabulous as the collection.

Our vote for France's most beautiful "*village perché*," Haut-de-Cagnes is an enchanting place filled with tiny piazzas, winding alleys, and staircase streets.

★ Many people come to St-Paul just to visit the **Fondation Maeght,** founded in 1964 by art dealer Aimé Maeght and set on a wooded cliff top high above the medieval town. It's not just a small modern art museum but also an extraordinary marriage of the arc-and-plane architecture of José Sert; the looming sculptures of Miró, Moore, and Giacometti; and a humbling hilltop perch of pines, vines, and flowing planes of water. On display is an intriguing and ever-varying parade of the work of modern masters, including the wise and funny late-life masterwork *La Vie* (*Life*), by Chagall. On the extensive grounds, the fountains and impressive vistas help to beguile even those who aren't into modern art. ✉ *Pl. du Frêne* ☎ *04–93–32–81–63* 🌐 *www.fondation-maeght.com* 🎫 *€11* 🕒 *July–Sept., daily 10–7; Oct.–June, daily 10–6.*

WHERE TO EAT AND STAY

¢–$ **Hostellerie les Remparts.** With original stone walls, coved ceilings, light-color fabrics, a warm welcome, and perfect location in the center of the Vieille Ville, this small medieval hotel is an uncut gem. Its restaurant serves good regional specialties. In summer expect to book at least two months in advance, and at least 10 days in advance for a table. **Pros:** an inexpensive and friendly hotel with a lot of charm; rooms are airy and big; the location in the center of the old town is ideal. **Cons:** hotel is usually full, so you need to book way in advance; often, even if you reserve, there is a longish wait for a table in the restaurant, especially in the summertime. ✉ *72 rue Grande* ☎ *04–93–32–09–88* *9 rooms* *In-room: no a/c, no TV. In-hotel: restaurant, some pets allowed* *AE, MC, V.*

$$$$ Fodor's Choice ★ **La Colombe d'Or.** Considered by many to be the most beautiful inn in France, "the golden dove" occupies a lovely, rose-stone Renaissance mansion set just outside the walls of St-Paul. Walk into the dining room and you'll do a double take—yes, those are real Mirós, Bonnards, and Légers on the walls, given in payment in hungrier days when this inn was known as the heart of St-Paul's artistic revival. Back then, it was the cherished retreat of Picasso and Chagall, Maeterlinck and Kipling, Yves Montand and Simone Signoret (who met and married here). Today, a ceramic Léger mural still lords it over the famous fig-tree luncheon terrace, a Calder stabile soaks in the giant pool, and there's even a Braque in the bar. The food is yumptious if not as four-star as the crowd (this is one of the very few places where movie stars enjoy being recognized). Upstairs, the guest rooms are bewitching, replete with Louis XIII armoires, medieval four-posters, wood beams, Provençal borders, and painted murals (even rooms in the two annexes are flawless in taste). Henri Matisse once called La Colombe "a small paradise," and who are we to argue? Simply put: if you haven't visited La Colombe, you really haven't been to the French Riviera. **Pros:** where else can you have an aperitif under a real Picasso? Where else can you wander in the garden, glass of wine in hand, and stare at a real Rodin? **Cons:** the menu is give or take: sometimes there are moments of brilliance but often menu items are outshone by the art; service is quite slow, which can be a good thing if you have the time to sit back and enjoy the atmosphere. ✉ *Pl. Général-de-Gaulle* ☎ *04–93–32–80–02* ⊕ *www.la-colombe-dor.com* *16 rooms, 10 suites* *In-room: a/c (some), refrigerator. In-hotel: restaurant, bar, pool, Wi-Fi hotspot, some pets allowed* ▭ *AE, DC, MC, V* ⊗ *Closed Nov. and 2 wks in Jan.* ¶◎¶ *MAP.*

HAUT-DE-CAGNES

Fodor's Choice ★ *6 km (4 mi) south of St-Paul-de-Vence, 21 km (13 mi) northeast of Cannes, 10 km (6 mi) north of Antibes, 14 km (9 mi) west of Nice.*

Although from N7 you may be tempted to give wide berth to **Cagnes-sur-Mer**—with its congested sprawl of freeway overpasses, beachfront pizzerias, and train station—don't. Just follow the brown signs inland touting BOURG MÉDIÉVAL and up into one of the most beautiful *villages perchés* (perched villages) along the Riviera: Haut-de-Cagnes. Alice, of Wonderland fame, would adore this steeply cobbled Old Town, honeycombed as it is with tiny little piazzas, return-to-your-starting-point-twice alleys, and winding streets that abruptly change to stairways. This town is so pretty you'll wish you could paint, not photograph, it!

GETTING HERE

Cagnes-sur-Mer is the station stop on the main Marseilles–Ventimiglia coastal train line. More than two-dozen trains pull into the station at Avenue de la Gare in the commercial sector called Cagnes-Ville. Sample trips: from Nice (13 mins, €5) and from Cannes (23 mins, €6). A free shuttle bus (*navette*) connects Place du Général-du-Gaulle in the center of Cagnes-Ville (turn right out of train station and walk about 9 blocks) to Haut-de-Cagnes at least once an hour; if the navette isn't running in low season, there's also a municipal bus that goes to the hilltop village from a stop across the street and about three blocks west of the station (ask at the train station). Les Collettes, Renoir's villa, is walkable from Place du Général-du-Gaulle.

Visitor Information Haut-de-Cagnes Tourist Office ⌧ *6 bd. Marechal Juinm B.P.* ☎ *04–93–20–61–64* 🌐 *www.cagnes-tourisme.com.*

EXPLORING

Anyone would find it a pleasure to wander the old byways of Haut-de-Cagnes, some with cobbled steps, others passing under vaulted arches draped with bougainvillea. Many of the pretty residences are dollhouse-size (especially the hobbit houses on Rue Passebon) and most date from the 14th and 15th centuries. There's nary a shop, so the commercial horrors of Mougins or St-Paul-de-Vence are left far behind. It's little wonder the rich and literate—Soutine, Modigliani, and Simone de Beauvoir, among them—have long kept Haut-de-Cagnes a secret forgetaway. Or almost: enough cars now arrive that a garage (Parking du Planastel) has been excavated out of the hillside.

★ Haut-de-Cagnes's steep-cobbled Vieille Ville is crowned by the fat, crenellated **Château Grimaldi,** built in 1310 by the Grimaldis (who now rule over Monaco) and reinforced over the centuries. You are welcomed inside the château by a grand Renaissance courtyard, off which are vaulted medieval chambers, adorned with, among other things, a vast Renaissance fireplace, a splendid 17th-century trompe-l'oeil fresco of the fall of Phaëthon from his sun-chariot, and three small specialized collections: the history of the olive, memorabilia of the cabaret star Suzy Solidor, and a collection of modern Mediterranean artists, including Cocteau and Dufy. Across the château's plaza, take some time to explore the grand **Chapelle Notre-Dame-de-la-Protection,** nearly hidden inside some medieval buildings, although its Italianate bell-tower gives it away. ⌧ *Pl. Grimaldi* ☎ *04–92–02–47–30* 🎟 *€3, €4.50 joint ticket with Musée Renoir* ⏲ *Oct and Dec.–Apr., Wed.–Mon. 10–noon and 2–5; May–Sept., Wed.–Mon. 10–noon and 2–6.*

★ After staying up and down the coast, Auguste Renoir (1841–1919) settled in a house in Les Collettes, just east of the Vieille Ville, now the **Musée Renoir.** Here, he passed the last 12 years of his life, painting the landscape around him, working in bronze, and rolling his wheelchair through the luxuriant garden tiered with roses, citrus groves, and some of the most spectacular olive trees along the coast. You can view this sweet and melancholic villa as it has been preserved by Renoir's children, and admire 11 of his last paintings. Although up a steep hill, Les Collettes is walkable from Place du Général-du-Gaulle in central Cagnes-Ville. ⌧ *Chemindes Collettes* ☎ *04–93–20–61–07* 🎟 *€3, €4.50 joint ticket with Château Grimaldi* ⏲ *Oct. and Dec.–Apr., Wed.–Mon. 10–noon and 2–5; May–Sept., Wed.–Mon. 10–noon and 2–6. Guided tours in English, Thurs. in July and Aug.*

WHERE TO EAT AND STAY

$$ Fodor's Choice ★ 🏨 **Hôtel Le Cagnard.** Housed in a 14th-century residence built on the outer walls of the Grimaldi castle, this lovely hideaway is a modern escape to a medieval world. Faithful to old-world style in antiques-abounding decor, the guest rooms are very elegant but everyone heads

here because of the superlative restaurant. The lavish menu (no lunch Monday, Tuesday, and Thursday; reservations recommended) lives up to the surrounding splendor with dishes like foie gras cooked with figs, peaches, apricots, and rosemary, or—*Dieu!*—the black-truffle lasagna. Lunch is mainly served in a soaring and coved hall covered with "romantic"-era frescoes; dinner is offered in a salon glittering with Renaissance-style boiserie and its famous, retractable ceiling, which often shows off the night sky. If you're arriving on the town square by the shuttle bus, the hotel's *voiturier* will be sent to pick up your luggage; there's also an alley where cars can drop off guests. **Pros:** fabulous food; evocative décor; service is friendly and prompt; the owners Jean-Marc and Françoise Laroche are truly welcoming. **Cons:** rooms can be a bit dark. ✉ *54 rue Sous Barri* ☎ *04–93–20–73–21* 🌐 *www.le-cagnard.com* *15 rooms, 6 suites* *In-room: a/c, refrigerator, Internet (some), Wi-Fi (some). In-hotel: restaurant, bar, parking (free), some pets allowed* *AE, DC, MC, V* *Closed Nov.–mid-Dec.*

NICE

Nowadays Nice strikes an engaging balance between historic Provençal grace, port-town exotica, urban energy, whimsy, and high culture. You could easily spend your vacation here, attuned to Nice's quirks, its rhythms, its very multicultural population, and its Mediterranean tides. The high point of the year falls in mid-February, when the city hosts one of the most spectacular Carnival celebrations in France (🌐 *www.nicecarnaval.com*).

As the fifth-largest city in France, this distended urban tangle is sometimes avoided, but that decision is one to be rued: Nice's waterfront, paralleled by the famous Promenade des Anglais and lined by grand hotels, is one of the noblest and most gorgeous in France. It's capped by a dramatic hilltop château, below which the slopes plunge almost into the sea and at whose base a bewitching warren of ancient Mediterranean streets unfolds.

It was in this old quarter, now Vieux Nice, that the Greeks established a market-port in the 4th century BC and named it Nikaia. After falling to the Saracen invasions, Nice regained power and developed into an important port in the early Middle Ages. In 1388, under Louis d'Anjou, Nice, along with the hill towns behind, effectively seceded from the county of Provence and allied itself with Savoie as the Comté de Nice (Nice County). It was a relationship that lasted some 500 years, and added rich Italian flavor to the city's culture, architecture, and dialect.

GETTING HERE

From the airport, you can take a bus to almost anywhere along the Riviera. There are a few options: RCA (☎ *04–93–85–64–44* 🌐 *www.rca.tm.fr*), which is more comfortable and more expensive (*€6*) to Nice or the Transport Alpes Maritimes (TAM) buses (☎ *08–10–06–10–06* 🌐 *www.lignedazur.com*), which service the same destinations and are cheaper (*€1*). To go to the center of Nice, take the No. 98 TAM bus from the airport (*€1*), which will take you to the main *Gare Routière,* or bus station (✉ *5 bd. Jean Jaurés* ☎ *04–93–85–61–81*). The other option from the airport is a taxi (☎ *04–93–13–78–78*), costing €10. In Nice, the Sunbus is a convenient way to cut across town; a day pass costs €4, and a one-way ticket is €1.30, available at tabacs, their ticket office at 10 avenue Félix Faure, or their Station Centrale (☎ *08–10–06–10–06* 🌐 *www.lignedazur.com*) on Square Général Leclerc. Their main routes include No. 12 to Promenade des Anglais, and No. 30 to Vieux Nice.

Visitor Information Nice Tourist Office ✉ *5 promenade des Anglais* ☎ *04–92–14–48–00* 🌐 *www.nicetourism.com.*

VIEUX NICE

Framed by the "château"—really a rocky promontory—and Cours Saleya, Nice's Vieille Ville is its strongest drawing point and, should you only be passing through, the best place to capture the city's historic atmosphere. Its grid of narrow streets, darkened by houses five and six stories high with bright splashes of laundry fluttering overhead and jewel-box Baroque churches on every other corner, creates a magic that seems utterly removed from the French Riviera fast lane.

TOP ATTRACTIONS

3 **Chapelle de la Miséricorde.** A superbly balanced *pièce-montée* (wedding cake) of half-domes and cupolas, this chapel is decorated within an inch of its life with frescoes, faux marble, gilt, and crystal chandeliers. A magnificent Bréa altarpiece crowns the ensemble. ✉ *Cours Saleya, Vieux Nice.*

9 **Colline de Château** *(Château Hill)*. Though nothing remains of the once-massive medieval stronghold but a few ruins left after its 1706 dismantling, this park still bears its name. From here take in extraordinary views of the Baie des Anges, the length of the Promenade des Anglais, and the red-ocher roofs of the Vieille Ville. ⏲ *Daily 7–7.*

1 ★ **Cours Saleya.** This long pedestrian thoroughfare, half street, half square, is the nerve center of Old Nice, the heart of the Vieille Ville and the stage-set for the daily dramas of marketplace and café life. Framed with 18th-century houses and shaded by plane trees, the long, narrow square bursts into a fireworks-show of color Tuesday through Sunday, when flower-market vendors roll armloads of mimosas, irises, roses, and orange blossoms into *cornets* (paper cones) and thrust them into the arms of shoppers. Cafés and restaurants, all more or less touristy, fill outdoor tables with onlookers who bask in the sun. At the far-east end, antiques and *brocantes* (collectibles) draw avid junk-hounds every Monday morning. At this end you can also find Place Félix. Little wonder the great painter Matisse lived (from 1921 to 1938) in the

> **WORD OF MOUTH**
>
> "Go to Nice. Stay on the Promenade des Anglais near Vieux Nice, where you'll be close to both shopping and many good restaurants. The beach will be on the other side of the Promenade; it's worth paying for a hotel room with that view." —Underhill

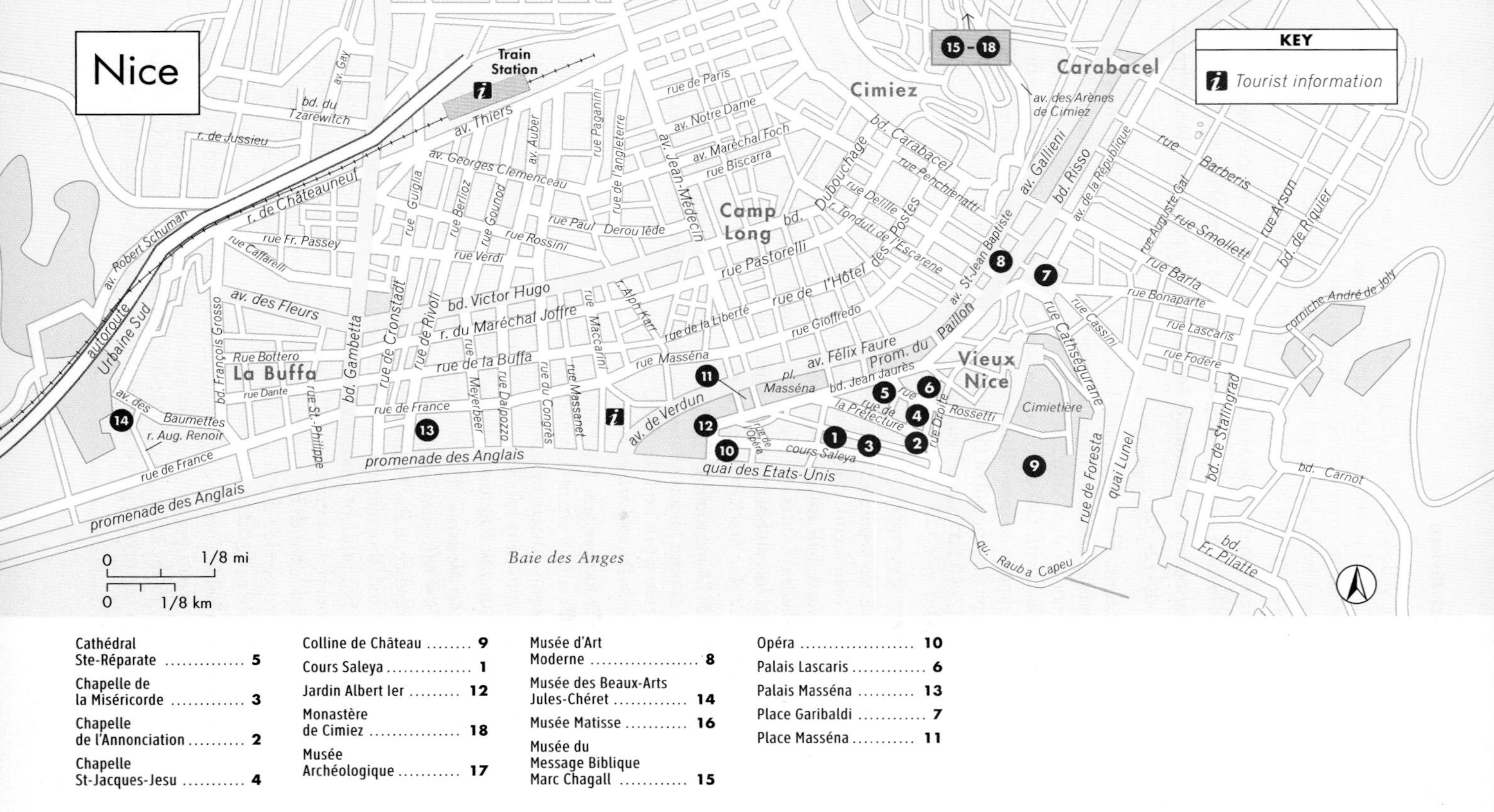

Nice
KEY
Tourist information
Train Station
Cimiez
Carabacel
Camp Long
Vieux Nice
La Buffa
Baie des Anges
15 - 18
av. des Arènes de Cimiez
av. Thiers
r. de Châteauneuf
av. Robert Schuman
autoroute Urbaine Sud
bd. du Tzarewitch
av. Gay
r. de Jussieu
av. Georges Clemenceau
av. Auber
rue Paganini
rue de l'angleterre
av. Jean-Médecin
rue de Paris
av. Notre Dame
av. Maréchal Foch
rue Biscarra
bd. Dubouchage
bd. Carabacel
rue Penchienatti
rue Delille
r. Tonduti de l'Escarène
rue des Postes
av. Gallieni
bd. Risso
av. de la République
rue Barberis
rue Auguste Gal
rue Smollett
rue Arson
bd. de Riquier
rue Barla
rue Bonaparte
rue Lascaris
rue Fodéré
corniche André de Joly
bd. de Stalingrad
bd. Carnot
bd. Fr. Pilatte
qu. Rauba Capeu
quai Lunel
rue de Foresta
rue Cathségurane
rue Cassini
Cimietière
av. St-Jean Baptiste
Paillon
Prom. du Paillon
av. Félix Faure
bd. Jean Jaurès
pl. Masséna
rue de la Préfecture
rue Droite
rue Rossetti
cours Saleya
rue de l'Opéra
quai des Etats-Unis
av. de Verdun
rue Masséna
rue Gioffredo
rue de la Liberté
rue de l'Hôtel des Postes
rue Pastorelli
r. Alph Karr
rue Maccarini
rue Massanet
rue du Congrès
rue Dalpozzo
rue Meyerbeer
rue de la Buffa
r. du Maréchal Joffre
bd. Victor Hugo
rue de Rivoli
rue de Cronstadt
bd. Gambetta
rue Paul Deroulède
rue Rossini
rue Verdi
rue Gounod
rue Berlioz
rue Guiglia
rue de France
promenade des Anglais
rue St.-Philippe
bd. François Grosso
Rue Bottero
rue Dante
av. des Fleurs
rue Fr. Passey
rue Caffarelli
av. des Baumettes
r. Aug. Renoir
0 1/8 mi
0 1/8 km
Cathédral Ste-Réparate 5
Chapelle de la Miséricorde 3
Chapelle de l'Annonciation 2
Chapelle St-Jacques-Jesu 4
Colline de Château 9
Cours Saleya 1
Jardin Albert Ier 12
Monastère de Cimiez 18
Musée Archéologique 17
Musée d'Art Moderne 8
Musée des Beaux-Arts Jules-Chéret 14
Musée Matisse 16
Musée du Message Biblique Marc Chagall 15
Opéra 10
Palais Lascaris 6
Palais Masséna 13
Place Garibaldi 7
Place Masséna 11

imposing yellow stone building that looms over the square. Indeed, you don't need to visit the city's famous Musée Matisse to understand this great artist: simply stand in the doorway of his former apartment (at 1 Place Charles Félix) and study the Place de l'Ancien Senat 10 feet away—it's a golden Matisse pumped up to the nth power.

NEED A BREAK?

Choose from a fantastic array of colorful sorbets, gelati, and ice creams and settle in to do some serious people-watching at one of the patio tables overlooking the fountain at Fennocchio (⊠ *2 pl. Rossetti, Vieux Nice* ☎ *04–93–80–72– 52*).

❻ **Palais Lascaris.** The aristocratic Lascaris Palace was built in 1648 for Jean-Baptiste Lascaris-Vintimille, *marechal* to the duke of Savoy. The magnificent vaulted staircase, with its massive stone balustrade and niches filled with classical gods, is surpassed in grandeur only by the Flemish tapestries (after Rubens) and the extraordinary trompe-l'oeil fresco depicting the fall of Phaëthon. ⊠ *15 rue Droite, Vieux Nice* ☎ *04–93–62–72–40* *Free; €5 guided tour, including Vieille Ville* ⏲ *Wed.–Mon. 10–1 and 2–6.*

WORTH NOTING

❺ **Cathédrale Ste-Réparate.** An ensemble of columns, cupolas, and symmetrical ornaments dominates the Vieille Ville, flanked by its own 18th-century bell tower and capped by its glossy ceramic-tile dome. The cathedral's interior, restored to a bright palette of ocher, golds, and rusts, has elaborate plasterwork and decorative frescoes on every surface. ⊠ *Rue Ste-Réparate, Vieux Nice.*

❷ **Chapelle de l'Annonciation.** This 17th-century Carmelite chapel is a classic example of pure Niçoise Baroque, from its sculpted door to its extravagant marble work and the florid symmetry of its arches and cupolas. ⊠ *Rue de la Poissonerie, Vieux Nice.*

❹ **Chapelle St-Jacques-Jesu.** If the Vieille Ville's other chapels are jewel boxes, this 17th-century chapel is a barn: broad, open, and ringing hollow, this church seems austere by comparison, but that's only because the theatrical decoration is spread over a more expansive surface. ⊠ *Corner of Rue Droite and Rue Gesu, Vieux Nice.*

❽ **Musée d'Art Moderne.** The assertive contemporary architecture of the Modern Art Museum makes a bold and emphatic statement regarding Nice's presence in the modern world. The art collection inside focuses intently and thoroughly on contemporary art from the late 1950s onward, but pride of place is given to sculptor Nikki de Saint Phalle's recent donation of more than 170 exceptional pieces. The rooftop terrace, sprinkled with minimalist sculptures, has stunning views over the city. ⊠ *Promenade des Arts, Vieux Nice* ☎ *04–97–13–42–01* 🌐 *www.mamac-nice.org* *Free* ⏲ *Tues.–Sun. 10–6.*

❼ **Place Garibaldi.** Encircled by grand vaulted arcades stuccoed in rich yellow, the broad pentagon of this square could have been airlifted out of Turin. In the center, the shrine-like fountain sculpture of Garibaldi seems to be surveying you as you stroll under the arcades and lounge in its cafés.

Like the Rio of France, Nice is lined with a gigantic crescent beach, whose prime spot, the Promenade des Anglais, is home to many palace-hotels.

ALONG THE PROMENADE DES ANGLAIS

Nice takes on a completely different character west of Cours Saleya, with broad city blocks, vast Neoclassical hotels and apartment houses, and a series of inviting parks dense with palm trees, greenery, and splashing fountains. From the Jardin Albert Ier, once the delta of the Paillon River, the famous Promenade des Anglais stretches the length of the city's waterfront. The original promenade was the brainchild of Lewis Way, an English minister in the then-growing community of British refugees drawn to Nice's climate. Nowadays it's a wide multilane boulevard thick with traffic—in fact, it's the last gasp of the N98 coastal highway. Beside it runs its charming parallel, a wide, sun-washed pedestrian walkway with intermittent steps leading down to the smooth-rock beach. A daily parade of *promeneurs,* rollerbladers, joggers, and sun baskers strolls its broad pavement, looking out over the hypnotic blue expanse of the sea. Only in the wee hours is it possible to enjoy the waterfront stroll as the cream of Nice's international society once did, when there was nothing more than hoofbeats to compete with the roar of the waves.

EXPLORING

12 **Jardin Albert Ier** *(Albert I Garden).* Along the Promenade des Anglais, this luxurious garden stands over the delta of the River Paillon, underground since 1882. Every kind of flower and palm tree grows here, thrown into exotic relief by night illumination.

14 ★ **Musée des Beaux-Arts Jules-Chéret** *(Jules-Chéret Fine Arts Museum).* Although the collection here is impressive, it's the 19th-century Italianate mansion that houses it that remains the showstopper. Originally built for a member of Nice's Old Russian community, the Princess Kotschoubey, this was a Belle Époque wedding cake, replete with one of the grandest staircases on the coast, salons decorated with Neo-Pompéienne frescoes, an English-style garden, and white columns and balustrades by the dozen. After the *richissime* American James Thompson took over and the last glittering ball was held here, the villa was bought by the municipality as a museum in the 1920s. Unfortunately, much of the period decor was sold but, in its place, are paintings by Degas, Boudin, Monet, Sisley, Dufy, and Jules Chéret, whose posters of winking *damselles* distill all the *joie* of the Belle Époque. From the Negresco Hotel area the museum is about a 15-minute walk up a gentle hill. ✉ *33 av. des Baumettes, Centre Ville* ☎ *04–92–15–28–28* 🌐 *www.musee-beaux-arts-nice.org* 🎫 *Free* 🕓 *Tues.–Sun. 10–6.*

10 **Opéra.** A half-block west of the Cours Saleya stands a flamboyant Italian-style theater designed by Charles Garnier, architect of the Paris Opéra. It's home today to the Opéra de Nice, with a permanent chorus, orchestra, and ballet corps. The season runs from mid-November to mid-June, and operas cost anywhere from €8 to €85. ✉ *4 rue St-François-de-Paule, Vieux Nice* ☎ *04–92–17–40–79* 🌐 *www.opera-nice.org.*

13 ★ **Palais Masséna** *(Masséna Palace).* This spectacular Belle Époque building, housing the **Musée d'Art et d'Histoire** *(Museum of Art and History)*, has finally reopened after years of renovations to spectacular results. Familiar paintings from French, Italian, and Dutch masters line the walls. A visit to the palace gardens set with towering palm trees, a marble bust of the handsome General Masséna, and backdropped by the wedding-cake trim of the Hôtel Negresco, is a delight; it's one of Nice's most imposing oases. ✉ *Entrance at 65 rue de France, Centre Ville* ☎ *04–93–91–19–10* 🕓 *Museum €4, gardens free* 🕓 *Tues.–Sun. 10–6.*

11 **Place Masséna.** As Cours Saleya is the heart of the Vieille Ville, so this broad square is the heart of the city as a whole. It's framed by an ensemble of Italian-style arcaded buildings first built in 1815, their facades stuccoed in rich red ocher. On the west flank sits the city's Belle Époque icon, the Hôtel Negresco.

CIMIEZ

Once the site of the powerful Roman settlement Cemenelum, the hilltop neighborhood of Cimiez—4 km (2½ mi) north of Cours Saleya—is Nice's most luxurious quarter (use Bus 15 from Place Masséna or Avenue Jean-Médecin to visit its sights).

EXPLORING

18 **Monastère de Cimiez.** This fully functioning monastery is worth the pilgrimage. You can find a lovely **garden,** replanted along the lines of the original 16th-century layout; the **Musée Franciscain,** a didactic museum tracing the history of the Franciscan order; and a 15th-century **church**

12

containing three works of remarkable power and elegance by Bréa. ✉ *Pl. du Monastère, Cimiez* ☎ *04–93–81–00–04* 🎫 *Free* ⏲ *Mon.–Sat. 10–noon and 3–6.*

> **WORD OF MOUTH**
>
> "While in Nice, try to make time for the Matisse and Chagall museums. I had the pleasure of visiting these two museums last summer and found them most enjoyable."
>
> —ExplorerB

17 **Musée Archéologique** *(Archaeology Museum)*. This museum, next to the Matisse Museum, has a dense and intriguing collection of objects extracted from the digs around the Roman city of Cemenelum, which flourished from the 1st to the 5th century. ✉ *160 av. des Arènes-de-Cimiez, Cimiez* ☎ *04–93–81–59–57* 🌐 *www.musee-archeologique-nice.org* 🎫 *€3* ⏲ *Wed.–Mon. 10–6.*

16 **Musée Matisse.** In the '60s the city of Nice bought this lovely, light-bathed 17th-century villa, surrounded by the ruins of Roman civilization, and restored it to house a large collection of Henri Matisse's works. Matisse settled along Nice's waterfront in 1917, seeking a sun cure after a bout with pneumonia, and remained here until his death in 1954. During his years on the French Riviera, Matisse maintained intense friendships and artistic liaisons with Renoir, who lived in Cagnes, and with Picasso, who lived in Mougins and Antibes. He eventually moved up to the rarefied isolation of Cimiez and took an apartment in the Hôtel Regina (now an apartment building, just across from the museum), where he lived out the rest of his life. Matisse walked often in the parklands around the Roman remains and was buried in an olive grove outside the Cimiez cemetery. The collection of artworks includes several pieces the artist donated to the city before his death; the rest were donated by his family. In every medium and context—paintings, gouache cutouts, engravings, and book illustrations—it represents the evolution of his art, from Cézanne-like still lifes to exuberant dancing paper dolls. Even the furniture and accessories speak of Matisse, from the Chinese vases to the bold-printed fabrics with which he surrounded himself. A series of black-and-white photographs captures the artist at work, surrounded by personal—and telling—details. ✉ *164 av. des Arènes-de-Cimiez, Cimiez* ☎ *04–93–81–08–08* 🌐 *www.musee-matisse-nice.org* 🎫 *€4* ⏲ *Wed.–Mon. 10–6.*

Fodor's Choice ★

15 ★ **Musée du Message Biblique Marc Chagall** *(Marc Chagall Museum of Biblical Themes)*. This museum has one of the finest permanent collections of Chagall's (1887–1985) late works. Superbly displayed, 17 vast canvases depict biblical themes, each in emphatic, joyous colors. ✉ *Av. du Dr-Ménard, head up Av. Thiers, then take a left onto Av. Malausséna, cross railway tracks, and take first right up Av. de l'Olivetto, Cimiez* ☎ *04–93–53–87–20* 🌐 *www.musee-chagall.fr* 🎫 *€7.50* ⏲ *May–Oct., Wed.–Mon. 10–6; Nov.–Apr., Wed.–Mon. 10–5.*

WHERE TO EAT

$$ FRENCH ✕ **Brasserie Flo.** Step into this three-piece costume drama: chef Michel Betis holds the starring role, the staff as his loyal support. Set in an old theater, the kitchen is literally center stage, and the best seats are on the upper balcony where you can watch every step of your meal being

prepared. Food is easy-to-eat Provençal, with a good late-night selection. Reserve well in advance. ✉ *24 rue Sacha Guitry, near Place Massena* ☎ *04–93–13–38–38* 🌐 *www.flonice.com* ✍ *Reservations essential for dinner on Fri. and Sat.* 💳 *AE, DC, MC, V.*

¢ FRENCH ✕ **Chez René/Socca.** This back-alley landmark is the most popular dive in town for *socca*, the chickpea-pancake snack food unique to Nice. Rustic olive-wood tables line the street, and curt waiters splash down your drink order. For the food, you get in line at the Socca, choose your €3 plate (or plates), and carry it steaming to the table yourself. It's off Place Garibaldi on the edge of the Vieille Ville, across from the *Gare Routière* (bus station). ✉ *2 rue Miralheti, Vieux Nice* ☎ *04–93–92–05–73* 💳 *No credit cards* ⏲ *Closed Mon.*

$$$ FRENCH ✕ **Don Camillo Creations.** In a complete turnabout, the once-fading Don Camillo has shed its staid, old maid–ish decor and introduced a swanky, modern look. The food, always good, is now even better with just a touch more inspiration; chef Marc Laville reinvents Niçois classiques that are as tasty as they are affordable. Try the lobster carpaccio with tempura battered zucchini flowers. ✉ *5 rue des Ponchettes, Vieux Nice* ☎ *04–93–85–67–95* 🌐 *www.doncamillo-creations.fr* 💳 *AE, MC, V* ⏲ *Closed Sun. and Mon.*

$$ SEAFOOD ✕ **Grand Café de Turin.** Whether you squeeze onto a banquette in the dark, low-ceiling bar or win a coveted table under the arcaded porticoes on Place Garibaldi, this is *the* place to go for shellfish in Nice: sea snails, clams, plump *fines de claires,* and salty *bleues* oysters, and urchins by the dozen. It's packed noon and night (and has been since it opened in 1910), so don't be too put off by the sometimes brusque reception of the waiters. ✉ *5 pl. Garibaldi, Vieux Nice* ☎ *04–93–62–29–52* 💳 *AE, DC, MC, V.*

$$$ FRENCH ✕ **Keisuke Matsushima.** One of the brightest voices in the gastronomic world, Keisuke Matsushima is collecting rave reviews (and Michelin stars) for his innovative Mediterranean cuisine and sleek minimalist presentation. A perfectly scrumptious menu may include a selection of asparagus—wild, purple, green, and lemon savory—followed by roasted sea bream served with spiky artichokes and mussels in a vegetable broth topped with capuchin flowers, and, la piece de résistance, pineapple cannelloni stuffed with coconut mousse, lime meringue, and pineapple-basil sorbet. If you're into nouvelle food and minimalist decor, you'll love this place. Lunch menus are a bargain at €28 or €35. ✉ *22 rue de la France, Vieux Nice* ☎ *04–93–82–26–06* 🌐 *www.keisukematsushima.com* ✍ *Reservations essential* 💳 *AE, MC, V* ⏲ *No lunch Mon. No lunch Sat. Closed Sun.*

$$$ FRENCH ★ ✕ **La Mérenda.** The back-to-bistro boom climaxed here when Dominique Le Stanc retired his crown at the Negresco to take over this tiny, unpretentious landmark of Provençal cuisine. Now he and his wife work in the miniature open kitchen, creating the ultimate versions of stuffed sardines, pistou, and slow-simmered *daubes* (beef stews). To reserve entry to the inner sanctum, you must stop by in person (there's no telephone). The prix-fixe dinner menu is €25 to €30. ✉ *4 rue Raoul Bosio, Vieux Nice* ☎ *No phone* 💳 *No credit cards* ⏲ *Closed weekends and 1st 2 wks in Aug.*

$$$ FRENCH ✕ **Terres de Truffes.** Celebrity chef Bruno Clément opened this stylish bistrot-deli in an effort to bring the exquisite but expensive taste of truffles to the masses. He has succeeded. Truffles come with everything, from caramelized truffle ice cream to truffle-infused baked Brie; and even the most budget-conscious can afford to indulge. ✉ *11 rue St-Francois-de-Paule, Vieux Nice* ☎ *04–93–62–07–68* 🌐 *www.terresdetruffes.com* 💳 *AE, MC, V* ⏲ *Closed. Sun. and Mon.*

WHERE TO STAY

$$$$ Fodor's Choice ★ **Boscolo Hotel Exedra Nizza.** Certainly the most stylish hotel in Nice—if not the Riviera—this magnificent extravaganza raises the hotel bar of southern France to brand new heights. Located seven blocks off the waterfront in a ritzy neighborhood, this is set in a wedding-cake, marble 1910 landmark building. But one step in the door and you've blasted off into the nether regions of the 21st century—think the white-on-white, Rococo-ed rooms at the end of Kubrick's *2001: A Space Odyssey*. Louis Quinze armchairs, minimal mod tables, soaring skylights (in this case, a redo of one originally fashioned by Gustave Eiffel himself), plus acres of teakwood walls, '50s kidney-shape sofas, and some of the biggest black-and-white Murano chandeliers in the world. A supermodel of a hotel, this also has guest rooms to die for, replete with cascading diamondlike ceiling lights, sculpted rose door handles, the very latest in push-button luxury, and a white-on-white color scheme. In the basement is one of the most striking spas around, the kind with plasma TVs in the saunas. A destination in itself, this is now the place to go in Nice. **Pros:** infinite chic; infinite taste. **Cons:** don't look for old-world Nice here; restaurant is a bit of a let-down, decor-wise. ✉ *12 bd. Victor Hugo, New Town* ☎ *04–93–16–75–70* 🌐 *www.boscolohotels.com* *100 rooms, 8 suites* *In-room: a/c, refrigerator, Internet, Wi-Fi. In-hotel: restaurant, bars, pool, gym, spa, Wi-Fi hotspot* 💳 *AE, DC, MC, V.*

$ **Felix.** On popular, pedestrian Rue Masséna and a block from the beach, this tiny hotel is owned by a hardworking couple (both fluent in English) who make you feel welcome. Rooms are compact but neat and bright, so they don't feel as small, and four have tiny balconies providing a ringside seat over the pedestrian thoroughfare. **Pros:** prime location of hotel makes perfect touring sense; owners are so nice that you feel right at home the minute you walk in the door. **Cons:** rooms can be noisy, especially those that face the street; some rooms are sparse. ✉ *41 rue Masséna, Place Masséna* ☎ *04–93–88–67–73* 🌐 *www.hotel-felix.com* *14 rooms, 5 suites* *In-room: a/c, refrigerator (some), Wi-Fi (some)* 💳 *AE, DC, MC, V.*

$$$$ ★ **Hôtel Negresco.** One of those names, like the Pierre or Claridges, which is synonymous with "Grand Hotel," the Negresco is a white-stucco slice of old-fashioned Riviera extravagance. Still the icon of Nice, it has hosted everyone from the Beatles to the Burtons. Built by Henri Negresco in 1912 as a wedding cake of plaster busts, marble columns, and gilded ceilings, it's the very epitome of La Belle Époque. Yes, the main hall is a bit forlorn, but its Gustave Eiffel glass ceiling still awes, as does its *qualité du Louvre* collection of old-master paintings. Happily, most guest rooms are traditionally elegant, replete with swagged drapes and fine antiques (plus a few unfortunate "with-it" touches like those

No wonder Matisse lived on the top floor of the golden yellow building seen here at the end of the Cours Saleya—this marketplace is one of France's most colorful.

plastic-glitter bathtubs). Downstairs, Le Chantecler ranks among the very finest restaurants in France, with young superchef Jean-Denis Rieubland at the helm adding some modern touches to the menu. The Carrousel Room—complete with merry-go-round horses and Folies Bérgère chandelier—is an over-the-top setting for your breakfast. For a touch of the Old Riviera, repair to the historic walnut-and-velour bar for a champagne cocktail. **Pros:** for those interested in the past, this hotel is a must; food at the famous Chantecler is very good. **Cons:** sincere need for renovations is glaringly apparent: paint is peeling in some parts, rooms need a freshening. ⊠ *37 promenade des Anglais* ☎ *04–93–16–64–00* 🌐 *www.hotel-negresco-nice.com* *145 rooms, 25 suites* *In-room: a/c, refrigerator. In-hotel: 2 restaurants, bar, beachfront, Wi-Fi hotspot, parking (free), some pets allowed* ▭ *AE, DC, MC, V.*

$$$–$$$$ ★ **La Perouse.** Just past the Vieille Ville, at the foot of the château, this hotel is a secret treasure cut into the cliff (an elevator takes you up to the reception). Some of the best rooms (including Raoul Dufy's favorite) not only have views of the azure sea but also look down into an intimate garden with lemon trees and a cliff-side pool. The excellent restaurant serves meals in the candlelight garden May–September. **Pros:** discreet elegance steps away from the Old Town, this hotel is the hideaway of lovers and artists; rooms are charming and large. **Cons:** decor is a bit bland, with monochrome colors and nondescript furniture; service can be a little snooty as well. ⊠ *11 quai Rauba-Capeau, Le Château* ☎ *04–93–62–34–63* 🌐 *www.hotel-la-perouse.com* *63 rooms* *In-room: refrigerator. In-hotel: restaurant, bar, room service, pool, gym, Wi-Fi hotspot* ▭ *AE, DC, MC, V.*

$$ ★ **Windsor.** This is a memorably eccentric hotel with a vision: most of its white-on-white rooms either have frescoes of mythological themes or are works of artists' whimsy. Try to avoid the "less expensive" rooms and insist on one decorated by a known artist like Ben—otherwise you may be disappointed. But the real draw of this otherworldly place is its astonishing city-center garden—a tropical oasis of lemon, magnolia, and palm trees. You can breakfast or dine here by candlelight. **Pros:** the welcome is enthusiastic and friendly; proud of their unique hotel, the staff are eager to share stories of its quirky history. **Cons:** decor is not for everyone; some of the rooms decorated by less famous artists are simply weird; Star Trek elevator is cool the first time, annoying by the end of the week. ✉ *11 rue Dalpozzo, Vieux Nice* ☎ *04–93–88–59–35* 🌐 *www.hotelwindsornice.com* *57 rooms* *In-room: a/c, safe, refrigerator, Wi-Fi. In-hotel: restaurant, bar, gym, Wi-Fi hotspot, some pets allowed* ▭ *AE, MC, V* *MAP.*

NIGHTLIFE AND THE ARTS

The **Casino Ruhl** (✉ *1 promenade des Anglais, Promenade* ☎ *04–97–03–12–22*), gleaming neon-bright and modern, is a sophisticated Riviera landmark. With sleek decor, a piano bar, and live bands, the **Dizzy Club** (✉ *26 quai Lunel, Port Nice* ☎ *04–93–26–54–79*) is consistently popular. If you're all dressed up and have just won big, invest in a drink in the intimate walnut-and-velour **Bar Le Relais** (✉ *37 promenade des Anglais, Promenade Nice* ☎ *04–93–16–64–00*), in the landmark Hôtel Negresco. The hottest gay club in Nice, **Le Klub** has the best dance music in town and is open to all clubbers in the know. The only criteria: be cool. (✉ *6 rue Halevy, Port Nice* ☎ *06–60–55–26–61* 🌐 *www.leklub.net*).

In July the **Nice Jazz Festival** (☎ *08–92–70–74–07* 🌐 *www.nicejazzfestival.fr*) draws performers from around the world. Classical music and ballet performances take place at Nice's convention center, the **Acropolis** (✉ *Palais des Congrès, Esplanade John F. Kennedy, Centre Ville* ☎ *04–93–92–83–00*). The season at the **Opéra de Nice** (✉ *4 rue St-François-de-Paule, Vieux Nice* ☎ *04–92–17–40–79*) runs from September to June.

THE OUTDOORS

Nice's **beaches** extend all along the Baie des Anges, backed full length by the Promenade des Anglais. Public stretches alternate with posh private beaches that have restaurants—and bar service, mattresses and parasols, waterskiing, parasailing, windsurfing, and jet-skiing. The general public can access the private beaches; mattresses cost on average €20 per, and you must buy any food or drink from the restaurant that controls the beach. One of the handiest private beaches is the **Beau Rivage** (☎ *04–92–47–82–82*), set across from the Opéra. The sun can also be yours for the basking at **Ruhl** (☎ *04–93–87–09–70*), across from the Casino.

SHOPPING

Olive oil by the gallon in cans with colorful, old-fashioned labels is sold at tiny **Alziari** (✉ *14 rue St-François-de-Paule, Vieux Nice*). A good source for crystallized fruit, a Nice specialty, is the **Confiserie Florian du Vieux Nice** (✉ *14 quai Papacino, Vieux Nice*), on the west side of the port. The venerable **Henri Auer** (✉ *7 rue St-François-de-Paule, Vieux Nice*) has sold crystallized fruit since 1820. For fragrances, linens, and pickled-wood furniture, head to **Boutique 3** (✉ *3 rue Longchamp, Vieux Nice*), run by three Niçoise women of rare talent and taste.

For every sort of hat imaginable, from the basic beret to huge creations with many a flower and ostrich plume, check out **La Chapellerie** (✉ *36 cours Saleya, Vieux Nice*). **Glove Me** (✉ *5 rue du Marché, Vieux Nice*) sells irresistible Italian-made leather gloves in every color imaginable.

Seafood of all kinds is sold at the **fish market** (✉ *Pl. St-François, Vieux Nice,*) every morning except Monday. At the daily **flower market** (✉ *Cours Saleya, Vieux Nice*) you can find all kinds of plants and fruits and vegetables. The **antiques and brocante market** (✉ *Pl. Robilante, Vieux Nice*), by the old port, is held Tuesday through Saturday.

THE EASTERN FRENCH RIVIERA

With the mistral-proof Alps and Pre-Alps playing bodyguard against inland winds, this stretch of the Riviera is the most reknowned and glamorous stretch of coastline in Europe. Here, coddled by mild Mediterranean breezes, waterfront resorts—Villefranche and Menton—draw energy from the thriving city of Nice, while jutting tropical peninsulas—Cap Ferrat, Cap Martin—frame the tiny principality of Monaco. Here the corniche highways snake above sparkling waters, their pink-and-white villas turning faces toward the sun. Cliffs bristle with palm trees and parasol pines, and a riot of mimosa, bougainvillea, jasmine, and even cactus blooms in the hothouse climate. Crowded with sunseekers and billionaires, the Riviera still reveals quiet corners with heart-stopping views of sea, sun, and mountains—all within one memorable frame.

The lay of the land east of Nice is nearly vertical, as the coastline is one great cliff, a corniche terraced by three parallel highways—the **Basse Corniche**, the **Moyenne Corniche**, and the **Grande Corniche**—that snake along its graduated crests. The lowest (*basse*) is the slowest, following the coast and crawling through the main streets of resorts—including downtown Monte Carlo, Cap-Martin, Beaulieu, and Villefranche-sur-Mer. The highest (*grande*) is the fastest, but its panoramic views are blocked by villas, and there are few safe overlooks. The middle (*moyenne*) runs from Nice to Menton and offers views down over the shoreline and villages—it passes through a few picturesque towns, most notably Èze.

VILLEFRANCHE-SUR-MER

Fodor's Choice ★ *10 km (6 mi) east of Nice.*

Nestled discreetly along the deep scoop of harbor between Nice and Cap Ferrat, this pretty watercolor of a fishing port seems surreal, flanked as it is by the big city of Nice and the assertive wealth of Monaco. Famed for its big harbor, this pretty and pleasant town is a somewhat overbuilt stage-set of brightly colored houses—the sort of place where Pagnol's *Fanny* could have been filmed.

GETTING HERE

Villefranche is a major stop on the Marseilles–Ventimiglia coastal train route, with more than 20 arrivals every day from Nice (30 mins). Buses connect with Nice and Monaco via Sun Bus's No. 100.

Visitor Information Villefranche-sur-Mer Tourist Office ✉ *Jardin Francois Binon* ☎ *04–93–01–73–68* 🌐 *www.villefranche-sur-mer.fr.*

EXPLORING

Whether it's just the force of gravity, or the fact that it remains picturesque, the harbor here relentlessly draws visitors down Villefranche's hillsides to the main waterfront. Here, genuine fishermen actually skim up to its docks in weathered-blue *barques*. They occasionally bid welcome to travelers who amble along the streets of the Vieille Ville, which tilt downhill just as they did in the 13th century. Some of the prettiest spots in town are around Place de la Paix, Rue du Poilu, and Place du Conseil, which looks out over the water. The deep harbor, in the caldera of a volcano, was once preferred by the likes of Onassis and Niarchos and royals on their yachts (today, unfortunately, these are usually replaced by warships as a result of the presence of a nearby naval base). The character of Villefranche was subtly shaped by the artists and authors who gathered at the Hôtel Welcome—Diaghilev and Stravinsky, taking a break from the Ballet Russe in Monaco; Somerset Maugham and Evelyn Waugh; and, above all, Jean Cocteau, who came here to recover from the excesses of Paris life.

So enamored was Jean Cocteau of this painterly fishing port that he decorated the 14th-century **Chapelle St-Pierre** with images from the life of St. Peter and dedicated it to the village's fishermen. ✉ *Pl. Pollanai Quai Courbet* ☎ *04–93–76–90–70* 🎫 *€2.50* ⏲ *Closed Mon. Mid-Mar.–mid-Sept. 10–noon and 3–7; mid-Sept.–mid-Mar. 10–noon and 2–6.*

Running parallel to the waterfront, the extraordinary 13th-century **Rue Obscure** (literally, "Dark Street") is entirely covered by vaulted arcades; it sheltered the people of Villefranche when the Germans fired their parting shots—an artillery bombardment—near the end of World War II.

The stalwart 16th-century **Citadelle St-Elme,** restored to perfect condition, anchors the harbor with its broad, sloping stone walls. Beyond its drawbridge lie the city's administrative offices and a group of minor gallery-museums, with a scattering of works by Picasso and Miró. Whether or not you stop into these private collections of local art (all free of charge), you're welcome to stroll around the inner grounds and to circle the imposing exterior.

WHERE TO EAT AND STAY

$$ FRENCH ✕ **La Grignotière.** Tucked down a narrow side street just a few steps away from the marketplace, this small and friendly local restaurant offers up top-quality, inexpensive dishes. The homemade lasagne is excellent, as is the spaghetti pistou. ✉ *3 rue du Poilu* ☎ *04–93–76–79–83* 💳 *AE, MC, V* ⏲ *Apr.–mid-Nov., daily lunch and dinner; mid-Nov.–Mar. No lunch.*

$$$ FRENCH ✕ **La Mayssa.** Perched high on the port building's large rooftop terrace, this newest place to see and be seen is consistently busy with the cocktail hour crowd. It offers up spectacular views of the bay and a nice selection

of cosmopolitan dishes, such as rack of lamb with sundried tomatoes and mixed herbs, or prawn ravioli with white wine and tarragon. ✉ *Pl. Wilson* ☎ *04–93–01–75–08* ▭ *AE, MC, V* ⊗ *Closed Mon.*

$$$–$$$$ ★ **Hôtel Welcome.** When Villefranche harbored a community of artists and writers, this waterfront landmark was their adopted headquarters. Somerset Maugham holed up in one of the tiny crow's-nest rooms at the top, and Jean Cocteau lived here while writing *Orphée*. Elizabeth Taylor and Richard Burton used to tie one on in the bar (now nicely renovated). It's comfortable and modern, with the best rooms brightened with vivid colors and stenciled quotes from Cocteau; some have spectacular views. **Pros:** its artistic heritage makes for a nostalgic trip into the Roaring Twenties, with photos of famous stars that have spent the night here adorning the walls; service is excellent. **Cons:** decor, especially on the top floor, is distinctly nautical in flavor; some rooms are oddly shaped—narrow and long—making for cramped quarters. ✉ *3 quai Courbet* ☎ *04–93–76–27–62* 🌐 *www.welcomehotel.com* *34 rooms, 2 suites* *In-room: a/c, safe, refrigerator. In-hotel: bar, Wi-Fi hotspot, parking (paid), some pets allowed* ▭ *AE, DC, MC, V* ⊗ *Closed mid-Nov.–late Dec.*

BEAULIEU

4 km (2½ mi) east of Villefranche, 14 km (9 mi) east of Nice.

With its back pressed hard against the cliffs of the corniche and sheltered between the peninsulas of Cap Ferrat and Cap Roux, this once-grand resort basks in a tropical microclimate that earned its central neighborhood the name *Petite Afrique*. The town was the pet of 19th-century society, and its grand hotels welcomed Empress Eugénie, the Prince of Wales, and Russian nobility. It's still a posh address, but if you're a picky atmosphere-hunter, you may find the town center too built-up with apartment buildings.

GETTING HERE

With frequent arrivals and departures, Beaulieu is a main stop on the Marseille–Ventimiglia coastal train line. From Beaulieu's train station hourly buses, for €2 a ticket, connect with neighboring St-Jean-Cap-Ferrat.

Visitor Information Beaulieu Tourist Office ✉ *Pl. Georges Clemenceau* ☎ *04–93–01–02–21* 🌐 *www.ot-beaulieu-sur-mer.fr.*

EXPLORING

One manifestation of Beaulieu's Belle Époque excess is the eye-knocking Fodor's Choice ★ **Villa Kerylos,** a mansion built in 1902 in the style of classical Greece (to be exact, of the villas that existed on the island of Delos in the 2nd century BC). It was the dream house of the amateur archaeologist Théodore Reinach, who originally hailed from a super-rich family from Frankfurt, helped the French in their excavations at Delphi, and became an authority on ancient Greek music. He commissioned an Italian architect from Nice, Emmanuel Pontremoli, to surround him with Grecian delights: cool Carrara marble, rare fruitwoods, and a dining salon where guests reclined to eat *à la grecque*. Don't miss this—it's one of the most unusual houses in the south of France. Not far from the house is the **Promenade Maurice Rouvier,** an enchanting coastal path that leads to St-Jean-Cap-Ferrat. A combination ticket allows you to also visit Villa Ephrussi del Rothschild in nearby St-Jean-Cap-Ferrat in the same week. ✉ *Rue Gustave-Eiffel* ☎ *04–93–01–01–44* 🌐 *www.villa-kerylos.com* 🎫 *€8.50, €15 for both villas* ⏲ *Mid-Feb.–June and Sept. and Oct., daily 10–6; July and Aug., daily 10–7; Nov.–mid-Feb., weekdays 2–6, weekends 10–6.*

ST-JEAN-CAP-FERRAT

2 km (1 mi) south of Beaulieu on D25.

This luxuriously sited pleasure port moors the peninsula of Cap Ferrat; from its port-side walkways and crescent of beach you can look over the sparkling blue harbor to the graceful green bulk of the corniches. Yachts purr in and out of port, and their passengers scuttle into cafés for take-out drinks to enjoy on their private decks. Unfortunately, Cap Ferrat is a vast peninsula and hides its secrets—except for the Villa Ephrussi, most fabled estates are hidden behind iron gates and towering hedges—particularly well.

★ Between the port and the mainland, the floridly beautiful **Villa Ephrussi de Rothschild** stands as witness to the wealth and worldly flair of the baroness who had it built. Constructed in 1905 in neo-Venetian style (its flamingo-pink facade was thought not to be in the best of taste by the local gentry), the house was baptized "Ile-de-France" in homage to the Baroness Bétrice de Rothschild's favorite ocean liner (her staff used to wear sailing costumes and her ship travel kit is on view in her bedroom). Precious artworks, tapestries, and furniture adorn the salons—in typical Rothschildian fashion, each room is given over to a different 18th-century "époque." Upstairs are the private apartments of Madame la Baronne, which can only be seen on a guided tour offered around noon. The grounds are landscaped with no fewer than seven theme gardens and topped off with a Temple of Diana (no less); be sure to allow yourself time to wander here, as this is one of the few places on the coast where you'll be allowed to experience the lavish pleasures characteristic of the Belle Époque Côte d'Azur. Tea and light lunches are served in a glassed-in porch overlooking the grounds and spectacular views of the coastline. A combination ticket allows you to also visit Villa Kerylos in nearby Beaulieu in the same week. ✉ *Av. Ephrussi* ☎ *04–93–01–33–09* 🌐 *www.villa-ephrussi.com* 🎫 *Access to ground floor and gardens €10; €15 for both villas; guided tour upstairs €3 extra* ⏲ *Mid-Feb.–June and Sept. and Oct., daily 10–6; July and Aug., daily 10–7; Nov.–mid-Feb., weekdays 2–6, weekends 10–6.*

While Cap Ferrat's villas are sequestered for the most part in the depths of tropical gardens, you can nonetheless walk its entire **coastline promenade** if you strike out from the port; from the restaurant Capitaine Cook, cut right up Avenue des Fossés, turn right on Avenue Vignon, and follow the Chemin de la Carrière. The 11-km (7-mi) walk passes through rich tropical flora and, on the west side, over white cliffs buffeted by waves. When you've traced the full outline of the peninsula, veer up the Chemin du Roy past the fabulous gardens of the **Villa des Cèdres,** owned by King Leopold II of Belgium at the turn of the last century. The king owned several opulent estates along the French Riviera, undoubtedly paid for by his enslavement of the Belgian Congo. His African plunder also stocked the private zoo on his villa grounds, today the town's **Parc Zoologique** (✉ *Bd. du Général-de-Gaulle* ☎ *04–93–76–07–60* *€15* *Mid-June–mid-Sept., daily 9:30–7; mid-Sept.–mid-June, daily 9:30–5:30*). Past the gardens, you can reach the **Plage de Passable,** from which you cut back across the peninsula's wrist. A shorter loop takes you from town out to the **Pointe de St-Hospice,** much of the walk shaded by wind-twisted pines. From the port, climb Avenue Jean Mermoz to Place Paloma and follow the path closest to the waterfront. At the point are an 18th-century prison tower, a 19th-century chapel, and unobstructed views of Cap Martin.

WORD OF MOUTH

"You must go to the Villa Ephrussi de Rothschild in Cap Ferrat—think the Isabella Stewart Gardner Museum times 1,000, plus Mediterranean views." —Mclaurie

WHERE TO EAT AND STAY

$$$ SEAFOOD **Le Sloop.** This sleek port-side restaurant caters to the yachting crowd and sailors who cruise into dock for lunch. The focus is fish, of course: *soupe de poisson* (fish soup), *St-Pierre* (John Dory) steamed with asparagus, roasted whole sea bass. Its outdoor tables surround a tiny "garden" of potted palms. The fixed menu is €37. Chef Alain Therlicocq has manned the kitchen for 25 years. ✉ *Port de Plaisance* ☎ *04–93–01–48–63* *Reservations essential in summer* *MC, V* *Closed Wed. mid-Sept.–June. No lunch Tues. and Wed. July–mid-Sept.*

$$$ ★ **Brise Marine.** With a glowing Provençal-yellow facade, bright blue shutters, and balustraded sea terrace, this lovely vision fulfills most desires for that perfect, picturesque Cap Ferrat hotel. Pretty pastel guest rooms feel like bedrooms in a private home—many offer window views of the gorgeous peninsula stunningly framed by statuesque palms. **Pros:** very quiet nights are lovingly caressed by the gentle pit-pat of the waves breaking along the shore; rooms are large and bright and airy. **Cons:** some rooms are small; some rooms in back are a bit dark. ✉ *58 av. Jean Mermoz* ☎ *04–93–76–04–36* *www.hotel-brisemarine.com* *18 rooms* *In-room: a/c, refrigerator. In-hotel: bar, Wi-Fi hotspot, parking (paid)* *AE, DC, MC, V* *Closed Nov.–Jan.*

$$–$$$ **Clair Logis.** With soft pastels, antique furniture, and large picture windows, this converted villa is perfectly framed by a sprawling garden park. The main house offers up subtle bourgeois elegance; for the budget-conscious there are other simpler, airy rooms scattered over several small buildings. Most have charming balconies looking out over gently swaying palms. There's no pool, but breakfast on the cobblestone terrace is lovely, and it's a good way to gear up for the 15-minute walk down to the beach. **Pros:** garden park is a nice escape from the crowds that trek along the coast; quiet evenings are a pleasure. **Cons:** distance from beach is significant; hike back up from town can be intimidating. ✉ *12 av. Centrale, Allee Des Brises* ☎ *04–93–76–51–81*

12

18 rooms In-room: a/c, refrigerator, Internet. In-hotel: parking (free), some pets allowed AE, MC, V Closed Nov.–mid-Dec. and early Jan.–early Feb.

$$$$ ★ **Grand Hôtel du Cap-Ferrat.** Completely refurbished and reopened late 2009, this stunning hotel is *the* new standard for discreet Cap-Ferrat moneyed luxury. Perched at the end of the peninsula with floor to ceiling windows leaning out over crashing waves, rooms have spectacular views far out sea. They are a glory of comfort: thick, stark-white and softer-than-soft comforters, mellow olive-green tones, hardwood floors, plasma screens, private terraces—some with their own pool—and acres of sculpted gardens. What more could one ask for? En plus is the newly Michelin starred restaurant headed up by wunderkind Didier Aniés, who whips up tasty dishes like Aquitaine caviar lasagna or the Saint Pierre (John Dory) with citrus confit. **Pros:** epitome of wealth and luxury, every detail is well thought out and promptly attended to. **Cons:** not a hotel for travelers on a budget; service can be a little snooty. *71 Blvd du Charles du Gaulle 04–93–76–50–50 www.grand-hotel-cap-ferrat.com 49 rooms, 24 suites (8 with private pools) In-room: a/c, refrigerator, Internet. In-hotel: 3 restaurants, room service, bar, tennis court, pools, gym, spa, bicycle, Wi-Fi hotspot, parking (paid) AE, DC, MC, V Restaurant closed mid Nov.–mid Dec.*

ÈZE

Fodor's Choice ★ *2 km (1 mi) east of Beaulieu, 12 km (7 mi) east of Nice, 7 km (4½ mi) west of Monte Carlo.*

Towering like an eagle's nest above the coast and crowned with ramparts and the ruins of a medieval château, preposterously beautiful Èze (pronounced *ehz*) is unfortunately the most accessible of all the perched villages—this means crowds, many of whom head here to shop in the boutique-lined staircase-streets. (Happily the shops are largely quite stylish, and there's a nice preponderance of bric-a-brac and vintage fabric dealers). But most travelers come here to drink in the views, for no one can deny that this is the most spectacularly sited of all coastal promontories.

GETTING HERE

Èze Village is the famous hilltop destination, but Èze extends down to the coastal beach and the township of Èze-sur-Mer. To get to the hilltop village from the train station, take bus No. 83 run by Lignes d'Azur (*08–10–06–10–06 www.lignedazur.com*). The trip, with its 1,001 switchbacks up the steep mountainside, takes 15 minutes; buses run hourly year-round (€1).

If you want to avoid the train entirely and are traveling on a budget, from the Nice Gare Routière (*5 bd. Jean Jaures www.rca.tm.fr*) you can take the Transport Alpes Maritimes's 100 TAM bus (*08–92–70–12–06*), which will take you directly to Èze-bord-de-Mer along the lower Corniche and costs €1. Otherwise, you can take the RCA bus No. 112 at Nice's Gare Routière, which goes from Nice to Beausoleil and stops at Èze Village. By car, you should arrive using the Moyenne Corniche, which deposits you near the gateway to Èze Village.

Visitor Information **Èze Tourist Office** ✉ *Pl. du Général de Gaulle* ☎ *04–93–41–26–00* 🌐 *www.eze-riviera.com.*

EXPLORING

If you can manage to shake the crowds and duck off to a quiet overlook, the village of Eze commands splendid views up and down the coast, one of the draws that once lured fabled visitors—lots of crowned heads, Georges Sand, Friedrich Nietzsche—and residents: Consuelo Vanderbilt, when she was tired of being duchess of Marlborough, traded in Blenheim Palace for a custom-built house here.

From the crest-top **Jardin Exotique** *(Tropical Garden)*, full of rare succulents, you can pan your videocam all the way around the hills and waterfront. But if you want a prayer of a chance at enjoying the magnificence of the village's arched passages, stone alleyways, and ancient fountains, come at dawn or after sunset—or (if you have the means) stay the night—but spend the midday elsewhere. The church of **Notre-Dame,** consecrated in 1772, glitters inside with Baroque altarpieces. Èze's tourist office, on Place du Général-de-Gaulle, can direct you to the numerous footpaths—the most famous being the **Sentier Friedrich Nietzsche**—that thread Èze with the coast's three corniche highways.

WHERE TO EAT AND STAY

$$ FRENCH ✕ **Loumiri.** Classic Provençal and regional seafood dishes are tastily prepared and married with decent, inexpensive wines at this cute little bistro near the entrance to the Vieille Ville. The best bet is to order *à l'ardoise*—that is, from the blackboard listing of daily specials. The lunch menu prix-fixe (€15) is the best deal in town. Prix-fixe dinner menus start at €23. ✉ *Av. Jardin Exotique* ☎ *04–93–41–16–42* ▭ *MC, V* ⊙ *Closed Mon. and mid-Dec.–mid-Jan. No dinner Wed.*

$$ FRENCH ✕ **Troubadour.** Amid the clutter and clatter, this is a wonderful find: comfortably relaxed, this old family house proffers pleasant service and excellent dishes like roasted scallops with chicken broth and squab with citrus zest and beef broth. Full-course menus range from €38 to €50. ✉ *4 rue du Brec* ☎ *04–93–41–19–03* ▭ *AE, DC, MC, V* ⊙ *Closed Sun. No lunch Mon., mid-Nov.–mid-Dec.*

$$$$ Fodor's Choice ★ **Château de la Chèvre d'Or.** Giving substance to Riviera fairy tales, this extraordinary Xanadu seems to sit just below cloud level like a Hilton penthouse, medieval-style. The "château of the Golden Goat" is actually an entire stretch of the village, streets and all, bordered by gardens that hang to the mountainside in nearly Babylonian style. The fanciest guest rooms come replete with stone boulder walls, peasant-luxe fireplaces, faux 15th-century panel paintings, and chandeliered rock-grotto bathrooms, but nearly all have exposed stone and exposed beams (even the cheapest have views over Èze's charming tile roofs). No fewer than three restaurants, ranging from the nicely affordable grill to the *haute gastronomique* grand dining room with its panoramic view, spoil you for choice. Children are in heaven with the hotel's fabulous Chicken in Coca-Cola sauce (€30). The swimming pool alone, clinging like a swallow's nest to the hillside, may justify the investment, as do the liveried footmen who greet you at the village entrance to wave you, VIP-style, past the cattle drive of tourists, or the breakfast on the spectacular

The "eagle's-nest" village of the Riviera, Eze perches 1,300 feet over the sea and travelers never fail to marvel at the dramatic setting.

terrace, which seems to levitate over the bay. **Pros:** spectacular setting is unique along the coast, with eagle nest views out to the sea and an infinity pool dropping off the cliff. **Cons:** service can be cool; be certain of the type of car you drive and of the label on your clothes. ✉ *Rue du Barri* ☎ *04–92–10–66–66* 🌐 *www.chevredor.com* *23 rooms, 9 suites* *In-room: a/c, safe, refrigerator, Wi-Fi. In-hotel: 3 restaurants, bar, tennis court, pool, gym, spa, Wi-Fi hotspot, some pets allowed* *AE, DC, MC, V.*

$$–$$$ ★ **La Bastide aux Camelias.** There are only four bedrooms in this lovely B&B, each individually decorated with softly draped fabrics and polished antiques. Set in Grande Corniche Park near Èze Village, it offers up the usual run of breathtaking views, but also has inviting, less precipitous ones of garden greenery. Have the complimentary breakfast on the picture-perfect veranda, indulge in a cooling drink by the gorgeous pool, or stretch out on the manicured lawn. Access to the hammam, Jacuzzi, and sauna is included in their price. It's gentle hospitality that's much in demand, however, so reserve well in advance. **Pros:** heartwarming welcome is down-home country genuine; breakfast is scrumptious. **Cons:** walking distance from the village is significant; few options for restaurants that do not require a car. ✉ *Rte. de l'Adret* ☎ *04–93–41–13–68* 🌐 *www.bastideauxcamelias.com* *4 rooms* *In-room: a/c, refrigerator. In-hotel: pool, Wi-Fi hotspot, parking (free), some pets allowed* *AE, MC, V* *BP.*

MENTON

Fodor's Choice ★

14 km (9 mi) east of Eze, 9 km (5½ mi) east of Monaco.

Menton, the most Mediterranean of the French resort towns, rubs shoulders with the Italian border and owes its balmy climate to the protective curve of the Ligurian shore. Its picturesque harbor skyline seems to beg artists to immortalize it, while its Cubist skew of terra-cotta roofs and yellow-ocher houses, Baroque arabesques capping the church facades, and ceramic tiles glistening on their steeples all evoke the villages of the Italian coast. Also worth a visit are the many exotic gardens set in the hills around the town.

GETTING HERE

RCA Menton (☎ *08–20–42–33–33* ⊕ *www.rca.tm.fr*) runs a regular daily bus service from Menton's main bus station (✉ *Gare Routière, Av. de Sospel* ☎ *04–93–35–93–60*). This route runs along the scenic Basse Corniche to the Nice bus station at 5 boulevard Jean Jaurés, making stops at all of the little villages along the way; tickets cost €17.50. The Ligne D'Azur bus No. 100 has direct service between Nice and Menton every 15 minutes, (€1) and takes just over an hour. Menton is serviced by regular trains on the Nice–Ventimiglia line (⊕ *www.voyages-sncf.com*); the trip from Nice takes 36 minutes and costs €4.20. The Menton Gare SNCF train station is within walking distance of the sea and the center of town.

Visitor Information Menton Tourist Office ✉ *Palais de l'Europe, Av. Boyer* ☎ *04–92–41–76–76* ⊕ *www.villedementon.com.*

EXPLORING

Set several miles to the east of Monaco (which we leapfrog over here; see our entry on Monaco below), Menton is the least pretentious of the French Riviera resorts and all the more alluring for its modesty.

The **Basilique St-Michel** (✉ *Parvis St-Michel*), a majestic Baroque church, dominates the skyline of Menton with its bell tower. Beyond the beautifully proportioned facade—a 19th-century addition—the richly frescoed nave and chapels contain several works by Genovese artists and a splendid 17th-century organ.

Just above the main church, the smaller **Chapelle de l'Immaculée-Conception** answers St-Michel's grand gesture with its own pure Baroque beauty, dating from 1687. Between 3 and 5 you can slip in to see the graceful trompe l'oeil over the altar and the ornate gilt lanterns early penitents carried in processions.

Two blocks below the square, **Rue St-Michel** serves as the main commercial artery of the Vieille Ville, lined with shops, cafés, and orange trees.

Between the lively pedestrian Rue St-Michel and the waterfront, the marvelous **Marché Couvert** (*Covered Market*) sums up Menton style with its Belle Époque façade decorated in jewel-tone ceramics. Inside, it's just as appealing, with merchants selling chewy bread, mountain cheeses, oils, fruit, and Italian delicacies in Caravaggesque disarray.

CLOSE UP

Menton's Magnificent Gardens

The French Riviera is famed for its grand villas and even grander gardens built by Victorian dukes, Spanish exiles, Belgian royals, and American blue bloods. Although its hothouse crescent blooms everywhere with palm and lemon trees and jungle flowers, nowhere else does it bloom so extravagantly as in Menton, famous for its temperate climes and 24-karat sun.

Menton attracted a great share of wealthy hobbyists during the 1920s and 1930s, including Major Lawrence Johnston, a gentleman gardener best known for his Cotswolds wonderland, Hidcote Manor. Fair-haired and blue-eyed, this gentle American wound up buying a choice estate in the village of Gorbio—one of the loveliest of all perched seaside villages, set 10 km (6 mi) west of Menton—and spent two decades making the **Serre de la Madone** one of the horticultural masterpieces of the coast. He brought back exotica from his many trips to South Africa, Mexico, and China, and planted them in a series of terraces, accented by little pools, vistas, and stone steps. Although most of his creeping plumbago, pink belladonna, and night-flowering cacti are now gone, his garden has been reopened by the municipality. Car facilities are very limited but the garden can also be reached from Menton via bus No. 7 (get off at Mers et Monts stop).

Back in Menton, green-thumbers will also want to visit the town's Jardin Botanique, the **Val Rahmeh Botanical Garden** (✉ *Av. St-Jacques* ☎ *04-93-35-86-72* ⏲ *Closed Tues.*), planted by Maybud Campbell in the 1910s, much prized by connoisseurs, bursting with rare ornamentals and subtropical plants, and adorned with water-lily pools and fountains.

The tourist office can also give you directions to other gardens around Menton, including the Fontana Rosa, the Villa Maria Serena, and the Villa Les Colombières.

✉ *Serre de la Madone: 74 rte. de Gorbio* ☎ *04-93-57-73-90* 🌐 *www.serredelamadone.com* 🎟 *€8 for Serre* ⏲ *Apr.-Oct. Tues.-Sun. 10-6; Dec.-Mar., Tues.-Sun. 10-5.*

On the waterfront opposite the market, a squat medieval bastion crowned with four tiny watchtowers houses the **Musée Jean-Cocteau.** Built in 1636 to defend the port, it was spotted by the artist-poet-filmmaker Jean Cocteau (1889–1963) as the perfect site for a group of his works. There are bright, cartoonish pastels of fishermen and wenches in love, and a fantastical assortment of ceramic animals in the wrought-iron vitrines he designed. ✉ *Vieux Port* ☎ *04-93-57-72-30* 🎟 *€3* ⏲ *Wed.–Mon. 10–noon and 2–6.*

The 19th-century Italianate **Hôtel de Ville** conceals another Cocteau treasure: it was he who decorated the **Salle des Mariages** *(Marriage Room)*, in which civil marriages take place, with vibrant allegorical scenes. ✉ *17 av. de la République* 🎟 *€2* ⏲ *Weekdays 8:30–12:30 and 1:30–5.*

At the far west end of town stands the 18th-century **Palais Carnolès** *(Carnolès Palace)* in vast gardens luxuriant with orange, lemon, and grapefruit trees. It was once the summer retreat of the princes of Monaco; nowadays it contains a sizable collection of European paintings from the Renaissance to the present day, plus some interesting temporary exhibits. ✉ *3 av. de la Madone* ☎ *04–93–35–49–71* 🎫 *Free* ⏲ *Wed.–Mon. 10–noon and 2–6.*

WHERE TO EAT AND STAY

$$$–$$$$ ★ **Aiglon.** Sweep down the curving stone stairs to the terrazzo mosaic lobby of this truly lovely 1880 garden villa for a drink or a meal by the pool, or settle onto your little balcony overlooking the grounds and a tiny wedge of sea. There's a room for every whim, all soft-edged, comfortable, and romantic, although you will be loath to leave the grand salon, a picture-perfect confection of 19th-century elegance that wouldn't shame some of the nobler houses in Paris. The poolside restaurant, Le Riaumont, serves candlelight dinners of fresh, local fish lightly steamed and sauced with a Provençal accent; breakfast is served in a shady garden shelter. It's a three-minute walk from the beach. Half-board prices are available. **Pros:** romantic air is highly contagious, with couples swinging by hand in hand; owners know this and play up to it, encouraging it with hidden beautiful spots like the salon, and love seats in archways. **Cons:** some rooms are small, with an almost cramped feel to them; bathrooms are tiny. ✉ *7 av. de la Madone* ☎ *04–93–57–55–55* 🌐 *www.hotelaiglon.net* *28 rooms, 2 apartments* *In-room: a/c. In-hotel: restaurant, bar, pool, Wi-Fi hotspot, some pets allowed* 💳 *AE, DC, MC, V* ⏲ *Restaurant closed mid-Nov.–mid-Dec.* *MAP.*

NIGHTLIFE AND THE ARTS

In August the **Festival de Musique de Chambre** *(Chamber Music Festival)* (☎ *04–92–41–76–95*) takes place on the stone-paved plaza outside the church of St-Michel. The **Fête du Citron** (*Lemon Festival* ☎ *04–92–41–76–76*) at the end of February, celebrates the lemon with floats and sculptures like those of the Rose Bowl Parade, all made of real fruit.

MONACO

7 km (4½ mi) east of Èze, 21 km (13 mi) east of Nice.

It's the tax system, not the gambling (actually, the latter helps pay for the former), that has made Monaco one of the most sought-after addresses in the world. It bristles with gleaming glass-and-concrete corncob-towers 20 and 30 stories high and with vast apartment complexes, their terraces, landscaped like miniature gardens, jutting over the sea. You now have to look hard to find the Belle Époque grace of yesteryear. But if you repair to the town's great 1864 landmark Hôtel de Paris—still a veritable crossroads of the buffed and befurred Euro-gentry—or enjoy a grand bouffe at its famous Louis XV restaurant, or attend the Opéra, or visit the ballrooms of the Casino (avert your eyes from the flashy gambling machines), you may still be able to conjure up Monaco's elegant past and the much-missed spirit of Princess Grace.

GETTING HERE

From the Nice airport, there's a direct bus service from Compagnie des Autobus de Monaco (☎ *377/97–70–22–22* 🌐 *www.cam.mc*) to the Place du Casino (in front of the Monte Carlo casino); it takes 50 minutes and costs €12.50. Both buses and trains connect Nice with Monaco.

RCA (☎ *04–93–85–64–44* 🌐 *www.rca.tm.fr*) has buses connecting with Nice's center-city bus station (✉ *Gare routière, 5 bd. Jean Jaures* ☎ *08–92–70–12–06*); tickets cost €1. The 100 TAM bus (*Transport Alpes Maritimes* ☎ *08–10–06–10–06* 🌐 *www.lignedazur.com*) costs €1 and leaves from the main bus station in Nice, but be prepared as it takes about two hours to get there. From Nice's train station (✉ *Gare SNCF, Av. Thiers* ☎ *36–35* 🌐 *www.voyages-sncf.com*), Monaco is serviced by regular trains along the Cannes–Ventimiglia line; Monaco's train station is on Avenue Prince Pierre. From Nice the journey costs €3.30 one-way and takes 20 minutes.

Visitor Information Monaco Tourist Office ✉ *2a bd. des Moulins, Monte Carlo* ☎ *377/92–16–61–66* 🌐 *www.monaco-tourism.com.*

EXPLORING

It's positively feudal, the idea that an ancient dynasty of aristocrats could still hold fast to its patch of coastline, the last scrap of a once-vast domain. But that's just what the Grimaldi family did, clinging to a few acres of glory and maintaining their own license plates, their own telephone area code (377—don't forget to dial this when calling Monaco from France or other countries), and their own highly forgiving tax system. Yet the Principality of Monaco covers just 473 acres and would fit comfortably inside New York's Central Park or a family farm in Iowa. And its 5,000 pampered citizens would fill only a small fraction of the seats in Yankee Stadium. The harbor district, known as **La Condamine,** connects the new quarter, officially known as **Monte Carlo,** with the Vieille Ville, officially known as **Monaco-Ville** (or Le Rocher). Have no fear that you'll need to climb countless steps to get to the Vieille Ville, as there are plenty of elevators and escalators climbing the steep cliffs.

Prince Rainier III, the family patriarch who famously wed Grace Kelly and brought Hollywood glamour to his toy kingdom, passed away in April 2005; his son, the eminently responsible Prince Albert, took over as head of the family and principality. Albert traces his ancestry to Otto Canella, who was born in 1070. The Grimaldi dynasty began with Otto's great-great-great-grandson, Francesco Grimaldi, also known as Frank the Rogue. Expelled from Genoa, Frank and his cronies disguised themselves as monks and in 1297 seized the fortified medieval town known today as Le Rocher *(the Rock)*. Except for a short break under Napoléon, the Grimaldis have been here ever since, which makes them the oldest reigning family in Europe.

TOP ATTRACTIONS

1 ★ **Casino.** Place du Casino is the center of Monte Carlo, and is a must-see, even if you don't bet a sou. Into the gold-leaf splendor of the Casino, the hopeful traipse from tour buses to tempt fate beneath the gilt-edge Rococo ceiling (but do remember the fate of Sarah Bernhardt, who lost her last 100,000 francs here). Jacket and tie are required in the back rooms, which open at 3 PM. Bring your passport (under-18s not admitted). Note that there are special admission fees to get into many of the period gaming rooms—only the Salle des Jeux Americains is free. ✉ *Pl. du Casino* ☎ *377/98–06–20–00* 🌐 *www.sbm.mc* 🕒 *Daily 2 PM–4 AM,*

8 **Jardin Exotique de Monaco** *(Monaco Exotic Garden)*. Carved out of

Fodor's Choice ★ the rock face and one of Monte Carlo's most stunning escape hatches, the gardens are studded with thousands of succulents and cacti, all set along promenades, belvederes over the sea, and even framing faux boulders (actually hollow sculptures). There are rare plants from Mexico and Africa, and the hillside plot, threaded with bridges and grottoes, can't be beat for coastal splendor. Thanks go to Prince Albert I, who started it all. Also on the grounds, or actually under them, are the **Grottes de l'Observatoire**—spectacular grottoes and caves a-drip with stalagmites and spotlighted with fairy lights. The largest cavern is called "La Grande Salle" and looks like a Romanesque rock cathedral. Traces of Cro-Magnon civilization have been found here, so the grottoes now bear the official name of the **Musée d'Anthropologie Préhistorique.** ✉ *62 bd. du Jardin Exotique* ☎ *377/93–15–29–80* 🌐 *www.jardin-exotique.mc* 🎫 *€6.90* ⏲ *Mid-May–mid-Sept., daily 9–7; mid-Sept.–mid-May, daily 9–6.*

3 **Musée National Automates et Poupées.** Here you'll find a beguiling collection of 18th- and 19th-century dolls and automatons. The museum is housed in a Garnier villa within a rose garden, in the Larvotto Beach complex—which is artfully created with imported sand. To get here, take the elevator down from Place des Moulins. ✉ *Villa Sauber, 17 av. Princesse Grace* ☎ *377/98–98–91–26* 🌐 *www.nmnm.mc* 🎫 *€6* ⏲ *Daily 10–6.*

7 **Musée Océanographique** *(Oceanography Museum)*. Perched dramatically on a cliff, this museum is a splendid Edwardian structure, built under ★ Prince Albert I to house specimens collected on amateur explorations. Jacques Cousteau (1910–97) led its missions from 1957 to 1988. The main floor displays skeletons and taxidermy of enormous sea creatures; early submarines and diving gear dating from the Middle Ages; and a few interactive science displays. The main draw is the famous **aquarium**, a vast complex of backlighted tanks containing every imaginable species of fish, crab, and eel. ✉ *Av. St-Martin* ☎ *377/93–15–36–00* 🌐 *www.oceano.mc* 🎫 *€13* ⏲ *July and Aug., daily 9:30–7:30; Apr.–June and Sept., daily 9:30–7; Oct.–Mar., daily 10–6.*

WORTH NOTING

6 **Cathédrale de l'Immaculée-Conception.** Follow the flow of crowds down the last remaining streets of medieval Monaco to this 19th-century cathedral, which has a magnificent altarpiece, painted in 1500 by Bréa, and the tomb of Princess Grace. ✉ *Av. St-Martin.*

5 **Collection des Voitures Anciennes** *(Collection of Vintage Cars)*. It's worth a stop to see this impressive collection of Prince Rainier's vintage cars, where you'll find everything from a De Dion Bouton to a Lamborghini Countach. Also on the Terrasses de Fontvieille is the **Jardin Animalier** *(Animal Garden)*, a mini-zoo housing the Grimaldi family's animal collection, an astonishing array of wild beasts including monkeys and exotic birds. ✉ *Terrasses de Fontvieille* ☎ *377/92–05–28–56 or 377/93–25–18–31* 🌐 *www.mtcc.mc* 🎫 *€6 Voitures; €4 Animalier* ⏲ *June–Sept., daily 9–noon and 2–7; Oct.–Feb., daily 10–noon and 2–5; Mar.–May, daily 10–noon and 2–6.*

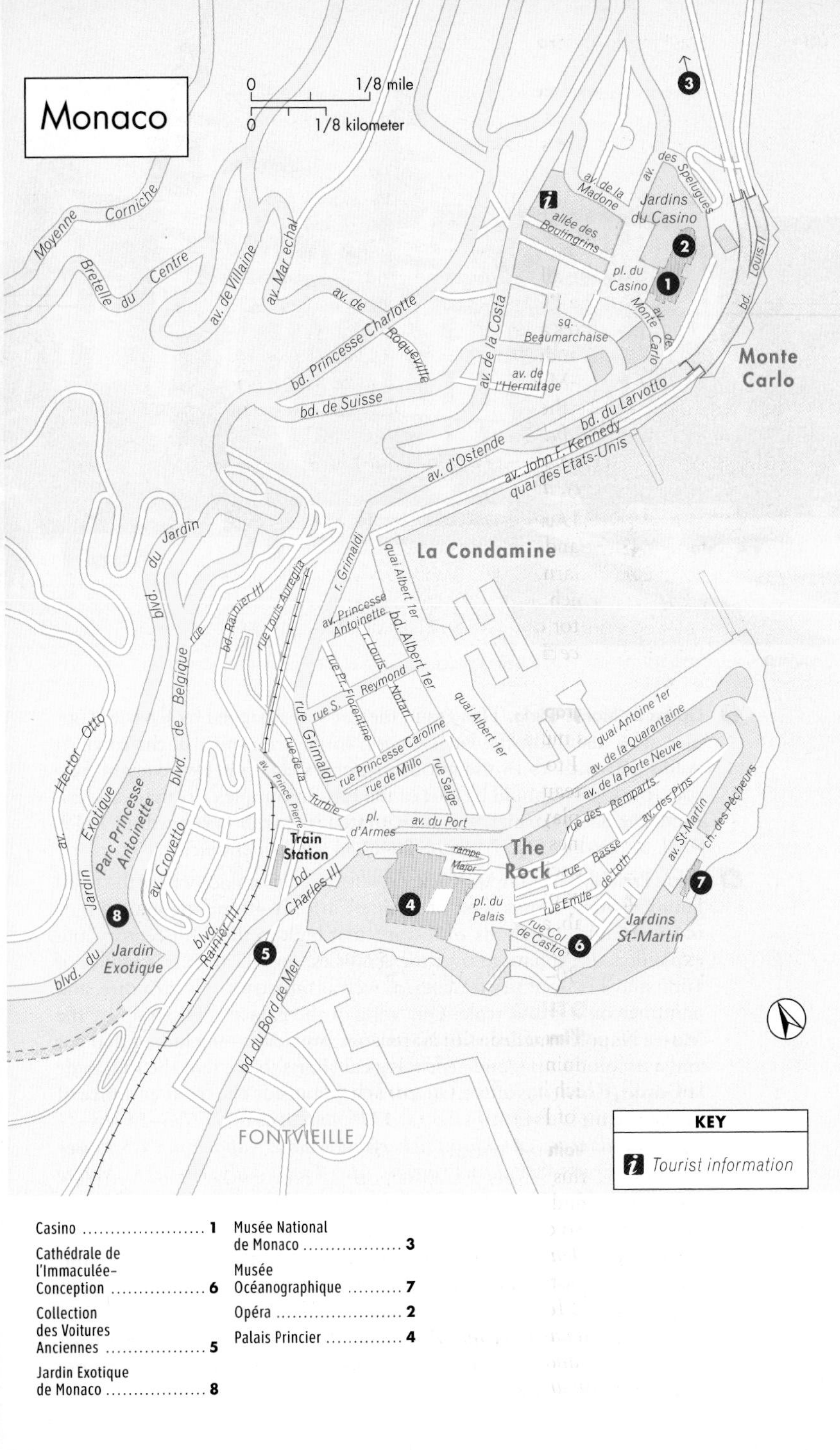

Casino 1
Cathédrale de l'Immaculée-Conception 6
Collection des Voitures Anciennes 5
Jardin Exotique de Monaco 8
Musée National de Monaco 3
Musée Océanographique 7
Opéra 2
Palais Princier 4

A golden ghetto for the rich, Monaco has a Belle Epoque opulence epitomized by its Opéra Monte Carlo, designed in 1879 by Garnier.

❷ **Opéra de Monte-Carlo.** This grand theater was designed by Charles Garnier, who also built the Paris Opéra. In the true spirit of the town, it seems that with its 18-ton gilt-bronze chandelier and extravagant frescoes, the Opéra should be part of the Casino complex. Its main auditorium, the Salle Garnier, was inaugurated by Sarah Bernhardt in 1879. ✉ *Pl. du Casino* ☎ *377/98–06–28–00* 🌐 *www.opera.mc.*

❹ **Palais Princier.** The famous Rock, crowned by this palace where the royal family resides, stands west of Monte Carlo. A 40-minute guided tour of this sumptuous chunk of history, first built in the 13th century and expanded and enhanced over the centuries, reveals an extravagance of 16th- and 17th-century frescoes, as well as tapestries, gilt furniture, and paintings on a grand scale. One wing of the palace is taken up by the **Musée Napoléon**, filled with Napoleonic souvenirs—including that hat and a tricolor scarf—and geneaological charts. Note that the **Relève de la Garde** *(Changing of the Guard)* is held outside the front entrance of the palace most days at 11:55 AM. ✉ *Pl. du Palais* ☎ *377/93–25–18–31* 🌐 *www.palais.mc* 🎫 *€9 joint ticket with Musée Napoléon, €4.5 Musée Napoléon only* ⏲ *Palais Princier: Apr.–Oct., daily 10–6:15; Musée Napoléon: Apr.–Oct., daily 10–6:15, Dec.–Mar., daily 10:30–5.*

WHERE TO EAT

$$$$ FRENCH ✕ **Bar Boeuf & Co.** For those wanting to try Alain Ducasse cuisine without having to pay Louis XVI prices, this bar (seabass) and boeuf (beef) concept restaurant is a treat. The sea views are gorgeous for those seated on the terrace, and the up-to-the-minute service is actually laid back enough for you to relax and simply enjoy. ✉ *Le Sporting, av Princesse*

Grace ☎ *377/98–06–71–71* 🌐 *www.alain-ducasse.com* 💳 *AE, DC, MC, V* ⏲ *Closed Oct.–Apr.*

$$$ FRENCH ✕ **Café de Paris.** This landmark Belle Époque brasserie, across from the Casino, offers the usual classics (shellfish, steak tartare, matchstick frites, and fish boned table-side). Supercilious, super-pro waiters fawn gracefully over titled preeners, gentlemen, jet-setters, and tourists alike. Happily, there's good hot food until 2 AM. ✉ *Pl. du Casino* ☎ *377/92–16–20–20* 💳 *AE, DC, MC, V.*

WORD OF MOUTH

"In Monaco, definitely see the changing of the guard, take the palace tour, and visit the cathedral during the day. But the casino is much more interesting at night. I enjoyed Monaco as two separate excursions—one time at night, and one time in the morning on a different day." —robertino

12

$$$$ FRENCH Fodor's Choice ★ ✕ **Le Louis XV.** Louis Quinze to the initiated, this extravagantly showy restaurant stuns with neo-Baroque details, yet it manages to be upstaged by its product: the superb cuisine of Alain Ducasse, one of Europe's most celebrated chefs. With too many tokens on his Monopoly board, Ducasse jets between his other, ever-growing interests leaving the Louis XV kitchen, for the most part, in the more-than-capable hands of chef Franck Cerutti, who draws much of his inspiration from the Cours Saleya market in Nice. Ducasse's absence is no great loss. Glamorous iced lobster consommé with caviar, and risotto perfumed with Alba white truffles slum happily with stockfish (stewed salt cod) and tripe. There are sole sautéed with tender baby fennel, salt-seared foie gras, milk-fed lamb with hints of cardamom, and dark-chocolate sorbet crunchy with ground coffee beans or hot wild strawberries on an icy mascarpone sorbet—in short, a panoply of delights using the sensual flavors of the Mediterranean. The decor is magnificent—a surfeit of gilt, mirrors, and chandeliers—and the waitstaff seignorial as they proffer a footstool for madame's handbag. In Ducasse fashion, the Baroque clock on the wall is stopped just before 12. Cinderella should have no fears. If your wallet is a chubby one, this is a must (the discovery menu is €280). ✉ *Hôtel de Paris, Pl. du Casino* ☎ *377/98–06–88–64* 🌐 *www.alain-ducasse.com* ✍ *Reservations essential* 💳 *AE, DC, MC, V* ⏲ *Closed Tues. and Wed. (summer schedule may vary) and Dec.*

$$$ FRENCH ✕ **Zebra Square.** An offshoot of its sister hot spot in Paris, this trendy bar-restaurant atop the Grimaldi Forum serves impeccable modern-Provençal cuisine on a lovely terrace looking out to the sea. Better yet, it turns into a late-night lounge after midnight and its low lighting and great selection of music are easy to *groove* to. ✉ *Grimaldi Forum, 10 av. Princess Grace* ☎ *377/93–99–25–50* 💳 *AE, MC, V* ⏲ *Closed Sun., and Dec. and Jan. No lunch Sat.*

WHERE TO STAY

$$$$ **Hôtel Metropole.** With its wonderfully impressive entrance, this fine Belle Époque palace is mouthwateringly beautiful. From the moment you walk through the colossal neo-Roman arch, down the cypress-studded lane, and into the cozy Jacques Garcia–designed lounge, you're swept away into Rothschild Renaissance–meets–contemporary style: the clever trompe-l'oeil bookcase in the bar is actually the door to the

bathroom, for example. Guest rooms are luxe and tastefully decorated in creams and beiges, but the main attraction here, especially for those with a healthy respect for creative and top-notch cuisine, is the restaurant. Headed up by much acclaimed chef Joël Robuchon, the menu varies from season to season but never fails to delight. The garden has also been transformed into an urban oasis, now harboring some 3,000 species of plants. Guests can choose from a number of chauffeur-driven half-day and full-day trips, plus children's programs and—*mais, oui*—dogs' programs. **Pros:** magical setting is only enhanced by the decor and the food, which is top-notch. **Cons:** level of service can be dependent on what you look like and how much you tip. ✉ *4 av. de la Madonne,* ☎ *377/93–15–15–15* 🌐 *www.metropole.com* *146 rooms, 10 suites* *In-room: a/c, refrigerator. In-hotel: 3 restaurants, bar, pool, gym, spa, Wi-Fi hotspot, parking (paid), some pets allowed* *AE, DC, MC, V* *MAP.*

$$–$$$ **Hotel Miramar.** Next to the port, but at a fraction of the price of other port hotels, this lovely little spot is one of the few real bargains in Monaco. The rooms are sweet—lots of burnished wood, beiges and creams—and all have wonderful views. Some even have small balconies, and those that don't can take advantage of the intimate rooftop lounge. **Pros:** staff are very friendly and there's a fun bar-brasserie downstairs. **Cons:** no pool, and some rooms are a little small. ✉ *1 av. President J-F Kennedy, La Condamine* ☎ *377/93–30–86–48* 🌐 *www.hotel-miramar.mc* *11 rooms* *In-room: a/c, refrigerator. In-hotel: restaurant, bar, Wi-Fi hotspot, some pets allowed* *MC, V* *BP.*

NIGHTLIFE AND THE ARTS

There's no need to go to bed before dawn in Monte Carlo when you can go to the **casinos.** Monte Carlo's spring arts festival, **Printemps des Arts** includes the world's top ballet, operatic, symphonic, and chamber-music performers (☎ *377/93–25–58–04* *www.printempsdesarts.com*). Year-round, opera, ballet, and classical music can be enjoyed at the magnificently sumptuous Salle Garnier auditorium of the **Opéra de Monte-Carlo** (✉ *Pl. du Casino* ☎ *337/98–06–28–28* 🌐 *www.opera.mc*), the main venue of the Opéra de Monte-Carlo and the Orchestre Philharmonique de Monte-Carlo, both worthy of the magnificent hall.

SPORTS

Held at the beautiful Monte Carlo Country Club, the **Monte Carlo Open Tennis Masters Series** (☎ *377/97–98–70–00* 🌐 *montecarlo.masters-series.com*) is held during the last two weeks of April every year. When the tennis stops, the auto racing begins: the **Grand Prix de Monaco** (☎ *377/93–15–26–00 for information* 🌐 *www.grand-prix-monaco.com*) takes place in mid-May.

The Midi-Pyrénées and Languedoc-Roussillon

WORD OF MOUTH

"Collioure is prettier, more 'real,' and busy all year-round because people actually live there. In other words, it is not just a holiday resort." —Pvoyageuse

"Carcassonne is the fortified medieval city of your dreams. My wife thinks it touristy but it has been that way for 800 years and that means it is a true, not touristy, experience." —Ira

WELCOME TO THE MIDI-PYRÉNÉES AND LANGUEDOC-ROUSSILLON

TOP REASONS TO GO

★ **Matisse Madness:** Captivating Collioure, the main town of the Côte Vermeille, was where Matisse and Derain went mad with color and created the Fauvist art movement in the early 20th century.

★ **Fairy-Tale Carcassonne:** With storybook towers, turrets, and battlements, medieval Carcassonne is the greatest sand castle ever built that didn't wash away.

★ **Tumultuous Toulouse:** With rosy roofs and red-brick mansions, the "pink city" of Toulouse is a place where high culture is an evening at an outdoor café, an art form perfected by the 80,000 students who make this city tick.

★ **Albi's Toulouse-Lautrec:** Presided over by its fortress-like Cathédrale Ste-Cécile, Albi honors its most famous native son, Toulouse-Lautrec, with the largest museum of his works.

★ **Abbey in the Sky:** At an altitude of nearly 3,600 feet, the picture-postcard medieval Abbaye St-Martin du Canigou enjoys a breathtaking (literally) perch.

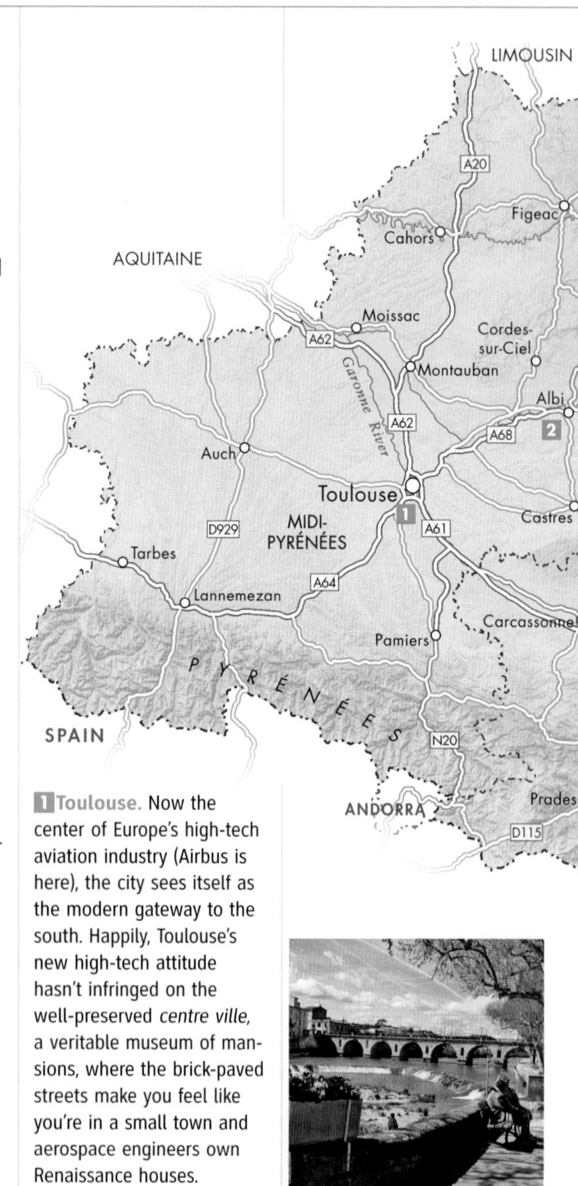

1 Toulouse. Now the center of Europe's high-tech aviation industry (Airbus is here), the city sees itself as the modern gateway to the south. Happily, Toulouse's new high-tech attitude hasn't infringed on the well-preserved *centre ville*, a veritable museum of mansions, where the brick-paved streets make you feel like you're in a small town and aerospace engineers own Renaissance houses.

2 Albi. Some 75 km (47 mi) northeast of Toulouse is Albi, set along the Tarn River and once a major center of the Cathars; the huge Cathédrale Ste-Cécile was a symbol of the church's victory over these heretics. Art lovers make a pilgrimage to the famed Musée Toulouse-Lautrec.

3 Languedoc-Roussillon. Studded with vineyards and art treasures, Languedoc is a vast province that ranges from Toulouse in the Pyrenean hills eastward to aristocratic Montpellier set on the Mediterranean. In between are famous sights like Carcassonne—the largest medieval town extant—and *le littoral languedocien* (the Languedoc coast), where France's "second Riviera" draws both artists and sun worshippers to Collioure and other towns along the Côte Vermeille.

GETTING ORIENTED

13

Spend some time in the Midi-Pyrénées, the country's largest region, and the term "the south of France" takes on new meaning. This western half of France's south is less glamorous (and much less expensive) than the Riviera and Provence but has an array of must-sees, beginning with lively Toulouse. South lies Languedoc, a province of contrasts—of rolling sun-baked plains around storybook Carcassonne, of stone-and-shrub-covered hills spiked with ruins of ancient civilizations. Stretching east to the Mediterranean is the southernmost province of Roussillon, so called from the red color of the earth and home to that artists' paradise, the Vermillion Coast.

THE MIDI-PYRÉNÉES AND LANGUEDOC-ROUSSILLON PLANNER

When to Go

You can expect pleasantly warm weather as early as April and as late as October, but be prepared for rainstorms and/or heat waves at almost any time.

The weather is especially unpredictable in the Pyrénées: a few passing clouds can rapidly turn into a full-blown storm.

Needless to say, during July and August towns high on tourist lists—like Albi, Carcassonne, and Collioure—are packed.

So perhaps opt for April and May, which are delightful months on the Côte Vermeille, and it's also the time when the Pyrenean flowers are at their best.

June and September (grape-picking season, or *vendange*) are equally good for the inland points. As October draws near, the chilly winds of winter begin to appear and frenzied mushroom hunters ferret amid the chestnut and pine trees.

No matter what the season, there's plenty to occupy the outdoors lover here, whether it be hiking the Grandes Randonnées (GRs) paths, scaling lofty peaks, or skiing sun-dappled snow fields.

The Grand Tour

The Midi-Pyrénées and Languedoc-Roussillon form the main body of France's traditional southwestern region. Sports and nature lovers flock here to enjoy the natural attributes of the area, of which Toulouse—a university town of rosy pink brick—is the cultural star.

Here, too, are Albi and its wonderful Toulouse-Lautrec Museum; the once-upon-a-timeliness of Carcassonne; and the relatively undiscovered city of Montpellier.

And when you see picturesque Collioure's stunning Mediterranean setting, you can understand why Matisse went color-berserk.

Getting to know this vast region would take several weeks, or even years. But it's possible to sample all its finest offerings in nine days, if that's all the time you have.

Begin by practicing your "Olé's" in Spanish-soul Toulouse; after two days and two nights in this exciting city, head west to the Gers département to spend Day 3 in Albi and take a virtual art class with Toulouse-Lautrec at the famous museum here devoted to his masterworks.

On Day 4, head some 112 km (70 mi) south to storybook Carcassonne to introduce your kids to the Puss in Boots fantasy of this castellated wonder.

After a night filled with medieval history and glamour, head southeast on Day 5 to the Vermilion Coast. It's time to pack your crayons for a trip to Matisse Country and head to the Roussillon's coastal town of Collioure to channel the spirits of the famous Fauve painters. Spend all of Day 6 here. Then on Day 7, drive north past Perpignan, the historic hub city of the Roussillon, and head to marvelous Montpellier.

After your seventh night, enjoy your Day 8 by touring this city's fascinating Vieille Ville, steeped in culture, history, and young blood (a famous university is based here). Add on a Day 9 to chill-out before returning to reality.

Finding a Place to Stay

Hotels range from Mediterranean modern to medieval baronial to Pyrenean chalet; most are small and cozy rather than luxurious and sophisticated.

Toulouse has the usual range of big-city hotels; make reservations well in advance if you plan to visit in spring or fall.

Look for *gîtes d'étape* (hikers' way stations) and *table d'hôtes* (bed-and-breakfasts), which offer excellent value and a chance to meet local and international travelers and sample life on the farm, as well as the delights of *cuisine du terroir* (country cooking).

As for off-season—if there is such a thing, since chic Parisians often arrive in November in their SUVs with a hunger for the authentic—call ahead and double-check when hotels close for their annual hibernation.

This usually starts sometime in winter, either before, or right after, the Christmas holidays.

Assume that all hotel rooms have air-conditioning, TV, telephones, and private bath, unless otherwise noted.

DINING AND LODGING PRICE CATEGORIES (IN EUROS)

	¢	$	$$	$$$	$$$$
Restaurants	under €13	€13–€17	€18–€24	€25–€32	over €32
Hotels	under €65	€65–€105	€106–€145	€146–€215	over €215

Restaurant prices are per person for a main course at dinner, including tax (5.5%) and service; note that if a restaurant offers only prix-fixe (set-price) meals, it has been given the price category that reflects the full prix-fixe price. Hotel prices are for a standard double room in high season, including tax (19.6%) and service charge.

Finding a Place to Eat

As a rule, the closer you get to the Mediterranean coast, the later you dine and the more you pay for your seafood platter and that bottle of iced rosé.

The farther you travel from the coast, the higher the altitude, the more rustic the setting you'll find yourself in, and the more reasonable the prices will be.

During the scorching summer months in sleepy mountain villages, lunches are light, interminable, and *bien arrosé* (French for "with lots of wine").

Here you can also find that small personal restaurant where the chickens roasting on spits above the open fire have first names and the cheese comes from the hippie couple down the road who came here in the '60s and love their mountains, their goats, and the universe in general.

GETTING AROUND

Visitor Information

The regional tourist office for the Midi-Pyrénées is the Comité Régional du Tourisme.

For Pyrénées-Roussillon information, contact the Comité Départemental de Tourisme du Pyrénées-Roussillon.

For Languedoc-Roussillon contact the Comité Régional du Tourisme du Languedoc-Roussillon.

Comité Régional du Tourisme (*CRT* ✉ *54 bd. de l'Embouchure, Toulouse* ☎ *05-61-13-55-48* 🌐 *www.tourisme-midi-pyrenees.com*).

Comité Départemental de Tourisme du Pyrénées-Roussillon (✉ *16 av. Des Palmiers, Perpignan* ☎ *04-68-51-52-53* 🌐 *www.cdt-66.com*).

Comité Régional du Tourisme du Languedoc-Roussillon (✉ *954 av. Jean Mermoz, Montpellier* ☎ *04-67-20-02-20* 🌐 *www.sunfrance.com*).

Handy Web sites for the regions in this chapter include: 🌐 *www.audetourisme.com* and 🌐 *www.tourisme-tarn.com*.

Train Travel

Most trains for the southwest leave from Paris's Gare d'Austerlitz. There are direct trains to Toulouse and Montauban. Carcassonne connects with either Toulouse or Montpellier.

Four trains leave Paris (Gare de Lyon) daily for Narbonne and one for Perpignan, although others connect with Montpellier. Most of these trips take between six and seven hours.

Note that at least three high-speed TGV (Trains à Grande Vitesse) per day leave Paris (Gare Montparnasse) for Toulouse; the journey time is five hours. A TGV line also serves Montpellier four times a day (departing from Paris's Gare de Lyon).

The regional French rail network in the southwest provides regular service to many towns, though not all.

Within the Midi-Pyrénées region, Toulouse is the biggest hub, with a major line linking Carcassonne (45 mins, €15), Béziers, Narbonne (1½ hrs, €21) (change here for Perpignan), and Montpellier (2 hrs, €32); trains also link up with Albi (1 hr, €11), Foix (1 hr, €12), Ax-les-Thermes (2 hrs, €15), and Montauban (30 mins, €8); the latter connects with Moissac.

Toulouse trains also connect with Biarritz (4 hrs, €35), Pau (2 hrs, €33), and Bordeaux (3 hrs, €39).

Montpellier connects with Carcassonne (1 hr, €12), Perpignan (2 hrs, €28), Narbonne, and other towns.

From Perpignan, take one of the dozen or so daily trains to Collioure (20 mins, €6).

Train Information **Gare SNCF Carcassonne** (✉ *Quai Riquet s/n* ☎ *08-92-35-35-35*). **Gare SNCF Montpellier** (✉ *Rue Jules Ferry* ☎ *08-36-35-35-35 [or 35-36]*). **Gare SNCF Perpignan** (✉ *Av. du Général de Gaulle* ☎ *35-36*). **SNCF** (☎ *36-35 [€0.34 per min]* 🌐 *www.voyages-sncf.com*). **SNCF Toulouse-Matabiau** (✉ *64 bd. Pierre Semard* ☎ *05-61-10-11-04*). **TGV** (🌐 *www.tgv.com*).

Bus Travel

As in most rural regions in France, there's an array of bus companies (in addition to SNCF buses, Intercars, Semvat, Courriers de la Garonne, Salt Autocars, Transnod, among others) threading the Midi-Pyrénées countryside. Toulouse's bus links include Albi (1½ hrs, €13), Auch, Castres, Foix (1 hr, €8), Carcassonne (2 hrs, €12), and Montauban; Albi connects with Cordes-sur-Ciel (summer only; other times take train to Cordes-Vindrac, 5 km [3 mi] away) and Montauban; Montauban with Moissac (20 mins, €4) and Auch; Montpellier with Narbonne. For Courriers Catalans, Cars Capeille, and Car Inter 66 buses to the Côte Vermeille, Collioure, Céret, Prades, and Font-Romeu depart from Perpignan. The train to Carcassonne is scenic and romantic, although buses (cheaper and faster) go there as well.

Bus Information **Gare Routière Carcassonne** (✉ *Bd. De Varsovie, Ville Basse*). **Gare Routière Montpellier** (✉ *Pl. du Bicentenaire*). **Gare Routière Perpignan** (✉ *Av. du Général Leclerc s/n* ☎ *04–68–35–29–02*). **Gare Routière Toulouse** (✉ *68 bd. Pierre Sémard* ☎ *05–61–61–67–67*).

Car Travel

The fastest route from Paris to Toulouse (677 km [406 mi] south) is via Limoges on A20, then A62; the journey time is about six hours. If you choose to head south over the Pyrénées to Barcelona, the Tunnel du Puymorens saves half an hour of switchbacks between Hospitalet and Porta, but in good weather and with time to spare the drive over the Puymorens Pass is spectacular. Plan on taking three hours between Toulouse and Font-Romeu and another three to Barcelona. The fastest route from Toulouse to Barcelona is the under-three-hour, 391-km (235-mi) drive via Carcassonne and Perpignan on A61 and A9, which becomes AP7 at Le Perthus.

A62/A61 slices through the region on its way through Carcassonne to the coast at Narbonne, where A9 heads south to Perpignan. At Toulouse, where A62 becomes A61, various highways fan out in all directions: N124 to Auch; A64 to St-Gaudens, Tarbes, and Pau; A62/A20 to Montauban and Cahors; N20 south to Foix and the Ariège Valley; A68 to Albi and Rodez. A9 (La Languedocienne) is the main highway artery that connects Montpellier with Beziers to the south and Nîmes to the north.

Air Travel

All international flights for Toulouse arrive at Blagnac Airport, 8 km (5 mi) northwest of the city. The airport shuttle (🌐 *www.navette-tisseo-aeroport.com*) runs every 20 minutes between 7:35 AM and 12:15 PM from the airport to the bus-train station in Toulouse (fare €4).

From the Toulouse bus station to the airport, buses leave every 20 minutes 5 AM–8:20 PM.

Airport Information **Airport Montpellier-Méditerranée** (☎ *04–67–20–85–00*). **Airport Carcassonne-Salvaza** (☎ *04–68–71–96–46*). **Airport International, Perpignan** (☎ *04–68–52–60–70*). **Blagnac Airport** (☎ *08–25–38–00–00*).

Carriers In addition, be sure to check out Ryanair, easyJet, and Flybe, who offer surprisingly cheap flights to Perpignan, Montpellier, Carcassonne, or Toulouse—often as low as €30 one-way.

Airlines and Contacts **Air France** (☎ *1800/992–3932* 🌐 *www.airfrance.com*). **easyJet** (🌐 *www.easyjet.com*). **Flybe** (☎ *44–13–92–26–85–29 in U.K.* 🌐 *www.flybe.com*). **Ryanair** (☎ *08–92–23–23–75* 🌐 *www.ryanair.com*).

Updated by John Fanning

Like the most celebrated dish of this area, cassoulet, the southwestern region of France is a feast of diverse ingredients. Just as it would be a gross oversimplification to refer to cassoulet merely as a dish of baked beans, southwestern France is much more than just Toulouse, the peaks of the Pyrénées, and the fairy-tale ramparts of Carcassonne.

For here you'll also find, like so many raisins sweetening up a spicy stew, the pretty seaside town of Collioure, the famed Côte Vermeille (where Matisse, Picasso, and Braque first vacationed to paint), and Albi, a hilltop town that honors its native son, Toulouse-Lautrec, with a great museum. But in most cases, every traveler heading to this area begins with the regional gateway: "La Ville Rose," so-called for Toulouse's redbrick buildings.

Big enough to be France's fourth-largest city and yet with a look and vibe of a gorgeous small town, Toulouse is all that more famous regional capitals would like to have remained, or to become. The cultural hub of this corner of France, the city remains alive with music, sculpture, architectural gems, and is vibrant with students. Sinuously spread along the romantic banks of the Garonne as it meanders north and west from the Catalan Pyrénées on its way to the Atlantic, Toulouse has a Spanish sensuality unique in all Gaul. The city began as the ancient capital of the province called Languedoc, so christened when it became royal property in 1270, meaning the country where *oc*—instead of the *oil* or *oui* of northeastern France—meant "yes."

If you head out in any direction from Toulouse you'll enjoy a feast for the eyes. Albi, with its Toulouse-Lautrec legacy, is a star attraction, while Céret is the gateway to a fabled "open-air museum" prized by artists and poets, the Côte Vermeille. The Vermilion Coast is centered around Collioure, the lovely fishing village where Matisse, Derain, and the Fauvists rewrote the rules of modern art in the early years of the 20th century. They were called the Fauves, or "wild beasts," partly because their colors were taken from the savage tones found in Mother Nature hereabouts. Sheer heaven for painters, the town's magic did not go unnoticed, and it soon drew vacationers by the boatload. They soon discover that everything around here seems to be asking to be immortalized in oil on canvas: the Mediterranean smooth and opalescent at dawn; villagers dancing Sardanas to the music of the raucous and ancient woodwind *flavioles* and *tenores*; and the flood of golden light so peculiar to the Mediterranean.

TOULOUSE: LA VILLE ROSE

The ebullient city of Toulouse is the capital of the Midi-Pyrénées and the fourth-largest city in France. Just 100 km (60 mi) from the border with Spain, Toulouse is in many ways closer in flavor to southern European Spanish than to northern European French. Weathered redbrick buildings line sidewalks, giving the city its nickname, "La Ville Rose" (the Pink City). Downtown, the sidewalks and restaurants pulse late into the night with tourists, workers, college students, and technicians from the giant Airbus aviation complex headquartered outside the city.

GETTING HERE

If you train to Toulouse you arrive at its Gare Matabiau (☎ *36–35*), which is right beside the Toulouse Gare Routiere (bus station), on Boulevard Pierré-Sémard. The Gare Routière (☎ *05–61–61–67–67*) is also where the airport shuttle, which departs every 20 minutes from Blagnac Airport (☎ *08–25–38–00–00*), leaves you off. If you want the TGV (🌐 *www.tgv.com*), there are around nine trains a day from Paris at about €75 a trip.

Visitor Information Toulouse Tourist Office. ✉ *Donjon du Capitole* ☎ *05–61–11–02–22* 🌐 *www.toulouse-tourisme.com.*

EXPLORING

Toulouse's bustling and new high-tech attitude hasn't infringed on the well-preserved *centre ville* (city center), the brick-paved streets between the Garonne river and the Canal du Midi. Here Toulouse still seems like a small town, where food, nouveau Beaujolais, and the latest rugby victory are the primary concerns. Here you can enjoy the Mediterranean pace, southern friendliness, and young spirit of the city.

Toulouse was founded in the 4th century BC and quickly became an important part of Roman Gaul. In turn, it was made into a Visigothic and Carolingian capital before becoming a separate county in 843. Ruling from this Pyrenean hub—one of the great artistic and literary capitals of medieval Europe—the counts of Toulouse held sovereignty over nearly all of the Languedoc, and maintained a brilliant court known for its fine troubadours and literature. In the early 13th century Toulouse was attacked and plundered by troops representing an alliance between the northern French nobility and the papacy, ostensibly to wipe out the Albigensian heresy (Catharism), but more realistically as an expansionist move against the power of Occitania, the French southwest. The counts toppled, but Toulouse experienced a cultural and economic rebirth thanks to the *woad* (dye) trade; consequently, wealthy merchants' homes constitute a major portion of Toulouse's architectural patrimony.

Toulouse, at the intersection of the Garonne and the Canal du Midi, midway between the Massif Central and the Pyrénées, became an important nexus between Aquitania, Languedoc, and the Roussillon. Today, Toulouse is France's second-largest university town after Paris and the center of France's aeronautical industry.

OLD TOULOUSE

The area between the boulevards and the Garonne forms the historic nucleus of Toulouse. Originally part of Roman Gaul and later the capital for the Visigoths and then the Carolingians, by AD 1000 Toulouse was one of the artistic and literary centers of medieval Europe. Despite its 13th-century defeat by the lords of northern France, Toulouse quickly reemerged as a cultural and commercial power and has remained so ever since. Religious and civil structures bear witness to this illustrious past, even as the city's booming student life mirrors a dynamic present. This is the heart of Toulouse, with Place du Capitole at its center. The huge garage beneath Place du Capitole is a good place to park, and offers easy walking distance to all the major sites. If you leave your car in another garage, you can take the subway that runs north–south to central Toulouse; it costs €1.40 (🌐 *www.tisseo.fr*).

TOP ATTRACTIONS

5 **Basilique St-Sernin.** Toulouse's most famous landmark and the world's largest Romanesque church once belonged to a Benedictine abbey, built in the 11th century to house pilgrims on their way to Santiago de Compostela in Spain. Inside, the aesthetic high point is the magnificent central apse, begun in 1080, glittering with gilded ceiling frescoes, which date from the 19th century. When illuminated at night, St-Sernin's five-tier octagonal tower glows red against the sky. Not all the tiers are the same: the first three, with their rounded windows, are Romanesque; the upper two, with pointed Gothic windows, were added around 1300. The ancient crypt contains the relics and reliquaries of 128 saints, but the most famous item on view is a thorn that legend says is from the Crown of Thorns. ✉ *Pl. Saint-Sernin,* ☎ *05–61–21–80–45* 🎫 *Crypt €3* 🕒 *Nov.–May, Mon.–Sat. 8:30–noon and 2–6, Sun. 8:30–12:30 and 2–5:30; June and Oct., Mon.–Sat. 8:30–12:30 and 2–6:30, Sun. 8:30-5:30; July–Sept., Mon.–Sat. 8:30–6:15, Sun. 8:30–5:30.*

Fodor's Choice ★

2 **Capitole/Hôtel de Ville** *(Capitol/Town Hall).* The 18th-century Capitole is home to the Hôtel de Ville and the city's highly regarded opera company. The reception rooms are open to the public when not in use for

GETTING AROUND

For the most part, Toulouse's hotels, restaurants, and sights are within walking distance of one another. The main square of the *centre ville* (town center) is Place du Capitole, a good 15-minute walk from the train station but only a few blocks away from the city's other focal points—Place Wilson, Place Esquirol, and Basilique St-Sernin. The métro still has only one line, but conveniently connects the Gare Matabiau with Place du Capitole and Place Esquirol. The Servat bus system is efficient, too.

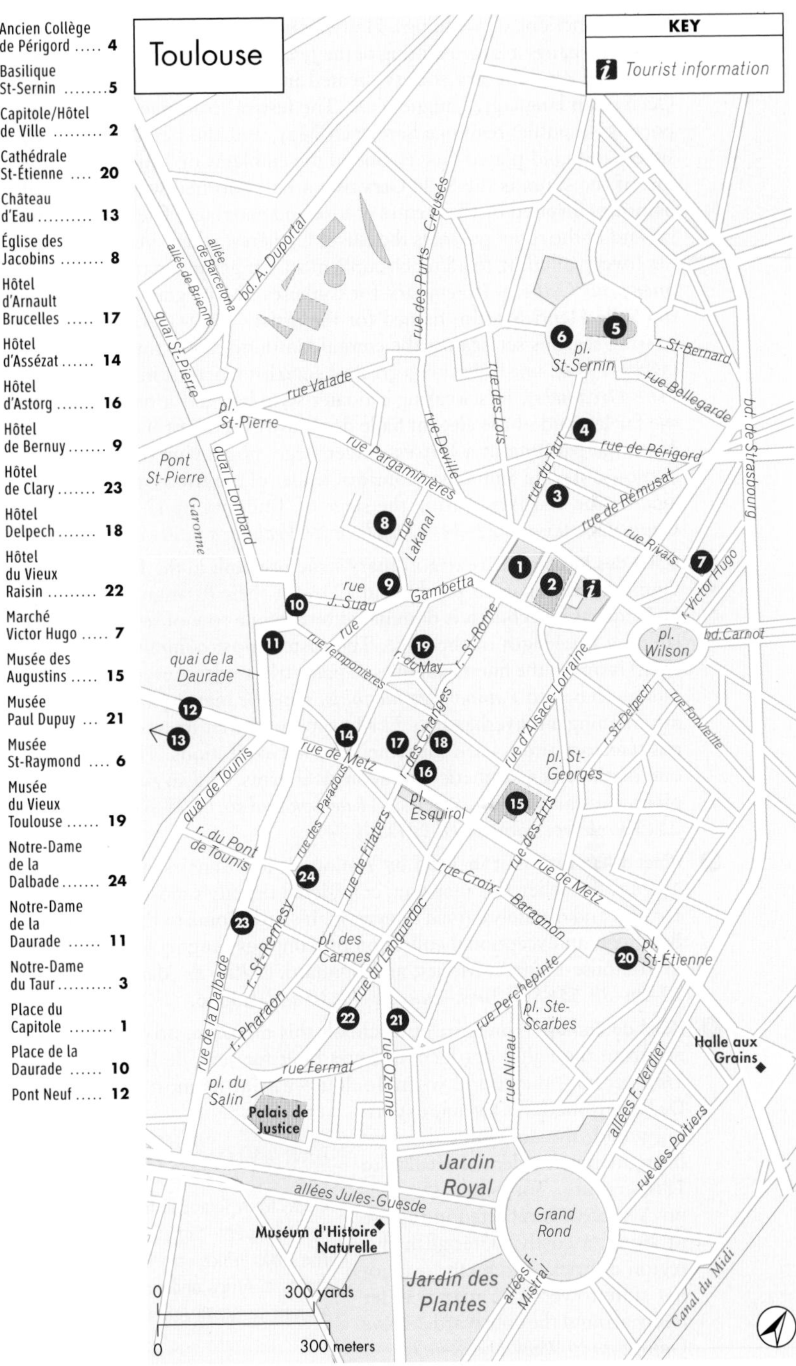

Toulouse
KEY
Tourist information
Ancien Collège de Périgord 4
Basilique St-Sernin 5
Capitole/Hôtel de Ville 2
Cathédrale St-Étienne 20
Château d'Eau 13
Église des Jacobins 8
Hôtel d'Arnault Brucelles 17
Hôtel d'Assézat 14
Hôtel d'Astorg 16
Hôtel de Bernuy 9
Hôtel de Clary 23
Hôtel Delpech 18
Hôtel du Vieux Raisin 22
Marché Victor Hugo 7
Musée des Augustins 15
Musée Paul Dupuy ... 21
Musée St-Raymond 6
Musée du Vieux Toulouse 19
Notre-Dame de la Dalbade 24
Notre-Dame de la Daurade 11
Notre-Dame du Taur 3
Place du Capitole 1
Place de la Daurade 10
Pont Neuf 12
bd. A. Duportal
allée de Barcelona
allée de Brienne
quai St-Pierre
rue des Purts Creusés
pl. St-Sernin
r. St-Bernard
rue Bellegarde
bd. de Strasbourg
rue Valade
pl. St-Pierre
rue des Lois
rue Deville
rue du Taur
rue de Périgord
rue Pargaminières
Pont St-Pierre
quai L.Lombard
Garonne
rue Lakanal
rue de Rémusat
rue Rivals
r. Victor Hugo
rue J. Suau
Gambetta
rue
r. St-Rome
pl. Wilson
bd.Carnot
rue Temponières
r. du May
quai de la Daurade
rue d'Alsace-Lorraine
r. St-Delpech
rue Fonvielle
r. des Changes
rue de Metz
quai de Tounis
pl. St-Georges
rue des Paradoux
pl. Esquirol
r. du Pont de Tounis
rue des Arts
rue de Filatiers
rue Croix-Baragnon
rue de Metz
r. St-Remesy
pl. des Carmes
rue du Languedoc
pl. St-Étienne
rue de la Dalbade
r. Pharaon
rue Perchepinte
pl. Ste-Scarbes
Halle aux Grains
rue Fermat
rue Ozenne
rue Ninau
allées F. Verdier
pl. du Salin
Palais de Justice
rue des Poitiers
Jardin Royal
allées Jules-Guesde
Grand Rond
Muséum d'Histoire Naturelle
Jardin des Plantes
allées F. Mistral
Canal du Midi
0
300 yards
0
300 meters

13

official functions or weddings. Halfway up the **Grand Escalier** (Grand Staircase) hangs a large painting of the *Jeux Floraux,* the "floral games" organized by a literary society created in 1324 to promote the local Occitanian language, Langue d'Oc. The festival continues to this day: poets give public readings here each May, and the best are awarded silver- and gold-plated violets, one of the emblems of Toulouse. At the top of the stairs is the **Salle Gervaise,** a hall adorned with a series of paintings inspired by the themes of love and marriage. The mural at the far end of the room portrays the Isle of Cythères, where Venus received her lovers, alluding to a French euphemism for getting married: *embarquer pour Cythères* (to embark for Cythères). More giant paintings in the **Salle Henri-Martin,** named for the artist (1860–1943), show the passing seasons set against the eternal Garonne. Look for Jean Jaurès (1859–1914), one of France's greatest socialist martyrs, in *Les Rêveurs* (*The Dreamers*); he's wearing a boater-style hat and a beige coat. At the far left end of the elegant **Salle des Illustres** (Hall of the Illustrious) is a large painting of a fortress under siege, portraying the women of Toulouse slaying Simon de Montfort, leader of the Albigensian crusade against the Cathars, during the siege of Toulouse in 1218. ✉ *Pl. du Capitole* ☎ *05–61–22–34–12* 🎫 *Free* ⏲ *Weekdays 8:30–5.*

8 ★ **Église des Jacobins.** An extraordinary structure built in the 1230s for the Dominicans (renamed Jacobins in 1216 for their Parisian base in Rue St-Jacques), the church is dominated by a single row of seven columns running the length of the nave. The easternmost column (on the far right) is one of the finest examples of palm-tree vaulting ever erected, the much-celebrated *Palmier des Jacobins,* a major masterpiece of Gothic art. Fanning out overhead, its 22 ribs support the entire apse. The original refectory site is used for temporary art exhibitions. The cloister is one of the city's aesthetic and acoustical gems, and in summer hosts piano and early music concerts. ✉ *Rue Lakanal s/n* ☎ *05–61–22–21–92* 🎫 *Church free, cloister €3* ⏲ *Daily 9–7.*

14 **Hôtel d'Assézat.** Built in 1555 by Toulouse's top Renaissance architect, Nicolas Bachelier, this mansion, considered the city's most elegant, has arcades and ornately carved doorways. It's now home to the **Fondation Bemberg,** an exceptional collection of paintings ranging from Tiepolo to Toulouse-Lautrec, Monet, and Bonnard. ✉ *Rue de Metz* ☎ *05–61–12–06–89* 🎫 *€5* ⏲ *Tues.–Sun. 10–12:30 and 1:30–6.*

9 **Hôtel de Bernuy.** Now part of a school, this mansion, around the corner from the Église des Jacobins, was built for Jean de Bernuy in the 16th century, the period when Toulouse was at its most prosperous. De Bernuy made his fortune exporting woad, the dark-blue dye that brought unprecedented wealth to 18th-century Toulouse. De Bernuy's success is reflected in the use of stone, a costly material in this region of brick, and by the octagonal stair tower. You may wander freely around the courtyard. ✉ *Rue Gambetta* ⏲ *Weekdays 8–6:30.*

PAR AVION

It was from Toulouse that Antoine de St-Exupéry—famed author of *The Little Prince*—pioneered mail flights to Africa and over the Atlantic to South America.

15 ★ **Musée des Augustins** *(Augustinian Museum)*. In this former medieval Augustinian convent, the museum uses the sacristy, chapter house, and cloisters for displaying an outstanding array of Romanesque sculpture and religious paintings. Built in Mediterranean-Gothic style, the architectural complex is vast and holds a collection rich with treasures and discoveries. ✉ *21 rue de Metz* ☎ *05–61–22–21–82* 🎫 *Museum €3; free 1st Sun. of month* ⏱ *Thurs.–Tues. 10–6, Wed. 10–9.*

TRIP TIP

If you intend to see a lot of Toulouse's sights, you should invest in a City Pass (Carte Privilegé). It's €10 and allows you half price on all the sites. Also, go to 🌐 *www.toulouse-tourisme.com* for details on the City Pass program for reduced bookings on selected hotels.

13

6 **Musée St-Raymond.** The city's archaeological museum, next to the basilica of St-Sernin, has an extensive collection of imperial Roman busts, as well as ancient coins, vases, and jewelry. ✉ *Pl. St-Sernin* ☎ *05–61–22–31–44* 🎫 *€3* ⏱ *Daily 10–6.*

19 **Musée du Vieux Toulouse** *(Museum of Old Toulouse)*. This museum is worthwhile for the building itself as much as for its collection of Toulouse memorabilia, paintings, sculptures, and documents. Be sure to note the ground-floor fireplace and wooden ceiling. ✉ *7 rue du May* ☎ *05–62–27–11–50* 🎫 *€2.50* ⏱ *Mid-May–mid-Oct., Mon.–Sat. 2–6.*

10 **Place de la Daurade.** On the Garonne, this is one of Toulouse's nicest squares. A stop at the Café des Artistes is almost obligatory. The corner of the quai offers a romantic view of the Garonne, the Hôtel Dieu across the river, and the Pont Neuf.

1 **Place du Capitole.** This vast, open square in the city center, lined with shops and cafés, is a good spot for getting your bearings or for soaking up some spring or winter sun. A parking lot is conveniently underneath.

WORTH NOTING

4 **Ancien Collège de Périgord** *(Old Périgord College)*. The wooden gallery-like structure on the street side of the courtyard is the oldest remnant of the 14th-century residential college. ✉ *56–58 rue du Taur.*

13 **Château d'Eau.** This 19th-century water tower at the far end of the Pont Neuf, once used to store water and build water pressure, is now used for photography exhibits (it was built in 1822, the same year Nicéphore Nièpce created the first permanent photographic images). ✉ *1 pl. Laganne* ☎ *05–61–77–09–40* 🎫 *€2.50* ⏱ *Tues.–Sun. 1–7.*

17 **Hôtel d'Arnault Brucelles.** One of the tallest and best of Toulouse's 49 towers can be found at this 16th-century mansion. ✉ *19 rue des Changes.*

16 **Hôtel d'Astorg et St-Germain.** This 16th-century mansion is notable for its lovely Romanesque wooden stairways and galleries and for its top-floor *mirande*, a wooden balcony. ✉ *16 rue des Changes.*

18 **Hôtel Delpech.** Look for the 17th-century biblical inscriptions carved in Latin in the stone under the windows. ✉ *20 rue des Changes.*

7 **Marché Victor Hugo** *(Victor Hugo Market)*. This hangarlike indoor market is always a refreshing stop. Consider eating lunch at one of the seven upstairs restaurants. **Chez Attila,** just to the left at the top of the stairs, is the best of them. ✉ *Pl. Victor Hugo.*

> **A TAXING MATTER**
>
> At the intersection of Rue des Changes and Rue des Temponiéres you can find a building with trompe l'oeil windows. These bricked-in apertures are a reminder of the window tax that all citizens of Toulouse struggled so mightily to avoid centuries ago.

11 **Notre-Dame de la Daurade.** Overlooking the Garonne is this 18th-century church. The name *Daurade* comes from *doré* (gilt), referring to the golden reflection given off by the mosaics decorating the 5th-century temple to the Virgin Mary that once stood on this site. ✉ *1 pl. de la Daurade.*

3 **Notre-Dame du Taur.** Built on the spot where St. Saturnin (or Sernin), the martyred bishop of Toulouse, was dragged to his death in AD 250 by a rampaging bull, this church is famous for its *cloche-mur,* or wall tower. The wall looks like an extension of the facade and has inspired many similar versions throughout the region. ✉ *Rue du Taur.*

12 **Pont Neuf** *(New Bridge)*. Despite its name, the graceful span of the Pont Neuf opened to traffic in 1632. The remains of the old bridge—one arch and the lighter-color outline on the brick wall of the **Hôtel-Dieu** (hospital)—are visible across the river. The 16th-century hospital was used for pilgrims on their way to Santiago de Compostela. Just over the bridge, on a clear day in winter, the snowcapped peaks of the Pyrénées are often visible in the distance, said to be a sign of imminent rain.

SOUTH OF RUE DE METZ

South of Rue de Metz you'll discover the cathedral of St-Étienne, the antiques district along Rue Perchepinte, and town houses and palaces along the way on Rue Ninau, Rue Ozenne, and Rue de la Dalbade—all among the top sights in Toulouse.

SIGHTS TO SEE

20 **Cathédrale St-Étienne.** The cathedral was erected in stages between the 11th and the 17th centuries, though the nave and choir languished unfinished because of a lack of funds. A fine collection of 16th- and 17th-century tapestries traces the life of St. Stephen. In front of the cathedral is the city's oldest fountain, dating from the 16th century. ✉ *Pl. St-Étienne* ☎ *05–61–52–03–82* ⏲ *Mon.–Sat. 8–5, Sun. 9–5.*

23 **Hôtel de Clary.** This mansion, known as the Hôtel de Pierre because of its unusually solid *pierre* (stone) construction—at the time considered a sign of great wealth—is one of the finest 16th-century mansions on the street. The ornately sculpted stone façade was designed by Nicolas Bachelier in the 16th century. ✉ *25 rue de la Dalbade.*

22 **Hôtel du Vieux Raisin.** Officially the Hôtel Beringuier Maynier, named for the original owner, the house became the Vieux Raisin (Old Grape) after the early name of the street and even earlier inn. Built in the 15th and

Seat of the municipal government, the Place du Capitole is an elegant square often transformed into an open market.

16th centuries, the mansion has an octagonal tower, male and female figures on the facade, and allegorical sculptures of the three stages of life—infancy, maturity, and old age—over the windows to the left. ✉ *36 rue de Languedoc.*

21 **Musée Paul Dupuy.** This museum, dedicated to medieval applied arts, is housed in the Hôtel Pierre Besson, a 17th-century mansion. ✉ *13 rue de la Pleau* ☎ *05–61–14–65–50* 🎫 *€3* ⏲ *Oct.–May, Wed.–Mon. 10–5; June–Sept., Wed.–Mon. 10–6.*

24 **Notre-Dame de la Dalbade.** Originally Sancta Maria de Ecclesia Alba, in Langue d'Oc (Ste-Marie de l'Église Blanche, in French, or St. Mary of the White Church—*alba* meaning "white"), the name of the church evolved into "de Albata" and later "Dalbade." Ironically, one of its outstanding features today is the colorful 19th-century ceramic tympanum over the Renaissance door. ✉ *Pl. de la Dalbade.*

WHERE TO EAT

$$ FRENCH ✕ **Au Bon Vivre.** This intimate restaurant lined with tables with red-check tablecloths fills up at lunch and dinner every day. Quick, unpretentious, and always good, the house specialties include such dishes as cod, wild boar (September–March), and cassoulet. ✉ *15 pl. Wilson* ☎ *05–61–23–07–17* ▭ *AE, MC, V.*

$$ FRENCH ✕ **Bistrot de l'Étoile.** Don't let the dismal exterior put you off, as it conceals a convivial and delightfully retro 1960s pub. With a great choice of dishes on the blackboard menu (including excellent grilled meats cooked on the fire in the center of the restaurant), fresh ingredients,

smiling staff, and fast service, this restaurant is well worth traipsing around the backstreets. The homemade desserts are great, too, especially the tiramisu. ✉ *6 rue de l'Étoile* ☎ *05–61–63–13–43* ✍ *Reservations essential* ▭ *AE, DC, MC, V* ⏲ *Closed weekends.*

$$ FRENCH ★ ✕ **Brasserie Flo "Les Beaux Arts."** Overlooking the Pont Neuf, this elegant brasserie is the place to be at sunset, as painters Ingres and Matisse knew all too well. Watch the colors change over the Garonne from a quayside window or a sidewalk table while enjoying delicious seafood, including six varieties of oysters. The house white wine, a local St-Lannes from the nearby Gers region, is fresh and fruity yet dry, and the service is impeccable. ✉ *1 quai de la Daurade* ☎ *05–61–21–12–12* ▭ *AE, MC, V.*

$$$ FRENCH ✕ **Jardins de l'Opéra**. Stephane Tournie's elegant restaurant next to the Grand Hôtel de l'Opéra is a perennial favorite. Intimate rooms and a covered terrace around a little pond make for undeniable charm, though some will find the grand flourishes—glass ceilings and mammoth chandeliers—a little too, well, operatic, and might prefer the adjacent brasserie, Grand Café de l'Opéra. The food is gastronomique local fare, with seductive nouvelle or Gascon touches that incorporate three different recettes (dishes) on each plate, albeit three different fish, or three different fowl. ✉ *1 pl. du Capitole* ☎ *05–61–23–07–76* ✍ *Reservations essential* ▭ *AE, MC, V* ⏲ *Closed Sun. and Mon.*

$$$ FRENCH ★ ✕ **La Corde**. This little hideaway is worth taking the time to find. Built into a lovely 15th-century corner tower hidden in the courtyard of the 16th-century Hôtel Bolé, La Corde claims the distinction of being the oldest restaurant in Toulouse. Try the grilled forest pigeon. ✉ *4 rue Jules-Chalande* ☎ *05–61–29–09–43* ▭ *AE, MC, V* ⏲ *Closed Sun.*

$$$$ FRENCH ✕ **Le 19**. Centrally placed across the street from the Hôtel Garonne and next to the Pont Neuf, this lovely former 16th-century fish market has vaulted ceilings that will take your breath (but not your appetite) away. Sleek contemporary design and international cuisine combine happily here. ✉ *19 descente de la Halle aux Poissons* ☎ *05–34–31–94–84* ▭ *AE, DC, MC, V* ⏲ *Closed Sun., Aug. 15–22 and Dec. 24–Jan. 6. No lunch Sat. or Mon.*

$$$$ VIETNAMESE ✕ **L'Empereur de Huê**. This sleek-lined contemporary space, open for dinner only, produces traditional Vietnamese cuisine at attractive prices. Soup dumplings and pea shoots are always excellent here, as are the duck-based dishes, without exception. ✉ *17 rue Couteliers* ☎ *05–61–53–55–72* ▭ *AE, DC, MC, V* ⏲ *Closed Sun. and Mon. No lunch.*

$$$$ FRENCH Fodor's Choice ★ ✕ **Michel Sarran**. This clean-lined post-nouvelle haven for what is arguably Toulouse's finest dining departs radically from traditional

TOURING TOULOUSE

Contact the **Toulouse Tourist Office** (✉ *Donjon du Capitole* ☎ *05-61-11-02-22* 🌐 *www.toulouse-tourisme.com*) for information about walking tours and bus tours in and around Toulouse. Ask for the English-speaking, encyclopedic, and superbly entertaining Gilbert Casagrande for a nonpareil tour of Toulouse. The Comité Régional du Tourisme has a brochure, "1,001 Escapes in the Midi-Pyrénées," with descriptions of weekend and short organized package vacations.

EATING WELL

Dining in France's Southwest is a rougher, heartier, and more rustic version of classic Mediterranean cooking—the peppers are sliced thick, the garlic and olive oil used with a heavier hand, the herbs crushed and served au naturel.

Expect *cuisine de marché*, market-based cooking, savory seasonal dishes based on the culinary trinity of the south—garlic, onion, and tomato—straight from the village market. Languedoc is known for powerful and strongly seasoned cooking.

Garlic and goose fat are generously used in traditional recipes. Be sure to try some of the renowned foie gras (goose or duck liver) and *confit de canard* (preserved duck). The most famous regional dish is cassoulet, a succulent white-bean stew with *confit d'oie* (preserved goose), duck, lamb, or a mixture of all three.

Keep your eyes open for festive *cargolades*—huge communal barbecues starting off with thousands of buttery-garlic snails roasted on open grills and eaten with your fingers, followed by cured bacon and lamb cutlets and vats (and vats) of local wine. In the Roussillon and along the Mediterranean coast from Collioure up through Perpignan to Narbonne, the prevalent Catalan cuisine features olive oil–based cooking and sauces such as the classic *aioli* (crushed and emulsified garlic and olive oil). When you're on the coast, it's fish of course, often cooked over wood coals.

13

stick-to-your-ribs southwest-France cuisine in favor of Mediterranean formulas suited to the rhythms and reasons of modern living. Foie-gras soup with Belon oysters and wild salmon in green curry sauce are two examples of Michel Sarran's light but flavorful cuisine. ✉ *21 bd. A. Duportal* ☎ *05–61–12–32–32* ✍ *Reservations essential* ▭ *AE, MC, V* ⏲ *Closed weekends and Aug. No lunch Wed.*

WHERE TO STAY

¢–$ **Grand Hôtel d'Orléans.** This picturesque former stagecoach relay station was built in 1867 and still retains a certain 19th-century charm. Four floors of wooden balustrades overhung with plants look down over a central patio. Guest rooms are small and cozy. **Pros:** good restaurant; close to train and bus stations. **Cons:** surrounding neighborhood is a little sketchy. ✉ *72 rue Bayard, near Matabiau railroad station* ☎ *05–61–62–98–47* 🌐 *www.grand-hotel-orleans.fr* *56 rooms* *In-room: a/c, Wi-Fi. In-hotel: restaurant, parking (paid), some pets allowed* ▭ *AE, MC, V.*

$$$–$$$$ ★ **Grand Hôtel de l'Opéra.** In a former 17th-century convent, this downtown doyen has an old-world feel with 21st-century amenities. Little wonder the likes of Deneuve, Pavarotti, and Aznavour favored this place. Grandeur is the keynote in the lobby, complete with soaring columns and Second Empire bergères and sofas of tasseled velvet. Guest rooms are plush, with rich fabrics, painted headboards, and the most *chaleureuse* (cozy and warm) colors, the best overlooking the grand

square outside. Even though you're on busy Place du Capitole, this hotel is a tranquil oasis. **Pros:** ideally situated on main street; within five minutes of the train station. **Cons:** the bar is a little too brightly lighted. ✉ *1 pl. du Capitole* ☎ *05–61–21–82–66* 🌐 *www.grand-hotel-opera.com* *41 rooms, 16 suites* *In-room: a/c, refrigerator, Wi-Fi. In-hotel: 2 restaurants, bar, gym, parking (paid)* *AE, MC, V.*

$–$$ **Hôtel Albert I.** The building may seem undistinguished and the reception hall is no Versailles, but the rooms are cheerful and spacious (especially the older ones with giant fireplaces and mirrors). The extremely warm and personable owner, Madame Hilaire, is on hand to give suggestions of all kinds. A continental breakfast is served, and nearby parking can be arranged by the hotel. **Pros:** great value for the location. **Cons:** parking lot is difficult to find. ✉ *8 rue Rivals* ☎ *05–61–21–17–91* 🌐 *www.hotel-albert1.com* *47 rooms* *In-room: a/c, Wi-Fi. In-hotel: parking (paid), some pets allowed* *AE, MC, V.*

$$$–$$$$ Fodor'sChoice ★ **Hôtel Garonne.** In the thick of the most Toulousain part of town, next to the Pont Neuf and the former fish market, this is a small but hyper-stylish spot. Modern guest rooms are strikingly done up in bold reds and blacks with rich wood trims; the best suite has a view of the Garonne. The restaurant, Le 19, is spectacular, set in a vast hemispherical brick-laid room, with soigné seating, high-art lighting, and nouvelle versions of regional dishes. A final plus: the staff is cheery and helpful. **Pros:** hip design wherein the moderne style actually works really well. **Cons:** far from town center; the lobby and rooms feel a bit small. ✉ *22 descente de la Halle aux Poissons* ☎ *05–34–31–94–80* 🌐 *www.hotelgaronne.com* *13 rooms, 1 suite* *In-room: a/c, refrigerator, Internet. In-hotel: parking (paid)* *AE, MC, V.*

NIGHTLIFE AND THE ARTS

For a schedule of events, contact the city tourist office. If you want to stay up late—as many do in Toulouse—a complete list of clubs and discos can be found in the annual *Toulouse Pratique* (🌐 *www.leguidetoulousepratique.com*), available at any newsstand. As for cultural highlights, so many opera singers perform at the **Théâtre du Capitole** and the **Halle aux Grains** that the city is known as the *capitale du bel canto.* The opera season lasts from October until late May, with occasional summer presentations as well. A wide variety of dance companies perform in Toulouse: the **Ballet du Capitole** stages classical ballets; **Ballet-Théâtre Joseph Russillo** and **Compagnie Jean-Marc Matos** put on modern-dance performances. The **Centre National Choréographique de Toulouse** welcomes international companies each year in the St-Cyprien quarter.

The most exciting music venue in Toulouse is the auditorium-in-the-round **Halle Aux Grains** (✉ *Pl. Dupuy* ☎ *05–61–63–13–13* 🌐 *www.onct.mairie-toulouse.fr*). **Théâtre du Capitole** (✉ *Pl. du Capitole* ☎ *05–61–22–31–31* 🌐 *www.theatre-du-capitole.org*) is the orchestra, opera, and ballet specialist. **Théâtre Daniel Sorano** (✉ *35 allée Jules-Guesde* ☎ *05–61–32–61–86* 🌐 *www.theatresorano.com*) stages dramatic productions and concerts. **Théâtre de la Digue** (✉ *3 rue de la Digue* ☎ *05–61–42–97–79* 🌐 *www.ladigue.org*) is a theater and dance venue.

Begin your night on the town at **Père Louis** (✉ *45 rue des Tourneurs* ☎ *05–61–21–33–45*), an old-fashioned winery (and restaurant), with barrels used as tables plus vintage photographs. **Bar Basque** (✉ *7 pl. St-Pierre* ☎ *05–61–21–55–64*) is one of the many good watering holes around Place St-Pierre. **Chez Ton Ton** (✉ *16 pl. St-Pierre* ☎ *05–61–21–89–54*), with a somewhat raucous crowd, is a very popular Place St-Pierre dive. **Le Bistro Étienne** (✉ *5 rue Riguepels* ☎ *05–61–25–20–41*), near the Cathedral of St-Étienne, is a hot spot for the third-Thursday-in-November Beaujolais Nouveau blowout. Brazilian guitarists perform at **La Bonita** (✉ *112 Grand-Rue St-Michel* ☎ *05–62–26–36–45*). Be sure to stop by the top jazz spot **Le Mandala** (✉ *23 rue des Aminodiers* ☎ *05–61–21–10–05*) for a bit of the bubbly and some of the best jazz in town.**Melting Pot** (✉ *26 bd. de Strasbourg* ☎ *05–61–62–82–98*) lives up to its title, with young people from around the world crowding the bar and dance floor.

Puerto Habana (✉ *12 port St-Étienne* ☎ *05–61–54–45–61*) is the place for salsa music. **Le Purple** (✉ *2 rue Castellane* ☎ *05–62–73–04–67*) is a hot multispace disco. Outside town is **Villa Garden** (✉ *157 av. de Lespinet* ☎ *05–62–17–38–80*), which is tricky to find but worth checking out. **L'Opera Bouffe** (✉ *5 rue Labeda* ☎ *04–62–30–89–49*) is always a lively spot. **Le Teatro** (✉ *1 pl. St-Cyprien* ☎ *05–61–59–50–00*) is frequented by Toulousains looking for everything: food, drink, and action.

If you're looking for a pretty terrace for lunch or a late dinner (until 10:30), head to **Les Terrasses de Saint-Rome** (✉ *39 rue St-Rome* ☎ *05–62–27–06–06*). Local glitterati and theater stars go to **Ubu** (✉ *16 rue St-Rome* ☎ *05–61–23–26–75*), the city's top nightspot for 20 years. For a midnight dinner over the Garonne, **Brasserie Flo "Les Beaux Arts"** (✉ *1 quai de la Daurade* ☎ *05–61–21–12–12*) is the place to be.

SHOPPING

Toulouse is a chic design outlet for clothing and artifacts of all kinds. **Rue St-Rome, Rue Croix Baragnon, Rue des Changes,** and **Rue d'Alsace-Lorraine** are all good shopping streets.

ALBI AND THE GERS

Along the banks of the Tarn to the northeast of Toulouse is Albi, Toulouse's rival in rose colors. West from Albi, along the river, the land opens up to the rural Gers *département*, home of the heady brandy Armagnac and heart of the former dukedom of Gascony. Studded with châteaux—from simple medieval fortresses to ambitious classical residences—and with tiny, isolated village jewels like Cordes-sur-Ciel, the Gers is an easy place to fall in love with, or in.

ALBI

75 km (47 mi) northeast of Toulouse.

Toulouse-Lautrec's native Albi is a well-preserved and busy provincial market town. In its heyday Albi was a major center for the Cathars, members of a dualistic and ascetic religious movement critical of the hierarchical and worldly ways of the Catholic Church.

GETTING HERE

About 12 trains daily (1 hr, €15) run between Toulouse and Albi's main station on Place Stalingrad (set in a somewhat isolated part of town). In summer months, you can catch infrequent buses to adjoining towns, including Cordes-sur-Ciel (1 hr) from the bus station on Place Jean Jaurès.

Visitor Information Albi Tourist Office. ✉ *Pl. Ste-Cecile* ☎ *05–63–49–48–80* 🌐 *www.albi-tourisme.com.*

EXPLORING

Pick up a copy of the excellent visitor booklet (in English) from the **tourist office** (✉ *Pl. Ste-Cécile* ☎ *05–63–49–48–80* 🌐 *www.albi-tourisme.fr*), and follow the walking tours—of the Vieille Ville (Old City), the old ramparts, and the banks of the River Tarn.

Fodor's Choice ★ One of the most unusual and dazzling churches in France, the huge **Cathédrale Ste-Cécile**, with its intimidating clifflike walls, resembles a cross between a castle and an ocean liner. It was constructed as a symbol of the Church's return to power after the 13th-century crusade that wiped out the Cathars. The interior is an astonishingly ornate contrast to the massive austerity of the outer walls. Maestro Donnelli and a team of 16th-century Italian artists (most of the Emilian school) covered every possible surface with religious scenes and brightly colored patterns—it remains the largest group of Italian Renaissance paintings in a French church. On the west wall you can find one of the most splendid organs in the world, built in 1734 and outfitted with 3,500 pipes, which loom over a celebrated fresco of the Last Judgment. ✉ *Pl. Ste-Cécile* ☎ *05–63–43–23–43* ⏲ *June–Sept., daily 9–6:30; Oct.–May, daily 9–noon and 2–6:30.*

Fodor's Choice ★ The **Musée Toulouse-Lautrec** occupies the landmark **Palais de la Berbie** (Berbie Palace), set between the cathedral and the Pont Vieux (Old Bridge) in a garden designed by the famed André Le Nôtre (creator of the "green geometries" at Versailles). Built in 1265 as a residence for Albi's archbishops, the fortresslike structure was transformed in 1922 into a museum to honor Albi's most famous son, Belle Époque painter Henri de Toulouse-Lautrec (1864–1901). Toulouse-Lautrec left Albi for Paris in 1882,

MY WAY OR THE HIGHWAY

Beneath Ste-Cécile's organ is an impressive 15th-century mural depicting punishments for the seven deadly sins in the Last Judgment. The scenes of torture and hellfire give an indication of how the Vatican kept its Christian subjects in line during the crusade against the Cathars and subsequent Inquisition trials.

and soon became famous for his colorful and tumultuous evocations of the lifestyle of bohemian glamour found in and around Montmartre. Son of a wealthy and aristocratic family (Lautrec is a village not far from Toulouse), the young Henri suffered from a genetic bone deficiency and broke both legs as a child, which stunted his growth. The artist's fascination with the decadent side of life led to an early grave at the age of 37 and Hollywood immortalization in the 1954 John Huston film *Moulin Rouge*. A 10-year renovation was completed in 2004, with vast new infrastructure and loan exhibition rooms excavated under the building. Upstairs, the collection of artworks (with more than a thousand, the world's largest Toulouse-Lautrec corpus) has been deftly organized into theme rooms, including galleries devoted to some of his greatest portraits and scenes from Paris's *maisons closées* (brothels), with paintings stylishly hung amid the palace's brick ogival arches. There are other masterworks here, including paintings by Georges de la Tour and Francesco Guardi. ✉ *Palais de la Berbie, just off Pl. Ste-Cécile* ☎ *05–63–49–48–70* 🌐 *www.museetoulouselautrec.net* 🎟 *€5.50, audio tour €8.50, gardens free* ⏲ *June and Sept., daily 9–noon and 2–6; July and Aug., daily 9–6; Apr. and May, daily 10–noon and 2–6; Oct. and Mar., Wed.–Mon. 10–noon and 2–5:30; Nov.–Feb., Wed.–Mon. 10–noon and 2–5.*

From the central square and parking area in front of the Palais de la Berbie, walk to the 11th- to 15th-century college and **Cloître de St-Salvy** (✉ *Rue Ste-Cécile*).

Next, take a look at Albi's finest restored traditional house, the **Maison du Vieil Albi** (*Old Albi House* ✉ *Corner of Rue de la Croix-Blanche and Puech-Bérenguer*).

If you're a real fan of Toulouse-Lautrec, you might view his birthplace, the **Maison Natale de Toulouse-Lautrec** (✉ *14 rue Henri de Toulouse-Lautrec*), although there are no visits to the house, the Hôtel du Bosc, which remains a private residence.

Rue de l'Hôtel de Ville, two streets west of the Maison Natale, leads past the Mairie (City Hall), with its hanging globes of flowers, to Albi's main square, **Place du Vigan**. Take a break in one of the two main cafés, Le Pontie or Le Vigan.

WHERE TO EAT AND STAY

$$ FRENCH ✕ **Le Jardin des Quatre Saisons.** A good-value menu and superb fish dishes are the reasons for this restaurant's excellent reputation. Chef-owner Georges Bermond's house specialties include *pot au feu* (stew) of the sea and *suprême de sandre* (a freshwater fish cooked in wine), and change with *les saisons*. ✉ *19 bd. de Strasbourg* ☎ *05–63–60–77–76* 💳 *AE, MC, V* ⏲ *Closed Mon. No dinner Sun.*

$$–$$$ 🏨 **Hostellerie St-Antoine.** Founded in 1734, this hotel in the center of town is one of the oldest in France. It's been run by the same family for five generations, a lineage attested to by the display of Toulouse-Lautrec sketches given to the owner's great-grandfather, a friend of the painter. Modern renovations have made it eminently comfortable. Room 30 has a pleasing view of the garden; pristine white furnishings give it a spacious feel. **Pros:** slightly off the beaten path in a quiet area; very

Albi honors native son Toulouse-Lautrec with a museum crammed with his masterpieces, including "Salon on the Rue des Moulins."

friendly staff. **Cons:** breakfast is very expensive; overall, doesn't quite live up to its four-star rating. ✉ *17 rue St-Antoine* ☎ *05–63–54–04–04* 🌐 *www.hotel-saint-antoine-albi.com* *38 rooms, 9 suites* *In-room: a/c, refrigerator, Wi-Fi. In-hotel: parking (paid)* *AE, DC, MC, V.*

$$–$$$ **Hôtel Chiffre.** A former stagecoach inn, this centrally located town house has impeccable rooms overlooking a cozy garden. The restaurant serves hearty regional cuisine such as excellent foie gras and *magret de canard* (breast of duck) and lamb in a parsley-and-garlic sauce. **Pros:** restaurant is good and a great value. **Cons:** foyer and rooms are sparsely decorated and lackluster; some beds need to be replaced. ✉ *50 rue Séré-de-Rivières* ☎ *05–63–48–58–48* 🌐 *www.hotelchiffre.com* *38 rooms, 1 suite* *In-room: a/c, refrigerator, Internet. In-hotel: restaurant, parking (paid)* *AE, MC, V* *MAP.*

¢ **La Régence–George V.** This little in-town B&B, with its affable staff, is near the cathedral and the train station. Each room is unique—one being particularly pink and thus probably best avoided, and some rooms share a bath. However, the garden makes for a pleasant retreat in summer. **Pros:** real bargain for the location. **Cons:** rooms are functional and no-frills. ✉ *27–29 av. Maréchal-Joffre* ☎ *05–63–54–24–16* 🌐 *www.laregence-georgev.fr* *24 rooms* *In-room: no a/c. In-hotel: some pets allowed* *AE, MC, V.*

SHOPPING

Around **Place Ste-Cécile** are numerous clothing, book, music, and antiques shops. The finest foie gras in town is found at **Alby Foie Gras** (✉ *29 rue Mariès*). **L'Artisan Chocolatier** (✉ *4 rue Dr-Camboulives, on Pl. du Vigan* ☎ *05–63–38–95–33*) is famous for its chocolate. Albi has many **produce**

markets: one takes place Tuesday to Friday and Sunday in the market halls near the cathedral; another is held on Saturday morning on Place Ste-Julien.A Saturday-morning **flea and antiques market** (✉ *Pl. du Castelviel*) is held in the Halle du Castelviel.

CORDES-SUR-CIEL

Fodor'sChoice ★ *25 km (15 mi) northwest of Albi, 80 km (50 mi) northeast of Toulouse.*

A must-stop for many travelers, the picture-book hilltop village of Cordes-sur-Ciel, built in 1222 by Count Raymond VII of Toulouse, is one of the most impressively preserved *bastides* (fortified medieval towns built along a strict grid plan) in France.

GETTING HERE

In July and August, a bus runs the 25 km (16 mi) from Albi's bus station on Place Jean Jaurès to the bottom of Cordes twice daily. At other times of the year, you'll have to take the train to Cordes-Vindrac, where it's frequently served from Toulouse (1¼ hrs) and Albi (1 hr); from Cordes-Vindrac, it's 3 km (1½ mi) to Cordes via bike, taxi, or walking. Note that traffic is banned in the upper town in summer and parking nearby is virtually impossible.

EXPLORING

When mists steal up from the Cérou Valley and enshroud the hillside, Cordes appears to hover in midair, hence its nickname, Cordes-sur-Ciel (Cordes-in-the-Sky/Heaven). Named after Andalusian Cordoba, it was built as a redoubt after the Occitan wars waged against the region's Cathars; its conical hill is studded with caves once used as granaries during times of siege. When peace arrived in the 15th century, the town thrived as a center for leather and fabric makers and many rich residents built pink-sandstone Gothic-style houses, a sizable number of which still line the main street, Grande-Rue Haute (also called Rue Droite). Today, many are now occupied by painters, sculptors, weavers, leatherworkers, and even creators of illuminated manuscripts, whose ateliers and stores lure the summer crowds. The annual blowout is the Fêtes Médiévales du Grand Fauconnier (named after the town's most historic abode; 🌐 *www.grandfauconnier.com*), a three-day festival held around mid-July, replete with an artisanal fair and costumed Bal Médiéval. The village's 14th-century St-Michel church and the venerable covered market, supported by 24 octagonal stone pillars, are also noteworthy, as is the nearby well, which is more than 300 feet deep. The small Musée Charles-Portail has relics from the town's medieval past while closer to the Haut de la Cité is the two-room Musée de la Sucre (Sugar), which showcases the works of the noted chef, Yves Thuriès, who presides over the town's famous inn and restaurant, Le Grand Écuyer.

WHERE TO STAY

$$–$$$ Fodor'sChoice ★ **Le Grand Écuyer.** The dramatic hilltop setting of this hotel suits it well—it's a perfectly preserved Gothic mansion, built as a hunting lodge for the count of Toulouse, Raymond VII, and now fitted out with time-burnished ancestral portraits, suits of armor, and four-poster beds. The

CLOSE UP

Crusading Cathars

Scorched by the southern heat, the dusty ruins perched high atop cliffs in southern Languedoc were once the refuges of the Cathars, the notoriously ascetic religious group persecuted out of existence by the Catholic Church in the 12th and 13th centuries. The Cathars inhabited an area ranging from present-day Germany all the way to the Atlantic Ocean. Adherents to this dualistic doctrine of material abnegation and spiritual revelation abstained from fleshly pleasures in all forms—forgoing procreation and the consumption of animal products. In some cases, they even committed suicide by starvation; diminishing the amount of flesh in the world was the ultimate way to foil the forces of evil. However, not thrilled by a religion that did not "go forth and multiply" (and that saw no need to pay taxes to the Church), Pope Innocent III launched the Albigensian Crusade (Albi was one of the major Cathar strongholds), and Pope Gregory IX rounded up the stragglers during a period of inquisition starting in 1233. All these forces had been given scandalously free rein by the French court, which allowed dukes and counts from northern France to build fortified bastide towns through the area to entrap the peasantry.

The counts were more than happy to oblige the pope with a little hounding, an inquisition or two, and some burnings at the stake. Entire towns were judged to be guilty of heresy and inhabitants were thrown by the dozens to their deaths from high town walls. The persecuted "pure" soon took refuge in the Pyrénées Mountains, where they survived for 100 years. Now all that remains of this unhappy sect are their former hideouts, with tour groups visiting the vacant stone staircases and roofless chapels of haunted places like Peyrepertuse and Quéribus. For more information, log on to 🌐 *www.cathar.info* or go hiking with medievalist Ingrid Sparbier (🌐 *www.guide-sud-france.com*).

best guest rooms—Planol, Horizon, and Ciel—have views of the rolling countryside, while the Raymond VII salon was a favorite of novelist Albert Camus ("In Cordes everything is beautiful, even regret"). Yves Thuriès is one of the region's best chefs and chocolatiers and his table has drawn such celebrities as King Juan Carlos of Spain and England's queen mother. Menus begin at €43 and culminate in a seven-course "rotating" gourmet extravaganza that costs €84. Delights include the codfish *demi-sel* with chickpea puree, the pan-seared Brittany lobster with roasted pear and pink grapefruit emulsion, and the white-chocolate-and-pistachio-marbled velouté. Thuriès also owns the town's stylish L'Hostellerie du Vieux Cordes, which takes over (at nicely lower prices) when Le Grand closes from fall to early spring every year. **Pros:** great food; central location. **Cons:** flamboyantly medieval decor and ambience isn't for everyone; hotel is a hike up a hill from parking area. ✉ *Haute de la Cité* ☎ *05–63–53–79–50* 🌐 *www.thuries.fr* *12 rooms, 1 suite* *In-room: a/c, refrigerator, Wi-Fi (some). In-hotel: restaurant, bar, some pets allowed* 💳 *AE, DC, MC, V* ⏲ *Closed mid-Oct.–early Apr.* *MAP.*

$–$$ ★ **L'Hostellerie du Vieux Cordes**. Sister hotel to Le Grand Écuyer, this lovely 13th-century house is built around a spectacular courtyard dotted with tiny white tables and shaded by a magnificent 300-year-old wisteria. Guest rooms are stylish decorated with tone-on-tone color schemes and antique accents. Downstairs, the bistro Tonin'ty has a 19th-century vibe, with delicious menus crafted around salmon and duck by famed chef Yves Thuriès (the restaurant is closed in January and on Monday for lunch from November to Easter). **Pros:** some rooms have views of the valley (book well in advance). **Cons:** Room 4 should be avoided; uphill hike to the hotel from parking area. ✉ *Rue St-Michel* ☎ *05–63–53–79–20* 🌐 *www.thuries.fr* *19 rooms* *In-room: no a/c, refrigerator, Wi-Fi (some). In-hotel: restaurant* ▭ *AE, DC, MC, V* ⊙ *Closed Jan.–mid-Feb.* 🍽 *MAP.*

13

LANGUEDOC-ROUSSILLON

One of the most idyllic regions in France, Languedoc-Roussillon extends along the southern Mediterranean coast of France to the Pyrénées. Draw a line between Carcassonne and Narbonne: the area to the south down to the Pyrénées, long dominated by the House of Aragon, the ruling family of adjacent Catalonia, is known as the Roussillon. Inland, the area, with its dry climate, is virtually one huge vineyard. The Canal du Midi flows through the region to Le Littoral Languedocien (the Languedoc Coast). Beaches stretch down the coast to Cerbère at the Spanish border. Immortalized by Matisse and Picasso, this strip is known as the Côte Vermeille (Vermilion Coast) and attracts droves of European sun worshippers even though the beaches are rocky. The farther south you go, the stronger the Spanish influence. Heading northward, Languedoc begins around Narbonne and extends to the region's hub, the elegant city of Montpellier. Life in this region—even in such urban centers as Perpignan—is distinctly relaxed and friendly. You'll probably be taking afternoon *siestes* (naps) before you know it.

CARCASSONNE

Fodor's Choice ★

88 km (55 mi) southeast of Toulouse, 105 km (65 mi) south of Albi.

Set atop a hill overlooking lush green countryside and the Aude River, Carcassonne is a spectacular medieval town that looks lifted from the pages of a storybook—literally, perhaps, as its circle of towers and battlements (comprising the longest city walls in Europe) is said to be the setting for Charles Perrault's classic tale *Puss in Boots*. With its turrets and castellated walls, it appeals to children and those who dream about the Middle Ages.

GETTING HERE

The shuttle to Salvaza Airport from the train station (beside the Canal du Midi on Avenue du Maréchal Joffre) also links you up with the Cité and Place Gambetta. Ryanair (🌐 *www.ryanair.com*) has daily flights to Stansted and Dublin. Due to the high volume of visitors, many trains arrive at Carcassone's station—17 trains from Narbonne and 24 from

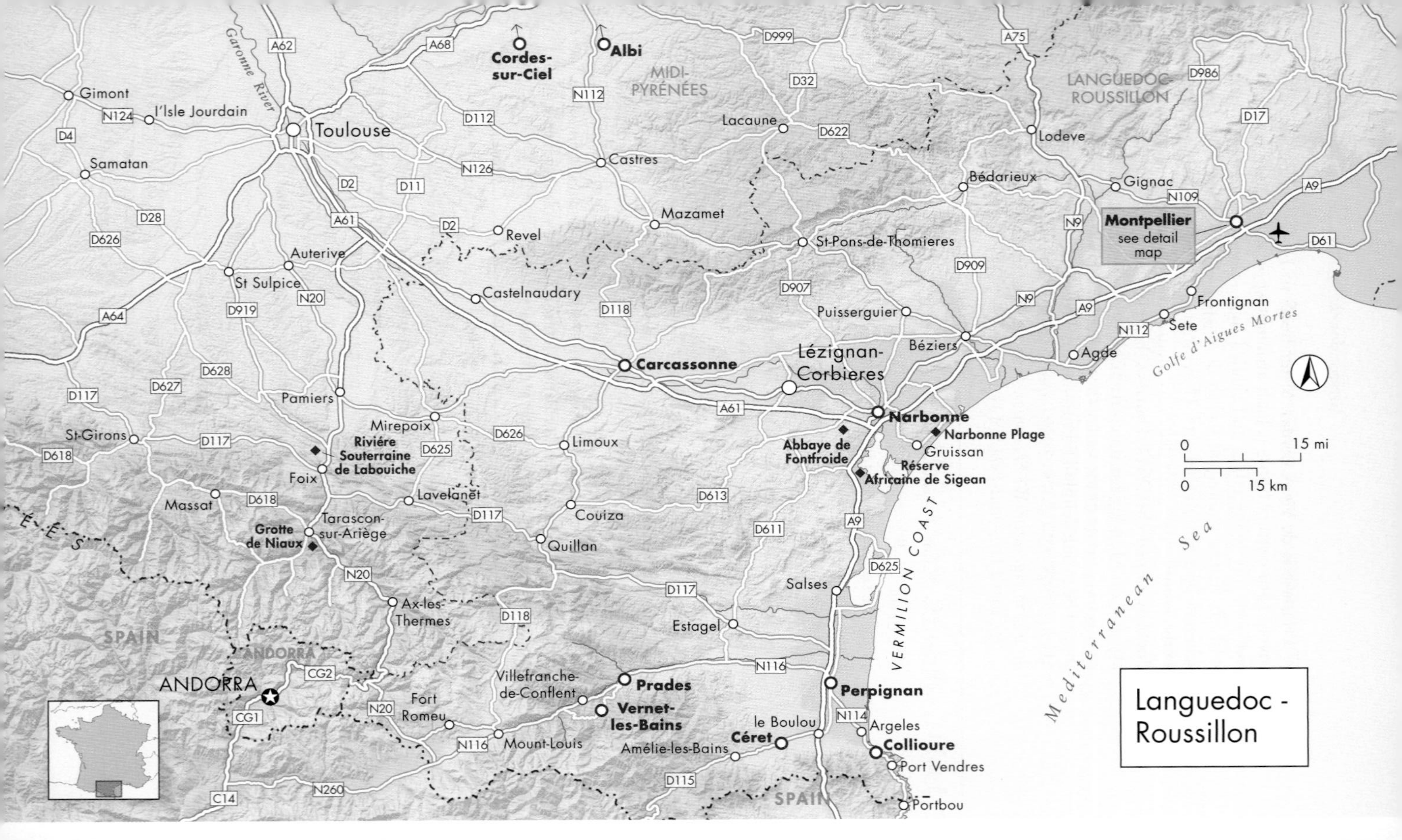

Languedoc -
Roussillon
Mediterranean Sea
Golfe d'Aigues Mortes
VERMILION COAST
0
15 mi
0
15 km
LANGUEDOC-
ROUSSILLON
MIDI-
PYRÉNÉES
ANDORRA
SPAIN
SPAIN
Cordes-
sur-Ciel
Albi
Gimont
l'Isle Jourdain
Toulouse
Garonne River
Samatan
Lacaune
Lodeve
Castres
Bédarieux
Gignac
Mazamet
Montpellier
see detail
map
Revel
St-Pons-de-Thomieres
Auterive
St Sulpice
Castelnaudary
Frontignan
Sete
Puisserguier
Béziers
Agde
Carcassonne
Lézignan-
Corbieres
Pamiers
Narbonne
Mirepoix
Narbonne Plage
St-Girons
Rivière
Souterraine
de Labouiche
Limoux
Abbaye de
Fontfroide
Gruissan
Réserve
Africaine de Sigean
Foix
Lavelanet
Massat
Couiza
Tarascon-
sur-Ariège
Grotte
de Niaux
Quillan
Salses
Ax-les-
Thermes
Estagel
Villefranche-
de-Conflent
Prades
Perpignan
Fort
Romeu
Vernet-
les-Bains
le Boulou
Argeles
Mount-Louis
Céret
Collioure
Amélie-les-Bains
Port Vendres
Portbou
A62
A68
D999
A75
D986
D32
N112
N124
D112
D17
D4
D622
N126
D2
D11
N109
A9
D28
A61
D2
N9
D626
D61
D909
N20
D907
A64
D919
D118
N9
A9
N112
D628
D627
D117
A61
D626
D117
D625
D618
D613
D618
D117
A9
D611
N20
D625
D117
D118
N116
CG2
N20
N114
CG1
N116
D115
N260
C14

Toulouse alone. Cars Tessier (☎ *04–68–25–85–45*) will bus you to all the same places as the trains, and at times a lot faster, too.

Visitor Information **Carcassonne Tourist Office** ✉ *28 rue de Verdun* ☎ *04–68–10–24–30* 🌐 *www.carcassonne-tourisme.com.*

EXPLORING

The town is divided by the river into two parts—La Cité, the fortified upper town, and the lower, newer city (the *ville basse*), known simply as Carcassonne. Unless you are staying at a hotel in the upper town, you are not allowed to enter it with your car; you must park in the lot (fee by the hour) across the road from the drawbridge. Be aware that the train station is in the lower town, which means either a cab ride, a 30-minute walk up to La Cité, or a ride on the *navette* shuttle bus. Plan on spending at least a couple of hours exploring the walls and peering over the battlements across sun-drenched plains toward the distant Pyrénées. Once inside the walls of the upper town, a florid carousel announces that 21st-century tourism is about to take over. The streets are lined with souvenir shops, crafts boutiques, restaurants, and tiny "museums" (i.e., a Cathars Museum, a Hat Museum), all out to make a buck and rarely worth that. Staying overnight within the ancient walls lets you savor the timeless atmosphere after the daytime hordes are gone.

As for the town history, legend has it that Charlemagne once set siege to the settlement in the 9th century, only to be outdone by one Dame Carcas, a clever woman who boldly fed the last of the city's wheat to a pig in full view of the conqueror. Charlemagne, thinking this indicated endless food supplies, promptly decamped, and the exuberant townsfolk named their city after her. During the 13th century, Louis IX (St. Louis) and his son Philip the Fair strengthened Carcassonne's fortifications—so much so that the town came to be considered inviolable by marauding armies and was duly nicknamed "the virgin of Languedoc."

A town that can never be taken in battle is often abandoned, however, and for centuries thereafter Carcassonne remained under a Sleeping Beauty spell. It was only awakened during the mid-19th-century craze for chivalry and the Gothic style, when, in 1835, the historic-monument inspector (and poet) Prosper Mérimée arrived. He was so appalled by the dilapidated state of the walls that he commissioned the architect, painter, and historian Viollet-le-Duc (who found his greatest fame restoring Paris's Notre-Dame) to restore the town. Today the 1844 renovation is considered almost as much a work of art as the medieval town itself. No matter if the town is more Viollet than authentic medieval, it still remains one of the most romantic sights in France.

The 12th-century **Château Comtal** is the last inner bastion of Carcassonne. It has a drawbridge and a museum, the **Musée Lapidaire,** where stone sculptures found in the area are on display. ☎ *04–68–11–70–70* 🎫 *€8* ⏲ *Apr.–Sept., daily 10–6:30; Oct.–Mar., daily 9:30–5.*

The real draw in the ville basse, built between the Aude and the Canal du Midi, is the **Musée des Beaux-Arts** *(Fine Arts Museum)*. It houses a nice collection of porcelain, 17th- and 18th-century Flemish paintings, and works by local artists—including some stirring battle scenes by Jacques

Gamelin (1738–1803). ✉ *1 rue de Verdun* ☎ *04–68–77–73–70* 🎟 *Free* ⏲ *Mid-Sept.–mid-June, Tues.–Sat. 10–noon and 2–6; mid-June–mid-Sept., daily 10–6.*

THE POSTCARD COMES TO LIFE

Carcassonne usually goes medieval in mid-August with **Les Médiévales** (🌐 *www.carcassonne-tourisme.com*), a festival of troubadour song, rich costumes, and jousting performances (some years the event isn't held; check with the tourist office). And don't forget the Bastille Day fireworks over La Cité—spectacular!

WHERE TO EAT AND STAY

$$$ FRENCH ✕ **Le Languedoc.** This restaurant in the ville basse (whose owners also own the Montsegur just down the road) serves up tempting versions of the region's specialties, from confit to game. In summer the flowery patio is a perfect spot for a long evening dinner. Be sure to try the quail with foie gras, if available. ✉ *32 allée d'Iéna* ☎ *04–68–25–22–17* 💳 *AE, DC, MC, V* ⏲ *Closed Mon. and Dec.–mid-Jan. No dinner Sun. Sept.–June.*

$ FRENCH ★ ✕ **Sire de Cabaret.** Nestled beneath the château of Roquefére, an unspoiled *village fleuri* in the Cabardés region of the Montagne Noire, this regional favorite serves up amazing steaks *à la Languedocienne.* Cooked over chestnut-wood fires, they're accompanied by mushrooms picked from nearby mountains by the genial chef Patrick Malea and served by his wife, Carmen (and a famously droll waiter, Jean-Pierre). With charcuterie *fait maison* (homemade sausages, pâtés, rillettes, and cured meats), this is a place worth visiting as much for its rustic charm as for its great food. In warm weather, ask for a table on the terrace and enjoy your *poisson à la plancha* (grilled fish) beneath olive trees amid hills cloaked with green oaks and chestnut trees. They also have a lovely B&B cottage next door, but make sure to reserve well in advance as it is nearly always booked. ✉ *Roquefére, 25 km (11 mi) north of Carcassonne* ☎ *04–68–26–31–89* 🌐 *www.auberge-siredecabaret.fr* 💳 *MC, V* ⏲ *Closed Jan.–Feb. 14. No dinner Wed. and Sun. Sept.–June.*

$ 🏨 **Château La Villatade.** Ensconced in the vines of this sprawling, verdant wine estate, you can enjoy La Villatade's exceptional reds (especially the special "Rituel") while soaking up the amazing views of the Montagne Noire, the Pyrénées, and Mont Canigou from one of the many terraces. With the ever-hospitable (and English-speaking) owner-vintners Sophie and Denis Morin to welcome you, and delightfully tasteful rooms to stay in, this is the place to come to escape the hectic tourist traffic of Carcassonne. **Pros:** real French living off the beaten tourist track; vineyard on-site. **Cons:** somewhat isolated—a car is essential, and there's no Internet service. ✉ *15 mins north of Carcassonne, Salleles* ☎ *04–68–77–57–51* 🌐 *www.villatade.com* 🛏 *2 rooms, 3 suites, 1 villa* 👍 *In-room: a/c* 💳 *MC, V* ⏲ *Closed 1 wk in Aug.*

$$$$ ★ 🏨 **Domaine d'Auriac.** This elegant 19th-century manor house southwest of Carcassonne offers an environment of superb grace and comfort. Room prices vary according to size and view; the largest look out onto a magnificent park and vineyards. Next to a terrace planted with mulberry trees, the restaurant, famed as one of the best in the area, offers superlative Languedoc cuisine; enjoy the Provençal-style salon

An entry to Fodor's "Show Us Your France" contest, this view of Carcassonne's ramparts was sent in by seeyourworld, a Fodors.com member.

festooned with copper pots while savoring truffled pigeon, John Dory in blueberry wine, and game dishes, in season, accompanied by rare regional vintages. **Pros:** excellent 18-hole golf course; beautiful views of the old city; delightful decor. **Cons:** few miles outside of Carcassonne's center. ✉ *Rte. de St-Hilaire, 4 km (2½ mi) southwest of Carcassonne, Carcassonne* ☎ *04–68–25–72–22* 🌐 *www.domaine-d-auriac.com* ⇨ *19 rooms, 5 suites* ♿ *In-room: a/c, Wi-Fi. In-hotel: restaurant, bar, golf course, tennis court, pool* ▭ *AE, DC, MC, V* ⊗ *Closed Jan., 1st wk of Feb. and 2nd wk of Nov.* 🍴 *MAP.*

$$$$ **Hôtel de la Cité**. Set within the walled upper town, this is *the* spot for celebrities in Carcassonne. The ivy-covered former Episcopal palace offers creature comforts the ascetic Cathars would have hated. Afternoon tea is in the library bar or rotunda lounge with its antique-tile floors, detailed woodwork, and leaded windows (with storybook views). Dining in sumptuous La Barbacane restaurant—all double-vaulted ceiling, ogival windows, and light tea-brown walls—is an event. For more casual fare, enjoy the charmingly cobbled square as you sip a pastis at the brasserie Chez Saskia. A pool, set like a sapphire in the garden, beckons on hot days. **Pros:** no better location in the old city. **Cons:** staff can be indifferent and aloof; pool is very small. ✉ *Pl. August-Pierre Pont, La Cité de Carcassonne* ☎ *04–68–71–98–71* 🌐 *www.hoteldelacite.com* ⇨ *40 rooms, 21 suites* ♿ *In-room: a/c, refrigerator, Wi-Fi. In-hotel: 3 restaurants,bar, pool, parking (paid)* ▭ *AE, DC, MC, V* ⊗ *Closed Dec. and Feb.* 🍴 *MAP.*

$–$$ **Hôtel Montségur**. With its ville basse location, this hotel is especially convenient. Rooms on the first two floors have Louis XV and Louis XVI furniture, some of it genuine; those above are more romantic, with gilt-iron bedsteads under sloping oak beams. **Pros:** Faugras family has been in the hotel business for over a century, so they know how to take care of their guests. **Cons:** central location is a big plus, but it also lends itself to street noise. ✉ *27 allée d'Iéna* ☎ *04–68–25–31–41* 🌐 *www.hotelmontsegur.com* *21 rooms* *In-room: a/c, Wi-Fi. In-hotel: some pets allowed, free parking* *AE, DC, MC, V* *Closed Dec. 27–Jan. 25.*

$–$$ **La Muse.** A manor house in the center of a village perched on a mountainside over a river valley, La Muse is a welcome respite from the oft-touristed environs of Cathar Country. Functioning primarily as an extended-stay retreat for artists and writers, the hostelry also accommodates shorter sojourns in Calliope, a spacious suite overlooking the valley, and in several neighboring stone village houses (€400–€600 per week). You can enjoy the extensive La Muse library, the expansive slate terrace and gardens, or a conversation with one of the many distinguished international artists or writers after "quiet hours." The village is 10 minutes north of Lastours and a 15-minute walk from a great meal at Roquefere's Sire de Cabaret. **Pros:** tranquil and quiet; special experience off the beaten tourist track; short drive from Château Villatade winery. **Cons:** car is essential for getting here; most accommodations require extended stays. ✉ *1 rue de la Place, Cabardes* ☎ *04–68–26–33–93* 🌐 *www.lamuseinn.com* *4 rooms, 1 suite, 3 villas* *In-room: a/c. In-hotel: Wi-Fi hotspot* *AE, V* *Closed Dec.*

THE ARTS

Carcassonne hosts a major arts festival in July, with dance, theater, classical music, and jazz; for details, contact the town's **Pole Culturel** (*10 rue de la Républic* ☎ *04–68–77–71–05* 🌐 *www.carcassone.org*).

PERPIGNAN

118 km (71 mi) southeast of Carcassonne, 27 km (17 mi) northwest of Collioure.

Salvador Dalí once called Perpignan's train station "the center of the world." That may not be true, but the city is certainly the capital hub of the Roussillon. No one can deny that its train routes, which helpfully connect with Montpellier and Narbonne, are the main magic carpets of the region.

GETTING HERE

Ryanair (🌐 *www.ryanair.com*) has a daily flight from London and Brussels to Perpignan. The airport has navettes (shuttles) from the train station (✉ *At end of Av. du Général de Gaulle*) an hour before each takeoff. The TGV from Paris takes about six hours for about €75. The bus station is to the north of town on Avenue Général Leclerc. While this is an important train hub, it shares these honors with Narbonne, found some 40 miles north. Narbonne's train station is on Boulevard Frédéric Mistral, north of the city center and adjacent to the Gare Routiere (bus station) on Avenue Carnot. Via train, it takes nearly an hour to get from Perpignan and Montpellier and an hour and a half to Toulouse. There are many connections: about six a day to Perpignan, as well as many others along the coast to the north and south. If you're coming from Paris on the TGV (🌐 *www.tgv.com*) to Perpignan, and then on the regular train to Narbonne, it'll cost you about €90 one-way.

Visitor Information Perpignan Tourist Office. ✉ *Pl. Armand Lanoux* ☎ *04-68-66-30-30* 🌐 *www.perpignantourisme.com.*

EXPLORING

Although Perpignan is big, you need stray no farther than the few squares of the *centre ville* grouped near the quays of the Basse River; this is the place to be for evening concerts and casual tapas sessions—you might even succumb to the "cosmological ecstasy" Dalí said he experienced here. In medieval times Perpignan was the second city of Catalonia (after Barcelona), before falling to Louis XIV's French army in 1659. The Spanish influence is evident in Perpignan's leading monument, the fortified **Palais des Rois de Majorque** *(Kings of Majorca Palace)* , begun in the 13th century by Jacques II of Majorca. Highlights here are the majestic **Cour d'Honneur** (Courtyard of Honor), the two-tier Flamboyant Gothic chapel of **Ste-Croix Marie-Madelene,** and the **Grande Salle** (Great Hall) with its monumental fireplaces. ✉ *Rue des Archers* ☎ *04-68-34-48-29* *€4* *Oct.–May, daily 9–5; June–Sept., daily 10–6.*

Perpignan's centre ville is sweet and alluring, lined with blooming rosemary bushes and landmarked by a medieval monument, the 14th-century **Castillet**, with its tall, crenellated twin towers. Originally this hulking brick building was the main gate to the city; later it was used as a prison. Now the **Casa Pairal,** a museum devoted to Catalan art and traditions, is housed here. ✉ *Pl. de Verdun* ☎ *04-68-35-42-05* *€4* *Oct.–May, Wed.–Mon. 11–5:30; June–Sept. 10–6.*

The **Promenade des Plantanes**, across Boulevard Wilson from Le Castillet, is a cheerful place to stroll among flowers, plane trees, and fountains.

To see other interesting medieval buildings, walk along the **Petite Rue des Fabriques d'En Nabot**—near Le Castillet, and to the adjacent Place de la Loge, the town's nerve center.

Note the frilly wrought-iron campanile and dramatic medieval crucifix on the **Cathédrale St-Jean** (✉ *Pl. Gambetta*).

WHERE TO EAT AND STAY

$–$$ FRENCH **Le France.** In the center of Perpignan in a 15th-century former stock market with exposed beams and arcades, this café-restaurant is perfect for a light meal or a glass of iced champagne under the parasols as you watch the world go by. Try the light appetizers such as scallop salad, or a foie gras with green beans and raisins. Grilled duck breast with apples and big plates of tapas are also served. ✉ *1 pl. de la Loge* ☎ *04-68-51-61-71* *MC, V.*

$ FRENCH ★ **Les Antiquaires.** With traditional Roussillon cooking served up in a rustic setting in a corner of old Perpignan, this friendly spot lives up to its title as a refuge for things antique. Duck à l'orange, a house favorite, has been on the menu here for 36 years, by popular demand. Foie gras in a Banyuls sauce is another staple in this pretty spot known for unpretentious yet refined cuisine. ✉ *Pl. Desprès* ☎ *04-68-34-06-58* *AE, DC, MC, V* *Closed Mon., last wk of June and 1st 2 wks of July. No dinner Sun.*

$$$–$$$$ **La Villa Duflot.** In a large park filled with olive and cypress trees, this hotel-restaurant complex serves some of the best meals in one of the calmest, prettiest settings in the city—too bad reports filter in about rude and snobbish hotel staff. Try to request a room with a view over the park—they're airy and comfortable, with warm, creamy colors; the rooms overlooking the patio aren't nearly as nice, although they are a bit more economical. Much of the finesse is saved for the food, and the food is *good*. The gastronomic restaurant popular with haute Perpignan serves light Mediterranean specialties around the pool—try the *parillade*, an assortment of the freshest catch of the day grilled to perfection and served with tangy aioli. **Pros:** restaurant is a local favorite; trees screen the property from the road. **Cons:** car is essential for getting into town; hotel gets traffic noise. ✉ *Rond Pont Albert Donnezan* ☎ *04–68–56–67–67* 🌐 *www.villaduflot.com* *23 rooms, 1 suite* *In-room: a/c, refrigerator, Wi-Fi. In-hotel: restaurant, bar, some pets allowed* 💳 *AE, DC, MC, V.*

SHOPPING

Rue des Marchands, near Le Castillet, is thick with chic shops. **Maison Quinta** (✉ *Rue Louis Blanc* 🌐 *www.maison-quinta.com*) is a top design and architectural artifacts store. Excellent local ceramics can be found at the picturesque **Sant Vicens Crafts Center** (✉ *Rue Sant Vicens, off D22 east of town center*).

PRADES

45 km (27 mi) west of Perpignan.

Visitor Information Prades Tourist Office. ✉ *4 rue des Marchands* ☎ *04–68–05–41–02* 🌐 *www.prades-tourisme.com.*

★ Once home to famed Catalan cellist Pablo Casals, the market town of Prades is famous for its annual summer music festival (from late July to mid-August), the **Festival Pablo Casals.** Founded by Casals in 1950, the music festival is primarily held at the medieval **Abbaye de St-Michel de Cuxa** (✉ *3 km [2 mi] on D27 south of Prades and Codalet* ☎ *04–68–96–15–35* 🌐 *www.prades-festival-casals.com* *€4* *May–Sept., daily 9:30–11:50 and 2–6; Oct.–Apr., daily 9:30–11:50 and 2–5*). One of the gems of the Pyrénées, the abbey's sturdy, crenellated bell tower is visible from afar. If the remains of the cloisters here seem familiar, it may be because you have seen the missing pieces in New York City's Cloisters Museum. The 10th-century pre-Romanesque church is the biggest in France, and a superb aesthetic and acoustical venue for the summer cello concerts. The six-voice Gregorian vespers service held (somewhat sporadically—call to confirm) at 7 PM in the monastery next door is hauntingly simple and medieval in tone and texture.

WHERE TO EAT AND STAY

¢ FRENCH ★ **Le Jardin d'Aymeric.** Locals swear by this semisecret gem, a charming little place that serves excellent cuisine du terroir in a relaxed and rustic setting. The menu changes seasonally, and the market rules supreme. On the walls you can find a changing show by local artists, as only befits this slightly bohemian refuge. ✉ *3 av. Général de Gaulle*

04–68–96–53–38 V *Closed Mon., and June 25–July 3 and Feb. 27–Mar. 3. No dinner Sun. and Wed.*

¢ **Les Glycines.** This flower-wreathed, traditional hotel in the middle of Prades offers small but charming rooms of impeccable cleanliness and simplicity. After a healthy hike to St-Michel-de-Cuxa, you can come to its rambling restaurant to savor fine home cooking and plenty of friendly good cheer. **Pros:** two blocks from the main square and close to shopping and Tuesday market; hidden away in a cul-de-sac. **Cons:** foyer could use a makeover. *129 av. Général de Gaulle* *04–68–96–51–65* *19 rooms* *In-room: no a/c, Wi-Fi. In-hotel: restaurant, parking (paid)* *MC, V.*

VERNET-LES-BAINS

12 km (7 mi) southwest of Prades, 55 km (34 mi) west of Perpignan.

Visitor Information Vernet-les-Bains Tourist Office *2 rue de la Chapelle* *05–62–05–55–35* *www.vernet-les-bains.fr.*

Fodor's Choice ★ A long-established spa town dwarfed by imposing Mont Canigou, Vernet-les-Bains's waters were so famed that many celebs, including English writer Rudyard Kipling, came to take the cure.But the reason to head here is to make a pilgrimage, esthetic or spiritual, to the celebrated medieval abbey, **Abbaye St-Martin du Canigou.** A steep 30-minute climb up from the parking area in Casteil, 2 km (1 mi) south of Vernet-les-Bains, this remains one of the most photographed abbeys in Europe thanks to its sky-kissing perch atop a triangular promontory at an altitude of nearly 3,600 feet.St-Martin du Canigou's breathtaking (literally) mountain setting was due, in part, to an effort to escape the threat of marauding Saracens from the Middle East. First constructed in 1009 by Count Guifré of Cerdagne and then damaged by an earthquake in 1428 and abandoned in 1783, the abbey was (perhaps too) diligently restored by the bishop of Perpignan early in the 20th century. Parts of the cloisters, along with the higher (and larger) of the two churches, date from the 11th century. The lower church, dedicated to Notre-Dame-sous-Terre, is even older. Rising above is a stocky, fortified bell tower. Although the hours vary, masses are sung daily; call ahead to confirm. Easter Mass here is especially joyous and moving. Note that the abbey is closed January and also on Monday from October to May. *04–68–05–50–03* *€5* *stmartinducanigou.org* *Oct.–May, tours Tues.–Sun. at 10, 11, 2, 3, 4; June–Sept., tours daily at 10, 11, noon, 2, 3, 4, 5. No visits at 10 on Sun.*

THE LITTLE TRAIN THAT COULD

Le petit train jaune ("Little Yellow Train") is a fun way to see some of the most spectacular countryside in the Pyrénées. This life-size toy train makes the 63-km (40-mi) three-hour trip from Villefranche to La Tour de Carol about five times a day. When the weather is nice, ride in one of the open-air cars. For information about hours and prices, contact the Vernet-les-Bains tourist office (*04–68–05–55–35*) or the SNCF Web site (*www.trainstouristiques-ter.com*).

As color-splashed as a Matisse or Braque painting, Collioure's harbor once inspired those masters and continues to seduce today's artists.

CÉRET

★ *68 km (41 mi) southeast of Prades, 35 km (21 mi) west of Collioure, 31 km (19 mi) southwest of Perpignan.*

Visitor Information Céret Tourist Office. ✉ *1 av. Georges Clemenceau* ☎ *04–68–87–00–53* 🌐 *www.ot-ceret.fr.*

Fodor's Choice ★ The "Barbizon of Cubism," Céret achieved immortality when leading artists found this small Catalan town irresistible at the beginning of the 20th century. Here in this medieval enclave set on the banks of the Tech River, Picasso and Gris developed a vigorous new way of seeing that would result in the fragmented forms of Cubism, a thousand years removed from the Romanesque sculptures of the Roussillon chapels and cloisters. Adorned by cherry orchards—the town famously grows the first and finest crop in France—the town landscapes have been captured in paintings by Picasso, Gris, Dufy, Braque, Chagall, Masson, and others. Some of these are on view in the fine collection of the **Musée d'Art Moderne** *(Modern Art Museum).* ✉ *8 bd. Maréchal-Joffre* ☎ *04–68–87–27–76* 🌐 *www.musee-ceret.com* 🎫 *€8* ⏲ *Mid-June–Sept., daily 10–7; Oct.–mid-June, daily 10–6. Closed Tues. Oct.–Apr. 12.*

The heart of town is, not surprisingly, the Place Picasso. Céret is proud of its Catalan heritage and it often hosts sardana dances. Be sure to stroll through pretty **Vieux Céret** *(Old Céret)*: find your way through **Place et Fontaine de Neuf Jets** (Nine Fountains Square), around the church, and out to the lovely fortified **Porte de France** gateway. Then walk over the single-arched **Vieux Pont** (Old Bridge).

WHERE TO STAY

$$$–$$$$ **La Terrasse au Soleil**. Sitting high above Céret, this hostelry is where the famous French singer Charles Trenet lived for a long time. It's easy to see why—the views from the terrace feature Mont Canigou in the distance and the verdant valley below. If your budget allows, opt for one of the villa apartments, as their views are all the more opulent. **Pros:** amazing views; on-site Turkish bath perfumed by organic essential oils. **Cons:** facilities don't quite live up to the high prices; difficult to find. ✉ *Rout de Fontfrede, Céret* ☎ *04–68–87–01–94* 🌐 *www.terrasse-au-soleil.com* *37 rooms, 2 suites* *In-room: a/c. In-hotel: restaurant, pool* 💳 *AE, MC, V* *Closed Jan. and mid-Feb–Mar. 1.*

¢–$ ★ **Les Arcades**. This comfortable spot in mid-Céret looks, smells, and feels exactly the way an inn ensconced in the heart of a provincial French town should. That the world-class collection of paintings of the Musée d'Art Moderne and the top-rated Les Feuillants restaurant are both just across the street puts it over the top. **Pros:** family-run business with great customer service; great art in the public areas. **Cons:** some rooms are small, so check them out first. ✉ *1 pl. Picasso* ☎ *04–68–87–12–30* 🌐 *www.hotel-arcades-ceret.com* *30 rooms* *In-room: no a/c (some), Internet. In-hotel: parking (paid)* 💳 *MC, V.*

13

COLLIOURE

Fodor's Choice ★ *35 km (21 mi) east of Céret, 27 km (17 mi) southeast of Perpignan.*

The fishing village where famed painters Henri Matisse, André Derain, and the Fauvists committed chromatic mayhem in the early 20th century, Collioure remains the jewel of the Vermilion Coast. A town of espadrille merchants, anchovy packers, and lateen-rigged fishing boats in the shadow of its 13th-century Château Royal, it is now as much a magnet for travelers (beware the crowds in July and August) as it once was and still is a lure for artists.

GETTING HERE

Collioure has about a dozen trains (☎ *04–68–82–05–89*) and many buses that make the trip to and from Perpignan (20 mins away). The train station is at the end of Avenue Aristide Maillol, and buses leave year-round from the car parks at Place du 8 Mai and Place Jean Jaurés. For specific times: 🌐 *www.voyages-sncf.com.*

Visitor Information **Collioure Tourist Office**. ✉ *Pl. du 18-Juin* ☎ *04–68–82–15–47* 🌐 *www.collioure.com.*

EXPLORING

Today Collioure—composed of narrow, cobbled streets and pink-and-mauve houses—is a living museum, as you can discover by touring its Chemin du Fauvisme, where 20 points along a route through town compare reproductions of noted Fauvist canvases with the actual scenes that were depicted in them. View-finder picture frames let you see how delightfully little has changed in eight decades. The views the artists once admired remain largely unchanged today: to the north, the rocky Îlot St-Vincent juts out into the sea, a modern lighthouse at its tip, whereas inland the Albères mountain range rises to connect the

Pyrénées with the Mediterranean. The town harbor is a painting unto itself, framed by a 12th-century royal castle and a 17th-century church fortified with a tower.

Matisse set up shop here in summer of 1905 and was soon inspired by the colors of the town's terra-cotta roofs (⇨ *see "Matisse Country" below*). André Derain, Henri Martin, and Georges Braque—who were dubbed Fauves for their "savage" (*fauve* means "wild beast") approach to color and form—quickly followed. The information center, behind the Plage Boramar, has an excellent map that points out the main sites once favored by the Fauve painters, now organized into the **Chemin du Fauvisme** (originating at the Espace Fauve at the Quai de l'Amirauté) pedestrian trail. Detour to the streets behind the Vieux Port to find former fishermen's stores now occupied by smart boutiques and restaurants.

To discover tomorrow's Matisses and Derains, head to the streets behind the Place du 18-Juin and to the old quarter of Le Mouré, set under Fort Miradou—the studios here are filled with contemporary artists at work. Today the most prized locales in town are the café-terraces overlooking the main beach or the fashionable Rue Camillle Pelletan by the harbor, where you can feast on Collioure's tender, practically boneless anchovies and the fine Rivesaltes and other local wines from the impeccably cultivated vineyards surrounding the town. Although nearby villages are apparently only rich in quaintness, Collioure is surprisingly prosperous, thanks to the cultivation of *primeurs*, early ripe fruit and vegetables, shipped to the markets of northern France.

At the end of Boulevard du Boramar is the 17th-century church of **Notre-Dame-des-Anges** (✉ *Pl. de l'Église*). It has exuberantly carved, gilded Churrigueresque altarpieces by celebrated Catalan master Joseph Sunyer and a pink-dome bell tower that doubled as the original lighthouse.

A slender jetty divides the Boramar Beach, beneath Notre-Dame-des-Anges, from the small landing area at the foot of the **Château Royal**, a 13th-century castle, once the summer residence of the kings of Majorca (from 1276 to 1344), and remodeled by Vauban 500 years later. ☎ *04–68–82–06–43* 🎫 *€4* ⏲ *June and Sept., daily 10–5:15; Oct.–May, daily 9–4:15; July and Aug., daily 10–6:15.*

No Matissses hold pride of place at the town's **Musée d'Art Moderne Fonds Péské** but the collection of 180 works deftly sums up the influence the painter had on this *cité des peintures*. Works by Cocteau, Valtat, and other artists are impressively housed in a picturesque, ivy-shrouded villa (built by Senator Gaston Pams) on a beautiful hillside site. ✉ *Rte. de Porte-Vendres,* ☎ *04–68–82–10–19* 🌐 *www.collioure.com* 🎫 *€2* ⏲ *July and Aug., daily 10–noon and 2–6; Sept. and June, daily 10–noon and 2–6; Oct.–May, Wed.–Sun. 10–noon and 2–6.*

WHERE TO STAY

$$–$$$ 🏨 **Casa Païral.** An idyllic, palm-shaded 19th-century town house surrounded by a leafy garden, this small oasis is a handy address in often tumultuous (for all its idyllic reputation) Collioure. The main house is more charming than the annex, but all rooms are comfortable and tastefully appointed. A five-minute walk from the water's edge, the hotel

CLOSE UP

Matisse Country

The little coastal village of Collioure continues to play the muse to the entire Côte Vermeille—after all, it gave rise to the name of the Vermilion Coast, because the great painter Henri Matisse daringly painted Collioure's yellow-sand beach using a bright red terra-cotta hue.

For such artistic daredevilry, he was branded a "wild beast"—or Fauve—and then rewrote the history of art in the process. Considered, along with Picasso, one of the most influential artists of the modern period, Matisse (1869–1954), along with fellow painter and friend André Derain (1880–1954), discovered "Fauvism" *en vacances* in Collioure in 1905.

In search of inspiration, he and Derain holed up here during that summer, seduced by its pink and mauve houses, ocher rooftops, and the dramatic combination of sea, sun, and hills. Back then, the final touches of color were added by the red and green fishing boats. With nature's outré palette at hand, Matisse was inspired to passionate hues and a brash distortion of form.

At summer's end, Matisse made the trip to Paris to show his Collioure works at the Salon d'Automne, the season's biggest art event. Because the canvases of Matisse, Derain, Vlaminck, and Marquet were so shockingly hued, they were made to hang their paintings in a back room, Room 7. The public jeered at their work, saying they were primitive, coarse, and extreme. Room 7 became known as "the cage."

Before long, their *sucess de scandale* quickly won them new adherents, including the painters Rouault, Van Dongen, Braque, and Dufy. Fauvism

became the rage from 1905 to 1908; by 1909 Matisse was famous all around the world.

Today Matisse's masterpieces grace the walls of the greatest museums in the world. In a sense, Collioure has something better: a host of virtual Matisses, 3-D Derains, and pop-up Dufys. Realizing this, the mayor decided to create the Chemin du Fauvisme (The Fauvist Way) a decade ago, erecting 20 reproductions of Matisse's and Derain's works on the very spots where they were painted.

Matisse could return today and find things little changed: the Château Royal still perches over the harbor, the Fort Saint-Elme still makes a striking perspectival point on its hilltop, and the Plage Boramar still looks like a 3-acre "Matisse."

Pick up the Chemin's trail at the town's Espace Fauve by going to Quai de l'Amiraute (☎ *04–68–98–07–16*) or check out its history at 🌐 *www.collioure.net*.

13

is comfortingly traditional, while the alluring courtyard, garden, and pool are relaxing and intimate. **Pros:** in the center of Collioure; very helpful staff. **Cons:** very difficult to find (call ahead for explicit directions). ✉ *Impasse des Palmiers* ☎ *04–68–82–05–81* 🌐 *www.hotel-casa-pairal.com* *27 rooms* *In-room: a/c, Wi-Fi. In-hotel: pool, parking (paid)* 💳 *AE, DC, MC, V.*

OLÉ!

If you're around Collioure's Place du 18-Juin on the weekends from April to June and during September, you can enjoy a festival of Catalan dance and music. Contact the town tourist office (☎ *04–68–82–15–47*) for full information. Throughout the region, in neighboring towns like Céret, other Sardane events are also held during this time of year.

$–$$ Fodor's Choice ★ **Les Templiers.** Universally considered the "soul" of Collioure, this place merits a visit on every itinerary. Way back when, Matisse, Maillol, Dalí, Picasso, and Dufy used to hang out here. Today owner Jojo Pous, son of the force behind Collioure's art colony, is proud to show off the more than 2,500 original works hanging from every nook and cranny (including the ceiling and stairs)—one of the most glorious sights in Languedoc-Roussillon. The bar itself is a work of art, curved like the hull of a skiff and ending with a wood sculpture of a mermaid suckling an infant sailor. Collioure is Catalan in all senses but cartographically, so the food here is mostly Catalan and usually excellent; be sure to try dishes that feature the town's fabled anchovies. The rooms overlooking the château are cozy, but be sure yours is not in the annex. **Pros:** in the center of town, close to a bus stop and an easy walk from the train station; great breakfasts. **Cons:** no access for cars (on a pedestrian alley); a bit noisy during the hustle and bustle of August. ✉ *12 quai de l'Amirauté* ☎ *04–68–98–31–10* 🌐 *www.hotel-templiers.com* *47 rooms, 1 suite* *In-room: no a/c (some), Wi-Fi. In-hotel: restaurant, bar* 💳 *AE, DC, MC, V* ⊗ *Closed Jan., 1st wk of Feb., and last wk of Nov.* *FAP.*

$$$–$$$$ **Relais des Trois Mas.** The vistas are priceless, and the rooms very pricey indeed at the Relais. Overlooking the harbor from the cliffs south of town, this hotel enjoys a perfect perch. Inside are small but interestingly furnished rooms—headboards, for example, are made from delightful wooden motifs. Rooms are named for painters whose work appears on the bathroom tiles. Below is a pebbled beach, though you may prefer the small pool (hewn from rock) or the huge Jacuzzi. Dine at the restaurant, La Balette, on the terrace or in one of the two small dining rooms overlooking the harbor. **Pros:** breathtaking views of Collioure. **Cons:** some standard rooms are very small; accommodations are very basic for the price; no lobby, sitting area, or bar. ✉ *Rte. de Port-Vendres* ☎ *04–68–82–05–07* 🌐 *www.relaisdestroismas.com* *19 rooms, 4 suites* *In-room: refrigerator. In-hotel: restaurant, pool, beachfront, Internet terminal* 💳 *AE, MC, V* ⊗ *Closed Nov. 15–Feb. 4* *FAP.*

NARBONNE

61 km (38 mi) north of Perpignan, 60 km (37 mi) east of Carcassonne, 94 km (58 mi) south of Montpellier.

In Roman times, bustling, industrial Narbonne was the second-largest town in Gaul (after Lyon) and an important port, though today little remains of its Roman past. Until the sea receded during the Middle Ages, Narbonne prospered.

GETTING HERE

Narbonne is an important rail junction for the region. The train station is on Boulevard Frédéric Mistral, north of the city center and adjacent to the Gare Routiere (bus station) on Avenue Carnot. Via train, it takes nearly an hour to get from Perpignan and Montpellier and an hour and a half to Toulouse. There are many connections: about six a day to Perpignan, as well as many others along the coast to the north and south. If you're coming from Paris on the TGV (🌐 *www.tgv.com*) to Perpignan, and then on the regular train to Narbonne, it'll cost you about €90 one-way.

Visitor Information **Narbonne Tourist Office.** ✉ *31 rue Jean Juares* ☎ *04-68-65-15-60* 🌐 *www.narbonne-tourisme.com.*

EXPLORING

The town's former wealth is evinced by the 14th-century **Cathédrale St-Just-et-St-Pasteur** (✉ *Rue Armand-Gauthier*); its vaults rise 133 feet from the floor, making it the tallest cathedral in southern France. Only Beauvais and Amiens, in Picardy, are taller, and as at Beauvais, the nave at Narbonne was never built. The "Creation" tapestry is the cathedral's finest treasure.

Richly sculpted cloisters link the cathedral to the former **Palais des Archevêques** *(Archbishops' Palace)*, now home to **museums** of archaeology, art, and history. Note the late-13th-century keep, the Donjon Gilles-Aycelin; climb the 180 steps to the top for a view of the region and the town. ✉ *Palais des Archevêques* ☎ *04-68-90-30-54* 💳 *€7.50, includes all town museums* ⏲ *May-Sept., daily 9:30-noon and 2-6; Oct.-Apr., Tues.-Sun. 10-noon and 2-5.*

WHERE TO STAY

$-$$ **Hôtel La Résidence.** One block from the Canal de la Robine and another single block from the Place Salengro and the cathedral, this traditional favorite has housed France's artistic crème de la crème from Georges Brassens to Michel Serrault. The 19th-century building is charming, while rooms combine old-fashioned warmth with modern comforts. **Pros:** centrally located for shops, restaurants, and museums. **Cons:** parking area can be difficult to navigate and can fill up. ✉ *6 rue Premier Mai* ☎ *04-68-32-19-41* 🌐 *www.hotelresidence.fr* *26 rooms* *In-room: a/c. In-hotel: Internet terminal, parking (paid)* ▬ *AE, DC, MC, V* ⏲ *Closed mid-Jan.-mid-Feb.*

MONTPELLIER

140 km (87 mi) northeast of Perpignan, 42 km (26 mi) southwest of Nîmes.

Vibrant Montpellier (pronounced monh-pell-*yay*), capital of the Languedoc-Roussillon region, has been a center of commerce and learning since the Middle Ages, when it was a crossroads for pilgrims on their way to Santiago de Compostela, in Spain, and an active shipping center trading in spices from the East. With its cargo of exotic luxuries, it also imported Renaissance learning, and its university—founded in the 13th century—has nurtured a steady influx of ideas through the centuries. Though the port silted up by the 16th century, Montpellier never became a backwater, and as a center of commerce and conferences it keeps its focus on the future.

GETTING HERE

British Airways and Air France fly out of the Airport Montpellier-Méditerranée (☎ *04–67–20–85–00*), set southeast of Montpellier. Shuttles *(€5)* leave the bus station about every hour for the airport from Place du Europe (🌐 *www.montpellier.aeroport.fr*). The TGV takes 4 hours, 40 minutes from Paris for about €85, and there are direct trains as far afield as Avignon, Nice, and Marseille. If you're trying to get to the sea, hail bus No. 17 (which passes every half hour for Palavas).

Visitor Information Montpellier Tourist Office. ✉ *30 allée Jean de Lattre de Tassigny, Esplanade Comédie* ☎ *04–67–60–60–60* 🌐 *www.ot-montpellier.fr.*

EXPLORING

An imaginative urban planning program has streamlined Montpellier's 17th-century Vieille Ville, and monumental perspectives dwarf passersby on the 17th-century Promenade du Peyrou. An even more utopian venture in urban planning is the Antigone district: a vast, harmonious 100-acre complex designed in 1984 by Barcelona architect Ricardo Bofill. A student population of some 75,000 keeps things lively, especially on the Place de la Comédie, the city's social nerve center. Happily, the Vielle Ville (Old Town) is a pedestrian paradise, and you can travel around the entire city on the excellent bus system (the Gare Routière station is by the train terminal on Rue Jules Ferry).

TOURING MONTPELLIER

In addition to publishing map itineraries that you can follow yourself, the **Montpellier Tourist Office** (✉ *30 allée Jean de Lattre de Tassigny, Esplanade Comédie* ☎ *04–67–60–60–60*) provides guided walking tours of the city's neighborhoods and monuments daily in summer and on Wednesday and Saturday during the school year (roughly, September–June). They leave from the Place de la Comédie. A small **tourist train** (☎ *04–67–51–27–37 information*) with broadcast commentary leaves from the Esplanade Charles de Gaulle daily at 11, noon, 2, 3, and 4 and more frequently in high season.

TOP ATTRACTIONS

2 **Arc de Triomphe.** Looming majestically over the peripheral highway that loops around the city center, this enormous arch is the centerpiece of the Peyrou. Designed by

Antigone 8
Arc de Triomphe 2
Cathédrale St-Pierre 4
Faculté de Médecine 5
Jardin des Plantes 3
Musée Fabre 7
Place de la Comédie 6
Promenade du Peyrou 1

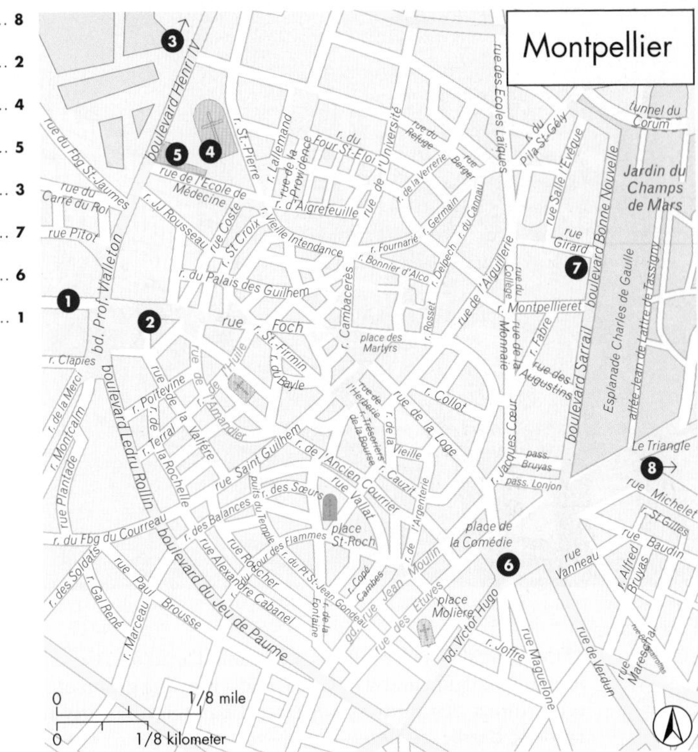

d'Aviler in 1689, it was finished by Giral in 1776. Together, the noble scale of these harmonious stone constructions and the sweeping perspectives they frame make for an inspiring stroll through this posh stretch of town. At the end of the park is the **Château d'Eau,** a Corinthian temple and the terminal for **les Arceaux,** an 18th-century aqueduct; on a clear day the view from here is spectacular, taking in the Cévennes Mountains, the sea, and an ocean of red-tile roofs (it's worth it to come back here at night to see the entire promenade lighted up).

7 ★ **Musée Fabre.** From crowd-packed Place de la Comédie, Boulevard Sarrail leads north past the shady Esplanade Charles de Gaulle to this famous museum. Renovated in 2006, it is a mixed bag of architectural styles (a 17th-century *hôtel,* a vast Victorian wing with superb natural light, and a remnant of a Baroque Jesuit college). This rich art museum has a surprisingly big collection, thanks to its namesake. François-Xavier Fabre, a native of Montpellier, was a student of the great 18th-century French artist David, who established roots in Italy and acquired a formidable collection of masterworks—which he then donated to his hometown, supervising the development of this fine museum. Among his gifts were the *Mariage Mystique de Sainte Catherine,* by Veronese, and Poussin's coquettish *Venus et Adonis.* Later contributions include a superb group of 17th-century Flemish works (Rubens, Steen), a collection of

The Three Graces fountain and the Opéra Comédie theater both anchor the Place de la Comédie, the social and cultural hub of Montpellier.

19th-century French canvases (Géricault, Delacroix, Corot, Millet) that inspired Gauguin and Van Gogh, and a growing group of 20th-century acquisitions that buttress a legacy of paintings by early Impressionist Frédéric Bazille. ✉ *39 bd. Bonne Nouvelle* ☎ *04–67–14–83–00* 🌐 *museefabre.montpellier-agglo.com* 🎫 *€8* 🕐 *Tues., Thurs., Fri., and Sun. 10–6, Wed. 1–9, Sat. 11–6.*

6 **Place de la Comédie.** The number of bistros and brasseries increases as you leave the Vieille Ville to cross Place des Martyrs; if you veer right down Rue de la Loge, you spill out onto the festive gathering spot known as Place de la Comédie. Anchored by the Neoclassical 19th-century **Opéra-Comédie,** this broad square is a beehive of leisurely activity, a cross between Barcelona's Ramblas and a Roman *passeggiata* (afternoon stroll, en masse). Brasseries, bistros, fast-food joints, and cinemas draw crowds, but the pleasure is getting here and seeing who came before, in which shoes, and with whom.

7 ★ **Promenade du Peyrou.** Montpellier's grandest avenue, this was built at the end of the 17th century and dedicated to Louis XIV.

WORTH NOTING

8 **Antigone.** At the far-east end of the city loop, Montpellier seems to transform itself into a futuristic ideal city, all in one smooth, low-slung postmodern style. This is the Antigone district, the result of city planners' efforts (and local industries' commitment) to pull Montpellier up out of its economic doldrums. It worked. This ideal neighborhood, designed by the Catalan architect Ricardo Bofill, covers 100-plus acres with plazas, esplanades, shops, restaurants, and low-income housing, all constructed out of stone-color, prestressed concrete. Be sure to visit

Place du Nombre d'Or—symmetrically composed of curves—and the 1-km-long (½-mi-long) vista that stretches down a mall of cypress trees to the glass-front **Hôtel de Region** (✉ *Rue de Pompegnane*).

4 **Cathédrale St-Pierre.** After taking in the broad vistas of the Promenade de Peyrou, cross over into the Vieille Ville and wander its maze of narrow streets full of pretty shops and intimate restaurants. At the northern edge of the Vieille Ville, visit this imposing cathedral, its fantastical and unique 14th-century entry porch alone worth the detour: two cone-top towers—some five stories high—flank the main portal and support a groin-vaulted shelter. The interior, despite 18th-century reconstruction, maintains the formal simplicity of its 14th-century origins. ✉ *Pl. St-Pierre 9.*

13

5 **Faculté de Médecine.** Next door to Cathédrale St-Pierre (on Place St-Pierre), peek into this noble institution, on Rue de l'École de Médecine, one of France's most respected medical schools, founded in the 13th century and infused with generations of international learning—especially Arab and Jewish scholarship.

3 **Jardin des Plantes.** Boulevard Henri IV runs north from the Promenade du Peyrou to France's oldest botanical garden, which was planted on order of Henri IV in 1593. An exceptional range of plants, flowers, and trees grows here. *Free ⏲ Gardens Tues.–Sat. 9–noon and 2–5. Greenhouses June–Sept., Tues.–Sun. noon–8; Oct.–May, Tues.–Sun. noon–6.*

WHERE TO EAT

$$ FRENCH **Le Chat Perché.** People flock here for the warm bistro ambience, the terrace overlooking the square below, the carefully selected regional wines, and the traditional dishes served with flair. The cuisine varies with the seasons, the markets, and the humor of the chef. *Everything here is homemade and reasonably priced.* ✉ *10 rue college Duvergier, Place de la Chapelle Neuve* ☎ *04–67–60–88–59* *Reservations essential* ▭ *MC, V* ⏲ *Closed Sun. and Jan. No lunch Mon.*

$$$$ FRENCH Fodor's Choice ★ **Le Jardin des Sens.** Blink and look again: twins Laurent and Jacques Pourcel, trained under separate masters, combine forces here to achieve a quiet, almost cerebral cuisine based on southern French traditions. At every turn are happy surprises: foie-gras crisps, dried-fruit risotto, and lamb sweetbreads with *gambas* (prawns). A modest lunch menu (in the $$$$ category) lets you indulge at la lower cost. Decor is minimal stylish, with steel beams and tables on three tiers. Truth is, the restaurant is in a rather *delabré* working-class neighborhood, and from the outside looks like an anonymous warehouse. ✉ *11 av.*

GETTING AROUND

Montpellier's historic *centre ville* is a pedestrian's paradise, with a labyrinth of stone paths and alleys leading from courtyard to courtyard. Hotels, restaurants, and sights are all within walking distance of Place de la Comédie, but the town also has a comprehensive bus system, SMTU, which starts out from the Gare Routière on Place du Bicentenaire. With thousands of college students in town, bike rentals are another easy way to get around.

St-Lazare ☎ 04–99–58–38–38 🌐 www.jardindessens.com 💳 AE, DC, MC, V ⊙ Closed Sun. and Jan. No lunch Mon. and Wed.

$ FRENCH ★ ✕ **Le Petit Jardin.** On a quiet Vieille Ville backstreet, this simple restaurant lives up to its name: you dine looking over (or seated in) a lovely, deep-shaded garden with views of the cathedral. A simple omelet with pepper sauce, fresh foie gras in a rhubarb sauce, or turbot in a honey and balsamic vinegar sauce mirrors the welcome, which is warm and unpretentious. ✉ *20 rue Jean-Jacques-Rousseau* ☎ *04–67–60–78–78* 💳 *AE, MC, V* ⊙ *Closed Mon. and Jan.*

¢ MEDITERRANEAN ✕ **Le Petit Mickey.** Since 1885 this eatery—the oldest in the city, known historically as Casimir—has been feeding locals fine Mediterranean fare such as bull stew and fish of the day *à la plancha* (grilled with olive oil, garlic, and herbs) at great prices. You might have to endure the crowds and a sometimes irascible owner, but when the copious traditional plates hit the table you'll quickly forget the wait at lunchtime. ✉ *15 rue du Petit Jean* ☎ *04–67–60–60–41* 💳 *MC, V* ⊙ *Closed Aug. No dinner Sun.*

$$$$ FRENCH ★ ✕ **L'Olivier.** For a great taste of Provence right in the heart of Montpellier, this is the place to go. The decor is nothing to write home about—spartan Provençal feel, even with the odd splash of a painting on the wall—but the cuisine proves a very satisfying gastronomic surprise. You come to L'Olivier for the good food. The *filet de sole aux homard et morilles* (sole and lobster in a wild mushroom sauce) and the slow-cooked *Costières du Gard pigeon aux cepes* (regional pigeon in a wild mushroom sauce) might not equal the three-star extravaganzas served up at Le Jardin des Sens, but they are well worth the price. ✉ *12 rue Aristide Olivier* ☎ *04–67–92–86–28* 💳 *AE, MC, V* ⊙ *Closed Sun., Mon., and July 24–Aug.*

WHERE TO STAY

$$–$$$ ★ 🏨 **Le Guilhem.** On the same quiet backstreet as the restaurant Le Petit Jardin, this jewel of a *hôtel de charme* is actually a series of 16th-century houses. Rebuilt from ruins to include an elevator and state-of-the-art white-tile baths, it nonetheless retains original casement windows (many overlooking the extraordinary old garden), slanting floors, and views toward the cathedral. Soft yellows and powder blues add to its *temps perdu* gentleness. Tiny garret-style rooms at the top are great if you're traveling alone; if not, ask for the largest available. **Pros:** location close to Cathedrale St-Pierre, Jardin des Plantes, and the Promenade du Peyrou. **Cons:** breakfasts are overpriced; if you have kids in tow, it's a long walk from the Place de la Comédie. ✉ *18 rue Jean-Jacques-Rousseau* ☎ *04–67–52–90–90* 🌐 *www.leguilhem.com* *35 rooms* *In-room: a/c, Wi-Fi. In-hotel: parking (paid)* 💳 *AE, DC, MC, V.*

NIGHTLIFE AND THE ARTS

Opera and orchestral concerts are performed in the very imposing **Salle MolièreOpéra de Montpellier** (✉ *11 bd. Victor Hugo* ☎ *04–67–60–19–99* 🌐 *www.opera-montpellier.com*). The resident **Orchestre National de Montpellier** is a young and energetic group of some reputation, performing regularly in the Salle Molière as well as the Opéra Berlioz in the Corum conference complex.

14

The Basque Country, Gascony, and Hautes-Pyrénées

WORD OF MOUTH

"Spring in the French Pyrénées is simply spectacular. But I did not care for Lourdes—it can make you lose your faith in humanity!—and St-Jean-Piéd-de-Port, because it gets so many tour buses."

—Zeppole

WELCOME TO THE BASQUE COUNTRY, GASCONY, AND HAUTES-PYRÉNÉES

TOP REASONS TO GO

★ **Biarritz, Big Sur à la Mode:** Today Biarritz is Europe's surf capital, a far cry from its start as the favorite watering place of Empress Eugénie, but, face it, this is one party everyone is invited to.

★ **Basque Chic:** Ainhoa, Sare, and St-Jean-de-Luz show off quirky and colorful, irregular, and asymmetric Basque rural village architecture.

★ **Michel Guérard's Les Prés d' Eugénie:** The co-father (with Paul Bocuse) of nouvelle cuisine still creates glorious meals in tucked-away Eugénie-les-Bains.

★ **Gorgeous Gavarnie:** Victor Hugo called the 1,400-foot-high waterfall here "the greatest architect's greatest work."

★ **Pretty Pau:** Set with a panoramic view of the Pyrénées, Pau is the historic capital of Béarn (as in Béarnaise sauce)—regal monuments recall its royal past as the birthplace of King Henri IV.

1 The Atlantic Pyrénées. From the first important height at 2,969-foot La Rhune, towering over the edge of the Atlantic, the Basque Pyrénées rise eastward through picturesque valleys and villages to the Iparla Ridge above Bidarrai and the range's first major peak at the 6,617-foot Orhi. The hills cosset cozy villages like Sare and Ainhoa. Colorful architecture and flower-festooned balconies help preserve St-Jean-Pied-de-Port's charm. Gateway to the Pyrénées, Pau is the most culturally vibrant city in Gascony, with elegant *hôtels particuliers* and a royal château.

2 Hautes-Pyrénées. The Hautes-Pyrénées include the most spectacular natural wonders in the cordillera. Although mountains soar in this region, they have always attracted cultural luminaries including Victor Hugo, Montaigne, and Rossini, who came to marvel at the Cirque de Gavarnie, a natural mountain amphitheater. Millions of others venture here to the healing holy waters of Lourdes.

3 The Basque Coast. Fine-sand beaches in tawny yellows and red, green, and blue fishing boats and villages keep your eyes busy with their competing palettes on the lush Basque Coast, with world-class chefs making the most of local produce. Bayonne as the graceful French provincial city, Biarritz as the imperial beach domain, and St-Jean-de-Luz as the colorful fishing port all play their parts to perfection along this southwestern coastline backed by the soft green pastures of the Basque hills.

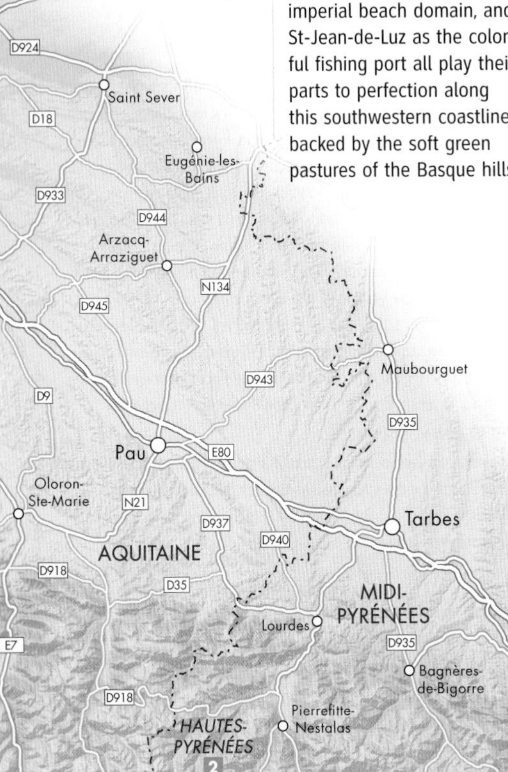

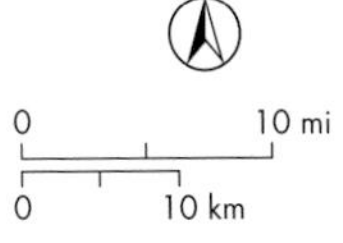

GETTING ORIENTED

The most southwestern corner of France's sprawling "Southwest," the rolling hills of the French Basque provinces stretch from the Atlantic beaches of glittering Biarritz to the first Pyrenean heights: the hills and highlands of Gascony around the city of Pau. These are mere stepping-stones compared to the peaks of the Hautes-Pyrénées, which lie to the east and sit in the center of the towering barrier historically separating the Iberian Peninsula from continental Europe.

14

THE BASQUE COUNTRY, GASCONY, AND HAUTES-PYRÉNÉES PLANNER

Transportation Basics

A car is best for getting around the Basque Coast and the Pyrénées.

Train and bus connections will get you from Bayonne to Biarritz and Hendaye and up to St-Jean-Pied-de-Port easily.

Unfortunately, less pivotal destinations will entail much waiting and loss of valuable time.

The roads are good, albeit slow, and you shouldn't plan on doing much better than 60 km–70 km an hour on average.

For walking the hills or long-distance hikes across the GR10 or the Haute Randonnée Pyrénéenne along the crest of the cordillera, bus and trains such as the SNCF Bayonne to St-Jean-Pied-de-Port connection are the first step.

They will then drop you off and pick you up at trailheads such as the one at Bidarrai's Pont d'Enfer.

Bus lines from St-Jean-Pied-de-Port will take you east to Larrau, Mauleon, and Pau.

From Pau there are SNCF connections up into the Pyrénées, with subsequent SNCF buses to points such as Gavarnie.

Making the Most of Your Time

Unless you prefer rising with the sun, traveling west to east, with the sun behind you as the shadows lengthen, is the best way to approach this part of the Pyrénées. Bayonne is the natural starting point, at the mouth of the Atlantic Pyrenean watershed, with the Basque Museum as an instructive primer for the culture of the villages you are about to go through. Biarritz and St-Jean-de-Luz offer opportunities for beach time and glamour. The picturesque villages of Sare and Ainhoa guide you into the mountains and valleys, threaded by rivers flowing into the Nive. St-Jean-Pied-de-Port is a Pyrenean hub from which Eugénie-les-Bains, Sauveterre de Béarn, and Navarrenx are short detours before continuing east to Pau, the Hautes-Pyrénées, and their crowning glory, Gavarnie.

Wherever you head, make haste slowly: this region's proximity to Spain comes to life in its architecture, in the expressive Midi accent, which turns the word *demain* (tomorrow) into "demaing," and the slow-paced lifestyle.

Gonzo Over Games

Perhaps the best-known and most spectacular of Basque sports is the ancestral ball game of pelota, a descendant of the medieval *jeux de paume* (literally, palm games), a fundamental element of rural Basque culture. A Basque village without a fronton (backboard and pelota court) is as unimaginable as an American town lacking a baseball diamond. There are many versions and variations on this graceful, fast-paced sport, played with the bare hand, with wooden bats, or with curved basketlike gloves; a real wicker *chistera*—the wicker bat used in the game—is an interesting souvenir to buy (and makes a very pretty fruit basket, but let no Basque hear that bit of heresy). Other rural Basque sports include scything, wood-chopping and -sawing, sack hauling, stone lifting, tug-of-war, competitive whaleboat rowing, and, for those who really want to take the weight of the world on their shoulders, *orga yoko,* or cart lifting—hefting and moving a 346-kilo (761-pound) hay wagon (you read it here). *See our special photo-feature, "Basque Spoken Here," for more details.*

Dining and Lodging

Dining in the regions of the Basque Country is invariably a feast, whether it's on seafood or the famous migratory *palombes* (wood pigeons).

Dishes to keep in mind include *ttoro* (hake stew), *pipérade* (tomatoes and green peppers cooked in olive oil, and often scrambled eggs), *bakalao al pil-pil* (cod cooked in oil "al pil-pil"—the bubbling sound the fish makes as it creates its own sauce), *marmitako* (tuna and potato stew), and *zikiro* (roast lamb).

Home of the eponymous *sauce bérnaise,* Béarn is also famous for its *garbure,* thick vegetable soup with *confit de canard* (preserved duck) and *fèves* (broad beans).

Civets (stews) made with *isard* (wild goat) or wild boar are other specialties. La Bigorre and the Hautes-Pyrénées are equally dedicated to garbure, though they may call their version *soupe paysanne bigourdane* (Bigorran peasant soup) to distinguish it from that of their neighbors.

The Basque Coast's traditional fresh seafood is unsurpassable every day of the week except Monday, the fleet having stayed in port on Sunday.

The inland Basque Country and upland Béarn is famous for game in fall and winter and lamb in spring. In the Hautes-Pyrénées, the higher altitude makes power dining attractive and thick bean soups and wild-boar stews come into their own.

From palatial beachside splendor in Biarritz to simple mountain auberges in the Basque country to Pyrenean refuges in the Hautes-Pyrénées, the gamut of lodging in southwest France is conveniently broad.

Be sure to book summertime lodging on the Basque Coast well in advance, particularly for August. In the Hautes-Pyrénées, only Gavarnie during its third-week-of-July music festival presents a potential booking problem.

DINING AND LODGING PRICE CATEGORIES (IN EUROS)

	¢	$	$$	$$$	$$$$
Restaurants	under €13	€13–€17	€18–€24	€25–€32	over €32
Hotels	under €65	€65–€105	€106–€145	€146–€215	over €215

Restaurant prices are per person for a main course at dinner, including tax (5.5%) and service; note that if a restaurant offers only prix-fixe (set-price) meals, it has been given the price category that reflects the full prix-fixe price. Hotel prices are for a standard double room in high season, including tax (19.6%) and service charge.

When to Go

The Basque Country is known for its wet climate, but when the skies clear the hillsides are so green and the air so clear that the rain gods are immediately forgiven.

Late fall and winter are generally rainier than the early autumn or late spring. The Pyrenean heights such as Brèche de Roland and Gavarnie, on the other hand, may only be approached safely in midsummer. Treacherous ice and snow plaques can be present even in mid-June, and summer blizzards are never impossible. Climate change may be shrinking glaciers and extending the Pyrénées's safety period, but freak conditions, the reverse side of the same coin, may be creating even more unpredictable and dangerous weather patterns. Beach weather is from May through September, and sometimes lasts until mid-October's *été de la Sant-Martin* (Indian Summer). Skiing conditions are reliable from December through March and, on occasion, into April.

GETTING AROUND

Car Travel

A64 connects Pau and Bayonne in less than an hour, and A63 runs up and down the Atlantic coast.

N117 connects Hendaye with Toulouse via Pau and Tarbes.

N134 connects Bordeaux, Pau, Oloron-Ste-Marie, and Spain via the Col de Somport and Jaca.

The D918 from Bayonne through Cambo and along the Nive River to St-Jean-Pied-de-Port is a pretty drive, continuing on (as D919 and D920) through the Béarn country to Oloron-Ste-Marie and Pau.

Roads are occasionally slow and tortuous in the more mountainous areas, but valley and riverside roads are generally quite smooth and fast.

D132, which goes between Arette and Pierre-St-Martin, can be snowed in between mid-November and mid-May.

This can also be the case for N134 through the Valley d'Aspe and the Col de Somport into Spain.

Train Travel

High-speed trains (TGVs, Trains à Grande Vitesse) cover the 800 km (500 mi) from Paris to Bayonne in 4½ hours. Biarritz's La Négresse train station (3 km [2 mi] southeast of the town center) has trains connecting with Bayonne, Bordeaux, St-Jean-de-Luz, and many other places. Bayonne and Toulouse are connected by local SNCF trains via Pau, Tarbes, and Lourdes. You can take the train from Pau to Lourdes, Bayonne, and Biarritz. From Bayonne, trains connect with many destinations, including St-Jean-de-Luz, St-Jean-Pied-de-Port, Toulouse, Bordeaux, and Pau. Local trains go between Bayonne and Biarritz and from Bayonne into the Atlantic Pyrénées, a slow but picturesque trip. A local train runs along the Nive from Bayonne to St-Jean-Pied-de-Port. Hendaye is connected to Bayonne and to San Sebastián via the famous *topo* (mole) train, so called for the number of tunnels it passes through.

Train Information Gare Ville Bayonne (✉ *Quartier St-Esprit* ☎ *08–36–35–35–35*). **Gare Ville Biarritz La Négresse** (✉ *18 allée Moura* ☎ *05–59–23–04–84*). **SNCF** (☎ *36–35 [€0.34 per minute]* 🌐 *www.voyages-sncf.com*). **TGV** (🌐 *www.tgv.com*).

Le Surfing

The area around Biarritz has become Europe's hot-cool surfing center. The season kicks off big-time every summer with the Roxy Jam long-board world women's championship (usually held July 1–8 🌐 *www.roxy.com*). For more real action head to the coast north of Biarritz and the towns of Anglet and Hossegor. La Barre beach in the north doubles as the hangout for dedicated surfers who live out of their vans. On the southern end (by the Anglet-Biarritz border) are surf shops, snack bars, and one *boulangerie.* These give the main beach drag, Chambre d'Amour, a decidedly California flair. If you're coming by train, get off in Bayonne or Biarritz and transfer to a STAB bus to Anglet. The main tourist office (✉ *1 av. de la Chambre d'Amour* ☎ *05–59–03–77–01* 🌐 *www.ville-anglet.fr*) is closed off-season. Hossegor, 20 km (12 mi) north of Bayonne, hosts the RipCurl Pro and the International Surf Championships every August.

Bus Travel

Various private bus concerns—**STAB** (serving the Bayonne–Anglet–Biarritz metropolitan areas) and **ATCRB** (up and down the coast and inland to many Basque towns, such as Bayonne, Biarritz, St-Jean-de-Luz, and Bidart)—service the region. Where they don't, the trusty **SNCF** national bus lines can occasionally come to the rescue. Other bus companies also thread the area. **T.P.R. Buses** head out from Pau to Lourdes (1 hr, 15 mins; €5.20 six times a day). From Lourdes, SNCF buses go to Cauterets and to Luz-St-Sauveur, where you can grab one of two daily buses for the 20-km (12-mi), 40-minute (€5.20) ride up the valley to Gavarnie. Other buses leave from the train station in St-Jean-de-Luz and go to villages like Sare (no public transport goes to Ainhoa). Beware of peak-hour traffic on roads in summer, which can mean both delays in transport time and few seats on buses. Check in with the local tourist office for handy schedules or ask your hotel concierge for the best advice.

Bus Information **STAB–Biarritz** (☒ *Rue Louis Barthou, Biarritz* ☎ *05–59–24–26–53*). **ATCRB** (☎ *05–59–26–06–99*). **Transports Basques Associés** (☒ *Pl. St-André, Bayonne* ☎ *05–59–59–49–00*). **R.D.T.L. Buses** (☒ *Pl. des Basques, Bayonne* ☎ *05–59–35–17–59*).

Getting on Top of Things

Supping on the hearty regional cuisine makes perfect sense after a day of hiking the Pyrénées, which are best explored on foot. Day trips to La Rhune overlooking Biarritz and the Basque Coast or the walk up to Biriatou from the beach at Hendaye are great ways to get to know the countryside.

Hiking the Pyrénées end-to-end is a 43-day trip. The GR (Grande Randonnée) 10, a trail signed by discreet red-and-white paint markings, runs from the Atlantic at Hendaye to Banyuls-sur-Mer on the Mediterranean, through villages and mountains, with refuges along the way. The HRP (Haute Randonnée Pyrénéenne, or High Pyrenean Hike) follows terrain in France and Spain irrespective of borders. Local trails are well indicated, with blue or yellow markings. Some classic walks in the Pyrénées include the Iparla Ridge walk between Bidarrai and St-Étienne-de-Baïgorry, the Santiago de Compostela Trail's dramatic St-Jean-Pied-de-Port to Roncesvalles walk over the Pyrénées, and the Holçarté Gorge walk between Larrau and Ste-Engrâce. Get trail maps at local tourist offices.

Tour Options

In Biarritz, Aitzin organizes tours of Bayonne, Biarritz, the Basque Coast, and the Basque Pyrénées.

The Association des Guides, in Pau, arranges guided tours of the city, the Pyrénées, and Béarn and Basque Country.

The Bayonne tourist office gives guided tours of the city.

La Guild du Tourisme des Pyrénées-Atlantiques offers information on and organizes visits and tours of the Basque Country and the Pyrénées.

Guides Culturels Pyrénéens, in Tarbes, arranges many tours, including explorations on such themes as cave painting, art and architecture, Basque sports, hiking, and horseback riding.

Contacts **Aitzin** (☎ *05–59–24–36–05*).

Association des Guides (☎ *05–59–30–44–01*).

Bayonne tourist office (☎ *05–59–46–01–46*).

Guides Culturels Pyrénéens (☎ *05–62–44–15–44*).

La Guild du Tourisme des Pyrénées-Atlantiques (☎ *05–59–46–37–05*).

14

Updated by George Semler

A pelota-playing mayor in the province of Soule recently welcomed a group of travelers with the following announcements: that the Basque Country is the most beautiful place in the world; that the Basque people were very likely direct descendants of Adam and Eve via the lost city of Atlantis; that his own ancestors fought in the Crusades; and that Christopher Columbus was almost certainly a Basque. There, in brief, was a composite picture of the pride, dignity, and humor of the Basques.

And if Columbus was not a Basque (a claim very much in doubt), at least historians know that whalers from the regional village of St-Jean-de-Luz sailed as far as America in their three-mast ships, and that Juan Sebastián Elkano, from the Spanish Basque village of Guetaria, commanded the completion of Magellan's voyage around the world after Magellan's 1521 death in the Philippines. The distinctive culture—from berets and pelota matches to Basque cooking—of this little "country" has cast its spell over the corners of the earth.

The most popular gateway to the entire region is Biarritz, the queen of France's Atlantic coast retreats, whose refinements once attracted the crowned heads of Europe to the area. It was Empress Eugénie who gave Biarritz its coming-out party, transforming it, in the era of Napoléon III, from a simple bourgeois town into an international glitterati favorite. Today, after a round of sightseeing, you can still enjoy the Second Empire trimmings from a perch at the roulette table in the town's casino. Then work on your suntan at Biarritz's famous beach or, a few miles away, really bask under the Basque sun at the picturesque port of St-Jean-de-Luz. As for the entire Pays Basque (Basque Country), it's happily compact: the ocher sands along the Bay of Biscay are less than an hour from the emerald hills of St-Jean-Pied-de-Port in the Basque Pyrénées.

Heading eastward toward the towering peaks of the central Pyrenean cordillera lies the Béarn region, with its splendid capital city of Pau, while northward lies a must-detour for lovers of the good life: Eugénie-les-Bains, where you can savor every morsel of a Michel Guérard feast at one (or all!) of his magnificently stylish restaurants and hotels. East through the Aubisque Pass, at the Béarn's eastern limit, is the heart of the Hautes-Pyrénées, where the mountains of Vignemale and Balaïtous compete with the Cirque de Gavarnie, the world's most spectacular cirque (or natural amphitheater), centered around a 1,400-foot waterfall. Whether you finish up with a vertiginous Pyrenean hike or choose to pay your respects to the religious shrine at Lourdes, this region always winds up lifting your spirits.

THE BASQUE COAST

La Côte Basque—a world unto itself with its own language, sports, and folklore—occupies France's southwest corner along the Spanish border. Inland, the area is laced with rivers: the Bidasoa River border with Spain marks the southern edge of the region, and the Adour River, on its northern edge, separates the Basque Country from the neighboring Les Landes. The Nive River flows through the heart of the verdant Basque littoral to join the Adour at Bayonne, and the smaller Nivelle River flows into the Bay of Biscay at St-Jean-de-Luz. Bayonne, Biarritz, and St-Jean-de-Luz are the main towns along the coast, all less than 40 km (25 mi) from the first peak of the Pyrénées.

BAYONNE

48 km (30 mi) southwest of Dax, 184 km (114 mi) south of Bordeaux, 295 km (183 mi) west of Toulouse.

At the confluence of the Adour and Nive rivers, Bayonne, France's most indelibly Basque city, was in the 4th century a Roman fort, or *castrum,* and for 300 years (1151–1451) a British colony. The city gave its name to the bayonet blade (from the French *baïonnette*), invented here in the 17th century, but today's Bayonne is more famous for its ham (*jambon de Bayonne*) and for the annual Basque pelota world championships held in September.

GETTING HERE

SNCF connects Bayonne with Paris (5 hrs, €45.50) with four TGV (Trains à Grande Vitesse) trains daily. Train connections from Bayonne include St-Jean-de-Luz (22 mins, €4.80), St-Jean-Pied-de-Port (1 hr, 13 mins; €9.20), Toulouse (3 hrs, 16 mins; €39.20), Bordeaux (1 hr, 43 mins; €29.90), and Pau (1 hr, 8 mins; €16); trains make the short jaunt to Biarritz frequently in summer; in winter, take a bus. The bus company STAB, or Société Transports en comun de l'Agglomération de Bayonne (☎ *05–59–14–15–16* 🌐 *www.bus-stab.com*) connects Bayonne with towns on the French Basque Coast, notably Biarritz (15 mins, €2.50) and Pau. The STAB shuttle connects the airport with Biarritz, Bayonne, and the surfing mecca of Anglet (20 mins, €1.50).

Visitor Information Bayonne Tourist Office. ✉ *Pl. des Basques* ☎ *05–59–46–01–46* 🌐 *www.ville-bayonne.fr.*

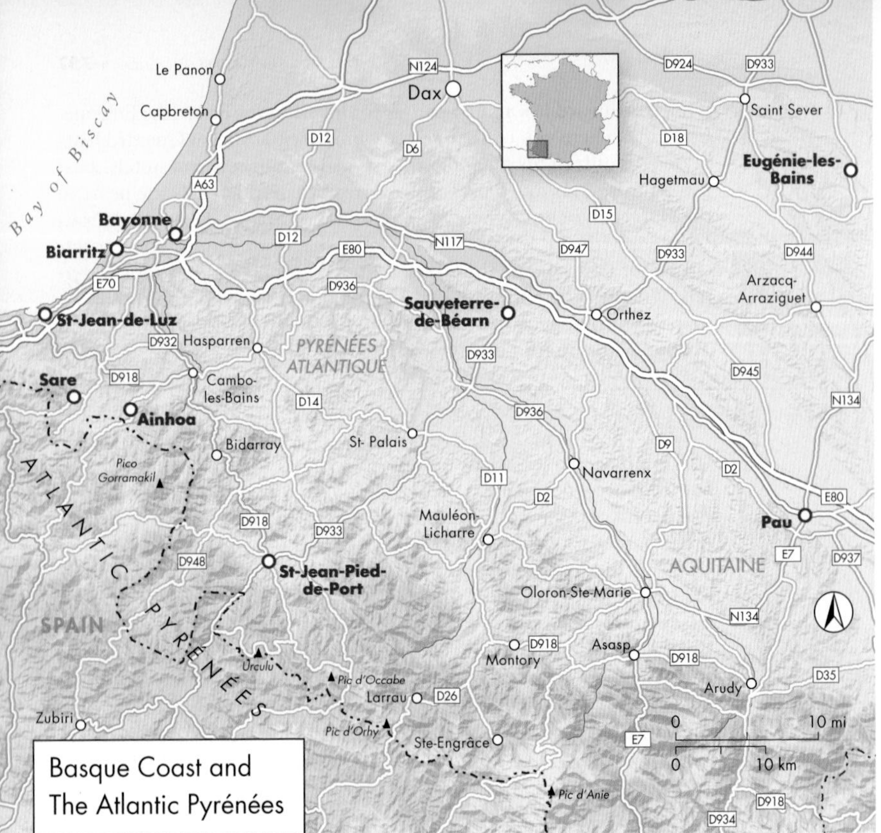

Basque Coast and The Atlantic Pyrénées

EXPLORING

A small port city, Bayonne remains the capital of the Pays Basque. Even though its port is spread out along the Adour estuary some 5 km (3 mi) inland from the sea, the two rivers and five bridges lend this small gem of a city a definite maritime feel. The houses fronting the quay, the intimate Place Pasteur, the Château-Vieux, the elegant 18th-century homes along Rue des Prébendés, the 17th-century ramparts, and the cathedral are some of the town's not-to-be-missed sights. Les Halles market in the Place des Halles on the left bank of the Nive is also a must-visit.

The **Cathédrale** (called both Ste-Marie and Notre-Dame) was built mainly in the 13th century, and is one of France's southernmost examples of Gothic architecture. Its 13th- to 14th-century cloisters are among its best features.

The airy, modernized **Musée Bonnat**, in itself reason enough to visit Bayonne, has a notable treasury of 19th-century paintings collected by French portraitist and historical painter Léon Bonnat (1833–1922). *5 rue Jacques-Lafitte 05–59–59–08–52 www.musee-bonnat.com €6.50 June–Sept., Wed.–Mon. 10:30–6:30; Oct.–May, 10–12:30 and 1:30–5:30.*

The handsomely designed and appointed **Musée Basque** on the right bank of the Nive offers an ethnographic history of the Basque Country and culture. ✉ *37 quai des Corsaires* ☎ *05–59–46–61–90* 🌐 *www.musee-basque.com* 🎫 *€6.50* ⏲ *July and Aug., daily 10–6:30, free Wed. evenings 6:30– 9:30; Sept.–June, Tues.–Sun. 10–6:30; free 1st Sun. of month; ticket window closes 1 hr before closing time.*

WHERE TO EAT AND STAY

$$$ FRENCH ★ ✕ **L'Auberge du Cheval Blanc.** Run by the Tellechea family since 1715, this former stagecoach inn in the Petit Bayonne quarter near the Musée Bonnat serves a combination of *cuisine du terroir* (home-style regional cooking) and original recipes in contemporary surroundings. Jean-Claude Tellechea showcases fresh fish as well as upland specialties from the Basque hills, sometimes joining the two in dishes such as the *merlu rôti aux oignons et jus de volaille* (hake roasted in onions with essence of poultry). The local Irouléguy wines offer the best value on the wine list. ✉ *68 rue Bourgneuf* ☎ *05–59–59–01–33* ▭ *AE, DC, MC, V* ⏲ *Closed Mon., and July 3–July 11 and Aug. 2–7. No lunch Sat. or dinner Sun., except Aug.*

$ **Le Grand Hôtel.** Just down the street from the Château-Vieux, this central spot has pleasant, comfortable rooms with an old-world feel. Expect little efficiency and only average comfort here; the draw is living in the heart of a lovely provincial French town. **Pros:** location; traditional French vibe; relaxed spirit. **Cons:** a little too relaxed; worn around the edges; hefty fees for everything, from parking to breakfast, build up fast. ✉ *21 rue Thiers* ☎ *05–59–59–62–00* 🌐 *www.bw-legrandhotel.com* *54 rooms* *In-room: a/c, refrigerator, Wi-Fi. In-hotel: bar, Internet terminal, Wi-Fi hotspot, parking (paid), some pets allowed* ▭ *AE, DC, MC, V* 🍽 *BP.*

BIARRITZ

Fodor's Choice ★ *8 km (5 mi) south of Bayonne, 190 km (118 mi) southwest of Bordeaux, 50 km (31 mi) north of San Sebastián, 115 km (69 mi) west of Pau.*

Biarritz may no longer lay claim to the title "the resort of kings and the king of resorts"; however, today there's no shortage of deluxe hotel rooms or bow-tie gamblers ambling over to the casino. The old, down-to-earth charm of the former fishing village has been thoroughly trumped by Biarritz's glitzy Second Empire 19th-century aura, and you won't find the bathing beauties and high rollers here complaining. Though nowhere near as drop-dead stylish as it once was, the town is making a comeback as a swank surfing capital with its new casino and convention center.

GETTING HERE AND AROUND

At 18 allée Moura, Biarritz's La Négresse train station (3 km [2 mi] southeast of the *centre ville [city center]*, so hop on bus No. 2 to reach the centrally located Hôtel de Ville near the main beach) has trains connecting with St-Jean-de-Luz (9 mins, €1.50), Bordeaux (1 hr, 55 mins; €31.50), and many other places, including San Sebastián, Spain (30 mins, €3.50). From Bayonne airport, bus No. 6 runs hourly to the Biarritz city center from 6 AM to 7 PM. Up to 10 trains arrive from Bayonne (9 mins, €1.50), a hub for trains connecting with Paris and other big cities in France. Most buses to Bayonne and Anglet run from the STAB bus booth (Rue Louis Barthous), near the main tourist office. Tickets cost €1.20 for a single ride, €5.60 for an eight-ride card. The ATCRB bus has regular service to other Basque towns, including St-Jean-de-Luz. SNCF connects Biarritz with Paris by TGV (5 hrs, 21 mins; €85.60) with six trains daily.

Visitor Information **Biarritz Tourist Office.** ✉ *1 sq. Ixelles* ☎ *05–59–22–37–10* 🌐 *www.biarritz.fr.*

EXPLORING

Once a favorite resort of Charlie Chaplin, Coco Chanel, and exiled Russian royals, Biarritz first rose to prominence when rich and royal Carlist exiles from Spain set up shop here in 1838. Unable to visit San Sebastián just across the border on the Basque Coast, they sought a summer watering spot as close as possible to their old stomping ground. Among the exiles was Eugénie de Montijo, soon destined to become empress of France. As a child, she vacationed here with her family, fell in love with the place, and then set about building her own palace once she married Napoléon III. During the 14 summers she spent here, half the crowned heads of Europe—including Queen Victoria and Edward VII—were her guests in Eugénie's villa, a gigantic wedding-cake edifice, now the **Hôtel du Palais,** set on the main sea promenade of town, the **Quai de la Grande Plage,** where the fashionable set used to stroll in Worth gowns and picture hats. Whether you consider Napoléon III's bombastic architectural legacies an eyesore or an eyeful, they at least have the courage of their convictions.

If you want to rediscover yesteryear Biarritz, start by exploring the narrow streets around the cozy 16th-century church of **St-Martin.** Adjacent to the Grand Plage are the set-pieces of the Hôtel du Palais and the **Église Orthodoxe Russe,** a Byzantine-style church built by the White Russian community that considered Biarritz their 19th-century Yalta-by-the-Atlantic. The duchesses often repaired to the terraced restaurants of the festive **Place Ste-Eugénie,** still considered the social center of town. A lorgnette view away is the harbor of the **Port des Pêcheurs** (Fishing Port), which provides a tantalizing glimpse of the Biarritz of old. Biarritz's beaches attract crowds—particularly the fine, sandy beaches of **La Grande Plage** and the neighboring **Plage Miramar,** both set amid craggy natural beauty. A walk along the beach promenades gives a view of the foaming breakers that beat constantly upon the sands, giving the name Côte d'Argent (Silver Coast) to the length of this part of the French Basque Coast.

★ If you wish to pay your respects to the Empress Eugénie, visit **La Chapelle Impériale,** which she had built in 1864 to venerate a figure of a Mexican Black Virgin from Guadalupe (and perhaps to expiate her sins for furthering her husband's tragic folly of putting Emperor Maximilian and Empress Carlotta on the "throne" of Mexico). The style is a charming hybrid of Roman-Byzantine and Hispano-Mauresque. ✉ *Rue Pellot* ⏲ *Mid-Apr.–mid-July and mid-Sept.–mid-Oct., Mon., Tues., and Sat. 3–7; mid-July–mid-Sept., Mon.–Sat. 3–5; mid-Oct.–Dec., Sat. 3–5.*

Continued on page 765

BASQUE SPOKEN HERE

Bilbao
Bilbo
Saint-Sébastien
Donostia
Bayonne
BISCAYE
LABOURD
(FRANCE)
GUIPEÚZUOA
BASSE-NAVARRE
ÁLAVA
Vitoria
Gasteiz
(SPAIN)
SOULE
Pampelune
Irunea
NAVARRE
FRANCE
SPAIN

While the Basque Country's future as an independent nation-state has yet to be determined, the quirky, fascinating culture of the Basque people is not restricted by any borders. Experience it for yourself in the food, history, and sport.

Basque solar cross

The cultural footprints of this tiny corner of Europe, which straddle the Atlantic end of the border between France and Spain, have already touched down all over the globe. The sport of jai-alai has come to America. International magazines give an ecstatic thumbs-up to Basque cooking. Historians are pointing to Basque fishermen as the true discoverers of North America. And bestsellers, not without irony, proclaim *The Basque History of the World*. As in the ancient 4 + 3 = 1 graffiti equation, the three French (Labourd, Basse Navarre, and Soule) and the four Spanish (Guipúzcoa, Vizcaya, Alava, and Navarra) Basque provinces add up to a single people with a shared history. Although nationless, Basques have been Basques since Paleolithic times.

Stretching across the Pyrénées from Bayonne in France to Bilbao in Spain, the New Hampshire-sized Basque region retains a distinct culture, neither expressly French nor Spanish, fiercely guarded by its three million inhabitants. Fables stubbornly connect them with Adam and Eve, Noah's Ark, and the lost city of Atlantis, but a leading genealogical theory points to common bloodlines with the Celts. The most tenable theory is that the Basques are descended from aboriginal Iberian peoples who successfully defended their unique cultural identity from the influences of Roman and Moorish domination.

It was only in 1876 that Sabino Arana—a virulent anti-Spanish fanatic—proposed the ideal of a "pure" Basque independent state. That dream was crushed by Franco's dictatorial reign (1939–75, during which many Spanish Basques emigrated to France) and was immortalized in Pablo Picasso's *Guernica*. This famous painting, which depicts the catastrophic Nazi bombing of the Basque town of Guernika stands not only as a searing indictment of all wars but as a reminder of history's brutal assault upon Basque identity.

"THE BEST FOOD YOU'VE NEVER HEARD OF"

(left) Zurrukutuna, garlic soup with codfish. (right) Preparing canapes.

So says *Food & Wine* magazine. It's time to get filled in.

An old saying has it that every soccer team needs a Basque goaltender and every restaurant a Basque chef. Traditional Basque cuisine combines the fresh fish of the Atlantic and upland vegetables, beef, and lamb with a love of sauces that is rare south of the Pyrénées. Today, the *nueva cocina vasca* (new Basque cooking) movement has made Basque food less rustic and much more nouvelle. And now that pintxos (the Basque equivalent of tapas) have become the rage from Barcelona to New York City, Basque cuisine is being championed by foodies everywhere. Even superchef Michel Guérard up in Eugénie-les-Bains has, though not himself a Basque, influenced and been influenced by the master cookery of the Pays Basque.

WHO'S THE BEST CHEF?

Basques are so naturally competitive that meals often turn into comparative rants over who is better: Basque chefs based in France or in Spain. Some vote for Bayonne's Jean-Claude Tellechea (his L'Auberge du Cheval Blanc is famed for groundbreaking surf-and-turf dishes like hake roasted in onions with essence of poultry) or St-Jean-Pied-de-Port's Firmin Arrambide (based at his elegant Les Pyrénées inn). Others prefer the postmodern lobster salads found over the border in San Sebastián and Bilbao, created by master chefs Juan Mark Arzak, Pedro Subijana, and Martin Berasategui, with wunderkind Andoni Aduriz and the Arbelaitz family nipping at their culinary heels.

SIX GREAT DISHES

Angulas. Baby eels, cooked in olive oil and garlic with a few slices of guindilla pepper.

Bacalao al pil-pil. Cod cooked at a low temperature in an emulsion of olive oil and fish juices, which makes a unique pinging sound as it sizzles.

Besugo. Sea bream, or besugo, is so revered that it is a traditional Christmas dish. Enjoy it with sagardo, the signature Basque apple cider.

Marmitako. This tuna stew with potatoes and pimientos is a satisfying winter favorite.

Ttoro. Typical of Labourd fishing villages such as St-Jean-de-Luz, this peppery Basque bouillabaisse is known as *sopa de pescado* (fish soup) south of the French border.

Txuleta de buey. The signature Basque meat is ox steaks marinated in parsley and garlic and cooked over coals.

BASQUE SPORTS: JAI-ALAI TO OXCART-LIFTING

Sports are core to Basque society, and virtually no one is immune to the Basque passion for competing, betting, and playing.

Over the centuries, the rugged physical environment of the Basque hills and the rough Cantabrian sea traditionally made physical prowess and bravery valued attributes. Since Basque mythology often involved feats of strength, it's easy to see why today's Basques are such rabid sports fans.

PELOTA

A Basque village without a frontón (pelota court) is as unimaginable as an American town without a baseball diamond. "The fastest game in the world," pelota is called *jai-alai* in Basque (and translated officially as "merry festival"). With rubber balls flung from hooked wicker gloves at speeds up to 150 mph—the impact of the ball is like a machine-gun bullet—jai-alai is mesmerizing. It is played on a three-walled court 175 feet long and 56 feet wide with 40-foot side walls.

Whether singles or doubles, the object is to angle the ball along or off of the side wall so that it cannot be returned. Betting is very much part of pelota and courtside wagers are brokered by bet makers as play proceeds. While pelota is the word for "ball," it also refers to the game. There was even a recent movie in Spain entitled *La Pelota Vasca*, used metaphorically to refer to the greater "ball game" of life and death.

HERRIKIROLAK

Herrikirolak (rural sports) are based on farming and seafaring. Stone lifters (*harrijasotzaileak* in Euskera) heft weights up to 700 pounds. *Aizkolari* (axe men) chop wood in various contests, *Gizon proba* (man trial) pits three-man teams moving weighted sleds; while *estropadak* are whaleboat rowers who compete in spectacular regattas (culminating in the September competition off La Concha beach in San Sebastián). *Sokatira* is tug of war, and *segalariak* is a scything competition. Other events include oxcart-lifting, milk-can carrying, and ram fights.

SOCCER

When it comes to soccer, Basque goaltenders have developed special fame in Spain, where Bilbao's Athletic Club and San Sebastián's Real Sociedad have won national championships with budgets far inferior to those of Real Madrid or FC Barcelona. Across the border, Bayonne's rugby team is a force in the French national competition; the French Basque capital is also home to the annual French pelota championship.

PARLEZ-VOUS EUSKERA?

Although the Basque people speak French north of the border and Spanish south of the border, they consider Euskera their first language and identify themselves as the *Euskaldunak* (the "Basque speakers"). Euskera remains one of the great enigmas of linguistic scholarship. Theories connect it with everything from Sanskrit to Japanese to Finnish.

What is certain is where Euskera did not come from, namely the Indo-European family of languages that includes the Germanic, Italic, and Hellenic language groups.

Currently used by about a million people in northern Spain and southwestern France, Euskera sounds like a consonant-ridden version of Spanish, with its five pure vowels, rolled "r," and palatal "n" and "l." Basque has survived two millennia of cultural and political pressure and is the only remaining language of those spoken in southwestern Europe before the Roman conquest.

The Euskaldunak celebrate their heritage during a Basque folk dancing festival.

A BASQUE GLOSSARY

Aurresku: The high-kicking *espata danza* or sword dance typically performed on the day of Corpus Christi in the Spanish Basque Country.

Akelarre: A gathering of witches that provoked witch trials in the Pyrénées. Even today it is believed that *jentilak* (magic elves) inhabit the woods and the Olentzaro (the evil Basque Santa Claus) comes down chimneys to wreak havoc—a fire is kept burning to keep him out.

Boina: The Basque beret or *txapela,* thought to have developed as the perfect protection from the siri-miri, the perennial "Scotch mist" that soaks the moist Basque Country.

Eguzki: The sun worship was at the center of the pagan religion that, in the Basque Country, gave way only slowly to Christianity. The Basque solar cross is typically carved into the east-facing facades of ancient *caserios* or farmhouses.

Espadrilles: Rope-soled canvas Basque shoes, also claimed by the Catalans, developed in the Pyrénées and traditionally attached by laces or ribbons wrapped up the ankle.

Etxekoandre: The woman who commands all matters spiritual, culinary, and practical in a traditional Basque farmhouse. Basque matriarchal inheritance laws remain key.

Fueros: Special Basque rights and laws (including exemption from serving in the army except to defend the Basque Country) originally conceded by the ancient Romans and abolished at the end of the Carlist Wars in 1876 after centuries of Castilian kings had sworn to protect Basque rights at the Tree of Guernika.

Ikurriña: The Basque flag, designed by the founder of Basque nationalism, Sabino Arana, composed of green and white crosses over a red background and said to have been based on the British Union Jack.

Lauburu: Resembling a four-leaf clover, lau (four) buru (head) is the Basque symbol.

Twenty: Basques favor counting in units of twenty (*veinte duros*—20 nickels—is a common way of saying a hundred pesetas, for example).

Txakolí: A slightly fizzy young wine made from grapes grown around the Bay of Biscay, this fresh, acidic brew happily accompanies tapas and fish.

WHERE TO EAT

$$ SEAFOOD **Chez Albert.** In summer it's nearly impossible to find a place on the terrace of this easygoing and popular seafood restaurant. Views of the fishing port and the salty harborside aromas of things maritime make the hearty fish and seafood offerings all the more irresistible here. *Port des Pêcheurs s/n 05–59–24–43–84 AE, DC, MC, V Closed Nov. 28–Dec. 12, Jan. 4–Feb. 9, and Wed. except in July and Aug.*

$$$ FRENCH ★ **L'Atelier.** Alexandre and Isabelle Bousquet have been a big success since moving to Biarritz from Aveyron. This hot new restaurant in the Quartier Saint-Charles a few steps from the Grande Plage is the *dernier cri* in a town surrounded by, but not known for, great cuisine (beyond the Hôtel du Palais). Tuna *tartare et croustillant* (raw and cooked) in a mustard sauce is a house specialty, as is the *pigeonneau* (wood pigeon). The wine list includes a range of selections from Bordeaux and Spain's Ribera de Duero. The €25 lunch *formule* (menu) is one of the best bargains in Biarritz. *18 rue Bergerie 05–59–22–09–37 AE, DC, MC, V Closed Mon. No dinner Sun.*

14

$$$$ ★ **Château de Brindos.** Take Jazz Age glamour, Renaissance stonework, and the luxest of guest rooms and you have this Pays Basque Xanadu—a large, rambling, white-stone manor topped with a Spanish belvedere tower set 4 km (2½ mi) east of Biarritz in Anglet. This was originally the home of Sir Reginald Wright, whose great soirées held here in the 1920s and '30s are conjured up in the saloon, now presided over by that premier mixologist, bartender Marc Pony. In recent years, interiors have been lovingly restored by Serge Blanco, who has managed to honor the mansion's history while installing state-of-the-art technology and comfort. Tapestries, wrought-iron Spanish wall sconces, Louis XIV–style armchairs, and dramatic stone fireplaces all dazzle the eye, as do views of the estate's private lake from guest rooms rife with quilted fabrics and overstuffed chaise longues. In summer dine out under the willows at the edge of the water at the grand restaurant (closed Monday, no dinner Sunday). Chef Antoine Antunès has trained with the best, from Guérard to Arrambide, and offers a guarantee of creative dining. **Pros:** flawless performance by staff; excellent dining; ultimate comfort. **Cons:** fitness facilities limited; addictively grande luxe; having to leave. *1 allée du Château 05–59–23–89–80 www.chateaudebrindos.com 24 rooms, 5 suites In-room: a/c, refrigerator, Wi-Fi (some). In-hotel: restaurant, bar, pool, Internet terminal, Wi-Fi hotspot, parking (paid), some pets allowed AE, DC, MC, V Closed Nov 28.–Dec. 11 and Feb. 15–Mar. 4 MAP.*

$$$$ ★ **Hôtel du Palais.** Set on the beach, this majestic, colonnaded redbrick hotel with an immense driveway, lawns, and a grand semicircular dining room, still exudes an opulent, aristocratic air, no doubt imparted by Empress Eugénie when she built it in 1855 as her Biarritz palace. Napoleonic frippery is everywhere in the public areas, but don't go looking for it in the more standard guest rooms, none of which have sea views. Still, the lobby alone may be worth the price of admission. The three restaurants—Hippocampe (where lunch is served beside the curved pool above the Atlantic), the regal dinner spot Villa Eugénie, and La Rotonde (with its spectacular soaring columns, gilt trim, and sea views)—are all

creatively directed by star chef Jean-Marie Gautier. Don't miss out on his *gazpacho de homard au piment d'Espelette* (lobster gazpacho with Espelette red pepper). **Pros:** historic grounds; gastronomical nirvana; perfect location. **Cons:** staff obsessed with hotel rules; slightly stuffy; magisterially expensive. ✉ *1 av. de l'Impératrice* ☎ *05–59–41–64–00* 🌐 *www.hotel-du-palais.com* *124 rooms, 30 suites* *In-room: a/c, refrigerator, Wi-Fi (some). In-hotel: 3 restaurants, bar, pool, Internet terminal, Wi-Fi hotspot, parking (paid), some pets allowed* ▭ *AE, DC, MC, V* ⊙ *Closed Feb. 11–21* *MAP.*

$ **Le Petit Hôtel**. A few steps from the main beach in front of the casino, this small but cozy hotel offers good value and carefully maintained comfort. Guest rooms are small, but the beds are not. Decor is fetching for the price—rooms in bright daffodil yellows and sleek teal blues lend a stylish note. **Pros:** near the beach; bright and breezy rooms; huge beds. **Cons:** small rooms; no restaurant. ✉ *11 rue Gardères* ☎ *05–59–24–87–00* 🌐 *www.petithotel-biarritz.com* *12 rooms* *In-room: no a/c. In-hotel: Internet terminal* ▭ *AE, MC, V* ⊙ *Closed Feb. 3–18.*

$ **Maïtagaria**. This typical Basque town house 400 yards from the beach is a handy and comfortable family operation that makes you feel more like a guest in a private home than a hotel client. The main drawing room is friendly and well-bred, replete with comfy chairs, yellow drapes, and a fine fireplace, and it sweetly overlooks the lush patio, which is a fine breakfast spot in summer. Guest rooms are efficient and well equipped. **Pros:** value; location; intimacy; leafy garden. **Cons:** somewhat cramped quarters; limited soundproofing (and thus privacy). ✉ *34 av. Carnot* ☎ *05–59–24–26–65* 🌐 *www.hotel-maitagaria.com* *17 rooms* *In-room: no a/c, Wi-Fi (some). In-hotel: Internet terminal, Wi-Fi hotspot, some pets allowed* ▭ *AE, DC, MC, V* ⊙ *Closed Dec. 1–15.*

$$$–$$$$ **Windsor**. This hotel, built in the 1920s, is close to the casino and overlooks the Grand Plage—the main beach of Biarritz. Guest rooms are modern and spiffy—those called Classique are done in cheery oranges and reds, while those named Harmonie will make fans of minimal grays and off-whites happy. In either case, rooms with sea views cost about twice as much as the ones facing the inner courtyard and street. The restaurant, Le Galion, serves up a fine terrine de foie gras with Armagnac, and ravioli stuffed with crab along with some grand panoramic views of the beach. **Pros:** central beachfront location; sea views if you can get them; excellent restaurant. **Cons:** '80s decor; those monotone Harmonie color schemes. ✉ *19 bd. du Général-de-Gaulle* ☎ *05–59–24–08–52* 🌐 *www.hotelwindsorbiarritz.com* *48 rooms* *In-room: no a/c (some), Wi-Fi. In-hotel: restaurant, bar, Internet terminal, Wi-Fi hotspot, parking (paid), some pets allowed* ▭ *AE, DC, MC, V.*

NIGHTLIFE AND THE ARTS

In September the three-week **Le Temps d'Aimer** festival presents dance performances, from classical to hip-hop, in a range of venues throughout the city. They're often at the Théâtre Gare du Midi, a renovated railway station. Troupes such as the Ballets Biarritz, Les Ballets de Monte-Carlo, and leading *étoiles* from other companies take to the stage in an ambitious schedule of events. At the **Casino de Biarritz** (✉ *1 av. Edouard-VII* ☎ *05–59–22–77–77*) you can play the slots or blackjack, or go dancing at the Flamingo. **Le Caveau** (✉ *4 rue Gambetta* ☎ *05–59–24–16–17*) is a mythical Biarritz dance club with guaranteed action every night. **Le Copa** (✉ *24 av. Édouard-VII* ☎ *05–59–24–65–39*) is a popular bar-restaurant-disco complex near the center of town. **Cayo Coco** (✉ *5 rue Jaulerry* ☎ *05–59–22–53–31*) is the Cuban connection, complete with mojitos and salsa classes. **Ibiza** (✉ *1 rue de la Poste* ☎ *05–59–22–33–10*) stays open late and, like its namesake Balearic island, rocks. **Newquay** (✉ *20 pl. Georges Clemenceau* ☎ *05–59–22–19–90*) is a midtown hub of nocturnal activity. **Le Playboy** (✉ *15 rue Clemenceau* ☎ *05–59–24–38–46*) fills with the surfing crowd in season. **Le Queen's Bar** (✉ *25 pl. Clemenceau* ☎ *05–59–24–70–65*) is a comfortable hangout both day and night.

14

SPORTS AND THE OUTDOORS

France's Atlantic Coast has become one of the hottest surfing destinations in the world. The "Endless Summer" arrives in Biarritz every year in late July for the **Roxy Jam** championships and concludes with other events in August. **Désertours Aventure** (✉ *65 av. Maréchal-Juin* ☎ *05–59–41–22–02*) organizes rafting trips on the Nive River and four-wheel-drive-vehicle tours through the Atlantic Pyrénées. **Golf de Biarritz** (✉ *2 av. Edith-Cavell* ☎ *05–59–03–71–80*) has an 18-hole, par-69 course. **Pelote Basque: Biarritz Athletic-club** (✉ *Parc des Sports d'Aguilera* ☎ *05–59–23–91–09*) offers instruction in every type of Basque pelota including *main nue* (bare-handed), *pala* (paddle), *chistera* (with a basketlike racquet), and *cesta punta* (another game played with the same curved basket).

On Wednesday and Saturday at 9 PM in July, August, and September, you can watch pelota games at the **Parc des Sports d'Aguilera** (☎ *05–59–23–91–09*).

ST-JEAN-DE-LUZ

Fodor's Choice ★

23 km (16 mi) southwest of Bayonne, 24 km (18 mi) northeast of San Sebastián, 54 km (32 mi) west of St-Jean-Pied-de-Port.

Back in 1660, Louis XIV chose this tiny fishing village as the place to marry the Infanta Maria Teresa of Spain. Ever since, travelers have journeyed here to enjoy the unique coastal charms of St-Jean. Along the coast between Biarritz and the Spanish border, it remains memorable for its colorful harbor, old streets, curious church, and elegant beach. Its iconic port shares a harbor with its sister town Ciboure, on the other side of the Nivelle River. The glorious days of whaling and cod fishing are long gone, but some historic multihue houses around the docks are evocative enough.

GETTING HERE

The train station (✉ *Av. de Verdun*) has frequent service to Biarritz (11 mins, €5.20) and Bayonne (23 mins, €6.80). Regional ATCRB buses (☎ *05–59–26–06–99*) leave from Place Maréchal Foch by the tourist office. They're slower but cheaper than the train, and give you more beach-town options, including Bayonne (40 mins, €3.50) and Biarritz (35 mins, €3.50).

Visitor Information St-Jean-de-Luz Tourist Office. ✉ *Pl. Foch* ☎ *05–59–26–03–16* 🌐 *www.saint-jean-de-luz.com.*

EXPLORING

The tree-lined **Place Louis-XIV,** alongside the Hôtel de Ville (Town Hall), with its narrow courtyard and dainty statue of Louis XIV on horseback, is the hub of the town. In summer, concerts are offered on the square, as well as the famous "Toro de fuego" festival, which honors the bull with a parade and a papier-mâche beast. Take a tour of the twin-tower **Maison Louis-XIV**. Built as the Château Lohobiague, it housed the French king during his nuptials and is austerely decorated in 17th-century Basque fashion. ✉ *Pl. Louis XIV* ☎ *05–59–26–01–56* 🎫 *€6* ⏲ *June–Sept., daily 10–noon and 2:30–6; Oct.–May by appointment.*

The marriage of the Sun King and the Infanta took place in 1660 in the church of **St-Jean-Baptiste** (✉ *Pl. des Corsaires*). The marriage tied the knot, so to speak, on the Pyrénées Treaty signed by Mazarin on November 7, 1659, ending Spanish hegemony in Europe. Note the church's unusual wooden galleries lining the walls, creating a theater-like effect. Fittingly, St-Jean-Baptiste hosts a "Musique en Côte Basque" festival of early and Baroque music during the first two weeks of September. The church is open daily from 9 to 6, with a three-hour closure for lunch.

Of particular note is the Louis XIII–style **Maison de l'Infante** *(Princess's House)*, between the harbor and the bay, where Maria Teresa of Spain, accompanied by her mother, Queen Anne of Austria and a healthy entourage of courtiers, stayed prior to her marriage to Louis XIV. ✉ *Quai de l'Infante.*

WHERE TO EAT AND STAY

$$$ SEAFOOD ✕ **Chez Dominique.** A walk around the picturesque fishing port to the Ciboure side of the harbor will take you past the house where Maurice Ravel was born (No. 27), and to this rustic maritime eatery. The simple, home-style menu here is based on what the fishing fleet caught that morning; in cold weather, try the hearty *marmitako* (tuna stew). The views over the harbor are unbeatable. ✉ *15 quai M. Ravel* ☎ *05–59–47–29–16* 💳 *AE, DC, MC, V* ⏲ *Closed Mon. and Tues. (except mid-June–Aug.), and mid-Feb.–mid-Mar. No dinner Sun.*

$$ SEAFOOD ✕ **La Taverne Basque.** This well-known midtown standard is one of the old-faithful local dining emporiums, specializing in Basque cuisine with a pronounced maritime emphasis. Try the *ttoro* (a rich fish, crustacean, potato, and vegetable soup). ✉ *5 rue République* ☎ *05–59–26–01–26* 💳 *AE, DC, MC, V* ⏲ *Closed Mon. and Tues. (except July and Aug.), and Mar.*

$ FRENCH ✕ **Txalupa.** The name is Basque for "skiff" or "small boat," and you can feel like you're in one when you're this close to the bay—yachts and fishing vessels go about their business just a few yards away. This well-known haunt with a terrace over the port serves the famous *jambon de Bayonne* (Bayonne ham) in vinegar and garlic sauce, as well as fresh fish and natural produce such as wild mushrooms. ✉ *Pl. Louis-XIV* ☎ *05–59–51–85–52* 💳 *AE, DC, MC, V.*

$$$$ 🏨 **Le Grand Hôtel.** Frequented by high rollers and well-to-do from around the globe, this is the place to stay in this colorful beach town.

Biarritz's main beach, the Grande Plage, is the town's focal point, especially for those who don't have money to lose in the resort casinos.

Traditionally famed as St-Jean-de-Luz's premier hotel, this elegant spot originally built in the 1920s offers panoramic ocean views, intimacy, and a sense of being where the action is. Guest rooms have been redesigned in colorful pastels, wood, and marble, and the unbeatable location at the northern end of the St-Jean-de-Luz beach will make you feel like the Sun King himself. **Pros:** views; comforts; action center. **Cons:** expensive; not too relaxing unless your pockets are *très* deep; slightly self-absorbed staff. ✉ *43 bd. Thiers* ☎ *05–59–26–35–36* 🌐 *www.luzgrandhotel.fr* ⇨ *50 rooms* ♿ *In-room: a/c, refrigerator, Wi-Fi. In-hotel: restaurant, bar, pool, gym, Internet terminal, Wi-Fi hotspot, some pets allowed* ▭ *AE, DC, MC, V* ⊙ *Closed Nov. 27–Dec. 18.*

THE ATLANTIC AND HAUTES-PYRÉNÉES

The Atlantic Pyrénées extend eastward from the Atlantic to the Col du Pourtalet, and encompass Béarn and the mountainous part of the Basque Country. Watching the Pyrénées grow from rolling green foothills in the west to jagged limestone peaks in the Béarn to glacier-studded granite massifs in the Hautes-Pyrénées makes for a dramatic progression of scenery. The Atlantic Pyrénées' first major height is at La Rhune (2,969 feet), known as the Balcon du Côte Basque (Balcony of the Basque Coast). The highest Basque peak is at Orhi (6,617 feet); the Béarn's highest is Pic d'Anie (8,510 feet). Not until Balaïtous (10,375 feet) and Vignemale (10,883 feet), in the Hautes-Pyrénées, does the altitude surpass the 10,000-foot mark. Starting east from St-Jean-de-Luz up the Nivelle River, a series of villages—including Ascain, Sare,

Ainhoa, and Bidarrai—are picturesque stepping stones leading up to St-Jean-Pied-de-Port and on into the Hautes-Pyrénées.

This journey ends in Pau, in the Béarn region, far from the Pays Basque. The Béarn is akin in temperament to the larger region which enfolds it, Gascony. Gascony may be purse-poor, but is certainly rich in scenery and lore. Its proud and touchy temperament is typified in literature by the character d'Artagnan in Dumas's *The Three Musketeers,* and in history by the lords of the château of Pau. An inscription over the château's entrance, TOUCHEZ-Y, SI TU L'OSES—"Touch this if you dare"—was left by the golden-haired Gaston Phoebus (1331–91), 11th count of Foix and viscount of Béarn, a volatile arts lover with a nasty temper who murdered his brother and his only son.

Farther east, past Lourdes, the Hautes-Pyrénées include the highest and most spectacular natural wonders in the cordillera: the legendary Cirque de Gavarnie (natural mountain amphitheater), the Vignemale and Balaïtous peaks, and the Brèche de Roland are the star attractions. Trans-Pyrenean hikers (and drivers) generally prefer moving from west to east for a number of reasons, especially the excellent light prevailing in the late afternoon and evening during the prime months of May to October.

SARE

14 km (8 mi) southeast of St-Jean-de-Luz, 9 km (5½ mi) southwest of Ainhoa on D118: take first left.

The memorably picturesque village of Sare is built around a large fronton, or backboard, where a permanent pelota game rages around the clock. Not surprisingly, the Hôtel de Ville (town hall) offers a permanent exhibition on Pelote Basque (*July and Aug., daily 9–1 and 2–6:30; Sept.–June, daily 3–6*).

GETTING HERE

Buses leave from the train station in St-Jean-de-Luz and go to Sare (30 mins, €3) and neighboring villages.

Visitor Information **Sare Tourist Office.** *Mairie* *05–59–54–20–14.*

EXPLORING

Sare's chief attractions are colorful wood-beam and whitewashed Basque architecture, the 16th-century late-Romanesque church with its lovely triple-decker interior, and the **Ospitale Zaharra** pilgrim's hospice behind the church. More than a dozen tiny chapels sprinkled around Sare were built as ex-votos by seamen who survived Atlantic storms. The town also has several interesting buildings constructed when it was a busy smuggling hub throughout the 19th century. Not to miss is the typical Basque house **Ortillopitz** (*Mar.–Nov., daily 9–1 and 2–6:30* *www.ortillopitz.com*), a 16th-century country manor offering farmhouse charm and scenic vistas. The **Musée du Gâteau Basque** (*www.legateaubasque.com* *Daily 9–1 and 2–6:30*), tracing the evolution of the most famous of Basque pastries, is another Sare treat.

Up the Sare Valley are the panoramic Col de Lizarrieta and the **Grottes de Sare**, where you can study up on Basque culture and history at the

Musée Ethnographique (Ethnographic Museum) and take a guided tour (in five languages) for 1 km (½ mi) underground and see a son-et-lumière (sound-and-light) show. *05–59–54–21–88* *www.sare.fr* *€8* *Feb.–Dec., weekdays 2–5, weekends 1–5.*

Fodor's Choice ★ West of Sare on D4, at the Col de St-Ignace, take the **Petit Train de la Rhune**, a tiny wood-panel cogwheel train (one of only three in France) that reaches the less-than-dizzying speed of 5 mph while climbing up La Rhune peak. The views of the Bay of Biscay, the Pyrénées, and the grassy hills of the Basque farmland are wonderful. Most round-trips last 90 minutes. *05–59–54–20–26* *www.rhune.com* *€14* *Daily, Mar. 28–Nov. 5 (closed Mon. and Thurs. Oct. 1–27).*

WHERE TO STAY

¢–$ ★ **Baratxartea.** This little inn 1 km (½ mi) from the center of Sare in one of the town's prettiest and most ancient *quartiers* is a beauty. Monsieur Fagoaga's family-run hotel and restaurant occupy a 16th-century town house complete with exposed wood-beam framework and surrounded by some of the finest rural Basque architecture in Labourd. **Pros:** upland location 20 minutes from beach; personalized family service; splendid dining. **Cons:** can get steamy in the August canicule; no Internet connection. *Quartier Ihalar* *05–59–54–20–48* *www.hotel-baratxartea.com* *14 rooms* *In-room: no a/c, Wi-Fi. In-hotel: restaurant, Wi-Fi hotspot, some pets allowed* *AE, DC, MC, V* *Closed mid-Nov.–mid-Mar.* *MAP.*

AINHOA

Fodor's Choice ★ *9 km (5½ mi) east of Sare, 23 km (14 mi) southeast of St-Jean-de-Luz, 31 km (19 mi) northwest of St-Jean-Pied-de-Port.*

The Basque village of Ainhoa is officially registered among the villages selected by the national tourist ministry as the prettiest in France. A showcase town for the Labourd region established in the 13th century, the streets of Ainhoa are lined with lovely 16th- to 18th-century houses graced with whitewashed walls, flower-filled balconies, brightly painted shutters, and carved master beams. The Romanesque church of **Notre-Dame de l'Assomption** has a traditional Basque three-tier wooden interior with carved railings and ancient oak stairs. Explore Ainhoa's little streets, dotted with artisanal ateliers and art galleries. Unfortunately, you'll need your own wheels to get to Ainhoa.

WHERE TO STAY

$$–$$$ Fodor's Choice ★ **Ithurria.** A registered historic monument, this was once a staging post on the fabled medieval pilgrims' route to Santiago de Compostela. If you're doing a modern version of the pilgrims' journey or just need a stopover on your way deeper into the mountains, the Ithurria—set in a 17th-century building in the prevailing Basque style and surrounded by a lovely garden—will give you a fine atmospheric night. All wood beams and antique accents, the rustic dining room (no lunch Thursday, except in July and August) is the gemstone here, with fare to match, combining inland game and fresh seafood from the Basque Coast in creative ways. Guest rooms are modern, comfortable, and tastefully decorated. **Pros:**

spotless; rustic charm; cheery and friendly family service. **Cons:** you'll understand why they call it luggage while hauling your gear from car to room; room decor undistinguished. ✉ *Rue Principale* ☎ *05–59–29–92–11* 🌐 *www.ithurria.com* *27 rooms* *In-room: refrigerator, Wi-Fi. In-hotel: restaurant, bar, pool, gym, Internet terminal, Wi-Fi hotspot, some pets allowed* *AE, DC, MC, V* *Closed Nov.–Apr.*

$–$$ **Oppoca.** This 17th-century *relais,* or stagecoach relay station, on Ainhoa's main square and pelota court remains one of the loveliest Basque houses in town. Guest rooms are small but adequate and the owners are a jolly group, always ready to share their knowledge about the locals and the locale. The restaurant serves creative interpretations of traditional Basque specialties. **Pros:** helpful service; superb fare; historic site. **Cons:** cramped spaces in some rooms; center of town can be resonant on weekends and holiday eves. ✉ *Pl. du Fronton s/n* ☎ *05–59–29–90–72* 🌐 *www.oppoca.com* *10 rooms* *In-room: Wi-Fi. In-hotel: restaurant, bar, Internet terminal, some pets allowed* *AE, DC, MC, V* *Closed mid-Nov.–mid-Dec.* *MAP.*

ST-JEAN-PIED-DE-PORT

54 km (33 mi) east of Biarritz, 46 km (28 mi) west of Larrau.

St-Jean-Pied-de-Port, a fortified town on the Nive River, got its name from its position at the foot (*pied*) of the mountain pass (*port*) of Roncevaux (Roncesvalles). The pass was the setting for *La Chanson de Roland* (*The Song of Roland*), the anonymous 11th-century epic poem considered the true beginning of French literature. The bustling town center, a major stop for pilgrims en route to Santiago de Compostela, seems, after a tour through the Soule, like a frenzied metropolitan center—even in winter. In summer, especially around the time of Pamplona's San Fermin blowout (the running of the bulls, July 7–14), the place is filled to the gills and is somewhere between exciting and unbearable.

GETTING HERE

SNCF trains between Bayonne and St-Jean-Pied-de-Port (1 hr, 13 mins; €8.30) depart six times daily in each direction. The bus company STAB (☎ *05–59–14–15–16* 🌐 *www.bus-stab.com*) connects Bayonne with St-Jean-Pied-de-Port and towns in between.

Visitor Information **St-Jean-Pied-de-Port Tourist Office.** ✉ *14 pl. Charles-de-Gaulle* ☎ *05–59–37–03–57.*

EXPLORING

Walk into the old section of St-Jean-Pied-de-Port through the Porte de France, just behind and to the left of the tourist office; climb the steps on the left up to the walkway circling the ramparts, and walk around to the stone stairway down to the Rue de l'Église. The church of **Notre-Dame-du-Bout-du-Pont** *(Our Lady of the End of the Bridge)*, known for its magnificent doorway, is at the bottom of this cobbled street. The church is a characteristically Basque three-tier structure, designed for women to sit on the ground floor, men to be in the first balcony, and the choir in the loft above.

From the **Pont Notre-Dame** *(Notre-Dame Bridge)* you can watch the wild trout in the Nive (also an Atlantic salmon stream) as they pluck mayflies off the surface. Note that fishing is *défendu* (forbidden) in town. Upstream, along the left bank, is another wooden bridge. Cross it and then walk around and back through town, crossing back to the left bank on the main road.

On **Rue de la Citadelle** are several sights of interest: the **Maison Arcanzola** (Arcanzola House), at No. 32 (1510); the **Maison des Évêques** (Bishops' House), at No. 39; and the famous **Prison des Évêques** (Bishops' Prison), next door to it.

WORD OF MOUTH

"And that Monday outdoor farmers' market in St. Jean Pied de Port merits another visit. All the very best purveyors of *brebis* (ewe's cheeses), Les Aldudes hams, honey, black cherry preserves, gâteau basque, wines, spirits, come to you—you don't have to go to every farm to visit them (although that's quite fun)—you have them together under one "canopy." Ditto to the wonderful indoor markets in St. Jean de Luz and Biarritz." —Robert2533

14

Continue up along Rue de la Citadelle to get to the **Citadelle**, a classic Vauban fortress, now occupied by a school. The views from the Citadelle, complete with maps identifying the surrounding heights and valleys, are panoramic.

WHERE TO EAT AND STAY

$$ FRENCH ✕ **Chez Arbillaga**. Tucked inside the citadel ramparts, this lively bistro is a sound choice for lunch or dinner. The food represents what the Basques do best: simple cooking of excellent quality, such as *agneau de lait à la broche* (roast lamb) in winter, or *coquilles St-Jacques au lard fumé* (scallops with bacon) in summer. ✉ *8 rue de l'Église* ☎ *05–59–37–06–44* 💳 *AE, DC, MC, V* ⊗ *Closed 1st 2 wks of June and Oct., and Wed. Jan.–May.*

$$$$ FRENCH Fodor's Choice ★ ✕ **Les Pyrénées**. A former stagecoach inn on the route to Santiago de Compostela now houses the best restaurant in the Pyrénées, directed by renowned master chef Firmin Arrambide. Specializing in contemporary *cuisine d'auteur,* Arrambide's flair is characterized by refined interpretations of Pays Basque cooking based on local Pyrenean delicacies, such as wine sauces from the nearby Irouléguy vineyards, the famous *fromage de brebis* sheep's milk cheese, and the best sweet and spicy bell peppers in France. Add in luxury—*saumon frais de l'Adour grillé à la béarnais* or his dishes featuring wood pigeon, langoustines, and truffles—and you know why everyone is talking. The desserts are almost more fabulous: Arrambide's recipe for gâteau basque has circled the world. The restaurant is closed Tuesday from late September to the end of June; no dinner Monday November to March. For the closest beds to the best cuisine in the Pyrénées, opt for one of the 14 rooms at this inn; some are small, four have balconies, the decor is Relais & Châteaux–modern, and facilities include public Internet and Wi-Fi and a pool. Needless to say, you'll want to invest in one of the board plans! ✉ *19 pl. Charles-de-Gaulle* ☎ *05–59–37–01–01* 🌐 *www.relais-chateaux.com/pyrenees* 💳 *AE, DC, MC, V* ⊗ *Closed Jan. 5–28 and Nov. 20–Dec. 22.*

$ **Central Hôtel.** Get the best quality for the price in town at this family-run hotel and restaurant (no dinner Monday; closed Tuesday March to June) over the Nive, where trout could be literally—though illegally—caught from certain rooms. The wonderfully musical 200-year-old oak staircase is another memorable detail. The owners speak Basque, Spanish, French, English, and some German, so communicating is rarely a problem. The cuisine is superb, especially the lamb and *magret de canard* (duck breast). **Pros:** location (as suggested by the name of the hotel); personal family service; river sounds and views. **Cons:** creaky bedsprings; can be hot in midsummer; village life starts early and here you are at the hub of it all. ✉ *1 pl. Charles-de-Gaulle* ☎ *05–59–37–00–22* *14 rooms* *In-room: no a/c. In-hotel: restaurant, Internet terminal* *AE, DC, MC, V* *Closed Dec.–Feb.* *MAP.*

SAUVETERRE-DE-BÉARN

Fodor's Choice ★

39 km (23 mi) northeast of St-Jean-Pied-de-Port.

Visitor Information Sauveterre-de-Béarn Tourist Office. ✉ *Mairie* ☎ *05–59–38–58–65* *www.tourisme.fr/office-de-tourisme/sauveterre-de-bearn.htm.*

EXPLORING

Enchantingly picturesque, the Romanesque-turning-into-Gothic church here crowns a hill from which unfolds a storybook vista—in the foreground is a postcard-perfect group of buildings—the Gave d'Oloron, the fortified 12th-century drawbridge, the lovely Montréal Tower, while the Pyrénées rise romantically in the distance. You cannot come to this region and miss this town.

The bridge, known both as the **Vieux Pont** *(Old Bridge)* and the Pont de la Légende (Bridge of the Legend), is associated with the legend of Sancie, widow of Gaston V de Béarn. Accused of murdering a child after her husband's death in 1170, Sancie was subjected to the "Judgment of God" and thrown, bound hand and foot, from the bridge by order of her brother, the king of Navarre. When the river carried her safely to the bank, she was deemed exonerated of all charges.

WHERE TO STAY

$ **La Maison de Navarre.** A pink-hue and green-shutter "maison de maître," this charming town house in the Saint Marc quarter of Sauveterre-de-Béarn is imbedded in a lush garden a five-minute walk from the *gave* (river). The cuisine is Béarnais with cosmopolitan touches, and the guest rooms are cozy and colorful. **Pros:** nonpareil dining; views over the rooftops of Sauveterre; intimate and personal service. **Cons:** better for a single night than a prolonged stay; slightly claustrophobic. ✉ *Rte. Départementale 933* ☎ *05–59–38–55–28* *www.lamaisondenavarre.com* *7 rooms* *In-room: a/c, refrigerator, Wi-Fi. In-hotel: restaurant, pool, Internet terminal, Wi-Fi hotspot* *AE, DC, MC, V* *Closed Aug. 17–Sept. 3, Nov. 1–30, and Feb. 25–Mar. 9* *MAP.*

EUGÉNIE-LES-BAINS

92 km (53 mi) northeast of Sauveterre-de-Béarn, 56 km (34 mi) north of Pau, 140 km (87 mi) south of Bordeaux.

GETTING HERE

For transport to Eugénie-les-Bains from Pau, CITRAM Pyrénées (☎ *05–59–27–22–22* ⊕ *www.annuaire-des-autocaristes.com*) dispatches three daily buses from Pau to the town of Aire-sur-l'Adour (1 hr, 15 mins; €13.50). For transport from Aire-sur-l'Adour to Eugénie-les-Bains, RDTL (*Réseau Départementale des Transports des Landes* ☎ *05–58–56–80–80* ⊕ *www.rdtl.fr*) offers regular bus connections (20 mins, €6.50). For transport to Eugénie-les-Bains via Dax (71 km), SNCF (⊕ *www.sncf.com*) offers 20 trains daily from Bayonne to Dax (41 mins, €8.75). For transport from Dax to Eugénie-les-Bains, contact RDTL (☎ *05–58–56–80–80* ⊕ *www.rdtl.fr*). The Dax to Hagetmau bus connects with the Hagetmau to Aire-sur-l'Adour line, which stops in Eugénie-les-Bains (1 hr, 30 mins; €14.80).

EXPLORING

Empress Eugénie popularized Eugénie-les-Bains at the end of the 19th century, and in return the villagers renamed the town after her. Michel and Christine Guérard brought the village back to life in 1973 by putting together one of France's most fashionable thermal retreats, which became the birthplace of nouvelle cuisine, thanks to the great talents of chef Michel. Their little kingdom now includes two restaurants, two hotels, a cooking school, and a spa. The 13 therapeutic treatments address everything from weight loss to rheumatism. Two springs are certified by the French Ministry of Health: L'Impératrice and Christine-Marie, whose 39°C (102°F) waters come from nearly 1,300 feet below the surface.

WHERE TO STAY

$$–$$$ ★ **La Maison Rose.** A (relatively) low-cost, low-calorie alternative to Les Prés d'Eugénie, Michel and Christine Guérard's "Pink House" beckons with a sybaritically simple spa approach. Set in a renovated, super-stylish 18th-century farmhouse adorned with old paintings hung with ribbons, rustic antiques, and Pays Basque handicrafts, this is a retreat that would have delighted the sober Madame de Maintenon—if she had wanted to lose weight, that is. This is a serious spa, complete with slimming cures and the most stylish relaxation room in France. No room service—everyone eats in the main dining room, a two-story, beam-ceiling delight. The kitchen's touch remains an inventive benediction to local produce. **Pros:** much easier on the plastic; more relaxed; superb dining without stuffing. **Cons:** cravings for the foie-gras treatment next door. ✉ *Eugénie-les-Bains* ☎ *05–58–05–06–07* ⊕ *www.michelguerard.com* *26 rooms, 5 studios* *In-room: no a/c, kitchen, refrigerator, Wi-Fi. In-hotel: restaurant, pool, gym, Internet terminal, Wi-Fi hotspot, some pets allowed* ▭ *AE, DC, MC, V* ¶◎| *MAP.*

$$$$ Fodor's Choice ★ **Les Prés d'Eugénie.** Ever since Michel Guérard's eponymous restaurant fired the first shots of the nouvelle revolution in the late 1970s, the excellence of this suave culinary landmark has been a given (so much so that the breakfast here outdoes dinner at most other places).

The Hautes-Pyrénées have some of the best hiking trails in Europe, especially those found on the way to the Cirque de Gavarnie.

Thanks to Guérard's signature flair, *cuisine minceur*—the slimmer's dream—collides with the lusty fare of the Landes region (langoustines garnished with foie gras and mesclun greens, lobster with confettied calf's head). In the lovely Second Empire–style hotel, set in a fine garden, grandeur prevails and rooms are formal. However, rooms in the "annex"—the former 18th-century **Couvent des Herbes**—have an understated luxe and look out over the herb garden. To top it all off, the complex includes an excellent spa, dance studio, two pools, and a 9-hole golf course, while "theme" weeks are devoted to cooking, perfumes, wines, or gardening. **Pros:** Guérard in full; magical cuisine; intelligent and attentive service. **Cons:** too beautiful to close your eyes and go to sleep (fortunately, Bacchus comes to your rescue). ✉ *Eugénie-les-Bains* ☎ *05–58–05–06–07, 05–58–05–05–05 restaurant reservations* 🌐 *www.michelguerard.com* *22 rooms, 6 suites* *In-room: no a/c, refrigerator, Wi-Fi. In-hotel: restaurant, bar, golf course, tennis courts, pools, gym, Internet terminal, Wi-Fi hotspot, some pets allowed* 💳 *AE, DC, MC, V* 🍽 *MAP.*

PAU

66 km (36 mi) southeast of Eugénie-les-Bains, 106 km (63 mi) east of Bayonne and Biarritz.

The stunning views, mild climate, and elegance of Pau—the historic capital of Béarn, a state annexed to France in 1620—make it a lovely place to visit and a convenient gateway to the Pyrénées. The birthplace of King Henri IV, Pau was "discovered" in 1815 by British officers returning from the Peninsular War in Spain, and it soon became a prominent winter resort town. Fifty years later English-speaking inhabitants made up one-third of Pau's population, many believing in the medicinal benefits of mountain air (later shifting their loyalties to Biarritz for the sea air). They started the Pont-Long Steeplechase, still one of the most challenging in Europe, in 1841; created France's first golf course here in 1856; introduced fox hunting to the region; and founded a famous British tea shop where students now smoke strong cigarettes while drinking black coffee.

GETTING HERE

Set 12 km (7 mi) north of Pau, the Pau-Pyrénées airport (✉ *Aéroport Pau-Pyrénées, Uzein* ☎ *05–59–33–33–00* 🌐 *www.pau.aeroport.fr*) receives daily flights from Paris, London, Lyon, and Amsterdam, among other points. SNCF connects Pau with Paris (5 hrs, 34 mins; €81.50) with four trains daily. Trains connect with Biarritz (1½ hrs, €18.10) five times daily. In addition, you can take the train to Lourdes (29 mins, €7.50), Bayonne (1 hr, 19 mins; €16), and Toulouse (2 hrs, 24 mins; €28.40). STAP buses (☎ *05–59–14–15–16* 🌐 *www.bus-stap.com*) connects Pau with Bayonne and Toulouse. To reach the center of Pau from the train station on Avenue Gaston-Lacoste, cross the street and take the funicular up the hill to Place Royale.

Visitor Information Pau Tourist Office. ✉ *Pl. Royale* ☎ *05–59–27–27–08* 🌐 *www.ville-pau.fr.*

EXPLORING

Fodor's Choice ★ Pau's regal past is commemorated at its **Musée National du Château de Pau**, begun in the 14th century by Gaston Phoebus, the flamboyant count of Béarn. The building was transformed into a Renaissance palace in the 16th century by Marguerite d'Angoulême, sister of François I. A woman of diverse gifts, she wrote pastorals, many performed in the château's sumptuous gardens. Her bawdy *Heptameron*—written at age 60—furnishes as much sly merriment today as it did when read by her doting kingly brother. Marguerite's grandson, the future king of France Henri IV, was born in the château in 1553. Exhibits connected to Henri's life and times are displayed regularly, along with portraits of the most significant of his alleged 57 lovers and mistresses. His cradle, a giant turtle shell, is on exhibit in his bedroom, one of the sumptuous, tapestry-lined royal apartments. ✉ *Rue du Château* ☎ *05–59–82–38–00* 🌐 *www.musee-chateau-pau.fr* 🎟 *€6, free 1st Sun. of month* ⏲ *Apr.–Oct., daily 9:30–11:30 and 2–5:45; Nov.–Mar., daily 9:30–11:30 and 2–4:30.*

To continue on your royal path, follow the **Sentiers du Roy** (King's Paths), a marked trail just below the Boulevard des Pyrénées. When you reach the top, walk along until the sights line up with the mountain peaks you see. For some man-made splendors instead, head to the **Musée des Beaux-Arts** and feast on works by El Greco, Degas, and Rodin. ✉ *Rue Mathieu-Lalanne* ☎ *05–59–27–33–02* 🎟 *€3* ⏲ *Tues.–Sun. 10–noon and 2–6.*

WHERE TO EAT AND STAY

$$$ FRENCH Fodor's Choice ★ ✕ **Chez Ruffet.** Well worth the short drive (or, even better, a 2-km [1-mi] hike) out to Jurançon, this 18th-century farmhouse with its classically lovely dovecote and ancient beams, floorboards, and fireplace is the best restaurant in or near Pau. Chef Stéphane Carrade has imbibed deeply from the masters—Bocuse, Guérard, Troisgros—and promptly taken off in all directions, mostly his own. Fascinated with worldwide products and preparations, Carrade unabashedly rolls out his *agneau d'Aragón clouté au lomo Ibérico et badigeonné au miso et gingembre* (lamb from Aragón with Ibérico fillet daubed with miso and ginger), combining Aragonese, Andalusian, Japanese, and Moorish flavors. His *fois frais de canard cuit à l'étouffé aux feuilles de citronnier et sarments de vignes* (fresh foie stewed with lemon leaves and grapevine cuttings) is another signature offering. ✉ *3 av. Ch. Touzet, Jurançon* ☎ *05–59–06–25–13* 🌐 *www.restaurant-chezruffet.com* 💳 *AE, DC, MC, V* ⊙ *Closed Sept. 12–19 and Dec. 20–Jan. 14. No dinner Sun. No lunch Wed. or Sat.*

TOUT SWEET

While in Pau, enjoy some of life's sweetest pleasures at **Confiserie Francis Miot** (✉ *48 rue Joffre* ☎ *05–59–27–69–51*) with his signature delicacies, "Les Coucougnettes du Vert Galant"—small, red, tender bonbons made from almond paste. At the gates of Pau in the village of Uzos, Miot has his own **Musée des Arts Sucrés** (✉ *Rte. de Nay, Uzos* ☎ *05–59–35–05–56* 🌐 *www.feerie-gourmande.com* 🎫 *€5* ⊙ *Mon.–Sat. 10–noon and 2–5*).

$$ FRENCH ✕ **Henri IV.** On a quiet pedestrian street near the château, this dining room with its open fire is a cozy find for a wet and freezing night in winter, while the terrace is a shady place to cool off in summer. Traditional Béarn cooking here stars *magret de canard* (breast of duck) cooked over coals and *cuisses de grenouille* (frogs' legs), sautéed dry and crunchy in parsley and garlic. ✉ *18 rue Henri IV* ☎ *05–59–27–54–43* 💳 *AE, DC, MC, V.*

$ **Hôtel de Gramont.** Frequented by a mixed bag of travelers young and old seeking respectable lodging at reasonable prices, this 17th-century stagecoach stop is Pau's oldest inn and a cozy and convenient base. Ask for one of the *chambres mansardées* (dormered bedrooms) under the eaves overlooking the Hédas. **Pros:** a short walk from the Château de Pau and overlooking the oldest part of town; relaxing and unpretentious; easy on the wallet. **Cons:** breakfast to be avoided; small rooms. ✉ *3 pl. de Gramont* ☎ *05–59–27–84–04* 🌐 *www.hotelgramont.com* *34 rooms* *In-room: a/c (some), Wi-Fi* 💳 *AE, DC, MC, V.*

NIGHTLIFE AND THE ARTS

During the music and arts **Festival de Pau**, theatrical and musical events take place almost every evening from mid-July to late August, nearly all of them gratis. Nightlife in Pau revolves around the central Triangle area (surrounded by Rue Lespy, Rue Émile Garet, and Rue Castetnau). The streets around Pau's imposing château are sprinkled with cozy pubs and dining spots, although the **casino** (✉ *Parc Beaumont* ☎ *05–59–27–06–92*) offers racier entertainment.

LOURDES

41 km (27 mi) southeast of Pau, 19 km (12 mi) southwest of Tarbes.

The mountain town of Lourdes is probably the most famous Catholic pilgrimage site (and sight) in the world. Some 5 million visitors come each year from every corner of the globe, many of them not Christians, with most in quest of a miraculous cure for sickness or disability.

GETTING HERE AND AROUND

Lourdes's train station on the Avenue de la Gare is one of the busiest in the country. So many pilgrim trains arrive between Easter and October that the station has a separate entrance to accommodate the religious masses. From the train station, local buses take anxious visitors to the grotto every 20 minutes (Easter–October). Trains go directly to Pau (22 mins, €7.20), Bayonne (2 hrs, 4 mins; €21.20), and Toulouse (1 hr, 38 mins; 2 hrs; €20.50).

Visitor Information Lourdes Tourist Office. ✉ *Pl. Beyramalu* ☎ *05–62–42–77–40* 🌐 *www.lourdes-france.com.*

EXPLORING

The origin of what is now a huge pilgrimage center (and business) lies in the humblest of origins. In February 1858 Bernadette Soubirous, a 14-year-old miller's daughter, claimed she saw the Virgin Mary in the **Grotte de Massabielle**, near the Gave de Pau (in all, she had 18 visions). Bernadette dug in the grotto, releasing a gush of water from a spot where no spring had flowed before. From then on, pilgrims thronged the Massabielle rock for the water's supposed healing powers, though church authorities reacted skeptically. It took four years for the miracle to be authenticated by Rome and a sanctuary erected over the grotto. In 1864 the first organized procession was held. Today there are six official annual pilgrimages between Easter and All Saints' Day, the most important on August 15. In fall and winter there are far fewer visitors, but that will be a plus for those in search of peace and tranquillity.

Lourdes celebrated the centenary of Bernadette Soubirous's visions by building the world's largest underground church, the **Basilique Souterraine St-Pie X**, with space for 20,000 people—more than the town's permanent population. The Basilique Supérieure (1871), tall and white, hulks nearby.

The **Pavillon Notre-Dame**, across from St-Pie X, houses the **Musée Bernadette** (Museum of Stained-Glass Mosaic Religious Art), with mementos of Bernadette's life and an illustrated history of the pilgrimages. In the basement is a collection devoted to religious gem-work relics. ✉ *72 rue de la Grotte* ☎ *05–62–94–13–15* 🎫 *Free* ⏲ *July–Nov., daily 9:30–11:45 and 2:30–6:15; Dec.–June, Wed.–Mon. 9:30–11:45 and 2:30–5:45.*

Across the river is the **Moulin de Boly** *(Boly Mill)*, where Bernadette was born on January 7, 1844. ✉ *12 rue Bernadette-Soubirous* 🎫 *Free* ⏲ *Easter–mid-Oct., daily 9:30–11:45 and 2:30–5:45.*

The **cachot**, a tiny room where, in extreme poverty, Bernadette and her family took refuge in 1856, can also be visited. ✉ *15 rue des Petits-Fos-*

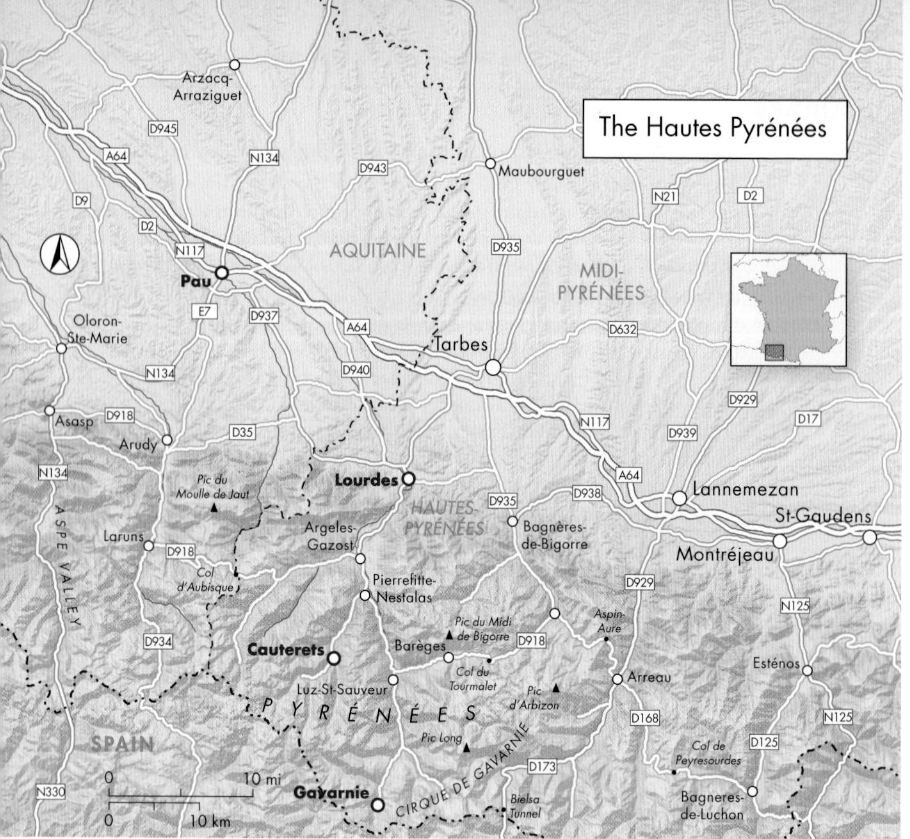

sés ☎ *05–62–94–51–30* 🎟 *Free* 🕑 *Easter–mid-Oct., daily 9:30–11:45 and 2:30–5:30; mid-Oct.–Easter, daily 2:30–5:30.*

Fodor's Choice ★ The **château** on the hill above town can be reached by escalator, by 131 steps, or by the ramp up from Rue du Bourg (from which a small Basque cemetery with ancient discoidal stones can be seen). Once a prison, the castle now contains the **Musée Pyrénéen**, one of France's best provincial museums, devoted to the popular customs, arts, and history of the Pyrénées. ✉ *25 rue du Fort* ☎ *05–62–94–02–04* 🎟 *€5* 🕑 *Easter–mid-Oct., daily 9–noon and 2–7, last admission at 6; mid-Oct.–Easter, Wed.–Mon. 9–noon and 2–7, last admission at 6.*

WHERE TO STAY

¢ 🏨 **Hôtel Albret/La Taverne de Bigorre.** The Dubreuil family's popular establishment serves traditional French mountain cooking such as hearty garbure in a large dining salon warmed up by cheerful print drapes. Guest rooms, in whites and grays, are clean and comfortable, with a personal touch that is very welcome in Lourdes. **Pros:** simple country lodging; family touch; kind to your budget. **Cons:** sometimes cramped rooms; devoid of modern technology such as Internet. ✉ *21 pl. du Champ Commun* ☎ *05–62–94–75–00* 🌐 *www.lourdes-hotelalbret.com* 🛏 *26 rooms* 👍 *In-room: no a/c. In-hotel: restaurant, bar, parking (paid)* 💳 *AE, DC, MC, V* 🕑 *Closed Jan.*

CAUTERETS

30 km (19 mi) south of Lourdes, 49 km (30 mi) south of Tarbes.

GETTING HERE

Unless you're coming to Cauterets from a hiking path, only one road leads into town, on which SNCF buses travel to and from Lourdes seven times a day (1 hr, €6.80).

Visitor Information Cauterets Tourist Office. ✉ *15 Cauterets* ☎ *05–62–92–50–27.*

EXPLORING

Cauterets (which derives from the word for hot springs in the local *bigourdan* dialect) is a spa and resort town (for long-term treatments) high in the Pyrénées. It has been revered since Roman times for thermal baths thought to cure maladies ranging from back pain to female sterility. Novelist Victor Hugo (1802–85) womanized here; Lady Aurore Dudevant—better known as the writer George Sand (1804–76)—is said to have discovered her feminism here. Other famous visitors include Gastón Phoébus, Chateaubriand, Sarah Bernhardt, King Edward VII of England, and Spain's King Alfonso XIII.

GAVARNIE

30 km (19 mi) south of Cauterets on D921, 50 km (31 mi) south of Lourdes.

Geologists point to the famous natural wonder that is the Cirque de Gavarnie as one of the world's most formidable examples of the effects of glacial erosion; the cliffs were worn away by the advancing and retreating ice sheets of the Pleistocene epoch. Seeing it, one can understand its irresistible appeal for mountain climbers—it is only fitting that there is a statue of one of the first of these, Lord Russell, in the village.

GETTING HERE

From Lourdes SNCF buses connect to Luz-St-Sauveur (34 mins, €4.50); Gavarnie is 20 km (12 mi) south of Luz-St-Sauveur by taxi or Capou bus service (30 mins, €4.50).

Visitor Information Gavarnie Tourist Office. ✉ *In center of village* ☎ *05–62–92–49–10* 🌐 *www.gavarnie.com.*

EXPLORING

Fodor's Choice ★ A spectacular natural amphitheater, the **Cirque de Gavarnie** has been dubbed the "Colosseum of nature" and inspired many writers, including Victor Hugo. At its foot is the village of Gavarnie, a good base for exploring the mountains in the region. The Cirque is a Cinerama wall of peaks that is one of the world's most remarkable examples of glacial erosion and a daunting challenge to mountaineers. Horses and donkeys, rented in the village, are the traditional way to reach the head of the valley (though walking is preferable), where the Hôtel du Cirque has hosted six generations of visitors. When the upper snows melt, numerous streams tumble down from the cliffs to form spectacular waterfalls;

the greatest of them, Europe's highest, is the **Grande Cascade,** dropping nearly 1,400 feet.

Another dramatic sight is 12 km (7 mi) west of the village of Gavarnie. Take D921 up to the Col de Boucharo, where you can park and walk five hours up to the **Brèche de Roland** glacier (you cross it during the last two hours of the hike). For a taste of mountain life, have lunch high up at the Club Alpin Français's **Refuge de Sarradets ou de la Brèche.** This is a serious climb, only feasible from mid-June to mid-September, for which you need (at least) good hiking shoes and sound physical conditioning. Crampons and ice axes are available for rent in Gavarnie; check with the **Gavarnie Tourist Office** (✉ *Pl. de la Bergère* ☎ *05–62–92–49–10*) for weather reports and for information about guided tours.

WHERE TO EAT AND STAY

$ FRENCH ★ ✕ **Hôtel du Cirque.** With its legendary views of the Cirque de Gavarnie, this spot is magical at sunset. Despite its name, it's just a restaurant, but not just any old eating establishment: the *garbure* here is as delicious as the sunset is grand. Seventh-generation owner Pierre Vergez claims his recipe using water from the Cirque and *cocos de Tarbes,* or *haricots tarbais* (Tarbes broad beans) is unique. ✉ *1-hr walk above village of Gavarnie* ☎ *05–62–92–48–02* ▭ *MC, V* ⏲ *Closed mid-Sept.–mid-June.*

$$$ **Hotel Vignemale.** Behind an imposing granite facade with steep rooflines reflecting the towering Hautes Pyrénées to the south, this spacious château-like hotel overlooks the rushing Gave (river) de Gavarnie. Guest rooms are ample and sunny, with floor-to-ceiling windows and gleaming tile floors, while the sunny breakfast terrace out front is the ideal way to start a day in the mountains. Views over the Cirque de Gavarnie and the 3,250-meter (10,725-foot) Marbore peak beyond are mesmerizing. **Pros:** rushing water music provided by the stream; a sense of space; a small hotel's personalized service. **Cons:** small balconies; decor somewhat dated; bathrooms not as splendid as the facade might suggest. ✉ *Village de Gavarnie* ☎ *05–62–92–40–00* 🌐 *www.hotel-vignemale.com* *7 rooms* *In-room: no a/c, Wi-Fi. In-hotel: restaurant, bar, Wi-Fi hotspot* ▭ *AE, DC, MC, V* ⏲ *Closed Nov. 4–Dec. 20* *MAP.*

NIGHTLIFE AND THE ARTS

Every July Gavarnie holds an outdoor ballet and music performance, **La Fête des Pyrénées** (☎ *05–62–92–49–10 information*), using the Cirque de Gavarnie as a backdrop; showtime is at sunset. For information contact the tourist office.

15

Bordeaux and the Wine Country

WORD OF MOUTH

"Some areas of France are dripping with 'über-quaint' sites. They're also dripping with tourists. Bordeaux has a more real-life feel than most of Provence does—the only exception is the town of St-Emilion."

—Josh

WELCOME TO BORDEAUX AND THE WINE COUNTRY

TOP REASONS TO GO

★ **La Route de Médoc:** With eight appellations alone in this one small area and names like Rothschild, Latour, and Margaux on the bottles, this is one itinerary that leaves no sour grapes.

★ **Bordeaux, Wine Mecca:** Flourishing around the banks of the Gironde estuary, Bordeaux's great wine shippers gave their city center a nearly royal 18th-century elegance.

★ **Buy a Rothschild:** While the family's Château Lafite is often locked, the arms are wide open to oenophiles at Château Mouton-Rothschild, thanks to its visitor center and museum.

★ **St-Émilion, Medieval Jewel:** With its 13th-century ramparts, cobblestone streets, and rock-face hermitage, this fortified hilltop town presides over one of the Bordeaux region's richest wine districts.

★ **Bordeaux Bacchanal:** Don't miss the four-day wine extravaganza at the end of June, when the appellations come to party on Bordeaux's biggest square.

1 Bordeaux. Dominated geographically by the nearby Atlantic Ocean and historically by great wine merchants and shippers, Bordeaux has long ranked among France's largest cities. There is considerable, if concentrated, affluence, which hides behind dour 18th-century facades. Showing off may not be a regional trait but, happily, the city fathers did provide a bevy of cultural riches to discover, including the spectacular Place de la Bourse, the Grand Théâtre, and the Musée des Beaux-Arts.

2 The Médoc. Northwest of Bordeaux, this triangulated peninsula extends from the Garonne River to the Atlantic coast. Dutch engineers drained this marshy landscape in the 18th century to expose the gravelly soil that is excellent for growing grapes, and today the Médoc is fabled as the home of several of the *grands crus classés*, including Château Margaux, Château Latour, Château Lafite-Rothschild, and Château Mouton-Rothschild. Public buses run here but stops are often in the middle of nowhere—a car, bike, or guided tour may be the best option.

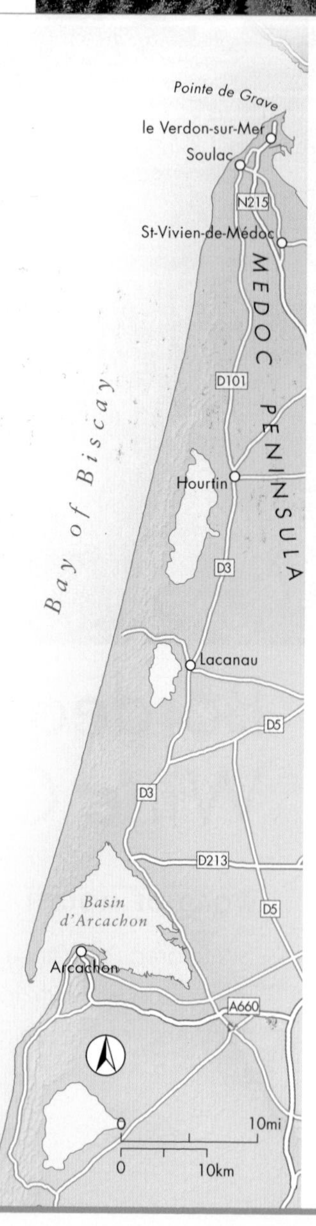

3 The Libournais. Set on the right bank of the Dordogne, this region was put on the map by two great wine districts—St-Émilion and Pomerol. Crowds head here because the town of St-Émilion looks as delicious as its wines taste: a UNESCO World Heritage Site, this open-air museum was constructed out of a limestone plateau honeycombed with vast caves and passageways, the source for the golden stonework of its 19th-century houses and steep streets. During summer, the small town is often swamped with visitors—plan your parking and hotels carefully.

GETTING ORIENTED

Along with Burgundy and Champagne, Bordeaux is one of the great wine regions of France. As the capital of the Gironde *département* and of the historic province of Aquitaine, the city of Bordeaux is both the commercial and cultural center of southwest France and an important transportation hub. It is smack-dab in the middle of one of the finest wine-growing areas in the world: Sauternes lies to the south, flat and dusty Médoc to the west, and Pomerol and St-Émilion to the east.

BORDEAUX AND THE WINE COUNTRY PLANNER

Transportation Basics

Bordeaux is one of France's main transportation hubs. However, once you get out into the surrounding Gironde—the "Wine Country"—you can find its seven regions (divided according to geography and the types of wine produced) difficult to reach without a car. Public buses run frequently through the countryside, but stops often appear in the middle of nowhere and schedules are irregular. Get very specific information from Bordeaux's main tourist office and from the bus ticket window on the Esplanade des Quinconces, before boarding a bus. If you have access to a car, you'll find life much easier, particularly if you purchase a Michelin map; Map No. 234 covers a large portion of the southwest. Another option is to go on a bus tour organized by the Bordeaux

A Bordeaux Baedeker

How to find the best vineyards (also referred to as *crus, clos,* and *domaines*) if you're based in Bordeaux? Easy—just head in any direction. The city is at the hub of a patchwork of vineyards: the Médoc peninsula to the northwest; Bourg and Blaye across the estuary; St-Émilion inland to the east; then, as you wheel around clockwise, Entre-Deux-Mers, Sauternes, and Graves.

The nearest vineyard to Bordeaux itself is one of the best: Haut-Brion, on the western outskirts of the city, and one of the five châteaux to be officially recognized as a *premier cru,* or first growth. There are only five premiers crus in all, and Haut-Brion is the only one not in the Médoc (Château Mouton-Rothschild, Château Margaux, Château Latour, and Château Lafite-Rothschild complete the list). The Médoc is subdivided into various appellations, or wine-growing districts, with their own specific characteristics and taste. Pauillac and Margaux host premiers crus; St-Julien and St-Estèphe possess many domaines of almost equal quality, followed by Listrac and Moulis; wines not quite so good are classed as Haut-Médoc or, as you move farther north, Médoc, pure and simple.

The Médoc wine region begins at the meeting point of the Dordogne and Garonne rivers just north of the city. The D2, or Route des Châteaux, to the north of the city cuts northwest through the majority of the wine country along the Gironde all the way to Talais, and the N215 farther west runs through the other side of the region entering appellations like Listrac and Moulis, which the D2 bypasses.

Eastward lies the Libournais and St-Émilion regions, with Libourne as your main transportation (train) hub if heading to the stunning Vieille Ville of St-Émilion. The surrounding vineyards see the merlot grape in control, and wines here often have more immediate appeal than those of the Médoc. There are several small appellations apart from St-Émilion itself, the most famous being Pomerol, whose Château Pétrus is the world's most expensive wine. South of St-Émilion is the region known as Entre-Deux-Mers ("between two seas"—actually two rivers, the Dordogne and Garonne), whose dry white wine is particularly flavorsome. This region is famed for its sweet wines, including the world's best, which hail from legendary Sauternes.

Bordelais Banquet

While countryside Médoc eateries are few, the city of Bordeaux is jammed with restaurants (especially around Place du Parlement) and many cafés (in the Quartier St-Pierre especially) and bars (Place de la Victoire and Cours de la Somme).

Not surprisingly, the wines of the region are often used as a base for regional food specialties. Lamprey, a good local fish, is often served in a red wine sauce as *lamproie à la Bordelaise* and another, in a white wine, as *esturgeon à la Libournaise,* or sturgeon cooked Libourne-style.

As for meat, the lamb from Pauillac and the beef from Bazas and Aquitaine are rightly famous, as is the wood pigeon (*palombe*).

And Bordeaux has spectacular desserts, such as *fanchonnette bordelaise* (puff pastry in custard covered by meringues), the *cannelé de Bordeaux* (small cakes made in fluted molds that can only be found here), and the famed macaroons from Saint-Émilion, invented there by the town's Ursuline nuns in the 17th century.

Finding a Place to Stay

Especially in winter, when many rural places are closed, your best strategy might be to base yourself in Bordeaux city. While the high-roller set will adore the city's new Regent Grand Hotel Bordeaux, countryside hotels can be gorgeous here. And many can create wine-country tours for you, as Gradyghost notes on Fodor's Talk Forum: "The concierge at the Hotel Burdigala arranged individual guided tours at First Growth vineyards like Lafite, Mouton-Rothchild, and Château Margaux. Needless to say, those were memorable experiences."

DINING AND LODGING PRICE CATEGORIES (IN EUROS)

	¢	$	$$	$$$	$$$$
Restaurants	under €13	€13–€17	€18–€24	€25–€32	over €32
Hotels	under €65	€65–€105	€106–€145	€146–€215	over €215

Restaurant prices are per person for a main course at dinner, including tax (5.5%) and service; note that if a restaurant offers only prix-fixe (set-price) meals, it has been given the price category that reflects the full prix-fixe price. Hotel prices are for a standard double room in high season, including tax (19.6%) and service charge.

When to Go

West coast weather—even as close to Southern France as this—can have bad storms even during the summer because of the nearby Atlantic, but this is the case with a lot of the south of France. Happily, storms or bad days don't hang around for long.

The factor to keep in mind is when you come. French people usually vacation within their own national borders, so that means mid-July to the end of August is when you'll have company, and lots of it, especially in the more famous destinations.

Spring and fall are the best times to visit—there aren't as many tourists around, and the weather is still pleasant.

The *vendanges* (grape harvests) usually begin about mid-September in the Bordeaux region (though you can't visit the wineries at this time), and two weeks later in the Cognac region, to the north.

15

VISITING THE VINEYARDS

Château Smith-Haut-Lafitte is a famous name in Bordeaux (above); the tower of Château Latour (right, above); Château Margaux has Bordeaux's greatest house (right, bottom).

Touring a region with more than a thousand square kilometers of wine-growing country, 5,000 châteaux, and 100,000 vineyards producing around 70 million annual gallons of wine, you'll find it hard not to resist sampling Bordeaux's ample liquid bounty—but where do you start?

Best bet is to head north for the Route de Médoc (also called the Route des Châteaux or the Route des Grands-Crus), stocked with maps and pointers from the very helpful Bordeaux tourist office (the *tourisme de viticole* desk is the place for this)—they're at 12 cours du 30-Juillet in the city center of Bordeaux. Or check out the "Wine Tours" section of the Bordeaux tourist Web site before you travel: 🌐 *www.bordeaux-tourisme.com*. A map is essential, as signage is poor and many "châteaux" are small manors hidden in the hills. Three main wine regions surround the city: Médoc to the northwest, St-Emilion to the east, and Graves-Sauternes to the south. Each boasts fabled vineyards but remember that Baron Philippe de Rothschild, owner of Mouton-Rothschild, was famed for drinking *vin ordinaire* at most meals.

I HEARD IT THROUGH THE GRAPEVINE

For tips log on to the Forums at www.fodors.com. "Remember that almost all châteaux are closed from noon to 2 PM for lunch."—at. "We had a 3-hour private tour at Latour, with a movie, a tour, and a wine tasting. Everything was first class—especially the wine! We also made same-day reservations at Pichon-Longeville (beautiful château) and Lynch-Bages."

—oforparis!

BY APPOINTMENT ONLY

If you're planning on visiting any of the more famous growers (but this also includes other vineyards), make sure to call or e-mail ahead of time and arrange a dégustation (wine tasting)—many of the labels are "by appointment only" because they're too small to have full-time guides.

Even the famous Château Mouton-Rothschild—visited by thousands—requires reservations, at least a week in advance for a regular tour and several weeks for a tour that includes the cellars.

VINEYARD TOURS

Everyone knows that the staff at Bordeaux's tourist office can help with questions. And since many vineyards are inaccessible without a car or bike, the easiest way to tour those of the Route de Médoc and Gironde is to join one of the nearly daily bus tours sponsored by the city's tourist office (☎ *05–56–00–66–00* 🌐 *www.bordeaux-tourisme.com*).

Here's the main scoop: These tours depart from (and return to) the Office du Tourisme at 12 cours XXX-Juillet. In low season, reservations can be had by the day; in high season, make them in advance.

There are one-day trips and also half-day trips (usually, from 2 to 6 in the afternoon). In high season there's a tour every day; in low, just a few a week.

Most tours stop at two châteaux only—for instance, in the Médoc, you can visit the Château Palmer (Troisième Cru Classé) and the Château Lanessan (Cru Bourgeois)—but there are so many different tours that you can go on a different one each day for a week and not see the same domains.

Tours are offered in several languages, including English, and usually a bus holds 40 participants.

THE GRAPE ESCAPE

Want to be *vigneron* (vintner) for a day or night? Some great vineyards now welcome guests: here's the crème de la crème.

The 14th-century estate of Château Smith Haut-Lafitte (☎ *05–57–83–83–83* 🌐 *www.sources-caudalie.com*) now houses the very successful Les Sources de Caudalie spa (wine-based treatments), complete with hotel and restaurant. The Château Pichon-Longueville Baron (☎ *05–56–73–17–17* 🌐 *www.piclonlongueville.com*) has accommodations available in its storybook castle, along with tastings, all by reservation.

Wine king Bernard Magrez has seven rooms available at his 17th-century Château Fombrauge; book through his big Luxury Wine Tourism company (🌐 *www.luxurywinetourism.com*).

15

GETTING AROUND

Air Travel

Frequent daily flights on Air France link Bordeaux and the domestic airport at Limoges with Paris. Flybe has six direct flights a week from Southampton to Bordeaux and Ryanair flies into Pau and Biarritz farther south.

Airport Information **Aéroport de Bordeaux-Mérignac** (☎ *05–56–34–50–50* 🌐 *www.bordeaux.aeroport.fr*).

Visitor Information

The Office de Tourisme in Bordeaux is the first place to head for further information on local and regional sights, including wine tours and tastings; a round-the-clock phone service in English is available. The office also organizes daylong coach tours of the surrounding vineyards every day in high season and nearly every Wednesday, Saturday, and Sunday in low season. The office also has branch offices at the Gare de Bordeaux train station and the airport.

Contact **Office de Tourisme** (✉ *12 cours du XXX-Juillet, Bordeaux cedex* ☎ *05–56–00–66–00* 🌐 *www.bordeaux-tourisme.com*).

Bus Travel

The regional bus operator is Citram Aquitaine; the main Gare Routière (bus terminal) in Bordeaux is on Allées de Chartres (by Esplanade des Quinconces), near the Garonne River. Citram Aquitaine buses cover towns in the wine country and beach areas not well served by rail (i.e., Pauillac). Use Cars de Bordeaux to get to the ocean or airport—buses leave for the latter every 45 minutes from Bordeaux's rail station.

Cars de Bordeaux (✉ *8 rue d'Artagnan, Bordeaux* ☎ *05–57–77–58–78* 🌐 *www.groupe-sera.com*). **Citram Aquitaine** (✉ *8, rue de Corneille, Bordeaux* ☎ *05–56–43–68–43* 🌐 *www.citram.com*).

Car Travel

As the capital of southwest France, Bordeaux has superb transport links with Paris, Spain, and even the Mediterranean (A62 expressway via Toulouse links up with the A61 to Narbonne). The A10, the Paris–Bordeaux expressway, passes close to Poitiers and Saintes before continuing toward Spain as A63. The A20 south is the main route from Paris to just before Cahors. The A20 also connects with the N21 at Limoges, which brings you down to Bordeaux.

Train Travel

The superfast TGV (Train à Grande Vitesse) Atlantique service links Paris (Gare Montparnasse) to Bordeaux—585 km (365 mi) in 3½ hours. Trains link Bordeaux to Lyon (6 hrs) and Nice (8½ hrs) via Toulouse. Around five trains a day leave from Bordeaux for St-Émilion, taking anywhere from 30 to 55 minutes. If you're heading north to Pauillac there are at least three trains (around 80 mins) a day from Bordeaux.

SNCF (☎ *08–92–35–35–35* 🌐 *www.sncf.fr*). **Gare de Bordeaux** (✉ *Rue Charles Domercq* ☎ *05–47–47–10–00*).

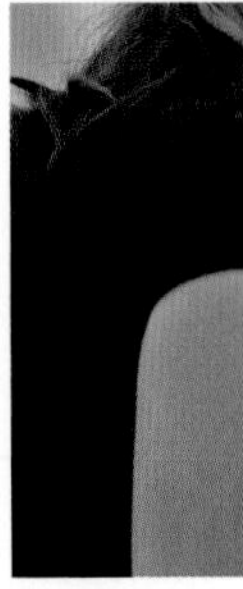

Updated by
John Fanning

When travelers arrive here, Bordeaux's countryside enchants them without their quite knowing why: what the French call *la douceur de vivre* (the sweetness of living) may have something to do with it.

To the east, extending their lush green rows to the rising sun, the fabled vineyards of the Route de Médoc entice visitors to discover such enchanting medieval wine towns as St-Émilion. To the north, the Atlantic coast offers elite enclaves of white-sand beach. In between is the metropolis of Bordeaux, replete with 18th-century landmarks and 20-year-old college students. Some complain that Bordeaux is like Paris without the good stuff. If you're a wine lover, however, it's still the doorway to paradise.

From the grandest *premiers grands crus*—the Lafite-Rothschilds, the Margaux—to the modest *supérieur* in your picnic basket, Bordeaux wines still command respect around the world. So much so that fans and oenophiles by the thousand come here to pay homage: to gaze at the noble symmetries of estate châteaux, whose rows of green-and-black vineyards radiate in every direction; to lower a nose deep into a well-swirled glass to inhale the heady vapors of oak and almond and leather; and, finally, to reverently pack a few bloodline labels into a trunk or a suitcase for home.

The history, economy, and culture of Bordeaux have always been linked to the production and marketing of wine. The birth of the first Bordeaux winery is said to have occurred between AD 37 and 68, when the Romans called this land Burdigala. By the Middle Ages a steady flow of Bordeaux wines was headed to England, where it's still dubbed "claret," after *clairet,* a light red version from earlier days. During these centuries the region was also put on the tourist radar because it had become a major stopping-off point on the fabled Santiago de Compostela pilgrimage road. With all these allurements, it's no wonder the English fought for it so determinedly throughout the Hundred Years' War. This coveted corner of France became home to Eleanor of Aquitaine, and when she left her first husband, France's Louis VII, to marry Henry II of Normandy (later king of England), both she and the land came under English rule. Henry Plantagenet was, after all, a great-grandson of William the Conqueror, and the Franco-English ambiguity of the age exploded in a war that defined much of modern France and changed its face forever. Southwestern France was the stage upon which much of the war was conducted—hence the region's many castles and no end of sturdy churches dedicated to the noble families' cause.

What they sought, the world still seeks. The wines of Bordeaux set the standard against which other wines are measured, and to truly savor them you should drink them on-site, from the mouthful of golden Graves that eases the oysters down to the syrupy sip of Sauternes that civilizes the smooth gaminess of the foie gras to the last glass of Médoc paired with the salt-marsh lamb that leads to pulling the cork on a Pauillac—because there is, still to come, the cheese tray. With a smorgasbord of 57 wine appellations (areas) to choose from, the revitalized city of Bordeaux, and the wine country that surrounds it with a veritable army of varietals, the entire region intoxicates with good taste.

BORDEAUX: CITY OF WINE

Bordeaux as a whole, rather than any particular points within it, is what you'll want to visit in order to understand why Victor Hugo described it as Versailles plus Antwerp, and why, when he was exiled from his native Spain, the painter Francisco de Goya chose it as his last home (he died here in 1828). The capital of southwest France and the region's largest city, Bordeaux remains synonymous with the wine trade: wine shippers have long maintained their headquarters along the banks of the Garonne, while buyers from around the world arrive for the huge biannual Vinexpo show (held in odd-number years). Today, much in the city is spanking new, courtesy of France's former prime minister, Alain Juppé, who became mayor of the city several years ago. As the gateway to marvelous Margaux and superlative Sauternes, Bordeaux—best entered from the south by the river—is 580 km (360 mi) southwest of Paris, 240 km (150 mi) northwest of Toulouse, and 190 km (118 mi) north of Biarritz.

GETTING HERE

If you're taking a train you'll arrive at one of France's major hubs, the Gare de Bordeaux, St-Jean (☎ *05–47–47–10–00* 🌐 *www.ter-sncf.com*), about 3 km (2 mi) from the city center. Bordeaux's urban buses (Nos. 7 and 8) will take you from the train station into the city center for less than €1.50 one-way. Citram Aquitaine (✉ *8 rue de Corneille* ☎ *05–56–43–68–43* 🌐 *www.citram.com*) is the main bus operator for farther afield in the Gironde, and even to other nearby *départements* (provinces). You can get here by train in about three hours from Paris, and even faster (about 90 mins)—at least 16 times a day—if you hop on a TGV (🌐 *www.tgv.com*) for about €55 one-way. Every 35 minutes (weekdays) you can get to the airport from the train station for €6.50; it takes about 45 minutes. The Aéroport de Bordeaux-Mérignac (☎ *05–56–34–50-50* 🌐 *www.bordeaux.aeroport.fr*) is 10 km (7 mi) west of the city center in Mérignac.

CLOSE UP

Red Gold: The Wines of Bordeaux

Everyone in Bordeaux celebrated the 2000 vintage as the "crop of the century," a wine that comes along once in a lifetime. But bringing everything down to earth are some new sour grapes: the increasingly loud whispers that Bordeaux may be "over."

In this world of nouvelle cuisine and uncellared wines, some critics feel the world has moved away from pricey, rich, red wines and more people are opting for lighter choices from other lands. Be that as it may, if you have any aspirations to being a wine connoisseur, Bordeaux will always remain the top of the pyramid, the bedrock of French viticulture.

It has been considered so ever since the credentials of Bordeaux wines were traditionally established in 1787. That year, Thomas Jefferson went down to the region from Paris and splurged on bottles of 1784 Château d'Yquem and Château Margaux, for prices that were, he reported, "indeed dear."

Jefferson knew his wines: in 1855, both Yquem and Margaux were officially classified among Bordeaux's top five. And two centuries later, some of his very bottles (the authenticity of their provenance has since been disputed, as well document in the controversial book *The Billionaire's Vinegar*), fetched upward of $50,000 when offered in a high-flying auction in New York City.

As it turns out, Bordeaux's reputation dates from the Middle Ages. From 1152 to 1453, along with much of what is now western France, Bordeaux belonged to England. The light red wine then produced was known as *clairet,* the origin of our word "claret." Today no other part of France has such a concentrated wealth of top-class vineyards.

The versatile Bordeaux region yields sweet and dry whites and fruity or full-bodied reds from a huge domain extending on either side of the Gironde (Blaye and Bourg to the north, Médoc and Graves to the south) and inland along the Garonne (Sauternes) and Dordogne (St-Émilion, Fronsac, Pomerol) or in between these two rivers (Entre-Deux-Mers).

At the top of the government-supervised scale—which ranks, from highest to lowest, as Appellation d'Origine Contrôlée (often abbreviated AOC); Vin Délimité de Qualité Supérieur (VDQS); Vins de Pays, and Vin de Table—are the fabled vintages of Bordeaux, leading off with Margaux. Sadly, vineyards of Margaux are among the ugliest in France, lost amid the flat, dusty plains of Médoc.

Bordeaux is better represented at historic St-Émilion, with its cascading cobbled streets, or at Sauternes. Nothing in that grubby village would suggest that mind-boggling wealth lurks amid the picturesque vine-laden slopes and hollows. The village has a wineshop where bottles gather dust on rickety shelves, next to handwritten price tags demanding small fortunes.

Making Sauternes is a tricky business. Autumn mists steal up the valleys to promote *Botrytis cinerea,* a fungus known as *pourriture noble* or noble rot, which sucks moisture out of the grapes, leaving a high proportion of sugar. Sauternes's liquid gold is harvested in *vendanges* beginning in September and lasting to December. *Santé!*

Visitor Information Bordeaux Tourist Office. ✉ *12 cours du XXX-Juillet* ☎ *05–56–00–66–00* 🌐 *www.bordeaux-tourisme.com.*

BORDEAUX'S BIG WINE BLOWOUT

The four-day Fête du Vin (Wine Festival) at the end of June sees glass-clinking merriment along the banks of the Garonne. The city's grandest square gets packed with workshops, booths, and thousands of wine lovers. Log on to 🌐 *www.bordeaux-fete-le-vin.com* for all the heady details.

EXPLORING

Bordeaux is a less exuberant city than many others in France but lively and stylish elements are making a dent in the city's conservative veneer. The cleaned-up riverfront is said by some, after a bottle or two, to exude an elegance redolent of St. Petersburg and that stylish aura of 18th-century elan also permeates the historic downtown sector—"le vieux Bordeaux"—where fine shops invite exploration. To the south of the city center are old docklands undergoing gradual renewal—one train station has now been transformed into a big multiplex cinema—but the area is still a bit shady. A multibillion-euro tramway system was completed in 2008. To get a feel for the historic port of Bordeaux, take the 90-minute boat trip that leaves Quai Louis-XVIII every weekday afternoon, or the regular passenger ferry that plies the Garonne between Quai Richelieu and the Pont d'Aquitaine in summer. A nice time to stroll around the city center is the first Sunday of the month, when it's pedestrian-only and cars are banned.

TOP ATTRACTIONS

6 **Cathédrale St-André.** This may not be one of France's finer Gothic cathedrals but the intricate 14th-century chancel makes an interesting contrast with the earlier nave. Excellent stone carvings adorn the facade of this hefty edifice. You can climb the 15th-century, 160-foot **Tour Pey-Berland** for a stunning view of the city; it's open Tuesday–Sunday 10–noon and 2–5. ✉ *Pl. Pey-Berland* ☎ *05–56–81–26–25* 🎫 *€5.*

5 ★ **Grand Théâtre.** One block south of the Maison du Vin is the city's leading 18th-century monument: the Grand Théâtre, designed by Victor Louis and built between 1773 and 1780. It's the pride of the city, with an elegant exterior ringed by graceful Corinthian columns and a dazzling foyer with a two-winged staircase and a cupola. The theater hall has a frescoed ceiling with a shimmering chandelier composed of 14,000 Bohemian crystals. ✉ *Pl. de la Comédie* ☎ *05–56–00–85–95* 🌐 *www.opera-bordeaux.com* 🎫 *€6.50* ☞ *Contact tourist office for guided tours.*

9 **Haut-Brion.** One of the region's most famous wine-producing châteaux is actually within the city limits: follow N250 southwest from central Bordeaux for 3 km (2 mi) to the district of Pessac, home to Haut-Brion, producer of the only non-Médoc wine to be ranked a *premier cru* (the most elite wine classification). It's claimed the very buildings surrounding the vineyards create their own microclimate, protecting the precious grapes and allowing them to ripen earlier. The white château looks out over the celebrated pebbly soil. The wines produced at **La Mission–Haut Brion**

Cathédrale St-André 6
Grand Théâtre 5
Haut-Brion 9
Maison du Vin (CIVB) 4
Musée d'Aquitaine 8
Musée d'Art Contemporain ...3
Musée des Beaux-Arts 7
Place de la Bourse 2
Pont de Pierre 1

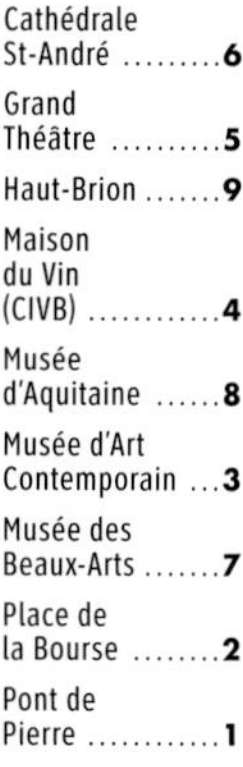

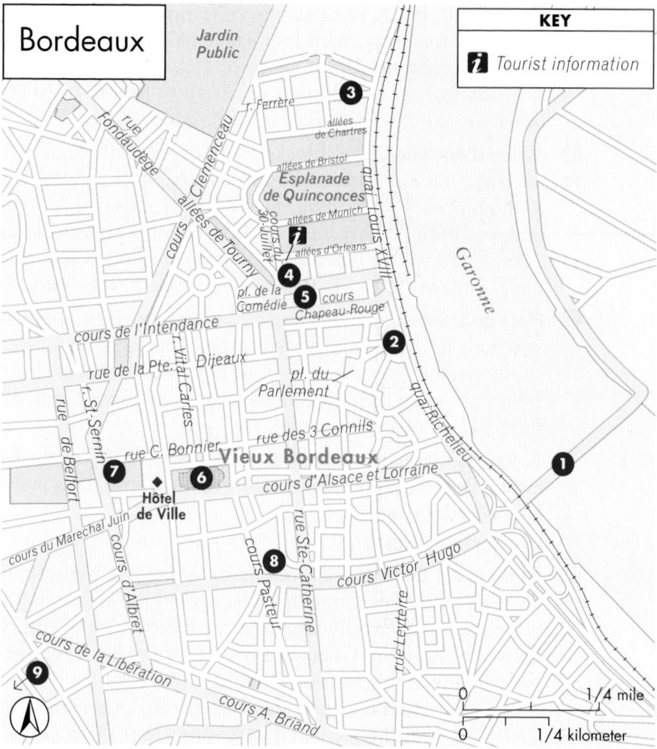

(**Domaine Clarence Dillon**), across the road, are almost as sought-after. ✉ *133 av. Jean-Jaurès, Pessac* ☎ *05–56–00–29–30* 🌐 *www.haut-brion.com* 🎫 *Free 1-hr visits by appointment, weekdays only, with tasting* ⏲ *Closed mid-July–mid-Aug.*

4 ★ **Maison du Vin.** Not far from the banks of the Garonne and the main artery of the Esplanade des Quinconces sits tree-lined Cours du XXX-Juillet and the important Maison du Vin, or House of Wine, run by the CIVB (Conseil Interprofessionnel des Vins de Bordeaux), the headquarters of the Bordeaux wine trade (note that the city tourist office is just across the street). Before you set out to explore the regional wine country, stop at the Maison to gain clues from the person at the Tourisme de Viticole desk (English-speaking), who has helpful guides on all the various wine regions. More important, tasting a red (like Pauillac or St-Émilion), a dry white (like an Entre-Deux-Mers, Graves, or Côtes de Blaye), and a sweet white (like Sauternes or Loupiac) will help you decide which of the 57 wine appellations (areas) to explore. You can also make purchases at the **Vinothèque** opposite. ✉ *8 cours du XXX-Juillet* ☎ *05–56–52–32–05* 🌐 *www.la-vinotheque.com* 🎫 *Free* ⏲ *Mon.–Sat. 10–7:30.*

7 **Musée des Beaux-Arts.** Not far from the Cathédrale St-André is this museum, found adorning tidy gardens behind the ornate Hôtel de Ville

(town hall). Inside is a fetching collection of works spanning the 15th to the 21st century, with important paintings by Paolo Veronese (*St. Dorothy*), Camille Corot (*Bath of Diana*), and Odilon Redon (*Apollo's Chariot*), and sculptures by Auguste Rodin. ⊠ *20 cours d'Albret* ☎ *05–56–10–20–56* 🎟 *Free* ⏲ *Wed.–Mon. 11–6.*

8 ★ **Musée d'Aquitaine.** Two blocks south of the Cathédrale St-André is this excellent museum that takes you on a trip through Bordeaux's history, with emphases on Roman, medieval, Renaissance, port-harbor, colonial, and 20th-century daily life. The detailed prehistoric section almost saves you a trip to Lascaux II, which is reproduced here in part. ⊠ *20 cours Pasteur* ☎ *05–56–01–51–00* 🎟 *Free* ⏲ *Tues.–Sun. 11–6.*

2 **Place de la Bourse.** Centerpiece of the left bank is this open square which was built 1729–33. Ringed with large-windowed buildings, it was beautifully designed by the era's most esteemed architect, Jacques Gabriel, father of the architect Jacques-Ange Gabriel (who went on to remodel Paris's Place de la Concorde).

A few blocks to the southeast of Place de la Bourse is **Place du Parlement**, also ringed by elegant 18th-century structures and packed with lively outdoor cafés.

WORTH NOTING

3 **Musée d'Art Contemporain** *(Contemporary Art Center)*. Just north of the Esplanade des Quinconces, a sprawling square, is this two-story museum, imaginatively housed in a converted 19th-century spice warehouse, the Entrepôt Lainé. Many shows here showcase cutting-edge artists who invariably festoon the huge expanse of the place with hanging ropes, ladders, and large video screens. ⊠ *7 rue Ferrère* ☎ *05–56–00–81–50* 🎟 *Free* ⏲ *Tues. and Thurs.–Sun. 11–6, Wed. 11–8.*

1 **Pont de Pierre.** For a view of the picturesque quayside, stroll across the Garonne on this bridge, built on the orders of Napoléon between 1810 and 1821, and until 1965 the only bridge across the river.

WHERE TO EAT

$$ FRENCH ✕ **Café Français.** For more than 30 years, Madame Jouhanneau presided over this venerable bistro in the heart of the Vieille Ville (Old Town), right by the Cathédrale St-André. Now Madame Mesnard has taken over and renovated the place but has kept the cuisine as it was: solidly based on fresh regional specialties. For solid sustenance at reasonable prices, it's hard to beat. Try for a table on the terrace: the view over Place Pey-Berland is never less than diverting. ⊠ *5–6 pl. Pey-Berland* ☎ *05–56–52–96–69* ▭ *AE, DC, MC, V.* ⏲ *Closed Mon.*

$$$–$$$$ FRENCH ★ ✕ **La Tupina.** With much glory stolen by its noble cellars, Bordeaux has struggled mightily against its reputation as a culinary backwater. Happily, earthy spins on *cuisine de terroir* are served up at this lovely restaurant (the name means "kettle") on one of Bordeaux's oldest streets, under the eye of flamboyant owner Jean-Pierre Xiradakis. Dried herbs hang from the ceiling, a Provençal grandfather clock ticks off the minutes, and an antique fireplace sports a grill bearing sizzling morsels of duck and chicken. Like the room itself, the menu aspires to the "*nostalgie des anciennes menus,*" and it succeeds. On the same street (No. 34) is the owner's fetching—and cheaper—Bar Cave de la Monnaie bistro

At the end of June, Bordeaux becomes one big party thanks to the four-day Fête du Vin (Wine Festival).

as well as his épicerie, Au Comestible, where you can buy a selection of La Tupina's fare in a can or jar, or even the chef's southwest cookbook. ✉ *6 rue Porte-de-la-Monnaie* ☎ *05–56–91–56–37* 🌐 *www.latupina.com* ✍ *Reservations essential* ▭ *AE, DC, MC, V.*

$$$$ FRENCH Fodor's Choice ★ ✕ **Le Chapon-Fin.** With all the laurels and stars thrown at Thierry Marx, the culinary wizard ensconced at Pauillac's Château Cordeillan-Bages, it was just a matter of time before he would swoop in and give Bordeaux's own landmark restaurant an all-out reenergizing shot in the arm. It needed one: founded in 1825, favored by such VIPs as Sarah Bernhardt, Toulouse-Lautrec, and Edward VII, and graced with an extraordinary decor (half winter-garden, half Rococo-grotto), the Chapon-Fin had hardened with age, but it has come back to glorious life these days. The current chef in charge is Nicolas Frion, who trained with Marx and has a winning moderne touch. Try his panfried fillet of beef with aubergine cannelloni in an onion and tomato compote surrounded by a bay leaf stock, or his veal sweetbreads and kidney charlotte with a salsify confit and garlic cream sauce. You haven't really been to Bordeaux until you've been here—so be sure to feast here. ✉ *5 rue Montesquieu* ☎ *05–56–79–10–10* 🌐 *www.chapon-fin.com* ✍ *Reservations essential* ▭ *AE, V* ⏲ *Closed Sun. and Mon., last wk in July, and 1st 3 wks in Aug.*

$$ FRENCH ✕ **L'Estacade.** *Le tout Bordeaux* now congregates at this fashionable spot, spectacularly set in a pierlike structure right on the Garonne River. Enormous bay windows allow you to drink in a beautiful panorama of the 18th-century Place de la Bourse on the opposite bank. The cuisine is creative (prawn risotto, Saint-Jacques with pineapple and chorizo) while the wine list focuses on young Bordeaux. ✉ *Quai de Queyries* ☎ *05–57–54–02–50* 🌐 *www.lestacade.com* ▭ *AE, MC, V.*

Bordeaux doesn't have many grand châteaux-hotels but when it does, it's a winner, as the Grand Barrail Château Resort and Spa proves.

WHERE TO STAY

$$$$ **Burdigala.** Of the three luxury hotels in Bordeaux, Burdigala (Latin for "Bordeaux") is the only one within walking distance of the center of town. Although the modern exterior is unappealing, the inside is comfortable, with guest rooms crammed with smart modern furniture, fancy bedspreads, and comfy seats. The soundproof rooms are neat; No. 416 is especially quiet and sunny. Deluxe rooms have marble bathrooms with whirlpool baths. The Jardin du Burdigala restaurant serves nouvelle cuisine. **Pros:** in the heart of Bordeaux; close to Gambetta Square. **Cons:** styles of rooms are very different—make sure you know what you're getting by taking a look around first. ✉ *115 rue Georges-Bonnac* ☎ *05–56–90–16–16* 🌐 *www.burdigala.com* *75 rooms, 8 suites* *In-room: a/c, refrigerator, Wi-Fi. In-hotel: restaurant, bar, some pets allowed* *AE, MC, V* *MAP.*

$–$$ **Des Quatre Sœurs.** In an elegant 1840 town house near the Grand Théâtre, this hotel has sober, well-kept rooms of varying sizes, all with air-conditioning. Believe it or not, Richard Wagner once stayed here—unfortunately, you'll never know it from the minimal-style, uninspired furnishings. **Pros:** only a few steps from the tourist office. **Cons:** guest room decor, right down to the naked walls, leaves something to be desired. ✉ *6 cours du XXX-Juillet* ☎ *05–57–81–19–20* 🌐 *4soeurs.free.fr* *29 rooms, 5 suites* *In-room: a/c. In-hotel: Wi-Fi hotspot, some pets allowed* *AE, MC, V* *MAP.*

$–$$ **Quality Hôtel Sainte-Catherine.** At the heart of Bordeaux's pedestrian center, this fully modernized hotel is in a 19th-century building in the old part of town. Service is limited, but the reception staff is helpful. The compact, pastel-tone rooms are decorated with light floral fabrics while the breakfast room has large windows, letting the light give you a real wake-up call. **Pros:** convenient location; right beside the Grand Théâtre. **Cons:** generic furnishings; parking is five minutes away. ✉ *27 rue du Parlement-Ste-Catherine* ☎ *05–56–81–95–12* 🌐 *www.quality-hotel-sainte-catherine-bordeaux.federal-hotel.com* *82 rooms* *In-room: a/c, refrigerator, Wi-Fi. In-hotel: bar, Wi-Fi hotspot, some pets allowed* *AE, DC, MC, V* *BP.*

$$$$ ★ **Regent Grand Hotel Bordeaux.** Bordeaux—a stylish city with a decided dearth of stylish hotels—was rescued in 2006 by the opening of this extravaganza. Designed by Jacques Garcia (Paris's gorgeous Hôtel Costes and Deauville's Normandy-Barrière), the Regent is festooned in luxury fabrics, 19th-century French furnishings, and stunning marble bathrooms. If anyone can redefine and resurrect Bordelais style it is über-chic Garcia—for this complex of buildings anchored by a historic *palais,* he has taken inspiration from the gilded Opéra National de Bordeaux, set just across the square. Add in Regent-brand luxe (flat-screen TVs, Bose Wave radios, etc.), a location that is steps from Bordeaux's Golden Triangle luxury shopping district, and a veritable army of restaurants and bars—ranging from the haute seafood and multistory wine cave on tap at Le Pressoir d'Argent to Brasserie L'Europe, a Belle Époque–style wine bar with regional food—and this place comes up a winner. **Pros:** *le style, c'est le Garcia*; Bordeaux has waited for these mod-cons for years. **Cons:** guest room decor is actually mod-ish and not as historic as the venerable surrounds. ✉ *2 pl. de la Comédie* ☎ *05–57–30–44–44* 🌐 *www.theregentbordeaux.com* *128 rooms, 22 suites* *In-room: a/c, refrigerator, Wi-Fi. In-hotel: 2 restaurants, bar, some pets allowed* *AE, DC, MC, V* *EP.*

NIGHTLIFE AND THE ARTS

L'Aztécal (✉ *61 rue Pas-St-Georges* ☎ *05–56–44–50–18*) is a comfortable spot for a drink or a disco soireé in the cavernous club downstairs. **Comptoir du Jazz** (✉ *59 quai Paludate* ☎ *05–56–49–15–55*), near the station, is the place for jazz. Neighboring **Le Sénéchal** (✉ *57 bis, quai Paludate* ☎ *05–56–85–54–80*) is the place to dance the night away.

★ Arguably one of the most beautiful historic theaters in Europe, the **Grand Théâtre** (✉ *Pl. de la Comédie* ☎ *05–56–00–85–95* 🌐 *www.opera-bordeaux.com*) puts on performances of French plays and occasionally operas. The theater (which can be visited on guided tours) is an 18th-century showpiece studded with marble muses.

SHOPPING

Between the cathedral and the Grand Théâtre are numerous pedestrian streets (Rue Ste. Catherine being the biggest) where stylish shops and clothing boutiques abound—Bordeaux may favor understatement, but there's no lack of elegance in and around its Golden Triangle shopping district. For an exceptional selection of cheeses, go to **Jean d'Alos Fromager-Affineur** (✉ *4 rue Montesquieu* ☎ *05–56–44–29–66*). With five stores in Bordeaux alone, **Baillardran** (✉ *55 cours de l'Intendance* ☎ *05–56–52–92–64* 🌐 *www.baillardran.com*) is going to be hard to walk by without at least looking in its windows at those indigenous sweet delights——Bordelais canelés! A small indented cake, much like a Doric column in miniature, canelés are delicious regional carmelized cakes made with vanilla and a dash of Rum.Set within the shadow of the church of Saint Michel (a few blocks south of the Pont de Pierre, just off the river), the **Grand Déballage de Brocante** (✉ *Place St-Michel*) is one of the country's largest flea markets, taking place every second Sunday during the months of March, June, September, and December all day long; all year long, a weekly flea market is also held here, just the ticket for those looking for real bargains away from the storefronts and a nice invitation to explore the historic St-Michel quartier, loaded with shops. The **Vinothèque** (✉ *8 cours du XXX-Juillet* ☎ *05–56–52–32–05*) sells top-ranked Bordeaux wines.Bear in mind that the *soldes* (sales) start in France at the height of summer, especially just before Bastille (July 14) weekend!

ROUTE DU MÉDOC AND THE WINE COUNTRY

Northwest of Bordeaux city is the most famous wine district. All along the west coast of the Gironde estuary south, until you hit the meeting point of the Dordogne and Garonne rivers just north of the city, you will encounter the Médoc wine region. The farthest north is the Médoc appellation itself with, to the south of it, the Paulliac appellation, which surrounds the Saint-Estéphe and Saint Julien appellations, nearer to the estuary. Nearer Bordeaux and just south of the Paulliac region is the conglomeration of the Listrac, Moulis, Margaux, and (nearest to the city along the Garonne) the Haut-Médoc appellations. The D2, or Route des Châteaux, to the north of the city cuts northwest through the majority of the wine country along the Gironde all the way to Talais, and the N215 farther west runs through the other side of the region entering appellations like Listrac and Moulis, which the D2 bypasses.

Wines from the Médoc are made predominantly from the cabernet sauvignon grape, and can taste dry, even austere, when young. The better ones often need 15 to 25 years before "opening up" to reveal their full spectrum of complex flavors. More fabled vintages are found 35 km (36 mi) to the east of the city in the medieval region of St-Émilion. Here, vineyards that are family owned and relatively small (with on average 7 hectares to each property) are divided into two appellations, St-Émilion and St-Émilion Grand Cru. At the region's heart lies the beautiful wine town of St-Émilion.

GETTING HERE

If you're heading north, you'll have to make your way to or through Pauillac (try to ignore the oil refinery). The buses of Citram Aquitaine (☎ *05–56–43–68–43*) operate in this region as well as the more unreliable SNCF buses. It takes about 50 minutes from Bordeaux to Pauillac. Citram Aquitaine also connects Bordeaux with Margaux (90 minutes) and as far north as Pointe de Grave (150 minutes). The train will drop you off at the Gare de Pauillac on 2 bis place Verdun. You can also train it around four times a day as far as Soulac (9 km [5½ mi] below Pointe de Grave), by changing at Lesparre for around €15 one-way. If you want to get into the Médoc from Bordeaux by car make sure to get off the road that encircles Bordeaux (the "Rocade") using Sortie (Exit) 7.

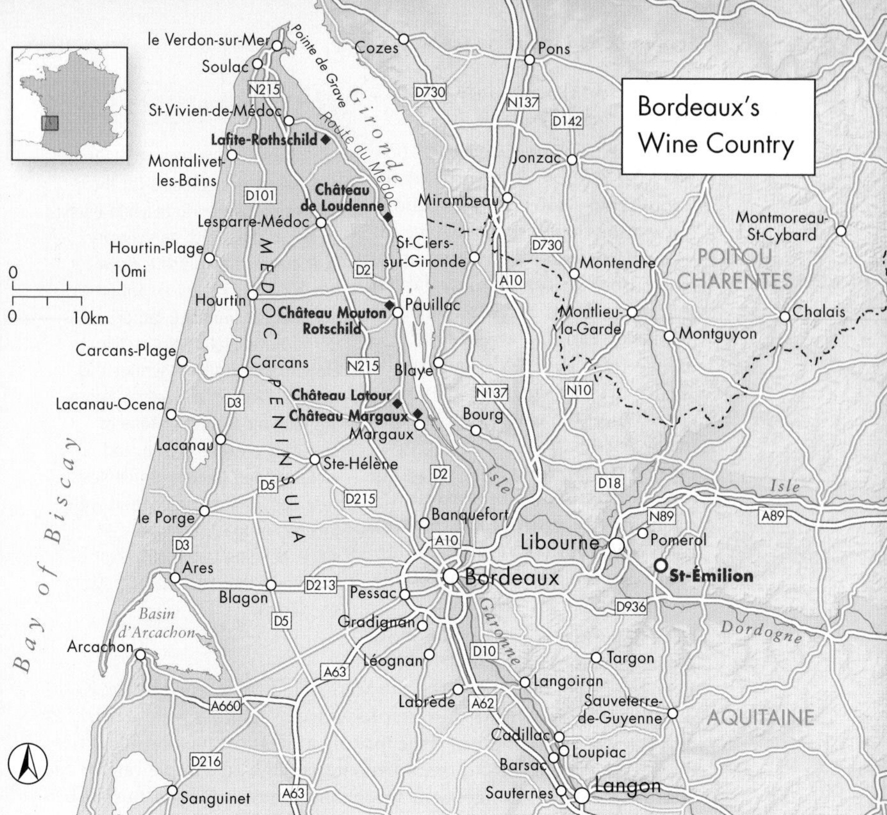

Visitor Information Pauillac Tourist Office. ✉ *La Verrerie* ☎ *05–56–59–03–08* 🌐 *www.pauillac-medoc.com.*

EXPLORING

North of Bordeaux, the Route du Médoc wine road (D2)—sometimes called the Route des Châteaux—winds through the dusty Médoc Peninsula, past the townships of Margaux, St-Julien, Pauillac, and St-Estèphe. Even the vines in Médoc look dusty, and so does the ugly town of **Margaux**, the area's unofficial capital, 27 km (17 mi) northwest of Bordeaux. Yet **Château Margaux** (☎ *05–57–88–83–83* 🌐 *www.chateau-margaux.com*), housed in a magnificent Neoclassical building from 1810, is recognized as a producer of premiers crus, whose wine qualifies with Graves's Haut-Brion as one of Bordeaux's top five reds. As with most of the top Bordeaux châteaux, visits to Château Margaux are by appointment only.

The well-informed, English-speaking staff at the tourist office can direct you to other châteaux such as **Lascombes** (☎ *05–56–00–66–00*) and **Palmer,** which have beautiful grounds, reasonably priced wines, and are open without reservations. In nearby Cussac, visit the winery and carriage museum at **Château Lanessan.**

★ Some 90 km (56 mi) north of Bordeaux on highway D2 is **Pauillac**, home to the three wineries—Lafite-Rothschild, Latour, and Mouton-

Rothschild—that produce Médoc's other top reds.

★ Renowned **Château Latour** (☎ *05–56–73–19–80* 🌐 *www.chateau-latour.com*) sometimes requires reservations a month in advance for its wine tastings (weekdays only). If the posh prices of these fabled grands crus are not for you, rent a bike in Pauillac at **Avia** (☎ *05–56–59–04–53*), and visit any of the slightly less expensive nearby wineries. Of all the towns and villages in the Médoc, Pauillac is the prettiest; you may want to stroll along the riverfront and stop for refreshments at one of its restaurants. A train line connects Pauillac to Bordeaux, running several times daily in summer.

LE STYLE ROTHSCHILD

Famed artists like Picasso, Balthus, and Bacon designlabels for the bottles of Mouton-Rothschild each. To honor the 150th anniversary of Rothschild ownership, however, the 2003 label is an exception—it spotlights founding father Baron Nathaniel de Rothschild. Le Mouton's Web site describes this vintage: "Full on the palate, showing roundness and refinement on nicely present, stylish, and well-rounded tannins, it mingles very ripe, almost jammy fruit with touches of toast, caramel, and spice, building to a highly expressive finish that has charm, power, and length."

★ **Lafite-Rothschild** is among the most resonant names of the wine world. Even by the giddy standards of the Médoc, Lafite—owned by the Rothschild family since 1868 (but first recorded as making wine as early as 1234)—is a high temple of wine making at its most memorable. Prices may be sky-high, but no one fortunate enough to sample one of the château's classic vintages will forget the experience in a hurry. Too bad you can't visit the family château on the grounds—its rooms are the defining examples of *le style Rothschild,* one of the most opulent styles of 19th-century interior decoration. ✉ *Pauillac* 🌐 *www.lafite.com* 🎫 *Free* 🕑 *By appointment only at 2 and 3:30, reserve at least 2 wks in advance; closed Aug.–Oct.*

Most of the great vineyards in this area are strictly private (although the owners are usually receptive to inquiries about visits from bona fide wine connoisseurs). One vineyard, however, has long boasted a welcoming visitor center: **Mouton-Rothschild**, whose eponymous wine was brought to perfection in the 1930s by that flamboyant figure Baron Philippe de Rothschild, whose wife, Pauline, was a great style-setter of the 1950s. The baron's daughter, Philippine, continues to lavish money and love on this growth, so wine lovers flock here for either the one-hour visit, which includes a tour of the cellars, *chai* (wine warehouse), and museum, or the slightly longer visit that tops off the tour with a tasting. ✉ *Le Pouyalet, Pauillac* ☎ *05–56–73–21–29* 🌐 *www.bpdr.com* 🎫 *€6.50; with tasting, €16* 🕑 *Mon.–Thurs. 9:30–11 and 2–4, Fri. 9:30–11 and 2–3, by appointment only, reserve at least 2 wks in advance.*

At the tip of the Gironde peninsula, near a memorial commemorating the landing of U.S. troops in 1917, is the Pointe de Grave, where you can take the **bac** (*ferry* ☎ *05–56–73–37–73*) across the Gironde from Le Verdon to Royan; it runs at least six times daily and costs €22.30

per car and €3.10 per passenger. During the 20-minute crossing, keep an eye out for the **Phare de Cordouan** on your left, a lighthouse that looks as if it's emerging from the sea (at low tide, its base is revealed to rest on a sandbank).

WHERE TO STAY

$$$–$$$$ ★ **Château Cordeillan-Bages.** This stone-face, single-story 17th-century "chartreuse" just outside Pauillac is surrounded by the vines that produce its own *cru bourgeois*. Paris-trained Thierry Marx is considered the highest-rated chef in the region, no mean accolade in a part of France where food can take second place to world-class wine. His fortes range from local salt-meadow lamb and "liquid" quiche lorraine to spaghetti with an oxtail, truffle, and cêpe sauce. Of course, who will be able to resist the accompaniment of one of the 1,000-plus Bordeaux from the cellars? The dining room is cookie-cutter modern, but the guest rooms are comfortable and Relais-&-Châteaux stylish. **Pros:** lovely marble building; away-from-it-all location; cooking school here is a perfect way to get to know region wines. **Cons:** uninspired modern decor messes with the period vibe; access isn't exactly convenient with the airport 45 km (27 mi) away—unless you want to use their helipad! ✉ *Rte. des Châteaux, 1½ km (1 mi) south of town, Pauillac* ☎ *05–56–59–24–24* 🌐 *www.cordeillanbages.com* *24 rooms, 4 suites* *In-room: a/c, refrigerator, Wi-Fi. In-hotel: restaurant, bar* *AE, DC, MC, V* *Closed late Dec.–mid-Feb.* *MAP.*

$ **France & Angleterre.** Set in an interesting, low-slung 19th-century building and a convenient choice if you wish to explore Pauillac's winding streets, this low-key spot overlooks the quaint waterfront and Gironde estuary. The restaurant (decor: underwhelming plain white walls hung with framed prints) serves local specialties such as lamprey in a Médoc wine and shallot sauce. **Pros:** you can wheel about Pauillac from here very easily. **Cons:** too much yellow in guest rooms? ✉ *3 quai Albert-Pichon, Pauillac* ☎ *05–56–59–01–20* 🌐 *www.hoteldefrance-angleterre.com* *29 rooms* *In-room: no a/c, Internet. In-hotel: restaurant, Wi-Fi hotspot* *AE, DC, MC, V* *Closed mid-Dec.–mid-Jan.* *MAP.*

ST-ÉMILION

Fodor's Choice ★ *74 km (41 mi) southeast of Pauillac, 35 km (23 mi) east of Bordeaux.*

Suddenly the sun-fired flatlands of Pomerol break into hills and send you tumbling into St-Émilion. This jewel of a town has old buildings of golden stone, ruined town walls, well-kept ramparts offering magical views, and a church hewn into a cliff. Sloping vineyards invade from all sides, and thousands of tourists invade down the middle, many thirsting for the red wine and macaroons that bear the town's name. The medieval streets, delightfully cobblestone (though often very steep), are filled with wine stores (St-Émilion reaches maturity earlier than other Bordeaux reds and often offers better value for the money than Médoc or Graves), crafts shops, bakeries, cafés, and restaurants.

A Fodor's.com member, t56gf, submitted this photo redolent of the medieval beauty of cobblestoned St-Émilion.

GETTING HERE

To take a train to St-Émilion you first need to head to Libourne—a 10-minute ride away. There are two direct trains from Paris to Libourne and another three that connect with Angoulême to Libourne. Trains from Bordeaux (40 mins) run three times a day for about €7 and twice a day on weekends and holidays. Citram Aquitaine (🌐 *www.citram.com*) will bus you to St-Émilion five times a day, the trip being a two-pronged affair: 45 minutes to Libourne for around €6, and from here on a Marachesseau bus (10 mins) to St-Émilion for €2.

St-Émilion Tourist Office. ✉ *Place des Cerneaux* ☎ *05–57–55–28–28* 🌐 *www.saint-emilion-tourisme.com.*

EXPLORING

The **Office de Tourisme** (*Tourist Office* ✉ *Pl. des Créneaux* ☎ *05–57–55–28–28* 🌐 *www.saint-emilion-tourisme.com*) hires out bikes (€15 per day) and organizes tours of the pretty local vineyards—the fabled **Château Angelus** and **Château Belair,** among others—including wine tastings and train rides through the vineyards. Note that it's best to hit the road on a weekday, when more châteaux are open.

A stroll along the 13th-century ramparts takes you to the **Château du Roi** *(King's Castle)*. To this day nobody knows whether it was Henry III of England or King Louis VIII of France who chose the site and ordered its building.

From the castle ramparts, cobbled steps lead down to **Place du Marché**, a leafy square where cafés remain open late into the balmy summer night. Beware of the inflated prices charged at the café tables.

The **Église Monolithe** *(Monolithic Church)* is one of Europe's largest underground churches, hewn out of the rock face between the 9th and the 12th century. The church was built by monks faithful to the memory of St-Émilion, an 8th-century hermit and miracle worker. Its spire-top *clocher* (bell tower) rises out of the bedrock, dominating the center of town. ✉ *Pl. du Marché* 🎟 *€6.50* ⏲ *Tours leave from tourist office, daily 10–noon and 2–5.*

Just south of the town walls is **Château Ausone**, an estate that is ranked with Château Angelus as a producer of St-Émilion's finest wines.

WHERE TO EAT AND STAY

$ FRENCH ✕ **Chez Germaine**. Family cooking and regional dishes are the focus at this central St-Émilion eatery, which serves lunch only. The candle-lighted upstairs dining room and the terrace are both pleasant places to enjoy the reasonably priced set menus. Grilled meats and fish are house specialties; for dessert, go for the almond macaroons. ✉ *13 pl. du Clocher* ☎ *05–57–74–49–34* 💳 *AE, DC, MC, V* ⏲ *No dinner.*

$$–$$$ 🏨 **Auberge de la Commanderie**. Close to the ramparts, this 19th-century two-story hotel has a gorgeous, white-shuttered facade that blends in beautifully with St-Émilion's fabled stonework. Public rooms overlook some vineyards. As for guest rooms, they range from tiny and barebones to large and decorated with colorful prints; some have exposed historic stonework. Try for Rooms 2, 3, 7, or 8, as they overlook the small garden. **Pros:** free parking; some room deals push this back into the $ category. **Cons:** know what you're getting—rooms are very different from one another. ✉ *Rue des Cordeliers* ☎ *05–57–24–70–19* 🌐 *www.aubergedelacommanderie.com* 🛏 *17 rooms* 👍 *In-room: a/c (some), Wi-Fi* 💳 *MC, V* ⏲ *Closed mid-Dec.–mid-Feb.*

$$$–$$$$ ★ 🏨 **Château Lamothe du Prince Noir**. Magically set on a circular moat, fitted out with a storybook turret, and covered in an ambuscade of ivy, this manor house is a real charmer. It's also one of the oldest estates—Edward, "the Black" Prince of Wales, reputedly set up shop here in the 14th century. Set halfway between St-Émilion and Bordeaux, it has spacious guest rooms with large four-poster beds; styles range from Empire to 19th-century "Romanticisme," and most are done with lush accents (such as a tub with gilded feet). Owner Jacques Bastide speaks English and is extremely helpful. **Pros:** if you want privacy and a place to get away from it all, *c'est ici*. **Cons:** no dining facilities. ✉ *6 rte. du Stade, 25 km (16 mi) west of St-Émilion, 20 km (12 mi) northeast of Bordeaux, St-Sulpice-et-Cameyrac* ☎ *05–56–30–82–16* 🌐 *www.chateaux-france.com/lamotheprincenoir* 🛏 *5 suites*

MÉDOC MARATHON

The Médoc Marathon (🌐 *www.marathondumedoc.com*), on the first or second Saturday of September, is more than just a 42-km (26-mi) race through the vineyards: 52 other events appear along the way with at least 90% of the runners in disguise indulging in no fewer than 21 giant buffets of local fare, and from 22 refreshment stands en route. Speed is not exactly of the essence for most taking part in the competition; 2010 sees the 26th running of this hybrid athletic-alcoholic event.

In-room: a/c, Wi-Fi. In-hotel: pool ▭ *AE, MC, V* ⊙ *Closed Nov.–Mar.* *BP.*

$$$$ Fodor's Choice ★ **Grand Barrail Château Resort & Spa.** In a region with lackluster hotel options, this pretty-as-a-picture 19th-century château happily conjures up all your dreams of the good life. Following a refurbishment in early 2010, it is now even prettier. The storybook towers, turrets, and neo-Renaissance stone trim make the main building almost Disney-esque and inside the Belle Époque magic continues in the stained glass-topped dining rooms. Here talented chef Romain Gondrasserves various succulent selections of fresh foie gras seared in ever-changing sauces (no lunch Monday–Tuesday). Whether in the château or new modern wing, most guest rooms are large and smartly furnished with couture fabrics and soigné woods. **Pros:** fairy-tale château; special spa packages, golf and hot-air balloon rides nearby. **Cons:** pricey—but you're worth it. ✉ *Rte. Lebourne, 4 km (2½ mi) northwest of St-Émilion on D243* ☎ *05–57–55–37–00* ⊕ *www.grand-barrail.com* *41 rooms, 5 suites* *In-room: a/c, refrigerator. In-hotel: restaurant, bar, pool, Wi-Fi hotspot, some pets allowed* ▭ *AE, DC, MC, V* *MAP.*

$$$$ Fodor's Choice ★ **L'Hostellerie de Plaisance.** Part of the Relais & Châteaux group, this sumptuous hotel has long been considered the top and priciest address in St.-Émilion. Set next to the tourist office in the upper part of town in a stunningly elegant limestone Italianate mansion, it's just across the way from the town's famous stone Église Monolithe. The decor is an extravaganza masterminded by Alberto Pinto, decorator to the rich and famous, with main salons symphonies in tangerines, beiges, and blacks (too bad about the gaudy paintings); the dining room is luxuriously understated and makes an elegant stage for chef Philippe Etchebest's exotic menu: the crab stuffed with cabbage, pork with mango chutney, or the truffled bananas are all home runs. Warm and appealing, many rooms come with terraces overlooking the tile roofs of the town; some have excellent views of the vineyards. **Pros:** superstar decor; ideally situated in St.-Émilion for those wine excursions. **Cons:** certain rooms can be quite small for the price. ✉ *3 pl. du Clocher* ☎ *05–57–55–07–55* ⊕ *www.hostellerie-plaisance.com* *18 rooms, 3 suites* *In-room: a/c, refrigerator, Wi-Fi. In-hotel: restaurant, some pets allowed* ▭ *AE, DC, MC, V* ⊙ *Closed mid-Dec.–Feb.* *MAP.*

16

The Dordogne

WORD OF MOUTH

"I am going back to the Dordogne again this fall (and I can't wait). Why? Because it is so beautiful around there—and all of it is steeped in history . . . and they all speak French (and tolerate my efforts at it). I don't think any place of historical standing calls to me quite so strongly. It is like living in a novel or better."

—JoeCal

WELCOME TO THE DORDOGNE

TOP REASONS TO GO

★ **Fantastic Food:** Périgord truffles, foie gras, walnuts, plums, and myriad species of mushrooms jostle for attention on restaurant menus here—and the goose-liver pâté is as good as it gets.

★ **Rock Stars:** Lascaux is the "Louvre" of Paleolithic man and millions have witnessed prehistory writ large on its spectacularly painted cave walls.

★ **Religious Rocamadour:** Climb toward heaven up the towering cliff to Place St-Amadour's seven chapels and you might be transported to a better place.

★ **Sarlat's Cité Médiévale:** Feast your eyes on Sarlat's honey-color houses and 16th-century streets and then just feast at the hundred or so wine and foie-gras shops.

★ **Versailles in the Sky:** Set 400 feet above the Dordogne River, the ancestral garden of the Marquises de Marqueyssac is a 3-km (2-mi) maze of topiaries, parterres, and hedges.

1 Western Dordogne to Rocamadour. The Western Dordogne countryside is studded with Renaissance castles, like those at Monbazillac and Biron. Surrounded by lands cultivated by peasant farmers for centuries, *bastide* towns such as Monpazier were once heavily fortified. Heading southeast, the Lot Valley welcomes travelers with the lively town of Cahors, noted for its Romanesque cathedral in the Aquitaine dome style, and St-Cirq-Lapopie, a Renaissance-era time machine. Have your Nikon ready for Rocamadour's sky-touching Cité Religieuse, one of France's most famous pilgrimage shrines.

GETTING ORIENTED

Just northeast of Bordeaux, the region of Périgord is famed for its prehistoric art, truffle-rich cuisine, and once-upon-a-timefied villages. The best of these delights are found in the beloved *département* called the Dordogne. Part of the Aquitaine region, this living postcard is threaded by the Dordogne River, which, after its descent from the mountainous Massif Central, weaves westward past prehistoric sites like Lascaux. Astounding, too, are the medieval cliff-hewn villages like Rocamadour—provided that you manage to peer through the crowds in high season.

2 Eastern Périgord to Brantôme. You'll have a fight on your hands figuring out which sector of the Dordogne is the most beautiful, but many give the prize to the Périgord Noir. Immerse yourself in the past at Sarlat-la-Canéda, the golden-stone regional capital so beautifully preserved that film crews flock here for its 16th- and 17th-century turrets and towers. Nearby are the prehistoric grotto at Domme, the riverside village of La Roque-Gageac, and the hilltop castle at Beynac. To the north is the Vézère Valley, the prehistoric capital of France, home to fabled Lascaux. Beyond lies the thriving city of Périgueux.

DORDOGNE PLANNER

Taken to Cask

To the world, Cognac is not a place but a drink. That's cool with the locals of Cognac, who are perfectly content to take a back seat to the liquor that is lovingly aged in their cellar casks and pumps their economy.

A trip 49 km (56 mi) northwest of Brantôme makes a fitting finale to a tour of the Dordogne's countryside. Heading up into the Poitou-Charentes region, the black-wall town of Cognac seems an unlikely home for one of the world's most celebrated drinks.

Cognac owed its development to the transport of salt and wine along the Charente River. When 16th-century Dutch merchants discovered that the local wine was both tastier and easier to transport when distilled, the town became the heart of the brandy industry. From April to September most cognac houses organize visits of their premises and *chais*, the local name for cognac warehouses. Otard wins the history prize for being housed in the Château de Cognac, where King François I was born in 1494. Wherever you decide to go, you'll be inhaling the atmosphere of cognac: 3% of the cask-bound liquid evaporates every year. It's known as *la part des anges*, the angels' share.

Saying Hi to the Flintstone Clan

Perhaps the most famous cultural sights in the Dordogne are the prehistoric caves and grottos, such as Lascaux II, Grotte du Pech-Merle, the Domme grottoes, and Grotte du Grand-Roc.

Lascaux can take up to 2,000 people a day, but others—such as the Grotte des Combarelles in Les Eyzies-de-Tayac—only take six people on a tour at any given time (guaranteeing an intimate look).

Either because demand far outstrips supply, or because tickets are so limited, it's recommended you call or e-mail to prebook tickets.

For places like Lascaux, book as far in advance as possible (up to a year).

For less popular sights, a couple of days ahead of time should do, or you can sign up for a tour as early in the morning as possible.

The main tourist offices in the region, such as the one at Les Eyzies-de-Tayac, have the lowdown on all the caves and prehistoric sights in the area.

If you were not able to call ahead for tickets, it's worth stopping by the cave of your choice even if the office says tickets are sold out—space often opens up.

Be forewarned: you might get signed onto a tour that starts in a couple of hours, leaving you with time to kill, so have a game plan handy for other places to visit nearby.

DINING AND LODGING PRICE CATEGORIES (IN EUROS)

	¢	$	$$	$$$	$$$$
Restaurants	under €13	€13–€17	€18–€24	€25–€32	over €32
Hotels	under €65	€65–€105	€106–€145	€146–€215	over €215

Restaurant prices are per person for a main course at dinner, including tax (5.5%) and service; note that if a restaurant offers only prix-fixe (set-price) meals, it has been given the price category that reflects the full prix-fixe price. Hotel prices are for a standard double room in high season, including tax (19.6%) and service charge.

Making the Most of Your Time

From a practical perspective, staying in Sarlat or thereabouts would be your best plan of attack for getting to really appreciate this diverse and wonderful region.

Not only is this historic town a great place to enjoy, but it's also near the caves with Lascaux and Montignac to its north; Les Eyzies de Tayac to its west; Beynac-et-Cazenac, La Roque-Gageac, and Domme immediately to its south; and Rocamadour a little farther to the southeast.

Also, Sarlat is just off the A20 highway, which brings you right into Cahors to the south, and north to the regional airport in Brive La Gaillarde (the Bergerac airport to the east on the D703/D660 is a little bit farther afield).

After getting yourself situated, the first thing to do is eat, because even before enjoying those awe-inspiring views from Rocamadour and La Roque-Gageac, there's the important task of savoring foie gras and truffles.

After all, scenery and history are not the only things the Dordogne is famous for!

If you prefer solitude, you won't have any trouble finding it in the vast, sparsely populated spaces stretching inland and eastward in the rolling countryside of the Dordogne, chock-full of storybook villages, riverside châteaux, medieval chapels, and prehistoric sites.

Best bet is to get out of the overpopulated places such as Périgueux and Bergerac and head for the hills, literally.

The cathedral in Périgueux is something to see, but the châteaux and villages that sprinkle this region like so much historical and cultural confetti (in places such as Biron, Hautefort, Beynac, and Rocamadour) are sites you'll kick yourself for not seeing before the attractions of the big towns.

À la Périgourdine

If you're traveling in the Dordogne between October and March, it's essential to call restaurants ahead of time to avoid disappointment, as some shut for the slow season.

Closing times, too, can be variable, but when you do sit down somewhere, don't leave without tasting the regional delicacies of foie gras, truffles, walnuts, and chestnuts. When you snag your table, hone in on the menu's listing for dishes *à la périgourdine.*

These delights usually mean you're about to enjoy truffles or foie gras, or, heaven forbid, both!

Finding a Place to Stay

Advance booking is particularly desirable in the highly popular Dordogne, where hotels fill up quickly, in midsummer.

Many country or small-town hotels expect you to have at least one dinner with them, and if you have two meals a day with your lodging and stay several nights, you can save money. Prices off-season (October–May) often drop as much as 20%, but note that a number of hotels are closed from the end of October through March.

Assume that all hotel rooms have air-conditioning, TV, telephones, and private bath, unless otherwise noted.

GETTING AROUND

Car Travel

As the capital of southwest France, Bordeaux has superb transport links with Paris, Spain, and even the Mediterranean (A62 expressway via Toulouse links up with the A61 to Narbonne).

The A20 is the main route from Paris to just before Cahors.

It connects with the N21 at Limoges, which brings you down into Périgueux and Bergerac.

N89 links Bordeaux to Périgueux and D936 runs along the Dordogne Valley from Libourne to Bergerac continuing as D660 toward Sarlat.

Around the Whirl

The Dordogne is prime biking territory. In particular, the hour-long bike ride between Rocamadour and the Gouffre de Padirac might just be one of your most memorable experiences in France. And let's not forget daylong bike trips through the neighboring Célé valley and the 35-km (22-mi) trip to the prehistoric Grotte du Pech-Merle outside the town of Cabrerets. Happily, Cahors has plenty of places for bike rentals and picnic fixings (head for the town's covered and outdoor markets).

Air Travel

Frequent daily flights on Air France link Bordeaux and the domestic airport at Limoges with Paris (from several provincial airports), but if you're not interested in making the trip from Bordeaux then there's also Bergerac airport, which has about 28 flights a week from such diverse English cities as Southampton, Leeds Bradford, Edinburgh, Exeter, and Birmingham on Flybe and on Ryanair (London Stansted, East Midlands, and Liverpool). Also, there's the regional supplier, Airlinair (🌐 *www.airlinair.com*), which flies from Paris into nearby Brive La Gaillarde two times a day during the week and once on Sunday.

Airport Information **Aéroport de Bergerac-Périgord-Dordogne** (☎ *05–53–22–25–25* 🌐 *www.bergerac.aeroport.fr*). **Aéroport de Bordeaux-Mérignac** (☎ *05–56–34–50–50* 🌐 *www.bordeaux.aeroport.fr*).

Airlines and Contacts **Air France** (☎ *09–69–39–02–15* 🌐 *www.airfrance.com*). **Airlinair** (🌐 *www.airlinair.com*). **Flybe** (☎ *0044/1392–268513* 🌐 *www.flybe.com*). **Ryanair** (🌐 *www.ryanair.com*).

Bus Travel

The regional bus operator in the Dordogne is the Trans-Périgord network. It connects the main towns in the Dordogne with 13 bus lines, operated by eight different outfits. The maximum fare is €2, and there are reduced rates for people who buy 10 passes for €14, so traveling by bus in the Dorgdogne could save you a lot of money. The Périgueux to Angoulême route is operated by C.F.T.A Périgueux and the Périgueux to Hautefort route by Périgord Voyages/Cheze. For urban transport in Périgueux town use Peribus, and in Bergerac use TUB (Transports Urbains Bergeracois).

Bus Information **C.F.T.A. Périgueux** (✉ *Gare Routière, 19 rue Denis-Papin, Périgueux* ☎ *05–53–08–43–13*). **Peribus** (✉ *Pl. Montaigne Périgueux, Périgueux* ☎ *05–53–53–30–37*). **Périgord Voyages** (✉ *Lafeuillade, Carsac* ☎ *05–53–59–01–48*). **Trans-Périgord** (✉ *Carbanat, Veyrines-de-Domme* ☎ *05–53–28–52–20*).

Train Travel

The superfast TGV (Train à Grande Vitesse) Atlantique service links Paris (Gare Montparnasse) to Bordeaux—585 km (365 mi) in 3½ hours—with stops at Poitiers and Angoulême.

Trains link Bordeaux to Lyon (6 hrs) and Nice (8½ hrs) via Toulouse. Five trains daily make the 3½-hour, 400-km (250-mi) trip from Paris to Limoges.

Bordeaux is the region's major train hub. Trains run regularly from Bordeaux to Bergerac (80 mins), with occasional stops at St-Émilion, and four times daily to Sarlat (nearly 3 hrs).

At least six trains daily make the 90-minute journey from Bordeaux to Périgueux, and four continue to Limoges (2½ hrs).

A handy hint is to go to the Raileurope Web site *www.raileurope.com* and hit the tab for "Train Tickets & Passes" and then just enter your desired destination.

Remember that these train tickets are much cheaper in France, but the site makes for a great preparation search tool instead of the exceedingly labor-intensive SNCF site, which is replete with complex details and short on basic facts.

Train Information **SNCF** (*08–36–35–35–35* *www.sncf.fr*).

Tour Options

The Office de Tourisme in Sarlat offers general guided tours of the town in English every Wednesday from mid-May to mid-October at 11 AM and from July to August at 10:30 AM every Wednesday. The guided tours in French are much more frequent and the cost is €5.

If it's truffles you're after, you should go on a guided tour of the truffle groves in Sorges (a picturesque village to the northeast of Périgueux) every Tuesday and Thursday in July and August.

The tours can be arranged and leave from the **Sorges Truffle Museum** (*05–53–05–90–11* *Tues.–Sun., 10–noon and 2–5*) at 3:30 and last around an hour. The rest of the year, reservations can be made to go on guided tours for more than 20 people.

Office de Tourisme (*Ecomusée de la Truffe, Sorges* *05–53–05–90–11*).

The Rocky Road to Lascaux

Reaching Lascaux II is a major production without a car. If driving from Sarlat, head to Montignac, 26 km (16 mi) north on Route D704; Lascaux II is 1 km (½ mi) south of Montignac on Route D704. If using public transport, get yourself to Montignac by bus from Sarlat (on the Bordeaux-Brive line), the nearest town with a train station. Sarlat has early-morning buses (7 and 9 AM), which leave from Place de la Petite Rigandie. In Montignac you can buy tickets for Lascaux II next to the tourist office on Place Bertran.

Row, Row, Row Your Boat

One popular way to see the Dordogne's landscape is by canoe or kayak. Rental depots spring up frequently along the rivers of the region, especially near campsites. The curving and winding Vézère river is an especially boat-friendly stretch, while the Lot River valley gorge is famous for its dreamy dawn mists. One-person boats go for about 10 to 20 euros an hour, about twice that for two-person boats. Some rental companies will take you upstream by car to let you off, and some will even provide tents and waterproof casings for overnight stays. For more information, pick up boating brochures at any tourist office in the region.

EATING AND DRINKING WELL IN THE DORDOGNE

The best pâté de fois gras comes from the Dordogne (above); this region is truffle heaven (right, top); top wines hail from Cahors.

The Dordogne, or as the French like to call it, the Périgord, is considered by those in the know as one of the best regional cuisines in the country. Local chefs celebrate the area's abundant natural bounty in gourmet preparations and simple peasant dishes alike.

The rich natural resources of the Périgord are legendary: forests and fields are alive with wild game feasting on the nuts and leaves of chestnut, walnut, and oak trees. These trees encourage the growth of gourmet mushrooms and coveted truffles. The picturesque, winding rivers are home to trout and crayfish. Rolling fields are filled with grains and vegetables, running alongside groves of stone fruit.

There are not many regions in France that can boast such a wide selection of local meats (especially the famed Dordogne *foie gras*, as well as the equally famous pork, duck, and goose dishes); cheeses like Cabécou, Cujassous, Dubjac, Thieviers, and Échougnac; as well as distinctive wines, liqueurs, and brandies. This amazing variety of ingredients enables chefs here to create nearly everything from local products. —John Fanning

REGIONAL SPECIALTIES

Many well-known French meat dishes are named after surrounding villages and towns. Don't miss steak *à la Sarladaise* (stuffed with foie gras pate) or chicken *à la mode de Sorges* (stuffed with a mixture of chicken liver, mustard, bacon, and herbs). And for a sure dose of truffles, try any dish with *sauce Périgueux* or *à la périgourdine* in its name.

FOIE GRAS

Goose liver may not sound too enticing, but once you've had it there's no denying this delicious delicacy. The region has numerous farms with advertisements for foie gras everywhere you go, in shop windows and on road signs, portraying plump geese and ducks happily meandering toward you. At any food shop, you'll find containers of fresh and frozen foie gras, and it is an ever-present restaurant offering, prepared pôelé (pan fried, usually accompanied by a sweet side), in a terrine (pâté), or otherwise incorporated into your salads and main courses.

WALNUTS

Walnuts, or noix in French, are everywhere. Nuts mature throughout the summer, and usually start falling from the trees in October. The importance of walnuts in the Dordogne and France cannot be overstated. To the French the walnut is *the* nut (in fact, the translation of noix is simply "nut"). The French make walnut oil for cooking and drizzling on salads, incorporate walnut meats into savory and sweet dishes, and even make alcoholic beverages infused with walnut flavor. In fact, the aperitif of choice in the Dordogne is a sweet dark wine made from green walnuts picked in summer. The immature nuts impart a unique flavor to the wine.

TRUFFLES

During the months of October and November, and sometimes into December, the region's black gold—a fungi called *tuber melanosporum*—is unearthed and sold for exorbitant prices.

Found at the roots of oak trees by trained dogs and pigs, truffles contribute to the local economy, and to the region's celebrated cuisine.

Their earthy perfume and delicate flavor have inspired countless dishes prepared by home cooks and restaurant chefs alike.

WINE AND LIQUOR

If you are dining on the region's fabulous bounty, the best accompaniment is a local wine, liqueur, or brandy.

Bergerac is known for its white wines made from Sémillon and Sauvignon Blanc, and for its reds made from Merlot, Cabernet Sauvignon, and Cabernet Franc.

The area also produces excellent white dessert wines from the Sémillon grape.

The *fait maison*, or homemade, liqueurs are made from many fruits, including plum, quince, and blackcurrant.

Fruit is also favored here for distilling brandies. Some of the best-known are made from cherries, grapes, pears, and plums.

Introduction by John Fanning

Want to smile happily ever after? Discover a picture-postcard fantasy of castles, cliff-top châteaux, geese flocks, storybook villages, and prehistoric wonders? Join the club. Since the 1990s the Dordogne region has become one of the hottest destinations in France. Formerly one of those off-the-beaten-path areas, it's now in danger of getting four-starred, boutiqued, and postcarded to death. But scratch the surface and you can find one of the most authentic and appealing regions of rural France.

What's more (and unlike the Loire Valley, for example, where attractions are often far apart), you can discover romantic riverside château after château with each kilometer traveled. Then factor in four troglodyte villages, numerous natural *gouffres* (chasms), the sky-kissing village of Rocamadour, and the most famous prehistoric sights in the world, and you can see why all these attractions have not gone unnoticed: in July and August even the smallest village is often packed with sightseers.

The Dordogne département (province) is in the Aquitaine region of southwest France, where, above the river valleys, oak and chestnut forests crowd in on about 1,200 castles and châteaux, most of them from the 13th and 14th centuries. The area is marked by rich, luxuriant valleys through which flow clear-water rivers, such as the Dordogne, Isle, Dronne, Vézére, and the Lot. Separating the valleys are rugged plateaus of granite and limestone, sharp outcroppings of rock, and steep, sheer cliffs. Happily, the 10-km (6-mi) stretch of the Dordogne River from Montfort to Beynac is easily accessible by car, bike, canoe, or on foot, and shouldn't be missed, especially when fields of sunflowers line the banks in season. Offering a nice contrast to the region's rugged physiognomy and *nature sauvage* (wilderness) are hyper-picturesque villages such as La Roque-Gageac, wedged between rocky cliffs and the Dordogne River.

The region is centered around Sarlat, whose impeccably restored medieval buildings make it a great place to use as a base. Even better, the area around this town is honeycombed with dozens of *grottes* (caves) filled with Paleolithic drawings, etchings, and carvings. Just north of Sarlat is Lascaux, the "Louvre" of Cro-Magnon man and perhaps the most notable sight ever created by the Flintstone clan.

Fast-forward 30,000 years. The modern era dawns as the region comes under Merovingian rule in the 9th century. Divided up later by the dukes of Aquitaine, the region later went to England and then around 1370 was returned to the French crown. The crown complicated matters further by giving the area to the house of Bourbon in 1574, which meant Henry of Navarre inherited it. But Henry became Henry IV, king of France, in 1589, so the region returned to the crown again. Well, history is repeating itself, at least from an English perspective, as over the last several decades the British have moved back here in droves. They see the Dordogne as the quintessential French escape—and now the rest of the world is following in their footsteps.

WESTERN DORDOGNE TO ROCAMADOUR

From a bird's-eye view the geographic area in this chapter is known in France by four colors: the Périgord Noir, Blanc, Poupre, and Vert. Sarlat and its environs are known as the Périgord Noir, or Black Périgord; Périgueux to the north is based in the Périgord Blanc (white) region; Bergerac to the southwest is the Périgord Pourpre (purple); and Brantôme in the far north is in the Périgord Vert (green) region. With more than 2 million visitors every year, the Périgord Noir is the most frequented. But the entire Dordogne relies heavily on travelers, so the local tourist offices have plenty of informative guides and maps to help you enjoy whatever "color" you choose. Many first opt for "purple," since Bergerac is the main hub for flights (after Bordeaux). Thus we kick things off in Western Dordogne and then head southwest down to the lovely Lot Valley, where dramatic Rocamadour lures 1½ million tourists and pilgrims every year.

BERGERAC

57 km (36 mi) east of St-Émilion via D936, 88 km (55 mi) east of Bordeaux.

Yes, this is the Bergerac of Cyrano de Bergerac fame—but not exactly. The real satirist and playwright Cyrano (1619–55) who inspired playwright Edmond Rostand's long-nosed swashbuckler was born in Paris and never set foot anywhere near this town. That hasn't prevented his legend from being preempted by the town fathers, who have plastered his schnoz all over the town's promotional materials.

GETTING HERE

About 5 km south of town, Aéroport Bergerac-Perigord-Dordogne (☎ *05–53–22–25–25*) has more than 20 Ryanair and Flybe flights a week. Unfortunately, there is yet no train or bus service to the airport, so you have to take a taxi (☎ *05–53–23–32–32*) into the town center.

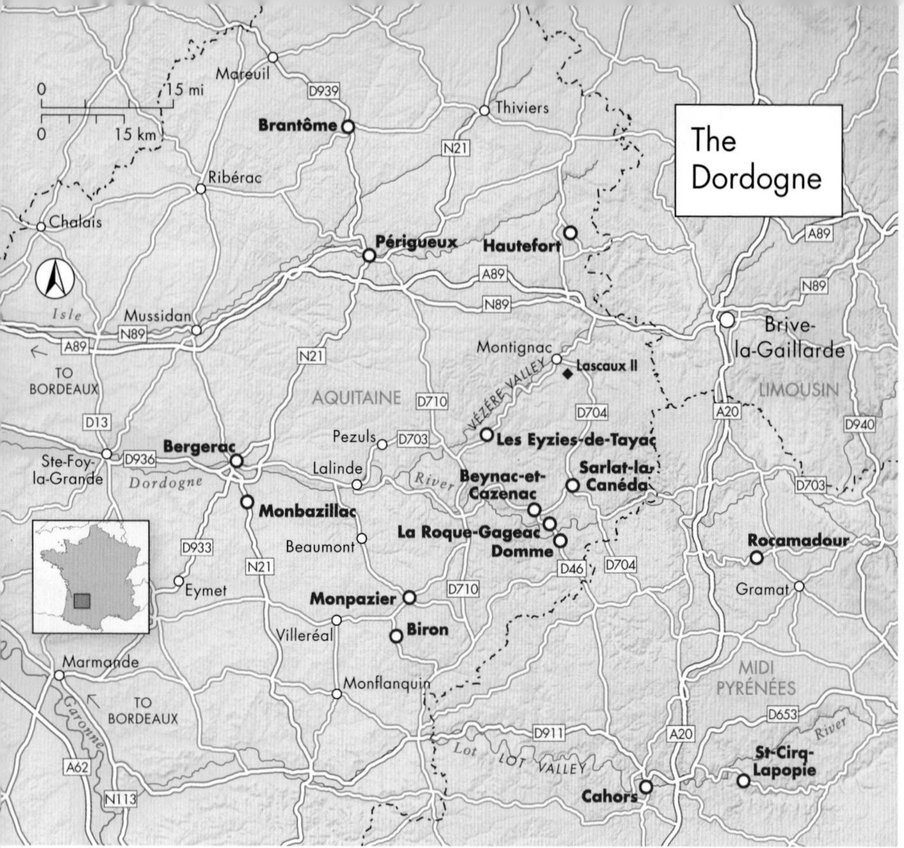

Transports Urbains Bergeracois (TUB ☎ *05–53–57–17–10*) is the urban bus service and costs €1 a ticket. Three bus operators leave the town for the surrounding region, Les Cars Bleus (☎ *05–53–23–81–92*) going to Eymet on two alternating routes through Sigoules or Issigeac; Boullet (☎ *05–53–61–00–46*) heading to Lalinde; and C.F.T.A. Perigueux (☎ *05–53–08–43–13*) traveling to Bergerac. Every trip costs €2. Bordeaux has five trains (taking anywhere from 1 hr, 15 mins to nearly 2 hrs) daily that run through Bergerac and hook up with Sarlat (1 hr, 15 mins); the rail station (☎ *05–53–63–53–80*) is on Avenue du 108e.

Visitor Information **Bergerac Tourist Office.** ✉ *97 rue Neuve d'Argenson* ☎ *05–53–57–03–11* 🌐 *www.bergerac-tourisme.com.*

EXPLORING

They needn't have bothered in erecting an exceedingly ugly statue of Cyrano in the middle of this town. Bergerac's gorgeous old half-timber houses, narrow alleys, riverside setting, and gastronomic specialties are more than enough to attract tourists staying in Bordeaux or Sarlat, both less than 100 km (62 mi) away. In the 14th century the English moved in, but in 1450 the French took over and, in time, Bergerac became a Protestant bastion. Today it's a lively farm-trade town with colorful markets held Wednesday and Saturday (the larger of the two).

Guided walking tours of the Vieille Ville (Old Town) in English (75–90 mins, €4.50) leave from the **tourist office** (✉ *97 rue Neuve d'Argenson* ☎ *05–53–57–03–11* 🌐 *www.bergerac-tourisme.com*).

There are also hour-long cruises along the Dordogne from 11 to 6, daily Easter through October (€7.50) in old wooden sailboats with **Périgord Gabarres** (☎ *05–53–24–58–80*).

The **Cloître des Récollets**, a former convent, is in the wine business. The convent's stone-and-brick buildings range in date from the 12th to the 15th century and include galleries, a large vaulted cellar, and a cloister where the **Maison des Vins** (Wine Center) provides information on, and samples of, local vintages of sweet whites and fruity young reds. ✉ *1 rue des Récollets* ☎ *05–53–63–57–57* *Free* *Feb.–Apr., Tues.–Sat. 10:30–12:30 and 4–6; May and June, Tues.–Sat. 10–12:30 and 4:30–7; July and Aug., daily 10–7.*

WHERE TO EAT AND STAY

$$ FRENCH **L'Imparfait.** In business in the heart of old Bergerac, this characterful restaurant has beamed ceilings, openwork stone and brick walls, large lamps, and tall, cane-back chairs. The lunch menu for €21 is good value, and for €43 in the evening you can start with warm oysters with saffron or a skewer of langoustine with honey and rosemary, then move on to ravioli in a citron sauce. ✉ *6–10 rue des Fontaines* ☎ *05–53–57–47–92* *AE, MC, V* *Closed late Dec.–late Jan.*

$ **Bordeaux.** Though in business since 1855 and occasional host to some famous clientele (Francis Bacon, François Mitterand, Georges Simenon), the Bordeaux of today has contemporary furnishings and simple, tidy rooms. Request one on the garden courtyard—or No. 22, which is slightly more spacious. The owner, Monsieur Manant, is very helpful. **Pros:** good location close to the Friday market, the old town, and the train station. **Cons:** rooms are a little too "understated" and are in need of some updating. ✉ *38 pl. Gambetta* ☎ *05–53–57–12–83* 🌐 *www.hotel-bordeaux-bergerac.com* *40 rooms* *In-room: a/c (some), Wi-Fi. In-hotel: pool, some pets allowed* *AE, DC, MC, V* *FAP.*

16

MONBAZILLAC

6 km (4 mi) south of Bergerac via D13.

★ From the hilltop village of Monbazillac are spectacular views of the sweet wine–producing vineyards tumbling toward the Dordogne. The storybook corner towers of the beautifully proportioned 16th-century gray-stone **Château de Monbazillac** pay tribute to the fortress tradition of the Middle Ages, but the large windows and sloping roofs reveal a Renaissance influence. Regional furniture and an ornate early-17th-century bedchamber enliven the interior. A wine tasting is included to tempt you into buying a case or two of the famous but expensive bottles. ☎ *05–53–63–65–00 weekdays, 05–53–61–52–52 weekends* 🌐 *www.chateau-monbazillac.com* *€6.30* *Apr., daily 10–noon and 2–6; May and Oct., daily 10–12:30 and 2–6; June and Sept., daily 10–7; July and Aug., daily 10–7; Nov., Dec., Feb., and Mar., Tues.–Sun. 10–noon and 2–5.*

MONPAZIER

Fodor's Choice ★ *45 km (28 mi) southeast of Bergerac via D660.*

Monpazier, on the tiny Dropt River, is one of France's best-preserved and most photographed bastide (fortified) towns. It was built in ocher-color stone by English king Edward I in 1284 to protect the southern flank of his French possessions. The bastide has three stone gateways (of an original six), a large central square, and the church of **St-Dominique,** housing 35 carved-wood choir stalls and a would-be relic of the True Cross.

Opposite the church is the finest medieval building in town, the **Maison du Chapître** *(Chapter House)*, once used as a barn for storing grain. Its wood-beam roof is constructed of chestnut to repel insects.

WHERE TO STAY

¢–$ **France.** Once an outbuilding on the estates of the Château de Biron, the Hôtel de France has never capitalized on its 13th-century heritage or its 15th-century staircase. Instead, it remains a small, modest family-run hotel that caters less to tourists than to locals, especially at its bar and restaurant ($), which serves rich regional food. Rooms are a clutter of old furniture (with a plastic-cabinet shower and toilet squeezed into the corner); some are quite large. **Pros:** central location; great restaurant; helpful staff. **Cons:** rooms are not nearly as impressive as the restaurant; no Internet service. ✉ *21 rue St-Jacques* ☎ *05–53–22–66–01* 🌐 *www.hoteldefrancemonpazier.fr* *10 rooms* *In-room: no a/c, no TV. In-hotel: restaurant, bar* 💳 *MC, V* ⏲ *Closed Nov.–Mar.* *MAP.*

BIRON

8 km (5 mi) south of Monpazier via D2/D53.

★ Stop in Biron to see its massive hilltop castle, the **Château de Biron**. Highlights of the château, which with its keep, square tower, and chapel dates from the Renaissance, include monumental staircases, Renaissance-era apartments, the kitchen with its huge stone-slab floor, and a gigantic dungeon, replete with a collection of scarifying torture instruments. The classical buildings were completed in 1760. The Gontaut-Biron family—whose ancestors invented great typefaces centuries ago—has lived here for 14 generations. ☎ *05–53–63–13–39* *€6.50* ⏲ *Apr.–June, Sept.–Nov., Tues.–Sun. 10–12:30 and 2–6; July and Aug., daily 10–7.*

CAHORS

60 km (38 mi) southeast of Monpazier via D811.

Less touristy and populated than most of the Dordogne, the Lot Valley has a subtler charm. The cluster of towns along the Lot River and the smaller rivers that cut through the dry, vineyard-covered plateau has a magical, abandoned feel. Just an hour north of southwestern France's main city, Toulouse, Cahors is the Lot area's largest town, hosts the helpful **regional information center** (✉ *107 quai Cavaignac* ☎ *05–65–35–07–09* 🌐 *www.tourisme-lot.com*), and makes a fine base from which to explore the Lot River valley, a 50-km (31-mi) gorge punctuated by medieval villages. Here and on other routes—notably the GR46, which spans the interior of the Lot region, with breathtaking views of the limestone plateaus and quiet valleys between Rocamadour and St-Cirq-Lapopie—*cyclotourisme* (biking) rules supreme.

GETTING HERE

If you're taking a train to Cahors you'll arrive at the station (☎ *08–36–35–35–35*) on Place Jouinot Gambetta from Paris's Gare d'Austerlitz in around five hours for about €60 one-way. Trains run frequently between Toulouse and Cahors, and the shuttle (€5) between the Toulouse airport and Toulouse bus station (next door to the railway station) run every 20 minutes. So you should consider flying into Toulouse as opposed to Bergerac, from which it is difficult to reach Cahors, or even into the regional airport of Brive La Gaillarde (🌐 *www.airlinair.com*) and then heading south to Cahors. Buses leave from the train station and, as within the rest of the Dordogne, can be erratic, although they cost only €2 a trip.

Visitor Information Cahors Tourist Office. ✉ *Pl. François-Mitterand* ☎ *05–65–53–20–65* 🌐 *www.tourisme-cahors.com.*

EXPLORING

Modern Cahors encircles its *Ville Antique* (Old Town), which dates from 1 BC. Once an opulent Gallo-Roman town, Cahors, sitting snugly within a loop of the Lot River, is famous for its vin de Cahors, a tannic red wine known to the Romans as "black wine." It was the Romans who introduced wine to Cahors, and Caesar is said to have brought Cahors wine back to Rome, but perhaps the region's biggest booster was the former bishop of Cahors who went on to become Pope John XXII. This second Avignon pope of the 14th century made sure his hometown wine became the communion wine of the Avignon church. Malbec is the most common grape used, which produces, according to recent studies, one of the most potent anticarcinogenic and heart-healthy wines on the planet—Madiran. There's also a growing amount of merlot in the region and the local jurançon noir grape to be tasted. Many of the small estates in the area offer tastings, and the town tourist office on Place François-Mitterrand (☎ *05–65–53–20–65*) can point you in the direction of some of the more notable vineyards, including the Domaine de Lagrezette (in Caillac) and the Domaine de St-Didier (in Parnac).

Cahors was also an early episcopal see and the capital of the old region of Quercy. Ruled by bishops until the 14th century, the university here was founded by Pope John XXII in 1322. The old parts of the town are interesting from an architectural perspective.

Fodor's Choice ★ The town's finest sight is the 14th-century **Pont Valentré**, a bridge with three elegant towers that constitutes a spellbinding feat of medieval engineering.

Also look for the fortresslike **Cathédrale St-Étienne** (✉ *Off Rue du Maréchal-Joffre*), with its Byzantine style and cloisters connecting to the courtyard of the archdeaconry, which is awash with Renaissance decoration and thronged with townsfolk who come to view art exhibits.

WHERE TO STAY

$$$–$$$$ **Château de Mercuès.** The former home of the count-bishops of Cahors, on a rocky spur just outside town, has older rooms in baronial splendor (ask for one of these), as well as unappealing modern ones (which tend to attract midges). One of the best is "Tour," with a clever ceiling that slides back to expose the turret. Duck, lamb, and truffles reign in the restaurant ($$$$), but the high prices lead you to expect more creativity from chef Philippe Combet than is delivered. The restaurant is closed Monday, and there's no lunch Tuesday–Thursday. **Pros:** unbeatable view; great pool. **Cons:** mix of French moderne and medievalesque furniture in the rooms can be jarring. ✉ *8 km (5 mi) northwest of Cahors on road to Villeneuve-sur-Lot, Mercuès* ☎ *05–65–20–00–01* 🌐 *www.chateaudemercues.com* *24 rooms, 6 suites* *In-room: no a/c, refrigerator, Internet. In-hotel: restaurant, tennis courts, pool, Internet terminal, some pets allowed* *AE, DC, MC, V* *Closed mid-Nov.–Easter* *MAP.*

ST-CIRQ-LAPOPIE

Fodor's Choice ★ *32 km (20 mi) east of Cahors via D653, D662, and D40.*

Perched on the edge of a cliff 330 feet up, the beautiful 13th-century village of St-Cirq (pronounced san-*sare*) looks as though it could slide right into the Lot River. Filled with artisans' workshops and not yet renovated à la Disney, the town has so many dramatic views you may end up spending several hours here. Traversing steep paths and alleyways among flower-filled balconies, you'll realize it deserves its description as one of the most beautiful villages in France.

GETTING HERE

The easiest way to reach St-Cirq-Lapopie from Cahors's train station is to take the SNCF bus bound for Figeac (40 mins); St-Cirq is a 25-minute walk from where the bus drops you. From the bus stop Tour de Faure, go back to the D181 (sign says ST-CIRQ 2 KM), cross the bridge, and walk uphill. It's a haul, but worth the hike.

Visitor Information St-Cirq-Lapopie Tourist Office. ✉ *Pl. du Sombral* ☎ *05–65–31–29–06* 🌐 *www.saint-cirqlapopie.com.*

EXPLORING

Residents happily still outnumber travelers here. Still, visitors are highly welcomed at the tourist office, in the center of town, which can give you tips for finding the beauty spots, including the mostly ruined 13th-century château can be reached by a stiff walk along the path that starts near the Hôtel de Ville. Morning hikes in the misty gorges in the valley are beyond beautiful.

★ Discovered in 1922, the **Grotte du Pech-Merle** displays 4,000 square feet of prehistoric drawings and carvings. Particularly known for its peculiar polka-dot horses, impressions of the human hand, and footprints, this is the most impressive "real-thing" prehistoric cave that is open to the public in France. The admission charge includes a 20-minute film, an hour-long tour, and a visit to the adjacent museum. Take a great bike ride here from St-Cirq-Lapopie or the SNCF bus from Cahors—getting

CLOSE UP

Nobody Knows the Truffles I've Seen

The Dordogne is a land of foie gras and cognac, so travelers get to eat (and quaff) like the kings (and queens) who once disputed this coveted corner, staking it out with châteaux-forts and blessing it with Romanesque churches.

Begin by following the winding sprawl of the Dordogne River into duck country. This is the land of the *gavée* goose, force-fed extravagantly to plump its liver into one of the world's most renowned delicacies.

Duck or goose fat glistens on potatoes, on salty confits, and on *rillettes d'oie*, a spread of potted duck that melts on the tongue as no mere butter ever could.

Wild mushrooms and truffles (referred locally to as "black diamonds") weave their musky perfume through dense game pâtés.

Although truffle production is nothing like it used to be, this subterranean edible fungus has been beguiling chefs and foodies for centuries.

The truffle forms a symbiotic relationship with the roots of certain trees (in the Périgord region they are mainly found growing from green oaks) and plants to form a part that is technically known as the *ascoma*, the fruiting body of a fungus.

Mysteriously appearing anytime from November to February in the forests of Périgord (and other areas of western Europe), the region's *truffes* (truffles) have been highly respected since the 15th century. The more famous truffles are black, but there are also white varieties—hundreds of species in all.

Truffles are savory, zesty, and extremely aromatic, and because of this they have been glorified as a delicacy in recipes for thousands of years (if we are to believe old Greek and Roman writings on the subject). They can be canned for export and are often infused into oils.

Traditionally, pigs hunted for truffles, but nowadays dogs are more commonly used—they can be taught to point for truffles.

Also, as the dogs don't eat the truffles when they find them, they make for much better hunters than the avaricious piglets.

Cultivation of the famous fungus by way of inoculating the roots of a host plant seedling with fungal spores has had success, though the manufactured truffles are still thought to taste inferior to the ones found in the forests.

To stand up to such an onslaught of earthy textures and flavors, the best Dordogne wines, such as Bergerac and Cahors, have traditionally been known as coarser brews.

However, since the 1970s the winegrowers around Cahors have succeeded in mellowing those coarser edges.

And to round it all off? A snifter of amber cognac—de rigueur for the digestion.

Dining thus, in a vine-covered stone *ferme auberge* deep in the green wilds of Dordogne, replete with a feast of pâtés, truffles, and cognacs, you begin to see what the 13th-century Plantagenets invaders from England were fighting for.

Draped on a cliff 1,500 feet over the Alzou River gorge, Rocamadour is one of the most spectacular towns of the Dordogne.

off at Conduché (before St-Cirq) and walking the 7 km (4 mi) along D41—or just drive (from Cahors take D653, 7 km [4 mi] to the right turn by Vers). On peak summer days tickets are at a premium (there's a daily limit of 700 visitors), so book them in advance. ✉ *10 km (6 mi) north of St-Cirq-Lapopie, 3 km (2 mi) west of Cabrerets* ☎ *05–65–31–27–05* 🌐 *www.pechmerle.com* 🎫 *€7.50* 🕒 *Early Apr.–early Nov., daily 9:30–noon and 1:30–5.*

WHERE TO STAY

¢–$ **L'Auberge du Sombral.** If location and views are what you're after then you've found the place! Sitting on a quaint cobbled square in the center of the town, this old house is covered in grapevines and roses. Although the auberge has all the local culinary specialties served up to you in a charming dining room (open for lunch daily and for dinner on Saturday to Friday), one should really try Le Gourmet Quercynois just down the street first. **Pros:** can't beat the location. **Cons:** clean the bathrooms, and bedroom decor could do with a face-lift. ✉ *St-Cirq-Lapopie* ☎ *05–65–31–26–08* 🌐 *www.lesombral.com* *8 rooms* *In-room: no a/c. In-hotel: restaurant, Wi-Fi hotspot* 💳 *AE, MC, V* *MAP.*

ROCAMADOUR

72 km (45 mi) north of St-Cirq via Labastide-Murat.

A medieval village that seems to defy the laws of gravity, Rocamadour surges out of a cliff 1,500 feet above the Alzou River gorge—an awe-inspiring sight that makes this one of the most-visited tourist spots in France.

GETTING HERE

Bergerac airport is a bit far from this famous village, so it might be easier to take regional carrier Airlinair (🌐 *www.airlinair.com*) to nearby Brive La Gaillarde directly north of Rocamadour (for as little as €40 one-way from Paris two times a day during the week and once on Sunday), or to the Toulouse airport. If you're getting here by train—direct connections are available to Toulouse (1½ hrs) and Brive (40 mins, €7)—you'll want to have your walking shoes on, because the Rocamadour-Padirac station (☎ *05–65–33–63–05*) is a shared affair with the neighboring village of Padirac and is 4 km (3 mi) away from the village. Walking takes about an hour, biking 15 minutes, or you can call Taxi Pascal Herbert (☎ *05–65–50–14–82, 06–81–60–14–60 cell*).

WORD OF MOUTH

While it would be easy to quote kind remarks from Fodor's Web site about St-Cirq, we will let André Breton (1896–1966)—theorist of the Surrealist movement—do the honors: "Beyond any other site of Europe or the Americas, Saint-Cirq put the spell on me—the one which binds you forever. I have stopped wanting to be elsewhere. Every morning, when I get up, I have the impression of contemplating through my window the very best of art, nature, and life."

16

Visitor Information Rocamadour Tourist Office. ✉ *Maison du Tourisme* ☎ *05–65–33–22–00* 🌐 *www.rocamadour.com.*

EXPLORING

Rocamadour got its name after the discovery in 1166 of the 1,000-year-old body of St. Amadour "quite whole." The body was moved to the cathedral, where it began to work miracles. Legend has it that the saint was actually a publican named Zacheus, who, after the honor of entertaining Jesus in his home, came to Gaul after the crucifixion and, under the name of Amadour, established a private chapel in the cliff here. Pilgrims have long flocked to the site, climbing the 216 steps to the church on their knees. Making the climb on foot is a sufficient reminder of the medieval penchant for agonizing penance; today two elevators lift weary souls. Unfortunately, the summer influx of a million tourists has brought its own blight, judging by the dozens of tacky souvenir shops. Cars are not allowed; park in the lot below the town.

The town is split into four levels joined by steep stairs. The lowest level is occupied by the village of Rocamadour itself, and mainly accessed through the centuries-old Porte du Figuier (Fig Tree Gate). Past this portal, the **Cité Médiévale**, or the **Basse Ville**, though in parts grotesquely touristy, is full of beautifully restored structures, such as the 15th-century **Hôtel de Ville**, near the Porte Salmon, which houses the **tourist office** and an excellent collection of tapestries. ☎ *05–65–33–22–00* 🎫 *€2* ⏲ *July and Aug., daily 9:30–7; Jan. and Feb., and Nov. and Dec., daily 2–5; Mar.–June, and Sept. and Oct., daily 9:30–12:30 and 2–6.*

Fodor's Choice ★ The Basse Ville's Rue Piétonne, the main pedestrian street, is lined with creperies, tea salons, and hundreds of tourists, many of whom are heading heavenward by taking the **Grand Escalier** staircase or elevator (fee) from Place de la Carreta up to the **Cité Religieuse**, set halfway up the cliff. If you walk, pause at the landing 141 steps up to admire the fort. Once up, you can see tiny Place St-Amadour and its seven chapels: the basilica of **St-Sauveur** opposite the staircase; the **St-Amadour crypt** beneath the basilica; the chapel of **Notre-Dame,** with its statue of the Black Madonna, to the left; the chapels of **John the Baptist, St-Blaise,** and **Ste-Anne** to the right; and the Romanesque chapel of **St-Michel** built into an overhanging cliff. St-Michel's two 12th-century frescoes—depicting the Annunciation and the Visitation—have survived in superb condition.

GOD'S VIEW

On the uppermost plateau of the Cité Réligieuse stands the Château de Rocamadour, a private residence of the church fathers. Open to the public for an admission fee are its ramparts, which have spectacular views of the gorge. However, you can enjoy the same views for free just by walking the Chemin de la Croix up to the castle.

WHERE TO STAY

$$$–$$$$ Fodor's Choice ★ **Château de la Treyne.** Certainly the most spectacular château-hotel in the Dordogne, this Relais & Châteaux outpost sits in splendor in enchantingly Baroque gardens that are perched over the Dordogne River. Set in Lacave, 6 km (3½ mi) northwest of Rocamadour, La Treyne was nearly destroyed in the 16th-century Wars of Religion but happily reconstructed under Louis XIII. Today the Great Lounge restaurant (no lunch Tuesday to Friday) is a symphony of chandeliers, oak panels, and Louis Treize chairs. Guest rooms are stylish, ranging from the Prison Doreé, or "Golden Prison" (set atop the castle tower, replete with centuries-old stone walls and panoramic views) to the hyper-charming Soleil Levant (the former chapel, now glowing in historic limes and yellow). As for modern luxe, delights range from Jacuzzis to minibars. **Pros:** the château has been sparklingly renovated; half-board included in room price. **Cons:** pricey. ✉ *La Treyne, 21 km (13 mi) northwest of Rocamadour, Lacave* ☎ *05–65–27–60–60* 🌐 *www.chateaudelatreyne.com* *12 rooms, 4 suites* *In-room: a/c, refrigerator, Internet (some). In-hotel: restaurant, bar, tennis court, pool, Wi-Fi hotspot, some pets allowed* *AE, DC, MC, V* *Closed early Nov.–late Dec. and early Jan.–late Mar.* *MAP.*

¢ **Lion d'Or.** In the center of Rocamadour, this simple, bargain-price, family-run hotel has a restaurant with panoramic views of the valley, where genial owners Emmanuel and Sally Vernillet serve up delicious truffle omelets and homemade foie gras au Noilly. **Pros:** location in the Old Town; amazing views from restaurant. **Cons:** rooms have floral wallpaper and linens that might not be to everyone's taste. ✉ *Cité Médiévale* ☎ *05–65–33–62–04* 🌐 *www.liondor-rocamadour.com* *36 rooms* *In-room: no a/c, Wi-Fi (some). In-hotel: restaurant* *MC, V* *Closed Nov.–Easter* *FAP.*

EASTERN PERIGORD TO BRANTÔME

Entering the Perigord Noir, a trifecta of top Dordogne sights awaits: the cliff-face village of La Roque-Gageac, the prehistoric grottoes of Domme, and the storybook castle at Beynac. Just eastward lies Sarlat, the regional center and a town famed for its half-timber pastoral and medieval vibe. Northward lies the Vézère Valley, the prehistoric capital of France, celebrated for its locales settled by primitive man, such as Lascaux. Continuing north, the traveler arrives at the bustling city of Périgueux and numerous riverside towns, including historic Brantôme. For three centuries during the Middle Ages, this entire region was a battlefield in the wars between the French and the English. Of the castles and châteaux dotting the area, those at Hautefort and Beynac are among the most spectacular. Robust Romanesque architecture is more characteristically found in this area than the airy Gothic style in view elsewhere in France, and can be admired at Périgueux Cathedral and in countless village churches.

LA ROQUE-GAGEAC

Fodor's Choice ★ *55 km (36 mi) west of Rocamadour via Payrac, 10 km (6 mi) southwest of Sarlat via D703.*

Across the Dordogne from Domme, in the direction of Beynac, romantically huddled beneath a cliff, is strikingly attractive La Roque-Gageac, one of the best-restored villages in the valley. Crafts shops line its narrow streets, dominated by the outlines of the 19th-century mock-medieval Château de Malartrie and the Manoir de Tarde, with its cylindrical turret. If you leave the main road and climb one of the steep cobblestone paths, you can check out the medieval houses on their natural perches and even hike up the mountain for a magnificently photogenic view down to the village.

WHERE TO STAY

$ ★ **La Plume d'Oie.** This lovely small inn overlooks the river and the limestone cliffs. Guest rooms, in light fabrics and wicker furniture, vary in size and price—views over the Dordogne also face the busy road (light-sleepers should ask for rooms in the back). La Plume d'Oie's major raison d'être, however, is the cheery stone-wall, wood-beam restaurant ($$$–$$$$), at which you are expected to have at least one meal. Chef–owner Marc-Pierre Walker prepares classic regional cuisine, such as roasted duckling in a pepper shallot sauce and the ever popular panfried foie gras (the restaurant is closed Monday and does not serve dinner Sunday or lunch Tuesday; reservations are essential). **Pros:** great view; top eatery. **Cons:** hotel is noisy; no Internet service. ✉ *La Roque-Gageac* ☎ *05–53–29–57–05* 🌐 *www.arachnis.asso.fr/dordogne/vitrines/plume/index1.html* *4 rooms* *In-room: no a/c. In-hotel: restaurant* MC, V *Closed late Nov.–mid-Dec. and mid-Jan.–mid-Feb.*

DOMME

5 km (3 mi) east of La Roque-Gageac.

The historic cliff-top village of Domme is famous for its **grottoes**, where prehistoric bison and rhinoceros bones have been discovered. You can visit the 500-yard-long illuminated galleries, which are lined with stalactites. ✉ *Pl. de la Halle* 🎫 *€8* ⏲ *Feb.–June and Sept.–Nov., daily 10:15–noon and 2:15–6; July and Aug., daily 10–6.*

BEYNAC-ET-CAZENAC

11 km (7 mi) west of La Roque-Gageac via D703.

Visitor Information **Beynac-et-Cazenac Tourist Office.** ✉ *La Balme* ☎ *05-53-29-43-08* 🌐 *www.cc-perigord-noir.fr.*

EXPLORING

One of the most picturesque sights in the Dordogne is the medieval castle that sits atop the wonderfully restored town of Beynac. Perched atop a sheer cliff face beside an abrupt bend in the Dordogne River, the muscular 13th-century **Château de Beynac** has unforgettable views from its battlements. During the Hundred Years' War this castle often faced off with forces massed directly across the way at the fort of Castenaud. Star of many films, Beynac was last featured in Luc Besson's 1999 life of Joan of Arc, *The Messenger.* Tours of the castle are in English for groups by reservation. ☎ *05-53-29-50-40* 🎫 *€7:50* ⏲ *May–Sept., daily 10–6:30; Oct.–Apr., daily 10–6.*

With a fabulous mountaintop setting, the now-ruined castle of **Castlenaud**, containing a large collection of medieval arms, is just upstream from Beynac across the Dordogne. Make sure to give yourself at least an hour to visit. ☎ *05-53-31-30-00* 🎫 *€7.80* ⏲ *Apr.–June, and Sept., daily 10–7; July and Aug., daily 9–8; Nov.–Jan., daily 2–5; Oct. and Feb.–Mar., daily 10–6.*

★ Five kilometers (3 mi) from Castlenaud is the turreted **Château des Milandes**. Built around 1489 in Renaissance style, it has lovely terraces and gardens and was once owned by the American-born cabaret star of Roaring '20s Paris, Josephine Baker. Here she housed her "rainbow family," a large group of adopted children from many countries. Today there's a museum devoted to her memory and, from April to October, falconry displays. From here D53 (via Belvès) leads southwest to Monpazier. ☎ *05-53-59-31-21* 🌐 *www.milandes.com* 🎫 *€8* ⏲ *May, June, and Sept., Sun.–Fri. 10–6:30; July and Aug., daily 9:30–7:30; Apr. and Oct., daily 10–6:15.*

Fodor's Choice ★ For Périgord Noir at its most enchanting, head to the garden of the **Château de Marqueyssac**, set in Vézac, about 3 km (1½ mi) south of Beynac-et-Cazenac. The park was founded in 1682, and its design, including a parterre of cut topiaries, was greatly influenced by the designs of André le Nôtre, the "green geometer" of Versailles. Shaded paths bordered by 150,000 hand-pruned boxwoods are graced with breathtaking viewpoints, rock gardens, waterfalls, and verdant glades. From the belvedere 400 feet above the river, there's an exceptional view of the Dordogne valley, with its castles and beautiful villages such as Beynac, Fayrac, Castelnaud, Roque-Gageac, and Domme. A tea salon is open from March to mid-November and is just the place to drink in the panoramic views from the parterre terrace. To get a dazzling preview, log on to the Web site. ✉ *Belvédère de la Dordogne, Vézac, 9 km (5 mi) southwest of Sarlat* ☎ *05–53–31–36–36* 🌐 *www.marqueyssac.com* 🎫 *€7.20* ⏲ *July and Aug., daily 9–8; Feb., Mar., and Oct.–mid-Nov., daily 10–6; mid-Nov.–Jan., daily 2–5; Apr., May, June, and Sept., daily 10–7.*

WHERE TO STAY

¢–$ **Pontet.** A few blocks from the Dordogne River and within the shadow of cliff-top Château de Beynac, this is one of the hotel mainstays of the adorably Dordognesque town of Beynac. Guest rooms are sweet and simple, and a short hike down to the river will bring you to the hotel's Hostellerie Maleville, a big riverside restaurant ($$–$$$), where you'll want to forgo a table in the modern, wood-beam dining room for a blissfully magical perch on the riverbank itself. Here umbrellas and willow trees shade diners happily tucking into such fare as goose neck stuffed with truffles and Beynacoises potatoes. **Pros:** charming old stone house surrounded by winding old streets. **Cons:** parking's not provided; no Internet service (although tentative plans are underway to add it). ✉ *Beynac-et-Cazenac* ☎ *05–53–29–50–06* *13 rooms* *In-room: no a/c. In-hotel: restaurant* *AE, MC, V.*

16

SARLAT-LA-CANÉDA

Fodor's Choice ★ *10 km (6 mi) northeast of Beynac via D57, 74 km (46 mi) east of Bergerac.*

Sarlat (as it's usually known) defines enchantment. If you're planning a trip to the many prehistoric caves and the amazing perched villages near this gorgeous town, then this capital of the Périgord Noir is the place to stay. It's ideally located, with Les Eyzies de Tayac, Montignac, and Lascaux to its north and Beynac-et-Cazenac, Domme, and La Roque-Gageac just to its south. Even Rocamadour, to the southeast on the D704, which connects with the D673 isn't all that far from here and Cahors is a straight shot south on the A20 *péage* (toll road) or the more scenic (and longer) N20.

GETTING HERE

Flying here usually means coming into Bergerac airport but there's also the regional supplier, Airlinair, which flies from Paris into nearby Brive La Gaillarde to the north (for as little as €40 one-way two times a day during the week and once on Sunday). A half-hour walk out of town, **Sarlat train station** (✉ *2 rue Stade,*) on the northeast side of town is poorly linked with the rest of the Dordogne. For trains to Les Eyzies (1 hr) and Périgueux (1½ hrs) you'll need to change at Le Buisson. There are trains to Sarlat from Bordeaux twice a day. To get to Paris you have to change at Souillac, and the trip takes about 5½ hours for about €70 one-way. Buses, again minimal, are operated by **Effia Transports Belmon** (☎ *05–56–33–03–80*) on the Souillac route and **Périgord Voyages/Cheze** (☎ *05–53–59–01–48*) on the Périgueux one. However, Sarlat proper does have the claim to fame (for a town of less than 10,000 people) of having three bus lines (Sarlat Bus). Don't get off at the train station, but at the stops at Place Pasteur or Rue de la République.

Visitor Information **Sarlat-la-Canéda Tourist Office.** ✉ *3 rue Tourny* ☎ *05-53-31-45-45* 🌐 *www.sarlat-tourisme.com.*

EXPLORING

Tucked among hills adorned with corn and wheat, Sarlat is a beautiful, well-preserved medieval town that, despite attracting huge numbers of visitors, has managed to retain some of its true character. With its storybook streets, Sarlat's **Cité Médiévale** is filled most days with tour groups, and is especially hectic on Saturday, market day: all the geese on sale are proof of the local addiction to foie gras. To do justice to the town's golden-stone splendor, wander through its medieval streets in the late afternoon or early evening, aided by the tourist office's walking map. The tourist office (✉ *Rue Tourny* ☎ *05–53–31–45–45*) also organizes walking tours, which for €5 give you an in-depth look at the town's medieval buildings.

The end of the Hundred Years' War (1453) favored the construction of beautiful urban architecture in the Dordogne, but Sarlat was especially favored: when the region was handed back to the French king by the English, he rewarded the town with royal privileges for its loyalty to his crown. Before long, a new merchant class sprang up, building gabled and golden-stone mansions in the latest French Renaissance style. It's no surprise to learn that only Nice and Paris have had more films shot in their locales than Sarlat; Lasse Hallstrom's *Chocolat* (2000) and Luc Besson's *The Messenger* (1999) are some of the better known of the more than 45 movies that have used the town as a backdrop. Also, every year in November the town actually has its own film festival with comedians, film stars, producers, and film technicians arriving to host an informational get-together for 500 students. In addition, there's a theater festival here mid-July to the end of August.

Sarlat's Cité Médiévale has many beautiful photo-ops. Of particular note is Rue de la Liberté, which leads to **Place du Peyrou**, anchored on one corner by the steep-gabled Renaissance house where writer-orator Étienne de la Boétie (1530–63) was born.

The elaborate turreted tower of the **Cathédrale St-Sacerdos** (✉ *Pl. du Peyrou*), begun in the 12th century, is the oldest part of the building and, along with the choir, all that remains of the original Romanesque structure.

The sloping garden behind the cathedral, the **Jardin des Enfers**, contains a strange, conical tower known as the Lanterne des Morts (Lantern of the Dead), which was occasionally used as a funeral chapel.

Running the length of the Enfer gardens is the **Rue Montaigne**, where the great 16th-century philosopher Michel de Montaigne once lived—some of the half-timber houses that line this street cast a fairy-tale spell. Rue d'Albusse, adjoining the garden behind the cathedral, and Rue de la Salamandre are narrow, twisty streets that head to Place de la Liberté and the 18th-century **Hôtel de Ville.**

DID YOU KNOW?

Sarlat's tourist office has walking tours that allow travelers to fully savor the town's golden-stoned splendor—heading out from Rue Tourny, these walks include beauty-spots wanderers might miss.

Opposite the town hall is the rickety Gothic church of **Ste-Marie**, with its picturesque gargoyles overlooking Place du Marché aux Oies.

Ste-Marie points the way to Sarlat's most interesting street, **Rue des Consuls**. Among its medieval buildings are the Hôtel Plamon, with broad windows that resemble those of a Gothic church, and, opposite, the 15th-century Hôtel de Vassal.

WHERE TO STAY

¢–$ ★ **Hostellerie La Couleuvrine.** Sarlat is not overly blessed with beautiful historic hotels, so this one is a true standout. Topped with a massive crenellated tower and built into the town's ancient ramparts, this imposing structure once held off besieging forces during the Wars of Religion thanks to its tower *couleuvrines* ("long cannons"). Inside, the atmosphere is richest in the medieval restaurant (closed January): a vast half-timber, 13th-century stone hall where the town council once presided. Even more delicious is the food, such as the brick-pressed duck with coriander artichokes and the fresh-fruit kebab with Sauternes zabaglione. Guest rooms are simply but elegantly furnished; the showpiece is the tower room complete with a crenellated Cinerama view out the windows. **Pros:** like a Relais & Chateaux property at one-quarter the price! **Cons:** a few blocks east of the Cite Médiévale. ✉ *1 pl. de la Bouquerie* ☎ *05–53–59–27–80* 🌐 *www.la-couleuvrine.com* *25 rooms, 3 suites* *In-room: no a/c, Wi-Fi. In-hotel: restaurant* *AE, DC, MC, V* *EP, MAP.*

$–$$ **Hôtel de la Madeleine.** This sturdy stone 19th-century building just to the north of the Old Town has small but cozy pastel-color bedrooms with floral quilts; three have a balcony. Note that at the end of 2009 the new owners Monsieur and Madame Florent made extensive renovations on the hotel; they added on great extras such as a swimming pool, hamman, and spa. **Pros:** lovely, spacious lounge is a great place to read and relax. **Cons:** very hard to find parking near the hotel. ✉ *1 pl. de la Petite-Rigaudie* ☎ *05–53–59–10–41* 🌐 *www.hoteldelamadeleine-sarlat.com* *39 rooms* *In-room: a/c. In-hotel: pool, Wi-Fi hotspot, some pets allowed* *AE, DC, MC, V* *Closed late Nov.–Feb.* *MAP.*

¢–$ **Hôtel des Recollets.** One of Sarlat's time-burnished hotels, this is in the southern section of the town's Cité Médiévale, side by side with the 17th-century Chapelle des Recollets and its convent. Today, the hotel—blessed with a golden-stone facade—is centered around the convent's ancient cloister, which makes an exquisite setting for breakfast. Guest rooms are extremely simple, befitting the rates, which also include such pluses as air-conditioning, minibars, and the nice location. **Pros:** good value for money; secure parking provided nearby. **Cons:** if you're not into French moderne decor then this is not the place for you. ✉ *1 pl. de la Bouquerie* ☎ *05–53–31–36–00* 🌐 *www.hotel-recollets-sarlat.com* *18 rooms* *In-room: a/c, refrigerator, Wi-Fi* *MC, V* *EP.*

LES EYZIES-DE-TAYAC

21 km (13 mi) northwest of Sarlat via D47.

Visitor Information **Eyzies-de-Tayac Tourist Office** ✉ *19 rue de la Préhistoire* ☎ *05–53–06–97–05* 🌐 *www.leseyzies.com.*

EXPLORING

Sitting comfortably under a limestone cliff, Les Eyzies is the doorway to the prehistoric capital of France. Early Homo sapiens (the species to which humans belong) lived about 40,000 years ago and skeletal remains and other artifacts of this Aurignacian culture were first found here in 1868. Many signs of Cro-Magnon man have been discovered in this vicinity; a number of excavated caves and grottoes, some with wall paintings, are open for public viewing, including the Grotte-Font-de-Gamme, just south of the town, with very faint drawings to be seen on a tour, and the Grotte des Combarelles. Stop by the town tourist office for the lowdown on all the caves in the area—the office also sells tickets for most sites and you should reserve here because a surprising number of tours sell out in advance (sometimes there are only six people allowed at any one time in a cave).

ARE YOU NUTTY?

If you're nuts about nuts, Sarlat is your town—the Périgord is the second-biggest producer of walnuts in France, and those from the Sarladais region are prized. The nuts are sold in the markets in October and November and walnut wood (often preferred here to oak) is used to make beautiful furniture. Visit the Eco-Musée de la Noix (⊕ *www.ecomuseedelanoix.site.voila.fr* ⊙ *Closed Apr.–mid-Nov.*), just south of Sarlat in Castelnaud-la-Chapelle, for a nutty detour!

16

Amid the dimness of the **Grotte du Grand-Roc** you can view weirdly shaped crystalline stalactites and stalagmites—not for the claustrophobic. At the nearby **Abri Préhistorique de Laugerie,** you can visit caves once home to prehistoric man. ✉ *Rte. du Périgueux* ☎ *05–53–06–92–70* 🎫 *€6* ⊙ *Feb.–Mar., Mon.–Thurs. 10–12:30 and 2–5:30; Apr.–June and Sept. and Oct., Sun.–Fri. 10–12;30 and 2–6; July and Aug., daily 10–7.*

To truly enhance your understanding of the paintings at Lascaux and other caves in the Dordogne, visit the **Musée National de Préhistoire** *(National Museum of Prehistory)*, which attracts large crowds to its renowned collection of prehistoric artifacts, including primitive sculpture, furniture, and tools. You can also get ideas at the museum about excavation sites to visit in the region. ✉ *1 rue du Musée* ☎ *05–53–06–45–45* ⊕ *www.musee-prehistoire-eyzies.fr* 🎫 *€5* ⊙ *July and Aug., daily 9:30–6:30; Sept. and June, Wed.–Mon. 9:30–6; Oct.–May, Wed.–Mon. 9:30–12:30 and 2–5:30.*

Fodor's Choice ★ As you head north from Les Eyzies-de-Tayac toward Lascaux, stop off 7 km (4 mi) north of Les Eyzies near the village of Tursac to discover the mysterious troglodyte "lost village" of **La Madeleine**, found hidden in the Valley of Vézère at the foot of a ruined castle and overlooking the Vézère River. Human settlement here dates to 15,000 BC, but what is most eye-catching now is its picturesque cliff-face chapel—seemingly half Cro-Magnon, half Gothic, it was constructed during the Middle Ages. The "Brigadoon" of the Dordogne, La Madeleine was abandoned in the 1920s. Guided visits tour the site (call ahead, English available). ✉ *Tursac, 7 km (4 mi) north of Les Eyzies-de-Tayac* ☎ *05–53–46–36–88* 🎫 *€5.50* ⊙ *July and Aug., daily 10–8; Sept.–June, daily 11–6.*

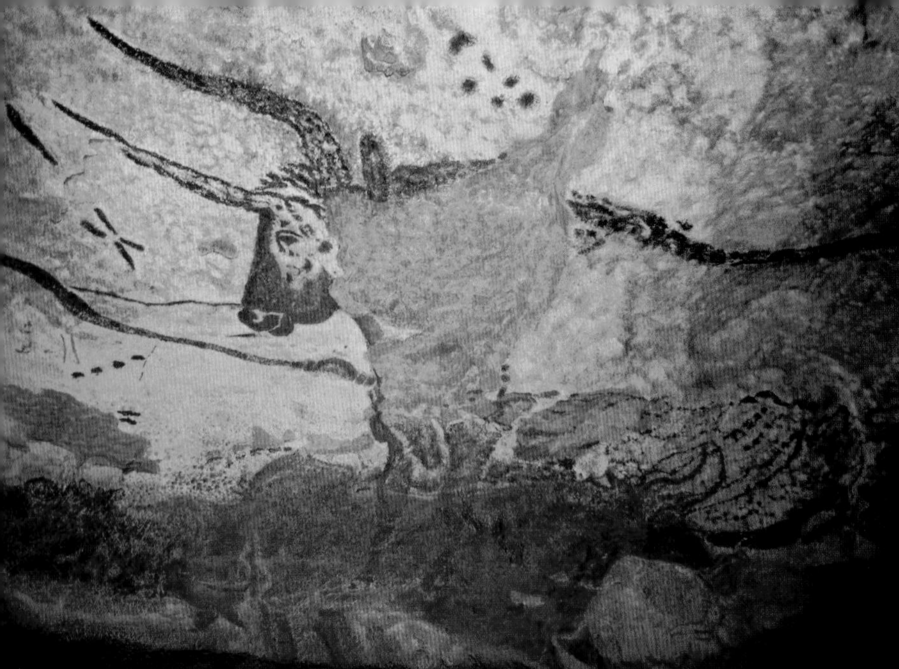

The Raphaels, Leonardos, and Picassos of prehistoric art are on view in the amazing caves of Lascaux II.

WHERE TO STAY

$$–$$$ **Le Centenaire.** Though it's also a stylish, modern Relais & Châteaux hotel, Le Centenaire is known foremost as a restaurant. Chef Richard Labbe adds flair to the preparation of local delights: risotto with truffles or snails with ravioli and gazpacho. The dining room's golden stone and wood beams retain local character (open daily; a jacket is required). **Pros:** leafy terraces make it a great place to dine and relax after touring. **Cons:** hotel staff can be rude; restaurant suffers from poor service. ✉ *Les Eyzies-de-Tayac* ☎ *05–53–06–68–68* 🌐 *www.hotelducentenaire.fr* *20 rooms, 4 suites* *In-room: a/c, refrigerator, Wi-Fi. In-hotel: restaurant, pool, gym, some pets allowed* ▭ *AE, DC, MC, V* ⊗ *Closed mid-Nov. and Jan.–mid-Feb.* *MAP.*

$$$–$$$$ ★ **Le Vieux Logis.** Built around the most gorgeous dining room in the Dordogne, this vine-clad manor house in Trémolat remains one of the best hotels of the region. The warm guest rooms vary in size; most face the well-tended garden and a rushing brook. The best have terra-cotta tile floors, stone walls, and suitelike bathrooms. The lounge is très chic, with exposed beams, Louis Treize–style exposed beams, and mounted faïence plates over the fireplace. Be sure to enjoy a meal in the restaurant, a stunning vision in half-timber and pink and red paisley fabrics. For dinner, the six-course dinner menu (€70) might include the chef Vincent Arnauld's forte, veal in a mustard sauce. Cheaper fare is available from a second restaurant, Le Bistrot, which is wildly popular and set in a house at the gates to the property. **Pros:** breathtaking grounds; Le Bistrot offers a value version of the restaurant's delectable food. **Cons:** swimming pool is small. ✉ *Le Bourg, 24 km (15 mi) west of Les Eyzies, Trémolat* ☎ *05–53–22–80–06* 🌐 *www.vieux-logis.com* *17 rooms, 9*

suites ♿ *In-room: a/c, refrigerator. In-hotel: 2 restaurants, pool, Wi-Fi hotspot, some pets allowed* 💳 *AE, DC, MC, V* 🍽 *MAP.*

LASCAUX

27 km (17 mi) northeast of Les Eyzies via D706. For information on getting here, see the Getting Around section at the front of this chapter.

Visitor Information Lascaux Tourist Office. ✉ *Pl. Bertran-de-Born* ☎ *05–53–51–82–60* 🌐 *www.tourisme-lascaux.fr.*

EXPLORING

Fodor's Choice ★ Just south of Montignac, the famous **Grotte de Lascaux** *(Lascaux Caves)* contain hundreds of prehistoric wall paintings—between 15,000 and 20,000 years old, making them the oldest known paintings in the world. The undulating horses, cow, black bulls, and unicorn on their walls were discovered by chance by four school kids looking for their dog in 1940. Unfortunately, the original Lascaux caves began to deteriorate due to the carbon dioxide exhaled by thousands of visitors. To make the colorful mosaic of animals accessible to the general public, the French authorities built Lascaux II, a formidable feat in itself. They spent 12 years perfecting the facsimile, duplicating every aspect of two of the main caves to such a degree that the result is equally awesome. Painted in black, purple, red, and yellow, the powerful images of stags, bison, and oxen are brought to life by the curve of the stone walls; many of them appear pregnant, and historians think these caves were shrines to fertility (not living quarters—no tool implements were ever found). Unlike caves marked with authentic prehistoric art, Lascaux II is completely geared toward visitors, and you can watch a fancy presentation about cave art or take a 40-minute tour in the language of your choice. This is one of the most visited sites in the Dordogne and, in summer, tickets can be at a premium. To be sure of admittance, arrive early, as tickets can sell out by midday. During the winter season, you are permitted to purchase tickets at the site, but from April to October tickets are available only at a booth beside the tourist office in Montignac (✉ *Pl. Bertran-de-Born*). Even better, make reservations via e-mail as soon as you know you're heading to the Dordogne. ✉ *Rte. de la Grotte de Lascaux* ☎ *05–53–51–95–03* 🌐 *www.semitour.com* 🎫 *€8.80* ⏲ *Early Feb.–early Apr., Tues.–Sun. 10–12:30 and 2–5:30; mid-Apr.–June, and Sept., daily 9–6:30; July and Aug., daily 9–8; Oct.–early Nov., daily 10–12:30 and 2–6; mid-Nov.–early Jan., Tues.–Sun. 10–12:30 and 2–5:30.*

WHERE TO STAY

$$$–$$$$ 🏨 **Manoir d'Hautegente.** This old, ivy-covered manor (originally a forge) enjoys a pastoral nook by the Coly River. Inside, the modernized rooms have beige-fabric wall coverings, and the colorful curtains match the bedspreads. Four duplexes can be found in the old miller's home nearby. Chef Ludovic Lavud's specialties include all things foie gras. If you're not convinced, check out the array of it at the hotel shop. The restaurant is closed Monday through Wednesday and there's no lunch Thursday. **Pros:** cozy family feel; close to Sarlat. **Cons:** bathrooms need updating;

rooms suffer somewhat from an attack of French moderne decor. ✉ *Haute Gente, 12 km (7 mi) east of Lascaux, Coly* ☎ *05–53–51–68–03* 🌐 *www.manoir-hautegente.com* ⇨ *11 rooms, 6 suites* ✋ *In-room: a/c (some), refrigerator. In-hotel: restaurant, pool, Internet terminal* 💳 *DC, MC, V* ⏲ *Closed Nov.–Easter.*

HAUTEFORT

25 km (15½ mi) north of Lascaux via D704.

The reason to come to Hautefort is its castle, which presents a disarmingly arrogant face to the world.

★ The silhouette of the **Château de Hautefort** bristles with high roofs, domes, chimneys, and cupolas. The square-line Renaissance left wing clashes with the muscular, round towers of the right wing, and the only surviving section of the original medieval castle—the gateway and drawbridge—plays referee in the middle. Adorning the inside are 17th-century furniture and tapestries. ✉ *Hautefort* ☎ *05–53–50–51–23* 🌐 *www.chateau-hautefort.com* 🎫 *€8.50* ⏲ *Apr. and May, daily 10–12:30 and 2–6:30; June–Aug., daily 9:30–7; Sep., daily 10-6; Mar. and Oct., daily 2–6; Nov. 1–11, weekends 2–6.*

PÉRIGUEUX

46 km (27 mi) west of Hautefort via D5, 120 km (75 mi) northeast of Bordeaux.

For anyone tired of the bucolic delights of the Périgord, even a short visit to this thriving city may prove a welcome re-immersion in classy urban ways.

GETTING HERE

As opposed to using the Bergerac airport, fly on regional carrier Airlinair (🌐 *www.airlinair.com*) to Brive la Gaillarde, to the west of Périgueux (for as little as €40 one-way from Paris two times a day during the week and once on Sunday). The bus station on Rue Denis Papin houses C.F.T.A. Périgueux (☎ *05–53–08–43–13*), which is part of the Transpérigord bus system. Bus lines (1, 1A, 2, 3, 10) leave here for Angouleme, Brantôme, and Bergerac for €2 a trip. Peribus (☎ *05–53–53–30–37*) on Place Montaigne is where you can catch a city bus. The train station is also on Rue Denis Papin. It takes 4½ hours to get here from Paris's Gare d'Austerlitz (connecting in Bordeaux) and will cost you around €60. If you're training it to Cahors from Perigueux you'll have to travel the 50 minutes east first to Brive La Gaillard and then head south to Cahors, which is another hour, all for around €25 one-way. It'll take you less time to get to Bergerac (70 mins) to the southeast, but you'll still have to connect at Le Buisson.

Visitor Information **Périgueux Tourist Office.** ✉ *26 place Francheville* ☎ *05–53–35–10–63* 🌐 *www.tourisme-perigueux.fr, www.arachnis.asso.fr.*

EXPLORING

As Périgueux is a commercial center for the region and a transportation nexus, the shops are stylish and sophisticated—some consider them the best reason for visiting this thriving town. Specialty-food shops proliferate (pâtés are the town's chief export), as do dimly lighted cafés and elegant fashion haunts. Don't forget the open-air markets in the heart of the medieval cité though, as this is the capital of the Périgord and that means one of the capitals of produce. Farmers' markets are held every day from eight in the morning to one in the afternoon on the Place du Coderc. Every Wednesday and Saturday you can catch the big markets, which spill over from the Place du Coderc to the front of the Mairie town hall. And for those of you who love your gras (fat) as the locals do, then you'll have to witness, every Wednesday and Saturday from November to March, one of the many marchés de gras!

With more than 2,000 years of history, from its Gallo-Roman cité to its medieval town, Périgueux is best known for its weird-looking cathedral that was associated with the routes to Santiago de Compostela. Finished in 1173 (although certain archaeologists date it as early as 984) and fully and fancifully restored in the 19th century, the **Cathédrale St-Front** looks like it might be on loan from Istanbul, given its shallow-scale domes and elongated conical cupolas sprouting from the roof like baby minarets. You may be struck by similarities with the Byzantine-style Sacré-Coeur in Paris; that's no coincidence—architect Paul Abadie (1812–84) had a hand in the design of both. Mandatory visit to the cathedral over, you can make for the cluster of tiny pedestrian-only streets that run through the heart of Périgueux.

16

BRANTÔME

Fodor's Choice ★ *27 km (17 mi) north of Périgueux via D939.*

Visitor Information Brantôme Tourist Office. ✉ *Bd. Charlemagne* ☎ *05–53–05–80–52* 🌐 *www.ville-brantome.fr.*

EXPLORING

When the reclusive monks of the abbey of Brantôme decided the inhabitants of the village were getting too nosy, they dug a canal between themselves and the villagers, setting the *brantômois* adrift on an island in the middle of the River Dronne. How happy for them, or at least for us. Brantôme has been unable to outgrow its small-town status and remains one of the prettiest villages in France. Today it touts itself as the "Venice of Périgord." Enjoy a walk along the river or through the old, narrow streets. The meandering river follows you wherever you stroll. Cafés and small shops abound.

At night the **Abbaye Benedictine** is romantically floodlighted. Possibly founded by Charlemagne in the 8th century, it has none of its original buildings left, but its bell tower has been hanging on since the 11th century (the secret of its success is that it's attached to the cliff rather than the abbey, and so withstood waves of invaders). Fifth-century hermits carved out much of the abbey and some rooms have sculpted reliefs of the Last Judgment. Also here is a small museum devoted to the

19th-century painter Fernand-Desmoulin. ✉ *Bd. Charlemagne* ☎ *05–53–05–80–63* 🎫 *€4* ⏲ *July and Aug., daily 10–7; Apr.–June and Sept., daily 10–12:30 and 2–6; Oct.–Dec. and Feb.–Mar. 10–noon and 2–5.*

WHERE TO STAY

$$$$ ★ **Le Moulin de l'Abbaye.** Storybook-perfect and set in the heart of Brantôme, this ivy-covered, turquoise-shuttered stone building looks directly over the placid waters of the Dronne, making this the ideal place to sample the watery charms of this little town. All the lovely and stylish rooms—named after wine châteaux—are individually decorated. Both Château Montrose and Château Cheval-Blanc have four-poster beds. The restaurant, run by chef Alexis Chaillou, has eight magnificent arched windows with views of the river—a truly memorable setting for delights such as young pigeon glazed in a Szechuan pepper sauce accompanied by foie gras ravioli with celery root. The food is so good, you'll probably want to splurge on the half-board rates (which raises the tab here considerably), but set some time aside for feasts at the nearby fishermen's bistro, Au Fil de l'Eau (🌐 *www.fildeleau.com*), which has an exquisite riverside terrace. For even more luxe and prettier guest rooms, explore the owner's other Brantôme hostelries, set nearby—the riverbank Maison de l'Abbé and the cliff-side Maison du Meunier, which has an eye-dazzling, two-story drawing room. **Pros:** proximity to several excellent restaurants. **Cons:** with the cheapest room at €220, you'll pay for your luxurious stay. ✉ *1 rte. des Bourdeilles* ☎ *05–53–05–80–22* 🌐 *www.moulinabbaye.com* *19 rooms* *In-room: a/c. In-hotel: restaurant, Wi-Fi hotspot, some pets allowed* 💳 *AE, DC, MC, V* ⏲ *Closed mid-Nov.–mid-Apr.* 🍽 *BP.*

FRENCH VOCABULARY

One of the trickiest French sounds to pronounce is the nasal final *n* sound (whether or not the n is actually the last letter of the word). You should try to pronounce it as a sort of nasal grunt—as in "huh." The vowel that precedes the *n* will govern the vowel sound of the word, and in this list we precede the final *n* with an *h* to remind you to be nasal.

Another problem sound is the ubiquitous but untransliterable eu, as in bleu (blue) or deux (two), and the very similar sound in je (I), ce (this), and de (of). The closest equivalent might be the vowel sound in "put," but rounded. The famous rolled *r* is a glottal sound. Consonants at the ends of words are usually silent; when the following word begins with a vowel, however, the two are run together by sounding the consonant. There are two forms of "you" in French: vous (formal and plural) and tu (a singular, personal form). When addressing an adult you don't know, vous is always best.

BASICS

ENGLISH	FRENCH	PRONUNCIATION
Yes/no	Oui/non	wee/nohn
Please	S'il vous plaît	seel voo play
Thank you	Merci	mair-**see**
You're welcome	De rien	deh ree-**ehn**
Excuse me, sorry	Pardon	pahr-**don**
Good morning/ afternoon	Bonjour	bohn-**zhoor**
Good evening	Bonsoir	bohn-**swahr**
Good-bye	Au revoir	o ruh-**vwahr**
Mr. (Sir)	Monsieur	muh-**syuh**
Mrs. (Ma'am)	Madame	ma-**dam**
Miss	Mademoiselle	mad-mwa-**zel**
Pleased to meet you	Enchanté(e)	ohn-shahn-**tay**
How are you?	Comment allez-vous?	kuh-mahn- tahl-ay **voo**
Very well, thanks	Très bien, merci	tray bee-ehn, mair-**see**
And you?	Et vous?	ay voo?

NUMBERS

ENGLISH	FRENCH	PRONUNCIATION
one	un	uhn
two	deux	deuh
three	trois	twah

ENGLISH	FRENCH	PRONUNCIATION
four	quatre	**kaht**-ruh
five	cinq	sank
six	six	seess
seven	sept	set
eight	huit	wheat
nine	neuf	nuf
ten	dix	deess
eleven	onze	ohnz
twelve	douze	dooz
thirteen	treize	trehz
fourteen	quatorze	kah-torz
fifteen	quinze	kanz
sixteen	seize	sez
seventeen	dix-sept	deez-**set**
eighteen	dix-huit	deez-**wheat**
nineteen	dix-neuf	deez-**nuf**
twenty	vingt	vehn
twenty-one	vingt-et-un	vehnt-ay-**uhn**
thirty	trente	trahnt
forty	quarante	ka-**rahnt**
fifty	cinquante	sang-**kahnt**
sixty	soixante	swa-**sahnt**
seventy	soixante-dix	swa-sahnt-**deess**
eighty	quatre-vingts	kaht-ruh-**vehn**
ninety	quatre-vingt-dix	kaht-ruh-vehn-**deess**
one hundred	cent	sahn
one thousand	mille	meel

COLORS

black	noir	nwahr
blue	bleu	bleuh

ENGLISH	FRENCH	PRONUNCIATION
brown	brun/marron	bruhn/mar-**rohn**
green	vert	vair
orange	orange	o-**rahnj**
pink	rose	rose
red	rouge	rouge
violet	violette	vee-o-**let**
white	blanc	blahnk
yellow	jaune	zhone

DAYS OF THE WEEK

Sunday	dimanche	dee-**mahnsh**
Monday	lundi	luhn-**dee**
Tuesday	mardi	mahr-**dee**
Wednesday	mercredi	mair-kruh-**dee**
Thursday	jeudi	zhuh-**dee**
Friday	vendredi	vawn-druh-**dee**
Saturday	samedi	sahm-**dee**

MONTHS

January	janvier	zhahn-vee-**ay**
February	février	feh-vree-**ay**
March	mars	marce
April	avril	a-**vreel**
May	mai	meh
June	juin	zhwehn
July	juillet	zhwee-**ay**
August	août	ah-**oo**
September	septembre	sep-**tahm**-bruh
October	octobre	awk-**to**-bruh
November	novembre	no-**vahm**-bruh
December	décembre	day-**sahm**-bruh

ENGLISH	FRENCH	PRONUNCIATION

USEFUL PHRASES

ENGLISH	FRENCH	PRONUNCIATION
Do you speak English?	Parlez-vous anglais?	par-lay **voo ahn**-glay
I don't speak . . .	Je ne parle pas . . .	zhuh nuh parl pah
French	français	frahn-**say**
I don't understand	Je ne comprends pas	zhuh nuh kohm-**prahn** pah
I understand	Je comprends	zhuh kohm-**prahn**
I don't know	Je ne sais pas	zhuh nuh say **pah**
I'm American/ British	Je suis américain/ anglais	a-may-ree-**kehn**/ ahn-**glay**
What's your name?	Comment vous ap pelez-vous?	ko-mahn voo za-pell-ay-**voo**
My name is . . .	Je m'appelle . . .	zhuh ma-**pell** . . .
What time is it?	Quelle heure est-il?	kel air eh-**teel**
How?	Comment?	ko-**mahn**
When?	Quand?	kahn
Yesterday	Hier	yair
Today	Aujourd'hui	o-zhoor-**dwee**
Tomorrow	Demain	duh-**mehn**
Tonight	Ce soir	suh **swahr**
What?	Quoi?	kwah
What is it?	Qu'est-ce que c'est?	kess-kuh-**say**
Why?	Pourquoi?	**poor**-kwa
Who?	Qui?	kee
Where is . . .	Où est . . .	oo ay
the train station?	la gare?	la gar
the subway station?	la station de métro?	la sta-**syon** duh may-**tro**
the bus stop?	l'arrêt de bus?	la-**ray** duh **booss**
the post office?	la poste?	la post
the bank?	la banque?	la bahnk

ENGLISH	FRENCH	PRONUNCIATION
the . . . hotel?	l'hôtel . . .?	lo-**tel**
the store?	le magasin?	luh ma-ga-**zehn**
the cashier?	la caisse?	la **kess**
the . . . museum?	le musée . . .?	luh mew-**zay**
the hospital?	l'hôpital?	lo-pee-**tahl**
the elevator?	l'ascenseur?	la-sahn-**seuhr**
the telephone?	le téléphone?	luh tay-lay-**phone**
Where are the restrooms?	Où sont les toilettes?	oo sohn lay twah-**let**
(men/women)	(hommes/femmes)	(**oh**-mm/**fah**-mm)
Here/there	Ici/là	ee-**see**/la
Left/right	A gauche/à droite	a goash/a draht
Straight ahead	Tout droit	too drwah
Is it near/far?	C'est près/loin?	say pray/lwehn
I'd like . . .	Je voudrais . . .	zhuh voo-**dray**
a room	une chambre	ewn **shahm**-bruh
the key	la clé	la clay
a newspaper	un journal	uhn zhoor-**nahl**
a stamp	un timbre	uhn **tam**-bruh
I'd like to buy . . .	Je voudrais acheter . . .	zhuh voo-**dray ahsh**-tay
cigarettes	des cigarettes	day see-ga-**ret**
matches	des allumettes	days a-loo-**met**
soap	du savon	dew sah-**vohn**
city map	un plan de ville	uhn plahn de **veel**
road map	une carte routière	ewn cart roo-tee-**air**
magazine	une revue	ewn reh-**vu**
envelopes	des enveloppes	dayz ahn-veh-**lope**
writing paper	du papier à lettres	dew pa-pee-**ay** a **let**-ruh
postcard	une carte postale	ewn cart pos-**tal**
How much is it?	C'est combien?	say comb-bee-**ehn**

ENGLISH	FRENCH	PRONUNCIATION
A little/a lot	Un peu/beaucoup	uhn peuh/bo-**koo**
More/less	Plus/moins	plu/mwehn
Enough/too (much)	Assez/trop	a-say/tro
I am ill/sick	Je suis malade	zhuh swee ma-**lahd**
Call a . . .	Appelez un . . .	a-play uhn
doctor	Docteur	dohk-**tehr**
Help!	Au secours!	o suh-**koor**
Stop!	Arrêtez!	a-reh-**tay**
Fire!	Au feu!	o fuh
Caution!/Look out!	Attention!	a-tahn-see-**ohn**

DINING OUT

ENGLISH	FRENCH	PRONUNCIATION
A bottle of . . .	une bouteille de . . .	ewn boo-**tay** duh
A cup of . . .	une tasse de . . .	ewn tass duh
A glass of . . .	un verre de . . .	uhn vair duh
Bill/check	l'addition	la-dee-see-**ohn**
Bread	du pain	dew pan
Breakfast	le petit-déjeuner	luh puh-**tee** day-zhuh-**nay**
Butter	du beurre	dew burr
Cheers!	A votre santé!	ah vo-truh sahn-**tay**
Cocktail/aperitif	un apéritif	uhn ah-pay-ree-**teef**
Dinner	le dîner	luh dee-**nay**
Dish of the day	le plat du jour	luh plah dew **zhoor**
Enjoy!	Bon appétit!	bohn a-pay-**tee**
Fixed-price menu	le menu	luh may-**new**
Fork	une fourchette	ewn four-**shet**
I am diabetic	Je suis diabétique	zhuh swee dee-ah- bay-**teek**
I am vegetarian	Je suis végétarien(ne)	zhuh swee vay-zhay-ta-ree-**en**
I cannot eat . . .	Je ne peux pas manger de . . .	zhuh nuh **puh** pah mahn-**jay** deh

ENGLISH	FRENCH	PRONUNCIATION
I'd like to order	Je voudrais commander	zhuh voo-**dray** ko-mahn-**day**
Is service/the tip included?	Est-ce que le service est compris?	ess kuh luh sair-**veess** ay comb-**pree**
It's good/bad	C'est bon/mauvais	say bohn/mo-**vay**
It's hot/cold	C'est chaud/froid	Say sho/frwah
Knife	un couteau	uhn koo-**toe**
Lunch	le déjeuner	luh day-zhuh-**nay**
Menu	la carte	la cart
Napkin	une serviette	ewn sair-vee-**et**
Pepper	du poivre	dew **pwah**-vruh
Plate	une assiette	ewn a-see-**et**
Please give me . . .	Donnez-moi . . .	doe-nay-**mwah**
Salt	du sel	dew sell
Spoon	une cuillère	ewn kwee-air
Sugar	du sucre	dew **sook**-ruh
Waiter!/Waitress!	Monsieur!/ Mademoiselle!	muh-**syuh**/ mad-mwa-**zel**
Wine list	la carte des vins	la cart day vehn

MENU GUIDE

FRENCH	ENGLISH

GENERAL DINING

FRENCH	ENGLISH
Entrée	Appetizer/Starter
Garniture au choix	Choice of vegetable side
Plat du jour	Dish of the day
Selon arrivage	When available
Supplément/En sus	Extra charge
Sur commande	Made to order

PETIT DÉJEUNER (BREAKFAST)

FRENCH	ENGLISH
Confiture	Jam
Miel	Honey

FRENCH	ENGLISH
Oeuf à la coque	Boiled egg
Oeufs sur le plat	Fried eggs
Oeufs brouillés	Scrambled eggs
Tartine	Bread with butter

POISSONS/FRUITS DE MER (FISH/SEAFOOD)

Anchois	Anchovies
Bar	Bass
Brandade de morue	Creamed salt cod
Brochet	Pike
Cabillaud/Morue	Fresh cod
Calmar	Squid
Coquilles St-Jacques	Scallops
Crevettes	Shrimp
Daurade	Sea bream
Ecrevisses	Prawns/Crayfish
Harengs	Herring
Homard	Lobster
Huîtres	Oysters
Langoustine	Prawn/Lobster
Lotte	Monkfish
Moules	Mussels
Palourdes	Clams
Saumon	Salmon
Thon	Tuna
Truite	Trout

VIANDE (MEAT)

Agneau	Lamb
Boeuf	Beef
Boudin	Sausage
Boulettes de viande	Meatballs

FRENCH	ENGLISH
Brochettes	Kebabs
Cassoulet	Casserole of white beans, meat
Cervelle	Brains
Chateaubriand	Double fillet steak
Choucroute garnie	Sausages with sauerkraut
Côtelettes	Chops
Côte/Côte de boeuf	Rib/T-bone steak
Cuisses de grenouilles	Frogs' legs
Entrecôte	Rib or rib-eye steak
Épaule	Shoulder
Escalope	Cutlet
Foie	Liver
Gigot	Leg
Porc	Pork
Ris de veau	Veal sweetbreads
Rognons	Kidneys
Saucisses	Sausages
Selle	Saddle
Tournedos	Tenderloin of T-bone steak
Veau	Veal

METHODS OF PREPARATION

A point	Medium
A l'étouffée	Stewed
Au four	Baked
Ballotine	Boned, stuffed, and rolled
Bien cuit	Well-done
Bleu	Very rare
Frit	Fried
Grillé	Grilled
Rôti	Roast

FRENCH	ENGLISH
Saignant	Rare

VOLAILLES/GIBIER (POULTRY/GAME)

Blanc de volaille	Chicken breast
Canard/Caneton	Duck/Duckling
Cerf/Chevreuil	Venison (red/roe)
Coq au vin	Chicken stewed in red wine
Dinde/Dindonneau	Turkey/Young turkey
Faisan	Pheasant
Lapin/Lièvre	Rabbit/Wild hare
Oie	Goose
Pintade/Pintadeau	Guinea fowl/Young guinea fowl
Poulet/Poussin	Chicken/Spring chicken

LÉGUMES (VEGETABLES)

Artichaut	Artichoke
Asperge	Asparagus
Aubergine	Eggplant
Carottes	Carrots
Champignons	Mushrooms
Chou-fleur	Cauliflower
Chou (rouge)	Cabbage (red)
Laitue	Lettuce
Oignons	Onions
Petits pois	Peas
Pomme de terre	Potato
Tomates	Tomatoes

Travel Smart France

WORD OF MOUTH

"If you can handle French, book on voyages-sncf.com. To book in English and get the same full range of fares go to tgv-europe.com. To keep the site in English and avoid being bumped to the Rail Europe site (which doesn't offer discount fares), just choose Great Britain as country of residence."

—TimS123

"Where to go? I believe I could stick a map of France on the wall, throw a dart, and be very happy wherever it landed!"

—Nikki

www.fodors.com/community

GETTING HERE AND AROUND

AIR TRAVEL

Flying time to Paris is 7½ hours from New York, 9 hours from Chicago, 11 hours from Los Angeles, and 1 hour from London. Flying time between Paris and Nice is 1 hour.

As one of the world's most popular destinations, Paris is serviced by many international carriers. Air France, the French flag carrier, offers numerous flights between Paris's Charles de Gaulle Airport and New York City's JFK Airport; Newark, New Jersey; and Washington's Dulles Airport; as well as Boston, Philadelphia, Atlanta, Miami, Chicago, Houston, Seattle, San Francisco, and Los Angeles. Most other North American cities are served through Air France partnerships with Delta. American-based carriers are usually less expensive, but offer fewer nonstop flights. Delta Airlines has flights to Paris from Atlanta, Cincinnati, Philadelphia, and New York City's JFK. Continental Airlines has nonstop flights to Paris from Newark and Houston. Another popular carrier is United, with nonstop flights to Paris from Chicago, Denver, Los Angeles, Miami, Philadelphia, Washington, and San Francisco. American Airlines offers daily nonstop flights to Paris's Charles de Gaulle Airport from numerous cities, including New York City's JFK, Miami, Chicago, and Dallas/Fort Worth.

Airline Contacts **Air France** (☎ *800/237–2747 in U.S., 36–54 in France [€0.34 per min]* 🌐 *www.airfrance.com*). **American Airlines** (☎ *800/433–7300 in U.S., 01–55–17–43–41 in France* 🌐 *www.aa.com*). **Continental Airlines** (☎ *800/523–3273 for U.S. reservations, 800/231–0856 for international reservations, 01–71–23–03–35 in France* 🌐 *www.continental.com*). **Delta Airlines** (☎ *800/221–1212 for U.S. reservations, 800/241–4141 for international reservations, 08–11–64–00–05 in France* 🌐 *www.delta.com*). **United Airlines** (☎ *800/864–8331 for U.S. reservations, 800/538–2929 for international reservations, 08–10–72–72–72 in France* 🌐 *www.united.com*).

Within Europe **EasyJet** (☎ *0905/560–7777 in U.K. [£1 per min] 08–26–10–26–11 in France [€1.34 per call and €0.34 per min]* 🌐 *www.easyjet.com*). **Ryan Air** (☎ *0871–246–0000 in U.K. [£0.10 per min] 08–92–78–02–10 in France [€0.34 per min]* 🌐 *www.ryanair.com*).

Airlines and Airports **Airline and Airport Links.com** (🌐 *www.airlineandairportlinks.com*) has links to many of the world's airlines and airports.

Airline Security Issues **Transportation Security Administration** (🌐 *www.tsa.gov*) has answers for almost every question that might come up.

AIRPORTS

There are two major gateway airports to France, both just outside the capital: Orly, 16 km (10 mi) south of Paris, and Charles de Gaulle, 26 km (16 mi) northeast of the city. The smaller Beauvais Airport, 75 km (46 mi) north of Paris, is used by European budget airlines. At Charles de Gaulle, also known as Roissy, there's a TGV station at Terminal 2, where you can connect to trains going all over the country. Many airlines have less frequent flights to Lyon, Lourdes, Perpignan, Biarritz, Nantes, Nice, Marseille, Bordeaux, and Toulouse.

Airport Information **Charles de Gaulle/Roissy** (☎ *01–48–62–22–80* 🌐 *www.adp.fr*). **Orly** (☎ *01–49–75–15–15* 🌐 *www.adp.fr*).

GROUND TRANSPORTATION

From Charles de Gaulle, the fastest and least expensive way to get into Paris is on the RER-B line, the suburban express train, which runs daily from 5 AM to 11:30 PM. The free CGDVal lightrail connects each terminal to the Roissypôle RER station in less than 8 minutes, running daily nonstop 24/7. There is also a free "navette" shuttle bus, although you have to wait for it outside each terminal, and traffic can make travel time up to 30 minutes to the RER station. Trains to central Paris (Gare du Nord, Les Halles, St-Michel, Luxembourg) depart every 15 minutes. The fare (including métro connection) is €8.50, and journey time is about 30 minutes.

The Air France shuttle is a comfortable option to get to and from the city—you don't need to have flown the carrier to use this service. Line 2 goes from the airport to Paris's Charles de Gaulle Étoile and Porte Maillot from 5:45 AM to 11 PM. It leaves every 15 minutes and costs €15, which you can pay on board. Passengers arriving in Terminal 1 need to take Exit 34; Terminals 2B and 2D, Exit 6; Terminals 2E and 2F, Exit 3. Line 4 goes to Montparnasse and the Gare de Lyon from 7 AM to 9 PM. Buses run every 30 minutes and cost €16.50. Passengers arriving in Terminal 1 need to look for Exit 34, Terminals 2A and 2C need to take Exit C2, Terminals 2B and 2D Exit B1, and Terminals 2E and 2F Exit 3.

Another option is to take Roissybus, operated by the Paris Transit Authority, which runs between Charles de Gaulle and the Opéra every 20 minutes from 6 AM to 11 PM; the cost is €9.10. The trip takes about 45 minutes in regular traffic, about 90 minutes in rush-hour traffic.

Taxis are your least desirable mode of transportation into the city. If you're traveling at peak tourist times, you may have to stand in a very long line with a lot of other disgruntled European travelers. Journey times, and as a consequence, prices, are therefore unpredictable. At best, the journey takes 30 minutes, but it can take as long as 90 minutes during rush hour. Count on a €40 to €50 fare.

Airport Connection is the name of just one of a number of van services that serve both Charles de Gaulle and Orly airports. Prices are set, so it costs the same no matter how long the journey takes. To make a reservation, call, e-mail, or fax your flight details at least one week in advance to the shuttle company and an air-conditioned van with a bilingual chauffeur will be waiting for you upon your arrival. Note that these shuttle vans pick up and drop off other passengers.

From Orly, the most economical way to get into Paris is to take the RER-C or Orlyrail line. Catch the free shuttle bus from the terminal to the Pont de Rungis train station. Trains to Paris leave every 15 minutes. Passengers arriving in either the South or West Terminal need to use Exit G. The fare is €6.20, and journey time is about 35 minutes. Another option is to take the monorail service, Orlyval, which runs between the Antony RER-B station and Orly Airport daily every 4 to 8 minutes from 6 AM to 11 PM. Passengers arriving in the South Terminal should look for Exit K, those arriving in the West Terminal, Exit W. The fare to downtown Paris is €9.85.

You can also take an Air France bus line 1 from Orly to Les Invalides on the Left Bank and Montparnasse, the line 1* also stops at Etoile and Porte d'Orleans on request; these run every 15 minutes from 6 AM to 11 PM. (You need not have flown on Air France to use this service.) The fare is €11.50, and the trip takes between 30 and 45 minutes, depending on traffic. Those arriving in Orly South need to look for Exit L; those arriving in Orly West, Exit D. The Paris Transit Authority's Orlybus is yet another option; buses leave every 15 minutes for the Denfert-Rochereau métro station; the cost is €6.40. You can economize using RATP Bus 183, which shuttles you from the airport to Line 7, métro Porte de Choisy station, for the price of a city bus ticket. It operates daily from 5:30 AM to 8:30 PM at the Orly Sud terminal.

Contacts **Air France Bus** (☏ *08–92–35–08–20 recorded information in English* 🌐 *www.cars-airfrance.com*). **Airport Connection** (☏ *01–43–65–55–55* 🌐 *www.airport-connection.com*). **Paris Airport Service** (☏ *01–55–98–10–80* 🌐 *www.parisairportservice.com*). **RATP (including**

Roissybus, Orlybus, Orlyval) (☎ *3246 in France [€0.34 per min]* 🌐 *www.ratp.com*).

BARGE AND YACHT TRAVEL

Canal and river trips are popular in France, particularly along the picturesque waterways in Brittany, Burgundy, and the Midi. For further information, ask for a "Tourisme Fluvial" brochure at any French tourist office. It's also possible to rent a barge or crewed sailboat to travel around the coast of France, particularly along the Côte d'Azur.

Barge Companies **Abercrombie & Kent** (☎ *630/954–2944 or 800/554–7016* 🌐 *www.abercrombiekent.com*). **En-Bateau** (☎ *04–67–13–19–62* 🌐 *en-bateau.com*). **European Waterways** (☎ *800/394–8630 in U.S., 888/342–1917 in Canada* 🌐 *www.gobarging.com*). **French Country Waterways** (☎ *781/934–2454 or 800/222–1236* 🌐 *www.fcwl.com*). **Maine Anjou Rivières** (☎ *08–05–80–10–83* 🌐 *www.maine-anjou-rivieres.com*). **Viking River Cruises** (☎ *800/304–9616* 🌐 *www.rivercruises.com*).

BOAT TRAVEL

A number of ferry and hovercraft routes link the United Kingdom and France. Prices depend on the length of the journey and the number of people traveling. Driving distances from the French ports to Paris are as follows: from Calais, 290 km (180 mi); from Cherbourg, 358 km (222 mi); from Caen, 233 km (145 mi); from St-Malo, 404 km (250 mi).

Dover–Calais **P&O European Ferries** (☎ *0825/120–156* 🌐 *www.poferries.com*) has up to 25 sailings a day; the crossing takes 90 minutes. **Seafrance** (☎ *44–8451–458–0666 from outside the U.K.* 🌐 *www.seafrance.fr*) operates up to 15 sailings a day; the crossing takes about 90 minutes.

Portsmouth & Poole–Cherbourg, Caen & St-Malo **Brittany Ferries** (☎ *0871/244–0744* 🌐 *www.brittany-ferries.co.uk*) has four sailings per day between Caen and Portsmouth, three crossings daily between Portsmouth and Cherbourg, one crossing daily between St-Malo and Portsmouth, and three crossings daily between Poole and Cherbourg.

BUS TRAVEL

If you're traveling to or from another country, train service can be just as economical as bus travel, if not more so. The largest international operator is Eurolines France, whose main terminal is in the Parisian suburb of Bagnolet (a half-hour métro ride from central Paris, at the end of métro Line 3). Eurolines runs many international routes to more than 37 European destinations, including a route from London to Paris, usually departing at 8 AM, arriving at 4:30 PM; noon, arriving at 9:30 PM; and 9:30 PM, arriving at 7:15 AM. Fares are £57 round-trip (under-25 youth pass £53). Other Eurolines routes include: Amsterdam (7 hrs, €67); Barcelona (15 hrs, €139); and Berlin (10 hrs, €137). There are economical passes to be had—15-day passes run €175–€310, a 30-day pass will cost €240–€410. These passes offer unlimited coach travel to all Eurolines European destinations.

France's excellent train service means that long-distance bus routes in France are rare; regional buses are found mainly where train service is spotty. In rural areas the service can be unreliable, and schedules can be incomprehensible for those who don't speak French. Your best bet is to contact local tourism offices.

Bus Information **Eurolines France** (☎ *08–92–89–90–91 in France [€0.34 per min]* 🌐 *www.eurolines.fr*).

CAR TRAVEL

An International Driver's Permit, valid for trips of less than 90 days, is not required but can prove useful in emergencies such as traffic violations or auto accidents, particularly when a foreign language is involved. Drivers in France must be over

18 years old to drive, but there is no top age limit (if your faculties are intact).

If you're driving from the United Kingdom to the Continent, you have a choice of either the Channel Tunnel or ferry services. Reservations are always a good idea, but are essential at peak times.

GASOLINE

Gas is expensive, especially on expressways and in rural areas. When possible, buy gas before you get on the expressway and keep an eye on pump prices as you go. These vary—anything from €1.20 to €1.40 per liter. The cheapest gas can be found at *hypermarchés* (large supermarkets). Credit cards are accepted everywhere. In rural areas it's possible to go for miles without passing a gas station, so don't let your tank get too low.

PARKING

Parking is a nightmare in Paris and many other metropolitan areas. "Pay and display" metered parking is usually limited to two hours in city centers. Parking is free on Sunday and national holidays. Parking meters showing a dense yellow circle indicate a free parking zone during the month of August. In smaller towns, parking may be permitted on one side of the street only—alternating every two weeks—so pay attention to signs. In France, illegally parked cars are likely to be impounded, especially those blocking entrances or fire exits. Parking tickets start at €11, topping out at €135 in a handicapped zone, for a first offense, and there's no shortage of the blue-uniformed parking police. Parking lots, indicated by a blue sign with a white P, are usually underground and are generally expensive.

ROAD CONDITIONS

France has 8,000 km (5,000 mi) of expressway and 808,000 km (502,000 mi) of main roads. For the fastest route between two points, look for roads marked A for *autoroute*. A *péage* (toll) must be paid on most expressways: the rate varies but can be steep. The N (*route nationale*) roads—which are sometimes divided highways—and D (*route départementale*) roads are usually also wide and fast.

There are excellent links between Paris and most French cities, but poor ones between the provinces (the principal exceptions are A26 from Calais to Reims, A62 between Bordeaux and Toulouse, and A9/A8 the length of the Mediterranean coast).

Though routes are numbered, the French generally guide themselves from city to city and town to town by destination name. When reading a map, keep one eye on the next big city toward your destination as well as the next small town; most snap decisions will have to be based on town names, not road numbers.

ROADSIDE EMERGENCIES

If you have car trouble on an expressway, go to a roadside emergency telephone. If you have a breakdown anywhere else, find the nearest garage or contact the police. There are also 24-hour assistance hotlines valid throughout France (available through rental agencies and supplied to you when you rent the car), but don't hesitate to call the police in case of any roadside emergency; they're quick and reliable, and the phone call is free. There are special phones just for this purpose on all highways; you can see them every few kilometers—just pick up the bright orange phone and dial 17. The French equivalent of the AAA is the Club Automobile de l'Ile de France, but it only takes care of its members and is of little use to international travelers.

Emergency Services Police (☎ *17*).

RULES OF THE ROAD

Drive on the right and yield to drivers coming from streets to the right. However, this rule does not necessarily apply at traffic circles, where you should watch out for just about everyone. You must wear a seat belt, and children under 12 may not travel in the front seat. Speed limits are 130 kph (80 mph) on expressways (*autoroutes*), 110 kph (70 mph) on divided highways (*routes nationales*), 90 kph (55 mph) on other roads (*routes*), 50 kph (30 mph) in cities and towns (*villes* and *villages*). French drivers break these limits all the time, and police dish out hefty on-the-spot fines with equal abandon. Do not expect to find traffic lights in the center of the road, as French lights are usually on the right- and left-hand sides.

You might be asked by the Police National to pull over at busy intersections. You will have to show your papers (*papiers*)—including car insurance—and may be submitted to an alcotest (you guessed it, a Breathalyzer test). The rules in France have become stringent because of the high incidence of accidents on the roads; anything above 0.5 grams of alcohol in the blood—which, according to your size, could simply mean two to three glasses of wine—and you are over the limit. This does not necessarily mean a night in the clinker, but your driving privileges in France will be revoked on the spot and you will pay a hefty fine. Don't drink and drive, even if you're just crossing town to the sleepy little inn on the river. Local police are notorious for their vigilance.

Some important traffic terms and signs to note: SORTIE (exit); SENS UNIQUE (one-way); STATIONNEMENT INTERDITE (no parking); and IMPASSE (dead end). Blue rectangular signs indicate a highway; green rectangular signs indicate a major direction; triangles carry illustrations of a particular traffic hazard; speed limits are indicated in a circle with the maximum limit circled in red.

TRAIN TRAVEL

The French national train agency, the Sociète Nationale de Chemins de Fer, or SNCF, is fast, punctual, comfortable, and comprehensive. Traveling across France, you have various options: local trains, overnight trains with sleeping accommodations, and the high-speed Trains à Grande Vitesse, known as the TGV.

TGVs average 255 kph (160 mph) on the Lyon–southeast line and 300 kph (190 mph) on the Lille and Bordeaux–southwest lines and are the best and the fastest domestic trains. They operate between Paris and Lille/Calais, Paris and Brussels, Paris and Amsterdam, Paris and Lyon–Switzerland–Provence, Paris and Angers–Nantes, and Paris and Tours–Poitiers–Bordeaux. As with other main-line trains, a small supplement may be assessed at peak hours.

It's usually fast and easy to cross France without traveling overnight, especially on TGVs, which are generally affordable and efficient. Be aware that trains fill fast on weekends and holidays, so purchase tickets well in advance at these times. Otherwise, you can take a slow overnight train, which often costs more than a TGV. There's a choice between high-price *wagons-lit* (sleeping cars) and slightly more affordable *couchettes* (bunks, six to a compartment in second class, four to a compartment in first).

In Paris there are six international rail stations: Gare du Nord (northern France, northern Europe, and England via Calais or Boulogne); Gare St-Lazare (Normandy and England via Dieppe); Gare de l'Est (Strasbourg, Luxembourg, Basel, and central Europe); Gare de Lyon (Lyon, Marseille, Provence, Geneva, and Italy); Gare d'Austerlitz (Loire Valley, southwest France, and Spain); and Gare Montparnasse for trains bound for southwest France.

BOOKING AND BUYING TICKETS

There are two classes of train service in France; first (*première*) or second (*deuxième*). First-class seats offer more legroom, plusher upholstery, private reading lamps, and computer plugs on the TGV, not to mention the hush-hush environment for those who want to sleep. The price is also nearly double.

It is best—and in many cases, essential—to prebook your train tickets. This requires making a reservation (which carries an additional charge of about 10 euros a person) online, by phone, or at the train station. Rail Europe does an excellent job providing train tickets to those in the US. They offer a service and their prices reflect that. There is nothing wrong with booking with them. However if you want to save money and don't mind doing it yourself, booking with the SNCF is much cheaper.

BUYING SNCF TICKETS ONLINE

Go to *www.voyages-sncf.com* (and when you click on the U.K. flag you get to *www.tgv-europe.com*). Find "advanced search," and then you'll be taken through a series of steps that will allow you to choose your outbound trip, followed by your inbound trip. Fares with the yellow background are the cheapest, a blue background is the mid price and gray is most expensive and tends to be flexible. Green background tends to be a class upgrade suggestion.

Whether you decide to print tickets yourself or pick them up at a station (do not have them sent by mail), select "France" as the country where you will collect your tickets. Do not select the U.S. or you will be redirected to the RailEurope Web site.

Know that certain fares or mix of fares may require you to pick up tickets at the station ticket window rather than print them yourself; make sure to factor in extra time as lines tend to be long throughout the day and be sure to bring ID and the credit card used to make the reservation. While there's the option to pick them up from one of the automatic machines, they only work with French credit cards that contain a special chip. You may book 90 days in advance for the TGV.

RAIL PASSES TO CHOOSE FROM

There are two kinds of rail passes: those you must purchase at home before you leave for France, including the France Rail Pass, the Eurail Selectpass, and those available in France from SNCF. The SNCF passes are available at any train station in France. Your rail pass does not guarantee you a seat on the train you wish to ride, however. You need to book ahead even if you're using a rail pass.

If you plan to travel outside of Paris, consider purchasing a France Rail Pass, which allows three days of unlimited train travel in a one-month period. If you travel solo, first class will run you $305, second class is $261: you can add up to six days on this pass for $46 (first class) or $39 (second class) a day. For two people traveling together on a Saver Pass, the cost in first class is $259, second class is $224; each additional day costs $40 (first class) or $33 (second class). Another option is the France Rail 'n Drive Pass (combining rail and rental car).

France is one of 18 countries in which you can use EurailPasses, which provide unlimited first-class rail travel in all of the participating countries for the duration of the pass. If you plan to rack up the miles, get a Eurail Global Pass. These are available for various time periods from 15 days ($767 first class, $384 second class) up to three months ($2,151 first class, $1,150 second class). If your plans call for only limited train travel between France and another country, consider a two-country pass, which costs less than a EurailPass. With the two-country pass you can get four flexible travel days between France and Italy, France, Spain, Germany, or Switzerland for $371 to $296. In addition to standard EurailPasses, ask about special plans. Among these are the Eurail Selectpass Youth (for those under age 26) and the Eurail Selectpass Saver (which gives a discount for two or more people traveling together). Whichever of the above passes you choose, remember that you must purchase your Eurail passes before leaving for France.

With an advance arrangement, SNCF will pick up and deliver your luggage at a given time. For instance, if you're planning on spending a weekend in Nice, SNCF will pick up your luggage at your hotel in Paris in the morning before checkout and deliver it to your hotel in Nice,

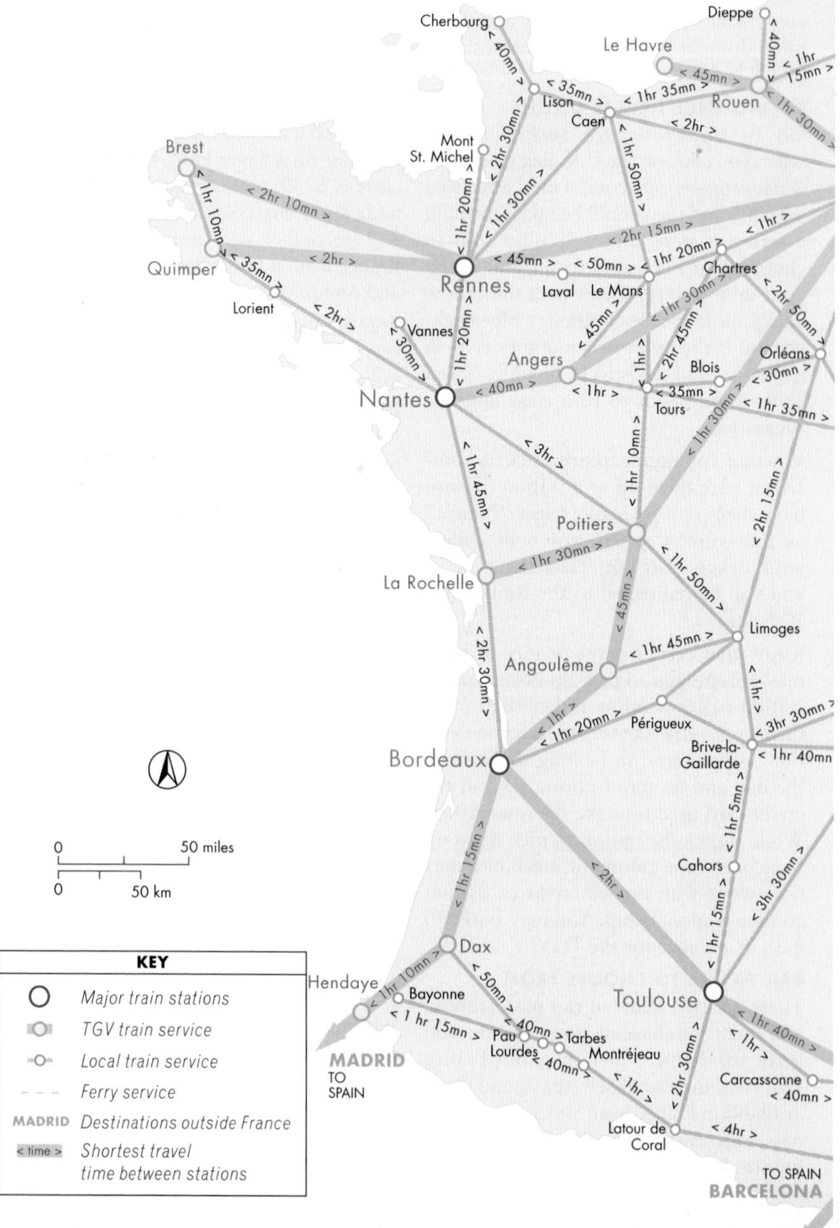
TO U.K.
LONDON
Boulogne
Cherbourg
Dieppe
Le Havre
Rouen
Lison
Caen
Mont St. Michel
Brest
Quimper
Lorient
Rennes
Laval
Le Mans
Chartres
Vannes
Angers
Blois
Orléans
Nantes
Tours
Poitiers
La Rochelle
Limoges
Angoulême
Périgueux
Brive-la-Gaillarde
Bordeaux
Cahors
Dax
Hendaye
Bayonne
Toulouse
Pau
Tarbes
Lourdes
Montréjeau
Carcassonne
Latour de Coral
MADRID
TO SPAIN
TO SPAIN
BARCELONA
0 50 miles
0 50 km
KEY
Major train stations
TGV train service
Local train service
Ferry service
MADRID Destinations outside France
< time > Shortest travel time between stations

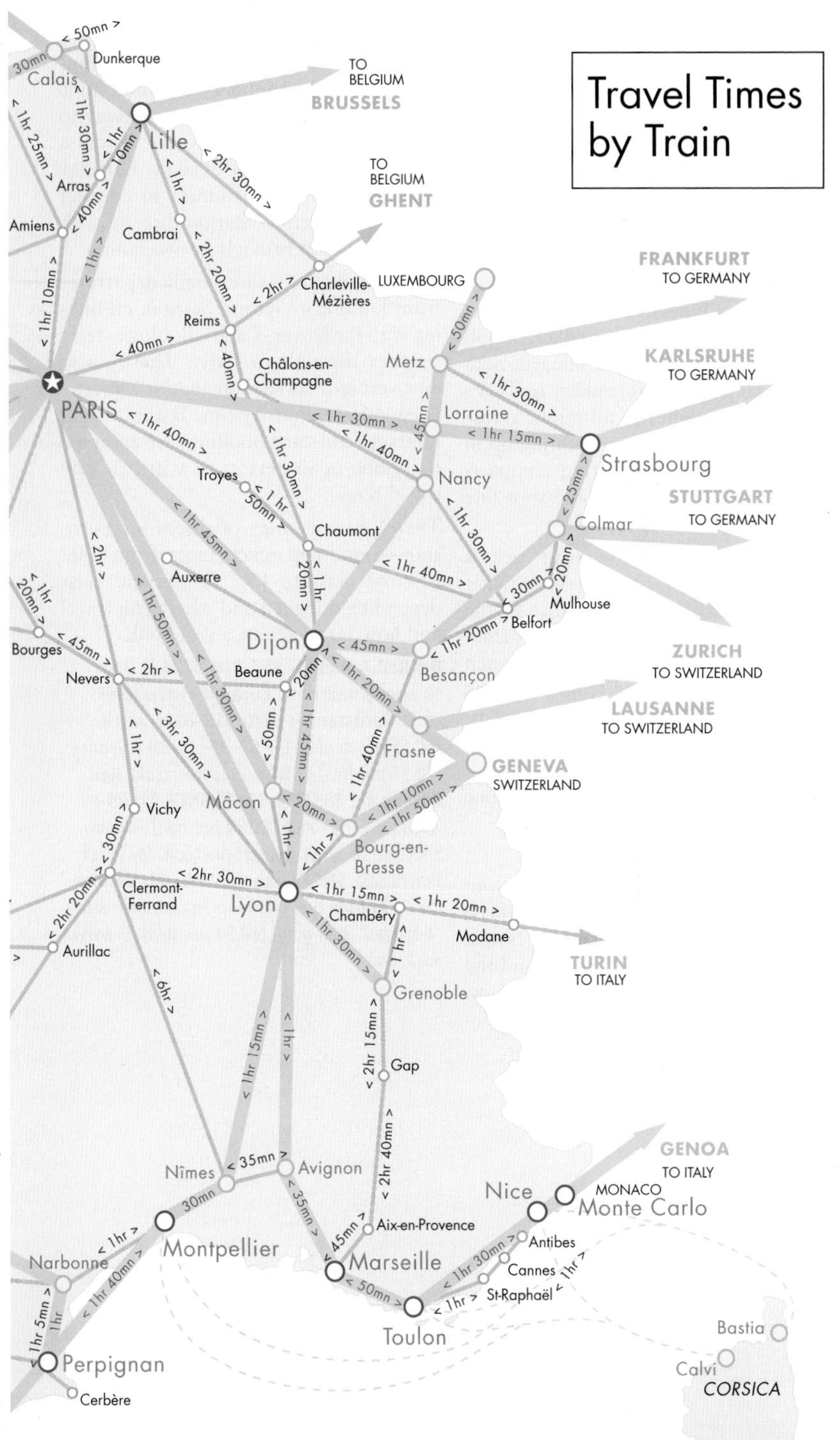

Travel Times by Train
TO BELGIUM BRUSSELS
TO BELGIUM GHENT
FRANKFURT TO GERMANY
KARLSRUHE TO GERMANY
STUTTGART TO GERMANY
ZURICH TO SWITZERLAND
LAUSANNE TO SWITZERLAND
GENEVA SWITZERLAND
TURIN TO ITALY
GENOA TO ITALY
LUXEMBOURG
MONACO Monte Carlo
CORSICA
PARIS
Calais
Dunkerque
Lille
Arras
Amiens
Cambrai
Charleville-Mézières
Reims
Châlons-en-Champagne
Metz
Lorraine
Nancy
Strasbourg
Colmar
Mulhouse
Belfort
Troyes
Chaumont
Auxerre
Dijon
Besançon
Frasne
Bourges
Nevers
Beaune
Vichy
Mâcon
Bourg-en-Bresse
Clermont-Ferrand
Lyon
Chambéry
Modane
Aurillac
Grenoble
Gap
Nîmes
Avignon
Montpellier
Aix-en-Provence
Marseille
Toulon
Nice
Antibes
Cannes
St-Raphaël
Narbonne
Perpignan
Cerbère
Bastia
Calvi

where it will be awaiting your arrival. The cost is €23 for the first bag, and €10 for two additional bags, with a maximum of three bags per person.

BOARDING THE TRAIN

Get to the station a half-hour before departure to ensure you'll have a good seat. Before boarding, you must punch your ticket (but not EurailPass) in one of the orange machines at the entrance to the platforms, or else the ticket collector will fine you €15. Once you're aboard, note that smoking is now forbidden in TGVs (the ban now applies to all public transportation in France). Even lighting up in the bathrooms or connecting compartments will land you an on-the-spot fine starting at €65.

Don't forget to validate your tickets (*composter le billet*) at the yellow ticket punchers, usually at the entrance to the platforms (*quais*). If you board your train on the run and don't have time to punch it, look for a conductor (*contrôleur*) as soon as possible and get him to sign it. Otherwise, you're in for a nasty fine (*amende*). Tickets printed by the SNCF must be validated; tickets printed at home don't need validation.

TO AND FROM THE U.K.

When you factor in travel time to and from the airport, not to mention flight delays, taking the Channel Tunnel is the fastest and easiest way between France and the U.K. It'll take you 2 hours and 15 minutes on the high-speed Eurostar train from Paris' Gare du Nord to London's St. Pancras Station; 35 minutes from Folkestone to Calais, 60 minutes from motorway to motorway. The Belgian border is just a short drive northeast of Calais. Eurostar trains use the same tunnels to connect London's Waterloo Station directly with Midi Station in Brussels in two hours.

British Rail also has four daily departures from London's Victoria Station, all linking with the Dover–Calais–Boulogne ferry services through to Paris. There's also an overnight service on the Newhaven–Dieppe ferry. Journey time is about eight hours. Credit-card bookings are accepted by phone or in person at a British Rail travel center.

There's a vast range of prices for Eurostar—round-trip tickets range from €600 for first class to €77 for second class depending on when and where you travel and how far in advance you book.

BritRail Travel (☎ *866/274–8724 in U.S.* 🌐 *www.britrail.com*). **Eurail** (🌐 *www.eurail.com*). **Eurostar** (☎ *0870/518–6186 in U.K. [€0.15 per min] or 08–92–35–35–39 in France [€0.17 per min]* 🌐 *www.eurostar.co.uk*). **Rail Europe** (☎ *888/382–7245*). **SNCF** (☎ *08–92–35–35–35 in France [€0.34 per min]* 🌐 *www.sncf.com or www.voyages-sncf.com for ticket purchases*). **SNCF Luggage Delivery Service** (☎ *3635 from any phone in France, then say "bagages" [bah-gahj] [€0.34 per min]* 🌐 *www.sncf.com*).

ESSENTIALS

ACCOMMODATIONS

The following is the price chart used throughout this book to determine price categories for most hotels listed. Paris remains the pricey exception: for that city, the highest category is over €250 and the lowest is under €80. Prices are for a standard double room in high season, including tax (19.6%) and service charge; rates for any board plans will be higher.

CATEGORY	PARIS	ALL REGIONS EXCLUDING PARIS
$$$$	over €250	over €215
$$$	€176–€250	€146–€215
$$	€121–€175	€106–€145
$	€80–€120	€65–€105
¢	under €80	under €65

APARTMENT AND HOUSE RENTALS

If you know the region you want to visit, contact the departmental branch directly and order a photo catalog that lists every property. If you specify which dates you plan to visit, the office will narrow down the choice to rentals available for those days. Be sure to plan early: renting gîtes has become one of the most popular ways to discover France.

Individual tourist offices often publish lists of *locations meublés* (furnished rentals); these are often inspected by the tourist office and rated by comfort standards. Usually they're booked directly through the individual owner, which generally requires some knowledge of French. Rentals that are not classified or rated by the tourist office should be undertaken with trepidation, as they can fall well below your minimum standard of comfort.

Vacation rentals in France always book from Saturday to Saturday (with some offering weekend rates off-season). Most do not include bed linens and towels, but make them available for an additional fee. Always check on policies on pets and children and specify if you need an enclosed garden for toddlers, a washing machine, a fireplace, and so on. If you plan to have overnight guests during your stay, let the owner know; there may be additional charges. Insurance restrictions prohibit loading in guests beyond the specified capacity.

Contacts **At Home Abroad** (☎ *212/421-9165* 🌐 *www.athomeabroadinc.com*). **Barclay International Group** (☎ *516/364-0064 or 800/845-6636* 🌐 *www.barclayweb.com*). **Drawbridge to Europe** (☎ *541/482-7778 or 888/268-1148* 🌐 *www.drawbridgetoeurope.com*). **Fédération Nationale des Gîtes de France** (☎ *01-49-70-75-75* 🌐 *www.gites-de-france.com*). **French Government Tourist Office** (⇨ *Visitor Information, below*). **Homes Away** (☎ *416/920-1873 or 800/374-6637* 🌐 *www.homesaway.com*). **Interhome** (☎ *954/791-8282 or 800/882-6864* 🌐 *www.interhome.us*). **Villanet** (☎ *206/417-3444 or 800/964-1891* 🌐 *www.rentavilla.com*). **Villas & Apartments Abroad** (☎ *212/213-6435* 🌐 *www.vaanyc.com*). **Villas International** (☎ *415/499-9490 or 800/221-2260* 🌐 *www.villasintl.com*). **Villas of Distinction** (☎ *707/778-1800 or 800/289-0900* 🌐 *www.villasofdistinction.com*). **Wimco** (☎ *800/449-1553* 🌐 *www.wimco.com*).

BED-AND-BREAKFASTS

Reservation Services **Bed & Breakfast.com** (☎ *512/322-2710 or 800/462-2632* 🌐 *www.bedandbreakfast.com*) also sends out an online newsletter. **Bed & Breakfast Inns Online** (☎ *615/868-1946 or 800/215-7365* 🌐 *www.bbonline.com*). **Chambres Hôtes France** (☎ *03-87-37-53-97* 🌐 *www.chambres-hotes-france.org*). **Fédération Nationale des Gîtes de France** (☎ *01-49-70-75-75* 🌐 *www.gitesdefrance.fr*). **Hôtes Qualité Paris** (☎ *08-92-68-30-00* 🌐 *www.parisinfo.com*).

HOME EXCHANGES

With a direct home exchange you stay in someone else's home while they stay in yours. Some outfits also deal with vacation homes, so you're not actually staying in someone's full-time residence, just their vacant weekend place.

Exchange Clubs **Home Exchange.com** (☎ *800/877–8723* 🌐 *www.homeexchange.com*); $99.95 for a one-year online listing. **HomeLink International** (☎ *800/638–3841* 🌐 *www.homelink.org*); $110 yearly for a Web-only membership; $170 includes Web access and two catalogs. **Intervac U.S.** (☎ *800/756–4663* 🌐 *www.intervacus.com*); $95 for membership; $195 includes two consulting calls from an Intervac rep.

HOTELS

The quality of accommodations, particularly in older properties and even in luxury hotels, can vary greatly from room to room; if you don't like the room you're given, ask to see another.

Hotels operate on the European Plan (EP, with no meal provided) unless we note that they offer a Breakfast Plan (BP), Modified American Plan (MAP, with breakfast and dinner daily, known as *demi-pension*), or Full American Plan (FAP, or *pension complète*, with three meals a day). Meal plans, which are usually an option offered in addition to the basic room plan, are generally only available with a minimum two- or three-night stay and are, of course, more expensive than the basic room rate. Inquire about meal plans when making reservations; details and prices are often stated on hotel Web sites.

It's always a good idea to make hotel reservations in Paris and other major tourist destinations as far in advance as possible, especially in late spring, summer, or fall. E-mail is the easiest way to contact the hotel (the staff is probably more likely to read English than to understand it spoken over the phone long-distance), though calling also works. But whether by fax, phone, or e-mail, you should specify the exact dates you want to stay (don't forget to notify your hotel of a possible late check-in to prevent your room from being given away); the size of the room you want and how many people will be sleeping there; the type of accommodations you want (two twins, double, etc.); and what kind of bathroom (private with shower, tub, or both). You might also ask if a deposit (or your credit-card number) is required, and if so, what happens if you cancel later. Request that the hotel fax you back so you have a written confirmation of your reservation.

If you arrive without a reservation, the tourist offices in major train stations and most towns can probably help you find a room.

Many hotels in France are small, and many are family-run establishments. Some are affiliated with hotel groups, such as Logis de France, which can be relied on for comfort, character, and regional cuisine (look for its distinctive yellow-and-green sign). A Logis de France paperback guide is widely available in bookshops. Two prestigious international groups with numerous converted châteaux and manor houses among its members are Relais & Châteaux and Small Luxury Hotels of the World; booklets listing members are available from these organizations. France also has some hotel chains. Examples in the upper price bracket are Frantel, Novotel, and Sofitel as well as Inter-Continental, Marriott, Hilton, Hyatt, Westin, and Sheraton. The Best Western, Campanile, Climat de France, Ibis,

WORD OF MOUTH

Did the resort look as good in real life as it did in the photos? Did you sleep like a baby, or were the walls paper thin? Did you get your money's worth? Rate hotels and write your own reviews in Travel Ratings or start a discussion about your favorite places in Travel Talk on www.fodors.com. Your comments might even appear in our books. Yes, you, too, can be a correspondent!

and Timhotel chains are more moderate. Typically, chains offer a consistently acceptable standard of modern features (modern bathrooms, TVs, etc.) but tend to lack atmosphere, with some exceptions (Best Western, for instance, tries to maintain the local character of the hotels it manages).

Here is a sample letter you may use when making a written or e-mailed reservation:

Cher (Dear) *Madame, Monsieur:*

Nous voudrions réserver une chambre pour (We wish to reserve a room for) _____ (number of) *nuit(s)* (nights), *du* (from) ______ (arrival date) *au* ______ (departure date), *à deux lits* (with twin beds), or *à lit-double* (with a double bed), or *une chambre pour une seule personne* (a room for a single person), *avec salle de bains et toilette privées* (with a bathroom and private toilet). *Si possible, nous voudrions une salle de bains avec une baignoire et aussi une douche.* (If possible, we would prefer a bathroom with a tub as well as a shower.) *Veuillez confirmer la réservation en nous communicant le prix de la chambre, et le dépot forfaitaire que vous exigez. Dans l'attente de votre lettre, nous vous prions d'agréer, Madame, Monsieur, l'expression de nos sentiments amicales.* (Can you please inform us about availabilities, the room rate, and if any deposit is needed? With our friendliest greetings, we will await your confirmation.)

COMMUNICATIONS

INTERNET

If you use a major Internet provider, getting online in France shouldn't be difficult. Most hotels have in-room broadband connections or wireless access. If you need to spend a lot of time online, make sure to ask when you book a room if there's a charge for the service. Remember to bring an adapter for the European-style plugs.

If you're not at your hotel, there are still many places to get online. Wi-Fi hot spots can be found at many of the cafés and public libraries in Paris and other metropolitan areas. In smaller towns ask at the local tourism office where you can get connected.

Access Numbers in Paris **AOL** (☎ *08-60-37-60-37*).

Contacts **Cybercafes** (🌐 *www.cybercafes.com*) lists more than 4,000 Internet cafés worldwide. **Hotspot Zone** (🌐 *cnet.jiwire.com*) lists the Wi-Fi zones throughout France (for Paris, search the region "Ile de France").

PHONES

The good news is that you can now make a direct-dial telephone call from virtually any point on earth. The bad news? You may pay dearly for the convenience. Calling from a hotel is almost always the most expensive option; hotels usually add huge surcharges to all calls, particularly international ones. In some countries you can phone from call centers or even the post office. Calling cards usually keep costs to a minimum, but only if you purchase them locally. And then there are mobile phones (⇨ *below*), which are sometimes more prevalent—particularly in the developing world—than landlines; as expensive as mobile phone calls can be, they are still usually a much cheaper option than calling from your hotel.

The country code for France is 33. The first two digits of French numbers are a prefix determined by zone: Paris and Ile-de-France, 01; the northwest, 02; the northeast, 03; the southeast, 04; and the southwest, 05. Numbers that begin with 06 are for mobile phones (and are notoriously expensive). Pay close attention to the numbers beginning with 08; 08 followed by 00 is a toll-free number but 08–36 numbers can be costly, usually €0.34 per minute but sometimes €1 and up.

Note that when dialing France from abroad, drop the initial 0 from the number. For instance, to call a telephone number in Paris from the United States, dial 011–33 plus the phone number minus the initial 0 (phone numbers in this book are listed with the full 10 digits, which you use to make local calls).

CALLING WITHIN FRANCE

The French are very fond of their mobile phones (*portables*) meaning that telephone booths are more scarce than ever. Look for public phones in airports, post offices, train stations, on the street, and subway stations. You can use your own credit card, but keep in mind that you will be charged a €20 minimum, and you'll have 30 days after the first call to use up the credit. Or pick up a discounted calling card (*carte téléphonique*) at newsstands, cafés with a TABAC sign, or post offices. There are two types of cards: one can be used on any phone, the other has a microchip (*puce*) that works only on public phones (*les cabines*). Insert your card and follow directions on the screen (it should give you the option to read in English). Or dial the toll-free number on the back of the card, enter the identification number from the back of the card, and follow the instructions in English.

CALLING OUTSIDE FRANCE

To make a direct international call out of France, dial 00, then the country code (1 for the United States), the area code, and number.

Telephone rates have decreased recently in France because the French Telecom monopoly finally has some competition. As in most countries, the priciest calls are between 8 AM and 7 PM; you can expect to pay €0.26 per minute for a call to the United States, Canada, or some of the closer European countries such as Great Britain, Belgium, Italy, and Germany. Rates are slashed in half when you make that same call between 7 PM and 8 AM, at just €0.12 per minute. To call home with the help of international directory assistance costs a hefty €3 per call; if this doesn't dissuade you, dial 118–700 and a bilingual operator will come on the line and ask which country you are calling. Hotels tack on hefty fees for even local calls, plus a surcharge for international calls, so steer clear of the phone in your room unless you're using an international phone card (*télécarte international*), which you can find at the same places as a local calling card. The cards cost about €12 for 50 units or €20 for 120 units.

Access Codes AT&T Direct (☎ *08–00–99–00–11, 800/222–0300 for information*). **MCI WorldPhone** (☎ *08–00–99–00–19, 800/444–4444 for information*). **Sprint International Access** (☎ *08–00–99–00–87, 800/793–1153 for information*).

MOBILE PHONES

If you have a multiband phone (some countries use different frequencies than what's used in the United States) and your service provider uses the world-standard GSM network (as do T-Mobile, AT&T, and Verizon), you can probably use your phone abroad. But be warned: this is often the most expensive calling option, with hefty toll charges on incoming and outgoing calls, sometimes as high as $4 per call. Roaming fees can be steep, too: 99¢ a minute is considered reasonable. Sending an international text message is usually a cheaper option, but be aware that fees abroad vary greatly (from 15¢ to 50¢ and up), and there's usually a charge for incoming messages.

If you just want to make local calls, consider buying a local SIM card for about €30 (note that your provider may have to unlock your phone for you to use a different SIM card) or a cheap pay-as-you-go phone (*sans abonnement*). You can then have a local number and can make local calls at local rates. If your trip is extensive, you could also simply buy a new cell phone in your destination, as the initial cost will be offset over time.

■ TIP→ If you travel internationally frequently, save one of your old mobile phones or buy a cheap one on the Internet; ask your cell phone company to unlock it for you, and take it with you as a travel phone, buying a new SIM card with pay-as-you-go service in each destination.

Contacts Cellular Abroad (☎ *800/287–5072* 🌐 *www.cellularabroad.com*) rents and sells

GMS phones and sells SIM cards that work in many countries with inexpensive per-minute rates. **Mobal** (☎ *888/888–9162* 🌐 *www.mobalrental.com*) rents mobiles and sells GSM phones (starting at $49) that will operate in 140 countries. Per-call rates are competitive but each sms (text messages) costs 80¢. **Planet Fone** (☎ *888/988–4777* 🌐 *www.planetfone.com*) rents cell phones, but the per-minute rates are expensive.

EATING OUT

All establishments must post their menus outside, so study them carefully before deciding to enter. Most restaurants have two basic types of menu: à la carte and fixed-price (prix-fixe or *un menu*). The prix-fixe menu is usually the best value, though choices are more limited. Most menus begin with a first course (*une entrée*), often subdivided into cold and hot starters, followed by fish and poultry, then meat; it's rare today that anyone orders something from all three. The restaurants we review in this book are the cream of the crop in each price category.

A few pointers on French dining etiquette: diners in France don't negotiate their orders much, so don't expect serene smiles when you ask for sauce on the side. Order your coffee after dessert, not with it. When you're ready for the check, ask for it: no professional waiter would dare put a bill on your table while you're still enjoying the last sip of coffee. And don't ask for a doggy bag; it's just not done. The French usually drink wine or mineral water—not soda or coffee—with their food. You may ask for a carafe of tap water if you don't want to order wine or pay for bottled water.

MEALS AND MEALTIMES

What's the difference between a bistro and a brasserie? Can you order food at a café? Can you go to a restaurant just for a snack? The following definitions should help. Many say that bistros served the world's first fast food. After the fall of Napoléon, the Russian soldiers who occupied Paris were known to bang on zinc-top café bars, crying "*bistro*"—"quickly"—in Russian. In the past, bistros were simple places with minimal decor and service. Although nowadays many are quite upscale, with beautiful interiors and chic clientele, most remain cozy establishments serving straightforward, frequently gutsy cooking. Brasseries—ideal places for quick, one-dish meals—originated when Alsatians fleeing German occupiers after the Franco-Prussian War came to Paris and opened restaurants serving specialties from home. Pork-based dishes, *choucroute* (sauerkraut), and beer (*brasserie* also means brewery) were, and still are, mainstays here. The typical brasserie is convivial and keeps late hours. Some are open 24 hours a day, a good thing to know since many restaurants stop serving at 10:30 PM.

Like bistros and brasseries, cafés come in a confusing variety. Often informal neighborhood hangouts, cafés may also be veritable showplaces attracting chic, well-heeled crowds. At most cafés the regulars congregate at the bar, where coffee and drinks are cheaper than at tables. At lunch tables are set, and a limited menu is served. Sandwiches, usually with *jambon* (ham), *fromage* (cheese), or *mixte* (ham and cheese), are served throughout the day. *Casse croûtes* (snacks) are also offered. Cafés are for lingering, for people-watching, and for daydreaming. If none of these options fit the bill, head to the nearest *traiteur* (deli) for picnic fixings.

See the Menu Guide at the end of the book for guidance with menu items that appear frequently on French menus and throughout the reviews in this book.

Breakfast is usually served from 7:30 AM to 10 PM, lunch from noon to 2 PM, and dinner from 7:30 PM to 10 PM. Restaurants in Paris usually serve dinner until 10:30 PM.

PAYING

By French law, prices must include tax and tip (*service compris* or *prix nets*), but pocket change left on the table in basic places, or an additional 5% in better restaurants, is always appreciated. Beware of bills stamped *service not included* in English. The following is the price chart used throughout this book to determine price categories for all restaurants. Prices are per person for a main course at dinner, including tax (5.5%) and service; note that if a restaurant offers only prix-fixe (set-price) meals, it is given a price category that reflects the full prix-fixe price.

CATEGORY	COST
$$$$	Over €32
$$$	€25-€32
$$	€18-€24
$	€13-€17
¢	under €13

ELECTRICITY

The electrical current in France is 220 volts, 50 cycles alternating current (AC); wall outlets take Continental-type plugs, with two round prongs.

Consider making a small investment in a universal adapter, which has several types of plugs in one lightweight, compact unit. Most laptops and mobile phone chargers are dual voltage (i.e., they operate equally well on 110 and 220 volts), so require only an adapter. These days the same is true of small appliances such as hair dryers. Always check labels and manufacturer instructions to be sure. Don't use 110-volt outlets marked FOR SHAVERS ONLY for high-wattage appliances such as hair dryers.

Contacts Steve Kropla's Help for World Traveler's (🌐 *www.travelnow.com*) has information on electrical and telephone plugs around the world. **Walkabout Travel Gear** (🌐 *www.walkabouttravelgear.com*) has good coverage of electricity under "adapters."

EMERGENCIES

For minor emergencies, contact a generalist who will actually visit you in your home or hotel, medical bag in hand, at any hour of the day or night, whether you're in the city or on the outskirts of a tiny town. Hospital emergency rooms should be used only for emergencies.

France's emergency services are conveniently streamlined. Every town and village has a *médecin de garde* (on-duty doctor) for flus, sprains, tetanus shots, and similar problems. Larger cities have a remarkable house-call service called "SOS Médecins" (SOS Doctors, or "SOS Dentistes" for dental emergencies); dial ☎ *08–20–33–24–24*. The cost is minimal, compared to the United States, about €60 for a house call. If you need an X-ray or emergency treatment, call an ambulance (dial ☎ *15*). Note that outside Paris it's difficult to find English-speaking doctors.

Pharmacies can be helpful with minor health problems and come equipped with blood-pressure machines and first-aid kits. They also can be consulted for a list of practicing doctors in the area, nearby hospitals, private clinics, or health centers.

On the street the French phrases that may be needed in an emergency are: *Au secours!* (Help!), *urgence* (emergency), *samu* (ambulance), *pompiers* (firemen), *poste de station* (police station), *médecin* (doctor), and *hôpital* (hospital).

HOLIDAYS

With 11 national *jours feriés* (holidays) and at least five weeks of paid vacation, the French have their share of repose. In May there's a holiday nearly every week, so be prepared for stores, banks, and museums to shut their doors for days at a time. Be sure to call museums, restaurants, and hotels in advance to make sure they'll be open.

Note that these dates are for the calendar year 2010: January 1 (New Year's Day); April 24 and 25 (Easter Sunday and Monday); May 1 (Labor Day); May 8 (V.E. Day); May 13 (Ascension); June 12 (Pentecost Sunday); July 14 (Bastille Day); August 15 (Assumption); November 1 (All Saints); November 11 (Armistice); December 25 (Christmas).

MAIL

Post offices, or PTT, are found in every town and are recognizable by a yellow LA POSTE sign. They're usually open weekdays 8 AM to 7 PM, Saturday 8–noon. The **main Paris post office** (✉ *52 rue du Louvre*) is open 24 hours, seven days a week.

SHIPPING PACKAGES

Letters and postcards to the United States and Canada cost €0.85 for 20 grams. Letters and postcards within France cost €0.55. Stamps can be bought in post offices and in cafés displaying a red TABAC sign outside. It takes, on the average, three days for letters to arrive in Europe, and five days to reach the United States.

If you're uncertain where you'll be staying, have mail sent to the local post office, addressed as poste restante, or to American Express, but remember that during peak seasons American Express may refuse to accept mail. The French postal service has a €0.55 per item service charge.

Sending overnight mail from major cities in France is relatively easy. Besides DHL, Federal Express, and UPS, the French post office has overnight mail service, called Chronopost, which is much cheaper for small packages. Keep in mind that certain things cannot be shipped from France to the United States, such as perfume and any meat products.

Express Services DHL (☎ *01-53-96-52-30, 01-45-01-91-00, 08-20-20-25-25 for information all over France* 🌐 *www.dhl.com*). **Federal Express** (☎ *01-40-06-90-16* 🌐 *www.fedex.com*). **UPS** (☎ *08-00-87-78-77 for information all over France [€0.12 per min]* 🌐 *www.ups.com*).

MONEY

The following prices are for Paris; other areas are often cheaper (with the notable exception of the Côte d'Azur). Keep in mind that it's less expensive to eat or drink standing at a café or bar counter than to sit at a table. Two prices are listed, *au comptoir* (at the counter) and *à salle* (at a table). Sometimes orders cost even more if you're seated at a terrace table. Coffee in a bar: €1–€2.50 (standing), €1.50–€6 (seated); beer in a bar: €2 (standing), €3–€8 (seated); Coca-Cola: €2–€4 a bottle; ham sandwich: €3–€5; 2-km (1-mi) taxi ride: €6; movie-theater seat: €9.90 (morning shows are always cheaper); foreign newspaper: €1–€5.

Prices throughout this guide are given for adults. Substantially reduced fees are almost always available for children, students, and senior citizens.

ATMS AND BANKS

Your own bank will probably charge a fee for using ATMs abroad; the foreign bank you use may also charge a fee. Nevertheless, you can usually get a better rate of exchange at an ATM than you will at a currency-exchange office or even when changing money in a bank. And extracting funds as you need them is a safer option than carrying around a large amount of cash.

TIP→ PIN numbers with more than four digits are not recognized at ATMs in many countries. If yours has five or more, remember to change it before you leave.

Easily found throughout France, ATMs are one of the easiest ways to get euros. Don't, however, expect to find ATMs in rural areas.

Note that the ATM machine will give you two chances to enter your correct PIN number; if you make a mistake on the third try, your card will be held, and you'll have to return to the bank the next morning to retrieve it. You may have better luck with ATMs with a credit or debit

TOP 10 MONEY SAVING TIPS

Heading to France this summer but not sure you can afford it?

Travelers are questioning just how far their dollars will go, so we asked our community of Fodorites on Fodor's Travel Talk Forum (🌐 *www.fodors.com*) to reveal their insider tips on how to get the biggest bang for your buck and still have a fabulously rich travel experience.

1. "Watch for new train routes opening up from Paris and plan a trip around 'introductory' prices for the new routes.

Trains can be a low cost and comfortable means of point to point travel in France."
—DeborahAnn

2. "People who stay farther from the center are not only spending much less money, but they are seeing a lot more of the city... a lot of the people who are already staying in the center will not necessarily venture to outer neighborhoods." —Kerouac

3. "We have found that a rental car frequently turns out to be cheaper for two people than taking the train.

If you drive, be sure to get a really good Michelin map for the area." —julies

4. "A restaurant lunch is cheaper than a restaurant dinner. One day we'll eat a restaurant lunch followed by a bread-cheese-pastry dinner.

The next day we'll have the bread-cheese lunch followed at dinner by salad and something to heat up from Leclerc." —Coquelicot

5. "Rent a gîte in a centrally located and interesting place. Outside of peak season, these can be remarkably inexpensive.

You can eat in (this saves a ton of money) without actually doing a lot of cooking by shopping at local markets, charcuteries, etc., for prepared foods that can be eaten cold or just warmed up." —julies

6. "In restaurants order 'robinet' not 'd'eau.' You will end up with tap water, which is free.... Look out for 'Les Routiers' [signs]. This is the traditional sign for lorry drivers but of course being French this is a sign of large amounts of local food at very low prices. This lunch deal normally starts at 12:00 (say until 12:15), wine included, and again no menu—just eat what is put in front of you." —bilboburgler

7. "If using a car, the cheapest fuel rates are at the *supermarchés* usually located at the edge of town. There are usually large billboards advertising the location.

Make sure to fill the tank on Saturday. They usually do not have staffed fuel stops on Sunday and your credit card won't work in the automatic machines." —ira

8. "Outside of Paris, if you're driving around, look for wine cooperatives where you can buy wine 'en vrac.'

Bring your own liter bottle and they will fill it for you." —petitepois

9. "For really cheap rail fares book early online—90–92 days before travel. Great if you're sure of your travel dates.... I got Nice-Paris €25 (TGV) single 92 days before traveling—they soon went to €45, then €60."
—Ricardo_215

10. "I agree with staying in B&Bs. You can often find them from 50 euros or less in rural areas." —dgassa

card that is also a Visa or MasterCard, rather than just your bank card.

CREDIT CARDS

France is a debit-card society. Debit cards are used for just about everything, from the automatic gas pumps, to the tolls on highways, payment machines in underground parking lots, stamps at the post office, and even the most minor purchases in the larger department stores. A restaurant or shop would either have to be extremely small or remote not to have some credit-card or debit-card capability. However, some of the smaller restaurants and stores do have a credit-card minimum, usually around €15, which normally should be clearly indicated; to be safe, ask before you order. Do not forget to take your credit-card receipt, as fraudulent use of credit-card numbers taken from receipts is on the rise. Note that while MasterCard and Visa are usually welcomed, American Express isn't always accepted.

It's a good idea to inform your credit-card company before you travel, especially if you're going abroad and don't travel internationally very often. Otherwise, the credit-card company might put a hold on your card because of unusual activity—not a good thing halfway through your trip. Record all your credit-card numbers—as well as the phone numbers to call if your cards are lost or stolen—in a safe place, so you're prepared should something go wrong. MasterCard and Visa have general numbers you can call (collect if you're abroad) if your card is lost, but you're better off calling the number of your issuing bank, since MasterCard and Visa usually just transfer you to your bank; your bank's number is usually printed on your card.

If you plan to use your credit card for cash advances, you'll need to apply for a PIN at least two weeks before your trip. Although it's usually cheaper (and safer) to use a credit card abroad for large purchases (so you can cancel payments or be reimbursed if there's a problem), note that some credit-card companies *and* the banks that issue them add substantial percentages to all foreign transactions, whether they're in a foreign currency or not. Check on these fees before leaving home, so there won't be any surprises when you get the bill.

■ TIP→ Before you charge something, ask the merchant whether he or she plans to do a dynamic currency conversion (DCC). In such a transaction the credit-card processor (shop, restaurant, or hotel, not Visa or MasterCard) converts the currency and charges you in dollars. In most cases you'll pay the merchant a 3% fee for this service in addition to any credit-card company and issuing-bank foreign-transaction surcharges.

Dynamic currency conversion programs are becoming increasingly widespread. Merchants who participate in them are supposed to ask whether you want to be charged in dollars or the local currency, but they don't always do so. And even if they do offer you a choice, they may well avoid mentioning the additional surcharges. The good news is that you *do* have a choice. And if this practice really gets your goat, you can avoid it entirely thanks to American Express; with its cards, DCC simply isn't an option.

In this guide, the following abbreviations are used: **AE,** American Express; **DC,** Diners Club; **MC,** MasterCard; and **V,** Visa.

Reporting Lost Cards American Express (☎ *800/992–3404 in U.S., 336/393–1111 collect from abroad* 🌐 *www.americanexpress.com*). **Diners Club** (☎ *800/234–6377 in U.S., 303/799–1504 collect from abroad* 🌐 *www.dinersclub.com*). **Discover** (☎ *800/347–2683 in U.S., 801/902–3100 collect from abroad* 🌐 *www.discovercard.com*). **MasterCard** (☎ *800/622–7747 in U.S., 636/722–7111 collect from abroad* 🌐 *www.mastercard.com*). **Visa** (☎ *800/847–2911 in U.S., 410/581–9994 collect from abroad* 🌐 *www.visa.com*).

CURRENCY AND EXCHANGE

The advent of the euro makes any whirlwind grand European tour all the easier. From France you can glide across the borders of Austria, Germany, Italy, Spain, Holland, Ireland, Greece, Belgium, Finland, Luxembourg, and Portugal with no pressing need to run to the local exchange booth to change to yet another currency before you even had the time to become familiar with the last. You'll be able to do what drives many tourists crazy—to assess the value of a purchase (for example, to realize that eating a three-course meal in a small restaurant in Lisbon is cheaper than that ham sandwich you bought on the Champs Élysées). Initially, the euro had another benefit because it was created as a direct competitor with the U.S. dollar, and was envisioned to be, therefore, of nearly equal value. Unfortunately, exchange rates have seen the euro soar and the dollar take a hit. At this writing, one euro equals U.S. $1.49.

These days, the easiest way to get euros is through ATMs; you can find them in airports, train stations, and throughout the city. ATM rates are excellent because they're based on wholesale rates offered only by major banks. It's a good idea, however, to bring some euros with you from home and always to have some cash on hand as backup.

Currency Conversion X-Rates (🌐 *www.x-rates.com*). **Oanda.com** (🌐 *www.oanda.com*). **XE.com** (🌐 *www.xe.com*).

PASSPORTS

All Canadian, U.K., and U.S. citizens, even infants, need only a valid passport to enter France for stays of up to 90 days.

We're always surprised at how few Americans have passports—only 25% at this writing. This number is expected to grow in coming years, when it becomes impossible to re-enter the United States from trips to neighboring Canada or Mexico without one. U.S. passports are valid for 10 years. You must apply in person if you're getting a passport for the first time; if your previous passport was lost, stolen, or damaged; or if your previous passport has expired and was issued more than 15 years ago or when you were under 16. All children under 18 must appear in person to apply for or renew a passport. Both parents must accompany any child under 14 (or send a notarized statement with their permission) and provide proof of their relationship to the child.

There are 13 regional passport offices, as well as 7,000 passport acceptance facilities in post offices, public libraries, and other governmental offices. If you're renewing a passport, you can do so by mail. Forms are available at passport acceptance facilities and online. The cost to apply for a new passport is $100 for adults, $85 for children under 16; renewals are $75. Allow six weeks for processing, both for first-time passports and renewals. For an expediting fee of $60 you can reduce this time to about two weeks. If your trip is less than two weeks away, you can get a passport even more rapidly by going to a passport office with the necessary documentation. Before your trip, make two copies of your passport's data page (one for someone at home and another for you to carry separately). Or scan the page and e-mail it to someone at home and/or yourself.

U.S. Passport Information U.S. Department of State (☎ *0877/487–2778* 🌐 http://travel.state.gov/passport/).

SAFETY

Beware of petty theft—purse snatching, pickpocketing, and the like—throughout France, particularly in Paris and along the Côte d'Azur. Use common sense: avoid pulling out a lot of money in public; wear a handbag with long straps that you can sling across your body, bandolier style, with a zippered compartment for your money and passport. Men should keep their wallets up front. When withdrawing money from cash machines, be especially aware of your surroundings and anyone standing too close. If you feel uneasy, press the cancel button (*annuler*) and walk to an area where you feel more comfortable.

Incidents of credit-card fraud are on the rise in France, especially in urban areas; be sure to collect your receipts, as these have recently been used by thieves to make purchases over the Internet. Car break-ins, especially in isolated parking lots where hikers set off for the day, are on the rise. It makes sense to take valuables with you or leave your luggage at your hotel.

Note one cultural difference: a friendly smile or steady eye contact is often seen as an invitation to further contact; so, unfortunately, you should avoid being overly friendly with strangers—unless you feel perfectly safe.

TIP→ Distribute your cash, credit cards, IDs, and other valuables between a deep front pocket, an inside jacket or vest pocket, and a hidden money pouch. Don't reach for the money pouch once you're in public.

TAXES

All taxes must be included in posted prices in France. The initials TTC (*toutes taxes comprises*—taxes included) sometimes appear on price lists but, strictly speaking, they're superfluous. By law, hotel prices must include 19.6% taxes and a service charge of 5.5% is charged for food in restaurants. If they show up as extra charges, complain.

Many shops offer V.A.T. refunds to foreign shoppers. Non-EU residents (including U.S. and Canada residents) can claim a refund of the 19.6% tax (less a 3% administrative fee) for any goods totaling €175.01 purchased in the same store. Request a détaxe form in the store. You will be asked to show your passport. At the airport or border crossing, present the form, plus the goods purchased, to customs officials, who will issue a stamp. Proceed to the cash refund office. You may also return the form to Global Refund by mail.

Global Refund is a Europe-wide service with 225,000 affiliated stores and more than 700 refund counters at major airports and border crossings. Its refund form, called a Tax Free Check, is the most common across the European continent. The service issues refunds in the form of cash, check, or credit-card adjustment.

V.A.T. Refunds Global Refund (*www.globalrefund.com*). **Detaxe TaxFree** (*01-42-60-29-29* *www.detaxe.com*).

TIME

The time difference between New York and Paris is six hours (so when it's 1 PM in New York, it's 7 PM in Paris). France, like the rest of Europe, uses the 24-hour clock, which means that after noon you continue counting forward: 13h00 is 1 PM, 22h30 is 10:30 PM. The European format for abbreviating dates is day/month/year, so 7/5/05 means May 7, not July 5.

Time Zones Timeanddate.com (*www.timeanddate.com/worldclock*) can help you figure out the correct time anywhere in the world.

TIPPING

The French have a clear idea of when they should be tipped. Bills in bars and restaurants include a service charge incorporated into the prices, but it's customary to round out your bill with some small change unless you're dissatisfied. The amount varies: anywhere from €0.50, if you've merely bought a beer, to €1–€3 (or more) after a meal. Tip taxi drivers and hair stylists about 10%. In some theaters and hotels, coat-check attendants may expect nothing (if there's a sign saying POURBOIRE INTERDIT—tips forbidden); otherwise give them €0.50–€1. Washroom attendants usually get €0.50, though the sum is often posted.

If you stay in a hotel for more than two or three days, it's customary to leave something for the chambermaid—about €1.50 per day. In expensive hotels you may well call on the services of a baggage porter (bellhop) and hotel porter and possibly the telephone receptionist. All expect a tip: plan on about €1.50 per item for the baggage porter, but the other tips will depend on how much you've used their services—common sense must guide you here. In hotels that provide room service, give €1 to the waiter (this does not apply to breakfast served in your room). If the chambermaid does some pressing, give her €1 on top of the charge made. If the concierge has been helpful, it's customary to leave a tip of €10–€20.

Museum guides should get €1–€1.50 after a guided tour.

VISITOR INFORMATION

All major cities and most small towns have tourism offices that can provide information on accommodation and sightseeing and maps.

France Tourism Information **Maison de la France** (☎ *514/288–1904* 🌐 *www.franceguide.com*) is the national site for French tourism.

FODORS.COM CONNECTION

Before your trip, be sure to check out what other travelers are saying in "Talk" on www.fodors.com.

Tourism Web Sites **Tourism in France** (🌐 *www.tourisme.fr*) has links to 3,500 tourist offices.

ONLINE TRAVEL TOOLS

All About France The **Centre des Monuments Nationaux** (🌐 *www.monum.fr*) runs 200 monuments—from the Arc de Triomphe to Chambord—and is chock-full of information. If you're château hopping, **Chateaux and Country** (🌐 *www.chateauxandcountry.com*) has a brief overview of hundreds of châteaux all over France. The **French Ministry of Culture** (🌐 *www.culture.fr*) provides a portal to all the cultural happenings and institutions throughout France. **French National Museums** (🌐 *www.rmn.fr*) is the main site for the Réunion des musées nationaux, which administers the country's biggest museums.

INDEX

C

D

E

F

M

N

Q

R

U

V

W

Y

Z

PHOTO CREDITS

1, Lane Clark, Fodors.com member. 2-3, dthomasdupont, Fodors.com member. 5, iStockphoto. Chapter 1: Experience France: 8-9, Jon Arnold/Agency Jon Arnold Images/age fotostock, 10, Lisa Ferguson, Fodors.com member. 11 (left), Michael Gwyther-Jones/Flickr, 11 (right), Betty H, Fodors.com member.12 (left), Leigh, Fodors.com member. 12 (right), Bob Lawson, Fodors.com member. 13, Doug Pearson/Agency Jon Arnold Images/age fotostock. 14 (left), Chris Christensen, Fodors.com member. 14 (right), AJ Kersten, Fodors.com member. 15 (left), SGM/age fotostock. 15 (right), Peter Allen, Fodors.com member. 20 (left), Pete Labrozzi, Fodors.com member. 20 (center), Tiffany Weir, Fodors.com member. 20 (bottom), Claudio Giovanni Colombo/Shutterstock. 20 (right), elaine, Fodors.com member. 21 (left), Elena Elisseeva/Shutterstock. 21 (center), Holly McKee, Fodors.com member. 21 (bottom), Tangata, Fodors.com member. 21 (right), james incorvaia, Fodors.com member. 22, basingstoke2, Fodors.com member. 23 (left), smugman, Fodors.com member. 23 (right), Judy J. Potrzeba, Fodors.com member. 24, SuperStock/age fotostock. 25, Anna McClain, Fodors.com member. 26, Le Buerehiesel. 27 (left), GLong2027, Fodors.com member. 27 (right), dthomasdupont, Fodors.com member. 28, Shannon McShane, Fodors.com member. 29 (left and right), Robert Fisher. 30, Zyankarlo/Shutterstock. 31 (left), LadyofHats/wikipedia.org. 31 (right), Elizabeth A. Miller, Fodors.com member. 32, dspiel, Fodors.com member. 33 (left), nfldbeothuk, Fodors.com member. 33 (right), schlegal1, Fodors.com member. 36, Juan Carlos Muñoz/age fotostock. 37, von Essen Hotels. 38, James Dunn, Fodors.com member. Chapter 2: Paris: 39, ajkarlin, Fodors.com member. 40, equiles28, Fodors.com member. 41 (left), Andrea Schwab, Fodors.com member. 41 (right), Ann Forcier, Fodors.com member. 46 (left and right), christinaaparis, Fodors.com member. 51, fabio chironi/age fotostock. 52, P. Narayan/age fotostock. 55, Ewan Chesser/Shutterstock. 56, Fabien1309/wikipedia.org. 57, Renaud Visage/age fotostock. 58 (left), Frank Peterschroeder / Bilderberg/Aurora Photos. 58 (right), ostill/Shutterstock. 64, Directphoto.org / Alamy. 65, Directphoto.org / Alamy. 69, wikipedia.org. 73, Kevin George / Alamy. 76, Marisa Allegra Williams/iStockphoto. 81, ImageGap / Alamy. 85 (top), Paul Hahn/laif/Aurora Photos. 85 (bottom), SuperStock/age fotostock. 86 (left), Renaud Visage/age fotostock. 86 (right), Ivan Vdovin/Shutterstock. 87 (top left), Stevan Stratford/iStockphoto. 87 (bottom), Paul Hahn/Laif / Aurora Photos. 87 (top right), Robert Haines / Alamy. 88 (left), © Renaud Visage/age fotostock. 88 (right), Carsten Madsen/iStockphoto. 89 (top left), xc/Shutterstock. 89 (top right), Corbis. 89 (bottom), Mehdi Chebil / Alamy. 90, Elena Elisseeva/Shutterstock. 96, rfx/SHutterstock. 106, P. Narayan/age fotostock. 115, Roger Salz/Flickr. 130 (top), Fabrice Rambert. 130 ((bottom left), Hôtel Langlois. 130 (bottom right), Francis Amiand. 137 (top), Jaime Ardiles-Arce/Four Seasons Hotels and Resorts. 137 (bottom), Hôtel Odéon Saint-Germain. 142, L F File/Shutterstock. 149, Paradis Latin Cabaret. 153, Cezary Piwowarski/wikipedia.org. 156, Elizabeth A. Miller, Fodors.com member. Chapter 3: Ile-de-France: 161, Wojtek Buss/age fotostock. 162, Judith Nelson, Fodors.com member. 163 (top), elaine, Fodors.com member. 163 (bottom), TravelChic10, Fodors.com member. 168, Ivan Bastien/iStockphoto. 172, AM Corporation / Alamy .174 (first), Elias H. Debbas II/Shutterstock. 174 (second), Jason Cosburn/Shutterstock. 174 (third), Public Domain. 174 (fourth), Michael Booth / Alamy. 174 (fifth), Michael Booth / Alamy. 175 (left), Jens Preshaw/age fotostock. 175 (top right), Public Domain. 175 (bottom right), The Print Collector / Alamy. 176 (top), michel mory/iStockphoto. 176 (center), Mike Booth/Alamy. 176 (bottom), Tommaso di Girolamo/age fotostock. 177, Hemis/Alamy. 178 (first), Public Domain. 178 (second), Jason Cosburn/Shutterstock. 178 (third), Guy Thouvenin/age fotostock. 178 (fourth), Visual Arts Library (London) / Alamy. 179 (top), Guy Thouvenin/age fotostock. 179 (bottom), Public Domain. 180, Jim Tardio/iStockphoto. 185, Jose Ignacio Soto/Shutterstock. 188, ShutterbugBill, Fodors.com member. 199, bobyfume/wikipedia.org. 202, Jean-Luc Bohin / age fotostock. Chapter 4: The Loire Valley: 209, Kevin Galvin/age fotostock. 210, P. Narayan/age fotostock. 211 (top left), P. Narayan/age fotostock. 211 (top right), Michael McClain, Fodors.com member. 211 (bottom), Connie28, Fodors.com member. 212, Patrick Giraud/wikipedia.org. 216, Per Karlsson - BKWine.com / Alamy. 217 (left), J.Bilic/age fotostock. 217 (right), Kelly Cline/iStockphoto. 218, caspermoller/Flickr. 225, © vittorio sciosia / age fotostock. 228 (top), SuperStock/age fotostock. 228 (bottom), David Lyons / Alamy. 230 (top left), P. Narayan/age fotostock. 230 (top right), Public Domain. 230 (bottom), P. Narayan/age fotostock. 231 (top left), Duncan Gilbert/iStockphoto. 231 (bottom left), Public Domain. 231 (top right), S. Greg Panosian/iStockphoto. 231 (bottom center), Public Domain. 231 (bottom right), Visual Arts Library (London) / Alamy. 232 (bottom left), Images Etc Ltd / Alamy. 232 (top left), Marc Dantan. 232 (bottom right), vittorio sciosia / Alamy. 232 (top right), Sylvain Grandadam/age fotostock. 236-37, © Travel Pix Collection / age fotostock. 242, Château de Colliers. 251, Edyta Pawlowska/Shutterstock. 258, Steve Vidler / SuperStock. Chapter 5: Normandy: 267, San Rostro/age fotostock. 268, Anger O./age fotostock. 269, paolo siccardi/age fotostock. 271, Steve Vidler / SuperStock. 274, Sylvain Grandadam/age fotostock. 275 (left), Robert Fried / Alamy. 275 (right), Puku/SIME/eStock Photo. 276,

Barbs44, Fodors.com member. 283, JTB Photo / age fotostock. 291, Renaud Visage / age fotostock. 296, Matz Sjöberg / age fotostock. 306, S Tauqueur / age fotostock. 307, iStockphoto. 308, impact productions / Alamy. 309 (top left), Sylvain Grandadam/age fotostock. 309 (bottom left), Martin Florin Emmanuel / Alamy. 309 (top right), Wojtek Buss/age fotostock. 309 (bottom right), Visual Arts Library (London) / Alamy. 310, fanotravel, fodors.com member. 311, Renaud Visage/age fotostock. 312, Wojtek Buss/age fotostock. Chapter 6: Brittany: 313, danilo donadoni/age fotostock. 314, iStockphoto. 315 (top), Chris Marlow, Fodors.com member. 315 (bottom), Steve Vidler / SuperStock. 316, schwaja, Fodors.com member. 319, GUIZIOU Franck / age fotostock. 320, SGM / age fotostock. 321 (left), SUDRES Jean-Daniel / age fotostock. 321 (right), psd/Flickr. 322, Guillaume Dubé/iStockphoto. 328, MATTES René / age fotostock. 335, Guy Thouvenin / age fotostock. 342, Christophe Boisvieux / age fotostock. 349, clu/iStockphoto. 350, Elena Elisseeva/iStockphoto. Chapter 7: Champagne Country: 357, Doug Pearson/age fotostock. 358, Jean-Pierre Lescourre/age fotostock. 359 (top), Steve Vidler / SuperStock. 359 (bottom), teresaevans, Fodor.com member. 361, mbritt275, Fodors.com member. 363, Claudio Giovanni Colombo/Shutterstock. 367, Michel de Nijs/iStockphoto. 372, David W Hughes/ Shutterstock. 373, John Miller / age fotostock. 374 (left), Cephas Picture Library / Alamy. 374 (right), Eric Baccega/age fotostock. 375 (top left), Public Domain. 375 (center left), Gryffindor/Wikimedia Commons. 375 (top right), Public Domain. 375 (bottom), Ray Roberts / Alamy. 375 (center right), PlatinumSunlight/Wikimedia Commons. 376, Clay McLachlan/Aurora Photos. 377 (left), Bramus!/ Flickr. 377 (right), Clay McLachlan/Aurora Photos. 380, Sylvain Grandadam / age fotostock. 385, Yann Guichaoua / age fotostock. Chapter 8: Alsace-Lorraine: 389, SGM/age fotostock. 390 (left), Mary Jane Glauber, Fodors.com member. 390 (right), busterx, Fodors.com member. 391, Mary Jane Glauber, Fodors.com member. 395, David Hughes / age fotostock. 396, klondike, Fodors.com member. 397 (left), Robert Harding Picture Library Ltd / Alamy. 397 (right), wikipedia.org. 398, Brian Ferrigno, Fodors.com member. 402, Picture Contact / Alamy. 405, Kevin O'Hara / age fotostock. 411, Mary Jane Glauber, Fodors.com member. 419, ARCO/G Lenz / age fotostock. 424, RIEGER Bertrand/age fotostock. 430-31, BODY Philippe / age fotostock. Chapter 9: Burgundy: 435, Sylvain Grandadam/age fotostock. 436 (top), R. Matina/age fotostock. 436 (bottom), Tristan Deschamps/age fotostock. 437, Christopher Redo, Fodors.com member. 439, Doug Pearson/age fotostock. 441, RIEGER Bertrand / age fotostock. 442, Simon Reddy / Alamy. 443 (left), beltsazar/Shutterstock. 443 (right), Per Karlsson - BKWine.com / Alamy. 444, Cynthia Stalker, Fodors.com member. 449, RIEGER Bertrand / age fotostock. 456, lynnlin/Shutterstock. 459, Clay McLachlan/IPN/Aurora Photos 460 (left), Alain DOIRE - CRT Bourgogne. 460 (right), Ernst Fretz/iStockphoto. 462, LOOK Die Bildagentur der Fotografen GmbH / Alamy. 473, RIEGER Bertrand / age fotostock. 479, Steve Vidler / SuperStock. 480, Austrophoto / age fotostock. 485, R. Matina / age fotostock. Chapter 10: Lyon and the Alps: 487, AJ Kersten, Fodors.com member. 488, Boyer/age fotostock. 489, wug, Fodors.com member. 493, Minerva Bloom, Fodors.com member. 498, MOIRENC Camille / age fotostock. 503, Matz Sjöberg / age fotostock. 504 (top), bocuse.com. 504 (bottom), bocuse.com. 505 (left), Thierry Vallier. 505 (top right), Matthieu Cellard. 505 (bottom right), Matthieu Cellard. 506 (top), Hemis / Alamy. 506 (bottom), Cesar Lucas Abreu / age fotostock. 507 (left), Homer W Sykes / Alamy. 507 (right), Lourens Smak / Alamy. 511, Saillet Erick / age fotostock. 516, CHICUREL Arnaud / age fotostock. 523, von Essen Hotels. 528, GUIZIOU Franck / age fotostock. 537, Lazar Mihai-Bogdan/Shutterstock. 540, Lazar Mihai-Bogdan/ Shutterstock. 543, Walter Bibikow / age fotostock. Chapter 11: Provence: 547, Sylvain Grandadam / age fotostock. 548, Earl Eliason/iStockphoto. 549 (left), Carson Ganci/age fotostock. 549 (right), xms, Fodors.com member. 554, Guillaume Piolle/wikipedia.org. 555 (left), anjƒçi/Flickr. 555 (right), Andy Hawkins/Flickr. 556, SGM/age fotostock. 563, © JTB Photo / age fotostock. 566, © JTB Photo / age fotostock. 574, Mike Tumchewics, Fodors.com member. 581, JACQUES Pierre / age fotostock. 589, Minerva Bloom, Fodors.com member. 592, Zyankarlo/Shutterstock. 595 (top), Chad Ehlers/age fotostock. 595 (bottom), Renaud Visage/age fotostock. 596 (left), David Barnes/age fotostock. 596 (right), Craig Lovell/viestiphoto.com. 597 (left), Bruno Morandi/age fotostock. 597 (right), David Buffington/ age fotostock. 598 (top), Susan Jones/age fotostock. 598 (bottom), Plus Pix/age fotostock. 599 (bottom), Plus Pix/age fotostock. 599 (top), Sergio Cozzi/viestiphoto.com. 600, Doug Scott/age fotostock. 601 (top), David Hughes/Shutterstock. 601 (center), SGM/age fotostock. 601 (bottom), Doug Scott/age fotostock. 602, L'Occitane en Provence. 607, Peter Adams/age fotostock. 615, MOIRENC Camille / age fotostock. 620, Brasil2/iStockphoto. 624, Johan Sjolander/iStockphoto. Chapter 12: The French Riviera: 629, mkinct, Fodors.com member. 630, Kathy Jensen, Fodors.com member. 631 (bottom left), Walter Bibikow/age fotostock. 631 (top), annerev, Fodors.com member. 631 (bottom right), flauta, Fodors.com member. 633, Christian Musat/Shutterstock. 636, Perov Stanislav/Shutterstock. 643, Priamo Melo/iStockphoto. 651, Alan Copson / age fotostock. 656, GARDEL Bertrand / age fotostock. 661, MOIRENC Camille / age fotostock. 665, Owen Franken. 666 (bottom), Owen Franken. 666 (top left),

Susana Guzmán Martínez/iStockphoto. 666 (top right), Colin & Linda McKie/iStockphoto. 667 (left), Le Jardin du Quai. 667 (right), Alain Llora- Le Moulin de Mougins. 668 (left), TATIANA FUENTES/iStockphoto. 668 (right), Corbis. 669 (left), Owen Franken. 669 (right), javarman/Shutterstock. 674, Renaud d'Avout d'Auerstaedt/wikipedia.org. 681, Jose Fuste Raga / age fotostock. 686, Richard L'Anson / age fotostock. 695, Giancarlo Liguori/Shutterstock. 702, Britrob/Flickr. Chapter 13: The Midi-Pyrénées and Languedoc-Roussillon: 705, Javier Larrea/age fotostock. 706, dcazalet, Fodors.com member. 707 (top), wikipedia.org. 707 (bottom), Alan Copson/age fotostock. 709 (top), flauta, Fodors.com member. 709 (bottom), Elin B/Flickr. 712, Mike Tumchewics, Fodors.com member. 719, FELIX Alain / age fotostock. 726, wikipedia.org. 733, seeyourworld, Fodors.com member. 738, Christian Musat/iStockphoto. 741, dan talson/iStockphoto. 746, José Antonio Moreno / age fotostock. Chapter 14: The Basque Country, Gascony, and Hautes-Pyrénées: 749, Josu Altzelai / age fotostock. 751 (left), Botond Horváth/Shutterstock. 751 (right), Jens Buurgaard Nielsen/wikipedia.org. 753, Juan Carlos Muñoz/age fotostock. 756, Roger Bruton, Fodors.com member. 761, BERNAGER E./age fotostock. 762 (left), Javier Larrea/age fotostock. 762 (right), Javier Larrea/age fotostock. 763 (left), Le Naviose/age fotostock. 763 (right), Mark Baynes / Alamy. 763 (top), Robert Fried / Alamy. 763 (bottom), Mark Baynes / Alamy. 764, Mark Baynes / Alamy. 769, Gonzalo Azumendi / age fotostock. 776, GUIZIOU Franck / age fotostock. Chapter 15: Bordeaux and the Wine Country: 783, J.D. Dallet / age fotostock. 784, salciccioli, Fodors.com member. 785, The BORDEAUX WINE FESTIVAL /Laurent WANGERMEZ. 786, The BORDEAUX WINE FESTIVAL / Dominique LE LANN. 787, The BORDEAUX WINE FESTIVAL / Gilles ARROYO. 788, Benjamin Zingg/wikipedia.org. 789 (top), Benjamin Zingg/wikipedia.org. 789 (bottom), Benjamin Zingg/wikipedia.org. 791, The BORDEAUX WINE FESTIVAL / Jean-Bernard NADEAU. 797, The BORDEAUX WINE FESTIVAL / Jean-Bernard NADEAU. 798, Fabrice RAMBERT. 804, t56gf, Fodors.com member. Chapter 16: The Dordogne: 807, P. Narayan/age fotostock. 808, Public Domain. 809 (top), Lagui/Shutterstock. 809 (bottom), S. Greg Panosian/iStockphoto. 811, Iain Frazer/Shutterstock. 814, aleske/Flickr. 815 (left), titanium22/Flickr. 815 (right), wikipedia.org. 816, deanh, Fodors.com member. 824, Peter Garbet/iStockphoto. 831, BODY Philippe / age fotostock. 834, CINTRACT Romain / age fotostock

NOTES

NOTES